HOUGHTON MIFFLIN SOCIAL STUDIES

A More Perfect Union

*W*e the people of the United States,
in order to form **a more perfect union,**
establish justice, insure domestic tranquility,
provide for the common defense,
promote the general welfare,
and secure the blessings of liberty to
ourselves and our posterity,
do ordain and establish this Constitution for
the United States of America.

Preamble to the U.S. Constitution

Beverly J. Armento
Gary B. Nash
Christopher L. Salter
Karen K. Wixson

A More Perfect Union

Houghton Mifflin Company • Boston

Atlanta • Dallas • Geneva, Illinois • Princeton, New Jersey • Palo Alto • Toronto

Consultants

Program Consultants

Catherine Clinton
Visiting Professor
Department of Afro-American Studies
Harvard University
Cambridge, Massachusetts

Edith M. Guyton
Associate Professor of Early
  Childhood Education
Georgia State University
Atlanta, Georgia

Gail Hobbs
Associate Professor of Geography
Pierce College
Woodland Hills, California

Charles Peters
Reading Consultant
Oakland Schools
Pontiac, Michigan

Cathy Riggs-Salter
Social Studies Consultant
Hartsburg, Missouri

Alfredo Schifini
Limited English Proficiency Consultant
Los Angeles, California

George Paul Schneider
Associate Director
  of General Programs
Department of Museum Education
Art Institute of Chicago
Chicago, Illinois

Twyla Stewart
Center for Academic Interinstitutional
  Programs
University of California—Los Angeles
Los Angeles, California

Scott Waugh
Associate Professor of History
University of California—Los Angeles
Los Angeles, California

Teacher Reviewers

David E. Beer (Grade 5)
Weisser Park Elementary
Fort Wayne, Indiana

Jan Coleman (Grades 6–7)
Thornton Junior High
Fremont, California

Shawn Edwards
  (Grades 1–3)
Jackson Park Elementary
University City, Missouri

Barbara J. Fech (Grade 6)
Martha Ruggles School
Chicago, Illinois

Deborah M. Finkel
  (Grade 4)
Los Angeles Unified
  School District,
  Region G
South Pasadena,
  California

Jim Fletcher (Grade 5)
La Loma Junior High
Modesto, California

Susan M. Gilliam
  (Grade 1)
Roscoe Elementary
Los Angeles, California

Vicki Stroud Gonterman
  (Grade 2)
Gibbs International
  Studies Magnet School
Little Rock, Arkansas

Lorraine Hood (Grade 2)
Fresno Unified School
  District
Fresno, California

Jean Jamgochian
  (Grade 5)
Haycock Gifted and
  Talented Center
Fairfax County, Virginia

Michael Kerwin (Grade 8)
Nativity School
Orchard Park, New York

Susan Kirk-Davalt
  (Grade 5)
Crowfoot Elementary
Lebanon, Oregon

Mary Molyneaux-Leahy
  (Grade 3)
Bridgeport Elementary
Bridgeport, Pennsylvania

Sharon Oviatt
  (Grades 1–3)
Keysor Elementary
Kirkwood, Missouri

Jayne B. Perala (Grade 1)
Cave Spring Elementary
Roanoke, Virginia

Carol Siefkin (K)
Garfield Elementary
Sacramento, California

Norman N. Tanaka
  (Grade 3)
Martin Luther King Jr.
  Elementary
Sacramento, California

John Tyler (Grade 5)
Groton School
Groton, Massachusetts

Portia W. Vaughn
  (Grades 1–3)
School District 11
Colorado Springs,
  Colorado

ISBN: 0-395-80940-1
123456-VH-99 98 97 96

Development by Ligature, Inc.

Acknowledgments

Grateful acknowledgment is made
for the use of the material listed below.
The material in the Minipedia is
reprinted from *The World Book*
Encyclopedia with the expressed permission of the publisher. © 1990 by World
Book, Inc.

–Continued on page 733.

From Your Authors

*J*ames Madison of Virginia was always early. A short man with a serious expression, he was the first delegate to ride into Philadelphia in May 1787. Deeply concerned about the politics of the new nation, Madison had been reading and reflecting on the subject of constitutional government day and night.

So begins an account of the writing of the Constitution of the United States. Twelve of the original 13 states sent delegates to the convention. In Chapter 4 of this book, you will read more about the debates and the compromises that resulted in the signing of this important document. The Constitution continues to this day to direct the running of our nation.

Most of the people you will meet in this book lived long ago in places that may seem very far away from home. But they all had feelings just like yours and faced many of the same challenges you will face in your life. And whether they were great leaders or ordinary people, their decisions and actions helped shape the world you live in.

As you read about these people, places, and events, we hope you will ask many questions. Some questions may be about history: "What caused these people to make the decisions they did?" or "How do we know about these events?" Other questions may be about geography: "What are the land and weather like in that place?" or "Why did people choose to settle there?" Still other questions may be about economics: "How did people meet their needs for food and shelter?" or "How did people work out ways for using scarce resources?"

Most of all, we hope you catch the excitement of thinking, questioning, and discovering answers about your world— now and in the twenty-first century.

Beverly J. Armento

Beverly J. Armento
Professor of Social Studies
Director, Center for Business and
Economic Education
Georgia State University

Christopher L. Salter

Christopher L. Salter
Professor and Chair
Department of Geography
University of Missouri

Gary B. Nash

Gary B. Nash
Professor of History
University of California—Los Angeles

Karen Wixson

Karen K. Wixson
Associate Professor of Education
University of Michigan

Contents

About Your Book   xii

Unit 1   1
A Land of Promise

Chapter 1   2
Reviewing Exploration and Settlement

Lesson 1   *The American Land*   4
Lesson 2   *European Exploration and Settlement*   16
Lesson 3   *Europeans and Native Peoples*   26
Lesson 4   *Life in the English Colonies*   33

Chapter 2   46
Reviewing the American Revolution

Lesson 1   *An Emerging American Identity*   48
Lesson 2   *Growing Conflict with England*   54
Lesson 3   *Fighting the American Revolution*   62
Lesson 4   *Fighting the War at Home*   71

Unit 2   78
The Constitution of the United States

Chapter 3   80
Toward the Constitution

Lesson 1   *Roots of Government*   82
Lesson 2   *The Articles of Confederation*   90
Lesson 3   *The Crisis of Confederation*   95

Chapter 4   104
The Constitutional Convention

Lesson 1   *The Constitutional Convention*   106
Lesson 2   *The Ratification Debate*   118
Lesson 3   *The Bill of Rights*   124

Unit 3   130
Establishing the New Nation

Chapter 5   132
The Creation of a Party System

Lesson 1   *Internal Conflict*   134
Lesson 2   *Jefferson and the Republicans*   146
Lesson 3   *The United States and the World*   153

Chapter 6   162
The Maturing Republic

Lesson 1   *Republicanism and Culture*   164
Lesson 2   *The First Western President*   172
Lesson 3   *How Others Saw Us*   179

Chapter 7   188
People of the New Nation

Lesson 1   *Life Changes Along the Atlantic Seaboard*   190
Lesson 2   *The Trans-Appalachian Frontier*   196
Lesson 3   *The Changing World of American Indians*   201
Lesson 4   *The Next Wave of Immigrants*   210

Unit 4   218
The Development of America's Regions

Chapter 8   220
The West

Lesson 1   *Exploring Beyond the Mississippi*   222
Lesson 2   *Achieving Manifest Destiny*   230
Lesson 3   *Settling the West*   236
Lesson 4   *Surviving on the Frontier*   241

Chapter 9   252
The North

Lesson 1   *The Industrial Revolution*   254
Lesson 2   *The Urban North*   261
Lesson 3   *Seeking a Better Way*   267

Chapter 10   282
The South

Lesson 1   *The Cotton Kingdom*   284
Lesson 2   *Life on the Plantation*   290
Lesson 3   *The Other Souths*   298

Unit 5 **The Nation** **Divides** **and Reunites**	310	**Chapter 11** *Causes of* *the Civil War*	312	Lesson 1 *The Sectional Conflict* — 314 Lesson 2 *The Antislavery Movement* — 320 Lesson 3 *The Road to Bleeding Kansas* — 325 Lesson 4 *The House Divided* — 330
		Chapter 12 *A Nation Divided*	340	Lesson 1 *North Versus South* — 342 Lesson 2 *A Nation at War* — 347 Lesson 3 *War on the Home Front* — 355 Lesson 4 *The Long March to Surrender* — 362
		Chapter 13 *Reconstruction*	374	Lesson 1 *A Time for Reconciliation* — 376 Lesson 2 *Radical Reconstruction* — 385 Lesson 3 *Southern Life Under Reconstruction* — 391
Unit 6 **A Time of** **Transformation**	406	**Chapter 14** *Reshaping* *the Great Plains*	408	Lesson 1 *A Time of Change* — 410 Lesson 2 *Culture of the Plains Indians* — 415 Lesson 3 *Indian Lands Lost* — 422 Lesson 4 *Resettlement of the Land* — 427
		Chapter 15 *Industry and* *Workers*	440	Lesson 1 *Building the American Dream* — 442 Lesson 2 *Moving into Industrial Cities* — 447 Lesson 3 *The Workers' Changing World* — 455 Lesson 4 *Destination: America* — 462
		Chapter 16 *The Gilded Age*	470	Lesson 1 *The Politics of Corruption* — 472 Lesson 2 *The Reforming Impulse* — 477 Lesson 3 *The Populist Revolt* — 486
		Chapter 17 *The Reform Era*	496	Lesson 1 *The Shame of the Cities* — 498 Lesson 2 *Progressive Reform* — 507 Lesson 3 *Competing Crusades* — 513
		Chapter 18 *America Emerges* *as a World Power*	526	Lesson 1 *International Expansion* — 528 Lesson 2 *Conflict and Conquest* — 533 Lesson 3 *America at War* — 541 Lesson 4 *Impact of the War* — 547
Unit 7 **The Promise** **Continues**	560	**Chapter 19** *Pluralism*	562	Lesson 1 *A Land of Immigrants* — 564 Lesson 2 *America's Many Cultures* — 571 Lesson 3 *The Gates Reopened* — 578
		Chapter 20 *Modern American* *Democracy*	590	Lesson 1 *A Government of Citizens* — 592 Lesson 2 *Putting the Constitution to Work* — 600 Lesson 3 *Making a Difference* — 609
Time/Space **Databank**	621	Our Constitution Today — 622 Constitution — 636 Declaration of Independence — 656 Primary Sources — 660		Minipedia — 670 Atlas — 694 Gazetteer — 709 Glossary of Geographic Terms — 712 Biographical Dictionary — 714 Glossary — 718 Index — 725 Acknowledgments — 745

vii

Understanding Skills

Each "Understanding Skills" feature gives you the opportunity to learn and practice a skill related to the topic you are studying.

Reference Materials: Using Specialized Resources	32
Timelines: Charting Pre-Revolutionary Events	60
Primary Sources: Reading Abigail Adams's Letters	88
Group Activities: Reaching a Compromise	123
Bibliography Cards: Researching Aaron Burr	152
Political Cartoons: Analyzing Jackson-Clay Cartoons	184
Mapmaking: Designing a City Map	208
Information Organization: Chronological Outlining	228
Reference Materials: Using Computerized Sources	274
Graphs: Choosing Appropriate Graphs	306
Point of View: Analyzing Viewpoints on Slavery	336
Written Reports: Reporting on Antietam	368
Cause and Effect: Analyzing the Civil War	398
Topographical Maps: Tracing Routes West	433
Thematic Maps: Comparing Population Maps	454
Period Literature: Reading Mark Twain	492
Visual Information: Analyzing Historical Photographs	520
Written Propaganda: Supporting the War Effort	556
Information Collection: Conducting an Interview	577
Written Arguments: Analyzing Editorials	598

Understanding Concepts

Each "Understanding Concepts" feature gives you more information about a concept that is important to the lesson you are reading.

Eurocentrism	28
Pluralism	50
Government Revenues	93
Origins of the Constitution	109
Leadership	138
Neoclassicism	168
Immigration	214
Regionalism	246
Cultural Institutions	270
Social Class	304
Sectionalism	317
Civil War	344
Constitutional Amendments	396
Ecology	424
Labor Unions	460
Monopolies	484
Reform	503
Imperialism	534
Assimilation	575

Making Decisions

Much of history is made of people's decisions. These pages take you step-by-step through fascinating problems from history and today. What will you decide?

Environment or Energy	14
The Shakers and the Civil War	360
Where the Buffalo Roam	436

Exploring

The story of the past is hidden all around you in the world of the present. "Exploring" pages tell you the secrets of how to find it.

American Coins	100
The Role of the First Lady	170
Sports in the United States	278
Work Past and Present	614

Literature

Throughout history people have expressed their deepest feelings and beliefs through literature. Reading these stories, legends, poems, and shorter passages that appear in the lessons will help you experience what life was like for people of other times and places.

"The Seven Devils Mountains" from *Indian Legends of the Northwest* edited by Ella E. Clark — 24

"The Witch of Blackbird Pond" from *The Witch of Blackbird Pond* by Elizabeth G. Speare — 40

"First Day in Philadelphia" from *The Autobiography* by Benjamin Franklin — 114

"Moral Algebra" letter by Benjamin Franklin — 115

"Maxims" from *Poor Richard's Almanac* by Benjamin Franklin — 116

"Rip Van Winkle" by Washington Irving — 140

"The Oregon Trail" from *The Oregon Trail* by Francis Parkman — 248

"Susan's Trial" from *Mother, Aunt Susan, and Me* by William Jay Jacob — 276

"Slave Life" from *Narrative of the Life of Frederick Douglass* by Frederick Douglass — 296

"The Slopes of War" from *The Slopes of War* by Norah A. Perez — 370

"The Lincoln Poems" from *Leaves of Grass* by Walt Whitman — 400

"It Was a Glorious Day!" from *Journal* by Charlotte Forten — 402

"The World of the Buffalo Comes to an End" from *American Indian Mythology* edited by Alice Marriott and Carol K. Rachlin — 420

"A New Home" from *My Antonia* by Willa Cather — 434

"Summer in New York" from *East River* by Sholem Ash — 522

"American War Songs" by George M. Cohen and Edward Bushnell — 554

"A Family Learns English" from *Hunger of Memory* by Richard Rodriguez — 584

"The Lower East Side" from *America's Immigrants,* edited by Rhoda Hoff — 586

"A Call for Civil Rights" speech by John F. Kennedy — 616

"Dreams of Freedom" from *Selected Poems* by Langston Hughes — 618

Primary Sources

Reading the exact words of the people who made and lived history is the best way to get a sense of how they saw themselves and the times in which they lived. You will find more than 50 primary sources throughout this book including the following:

John and Abigail Adams, letters — 88

James Madison, Franklin's "Rising Sun" speech — 113

Carl Schurz, reminiscences — 210

Solomon Northup, on slavery — 285

Lucretia Mott, antislavery arguments — 336

Abraham Lincoln, Gettysburg Address — 355

Walt Whitman, on government corruption — 474

William Jennings Bryan, "Cross of Gold" speech — 486

Mary Lease, on Populism — 489

Jade Snow Wong, on the Chinese immigrant experience — 574

Unnamed Vietnamese refugee, journey to America — 578

Martin Luther King, Jr., excerpt from "I Have a Dream" speech — 602

The Constitution of the United States — 636

The Declaration of Independence — 656

A Letter from Columbus — 660

Mayflower Compact — 663

Patrick Henry, "Give me Liberty or Give me Death" — 664

Thomas Paine, *Common Sense* — 666

Monroe Doctrine — 668

A Closer Look

Take a closer look at the objects and pictures spread out on these special pages. With the clues you see, you'll become a historical detective.

The Colonial Farm	36
The Federalist Papers	121
The Battle of New Orleans	157
Cities—Old and New	182
The Battle of the Alamo	233
Appalachian Crafts	300
Civil War Technology	364
The Rebuilding of Richmond	380
Plains Indian Culture	416
Ellis Island Immigrants	464
Gilded Age Elections	478
Sweatshops	500
Building the Panama Canal	538
The March on Washington	603

A Moment in Time

A person from the past is frozen at an exciting moment. You'll get to know these people by reading about where they are, what they're wearing, and the objects around them.

A Minuteman	64
A China-bound Sailor	97
A Cherokee Mother and Son	206
A Telegraph Operator	265
A Quaker Abolitionist	323
A Chicago Newsboy	450
A Hmong Woman	573

Charts, Diagrams, and Timelines

These visual presentations of information help give you a clearer picture of the people, places, and events you are studying.

Ethnic Population, 1775	49
The 1980 U.S. Census	50
Major Battles of the Revolution	66
Exports and Imports, 1770 to 1782	73
British Influences on the American Government	84
Delivery! The Journey of a Letter in 1790	92
Federal Government Funding, 1989	93
The Connecticut Compromise	110
The Road to Ratification: 1787 to 1790	122
Two Approaches to Government	136
Judicial Review Process	151
Voter Participation, 1824 to 1832	174
Advances in Wheat Production	191
Texas Towns: A Varied Heritage	231
The First Industrial Revolution, 1790 to 1860	256
Comparing the North and the South, around 1850	287
Missouri Compromise	315
Political Parties	326
Union and Confederate Resources, 1860	346
Major Battles of the Civil War	350
Reconstruction Amendments	384
Reconstruction, 1865 to 1877	395
Black Population in Chicago	453
Immigrant Populations, 1920	467
Owners of the Railroads, 1904	481
U.S. Monopolies, 1870 to 1900	485
Commission Plan/Council Manager Plan	506
American Foreign Trade, 1876 to 1914	529
U.S. Foreign Born Population, 1850 to 1980	569
The Changing Tide of U.S. Immigration	580
Citizenship and Voting Rights, 1790 to 1970	595
Voter Turnout for Presidential Elections, 1952 to 1988	612
The Federal System	623
Checks and Balances	625
Race for the White House	629
The Executive Branch	631
A Bill Becomes Law	633
The Federal Judiciary	635

Maps

The events of history have been shaped by the places in which they occurred. Each map in this book tells its own story about these events and places.

Geographical Regions of the United States	5
European Exploration of the New World, 1492–1610	19
Settlements in the New World, 1650	21
The English Colonies, 1750	38
European Land Claims in North America, 1763	55
Major Battles of the Revolutionary War	69
An Imaginary United States, 1777	83
Western Land Claims and Cessions	86
The Constitutional Convention Delegates from Each State	112
Mississippi River Valley, 1803	150
The Americans Emerge from European Ownership, 1823	159
Adding States to the Republic, 1821	167
Jackson's Land Slide Victory, 1828	175
Where Free Blacks Were Living, 1810	194
The First Roads West, 1838	198
Relocation of Several American Indian Tribes, 1800–1840	203
Cherokee Trail of Tears, 1840	207
Where German Immigrants Settled, 1860	213
Where Irish Immigrants Settled, 1860	213
Expanding United States, 1810	223
Routes of Western Explorers, 1804–1845	227
Mexican War, 1846–1848	234
Expanding United States, 1853	235
A Journey on the Overland Trail	244
Northern Railroad and Canal Network, 1850	258
Cash Crop Economy of the South	288
Missouri Compromise, 1820	316
Compromise of 1850	318
Free and Slave States and Territories, 1854	327
Slave Population, 1860	332
Slave Routes to Freedom, 1861	333
Secession of Confederate States, 1861	343
Major Battles of the Civil War	350
States' Readmission to the Union, 1870	386
Geographical Regions of the West	411
Railroad Network, 1893	412
American Indian Lands in 1850	419
Conflict on the Western Frontier, 1864–1898	423
American Indian Lands in 1890	425
Moving Western Beef to Market	430
Western Regions and Railroad Routes	433
Comparing Major Cities in the United States	452
Development of Industrial Cities, 1910–1920	454
Immigration to the United States, 1870–1920	463
Election of 1896	491
Election of 1912	511
Spanish-American War in Cuba	536
Spanish-American War in Philippines	536
The Western Front, 1918	546
Europe after World War I	550
American Ancestry, 1980	572
World: Political	694
World: Physical	696
United States: Political	698
United States: Physical	700
North America: Political	702
North America: Physical	703
United States: Population Density, 1700	704
United States: Population Density, 1870	704
United States: Population Density, 1910	705
United States: Population Density, 1990	705
United States: Climate	706
United States: Vegetation	706
United States: Precipitation	707
United States: Land Use and Resources	707
World: Gross National Product	708
United States: Time Zones	708

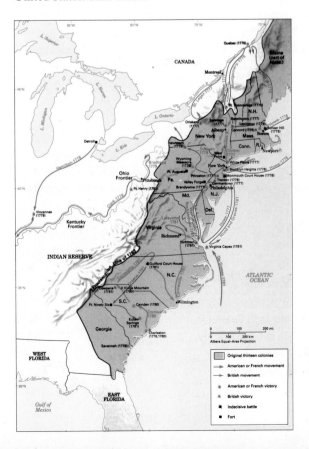

ABOUT YOUR BOOK

Starting Out

What makes this textbook so much more interesting than others you've used before? In this book, the people of the past speak directly to you, through their actual words and the objects they used. You'll walk inside their houses and look inside their cooking pots. You'll follow them as they go to school, build cities, fight wars, work out settlements for peace.

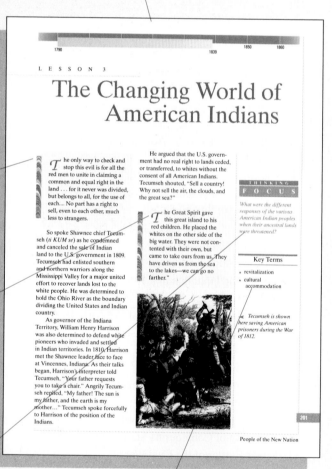

When and what? The timeline at the beginning of each lesson tells you when these events took place. The lesson title tells you what the lesson is about.

From unit to chapter to lesson—each step lets you see history in closer detail. The photos show you where events happened. The art introduces you to the people. The lower timeline on the chapter opener names the U.S. presidents of this period.

Right from the beginning the lesson opener pulls you into the sights, the sounds, the smells of what life was like at that time, in that place.

Every age has its great storytellers. Each chapter includes short examples of fine writing from or about the period. Here Tecumseh's words are part of the oral tradition, but are literature nevertheless. The literature is always printed on a tan background with a blue initial letter and a multicolored bar.

Like a road sign, the question that always appears here tells you what to think about while you read the lesson.

Look for these terms. They are listed here so that you can watch out for them. The first time they appear in the lesson they are shown in heavy black print and defined. Key terms are also defined in the Glossary.

xii

The titles outline the lesson. The red titles tell you the main topics discussed in the lesson on "The Changing World of American Indians." The blue titles tell you the subtopics.

Every map tells a story. The maps in this book tell the story of where people like the relocated Indian tribes came from, where they went, and what the land was like.

Indian Territories Invaded by the Push Westward

Ever since the first Europeans arrived, whites had gotten land by defeating American Indians. By the 1780s, few of the Indian tribes that had once flourished along the Atlantic seaboard survived. Entire tribal groups had been killed off by war, starvation, and disease.

Farther inland, however, Indian tribes still occupied much of the land. Many wanted to make sure that they would not share the fate of the coastal Indian peoples. The Shawnee, Delaware, Miami, and Potawatomi (*POT a WOT a mee*) of the Old Northwest, for example, formed a confederacy at the time of the Revolutionary War.

Led by Miami chief Little Turtle, the warriors of this powerful alliance raided white settlements on Indian lands. In the late 1780s and early 1790s, they were able to halt white advances. The Indians defeated the territorial militias that marched into their lands.

Then in 1793, President Washington sent federal troops commanded by the Revolutionary War hero General Anthony Wayne. In 1794, at the Battle of Fallen Timbers in what is now northern Ohio, General Wayne defeated Little Turtle's allied warriors. The next year, members of the confederacy were forced to sign the Treaty of Greenville. As a result, the Indians ceded to the United States the southeastern quarter of the Northwest Territory—about half the present state of Ohio.

Hunger for Land

In the Treaty of Greenville, the United States broke a promise it had made to the Indian peoples only eight years before. The Northwest Ordinance of 1787 had promised security for the Indians in their ancestral lands. But the policy of the U.S. government from the 1790s onward was to recognize the Indian tribes as independent nations. Each "nation" was seen as the sole "owner" of distinct territories. The Indians did not see themselves this way. But this policy enabled the government to obtain land by negotiating treaties with each separate Indian "nation."

And so began a series of treaties whereby the Indian tribes "freely consented" to cede their lands, sometimes receiving only pennies an acre for it. By making treaties, the U.S. government made it seem as though the Indians were voluntarily moving off the land. In fact, many treaties were obtained through the use of fraud and violence. Many treaties were signed by individuals who did not speak for all of the Indians or who had no authority to sign over the land. The U.S. government used any means to force Indian

► The land Tecumseh defended was long ago divided up among individuals. Now only a little land of the Old Northwest, like this state park, is "for the use of all."

202
Chapter 7

Relocation of Several American Indian Tribes, 1800–1840

◄ These lines show the relocation of selected Indian tribes to the new Indian Territory. Few Indians could pursue their traditional ways of living in the Indian Territory.

tribes off desirable frontier land onto more distant, less desirable land. "Indian Territory," as it is shown on the map, got smaller and smaller.

After the Treaty of Fort Wayne was signed in 1809, all of the Northwest Territory was legally open to white settlement. Tens of thousands of settlers were now entering yet another environment where Indians had lived for centuries. The ways of the Indians had been closely connected to the plants, the animals, the rivers, and the soil of a particular area. When white settlers cut down many square miles of forest to clear new farmland, they destroyed a way of life. They drove off the game—bear, deer, and buffalo—that had been a major food source for the Indian. Settlement of Indian lands also broke up networks of intertribal trade. But the pioneers did not particularly care what happened to the former inhabitants of the land.

Indian Resistance

Realizing that only drastic measures could save them, many Indian leaders saw the War of 1812 as an opportunity to strike out against the settlers. Along the southern frontier, more than 2,000 militant Creeks, called "Red Sticks," rose up as a unified force of warriors. But in 1814, after months of bloody fighting, General Andrew Jackson finally defeated the Red Sticks in Tennessee. The treaty that ended the conflict brought

▲ These war clubs were used by Tecumseh's warriors in defending their lands.

203

People of the New Nation

A picture is worth a thousand words. But just a few words in a caption can help you understand a picture, an illustration, a map, or in this case, a photograph of the land Tecumseh defended.

The things people make and use tell a great deal about them. In this book you'll find lots of photographs of the paintings and statues people made and the tools, jewelry, and weapons they used.

LESSON 2

Achieving Manifest Destiny

THINKING FOCUS

How did Texas become the center of a conflict that gave the United States its new lands?

Key Terms
- expansionist
- buffer zone
- annex

I n a stirring speech in 1846, Democratic politician Major Auguste Davezac stated as follows his belief that the United States should expand:

L *and enough—land enough! Make way, I say, for the young American buffalo—he has not yet got land enough; he wants more land as his cool shelter in summer—He wants more land for his beautiful pasture grounds. I tell you, we will give him Oregon for his summer shade, and the region of Texas as his winter pasture. [Applause] Like all of his race, he wants salt too. Well, he shall have the use of two oceans, the mighty Pacific and the turbulent Atlantic shall be his. He shall not stop his career until he slakes his thirst in the frozen ocean.*

Expansion was part of the concept of Manifest Destiny. Its roots went back to colonial days. In the mid-1600s, Governor John Winthrop of Massachusetts established the idea

that if people did not improve land—that is, farm, mine, or change it in some way—they lost all right to it.

This idea grew into the view that the United States had the right to settle all of the continent of North America. **Expansionists**—those who wanted to increase U.S. territory—did not explain how the United States received the right to take over the entire North American continent.

Some people said Americans had the duty to extend white American culture—especially the ideals of democratic government, Christianity, and economic growth—to all who lacked them. From this idea it was but a short step to the claim that white American culture was superior to all others.

In 1845, editor John L. O'Sullivan came up with the name "Manifest Destiny" for the complex of expansionist ideas. Manifest Destiny was a thread that wove through the political fabric of the nation in the 1800s. Nowhere did it become more evident than in United States relations with Spain and later with Mexico.

Development of Texas

Spain claimed vast North American lands, among them what are now Texas, New Mexico, Arizona, and California. In a hundred years of colonization, however, few people had settled north of Mexico. Only 3,500

non-Indian people were scattered across the Southwest by 1820. In California and Texas, many were rancheros—cattle ranchers who grazed their herds on the unfenced range. In New Mexico, many colonists herded sheep.

270
Chapter 8

Letters, diaries, books—short passages from these primary sources let people from the past speak to you. When you see a tan background, a red initial letter, and a gray bar, you know that the quotation is a primary source.

xiii

Continuing On

As you get to know the people of the past, you'll want ways of understanding and remembering them better. This book gives you some tools to use in learning about people and places and remembering what you've learned.

You're in charge of your reading. See the red square at the end of the text? Now find the red square over in the margin. If you can answer the question there, then you probably understood what you just read. If you can't, perhaps you'd better go back and read that part of the lesson again.

two-thirds of the Creek lands into the United States. The remaining Creeks withdrew to southern and western Alabama.

In the Old Northwest, the alliance led by Shawnee chief Tecumseh and his brother Elskwatawa *(el-SKWA ta wa)*, known as "The Prophet," also tried to push back white settlement. In 1811, Governor William Henry Harrison fought a large force of The Prophet's warriors at the Indian stronghold of Tippecanoe *(tip ee ka NOO)*, in Indiana Territory. White

■ *Find evidence to support this statement: The U. S. government did not deal fairly when signing land cession treaties with American Indians.*

losses were much higher than those of the Indians. But Harrison's army managed to burn the village of Tippecanoe, the stronghold of the Indians. Harrison claimed a victory.

Tecumseh sided with the British in the War of 1812. Together their forces scored several dramatic victories. But Tecumseh died in 1813, at the Battle of the Thames *(temz)* in Ontario, Canada. This loss put an end to most Indian resistance in the Old Northwest. ■

Various Indian Responses

By the early 1800s, more was at stake for the Indians than ownership of land. Constant pressure from white settlers and the U.S. government threatened their traditional culture and their livelihood. The Indians stood in danger of losing their entire way of life.

Cultural Revival

In his youth, The Prophet had fallen "victim," as he saw it, to the evils of white culture. He had become an alcoholic and had left his people's customs. As a result of the wars and the invasions of the whites, many Indians had left their traditions. But The Prophet recovered from alcoholism. Then he began a movement to

▼ *This drawing of The Prophet shows him in the traditional dress of the Shawnee warrior. The Prophet shunned white culture.*

bring back the old beliefs and traditional ways of the American Indians. The effort to renew a people's culture is called **revitalization.** The Prophet preached that the Indians would get back their power if they rejected alcohol and other white trading goods and cultural habits.

The Prophet's message was appealing. He converted many among the Shawnee, Potawatomi, and other Indians of the Old Northwest. Many warriors, however, looked instead to his brother Tecumseh for political leadership. But after Tecumseh's death in 1813, Indian unity crumbled and The Prophet's movement dissolved.

Cultural Compromises

Other Indians believed that violent opposition to whites was no solution. The Cherokee, for example, recognized that the white presence in America was permanent. The Cherokee favored **cultural accommodation,** or peaceful compromises, with white society. They tried to combine the best features of both European and Cherokee culture.

Cultural accommodation brought about a remarkable period in Cherokee history. During the early 1800s, many Cherokee gave up hunting to become farmers. Some even became

204

rich plantation owners with dozens of black slaves. Other Cherokee turned to commerce—managing stores, mills, and other businesses.

At this time, boarding schools run by Christian missionaries taught Cherokee children everything from geography to arithmetic. But the Cherokee educational system took even greater steps forward because of the achievements of Sequoya *(si KWOI a)*, a Cherokee silversmith.

Sequoya saw the advantages whites enjoyed because of their ability to read and write. He set out to make an alphabet for writing the Cherokee language. After years of work, he made an alphabet of 85 symbols that stood for the different syllables of the Cherokee language.

Sequoya's system was easy to learn. In fact, most Cherokee were able to read and write effectively in about a week. The Cherokee also

Cherokee leadership was especially during this period. The were run by

▲ *Sequoya is shown here with his alphabet. Note that his clothes are like those of the white settlers*

A MOMENT IN TIME

A Cherokee Mother and Son

*1:37 P.M. December 15, 1838
Along the Trail of Tears, on a frozen dirt path
outside Greenville, Missouri*

Leg Rattles
At the Green Corn Dance, she created loud rhythms by dancing while wearing these. She carries them in an oak basket to remind her of happier times.

Blowgun
This morning, the boy shot a pheasant with this simple gun. Georgia wild turkey is his favorite target.

Basket
An expert basket-maker, the boy's mother has taught many young girls to weave. In this basket, he now carries a few tools and dried fruit.

Hymnal
Methodist missionaries gave her this book of hymns. It is printed in Cherokee, so she can use it to teach her son to read after they reach Oklahoma.

Copper Pan
She had many fine pieces of copper cookware at home, but she can only carry one as she walks.

Red Clay
By carrying a handful of clay from Georgia and mixing it with the soil of his new home, the boy will keep part of his past alive.

206

Frozen at a moment in time, the Cherokee woman and her son give you a glimpse of a powerful moment in American history. You learn all about them, through the clothes they wear, the things they carry, and the trail they walk.

Some tools you'll always use.
The Understanding pages walk you through skills that you will use again and again, as a student and later on in life.

UNDERSTANDING POLITICAL CARTOONS

Analyzing Jackson-Clay Cartoons

UNDERSTANDING IMMIGRATION

Giving you the inside story is the purpose of two special paragraphs. Across Time & Space connects what you're reading to things that happened centuries ago or continents away. Its companion, How Do We Know?, tells you where information about the past comes from. (See page 199 for an example.)

A special kind of Understanding page looks at concepts—the big ideas that help put all the pieces together. This section helps you understand ideas like Pluralism, Leadership, and in this case, Immigration.

Cherokee Trail of Tears, 1838–1840

Take a closer look, in this case at the cities that were taking the place of Indian settlements. Look at the shopkeepers' signs; compare American cities to those in Europe.

After you read the lesson, stop and review what you've read. The first question is the same one you started out with. The second question connects the lesson to what you've studied earlier. Other questions and an activity help you think about the lesson you've read. Chapter Review questions help you tie the lessons together. (See pages 216 and 217 for an example.)

A CLOSER LOOK

Cities—Old and New

Also Featuring

Some special pages show up only once in every unit, not in every lesson in the book. These features continue the story by letting you explore an idea or activity, or read a story about another time and place. The Time/Space Databank in the back of the book brings together resources you will use again and again.

School isn't the only place where you can learn social studies. This feature gives you a chance to explore history and geography outside the classroom—at home or in your own neighborhood.

EXPLORING

American Coins

(For more background information on money, see pages 674-677 in the Minipedia.)

Find Out
Select one American coin that interests you. It could be a new coin from your pocket, an older one someone in your family has set aside, or an unusual coin whose picture you've come across in a book.

Look very carefully at both sides of that coin. Use your magnifying

◄ *Susan B. Anthony dollar, 1979. Because this coin was only slightly larger than a quarter, people did not like it since they often confused the two. Minting of the coin was stopped in 1981.*

• What is it made out of?

► *Above right is the Nova Caesara ("New Jersey") cent, minted in 1786. During the first years after independence, individual states minted their own coins. This penny was produced by private metal crafters under contract to the state of New Jersey.*

► *This is the first penny issued by the U.S. government.*

MAKING DECISIONS

Where the Buffalo Roam

Buffalo Bill, Buffalo Bill
Never missed and never will;
Always aims and shoots to kill
And the company pays his buffalo bill.

Popular jingle in the late 1800s about "Buffalo Bill" Cody

I moved up a dead buffalo and got in several good shots . . . I moved again, on through the dead ones, to the farthermost one, and fired three more shots and quit. As I walked back through where the carcasses lay the thickest, I could not help but think that I had done wrong to make such a slaughter for the hides alone.

John Cook, buffalo hunter

Background

During the early 1800s, enormous herds of buffalo roamed the Great Plains of America. Daniel Boone followed a buffalo trail through the Appalachian Mountains. This trail became the National Road, or so-called Cumberland Trail, which opened up the American West to settlement. As settlers moved slowly westward, they used buffalo meat as a source of food, buffalo hides for clothing and shelter, and buffalo droppings for heat and cooking fuel.

The buffalo helped in other ways as well. Guides and scouts used the trails of migratory buffalo to identify water holes as well as shallows in rivers where the settlers' heavy wagons could cross. Occasionally, a ribbon of greener, taller, grass fertilized by buffalo droppings marked the path to a water hole.

Western settlers were often amazed at the size of buffalo herds. One traveler in Kansas reported driving a wagon for 25 miles through one continuous herd. (Scientists estimate that the total number of buffalo in the early 1800s was between 50 and 70 million animals.) A great buffalo slaughter, however, began in 1871.

► *Between 50 and 70 million buffalo roamed the Great Plains during the early 1800s. By the early 1870s, only 7 million remained.*

100

Chapter 3

A Resource or a Nuisance?

There were so many buffalo the supply must have seemed endless. Often settlers would shoot several buffalo weighing 1,800 pounds and take only 50 or 75 pounds of meat from each animal. One hunter could kill over 100 buffalo in an hour while standing in one spot. The invention of the Sharp's rifle in 1871 made shooting buffalo even easier, since now the buffalo could be shot from a greater distance.

As the plains became more settled, farming and ranching brought further harm to the buffalo. In order to keep buffalo away from their cattle and crops, farmers used barbed wire. This also served to cut the buffalo off from their water supply.

Buffalo were no longer regarded as a resource, but as a nuisance. Migrating herds often blocked shipping on rivers for days as they swam across, or stopped railroads in their tracks. Angry buffalo bulls were capable of overturning a locomotive. Professional hunters were hired by the railroad companies to guard water holes, shooting the animals when they came to drink.

By 1865, there were only 15 million buffalo remaining, and by 1872 only 7 million. In 1883, a herd of 10,000 animals, the largest in Montana, was exterminated in just a few days. It was while working as such a professional buffalo hunter that William Cody earned his nickname, "Buffalo Bill."

Realizing that the buffalo were in danger of extinction, Walking Coyote, an Indian of the Pend d'Oreille tribe, captured, protected, and bred two pair of buffalo. They became the basis for two herds living in Montana today.

In 1905, Theodore Roosevelt and others founded the American Bison Society to create a buffalo sanctuary. Today, 35,000 buffalo live in the U.S. and Canada. Although this is a tiny fraction of their former number, they are no longer in danger of extinction.

Should animals be protected?

Animals should be protected because:
• they are natural resources
• even when they are numerous, they can become endangered

Animals should not be protected because:
• they provide many resources for humans
• they are so numerous that eliminating some will not endanger the species
• they can get in the way of economic progress

Yes, animals should be protected.

No, animals should not be protected.

Decision Point

1. Compare the goals and values of those who wanted to protect the buffalo with those who hunted the buffalo.
2. Buffalo herds require enormous amounts of range land—land that could be used for farming or ranching. Which use is more

important? Can you think of a compromise to allow for both?
3. Identify an issue in your state or region that involves a conflict between protecting wildlife and meeting peoples' needs. Collect news articles about the issue and discuss it in class.

437

Reshaping the Great Plains

What would you do? The Making Decisions pages show you an important decision from the past. Then you practice the steps that will help you to make a good choice.

Stories have always been important parts of people's lives. Each unit in the book has at least one story about the time and place you're studying. In this case, it's a retelling of an American Indian legend. Some Indian boys and girls probably listened to this legend too.

LITERATURE

The Seven Devils Mountains

An American Indian Legend

As you read in Lesson 2, there are dozens of different American Indian cultures in North America at the time of European settlement. Each of these Indian cultures had its own myths and legends, one of which is reprinted here.

The Seven Devils Gorge acts as part of the border between Oregon and Idaho. The high peaks along the Idaho side of the gorge are called the Seven Devils Mountains. Caleb Whitman, a Nez Perce on the Umatilla Reservation, told the legend of these mountains to Ella E. Clark, the editor of a collection of Indian legends, in 1950. Legends are passed from generation to generation and have been passed down to you that reveal something about your family?

Long, long ago, when the world was very young, seven giant brothers lived in the Blue Mountains. These giant monsters were taller than the tallest pines and stronger than the strongest oaks.

The ani . . .

The **Time/Space Databank** is like a reference section of a library at your fingertips. It's the place to go for more information about the places, people, and key terms you meet in this book. Some of your country's most prized documents are reproduced here too.

What's a minipedia? It's a small version of an encyclopedia, one that you don't have to go to your library to use. It's bound right into the back of your book so you can quickly look up its articles, charts, and graphs.

The Atlas maps out the world. Special maps tell you about the climate, vegetation, precipitation, and resources of the United States. Historical maps let you compare the nation's population at different times in its history.

that no one dared to attack them. Coyote and Fox watched from behind some rocks and shrubs.

Down, down, down the seven giants went into the seven deep holes of boiling liquid. They struggled and struggled to get out, but the holes were very deep. They fumed and roared and splashed. As they struggled, they scattered the reddish liquid around them as far as a man can travel in a day.

Then Coyote came out from his hiding place. The seven giants stood still. They knew Coyote.

"You are being punished for your wickedness," Coyote said to the seven giants. "I will punish you even more by changing you into seven mountains. I will make you very high, so that everyone

Unit 1

A Land of Promise

America was different promises to different people. For Columbus, it was the hope of a faster trade route to Asia. For the Spanish explorers, it was an opportunity for fame and fortune. For the Pilgrims, it was a refuge from religious persecution. And for thousands of European settlers, it was a chance for political freedom and economic opportunity. Whatever the promise, the wilderness land that greeted these newcomers seemed as large and grand as their dreams.

1492

The Rocky Mountains in Colorado. Photograph by Grant Heilman.

1783

Chapter 1

Reviewing Exploration and Settlement

European explorers set sail with dreams of glory and discovery in the late 1400s. What they hoped to find was a quicker trade route to Asia. Instead they found a new land and a people whose existence had not been known. By the 1600s, thousands of Europeans were taking the long ocean voyage to the Americas, drawn by the excitement of discovery and the promise of life in a New World.

1543-45 Battista Agnese's world map includes both the New World and the routes of Spanish explorers.

1450	1500	1550	1600

1492

The development of a new kind of ship, the Portuguese caravel pictured in the 16th century painting above, made the long voyages of the early explorers possible. These explorers used navigational instruments such as the quadrant, shown at left, to chart their courses.

The Pilgrims founded a small settlement in Massachusetts called Plymouth, shown above in a modern reconstruction.

1650   1700   1750   1800

1775

The American Land

Key Terms

- landform
- physical geography
- human geography
- estuary
- precipitation
- prairie
- plateau

Even after hundreds of years of exploring, Americans continue to make many discoveries about the land they inhabit. In 1974, for example, a team of archaeologists working in southeastern Missouri unearthed the remains of a culture of people who lived along the Mississippi River centuries ago. The tools, weapons, and broken pottery they found shed new light on the lives of the mound builders of the Mississippi Valley.

Mound builders were not a single group of people. They were many groups of early North American Indians who built monuments out of earth. The mounds they constructed served as burial places and as platforms to hold either temples or the homes of their leaders. Most mound builders lived in the Great Lakes region or in the valleys of the Ohio and Mississippi rivers, where thousands of burial mounds still stand.

The culture of the Mississippian mound builders lasted from roughly 700 to 1600 A.D. In addition to raising livestock and growing crops, these Indians built some of the earliest cities in North America. Cahokia, which is located in present-day Illinois, was the largest of these cities with a population of nearly 40,000.

Like the Mexican Indians, the Mississippian mound builders built their flat-topped mounds in the center of their cities and used them for religious ceremonies. The largest of these temple mounds, Monk's Mound in Cahokia, has a larger base than the Great Pyramid of Egypt and stands 100 feet tall.

By the time the Spanish explorers arrived in the early 1500s, the civilization of the mound builders was already in serious decline. Diseases brought by the Spanish wiped out most of the remaining mound builders in the Mississippi Valley. Although the 1974 discovery in Missouri added another piece to the story of this fascinating people, much remains to be learned about the early inhabitants of the central river valley of North America.

The Relationship Between Geography and History

Like the history of the mound builders, the history of the United States is a story filled with discoveries: the discovery of the New World; the discovery of a previously unknown race of human beings; the discovery of the Pacific Ocean; the discovery of the St. Lawrence, Hudson, and Mississippi Rivers; the discovery of the Great Lakes and the Rocky Mountains; the discovery of corn, tomatoes, potatoes, and squash; the discovery of buffalo, mountain lions, and coyotes—the list could go on for pages. Unlike Europe, which contained no more wilderness, America was a land of mystery—the great unknown. The people who settled there became a nation of explorers, continually looking beyond the next river or hill for new adventures.

Geography: History's Stage

Any list of the most important discoveries in American history will share a central element: geography. Geography is the place where history happens. Just as the events of a play take place on a specially designed stage, the events of history occur in a specific geographic setting from which they cannot be separated.

Geography involves more than just the study of **landforms** such as mountains, plains, and valleys. In fact, geographers have divided their field into two main branches to take into account geography's varied concerns. **Physical geography** involves the study of the natural world, including the earth's climate, landforms, bodies of water, plants, animals, and resources. **Human geography**, on the other hand, explores how people and places influence one another. Someone interested in the human geography of a region, for instance, might look at the growth and movement of the population, the use of resources, land-use patterns, and the impact of such human-made objects as cities, reservoirs, dams, highways, mines, bridges, and canals.

Geography and American History

To understand American history, then, one must also have a solid grasp of the geography of North America. The briefest survey of U.S. history soon illustrates this point.

For example, geography was partly responsible for the variation in custom and lifestyle that distinguished American Indian societies from one another. Geography also influenced how North America was settled and the particular way in which the continent's population spread westward after 1492. In addition, geography played a role in determining why some towns grew and prospered while others failed.

Geography did more, however, than simply influence certain events and patterns of the nation's history. It also helped shape the character of the American people. Few Europeans knew what to expect when they came to America in the 1600s, and they were continually surprised by what

Mountain lions like the one pictured above were among the many new animals Europeans encountered in the New World.

The map below indicates the most significant physical regions of the United States.

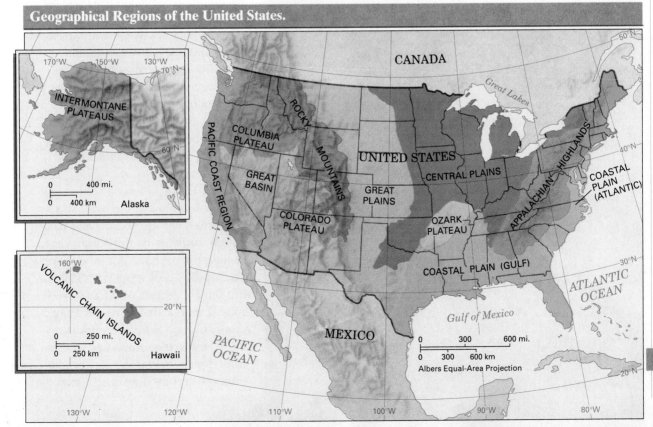

Geographical Regions of the United States.

INTERMONTANE PLATEAUS

0   400 mi.
0   400 km   Alaska

VOLCANIC CHAIN ISLANDS

0   250 mi.
0   250 km   Hawaii

CANADA

Great Lakes

PACIFIC COAST REGION

COLUMBIA PLATEAU

ROCKY MOUNTAINS

GREAT BASIN

UNITED STATES

GREAT PLAINS

CENTRAL PLAINS

COLORADO PLATEAU

OZARK PLATEAU

APPALACHIAN HIGHLANDS

COASTAL PLAIN (ATLANTIC)

COASTAL PLAIN (GULF)

ATLANTIC OCEAN

Gulf of Mexico

MEXICO

PACIFIC OCEAN

0   300   600 mi.
0   300   600 km
Albers Equal-Area Projection

they found here. Despite its rich and varied resources, the land proved a constant challenge to these new settlers, demanding all their courage, ingenuity, hard work and perseverance. It is not really surprising, therefore, that while learning to live in this new landscape, these settlers developed a strong sense of self-reliance and independence.

Above all, the sheer size and diversity of the American land amazed most newcomers from Europe. And while the vastness of the land was in one sense yet another challenge, it also fired the imaginations of those who chose to settle in the New World. Just as there seemed no limit to the land, there seemed no limit to the freedom and discoveries it promised. Or, as Archibald MacLeish put it in his 1938 poem, "Land of the Free": "We looked west from a rise and we saw forever." ■

■ *In what ways is geography important to the study of history?*

The Eastern and Southern United States

Three major physical regions dominate the eastern portion of the United States: the Atlantic and Gulf Coastal Plains, the Piedmont, and the Appalachian Highlands. Stretching from Maine to Texas, these regions include the original 13 colonies that eventually became the United States.

As you read further in this lesson, refer regularly to the physical map of the United States on pages 700–701 in the Atlas. Refer also to the climate and vegetation maps on page 706 and the precipitation and land use maps on page 707.

Coastal Plains

From Maine southward, the Atlantic seaboard has a steadily widening coastal plain. Much of the immediate coast is low-lying and swampy, with many offshore islands. Further inland, the coastal plain is a bit higher and better drained.

The jagged shoreline of the east coast contains many natural harbors. In addition, a rise in sea level centuries ago formed numerous **estuaries**, or submerged river mouths, which also provide excellent shelter for ships. Two of the most important of these estuaries are the Chesapeake and Delaware bays.

The Europeans who settled the eastern seaboard in the early 1600s stayed close to the coast. Their chief reason for living by the ocean was to be near the harbors that brought people, supplies, and news from Europe. But the abundance of sea life in coastal waters also provided a steady supply of food for these settlers.

A low, flat continuation of the coastal plain begins in Florida and extends through the South, along the

▼ *Early settlers from Europe made their homes along the Atlantic seaboard. Pictured below is the rocky coast of Maine.*

Gulf of Mexico, to Texas. This area was the site of many Spanish settlements in the 16th and 17th centuries. Although similar to the plain along the Atlantic seaboard, the Gulf Coastal Plain is lower and swampier and contains fewer excellent harbors.

The Piedmont

Inland from the coastal plain lies the "Upper Country," or Piedmont ("foot of the mountains"), as it was later named. This rolling, hilly area—running from New Jersey to Alabama—forms a transition between the plains to the east and the mountains to the west. The place where the harder rocks of the Piedmont meet the softer coastal plain was the former Atlantic shoreline, referred to as the "fall line." The streams flowing out of the hills onto the flat plain produce small waterfalls, which early settlers turned into a source of energy by building waterwheels.

The Appalachian Highlands

West of the Piedmont is the most prominent feature of the eastern section of the country. The Appalachian Highlands, as this region is called, extend from northern Alabama to Maine. At first these mountains were thought to be a barrier to communication and movement, but frontiersmen found "gaps," such as the Cumberland Gap in Kentucky, through which west-

ward movement took place.

A northern section of the Appalachians covers much of New England, meeting the Atlantic Coast in Maine. Because the thin, stony soil was poor for farming, New England's economy depended more on trade and fishing than agriculture in colonial times.

Climate

The Europeans who settled the eastern section of North America encountered greater extremes of temperature than they were accustomed to in Europe. The summers were longer and much hotter, while the winters were colder and harsher.

The entire east coast was said to

The Appalachian Mountains made western expansion difficult for the English colonists.

A low coastal plain and wet climate have created many swamps in the southeastern United States. Alligators like the one shown below populate many of these swamps.

▲ *Black bears were a common sight in the forests of the eastern United States in the 1600s and 1700s.*

➤ *Deer provided the early settlers with an important source of food.*

■ *What are the main geographic features of the eastern and southern United States?*

be "well watered," meaning that there was adequate and dependable rainfall. While western Europe received **precipitation**, or rainfall, in fairly even amounts throughout the year, the settlers found heavier precipitation in the warmer months, coinciding with the growing season.

The further south you go along the eastern seaboard of the United States, the warmer the climate becomes and the milder the winters. The Gulf Coast Plain has a humid subtropical climate. The weather there is hotter and rainier than that found along the Atlantic coast. These conditions provide a longer growing season for such crops as cotton.

Vegetation and Wildlife

Forests were the dominant vegetation in the eastern and southern United States in the early 1600s. Plentiful lumber made the log cabin the most practical form of housing for many settlers. Coniferous, or needleleaf, trees such as cedar, spruce, and pine mixed with deciduous, or leaf-shedding,

hardwoods such as elm, oak, maple, ash, and hickory in the colder north. Broadleaf hardwoods were dominant in the middle section of the eastern seaboard and gradually gave way to pines and cypress along the sandy southern coasts. Thicker, tropical vegetation thrived in the swamps of the Gulf Coast.

The first settlers went to work clearing thousands of acres of land for their farms. Despite the massive amounts of land clearing that occurred in the 17th and 18th centuries, new forests now cover large portions of the eastern and southern United States that were once farmland.

In the same way that the rich sea life in the Atlantic attracted people to the coast, the abundant wildlife in the forests soon drew many settlers further inland. French and Dutch fur traders were the first to venture westward in search of beaver, mink, and otter. They soon discovered that the eastern forests of the New World were teeming with such wildlife as black bears, deer, moose, foxes, wildcats, and muskrats. ■

The Central Heartland

In the 1700s, the first brave settlers pushed their way westward over the Appalachian Mountains into present-day Kentucky, Ohio, and Indiana. Eventually some of these settlers moved farther west to what is now Indiana and Illinois. What they found

was the enormous plain that forms the central heartland of America. Most of this plain consisted of **prairie**, an expanse of flat or rolling grassland.

Writer Washington Irving captured the landscape of the prairie in his 1835 book *A Tour on the Prairies:*

*A*fter a toilsome march of some distance through a country cut up by ravines and brooks, and entangled by thickets, we emerged upon a grand prairie. Here one of the characteristic scenes of the Far West broke upon us. An immense extent of grassy, undulating, or, as it is termed, rolling country, with here and there a clump of trees, dimly seen in the distance like a ship at sea; the landscape deriving sublimity (majesty) from its vastness and simplicity.

The Central and Great Plains

From the Appalachians westward to the Rockies lies the region drained by the Mississippi River system. Geographers generally divide this great interior plain into two areas: the Central Plains in the east and the Great Plains in the west.

The early explorers of the Central Plains either came north from the mouth of the Mississippi River or south from the Great Lakes. What they discovered was a huge expanse of rolling grasslands that rose gradually toward the forested foothills of the Appalachian Mountains in the east.

The south-central portion of the Central Plains is interrupted by the Ozark Mountains, which cover a wide area of present-day Arkansas and Missouri. The northern reaches of this interior region are occupied by the Great Lakes, the enormous water system that allowed early explorers and traders to penetrate the interior.

Like the Central Plains, the Great Plains are an enormous expanse of grassland, though they are bleaker and emptier than the eastern prairies. From their starting point in the western sections of the Dakotas, Nebraska, and Kansas, the Great Plains rise gradually to meet the Rocky Mountains in the west. Stretching from North Dakota to Texas, the Great Plains are briefly interrupted in South Dakota by a series of steep hills and gullies known as the Badlands.

Climate

The climate of the central heartlands is a climate of extremes. In the summer, temperatures often top 100° F. In the winter, they may drop as low as -40° F. The distance of the plains from any oceans, which have a moderating influence on weather patterns, is largely responsible for these extreme temperatures.

The average annual rainfall in the Central Plains is moderate, though it is less plentiful than that found along the Atlantic seaboard. To the west of the Mississippi, however, the amount of rainfall diminishes steadily. Rainfall

▼ *Coyotes like the one shown below roamed the tall grasslands of the prairies long before the first Europeans arrived on the scene.*

in the Great Plains is so limited that parts of that region are semidesert.

Vegetation and Wildlife

The humid, wetter areas just west of the Appalachians supported forests of broadleaf hardwoods. The Great Lakes territory and the Ozark Highlands were also heavily forested. But starting in Indiana and Illinois, the forests gave way to grasslands.

The first pioneers who saw the prairies described them as a "sea of grass." This description particularly suited the prairies of the Central Plains, which received sufficient rainfall to support a lush cover of tall grass that was often higher than a horse's back. In addition, the streams and rivers of the eastern plains were lined in many places with trees.

To the west, the limited moisture of the Great Plains provided only enough moisture for shorter grasses, one to two feet high. But these "buffalo" grasses, as the early settlers called them, played a crucial role in the environment of the plains. By holding the soil in place, they kept the Great Plains from becoming a real desert.

Early visitors to the prairies did not realize the rich agricultural potential of these grasslands. In addition, the wooden plow of that time was not capable of cutting through the thick root system of the grasses. The invention of the steel plow in the 1830s enabled the pioneers of that era to subdue and farm the land of the Central Plains. Even the Great Plains, once called the "Great American Desert," became prime grazing land for cattle and a major producer of wheat in the late 1800s.

Before 1800, the American bison, or buffalo, roamed as far east as Ohio and Kentucky. As late as the 1870s, millions of buffalo still crowded the western plains, along with a number of other forms of wildlife unique to that region. The pronghorn (American antelope), prairie dog, ground squirrel, jack rabbit, coyote, mountain lion, and wolf were some of the wildlife encountered by pioneers on their western journeys. ■

The American West

The American West, or Far West as it is sometimes called, contains three major physical regions: the Rocky Mountains, the Intermountain region, and the Pacific Coast. It also contains some of the most dramatic and varied landscape in the United States.

The Rocky Mountains

Running more than 3,000 miles, north and south, through the United States and Canada, the Rocky Mountains cover parts of New Mexico, Colorado, Utah, Wyoming, Idaho, Montana, Washington, and Alaska. They were long seen as an immense barrier between the eastern two-thirds of the United States and the western coast. Tall and rugged, the Rockies contain 52 peaks that are higher than 14,000 feet. Crossing these mountains created many hardships for pioneers in the 1800s.

The crest of the Rockies forms an important dividing line on the North

American continent. Called the Continental Divide, this ridge separates rivers that flow east into the Mississippi and the Gulf of Mexico—the Missouri, the Arkansas, the Platte, the Rio Grande—from those that flow west into the Pacific Ocean—the Colorado and the Columbia.

The Intermountain Region

The Intermountain region, as the area between the Rockies and the Sierra Nevada is sometimes called, contains high plateaus and basins, deep canyons, and wide deserts. The largest and most important geographical areas in the Intermountain region are the Great Basin and the Colorado Plateau.

Although the term basin often applies to a low-relief, low-elevation landscape, such is not the case with the Great Basin, whose average elevation is 4,000–5,000 feet above sea level. Located as it is between the Rocky Mountains on the east and the even taller Sierra Nevada on the west, however, the Great Basin does have the appearance of an enormous bowl.

Because the region is an interior basin, rivers flowing into the Great Basin from the surrounding mountains have no outlet to the ocean. As a result, these streams either dry up, disappear underground, or flow into lakes that become salty. The most famous of these lakes is Great Salt Lake in Utah.

A **plateau** is an area of high, flat land. One of the largest plateaus in the United States is the Colorado Plateau, which includes much of Arizona, parts of Utah, and smaller areas of Colorado and New Mexico. Long the home of the Hopi, Navajo, and Zuni Indians, this region was later settled by the Spanish and Mexicans.

Rugged deserts and deep canyons make up most of the land in the Colorado Plateau. Among the most famous natural features of the region are the Grand Canyon of the Colorado River and the Painted Desert.

The Pacific Coast

Unlike the eastern seaboard, the Pacific Coast contains few natural harbors. But with its rugged coastline and nearby mountain ranges, it does possess some of the most dramatic scenery in North America.

Apart from a break at San Francisco Bay, the mountains of the Coastal Ranges run parallel to the coast from central California through Oregon to Washington state. Further inland are the much higher peaks of the Klamath Mountains and the Sierra Nevada in California, and the Cascades in California, Oregon, and Washington. The most important rivers in the region—the Columbia, the Sacramento, the San Joaquin, and

Across Time & Space

Today the states in the Great Plains produce more wheat than any other region in the world. In addition to being the "breadbasket" of the United States, this area provides wheat to many other nations as well.

▼ *The Rocky Mountains proved to be a serious obstacle for pioneers traveling west. The region is still rich in wildlife such as the elk pictured below.*

Although the Pacific Coast contains many dramatic cliffs and beautiful beaches, it has few natural harbors.

Seals are among the most common form of marine life found in the waters off the California coast.

the Colorado—are important sources of water and water power. The Grand Coulee Dam on the Columbia River and the Hoover Dam on the Colorado produce a large portion of the region's electrical power.

The other significant landform in the region is the great Central Valley of California. This valley runs more than half the length of the state. Many of California's early settlers chose the rich land of the Central Valley for their new home.

Climate

The highlands climate of the Rocky Mountains is characterized by cool, short summers and cold winters. Rainfall varies with elevation, with the higher elevations receiving heavy amounts of precipitation.

The chief climatic feature of the Intermountain region is the lack of rainfall. In fact, roughly half of the land in this area is actual desert, more suitable for mining than for agriculture. Temperature ranges from summer to winter are extreme throughout the region, particularly in the Great Basin.

Much of California has a Mediterranean climate, with mild, wet winters, and sunny, dry summers. Since it mirrored the weather patterns of Spain, this climate was especially attractive to Spanish settlers.

The Pacific Northwest, which includes northern California and the Oregon and Washington coasts, has what is known as a marine climate. Although this climate is cooler and wetter than that of central and southern California, it is also much milder than the climate of New England.

Vegetation and Wildlife

The lower slopes of the Rocky Mountains are covered with junipers, piñon pines, and aspen. At higher elevations, coniferous forests of fir, pine, and spruce flourish. Above a certain point called the "tree line," however, the climate is too harsh to support trees.

Because of the lack of rainfall there, the vegetation of the Great Basin is sparse. Plant life consists mainly of scrub, broken here and there by occasional patches of steppe grasses. Trees are rare and are confined to narrow strips along riverbanks.

In addition to scrub, sagebrush,

and mesquite trees, the deserts of the Colorado Plateau support a variety of species of cactus. During dry periods, the vegetation of the desert is sparse. But after a rainfall, colorful flowers and lush vegetation may cover parts of the desert for a brief period.

The Pacific Coast supports a wide variety of plant life. In the southern sections of California, for example, tropical plants such as palm trees thrive. In the Central Valley, on the other hand, Mediterranean crops such as grapes and olives have replaced the earlier cover of short grasses. Scrub vegetation and coniferous forests of fir and redwoods cover the mountains of the Coastal Ranges, while coniferous forests of fir and pine are the rule in the higher Sierra Nevada and Cascades. The thick forests of the Pacific Northwest are a major source of timber for the United States.

The American West contains numerous forms of wildlife that are not found elsewhere on the continent. The Rocky Mountains, for example, serve as the home for grizzly bears, wild goats, and longhorn sheep. The deserts of the American southwest contain such wildlife as roadrunners, peccaries (wild pigs), kangaroo rats, Gila monsters, and many other species of birds and lizards that are unique to the desert. Columbian black-tailed deer and Roosevelt elk are unique to the Pacific Coast. The rich marine life of the west coast includes salmon, abalones, otters, and sea lions.

In the mid-1800s, thousands of pioneers traveling west thought of the Pacific Coast as a kind of promised land. Just two centuries earlier, many Europeans viewed the eastern seaboard of North America in exactly the same way. In the late 1400s, however, most Europeans did not even dream, let alone know, of the existence of a New World far to their west. America was still a wilderness land waiting to be discovered. ■

▲ *The jack rabbit, shown left, and the cactus, shown above, are two of the most distinctive features of the American desert.*

■ *What are the main geographic features of the western United States?*

R E V I E W

1. **FOCUS** How does the geography of the United States vary from one part of the nation to another?

2. **GEOGRAPHY** In what kinds of events or objects would a human geographer be interested?

3. **GEOGRAPHY** How did geography influence the way the eastern section of the United States was settled?

4. **CRITICAL THINKING** Look at the population density map for 1980 on page 705 in the Atlas. How did geography contribute to the creation of both the most densely and least densely populated regions of the United States?

5. **WRITING ACTIVITY** Imagine you are a pioneer who has moved from New England to the Great Plains. Write a journal entry in which you compare your new life to your old and explain how it is influenced by geography.

Environment or Energy

T he facts point to the urgent need to open 1.5 million acres of the Coastal Plain of the Arctic National Wildlife Refuge [ANWR] to exploration. The facts also highlight the industry's ability to develop arctic oil in an environmentally sound manner.

Oil Company Publication,
Winter 1989

I f we're going to develop this [the ANWR coastal plain] we might as well go ahead and dam the Grand Canyon. You can make the same arguments for national energy needs. So why don't we? Because the nation has decided it's in its own best interest to preserve the Grand Canyon and find our energy elsewhere.

Tim Mahoney, "An Arctic Dilemma,"
National Geographic, December 1980

Background

▼ *Environmentalists say that exploration of the coastal plain could harm the habitats of wildlife such as the Dall sheep.*

The wild and remote lands of northeast Alaska are home to a variety of wildlife—grizzly bears, wolverines, Dall sheep, foxes, moose, and North America's largest caribou herd.

These lands are also the summer nesting places of snowy owls, peregrine falcons, golden eagles, and many other birds.

In 1960, to protect the wildlife in this unspoiled region, Congress set aside 8.9 million acres as the Arctic National Wildlife Range. Twenty years later, in 1980, Congress added 10 million acres to the protected area, and renamed it the Arctic National Wildlife Refuge (ANWR). Congress also said that 1.5 million acres of the refuge could be studied as a possible source of oil and gas. The area to be studied was the coastal plain—the flat, marshy land between the rugged mountains of the Brooks Range and the Arctic Ocean.

In early 1987, the U.S. Department of the Interior released the results of a six-year study of the ANWR coastal plain. Their report stated that the region might contain as much as 9.2 billion barrels of oil.

Conflict Over the Land

The report recommended beginning oil exploration as soon as possible, and touched off a heated debate between oil companies and environmentalists. Producers argue that the nation needs the energy and that the ANWR region is the most promising oil exploration site in the country. Developing the site, they say, would eliminate the need to purchase imported oil. It would also help the Alaskan economy by bringing in money and jobs. They cite polls showing that most Alaskans want to develop the state's mineral resources.

Environmentalists argue that oil drilling would be harmful to the environment, destroy wildlife habitats, and disturb the fragile balance of the Alaskan wilderness. The oil industry cannot be trusted to protect the environment, they say, pointing to the oil spills that happened around the world, despite the industry's assurances that such events will not happen.

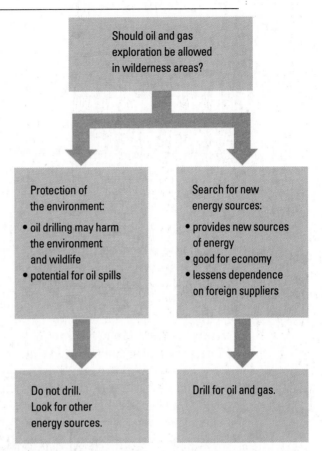

Should oil and gas exploration be allowed in wilderness areas?

Protection of the environment:
- oil drilling may harm the environment and wildlife
- potential for oil spills

Search for new energy sources:
- provides new sources of energy
- good for economy
- lessens dependence on foreign suppliers

Do not drill. Look for other energy sources.

Drill for oil and gas.

Decision Point

1. What are the benefits of drilling for oil on the coastal plain?
2. What are the benefits of leaving the coastal plain undisturbed?
3. If you were going to vote on whether drilling should be allowed on the coastal plain, what other information would you want?
4. What alternatives to drilling can you think of that would be good for the economy and less harmful to the environment? Discuss this question in small groups, then report to your class.

◄ *Oil producers believe that the ANWR region offers the most promising oil exploration site in the United States.*

L E S S O N   2

European Exploration and Settlement

THINKING
F O C U S

Why did Europeans leave their homes in the 1500s and 1600s to explore and settle new continents?

Key Terms

- navigation
- conquistador
- sect

Thunderclouds rise like mountains off to the east. The once calm ocean has suddenly grown restless, loudly thumping the ship's prow.

You're crossing the Atlantic Ocean in the mid-1500s. Nearby you can hear the crew member on watch calling out worried instructions to the man at the helm. Already the sky has turned black, and the seas begin to run high. Suddenly the storm erupts. You witness a wild fury you've never seen before in nature.

Indeed, dangerous storms were just one of the hardships facing the brave women and men who left Europe in search of new lives in a New World. They came in boats not much longer than your classroom. The ships had weak rigging and small hulls. To plot their course, sailors depended on simple navigational equipment such as the astro-labe, an instrument used to calculate the position of the sun and stars. Conditions on board these early ships were not pleasant. A Spanish priest named Father Thomas de la Torre, who made the long voyage to America in 1544, described his experience in this way:

> We soon realized that the sea was not man's natural habitat. Everyone became so seasick that nothing in the world could induce us to move from where we lay. A more befouled hospital and one so filled with the moans of the sick can hardly be imagined. Some sufferers were cooked alive in the heat below decks. The sun roasted others, where they were trod upon and trampled, and where they were so filthy that words cannot describe the scene. . . .

Europeans Look to New Worlds

Despite the hardships of the two-month Atlantic crossing, Europeans made it their business to stretch the boundaries of their world. The hunger for new lands came in many forms and for many reasons.

First of all, a revival of classical art, literature, and learning known as the Renaissance *(REHN i sahns)*, was taking place in Europe in the 15th and 16th centuries. It sparked people's imaginations and made them more eager to explore the world around them. At roughly the same time there was a revolution in religion known as the Protestant Reformation. This movement challenged the Catholic religious authorities, who in turn persecuted the Protestants. The Protestants longed for a place where they could worship as they thought best.

Several European nations also began to form strong, stable governments during this period. Spain, Portugal, France, England, and the Netherlands gradually resolved internal power struggles that had weakened and preoccupied them. They also gathered the wealth, ships, and armies needed to take ambitious leaps into new worlds.

All of these nations were interested in finding quicker routes to Asia in order to take advantage of the rich trade with that continent. They got help from new developments in sea travel. The Portuguese designed a more maneuverable ship called the *caravel,* shown below. Larger than earlier ships, a caravel had sails that allowed it to move both with and against the wind. The caravels sailed under the command of men who had an improved understanding of **navigation,** or the charting of a course at sea. Instruments such as the astrolabe, the quadrant, and the cross-staff helped sailors to navigate on long voyages. ■

◄ *Until the invention of the sextant, navigators relied on the astrolabe, shown at left, to measure the angle of the stars above the horizon and to determine the exact location of their ships.*

■ *What historical events and developments led Europeans to explore the world beyond their borders?*

Spain Leads the Way

Even more than the desire for exploration, the search for wealth turned Spain into the leading nation of what is now called the Age of Discovery. Spanish rulers and merchants desperately wanted to find a way around the land routes to Asia. They had become tired of paying the middlemen who were raking large profits from overland caravans to the Far East. They desired not only exotic goods such as gold, silk, and jewels, but also Asian spices to enhance their plain European diet.

Some people thought there might be a better and faster way to Asia. One of them was an Italian named Christopher Columbus.

Columbus Stumbles on a New World

Many educated people in the 1400s knew that the world was round. Christopher Columbus set out to prove this fact to those Europeans who still had doubts. First he tried to persuade the rulers of Portugal, France, and England to provide the men and ships needed to make a trip to Asia. When they turned him down, he moved to Spain, where he took his case to the Spanish court. Here, too, he almost gave up. But after six years of indecision, Queen Isabella agreed to arrange an expedition for the 41-year-old navigator.

Two of Columbus's ships—the Nina and the Pinta—were only 50 feet long. The flagship, the Santa Maria, was much larger but less maneuverable. In all, 90 men went on the voyage. Favorable winds carried them westward from the time they set sail on August 3, 1492.

After two months at sea, Columbus's men became restless. Because he feared mutiny, Columbus concealed from his men the distance they

Sebastiano del Piombo painted this famous portrait of Christopher Columbus after the explorer's death.

➤ *Conquistador Hernando Cortés presented this Aztec sculpture, a double-headed snake made of turquoise mosaic, to Emperor Charles V of Spain.*

in 1493, 1498, and 1502—Columbus never learned that it wasn't India he had reached, but a New World.

Seekers of Gold and Glory

Columbus' discovery set off a wave of exploration. As the map on page 19 shows, other daring explorers were soon following in his wake, drawn by the promise of wealth and fame. Along the way, these explorers made some exciting new discoveries.

In 1499, an Italian merchant named Amerigo Vespucci *(vehs POOT chee)* made the first of two voyages to the New World. Vespucci soon realized that the land he had explored was not Asia but "a very great continent, until [now] unknown." A few years later a map-maker named this new continent "America" in Vespucci's honor.

Vasco Núñez de Balboa, a Spanish explorer, confirmed Vespucci's conclusion in 1513. That year Balboa led a party across the Isthmus of Panama, the narrow strip of land connecting North and South America. After weeks of hacking through thick rain forest, Balboa emerged on a cliff and became the first European to look out upon the Pacific Ocean.

The discoveries explorers made were often accidental. Explorers were more interested in acquiring gold and power than in finding new lands. New World or old, they were set on plundering it. Armed with swords, firearms, and lances, these Spanish **conquistadors** *(kohn KEES tah dohrs)*, or conquerors, subdued whole civilizations of native peoples.

had traveled. Finally, he agreed that if they did not reach Asia in three days, he would turn back.

On the third day, they sighted land. Columbus mistakenly believed that the land they had reached was India, so he called the native people he found there Indians. In reality, he had landed on an island in the Bahamas that he named San Salvador. On October 12, 1492, the Spanish flag was hoisted and flew over San Salvador. Although he returned three times—

The most famous of the Spanish conquistadors was Hernando Cortés *(kohr TESS)*, who in 1519 marched into the interior of Mexico with 600 men. There he found a thriving civilization with huge pyramids in its elaborate capital city, Tenochtitlán *(tay noch tee TLAHN)*. More than 150,000 people lived in the Aztec capital, which was larger than any Spanish city at that time. The emperor Montezuma ruled over these people. In a few short years, Cortés used his superior arms and the discontent of many of Montezuma's subjects to destroy much of Tenochtitlán and topple the Aztec empire.

Another Spanish conqueror, Francisco Pizarro, led 180 men southward into the heart of Peru in 1531. Pizarro soon captured the Incas' ruler, Atahualpa, and by 1535 had brought down the entire Incan empire.

A steady stream of explorers and warriors followed these early conquistadors. They were men bent on conquest and the discovery of gold. Focusing first on Central and South America, they eventually reached as far as the southern regions of North America.

Two such Spanish explorers were Francisco Vásquez de Coronado, and Hernando de Soto. On an expedition through the American Southwest in 1540–1542, Coronado discovered the Grand Canyon. De Soto explored what is now the southern United States and was the first European to reach the Mississippi River.

Although their names and discoveries live on in romantic stories, most of the conquistadors acted ruthlessly in their search for riches and power. They treated the native inhabitants of America cruelly, enslaving them and often killing them. The conquistadors left a trail of slaughter as they searched for lost cities of gold. Nobody ever found a single city of gold, but the silver and gold the conquistadors did find—and the sugar they grew—made them and Spain fabulously wealthy. At the same time, they opened up a vast area for Spanish settlement. ■

■ *What was the chief motive of Spanish explorers in going to the New World?*

▼ *As the exploration map below illustrates, geography played a key role in determining the pattern of European exploration. Explorers from southern Europe tended to focus on Central and South America, while explorers from northern Europe tended to concentrate on North America.*

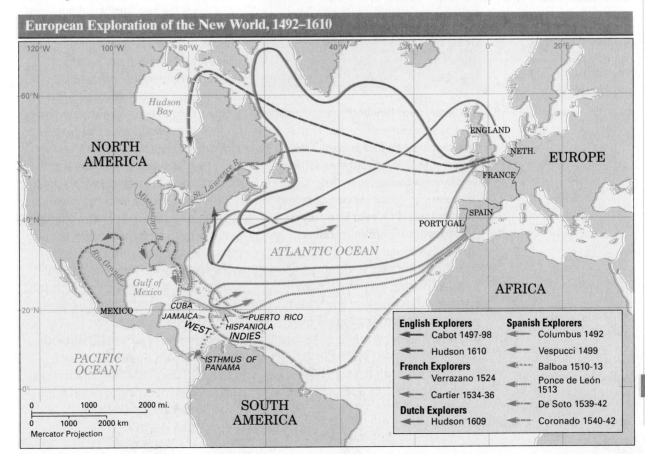

European Exploration of the New World, 1492–1610

English Explorers	Spanish Explorers
← Cabot 1497-98	← Columbus 1492
← Hudson 1610	← Vespucci 1499
French Explorers	← Balboa 1510-13
← Verrazano 1524	← Ponce de León 1513
← Cartier 1534-36	← De Soto 1539-42
Dutch Explorers	← Coronado 1540-42
← Hudson 1609	

NORTH AMERICA

EUROPE

ENGLAND

NETH.

FRANCE

SPAIN

PORTUGAL

AFRICA

ATLANTIC OCEAN

Hudson Bay

St. Lawrence R.

Mississippi R.

Rio Grande

Gulf of Mexico

MEXICO

CUBA

JAMAICA

WEST INDIES

PUERTO RICO

HISPANIOLA

ISTHMUS OF PANAMA

PACIFIC OCEAN

SOUTH AMERICA

0   1000   2000 mi.

0   1000   2000 km

Mercator Projection

19

England, France, and the Netherlands Stake Claims

Spain had caught the rest of the world napping. Most of Europe was too entangled in its own internal problems to conquer new worlds. But Spain's growing power made the rest of Europe nervous—especially England, a Protestant nation and Catholic Spain's chief rival. Spain might soon take over most of the New World, leaving no room for other nations to stake a claim.

➤ *This engraving shows John Cabot somewhere off the coast of Canada during his 1497 voyage.*

The Search for the Northwest Passage

Like the Spanish, other Europeans wanted to find a quick trade route to Asia. They hoped to find a Northwest Passage, a northern waterway connecting the Atlantic Ocean and the Pacific Ocean. Even after they knew more about the New World, European explorers kept on searching for a northern shortcut to Asia. As late as 1847, the British explorer John Franklin and all his men died while trying to find their way through the Northwest Passage. But it was not until 1906 that the first successful trip through the frozen waters north of Canada occurred.

A Series of Discoveries

England's first exploration had limited results. John Cabot, an Italian working for the English king, sailed to Newfoundland and Nova Scotia in 1497. Cabot found waters teeming with fish, highly valuable in Europe. However, England was too preoccupied with internal affairs to take advantage of his discoveries.

Two explorers, Giovanni da Verrazano of Italy and Jacques Cartier *(kahr tee YAY)* of France, voyaged even farther than Cabot. In 1524, Verrazano explored the eastern coastline of North America from what is now North Carolina to Newfoundland. Eleven years later, in 1535, Cartier explored the Gulf of St. Lawrence. His discovery of the St. Lawrence River on a second voyage marked the beginning of France's dominance of the territory that later became Canada.

Henry Hudson, an Englishman, made several trips to the New World. On a 1609 voyage for the Dutch, Hudson found the river now named after him. His discovery planted the seeds of New Netherland, the powerful Dutch settlement in what is now New York. On later voyages for the English, Hudson discovered two more bodies of water that bear his name: Hudson's Strait and Hudson's Bay.

Hudson's desire to find a Northwest Passage led to his downfall. After a long, hard winter, during which Hudson's ship became trapped in the ice, his men mutinied. When they broke free from the ice in June 1611, the crew set Hudson, his son John, and seven other sailors adrift without food in a tiny boat. Hudson and his party were never seen again.

Explorers blaze paths. But if the lands are promising, settlers soon move in. This pattern of exploration and settlement is exactly what happened in North America. ■

■ *Why did European nations other than Spain begin sending explorers to the New World?*

Europeans Settle the New World

Many problems in Europe drove people to seek a new life across the ocean in the late 1500s and early 1600s. A new spurt in population growth crowded European cities. Religious intolerance led to the persecution of minority **sects,** small religious groups that had separated from larger denominations. In addition, changing economic conditions had left many people without jobs or land.

Thus, when news of a new continent with limitless opportunities spread throughout Europe, many people responded. Despite the dangers and uncertainties, Europeans began to leave their homelands—first in a trickle and then in a steady stream—to begin a challenging life in the New World. The map below shows where they settled.

Spanish Settlements

Spain was the first nation to settle the New World, and it had been the first to conquer parts of it. Following the conquistadors, Spanish missionaries brought their religious faith to the New World. These Catholic priests established missions in South America, Central America, and Mexico in the 1500s. During the next two centuries they expanded their activities into the American Southwest and West. The Spanish priests forced many American Indians into labor and

◄ *Compare the map at left with the European exploration map on page 19. Notice that European nations tended to settle those areas of the New World where they had originally sent explorers.*

Settlements in the New World, 1650

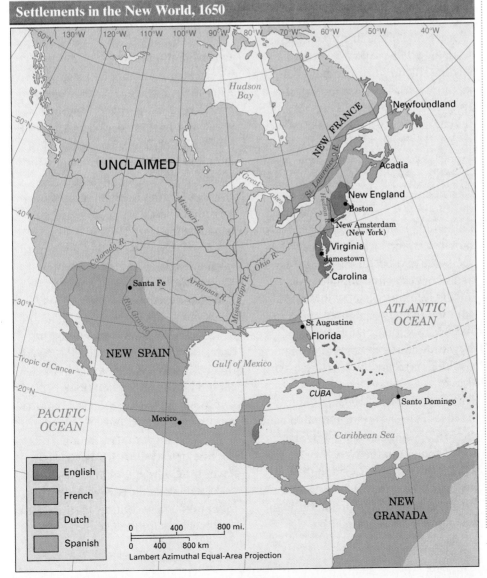

English
French
Dutch
Spanish

0   400   800 mi.
0   400   800 km
Lambert Azimuthal Equal-Area Projection

Early Spanish and English settlements differed greatly in physical appearance. On these two pages are shown the English settlement at Jamestown (facing page) and the Spanish mission at San Carlos de Rio Carmelo (above).

taught them Christianity. The missions became the centers of the Spanish settlements.

The Spanish established armed presidios, or forts, wherever they needed to defend their claims to new lands. But the Spanish mission played a larger role in the history of Spanish settlement. The man who played a leading role in starting many of these missions was Padre Junípero Serra, a Franciscan friar. Serra lived among the Indians in Baja California for twenty years. Then he journeyed into Alta (upper) California, establishing missions along the way and teaching Christianity. Serra started nine missions between San Diego and San Francisco before retiring to his mission at Carmel, New Spain, in 1784.

Serra and his fellow missionaries had strong religious motives for making the journey to the New World. In addition to converting thousands of American Indians, they also paved the way for Spanish settlement of Mexico and what is today the American West.

French and Dutch Settlements

The French settlers who first came to North America hoped to make their fortunes in the New World. They sought the fish that swam in the waters of the western Atlantic and the furs of animals that scurried through the dense inland forests. Like the Spanish, the French taught Christianity, but their settlements were trading posts and forts rather than missions. These settlements sprang up along the St. Lawrence River. Later the French expanded into the Great Lakes region and the Mississippi River Valley.

Following in the wake of Henry Hudson's 1609 voyage, the Dutch came to establish a powerful colony in what is now New York State. Settling first on Manhattan Island in 1623, the Dutch established the city of New Amsterdam there. By offering large tracts of land to anyone who brought fifty or more settlers with them, the Dutch soon built up a sprawling colony which extended up the Hudson River Valley to the present-day city of Albany. They called this colony New Netherland. The Dutch held New Netherland until the English fleet seized the colony in 1664.

English Settlements

An early attempt by England to establish a settlement in the New World resulted in one of history's great unsolved mysteries. In 1584, Sir Walter Raleigh received permission from Queen Elizabeth to found a colony on Roanoke Island off the coast of North Carolina. Raleigh sent a group of settlers to colonize the island in 1587.

Unfortunately, Spain's attempt to invade England in 1588 prevented Raleigh from sending supplies to this new colony for nearly three years. When a ship finally reached Roanoke in 1590, the settlers were gone. The only clue to their disappearance was the word *CROATOAN* that had been carved on the door post of the ruined fort. Some people speculated that the settlers had fled to another island or had joined the Croatan Indians. But the fate of the "Lost Colony" was never discovered.

England's first permanent settlement in the new continent was small and nearly as ill-fated as the Roanoke

Colony. The settlement of Jamestown survived, but at a great cost in human suffering.

On May 14, 1607, native inhabitants of what is now Virginia saw the first permanent European settlers heave their boats up onto the beaches of Jamestown Island. These colonists had come seeking economic gain. However, the settlement they founded, Jamestown, sat in marshy land that was not only poor farmland but was also a breeding ground for malaria-carrying mosquitoes.

As a result of malnutrition and disease, only 32 of the 105 original settlers at Jamestown survived the first seven months. To make matters worse, relations with surrounding American Indians quickly deteriorated, often as a result of harsh treatment by the new white settlers. Almost the entire colony perished in "the starving time" during the winter of 1609–1610.

During the next twenty years, the Jamestown settlers scratched out a living for themselves, endured hostile Indian attacks, and struggled with deadly diseases. By the 1630s, they had established a successful colony, where tobacco provided enough cash return to keep the settlement going.

Keeping the first settlement in New England going proved almost as difficult. Half of the passengers who sailed from England on the Mayflower perished during the first hard winter of 1620–1621. Unlike the colonists at Jamestown, the Pilgrims had come to the rocky shores of Massachusetts to escape religious persecution. But the conditions they faced were every bit as harsh as those that had confronted the settlers at Jamestown.

The Pilgrim settlement at Plymouth did survive, but it was eventually absorbed by the far larger Puritan settlement to its north. The Puritans left England in eleven ships with roughly one thousand prospective settlers in 1630, searching for a place to establish a strict religious community. By 1642, about 12,000 of them had settled in the Massachusetts Bay Colony in the general area where the city of Boston now lies. They, too, faced death in their first winter, and they struggled to keep a community alive as well. But, like Jamestown, the Puritan settlement in Massachusetts took root, flourished, and grew steadily. With each passing year, more and more Europeans came to the strange new continent and made it their home. ■

▲ *Founded in 1607, Jamestown (shown above) was the first successful English settlement in North America.*

■ *What factors led English settlers to leave their home for the New World?*

REVIEW

1. **FOCUS** Why did Europeans leave their homes in the 1500s and 1600s to explore and settle new continents?

2. **CONNECT** How did the geography of the New World frustrate early European explorers in their attempts to find a new trade route to East Asia?

3. **GEOGRAPHY** If land routes to Asia had been shorter and safer, would the Age of Discovery have occurred sooner or later than it did?

4. **CRITICAL THINKING** Judging from their behavior, what can you infer about the way the Spanish conquistadors viewed the native inhabitants of the Americas?

5. **ACTIVITY** Imagine you are a European farm laborer in the mid-1600s. Years of bad crops have left you with no work. Make a list of the pros and cons of leaving your homeland.

The Seven Devils Mountains

An American Indian Legend

The Seven Devils Gorge acts as part of the border between Oregon and Idaho. The high peaks along the Idaho side of the gorge are called the Seven Devils Mountains. Caleb Whitman, a Nez Perce on the Umatilla Reservation, told the legend of these mountains to Ella E. Clark, the editor of a collection of Indian legends, in 1950. Legends are passed from generation to generation and belong to the long oral heritage of the Indians. Do you have stories that have been passed down to you that reveal something about your family?

As you read in Lesson 2, there were dozens of different American Indian cultures in North America at the time of European settlement. Each of these Indian cultures had its own myths and legends, one of which is reprinted here.

*L*ong, long ago, when the world was very young, seven giant brothers lived in the Blue Mountains. These giant monsters were taller than the tallest pines and stronger than the strongest oaks.

The ancient people feared these brothers greatly because they ate children. Each year the brothers traveled eastward and devoured all the little ones they could find. Mothers fled with their children and hid them, but still many were seized by the giants. The headmen in the villages feared that the tribe would soon be wiped out. But no one was big enough and strong enough to fight with seven giants at a time.

At last the headmen of the tribe decided to ask Coyote to help them. "Coyote is our friend," they said. "He has defeated other monsters. He will free us from the seven giants."

So they sent a messenger to Coyote. "Yes, I will help you," he promised. "I will free you from the seven giants."

But Coyote really did not know what to do. He had fought with giants. He had fought with monsters of the lakes and the rivers. But he knew he could not defeat seven giants at one time. So he asked his good friend Fox for advice.

"We will first dig seven holes," said his good friend Fox. "We will dig them very deep, in a place the giants always pass over when they travel to the east. Then we will fill the holes with boiling liquid."

So Coyote called together all the animals with claws—the beavers, the whistling marmots, the cougars—the bears, and even the rats and mice and moles—to dig seven deep holes. Then Coyote filled each hole with a reddish-yellow liquid. His good friend Fox helped him keep the liquid boiling by dropping hot rocks into it.

Soon the time came for the giants' journey eastward. They marched along, all seven of them, their heads held high in the air. They were sure that no one dared to attack them. Coyote and Fox watched from behind some rocks and shrubs.

Down, down, down the seven giants went into the seven deep holes of boiling liquid. They struggled and struggled to get out, but the holes were very deep. They fumed and roared and splashed. As they struggled, they scattered the reddish liquid around them as far as a man can travel in a day.

Then Coyote came out from his hiding place. The seven giants stood still. They knew Coyote.

"You are being punished for your wickedness," Coyote said to the seven giants. "I will punish you even more by changing you into seven mountains. I will make you very high, so that everyone can see you. You will stand here forever, to remind people that punishment comes from wrong-doing.

"And I will make a deep gash in the earth here, so that no more of your family can get across to trouble my people."

Coyote caused the seven giants to grow taller, and then he changed them into seven mountain peaks. He struck the earth a hard blow and so opened up a deep canyon at the feet of the giant peaks.

Today the mountain peaks are called the Seven Devils. The deep gorge at their feet is known as Hell's Canyon of the Snake River. And the copper scattered by the splashings of the seven giants is still being mined.

Further Reading

Indian Legends of the Pacific Northwest. Ella E. Clark. The legend reprinted above as well as other Indian legends are contained in this book.

A Girl Who Married a Ghost and Other Tales of North American Indians. John Bierhorst.

Doctor Coyote: A Native American Aesop's Fables. John Bierhorst. These two books contain more American Indian legends.

L E S S O N   3

Europeans and Native Peoples

THINKING FOCUS

What impact did European exploration and settlement have on the native inhabitants of the Americas?

Key Terms

- nomad
- alliance

▼ *The horse helped Plains Indians become efficient buffalo hunters.*

You are standing in the empty expanses of the Great Plains on a hot summer afternoon in the late 1600s. The sun hangs low in the sky, and the heat rises in eerie waves off the land.

Suddenly a thundering noise arises in the west, and black specks appear along the horizon. A few minutes later a herd of buffalo sweeps past you, followed by several men riding on the backs of strange beasts. With their hair streaming behind them, these men look like gods who have captured the wind.

As you may have realized, the men described in the above passage were riding horses. But if you had been a Plains Indian in the 1600s, you might have been seeing a horse for the first time. Before the Spanish conquistador Hernando Cortés brought horses to the New World in 1519, Indians did not even know that these animals existed. Soon, however, horses changed the way Plains Indians had lived for centuries.

Before the arrival of the horse, Plains Indians lived in villages along the Missouri River and its tributaries. The men hunted on foot, and the women cultivated crops. Horses changed all that. They gave Plains Indians the ability to move around more easily and turned them into full-time buffalo hunters. Before long, these Indians adopted new methods of hunting and developed new rituals. Their entire way of life came to center around the great shaggy beasts that blanketed the plains. The meeting of two cultures had dramatically transformed the lives of a people.

The First Americans

Europeans were not the first to discover the "new" world. Thousands of years before Columbus arrived, peoples from northern Asia crossed over the land bridge that once connected Asia and North America. By the time the Europeans arrived, hundreds of Indian cultures existed throughout the Americas. In Mexico, Central America, and South America, the Mayas *(MY uz)*, the Incas, and the Aztecs developed sophisticated civilizations with elaborate cities. In North America, Indians lived in literally hundreds of tribal groups as different as any of the nations of Europe.

Different Ways of Life

Some Indians were **nomads,** wandering the countryside in search of water and wild food rather than establishing a home in one place. Many more settled down near lakes and streams, living off the fruits, berries, roots, and game they could gather and hunt near their camps.

However, most Indian groups became very successful farmers. Indians developed almost half the crops grown for food in the world today, including potatoes, corn, squash, pumpkins, and a variety of beans. Some Indian nations built irrigation systems to provide water for their crops, and many Indian societies cleared land for farming.

A Variety of Cultures

Whether they were farmers or hunters, the native inhabitants of the Americas did not see themselves as a single unified people. A Hopi was not a Blackfoot, who was not an Ojibwa, who was not a Shawnee. They spoke languages as foreign to each other as French is to English. They formed **alliances**—organizations to promote the common interests or defense of their members—fought wars, and recognized their cultural differences. Some of their alliances were highly complex. In the east, five tribes—the Mohawk, Seneca, Oneida, Onondaga, and Cayuga—joined together in the 1500s to form the Iroquois League, an alliance based on their common languages and interests.

More often, language differences and competition maintained sharp divisions between the peoples of the Americas. In time, European colonists would exploit these differences. ■

◄ *English settler John White painted this watercolor of an Indian village in 1585.*

■ *In what ways were Indian tribes similar to European nations?*

Early Contacts with American Indians

The first meetings between Indians and Europeans varied greatly from place to place. In some places Indians kept a cautious distance from the intruders. Elsewhere, they came forward eagerly to greet and trade with the strange new people who came on giant boats from across the ocean. Whenever they did make contact with Europeans, Indians got something they hadn't counted on: deadly diseases.

Destructive New Diseases

A great, invisible death walked among the Indians of the Americas after the Europeans came to stay. For many centuries, Europeans had been building up immunity to typhoid, diphtheria, smallpox, and other plagues. But Indians had lived untouched by these diseases, until the European settlers brought the germs to the New World. With no immunity against the silent killers, many Indians died of such mild diseases as influenza and the common cold.

By far, the deadliest of the diseases Europeans brought to the Americas was smallpox. Spanish conquistadors spread smallpox throughout Central and South America. The results were devastating. During the century after Columbus arrived in the New World, the Indian population of Central America and Mexico dropped from more than 25 million to just one million people. Although warfare and enslavement caused some of these deaths, many more were the result of disease.

Smallpox also nearly wiped out the Indians of North America. Everywhere it touched, the disease killed Indians by the thousands. It is said to have slain over half the Indian population of North America. When the time came to defend their lands against the spread of European invaders, many Indian societies found themselves so weakened in numbers by various plagues that they were unable even to defend themselves in war.

Religion and Trade

Europeans brought more than just diseases to the New World. They brought Christianity and European goods as well.

You have already read how the Spanish sent hundreds of missionaries to the Americas in the 1600s and

UNDERSTANDING EUROCENTRISM

When Europeans first reached the land of the Western Hemisphere, they called it the New World. In fact, it was a new world for them, but it wasn't new at all for the native inhabitants who had been living there for thousands of years. The Europeans called them "Indians," because the first explorers had thought they had arrived in India.

Terms such as "New World" and "Indians" reflect a European point of view. Today we use the word Eurocentrism to refer to the tendency to see things in terms of European culture and civilization.

Europe in the World

Eurocentrism is more than just a love of European culture. It is the notion that Europe is the center of the world. And for a long period of time, it seemed to be. From the 1500s to the early 1900s, European countries controlled a large part of the world.

During this period, European nations forced their rule on people throughout Africa and Asia as well as the Americas. In the 1900s, these colonized peoples began their struggle for independence. After years of wars and independence movements, they regained their right to rule.

Effects of Eurocentrism

Even today, some of the geographic terms we use reflect a Eurocentric point of view. Consider the terms Middle East and Far East. People from the United States actually travel west to reach Japan and China, but we still call that part of the world the Far East.

As you read more about the colonial period, try to imagine how American history might have been different if European settlers had been more open to the ways of other cultures. What might they have learned from native peoples in America?

1700s to bring the Roman Catholic faith to the New World. The Spanish saw the Indians as souls to be saved by Christianity, but also as potential slaves. The Spanish used both religion and force to control the Indians.

The French also sent missionaries to the New World, though they had less impact than the Spanish missions. The most famous of the French missionaries was a Jesuit named Jacques Marquette *(mahr KEHT)*, who explored much of the Missouri and Mississippi rivers in the early 1670s. Marquette won converts from Quebec to Arkansas.

Marquette traveled with a fur trader named Louis Joliet. In fact, wherever the French, Spanish, and English went in the New World, they brought trade with them. It wasn't long before tools such as fishhooks, kettles, knives, needles, and guns were introduced into the daily life of many Indian villages. In return, Europeans were transporting beaver and deer hides back across the ocean. They were also growing crops and eating foods they had never tasted in their homelands.

Where trade flourished, European settlers and Indians often got along quite well; they had a mutual interest in remaining friendly in these situations. But relations between settlers and Indians varied widely from region to region, and from time to time, from group to group. ■

■ *How did trade between whites and native peoples affect the daily lives of both Europeans and Indians?*

▼ *The Pilgrims learned about new vegetables such as maize (corn) and squash. These foods helped the Pilgrims survive the cold New England winters.*

Relations with English Colonists

The Pilgrims struggled through the terrible winter of 1620–1621 at Plymouth, half of them dying in the process. They did not seek contact with Indians, whom they feared and mistrusted. When spring came, they had run out of food and were too weak to begin planting.

Just as the Pilgrims' situation was getting desperate, Samoset, a Pemaquid Indian, made his appearance. To the Pilgrims' astonishment, he spoke some English, which he said he had learned from English fishermen. He made his tribe's peaceful intentions known and introduced them to Squanto, an Indian who had been enslaved in Spain and had spent two years in England. Squanto showed the colonists where to fish and hunt and taught them to plant native crops such as corn, beans, and squash.

After the 1621 harvest, the Pilgrims wanted to give thanks to God, whom they felt had provided them with plentiful crops. Consequently, they invited their Indian neighbors to a common feast of "thanksgiving," as the colony's governor, William Bradford, proclaimed it. The peaceful relations between the Pilgrims and the Pemaquids lasted for years, and Americans have continued to celebrate Thanksgiving to this day.

Friendship and Cooperation

Peace wasn't always won that easily. Generally, disagreements about land were the cause of the tension between European settlers and native inhabitants. When the leaders of the Massachusetts Bay Colony wanted Indian land, for instance, they simply decided to take it.

Roger Williams, a fiery, religious man from Salem, accused the colonists of

taking what the Indians had every right to keep. Because they didn't like his attitude toward the Indians and his belief in religious tolerance, the Puritans banished Williams from the colony. He went south with his followers to live in Rhode Island, where they lived peacefully with the Narragansett Indians.

Probably the greatest success story of European-Indian cooperation was the colony of William Penn and the Quakers. A Quaker leader, Penn recived a vast grant of land in what is now Pennsylvania from King Charles II in 1681. The Quakers, a sect much persecuted in England, respected Indians as fellow children of God. It was not surprising, therefore, that Penn set out to establish a colony in which Indians and colonists could live together in peace. Penn promised never to occupy any land without the agreement of the Indians. Remarkably, Quakers and Indians did live in peace for almost 70 years.

Competition for Land

In the early 1600s, Virginia settlers staked out huge tracts of land to build tobacco plantations, thereby creating tension with local Indians. When the colonists murdered a popular Indian religious leader, his people sought revenge. The Indians' surprise raid in 1622 killed one-third of Virginia's white settlers and devastated the colony's economy. The colonists responded by slaughtering the inhabitants of many Indian villages.

The fighting in Virginia was only one battle in a complicated pattern of wars that would engulf the English colonies. In 1637, for example, English settlers in New England, helped by their Narragansett allies, set fire to the main village of the Pequot on the Mystic River. This battle destroyed the Pequot tribe. The Pequot War had begun over a series of land disputes.

Several decades later, in 1675, the Narragansett found themselves in the

American painter William Hicks's "The Peaceable Kingdom" shows William Penn signing a peace treaty with Pennsylvania's Indians.

same position as the Pequot. To defend themselves against advancing English settlers, the Narragansett allied themselves with the Wampanoag in Metacom's War. This war is known as King Philip's War, since the Wampanoag leader, Metacom, was called King Philip by the English. The Indians destroyed 13 Puritan towns and killed thousands of settlers, but the Narragansett were nearly wiped out. When Metacom died in battle in 1676, his head was brought back to Plymouth and put on display for 25 years.

While Metacom's War was being fought in New England, friction between poor frontier farmers and rich coastal planters started a civil war in Virginia. Virginia's native inhabitants were the final losers of this war.

The small planters of Virginia's frontier desired the rich lands that belonged to the Susquehannock and other Indian nations. These settlers strongly opposed the colonial governor's policy of peaceful relations with Virginia's Indian tribes. In 1676, a group of these planters decided to take matters into their own hands. Led by a hot-tempered immigrant named Nathaniel Bacon, they began to attack any Indians they could find, friendly or hostile.

When the colonial governor spoke against these attacks, Bacon led his forces against Jamestown. After burning much of the capital to the ground, the rebels took control of Virginia's government. However, their victory was short-lived. Six months later, Bacon lay dead of fever, the colonial governor had returned to power, and 23 of Bacon's followers were hanging from the gallows.

Even though Bacon's Rebellion failed, the backcountry planters had made their point. In the years following the rebellion, the colonial government allowed the white settlers of the frontier to conduct a war of extermination against local Indians.

A Variety of Alliances

In many of the conflicts between European settlers and native inhabitants, the colonists turned Indian nations against each other. Often they tried to make alliances that led Indians to do much of the colonists' fighting for them. The clearest example of this strategy occurred during the 1715 Yamasee War. During this conflict, the English in the Carolinas persuaded the Cherokee to join them in fending off the Yamasee and their allied nations. Only two years earlier, these same Yamasee had helped the colonists wipe out the Tuscarora. By dividing their Indian enemies, white settlers often succeeded in conquering and eliminating their chief competitors for land.

By the late 1600s, a pattern had been established. Whether sold into slavery, killed or dispersed, the native inhabitants of the English colonies fell victim to the settlers' seemingly endless hunger for land. ◼

▲ *Using mostly primitive weapons American Indians lost most battles with colonists.*

◼ *What caused most of the conflicts between European colonists and American Indians?*

R E V I E W

1. **FOCUS** What impact did European exploration and settlement have on the native inhabitants of the Americas?
2. **CONNECT** European explorers and settlers did not hesitate to claim large expanses of land in the New World for themselves. How do you think this attitude affected relations with the Indians of these regions?
3. **CULTURE** What European objects soon became a part of the daily lives of many American Indian societies?
4. **CRITICAL THINKING** If the native peoples of the Americas had not been so susceptible to European diseases, how might the history of the colonial settlement of the New World have been different?
5. **WRITING ACTIVITY** Imagine that you are an American Indian watching the arrival of a European ship. Write a paragraph describing the ship and the landing of the settlers inside it. How do you feel about these people?

Reviewing Exploration and Settlement

Using Specialized Resources

Here's Why

As you have read in this chapter, the history of the United States is still being written. Each time archaeologists find unfamiliar tools, weapons, or pieces of pottery, they uncover more information about the background of this country. In order to keep track of both historical information and new information, historians use a number of different reference sources.

As a student of American history, you too will need to use a number of different reference sources. The most familiar reference sources are dictionaries and encyclopedias. You may also use the card catalog to locate books on a specific topic. In addition, however, most libraries have special reference materials that contain a wealth of information about American history.

Suppose you want to research a particular topic, such as the origin and use of the hoe pictured on this page. Becoming familiar with these references can help you find answers quickly and also expand your ability to locate information and documents that you need.

Here's How

Spend some time in the reference section of your school or local library. Locate one or more of the following kinds of reference materials:

Historical Atlases: In a historical atlas, you can find maps that show information about people, events, and conditions at different points in history. Some atlases, such as the *National Geographic Historical Atlas of American History,* also contain timelines and informative articles.

Chronologies: If you need to verify a date or find out about the important events that happened in a particular year, you might use a chronology like the one in Richard Morris's *Encyclopedia of American History.* Morris's book contains a summary chronology of the major events of American history plus separate chronologies on such topics as territorial expansion, transportation, and communication. The final section of the book presents biographical information about 500 notable Americans.

Statistical Sources: Often you may want statistical information about the population or economic activities at specific times in our past. Each year since 1878 the United States Bureau of the Census has published a *Statistical Abstract of the United States.* This book provides data about more than 30 topics. Much of it is about the United States today, but the book also includes much statistical information from as far back as 1790, when the first census was conducted. Many almanacs also provide some limited data about United States history.

Try It

Below is a list of items to research. Identify which of the reference sources described above would be the best source for information about each of the following items:

1. the text of a speech by an Indian leader
2. a map of areas of European settlement in 1700
3. a list of the U. S. cities with the largest populations in 1800
4. a summary of the key events in Metacom's War
5. William Penn's date and place of birth
6. the text of the Articles of Confederation

Apply It

Consider what you have read about the geography of the United States and about the Indians and colonists in the 1600s and 1700s. Choose a topic that interests you for further research. Write a short paragraph that defines the topic and outlines what specialized history references you would use in your school or community library.

LESSON 4

Life in the English Colonies

The summer heat turned the forest into an open oven. Lifting an ax high across his shoulders, the farmer swung it into the trunk of the tree and then wrestled it out again. Lift, stroke, heave, pull—this backbreaking work went on hour after hour, until the farmer was aching and drenched with sweat.

The stumps of fallen trees lay on the ground until spring, when the felled wood was burned and the stumps set on fire. Settlers all over the English colonies used this process to clear away forests and prepare the land for farming.

Farther south, in the Chesapeake region, farmers used a system called girdling. First, they cut a deep notch all the way around the trunk of a tree and pulled away the bark around this notch. Because the tree could no longer grow leaves and block the sun, farmers could plant crops sooner. A year later, they would chop down the ghostly gray trees that stood dead in their fields.

Whatever method a farmer chose, clearing the land was a slow pro-cess. In a year, a man could clear only one or two acres. If he worked alone, he could spend a lifetime clearing enough ground to make a decent-sized farm.

Intermingled with the many other daily tasks of colonial farm life, the clearing of ground became a grueling chore, always waiting to be done. It could not be left undone, because in those days you "bought" your farmland from the wilderness—that is, you carved it out with your own bare hands.

THINKING FOCUS

What were some of the main characteristics of daily life in the English colonies in the early 1700s?

Key Terms

- indentured servant
- subsistence farmer

◄ *The painting at left shows settlers burning trees that they had "girdled" the previous year.*

33

The Demand for Labor

Clearing the land, tilling, planting, and harvesting the crops all required weeks and months of labor. The labor-intensive plantations of the South had a special need for workers to keep them going. Plantation owners relied first on indentured servants and then on slaves to do much of this work.

Indentured Servants

Indentured servants were people who agreed to work for a specified period of time in exchange for payment of their passage from Europe to the English colonies and for food, clothing, and shelter. Their period of servitude could last anywhere from four to seven years. The contract indentured servants signed promised them tools, seed, and sometimes even land when the period of indenture was over.

In the 1600s, most indentured servants settled in the Southern colonies where their labor was most needed. For example, as many as 80 percent of the immigrants to Virginia and Maryland were indentured servants at this time. In fact, these workers accounted for more than one-third of the immigrants to the English colonies during that century.

Indentured servants could be bought and sold like property. Some planters even gambled them away in card games. Often, they were worked hard and fed poorly.

Given these conditions, it is not surprising that many indentured servants died before they finished their servitude. Still, however bad their lot in life, it was generally much better than that of the African slave.

The Growth of Slavery

As late as 1671, white indentured servants outnumbered black slaves in Virginia by three to one. But the pressure to shift to a black labor force was already strong. Three main factors created this pressure. First, England became increasingly involved in the slave trade during the late 1600s, making it easier for colonial planters to acquire slaves. At the same time, the supply of white indentured servants began to decline sharply as economic conditions improved in England. Finally, wealthy planters feared that a growing population of bitter ex-servants would increase the likelihood of more uprisings like Bacon's rebellion.

To meet the growing demand by Southern planters for slaves, England set up the Royal African Company in 1672. Colonial merchants, many from New England, also entered the business of transporting slaves to the colonies. These merchants traveled to the coast of West Africa to trade for slaves. Then began the terrible "middle passage"—the journey across the Atlantic. Packed into the holds of ships like cargo and chained together like criminals, slaves suffered through intense heat, painful illnesses, and rough seas. Not surprisingly, one out of every seven died on these grueling journeys of four to six weeks.

The Africans who did survive were quickly sold at slave auctions.

Slave traders used loading plans like the one shown below right to pack as many African slaves into the smallest space possible. The poster announces the auction of a new cargo of slaves.

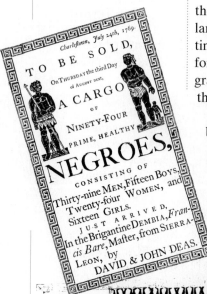

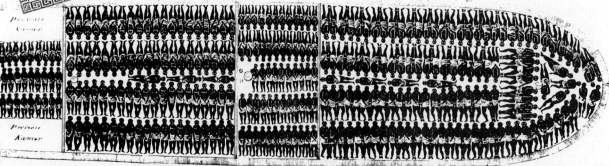

> *T*he sale began—young girls were there,
>   Defenceless in their wretchedness,
>   Whose stifled sobs of deep despair
> Revealed their anguish and distress.
> And mothers stood with streaming eyes,
> And saw their dearest children sold;
> Unheeded rose their bitter cries,
> While tyrants bartered them for gold.

Frances Harper from Slave Auction

In her 1854 poem, "Slave Auction" (above), reformer and author Frances Harper captured the sense of grief that slaves experienced.

Torn from their homelands and loved ones, most slaves ended up on Southern plantations where their numbers increased rapidly in the late 1600s. Whereas fewer than 5,000 slaves lived in the English colonies in 1670, three decades later that number had jumped to 28,000. Still, the slave trade did not reach its peak until around 1730. By that time slave traders were bringing roughly 5,000 new slaves to the colonies each year. By 1775, roughly 500,000 slaves toiled in the colonies. ■

■ *What factors led to the rapid growth of slavery in the English colonies?*

Regional Differences

The Northern colonies had far fewer slaves than the Southern colonies. But this was just one of many differences in the way life was lived from colony to colony.

New England Colonies

Most New Englanders shared a common heritage. The great majority of the settlers there came from England or Scotland. As a result, the colonies of New England—New Hampshire, Massachusetts, Connecticut, and Rhode Island—all developed in similar ways.

Despite the region's poor, rocky soil, many New Englanders were farmers. Both to promote a sense of religious community and to protect themselves from Indians, New England farmers settled in small villages rather than scattered farms. While they went out to work in their fields during the day, their cattle grazed on the common, a shared area of land in the middle of the village. These hardy settlers were **subsistence farmers**, producing just enough food for their own needs. The Closer Look on pages 36–37 shows more about these farms.

◄ *Linton Park's painting, "The Scutching Bee," shows that scutching flax could be fun as well as work.*

35

Many of those who weren't farmers lived in one of the busy seaports that dotted New England's coast. Shipbuilding flourished in these seaports, as did the fishing and whaling industries. Soon, the cutting and shipping of timber became a major commercial activity as well.

As elsewhere in the colonies, life in New England was often difficult and primitive. Cutting and dragging wood, working the fields, tending the livestock, making and fixing clothes, mending the fences—all these tasks made life a constant round of toil for men, women, and children.

Even the popular forms of entertainment tended to involve work. Groups of farm women would often get together in a quilting bee where they made large quilted blankets. Or men, women, and children would gather for a scutching bee, in which the participants would break stalks of flax, a cotton-like plant, into fiber.

Music and dancing generally enlivened all these gatherings.

Middle Colonies

Life wasn't much easier in the Middle colonies—Pennsylvania, Delaware, New Jersey, and New York—with two important exceptions. The soil was richer, and much of the land had already been cleared by Indian farmers. As a result, the farmers in these colonies were able to grow small surpluses, or cash crops, which they could then sell to others. Travelers along the country roads of the Middle colonies could see farmers bringing corn, wheat, beef, and pork to trade in cities like New York and Philadelphia, the largest seaport in America at the time.

Unlike farmers in New England, farmers in the Middle colonies did not settle in small villages. Relations with the Indians in this part of the colonies were generally friendly, and good land

A Closer Look

The Colonial Farm

Imagine the Pennsylvania farmers' rough hands. Women's were blistered from churning butter. Men's stung with splinters from chopping wood. On colonial farms, men and women filled clearly defined roles.

Women used decorative butter molds to stamp butter with garden designs such as strawberries or wheat.

Women cooked meals in iron pots over coals and flames.

Women spun cotton and wool to make the family's clothes.

It took three to four hours to churn three pounds of butter.

Chickens in the Chimneys!
To remove soot, women dropped live chickens down kitchen chimneys. The frantic wing-beating cleaned the chimney and the chicken was no worse for the trip.

was more abundant. As a result, settlers built up large farms in the fertile, rolling countryside.

Farming wasn't the only way to make a living in the Middle colonies. The region also employed a large number of workers in a variety of manufacturing jobs involving the production of glass, textiles, and paper. In addition to working in shipyards and iron mines, thousands worked as craftsmen—shoemakers, tailors, blacksmiths, carpenters, watchmakers, printers, and many others.

Whereas most New Englanders came from England or Scotland, people from a variety of different nations settled in the Middle colonies. Immigrants from England, Ireland, Germany, Scotland, Sweden, and the Netherlands made the population of this region more diverse than anywhere else in the English colonies. Some of these immigrants chose to settle inland, on the eastern slopes of the Appalachian Mountains, an area that came to be known as the backcountry. Life in the backcountry was rough and dangerous, but the people who settled on the frontier enjoyed an unusual degree of independence.

Southern Colonies

The contrast between life along the coast and life in the backcountry was even sharper in the Southern colonies. In the tidewater region of the South—the rich coastal plains where ocean tides swept up the rivers—a system of large plantations grew up in the 1600s. In the forested backcountry, on the other hand, a society of small farmers emerged.

Settlers in Virginia began to grow tobacco in the early 1600s. Soon they discovered that they could increase profits by cultivating tobacco on a large scale. The great tobacco plantations that resulted became the hallmark not only of the Chesapeake

Across Time & Space

Today developers in Brazil use great earth-moving machines to gouge out huge bites from the nation's forests. In an effort to obtain rich farmlands, these developers displace native peoples, destroy habitats, and threaten the extinction of innumerable species.

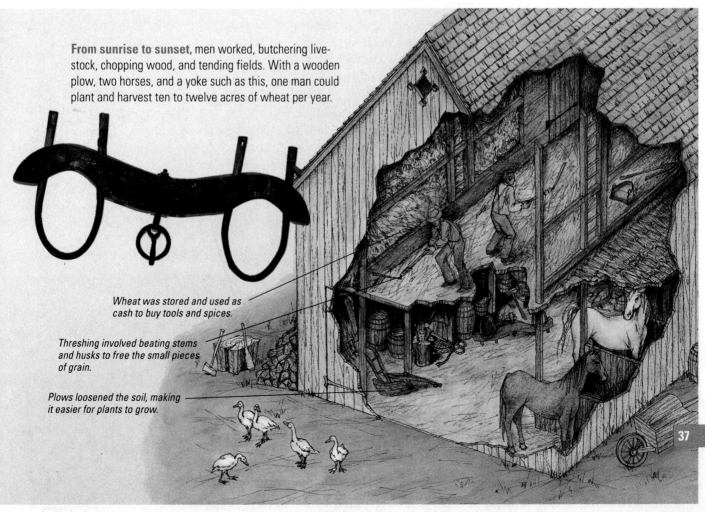

From sunrise to sunset, men worked, butchering livestock, chopping wood, and tending fields. With a wooden plow, two horses, and a yoke such as this, one man could plant and harvest ten to twelve acres of wheat per year.

Wheat was stored and used as cash to buy tools and spices.

Threshing involved beating stems and husks to free the small pieces of grain.

Plows loosened the soil, making it easier for plants to grow.

The English Colonies, 1750

CANADA

Maine (Part of Mass.)

(Claimed by N.Y. and N.H.)

L. Huron

L. Ontario

L. Erie

New York

N.H.

Mass. • Boston

Hartford •
New Haven • R.I.
Conn.

Pennsylvania

Philadelphia •

New York

New Jersey

Md.
Annapolis •   • Delaware

Virginia

Williamsburg •

ATLANTIC OCEAN

North Carolina

South Carolina

Georgia • Charleston
  • Savannah

0   250 mi.
0   250 km

Lambert Conformal Conic Projection

FLORIDA (Sp.)

North
New England
Middle
South
Chesapeake
South

> *Although they shared certain characteristics, the English colonies were divided by distinct regional differences. The map at left shows the different regions of the colonies.*

colonies of Virginia and Maryland, but of the Upper South colony of North Carolina as well.

A plantation system also developed in the Lower South colonies of South Carolina and Georgia. Here the chief crop was not tobacco but rice, which thrived in the swampy lowlands of the coast. In the 1740s, Eliza Lucas Pinckney, wife of a rich planter, successfully cultivated indigo, a plant from which blue dye is made. Indigo soon joined rice as a staple crop in the economy of the Lower South.

The typical Southern plantation was a more self-sufficient community than an ordinary farm. The planter and his family lived in a mansion known as the Great House. Other buildings on the plantation might include stables, a blacksmith's shop, a schoolhouse, a dairy, a bakehouse, a brickworks, and quarters for indentured servants or slaves.

Most planters managed the operation of the plantation themselves. Some hired overseers, or supervisors, to help them direct a work force of anywhere from 10 to 100 or more slaves. Women also played a major role in running the plantation. The planter's wife organized the household and supervised the house slaves and servants who worked there.

For the immigrants and former indentured servants who settled in the Southern backcountry, life was a continual struggle. Most backcountry people lived in log cabins or shacks and farmed at a subsistence level. Though

some farmers earned a little money raising cattle and pigs, many more waged a constant fight against poverty. Schools, churches, and towns were few and far between.

Backcountry settlers did not hide their hostility toward the wealthy colonists who lived along the coasts.

> *As this 1720 painting by Peter Cooper shows, Philadelphia was already a bustling port city by the early 1700s.*

The South East Prospect of the City of Philadelphia By Peter Cooper Painter

These poor farmers felt they were not fairly represented in the colonial governments and resented the taxes these governments imposed on them. Sometimes their resentment boiled over into open revolt, as in the case of Bacon's rebellion.

Although the population of the Southern colonies was less varied than that of the Middle colonies, it was more diverse than that of New England. The most distinctive feature of the South's population was, of course, the large number of African slaves living there—roughly 35 percent of the region's total population in 1750. The other distinctive feature was the sharp split between the coast and the back-country in terms of national origins. The large plantation owners tended to be English, while the small farmers of the frontier were mainly Germans and Scots-Irish, with a few English and French Protestants mixed in. ■

■ *What were the chief differences between life in the New England, Middle, and Southern colonies?*

Patterns of Colonial Life

Despite the distinct differences among the ways of life in the New England, Middle, and Southern colonies, these regions shared some important characteristics as well. Many of these shared characteristics involved transportation and communication.

The most common denominator of colonial life was travel. And travelers in the 1700s were often on their way to or from a port city. During the first half of the 18th century, many small trading villages blossomed into bustling port cities. The most important of these were Boston, Newport, New York, Philadelphia, and Charleston.

Port cities were centers of trade and consequently the lifeblood of the colonial economy. Out of them flowed the goods that the colonists exported to England and the Caribbean: tobacco, rice, indigo, fish, timber, and wheat, to name a few. Into the port cities came English goods that the colonists needed, including glass, paper, iron tools, cloth, and spices.

Port cities also became centers of transportation and communication. They were the hubs through which public coaches passed. They also published the most important colonial newspapers and were the places where news from the rest of the world arrived first. Farmers returning home from port cities would bring important information, which they would then pass on to their neighbors.

On a much smaller scale, the colonial tavern was the rural equivalent of the port city. Dotting lonely stretches of road, colonial taverns served as lodgings, restaurants, and gathering places. Travelers often had to put up with uncomfortable beds and simple meals in these taverns. Like port cities, however, these stopping-over places became centers of transportation and communication. They formed a complex network that bound the colonies closer together. ■

▲ *The signs hung outside colonial taverns were often distinctive and colorful, as the tavern sign above illustrates.*

■ *What features of daily life were common to all the English colonies?*

R E V I E W

1. **FOCUS** What were some of the main characteristics of daily life in the English colonies in the early 1700s?
2. **CONNECT** Look at the exploration map on page 19. How did the routes English explorers took affect the way England settled the New World?
3. **ECONOMICS** Why did Southern planters prefer to use slaves rather than indentured servants as laborers?
4. **CRITICAL THINKING** Why do you think some people chose to live in the backcountry of the Southern colonies rather than on the coastal plains?
5. **WRITING ACTIVITY** Write an eyewitness account of conditions on a slave ship in the late 1600s.

39

Reviewing Exploration and Settlement

The Witch of Blackbird Pond

Elizabeth G. Speare

Having grown up in exotic Barbados, 16-year-old Kit Taylor comes to live with relatives in Puritan Wethersfield, in the colony of Connecticut, in the late 1600s. There, she has a difficult time fitting in. She befriends an elderly woman, Hannah, who lives near Blackbird Pond with her cat and memories of her husband, Thomas. When an epidemic kills many in Wethersfield, the townspeople think there is witchcraft at work. As you read this excerpt from Elizabeth G. Speare's book, ask yourself why Kit , a young girl, shows so much compassion for Hannah, when the "religious" people of Wethersfield do not.

In Lesson 2 you learned about the Puritan settlement of New England, and in Lesson 3 you read about the Puritans' treatment of Roger Williams. In this story you will read about life in a Puritan village.

From without the house there was an approaching sound of stamping feet and murmuring voices, gathering volume in the roadway outside. There was a crashing knock on the outer door. The three women's eyes met in consternation. Matthew Wood reached the door in one stride and flung it open.

"How dare you?" he demanded in low-voiced anger. "Know you not there is illness here?"

"Aye, we know right enough," a voice replied. "There's illness everywhere. We need your help to put a stop to it."

"What do you want?"

"We want you to come along with us. We're going for the witch."

"Get away from my house at once," ordered Matthew.

"You'll listen to us first," shouted another voice, "if you know what's good for your daughter."

"Keep your voices down, then, and be quick," warned Matthew. "I've no time to listen to foolishness."

"Is it foolishness that there's scarce a house in this town but has a sick child in it? You'd do well to heed what we say, Matthew Wood. John Wetherell's boy died today. That makes three dead, and it's the witch's doing!"

"Whose doing? What are you driving at, man?"

"The Quaker woman's. Down by Blackbird Pond. She's been a curse on this town for years with her witchcraft!"

The voices sounded hysterical. "We should have run her out long ago."

"Time and again she's been seen consorting with the devil down in that meadow!"

"Now she's put a curse on our children. God knows how many

more will be dead before morning!"

"This is nonsense,"scoffed Matthew Wood impatiently. "There's no old woman, and no witchcraft either could bring on a plague like this."

"What is it then?" shrilled a woman's voice.

Matthew passed a hand over his forehead. "The will of God—" he began helplessly.

"The curse of God, you mean!" another voice screamed. "His judgment on us for harboring an infidel and a Quaker."

"You'd better come with us, Matthew. Your own daughter's like to die. You can't deny it."

"I'll have naught to do with it," said Matthew firmly. "I'll hold with no witch hunt."

"You'd better hold with it!" the woman's voice shrilled suddenly. "You'd better look to the witch in your own household!"

"Ask that high and mighty niece of yours where she spends her time!" another woman shouted from the darkness. "Ask her what she knows about your Mercy's sickness!"

The weariness dropped suddenly from Matthew Wood. With his shoulders thrown back he seemed to tower in the doorway.

"Begone from my house!" he roared, his caution drowned in anger. "How dare you speak the name of a good, God-fearing girl? Any man who slanders one of my family has me to reckon with!"

There was a silence. "No harm meant," a man's voice said uneasily. "'Tis only woman's talk."

"If you won't come there's plenty more in the town who will," said another. "What are we wasting our time for?"

The voices receded down the pathway, rising again in the darkness beyond. Matthew bolted the door and dashed back to the dumbfounded women.

"Did they wake her?" he asked dully.

"No," sighed Rachel. "Even that could not disturb the poor child."

For a moment there was no sound but that torrid breathing. Kit had risen to her feet and stood clinging to the table's edge. Now the new fear that was stifling her broke from her lips in an anguished whisper.

"What will they do to her?"

Her aunt looked up in alarm. Matthew's black brows drew together darkly. "What concern is that of yours?"

"I know her!" she cried. "She's just a poor helpless old woman! Oh, please tell me! Will they harm her?"

"This is Connecticut," answered Matthew sternly. "They will abide by the law. They will bring her to trial, I suppose. If she can prove herself innocent she is safe enough."

"But what will they do with her now —tonight —before the trial?"

"How do I know? Leave off your questions, girl. Is there not trouble enough in our own house tonight?" He lowered himself into a chair and sunk his head in his hands.

"Go get some sleep, Kit," urged Rachel, dreading any more disturbance. "We may need you later on."

Kit stared from one to the other, half frantic with helplessness. They were not going to do anything. Unable to stop herself she burst into tears and ran from the room.

Upstairs, in her own room, she stood leaning against the door, trying to collect her wits. She would have to get to Hannah. No matter what happened, she could not stay here and leave Hannah to face the mob alone. If she could get there in time to warn her—that was as far as she could see just now.

She snatched her cloak from the peg and, carrying her leather boots in her hand, crept down the stairs. She dared not try to unbolt the great front door but instead tiptoed cautiously through the cold company room into the back chamber and let herself out the shed door into the garden. She could hear shouts in the distance, and slipping hurriedly into her boots she fled along the roadway.

In Meeting House Square she leaned against a tree for an instant to get her bearing. The crowd was gathering, a good twenty men and boys and a few women, carrying flaring pine torches. In the hoarse shouting and the heedless screaming of the women there was a mounting violence, and a terror she had never known before closed over Kit's mind like a fog. For a moment her knees sagged and she caught at the tree for support. Then her mind cleared again, and skirting the square, darting from tree to tree like a savage, she made her way down Broad Street and out onto South Road.

She had never before seen the Meadows by moon light. They lay serene and still, wrapped in thin veils of drifting mist. She found the path easily, passed the dark clump of willows, and saw ahead the deep shining pool that was Blackbird Pond and a faint reddish glow that must be Hannah's window.

Hannah's door was not even bolted. Inside, by the still-flickering embers of the hearth, Hannah sat nodding in her chair, fast asleep. Kit touched the woman's shoulder gently.

"Hannah dear," she said, struggling to control her panting breath. "Wake up! 'Tis Kit. You've got to come with me, quickly."

"What is it?" Hannah jerked instantly awake. "Is it a flood?"

"Don't talk, Hannah. Just get into this cloak. Where are your shoes? Here, hold out your foot, quick! Now—"

There was not a moment to spare. As they stepped into the darkness the clamor of voices struck against them. The torches looked very near.

"Not that way! Down the path to the river!"

In the shelter of the dark bushes Hannah faltered, clutching at Kit's arms. She could not be budged. "Kit! Why are those people coming?"

"Hush! Hannah, dear, please—"

"I know that sound. I've heard it before. They're coming for the Quakers."

"No, Hannah, come—I—"

"Shame on thee, Kit. Thee knows a Quaker does not run away. Thomas will take care of us."

Desperately Kit shook the old woman's shoulders. "Oh, Hannah! What shall I do with you?" Of all times for Hannah to turn vague!

But Hannah's brief resolution suddenly gave way, and all at once she clung to Kit, sobbing like a child.

"Don't let them take me again," she pleaded. "Where is Thomas? I can't face it again without Thomas."

This time Kit succeeded in half dragging the sobbing woman through the underbrush. They made a terrible rustling and snapping of twigs as they went, but the noise behind them was still louder. The crowd had reached the cottage now. There was a crashing, as though the furniture were being hurled to splinters against the walls.

"She was here! The fire is still burning!"

"Look behind the woodpile. She can't have got far."

"There's the cat!" screeched a woman in terror. "Look out!"

There was a shot, then two more.

"It got away. Disappeared into thin air."

"There's no bullet could kill that cat."

"Here's the goats. Get rid of them too!"

"Hold on there! I'll take the goats. Witched or no, goats is worth twenty shillings apiece."

"Scotch the witch out!"

"Fire the house! Give us a light to search by!"

Desperately the two women pushed on, over a marshy bog that dragged at their feet, through a cornfield where the neglected shocks hid their scurrying figures, past a brambly tangle, to the shelter of the poplar trees and the broad moonlit stretch of the river. There they had to halt, crouching against a fallen log.

Behind them a flare of light, redder than the moonlight, lit up the meadows. There was a hissing and crackling.

"My house!" cried out Hannah, so heedlessly that Kit clapped a hand over her mouth. "Our own house that Thomas built!" With the tears running down her own cheeks, Kit flung both arms around the trembling woman, and together they huddled against the log and watched till the red glow lessened and died away.

For a long time the thrashing in the woods continued. Once voices came very close, and the search party went thwacking through the cornfield. Two men came out on the beach, not twenty feet from where they hid.

"Could she swim the river, think you?"

"Not likely. No use going on like this all night, Jem. I've had enough. There's another day coming." The men climbed back up the river bank.

When the voices died away it was very still. Serenity flowed back over the meadows. The veil of mist was again unbroken. After a long time, Kit dared to stretch her aching muscles. It was bitterly cold and damp here by the river's edge. She drew Hannah's slight figure closer against her, like a child's, and presently the woman's shuddering ceased, and Hannah drifted into the shallow napping of the very old.

Further Reading

The Seekers. Eilis Dillon. Based on firsthand accounts, this is the story of a young boy who sails to a Puritan colony in 1632 to follow his beloved to the New World.

Everyday Life in Colonial America. David Freemen Hawke. Diary accounts, curious facts, and illustrations give insight into the life of colonial Americans.

Chapter Review

Reviewing Key Terms

alliance (p. 27)
conquistador (p. 18)
estuary (p. 6)
human geography (p. 5)
indentured servant (p. 34)
landform (p. 5)
navigation (p. 17)

nomad (p. 27)
physical geography (p. 5)
plateau (p. 11)
prairie (p. 8)
precipitation (p. 8)
sect (p. 21)
subsistence farmer (p. 35)

A. In each of the following pairs, the two terms are related in some way. Write a sentence for each pair that clearly explains the relationship between the two terms.

1. human geography, physical geography
2. indentured servant, subsistence farmer
3. prairie, plateau
4. navigation, estuary
5. nomad, alliance

B. Based on what you have read in the chapter, decide whether each of the following statements is accurate. Write an explanation of each decision.

1. Conquistadors settled the New England colonies.
2. Human geography involves the study of the natural world, such as climate and rainfall.
3. Because of improvements in navigation, sailors were able to make more accurate and longer voyages.
4. Mountains, plains, and valleys are examples of landforms.
5. Most of the New England states consist of prairies.
6. Indentured servants paid someone else's passage to the New World in exchange for labor.

Exploring Concepts

A. Copy the timeline below on a separate sheet of paper. Use the information below to complete your timeline. Insert the name of each event in the correct time position.

- Jamestown founded
- John Cabot sails to New World
- Massachusetts Bay Colony founded
- Henry Hudson discovers Hudson River
- Cartier discovers Gulf of St. Lawrence
- Columbus's first voyage for Spain
- Plymouth founded
- Verrazano sails to New World
- Balboa finds Pacific
- Roanoke colony begun

B. Support each of the following statements with facts and details from the chapter.

1. The crossing of the Atlantic was usually a voyage filled with hardship.
2. Explorers had many reasons for braving the unknown.
3. The continental United States has a dramatically varied geographic landscape.
4. The Pilgrims owed their survival to the help of Indians.
5. The civilization Cortés founded in Mexico was a flourishing one.
6. The "middle passage" was a voyage of endless misery.

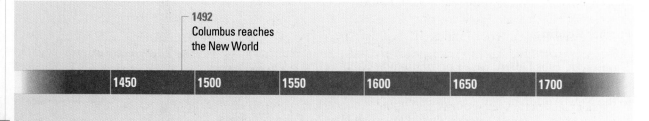

1492
Columbus reaches the New World

1450　1500　1550　1600　1650　1700

44

Reviewing Skills

1. What is the difference between a historical atlas and a world atlas?
2. The hoe pictured on page 32 was handmade by a colonial farmer or blacksmith. How might you find out (a) the date when factories began producing hoes and (b) the cost of handmade and factory-made hoes?
3. Which of the references listed on page 32 would help you to determine how the geography and climate of the area in which you live affected the way the area developed?
4. Suppose you wanted to find the state census for the year you were born, as well as a map that shows your state during that year. Which of the reference materials listed on page 32 could you use?

Using Critical Thinking

1. Are people in modern American society as ruled by geographic conditions as people in colonial society were? Keep in mind such considerations as modes of travel, how food is acquired, and types of houses built.
2. Do geography and climate affect the ways people in your town or city make their living? Explain your answer.
3. Which Europeans, in your opinion, treated the native inhabitants of America worse, the Spanish conquistadors or the English settlers? Why?
4. Did an indentured servant have basically the same status as a slave? Why or why not?
5. Even though the English colonies were all controlled by England, important differences soon arose among the colonies' various regions. Explain how the geography of each region—New England, the Middle Colonies, and the South—contributed to its distinctive qualities.
6. Europeans' treatment of Indians ranged from enslavement to acceptance of them as equals. What factors contributed to the Europeans' harsh treatment of the Indians? Why didn't more Europeans follow the example of William Penn and Roger Williams?

Preparing for Citizenship

1. **WRITING ACTIVITY** Many laws of colonial New England seem harsh to us today, but the leaders of communities believed that those laws were necessary to maintain order in an untamed land. Research and write a report on colonial laws and punishments.
2. **WRITING ACTIVITY** Imagine you have won a roundtrip one-day time-travel ticket to colonial New England. Keep a travel journal of what you eat, activities you engage in, clothes you wear, etc. Then write a short paper comparing your day in colonial New England with a typical day as a modern teenager.
3. **COLLECTING INFORMATION** Indians occupied most areas of North America at the time Europeans first came here. Traces of Indian life still survive in many communities. For example, New York City's major street, called Broadway, was originally an Indian path on Manhattan Island. Many place names also reflect the Indian heritage. Find out if any groups of Indians lived in your area. Report on their way of life and what happened to them. Include in your report any examples of the Indian heritage that still survive.
4. **ART ACTIVITY** Imagine you are an enterprising Englishman who wants to start your own colony in one of the three major areas of colonial America. Choose an area, and design an advertisement convincing people to leave their homes and settle in the New World.
5. **ART ACTIVITY** Conduct a class quilting bee. Make the quilt out of paper by having each student make a square of paper nine inches on each side. Decorate the square with a picture of one of the persons, events, or scenes from the chapter. When all are finished, paste them together in a large quilt for display.
6. **COLLABORATIVE LEARNING** As a class, make a list on the board of the landforms, climate, and major geographic features of the community in which you live. Then determine how people today control, change, utilize, or simply adapt to their geographic surroundings. Do we have greater control over geography than the colonists did?

Chapter 2

Reviewing the American Revolution

By the mid-1770s, a distinct American identity had begun to emerge. Along with this new identity came a growing spirit of independence from George III and the English government. When England tried to assert its authority over the colonies, the colonists first resisted and then rebelled. Out of the revolution a new nation emerged.

George III reigned as King of England from 1760 to 1811. His unpopular political and economic policies eventually stirred the colonists to revolt against British rule.

Thomas Paine's popular and influential pamphlet, *Common Sense*, aroused the colonists in the winter and spring of 1776 and prepared the way for revolution.

1690	1710	1730

1700

Artist Archibald M. Willard painted *The Spirit of '76* almost a century after the American Revolution. It portrays several patriots rallying to the cause of American independence.

1776 Thomas Jefferson designed and made the lap-top writing desk shown at left. On it he wrote the Declaration of Independence in the summer of 1776.

1750	1770	1790

1783

LESSON 1

An Emerging American Identity

THINKING FOCUS

How did many kinds of new immigrants help to create a distinct American culture?

Key Terms

- immigrant
- pluralism
- salutary neglect
- veto

W hen a young Scottish doctor named Alexander Hamilton visited Philadelphia for the first time in 1744, he was surprised by what he found there, as his diary entry illustrates:

> I dined at a tavern with a very mixed company of different nations and religions. There were Scots, English, Dutch, Germans, and Irish; there were Roman Catholics, Church men [Anglicans], Presbyterians, Quakers, Methodists, Seventh-Day men, Moravians, Anabaptists, and one Jew."

At the time of Hamilton's visit, Philadelphia was already the largest city in the colonies, and it was growing and changing fast. The city's population doubled from 15,000 to 30,000 between 1740 and 1775. It attracted people from Ireland, the German

states, and Scotland, as well as from other colonies.

Newcomers to Philadelphia found a booming, prosperous city. They marveled at its stone-paved streets, lit at night by whale oil lamps. The city's many rooming houses provided lodging for its fast-growing population. Wealthy merchants built great homes and decorated them with paintings, helping to make Philadelphia the cultural center of the colonies.

Dr. Hamilton was not the only European visitor to notice how many different kinds of people were living in Philadelphia in the mid-1700s. Through the city's streets, Quakers in their broad black hats walked side by side with Shawnee or Delaware Indians from the surrounding countryside. Free blacks traded with shopkeepers who spoke German and French. Boasting many of the features of a large European city, Philadelphia was also uniquely American in the variety of its inhabitants.

The Colonial Population Grows and Changes

What was happening in Philadelphia symbolized what was happening in all the English colonies of North America in the early to mid-1700s. An increasing number of **immigrants** arrived daily. They were people eager to find a home in a new land that valued hard work and ability more than high birth or position. Over time, the

presence of a variety of new peoples worked to change the character of the colonial population.

A New Wave of Immigrants

The largest group of new immigrants came from Northern Ireland. These were Scottish farmers whose families had moved to Ireland a

◄ *This engraving shows the downtown area of colonial Philadelphia. Philadelphia was one of the fastest growing cities in colonial times.*

century earlier. As a result of drought and disputes with the English government in the early 1700s, many of these Scots-Irish chose to try their luck in America. A majority of them settled in Pennsylvania, but the hardiest pushed farther west into the frontier.

Some crossed the Appalachians into what is now West Virginia. Others moved south to North Carolina and South Carolina.

Crop failures and constant wars in Europe drove many Germans to America. Germans soon developed improved versions of the rifle and the iron stove. Their efficient methods of farming were copied by other colonists. Swedes also moved to the timber-covered new land. They introduced the log cabin to the North American wilderness.

America was always a safe place for those running from religious persecution as well. French Protestants, or Huguenots, settled in cities along the coast. Jews from Portuguese colonies set up synagogues in the major port cities. Catholics made homes in Maryland. Lutherans from Germany and Sweden, Calvinists from Switzerland, and Quakers from England also enriched the American mix. The word

pluralism describes a nation in which many ethnic, religious, and cultural groups live together. As the chart below shows, American society became more pluralistic in the 1700s. See Understanding Pluralism on page 50.

A Growing Population of Slaves

The largest number of newcomers to America were black slaves brought from Africa against their will. As Southern plantations grew in size, the demand for slaves increased.

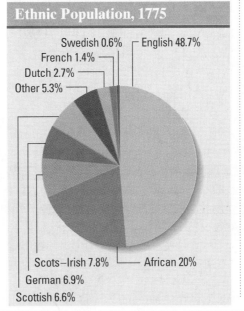

Ethnic Population, 1775

Swedish 0.6% — English 48.7%
French 1.4%
Dutch 2.7%
Other 5.3%

Scots–Irish 7.8% — African 20%
German 6.9%
Scottish 6.6%

◄ *This chart shows the great diversity in the population of the colonies. Notice that by 1775 less than half of the colonists were of English background.*

49

Since colonial times, first-time visitors to America have marveled at the broad diversity of its people. For many years, America has prided itself on its ability to accept—and to borrow from—the lifestyles and values of many different nationalities. It has also recognized and respected the practice of many different languages and religions. This belief that many cultures can co-exist in one country is called pluralism. In fact, our national motto expresses this fundamental belief: *E pluribus unum*, Latin for "out of many, one."

Many nations in the world are not pluralistic. For example, Japan has a very homogeneous population. That is, most of the Japanese people share the same language, customs, and ancestry. The Japanese celebrate their likeness rather than their differences. For more than 1,200 years, the Japanese have discouraged immigration to their country. They believe that their sameness—their *nihonjinron* or "Japaneseness" binds them together and makes them strong.

Present Day Pluralism

Today, the United States is becoming more pluralistic than ever before. The official 1980 census showed that the largest groups of American citizens are of British and German origin (22 percent each). Other large groups include Irish (18 percent); African (11.7 percent; Hispanic (6.4 percent); and Chinese, Japanese, and Filipino (1.2%). Since 1980, the diversity of our population has continued to increase through large-scale immigration, particularly from Asia and Latin America.

American Life Enriched

What does pluralism mean to the United States as a democratic society? It means that citizens of all cultural groups have a voice in the decision-making process of government. It means that people must compromise, or settle their differences by yielding on certain points. In addition, our pluralistic society challenges Americans to exercise tolerance, or respect, for the opinions, customs, traditions, and lifestyles of others. Today, as in the past, the diversity of our people greatly enriches American life and strengthens the nation.

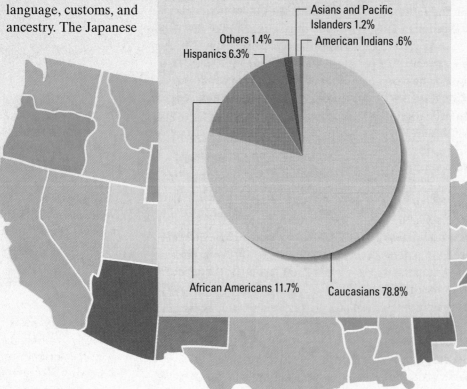

The 1980 U.S. Census

- Asians and Pacific Islanders 1.2%
- American Indians .6%
- Others 1.4%
- Hispanics 6.3%
- African Americans 11.7%
- Caucasians 78.8%

Slave traders brought over 250,000 Africans to the colonies between 1700 and 1775. On the eve of the Revolution, one in five Americans was black.

A few African Americans won their freedom and became farmers, artisans, and shopkeepers. In most places, however, laws limited the rights of free blacks, denying them full equality with whites.

African Americans made many valuable contributions to American life. They showed planters how to grow rice, which became South Carolina's most important food crop and product. They also brought improved methods for herding cattle and introduced African-style boats, baskets, and fishing nets. Large numbers of Africans converted to Christianity and joined their rich musical tradition with their new religion. Out of this blend of cultures came the spiritual, a distinctly American form of religious song. ■

■ *How did the make-up of the American population change between 1700 and 1775?*

A Varied Population Creates a Unique New Culture

Different immigrant groups brought their own special cultural traditions to America. Living closely together, people from different lands began to form a very distinct new culture. Most colonists continued to think of themselves as residents of a particular colony. By 1750, however, the term *American* was widely used to describe both the colonists and their culture.

A New American Dialect

Although English remained the principal language of the colonies, an "American" English began to evolve. Colonists often used the American Indian names for towns, rivers, and mountains. They also borrowed Indian words such as *squash, chipmunk, raccoon, skunk,* and *woodchuck* for new plants and animals.

New words from many different cultures became part of Americans' everyday speech. From African languages came the words *banjo, yam,* and *okra*. From the German language came *sauerkraut* and *beer*. Dutch settlers added *cole slaw, cookies,* and *waffles,* together with the words *boss, Santa Claus,* and *Yankee* to the American vocabulary. The Scots contributed *brae* and *plaid*. On top of all this, Americans made new words by combining older ones in new ways, such as *bullfrog* and *snowshoe*. In 1756, Dr. Samuel Johnson, the English author and dictionary writer, called the colonists' speech an "American dialect." The New World had produced a new form of English.

Growing Religious Tolerance

The great variety of religious traditions carried on in the colonies led to a growing spirit of toleration in the 1700s. A Swedish traveler, Peter Kalm, was impressed by the religious freedom he found in America. Such freedom was not easy to find in Europe at that time. "There are many Jews settled in New York, who possess great privileges," he wrote. "They have great synagogues and houses . . . and are allowed to keep shops. . . . They enjoy all the privileges common to the other inhabitants."

Even so, Jews, Catholics, and atheists could not hold office or vote in most colonies. But, for the most part, religious persecution had almost disappeared by the mid-1700s.

The Great Awakening

Between 1730 and 1750, a religious revival known as the Great Awakening swept through the colonies. Ministers responded to a long decline in church membership with a

▲ *The colonies had little industry. New arrivals found they needed a spinning wheel like this one to make yarn and thread.*

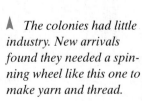

This needlepoint showing a colonial wedding scene was made in the period of the Great Awakening.

■ *What features of everyday life in the colonies were distinctly American?*

vivid description of the horrors of hell caused members of his congregation to rush to be "born again." They renewed their faith by declaring themselves newly converted.

George Whitefield *(WIT feeld)*, a British preacher, stormed through the colonies in 1739 and 1740. His outdoor sermons drew huge crowds. Whitefield was a powerful speaker, and spellbound audiences followed his exhortation to "fly to Christ."

During the Great Awakening, lay people, or non-clergy, played a greater role in religious matters. They rose in church to speak of their conversion. They even spread the Christian message as lay preachers. Some preachers stressed the equality of all people and attacked religious and political leaders who had great wealth and power.

The Great Awakening had a very strong effect on the colonies, influencing slaves as well as white colonists. By attacking the authority of the official church of England, it strengthened other religions. For the same reason, it wore down ties between church and state. The Awakening gave people a new sense of self-worth. They had been part of a powerful experience. They had challenged the authority of the established church beliefs. These experiences helped the colonists develop a greater sense of independence and helped to pave the way for the American Revolution. ■

new approach. They attempted to reach the hearts as well as the minds of their listeners.

In New England, Jonathan Edwards was the leading figure of the Awakening. He warned his congregation that sin placed their very souls in great danger: "O sinner! . . . You hang by a slender thread, with the flames of divine wrath flashing about it." His

Colonial Governments Seek Greater Independence

The 3,000-mile-wide Atlantic Ocean separated England from the colonies. It took five weeks or longer for a message to arrive from Great Britain. The gap in space and time allowed early American colonial governments to develop an important role.

In the first half of the 1700s, the British government was busy with European conflicts. It took little interest in its colonies. England seldom enforced the rules it set for its

colonies, a policy known as **salutary neglect.** For example, in 1733, England set a tax on molasses that the colonies imported from outside the British Empire. The colonists bribed customs officials to ignore the tax. The English government did nothing.

A governor, a council, and an assembly shared political power in each colony. Usually the governor received his appointment from the king. In turn, the governor named a

council of advisers. The colonists elected members to an assembly that represented them.

Not everybody could vote for the assembly. That right was limited to free white males over the age of 21. Voters also had to own land and, in some colonies, meet religious qualifications as well. These voting requirements were very much like England's. But because land ownership was more common in the colonies than in England, so was the right to vote. In New England, up to 75 percent of the white male population could vote. The percentage of eligible voters was generally smaller in the South.

Through the years, as the royal power grew weaker, the power of colonial assemblies increased. By the 1730s, they had won the right to approve plans for spending money. This right, "the power of the purse,"

was crucial. For example, if a colonial assembly did not vote funds for a road, the road would not be built. If a governor wanted to raise troops for the colony's defense, he had to ask the assembly to provide the money to make this possible.

In all colonies except Virginia, the assembly also controlled the salary of the governor. This power often made the governor less willing to oppose the assembly's demands.

The king had to approve any law passed by the assemblies. But a **veto**, or rejection of a bill from a colonial assembly, meant the assembly would often pass another bill that was similar to the one vetoed. Gradually it became clear that the assemblies held most of the power to make the colonies' laws. When England tried to reassert its authority in the 1760s, serious conflict resulted. ■

■ *How did the British policy of salutary neglect contribute to the development of colonial governments?*

1. **FOCUS** How did many kinds of new immigrants help to create a distinct American culture?

2. **CONNECT** In what ways were the English colonies different in the 1750s from what they had been in the 1650s?

3. **POLITICAL SYSTEMS** What was the "power of the purse," and how did it affect colonial politics?

4. **CRITICAL THINKING** How do you think the colonial leaders of the Anglican Church felt about the Great Awakening? Why?

5. **ACTIVITY** Using the maps on pages 672 and 698–699, make a list of at least 10 place names that are of American Indian origin.

LESSON 2

Growing Conflict with England

What were the causes of the colonists' growing resentment of British rule?

Key Terms

- writs of assistance
- boycott
- embargo

➤ *To show their disapproval of the 1765 Stamp Act, these citizens from Boston seized and burned stacks of the British government's official stamps.*

As the sun rose over Boston on August 14, 1765, a scarecrow-like figure clad in rags dangled from a large oak tree. This hanging effigy, or dummy, represented Andrew Oliver, stamp distributor for Boston. Underneath was a warning: "He that takes this down is an enemy to his country." The display was a protest against the Stamp Act, due to be enforced in November, which required stamps on nearly all printed materials. The colonists were enraged that they should be taxed without their consent or, at the very least, without their representation.

Throughout the day, Bostonians gathered at the spot to view the protest. At one point the sheriff arrived with orders to remove the effigy. But when a threatening crowd surrounded him, he quickly retreated.

At the end of a tense afternoon, the leaders of the mob cut down the figure of Oliver and nailed it to a board. Four men carried it through the streets, heading for a new brick building on the docks of Boston's South End. Word on the street said that this would be Oliver's office for distributing the hated stamps. In less than an hour, the mob tore the building down.

Led by Ebenezer MacIntosh, a poor 28-year-old shoemaker, the crowd then marched to Oliver's home. Warned by the sheriff, Oliver and his family had just slipped out the back way when the protesters arrived. While one group cut off the head of the effigy, others destroyed Oliver's stable and coach. Breaking into the house, the mob smashed the windows and tore apart the furniture. They emptied the bottles from Oliver's large and elegant wine cellar and tore up his gardens. Oliver got the message and resigned as stamp distributor the next day.

Boston was not alone in its hatred of the Stamp Act. More protests followed in other colonial towns and cities. The colonists would stoutly resist the efforts of the British government to tax them. "No taxation without representation" became their rallying cry.

Rivalry for North America Leads to Seven Years' War

To understand the reasons for the Stamp Act riots, you must first look at the Seven Years' War, also called the French and Indian War. This war was actually one in a series of wars fought between England and France beginning in the late 1600s. While competing for North American territory on the one hand, the two European nations were also battling for dominance of Europe.

Both England and France claimed territory along the Ohio River Valley. As English colonists from Virginia began to settle this area, they faced resistance from both the French and the Indians. In 1755, England sent soldiers under General Edward Braddock to the region, but the French and their Indian allies drove them back.

George Washington, a young Virginian, was part of Braddock's force. He noted that British soldiers in their bright red coats were easy targets for Indians who fired from hiding places in the forest. Washington was later able to put this knowledge to use during the American Revolution.

Braddock's defeat did not discourage the British. They sent the full might of their military force against the French empire in America. In 1759, three years after the war started, the British took the French outpost at Quebec, Canada. The following year, all of Canada was in British hands.

By the Treaty of Paris in 1763, England gained Canada and the French lands east of the Mississippi River, (as the map below shows). Because Spain had unwisely entered the war on France's side, it lost Florida to England. But Spain received French territory west of the Mississippi as compensation, or payment, for this loss. ■

■ *What did England gain as a result of the Seven Years' War?*

◄ *After defeating the French in the Seven Years' War, England controlled the entire eastern half of North America. Spain claimed much of what was left of the continent.*

European Land Claims in North America, 1763

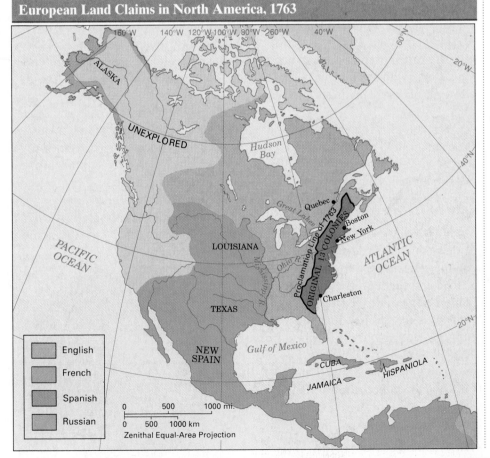

English
French
Spanish
Russian

0   500   1000 mi.
0   500   1000 km
Zenithal Equal-Area Projection

Reviewing the American Revolution

British Policies Stir Colonial Protests

As a result of the war, England's North American territory was doubled, but the war also plunged England into a huge debt. The British government believed the colonies should help pay this debt, but first England had to assert its right to control the colonists' economic affairs.

The Proclamation of 1763

The colonists expected to benefit from England's control over the western frontier. Many colonial farmers wanted to move into the area. They received a rude shock when the king issued the Proclamation of 1763. This act closed the newly won territory west of the Appalachians to all colonists. You can find the Proclamation Line on the map on page 55.

Chief Pontiac of the Ottawas was indirectly responsible for the Proclamation. Seeing the new British rulers as a threat, he had organized many tribes in a widespread attack on British forts in 1762. Pontiac's Rebellion was only partly successful. Nevertheless, the British wanted time to negotiate a treaty with the Indians before allowing any more colonists into the area.

The colonists felt cheated by the Proclamation. Many of them had fought with the British troops to drive out the French. They wanted to share in the fruits of victory.

The Quartering Act

England left an army in the colonies to guard the frontier. In order to feed and shelter those troops, Parliament passed the Quartering Act in 1765. This act required that colonial cities give lodging to the royal troops. The law also ordered local governments to pay for such supplies as firewood, bedding, candles, vinegar, and salt.

The British military commander had his headquarters in New York. At first, the New York Assembly refused to vote any money for his troops, saying that the Quartering Act placed an unfair burden on the colony. But when Parliament threatened to take away the powers of the assembly, it finally gave up the money.

The Stamp Act

Parliament also passed the Stamp Act in 1765—the most hated of its attempts to raise money. The act required colonists to buy a revenue stamp each time they registered a legal document or bought newspapers, pamphlets, almanacs, liquor licenses, or playing cards. Two revenue stamps are shown here. Another is shown on page 57. Most hard hit by the tax were lawyers, tavern owners, merchants, and printers.

When news of the Stamp Act reached America, the colonists became enraged. In Boston and other colonial cities, groups calling themselves the Sons of Liberty formed to protest the Stamp Act. Rioting broke out in a number of these cities, including New York and Philadelphia.

In October, representatives from nine colonies met in New York at the

THE REPEAL—
OR THE FUNERAL OF MISS AME STAMP

This British political cartoon, which pictures a funeral procession for the recently repealed Stamp Act, pokes fun at Parliament and British Prime Minister George Grenville (fourth from left).

Stamp Act Congress. There they wrote a Declaration of Rights. This declaration expressed their opposition both to taxation without representa-

tion in Parliament and to trial without jury in the courts. They asked the king to repeal the Stamp Act. They claimed that only colonial assemblies could legally impose taxes on them, except taxes meant to regulate trade.

In the face of strong colonial opposition, the British government backed down. Before the petition even reached England, Parliament repealed the Stamp Act in March 1766. When the news reached the colonies, people paraded in the streets. ■

■ *How did the Seven Years' War change the relationship between England and the colonies?*

Tensions Reach the Breaking Point

Despite the failure of the Stamp Act, England kept trying to control and tax the colonies. In 1767, Parliament passed the Townshend Acts, which taxed paint, glass, lead, paper, and tea. To enforce the act, customs officials were granted **writs of assistance.** These documents, issued by a court, gave them the power to enter private homes and businesses at any time, with no reasonable suspicion, to look for smuggled goods.

In response, men and women in the colonies launched a **boycott**—that is, they refused to buy the newly taxed

goods. Colonists made their own clothes, paper, and paint. Women organized the Daughters of Liberty and held public spinning bees to make American cloth. The boycott helped create a sense of unity.

The Boston Massacre

Anti-British feeling ran highest in the city of Boston where British troops had been stationed since 1768. Samuel Adams, a leader of the Sons of Liberty, whipped up crowds of protesters and wrote inflammatory newspaper articles.

Reviewing the American Revolution

Engrav'd Printed & Sold by PAUL REVERE BOSTON

▲ Silversmith Paul Revere's famous engraving of Boston's "Bloody Massacre" circulated widely in the colonies and stirred up anger against the British. A propaganda piece, Revere's picture refers to the British-controlled Customs House as "Butcher's Hall" and shows the British captain giving the order to fire.

Tensions came to a head on March 5, 1770. On that day a band of unemployed laborers attacked the guard of the Boston Customs House. When British soldiers came to his aid, the crowd pelted them with oyster shells and snowballs. In the scuffle that followed, someone started to shoot and five rioters were killed. The first to die was Crispus Attucks, a black man who had fled slavery to become a sailor.

Patriots immediately branded the incident a "massacre" to gain sympathy for their cause. Adams's articles about the incident spread news of the Boston Massacre throughout the colonies.

The Boston Tea Party

As a result of the colonists' boycott, the British government repealed the Townshend taxes on all items except tea in 1770. The news calmed most colonists.

However, Samuel Adams formed a Committee of Correspondence in Boston in 1772 to keep American complaints against England in the public eye. Towns in other colonies followed his lead and exchanged written complaints about British actions.

In 1773, Parliament passed the Tea Act, which allowed the British East India Company to sell tea directly to the colonists. Previously the company sold tea to British wholesalers,

who in turn sold tea to the colonists. By selling more tea at lower prices, England expected to benefit more from its tax on imported tea.

Protest was immediate. In Charleston, colonists locked the tea in warehouses. In North Carolina, women burned their tea in public. In some colonies, Americans prevented tea ships from landing.

On December 16, 1773, a band of men disguised as Indians boarded three tea ships in Boston harbor. While a crowd looked on, the leaders of the "Boston Tea Party" threw hundreds of chests of tea overboard.

King George III was furious. He said of the colonists, "We must master them or totally leave them to themselves and treat them as aliens."

The Intolerable Acts

In 1774, Parliament passed a series of measures designed to punish the colonists. It closed the port of Boston until the city paid for the destroyed tea. It increased the powers of the governor to the point that he could even ban town meetings. At the same time, a new Quartering Act allowed British commanders to station troops in private homes. Finally, the Quebec Act put much of the Ohio River Valley into the province of Quebec, cutting off this land from New York, Pennsylvania, and Virginia.

Colonists called these measures the Intolerable Acts. The Committees of Correspondence urged the colonies to hold a meeting about the crisis. Within months, the colonies had agreed to meet.

The First Continental Congress

Delegates from all 13 colonies except Georgia met at Carpenter's Hall in Philadelphia from September 5 to October 26, 1774. Calling themselves the First Continental Congress, they agreed to support Massachusetts and passed a resolution that declared the Intolerable Acts null and void. They also called for further acts of protest. But to soothe those who wanted to settle the crisis peacefully, the delegates sent a petition of their grievances to the British government.

The Congress also set up the Continental Association to enforce an **embargo,** or ban on trade, against England. The Congress set the stage for future developments when it called on each colony to begin training soldiers for defense.

Before the delegates adjourned, they scheduled another Congress for May of the following year. By the time the Second Continental Congress met, fighting had already begun. ■

◄ *This wooden chest, typical of the beautifully decorated tea chests of the period, was recovered from Boston harbor after the Boston Tea Party.*

■ *What actions taken by Parliament contributed to the growing tension between England and the colonies?*

R E V I E W

1. **FOCUS** What were the causes of the colonists' growing resentment of British rule?
2. **CONNECT** Did England continue its policy of salutary neglect after the Seven Years' War? Explain.
3. **ECONOMICS** In what sense were economic issues responsible for the outbreak of the American Revolution?
4. **CRITICAL THINKING** Why do you think it was so difficult for the British government to maintain tight control over the colonies?
5. **WRITING ACTIVITY** Imagine that you are a colonial printer. Write a letter to the King of England stating why you think the Stamp Act is unfair.

Reviewing the American Revolution

Charting Pre-Revolutionary Events

Here's Why

Timelines allow you to see a sequence of events and then to understand how these events affect one another. In this chapter you have read about a number of events that took place in England and the colonies before the Revolutionary War. The distance between England and the colonies delayed communication by months. There was often a definite connection, however, between what happened in one place and what happened in the other.

Suppose you wanted to find out how various events related to the onset of the war. Two parallel timelines—one of events in England and the other of events in the colonies—would help you to see the order and frequency of events on both sides of the conflict. By comparing the two timelines, you could more clearly see the relationship of one event to another. You could also see the progression of related events within that time period.

Here's How

Look at the two timelines on page 61. They are marked off in decades from 1740 to 1776. The events on the top timeline occurred in England, while the events in the line below occurred in the colonies.

You can see that a number of events in England and the colonies were happening at the same time. Identify the relationship between those events. For example, in 1765, Parliament passed the Stamp Act. That same year the colonists staged protests and petitioned for repeal of the act (see A. B. Frost's picture at the left of colonists in New York burning seized stamped papers). When England passed the Stamp Act, the colonies were quick to respond. By the next year, the act was repealed. There was a direct relationship between the colonists' protests and the act's repeal.

Now look at the frequency of events. Notice that there are more events listed on the timeline after 1760 than before. That could mean that conflicts between England the colonies were increasing at that time. Remember, however, that the analysis that you can conduct by using a timeline is dependent on the information that it contains. You need to be sure that all the information on the timeline is accurate and that all the relevant events that occurred between the colonies and England appear on the timeline.

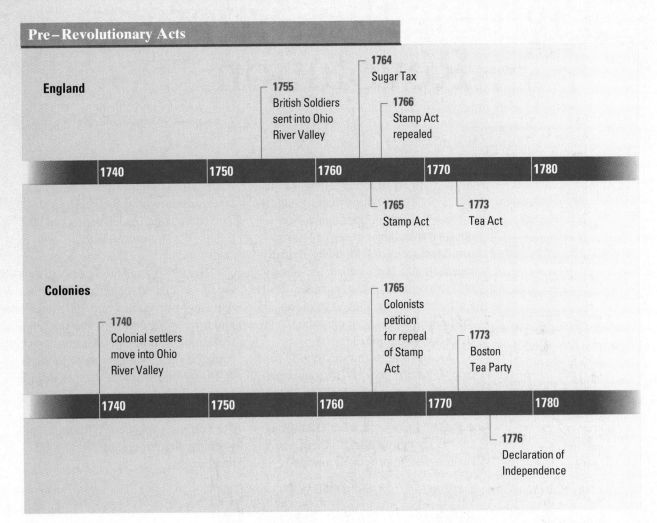

Pre–Revolutionary Acts

England

- **1755** British Soldiers sent into Ohio River Valley
- **1764** Sugar Tax
- **1766** Stamp Act repealed

1740 | 1750 | 1760 | 1770 | 1780

- **1765** Stamp Act
- **1773** Tea Act

Colonies

- **1740** Colonial settlers move into Ohio River Valley
- **1765** Colonists petition for repeal of Stamp Act
- **1773** Boston Tea Party

1740 | 1750 | 1760 | 1770 | 1780

- **1776** Declaration of Independence

Try It

Copy the timelines above onto a piece of paper. Read the following list of events, and go back to the chapter to find the dates of each event. Decide on which timeline they belong and enter them on your copy.

- Proclamation of 1763
- Quartering Act
- Stamp Act Congress
- Townshend Acts
- Boston Massacre
- Committees of Correspondence
- First Continental Congress
- Green Mountain Boys take Ticonderoga

Can you see that adding events to the timeline changes the conclusions you are able to reach? This new timeline now includes your researched additions. Which events happened first? Which events appear to be reactions to other events? What relationships do you see between the events you entered on the England timeline and those you entered on the colonies timeline?

Apply It

Create a pair of parallel timelines for the past year. Mark each one off in one-month segments. On one timeline enter important national events such as presidential elections, Supreme Court decisions, or scientific discoveries.

On the other timeline enter important events in the life of your family over the same time period. Can you see a relationship between the national events and your personal life?

L E S S O N 3

Fighting the American Revolution

How did the colonies manage to defeat the most powerful nation in the world?

Key Terms

- militia
- minuteman
- republic

On the afternoon of April 19, 1775, eight Patriots—supporters of American independence—lay dead on the village green at Lexington, Massachusetts, killed by British musket-balls. In Concord, the liberty pole—a symbol of the colonists' desire for freedom—lay hacked to pieces. The courthouse, burned by the British, still smoldered.

Meanwhile, along the bloody road from Concord back to Boston, curses and screams filled the air. The 700 British troops that had overrun Lexington and Concord were attempting an orderly march back to their base in Boston. But hundreds of enraged colonists, firing from houses and barns, from behind stone walls and trees, assaulted the British troops. The red-coated soldiers shrieked and fell as Patriot musket-balls found their marks.

The British suffered heavy losses. By the end of the day, 70 British soldiers had been killed and 200 more had been wounded. Outside Boston that night, hundreds of campfires surrounded the city. These were the fires of 16,000 Patriots who were beginning an armed vigil.

A spark had flown, and the powder keg had exploded. Without plan or warning, the American Revolution had begun.

➤ *In this color print of the Battle of Lexington, British soldiers and colonial minutemen engage in the first military encounter of what would be a seven-year war.*

Early Battles of the Revolution

The outbreak of armed conflict took many in the colonies by surprise. Less than a month before the fighting in Lexington and Concord, members of the Virginia Assembly had been shocked when they heard a proposal by Patrick Henry, politician and colonial leader, to prepare Virginia for war. Nevertheless, Henry's words proved to be prophetic:

> *Gentlemen may cry peace, peace—but there is no peace. The war is actually begun! The next gale that sweeps from the north will bring to our ears the clash of resounding arms! Our brethren are already in the field! Why stand we here idle? . . . I know not what course others may take; but as for me, give me liberty, or give me death!*

Lexington and Concord

In the fall of 1774, a group of middle-class Massachusetts colonists—including John Hancock and Paul Revere—met at Concord and decided to prepare for a possible war with Britain. They named Hancock, a wealthy merchant, to organize an armed force. His **militia,** or citizen army, called themselves **minutemen,** because they were ready to fight at a minute's notice. (See Moment in Time on page 64.)

The royal governor of Massachusetts, stationed at Boston, was General Thomas Gage. In April 1775, he sent 700 soldiers to Concord to arrest the Patriot leaders. Paul Revere learned of the plan. On the night of April 18, 1775, he prepared to warn the Patriots.

Boston was already an armed camp. Yet Revere slipped out of town and rode off on his horse down the road the British would travel. He shouted the alarm as he passed the houses of minutemen along the way.

A little before midnight, Revere reached Lexington, where Hancock was hiding. True to their name, 70 of Lexington's minutemen were waiting on the village green when the British marched in at dawn on April 19.

When the colonists refused to lay down their arms, the British soldiers rushed forward, firing several volleys. They killed eight minutemen and wounded ten others.

By noon, a larger force of minutemen had assembled at Concord. They blocked the North Bridge and this time fired from behind walls and trees. The "shot heard 'round the world" dealt the British their first casualties. Philosopher and poet Ralph Waldo Emerson later captured this moment in the following stanzas of his 1837 poem, "Concord Hymn":

> *By the rude bridge that arched the flood,*
> *Their flag to April's breeze unfurled,*
> *Here once the embattled farmers stood*
> *And fired the shot heard 'round the world.*
>
> *Spirit that made those heroes dare*
> *To die, and leave their children free,*
> *Bid Time and Nature gently spare*
> *The shaft we raise to them and thee.*

Ticonderoga

In the area that is now Vermont, Ethan Allen organized a group of tough frontiersmen called the Green Mountain Boys. In May 1775, they surprised the sleeping British troops at Fort Ticonderoga in New York. Allen captured the fort's 50 cannons. His Green Mountain Boys slowly dragged these cannon along backwoods trails to the Patriot forces in Boston, where Washington later used them to drive the British from the city.

▲ *This lantern, hung from the belfry of the Old North Church, sent Paul Revere on his midnight ride.*

How Do We Know?

Some of Patrick Henry's speeches–including his most famous "Give Me Liberty or Give Me Death" address–were never formally written down. The speeches exist only as they were remembered by people who heard them. A reconstruction of Henry's 'Liberty or Death' speech appears on page 664.

A Minuteman

11:12 A.M. April 19, 1775
Near the North Bridge
in Concord, Massachusetts

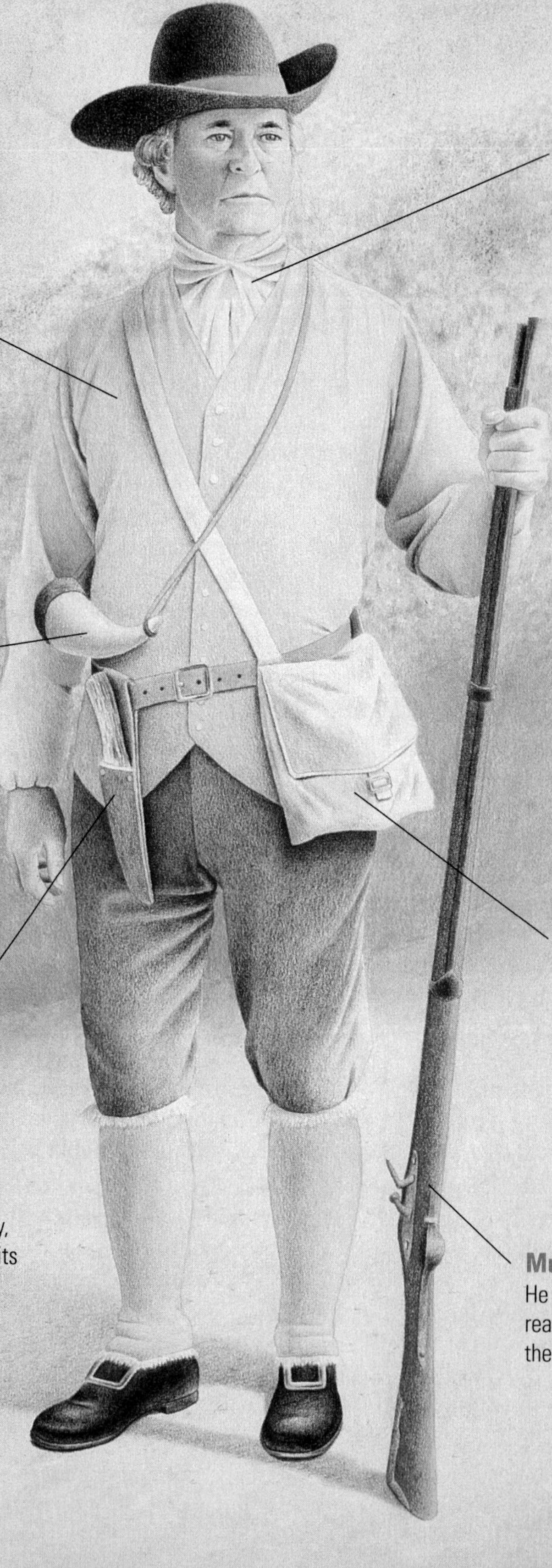

Homespun Shirt
He grabbed his favorite shirt off the clothesline. His wife spun the yarn herself and wove the cloth on her loom last winter.

Vest
His mother-in-law sewed this from the hide of a deer he shot last winter. It keeps him warm on cool spring mornings such as this one.

Powder Horn
This morning, a neighbor ran to tell him about the British troops coming from Boston. He quickly got dressed, filled this powder horn with gun powder and ran to join his fellow patriots.

Haversack
On his way out the door, he stuffed some dried apples and a biscuit in his heavy canvas bag.

Hunting Knife
When he dressed up as an Indian for the "Tea Party" in Boston back in '73, he used this knife to cut the ropes of the tea crates. Most recently, he used it to clean two rabbits for dinner last night.

Musket
He holds it proudly as he stands ready, wondering anxiously when the British troops will arrive.

View of The ATTACK on BUNKER'S HILL, with the Burning of CHARLES TOWN, June 17, 1775.

◄ *"Don't fire until you see the whites of their eyes" was the order given by an American general at the Battle of Bunker Hill, pictured here.*

The Battle of Bunker Hill

In order to defend Boston, General Thomas Gage decided to place troops on Bunker Hill. Once more the Americans learned of his plans. On the night of June 16, over a thousand Patriots moved to nearby Breed's Hill. Gage ordered his men to drive them off. "Don't fire until you see the whites of their eyes," ordered American General Israel Putnam, in an attempt to conserve ammunition. When the British troops were 100 feet away, the American guns roared, and the British front ranks fell. Yet the British surged forward, again and again, until the Patriots ran out of ammunition and retreated.

After the Battle of Bunker Hill, over 1,000 British soldiers lay dead or wounded, while the Americans lost only 397 men. Although the British technically won the battle because they forced the Patriots to retreat, the Americans had shown that the British faced a hard fight. ■

■ *Find evidence to support the following statement: The early battles showed that the Revolution was likely to be a long and difficult war.*

The Road to the Declaration of Independence

Despite the fighting, many colonists still wanted to avoid war. In July 1775, the Second Continental Congress sent the Olive Branch Petition to King George III. It blamed Parliament for the trouble and urged the king to intervene. Instead, he proclaimed that the colonies were in rebellion and gave orders "to bring the traitors to justice."

Common Sense Stirs Colonists

In January 1776, a pamphlet titled *Common Sense* appeared in the colonies. Its author, Thomas Paine, had moved to America from England only a year before. But the news of Lexington and Concord had inflamed him. Calling George III "the Royal Brute of Britain," Paine declared, "A government of our own is our natural right. . . ." He then urged the colonists to establish a **republic**, or system of representative government.

Common Sense sold half a million copies in six months. Arguments about the legality of Parliament's acts seemed pale and fussy in the face of Paine's outright demand for independence.

Writing the Declaration

In the late spring of 1776, public sentiment finally persuaded the Continental Congress to take the final step. The delegates named Thomas Jefferson to head a committee to write a declaration of independence. Jefferson, a brilliant young lawyer from Virginia, took pen in hand and wrote a first draft.

Jefferson's words stirred the colonists: "All men are created equal . . . with certain unalienable rights; that among these are life, liberty, and the pursuit of happiness."

On July 4, 1776, John Hancock, the president of the Congress, signed his name to the Declaration. Legend said he wrote it large enough for King George to read without his glasses. The delegates from the remaining colonies added their names. The English colonies had become the United States of America. (For the full text of the Declaration of Independence, see pages 656–659.) ■

■ *What events finally convinced many colonists that they should declare their independence from England?*

War in the North

If the Declaration were to become more than a piece of paper, an army had to defend its bold words. The year before, in 1775, Congress had asked George Washington to organize a Continental Army.

Washington's Early Campaign

When Washington led his small force toward Boston in March 1776, the British withdrew. But Washington knew that the British commander, General William Howe, eyed a bigger prize: New York City.

Howe's troops landed on Long Island in August 1776. By this time Washington had managed to assemble an army of roughly 20,000 men representing nearly every colony. When Washington tried to block Howe's forces, however, the experienced British troops routed the Americans. Only a desperate nighttime retreat saved the Continental Army.

▼ *Progress in the war was slow for both sides. The conflict dragged on for seven years.*

Major Battles of the Revolution

Lexington and Concord
April 19. Minutemen, warned by Paul Revere, open the war by confronting 700 British soldiers and forcing them to retreat to Boston.

Trenton
Dec. 26. Having crossed the icy Delaware river, George Washington and 2,400 men strike Hessian mercenaries and take 900 prisoners.

1775	1776	1777	1778

Bunker Hill
June 17. Colonial militia (see drum at left), dug in on the hill overlooking Boston harbor, are ousted by British soldiers. But in the process, the British suffer twice the losses of the colonists.

Ticonderoga
May 10. Surprise attack by Ethan Allen and his "Green Mountain Boys" on the British fort results in the capture of much-needed cannons. It also marks the first surrender by a British commander.

Saratoga
Oct. 17. British plans to isolate New England are thwarted when commander Burgoyne has to surrender to General Horatio Gates (below).

As winter came on, Howe rested his army in New Jersey. Washington struck back in a sneak attack. On Christmas night, 1776, he led his forces across the Delaware River to Trenton, New Jersey. Washington's men surprised and captured many Hessian mercenaries—German soldiers—hired to help the British. Ten days later, Washington captured Princeton, New Jersey. These victories raised the colonists' spirits.

Victory Brings French Support

In 1777, British General John Burgoyne worked out a plan to isolate New England by bringing his army south from Quebec to Albany, recapturing Fort Ticonderoga on the way. According to Burgoyne's ambitious plan, General Howe and his army would sail up the Hudson from New York City, thereby cutting off all land routes from New England to the other colonies.

A gambler, "Gentleman Johnny" Burgoyne had placed a bet of 50 pounds with a friend in London that he would return victorious from America by Christmas of 1777. After successfully retaking Fort Ticonderoga, however, Burgoyne experienced a summer of disastrous encounters in the wilderness of upper New York. But Howe had gone to Philadelphia. Burgoyne was left stranded.

At Saratoga, New York, American General Horatio Gates attacked Burgoyne's poorly positioned forces. Moving swiftly, Gates surrounded the British, cutting them off from supplies. On October 17, 1777, Burgoyne had to surrender his entire army of 6,000 men to General Gates.

At the time of the American victory at Saratoga, Benjamin Franklin was in Paris, trying to persuade the French government to help the colonies. The French wanted to see their British enemy defeated, but they also needed proof that the Americans could win the war. The news of Saratoga provided a convincing argument. Before long, French ships were carrying soldiers and supplies to the war-torn colonies.

Cowpens, S.C.
Jan 17. After the defeats of Savannah and Charleston, this battle is a crucial victory for the colonists under the brilliant Daniel Morgan, who receives the medal at left for his efforts.

1779	1780	1781	1782

Charleston
May 12. The situation at first looks bleak for the colonists in the second, Southern phase of the war. The British, having conquered Savannah in December 1779, now capture Charleston and its entire garrison.

Yorktown
Oct. 19. The war comes to an end when General Cornwallis, entrenched on the peninsula of Yorktown, is surrounded by Washington's troops on land and French ships on sea. "My God! It is all over," is the British response to the news of his surrender.

Valley Forge—a Low Point

Despite the victory at Saratoga, the winter of 1777–1778 proved to be a difficult time for the Continental Army. That winter, while the British occupied Philadelphia, Washington's men set up camp and endured the bitter cold in Valley Forge, Pennsylvania. The Continental Congress had no money left to feed and clothe its army, and many soldiers did not even have shoes. According to General Washington, "you might have tracked the army . . . to Valley Forge by the blood of their feet" Over 2,500 men died of disease or starvation that winter. Sometimes the troops had only bread and water to eat. Some began to slip away, heading for families and farms they had neglected in what now seemed like a lost cause.

Washington told his men they had to stay together. Each day he rode around the camp, reminding them of the cause for which they were fighting. By the sheer force of his personality, he kept his ragtag army from falling apart. ■

■ *Why did the French decide to enter the Revolution on the side of the colonists?*

War in the West and South

Valley Forge marked a turning point in the war. After the spring of 1778, as the map on the opposite page shows, the major fighting in the Revolution turned to the West and South.

Clark Drives British from the West

On the Ohio frontier, Lieutenant Colonel George Rogers Clark raised the money to supply an American force in early 1778. His aim was to take the British wilderness outposts. Clark's frontier fighters knew the paths through the forests and mountains. They marched down the Ohio River Valley and appeared without warning to attack British camps. When Clark's men captured the British fort at Vincennes in February 1779, their victory virtually ended British control of the frontier.

British Successes in the South

Late in 1778, the British captured Savannah, Georgia. Then, on May 12, 1780, they won in their second try to take Charleston, South Carolina. England continued to build on these successes in the following months. General Gates, the hero of Saratoga, took command of the American army in the South. But in August 1780, British General Charles Cornwallis dealt him a disastrous defeat at Camden, South Carolina. Cornwallis then moved west, plundering the large plantations as he went.

His only opposition came from Francis Marion, known as the Swamp Fox. Marion led a band of Carolina men in hit-and-run attacks on the British. Marion and his men harassed Cornwallis by destroying supplies, then disappearing into secret lairs.

In December 1780, Washington named General Nathanael Greene to replace Gates as head of the army in the South. General Greene followed Washington's strategy: strike the British where they were weak and retreat where they were strong. Greene lured Cornwallis into battle at carefully chosen spots, handing heavy losses to the British.

▼ *This is a typical cannon of the Revolutionary period.*

L. Superior

85°W

CANADA

L. Huron

45°N

L. Michigan

Montreal

St. Lawrence R.

Quebec (1775)

Burgoyne-1777

Montgomery-1775

Maine (part of Mass.)

Arnold-1775

St. Leger-1777

L. Ontario

80°W

Detroit

L. Erie

Ft. Ticonderoga (1775)

N.H.

Oriskany (1777)

Saratoga (1777)

Bennington (1777)

Lexington (1775)

Howe-1776

Hudson R.

Albany

Concord (1775)

Bunker Hill (1775)

Boston

New York

Mass.

Conn.

R.I.

Newton (1779)

Sullivan 1779

Clinton 1777

West Point

Newport

Wyoming Massacre (1778)

White Plains (1777)

Howe-1776

Hamilton-1778

Brodhead 1779

Ohio Frontier

Pittsburgh

Ft. Augusta

Pa.

Princeton (1777)

Monmouth Court House (1778)

Brooklyn Heights (1776)

Trenton (1776)

Germantown (1777)

New York

40°N

Ft. Henry (1782)

Valley Forge

Brandywine (1777)

Philadelphia

Md.

N.J.

Clark 1778

Del.

Howe-1777

Vincennes (1779)

Ohio R.

Kentucky Frontier

Lafayette 1781

Virginia

Washington, Rochambeau-1781

Hood and Graves-1781

Richmond

35°N

INDIAN RESERVE

Proclamation Line of 1763

Yorktown (1781)

Virginia Capes (1781)

Cornwallis 1781

Greene-1781

Guilford Court House (1781)

N.C.

Cornwallis-1781

De Grasse-1781

ATLANTIC OCEAN

Cowpens (1781)

Kings Mountain (1780)

Ft. Ninety Six

S.C.

Camden (1780)

Wilmington

Eutaw Springs (1781)

Cornwallis 1780

Georgia

Charleston (1776, 1780)

30°N

WEST FLORIDA

Savannah (1778)

EAST FLORIDA

Gulf of Mexico

| 0 | 100 | 200 mi. |
| 0 | 100 | 200 km |

Albers Equal-Area Projection

	Original thirteen colonies
→	American or French movement
→	British movement
✳	American or French victory
✳	British victory
✳	Indecisive battle
■	Fort

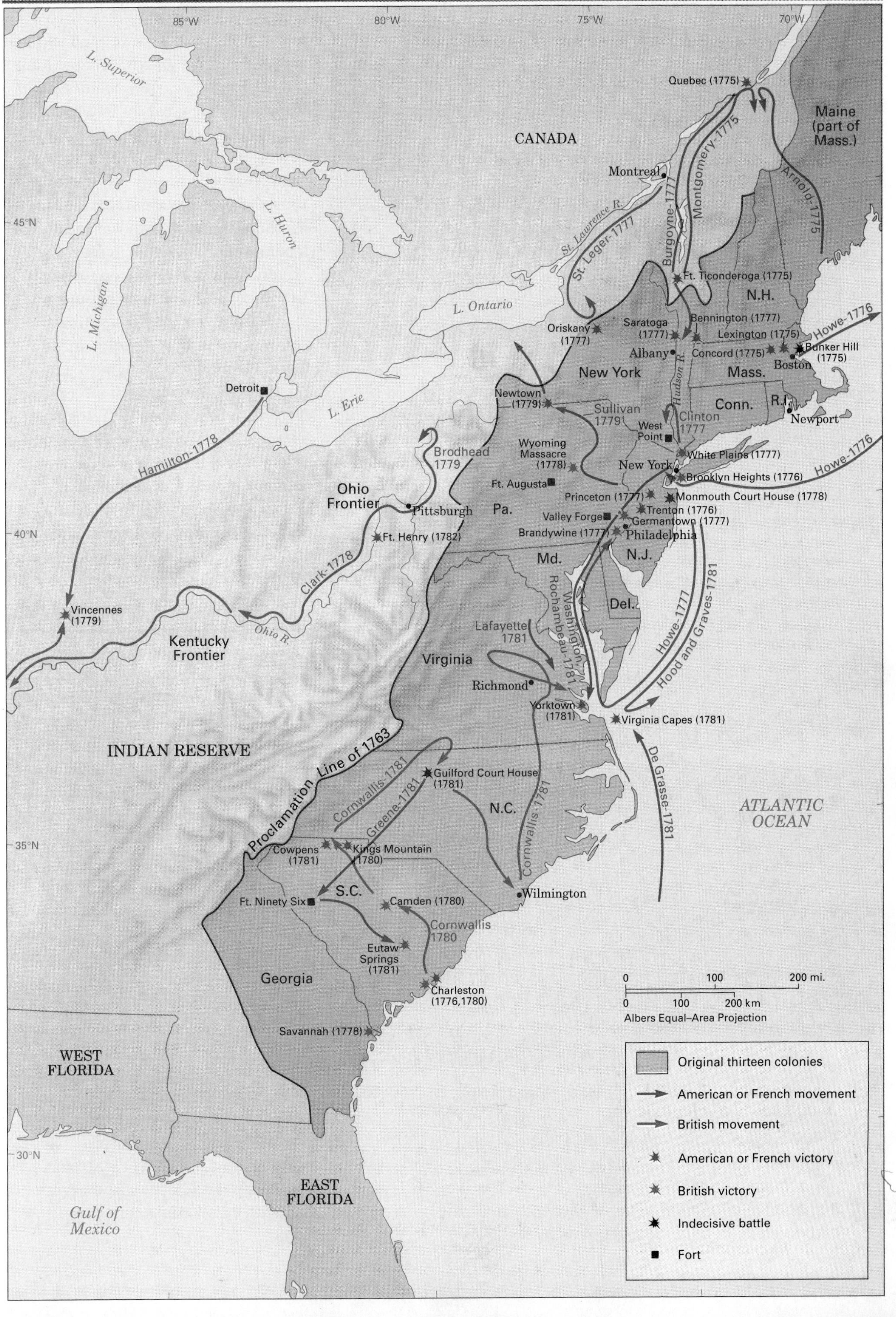

▲ *This painting shows General Washington receiving the surrender of the British at Yorktown.*

■ *What factors led to Cornwallis's surrender at Yorktown?*

Technically, Cornwallis won several victories over Greene's army, but he lost so many men that he eventually abandoned South Carolina. He then moved north to Virginia, where one final battle awaited him.

Victory at Yorktown

By 1781, French aid had strengthened the American cause. Washington's troops were now well fed and well armed. His close friend, the Marquis de Lafayette, a French nobleman inspired by the ideals of freedom, led a combined French-American army in Virginia. When Lafayette learned that Cornwallis's army was in Yorktown, he sent an urgent message to Washington. Yorktown was located on a peninsula. With enough men, the Americans could bottle up Cornwallis's forces and starve them out.

Washington led 7,000 soldiers south from his headquarters in New York. He marched them hard, knowing that this was a chance for a major victory. In September 1781, the trap snapped shut. Washington stood outside Yorktown with more than twice as many men as Cornwallis had.

British ships tried to rescue Cornwallis by sea, but French warships drove them off. Finally, on October 19, the British soldiers marched out of Yorktown and lay down their arms. ■

The Treaty of Paris

■ *Why did the delegates for the United States meet secretly with the British to negotiate the Treaty of Paris?*

Yorktown spelled the end of British control over the colonies. The defeat forced the British to ask for peace terms. In Paris, Benjamin Franklin and John Jay met with a British representative. They demanded independence and the withdrawal of all British troops. The Americans found that France wanted a treaty that would satisfy Spain, its ally. Spain did not want a strong United States to threaten its own American empire. Consequently, France tried to limit the territory that Britain would give up.

Meeting in secret, the Americans quickly hammered out an agreement with the British. It set the United States' western boundary at the Mississippi River. Franklin had hoped to get all of Canada as well, but he settled for the border that still exists between the two countries.

The Treaty of Paris, signed on September 3, 1783, officially ended the war. On December 4, the last British troops left their former colonies. The United States became the world's newest nation. ■

R E V I E W

1. **FOCUS** How did the colonies manage to defeat the most powerful nation in the world?
2. **CONNECT** How did the emergence of an American "identity" in the mid-1700s contribute to the colonists' decision to make the break from England?
3. **CITIZENSHIP** Why is the Declaration of Independence considered such an important American document?
4. **CRITICAL THINKING** How might the course of the Revolutionary War have been different if France had not entered the war on the side of the colonists?
5. **ACTIVITY** Imagine you are a member of the Second Continental Congress. Then make a chart listing the pros and cons of declaring the colonies' independence from England.

LESSON 4

Fighting the War at Home

Elizabeth Sandwith Drinker's 1777 diary account could have been written by thousands of women who survived the seven-year struggle for independence:

> November 1: . . . The Hessians go on plundering at a great rate such things as wood, potatoes, turnips, etc. Provisions are scarce among us.
>
> November 5: A soldier came to demand blankets. . . . Notwithstanding my refusal, he went upstairs and took one, and with seeming good nature begged I would excuse his borrowing it, as it was by Gen. Howe's orders.

As the Revolution wore on, the hardships of war intruded more and more deeply into domestic life:

> I will tell you what I have done. . . . retrenched [cut back on] every superfluous [extra] expense in my table and family; tea I have not drunk since last Christmas, nor bought a new gown. . . . I have learned to knit and am now making stockings of American wool for my servants, and this way do I throw in the mite [do a small part] to the public good. I know this, that as free I can die but once, but [unfree] I shall not be worthy of life.

So wrote a Philadelphia woman in a letter to a family member during the Revolution.

These women were not alone in their sacrifices. During the Revolution, daily life changed for nearly everyone. Women throughout the colonies shared the hardships of war. Women who stayed home plowed fields and harvested crops to keep farms going while their men went off to fight. They took over their husbands' businesses as shopkeepers and traders, becoming quite expert in traditionally masculine activities. After the war, many women were reluctant to give up their new roles.

When women took men's jobs, they found a new sense of self-reliance. Some learned to use guns to defend their homes. Many melted their pewter cups and plates to make bullets. Women sometimes took a direct role in the fighting to defend their homes. Nancy Morgan Hart lived in the back country of Georgia. She singlehandedly captured five British soldiers who had come to her home demanding a meal. She managed to grab one of their rifles, kill one soldier, and hold the others at bay while her daughter ran for help.

Mary Ludwig Hays, nicknamed Molly Pitcher, also became famous for her role as a fighter. When her husband fell at the Battle of Monmouth, she took his place and kept the Patriot cannon firing.

THINKING FOCUS

How did the American Revolution affect the people of the colonies?

Key Terms

- currency
- inflation
- cede

71

Local Impact of the War

The revolution was a destructive civil war as well as a rebellion against England. States, counties, towns, and even families were torn apart as Americans chose sides. About 10 to 20 percent of the colonists remained loyal to Britain. They called themselves Loyalists, but the Patriots called them Tories.

Loyalists Versus Patriots

Patriots jeered their Loyalist neighbors in the street and sometimes vandalized and burned their houses. Those suspected of aiding the British were often tarred and feathered by angry Patriots.

Patriots also formed organizations called Committees of Safety, which took the law into their own hands to find and to harass Loyalists. They demanded oaths of allegiance to the Revolution and jailed those who refused to take them. In 1777, the Continental Congress ordered that all Loyalist land be seized. If a family was split between Loyalists and Patriots, the Patriot members often lost their land anyway.

Some Loyalists fled to areas under British occupation. Others went to Canada, the British West Indies, or England. About 80,000 Loyalists had left the colonies by the end of the war. Some later regretted leaving home. One loyalist, Hannah Winslow, sadly wrote in England: "Sincerely wish I had never left Boston, but it is now too late and my unhappy fate is fix't."

Physical Devastation

As the fighting spread, civilians experienced the horrors of war first-hand. The armies lived off the land, taking what they needed and showing little mercy to those who opposed them. British and American troops burned settlements and crops. They committed brutal acts against civilians, driving many settlers from their homes.

The more populated coastal areas suffered the most damage during the war. The British attacked the tidewater region of Virginia, destroying plantations and capturing slaves. Ships raided New England towns. What the British could not take, they torched.

Many civilians lost their homes and belongings during the Revolution. In the painting below, British troops plunder and burn a colonial farm.

At some time during the war, British troops occupied all the major colonial cities—Boston, New York, Philadelphia, Charleston, and Savannah. When the British marched into New York in 1777, half of the city's population fled. The occupation troops plundered the city, taking the best housing and food for themselves. Poor citizens lived in makeshift huts made of sailcloth and timbers. A "canvas town" stretched along Broadway, New York's main street. When American troops entered New York at the end of the war, a soldier complained: "We took possession of a ruined city."

Economic Consequences

The loss of the major port cities dealt an economic blow to the Americans. These centers of shipping and trade had been the colonies' lifeline.

The colonies had enjoyed the benefits of being part of a great empire. Now they were cut off from their traditional trading partners. England and the West Indies would not buy New England fish, Pennsylvania grain, or Virginia tobacco. The British fleet no longer protected colonial trade. Instead it tried to sweep American merchant ships from the seas.

The American economy fell into chaos. The collapse of foreign trade wrecked once prosperous industries such as shipbuilding. It also affected farmers who produced goods for

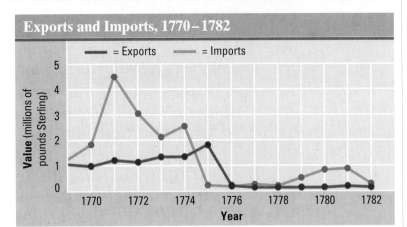

Exports and Imports, 1770–1782

= Exports   = Imports

(line graph: Value in millions of pounds Sterling (0 to 5) on vertical axis; Year from 1770 to 1782 on horizontal axis)

export. Many farms and shops were abandoned when people left to fight the war or to flee opposing armies.

During the Revolution the Continental Congress printed its own **currency**, or money, called a Continental dollar. As more money was printed, the value of the dollar decreased, causing rising prices, or **inflation**. Since the value of each dollar was less and the cost of goods higher, inflation caused more economic hardship.

In Massachusetts, the cost of a bushel of corn soared from less than a dollar to $80 in the first two years of the war. Angry women in Boston protested high prices by tossing a merchant into a cart and dragging him through the streets. Throughout the colonies, inflation made the wages of workers and soldiers virtually worthless. "Not worth a Continental" was a common complaint of the period. ■

▲ *What does this graph show about the growth or decline in imports and exports during the war?*

▲ *Shown here is Continental currency with a face value of eight dollars. Wartime inflation, however, made this paper money almost worthless.*

■ *How did the war affect American agriculture, manufacturing, and trade?*

The War's Impact on Some Social Groups

Although few Americans completely escaped the impact of the Revolution, the war affected different groups in the population in different ways. For example, the war had a unique impact on black Americans, American Indians, and women.

Black Soldiers Aid the Fight

African Americans took part in all the early battles of the Revolution. Ten black minutemen fought at Lexington and Concord. Salem Poor was commended for bravery at Bunker Hill, and Peter Salem received credit for killing the British commander in the battle. Despite this impressive record, the Continental Army barred blacks in November 1775.

The British attempted to win the support of blacks as soon as the war broke out. In 1775, the royal governor of Virginia, Lord Dunmore, promised freedom to all slaves who were "will-

Reviewing the American Revolution

ing to bear arms." Many slaves rushed to enlist, wearing sashes bearing the motto "Liberty to Slaves."

Lord Dunmore's action forced the Continental Army to accept free blacks in January 1776. About 5,000 of them served during the war, and African Americans saw action in every major battle.

The valuable service of blacks in the military nourished antislavery sentiments in the North, but little was done to improve the condition of blacks. Thousands of slaves took advantage of the war to flee their masters or to gain freedom through military service.

Whether slave or free, however, few blacks benefited from the high ideals set forth in the Declaration of Independence.

American Indians Lose an Ally

For the native inhabitants of North America, the American Revolution was a disaster. Most sympathized with the British, who had brought them trade and gifts and kept American settlers out of their lands.

In the South in 1776, Cherokees raided the farms of settlers who had moved into their territory. Carolina and Virginia militia retaliated by destroying Cherokee towns.

The most powerful American Indian group, the Iroquois Confederacy, split apart at the start of the war. All but the Oneidas and Tuscaroras joined the British side. British and Iroquois forces pillaged towns in central New York and along the Pennsylvania border. In revenge, the Americans burned Iroquois villages and killed men, women, and children.

After the war, the British withdrew from land they had formerly held and abandoned their Indian allies in the process. Both the Iroquois and Cherokees were forced to **cede,** or give, much of their territory to the new government of the United States.

Women Join the Battle

As many as 20,000 women marched with the armies of both sides. They served as cooks, laundresses, nurses, guides, and porters. One observer of American troops noticed "great numbers of women, who seemed to be the beasts of burden, having a bushel basket on their back, by which they were bent double. The contents seemed to be pots and kettles, various sorts of furniture." Some women disguised themselves as men in order to join the army. Deborah Sampson took a man's name and enlisted in the Continental Army. She was wounded twice but escaped detection and received an honorable discharge.

Mercy Otis Warren, shown here, published political pamphlets on the issues of the day. A friend of many

▼ *The portrait* (below) *of Mercy Otis Warren, author and Patriot, was painted by John Singleton Copley, the finest colonial portrait painter. Among the writings of Warren were two short plays in which the British and the Loyalists were the targets of her sharp wit.*

leaders of the Revolution, including Thomas Jefferson and Sam Adams, she was a strong supporter of American independence. She also wrote the first complete history of the Revolution, published in 1805. ■

■ *What impact did the war have on the Iroquois Confederacy?*

Colonies Form New Governments

During the war, the former colonies formed new state governments, a process that often divided people with different views about government. The first duty of these governments was to help fight the war. Each state formed its own militia. The states also turned over some of their tax revenues to the war effort. Like the Continental Congress, the state governments issued paper currency.

The states gave more people the right to vote by reducing property requirements for voters. In a few states, almost every white male over the age of 21 could vote.

The state governments set up during the war faced a new problem once the war ended: how to govern effectively in peacetime. The economy had to be pulled back together, and important matters of law had to be decided.

The particular traditions of government in each colony ran deep. Most colonists identified themselves as Virginians, New Yorkers, and so forth, rather than as Americans. Accustomed to acting as independent units, state governments resisted the compromises necessary to establish an effective central government. For a while, it looked as if the 13 states might split into many tiny nations. Some time would be required before they put aside their differences and formed a true national government. ■

■ *Why was it more difficult for the colonies to work together after the war than during the war?*

◄ *Independence Hall, Philadelphia, was built in 1732 as Pennsylvania's colonial state house. It was here that the Declaration of Independence (1776), the Articles of Confederation (1781), and the United States Constitution (1787) were adopted.*

REVIEW

1. **FOCUS** How did the American Revolution affect the people of the colonies?

2. **CONNECT** Which group do you think the Revolution hurt more: farmers in New England or farmers in the Middle Colonies? Explain.

3. **ECONOMICS** Discuss at least three ways in which the Revolution might have affected a wealthy merchant living in Philadelphia.

4. **CRITICAL THINKING** Do you think slaves would have been better off fighting for the British or the Americans during the American Revolution?

5. **ACTIVITY** Make a list of activities women engaged in during the American Revolution that were not part of their usual role in society. Share your list with the class.

Reviewing the American Revolution

Chapter Review

Reviewing Key Terms

boycott (p. 57)
cede (p. 74)
currency (p. 73)
embargo (p. 59)
immigrant (p. 48)
inflation (p. 73)
militia (p. 63)

minuteman (p. 63)
pluralism (p. 49)
republic (p. 65)
salutary neglect (p. 52)
veto (p. 53)
writs of assistance (p. 57)

A. In each of the following pairs, the two terms are related in some way. Write a sentence for each pair that clearly explains the relationship between the terms.

1. boycott, embargo
2. militia, minuteman
3. currency, inflation

B. Based on your reading in the chapter, decide whether each of the following statements is accurate. Write an explanation for each decision.

1. People of many nations and religious groups contributed to the pluralism of the colonies.
2. The British followed a policy of salutary neglect by not requiring colonists to salute statues and paintings of the king.
3. Colonial assemblies often responded to a veto by passing a law similar to the one that had been rejected.
4. The writs of assistance required colonial officials to provide food and shelter to British troops.
5. In a republic, elected officials represent the people.
6. The American Revolution broke out because the colonists refused to pay taxes to England.

Exploring Concepts

A. On a separate sheet of paper, make a chart like the one shown below. Complete it by identifying the contributions each event made to society .

Event	Contribution
Great Awakening	
Seven Years' War	
Passage of Stamp Act	
First Continental Congress	
Battle of Lexington	
Battle of Concord	
Battle of Saratoga	
Battle of Yorktown	

B. Support each of the following statements with facts and details from the chapter.

1. In the 1700s, new immigrants came to the colonies from many places besides England.
2. The American "dialect" reflected the wide variety of peoples who lived in the colonies.
3. The colonial assemblies increased their power in a variety of ways in the 1700s.
4. Although England won the Seven Years' War, the effects of the war created conflict between England and the colonies.
5. Opposition to British policies was stronger in Boston, Massachusetts than anywhere else in the colonies.
6. The written word proved as powerful a tool for the cause of independence as the muskets of the minutemen.
7. Women made important contributions to the revolutionary cause.
8. The newly independent nation faced serious economic problems as a result of the war.
9. Blacks and Indians took part in the war on both sides.

Reviewing Skills

1. Look at the timeline on pages 46-47. Identify the time period it covers. What is the earliest date shown on the timeline? What is the latest date? Into what segments of time is it divided?
2. Identify two different kinds of information you can gather from timelines. Explain how timelines provide that information.
3. Create a timeline of current events in the past month. Ask a friend or classmate to create his or her own timeline of current events. What are the similarities and differences between your timelines? Why do you think such differences occur?
4. What specialized resource would you use if you wanted to find out how much of North America Spain laid claim to after the Seven Years' War?
5. Suppose you wanted to see how all the events that have occurred in your life this month compare to all the events in your life this year. What kind of a timeline would you use?

Using Critical Thinking

1. The Boston Tea Party was an act of civil disobedience—the refusal to obey civil laws considered unjust. In many other parts of the colonies, people deliberately broke what they considered to be unjust laws as a way of protesting British policies. Can you suggest any recent examples of civil disobedience used by protesters? Do you agree that people should not obey laws they believe are unjust? Explain your answer.
2. Many colonists felt that they could obtain their demands through peaceful means. What do you think would have had to happen to prevent war between England and the colonies? Would the colonists have ever been content to remain part of the British Empire? How would our nation be different today if the American Revolution had not occurred?
3. The only colonists who benefited from the American Revolution were wealthy white males. Do you agree or disagree with this statement? Explain your answer, using specific examples from the chapter.
4. It has often been said, "The pen is mightier than the sword." Think about the writings of Thomas Paine and Thomas Jefferson. What effect did their publications have on the growing split with England? With that in mind, explain the quote above.

Preparing for Citizenship

1. WRITING ACTIVITY Imagine you are a colonist in 1776 reading the Declaration of Independence for the first time. (Turn to page 656 and read the complete text of the Declaration.) Then write a letter to the editor detailing what you think of the Declaration. Be specific in explaining whether you think the idea of breaking ties with England will be good or bad for the colonies.
2. COLLECTING INFORMATION In the 1760s and 1770s, the colonists formed citizens' groups such as the Sons of Liberty and the Committees of Correspondence. The purpose of these groups was to keep a close watch on the actions of the British government and protest those actions when they hurt the colonists' interests. Go to the library and do some research on modern citizens groups, such as Common Cause. Compare and contrast the methods used by today's groups with those used by the Sons of Liberty and the Committees of Correspondence.
3. COLLABORATIVE LEARNING Select eight or ten important leaders in the Revolutionary days and prepare a "clues" program for the class. Divide the class into two teams. Give each team a list of five leaders, and have each team then develop a set of ten or more clues to the identity of each leader. A spokesperson from each team then gives one clue at a time to the other team. See how many clues it takes to identify each Revolutionary leader.
4. COLLABORATIVE LEARNING Prepare a class trial of George III based on the list of accusations in the Declaration of Independence. Choose a judge, a jury, a committee for the prosecution, and a committee for the defense. Research the background of each accusation and prepare your case carefully before staging the trial.

The Constitution of the United States

After declaring their independence, the colonies joined together in a loose alliance of states. As these 13 states debated the best form for their government, they also debated the best symbols of their patriotic spirit. Although Benjamin Franklin favored the wild turkey as the national bird, Congress chose the bald eagle — a symbol of freedom and power. Artisans often decorated buildings and ships with wooden eagles, such as the one pictured here.

1775

Eagle carved from one piece of pine, found in Salem, Massachusetts. The Shelburne Museum, Shelburne, Vermont.

1791

Chapter 3

Toward the Constitution

The former colonists were now on their own as a new nation. Cautiously, the thirteen states joined together under a weak government. Having just fought a war over individual freedoms, the states were reluctant to surrender hard-won rights to their own central government. Could the new nation succeed—separate as states, but together as a country?

Robert Morris, a Pennsylvania merchant and banker (shown below, right), raised money to support the American Revolution. In 1782, he established the Bank of North America.

1776 The people of Pennsylvania ratify their first state constitution at a convention held in the Pennsylvania State House in Philadelphia.

1775

1779

1775

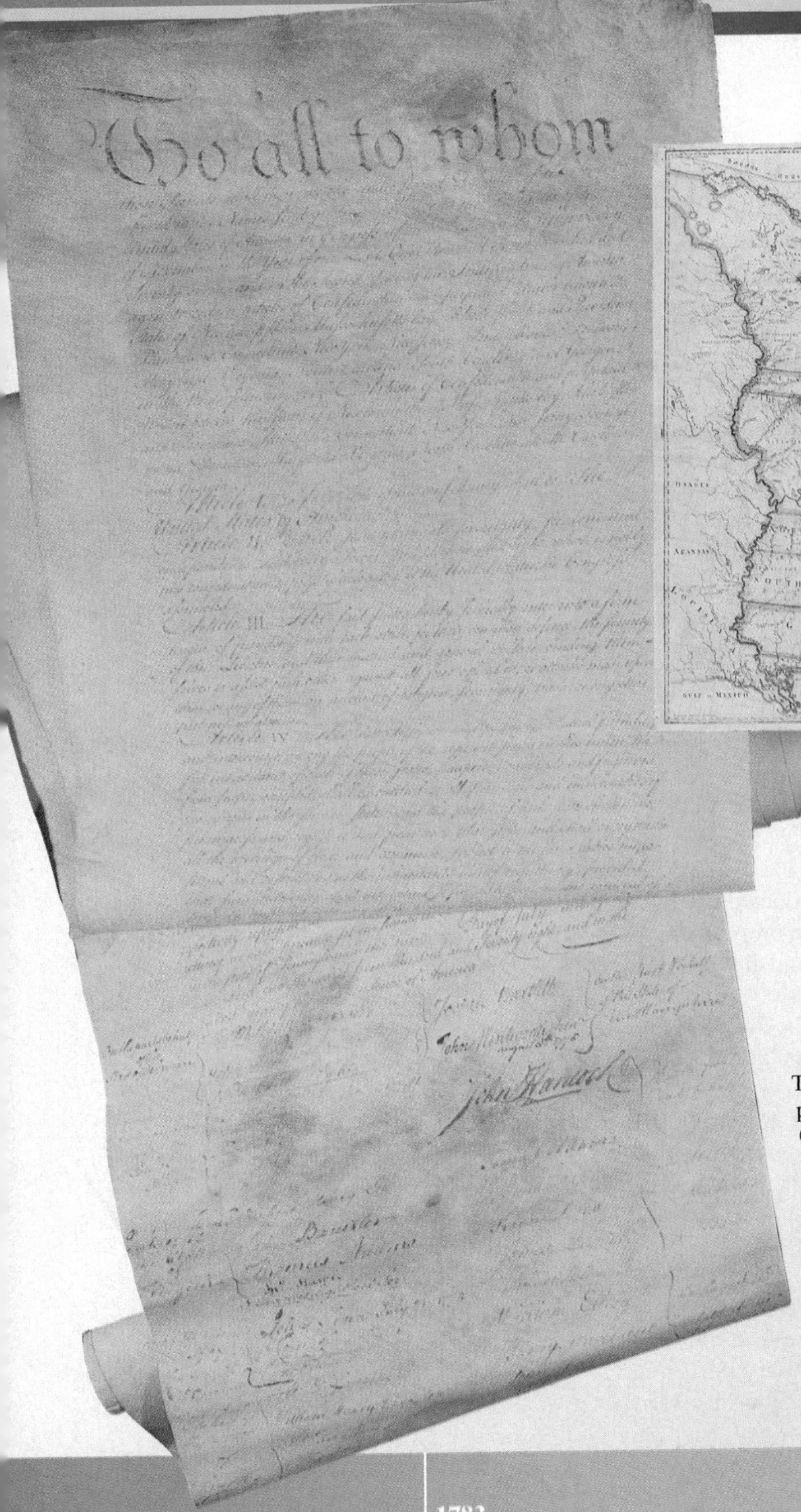

The first map of the new nation drawn by an American, Abel Buell, is based on the boundaries established by the Treaty of Paris in 1783.

The new central government plan, known as the Articles of Confederation, is designed to protect the power of each state. The states, however, soon begin to quarrel bitterly about land rights and inter-state trade.

1783

1787

1787

LESSON 1

Roots of Government

What major ideas went into the shaping of the new American government?

Key Terms

- constitution
- federal
- confederation
- executive
- legislature

➤ *American painter John Trumbull probably copied a French engraving to produce this oil portrait of Benjamin Franklin.*

Benjamin Franklin wore a rustic fur hat when he arrived in Paris in 1776 as the representative of his new nation. The Parisians saw Franklin as a self-taught frontiersman, and he charmed them with his witty conversation. Considered something of a curiosity, he was followed by crowds throughout Paris. Poets wrote flattering rhymes in his honor. And French shopkeepers sold snuffboxes and other trinkets bearing his portrait.

To the French, Franklin stood for a new citizen of the world—the American. During his long life he worked as a printer, author, inventor, philosopher, scientist, and diplomat. More than anything else, Franklin was a patriot, one of the first to dream that the colonies could become one nation.

In July 1775—a full year before the signing of the Declaration of Independence—he presented to the Second Continental Congress a plan

of government called "The Articles of Confederation and Perpetual Union." Most delegates to the Congress considered Franklin's proposal for a unifying central government too radical for the time. Many people still hoped that the colonies could settle their disputes with Britain and be left to rule themselves, individually.

Visions of a New Government

Franklin's ideas circulated throughout the colonies during the Revolutionary War as the colonists thought about creating a government. "We have it in our power to begin the world over again," Thomas Paine, the author of the pamphlet *Common Sense*, wrote enthusiastically.

An Age of Reason

Franklin and Paine, as well as Thomas Jefferson, were greatly influenced by the revolutionary ideas of

the Enlightenment—the philosophical movement taking place in Europe at that time. Its most important idea was that people could approach religious, social, political, and economic issues through reason and science. This meant that people should not follow authority blindly. Instead, progress and a better life—for both individuals and society—were possible through putting thoughts into action. According to Enlightenment thinkers, the right of people to revolt against oppressive authority followed from the use of individual reasoning.

Enlightenment thinkers in the American colonies were excited. Here they were, the first people in history to have the chance to create an entirely new government based on Enlightenment principles. But what form should the new American government be given in order to serve the different needs and desires of people in 13 separate colonies?

New World Possibilities

Today it is difficult to appreciate just how rare republicanism, or government based on the consent of the people, was in the late 1700s. At that time, kings and emperors ruled most of the world. The only models for republics were a few small countries such as Switzerland, Holland, and the city-states of Italy.

A group of George Washington's officers wanted him to become King of America. Imagine what our nation would be like now if the patriots had chosen to have a monarch! At the creation of an entirely new government, almost anything was possible. The familiar shape of the United States map in the Atlas on page 702 might even have been different if Great Britain's colonies in Canada had accepted a U.S. invitation to agree "to this confederation, joining in the measures of the united states" to become additional states.

The English Heritage

Even though they rejected the idea of having a monarchy, Americans did look to England for ideas for their new political system. Their English tradition had given the colonists a respect for government based on legal documents. In addition, many English writers of the time lent their voices to Enlightenment ideas. Americans naturally tried to adapt English tradition to suit their new country.

England did not have a single

written **constitution**, or document that defined its fundamental principles of government. But several historical documents contributed to English political structure. One such document was the Magna Carta of 1215. English nobles had won from King John the right to trial by people of a rank equal to their own. This early law formed the basis of what we know as trial by jury.

In 1689, the English Bill of Rights further limited the power of the monarchy and increased Parliament's say in ruling the country. Parliament gained the right to approve plans to spend money, and the king was forbidden to keep a standing, or permanent, army.

The English settlers had brought the idea of constitutional government to the New World. Before the *May-flower* landed in 1620, 41 of the men on board had agreed to abide by cer-

▲ *This crown, used for British coronations to this day, has long been a symbol of the British monarchy.*

▼ *Although the United States left the door open for Canada to "be admitted into, and entitled to all the advantages of this union," the invitation was rejected. This map never became real.*

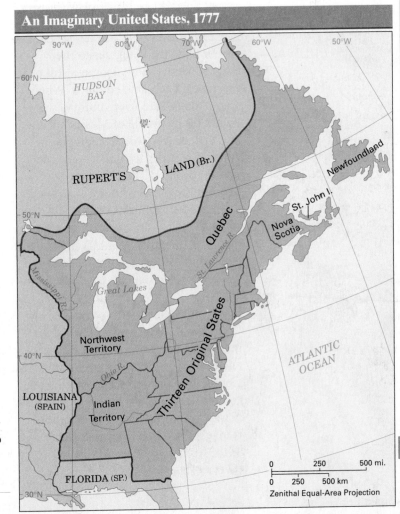

An Imaginary United States, 1777

HUDSON BAY

RUPERT'S LAND (Br.)

Newfoundland

St. John I.

Nova Scotia

Quebec

St. Lawrence R.

Mississippi R.

Great Lakes

Northwest Territory

Ohio R.

LOUISIANA (SPAIN)

Indian Territory

Thirteen Original States

ATLANTIC OCEAN

FLORIDA (SP.)

0 250 500 mi.

0 250 500 km

Zenithal Equal-Area Projection

British Influences on the American Government

1620, Mayflower Compact
- Agreed to form a self-governing body.
- Promised to frame, constitute, and enact just and equal laws.
- Agreed to promote general order and the good of all.

1689, English Bill of Rights
- Required King to have consent of Parliament to levy taxes.
- Provided for free election of members of lower house of Parliament.
- Restricted King from maintaining an army in peacetime.

1200	1300	1400	1500	1600	1700	1800

1215, Magna Carta
- Checked royal power.
- Required King to seek advice on laws and taxes.
- Granted due process of law.
- Provided for trial by jury of peers.

1628, Petition of Rights
- Rejected idea of absolute monarchy by divine right.
- Established supremacy of law over personal wishes.
- Forbade King from housing soldiers in private homes, setting up martial law, and imprisoning citizens illegally.

▲ *Unlike the other constitutional documents, which restricted powers of the king, the Mayflower Compact was written for life in an unknown wilderness.*

■ *How did Americans hope to improve upon the English tradition of constitutional law?*

tain rules for the general good of all. This Mayflower Compact was the most basic form of a constitution.

As Americans prepared to set up their own government in the late 1700s, they wanted a single document that would spell out their rights in clear terms. They hoped that by defining clearly their governing principles they could avoid the kinds of problems that had troubled the American colonies—such as the disputes they had had with the King and English Parliament. ■

One Nation United

In 1775, the delegates to the Second Continental Congress still represented 13 separate colonies. When John Adams said "our country," he meant his own state of Massachusetts. But in declaring their own independence, the states took a risk as one nation together. The concept of "Union" began as a military necessity, the united effort needed to defeat Great Britain—the greatest military power of the time. Soon the shared experience of fighting the Revolution would more closely bind the colonists.

Strong or Weak Government?

In June 1776 — just a few weeks before the Declaration of Independence would be signed—the Second Continental Congress appointed a committee to write a blueprint for a new government. Thirteen members were chosen—one from each "state," as the former colonies now called themselves.

A month later the committee presented a draft calling for a **federal** government, to be given a strong central authority by the states. They used Franklin's old title: "Articles of Confederation and Perpetual Union." As members of Congress debated, disagreements surfaced. Delegates feared a tyrannical national government might be too much like a monarchy. They therefore proposed that the new government be a **confederation**—a loose alliance of states.

The delegates argued about how to structure a congress. If the new congress were to represent the people of the new nation, large states should have more representatives. But as Roger Sherman of Connecticut argued, "We are representatives of states, not individuals."

After over a year of debate during which war raged, the Second Continental Congress adopted a list of thirteen items in 1777. Article III of the Articles of Confederation described the states' new relationship:

> T he said states hereby several-
> ly enter into a firm league of
> friendship with each other, for their
> common defence, the security of
> their Liberties, and their mutual
> and general welfare, binding them-
> selves to assist each other, against
> all force offered to, or attacks made
> upon them, or any of them, on
> account of religion, sovereignty,
> trade, or any other pretence
> whatever.

Each state would have equal power in the new congress. There was no national **executive**—that is, no one person in the government was given administrative authority. And there was no national court system.

Colonial Experiences

Based on their experience as colonial subjects of Great Britain, Americans were afraid of a central-ized government. They were especi-ally suspicious of any strong executive, such as the governor appointed by the king for each colony. Tensions often flared between these royal governors and many of the elected **legislatures** responsible for making some of the laws within the colonies. In New Jer-sey, for example, Governor William Franklin was imprisoned during the Revolutionary War because of his staunch Loyalist sympathies. Ironical-ly, he was the son of patriot Benjamin Franklin.

In their first attempts at represen-tative government, the colonists made sure that their local governments were strong. Throughout New England, local government took the form of town meetings—annual gatherings called to establish rules for each com-munity. Although the New England colonies had elected legislatures, such as the Great and General Court of Massachusetts, the people felt that they had additional control over their daily lives through participation in their town meetings. These annual town meetings still go on today.

In Virginia, laws were passed by the elected members of the colony's legislature, which was called the House of Burgesses. But Virginia law was also made at the local level by jus-tices of the peace who met in county courts.

Disputes over Western Lands

In November 1777, the Second Continental Congress presented the Articles of Confederation to the states. For the Articles to go into effect, all 13 states would have to approve them. But long-standing dis-putes over western lands delayed the Articles' passage.

The old colonial charters had granted states such as Massachusetts and the Carolinas all the land stretch-ing westward from the Atlantic Ocean. Virginia's charter mentioned

Across Time & Space

After the war, the Ameri-can branch of the Church of England cut its ties to the British monarchy and became the Episcopal Church. In 1786, Thomas Jefferson urged Virginia to pass a law separating all churches from state control and the state legis-lature did. Today, separa-tion of church and state is an established American principle.

land to the northwest as well. New York's land claims stretched from the Great Lakes south to Georgia. Look at the map on page 86 to find land claimed by more than one state.

The states that lacked such west-ern lands were not willing to let these

▲ *Colonel Nathaniel Heard and his militia, under orders of the New Jersey state provincial congress, arrested royal governor William Franklin in June 1776.*

85

Toward the Constitution

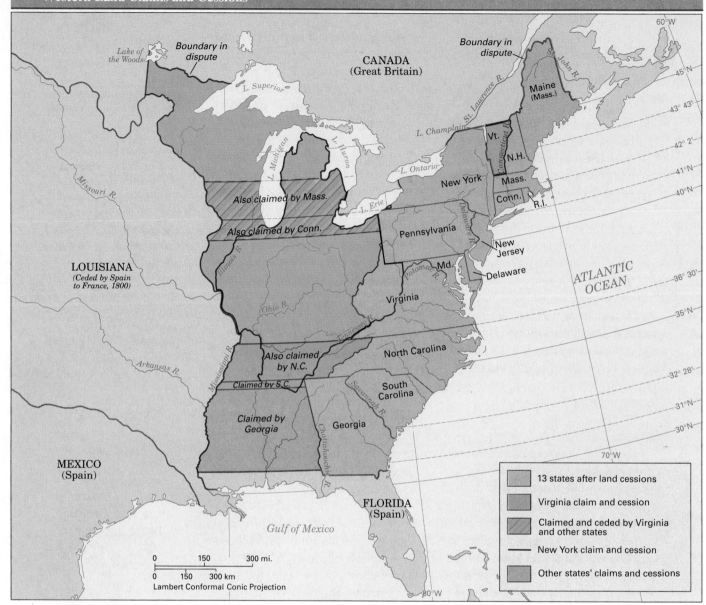

Boundary in dispute

Lake of the Woods

L. Superior

L. Michigan

L. Huron

CANADA (Great Britain)

St. Lawrence R.

Boundary in dispute

St. John R.

Maine (Mass.)

L. Champlain

Vt.

N.H.

Connecticut R.

L. Ontario

New York

Mass.

Conn.

R.I.

L. Erie

Also claimed by Mass.

Also claimed by Conn.

Pennsylvania

Delaware R.

New Jersey

Md.

Potomac R.

Delaware

ATLANTIC OCEAN

Missouri R.

Illinois R.

Ohio R.

Virginia

LOUISIANA (Ceded by Spain to France, 1800)

Tennessee R.

Arkansas R.

Mississippi R.

Also claimed by N.C.

Claimed by S.C.

North Carolina

South Carolina

Savannah R.

Claimed by Georgia

Georgia

Chattahoochee R.

MEXICO (Spain)

FLORIDA (Spain)

Gulf of Mexico

0   150   300 mi.
0   150   300 km
Lambert Conformal Conic Projection

60°W
45°N
43° 43'
42° 2'
41°N
40°N
36° 30'
35°N
32° 28'
31°N
30°N
70°W
80°W

13 states after land cessions

Virginia claim and cession

Claimed and ceded by Virginia and other states

New York claim and cession

Other states' claims and cessions

▲ *Seven states ceded land claims in the western territories. New York and New Hampshire also ceded claims to Vermont in 1791.*

■ *What issues contributed to the reluctance of Americans to establish a strong national government?*

claims stand. They argued that the western lands were "wrested from the common enemy by the blood and treasure of the thirteen states." Therefore, the states as one union should share the frontier territory.

Maryland refused to approve the

Articles unless all western lands were ceded, or transferred, to the central government. In 1781, after New York and Virginia agreed to the cession of their lands, Maryland accepted the proposal for a new government. The Articles were finally approved. ■

Emergence of State Governments

After declaring independence from Great Britain, the states tried not only to establish an effective national government. Each had to set up its own new government also. This was indeed an exciting time—a chance to develop plans for the future. "We are," said Benjamin Franklin, "on the

right road to improvement, for we are making experiments."

Republicanism in the States

Speaking to a state convention—made up of former members of the Virginia House of Burgesses—James Madison praised the emerging

Chapter 3

republican governments. "I go on this great republican principle, that the people will have the virtue and intelligence to select men of virtue and wisdom."

All the new state governments had elected legislatures. Republicanism demanded that the representatives had to be close to the voters who elected them. In most states, representatives had to stand for election annually. They had to live in the community they represented and have a stake in it by owning property there.

The state legislatures were usually more powerful than the executives of the states, the governors. In more than half the states, the legislature chose the governor, making him accountable to the wishes of the representatives.

Variety Among the States

Although the early state constitutions shared features of republicanism, some were more creative than others. Only Connecticut and Rhode Island kept their original colonial charters, after omitting references to the King and Parliament.

In 1776, Pennsylvania's new constitution eliminated the state executive so that there would be no governor at all, and established a unicameral, or one-house, legislature. Supporters of this constitution saw no need for an upper house—like the House of Lords in the English Parliament—to represent the wealthier people of the community. Pennsylvania, along with North Carolina, dropped any requirement for owning property in order to vote—a radical concept for the time.

Conservative political leaders were appalled by these democratic innovations. They succeeded in 1790 in replacing the first Pennsylvania constitution with a more moderate one.

Massachusetts established a two-step procedure for democratically adopting a new government. In the first step, a special convention gathered to write a constitution. In the second step, all Massachusetts voters—not just members of the state legislature—decided whether to approve their new constitution. Massachusetts' constitution, approved in 1780, was unusual in ending slavery and allowing both free black men and American Indians to vote.

The creation of the early state constitutions was a critical step in the evolution of a successful national government. Through their state governments, Americans learned more about the workings of republicanism as well as about ways to improve their national government. ■

▲ *After the British dissolved the House of Burgesses in 1774, many former members worked to create Virginia's constitution and became part of the new state government. The House of Burgesses is pictured above as it might have looked in the 1600s.*

■ *Predict which aspects of the early state constitutions would eventually be adopted for the national government.*

R E V I E W

1. **FOCUS** What major ideas went into the shaping of the new American government?

2. **CONNECT** Why were one-year terms for political offices thought to be a way to avoid a tyrannical government?

3. **POLITICAL SYSTEMS** How was Pennsylvania's constitution unusually democratic for the time?

4. **CRITICAL THINKING** Why would a politician like John Adams refer to his home state of Massachusetts as "his country"?

5. **WRITING ACTIVITY** Imagine that you represent Maryland in Congress in 1781. Prepare a brief speech arguing against approval of the Articles of Confederation while states still hold western land.

Reading Abigail Adams's Letters

Here's Why

Primary sources are the raw materials of history. Any document of daily life—a news article, a personal letter, even a laundry list—provides information about how people lived. Knowing how to use such primary sources is one way to get a view of individual people and events of the past.

In this chapter you read about the roots of our nation and how men like Benjamin Franklin, James Madison, and John Adams shaped our government. Primary sources are extremely useful because they give us a record of events by people who were there, and in their own words.

Suppose you wanted to get a closer perspective on the personal lives of the people affected by events in this chapter. Reading letters written by John Adams and by his wife Abigail Adams would provide that information.

Here's How

In order to use a particular item for historical information, you need to evaluate it as a primary source. On this page is a letter that Abigail Adams sent her husband in 1776. (Above the letter is what is traditionally thought to be a portrait of Abigail Adams). Ask the following questions to determine the accuracy and usefulness of this document.

1. **Who was the writer?**
   Abigail Adams educated herself by reading literature and history. She was a woman who took an

Abigail to John
March 31, 1776

I long to hear that you have declared an independency—and, by the way, in the new code of laws, which I suppose it will be necessary for you to make, I desire you would remember the ladies, and be more generous and favorable to them than [were] your ancestors. Do not put such unlimited power into the hands of the husbands. Remember all men would be tyrants if they could. If particular care and attention is not paid to the ladies, we are determined to [instigate] a rebellion, and will not hold ourselves bound by any laws in which we have no voice or representation. That your sex are naturally tyrannical is a truth so thoroughly established as to admit of no dispute. But such of you as wish to be happy willingly give up the harsh title of master for the more tender and endearing one of friend. Why, then, not put it out of the power of the vicious and the lawless to use us with cruelty and indignity. . . ? Men of sense in all ages abhor those customs which treat us only as the vassals of your sex. Regard us then as beings, placed by providence under your protection, and in imitation of the Supreme Being make us of that power only for our happiness.

John to Abigail
April 14, 1776

As to your extraordinary code of laws, I cannot but laugh. We have been told that our struggle has loosened the bands of government everywhere. . . .
Depend upon it, we know better than to repeal our masculine systems. Although they are in full force, you know they are little more than theory. We dare not exert our power in its full latitude. We are obliged to go fair and softly, and in practice, you know, we are the subjects. We have only the name of masters, and rather than give up this, which would completely subject us to the despotism of the petticoat, I hope General Washington, and all our brave heroes would fight. . . .

active interest in her husband's work. Since women of that time did not vote or work outside the home and usually did not attend political meetings, this letter does not present the ideas and feelings of the average woman of that time.

2. **When was the letter written?**
Notice that Adams wrote her letter in the same year that the Declaration of Independence was signed. It gives the reader a unique look at the issues that were being discussed. As a primary source, the letter provides more detailed information about the decisions involved in producing the Declaration than a document written many months or years later.

3. **Why was it written?**
The letter reveals that Abigail Adams hoped to convince her husband that he should create a certain kind of policy. She wanted him to grant rights to women, to "remember the ladies," and to treat women as friends rather than as possessions.

4. **What difficulties does this source present?**
Some sources present difficulties because they are incomplete or because they require special knowledge in order to be understood. In Adam's letter, the language may prove difficult. Look up the words *instigate*, *tyrannical*, and *vassals* in the dictionary. When you examine primary sources, you need to determine if the vocabulary or spelling were common for that time period. In this case, the vocabulary that Adams uses is an indication of how well-educated she was.

Try It
Now read the letter that John Adams sent to Abigail on April 14, 1776. Following the steps outlined above, answer the following questions. What is his first response? What does he think about his wife's concern for women's rights? Do you think that he shares her opinions? What does he mean when he says "We have only the name of masters . . .?" Compare John Adams's letter with Abigail Adams's. What do you think about the roles of men and women during that time?

Apply It
Ask your parents, grandparents, or other older relatives for a letter they have saved. Read through it several times. Look for information in the letter that helps you to learn about the writer and about the person being addressed, as well as about any event to which the letter refers.

LESSON 2

The Articles of Confederation

THINKING
FOCUS

How did the Articles of Confederation divide power between the new national government and the state governments?

Key Terms

- sovereignty
- term of office

I magine that you are a merchant in the new nation. One morning in 1785 as the tide goes out, your two-masted schooner slips away from a busy Philadelphia dock. It is bound for Charleston, South Carolina.

Your ship hugs the coastline during the trip south. With some of the profit from selling a cargo of wheat flour from Pennsylvania mills, you plan to buy indigo—a plant that produces a beautiful deep blue dye.

After a week, the ship finally docks in Charleston. Unlike Europe, where travel is restricted, the new nation allows you to enter another state freely without a passport.

Despite any differences between you and the people in Charleston, you will be doing business together as citizens of the same nation. The Articles of Confederation promise the "free inhabitants of each of these states . . . all privileges and immunities of free citizens in the several states."

You are anticipating difficulties, however. You can now trade freely with merchants from different states, without excessive import taxes and regulations. But you still face the problem of doing business with different money issued by each state. You worry that the money you will receive will not be equal to the value of your cargo, and you will not be able to spend it when you return home to Philadelphia. Often money issued by the states is worth only a fraction of its face value. You believe that the need for uniform currency—worth the same amount wherever it is spent—points to the need for a strong central government to issue that currency and to vouch for its value.

➤ *The docks and ship-yards of the Philadelphia waterfront spread out along the banks of the Delaware River.*

Confederation Works for Wartime

Even before all the states accepted the Articles, Congress had used them as a working plan of government. Americans desperately needed a system by which to raise and pay an army to fight Great Britain.

No member of Congress played a more important role in funding the Revolutionary army than the prominent Philadelphia merchant Robert Morris. As superintendent of finance, he borrowed money and bought supplies to keep Washington's troops on the battlefield. Morris was dedicated to strengthening the Confederation, at the same time making a profit for himself and his friends.

Congress also sent diplomats to Europe to gain support for the Confederation's military efforts against Great Britain. After the colonists' victory at Saratoga in 1777, American diplomats showed off a French translation of the Articles to demonstrate that the United States had a serious new government worthy of aid. Benjamin Franklin, John Adams, Thomas Jefferson, and John Jay impressed Europeans with their arguments. They gained diplomatic and financial support from France, Holland, Russia, and Spain.

After the war ended in 1781, the Confederation government sent three seasoned diplomats—Franklin, Adams, and Jay—to Paris to negotiate a peace treaty. They won not only Great Britain's recognition of Ameri-

This painting shows Franklin in the French royal court at Versailles surrounded by a crowd of admirers.

can independence but also all British territory south of the Great Lakes and east of the Mississippi River, the Northwest Territory, and the old Southwest Territory. The victory at the peace table in 1783 was as stunning as the battle at Yorktown. ∎

■ *How did the Articles help win support from Europeans for the American cause?*

The Articles Define Government

At first, most Americans found it difficult to think of their new confederation as a true union. The Articles were an attempt to create a national government that would unite 13 very diverse colonies. Although the new government was weak, Thomas Jefferson regarded it as a model—the best government "existing or that ever did exist."

Congressional Powers

The Articles did give the Congress a few of the powers typical of an independent, sovereign nation. For example, Congress alone had the **sovereignty**—the supreme authority and power—to conduct foreign affairs, send ambassadors, and negotiate treaties. The individual states had given up such powers when they signed the Articles. Congress controlled the national army and appointed its officers. It held the sole right to coin money, to establish weights and measures, and to operate a national postal system. The chart on the following page shows how the postal system worked.

The national government con-

Write
Sender writes in cramped script with a quill pen on single sheet because of paper shortage. No envelopes. The letter is folded, addressed and sealed with wax.

Post
Sender goes into town to hand letter to appointed post master, usually an innkeeper or merchant.

Deliver
Post rider travels between towns on the post road, often through wilderness. Road-side mile markers are used for setting postage.

Receive
Recipient claims letter from closest post-master, paying the postage at the rate of 6 cents per single sheet per 25 miles.

▲ *Parts of the postal system shown in the diagram were inherited from the British colonial system. This milestone was located along the old post road between New York and Boston.*

■ *What was the national government's most serious weakness under the Articles of Confederation?*

sisted only of Congress and the agencies created by it. Congress established four important departments: foreign affairs, war, finance, and the post office. These were forerunners of executive agencies that exist in the federal government today.

Limited Sovereignty

The Articles deliberately kept the central government weak so that the freedom of each state was not threatened. There was no executive branch to enforce the will of Congress. The "president" was merely a member of Congress appointed to preside over each congressional session. The lack

of a national court meant that disputes between states had to be settled either through negotiation in interstate commissions or in state courts. Because each state court tended to favor its own state, this policy did not work well.

All important decisions in Congress required the approval of at least nine states. Even so, resolutions of Congress were merely recommendations to the states, unless the resolution dealt with matters over which Congress had total control. For example, although Congress could make treaties, it could not enforce them. When New York took away lands owned by British Loyalists—a violation of the 1783 treaty—Congress could do nothing.

In addition, members of Congress were elected for only a year-long **term of office** and could not serve more than three of these limited periods within six years. Thus, by the time a delegate had acquired enough experience to be effective in Congress, he was forced to leave Congress for at least three years. ■

Morris Funds the National Treasury

Robert Morris had to deal with the government's biggest problem: Congress lacked the power under the Articles to tax its citizens directly. Congress assigned to each state a share of the funds needed by the national government. The share was

based on the value of that state's land. Congress could only hope that the state governments would be cooperative and collect money for them. The national government was often fortunate to receive even one-fourth of the funds requested from the states.

Robert Morris, the first Superintendent of Finance of the new Confederation, was the first to juggle one of the most challenging checkbooks around—that of the United States government. Morris had a hard time gathering enough funds to pay the bills, and things haven't changed since then. Today, the President, his financial advisers, and the Congress spend much time and energy trying to finance the needs of the American society. The money needed and spent by the government is called revenues.

Incoming Revenues

The term income refers to money collected, whether it be the income of an individual worker or of a huge government. The national and state governments receive their income from various sources. For example, some state government funds come from fees charged for the use of parks, for driver's licenses, or for permission to operate a business. The national, or federal, government can sell or lease some of the millions of acres of land it owns.

By far, the largest source of government income is taxes. Taxes take many forms. For example, many state and local governments collect sales tax, a percentage of each purchase made by citizens added on to the price of goods. Property owners pay taxes on their homes, cars, and land. In 1913, the Sixteenth Amendment to the Constitution allowed the federal government to make citizens pay a tax on a portion of their incomes. Today, this income tax is the chief source of income for the federal government.

Outgoing Revenues

From this variety of sources, the federal government collects many billions of dollars each year. In fact, by the late 1980s, the national budget exceeded $1 trillion per year.

Deciding how to spend all this money is one of the principal jobs of the Congress. Each year, Congress and the President must decide the relative importance, for example, of military spending, stopping the drug problem, or cleaning up the environment. These decisions affect all of our lives.

The Problem of Debt

Since the 1950s, Congress has been spending more money than it takes in. The government makes up the difference by borrowing money. By 1990, the national debt had ballooned to about $2.5 trillion. That translates to nearly $10,000 for every man, woman, and child in the country.

In one sense, government funding has improved since Morris's time. Today, taxes provide a huge and dependable source of income for our nation's government. On the other hand, we have continued to overspend our budgets year after year. As a result, more than $100 billion, or about 10 percent of the federal government's income goes simply to pay the interest on our debt. The growth of this debt has created a financial situation that Robert Morris could never have imagined.

Federal Government Funding, 1989

- Excise Taxes 3.5%
- Miscellaneous Deposits 2.2%
- Customs Duties 1.7%
- Estate and Gift Taxes .8%
- Corporation Income Taxes 10.9%
- Social Insurance Tax and Contributions 37.3%
- Individual Income Taxes 43.6%

Morris worked heroically to keep the government financially solvent, sometimes purchasing army supplies with his personal funds. Still, the national treasury was often bare. In a letter sent to Morris in 1783, General Washington wrote:

I have often reflected, with much Solicitude, upon the disagreeableness of your Situation and the Negligence of the several States, in not enabling you to do that Justice to the public Creditors, which their Demands require. I wish the Step you have taken, may sound the Alarm to their inmost Souls, and rouse them to a just Sense of their own Interest, honor and Credit.

Matters worsened as the Revolutionary War was ending. Soldiers grumbled about not being paid, and many

➤ *This gold coin, minted by New York in 1787, was called a doubloon. The face value of this paper money, printed by South Carolina in 1778, was five shillings. The names doubloon and shilling came from European money of the time.*

■ *If the states still issued their own money today, how would trade and travel within the country be different?*

feared that they would never receive their promised wages.

In March 1783, a group of soldiers and officers in Newburgh, New York, plotted to overthrow the government.

General Washington had to use his prestige to stop this revolt. As he put on his spectacles before speaking to the men at Newburgh, he said: "Gentlemen, I have grown gray in your service, and now I am going blind." He silenced the protesters, at least temporarily. Even so, other soldiers marched on Philadelphia three months later to demand payment for their services, forcing the government to flee to Princeton, New Jersey.

During this time, Congress had been printing money to pay for military supplies and salaries without having the gold to back up the paper. Many people would not accept the national government's paper currency —basically worthless—as payment for debts. So the states issued their own paper currency, backed only by "full faith and credit"—that is, people's confidence that the state could pay its debts. People who traveled from state to state had to carry or obtain different kinds of paper money. Naturally, this hampered trade between the states.

Many states wanted to create a strong currency, but the lack of gold and silver in circulation made this task difficult. The states set limits on the amount of currency that they put into circulation. They also raised taxes to pay their debts promptly. These measures made borrowing expensive and led to a crisis in western Massachusetts. Indeed, the problems of banking and currency would not be resolved for another 100 years. ■

1. **FOCUS** How did the Articles of Confederation divide power between the new national government and the state governments?
2. **CONNECT** Relate Washington's point of view in his letter to Morris to Washington's problems with feeding and clothing his army during the Revolutionary War.
3. **POLITICAL SYSTEMS** What are some aspects of the early

government that have been carried over into the twentieth century?
4. **CRITICAL THINKING** What are some advantages and disadvantages of a weak central government?
5. **WRITING ACTIVITY** Imagine that you are Robert Morris trying to persuade the states to pay their shares into the treasury. Write a convincing letter to them.

LESSON 3

The Crisis of Confederation

Five hundred angry farmers, armed with pitchforks and wooden boards, stood with their leader Daniel Shays, near Springfield, in western Massachusetts. They were attempting to intimidate the state's supreme court, which was hearing cases against farmers who could not pay their private debts and state property taxes.

It was September 1786, and the end of the war had not brought prosperity. The states were taxing the farmers heavily—in the gold and silver no one had—to pay off war debts. Turning to wealthy merchants, the farmers had borrowed the money they needed to pay their taxes. Then, unable to pay these private debts, many farmers faced having their farms auctioned off. Their many petitions for relief to the merchant-dominated state legislature in Boston had gone unanswered.

Daniel Shays had fought at Bunker Hill and Saratoga. In 1780, he had returned home to wait for payment for his military service. No payment came, and his debts piled up. He feared "the spectre of debtor's jail always . . . close by." Most of the men with him at Springfield were also angry veterans and, like him, were in debt.

The Massachusetts governor ordered the protesters to disband. When they refused, he called out a special militia financed by the state's rich merchants. Four months later, in January 1787, Shays again led his band, now over two thousand strong, to the federal arsenal in Springfield. Its defenders opened fire, killing four of the rebels, and Shays's force fled.

The governor's militia chased down the rebels—taking away for a period of three years their right to vote, hold elective office, and serve as jurors. By March 1787, six months after the rebellion began, it was over.

Shock waves from Shays's Rebellion spread beyond Massachusetts. Wealthy creditors around the nation wanted protection against future armed rebellion. Under the Articles of Confederation, the national government could not supply it.

THINKING FOCUS

Why did the Articles of Confederation fail?

Key Terms

- commerce
- territory

◀ *This engraving shows a group of angry farmers seizing a Massachusetts court house during Shays's Rebellion.*

95

Toward the Constitution

A Critical Period in Finance and Trade

Without a strong national government, each state went its own way under the Articles of Confederation. For example, trade among the states would have benefited if everyone had agreed to accept the uniform paper money of the national government. Instead, the states' paper money, each with a different rate of exchange, caused confusion and arguments. Often, currency issued by a state bank was nearly worthless and merchants would not accept it as payment for goods. Sometimes they would allow only $0.25 for a note with a face value of $1.00.

Congress Lacks Power

The states would not allow Congress to regulate **commerce**—the buying and selling of goods among states and with foreign nations. In the area of commerce, the states retained complete sovereignty. When Great Britain closed its West Indian colonies to American trade, Congress had no power to retaliate by banning British ships from American ports.

Nor could Congress collect import taxes on foreign goods. The states had kept this right for themselves. "Easy states" took trade from the others by offering lower import tax rates to importers.

Furthermore, the states resisted any plans for national taxation. Without the power to tax, the national government could not raise enough money to function effectively.

The weakness of the government under the Articles of Confederation also showed in foreign affairs. The Barbary Coast pirates had, since the 1500s, freely accepted payments in exchange for letting any merchant ships pass through the Mediterranean Sea. The pirates operated out of the region of North Africa that includes present-day Libya and Tunisia. They captured many American ships and sold their sailors into slavery. The U.S. Government was too poor to buy back its citizens' freedom and too weak to prevent such hostile acts.

International Trade Grows

Still, the new United States was able to develop trade with France, the Netherlands, and Morocco. American ships also began to travel to the markets of the Dutch and French West Indies.

A year after the Treaty of Paris ended the Revolutionary War, the ship *Empress of China* sailed from Philadelphia to Canton, China, with a cargo of cotton and fur. Its voyage opened what became known as the China trade. The China trade would become increasingly important to the United States in the 1800s. ■

Success in Land Policy

In the midst of financial chaos, the Confederation government achieved its greatest success. After two years of debate, Congress agreed on how to develop the Northwest Territory.

In 1785 Congress issued a land ordinance, a legal order subdividing the western **territories**—possessions of the United States that were not states—into pieces called townships.

A China-bound Sailor

10:16 A.M., August 18, 1789
Whampoa Beach, 4 miles from Canton, China

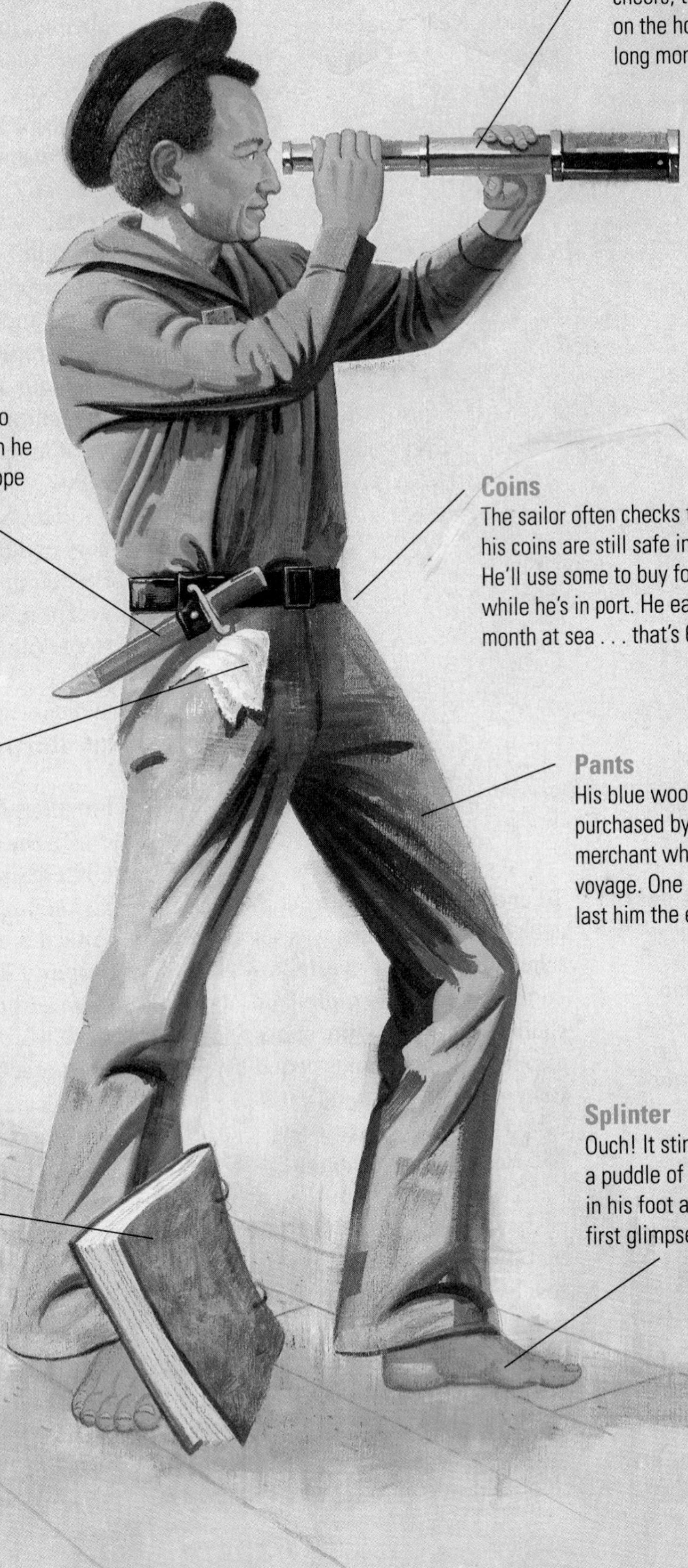

Spyglass
Land ho! He grabs the spyglass and runs to the side of the ship. The crew cheers, thrilled to see land on the horizon after eight long months at sea.

Knife
He uses this utensil to eat with, to clean fish he catches, and to cut rope for his hammock.

Coins
The sailor often checks to make sure his coins are still safe in his pocket. He'll use some to buy food and drink while he's in port. He earns $20 a month at sea . . . that's 67 cents a day.

Handkerchief
His girlfriend embroidered this linen handkerchief. With the money he makes from this voyage, they'll marry.

Pants
His blue woolen uniform was purchased by the New York merchant who financed this voyage. One pair of pants must last him the entire 14-month trip.

Splinter
Ouch! It stings as he stands in a puddle of salty water. It stuck in his foot as he ran to catch his first glimpse of China.

Sketchbook
With simple charcoal, he has drawn portraits of other crew members. After they reach Whompoa Beach, he'll draw temples, dragons, and chopsticks.

97

To encourage education, some land in each of the townships was set aside for schools. The western territories shown on the map are the same lands earlier claimed by some of the states. These also included the lands ceded by Britain in the Treaty of Paris.

▲ *This 1785 map shows the territories affected by the land ordinances. In the words in the upper right corner, the map-maker apologizes for the quality of his work.*

elected a legislature and nonvoting delegates to Congress. When a territory had a population of 60,000 free male inhabitants, step three was to apply to become a state. The Northwest Territory could eventually be divided into no more than five and no fewer than three states. The Northwest Territory included the present states of Ohio, Michigan, Indiana, Illinois, Wisconsin, and part of Minnesota.

Any new states would be on an equal footing with the original states. In addition, Congress promised to protect rights and liberties in the new states and territories. Therefore, people who moved west were guaranteed freedom of religion, the first time that the national government stood for what later became a basic American right.

The Northwest Ordinance was a very enlightened piece of legislation. By defining in writing a policy to accept new territories as states equal to the others, Congress avoided the problem of governing colonies. It also avoided conflicts between the East and the West.

The Northwest Ordinance

Two years later, in 1787, Congress passed the Northwest Ordinance, thereby creating the three-step process by which territories could become new states. In the first step, Congress appointed a governor, secretary, and three judges for a territory.

After 5,000 free male inhabitants moved into the territory, the second step went into effect. The people

■ *Why was the North-west Ordinance the crowning achievement of the Confederation?*

Promises Made

In the Northwest Ordinance, the United States promised that "utmost good faith shall always be observed toward the Indians; their land and property shall never be taken from them without their consent." With these words, the U.S. Government guaranteed sovereignty rights to the American Indians and respect for their territory. This promise would be broken in less than 10 years.

The ordinance also stated, "There shall be neither slavery nor involuntary servitude in the . . . territory." This had little effect on the slaves in the Northwest, but it encouraged anti-slavery feelings among most of the settlers. The states north of the Ohio River and east of the Mississippi River would later oppose extension of slavery into newer territories. ■

Government at a Standstill

While Congress was passing the Northwest Ordinance, Americans were also attempting to strengthen the government under the Articles. Even former supporters of the Articles now admitted that the government was too weak. The states regularly ignored resolutions of the Congress. George Washington remarked that the Confederation was "little more than the shadow without the substance."

Tax Plans Blocked

In 1783, Congress proposed a national tax based on state populations—an act for which it had no specific authority under the Articles. In addition, in 1784 Congress asked for two revisions to the Articles that would give the national government some control over commerce. In 1786, New York rejected the national tax plan. The commercial revisions did not come close to being approved.

All states had to agree unanimously on any revision of the original Articles. A single state could block change, making it difficult to come to agreement on any issue.

Reforms Attempted

James Madison, a delegate to Congress from Virginia, worked to reform the Articles. However, he could serve as a delegate for only three years. Returning to Virginia, he was elected to the state assembly in 1785. At his urging, Virginia organized a national convention on the problems of interstate commerce.

The commission chose Annapolis, Maryland, as the site. Yet when the Annapolis Convention opened in September 1786, only five states sent delegates. The few delegates who attended felt unable to proceed.

Alarmed by crises such as Shays's Rebellion, Madison and the other Virginia delegates tried again. They enlisted the support of Alexander Hamilton, a politically minded New York lawyer and an important wartime aide to General Washington, to call another convention the following spring. The experience of ineffective government under the Articles of Confederation made it clear to more Americans that they needed a stronger national authority. Congress, therefore, authorized a convention to meet in Philadelphia in May 1787, to consider all the defects of the Articles of Confederation.

Despite the problems of this first American attempt at a national government, the Articles did serve as the first constitution of the new nation. The Articles' greatest legacies were the victory in the Revolutionary War and the peace with Great Britain and especially Benjamin Franklin's concept of "perpetual union." In adopting this phrase, Congress fostered the idea that they had produced an unbreakable union out of many states —*E pluribus unum.* ∎

▲ *On June 20, 1782, Congress adopted the seal still used today. On the scroll in the eagle's beak is written* E pluribus unum—*also the motto on the gold coin minted by the state of New York (page 94).*

■ *Find evidence to support this statement: the Confederation was an inefficient and largely ineffective government.*

REVIEW

1. **FOCUS** Why did the Articles of Confederation fail?
2. **CONNECT** According to Benjamin Franklin, Americans were "on the right road to improvement, for we are making experiments." Why was government under the Articles a useful experiment in the long run?
3. **HISTORY** Explain how the three-step process of statehood in the Northwest Ordinance was far-sighted.
4. **CRITICAL THINKING** Why was it so difficult for Congress to move forward with its proposals for the government under the Confederation?
5. **WRITING ACTIVITY** Imagine you are a farmer in western Massachusetts in 1786 who has decided to participate in Shays's Rebellion. Write a petition to the governor that you want to pass around to your friends to sign.

American Coins

If you found an old coin in a pocketful of change, would you pull it out and wonder how much it is worth today? Would you wonder about its history? What do you know about the coins you see every day?

➤ *Above right is the Nova Caesara ("New Jersey") cent, minted in 1786. During the first years after independence, individual states minted their own coins. This penny was produced by private metal crafters under contract to the state of New Jersey.*

Get Ready

Coins are tokens of value, but they are also miniature monuments that reflect the pride of a nation. Most coins display images of national heroes or noble animals, and present mottoes expressing the ideals of a country. They also carry information about who designed the coin, where and when it was made, and its value. The study of coins is called *numismatics.*

Take a look at the coin below. (The coins on these pages are not actual size. They have been enlarged to help you see the details on the coins.) As a numismatist, you would find that this coin is the first penny issued by the United States government. On the front of the coin, the designer used a woman to represent liberty. On the back he used a circular chain to symbolize the union of the thirteen states. This design proved to be very unpopular. People said that Liberty looked terrified, and that the chain symbolized captivity, not unity—"Liberty in chains" would never do. Within a few months, a newly designed penny was produced instead. Today, this first penny is worth anywhere between $1,000–$20,000, depending on its condition.

For your own study of coins, you'll need a sketchbook and pencil to record the features of coins you decide to study. You may also want to carry a magnifying glass—it can help you discover symbols and letters on coins that are too small for most people to notice. You will also need a guidebook to U.S. coins, which you can find in the library.

➤ *This is the first penny issued by the U.S. government.*

100

(For more background information on money, see pages 674-677 in the Minipedia.)

Find Out

Select one American coin that interests you. It could be a new coin from your pocket, an older one someone in your family has set aside, or an unusual coin whose picture you've come across in a book.

Look very carefully at both sides of that coin. Use your magnifying glass to search for hidden details. Make a large sketch of what you see, and make notes about what you think the words and symbols mean. Then trace the coin or draw a circle to show its size, and write what metal or metals you think it is made of.

Move Ahead

Note what your coin is worth and the year it was made. Next, use your knowledge of history to make some notes about important events that happened during the era in which the coin was made.

Here are some questions to guide your research.

- Where was your coin made?
- Who designed it?
- What was the inspiration for its design?
- Why was it created?

- What is it made out of?
- What do the pictures on it represent? What do they symbolize?

Explore Some More

Whenever you come across an unusual coin, sketch its features in your notebook. If it has odd or unusual symbols on it, check in a coin book to see what those symbols mean. Do the same when you come across coins from other nations. Remember, each coin is a miniature national monument. If you can discover the meanings of the words and symbols on a coin, you will have learned something important about the ideals of the nation that produced it.

◄ *Susan B. Anthony dollar, 1979. Because this coin was only slightly larger than a quarter, people did not like it since they often confused the two. Minting of the coin was stopped in 1981.*

▼ *Trace the development of the United States half-dollar since the early 1900s. The Liberty half-dollar (left) was first issued in 1916. This coin shows Liberty walking toward a rising sun with 13 rays. The Liberty coin was replaced by the Benjamin Franklin half-dollar (middle) in 1948. In 1964, the John F. Kennedy half-dollar, (right) replaced the Benjamin Franklin half-dollar.*

Chapter Review

Reviewing Key Terms

commerce (p. 96)
confederation (p. 84)
constitution (p. 83)
executive (p. 85)
federal (p. 84)

legislature (p. 85)
sovereignty (p. 91)
term of office (p. 92)
territory (p. 96)

A. In each of the following pairs, the two terms are related in some way. Write a sentence for each pair that clearly explains the relationship between the two terms.

1. federal, confederation
2. confederation, sovereignty
3. executive, term of office

B. Based on what you have read in the chapter, decide whether each of the following statements is true or false. If it is false, change the sentence to a true statement.

1. The idea of sovereignty appealed to people who wanted to have a say in their own government.
2. A constitution could provide for either a weak or a strong central government.
3. Under the Articles of Confederation, the executive branch made the laws for the government.
4. Every member of the legislative branch was allowed to serve for a certain term.
5. The people in the western territory had no way of developing state governments.

Exploring Concepts

A. On a separate sheet of paper make a table like the one below. Decide whether each of the phrases listed at right belongs in either the "strengths" or "weaknesses" column. Place the number of the phrase in the proper column. Then next to the number, write a short explanation of your choice. For example, Number 1, "no national court," has been placed in the "weaknesses" box because without a national court there was no way for the government to settle disputes between states.

Articles of Confederation	
Strengths	**Weaknesses**
	1. No way to settle disputes between states.

1. no national court
2. no executive branch
3. Congress operates national postal service
4. Congress controls national army
5. republican form of government
6. member of Congress limited to three-year term
7. Congress unable to tax citizens directly
8. Congress unable to regulate commerce
9. Congress decides use of western territories
10. changes in the Articles required unanimous state agreement

B. Support each of the following statements with facts and details from the chapter. Then use your responses to write a statement about the beliefs and values people at that time had about government.

1. In creating a written plan of government, Americans found different models in their English and colonial heritages.
2. When the Articles of Confederation were written, Americans had several reasons for wanting a weak central government.
3. The new state governments provided additional models of republicanism.
4. Congress successfully used its few powers in several ways.

Reviewing Skills

I cannot say that I think you very generous to the ladies. For, whilst you are proclaiming peace and good will to men, emancipating all nations, you insist upon retaining an absolute power over wives. But you must remember that arbitrary power is like most other things which are very hard—very liable to be broken; and, notwithstanding all your wise laws and maxims, we have it in our power not only to free ourselves but to subdue our masters, and without violence throw both your natural and legal authority at our feet.

Abigail to John, May 7, 1776

1. What type of primary source material is shown above? Why are such documents important to historians?
2. Read the letter shown above from Abigail Adams to her husband John dated May 7, 1776. Look up any unfamiliar words such as *emancipating*, *arbitrary* and *liable*. As a primary source, what does this letter tell you about the relationship between John Adams and his wife?
3. In Abigail Adams's letter to her husband John dated March 31, 1776 (page 88), she asks him to "Regard us then as beings, placed by providence under your protection, and in imitation of the Supreme Being make use of that power only for our happiness." As a primary source, what does this letter tell you about how Abigail Adams felt about the roles of women at that time?
4. Create a timeline for the events in this chapter. Then identify any relationships you see among the events shown on your timeline.
5. Suppose you wanted to find out what daily life was like for a British soldier living in the colonies. What kind of source would you look for in your library?

Using Critical Thinking

1. Some people have suggested that the terms of today's Representative and Senators should be limited, as were those of the members of Congress under the Articles of Confederation. What would be the advantages and disadvantages of setting a limit on the number of terms someone could serve in Congress?
2. What important powers does the national government have today under the Constitution that it did not have under the Articles of Confederation?
3. Under the Articles of Confederation, states had to agree unanimously on any revision of the original Articles. Do you think this was fair? Why or why not? What are advantages and disadvantages of unanimous rule?
4. The United States has had two major political parties since the early 1800s. What are the advantages and disadvantages of a two-party system of government?

Preparing for Citizenship

1. **WRITING ACTIVITY** Robert Morris, once one of the richest men in the colonies, died penniless and forgotten. Find out more about his life and the contributions he made to the nation in its earliest years. Write a report on your findings.
2. **ART ACTIVITY** The United States flag has gone through a number of changes throughout its history. On June 14, 1777, the Second Continental Congress passed a flag resolution. It said that the flag of the United States would have 13 alternating red and white stripes and 13 white stars on a field of blue, but it did not say exactly how the stars should be arranged. Design your own flag for the United States, based on the information given in the flag resolution.
3. **COLLABORATIVE LEARNING** In small groups, make a list of expenses for which the government attempted to collect taxes during the time period covered in this chapter. Then research the range of programs and other efforts for which present-day federal taxes are paid.
4. **COLLABORATIVE LEARNING** Stage a class debate over the Articles of Confederation. One team will support the Articles, and the other will argue that they need to be changed. Follow Robert's Rules of Order in managing the debate.

Chapter 4

The Constitutional Convention

The plan was to meet in Philadelphia in 1787 to patch up an ailing government. But when the 55 delegates met, the arguments began. Tempers flared and bargains were made. The result? The new Constitution. The signing of the Constitution was only the beginning of even more debate.

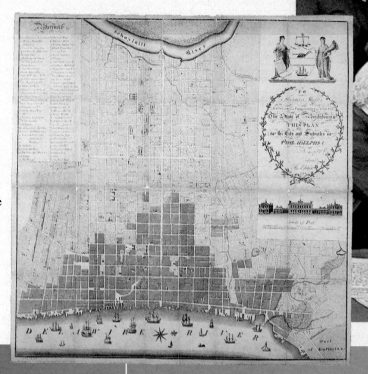

1787 The Constitutional Convention begins at the Pennsylvania State House, now Independence Hall. On the 1794 map at right, the State House is the red building on the gray block above the last E in Delaware.

1787	1788	1789

1787

SOCIETY of PEWTERERS

SOLID AND PURE

With the inkstand shown here, which had also been used for the signing of the Declaration of Independence, 39 delegates signed their names to the Constitution. The flag above commemorates the adoption of the Constitution by the new nation.

1790

1791

1792

1792

LESSON 1

The Constitutional Convention

What important compromises did delegates to the Constitutional Convention make?

Key Terms

- checks and balances
- legislative branch
- executive branch
- judicial branch
- bill of rights

➤ *Involved in politics since the 1770s, James Madison helped draft a new Virginia constitution and the Virginia Declaration of Rights.*

James Madison of Virginia was always early. A short man with a serious expression, he was the first delegate to ride into Philadelphia in May 1787. Deeply concerned about the politics of the new nation, Madison had been reading and reflecting on the subject of constitutional government day and night. He entered the city well prepared for the work ahead.

Madison worried that a national crisis was at hand. In its call for a federal convention, Congress had specified that this convention should have the "sole and express purpose of revising the Articles of Confederation." But Madison thought that simple changes could not solve the many problems of the ineffective Confederation government. He was planning to propose a totally new government at the convention—and he was worried that the other delegates would consider his plan to be radical, that is, too extreme for the time.

Madison planned his strategy carefully. To prepare for the convention, he asked his friend Thomas Jefferson to send him books about earlier confederations and other forms of government. Jefferson, who was serving as ambassador to France, responded by sending Madison more than 100 volumes by French and English philosophers. These books covered a wide range of political theory and the history of governments.

In the days before the convention began, Madison continued to work on his plans for the new government. But he worried about his chances for success. Could 13 states really come to agreement despite all their differences—different concepts of government, different natural resources, different cultural backgrounds, even different money?

Madison expected most of the delegates to be loyal to their own regions. He anticipated that many would be firmly committed to preserving the independence their states had enjoyed under the Articles of Confederation. But where were the other delegates? What if nobody showed up?

A New Government Debated

On May 13, the day before the federal convention was scheduled to begin, George Washington arrived in Philadelphia. Bells rang and cannons boomed to welcome him. The city's troops escorted him to the home of 81-year-old Benjamin Franklin, who was the "elder statesman" of the nation. General Washington, at the age of 55, was the most highly respected American of his time. His participation in the convention lent a special dignity to the proceedings.

The other delegates were also men from the highest levels of wealth and achievement—plantation owners from the South, merchants from the cities, college-educated professionals from all fields. When Thomas Jefferson later read the list of delegates, he called it, with understandable overstatement, "an assembly of demigods."

Although the average age of the delegates was only 42, most had extensive experience in government, and some had signed the Declaration of Independence. Jefferson and John Adams were missing because they were serving as ambassadors overseas. Also missing was Patrick Henry of Virginia, who was chosen as a delegate but refused to attend. Henry was part of a group of politicians who opposed any strengthening of the national government that might limit the powers of the states.

Slowly Delegates Gather

On May 14, which was 11 days after James Madison had arrived, only delegates from Virginia and Pennsylvania were at the Convention. A week of rain and muddy roads had delayed many of the delegates. Some were traveling hundreds of miles to get to Philadelphia, making uncomfortable, week-long trips by carriage or on horseback. Once they arrived, delegates were eager to deal with the nation's problems. But the Convention could not begin until at least seven of the thirteen states were represented.

All that the men could do was wait and worry about what, if anything, would happen at this meeting.

Finally, on May 25, delegates from seven states had arrived, and the convention began. The delegates unanimously elected George Washington as president of the convention. They also established rules for their debates, including a rule of strict secrecy. No one was to make the proceedings public until a final agreement had been reached.

◄ *Delegates to the Convention met in the same room of the Pennsylvania State House in which the Declaration of Independence had been signed. The building is now called Independence Hall.*

Even though Washington presided over the Convention, he was silent in debates. Why was his presence so important?

Edmund Randolph's family had been prominent in Virginia ever since his ancestors arrived from England in 1673.

The Virginia Plan

On the third day of the convention, Edmund Randolph took the floor to present 15 resolves, or formal proposals, drafted by the Virginia delegation. Why Randolph, when many of the ideas were actually those of Madison? The handsome, six-foot Randolph, governor of Virginia and the head of his delegation, made a more imposing figure than the shy, slight Madison.

"An individual independence of the States is utterly irreconcilable," Randolph announced. "Let national Government be armed with positive and complete authority."

As Randolph read his speech, the words *complete authority* sent shock waves through the hall. Although most of the delegates agreed that the nation needed a stronger central government,

most were not ready to give up the sovereignty, or independence, of the states.

The Virginia Plan, as it came to be known, proposed a supreme national government. The basis of this entirely new government would be three branches with a system of built-in **checks and balances**. Each branch of government would balance the power of the others in order to check, or protect, against any abuses of power. Although stunned by the far-reaching changes proposed, the delegates had been frustrated with the weaknesses of the Articles of Confederation. Most delegates agreed that the new plan had merit.

Reactions and Counterproposals

Charles Pinckney, a wealthy planter from South Carolina, started the debate by challenging the Virginia Plan. Did Randolph, asked Pinckney, mean to abolish state governments altogether? Many delegates were concerned that a strong central government would overpower the individual states. But they voted for a national government, despite their concerns.

The writers of the Constitution had done their homework. As you have learned, before coming to the convention, James Madison asked for and received a whole crate full of books from Thomas Jefferson, who was away in France. What do you think Jefferson might have included in his selection of books? What ideas influenced the authors of the Constitution?

British and European Origins

All of the delegates to the Constitutional Convention were once British citizens. The 35 lawyers and 8 judges among them were all steeped in the tradition of British law. Thomas Jefferson and Benjamin Franklin had both traveled widely in Europe. Thus it would not be surprising to find similarities between British and European traditions and the new U.S. Constitution.

To answer the question of who the most influential writers were among the colonists, a recent study looked at more than 15,000 political writings published in America between 1760 and 1805. A tally was made of the authors who were referred to or cited most often. Topping the list, cited three or four times more often than any other, was the French philosopher Baron de Montesquieu. The English philosophers David Hume and John Locke were the next two runners-up.

The Enlightenment

All three writers were a part of the Enlightenment, an intellectual movement that began in Europe in the eighteenth century. The Enlightenment is also sometimes called the Age of Reason. A central idea in this movement was the optimistic notion that humankind, by exercising its ability to use reason, could solve the problems of society.

The Enlightenment thinkers also gave a great deal of power to the individual. They believed that people should participate directly in their government. People had natural rights, they said, that belonged to them as a condition of being human, as part of the natural order of things. Locke identified these rights as life itself, liberty, and property. Note how closely this follows the wording of the Declaration of Independence:

"That all men. . . are endowed by their Creator with certain unalienable Rights, that among these are Life, Liberty and the pursuit of Happiness."

Locke, in his book *Two Theories of Government* (1690), wrote that government was a contract between the people and their ruler. If the ruler did not honor the contract and live up to its provisions, then the people had the right to replace him with another ruler.

At the time Locke wrote his book, England was working out an agreement known as the Bill of Rights of 1689. It guaranteed the right of the nobles and the gentry —the upper middle class—against the crown. Although some similarities can be seen between the English Bill of Rights and the U.S. Bill of Rights a century later, there are also some strong differences.

The U.S. document goes much further in guaranteeing the rights of the individual, not just of a single class of people.

Checks and Balances

A point that Montesquieu was fond of making was that "power should be a check to power." Therefore he was interested in looking for ways of maintaining checks and balances between powers. This also concerned the authors of the U.S. Constitution.

Montesquieu identified three centers of power: the legislative, the executive, and the executive in regard to civil law. (what is called in this country the judiciary). The Constitution, in its first three Articles, lays out the power of the legislative, the executive, and the judicial. The Constitution also establishes a system of checks and balances, so that each of the branches of government has some control over the others.

Here are some examples of how this works: Congress, the legislative branch, has the power to make the laws, but the President has the power to veto them—a check by the executive on the legislative. Congress, however, can override the veto—a check by the legislative on the executive. The Supreme Court can declare laws or executive actions unconstitutional— a check by the judicial on the legislative and the executive. The President appoints the Supreme Court justices and the Senate confirms the appointments—a check by the executive and the legislative on the judicial.

The Connecticut Compromise

Virginia Plan
- Representation in both houses of Congress based on population.
- Favored by large states.

New Jersey Plan
- One state, one vote; equal representation regardless of size.
- Favored by small states.

Connecticut Compromise
- Allows for the equal representation of each state in the Senate.
- Bases representation of states in the House on population.

> *The Connecticut Compromise was so important to the writing of the Constitution that it often has been called the Great Compromise.*

> *Find evidence to support this statement: Willingness to compromise helped the delegates settle the issue of how to represent each state in Congress.*

The new government would consist of a **legislative branch** (the Congress), an **executive branch** headed by the President, and a **judicial branch** (a national system of courts of law). Clearly the convention was no longer repairing the old Articles of Confederation. Instead the delegates were replacing the Articles with a constitution, a document defining a new government.

The delegates agreed quickly to a bicameral, or two-house, legislature. The Virginia Plan had proposed a lower house, the House of Representatives, to be elected by the people of each state. In turn, this lower house would select an upper, more selective house, the Senate. But a major disagreement arose between the states with large populations and the states with small populations. It concerned the election of representatives. Then the real struggle began.

Madison believed that representation in both houses should be proportional to population rather than equal for each state. This meant that a large state would have more representatives than a small state. James Wilson of Pennsylvania agreed. "We must bury all local interests and distinctions," he argued. The delegates from smaller states objected. They feared that they would lose their ability to prevent Congress from making any decisions the small states opposed.

William Paterson of New Jersey warned that his state would never give up its political independence. He then countered the Virginia Plan by proposing the New Jersey, or small-state, Plan. This plan was similar to the old Articles of Confederation in that each state—large or small—would get one vote in Congress. After three days of sharp debate, the delegates defeated the New Jersey Plan.

The Great Compromise

Spring gave way to summer, and the delegates still had many decisions to make. After the New Jersey defeat, the Connecticut delegation proposed a compromise. The people of each state would directly elect representatives to one house of Congress, the House of Representatives. The number of representatives for each state would be based on population. For the other house of Congress, each state legislature would choose two senators. After many days of impassioned debate, the delegates accepted the Connecticut Compromise. With this compromise all states were represented equally in the Senate, but representation in the House varied with each state's population. ■

The Slavery Issue

As the debate in the Pennsylvania State House heated up, so did the summer weather. The windows were sealed tight to protect the secrecy of the convention and to keep out flies, so the air in the meeting room became incredibly warm.

Debate soon turned to the issue of exactly how many representatives each state could send to the House of Representatives. As delegates argued their points of view, Madison observed that the states were "divided into different interests not by their difference of size . . . but principally from their having or not having slaves." How would populations be counted, especially in states with large numbers of slaves?

So far, the word *slavery* had been avoided at the convention. The delegates knew that a confrontation over this issue might ruin any chance they had of reaching a consensus. But it was impossible to avoid the issue of slavery entirely.

How to Count Slaves

Delegates from New England proposed that representation be based on the number of free inhabitants only. Delegates from the South wanted to increase their representation by counting everyone, including slaves.

The debate on this issue was lengthy. It touched on many concerns, including how to count a state's population for the purpose of setting that state's share of national taxes. During these debates, the Southern states defended their right to keep slaves.

The Three-Fifths Compromise

Eventually the delegates compromised. Representation would be in proportion to the whole number of white and other free citizens and three-fifths of all other persons. The

▼ *Taverns, such as the one shown in this John Lewis Krimmel oil painting of a Philadelphia inn, were often a gathering place for political discussion.*

"other persons" were, of course, slaves. For purposes of representation, all population counts included women.

The delegates reached two other compromises concerning slavery. Southerners insisted on treating slaves as property. They bought them to expand the labor force on their planta- tions. Delegates finally agreed to stop Congress from voting to end the slave trade until after 1808. This Slave Trade Clause was included in the text of the Constitution. The Fugitive Slave Clause, which allowed for the arrest of runaway slaves in any state, was also included. ■

The Constitution Is Signed

Throughout the four long months of debate, delegates came and went. Rhode Island had refused to send any delegates at all. At one point, two of the New York delegates walked out because they disagreed with the direc- tion of the Convention. The third, Alexander Hamilton—one of the original organizers of the federal con- vention—left also but later returned.

As the map below shows, other dele- gates had various reasons for being absent.

Finally, on September 17, 1787, a completed document was ready for signing. Of the 55 delegates who had attended at one time or another, 42 were present for the signing. Benjamin Franklin set the tone for the day: "I confess that there are several parts of

The Constitutional Convention: Delegates From Each State

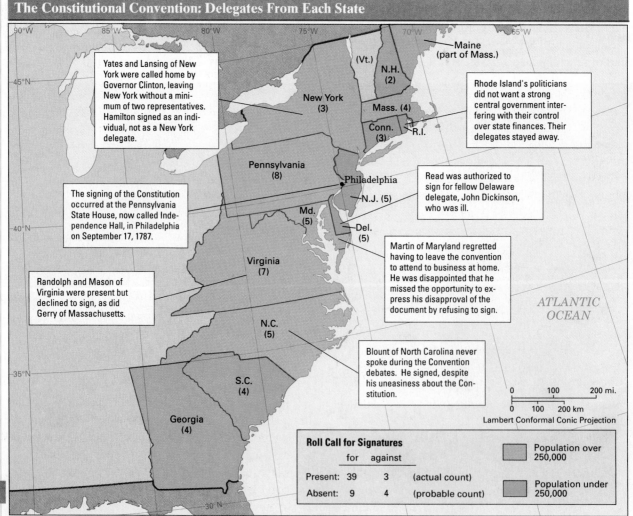

Maine (part of Mass.)

Yates and Lansing of New York were called home by Governor Clinton, leaving New York without a mini- mum of two representatives. Hamilton signed as an indi- vidual, not as a New York delegate.

(Vt.)

N.H. (2)

New York (3)

Mass. (4)

Conn. (3)

R.I.

Rhode Island's politicians did not want a strong central government inter- fering with their control over state finances. Their delegates stayed away.

Pennsylvania (8)

Philadelphia

N.J. (5)

Read was authorized to sign for fellow Delaware delegate, John Dickinson, who was ill.

The signing of the Constitution occurred at the Pennsylvania State House, now called Inde- pendence Hall, in Philadelphia on September 17, 1787.

Md. (5)

Del. (5)

Virginia (7)

Martin of Maryland regretted having to leave the convention to attend to business at home. He was disappointed that he missed the opportunity to ex- press his disapproval of the document by refusing to sign.

ATLANTIC OCEAN

Randolph and Mason of Virginia were present but declined to sign, as did Gerry of Massachusetts.

N.C. (5)

Blount of North Carolina never spoke during the Convention debates. He signed, despite his uneasiness about the Con- stitution.

S.C. (4)

Georgia (4)

| 0 | 100 | 200 mi. |
| 0 | 100 | 200 km |

Lambert Conformal Conic Projection

Roll Call for Signatures

	for	against	
Present:	39	3	(actual count)
Absent:	9	4	(probable count)

Population over 250,000

Population under 250,000

this constitution which I do not at present approve. . . ." But he went on to explain why he would sign it anyway, and he finished by offering a motion that the Constitution be accepted by unanimous consent of "the States."

◄ In objecting to the Constitution, George Mason said, "We are not indeed constituting a British Government, but a more dangerous monarchy, an elective one."

> W hilst the last members were signing it, Doctr. Franklin looking towards the President's chair, at the back of which a rising sun happened to be painted, observed to a few members near him, that painters had found it difficult to distinguish in their art a rising from a setting sun. I have, said he, often and often in the course of the session . . . looked at that [sun] behind the President without being able to tell whether it was rising or setting: But now at length I have the happiness to know that it is a rising and not a setting sun.
>
> James Madison, in *The Records of the Federal Convention of 1787*

Only three of the members present that day refused to sign. Edmund Randolph, who had proposed the Virginia Plan, wanted to remain uncommitted until his state had a chance to debate the Constitution. George Mason, a fellow Virginian, particularly objected to the absence of a **bill of rights**, a summary of the basic rights and liberties of the people. Elbridge Gerry of Massachusetts also refused to sign the Constitution without a bill of rights. He feared that the debate in

the states would result in civil war and said he "could not . . . pledge himself to abide by it at all events."

That night, according to Washington's diary, the delegates dined together at the City Tavern and then parted on friendly terms. After months of secret meetings, they felt relieved that a new constitution existed. But they also felt rather uneasy. The Congress—still operating under the Articles of Confederation—would now have to send the Constitution to the states. At least nine of the thirteen states would have to approve it.

In the minds of the delegates the question remained: what if no one agreed with what the delegates had worked out? There was still a chance that all those hot days and long hours of debate would add up to nothing. ■

How Do We Know?

HISTORY *We learned about the secret discussions at the Convention from the notes kept by a few delegates. Each night, after the long, tiring meetings, James Madison carefully wrote out in longhand his notes of what took place that day. Madison's journal was made public after his death in 1836.*

■ *Why didn't the signing of a document on September 17 finish the business of creating the Constitution?*

R E V I E W

1. **FOCUS** What important compromises did the delegates to the Constitutional Convention make?

2. **CONNECT** Considering the many problems with the Articles of Confederation, why were some delegates upset by the prospect of a supreme national government?

3. **SOCIAL SYSTEMS** How did the 13 states' differences on the issue of slavery contribute to the outcome of the Constitutional Convention?

4. **CRITICAL THINKING** Why did the disagreement among delegates over the election of representatives result in the Connecticut Compromise? Can you think of a different solution to the problem of representation?

5. **ACTIVITY** Assume the role of a delegate to the Convention of 1787 from a small state in the North or a large state in the South. Prepare a two-minute speech in which you report to your state legislature on the outcome of the Convention. Use an outline to organize your speech.

First Day in Philadelphia

Benjamin Franklin

In Chapter 3, Lesson 1, you read about Benjamin Franklin's contributions and his ideas about the form that a new government could take in America. In this selection you will meet the young Ben Franklin.

Benjamin Franklin (1706-1790) was an inventor, scientist, and statesman as well as a diplomat, editor, and publisher. Franklin was also a dedicated author whose writings about his thoughts, ideas, and accomplishments are both educational and entertaining. Below is a selection from his Autobiography. *It captures the thoughts of the young Ben Franklin as he arrives, alone, in Philadelphia for the first time. The second selection, a letter to Joseph Priestley written in 1772, is Franklin's practical reply to a request for his advice on decision-making. While reading these selections, think about what sort of person might have written these words.*

I have been the more particular in this description of my journey, and shall be so of my first entry into that city, that you may in your mind compare such unlikely beginnings with the figure I have since made there. I was in my working dress, my best clothes being to come round by sea. I was dirty from my journey; my pockets were stuff'd out with shirts and stockings, and I knew no soul nor where to look for lodging. I was fatigued with travelling, rowing, and want of rest, I was very hungry; and my whole stock of cash consisted of a Dutch dollar, and about a shilling in copper. The latter I gave the people of the boat for my passage, who at first refus'd it, on account of my rowing; but I insisted on their taking it. A man being sometimes more generous when he has but a little money than when he has plenty, perhaps thro' fear of being thought to have but little.

Then I walked up the street, gazing about till near the market-house I met a boy with bread. I had made many a meal on bread, and, inquiring where he got it, I went immediately to the baker's he directed me to, in Second-street, and ask'd for bisket, intending such as we had in Boston; but they, it seems, were not made in Philadelphia. Then I asked for a three-penny loaf, and was told they had none such. So not considering or knowing the difference of money, and the greater cheapness nor the names of his bread, I bad him give me three-penny worth of any sort. He gave me, accordingly, three great puffy rolls. I was surpriz'd at the quantity, but took it, and, having no room in my pockets, walk'd off with a roll under each arm, and eating the other. Thus I went up Market-street as far as Fourth-street, passing by the door of Mr. Read, my future wife's father; when she, standing at the door, saw me, and thought I made, as I certainly did, a most awkward, ridiculous appearance. Then I turned and went down Chestnut-street and part of Walnut-street, eating my roll all the way, and, coming round, found myself again at Market-street wharf, near the boat I came in, to which I went for a draught of the

bad   asked

draught   drink

river water; and, being filled with one of my rolls, gave the other two to a woman and her child that came down the river in the boat with us, and were waiting to go farther.

Thus refreshed, I walked again up the street, which by this time had many clean-dressed people in it, who were all walking the same way. I joined them and thereby was led into the great meeting-house of the Quakers near the market. I sat down among them, and, after looking round awhile and hearing nothing said, being very drowsy thro' labor and want of rest the preceding night, I fell fast asleep, and continued so till the meeting broke up, when one was kind enough to rouse me. This was, therefore, the first house I was in or slept in, in Philadelphia.

Moral Algebra

Dear Sir:

In the affair of so much importance to you, wherein you ask my advice, I cannot, for want of sufficient premises, advise you *what* to determine; but, if you please, I will tell you *how*. When these difficult cases occur, they are difficult, chiefly because, while we have them under consideration, all the reasons *pro* and *con* are not present to the mind at the same time; but sometimes one set present themselves, and at other times another, the first being out of sight. Hence the various purposes or inclinations that alternately prevail, and the uncertainty that perplexes us.

To get over this, my way is to divide half a sheet of paper by a line into two columns; writing over the one *pro*, and over the other *con*; then during three or four days' consideration, I put down under the different heads short hints of the different motives that at different times occur to me, *for* or *against* the measure. When I have thus got them all together in one view, I endeavor to estimate their respective weights; and, where I find two (one on each side) that seem equal, I strike them both out. If I find a reason *pro* equal to some two reasons *con*, I strike out the three. If I judge some two reasons *con*, equal to some three reasons *pro*, I strike out the five; and thus proceeding I find at length where the balance lies; and if, after a day or two of further consideration, nothing new that is of importance occurs on either side, I come to a determination accordingly. And though the weight of reasons cannot be taken with the precision of algebraic quantities, yet, when each is thus considered separately and comparatively, and the whole lies before me, I think I can judge better, and am less likely to make a rash step; and in fact I have found great advantage from this kind of equation, in what may be called *moral* or *prudential algebra*.

Wishing sincerely that you may determine for the best, I am ever, my dear friend, yours most affectionately,

—B. Franklin

premises details

alternately prevail take turns in being uppermost in one's mind

endeavor try

Maxims

This selection is from Poor Richard's Almanac, *a book written and published by Benjamin Franklin. An almanac provides practical advice, poems, jokes, and weather predictions. The practical advice is expressed in short sayings called maxims. The maxims selected here reflect Benjamin Franklin's ideas on thrift, hard work, and simplicity.*

Keep conscience clear,
Then never fear.

❦

Half the truth is often a great lie.

❦

Blessed is he that expects nothing, for he shall never be disappointed.

❦

Eat to live, and not live to eat.

❦

There are three things extremely hard: steel, a diamond, and to know one's self.

❦

To lengthen thy life, lessen thy meals.

❦

He that lieth down with dogs shall rise up with fleas.

❦

He that falls in love with himself will have no rivals.

❦

A flatterer never seems absurd;
The flattered always takes his word.

❦

The rotten apple spoils his companion.

❦

Tart words make no friends: a spoonful of honey will catch more flies than a gallon of vinegar.

❦

If you'd lose a troublesome visitor, lend him money.

❦

He's a fool that makes his doctor his heir.

❦

Three may keep a secret, if two of them are dead.

❦

All would live long, but none would be old.

❦

Dost thou love life? Then do not squander time;
for that's the stuff life is made of.

❦

Doing an injury puts you below your enemy;
Revenging one makes you but even with him;
Forgiving it sets you above him.

❦

If your head is wax, don't walk in the sun.

❦

Learn of the skilful: He that teaches himself
hath a fool for his master.

❦

For want of a nail the shoe is lost; for want of a shoe the horse is lost;
for want of a horse the rider is lost.

❦

Man's tongue is soft, and bone doth lack;
Yet a stroke therewith may break a man's back.

❦

Lost time is never found again.

❦

Time is an herb that cures all diseases.

❦

Better slip with foot than tongue.

Further Reading

The Autobiography and Other Writings. Benjamin Franklin. Edited and with an introduction by Peter Shaw. The three excerpts given here appear in this book along with many other of Franklin's writings.

The Many Worlds of Ben Franklin. Frank R. Donovan.

Benjamin Franklin. Robin McKowan. These two books contain biographical information about the life of this great man.

LESSON 2

The Ratification Debate

How did the ratification of the Constitution depend on the debates in each of the states?

Key Terms

- Federalist
- Antifederalist
- ratify

> *T*his proposal of altering our federal government is of a most alarming nature. You ought to be extremely cautious, watchful, jealous of your liberty, for instead of securing your rights, you may lose them forever. If a wrong step be now made, the republic may be lost forever.

The great orator Patrick Henry was speaking at Virginia's state convention. It was a sweltering June day in Richmond. Nine months had gone by since the delegates in Philadelphia had signed the Constitution, but Patrick Henry was still dead-set against its approval. In a thundering voice, he warned a roomful of his fellow Virginians about the dangers the Constitution presented.

Referring to the delegates at the Philadelphia Convention, he asked: "Who authorized them to speak the language of 'We, the People' instead of 'We, the States'? States are the characteristics and the soul of a confederation."

Henry feared that the national government could overpower the ability of the states to protect their own citizens. He asked his fellow Virginians to consider the rights they valued, such as trial by jury. "Will the abandonment of your most sacred rights tend to the security of your liberty?"

Speaking directly to the state convention's chairman, Henry compared the Constitution to the human face:

> *T*his Constitution is said to have beautiful features, but when I come to examine these features, sir, they appear to me horridly frightful. Among other deformities, it has an awful squinting; it squints [is inclined to a bias] towards monarchy.

➤ *In the noted 1763 lawsuit called the "Parson's cause," shown here in this painting, Patrick Henry first won fame as a brilliant speaker.*

The Debate Goes Public

Similar objections were raised in all the state conventions. After four months of secret deliberations, the Constitution had become the subject of widespread public debate.

When the Philadelphia Convention had submitted the Constitution to the Congress still meeting in New York City under the old Articles of Confederation, the document was accompanied by a letter signed by George Washington. He firmly supported the Constitution, writing:

> It is obviously impracticable, in the federal government of these states, to secure all rights of independent sovereignty to each, and yet provide for the interest and safety of all: Individuals entering into society must give up a share of liberty to preserve the rest.

After Congress agreed to turn the Constitution over to the states for ratification, newspapers throughout the country printed its full text. (You can read the Constitution starting on page 636.) Though Washington's stamp of approval carried great weight, opponents of a constitution rallied to defeat it at the state conventions.

Antifederalist Fears

The word *federal* refers to a union of states under a government with central authority. People who supported the Constitution were called **Federalists**. People who opposed the Constitution were called **Antifederalists**. Although their specific concerns varied, most Antifederalists looked to the historical legacy of the English Bill of Rights, designed to protect the basic liberties of the king's subjects. Why, asked the Antifederalists, had the framers of the Constitution failed to include an American bill of rights to protect individual citizens?

The Antifederalists also questioned the legality of the Constitution. What right had the Convention to go so far beyond its original purpose, which was simply to revise the Articles of Confederation?

Among the first Antifederalists to explain his position publicly was Elbridge Gerry. "Conceiving as I did that the liberties of America were not secured by the system," he wrote the Massachusetts legislature in October 1787, "it was my duty to oppose it."

Some of the most powerful leaders within the states—including George Clinton, governor of New York—had long opposed the idea of a strong central government. These men did not want the national government to have more power than the states.

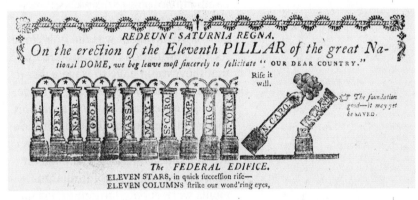

ELEVEN STARS, in quick succession rise—
ELEVEN COLUMNS strike our wond'ring eyes,

They had begun to publish the reasons for their opposition in newspapers and pamphlets as soon as the Constitution was in print.

Antifederalist writers aroused people's fears that a strong central government could not be trusted. Among the threats to personal freedom, argued the Antifederalists, were taxes, government regulations, and a standing army. A strong central government could take away the liberties they had fought so hard to achieve in the war against Great Britain.

Some Antifederalists believed that the Constitution established a government in which a small, select group would protect its own interests

In building the federal government, each state had to formally approve the new Constitution. This 1788 cartoon shows 11 columns—states—supporting approval. Two columns remained unsteady.

The Constitutional Convention

more than those of the common people. In their deepest fears, the Antifederalists worried that an elected government could turn out to be even worse than a monarchy. Publishing their "Reasons for Dissent" in the *Pennsylvania Packet and Daily Advertiser,* some delegates to the Pennsylvania convention claimed:

> The power of direct taxation will apply to every individual.... However oppressive, the people will have but this alternative, except to pay the tax, or let their property be taken, for all resistance will be in vain. The standing army and select militia would enforce the collection.

Selling the Constitution

The Federalists, on the other hand, did not share this sense of mistrust. They believed that a strong, central government was the only hope for the new nation. They soon realized that they would have to wage a war in the press to answer the charges made by the Antifederalists. To win support for the ratification of the Constitution, the Federalists resorted to newspaper articles and pamphlets. The page on the right shows how political arguments were debated in print.

Alexander Hamilton enlisted the aid of John Jay, another Federalist

from New York, and James Madison. Together they wrote a series of letters, starting in October 1787, that were printed in a New York newspaper under the name *Publius.* Political writers often used classical pen names, and Hamilton chose *Publius,* the hero who established a stable republican government in Rome.

The letters from *Publius* were later collected and republished in book form under the title *The Federalist.* In Number 29 of *The Federalist,* Alexander Hamilton ridiculed the Antifederalists' fears:

> There is something so far-fetched and so extravagant in the idea of danger to liberty from the militia that one is at a loss whether to treat it with gravity or with raillery [humor] .... Where in the name of common sense are our fears to end if we may not trust our sons, our brothers, our neighbors, our fellow-citizens?

The Federalist essays were an eloquent defense of the newly created Constitution, but they were only one of many political strategies used to win votes for the ratification of the document. The decisive battles were fought state by state in the ratifying conventions. ■

■ Explain how the Federalists used ridicule to respond to the arguments of the Antifederalists.

Ratification—Just Barely

The Federalists acted quickly to bring the Constitution to a vote in states in which they had a clear majority. The first states to debate the Constitution were Delaware and Pennsylvania. Delaware was the first state to **ratify**, or formally approve, with a unanimous vote on December 7, 1787. Pennsylvania followed with its approval in less than a week.

Those who opposed the Constitution were angry. They believed that the first state conventions had been

called too hastily. Antifederalists tried to delay the process.

The next three state conventions —in New Jersey, Georgia, and Connecticut—ratified the Constitution with little opposition. Massachusetts proved to be the first serious problem. Antifederalists probably had a majority in the state, but they lacked leadership. Massachusetts, after debating from early January to early February 1788, became the sixth state to ratify the Constitution by a vote of 187-168.

The Federalist Papers

Federalists versus Antifederalists. Alexander Hamilton wondered how to win people over to his Federalist thinking. How about a newspaper devoted to the cause? If the essays were persuasive enough, the new nation might choose to establish a strong central government.

Great writers unite!
For eight months, anonymous essays by some of America's greatest political thinkers—Alexander Hamilton, James Madison, and John Jay—sparked the attention of readers. Together, these essays explained why their authors thought the Constitution should be ratified.

The Federalist was printed on a press such as this. The printer set individual letters of type into a form by hand. Then the type was inked, and a piece of paper was placed on it. The printer pushed down on a lever so that a wooden block pressed the type to the paper.

Only 300 copies were printed because printers knew that people would post them on public buildings and read them aloud at public meetings. Soon after the newspapers were published, *The Federalist* was published as a book. Today, the essays are still studied around the world.

121

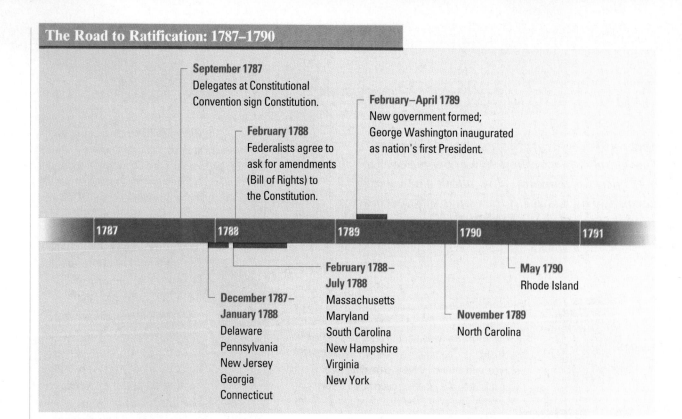

The Road to Ratification: 1787–1790

September 1787
Delegates at Constitutional Convention sign Constitution.

February 1788
Federalists agree to ask for amendments (Bill of Rights) to the Constitution.

February–April 1789
New government formed; George Washington inaugurated as nation's first President.

1787   1788   1789   1790   1791

December 1787–January 1788
Delaware
Pennsylvania
New Jersey
Georgia
Connecticut

February 1788–July 1788
Massachusetts
Maryland
South Carolina
New Hampshire
Virginia
New York

November 1789
North Carolina

May 1790
Rhode Island

North Carolina and Rhode Island finally ratified the Constitution after George Washington was sworn into office in April 1789 as the first President.

What were the strategies of the Federalists and the Antifederalists for winning votes in the states?

After overcoming strong opposition, New Hampshire — on June 21, 1788 — became the ninth and decisive state to ratify the Constitution.

Meanwhile, a grand debate was taking place in Richmond, Virginia, between James Madison, often called the Father of the Constitution, and Patrick Henry, its most articulate opponent. The vote for ratification was close: 89-79.

If the Antifederalists had moved more quickly in Virginia and New York, where they had strong leaders and much support, the Constitution might never have been ratified. In fact, the Antifederalists' decision to delay worked against them. Another factor was that less than 10 percent of

the newspapers supported them.

The Federalists had needed the approval of only nine states—not all thirteen. The fact that ratification did not require a unanimous vote, which had been a problem with the Articles of Confederation, kept the Constitution alive.

Even though the Antifederalists were defeated, they had won some support for the idea that the Constitution was not complete without a bill of rights. Still to be added to the Constitution was an official promise that the national government would not infringe on dearly valued liberties. Whether the Antifederalists would get such an addition to the Constitution was still uncertain. ■

R E V I E W

1. **FOCUS** How did the ratification of the Constitution depend on the debates in each of the states?

2. **CONNECT** How did Patrick Henry and other Antifederalists appeal to Americans' long-standing fear of the British monarchy?

3. **POLITICAL SYSTEMS** Examine the Federalist and Antifederalist positions. Which position gave greater value to the sovereignty of the nation and which gave greater value to the independence of the states?

4. **CRITICAL THINKING** Explain how printing political arguments in the newspapers of 1787–1788 was essential to carrying out the ratification debates.

5. **CRITICAL THINKING** Why do you think the Constitution was, in the end, ratified?

6. **ACTIVITY** Take a Federalist or an Antifederalist position, and draw and caption your own cartoon to illustrate your viewpoint. What sort of publication do you think would print your cartoon?

Reaching a Compromise

Here's Why

A compromise is a settlement of differences by agreement. Sometimes a number of people have to work together on a project, but each of them has different ideas about how to do the work. In order to finish the project, the group has to reach an agreement on how to do the work. The agreement they reach is called a compromise.

For example, although the delegates to the Constitutional Convention of 1787 wanted to do the best they could for America's 13 states, each had a very different idea of what should be done. The delegates had to reach a compromise in order to do the work of the convention. Families, businesses, and friends all use the process of compromise.

Suppose your class decided to have a surprise party for your teacher, but everyone had different ideas about how to do it. You would need to find a way for everyone to agree on the plans for the party.

Here's How

Each person in a group has to be willing to give up something in order for a group to reach an agreement. Therefore one of the most important parts of the compromise process is your individual decision on what you will go along with and what you won't.

Asking yourself questions is often a good way to decide where you stand on an issue. If you need to work with a group to plan a party for your teacher, you might want to ask yourself these questions:

1. **What part of this project is most important to me?**
    You may decide that the decorations are the most important part of the project for you.

2. **How many other people think that part of the project is important?**
    If many people want to do the decorating, it may be difficult for everyone to agree on who should be responsible for it.

3. **Why is that part important to me?**
    You need to evaluate how important decorating is for you, in order to see if it is something you can give up. Perhaps the decorations are the most important part for you because you enjoy drawing and making them. Or perhaps it is the only part of the project you feel you can do well.

4. **What is best for the group?**
    At this point, you need to look at the whole project. If you love decorating, but the party will not happen unless there are more people making food than decorating, you need to decide if it would be better for you to give up doing the decorating in order to get the job done. On the other hand, if you feel decorating is the only thing you could do well for the group, you may want to stick to your original goal of doing the decorating.

Try It

Whenever students work together in groups in the classroom, they have to agree on who will do what. Assume that your class has to produce a play. Use the questions to decide which part of the production you would choose to work on and how you would work with the group to reach an agreement.

Apply It

Choose an issue important to your class, such as the choice of school lunch menus. Make your individual decision, then divide into groups and go through the process of compromise. Write a short paragraph outlining what your original decision was, what the group decision was, and how the compromise was reached.

L E S S O N   3

The Bill of Rights

THINKING
F O C U S

How does the Bill of Rights balance governmental powers with the rights of individuals?

Key Terms

- free press
- amendment

▲ *Antifederalist Elbridge Gerry warned citizens that a bill of rights was necessary to protect individual liberties.*

Helping to fuel the strong feelings for the bill of rights in the 1780s were Americans' memories of New Yorker John Peter Zenger's fight for freedom of the press fifty years earlier. Every Monday in 1733, Zenger's *New York Weekly Journal* would appear with stinging articles criticizing the British colonial government: Governor William Cosby is a tyrant! An enemy of justice!

Government officials were outraged. Roughly one year after the newspaper was first published, British officials jailed Zenger for his criticism of the colonial government in New York. Although Zenger wrote few of the articles himself, he was held solely responsible since he was the newspaper's publisher. Zenger was kept in jail for more than 11 months since he could not afford to pay the bail. Still the newspaper appeared every Monday. With whispered instructions she received through a hole in the prison door, Zenger's wife, Anna, continued to publish the newspaper so hated by the British.

Finally, the case was brought to trial. The financial backers of Zenger's newspaper hired Andrew Hamilton of Philadelphia to represent Zenger. Hamilton was considered one of the most brilliant lawyers in the colonies. Hamilton argued that Zenger had only published the truth, and that he should not be punished for publishing the truth. The jury agreed and they found Zenger not guilty. After his release, Zenger printed a complete account of his trial and the British authorities didn't stop him. This was considered the first major victory for a **free press** that is, news media such as newspapers and magazines that are unrestricted by the government.

Americans did not forget the case. Nor did they forget other memories of British rule. The British army had forced the owners of private homes to house soldiers. Colonial customs officials had invaded homes to search for and seize smuggled goods. With a bill of rights, the new Constitution would guarantee that such governmental practices would be only memories of the past.

Why Massachusetts Resisted

"There is no declaration of rights." This was how George Mason had objected to the Constitution in 1787. And these words became the rallying cry of the Antifederalists back in the states. The debates at the Massachusetts state ratifying convention would prove to be the turning point for the adoption of the bill of rights.

"Beware! beware!—you are forging chains for yourselves and your children—your liberties are at stake," exclaimed Elbridge Gerry in November 1787, after he had returned to Massachusetts. The lack of a bill of rights was the most serious obstacle to winning the support of old patriots such as Samuel Adams and John

Hancock. Adams planned to oppose the Constitution at the Massachusetts state convention, because he was determined "to protect and cover the rights of Mankind" against the threat of a strong central government.

Wanted: Guaranteed Rights

After the Philadelphia Convention, most of the men who had written the Constitution could not understand why a bill of rights was a serious issue for many states. They believed that the Constitution, as it was, could stand on its own. On the last day of the Convention, George Mason proposed that a bill of rights be added to the Constitution. Elbridge Gerry agreed with him but other delegates had argued that the states' own declarations of rights would be sufficient to protect individual liberties. They had voted against the motion to add a bill of rights at the Convention.

A Winning Strategy

Although many Federalists continued to consider a bill of rights unnecessary, some were willing to compromise on this issue in order to establish a new government. The Federalists had already used compromise as a unifying force in Philadelphia. Because they feared defeat in the Massachusetts ratifying convention, Federalist leaders decided to gain support by drafting a list of **amendments,** additions meant to improve the Constitution. They persuaded John Hancock, the most popular man in Massachusetts, to present these

amendments to the state convention. The proposed amendments made the Constitution acceptable to many who had formerly opposed ratification.

The winning strategy of the Massachusetts Federalists turned the tide of ratification. As other states debated the Constitution, they too insisted on amendments that would guarantee a person's rights. ■

The British army occupied Boston in 1768 to enforce the writs of assistance, which gave officials blanket authority to carry out searches at any time and any place.

■ *What made some Federalists change their minds about including a bill of rights in the Constitution?*

Balancing the Constitution

The framers of the Constitution had worked hard to create a system that balanced the powers of the three branches of government—legislative, executive, and judicial. The amendments proposed by the state ratifying conventions were aimed at another kind of balance: balancing the rights of the states and of individual citizens against the powers of the central government.

James Madison was one of the Federalists who had expressed concerns about the protection of basic rights, through his part in writing *The Federalist.* During the debates in

Virginia, Madison promised to work for a bill of rights once the Constitution was ratified. After he was elected in 1789 to the first Congress, he pressed for passage of a series of amendments to the new Constitution.

Rights for the People

The amendments drafted at the state conventions listed the rights of individual citizens and the rights of the states. These were rights the national government could not take away. Many advocates of a bill of rights also wanted the Constitution to state clearly that any rights not given to the national government by the states be reserved to the states or to the people.

The first Congress under the Constitution met in New York in March 1789. Most men elected to Congress had been delegates to the Convention of 1787 or to the state ratifying conventions. Madison and other members of the first Congress combined the many proposed amendments into a list of twelve. Some amendments included more than one right. For example, the First Amendment was written to protect freedom of speech, press, assembly, and petition. Congress voted in favor of the twelve amendments in September 1789 and sent them to the states for ratification.

Ratification of Ten Amendments

Although the men who framed the original Constitution had not included a bill of rights at first, they did have the foresight to include ways to amend the Constitution. Americans are able to change the Constitution or add to it. An amendment may be proposed by two-thirds of both houses of

➤ *Of the twelve amendments proposed for a bill of rights, two were not ratified. One limited the size of the House of Representatives; the other forbade members of the House and Senate to raise their own salaries.*

Congress, or the legislatures of two-thirds of the states can propose a constitutional convention. If three-fourths of the states ratify a proposed amendment, it then becomes part of the Constitution.

Thomas Jefferson observed this amendment process from France. He commented proudly that "the example of changing a constitution by assembling the wise men of the state instead of assembling armies" would be worth "much to the world."

The system worked remarkably well. By December 15, 1791, the states had ratified ten out of the twelve proposed amendments to the Constitution, and the United States had its Bill of Rights. Look at page 647 of this book and find where the Bill of Rights now appears in the Constitution along with more recent amendments.

The Framework Completed

The Bill of Rights balances the Constitution by giving people legal protection against abuses of power. The First Amendment, for example, prohibits the government from attempting to control what people think, say, or write. It grants people the right to worship according to their own beliefs, without interference from the government. The Fourth Amendment protects people from unreasonable searches and seizures of their private property. The Sixth Amendment guarantees the right to a speedy and fair trial by jury. The Eighth Amendment prohibits cruel and unusual punishment. When these or any other declared rights are violated, individuals may appeal to the courts.

The first ten amendments brought the nation together under one federal government by removing most of the Antifederalists' fears. Now that the Constitution included the Bill of Rights, many Antifederalists became active in the new government. Edmund Randolph was named the first attorney general by Washington. George Clinton became Vice President under Jefferson and again under Madison. And James Monroe, an Antifederalist from Virginia, eventually became the fifth President of the United States.

The government created by the Constitutional Convention of 1787 has worked for more than 200 years because its wise authors made it both strong and flexible. With the addition of the Bill of Rights, the Constitution has also protected the basic freedoms and rights that Americans cherish.

The framers could not have foreseen all the conflicts, problems, and needs of a growing nation. The Constitution was indeed sketchy. But with its amendment procedure, it has provided a means to accommodate changes. As the U.S. Supreme Court's Chief Justice John Marshall once stated, the Constitution was "intended to endure for ages to come, and, consequently to be adapted to the various *crises* of human affairs. ■

▲ *The states still had to work out many details. There was not yet an official arrangement of the stars in the U.S. flag.*

■ *How did the amendment process provide the flexibility to make the Constitution strong?*

R E V I E W

1. **FOCUS** How does the Bill of Rights balance governmental powers with the rights of individuals?

2. **CONNECT** Why did Federalists first oppose the addition of a bill of rights? Why did most Antifederalists believe such a bill was absolutely necesssary?

3. **HISTORY** Explain why the strategy of the Federalists to compromise in Massachusetts also helped the Antifederalists in the other states.

4. **CONSTITUTIONAL HERITAGE** Describe the process by which the Bill of Rights was added to the Constitution.

5. **CRITICAL THINKING** In 1791, the Bill of Rights was ratified. Since then 16 amendments have been ratified. Why do you think Americans have continued to revise the Constitution?

6. **ACTIVITY** Prepare and deliver a one-minute presentation on the basic rights guaranteed by the Bill of Rights.

The Constitutional Convention

Chapter Review

Reviewing Key Terms

amendment (p. 125)
Antifederalist (p. 119)
bill of rights (p. 113)
checks and balances (p. 108)
executive branch (p. 110)

Federalist (p. 119)
free press (p. 124)
judicial branch (p. 110)
legislative branch (p. 110)
ratify (p. 120)

A. In each of the following pairs, the two terms are related in some way. Write a sentence for each pair that clearly explains the relationship between the two terms.

1. Antifederalist, Federalist
2. bill of rights, amendment
3. free press, bill of rights

B. Based on what you have read in the chapter, decide whether each of the following statements is accurate. Write an explanation for each decision.

1. The Constitution created a system of checks and balances to keep any one branch of government from becoming more powerful than the other two.
2. The judicial branch of the government is headed by the President.
3. The legislative branch of the government is made up of the Congress.
4. The framers of the Constitution provided for the passage of amendments to make sure that its provisions would never change.

Exploring Concepts

A. On a separate sheet of paper make a table like the one shown below. Then complete the table by briefly describing the Antifederalist position and the Federalist position on each of the issues listed on the left.

Issues	Anti-Federalist Position	Federalist Position
The power of state government		
The power of central government		
Importance of Bill of Rights		
Legality of the Constitution		

B. Decide whether each of the following statements is true or false. If it is false, correct the statement and provide facts from the chapter to support your correction.

1. A series of compromises helped the delegates to the Constitutional Convention agree on a final document.
2. Even though most of the delegates signed the Constitution, they were not sure it would be adopted.
3. Many people thought the Constitution was incomplete.
4. There were many reasons why people feared a strong central government.
5. The Federalists' actions won several quick victories in favor of the Constitution.
6. The Antifederalists' decision to delay votes worked for them.
7. The Antifederalists did not want the Constitution to have a bill of rights.
8. In order to gain ratification, the Federalists agreed they would soon add a bill of rights.
9. The decision to include a procedure for amending the Constitution was a mistake.
10. The delegates to the Constitutional Convention reached an easy compromise.

128

Reviewing Skills

1. Identify three situations in which you would want to use the process of compromise.
2. Using the process of reaching a compromise that you learned on page 123, write a short paragraph describing how you would decide whether you would have wanted to support the Federalist position on the Constitution or the Antifederalist position.
3. What compromise did the delegates to the Constitutional Convention of 1787 reach?
4. If you were looking for detailed information on the Constitutional Convention what kind of primary sources could you use?
5. Suppose you and your family are planning a vacation. You want to go someplace where you can go swimming, another person wants to go skiing, and another wants to go horseback riding. How would you reach a compromise?

Using Critical Thinking

1. If you had lived during the development of the Constitution, would you have been a Federalist or an Antifederalist? Explain your answer.
2. Why do you think the framers of the Constitution included a provision that ensured that there would be a free press?
3. Federalist Alexander Hamilton wrote that those who fought the Revolution "sought to obtain liberty for no particular state, but for the whole Union. . . connected under one controlling and supreme head." Do you agree with his position in this statement? Explain your answer.
4. Antifederalists in Pennsylvania wrote that "the powers vested in Congress by this Constitution must necessarily annihilate [wipe out] and absorb the legislative, executive, and judicial powers of the several states." Did this prediction come true? Explain your answer.
5. Read the Bill of Rights which begins on page 647 in the back of this book. Which of the rights or freedoms in the Bill of Rights is the most important to you? Why?
6. Thomas Jefferson, writing from France, said that "the example of changing a constitution by assembling the wise men of the state instead of assembling armies" was "worth much to the world." Find out what was happening in France at the time of the Constitutional Convention. With that information in mind, explain Jefferson's statement.

Preparing for Citizenship

1. WRITING ACTIVITY The Bill of Rights still causes controversy today. Choose one of the rights listed in the first ten amendments to the Constitution. Find some recent newspaper stories or magazine articles that describe disputes over its meaning. Write a summary of the arguments, giving both sides of the issue, and stating your position on the issue.
2. COLLECTING INFORMATION The Constitution originally allowed the state legislatures to choose the Senators for their state. Read the amendments to the Constitution, beginning on page 647 at the back of this book, and find which amendment changed the election process for the Senate. Write a paragraph explaining how the Senators are elected today and stating why you think the amendment was changed.
3 ART ACTIVITY Throughout history documents have been important graphic symbols as well as legal papers. Find a copy of the original Constitution. Create a contemporary design for the document. You may use advanced artistic techniques, such as computer graphics, if you would like.
4. ART ACTIVITY Make a chart showing the members of the national government who represent you. Include the President and Vice President as well as the senators and representatives from your district. If possible, include a picture of each one and a short biography.
5. COLLABORATIVE LEARNING Create a constitution for your class. Assuming that the teacher is the executive, create a system of checks and balances to ensure that necessary class work is done. Class duties such as cleaning the room, decorating the bulletin boards, and monitoring assignments should be taken into account. Make provisions for a free press, for individual rights, and for resolving disputes that may arise among classmates.

Establishing the New Nation

During the years in which its first Presidents served, the United States was a young nation — discovering its own identity, expanding along the western frontier, and defining the ideals it valued. Americans, rejoicing in the newness of their nation, chose July 4 — Independence Day — as an annual national celebration. In this 1819 painting of Philadelphia, artist John Lewis Krimmel portrays the excitement of an early Fourth of July.

Don't give up the Ship

1789

Fourth of July Celebration in Centre Square, Philadelphia, by John Lewis Krimmel, 1819. Historical Society of Pennsylvania.

1860

The Battle of New Orleans

VIRTUE LIBERTY INDEPENDENCE

The 4th of IULY 1819

Chapter 5

The Creation of a Party System

The people had launched a new government under the Constitution. The early Presidents worked to establish the nation at home and abroad. Many issues needed to be solved. What goals were best for the country? What role should the government play? Not all people agreed on one plan, and political parties began to form.

Thomas Jefferson (right) led the opposition to the policies of Alexander Hamilton, (left). Two separate political parties formed as a result of their differences.

1789 President Washington, shown on the button above, laid the foundation for a powerful central government. This mug commemorated Washington's first presidential inauguration.

1780	1790	1800

Presidents

1789-1797
Washington

1797-1801
Adams

1801-1809
Jefferson

1789

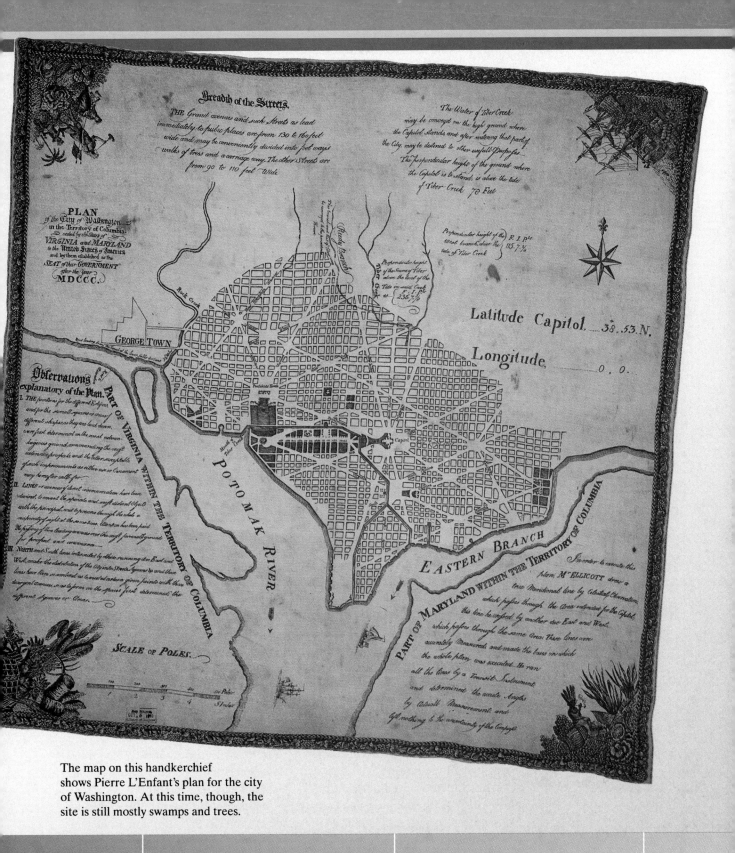

The map on this handkerchief shows Pierre L'Enfant's plan for the city of Washington. At this time, though, the site is still mostly swamps and trees.

1810

1820

1830

1809-1817
Madison

1817-1825
Monroe

133

1823

Internal Conflict

*What issues divided
Americans so much that
they formed separate
political parties?*

Key Terms

- Cabinet
- administration
- agrarian
- alien
- sedition

George Washington felt a mixture of dread and nervous anticipation as he left Mount Vernon for New York City on April 16, 1789. In New York, the first U. S. capital under the Constitution, he was to be inaugurated President of the United States. Great crowds along the way cheered the first President-elect. Unanimously elected on February 4, 1789, Washington had accepted the office only reluctantly. He doubted his ability as a political leader, but he felt he had a duty to serve the new nation.

On April 30, Washington, standing on the balcony of Federal Hall, took the oath of office and gave his inaugural address. He shared his feelings about taking on "the weighty and untried cares" before him. "The magnitude and difficulty of the trust to which the voice of my country called me," the President confessed, were overwhelming.

Washington's uneasiness was clear to everyone who heard him speak that day. Washington trembled as he spoke and at times seemed barely able to make out the speech he had in front of him. One senator remarked, "This great man was agitated and embarrassed more than ever he was by the leveled cannon or pointed musket."

Federalists Shape a Government

Imagine the burden on the first President. He had to work out the many details of the government's operation. He had to solve problems that had not been anticipated by the framers of the Constitution. An entire country depended on him to make the new system work.

The Constitution gave Washington a strong foundation for a new government. He wanted unity and stability for the United States, and the Constitution was his only guide. But what direction should the nation take? And how should it proceed?

Quest for Political Unity

As provided by law, Washington appointed assistants to head the departments of government: a secretary of state, a secretary of the treasury, a secretary of war, and a postmaster general. Together, these assistants who advise the President came to be known as the **Cabinet**. Since Washington's time, the President together with the Cabinet and the Vice President have been called the **administration.**

The men in the Washington administration were mostly Federalists. They believed in a powerful central government run by the elite, that is, men of wealth, education, and special talent. In their opinion, only such men were able to promote the public good and to make the wisest policies in government.

The Founding Fathers neither expected nor welcomed political parties. They believed that parties represented selfish interests that worked against the public good. "A division of the republic into two great parties," Vice President John Adams said, "is to be dreaded as the greatest political evil under our Constitution." But parties proved unavoidable. Soon it became clear that Alexander Hamilton was leading a party of Federalists.

Hamilton's Proposals

George Washington had named Hamilton as secretary of the treasury. Hamilton's extraordinary intelligence and ambition helped him become the most powerful figure in Washington's Cabinet. An unshakable Federalist, he favored a powerful national government. As secretary of the treasury he wanted to strengthen and stabilize the nation's economy by encouraging the growth of manufacturing and commerce as well as farming.

In his Report on Public Credit of 1790, Hamilton recommended that the national government pay off the debt left over from the Revolutionary War, including the debts of the states. Much of the debt took the form of government bonds, or notes, which had been given to soldiers as pay or bought by patriotic citizens. Hamilton proposed that anyone holding a government bond be paid in full, plus interest. Most of the original owners, however, had sold their bonds for hard money at far less than their face value. In addition, the real value of the debt

had decreased. Nonetheless, Hamilton argued that the program would establish the nation's credit and would give investors a good feeling about the new government.

Hamilton also called for the creation of a national bank. The bank would keep deposits of money for the government, regulate the state banks, and print bank notes that could be turned in for gold or silver. He believed that such a bank would strengthen the ties between rich Americans and the federal government. In other words, a national bank would lead to a more stable financial base for the country. ■

▲ *The National Bank is shown at its location on Third Street in New York City.*

■ *Hamilton favored government by the elite. Why would this make some Americans feel uncomfortable?*

Some Oppose Federalist Centralization

James Madison, who was known as the architect of the Constitution, now served as a congressman from Virginia. He questioned the fairness of Hamilton's credit proposals. He thought the national bank was not legal.

The credit program seemed to favor Northerners over Southerners, speculators over original bond holders, and the federal government over individual states. Merchants and investors from the North had bought

up most of the nation's bonds, often at low cost from the first holder. These Northerners would profit tremendously from the plan. Hamilton had also called for a federal tax on imported goods to pay off both federal and state debts. Madison felt that this tax was unfair to the Southern states, which generally had smaller debts than the Northern states. And nowhere, he claimed, did the Constitution give the federal government the power to create banks.

135

Two Approaches to Government

Federalists
(Hamilton)

- Favored strong, centralized government
- Advocated regulation of foreign and interstate trade
- Created national bank
- Promoted industry and manufacturing

Republicans
(Jefferson)

- Favored limited federal government
- Supported states' rights
- Encouraged western expansion
- Emphasized agricultural society

▲ *The Federalists and the Republicans held different views on most subjects.*

▼ *The painting below, made in 1822, idealizes the agrarian republic so dear to Jefferson.*

Jefferson's Vision

People who hated the favors that Hamilton's programs gave to Northern businessmen looked to Thomas Jefferson as their leader. As Washington's secretary of state, Jefferson believed in limited government and wished for a nation of landholding farmers. His ideal of a peaceful **agrarian,** or farm-based, nation seemed a sharp contrast to Hamilton's ideal of a complex, industrialized nation. In a letter to John Jay in 1785 Jefferson expressed his confidence in the common people:

> Cultivators of the earth are the most valuable citizens. They are the most vigorous, the most independent, the most virtuous, and they are tied to their country and wedded to its liberty and interests by the most lasting bonds.

Jefferson had greater faith in the people's ability to govern than Hamilton had. "The whole mass of the people," he believed, "are the only sure reliance for the preservation of our liberty."

The Rise of Republicanism

As tension mounted over Hamilton's financial program in 1790, Madison and Jefferson tried to discredit Hamilton. They even charged Hamilton with planning to replace republicanism with monarchy. To show their loyalty, Jefferson, Madison, and their followers began calling themselves Republicans. Meanwhile, Hamilton and his Federalist friends, claiming to be the correct followers of the Constitution, also started to form a party.

By 1791, Congress had approved Hamilton's credit program, and the Bank of the United States—the national bank suggested by him—had

GENERAL GEORGE WASHINGTON.
Reviewing the Western army at Fort Cumberland the 18th of Octob. 1794

◄ *The President also acts as Commander-in-Chief of the armed forces. President Washington actually led the army on the field against the Whiskey Rebellion.*

been established. Nevertheless, President Washington feared that the growing opposition to these changes threatened the strength of the government. He tried to promote unity by seeking a second term of office, and in 1792 he was re-elected without opposition. John Adams also won re-election as Vice President.

Despite Washington's leadership, a full-scale revolt was beginning. To get money to pay off the war debt, Hamilton had convinced Congress in 1791 to pass a 25 percent tax on whiskey. Many farmers made their grain into whiskey because it was easier to bring to market. Also, whiskey took the place of money in some places. Farmers felt they were being unfairly singled out to pay for Hamilton's programs. In protest, the angry farmers of western Pennsylvania tarred and feathered tax collectors, destroyed the whiskey stills of those who paid the tax, and stopped court proceedings. Frightened by the violence of the farmers, one chief collector of the whiskey tax quit his job.

President Washington was angry and shocked at the farmers' defiance of the federal government. In 1794, he led nearly 13,000 militia to Pennsylvania to make them obey. But the farmers were not an organized force. Washington found no army to fight against. Only a few rioters were arrested, and these were pardoned. The government's show of arms against the people helped to make the Republicans more popular. Understanding Concepts on page 138 explores the importance of leadership. ■

How Do We Know

HISTORY *Though they did not dislike each other personally, Jefferson and Hamilton were each convinced that the other's ideas were the source of all political evil. Their letters to each other and to friends about each other still exist—providing historians with plenty of evidence of their strong disagreements.*

■ *The policies Hamilton proposed were designed to create national unity. But instead they divided people. Why?*

Events in Europe Cause Tension at Home

The political events in Europe during this time served to divide the nation even more. Officially, the United States held a neutral position in all European wars. That is, it did not take sides. But in truth, Americans usually had strong feelings about European matters.

When the French Revolution began in 1789, almost all Americans rejoiced. The ideals of the American Revolution, it seemed, had spread to

The Creation of a Party System

France, where peasants lacked adequate land and the middle class lacked adequate political power. Dissatisfaction with the monarchy was growing. However, American feelings changed when the French beheaded King Louis XVI in 1793 and declared war on Great Britain. Federalists were horrified by the bloodiness of the revolution and sided with Great Britain. Republicans, however, refused to abandon the cause of liberty and remained sympathetic to France.

The French Revolution was not the only international event to concern the United States during this time. Americans were angry about Great Britain's harassment of American ships during its war with France. British occupation of American northwestern forts after the Revolutionary War also added to the tension. In 1794, Washington sent Chief Justice John Jay to London to negotiate a settlement of the nations' differences and thus to prevent war.

UNDERSTANDING LEADERSHIP

The early days of the new nation saw the rise of many political leaders: Washington, Hamilton, Jefferson, Franklin. What qualities did they possess that allowed them to become effective leaders? In other words, what is meant by leadership? To define the word very simply, leadership is both the position (or role) of a leader and the ability to lead.

Leadership exists at many levels: in schools; in your community, state, and nation; and in other nations. In addition, leadership is found in all kinds of groups and organizations.

Leadership Qualities

What qualities do people look for in a good leader? Some qualities of effective leaders are listed below. Think about these qualities. Are there any qualities you might add?

- knowledge of the responsibilities of his or her role

- ability to set goals, communicate a vision, and use effective plans to carry out goals and visions
- receptiveness to the ideas, viewpoints, and visions of others
- ability to organize and communicate ideas
- self-confidence and decisiveness
- willingness to let other people assume responsibility
- ability to weigh decisions carefully
- ability to get along well with people
- fairness and honesty

Washington's Leadership

George Washington stands out as an example of an effective leader. He served in many important leadership roles in the new nation, including Commander of the Continental Army, president of the Constitutional Convention, and first President of the United States. Through his responsible leadership in all three roles, Washington inspired

people and won their respect and confidence.

Leadership Today

When you think of modern leaders, what names come to mind? Some popular responses are Martin Luther King, Jr., John F. Kennedy, Mohandas Gandhi, Cesar Chavez, Ronald Reagan, and Mikhail Gorbachev. In the past only men held positions of political leadership. But in this century, many women have held important positions of world leadership. The most outstanding examples include Margaret Thatcher of Great Britain, Golda Meir of Israel, and Indira Gandhi of India.

Any leader is a representative of the large group that he or she leads. For that reason, people in the United States from the days of George Washington to today try to choose leaders carefully. Our leaders are people who not only "get the job done" but also represent beliefs in the present and hopes for the future.

138

The British agreed to take their troops out of the forts by 1796, but they refused to accept the U.S. demand for freedom of the seas. When the treaty's terms became known, protest swept the country and added to the growing power of the Republicans.

Vice President John Adams, a Federalist, narrowly won the presidential election of 1796, the first to have rival candidates for the presidency. As soon as Adams was inaugurated, he faced a problem with France. Angry because the United States had signed a treaty with Great Britain, the French took American ships and refused to talk with American officials. In 1798 Adams responded by ordering American ships to seize French vessels, thus starting an undeclared war at sea. Republicans protested and called for peace.

Suppression by Federalists

The battle for control of the nation went on. The Federalist-controlled Congress passed several laws meant to put down the Republican opposition. Immigrants, especially French ones, were suspected of being Republicans. The Naturalization Act lengthened the time required for foreigners—mostly common people supporting the Republicans—to gain citizenship. Naturalization, or the granting of full citizenship to foreigners, now took fourteen years instead of five. The Alien Acts authorized the President to imprison or expel any **aliens,** or foreigners, he considered dangerous.

The Sedition Act repressed **sedition**—rebellion against the government—by restricting freedom of speech and of the press. Anyone who wrote, printed, or said anything false or critical about the government of the United States could be fined or put in jail. Under this law Federalists imprisoned the editors of the five largest pro-Republican newspapers.

Republicans tried to block the Alien and Sedition Acts. The Virginia and Kentucky governments passed resolutions stating that the acts went against the Bill of Rights. Since the Constitution "resulted from the compact to which the states are parties," they argued, "the states have the right and . . . duty" to stop the federal government from using powers not allowed by the Constitution. Both states declared the Alien and Sedition Acts "altogether void and of no effect" and urged other states to join them in protest. The resolutions received no positive replies, but they served to rally Republicans everywhere in the country. ■

▲ *This cartoon illustrates a famous brawl that took place in Congress in 1798. Federalist Roger Griswold is at the right; Republican Matthew Lyon is in the center.*

■ *What motivated the Federalist Congress to pass the Alien and Sedition Acts—and why did they cause problems?*

1. **FOCUS** What issues divided Americans so much that they formed separate political parties?

2. **CONNECT** How were the Virginia and Kentucky Resolutions related to the positions taken by the Antifederalists ten years earlier?

3. **GEOGRAPHY** Why were Hamilton's programs not well received in the South?

4. **CRITICAL THINKING** In what ways might Jefferson's agrarian ideal have been short-sighted?

5. **WRITING ACTIVITY** Imagine you are a western Pennsylvania farmer and write an account of your experiences in the Whiskey Rebellion.

Rip Van Winkle

Washington Irving

During the first decades of the new republic, politics, economics, and social life all changed dramatically. The story of Rip Van Winkle cautions us not to fall out of touch with the changing world around us.

Washington Irving (1783-1859) was born in New York City and lived in this country until he was 32. He went to Europe in 1815 and stayed there for 15 years. During this time he traveled to many countries, collecting fairy tales from each one he visited. The story of Rip Van Winkle is loosely based on the German folktale "Peter Klaus." Irving set his story of Rip Van Winkle in the Revolutionary War period. He added descriptions of local customs and settings to create a uniquely American story of colonial life in the Catskill Mountains of New York. This tale of a ne'er-do-well who sleeps for 20 years helped the short story become established as a popular literary form. As you read this short story, ask yourself why fairy tales continue to be a part of our literary tradition.

As he approached the village he met a number of people, but none whom he knew, which somewhat surprised him, for he had thought himself acquainted with every one in the country round. Their dress, too, was of a different fashion from that to which he was accustomed. They all stared at him with equal marks of surprise, and whenever they cast their eyes upon him, invariably stroked their chins. The constant recurrence of this gesture induced Rip, involuntarily, to do the same, when, to his astonishment, he found his beard had grown a foot long!

He had now entered the skirts of the village. A troop of strange children ran at his heels, hooting after him, and pointing at his gray beard. The dogs, too, not one of which he recognized for an old acquaintance, barked at him as he passed. The very village was altered; it was larger and more populous. There were rows of houses which he had never seen before, and those which had been his familiar haunts had disappeared. Strange names were over the doors—strange faces at the windows—every thing was strange. His mind now misgave him; he began to doubt whether both he and the world around him were not bewitched. Surely this was his native village, which he had left but the day before. There stood the Kaatskill mountains—there ran the silver Hudson at a distance—there was every hill and dale precisely as it had always been—Rip was sorely perplexed—"That flagon last night," thought he, "has addled my poor head sadly!"

It was with some difficulty that he found the way to his own house, which he approached with silent awe, expecting every moment to hear the shrill voice of Dame Van Winkle. He found the house gone to decay—the roof fallen in, the windows shattered, and the doors off the

flagon jug

hinges. A half-starved dog that looked like Wolf was skulking about it. Rip called him by name, but the cur snarled, showed his teeth, and passed on. This was an unkind cut indeed—"My very dog," sighed poor Rip, "has forgotten me!"

He entered the house, which, to tell the truth, Dame Van Winkle had always kept in neat order. It was empty, forlorn, and apparently abandoned. This desolateness overcame all his connubial fears—he called loudly for his wife and children—the lonely chambers rang for a moment with his voice, and then all again was silence.

He now hurried forth, and hastened to his old resort, the village inn—but it too was gone. A large rickety wooden building stood in its place, with great gaping windows, some of them broken and mended with old hats and petticoats, and over the door was painted, "the Union Hotel, by Jonathan Doolittle." Instead of the great tree that used to shelter the quiet little Dutch inn of yore, there now was reared a tall naked pole, with something on the top that looked like a red night-cap, and from it was fluttering a flag, on which was a singular assemblage of stars and stripes—all this was strange and incomprehensible. He recognized on the sign, however, the ruby face of King George, under which he had smoked so many a peaceful pipe; but even this was singularly metamorphosed. The red coat was changed for one of blue and buff, a sword was held in the hand instead of a sceptre, the head was decorated with a cocked hat, and underneath was painted in large characters, GENERAL WASHINGTON.

connubial marital

yore time past
The "liberty cap," symbol of the French Revolution, was often displayed during the revolutionary period.
assemblage arrangement
buff pale yellow
sceptre a staff symbolizing a king's authority

141

disputatious inclined
to dispute
phlegm lack of energy

There was, as usual, a crowd of folk about the door, but none that Rip recollected. The very character of the people seemed changed. There was a busy, bustling, disputatious tone about it, instead of the accustomed phlegm and drowsy tranquillity. He looked in vain for the sage Nicholas Vedder, with his broad face, double chin and fair long pipe, uttering clouds of tobacco-smoke instead of idle speeches; or Van Bummel, the schoolmaster, doling forth the contents of an ancient newspaper. In place of these, a lean, bilious looking fellow, with his pockets full of handbills, was haranguing vehemently about rights of citizens—elections—members of congress—liberty—Bunker's Hill—heroes of seventy-six—and other words, which were a perfect Babylonish jargon to the bewildered Van Winkle.

The appearance of Rip, with his long grizzled beard, his rusty fowling-piece, his uncouth dress, and an army of women and children at his heels, soon attracted the attention of the tavern politicians. They crowded round him, eyeing him from head to foot with great curiosity. The orator bustled up to him, and, drawing him partly aside, inquired "on which side he voted?" Rip stared in vacant stupidity. Another short but busy little fellow pulled him by the arm, and, rising on tiptoe, inquired in his ear, "Whether he was Federal or Democrat?" Rip was equally at a loss to comprehend the question; when a knowing, self-important old gentleman, in a sharp cocked hat, made his way through the crowd, putting them to the right and left with his elbows as he passed, and planting himself before Van Winkle, with one arm akimbo, the other resting on his cane, his keen eyes and sharp hat penetrating, as it were, into his very soul, demanded in an austere tone, "what brought him to the election with a gun on his shoulder, and a mob at his heels, and whether he meant to breed a riot in the village?"—"Alas! gentlemen," cried Rip, somewhat dismayed, "I am a poor quiet man, a native of the place, and a loyal subject of the king, God bless him!"

akimbo hand on hip
and elbow bowed outward

Here a general shout burst from the by-standers—"A tory! a tory! a spy! a refugee! hustle him! away with him!" It was with great difficulty that the self-important man in the cocked hat restored order; and, having assumed a tenfold austerity of brow, demanded again of the unknown culprit, what he came there for, and whom he was seeking? The poor man humbly assured him that he meant no harm, but merely came there in search of some of his neighbors, who used to keep about the tavern.

austerity severity

"Well—who are they?—name them."

Rip bethought himself a moment, and inquired, "Where's Nicholas Vedder?"

There was a silence for a little while, when an old man replied, in a thin piping voice, "Nicholas Vedder! why, he is dead and gone these eighteen years! There was a wooden tombstone in the churchyard that used to tell all about him, but that's rotten and gone too."

"Where's Brom Dutcher?"

"Oh, he went off to the army in the beginning of the war; some say he was killed at the storming of Stony Point—others say he was drowned in a squall at the foot of Antony's Nose. I don't know—he never came back again."

"Where's Van Bummel, the schoolmaster?"

"He went off to the wars too, was a great militia general, and is now in congress."

Rip's heart died away at hearing of these sad changes in his home and friends, and finding himself thus alone in the world. Every answer puzzled him too, by treating of such enormous lapses of time, and of matters which he could not understand: war—congress—Stony Point;—he had no courage to ask after any more friends, but cried out in despair, "Does nobody here know Rip Van Winkle?"

"Oh, Rip Van Winkle!" exclaimed two or three, "Oh, to be sure! that's Rip Van Winkle yonder, leaning against the tree."

Rip looked, and beheld a precise counterpart of himself, as he went up the mountain: apparently as lazy, and certainly as ragged. The poor fellow was now completely confounded. He doubted his own identity, and whether he was himself or another man. In the midst of his bewilderment, the man in the cocked hat demanded who he was, and what was his name?

"God knows," exclaimed he at his wit's end; "I'm not myself—I'm somebody else—that's me yonder—no—that's somebody else got into my shoes—I was myself last night, but I fell asleep on the mountain, and they've changed my gun, and every thing's changed, and I'm changed, and I can't tell what's my name, or who I am!"

The by-standers began now to look at each other, nod, wink significantly, and tap their fingers against their foreheads. There was a whisper, also, about securing the gun, and keeping the old fellow from doing mischief, at the very suggestion of which the self-important man in the cocked hat retired with some precipitation. At this critical moment a fresh comely woman passed through the throng to get a peep at the gray-bearded man. She had a chubby child in her arms, which, frightened at his looks, began to cry. "Hush, Rip," cried she, "hush, you little fool; the old man won't hurt you." The name of the child, the air of the mother, the tone of her voice, all awakened a train of recollections in his mind. "What is your name, my good woman?" asked he.

"Judith Gardenier."

"And your father's name?"

"Ah, poor man, Rip Van Winkle was his name, but it's twenty years since he went away from home with his gun, and never has been heard of since—his dog came home without him; but whether he shot himself, or was carried away by the Indians, nobody can tell. I was then but a little girl."

Rip had but one question more to ask; but he put it with a faltering voice:

"Where's your mother?"

"Oh, she too had died but a short time since; she broke a blood-vessel in a fit of passion at a New-England peddler."

There was a drop of comfort, at least, in this intelligence. The honest man could contain himself no longer. He caught his daughter and her child in his arms. "I am your father!" cried he—"Young Rip Van Winkle once—old Rip Van Winkle now!—Does nobody know poor Rip Van Winkle?"

All stood amazed, until an old woman, tottering out from among the crowd, put her hand to her brow, and peering under it in his face for a moment, exclaimed, "Sure enough! it is Rip Van Winkle—it is himself! Welcome home again, old neighbor—Why, where have you been these twenty long years?"

Rip's story was soon told, for the whole twenty years had been to him but as one night. The neighbors stared when they heard it; some were seen to wink at each other, and put their tongues in their cheeks: and the self-important man in the cocked hat, who, when the alarm was over, had returned to the field, screwed down the corners of his mouth, and shook his head—upon which there was a general shaking of the head throughout the assemblage.

It was determined, however, to take the opinion of old Peter Vanderdonk, who was seen slowly advancing up the road. He was a descendant of the historian of that name, who wrote one of the earliest accounts of the province. Peter was the most ancient inhabitant of the village, and well versed in all the wonderful events and traditions of the neighborhood. He recollected Rip at once, and corroborated his story in the most satisfactory manner. He assured the company that it was a fact, handed down from his ancestor the historian, that the Kaatskill mountains had always been haunted by strange beings. That it was affirmed that the great Hendrick Hudson, the first discoverer of the river and country, kept a kind of vigil there every twenty years, with his crew of the Halfmoon; being permitted in this way to revisit the scenes of his enterprise, and keep a guardian eye upon the river, and the great city called by his name. That his father had once seen them in their old Dutch dresses playing at nine-pins in a hollow of the mountain; and that he himself had heard, one summer afternoon, the sound of their balls, like distant peals of thunder.

To make a long story short, the company broke up, and returned to the more important concerns of the election. Rip's daughter took him home to live with her; she had a snug, well-furnished house, and a stout cheery farmer for a husband, whom Rip recollected for one of the urchins that used to climb upon his back. As to Rip's son and heir, who was the *ditto* of himself, seen leaning against the tree, he was employed to work on the farm; but *evinced* an hereditary disposition to attend to any thing else but his business.

ditto exact copy
evinced demonstrated clearly

Rip now resumed his old walks and habits; he soon found many of his former cronies, though all rather the worse for the wear and tear of time; and preferred making friends among the rising generation, with whom he soon grew into great favor.

Having nothing to do at home, and being arrived at that happy age when a man can be idle with *impunity*, he took his place once more on the bench at the inn door, and was reverenced as one of the patriarchs of the village, and a chronicle of the old times "before the war." It was some time before he could get into the regular track of gossip, or could be made to comprehend the strange events that had taken place during his torpor. How that there had been a revolutionary war—that the country had thrown off the yoke of old England—and that, instead of being a subject of His Majesty George the Third, he was now a free citizen of the United States.

impunity exemption from punishment

Further Reading

The Legend of Sleepy Hollow. Washington Irving. A short story about a poor schoolmaster, Ichabod Crane, and his encounter with a headless horseman.

Knickerbocker's History of New York (A History of New York from the Beginning of the World to the End of the Dutch Dynasty). Washington Irving. A satirical account of New York state during the eighteenth and early nineteenth centuries, written under the pen name Diedrich Knickerbocker.

L E S S O N   2

Jefferson and the Republicans

How did the transfer of power to the Republicans in 1800 make a difference for the nation?

Key Terms

- electoral vote
- judicial review
- constitutional

➤ *This political cartoon from the election of 1800 shows Jefferson throwing the Constitution into the flames of "Gallic Despotism" (France). The eagle symbolizes the Federalists, who save the Constitution.*

President John Adams: "a fool, a gross hypocrite, and an unprincipled oppressor." His opponent, Thomas Jefferson: "an uncivilized atheist, anti-American, a tool for the godless French." The presidential election of 1800 was dirty business, with ugly insults coming from both sides. Newspapers of the time followed strict party lines. They printed nasty statements meant to entertain as well as persuade—like political bumper stickers and TV ads today.

Federalists urged their followers to join together and save their government "from the fangs of those who are tearing it to pieces." Republicans came back with the warning, "Now is the time when the heads of federal robbers shall be hunted from their den, when public indignation shall overtake them. . . ."

The worst attack came from a Federalist newspaper in Baltimore. Trying to dash Republican hopes, it printed a false rumor that Jefferson had died.

Jefferson Takes the Reins

The Republicans had begun soon after the election in 1796 to build a national party organization. They started state and local political groups everywhere in the nation. Federalists also tried to develop and coordinate local party organizations. But conflicts inside their party limited the Federalists' success. Alexander Hamilton disliked and disagreed with President Adams. As leader of the Federalist party, Hamilton tried to persuade the

Federalists to elect Charles C. Pinckney President. Adams would then become Vice President. But Hamilton's plan failed.

Close Presidential Race

Presidents are not elected directly by the people. Instead, **electoral votes**, cast by specially chosen people in each state, determine who gets elected. The people chosen to cast electoral votes are called electors. Each state has the same number of electors as it has representatives in Congress.

In the election of 1800, Jefferson and another Republican, Aaron Burr of New York, won the majority of electoral votes. They each had 73 votes, compared with 65 for John Adams and 64 for Charles C. Pinckney. In these early presidential elections, the person with the most votes became President and the first runner-up was made Vice President. The election showed that the people were tired of Federalist rule. The majority of ballots had been cast for the Republicans. But which Republican—Jefferson or Burr—would lead the country?

Because of the tie, the decision went to the House of Representatives. There the Federalists tried to give the presidency to Burr. Thirty-five times the representatives voted, and thirty-five times the ballots remained tied. Some feared that the government would dissolve. Delaware Federalist James Bayard finally broke the tie, and Jefferson became President.

Peaceful Transfer of Power

"I have this morning witnessed one of the most interesting scenes a free people can ever witness," Margaret B. Smith wrote to her sister-in-law after observing the inauguration ceremony of Thomas Jefferson. "The changes of administration, which in every government and in every age have most generally been epochs of confusion, villainy, and bloodshed, in this our happy country take place without any species of distraction or disorder."

Jefferson viewed his election as the "Revolution of 1800." But unlike the French Revolution, and contrary to the fears publicized by the Federalists only a short time before, it was not followed by a period of violence and political chaos. Indeed, the fact that Jefferson's inauguration was an occasion when control of the government was transferred peacefully from one political party to another may have been the most revolutionary thing about it.

On March 4, 1801, Jefferson became the first President to be inaugurated in Washington, D.C., the nation's new capital. At that time, Washington consisted of unfinished government buildings, boarding houses, muddy roads, and large tracts of wilderness. The building we know as the White House was called the President's House and was not white at all. The capitol building was less than

Across Time & Space

Throughout history other countries have experienced political transitions much more difficult than that of 1800 in the United States. In 1989, leaders in Panama were charged with fraud, following an election in which the government was challenged by a strong opposition. Chile and El Salvador have also found it difficult to accommodate dissent and protest during free elections.

◄ *Through an oversight, the voting laws of New Jersey allowed women to vote until 1808. Republican wives and daughters helped Jefferson win New Jersey in 1800.*

147

The Creation of a Party System

■ *Why did Jefferson think of his election as the Revolution of 1800?*

half-finished. Only the chamber for the House of Representatives was ready to be used. One British diplomat thought the primitive new capital was "scarce any better than a mere swamp." ■

The Republicans Make Some Changes

In his first inaugural address, Jefferson tried to play down his differences with the Federalists. "Every difference of opinion is not a difference of principle," he said. "We are all republicans, we are all federalists." Now that the election had been decided, all must "unite in common efforts for the common good."

Jefferson's goal was not to coexist peacefully with the Federalists, but to draw them into the Republican Party. Sharing the Federalists' dislike for parties, Jefferson hoped that all parties would sooner or later disappear. "Nothing shall be spared on my part to obliterate the traces of party and consolidate the nation," Jefferson wrote shortly after he was inaugurated.

The heart of Jefferson's strategy was not in what he did, but in what he did not do. Even though he disliked the Hamiltonian national bank, for example, he did not do away with it. Hamilton's system for paying off the debt remained in place, and the national bank went on operating until its charter ran out in 1811. Jefferson's moderation convinced many Federalists that the Republicans were not a danger to the nation.

Yet Jefferson, with the help of his Congress, reshaped the government to fit Republican goals. Most notably he appointed Republican judges. When the Alien and Sedition acts ran out in 1801, Congress refused to renew them. A new liberal naturalization law was adopted. Jefferson pardoned prisoners and gave back fines to those who had already been convicted under the Sedition Act. He also persuaded Congress to shorten the residency requirement for naturalization of citizens to its old level of five years. Once again, Jefferson hoped, the nation could serve as a new home for "oppressed humanity."

The new President trimmed a

▲ *This flag celebrates the victory of Thomas Jefferson in the election of 1800.*

great deal from the budget, particularly military costs. He also did away with all taxes on U.S.-made goods, including the tax on whiskey.

Jefferson set a tone of simplicity in the new Republican government and got rid of most of the stiff, formal ceremony that had characterized Federalist administrations. He liked to shake hands rather than bow, for example, and he rode around Washington on horseback instead of by carriage. He also paid no attention to the rules of protocol that gave a rank of dignity to every senator, representative, and diplomat. "When brought together in society, all are perfectly equal," Jefferson insisted. ■

■ *How did Jefferson earn the cooperation of the Federalists?*

The Nation Matures Under Jefferson

After cutting out Federalist excesses, Jeffersonian Republicans began to put in place a policy that worked toward their goal of a strong agrarian republic. The greatest accomplishment of the Jefferson administration was a major land purchase that helped make the new nation more independent. Other actions, especially an important Supreme Court case, tested and made clear procedures set up by the Constitution.

The Louisiana Purchase

Republicans believed the strength of a nation depended on liberty and on land ownership for all. Jefferson wanted to stop the concentration of wealth and power linked with manufacturing and big cities. He believed the answer lay in gaining new lands for farming.

When Jefferson learned that Spain had given Louisiana to France by a secret treaty in 1800, he was greatly upset. The presence in Louisiana of a powerful foreign country like France threatened future expansion by the United States. American trade on the Mississippi River could be endangered if the French owned New Orleans, the city at the river's mouth. Jefferson had always looked upon France as the nation's "natural friend." But even he

▼ *This 1803 painting of New Orleans celebrates the Louisiana Purchase. The eagle symbolizes the United States. Note the American flags on the ships and buildings. New Orleans gave the United States control of the Mississippi River, the most important transportation route for Western farmers.*

UNDER MY WINGS EVERY THING PROSPERS

considered an alliance with Britain to remove the French from Louisiana. As he told Robert Livingston, the American minister to France, "there is on the globe one single spot the possessor of which is our natural and habitual enemy. . . . The day that France takes possession of New Orleans, . . . we must marry ourselves to the British fleet and nation."

Jefferson tried to solve the problem through peaceful means. He had Livingston offer to buy New Orleans from France. Jefferson sent James Monroe to Paris in 1803 to help Livingston. To the surprise of the Americans, the French minister offered to sell the whole Louisiana Territory. It just happened that the French Emperor Napoleon needed money to fight Great Britain. Livingston and Monroe both jumped at the chance. For $15 million, the United States bought all of the Louisiana Territory. The

➤ *The Mississippi River provided transportation for the large and fertile interior of North America. This map shows the importance of the river to trappers and farmers.*

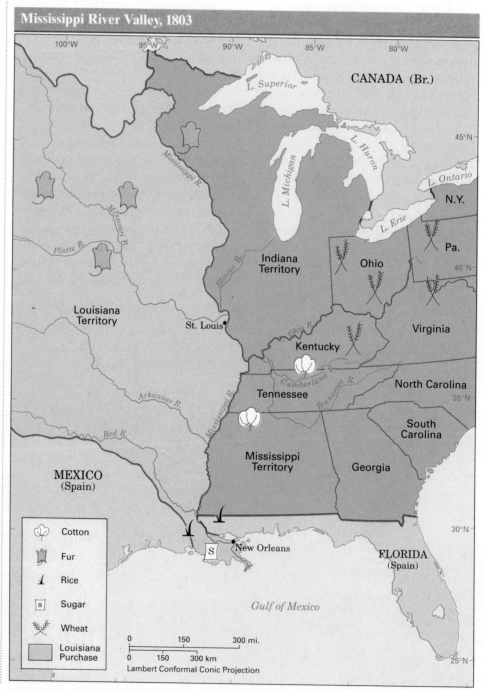

Mississippi River Valley, 1803

CANADA (Br.)

L. Superior

L. Huron

L. Michigan

L. Ontario

L. Erie

N.Y.

Pa.

100°W 95°W 90°W 85°W 80°W

45°N

40°N

35°N

30°N

25°N

Mississippi R.

Missouri R.

Platte R.

Illinois R.

Indiana Territory

Ohio

Virginia

Louisiana Territory

St. Louis

Ohio R.

Kentucky

Cumberland R.

Tennessee

Tennessee R.

North Carolina

Arkansas R.

Mississippi R.

Red R.

Mississippi Territory

Georgia

South Carolina

MEXICO (Spain)

S New Orleans

FLORIDA (Spain)

Gulf of Mexico

Cotton

Fur

Rice

S Sugar

Wheat

Louisiana Purchase

0   150   300 mi.
0 150 300 km

Lambert Conformal Conic Projection

purchase secured American control of the Mississippi River and provided transportation routes for the crops of western farmers. As you can see on the map on page 150, the purchase doubled the nation's land area and allowed Jefferson's vision of an agrarian republic to live on.

Strong Supreme Court

Also during Jefferson's administration, the Supreme Court decision in the case *Marbury* v. (versus) *Madison* made clear the part of the Constitution that defines the Court's powers. As a result, the Supreme Court became an equal branch of government, in fact as well as in theory.

Shortly before leaving office in 1800, President Adams had appointed a large number of Federalist judges, including John Marshall as chief justice of the Supreme Court and William Marbury justice of the peace in the District of Columbia. However, Marbury's commission, the paper entitling him to his job, had not been given to him before Jefferson became President. Jefferson wanted to appoint a Republican and thus asked his secretary of state, James Madison, to hold on to the paper. Marbury filed a suit against Madison. He wanted the court to order Madison to deliver the commission. A law passed by Congress had given the federal courts the power to order such an action by the executive branch.

Chief Justice Marshall dismissed the suit. He observed that Marbury had a right to his commission and that Jefferson and Madison had no right to keep it. More importantly, however, Marshall stated that the Supreme Court did not have the power to order the President to turn over the commission. Marshall ruled that the law giving the Supreme Court power to make such an order went against the Constitution and was therefore invalid.

By denying Marbury's request, Marshall handed Jefferson a victory. At the same time, he defined the process of **judicial review** as the Supreme Court's key function in the system of checks and balances. Through judicial review, the Court decides whether laws are **constitutional**—that is, in agreement with the principles and powers established by the Constitution. With Republicans controlling the other branches of government beginning in 1800, the heavily Federalist Supreme Court asserted its power as an independent and equal part of the government. ■

Judicial Review Process

Federal and state laws are contested by citizens

Federal and state court decisions are appealed

Supreme Court agrees to review select cases

Interprets how U.S. Constitution applies to law

Hands down decision regarding constitutionality

◀ *This chart shows how questions of constitutionality are resolved. Note that the Supreme Court only reviews laws that have been contested in lower courts.*

■ *Why did Americans consider control of the Mississippi River so*

R E V I E W

1. **FOCUS** How did the transfer of power to the Republicans in 1800 make a difference for the nation?
2. **CONNECT** Were Jefferson's actions as President consistent with the views he expressed while the Federalists were in power? Explain your answer.
3. **HISTORY** Explain how the Republican vice presidential candidate Aaron Burr was almost elected President.
4. **CRITICAL THINKING** What was the most important result of the *Marbury* v. *Madison* case?
5. **WRITING ACTIVITY** Write a news story for a television broadcast about the purchase of the Louisiana territory. Include in your story imaginary interviews with citizens of both the United States and France who give their opinions about the purchase and sale.

The Creation of a Party System

Researching Aaron Burr

Here's Why

Doing research is like being a private investigator. You have to follow clues. An article you read in a magazine may mention a book with more information on the subject. That book may refer to a news article. One step leads to another until you have found enough information on the topic to write a report.

Sometimes you can use short cuts. Researchers create bibliographies, or lists of books and articles they used in their research. You can use these bibliographies to do your own research. In turn, you should create a bibliography of your research for other investigators to use.

Suppose you were writing a report on Aaron Burr (pictured above), Thomas Jefferson's vice

president, who was tried for treason. You would need to create bibliography cards to keep track of your sources.

Here's How

1. Begin by using the library to locate information on Aaron Burr. Then use an index card to record the following bibliographic information on each card:

   • the title of the book or article
   • the author(s) or editor(s)
   • the publisher
   • the city of publication
   • the date of publication

   The publisher and publication dates are important, because they tell the reader exactly which edition of a book you used and how old the information is.

2. Now use index cards to take notes. At the top of each card, record the title of the book, magazine, or reference article from which you are taking information, along with the number of the page with which you are working.

3. Use as many cards as necessary. Just remember to write the title of your source and its page number at the top.

Try It

Look at the title page at left. Use it to create a bibliography card and a note card.

Apply It

Choose a contemporary political figure of interest to you. Follow the steps above to locate sources, create bibliography cards, and take notes.

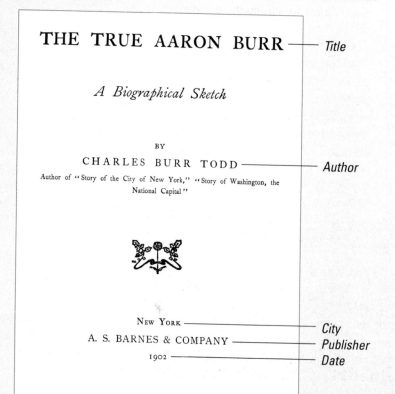

THE TRUE AARON BURR —— *Title*

A Biographical Sketch

BY

CHARLES BURR TODD —— *Author*

Author of "Story of the City of New York," "Story of Washington, the National Capital"

NEW YORK —— *City*

A. S. BARNES & COMPANY —— *Publisher*

1902 —— *Date*

LESSON 3

The United States and the World

S moke and flames engulfed the city of Washington, D.C., on the evening of August 24, 1814. British soldiers had stormed into the city, driving the small American army into the Virginia woods. In what became an unforgettable insult to the young nation, the troops set fire to all but one of the government buildings in the capital. The President's House and the Capitol survived but were scarred by smoke and flames.

When the attack began, First Lady Dolley Madison quickly gathered some of the treasures from the President's House and fled to Virginia.

Among the things she saved were some important Cabinet papers, the most famous portrait of George Washington, and the presidential silver service. President Madison also fled, finding shelter in houses and inns.

Americans were devastated by the loss of their capital. One woman declared, "Already in one night have hundreds of our citizens been reduced from affluence to poverty, for it is not to be expected Washington will ever again be the seat of Government." What had happened between the end of Jefferson's presidency and the beginning of Madison's to cause this humiliating attack by the British?

THINKING FOCUS

How well did the United States handle international conflicts?

Key Terms

- neutrality
- impressment

▲ *The portrait above is of First Lady Dolley Madison.*

◄ *This English engraving shows the burning city of Washington, D.C., in 1814.*

153

The Creation of a Party System

Jefferson's Foreign Policy Is Challenged

As President of a neutral nation during a period of European wars in the early 1800s, Jefferson had struggled to defend American freedom of the seas. He knew that overseas markets for agricultural exports were crucial; the prosperity of American farmers depended upon them. At the same time, manufactured goods from Europe were also important. The United States was then mostly a farming nation, unable to supply its own manufactured goods.

Caught in the Middle Again

America's struggle to maintain **neutrality,** the state of being a non-participant in war, was not a new issue. During Washington's presidency,

▼ *In this political cartoon, President Jefferson is robbed by King George of Great Britain and Emperor Napoleon of France (top). Certificates of citizenship like this one were issued to American sailors while Great Britain was at war with France (bottom).*

the French Revolution had put the United States in an awkward position with its old friend. Toward the end of the Adams administration, France's violations of American neutral rights had forced America into an undeclared war.

So when war between Great Britain and France resumed in 1803, American neutrality faced familiar challenges. Thanks to its powerful navy, Great Britain

ruled the seas. French armies quickly took control of the European continent. As a new country with little diplomatic or military power, the United States gained little respect from either side.

To keep its enemies from receiving goods by ship, Great Britain began a blockade of the European coast. In a blockade, hostile ships keep all other ships, usually neutrals, from going into or out of enemy ports. Sometimes only ships carrying war supplies are kept out. Ships caught in the British blockade were often taken for use by the British Navy. The French responded by blockading the British Isles. The French also seized neutral ships. Further restrictions from both Great Britain and France made it impossible for American ships to trade safely with either side. If American ships obeyed the wishes of one nation, they were subject to seizure by the other. By 1812, Great Britain had taken nearly 1,000 American ships; France had taken about 500.

The crisis was made worse by the policy of British **impressment.** This was the taking from American ships of sailors who might have been British deserters. The sailors were made to serve in the Royal Navy, which needed men to fight France. Although American sailors started to carry certificates of American citizenship with them, they were not safe from British impressment. As long as America was too weak to stop the British, the sailors would never be safe.

The Failure of Diplomacy

Jefferson answered British and French aggression by cutting off American trade. In 1807 he had Congress pass the Embargo Act, which prohibited American ships from sailing to any foreign ports. This kept Great Britain and France from getting

American goods even by buying them through neutral countries. But the law left American ships by the hundreds rotting at their wharves and sent the economy into a bad slump. Bitter opposition arose among farmers and merchants. As a result, Congress repealed the Embargo Act in 1809 and replaced it with the Non-Intercourse Act, which opened trade with all nations except France and Great Britain.

Both the Embargo Act and the Non-Intercourse Act failed as foreign policy measures. The government was not able to enforce the acts. Also, the European nations were able to get their supplies from other countries. ■

■ *Why was the war between Great Britain and France so harmful to the United States?*

Madison Pressured into War

In the election of 1808, James Madison won the presidency with no trouble. As President, he faced many of the same foreign policy dilemmas that had troubled Jefferson. Great Britain, the worst violator of neutral rights, went on to become the chief enemy of the United States during Madison's administration.

Madison also had troubles along the frontiers of the Northwest Territory. Shawnee chief Tecumseh had united many Indian tribes to resist white settlers who violated treaty boundaries. The growing militancy of the Indians alarmed the governor of the Indiana Territory, William Henry Harrison. At the Battle of Tippecanoe in 1811, Harrison destroyed the Indians' stronghold. The Indians fought back with devastating attacks all across the northwestern frontier.

Although the hostility of the Indians was largely due to their real anger about the whites' invasion of Indian lands, the attacks increased anti-British feelings. "I can have no doubt of the influence of British agents in keeping up Indian hostility," a Kentucky congressman said.

The trouble at sea and the perceived British influence on Indians led to an increase in war fever, particularly in the West and the South. A new group of Republican congressmen called War Hawks criticized Madison's ineffective diplomacy and called for stronger measures against the British. In June 1812, Madison tired of "the injuries and indignities which have been heaped upon our country." He then asked Congress for the nation's first declaration of war. Had news traveled faster, he might not have.

◄ *The U.S.S.* Constitution, *or "Old Ironsides," as it became known, is shown engaging the British frigate* Guerrière. *The* Guerrière *surrendered in half an hour. Today the* Constitution *is based at the Charlestown Naval Yard in Boston, Massachusetts. It has been restored and is now available for visits by the public. It sails on Independence Day.*

Washington and Baltimore, and in the south they attacked from the Gulf of Mexico into New Orleans.

During the British attack on Fort McHenry outside Baltimore, Francis Scott Key spent the night watching "bombs bursting in air," afraid for the lives of his fellow Americans. At dawn, the sight that "our flag was still there" inspired Key to write the verses to "The Star Spangled Banner." Popular for many years, the song became the national anthem in 1931.

> *O* say, can you see, by the
>   dawn's early light,
> What so proudly we hail'd at the
>   twilight's last gleaming?
> Whose broad stripes and bright
>   stars, thro' the perilous fight,
> O'er the ramparts we watch'd,
>   were so gallantly streaming.
>
> And the rockets' red glare, the
>   bombs bursting in air,
> Gave proof thro' the night, that
>   our flag was still there . . .

Finally, in January 1815, a scrappy army of American militiamen, including many free blacks, surprised the British in New Orleans. It would be the last battle of the war. Led by General Andrew Jackson, the Americans boldly fought off the British troops. For more details about the Battle of New Orleans, see A Closer Look.

New Englanders Resist

The decision to declare war had divided the nation. Even though the War of 1812 was fought to defend the rights of Americans on the seas, support for the war came from the agrarian states of the Mid-Atlantic, South, and West. New England, led by its merchants, was against the war. Mostly Federalists, New Englanders felt betrayed by the Republicans in power. The war had put an end to the illegal trade New Englanders had been carrying on.

▲ *Fort McHenry survived after suffering 400 direct hits during the bombardment of September 13–14, 1814. This painting shows the British launching huge 190-pound bombs at the fort (top). Francis Scott Key's original manuscript of "The Star Spangled Banner" (bottom).*

Unknown to Madison, the British had already officially ended their policy of impressment.

Americans Face the British

Americans were hopelessly unprepared for the War of 1812, but they still felt very sure of victory. To acquire new territory and to eliminate British support for the Indians, some Americans even wanted to conquer and annex Canada.

The first year of the war was a gloomy one for the United States. But in 1813, Captain Oliver Hazard Perry defeated the British on Lake Erie. "We have met the enemy and they are ours," he reported. By securing control of Lake Erie, Perry enabled an American general to capture part of Canada temporarily from the British. However, other invasions of Canada were failures.

After defeating French Emperor Napoleon in 1814, Great Britain strengthened its North American military force and planned a three-pronged invasion of the United States. In the north, British troops came from Canada by way of Lake Champlain. On the Atlantic coast they came through the Chesapeake Bay into

The Battle of New Orleans

When rumors of a British attack reached General Jackson in Mobile, he led his soldiers through the swamps to defend New Orleans. The British invaded, amid cattails and hanging moss, to fight for access to the Mississippi River. Ironically, the battle should never have happened: it actually took place after the Treaty of Ghent was signed.

American troops cut down bayou trees to block access to the city. They stacked them and added cotton bales for extra height. As this painting shows, most of the combat was hand-to-hand, but both sides used cannons to rip through enemy walls.

"Old Hickory" triumphs! Under the command of rough and determined Andrew Jackson, the Americans killed more than 2,600 British soldiers while losing only 21 men of their own.

Bales go up in thick black smoke. Americans discovered just how flammable cotton could be in this, the last battle of the War of 1812. Bales sizzled and hissed in the muddy water, sending thick smoke into the air. After this battle, soldiers always covered cotton bales with mud to prevent them from going up in flames.

In December 1814, while the last battles were being fought, New England delegates were holding a convention in Hartford, Connecticut, to discuss "public grievances and concerns" over Republican conduct of the war. A few extremists recommended withdrawing from the Union and forging a separate peace with Great Britain. Most, however, called for amendments to the Constitution designed to limit the power of the South, the West, and the Republican Party.

The Hartford Convention backfired fatally on the Federalists. In those days news could take weeks to reach the United States from Europe. The nation learned all at once of Andrew Jackson's incredible victory at New Orleans and of the signing of a peace treaty in Ghent, Belgium. The Federalists looked disloyal and foolish when the good news arrived. Soon afterwards, Federalism collapsed as a national political force.

War Ends, Problems Remain

The Treaty of Ghent had been signed on Christmas Eve, 1814—before the Battle of New Orleans. The treaty formally ended the war between Great Britain and the United States. But it included no statement about impressment and neutral rights. The treaty simply restored British-American relations and boundaries to what they had been before the war.

Although American military goals had not been met, nationalist goals had. In this way, the war was a success. An outpouring of national pride went on for 10 years after the war. Many people thought of the War of 1812 as a second war of independence. ■

■ *How did the War of 1812 help to bring Americans together?*

American Influence Expands

In the presidential election of 1816, Madison's secretary of state, James Monroe, easily defeated his Federalist opponent, Rufus King. When Monroe became President, the nation was at peace, feeling stronger, and ready to assert itself at home and abroad. Unlike earlier Presidents, Monroe made his greatest achievements in foreign affairs.

A Continental Nation

The negotiations with Spain after the War of 1812 dealt with both Florida and the western boundary of the Louisiana Territory. Monroe sent Secretary of State John Quincy Adams to bargain with the Spanish leader Luis de Onis. At the meeting, Spain agreed to the sale of the territory for $5 million. On February 22, 1819, Spain ceded Florida to the United States. In the boundary agreement, Spain gave up its claim to the Oregon country but held on to the lands of the Southwest. This area included what is now California, Texas, Arizona, and New Mexico. The resulting Transcontinental Treaty—also known as the Adams-Onis Treaty—transferred Florida to the United States and extended American territorial claims to the Pacific Ocean. In 1819, the United States became recognized as a continental nation.

➤ *This engraving shows James Monroe, a President noted for foreign policy achievements.*

JAMES MONROE,
Fifth President of the United States

The Monroe Doctrine

Just two years later, Mexico's colonial revolution shifted control of the southwestern territory from Spain to Mexico. Indeed, successful independence movements in Colombia, Mexico, Chile, Argentina, and Peru caused the Spanish empire to fall apart very rapidly during the early 1800s. Sympathizing with the newly independent republics, Monroe in 1822 suggested that the United States officially recognize them as nations. Congress quickly agreed.

The possibility that France or its friends would help Spain once again get control of these Latin American nations worried Monroe and Secretary of State Adams. The British foreign secretary suggested a joint Anglo-American policy to address the question. But Adams did not like the idea and called for independent action. The time for the United States to play the junior partner to Great Britain was over.

Monroe made Adams's ideas the official policy of the United States in a speech he delivered to the Congress of the United States on December 2, 1823. The Monroe Doctrine, as it came to be called, laid down two American foreign policy ideals: non-colonization and nonintervention. "The American continents," Monroe said, are closed to "future colonization by any European powers." Monroe further warned Europe against trying to oppress, or control the destiny of, the newly independent Latin American nations. In return, the United States promised "not to interfere in the internal concerns" of

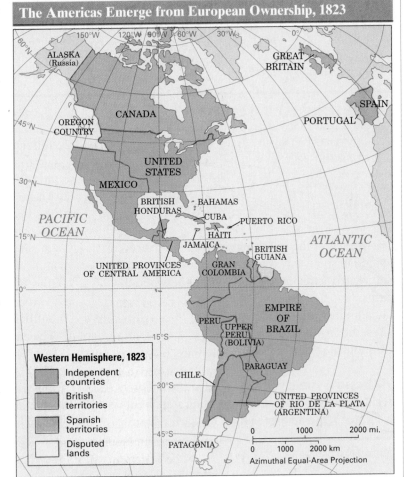

The Americas Emerge from European Ownership, 1823

Western Hemisphere, 1823
- Independent countries
- British territories
- Spanish territories
- Disputed lands

the European powers.

The Monroe Doctrine stated in clear terms the longstanding belief that the New World was separate from the Old World. It also stated that American ideals and interests in the Western Hemisphere were more important than European interests. Such a statement of diplomatic nationalism by the United States would have been impossible during Jefferson's administration of 1800 or even during the War of 1812. The nation had finally won the respect of Europe. ■

▲ *By 1823 much of the New World was free from European control.*

■ *Why was John Quincy Adams determined not to form a joint foreign policy with Great Britain?*

R E V I E W

1. **FOCUS** How well did the United States handle international conflicts?
2. **CONNECT** Why do you think many Americans considered the War of 1812 a second War of Independence?
3. **ECONOMICS** Explain the role of commerce in the origin of the War of 1812.
4. **GEOGRAPHY** Why did the British choose New Orleans as one of the targets in their three-pronged invasion?
5. **CRITICAL THINKING** Why was Monroe's foreign policy more successful than that of earlier Presidents?
6. **ACTIVITY** Draw a political cartoon that illustrates one of the policies established by the Monroe Doctrine.

The Creation of a Party System

Chapter Review

Reviewing Key Terms

administration (p. 134)
agrarian (p. 136)
alien (p. 139)
Cabinet (p. 134)
constitutional (p. 151)

electoral vote (p. 146)
impressment (p. 154)
judicial review (p. 151)
neutrality (p. 154)
sedition (p. 139)

A. In each of the following pairs, the two terms are related in some way. Write a sentence for each pair that clearly explains the relationship between the terms.
1. administration, Cabinet
2. sedition, alien
3. judicial review, constitutional

B. Based on what you have read in the chapter, decide whether each of the following statements is accurate. Write an explanation for each decision.

1. Jefferson wanted the United States to be an agrarian society in which most people worked and lived in cities.
2. Those who plan sedition are usually loyal to their government.
3. The United States maintained its neutrality during Jefferson's administration.
4. If a law is constitutional, you can find support for it in the language of the Constitution.
5. As a citizen of the United States, you are entitled to an electoral vote.
6. The army built up its forces by using impressment.
7. The Cabinet is where the President stores important foreign documents.
8. The Supreme Court conducts a judicial review of all laws every four years.

Exploring Concepts

A. On a separate sheet of paper, copy the timeline below. Complete your timeline by placing each of the following events in the correct time position.

- End of the Whiskey Rebellion
- Outbreak of the French Revolution
- Alien and Sedition Acts passed
- Louisiana Purchase
- Embargo Act
- Madison asks for declaration of war
- Battle of New Orleans
- Treaty of Ghent
- Adams-Onis Treaty
- Monroe Doctrine

B. Support each of the following statements with facts and details from the chapter.
1. Two different political parties grew up during Washington's administration.
2. In his administration Jefferson combined the programs of both the Federalists and Republicans.
3. Government policies between 1789 and 1814 caused differences of opinion between sections of the United States.
4. Support for the Alien and Sedition Acts dwindled as the Federalists lost power.
5. The causes of the War of 1812 developed during the Washington and Jefferson administrations.

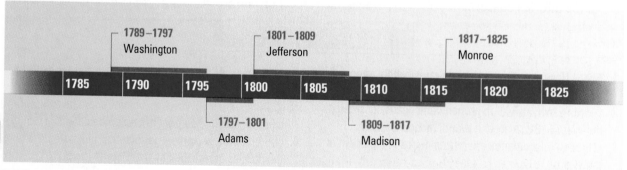

Chapter 5

Reviewing Skills

1. Look at the bibliography card at right. Identify each item and state where you would find it.
2. Create a bibliography card for this textbook.
3. Read the following passage taken from page 7 of the book *The True Aaron Burr* (shown on page 152). Look up any unfamiliar words and create a note card based on this passage:

   "It was here [New York City], while the army lay in New York, that Burr and Hamilton first met, and here began that unfriendliness which culminated twenty-eight years later in the action on the fatal shelf at Weehawken."

Wagons to the West

Jesse Wells
Houghton Mifflin Company
Boston
1982

4. Suppose you wanted to find out more information about the feud between Burr and Hamilton. Identify different ways you could do research on the feud.

Using Critical Thinking

1. In his inaugural address, Thomas Jefferson said, "Having banished from our land that religious intolerance under which mankind so long bled and suffered, we have yet gained little if we countenance [allow] a political intolerance as . . . capable of as bitter and bloody persecutions." What was the political situation Jefferson sought to correct? Are conflicts between political parties today as bitter as those Jefferson warned against? Give examples to support your answer.
2. Senator Samuel White of Delaware called the Louisiana Purchase "the greatest curse that could . . . befall us." White felt that Louisiana would draw settlers, draining the United States of its population. He feared that these settlers, separated by thousands of miles from Washington, D.C., would lose their loyalty to the United States. He preferred that France or Spain keep Louisiana, on condition that no United States citizens be allowed to settle there. What would the United States be like today if White's proposal had been adopted? Why didn't White's prediction come true?
3. Think about the expansion of the United States and the beliefs of certain political parties. Can you see any relationship between the concerns about the development of political parties and the policies the new government pursued?

Preparing for Citizenship

1. WRITING ACTIVITY Martha Washington, Abigail Adams, and Dolley Madison were wives of the presidents during the period covered in this chapter. Each became famous in her own right. Research and write a short biographical report on Martha Washington, Abigail Adams, or Dolley Madison. Explain how your subject contributed to the nation during those early years. Include quotations from the writings of the first lady to illustrate what she thought about the events of the time in which she lived.
2. ART ACTIVITY Draw a map that shows the territory controlled by the United States in 1824. Use colors to shade in the areas of the Louisiana Purchase and of the territory gained by the Adams-Onis Treaty. Use the map to predict any possible problems expansion could create for the United States.
3. ART ACTIVITY Make a chart that lists each presidential election from 1788 to 1820. Show who was elected President and Vice President in each election. Write a brief description of the major events of each president's administration.
4. COLLABORATIVE LEARNING As a class, write a skit about one or more of the events of the War of 1812. For example, you may choose the events leading to President Madison's decision to declare war, the burning of Washington, D.C., the bombardment of Fort McHenry, or the Battle of New Orleans. Then present the skit for another class or for a parents' evening.

Chapter 6

The Maturing Republic

"Who is this new person, the American?" foreigners asked. The young nation asked itself this same question. Who are we? What are our ideals? Everyone had a different opinion. Classical ideas from ancient civilizations competed with the rugged individualism of the frontier. Which cultural traditions would people keep? Which traditions would they throw aside in favor of new American values?

Creating schools was important to the Americans. Thomas Jefferson's architectural design for the University of Virginia reflected his love of classical ideas and values.

1775			1800	

Presidents

1789-1797
Washington

1801-1809
Jefferson

1782

1797-1801
J. Adams

1809-1817
Madison

American women gathered at quilting bees. Quilts like these embodied the patriotic spirit in a traditional craft.

New forms of music helped to define the American identity. This banjo, a uniquely American instrument that had its roots in Africa, was among the possessions of President Andrew Jackson's family.

1825

1850

1817-1825
Monroe

1825-1829
J. Q. Adams

1829-1837
Jackson

1837-1841
Van Buren

1840

LESSON 1

Republicanism and Culture

BY NOAH WEBSTER, L.L.D.

THINKING
FOCUS

How did Americans define their own national values in their new nation?

Key Terms

- household economy
- neoclassical
- market economy
- suffrage

"I am attached to America by berth, education, and habit. . . . I uze words that are most common and generally understood. . . . I rite from feeling, from obzervation, from experience." So wrote Noah Webster in 1800. This man, who compiled a spelling book and wrote the first American dictionary (shown at right), would certainly have trouble passing a spelling test today. But in 1800, spelling was a matter of individual preference.

Webster, like other Americans in the early republic, wanted to create a truly American version of the English language. He redefined words such as *congress* and *court*—words that had meant something different back in England. Before he started to experiment with his spellings, he wrote, "As an independent nation, our honor requires us to have a system of our own, in language as well as government." Webster wanted to break cultural ties with England. He also saw that a standardized language—in spelling and pronunciation—would help to unify the new nation.

Many of Webster's spelling changes are still in use today. He worked to simplify language so that words were spelled phonetically—that is, the way they are pronounced. For example, he changed the British *centre* to *center*, *colour* to *color*, and *shoppe* to *shop*. He was less successful with other changes; Americans would not accept *meen* for *mean* or *frend* for *friend*.

Creation of an American Identity

During the early 1800s, Americans deliberately went about establishing a national identity—through art and education as well as through Webster's American language. They talked about ideals for their republic, such as virtue and placing the public good above selfish interests. Americans valued the ideal of independence, the right to make their own decisions. But even after the Revolutionary War, they also accepted men from an elite social group as their political leaders. These leaders were nearly always the wealthiest and best educated members of society. Common people were not likely to run for office.

The household economy was yet another republican ideal. In the **household economy**, small, independent owners of land grew food for their own families and for exchange with others within their community. These farmers usually knew most of the people with whom they did business. Thus their desire for profit was balanced by a strong sense of responsibility to their neighbors and to their community's needs.

Washington: A Classical Hero

In establishing their own identity and values, well-educated Americans looked to classical models—those of the ancient republics of Greece and Rome. Writers at the time often compared their heroes to classical figures. George Washington was compared to Cincinnatus, the Roman general who returned to his farm after defending his country. Many statues of Washington were made that showed him in a Roman toga, wearing the classical hero's laurel-leaf crown.

In 1800, Mason Weems, a clergyman often referred to as "Parson" Weems, wrote a best-selling biography of Washington. Weems portrayed Washington as the perfect republican citizen. He made up many tall tales for his book, including the story of Washington and the cherry tree. In another tale, which used Washington's real experiences in the Seven Years' War to create a larger-than-life hero, Weems wrote:

A famous Indian warrior . . . was often heard to swear, that "Washington was not born to be killed by a bullet! For," continued he, "I had seventeen fair fires at him with my rifle, and after all could not bring him to the ground!" And indeed whoever considers that a good rifle, levelled by a proper marksman, hardly ever misses its aim, will readily conclude . . . that there was some invisible hand, which turned aside his bullets.

The real George Washington was, of course, not invulnerable to bullets. He also never said, "I can't tell a lie." But Weems made Washington seem

▲ *Washington was held up as a nearly godlike hero. In this work, the artist shows Washington entering heaven after his death.*

an example of heroic virtue. Adults of the time used such moral tales to teach their children republican ideals.

Republican Architecture

To help express the ideals of their new nation, some Americans adopted classical art and architecture. By adapting elements of the style of ancient Greece and Rome, they tried to forge a link with the ideals of those great republics. Thomas Jefferson was very impressed by the classical style buildings he had seen in Europe. In fact, Jefferson patterned his designs for the University of Virginia and his own home, Monticello, after classical buildings. Throughout the nation, people built town halls and state

The Maturing Republic

Emma Hart Willard promoted better education for young women.

How did Americans use classical models at the beginning of the 1800s?

of Rococo art. Read Understanding Concepts on page 168 for more about this art style.

Republican Motherhood

What role did women play in the new republic? The Constitution did not allow women to vote or to hold office. Instead, they were encouraged to be virtuous citizens within their own homes. The role of women in the new republic took shape through the ideal of "republican motherhood." Every patriotic woman's aim was to instill in her family the values that would make the republic strong.

"Who knows how great and good a race of men may yet arise from the forming hand of mothers . . .?" So wrote Emma Hart Willard in 1819. She was arguing the case for better women's education—education that would help young women become republican mothers. In the new nation, women were respected for the moral instruction they provided to guide their children into ethical public service. Although some women began to form associations to reform society, republican motherhood also served to limit their opportunities in the world outside the home.

capitols in what was called the **neo-classical,** or new classical, style. Majestic columns and bold , simple forms replaced the swirls and curves so popular in Europe in the earlier period

The New Individualism

During this period of a strengthening American identity, many people of the new republic began to move farther westward. Pioneers settled Kentucky and Tennessee in the 1790s. At the same time people started exploring the lands of the Old Northwest—the area that would become the states of Ohio, Indiana, Illinois, Michigan, and Wisconsin. Southern settlers moved into the Old Southwest—the area that would soon become the states of Alabama, Mississippi, and Louisiana.

Better transportation networks led to expanding American mobility and helped the nation grow. State governments had built some of the first roads, and under President Jefferson, the U.S. government began to build the National Road. It started in Cumberland, Maryland, and in 1818 reached Wheeling—now in West Virginia—on the Ohio River. An expanding canal system linked lakes and rivers. The newly invented steamboats moved along these waterways, making shipping quicker and cheaper than with hand-powered boats.

These changes brought about a great increase in trade and aided the growth of a **market economy**. That is, people began to send their goods to distant markets to be sold for cash.

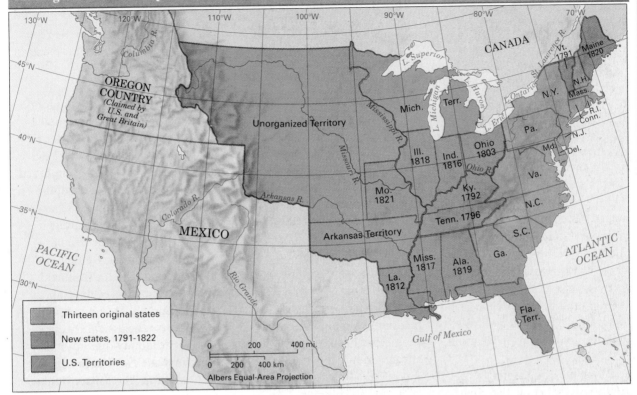

Thirteen original states

New states, 1791-1822

U.S. Territories

0   200   400 mi.
0   200   400 km
Albers Equal-Area Projection

The market economy was quickly replacing the household economy. People's social ties to their own community grew weaker, since buyers and sellers often no longer exchanged their goods face to face. As a result, individual material success was fast becoming more important than a person's responsibility to the community. ■

▲ *How many states did the United States add to the original 13 during 1791-1821?*

■ *Summarize the economic changes that led to the weakening of people's ties to their communities.*

Values in Conflict

One ideal that grew out of the new emphasis on individual success was the "self-made man." This was the man who succeeded through his own efforts. Self-help books, with titles such as *A Good Foundation for Riches and Honor*, became popular across the United States. Both religion and politics were beginning to reflect the conflict between the wish for personal gain and the need to sacrifice for the good of the community.

The Second Great Awakening

This clash of values was at the heart of a religious revival now known as the Second Great Awakening, which followed the Great Awakening by about 70 years. Church membership had gone down during the Revolutionary War. Now clergymen wanted to bring people back into a more active religious life. At huge outdoor revival meetings, preachers excited the crowds by calling on them to renew their dedication to Christianity. This plea appealed to people's growing self-awareness.

From 1800 to 1840, a religious fervor spread throughout Protestant America. At the same time, independent black churches were growing around the nation. The revival movement brought spiritual renewal to both white and black churches.

The revival movement found its greatest success in western New York. This area was called the "burnt-over district" because revivalism spread through it like a fire. The most popular and inspiring of the preachers was Charles Grandison Finney. Throughout the North, thousands gathered to hear him preach "perfectionism."

UNDERSTANDING NEOCLASSICISM

By 1750, Europeans had grown weary of the very ornate style of art known as rococo that had been popular for 50 years. They began examining ancient Roman and Greek sources for their art. Soon a new art movement, called neoclassicism, emerged and swept through Europe. Later it would reach the United States and greatly influence the architecture of many of the nation's public and private buildings. The movement was popular in America from about 1750 to 1830.

Just the opposite of the elaborate rococo, neoclassicism was literally a "new classical" form of art. It was both a movement and an artistic style that tried to imitate characteristics of classical Greek and Roman art and architecture that were popular in ancient cities from about 500 B.C. to about A.D. 475.

Origins

Interest in the neoclassical movement was sparked by archaeological excavations that began in 1738 at Herculaneum and in 1763 at Pompeii, Roman towns buried alive by an eruption of Mount Vesuvius in A.D. 79. The excavations revealed two well-preserved towns and provided an opportunity to view many aspects of everyday life in ancient Rome.

The neoclassical style was restrained and dignified, with simple, well-proportioned form and symmetrical parts. Color was either absent or in very light hues. Greek columns—the Doric, Ionic, and Corinthian—were commonly used. Some buildings had a rectangular ground plan; others had a central plan with dome. The neoclassical style was popular in the design of large structures, especially public buildings such as capitols and courthouses.

Examples

Thomas Jefferson, who himself was an architect, designed several outstanding examples of neoclassical architecture. These buildings include the Virginia State Capitol in Richmond, the University of Virginia at Charlottesville, and Jefferson's own home, Monticello (shown here).

Two architects, Benjamin Latrobe and Charles Bulfinch, transformed parts of the Capitol in Washington, D.C., to the new style. The neoclassical style is also reflected in other notable buildings such as the Bank of Pennsylvania, the Missouri State Capitol, and President James Polk's mansion in Tennessee.

Most of the plantation mansions in the South were built in a late phase of the neoclassical style known as Greek Revival. The North Carolina State Capitol is an outstanding example of this style, which became popular in all parts of the country.

Finney defined sin simply as selfishness. He stressed the emotional nature of religion and told his converts to try to be "useful in the highest degree possible."

The Second Great Awakening also inspired church members to become missionaries. "Penny" societies, whose members gave a penny a week, sought to Christianize the poor and the uneducated. Such groups sent missionaries to western cities, to communities of American Indians, and even to Hawaii and China.

In addition, the revival movement gave young women—and many teenage girls—the chance to take a more active role in society. Some women formed female associations to carry the religious message. The wives of the well-to-do also formed groups to raise money for the revival ministries.

Expansion of People's Politics

As more Americans became active in churches, politics also became more democratic. All over the nation, barriers to **suffrage,** or the right to vote, were done away with, at least for white males. For example, some states no longer required voters to own land. The new self-made men began to seek political power. They soon won election to local offices and to Congress.

Those who clung to the old republican values looked down on these independent men, calling them "coonskin Congressmen" because of their frontier caps made of raccoon skins. But the new breed of politician paid more attention to public opinion than had the old elite. The growing number of voters rewarded those who shared their views. ■

Across Time & Space

In 1920, an amendment to the Constitution prohibited the states from denying suffrage to women. Many Northern states had given free blacks the right to vote after the Revolutionary War but took away the right by the mid-1800s. Although a constitutional amendment in 1870 granted all African Americans the right to vote, many were prevented from exercising that right until the mid-1960s.

■ *What national values did the preachers of the Second Great Awakening draw on to revive their ministries?*

REVIEW

1. **FOCUS** How did Americans define their own national values in their new nation?
2. **CONNECT** How well did the change from a household economy to a market economy match Jefferson's vision of an agrarian republic?
3. **BELIEF SYSTEMS** Explain what characteristics the Second Great Awakening and the growth of people's politics have in common.
4. **CRITICAL THINKING** Why was it so important that the United States establish it own identity?
5. **ACTIVITY** Look around your community for examples of neoclassical architecture. You might also do some research on the buildings in your state capital. Compare your list of buildings with those of your classmates.

169

The Role of the First Lady

*T*hey are not elected. They have no official job description. Still, these women, the wives of the Presidents, have filled one of the most demanding positions in the United States. By searching in the spotlight and in the shadows, you can find how each defined her role to fit her unique personality.

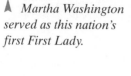

▲ *Martha Washington served as this nation's first First Lady.*

➤ *Dolley Madison was famous for being a very outgoing and fashionable Washington hostess.*

170

Get Ready

You will be researching the lives of some fascinating American women. To learn about more than just their public lives, however, you will need to look behind the headlines, beyond the publicity photographs, and into primary sources — letters, personal memoirs, and biographies. Keep a notebook handy to organize your information.

Find Out

Your school library or local public library will be the place to begin your research. Choose one First Lady and concentrate on her. Look in a good encyclopedia and read what it has to say about her. If there is a list of additional resources, make a note of them for future use. Did your First Lady ever write anything about herself? Look up those materials, if any are available to you. Check the biography shelves to see if someone else wrote about her life.

Move Ahead

Several of you can report on your First Ladies and then compare them. Did they seem to enjoy their role? Were they shy? Did their husbands consult with them? What were their interests?

Explore Some More

You can use the daily newspaper as a way to keep track of the current First Lady. Write down any direct quotes. What does she seem to be most interested in? Compare her to the First Lady you researched. Are there ways they are similar? How are they different?

Some First Ladies

The first First Lady, Martha Washington, did not have even the example of previous First Ladies to guide her, but she was still an effective partner to the first President. Throughout the Revolutionary War and the first presidency, she used her considerable charm, wit, intellect, and social skills to smooth over political differences between her husband and other early leaders. Although she defined the role of First Lady and carried it out enthusiastically, she treasured her privacy. On leaving office after President Washington's second term she wrote, "The General and I felt like children just released from school. . . ."

For marrying a non-Quaker, Dolley Madison was expelled from the Society of Friends (Quakers) and she made up for the long years of modest living by becoming the most fashionable and elegant hostess in Washington, establishing a tradition that continues today. She occasionally filled in as official hostess for the widowed Thomas Jefferson as well.

Perhaps the most remarkable of

all the First Ladies, Eleanor Roosevelt devoted herself to a wide variety of social causes on behalf of minorities and the poor, becoming a public leader in her own right. During her husband's presidency, she became so active in the country's affairs that one political opponent complained that the people were getting two Presidents instead of one. Following her husband's death in office, the new President (Truman) appointed Mrs. Roosevelt U.S. delegate to the United Nations, where she chaired the Commission on Human Rights, and was called by some, "First Lady of the World."

After Ellen Wilson died in 1914, President Woodrow Wilson met and married Edith Bolling Galt. When he became too ill to perform the duties of the presidency, she and a presidential aide took over many of them, without constitutional authority. The episode was called by her critics, "Mrs. Wilson's First Regency" and she herself was referred to as "acting First Man."

Barbara Bush, an active woman whose many interests include literacy, cancer research, and education, is an example of a contemporary First Lady. Her personal interest in literacy led her to write a book to help promote her efforts. The 1953 death of her four-year-old daughter from cancer led to her involvement in medical activities. Known for her warm, easy-going manner and clever sense of humor, Barbara Bush has faced the challenge of her role as our nation's First Lady with an energy and grace all her own.

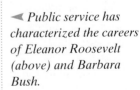

Public service has characterized the careers of Eleanor Roosevelt (above) and Barbara Bush.

171

L E S S O N   2

The First Western President

THINKING
FOCUS

How did Andrew Jackson's presidency reflect the politics of his time?

Key Terms

- tariff
- popular vote
- caucus
- spoils system
- states' rights
- nullify

➤ *In another mob gathering at the White House in 1837, visitors carved up the 1600-pound cheese sent to Andrew Jackson by some admirers. None of the cheese was left for the President.*

Throngs of well-wishers lined the streets of Washington, D.C., on Inauguration Day March 4, 1829—many of them dressed in rough, frontier clothing. With his white mane of hair blowing in the wind, the tall, lean Andrew Jackson—61 years old—took the oath of office as President. After reading his inaugural address, Jackson bowed to the roaring crowd and rode to the White House for a public reception.

Hordes of people swarmed into the White House. Ice cream, cake, and lemonade awaited the guests. In the scramble to get to the food, the crowd overturned tables, broke china, and stained satin-covered furniture with their muddy boots. Jackson had to escape the crush of people through a back door. Fistfights broke out and noses were bloodied. The White House was cleared only after servants placed tubs of punch on the lawn, and some of the men jumped out of windows to get at it.

Washington had never seen anything like this party. "It was a proud day for the people," reported a Kentucky newspaper. "General Jackson is their own President." Many others, however, were horrified. For Supreme Court Justice Joseph Story, "the reign of King Mob seemed triumphant."

The Rise of Jacksonian Politics

Andrew Jackson's election in 1828 —after his second presidential campaign—was the triumph of the self-made man. Born into a poor family in South Carolina, Jackson became wealthy through a successful law practice and the shrewd buying and selling of land. He had fought in the Revolutionary War at the age of 13, and he would always carry the scars from a British sword. Active in Tennessee politics, Jackson served briefly as its first congressman when Tennessee became a state in 1796. He won national fame in 1815 as a heroic

general at the Battle of New Orleans. Because of his toughness, his admiring soldiers called him "Old Hickory."

At the Hermitage, his luxurious mansion outside Nashville, Tennessee, Jackson kept many slaves. Yet he became the symbol of the common man in national politics. As a war hero and a Westerner from the land west of the original colonies, Jackson represented the new American ideal.

The 1824 Election

Jackson had first run unsuccessfully for the presidency in 1824. The presidential campaign that year was a free-for-all that attracted several other ambitious men: Secretary of State John Quincy Adams of Massachusetts, Speaker of the House Henry Clay of Kentucky, and Secretary of the Treasury William Crawford of Georgia. When the votes of the presidential

electors were counted, Jackson had more electoral votes than anyone else. But he did not have a majority. Again, as in the election of 1800, the House of Representatives would have to decide the election.

Through the influence of Henry Clay, the House elected Adams. When Adams then picked Clay to be his secretary of state, the Jackson supporters cried, "Corrupt bargain!" The Tennessee state legislature quickly made Jackson a candidate for the next election.

In the meantime, Adams was the President for the next four years. Adams stood for the old republican values. As John Adams's son he represented the ruling elite, the wealthy, and the well educated at a time when political values were changing. He was known as a harsh, stubborn person. As President, Adams wanted a high tax on imported goods, called a **tariff,** to raise money for important improvements such as roads and canals. He wanted to establish a national university.

◄ After the election of 1824 Andrew Jackson (portrait on left) considered John Quincy Adams (portrait on right) to be his personal enemy as well as his political rival.

173

He also wanted the government to give money for scientific studies. Despite these new ideas, Adams was not a strong leader because he received no popular support from the people.

The 1828 Campaign

In 1828, Adams faced Jackson again. Jackson's followers staged barbecues, picnics, and torchlight parades to bring new voters to the polls. Campaign songs put down Adams and praised "our Jackson." Sung to the tune of "Auld Lang Syne," the "Jackson Toast" began:

Though Adams now misrules the land,
And strives t'oppress the free,
He soon must yield his high
  command
Unto "Old Hickory."

Chorus:
Then toast our Jackson, good
  and great,
The man whom we admire,
He soon will mount the chair of
  state,
Which patriots desire.

And though Corruption's
  baleful voice
Did formerly prevail—
Once more he'll be the people's
  choice,
Though demagogues assail.

Now Johnny Q. and Henry Clay,
With all the people's foes,
Are giving as they pass away,
Their last convulsive throes.

Still angry about the 1824 "theft" of the presidency, Jackson supporters attacked Adams's reputation. Pro-Adams newspapers countered with false stories about Jackson's wife Rachel and about his mother. Adams supporters also handed out the so-called Coffin Handbill, which pictured the coffins of six men allegedly murdered by Jackson.

As a candidate, Jackson took stands favoring the common people over the rich and powerful. He did not like large banks and large factories. He believed such businesses would strengthen the national government and take power from the people. Settlers out west liked Jackson for his support of westward expansion. He swept to victory with 56 percent of the **popular vote**—the total number of votes by the people in all the states. He also won a large majority of the electoral votes.

Adams found it hard to accept his defeat. "It seemed," he said, "as if I was deserted by all Mankind."

The Second American Party System

Two new parties arose out of the bitter campaign of 1828. The Republican Party of Jefferson and Madison split. Jackson's followers became known as Democratic-Republicans, or Democrats. Those who opposed him formed the National-Republican Party, later called the Whig Party. The Whigs included business leaders

➤ Note in the first bar of the graph that the Republican Party had not yet split into two parties in 1824. Notice the increase in the number of people who voted in the 1828 national election.

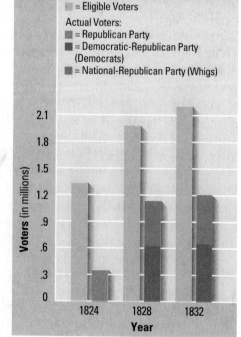

Voter Participation, 1824–1832

= Eligible Voters

Actual Voters:
= Republican Party
= Democratic-Republican Party (Democrats)
= National-Republican Party (Whigs)

Voters (in millions): 2.1, 1.8, 1.5, 1.2, .9, .6, .3, 0

Year: 1824, 1828, 1832

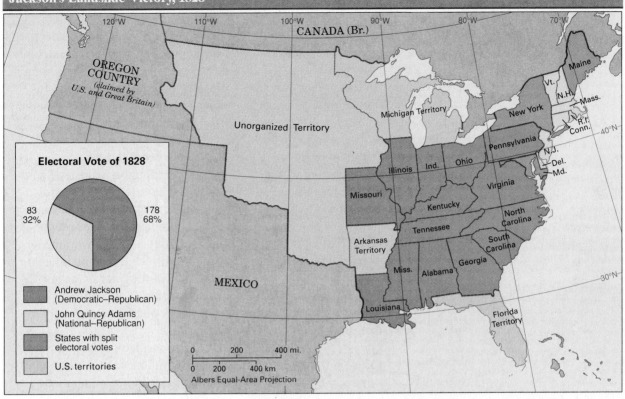

Electoral Vote of 1828

83
32%

178
68%

Andrew Jackson
(Democratic–Republican)

John Quincy Adams
(National–Republican)

States with split
electoral votes

U.S. territories

0   200   400 mi.
0   200   400 km
Albers Equal-Area Projection

from the North as well as the South, and many Protestant religious reformers. Among the Whig leaders were Henry Clay and Massachusetts senator Daniel Webster. After losing his reelection campaign for the presidency, John Quincy Adams—himself a Whig—won election to the House of Representatives and served there for 17 years. Adams was the only President to have served as an elected official after his presidential term.

Political procedures in national elections became more democratic in Jackson's time. The public was no longer willing to leave the nomination in the hands of the **caucus.** This group of Congressional leaders had met in secret to pick the presidential candidates. By the 1832 election, both parties would hold national nominating conventions that ensured greater participation, at least by the delegates from state party committees. ■

From what regions of the United States did Andrew Jackson draw his support in the election of 1828?

Find evidence to support this statement: The American people were ready for Jacksonian politics.

A Strong Presidency

After his overwhelming victory in 1828, Jackson entered office determined to take charge of the national government. He believed he had the people's support to put in place all of his own programs.

Political Supporters Rewarded

"To the victors belong the spoils" claimed a friend of Jackson after the election. The **spoils system** gave public jobs to the members of the party in power. The name that Jackson gave to his replacement of government offi-

cials was "rotation in office." He defended it, claiming that it simply allowed more people to serve their country. Government jobs were "so plain and simple," said Jackson. "No one man has any more . . . right to official station than another."

Jackson rewarded some of his friends with Cabinet posts. But the President's Tennessee "buddies" were his most important advisers. These men, who met informally with Jackson in the White House, were known as "the kitchen cabinet."

175

The Maturing Republic

Jackson's Indian Policy

President Jackson had strong feelings about many issues, and he acted on them. Indian policy was one such issue. Jackson knew that Indian lands would make very good farms for white settlers. To make room for these settlers, he wanted to force American Indians remaining in the area east of the Mississippi River further westward. Known as an Indian fighter, Jackson had built his reputation on his successful battles against the Creeks and the Seminole. He

Jackson, famed as an Indian fighter, is shown in this print accepting the surrender of a Creek chief, Red Eagle, in 1814 after the Battle of Horseshoe Bend.

This political cartoon shows Jackson in an emperor's robe, complete with crown and scepter. The Constitution lies shredded at his feet.

turned a deaf ear to all arguments about Indian rights; so did his selfish supporters.

Under U.S. treaties, the Cherokee in western Georgia—like other Indian peoples—were treated as an independent nation. In fact, a treaty of 1791 with the United States had guaranteed the Cherokee their lands in Georgia. When Georgians tried to take over Cherokee land, the Cherokee brought several unsuccessful legal actions against the state of Georgia to the Supreme Court. In the 1832 *Worcester* v. *Georgia* case, Chief Justice John Marshall ruled that state laws that violated federal treaties with the Indian people were invalid.

Jackson, however, encouraged Georgia to ignore the Court's ruling.

"John Marshall has made his decision; now let him enforce it," he said. Only a few years later, the U.S. government brutally forced the Cherokee and other Indians east of the Mississippi from their lands.

War on the Federal Bank

As the common people's champion against the rich and powerful, Jackson went to war with the Bank of the United States. The federal bank held deposits of government money, on which it paid no interest. It used the money to pay the government's bills. It also printed paper money and loaned money to other banks.

Jackson called the federal bank the "moneyed monster," claiming that it did not give fair treatment to the common people. Nicholas Biddle, head of the bank, was from a rich old Philadelphia family. He had long been Jackson's enemy

In 1832 Henry Clay was planning a presidential race. He had Biddle ask Congress to renew the federal bank's charter early. Clay expected Jackson to veto, or reject the charter renewal. Hoping such a show of Jackson's power would result in a good campaign issue, Clay felt he would then win the votes of the

BORN TO COMMAND.

OF VETO MEMORY.

HAD I BEEN CONSULTED.

KING ANDREW THE FIRST.

In this 1832 cartoon Jackson strikes at the many-headed monster of the Bank of the United States with his veto rod. The face with top hat is bank president Nicholas Biddle, and the monster's other heads represent bank branch directors. Jackson is being helped by Vice President Martin Van Buren (in the middle), while fictional backwoodsman Major Jack Downing (on the right), sneaks up on Biddle.

federal bank supporters. Jackson did veto the rechartering, but as a campaign issue, the veto worked to Jackson's advantage. He won the election in 1832 by an even larger margin than in 1828.

Thinking the people were supporting his policies, Jackson began to deposit government money in state banks run by his friends. Congress let the federal bank's charter run out in 1836. Clearly, Jackson had won his battle—but with disastrous results for the economy. No longer held in check by the federal bank, the state banks began to give out too many loans, printing a flood of almost worthless paper money. Eventually the economy crashed in what was called the Panic of 1837. It was up to Jackson's successor, Martin Van Buren, to deal with the financial crisis. ■

■ What specific attitudes serve to identify Jackson as a Western President?

The Federal Union Put to the Test

At the same time that he was waging war against Biddle and the Bank of the United States, Andrew Jackson also found himself engaged in a struggle with some of his own old supporters. At a Democratic Party dinner in 1830, President Jackson lifted his glass to offer a toast: "Our Union—it must be preserved." All eyes turned to Vice President John Calhoun of South Carolina. "The Union—next to our liberty, the most dear! May we always remember that it can only be preserved by distributing equally the benefits and burdens of the Union," answered Calhoun. This exchange made public their intense disagreement over how much power the federal government should hold over the states.

The Tariff of Abominations

In 1828, during the Adams administration, Congress had passed the highest tariff bill ever. The purpose of taxing imports so highly was to protect American industries from foreign competition.

➤ *One com-
mentator descri-
bed John
Calhoun as
"the cast iron
man who looks as
if he had never
been born, and
never could be
extinguished."*

Across Time & Space

*Protecting American
manufacturing from
foreign competition—
especially that of
Japanese industry—is
an important economic
issue today. Since the
1970s Congress has
debated various mea-
sures, such as setting
protective tariffs, limiting
the number of Japanese
cars sold in the United
States, and guaranteeing
that Japanese markets
are open to American
products.*

■ *How did the nullifica-
tion crisis test the doctrine
of states' rights?*

Factory owners and workers in
the North liked the bill because it protected their growing textile and clothing industries. Jackson himself
supported it. But the South had few
industries and imported manufactured
goods. Southerners resented the high
prices caused by what they called the
"Tariff of Abominations."

As spokesman for the Southern
point of view, Calhoun wrote a document called the *South Carolina Exposition* in 1828. In it he claimed that the
final source of government power
came from the states. This was the
first time that anyone had clearly
spelled out the doctrine of **states'
rights**. From this doctrine came another idea that the states could **nullify,** or
refuse to enforce, laws of Congress
within their state boundaries.

In January 1830, the Senate
debated the issue of states' rights.
Robert Y. Haynes from South Carolina defended the idea of nullification.
Daniel Webster, the most gifted
speaker in the Senate, replied in

defense of the federal government in
a speech that lasted four hours. He
ended with the ringing words, "Liberty and Union, now and for ever, one
and inseparable."

Jackson had supported the principle of states' rights with respect to his
Indian policy. But on the nullification
problem, he chose instead to support
the rights of the federal government
over the rights of the states.

Defense of the Union

In 1832, Congress lowered tariff
rates slightly. South Carolinians were
not satisfied, however, and Calhoun
resigned the vice presidency to lead
the anti-tariff fight. South Carolina
called a state convention that ruled for
nullification of the tariffs of 1828 and
1832 and prevented the collection of
tariffs in the state.

Jackson was outraged. In private,
he threatened to hang Calhoun. Publicly, he said that nullification was
treason. "The laws of the United
States must be executed," Jackson
said, and he strengthened the federal
forts in South Carolina.

In 1833, under Henry Clay's leadership, Congress worked out a compromise that substantially reduced
tariffs over a 10-year period. At the
same time, Congress passed the Force
Bill, which allowed the President to
use the army and navy to enforce the
laws. The South Carolina convention
repealed its nullification ordinance.
But to have the last word, the convention also nullified the Force Bill. The
nullification crisis had passed. Jackson
had temporarily silenced the Southerners and held the Union intact. ■

R E V I E W

1. **FOCUS** How did Andrew Jackson's presidency reflect the
politics of his time?

2. **CONNECT** Compare the presidential campaign of 1828
with the election of 1800.

3. **ECONOMICS** Explain how the federal bank's role in the
economy became a political issue.

4. **CRITICAL THINKING** How did Jackson's position in the
Georgia-Cherokee conflict exemplify his Indian policy?

5. **ACTIVITY** Make a chart to illustrate the argument over
states' rights. List in two separate columns the positions
of South Carolina and the federal government.

LESSON 3

How Others Saw Us

ow dare she slander and belittle us Americans!" This is probably how you would have reacted in 1832 if you had seen the new book everyone in the United States was reading. Copies of *Domestic Manners of the Americans* had just arrived in the United States from its London publisher.

The book's author, an English-woman named Frances Trollope (*TRAHL uhp*) did not mince words. Of Americans in general, she wrote, "I do not like them. I do not like their principles, I do not like their manners, I do not like their opinions." Who did this Mrs. Trollope think she was anyway?

Trollope had come to the United States in 1827. She opened a store in the bustling frontier town of Cincinnati, hoping that Americans would buy fine clothing from London and Paris. After her shop failed, she returned to England to write books.

Almost all Americans, Trollope declared, showed a "total and universal want of manners, both in males and females." She complained about their bad posture and poor manners:

*T*he loathsome spitting… the frightful manner of feeding with their knives, till the whole blade seemed to enter into the mouth; and the still more frightful manner of cleaning the teeth afterwards with a pocket knife…

As for American women, she wrote, they "powder themselves immoderately, face, neck, and arms, with pulverized starch; the effect is disagreeable by day-light and not very favorable at any time."

Trollope had been used to the social life of Europe, where age-old traditions and formalities dictated what people could say and how they could act. Trollope had found little to admire about the United States, and most Americans were outraged by the criticisms in her book. They fought back with nasty cartoons and stinging **satires**—witty literary pieces that put down "Dame Trollope" by showing her as old, ugly, and crazy.

THINKING
FOCUS

What can we learn about our history from Euro-peans who visited the young United States?

Key Terms

- satire
- social class

◄ *This illustration in Trollope's book was drawn by Auguste de Hervieu (air VYUH). Here he pictures an American woman who, according to Trollope, wears too much make-up.*

The American Defined

Trollope was only one of many curious foreigners who sailed across the ocean to see the new country. A Frenchman named Michel-Guillaume Jean de Crèvecoeur (*krehv KUR*) had arrived in 1759. (His pen name was J. Hector St. John.) After many travels, Crèvecoeur married an American and settled on a farm in New York. But his support for Great Britain caused him to leave this country during the Revolutionary War. He did not return until 1783, when France appointed him consul in Boston.

Meanwhile, Crèvecoeur had published *Letters from an American Farmer* in London in 1782. He wrote the book as a series of letters from "James," a fictional Pennsylvania farmer, to a fictional English friend. Crèvecoeur's work was popular in Europe because it tried to answer the question that puzzled Europeans of that time: "What, then, is the American—this new man?"

Crèvecoeur found much to admire in American society. Unlike Europe, the United States was not composed "of great lords who possess everything and of a herd of people who have nothing." In Europe, **social class,** the grouping of people according to their status in society, was much more rigidly defined. People were either born into the upper class or the lower class, and they usually remained at that level of society all their lives. Crèvecoeur believed that what united Americans was a respect for laws, because American laws applied equally to rich and to poor.

Crèvecoeur's "James" also saw disturbing situations in the new nation. He described the horrors of slavery and found the frontier a lawless place, where isolation dissolved the bonds of community. He warned against the trend toward selfishness.

To Crèvecoeur, the greatness of the new country was that "individuals of all nations are melted into a new race of men." What emerged was the American—"a new man, who acts upon new principles; he must therefore entertain new ideas and form new opinions." ■

How Do We Know?

HISTORY *While photography was not invented until 1839, artists like Hervieu and Beaumont did provide a visual record of what life was like in the early republic.*

■ *Summarize Crèvecoeur's definition of the new American.*

➤ *The landscape of the United States was mostly rural at the time Crèvecoeur lived here, as shown in this painting of Poestenkill, New York.*

Criticism of America

Harriet Martineau (*MAHR tuh noh*), yet another foreign observer, brought a different point of view. Martineau was already a well-known English author when she arrived in New York in 1834. Two years before, Americans had been stung by Trollope's book. This time they wanted to make a good impression. The U.S. newspapers warned their readers not to chew tobacco or praise themselves while Martineau was present.

But the Englishwoman assured her hosts that she had come to "rough it." Since she was almost deaf, Martineau had to ask people to shout into her ear horn. She dealt with Americans cordially, even though she thought that many of them talked too much and were hungry for flattery.

Americans, Martineau observed, were very aware of the opinions of others. "Worship of opinion" was the religion of the United States. Though Americans respected individualism, they were really conformists.

It was the practice of slavery that struck Martineau more than anything else. She wrote forcibly about what she saw as a hypocritical, or insincere, attitude toward slaves in the South: "A common question put to me by amiable ladies was, 'Do not you find the slaves generally very happy?' " To this, the outraged Englishwoman would answer, "Would you be happy with their means?"

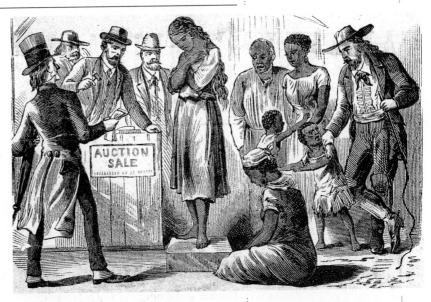

Martineau wrote, "Much that is dreadful ensues from the negro being subjected to toil and lash." She questioned the foundations of American society in her book *Society in America*:

> This discrepancy between principles and practice needs no more words. But the institution of slavery exists; and what we have to see is what the morals are of the society which is subject to it. What social virtues are possible in a society of which injustice is the primary characteristic? in a society which is divided into two classes, the servile [slavish] and the imperious [domineering]?

▲ *Shown above is a drawing of a slave auction. Many auctions were actually much more cruel, with slaves bound hand and foot.*

■ *In what ways was Martineau critical of American society?*

Tocqueville's America

In 1831, the Frenchman Alexis de Tocqueville (*TOHK vihl*) and his friend Gustave de Beaumont (*BOH mahn*) traveled throughout the United States to report on American prisons. Later, with that business done and out of the way, Tocqueville wrote a book about life in the new republic, *Democracy in America: 1835-39*. A historian and lawyer from an aristo-cratic French family, Tocqueville brought a fresh point of view and proved to be a sharp observer of the American scene. His outsider's view told Americans much about their own national identity. Look at the following Closer Look for more on the European viewpoint on American architecture, work habits, and social values.

Cities—Old and New

In 1859, Charles Dickens published a novel called A Tale of Two Cities. *It portrayed London and Paris, two of Europe's grandest cities. Yet another kind of city was growing up across the sea in America, one with a unique look, character, and charm.*

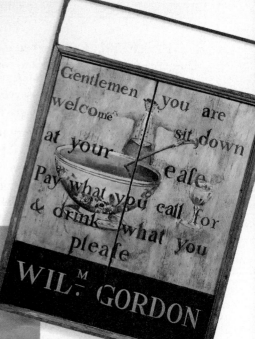

Hang Out Your Shingle!
To newcomers from Europe, the United States held out the promise of prosperity. Anyone could "hang out a shingle," that is, start a new business, just like this innkeeper.

Wide open spaces were a feature of many cities on this side of the Atlantic. This painting of Cincinnati shows simple, colonial architecture and low, square buildings. Streets were dirt or cobblestone; sidewalks were made of wooden planks. Practical Americans were busy building a country for themselves. They had no use for the architecture of kings.

Palaces, cathedrals, and towers graced the streets and squares of European cities. Tall columns, sculpted gardens and stately villas were a familiar sight. They were designed to impress passers-by with the majesty of kings and noblemen, the power of the church, or the sheer wealth of a city such as Venice.

Though Tocqueville did write about the horrors of slavery, he was also impressed by the lack of class distinctions he saw in rural white society. "Among the novel objects that attracted my attention," he wrote, "nothing struck me more forcibly than the general equality of condition among the people." This equality, he continued, "gives birth to new sentiments, founds novel customs, and modifies whatever it does not produce."

It was this new American society, in which all social classes "melted into a middle class," that caused Tocqueville to remark, "We are in a different world here." It was a world of constant change. The poor today could be rich tomorrow. And new ways and "feverish activity" prevailed.

As an example, Tocqueville wrote about this conversation :

I accost an American sailor and inquire why the ships of his country are built so as to last for only a short time; he answers without hesitation that the art of navigation is every day making such rapid progress that the finest vessel would become almost useless if it lasted beyond a few years.

Tocqueville saw the quest for perfection, whether in a better ship or in a better system of government, as a typically American trait.

Another result of the democratic climate in the United States, according to Tocqueville, was a new attitude toward women. American women received greater respect and esteem than women in Europe, though Tocqueville admitted that social inferiority of women did still continue in America. He wrote, "Although the women of the United States are confined within the narrow circle of domestic life, . . . I have nowhere seen women occupying a loftier position."

Like Martineau, Tocqueville found that public opinion ruled American thought, determining what the

general will was at the moment. In Tocqueville's words, "the people reign in the American political world as the Deity does in the Universe."

That the people reigned, as Tocqueville put it, was reflected in everyday values as well as in the growing influence of Jacksonian politics. The United States, a self-made nation defined by its commitment to democracy, was finally coming of age.

Tocqueville and the other foreign visitors helped Americans to see themselves. Their outsiders' observations still provide historians with insights into American character. ■

▼ Tocqueville's traveling companion Gustave de Beaumont kept a sketchbook of their 1831 trip. In this drawing he sketched their American Indian guide in the forests of Saginaw, now Michigan.

■ List four features that Tocqueville chose to describe as characteristic of American democracy.

Analyzing Jackson-Clay Cartoons

Here's Why

Reading political cartoons is an amusing way to uncover the politics that accompanied a particular event. Historical accounts of people and events relate when and where a particular situation occurred and usually also present why it occurred. What is often missing in such accounts is the general flavor of the times—the way the people and the press viewed the personalities of their day. Editorial drawings, or political cartoons, can provide that information while also giving a more detailed picture of what actually happened.

Cartoonists use dramatic symbols and characters and often exaggerate the images to make strong statements about events. As you have learned in this chapter, Andrew Jackson was a colorful and controversial president. His striking looks, strong personality, and decisive opinions on the issues of the day made him an easy target for the editorial cartoonists of his time.

Suppose you wanted to find out how events during Jackson's presidency were viewed by the people and the press. One good way to begin would be to examine how he was portrayed in the editorial cartoons of that era.

Here's How

You can use the following three steps to understand a political cartoon:

1. Identify the action in the cartoon.
2. Identify the symbols and possible exaggeration in the cartoon.
3. Interpret the cartoonist's purpose.

Look at the cartoon on this page, which was first published in 1834. The action here is Senator Henry Clay sewing President Jackson's mouth shut. Jackson was a very outspoken person who often did what he wanted without consulting Congress. The cartoonist was exaggerating how difficult it would be to change Jackson's behavior. You would have to wrestle him into a chair and sew his mouth shut.

PLAIN SEWING DONE HERE

SYMPTOMS OF A LOCKED JAW

"CLAY"

"Might stop a hole, to keep the wind away"

Race over Uncle Sam's Course.
4ᵗʰ March 1833

By showing Clay as the one doing the sewing, the cartoonist was making a statement about who wanted to silence Jackson. In March 1834 the Senate voted to censure, or officially express disapproval of, President Jackson for taking government money out of the bank without congressional approval. Clay was the person who pushed the Senate to censure Jackson. Censuring a person is one way of reducing that person's power.

In this cartoon Jackson's mouth is a symbol of his power. Clay's use of a needle and thread to sew the mouth shut is a symbol of Clay's use of the Senate vote against Jackson to shut off his power. The cartoonist is saying that Clay was trying to stop Jackson from taking action without consulting Congress.

Notice the quotation from Shakespeare's play *Hamlet*: "Might stop a hole, to keep the wind away." Wind can be very damaging if allowed to blow. Sewing up holes in clothing or stopping up holes in walls is one way of preventing the damage that wind can do. The quotation indicates that the cartoonist thinks Clay's action was good. Clay's attempt to "stop up the hole" (Jackson's power) kept Jackson's "wind" (or damaging actions) away.

Try It

Look at the political cartoon above. It shows Clay and Jackson racing toward the White House. Jackson's horse is shown running into a rock called the Bank U S. while Clay's horse pulls ahead. In the cartoon, Nicholas Biddle, head of the federal bank, is a monkey riding on the back of Jackson's horse, and Jackson is swinging a club labeled "veto."

Now go back to page 176, read "The War on the National Bank," and answer the following questions. Why did the cartoonist label the rock "Bank U S."? Why is Biddle portrayed as a monkey on Jackson's back? What was the cartoonist saying about the election of 1832? Was he right?

Apply It

Newspapers and magazines today are filled with editorial cartoons about colorful figures. Find a cartoon of a current event or national leader. Write a short paragraph identifying the use of symbols and exaggeration and explaining the cartoonist's purpose.

185

Chapter Review

Reviewing Key Terms

caucus (p. 175)
household economy (p. 164)
market economy (p. 166)
neoclassical (p. 166)
nullify (p. 178)
popular vote (p. 174)

satire (p. 179)
social class (p. 180)
spoils system (p. 175)
states' rights (p. 178)
suffrage (p. 169)
tariff (p. 173)

A. Use a dictionary to look up the meaning and derivation of each of the following key terms. Then write a complete sentence for each term, using the term correctly.

1. neoclassical
2. suffrage
3. nullify
4. satire
5. tariff
6. caucus

B. Based on what you have read in the chapter, decide whether each of the following statements is true or false. If a statement is false, rewrite it to make it true.

1. Because women had suffrage, they could not vote in the early years of the nation.
2. The tariff placed on imported goods made them more expensive for American shoppers.
3. In the caucus system, all voters could decide on the nomination of a presidential candidate.
4. The spoils system let a winning candidate reward his supporters.
5. Americans enjoyed reading satire about Mrs. Trollope and felt that it defended their government.
6. Tocqueville felt that because most Americans belonged to the middle class, there were no social class differences in the United States.

Exploring Concepts

A. On a separate sheet of paper, copy the cluster diagram shown below and fill in the empty circles with additional Republican Ideas and Values. Two circles have been already been filled in. You may add as many circles as you would like to your copy of the diagram.

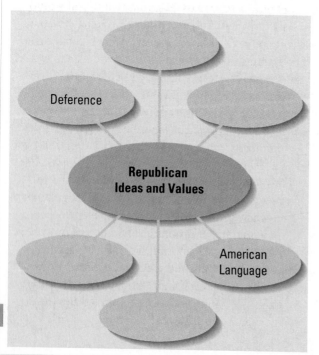

B. Support each of the following statements with facts and details from the chapter. Then write a short paragraph outlining connections among the categories of information presented in the statements below. For example, what did the new spirit of individualism, the Great Awakening, and the election of Andrew Jackson all have in common? How were they different?

1. The new spirit of individualism created values that conflicted with republican ideas.
2. Better means of transportation produced an increase in trade.
3. The Great Awakening increased people's participation in religion.
4. The election of Andrew Jackson as president stood for the triumph of the common man over the elite.
5. As president, Jackson used his power to make sweeping changes.

Reviewing Skills

1. Look at the cartoon on page 185. Why is the hat labeled "New Orleans"? Why is the box behind Clay labeled "American System"?
2. Look at the cartoon on page 176. It shows Andrew Jackson dressed as a king. Identify the symbols in the cartoon. What is the action in the cartoon? Define the major points in the cartoon and write a short paragraph explaining how the cartoon relates to an issue in Jackson's presidency.
3. Find a cartoon of a current event or a national personality in a newspaper or magazine. Mount the cartoon on a sheet of paper, and write your interpretation of the cartoon next to it, pointing out the symbols and action.
4. Thomas Nast was a famous political cartoonist. Use your library to find information on Nast. Take notes on the information you find, and create a bibliography card.
5. Suppose you wanted to look at political cartoons from other countries. In what kinds of publications would you look?

Using Critical Thinking

1. "Andrew Jackson was the first president who really represented the common man." Do you agree or disagree with this statement? Does Jackson's background and personality indicate that the spirit of American politics was changing in the 1820s? If so, how?
2. Andrew Jackson felt that the House should have elected him president in 1824, because he had received more electoral votes than any of his opponents. Do you agree? State your reasons. How do you think people would react today if the House of Representatives decided an election in favor of a candidate who did not receive the most electoral votes?
3. Frances Trollope wrote that in the United States, "Any man's son may become the equal of any other man's son." What did she mean by this statement? Based on her observation, how do you think the society of her country differed from that of the United States? Explain your answer.

Preparing for Citizenship

1. WRITING ACTIVITY Many people consider George Washington to be the first American hero. Identify someone you consider to be a modern American hero. What characteristics or deeds make a person a hero? Is your hero similar in any way to George Washington? Write a short essay defining *hero*, and explaining the similarities and differences between your choice of a modern hero and George Washington.
2. WRITING ACTIVITY The idea of the "self-made man" that became popular in the United States during the early 1800s, is still alive today. Identify current men or women who have achieved individual success in their lives. Choose one who interests you, and look up recent newspaper and magazine articles about the person. Write a short report defining the person's success and identifying how that success was "self-made."
3. ART ACTIVITY Cut out magazine images of events and people that you believe are examples of basic American values. Then create a collage or poster that illustrates how those values have or have not changed since the early 1800s.
4. COLLABORATIVE LEARNING Divide into groups and choose a school or community law you would like to see changed. Determine what the consequences would be if you "nullified," or refused to obey, that law. Then decide what steps would need to be taken in order to change that law. Compare group decisions.
5. COLLABORATIVE LEARNING Divide into four groups representing the car manufacturing and trade situation in the United States: Group 1 will be government representatives, Group 2 will be a consumer interest group, Group 3 will be foreign car dealers, and Group 4 will be American car manufacturers. Each group should come up with a list of arguments to support or oppose a proposed tariff on foreign cars. When the groups have finished, one representative from each group should state the group's position. Then the representatives should work together to reach a compromise.

Chapter 7
People of the New Nation

The political and economic freedom won in the Revolution released a torrent of creative energy in the new nation. The spirit of independence was reflected in rapid territorial expansion, population growth, and technological advances. Although people who had come from many nations enjoyed the benefit of this growth, the American Indians found that the growth was often at their expense.

Led by such men as former slave Absalom Jones (here in a painting by Raphael Peale), communities of free blacks formed in cities throughout the United States.

Increased prosperity freed women to devote themselves to more refined activities such as embroidery. Shown here is a sampler from 1826.

	1790	1800	1810	1820

Presidents

1789-1797 Washington

1797-1801 J. Adams

1801-1809 Jefferson

1809-1817 Madison

1817-1825 Monroe

1790

1856 From the Atlantic to the Great Plains, the country was dotted with towns and farms and crisscrossed by roads, canals, and railroads. Painter Henry Boese depicted this "Landscape with Stagecoach" in 1856.

1830

1840

1850

1860

1829-1837
Jackson

1841-1845
Tyler

1853-1857
Pierce

1857-1861
Buchanan

1825-1829
J. Q. Adams

1837-1841
Van Buren

1845-1849
Polk

1850-1853
Fillmore

1841
W. Harrison

1849-1850
Taylor

1860

L E S S O N 1

Life Changes Along the Atlantic Seaboard

THINKING FOCUS

How did economic growth in the new nation change family and community life?

Key Terms

- middle class
- working class

I n the late 1700s, a 77-year-old farmer in Andover, Massachusetts, sat with quill in hand, putting the finishing touches on his will. This farmer was John Abbot. For three generations, members of his family had divided the Abbot farmland among their sons.

"And here let it be further Observed that it is upon mature Deliberation and for Sundry good & weighty Reasons that I have [Bequeathed] & Willed to my Said Eldest Son as above Expressed," wrote John Abbot. By this will, Abbot transferred all of his land together with any buildings to his oldest son, John, Jr.

With the words "mature Deliberation" and "good & weighty Reasons,"

the elder Abbot apologized for not dividing the family homestead among all his sons. It had long been a tradition to give each son a sizeable portion of land. But John Abbot knew that if he divided his farm among all four of his boys, each portion would be too small to support a family. Therefore his second son, Barachias, had already received some cash and training as a shoemaker. Abiel, the third son, had been given an education at Harvard College. And Joseph, the youngest, was given some livestock and a few farm tools. He had already been given money for farmland in New Hampshire.

As the population of New England grew, many farmers found themselves in John Abbot's position.

Family Farms Become More Profitable

The Abbot family's experience was shared by many farm families in the northeastern United States. Well into the 1800s, farmers worked their land by hand, with the help of a few family members. But life was also changing for other American farmers. Two developments would drastically alter their way of life: the growing worldwide demand for wheat and the invention of new farming tools.

The Wheat Boom

Population growth and wars throughout Europe had a direct effect

on the American farm economy. Before the 1740s, European countries had been able to feed themselves. But the Napoleonic wars destroyed most of Europe's wheat crop. European demand for wheat increased greatly. As a result, wheat prices in the United States skyrocketed. Now huge quantities of grain and other farm produce were exported to Europe.

Farmers in the North and South planted as much wheat as they could. All wanted to make money on the booming wheat trade. Thousands of Americans sank their fortunes and

Advances in Wheat Production

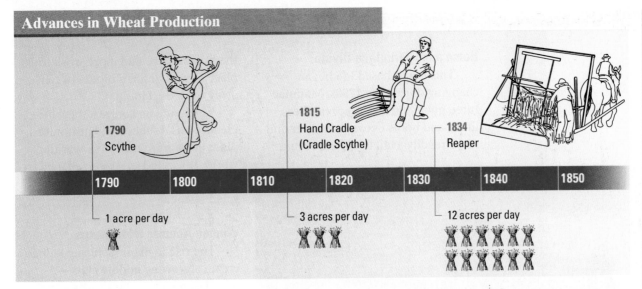

1790
Scythe

1815
Hand Cradle
(Cradle Scythe)

1834
Reaper

| 1790 | 1800 | 1810 | 1820 | 1830 | 1840 | 1850 |

1 acre per day

3 acres per day

12 acres per day

their plows into the fertile land of western New York, Pennsylvania, Virginia, and the territories of Tennessee and Kentucky. The grain trade, long the cornerstone of the nation's market economy, quickly made farmland of the old frontier.

Improved Farming Methods

Long after the turn of the 19th century, American farmers used the same simple tools and methods used by European farmers for hundreds of years. Typically, farmers had harvested their grain with the old-fashioned scythe, a single-edged blade on the end of a long, curved wooden handle.

In the 1830s, however, the way farmers worked the land changed very quickly. A new age began as machines entered the everyday world of nearly all Americans. With Cyrus McCórmick's revolutionary mechanical reaper, developed in 1831, farmers cut and tied wheat twelve times faster than they had with some traditional tools. The tough

steel-bladed plow, like the one shown below, was developed by John Deere in 1837. The plow sliced through even hard, rocky soil and turned it over into neat furrows.

With these machines American farms became more efficient and more profitable. It was now possible to plant many more acres of grain than before. With the cash from selling surplus wheat, farmers could afford to buy more ready-made products. Farm families were eager to buy items such as soap, shoes, pottery, and clothing. The merchants and craftspeople who made and sold these goods prospered as well. ■

This graph compares how many acres of wheat one man could harvest in one day using a sickle, a scythe with a cradle, and a McCormick reaper.

■ *How did wars in Europe and new farming tools help American farms become more profitable?*

One of the first steel-bladed plows, made by John Deere himself in 1838.

The American Economy Matures

Since colonial times, American farmers had been mostly self-sufficient. Most families grew their own food, wove their own cloth, and even made many of their own household tools. Boots, wooden plows, carved wooden utensils, and straw brooms were all homemade.

For these early American families, "work" was any farm or household task that had to be done. Very few people had jobs in the sense we now understand. And although men and women might have had different chores, their work was considered equally important.

191

People of the New Nation

Home and Workplace Divide

This home-based life began changing during the 1790s. Manufactured goods such as soap, candles, linen, and boots became cheaper and more readily available. As a result,

▲ *Etchings like this emphasized the importance of the woman's role as homemaker.*

American women spent fewer hours making these household goods. Farm women were then able to produce surplus dairy products and homegrown vegetables for sale to townspeople.

Many women took on "outwork" in their homes. They stitched and sewed raw materials provided by storekeepers. Women in one New Hampshire town made hats from imported palm leaves provided by a local merchant. Outwork paid little, but it enabled families to save some money. Often the savings bought farmland for the children.

Better transportation, increased manufacturing, and labor-saving inventions changed the work of men as well. A growing number of men, like John Abbot's younger sons, found work outside the home—in shops, factories, and offices. Manufacturers, especially of shoes and textiles, began to organize work into hourly units. Gradually men's work came to be viewed as something separate from

the home. More and more work took place in well-defined blocks of time away from the family.

The home, in contrast, became idealized as a sheltered, harmonious place away from the harsh working world. It was to be a haven shaped by women, just as public life would be ruled by men.

Women Acquire New Status

The rise in manufacturing helped create a growing **middle class**—a group of people of better-than-average education and income. This class held certain values in common. Chief among these middle-class values was education. For young women in financially stable families in the early 1800s, childrearing was now thought of as an educational mission.

Publishers offered hundreds of "how-to" books and articles for housewives. They covered topics such as cooking, family health, and infant care. Catharine Beecher's *A Treatise on Domestic Economy*, published in 1841, dealt with the noble task of children's education.

S urely it is a ...mistaken idea, that the duties which tax a woman's mind are petty, trivial, or unworthy of the highest grade of intellect and moral worth. Instead of allowing this feeling, every woman should imbibe, from early youth, the impression that she is training for the discharge of the most important, the most difficult, and the most sacred and interesting duties....

Literature such as Beecher's book was very popular at the time. It helped shape the ideals of generations of middle-class American women. These publications were also popular with women who were members of the **working class**—those who labored in mills and workshops for hourly wages. ■

■ *How were women and the American home affected by economic changes?*

Port Cities Provide Economic Opportunity

Just as life was changing for young women, young men were gaining opportunities. Younger sons of farming families often left home to pioneer new land farther west. Others of these young men were drawn to busy seaports like Baltimore, Philadelphia, and New York. In the years between 1790 and 1860, Boston, Charleston, and other port cities grew dramatically. Their populations doubled several times over.

In New England, a rise in textile manufacturing fueled the rapid growth of the port of Boston. Boston's harbor could hold up to 500 ships at a time, and its 80 wharves teemed with dockworkers, sailors, and peddlers. In addition to textiles, Boston ships carried grain, lumber, horses, onions, butter, cheese, and beeswax to European ports. This thriving city opened the first free public schools in the United States.

In the South, Charleston became an important center for trade and business. Lively banter in French and Spanish could be heard near the docks. In the markets the smells of Brazilian coffee, New England dried fish, and Cuban tobacco mingled.

During this period a change occurred in the way goods were produced in the port cities. Traditionally, goods were made by master craftsmen with years of experience. As they worked, they trained others in their craft. But this system broke down. The opening of the Old Northwest and of the southwest frontier, plus the inflow of immigrants, created a huge demand for crafted goods. When the craftsmen were not able to keep up, city merchants set up factories of their own. They hired less-skilled workers and used a crude production line to make the goods. Though not as good as products made by master craftsmen, they were cheaper.

By the 1840s, few craftsmen could compete with the factories. Factory workers earned more than some trainees. But few would ever become their own master. ■

■ How were master craftsmen affected by the booming economy in the port cities?

Some African Americans Experience Changes

The coastal cities, especially in the North, were the scene of important changes for many African Americans. Free blacks, African Americans who were no longer enslaved, were drawn to Philadelphia, Boston, New York, and Baltimore. The population of free blacks increased greatly, though not as greatly as the slave population. Out of the 1,800,000 African Americans in 1820, free blacks numbered 233,000, or 13 percent. In 1860, 488,000 out of 4,400,000 African Americans, or 11 percent, were free.

No Rights for Slaves

Most African Americans living in the first half of the 1800s were slaves, however. Legally, they were property, with no more legal rights than a horse or cow. A child's status—slave or free—was inherited from the mother. Unless a slaveholder chose to free his or her slave, a slave's status would not

◄ African Americans in Philadelphia formed a large and thriving community. Dating from 1800, this painting shows a black street vendor selling oysters.

change. Slaves could be bought or sold as their slaveholder wished.

Slaves could not legally marry. Nor could they testify in court—not even at an owner's request or in an owner's defense. Even though a slave had no legal rights, in most states a slave was held responsible for any crimes he or she might commit.

Slow Steps Toward Freedom

Because the Northern textile and shoe industries could hire workers very cheaply, slavery was economically far less important in the North. Moreover, many reformers who wanted to do away with slavery lived in Northern cities.

Rhode Island did away with slavery in 1774 and Vermont's constitution prohibited it in 1777. Court cases in Massachusetts had won African Americans the freedoms guaranteed in that state's constitution. Politicians in other Northern states tried to make up a legal system for freeing slaves. Such laws were hard to pass. Slave-

holders fought hard to protect their rights as "property owners."

Often, free black men worked on the docks or as seamen on merchant and naval ships. In fact, in the mid-1820s officials in South Carolina were afraid of the influence that free blacks from the crews of Northern ships might have on plantation slaves. These careful South Carolinians ordered that all black sailors be kept in prison while their ships were in port.

In Pennsylvania, politicians argued for two years before passing a law in 1780 to free slaves gradually. New York and New Jersey would later pass laws that were very much like the Pennsylvania law.

Such laws, however, meant little to existing slaves. Pennsylvania's law, for example, stated that slaves born before March 1, 1780, would remain slaves for life. Those born after that date were required to work as slaves until the age of 28. Slaveholders maintained that 28 years of service would pay them for the money they had spent to raise the slave. Once they received their freedom papers, free blacks worked hard to earn enough money to buy the freedom of their families and loved ones still in slavery.

African Americans Form Communities

Despite these problems, communities of African Americans continued to grow in American cities. Black families organized groups for protection and support, founding societies—such as the Boston African Society and the Free African Society in Philadelphia —to help with health insurance and funeral costs.

Free blacks started their own sections of established fraternal organizations, like the Black Freemasons. These groups did charitable work and the members took part in social activities. Blacks even created their own schools. Until then, the Quaker religious groups had run the only schools that were open to black students.

▼ *The population density of free blacks was greatest in the North and Middle Atlantic states. But as this map shows, by 1810 free blacks lived in every state and territory of the nation.*

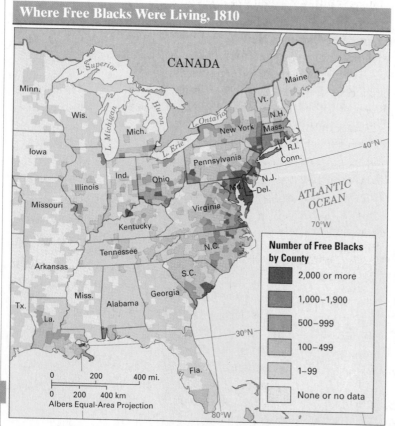

Where Free Blacks Were Living, 1810

CANADA

Number of Free Blacks by County

- 2,000 or more
- 1,000–1,900
- 500–999
- 100–499
- 1–99
- None or no data

0   200   400 mi.
0   200   400 km
Albers Equal-Area Projection

◄ *This blacksmith's shop is shown being moved to a new location, where it will function as Richard Allen's church. Allen is shown above.*

Schools for free blacks educated both children and adults who wanted to learn to read.

Free blacks also started their own churches. Richard Allen and Absalom Jones were former slaves who became leaders of Philadelphia's free black community. They wanted African churches to be able to support themselves. They did not want to be dependent on the well-meaning charity of their white friends. In time, African churches, such as the African Methodist Episcopal Church founded in 1816 by Allen, became a powerful voice for African American rights and freedom.

The dreams of many of the nation's free blacks were crushed by restricted opportunities for jobs and education. Their social mobility and participation in politics were limited by many hostile white people. As the two groups competed for jobs and housing, many free blacks met violence at the hands of poor white job seekers. During the 1820s and 1830s, for example, race riots broke out against free blacks in New York, Philadelphia, and other cities.

Not surprisingly, many free blacks headed west. Yet, even on the frontier, they met with hostility from white settlers. In Cincinnati, Ohio, racial tension almost led to the total expulsion of many of the city's free blacks in 1829. Nevertheless, westbound African Americans continued to seek the same opportunities enjoyed by white pioneers. ■

■ *Describe the process, as in the 1780 Pennsylvania law, by which slaves in some Northern states were freed.*

REVIEW

1. **FOCUS** How did economic growth in the new nation change family and community life?
2. **CONNECT** Explain why a "republican mother" of the early 1800s would have been a member of the middle class.
3. **CONNECT** How do you think the Embargo Act of 1807 affected the price of American wheat?
4. **CULTURE** Name several of the social and economic problems faced by free blacks before the Civil War.
5. **CRITICAL THINKING** Why did women become more widely seen as "homemakers" in the years between 1790 and 1840? Give evidence to support your answer.
6. **WRITING ACTIVITY** Imagine that you are a great-grandchild of John Abbot's. Make a family tree giving dates and places of birth for all of your relatives. Create any characters and details that you may need for a realistic family tree.

LESSON 2

The Trans-Appalachian Frontier

THINKING FOCUS

What was the sequence of events leading to established, settled communities in the trans-Appalachian frontier?

Key Terms

- migrate
- institution

Buchanan's Station was one of several small settlements on Tennessee's remote Cumberland frontier in 1792. Eight pioneer families, some with slaves, clustered within the high timber walls of its stockade—afraid of yet another Indian attack. They would go out to feed the horses, milk the cows, or work the fields, but always within running distance of the stockade's gates.

Sometime after midnight on September 30, an Indian war party attacked. Within seconds, all 17 men in the settlement were firing from scattered positions along the wooden walls. Through the dust and smoke they could see a ring of hundreds of Chickamauga and Creek warriors. From as little as 10 feet away, Indian bullets and arrows poured into the stockade.

The pioneers fired back, no one even pausing to clean a gun barrel between shots. The yells of Indians and the roar of rifles filled the air. The women huddled in the small log houses, their children under the beds. All except for Sally Ridley Buchanan, wife of the settlement's leader. Nine months pregnant, she raced bravely through the moonlight from defender to defender, passing out bullets and spreading good cheer. All night long she repeated her rounds.

Suddenly, an explosion rocked the air. A spark from a misloaded weapon set off the powder and ammunition stored in a blockhouse, sending flames and bullets down on the startled Indian warriors. The blockhouse explosion took the fight out of the attackers, and they finally retreated shortly after dawn. The siege at Buchanan's Station was over.

➤ *Settling the trans-Appalachian frontier caused conflicts between settlers and American Indians. This engraving shows an attack on a Cumberland Valley settlement.*

People Move Westward for New Opportunities

Reports of conflict with the Indians helped shape Americans' ideas about the trans-Appalachian frontier, the area between the Appalachian Mountains and the Mississippi River. Americans relished the tall tales that glorified the exploits of frontiersmen like Davy Crockett. In real life, a hunter, soldier, scout, and Tennessee congressman, Crockett himself wrote some of the stories on which his reputation was based. He jokingly claimed to be "half horse, half alligator."

Frontier scout Daniel Boone was another living legend. Boone led the first groups of pioneers across the Appalachian Mountains through the Cumberland Gap and into Kentucky. Boone was famous for his knowledge of the American Indians. He had been captured by the Shawnee and had lived for a time as an adopted son of their chief, Blackfish.

Author James Fenimore Cooper modeled Natty Bumppo, the hero of his hugely popular series of novels, *The Leatherstocking Tales*, on Daniel Boone. Also known by the names "Deerslayer," "Hawkeye," and "Pathfinder," Natty dressed like his Indian friends. He wore "a hunting-shirt of forest-green, fringed with faded yellow" and "a summer cap of skins." His moccasins were decorated in the "fashion of the natives," and he wore "a pair of buckskin leggings that laced at the sides."

Readers all over the world admired Cooper's hero. In fact, Natty Bumppo helped inspire thousands to join what Cooper called "that band of pioneers . . . opening the way for the march of the nation across the continent."

Along the Frontier

This westward march rapidly changed the frontier of the United States into settled land. As a result, the nation's population center, that point at which equal numbers of people could be found to the north, south, east, and west, shifted westward. In 1790, the population center of the United States was in Baltimore, Maryland, just 50 miles from the Atlantic Ocean.

Over the next 25 years, two million pioneers moved into two main areas of the trans-Appalachian frontier: the Old Northwest and the southern frontier. By 1820, newly formed states included Ohio, Indiana, and Illinois in the Old Northwest and Alabama, Mississippi, and Louisiana on the southern frontier. By 1860, the country's population center had shifted all the way to Chillicothe, Ohio, 500 miles from the Atlantic.

Why did so many people **migrate**—that is, move great distances—within the United States to take on the uncertain life of the frontier? Most pioneers sought land and better economic opportunity. For

◄ *James Fenimore Cooper's exciting tales encouraged many Americans to try life on the frontier.*

▼ *This powder horn, used to store gun powder, belonged to Daniel Boone, the legendary hunter.*

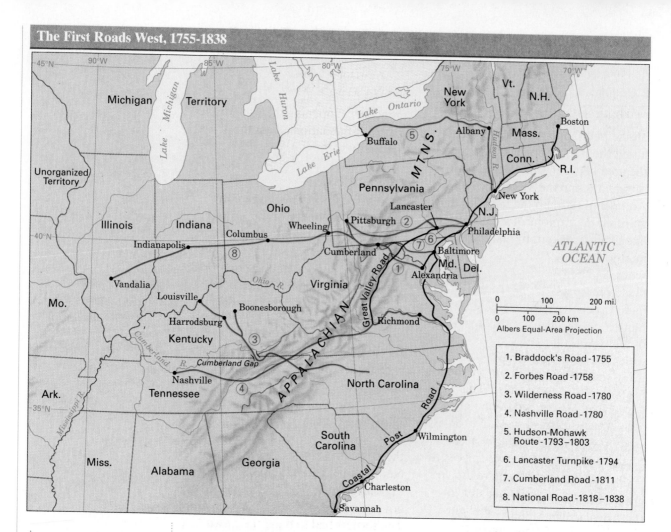

1. Braddock's Road - 1755
2. Forbes Road - 1758
3. Wilderness Road - 1780
4. Nashville Road - 1780
5. Hudson-Mohawk Route - 1793 – 1803
6. Lancaster Turnpike - 1794
7. Cumberland Road - 1811
8. National Road - 1818 – 1838

▲ *The first federally funded road was the stone-paved National Road, begun in 1811. Paid for in irregular installments by Congress, it began in Cumberland, Maryland and eventually ended, in 1830, in Vandalia, Illinois (then the state capital).*

example, New Englanders, like the sons of John Abbot in Lesson 1, left small farms that could not be further divided among family members. And Southern planters migrated west to grow cotton in the rich lower Mississippi River Valley.

Many pioneers such as Colonel Ridley, father of the heroine of the siege at Buchanan's Station, were veterans of the Revolutionary War. Soldiers had often been rewarded with land in Tennessee and Kentucky instead of being paid in cash for their military service.

The pioneers also included many African Americans. Southern planters took tens of thousands of slaves across the Appalachians to hack cotton plantations out of the wilderness. But hundreds of free blacks also migrated, especially into the Old Northwest and beyond the Mississippi into the Far West. There, they farmed or took jobs as cowhands and miners.

Roads to the West

For all Americans, westward overland travel was slow and difficult. At first, pioneers followed narrow pathways across the Appalachian Mountains. Even after roads were built, a full day's journey through dust or mud would cover fewer than 25 miles—as long as there were no rivers to cross. The first east-west roads are shown on the map above.

Many of the early roads were toll roads, built by private investors. Travelers had to stop at toll gates spaced every 6 to 10 miles to pay up to 25 cents per wagon. The first toll road, the Lancaster Turnpike, opened in 1794, between Philadelphia and Lancaster, Pennsylvania. The Lancaster Turnpike was surfaced with stone and gravel. It was the best road of its day. Many "roads," however, were only narrow dirt passages, with tree stumps cut off at 16 inches—just low enough for wagon axles to clear.

198

Chapter 7

Transportation routes were not limited to roads. Canals and rivers carried both settlers and cargo to the West. At first flatboats, which had to have oarsmen, crossed the Mississippi and Ohio rivers. After 1810, the flatboats were being replaced by the first crude steamboats. ■

■ *List four reasons for the migration of Americans into the trans-Appalachian frontier.*

Pioneers Settle the West

The frontier did not remain untamed for long. New settlers set about clearing the land, planting crops, and putting up houses and barns. In their new environment, settlers often had to find different ways to solve old problems.

Mapping and Planning Towns

Since the 1600s, Americans had been using an old surveying method called "metes and bounds." This meant that surveyors described the boundaries of a piece of land in terms of natural landmarks. These were often trees, rivers, and other pieces of property. For example, surveyors in 1784 used a huge black oak and 26 other large trees to define William Few's 887 acres in Georgia. Such boundaries were often unclear. Misunderstandings sometimes led to lawsuits that cost far more than the land itself was worth.

To do away with this confusion in the Northwest Territory, Thomas Jefferson suggested a new system for describing boundaries. Put into use by the Land Ordinance of 1785, this system set boundaries according to the lines of longitude and latitude. These measurements were internationally recognized, but they ignored natural boundaries such as rivers, lakes, and mountains.

Land of the Northwest Territory was divided first into townships, areas that were six miles on each side. Townships were divided into thirty-six square "sections" of 640 acres. Each section was further divided into 320-acre "halves," 160-acre "quarters," and even 40-acre "quarter quarters."

This system gave the Old Northwest square fields and arrow-straight city streets. As seen from above today, this regularity contrasts with the odd lots created by the old "metes and bounds" system.

The township system allowed pioneers to buy government land with clearly defined boundaries. Abraham Lincoln's father, for example, had lost his Kentucky farm in a lawsuit over boundaries. In 1816, the Lincoln family could settle in Indiana with clear borders for their land.

Building Schools and Churches

Establishing boundaries was just the beginning of settling the West. Newly arrived families found no public **institutions**—schools, churches, and governing bodies—waiting for them. The settlers had to build their own social organizations.

One of the first businesses in a new township was often a mill where corn and wheat could be ground into flour. Blacksmiths, wheelwrights, and

How Do We Know?

GEOGRAPHY *Town, county, and state governments have preserved millions of documents that help us understand how earlier Americans divided up the frontier. These documents, which include old maps, surveyors' records, and deeds showing property transfer, are kept in archives.*

▼ *This map shows the survey of lands near Dayton, Ohio, under the Land Ordinance of 1785.*

People of the New Nation

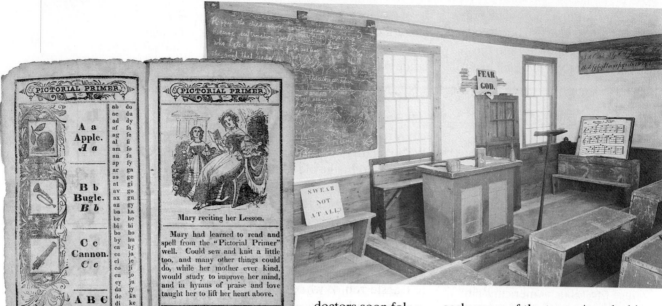

PICTORIAL PRIMER

A a
Apple.
𝒜 a

B b
Bugle.
ℬ b

C c
Cannon.
𝒞 c

A B C

PICTORIAL PRIMER

Mary reciting her Lesson.

Mary had learned to read and spell from the "Pictorial Primer" well. Could sew and knit a little too, and many other things could do, while her mother ever kind, would study to improve her mind, and in hymns of praise and love taught her to lift her heart above.

▲ *According to the Northwest Ordinance of 1787, a parcel of land in every township area was set aside for schools. This 1820 schoolhouse is actually a display from the Smithsonian Institute in Washington, D.C. Students used readers like this American Pictorial Primer in their daily studies.*

■ *How did the township system benefit the pioneers who moved west?*

doctors soon followed, providing important services. Such service businesses were a very important and necessary part of maintaining a community. They answered the many needs of settlers who worked the land.

The Northwest Ordinance of 1787 had set aside pieces of land in the new townships for public education. As soon as schools could be built, frontier children received a basic education in the 3 R's—"reading, 'riting, and 'rithmetic." Few teachers were available in the West, however. Well-known lecturer and writer Catharine Beecher dedicated herself to the goal of sending New England teachers westward. She also devoted her efforts to organizing "female colleges" in Wisconsin and nearby states, to train the teachers needed by the new communities.

Churches grew slowly during the early years of the trans-Appalachian frontier. "Circuit riders"—preachers riding from place to place on horseback—began to appear in small towns. Pioneers also went to "camp meetings," which became important religious and social events. Later, when the population could support a priest or a minister on a more regular basis, these loose congregations became organized churches.

By the 1840s, pioneers had turned the farmlands and forests of the Cherokee, Creek, Pawnee, and Kickapoo into heavily cultivated farms and growing cities. The valleys of the Cumberland, Ohio, and Mississippi rivers now had the same institutions and services that the settlers had known in the East. But there were still opportunities for more settlers, soon to include the next wave of immigrants from Europe. ■

R E V I E W

1. **FOCUS** What was the sequence of events leading to established, settled communities in the trans-Appalachian frontier?

2. **CONNECT** Relate the economic and social changes on the family farm of the early 1800s to the migration of Americans to the frontier.

3. **GEOGRAPHY** Explain how township lines affected the landscape of the Old Northwest, especially in terms of natural boundaries such as forests, mountains, and rivers.

4. **CRITICAL THINKING** Predict how later generations of settlers to the Old Northwest will benefit from the established township system.

5. **WRITING ACTIVITY** Write a news story for radio or TV broadcast about the completion of the Lancaster Turnpike.

LESSON 3

The Changing World of American Indians

*T*he only way to check and stop this evil is for all the red men to unite in claiming a common and equal right in the land . . . for it never was divided, but belongs to all, for the use of each.... No part has a right to sell, even to each other, much less to strangers.

So spoke Shawnee chief Tecumseh (*ti KUM se*) as he condemned and canceled the sale of Indian land to the U.S. government in 1809. Tecumseh had enlisted southern and northern warriors along the Mississippi Valley for a major united effort to recover lands lost to the white people. He was determined to hold the Ohio River as the boundary dividing the United States and Indian country.

As governor of the Indiana Territory, William Henry Harrison was also determined to defend white pioneers who invaded and settled in Indian territories. In 1810, Harrison met the Shawnee leader face to face at Vincennes, Indiana. As their talks began, Harrison's interpreter told Tecumseh, "Your father requests you to take a chair." Angrily Tecumseh replied, "My father! The sun is my father, and the earth is my mother..." Tecumseh spoke forcefully to Harrison of the position of the Indians.

He argued that the U.S. government had no real right to lands ceded, or transferred, to whites without the consent of all American Indians. Tecumseh shouted, "Sell a country! Why not sell the air, the clouds, and the great sea?"

*T*he Great Spirit gave this great island to his red children. He placed the whites on the other side of the big water. They were not contented with their own, but came to take ours from us. They have driven us from the sea to the lakes—we can go no farther."

THINKING FOCUS

What were the different responses of the various American Indian peoples when their ancestral lands were threatened?

Key Terms

- revitalization
- cultural accommodation

◄ *Tecumseh is shown here saving American prisoners during the War of 1812.*

Indian Territories Invaded by the Push Westward

Ever since the first Europeans arrived, whites had gotten land by defeating American Indians. By the 1780s, few of the Indian tribes that had once flourished along the Atlantic seaboard survived. Entire tribal groups had been killed off by war, starvation, and disease.

Farther inland, however, Indian tribes still occupied much of the land. Many wanted to make sure that they would not share the fate of the coastal Indian peoples. The Shawnee, Delaware, Miami, and Potawatomi (*POT a WOT a mee*) of the Old Northwest, for example, formed a confederacy at the time of the Revolutionary War.

Led by Miami chief Little Turtle, the warriors of this powerful alliance raided white settlements on Indian lands. In the late 1780s and early 1790s, they were able to halt white advances. The Indians defeated the territorial militias that marched into their lands.

Then in 1793, President Washington sent federal troops commanded by the Revolutionary War hero General Anthony Wayne. In 1794, at the Battle of Fallen Timbers in what is now northern Ohio, General Wayne defeated Little Turtle's allied warriors. The next year, members of the confederacy were forced to sign the Treaty of Greenville. As a result, the Indians ceded to the United States the south-eastern quarter of the Northwest Territory—about half the present state of Ohio.

Hunger for Land

In the Treaty of Greenville, the United States broke a promise it had made to the Indian peoples only eight years before. The Northwest Ordinance of 1787 had promised security for the Indians in their ancestral lands. But the policy of the U.S. government from the 1790s onward was to recognize the Indian tribes as independent nations. Each "nation" was seen as the sole "owner" of distinct territories. The Indians did not see themselves this way. But this policy enabled the government to obtain land by negotiating treaties with each separate Indian "nation."

And so began a series of treaties whereby the Indian tribes "freely consented" to cede their lands, sometimes receiving only pennies an acre for it. By making treaties, the U.S. government made it seem as though the Indians were voluntarily moving off the land. In fact, many treaties were obtained through the use of fraud and violence. Many treaties were signed by individuals who did not speak for all of the Indians or who had no authority to sign over the land. The U.S. government used any means to force Indian

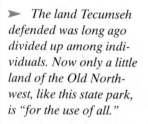

The land Tecumseh defended was long ago divided up among individuals. Now only a little land of the Old Northwest, like this state park, is "for the use of all."

Relocation of Several American Indian Tribes, 1800-1840

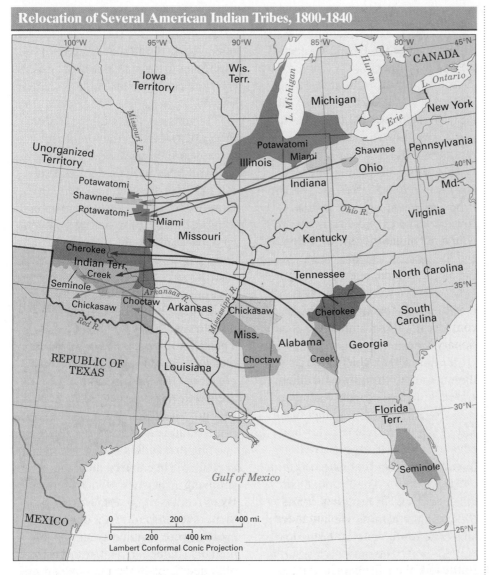

tribes off desirable frontier land onto more distant, less desirable land. "Indian Territory," as it is shown on the map, got smaller and smaller.

After the Treaty of Fort Wayne was signed in 1809, all of the Northwest Territory was legally open to white settlement. Tens of thousands of settlers were now entering yet another environment where Indians had lived for centuries. The ways of the Indians had been closely connected to the plants, the animals, the rivers, and the soil of a particular area. When white settlers cut down many square miles of forest to clear new farmland, they destroyed a way of life. They drove off the game—bear, deer, and buffalo— that had been a major food source for the Indian. Settlement of Indian lands also broke up networks of intertribal trade. But the pioneers did not particularly care what happened to the former inhabitants of the land.

Indian Resistance

Realizing that only drastic measures could save them, many Indian leaders saw the War of 1812 as an opportunity to strike out against the settlers. Along the southern frontier, more than 2,000 militant Creeks, called "Red Sticks," rose up as a unified force of warriors. But in 1814, after months of bloody fighting, General Andrew Jackson finally defeated the Red Sticks in Tennessee. The treaty that ended the conflict brought

▲ These war clubs were used by Tecumseh's warriors in defending their lands.

People of the New Nation

two-thirds of the Creek lands into the United States. The remaining Creeks withdrew to southern and western Alabama.

In the Old Northwest, the alliance led by Shawnee chief Tecumseh and his brother Elskwatawa *(el SKWA ta wa)*, known as "The Prophet," also tried to push back white settlement. In 1811, Governor William Henry Harrison fought a large force of The Prophet's warriors at the Indian stronghold of Tippecanoe *(tip ee ka NOO)*, in Indiana Territory. White losses were much higher than those of the Indians. But Harrison's army managed to burn the village of Tippecanoe, the stronghold of the Indians. Harrison claimed a victory.

Tecumseh sided with the British in the War of 1812. Together their forces scored several dramatic victories. But Tecumseh died in 1813, at the Battle of the Thames *(temz)* in Ontario, Canada. This loss put an end to most Indian resistance in the Old Northwest. ■

■ *Find evidence to support this statement: The U. S. government did not deal fairly when signing land cession treaties with American Indians.*

Various Indian Responses

By the early 1800s, more was at stake for the Indians than ownership of land. Constant pressure from white settlers and the U.S. government threatened their traditional culture and their livelihood. The Indians stood in danger of losing their entire way of life.

Cultural Revival

In his youth, The Prophet had fallen "victim," as he saw it, to the evils of white culture. He had become an alcoholic and had left his people's customs. As a result of the wars and the invasions of the whites, many Indians had left their traditions. But The Prophet recovered from alcoholism. Then he began a movement to bring back the old beliefs and traditional ways of the American Indians. The effort to renew a people's culture is called **revitalization.** The Prophet preached that the Indians would get back their power if they rejected alcohol and other white trading goods and cultural habits.

The Prophet's message was appealing. He converted many among the Shawnee, Potawatomi, and other Indians of the Old Northwest. Many warriors, however, looked instead to his brother Tecumseh for political leadership. But after Tecumseh's death in 1813, Indian unity crumbled and The Prophet's movement dissolved.

Cultural Compromises

Other Indians believed that violent opposition to whites was no solution. The Cherokee, for example, recognized that the white presence in America was permanent. The Cherokee favored **cultural accommodation**, or peaceful compromises, with white society. They tried to combine the best features of both European and Cherokee culture.

Cultural accommodation brought about a remarkable period in Cherokee history. During the early 1800s, many Cherokee gave up hunting to become farmers. Some even became

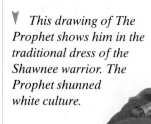

▼ *This drawing of The Prophet shows him in the traditional dress of the Shawnee warrior. The Prophet shunned white culture.*

rich plantation owners with dozens of black slaves. Other Cherokee turned to commerce—managing stores, mills, and other businesses.

At this time, boarding schools run by Christian missionaries taught Cherokee children everything from geography to arithmetic. But the Cherokee educational system took even greater steps forward because of the achievements of Sequoya *(si KWOI a)*, a Cherokee silversmith.

Sequoya saw the advantages whites enjoyed because of their ability to read and write. He set out to make an alphabet for writing the Cherokee language. After years of work, he made an alphabet of 85 symbols that stood for the different syllables of the Cherokee language.

Sequoya's system was easy to learn. In fact, most Cherokee were able to read and write effectively in about a week. The Cherokee also adopted English as a second language. By the 1820s, they had established written laws and a democratic constitution. They founded their own newspaper, the *Cherokee Phoenix*. The *Cherokee Phoenix* printed every article in Cherokee and English, side by side.

Cherokee leadership was especially strong during this period. The tribal and central councils were run by strong, able leaders like John and Lewis Ross, who helped govern the Cherokee people for almost forty years. ■

▲ *Sequoya is shown here with his alphabet. Note that his clothes are like those of the white settlers of the time.*

■ *Compare and contrast the attitudes of The Prophet and Sequoya toward American society.*

Defeat of the Cherokee

The Cherokee's success stirred up resentment among their white neighbors. The Cherokee adopted their constitution in 1827. Whites saw that the Cherokee were using their status as an independent nation to improve their situation.

Legal Battle over Removal

White settlers on the southern frontier hungered for the Cherokee lands. Not by coincidence, white demands for the removal of the Cherokee increased when gold was discovered on their lands.

Arguments went on for years, as did lawsuits. In time, some groups of Cherokee were pressured to give up their land and to move west. Others, under the leadership of John Ross, would not leave. They took their case all the way to the Supreme Court. Finally, in the 1832 case of *Worcester* v. *Georgia*, the Cherokee seemed to win. Chief Justice John Marshall recognized the right of the Cherokee people to their own nation and laws.

The victory, however, was hollow. Georgia, with the support of President Andrew Jackson, ignored Marshall and the Court. Other states joined Georgia in calling for the final removal of the remaining Cherokee from the southern frontier.

A Cherokee Mother and Son

1:37 P.M. December 15, 1838
Along the Trail of Tears, on a frozen dirt path
outside Greenville, Missouri

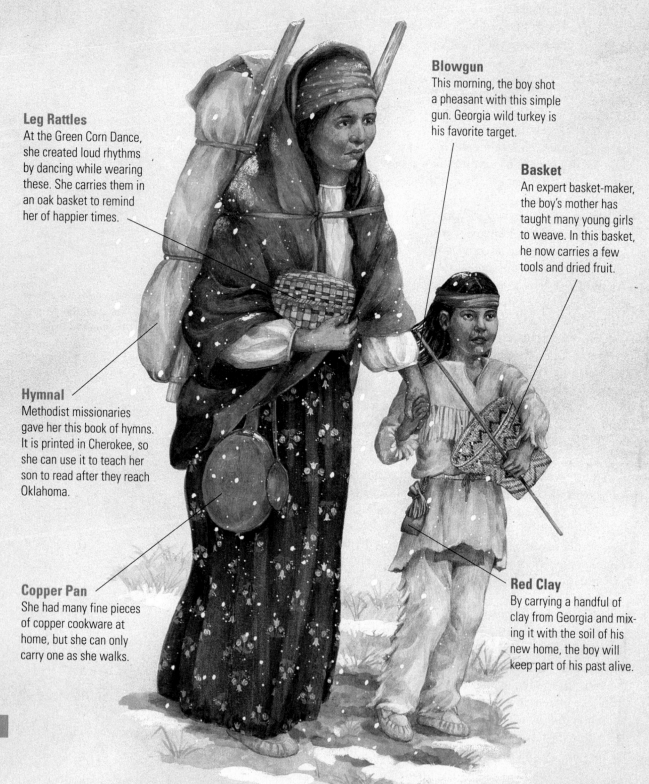

Leg Rattles
At the Green Corn Dance, she created loud rhythms by dancing while wearing these. She carries them in an oak basket to remind her of happier times.

Blowgun
This morning, the boy shot a pheasant with this simple gun. Georgia wild turkey is his favorite target.

Basket
An expert basket-maker, the boy's mother has taught many young girls to weave. In this basket, he now carries a few tools and dried fruit.

Hymnal
Methodist missionaries gave her this book of hymns. It is printed in Cherokee, so she can use it to teach her son to read after they reach Oklahoma.

Copper Pan
She had many fine pieces of copper cookware at home, but she can only carry one as she walks.

Red Clay
By carrying a handful of clay from Georgia and mixing it with the soil of his new home, the boy will keep part of his past alive.

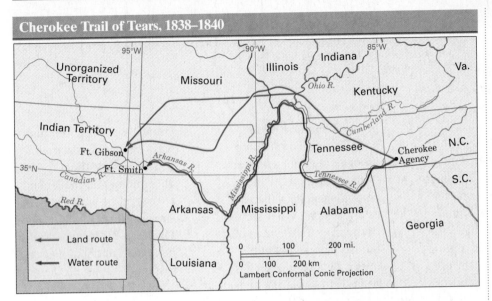

Cherokee Trail of Tears, 1838–1840

95°W 90°W 85°W

Unorganized Territory

Missouri

Illinois Indiana

Ohio R. Kentucky Va.

Indian Territory

Ft. Gibson Arkansas R. Cumberland R.

35°N Ft. Smith Canadian R. Tennessee Cherokee Agency N.C.

Red R. Tennessee R. S.C.

Arkansas Mississippi Alabama

Louisiana Georgia

→ Land route
→ Water route

0   100   200 mi.
0   100   200 km
Lambert Conformal Conic Projection

◄ *A rich civilization all but died on the 600-mile Trail of Tears. Most Cherokee were moved over land. Others went by flatboat along rivers.*

A minority party of Cherokee, led by Major Ridge and his son John, gave in to white harassment. They finally signed a treaty giving up all rights to their land in 1835.

The Trail of Tears

Many Cherokee continued to resist removal even after this treaty was signed. President Martin Van Buren finally gave the order in 1838 to round up the Cherokee, at the point of a gun or a bayonet if need be. "The Cherokees are nearly all prisoners," one Baptist minister reported. "They have been dragged from their houses and encamped at the forts and military posts."

The U.S. Army moved over 15,000 Cherokee west during the winter of 1838–1839. More than 4,000 people died on what came to be known as the "Trail of Tears." The lands of what had been the remarkable Cherokee nation became the property of whites. Only a few scattered groups of Indian peoples, including the Seminoles of Florida, remained. Despite orders to treat the Cherokee humanely, they went without adequate clothing, shelter, or food. An Army private recalled the trail:

> *T*he trail of the exiles was a trail of death. They had to sleep in the wagons and on the ground without fire. I have known as many as 22 of them to die in one night of pneumonia due to ill treatment, cold, and exposure.

The fate of the Cherokee suggested that there was little hope for the survival of Indian culture. No matter how they chose to approach the whites—with revitalization, resistance, or accommodation—Indians would eventually be overwhelmed by the white settlers flooding the West. ■

Across Time & Space

The United States has broken hundreds of treaties with American Indians. In 1946, the government set up the Indian Claims Commission. It heard and decided over 500 Indian claims against the United States for fraud and unfair treatment. Since 1978, the United States Claims Court has handled these claims. American Indians continue to fight for their legal rights.

■ *How was the Cherokee civilization finally destroyed?*

REVIEW

1. **FOCUS** What were the different responses of the various American Indian peoples when their ancestral lands were threatened?
2. **CONNECT** How did the U.S. policy toward American Indians from the 1790s onward differ from the policy of the British colonial governments? How were the Indians affected by this difference?
3. **CULTURE** What did the Cherokee lose or leave behind in western Georgia at the time of their removal?
4. **CRITICAL THINKING** Do you think that the possibility ever existed for the settlers and the American Indians to coexist peacefully? Explain your answer.
5. **ACTIVITY** Make a time line, beginning in 1827, that charts the events leading to the Trail of Tears.

Designing a City Map

Here's Why

You have already seen how maps play an important role in relating the history of an area to the actual land. In this chapter you have read that the Land Ordinance of 1785 changed the way cities were planned and mapped in the Old Northwest.

Knowing how to draw your own map can be useful for many purposes. You can present information about an area you know, show the distances between places, provide directions for someone else, illustrate a certain point in a report, or enhance the understanding of a project.

Suppose you wanted to draw a map of a city, like the port city shown on the facing page. First you would need to know what makes a successful map.

Here's How

You need to consider several steps in order to make an effective map.

1. **Scale**—In designing a map, scale is one of the most important things you need to consider. You must first decide the exact area you wish to show on the map, what size the map should be, and what information you need to include. The answers to these questions will help you determine the scale of the map. The smaller the area shown, the larger the scale.

2. **Orientation**—You need to place a compass on the map. The person reading the map may not know any of the places on the map. A compass will help the reader understand the direction of the map. In the map on the next page, you will notice that a compass has been included in the lower right-hand corner, so that you can see which direction is north.

3. **Labels**—You need to label the places, streets, land masses, waterways, countries, and cities, so that the person reading the map understands what is being shown. For example, notice in the port city map that the streets running northwest to southeast are numbered and that the streets running perpendicular to them are named.

4. **Symbols**—It is important to choose symbols that are easily understood. You can choose symbols that are direct representations like the lighthouse in the port city map. You can also choose ones that are more symbolic like the dollar sign representing the bank.

   Many symbols can change from one map to another. For example, a black dot may indicate a city on one map and an oil refinery on another. Therefore it is also important to draw a legend that includes all the symbols used on the map. On the port city map you will see that both highways and railroads are lines. It is necessary, then, to look at the colors on the legend to determine which is being shown.

5. **Distance**—It is important to be able to understand the distances between places on a map. So that these distances can be measured on your map, you need to include a scale. When you look at the port city map, you will see that the scale has been included in the lower right-hand corner. It shows that one-half mile in the city is represented by one inch on a ruler. Using a ruler, you will see that the distance between the center of the market and the city hall is two inches, or one mile.

Finally, it is important to be accurate when you use all of the above criteria to make your map. If you choose an appropriate scale for the area shown, orient your reader with a compass, give labels that are correct and easy to read, place your symbols accurately, and draw a correct scale for measuring distance, you will create a successful map.

Try It

Trace the map on the next page on another piece of paper. First choose names for the town and the bodies of water, and label them where they will be easy to read. Using the symbols

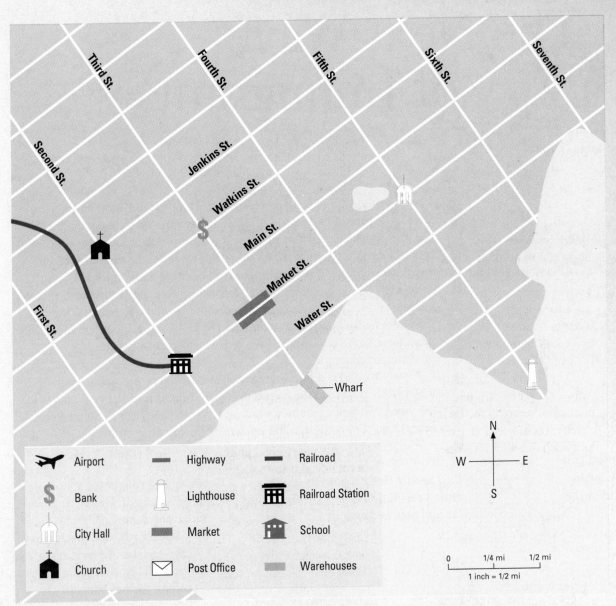

Legend

✈	Airport	▬	Highway	▬	Railroad
$	Bank	🗼	Lighthouse	🏛	Railroad Station
🏛	City Hall	▬	Market	🏫	School
✝	Church	✉	Post Office	▬	Warehouses

N
W — E
S

0   1/4 mi   1/2 mi
1 inch = 1/2 mi

provided, add a school on Jenkins Street three-quarters of a mile from the church. Include an industrial section with warehouses, and have it take up most of the city block three-quarters to one mile northwest of the lighthouse between Fourth and Fifth Streets. Add an airport on Main Street two miles east of the intersection of Main and Third Street, and include a major highway that intersects with the airport. Choose a partner to work with, and decide what other places of interest should be included on the map. Have your partner give you directions about where these new places are, and add those places on the map. Remember to design appropriate symbols and to include them in your legend.

Apply It

Suppose you want to give directions to your house to a friend who has never been to your town. Make a map of your neighborhood using the steps outlined on the previous page. Exchange your map with a friend or classmate, and have them take a trip to your house by following your map to see if you have created a successful map.

L E S S O N   4

The Next Wave of Immigrants

THINKING FOCUS

What experiences characterized German and Irish immigration to the United States in the 1840s and 1850s?

Key Terms

- emigrate
- famine
- nativism

*O*n the 17th of September, 1852, my young wife and I entered the harbor of New York. . . . Having determined to make the United States my permanent home, I was resolved to look at everything from the brightest side, and not to permit myself to be discouraged by any disappointment. . . I remember well our first walk to see the town: —the very bustle on the principal streets; the men, old and young, mostly looking serious and preoccupied, and moving on with energetic rapidity; the women also appearing sober-minded and busy, although many of them were clothed in loud colors, red, green, yellow, or blue of a very pronounced glare.

We observed huge banners stretched across the street, upon which were inscribed the names of . . . candidates for the presidency and the vice-presidency—names which at that time had, to me, no meaning, except that they indicated the existence of competing political parties.

Carl Schurz, *The Reminiscences of Carl Schurz*

Carl Schurz fled his native Germany after a revolution there failed in 1849. He and other educated Germans had fought for a more democratic government. Defeated, many sailed for America.

Schurz adjusted quickly to American society, farming in Wisconsin and learning English by reading the newspapers. By 1858, Schurz had left farming to practice law. His legal knowledge impressed many of the more established Wisconsin politicians in the Republican Party. In 1861, Schurz was appointed ambassador to Spain by President Lincoln. Later he served as a senator from Missouri and as secretary of the interior in the administration of President Rutherford B. Hayes.

➤ *Carl Schurz and his wife, Margaretha Meyer Schurz, in 1852. Margaretha established the first kindergarten in the United States.*

A New Generation of Europeans Arrives

During the 1820s, some 500,000 people arrived in the United States from Germany, Ireland, and other countries. But that number grew quickly. In the 1850s, 2.7 million people would **emigrate** from European countries. They left their homelands forever, to live in the United States. Like Schurz, many Germans who arrived after 1849 were running from the political turmoil of a failed revolution. But for the Irish, it was **famine,** a devastating food shortage, that drove them from their homeland.

While the situations in Germany and Ireland served to push people out of Europe, many also came because of what the United States had to offer. In America, as in few other places, people participated in their own government. There was plenty of land here and it was relatively easy to get. The discovery of gold in California in 1849 drew those who looked for riches. The rise of manufacturing promised the immigrants—the new arrivals—jobs and hope for a better life.

Germans Seek Democracy

By the mid-1800s, German intellectuals had lost patience with slow political reform in their country. Several years of bad crops and rising unemployment also caused great dissatisfaction. The intellectuals wanted a more democratic government, with representation for all Germans. But in 1849 their attempt to write a new constitution was put down. Government officials had rebels imprisoned, and soon afterward the "Parliament of Professors"—educated reformers—broke up. Intellectuals were not the only ones left discouraged. German tradespeople were not doing well because of competition from Great Britain's growing factory system.

The United States, especially the farmlands of the Midwest and the Great Plains, offered these immigrants

political freedom and the chance for economic independence. Selling their belongings and withdrawing their savings, they set sail for the United States.

Irish Flee Potato Famine

Economic conditions in Ireland had been getting worse for generations. It was not unusual for a person to live on a diet of half a dozen potatoes and a cup of milk each day. Sadly, this situation grew even more desperate. A destructive blight, or plant disease, struck the Irish potato fields in the 1840s and 1850s. The blight wiped out nearly the whole potato crop. In 1847, the Irish government sent agents into the countryside. One of them reported, "All I met told me they were going to give up the land, for they had neither food nor strength to till it."

With the mainstay of the Irish diet destroyed, hundreds of people died each month

This print, titled Helpless Mouths, *shows the conditions that caused many Irish people to come to America.*

The potato blight struck first at the plant below ground. The blight caused a major food shortage in Ireland in 1847.

211

from starvation and disease. Families barely survived in houses like the one Liam O'Flaherty described in his novel *Famine:*

> *T*he living-room was in a very sordid state, which was only natural on account of all those children romping about in a chamber that was only ten feet by eight, with a great deal of that space occupied by the furniture, cooking utensils, and farming tools. There was even some oat straw and a little heap of potatoes, all that was left of the year's crop.

Millions left Ireland, going anywhere that offered a chance for a better life. Over 1.5 million came to the United States.

Most Irish immigrants were poor tenant farmers and unskilled laborers. Since they had no land of their own to sell, most were not able to pay for their passage. But money came from relief organizations, relatives, and even local Irish governments. Some officials encouraged the poor to emigrate. This took some of the strain off public welfare budgets.

Immigrants Suffer En Route

No matter where they came from, most immigrants had a horrifying experience during their passage to the New World. A more prosperous passenger observed that the Irish people aboard his westbound ship were "full of wretchedness. Need and oppression stared within their eyes; upon their backs hung ragged misery. The world was not their friend."

They sailed in vessels known to people of the time as "plague ships" and "floating coffins." The trip could last three or four months. Hundreds of people crowded between the decks, and diseases spread rapidly. As of 1845, 20 percent of all those immigrating to America died during the voyage. One ship lost over 500 of the 1,100 German immigrants on board. ■

■ *What kind of hardships drive people from Europe to the United States?*

Immigrants Establish Themselves in the New Country

What awaited these immigrants when they finally stepped ashore? Their experiences would depend entirely on their individual situations.

Many Germans had worked in the old country as artisans or skilled laborers. They came to the United States with some savings and a valuable skill. In Germany, one's status was measured by the size of one's land holdings. Thus, many newly arrived Germans were eager to earn money quickly in order to buy land on the American frontier. Communities of

➤ *German immigrants tended to form close communities in their new home. In this 1856 drawing, German newcomers enjoy a Christmas gathering in an elegant New York building known as the Winter Garden.*

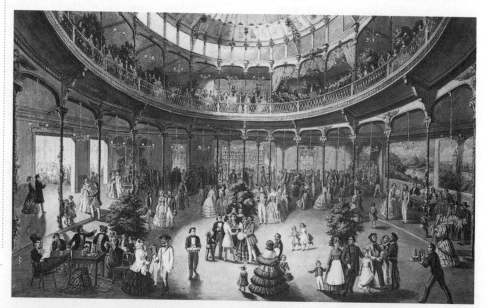

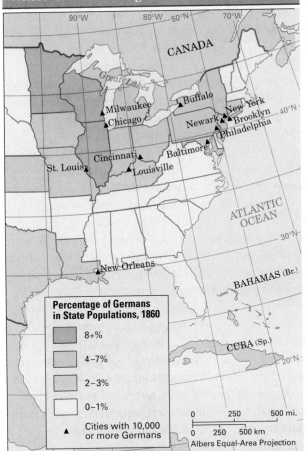

Where German Immigrants Settled, 1860

Percentage of Germans in State Populations, 1860
- 8+%
- 4–7%
- 2–3%
- 0–1%
- ▲ Cities with 10,000 or more Germans

0 250 500 mi.
0 250 500 km
Albers Equal-Area Projection

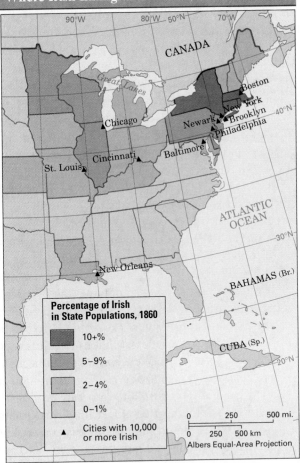

Where Irish Immigrants Settled, 1860

Percentage of Irish in State Populations, 1860
- 10+%
- 5–9%
- 2–4%
- 0–1%
- ▲ Cities with 10,000 or more Irish

0 250 500 mi.
0 250 500 km
Albers Equal-Area Projection

German immigrants grew in the seaport cities of the Northeast and in the midwestern cities of Cincinnati, St. Louis, Milwaukee, and Chicago.

Some immigrants already had cash from sales of their farms in Germany. They settled in the fertile countryside of Illinois, Michigan, Wisconsin, and the Great Plains.

For the most part, German immigrants were able to achieve a secure livelihood for themselves and their children. Though they sometimes met resentment from native-born Americans, they had little trouble with their neighbors.

The Irish, however, often had a far different experience. Penniless and unskilled, most Irish immigrants could not afford the cost of moving to the frontier of the United States. Compare the distribution of Irish and German immigrants in the two maps above.

The Irish immigrants often had to take whatever jobs they could find. Men collected rubbish, dug ditches and cellars, and labored in the building of canals and railroads. Women worked as cooks, laundresses, and servants. The housing they could afford was usually crowded and unhealthy. With hard work, Irish immigrants eventually gained some stability. ■

▲ *German immigrants tended to settle where good farm land was available. Generally, they stayed together as families. Irish immigrants tended to cluster in cities.*

■ *Why did most Germans find it easier to establish themselves in America than did most Irish?*

New Americans Perceived as a Threat

The new immigrants had arrived with high hopes. Many native-born Americans accepted the immigrants and helped them adjust to American society. But a backlash of fear and resentment also developed.

The same Americans who found the Irish useful as cheap labor feared that the immigrants would take away their own jobs. Others worried that voting immigrants might become a powerful and dangerous political force.

213

People of the New Nation

*I*n 1800, the population of Ohio was 45,365 people; in 1810, it was 230,760. The population of the state had expanded to more than five times its size in only 10 years. The reason for the state's enormous growth in such a short time are many, and included both emigration from the east coast and immigration from other countries.

You might find the similarity of these terms confusing. The general term *migration* refers to any permanent movement of people from one country or region to settle in another. *Emigration* is the act of moving away from one's country or region to another (*e* means "out"). *Immigration* means entering or settling in a new country other than one's own (*im* means "in"). Thus newcomers to this country are always both emigrants (for example, from Ireland) and immigrants (into the United States).

Of course, everyone in the United States is a descendant of someone who once immigrated here. Only American Indians, Inuits, and Hawaiians are considered natives of this country.

Reasons for Immigration

Scholars who study migration movements worldwide speak of the "push-pull factors." What they mean is that sometimes the "push factor," such as the failure of the Irish potato crop in 1847, is a major cause of emigration. At other times, the "pull factor," such as the lure of gold in California in 1849, is the main reason for immigration. More frequently, the reasons are multiple, and are a combination of push and pull.

When reviewing the history of immigration to the United States, the push-pull factor is a useful tool of analysis. For example, the Quakers who left England and Europe in the 1660s were fleeing from religious and political persecution in their homelands. At the same time, they were pulled to the New World by the hope of achieving religious and political freedom here.

To economic, religious, and political reasons for immigration must be added a fourth factor—the forced immigration up until 1808 of Africans as slaves. The Africans had no choice in selecting whether to stay or to immigrate, so the push-pull factor could not be said to work for them.

Immigration Today

The same push-pull factors can be applied to many foreigners who seek refuge in the United States today. The Jews and Pentecostal Christians who have left the Soviet Union for the United States exemplify the push-pull of religious persecution and opportunity. The displaced peoples of East Asia and of Central America come because of political persecution at home and hope for political freedom here.

After one year's residence, refugees may change their status to that of permanent residents, which is a necessary first step toward naturalization, or becoming a citizen. In 1988, 110,721 refugees adjusted their status to permanent residents.

This unusually high number was a result of changes in the immigration law that took effect during this period.

The economic and political reasons for entering a rich democracy such as the United States have been so compelling that millions have immigrated to this country illegally. As a corrective to this, and as a first step toward remedying its immigration programs, Congress passed in 1986 an Immigration Reform and Control Act.

The IRCA allowed for legal registration of aliens who had resided here continuously since before January 1, 1982. This amnesty, or pardon for illegal entrance, combined with the usual annual acceptance of refugees, pushed up the number of immigrants during the 1980s to a new high.

Destinations of Immigrants

The largest number of 1988 immigrants came to join family members who already lived in the United States. This tradition has existed in America since its earliest days of settlement.

Most immigrants, in the past as well as today, headed for the large urban centers. In the cities, immigrants can attach themselves to communities of people who share the same ethnic background. Still ahead is another decision—do the new immigrants take shelter with those who speak the same languages and eat the same foods, or do they let go of the ethnic identities they once had to begin the long, slow process of becoming American?

Anti-Catholic Feelings

America was at that time a nation of Protestants. The Irish, who were Catholics, were widely feared and hated because of their strong ties to the Pope. Protestants feared that the Pope would gain political power in America through his Irish Catholic supporters. These feelings led to signs reading "No Irish Need Apply." Even worse, in some cities mobs attacked Catholic churches and schools.

This rise of strong feelings against immigrants formed part of a social movement called **nativism**. In this movement, established, native-born Americans glorified their own culture and condemned immigrant cultures. A number of societies whose aim was to control the new immigrants began to form. In the Northeast, the Native American Association was founded in 1837. It grew into the Native American Party, which gathered political support in the West and South by 1845.

Several of these societies united to form the Supreme Order of the Star Spangled Banner in 1850 and the American Party in 1854. Even though members of these groups met openly, all the proceedings were conducted under strict rules of secrecy. These societies had a number of undemocratic goals. They wanted to ban Catholics and aliens from elected office, to cut down on immigration, and to establish requirements that would limit immigrants' voting rights. Clearly, some Americans felt very threatened by the arrival of new people from foreign lands.

The Know-Nothings

Members of the American Party were called "Know-Nothings" because they answered "I don't know" when asked about their policies. The Know-

Nothings influenced elections for several years. At one point, they even managed to control the Massachusetts government. But they remained weak in the West and never became a truly national political force.

By the late 1850s, the influence of the Know-Nothings was no longer very strong. The party's public image, it seemed, was hurt by its intense secrecy and hatred. The conflicts between native-born Americans and immigrants, between the East and the frontier, and between Indians and whites were being overshadowed by the great division between the Northern and Southern regions. ■

▲ *The Irish gradually overcame the troubles they found in America. This picture shows a lively St. Patrick's Day parade in New York City, a tradition that continues today.*

■ *Why did some Americans feel economically and politically threatened by the large immigrant population?*

R E V I E W

1. **FOCUS** What experiences characterized German and Irish immigration to the United States in the 1840s and 1850s?

2. **CONNECT** How was the social and economic position of Irish immigrants similar to that of free blacks?

3. **CRITICAL THINKING** Why might a German craftsman have been better off settling on the frontier than in Boston, New York, or Charleston?

4. **CULTURE** What advantages might immigrants gain by forming communities of their own? What might be the disadvantages?

5. **ACTIVITY** Prepare an oral report on an immigrant who has made important contributions to American society. Explain when and why the person came to the United States. Describe his or her achievements. Why was it possible for this person to succeed in the United States?

Chapter Review

Reviewing Key Terms

cultural accommodation (p. 204)
emigrate (p. 211)
famine (p. 211)
institutions (p. 199)
middle class (p. 192)

migrate p. 197)
nativism (p. 215)
revitalization (p. 204)
working class (p. 192)

A. In each of the following pairs, the two terms are related in some way. Write a sentence for each pair that clearly explains the relationship between the two terms.
1. institutions, working class
2. migrate, emigrate
3. revitalization, cultural accommodation
4. famine, emigrate

B. Based on your reading of the chapter, decide which of the following statements are accurate. Write an explanation of each decision.
1. Some settlers floated down the Mississippi in large institutions.
2. On the frontier, the settlers had to establish their own public institutions.
3. People of the working class were those in between the Republican and Democratic parties.
4. When crops fail because of bad weather, a famine sometimes results.
5. People who believed in nativism supported the rights of American Indians.

Exploring Concepts

A. On a separate sheet of paper, make a chart like the one shown below. Then complete the chart by listing examples from the chapter that show where members of each group moved during the early 1800s and why they moved.

Group	Moved to	Reason
Young Eastern farmers		
Free blacks		
Creek Indians		
Cherokee Indians		
German immigrants		
Irish immigrants		

B. Support each of the following statements with facts and details from the chapter.
1. Population growth and wars in Europe had many effects on the United States economy.
2. New inventions contributed to changes in the United States' economy during the 1800s.
3. Women's roles at home and in society underwent great changes during the 1800s.
4. Free blacks who moved to the cities started to develop their own institutions.
5. Many factors attracted great numbers of settlers to the land across the Appalachians.
6. The United States government followed a policy of forcing Indians off their lands to make room for settlers.
7. No matter what policy the Indians followed, they were treated unfairly by the United States.
8. Immigrants' experiences in the United States were shaped by their cultural traditions and education level.
9. Westward overland travel was very difficult for the pioneers because roads were not well-constructed.

Reviewing Skills

1. Name five important elements in mapmaking.
2. Look at a map of your state in an atlas. Identify the symbols that are used in the map, such as the symbols for railroads, rivers, and cities.
3. Select a map from this book and study it carefully. Then choose a partner and give that person directions that would enable him or her to draw the map that you have studied
4. What kind of primary sources did the early cartographers use to design maps of the far west?
5. Today pictures can be taken of the earth from satellites. How is that information helpful in designing maps?

Using Critical Thinking

1. Throughout American history, people have always migrated to other areas where opportunities were greater. What effect did the migrations you read about in this chapter have on the nation? What areas of the country have people migrated to, and away from, in recent years? Are their reasons for migrating today similar to those in the past? Explain.
2. It is quite possible that within your lifetime certain areas of the United States could become as densely populated as Europe is now. What areas of the country attract the most immigrants today? Why? Do you think our government's policy toward immigrants will change? If so, explain what kinds of changes might take place and why the government might enact them.
3. The United States' treatment of the Indians is one of the most shameful episodes in American history. What differences between the white and Indian ways of life caused conflict? Why was the United States government unsympathetic to the Indians? Do you think that if the Indians had been able to keep the lands on which they lived, they would have become part of American society as the immigrants did? Explain your answer.

Preparing for Citizenship

1. **WRITING ACTIVITY** Immigrants still come to the United States from all over the world. With a partner, gather information about current immigration from one country of your own choosing. Find out why the people are leaving their home country, why they chose the U.S. as their new home, what region of the U.S. they are settling in and why, and what kinds of jobs they are doing. Write a short report on your findings.
2. **COLLECTING INFORMATION** Interview three adults about your local community's policies toward immigrants. In your interview, ask your subjects to tell you what the policies are, as well as their own opinion of how those policies are working. Compare their responses with those of Americans of the 1850s. Do you see any similarities or differences? What are they?
3. **ART ACTIVITY** Make a copy of the family tree below. Enter the names and places of birth for your parents and grandparents. You may add onto the tree to go back further in your family history if you would like. Share your family tree with your classmates.

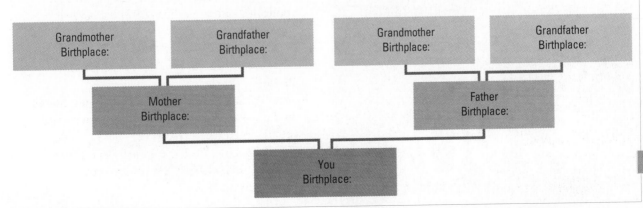

Grandmother Birthplace: Grandfather Birthplace: Grandmother Birthplace: Grandfather Birthplace:

Mother Birthplace: Father Birthplace:

You Birthplace:

Unit 4

The Development of America's Regions

The first half of the 1800s was a time of rapid expansion for the United States. The nation moved westward and acquired vast new territories. The economy grew as the nation became more industrialized. Rapid development of new roads, canals, and railroads produced a complex transportation network. As America grew, the nation's major regions developed as well. By 1860, the American West, North, and South each had its own special identity.

1790

Antique weathervanes from the 1800s.
The Shelburne Museum, Shelburne, Vermont.

1860

Chapter 8

The West

By 1850, the nation had pushed its boundaries to the shores of the Pacific Ocean. Explorers, eager to learn about the new land, crisscrossed unknown mountains and deserts. In their footsteps went daring men and women who built communities out of the wilderness.

Lieutenant Zebulon Pike ventures into the uncharted territory. Pike's Peak in Colorado is named after this brave explorer.

1804 William Clark's compass helps point the way on his journeys with Meriwether Lewis to explore the newly acquired lands west of the Mississippi River.

1790	1800	1810	1820

Presidents

1789-1797 Washington

1797-1801 J. Adams

1801-1809 Jefferson

1809-1817 Madison

1817-1825 Monroe

1790

The majesty of the western landscape dominated the people who challenged it. This painting by Albert Bierstadt shows the vastness of the Sierra Nevada mountain range in California.

1848 Explorer John Charles Frémont's expeditions supplied information and valuable maps. This map shows Oregon and northern California.

1830

1840

1850

1825-1829
J. Q. Adams

1829-1837
Jackson

1837-1841
Van Buren

1841-1845
Tyler

1841
W. Harrison

1845-1849
Polk

1849-1850
Taylor

1850-1853
Fillmore

1853-1857
Pierce

1857-1861
Buchanan

1860

LESSON 1

Exploring Beyond the Mississippi

Why did the U.S. government call for exploration west of the Mississippi?

Key Terms

- mountain man
- rendezvous
- continental divide
- Manifest Destiny

➤ *Many statues exist of Sacajawea (right), who carried her baby son Jean Baptiste all the way to the Pacific and back on the Lewis and Clark expedition. She lived only a few years after the expedition ended. Jean Baptiste became a fur trapper and gold miner.*

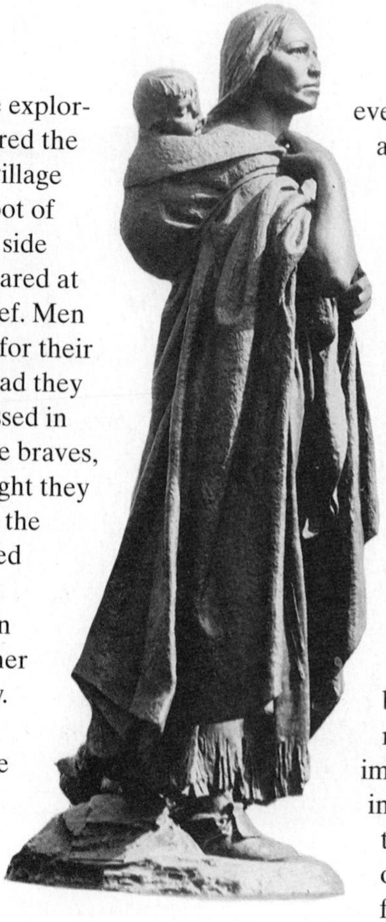

Warily the explorers entered the Indian village at the foot of the Rockies. On every side women and children stared at the strangers in disbelief. Men muttered and reached for their knives. Never before had they seen such people. Dressed in deerskin like the village braves, the men had skins so light they must have "come from the clouds." The air vibrated with tension.

Then a small Indian woman appeared. On her back she carried a baby. A sigh of relief swept through the village. The woman's presence signaled that the strangers were not hostile. No enemy war party ever traveled with women and children.

The explorers were Lewis and Clark. The Indian woman was Sacajawea *(sak uh juh WE uh)*. Then probably 16 years old, she was part of the Corps of Discovery that made its way west to the Pacific Ocean between 1804 and 1805. On the way, Sacajawea was reunited with her own people, the Shoshone, from whom she had been captured during a raid. She played an important role as an interpreter. Without her, the historic expedition of discovery might have failed.

The United States Expands

Sacajawea's Shoshone were among the many American Indian tribes that lived west of the Mississippi. As the map shows, part of this western land was known as the Louisiana Territory. President Jefferson was convinced this area was vital to the nation. He predicted that one day it would yield much of the nation's farm produce and "contain more than half of our whole population."

Jefferson believed that the independent farmer was the backbone of the United States. Since farmers needed land and the population was doubling every 25 years, territorial growth seemed a natural goal for the nation. In fact, the U.S. frontier had been moving westward ever since colonial times. Some foresaw the day when the republic would stretch from the Atlantic Ocean to the Pacific.

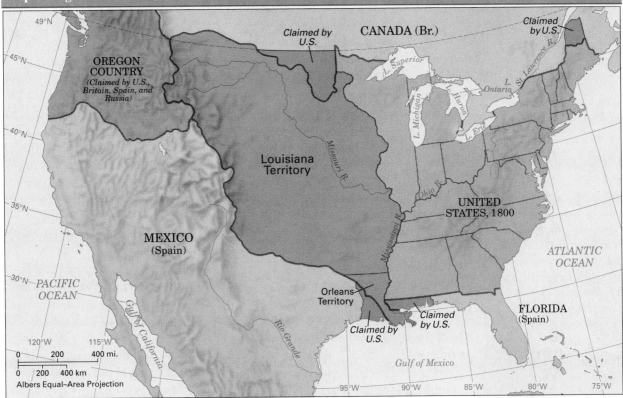

The western frontier in 1800 was east of the Mississippi River, although these lands were quickly settled in the next few years. By 1850 the United States had acquired enormous territory west of this river.

Preparing for Exploration

In 1803, Napoleon, France's powerful emperor, sold the Louisiana Territory to the United States for $15 million (Chapter 5). This acquisition protected the Western farmers who shipped their products down the Mississippi River to the port of New Orleans. It made sure that the port would remain open for commerce. The purchase also removed the threat of a powerful nation—France—that might stand in the way of U.S. expansion. Although the lands west of the Louisiana Territory were claimed by Spain, that country was weak and posed little threat to the United States. Finally, the purchase of the Louisiana Territory gave the United States vast new lands to explore.

Jefferson promptly called for an expedition to explore the new lands.

He chose as its leader his private secretary and friend, Captain Meriwether Lewis, then on leave from his military duties. The 29-year-old Lewis was well educated, resourceful, and skilled at living in the wilderness, but he was subject to swift changes of mood. In contrast, William Clark, the co-leader that Lewis chose, was even-tempered. He was the youngest brother of George Rogers Clark, who had helped the United States acquire the territory known as the Old Northwest.

Jefferson gave Lewis detailed instructions about the goals of the expedition. Its main object was to explore the Missouri River and the smaller rivers that flowed into it. Jefferson hoped that one of these rivers reached the Pacific Ocean. He was looking for "the most direct & practicable water communication across this continent, for the purposes of commerce." The all-water route he sought was the fabled Northwest Passage that explorers had been seeking since the discovery of America.

Jefferson also instructed Lewis and Clark to make accurate maps and

Compare this map with the modern political map of the United States in the Atlas, pages 698–699. In 1810, what foreign nations held or claimed territory in what is now the United States?

223

The West

■ *What instructions did Jefferson give Lewis and Clark?*

detailed observations about the region's geography, climate, plants, and animals. They were also to record every detail that could be learned about the native peoples. By having the explorers treat the Indians with respect, Jefferson hoped to make ties that could be used to promote trade. ■

Lewis and Clark Explore the West

On May 14, 1804, the expedition of 44 men pushed their boats into the Missouri River where it met the Mississippi in St. Louis. They were setting off for the unknown. Lewis, who had studied botany, anatomy, medicine, and zoology to prepare for the journey, took charge of scientific discoveries. Clark acted as mapmaker, navigator, and journalist. Although an erratic speller, Clark kept meticulous records, as Jefferson had instructed.

Across the Plains

As the explorers pushed their boats into the waters of the Missouri, they had little idea of what lay ahead. How far south did the Rocky Mountains extend? Did the Pacific coast lie just a hundred miles west of the Missouri's source, as rumor said it did?

The explorers used the river to cross the nearly treeless Great Plains, which seemed to stretch endlessly before them. The men had few complaints, observed Clark, except "the Ticks & Musquiters are very troublesome." To drive away the pests, the explorers rubbed their bodies with cooking grease.

When the explorers met Indians, they presented items from their store of gifts—calico shirts, razors, colored glass beads, American flags, small hand mirrors, and medals. Jefferson had ordered that the medals be given to chiefs as a sign of peace, and the chiefs valued them highly.

Toward the end of October, the expedition reached the walled villages of the Mandan tribe in what is now North Dakota. Planning to stay the winter, they built a log structure and named it Fort Mandan. In preparation for the next spring, they hired the fur trader Toussaint Charbonneau *(too SAN shar bon NOH)* to be their interpreter. Charbonneau agreed to take along his Shoshone wife, Sacajawea, who had been sold to Charbonneau as a slave. In addition to helping her husband translate various Indian languages, she cooked meals for the expedition and found wild plants for them to eat and use for medicine.

Over the Mountains and Back

In April 1805, as the ice was breaking up on the rivers, the expedition left Fort Mandan. They crossed the plains that sloped gently upward to the barrier of the Rocky Mountains. The Rockies' jagged peaks glittered with ice and snow. They were an awesome sight to people familiar with the green, rounded peaks of eastern mountains.

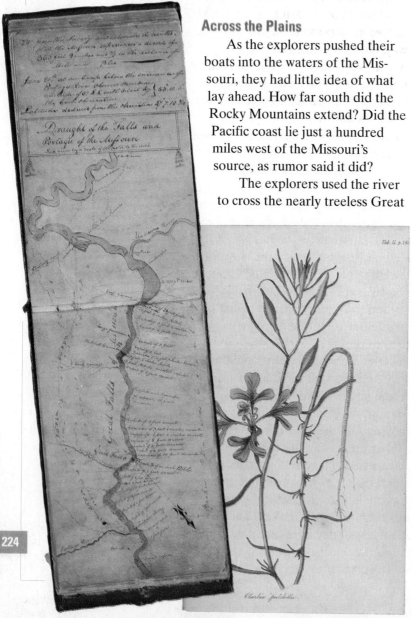

▼ *Clark's map of the great falls of the Missouri shows where the boats were carried around rapids and waterfalls. The evening primrose* (clarkia palchella), *drawn from a specimen Lewis collected, is one of the new genera named for the explorers.*

Olaf Seltze painted Lewis and Clark, Clark's servant York, and Sacajawea at Black Eagle Falls in Montana. The Friendship medals (below) were given to American Indian chiefs.

When the expedition reached the great falls of the Missouri, the water was often rough. The boats had to be unloaded and carried around the roughest stretches. The men were in and out of the water all day. Sharp rocks on the shore cut their feet. Round pebbles in the stream threw them off balance and into the water.

A memorable meeting with the Shoshone made up for these trials. Mounted on fine horses, the warriors dashed up to the explorers at a gallop. The overjoyed Shoshone were now led by Sacajawea's brother. They hugged the members of the expedition, delighted to see Sacajawea again.

Using horses provided by the Shoshone, the explorers struggled over the mountains. They left the weary horses with some of the Nez Perce *(nez purs)*, who promised to keep them over the winter. After the explorers slowly descended the western slopes of the Rockies, they made new boats and followed the watershed of the Columbia River to the Pacific Ocean. They spent the winter of 1805–1806 near the shore at Fort Clatsop, which they had built.

The expedition had counted on four deer or one buffalo a day for food. In the early spring, however, game was scarce. At times the explorers were reduced to eating squirrels or crows. On the return journey, the group split up to make sure they had not missed an important waterway. Otherwise, the return trip was mostly a repeat of the outward journey. The weary explorers finally reached St. Louis on September 23, 1806. As they fired their guns in salute, cheering crowds rushed to the river bank. Months earlier, they had given the explorers up for lost.

Achievements of the Expedition

The Lewis and Clark expedition was one of the most successful journeys of exploration in U.S. history. Although it did not find the Northwest Passage, the expedition added enormously to knowledge of the Western lands. Lewis and Clark were the first to map the watershed of the Columbia River, thereby strengthening American claims to the Oregon country. Clark's descriptions of abundant game spurred American fur trappers to move west. Perhaps the most lasting achievement of the expedition was the great interest in the West that it aroused in a people who already had a tradition of westward expansion. Clark's map, which was the first to show the Northwest accurately, became invaluable to later explorers. ■

How Do We Know?

HISTORY *Archaeological findings indicate how greatly the peace medals were valued. Archaeologists have found the Jefferson medals included in chiefs' burials along with other objects important to those Indians.*

■ *What were the achievements of the Lewis and Clark expedition?*

225

The West

Mountain Men Blaze Trails

Lewis and Clark were soon followed by other explorers. Many of them were solitary trappers drawn to the wilderness of the Rockies by the chance to trap fur-bearing animals.

World of the Mountain Men

Each **mountain man**—as the fur trapper was called—was molded by hardship and constant danger. Like many Indians, he was a skilled tracker and pathfinder.

The mountain man spent much of the year alone or with a few companions, trapping animals such as mink, otter, and especially beaver, whose fur brought high prices in the East. Each spring he packed up his furs and headed for the **rendezvous** (*RAHN day voo,* a French word meaning "meeting place"). Held each summer, the rendezvous took place at a location that was convenient for both fur trappers and traders. Instead of buying furs from the Indians, the traders hired a group of trappers and outfitted them.

As many as a hundred trappers and up to 5,000 Indians gathered at the rendezvous. For two or three weeks they swapped tall tales, caught up on the latest news, and enjoyed the rare chance to be sociable before returning to the wilderness trails.

Pathfinders of the West

Mountain men were colorful characters. Tall, gaunt Jedediah Smith carried a rifle in one hand and his Bible in the other. His face was deeply scarred because of his encounter with a grizzly bear that had tried to bite off his head. In 1824, he went through South Pass in what is now Wyoming and crossed the **continental divide**, the line that divides the rivers that flow west from those that flow east. Two years later Smith found the trail across the Great Basin to California. He also explored what are now the states of Oregon and Washington (see map, page 227).

Mountain men were keen observers, walking encyclopedias of the rivers, mountain passes, and Indian trails. The routes they found across the mountains and deserts in time became the overland trails for pioneers moving westward. Few mountain men, however, wrote down descriptions of the trails they knew. That task was done by U.S. government expeditions, which often used the mountain men as guides.

Government Expeditions

One of the first government explorers was General Zebulon Pike. In 1805–1806 Pike explored the upper Mississippi and the next year the land from central Colorado south. He also climbed halfway up Pikes Peak in Colorado, which is named in his honor.

In the 1840s, some people persuaded the government to sponsor scientific expeditions to the West. A member of the U.S. Army topographical corps, John C. Frémont, was married to Jessie Benton, the daughter of influential Senator Thomas Hart Benton. He was chosen to head several expeditions. On a steamboat chugging up the Missouri River in 1842, Frémont met and hired trapper Kit Carson. Calm, mild mannered Carson had little formal education but spoke French, Spanish, and several Indian dialects and was adept in Indian sign language. Frémont, in contrast, was well-educated in mathematics, topography, botany, and geology.

▲ Like the American Indians, mountain men wore clothing of deerskin and elkskin and carried small items in pouches decorated with beadwork.

Across Time & Space

Some of the land once explored by the mountain men remains in a wild state today. For example, the Jedediah Smith Wilderness covers over 116,500 acres in the Targhee National Forest in western Wyoming and eastern Idaho.

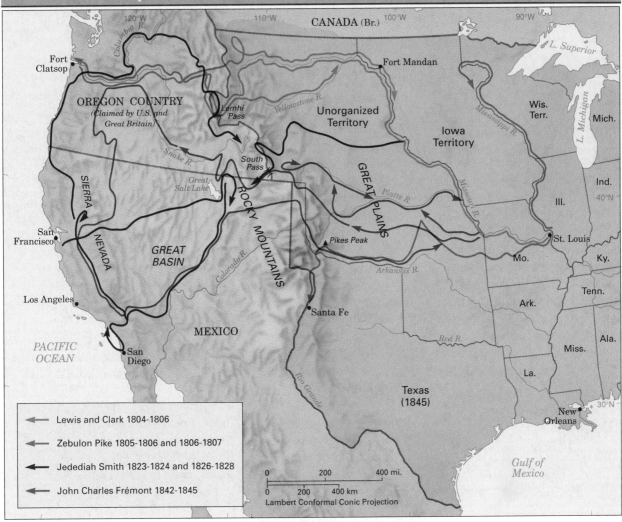

Legend:
- Lewis and Clark 1804-1806
- Zebulon Pike 1805-1806 and 1806-1807
- Jedediah Smith 1823-1824 and 1826-1828
- John Charles Frémont 1842-1845

Over the next few years Frémont and his mountain men guides explored almost all of the West, as the map shows. Frémont's carefully prepared descriptions and maps provided concrete information for people traveling west. His wife Jessie helped him turn his reports into dramatic accounts.

As more and more of the West became known, the movement to push the western border of the United States to the Pacific gained momentum. In 1845, the idea that the United States had a duty to expand from the Atlantic to the Pacific became known as **Manifest Destiny**. The Louisiana Purchase was just one step toward this goal. Between 1820 and 1850 the United States took other steps to achieve its objective. ■

▲ *The map shows some of the trails explorers found or made across the Rockies to the Pacific coast.*

■ *How did the activities of the mountain men encourage U.S. expansion?*

REVIEW

1. **FOCUS** Why did the U.S. government call for exploration west of the Mississippi?

2. **CONNECT** How did Jefferson's policy toward the Indians contrast with the way Jackson had dealt with the Cherokee and other tribes in the Southeast?

3. **GEOGRAPHY** Use the physical map of North America in the Atlas to help you describe the many geographical obstacles that the Lewis and Clark expedition faced.

4. **ECONOMICS** Why was the fur trade important?

5. **CRITICAL THINKING** The reports of Lewis and Clark aroused interest in the West among people in the East. How do you think this interest might have affected the American Indians in the West?

6. **ACTIVITY** Prepare an oral report of the meeting between the Lewis and Clark expedition and the Shoshone. Include imaginary interviews with Sacajawea, various Shoshone, and expedition members.

Chronological Outlining

Here's Why

As a student, you are exposed to a great deal of information, both specific and general. You need to organize this information so that you can understand how the many facts relate to one another. Organizing information into an outline is one good way to do that. It is often helpful to list items chronologically, in the order in which they occurred.

In this chapter you have learned how Lewis and Clark were sent to explore the Louisiana Purchase territory and to take detailed notes on what they found there. (You can see pictures of their journey on page 229.)

Suppose you wanted to prepare a report based on their findings. You would need to organize information about where and when they traveled, and all the descriptions of what they found. One way that you could do that would be to prepare a chronological outline.

Here's How

Look at the outline below. It is based on the expeditions of Lewis and Clark. Notice how the outline is organized:

1. All major topics are marked with Roman numerals (I, II).
2. All subtopics are marked with capital letters (A, B, C, D).
3. All supporting details and information are marked with numerals (1, 2, 3, 4).

Major Topics

Subtopics

Supporting Details

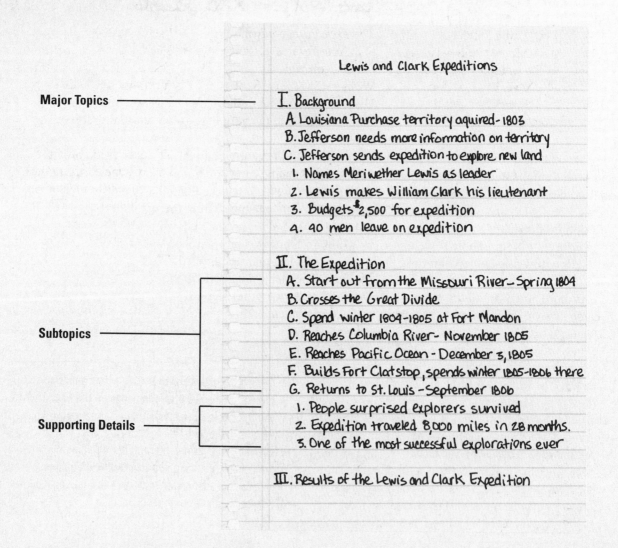

Lewis and Clark Expeditions

I. Background
   A. Louisiana Purchase territory aquired-1803
   B. Jefferson needs more information on territory
   C. Jefferson sends expedition to explore new land
      1. Names Meriwether Lewis as leader
      2. Lewis makes William Clark his lieutenant
      3. Budgets $2,500 for expedition
      4. 40 men leave on expedition

II. The Expedition
   A. Start out from the Missouri River—Spring 1804
   B. Crosses the Great Divide
   C. Spend winter 1804-1805 at Fort Mandon
   D. Reaches Columbia River- November 1805
   E. Reaches Pacific Ocean - December 3, 1805
   F. Builds Fort Clatstop, spends winter 1805-1806 there
   G. Returns to St. Louis -September 1806
      1. People surprised explorers survived
      2. Expedition traveled 8,000 miles in 28 months.
      3. One of the most successful explorations ever

III. Results of the Lewis and Clark Expedition

The outline is organized chronologically. First comes the background to the expedition, then the facts about the expedition itself, and then the results of the expedition. Within each of these major topics, subtopics are arranged. Supporting details are all arranged under their subtopics. When you are done arranging your information, this outline gives you all the facts that you need to write or present a report on this subject.

Try It

Look at the third major topic on the outline on page 228: "III. Results of the Lewis and Clark Expedition." Decide whether each fact in the following list is a subtopic or a detail. Label each subtopic with an "s" and each detail with a "d." Put all the facts in correct order. Then copy the outline from page 228 on a separate sheet of paper, and enter the facts in the proper place in the outline.

- The expedition confirmed the United States' claim to the Oregon region.
- William Clark carved the United States' claim to the Oregon region on the yellow pine tree.
- The expedition brought back the first maps to document the new land.
- Lewis's and Clark's maps showed that the Missouri River did not reach the Pacific Ocean.
- The Oregon region was first claimed by a Boston fur trapper, Robert Gray, who discovered the mouth of the Columbia River.
- The expedition brought back valuable information about the tribes of Indians living in the area.
- One map showed the watershed of the Columbia River.

Apply It

Research the life of a modern-day explorer or researcher such as Thor Heyerdahl, Jacques Cousteau, Sir Edmund Hillary, Jane Goodall, or another person who interests you. Organize the information that you find chronologically into an outline that includes at least three major topics.

L E S S O N   2

Achieving Manifest Destiny

How did Texas become the center of a conflict that gave the United States vast new lands?

Key Terms

- expansionist
- buffer zone
- annex

In a stirring speech in 1846, Democratic politician Major Auguste Davezac stated as follows his belief that the United States should expand:

Land enough—land enough! Make way, I say, for the young American buffalo—he has not yet got land enough; he wants more land as his cool shelter in summer—He wants more land for his beautiful pasture grounds. I tell you, we will give him Oregon for his summer shade, and the region of Texas as his winter pasture. [Applause] Like all of his race, he wants salt too. Well, he shall have the use of two oceans, the mighty Pacific and the turbulent Atlantic shall be his. He shall not stop his career until he slakes his thirst in the frozen ocean.

Expansion was part of the concept of Manifest Destiny. Its roots went back to colonial days. In the mid-1600s, Governor John Winthrop of Massachusetts established the idea that if people did not improve land—that is, farm, mine, or change it in some way—they lost all right to it.

This idea grew into the view that the United States had the right to settle all of the continent of North America. **Expansionists**—those who wanted to increase U.S. territory—did not explain how the United States received the right to take over the entire North American continent.

Some people said Americans had the duty to extend white American culture—especially the ideals of democratic government, Christianity, and economic growth—to all who lacked them. From this idea it was but a short step to the claim that white American culture was superior to all others.

In 1845, editor John L. O'Sullivan came up with the name "Manifest Destiny" for the complex of expansionist ideas. Manifest Destiny was a thread that wove through the political fabric of the nation in the 1800s. Nowhere did it become more evident than in United States relations with Spain and later with Mexico.

Development of Texas

Spain claimed vast North American lands, among them what are now Texas, New Mexico, Arizona, and California. In a hundred years of colonization, however, few people had settled north of Mexico. Only 3,500 non-Indian people were scattered across the Southwest by 1820. In California and Texas, many were rancheros—cattle ranchers who grazed their herds on the unfenced range. In New Mexico, many colonists herded sheep.

U.S. Settlers Welcomed

After the United States bought Louisiana, Americans had quickly settled the frontier along the Mississippi River. This rapid expansion caused Spain to fear for its northern lands. They had too few people and were too far away from Mexico City to be protected from adventurous settlers from the United States. For example, San Antonio de Bexar *(beh HAR)*, the center of government in Texas, had only 800 inhabitants in 1820.

Spain therefore agreed to a proposal made by a Missourian named Moses Austin. Austin wanted to settle a limited number of U.S. citizens in Texas. In exchange for low-priced land, he agreed that the U.S. settlers would be loyal to Spain and accept the Catholic religion. Spain felt that loyal colonists would help block U.S. expansion. It looked on the Texas colony as a **buffer zone**, a territory separating two opposing powers.

Moses Austin died before he could set up the colony, but his son Stephen took over the task. "I determined to fulfill rigidly all the duties of a Mexican citizen," he said, and remained faithful to his vow. The 300 settlers he brought from the United States in 1822 also lived up to the terms of the agreement.

Mexico gained its independence from Spain in 1821. It took Austin months to persuade the new government to maintain the grant in Texas.

Growing Tensions

In the next few years Austin's colony in Texas prospered. As more and more U.S. settlers moved into Texas, however, relations with the Mexican government became strained. The settlements grew much more rapidly than the Mexican government had expected. By 1830, 15,000 white settlers and over 1,000 black slaves lived in Texas, outnumbering the Mexican settlers by about four to one. The explosive growth of people from the United States alarmed Mexico. Instead of serving as a buffer zone, Texas itself had become the threat.

In addition, many of the newer settlers refused to honor the original agreement. Protestants were annoyed by the religious requirement. The inefficiencies of the Mexican government, torn by quarrels between different political parties, exasperated them. Many refused to obey Mexican laws. For example, Mexico tried to restrict U.S. settlement by abolishing slavery in Texas in 1824. The settlers freed their slaves and then forced them to sign agreements that made them slaves in all but name. Austin's one-man rule also angered settlers accustomed to the democratic practices found in the United States.

Control of Texas passed out of Austin's hands and into those of the newcomers, some of whom began to demand independence. To strengthen its control, the Mexican government sent troops to occupy Texas. It also forbade further immigration from the United States, but was unable to stop the flood of settlers. ■

Texas Towns: A Varied Heritage

San Antonio
- Founded as a Spanish mission and fort
- Named for Saint Anthony
- Planned around squares (plazas)
- Adobe buildings

Austin
- Founded as capital of Republic of Texas
- Named for Stephen F. Austin
- Planned along a grid of main streets and cross streets
- Log or wood frame buildings

▲ *Compare the two towns. Note what they tell about the mixture of cultures in Texas.*

■ *How did the white settlers' disregard for Mexican law and religion contribute to tension in Texas?*

Texas Gains Independence

On October 2, 1835, a group of volunteers refused an order to surrender a cannon to Mexican troops. Their refusal became the first step in a rebellion against Mexico. At first, the Texans acted as loyal Mexican citizens. They opposed not Mexico but its leader, General Antonio López de Santa Anna, who was doing away with the reforms of Mexico's constitution.

Battle of the Alamo

Early in December 1835, a group of 300 Texas volunteers drove 1,100 Mexican troops out of San Antonio. Santa Anna, vowing to crush the rebels, assembled an army. Few Texans took the threat seriously.

Some 180 rebels commanded by 26-year-old William Barret Travis occupied the Alamo, an old Spanish mission in San Antonio. On February 24, 1836, Santa Anna's army of more than a thousand men laid siege to the Alamo. As more troops joined the Mexicans, Travis realized the danger of his position:

> I am besieged by a thousand or more of the Mexicans under Santa Anna. . . . I shall never surrender or retreat. . . . I am determined to sustain myself as long as possible and die like a soldier who never forgets what is due to his own honor & that of his country—
> VICTORY OR DEATH.

A Closer Look on the next page deals with the battle. The rebels held out until March 6. When the Mexicans finally broke into the Alamo, Santa Anna ordered the Texans killed.

Independence Proclaimed

While the Alamo was under siege, a group of delegates met to write a constitution for Texas. Deciding that Texas could no longer accept rule by Mexico, they proclaimed their independence and drew up a constitution based upon the U.S. document.

The new republic was in a desperate position. Santa Anna was determined to end opposition to his rule. After the victory at the Alamo, he succeeded in defeating the Texans at Goliad. Once again, he ordered all prisoners killed. Sam Houston, commander of the disorganized Texan army, led his grumbling troops on a steady retreat (they wanted to stop and fight). At San Jacinto on April 21, 1836, Houston decided the Texans were ready to attack. They caught Santa Anna by surprise and defeated the Mexican soldiers in minutes. The Texans then took a bloody revenge for the men killed at the Alamo and Goliad.

Lone Star Republic

The next day Santa Anna was captured and forced to recognize the independence of Texas. The Mexican government, however, stated that the treaty was worthless because it had been obtained by threat. Texas, the Mexicans insisted, was still part of Mexico.

At the same time the United States refused to **annex** Texas, that is, add it to the Union. Texas was a slave state; if it joined the Union, representatives argued, it would upset the balance between the 13 slave states and the 13 free states.

For almost 10 years Texas was an independent republic. The United States hesitated to annex it. The Mexicans, troubled by unrest at home, were powerless to bring it back under their control. Texans called their country the Lone Star Republic, symbolized by a single star on its flag. An uneasy peace prevailed. Bands of Comanche sometimes raided isolated settlements, and clashes with Mexico continued.

▲ Susanna Dickinson was one of the few survivors of the Battle of the Alamo. After the battle, Santa Anna sent the 18-year-old widow to Sam Houston to tell him that further revolt would be crushed like that at the Alamo.

The Battle of the Alamo

When the Mexicans approached, the story goes, Colonel Travis drew a line in the dirt at the Alamo. He challenged his Texas volunteers, "I want everyone who's willing to die with me to come across this line. Who will be first?"

Bowie knives with bone handles were the weapons of the Texas volunteers. Popularized by adventurer Jim Bowie, they were no match for Mexican bayonets.

Sharpshooting and rugged, this flint-lock rifle was probably swung like a baseball bat during the hand-to-hand combat inside the fort.

After losing his life at the Alamo, Davy Crockett became a folk hero. Susanna Dickinson was one of only a few survivors of the battle. Afterward, she spread the news of the Alamo across the land.

Walls that were once battered by Mexican cannonballs still stand in San Antonio today. Now, the Alamo is surrounded by modern buildings, not horses.

233

Sam Houston, elected as first president, worked tirelessly to get rid of the huge debt. He encouraged people from the United States and Europe to move to Texas by offering them free land. The number of immigrants grew from 35,000 settlers in 1836 to about 147,000 people 10 years later. Most settled on the fertile land along the rivers and produced large cotton crops. Others raised cattle for their hides and meat. As settlements grew, the demand to be annexed to the United States continued. ■

■ *What events made Texas the Lone Star Republic?*

War with Mexico

U.S. presidential candidate James K. Polk made the annexation of Texas a major issue in the election of 1844. Annexing Texas, he argued, would help the United States achieve its Manifest Destiny. Just before Polk took office in 1845, Congress voted Texas into the Union.

Mexico Defeated

Polk also had his eye on the rest of the Mexican lands reaching from Texas to the Pacific Ocean. The United States, he argued, had yet to reach its territorial limits. To achieve this goal, Polk made several attempts to buy the territory from Mexico. When diplomacy failed, he provoked a war by sending troops to the area of the Rio Grande. Texas claimed that river was its southern boundary. Mexico insisted that the boundary was the Nueces (*noo AY sis*) River, 150 miles farther north. In Mexican eyes, the United States had committed a hostile act. It had annexed Mexican land (Texas) and had moved troops there.

When Mexican and U.S. troops clashed, Polk used the incident as an excuse. He proclaimed that Mexicans had "shed American blood on American soil." Expansionists applauded his claim, and the U.S. Congress declared war on Mexico on May 13, 1846. Some representatives, however, protested. Abraham Lincoln, a congressman from Illinois, asked Polk to show exactly where on American soil the incident had occurred.

Although the Mexican soldiers fought bravely, the war went badly for Mexico. The U.S. forces were better organized and equipped. The Mexicans were weakened by civil war.

Santa Fe, the capital of New Mexico, was quickly occupied by U.S. troops. In California, just before the war broke out, a group of U.S. settlers in Sonoma had seized Mexican General Mariano Vallejo (*vah YEH hoh*). Raising a homemade flag showing a bear and a single star, they proclaimed California to be the Bear Flag Republic. When the U.S. navy occupied California ports in July 1846, the Bear Flaggers joined its forces. Some Californios and New Mexicans later rebelled, but their uprisings were quickly halted.

▼ The Mexican forces, led by Santa Anna, faced U.S. troops commanded by experienced generals —Zachary Taylor, called "Old Rough and Ready," and Winfield Scott, "Old Fuss and Feathers." Find the invasion routes these generals took into Mexico.

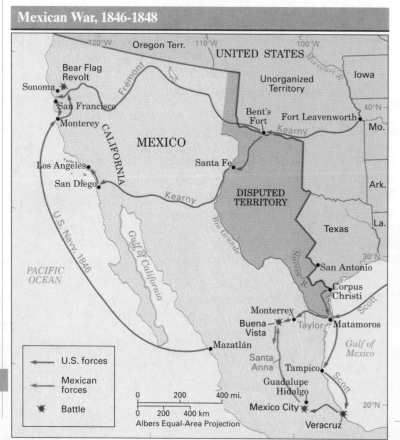

Mexican War, 1846-1848

- ← U.S. forces
- ← Mexican forces
- ✳ Battle

0   200   400 mi.
0 200 400 km
Albers Equal-Area Projection

234

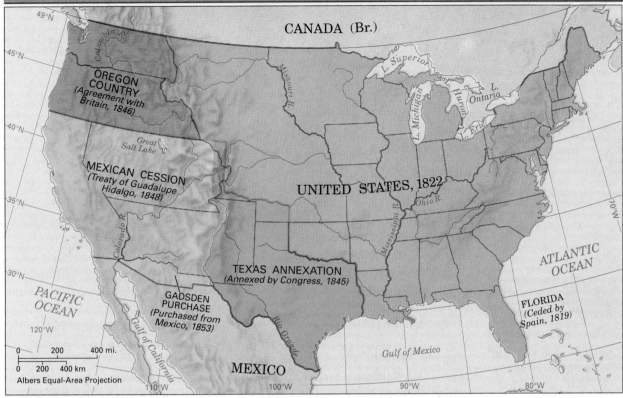

Manifest Destiny Achieved

U.S. troops also invaded Mexico south of the Rio Grande and won several victories (see map, page 234). After two years of war, the Mexican government conceded defeat.

In February 1848, Mexico and the United States signed the Treaty of Guadalupe Hidalgo. Under the terms of the treaty, the United States would pay Mexico $15 million and would assume up to $3.25 million in Mexican debts to American citizens. In return, Mexico would cede to the United States most of the land north of the Rio Grande. The Senate approved the treaty in March 1848. The United States had achieved its long-sought Manifest Destiny and now stretched "from sea to shining sea."

Although the nation had doubled in size, it had also acquired some new problems. The war caused hard feelings between Mexico and the United States. Mexico was humiliated by its defeat; U.S. expansionists were elated at their nation's victory. Some U.S. citizens, convinced that their civilization was superior, tended to look on Mexico as a backward nation, an attitude that has lasted into modern times. The land gained from Mexico included thousands of Mexicans who became U.S. citizens. As white settlers moved west, the treaty protecting Mexican Americans was often not enforced. ■

▲ *Included in the Mexican Cession were present-day Utah, California, Nevada, parts of Colorado and Wyoming, and most of New Mexico and Arizona. In 1853, Santa Anna sold the rest of New Mexico and Arizona to the United States.*

■ *How did the United States achieve Manifest Destiny through war with Mexico?*

R E V I E W

1. **FOCUS** How did Texas become the center of a conflict that gave the United States vast new lands?
2. **CONNECT** How did the concept of Manifest Destiny relate to Jefferson's territorial goals?
3. **CULTURE** List the factors that caused conflict between the U.S. settlers in Texas and the Mexican government.
4. **GEOGRAPHY** Compare the modern U.S. political map in the Atlas (pages 698–699) with the map above showing territory lost by Mexico. What present-day U.S. states were once part of Mexico?
5. **CRITICAL THINKING** What bias might result from the belief in Manifest Destiny?
6. **ACTIVITY** With a classmate, debate the desirability of Manifest Destiny. Be sure both sides of the argument are presented. Use relevant material from the lesson to support the presentation.

235

L E S S O N   3

Settling the West

Why did U.S. citizens begin to settle in the lands west of the Mississippi River?

Key Terms

• secularize

➤ *On the veranda of a California rancho a couple dances a fandango to the music of a guitar.*

Picture yourself a Yankee trader in the company of Walter Colton, a judge in Monterey, California. He has asked you to join him at a party on a nearby rancho or ranch.

As you watch the guests arrive, your eye is caught by a young couple riding together on a spirited chestnut horse. The ranchero's dark sombrero is tilted forward and tightly strapped under his chin. His dark blue suit shines with silver buttons, and his handsewn boots bear jingling spurs. The boots were probably part of the cargo a Yankee ship carried from New England. The leather for the boots may have originally come from hides of the ranchero's own cattle.

Sitting sideways in front of the ranchero is his wife, a wreath of tiny flowers in her dark braids, her dark eyes sparkling with excitement. Her rustling dress may also have come from New England, and her fine silk shawl may have come from China.

The couple greet friends and join others dancing to the music of a violin and guitar. In a quiet corner older women sit and gossip behind their fans. Rancheros boast about their horses. Indian servants bustle from kitchen to dining room. Children run back and forth, playing games and snatching tidbits from the table laden with food.

Although imaginary, the account above describes what a visitor to a rancho might have seen. The music, the food, the dress of the people, and the soft-spoken Spanish all indicate how California differed from New England in the 1830s.

Spaniards Settle in California

The difference between California and New England lies in their colonial backgrounds. California was settled by people from Catholic Spain, whereas New England's early settlers were Protestant English.

Mission California

The colony in California was set up in 1769. When officials in New Spain (now Mexico) set up outposts in places such as California and Texas, they sent soldiers to build forts, priests to establish churches, and settlers to grow food for the soldiers. Walled presidios, or forts, had quarters for troops, a jail, and storage rooms.

Food for the presidios was supposed to be grown by the settlers. Since few people in New Spain wanted to migrate to California, the government gave them land as an encouragement. Some settlers became rancheros; others were townspeople who ran small businesses or served as government officials.

The missions were much more successful than the towns. Each mission included a church, workshops and storerooms, rooms for the priests, and houses for the Indians who had become Christians. By 1823, 21 missions, each a day's walk from the next, stretched 600 miles along the coast from San Diego in the South to Sonoma, north of San Francisco. These missions were home to several thousand Indian converts. Some Indians labored in the fields of wheat, the fruit orchards, and the vineyards. Others tended the herds of sheep and cattle or worked in the kitchens and workrooms, grinding meal into flour, tanning hides, making tiles and adobe bricks for building, and weaving blankets and clothing. Indian artists created religious carvings and paintings for the mission church.

Most Indians found it hard to adjust to mission life. They were accustomed to living in small bands and wandering from place to place gathering food. The Indians resented the hard work they were forced to do at the mission, and many of them ran away. Moreover, diseases brought by the Spaniards often proved fatal to the Indians. By 1833, the Indian population of California was half what it had been in 1769 when the first mission was established.

This plan of Rancho del Ciénaga (Marsh Ranch) was used to register the land claimed by the ranchero.

California Ranchos

When Mexico gained its independence from Spain, it took over California. In 1833 the Mexican government began to **secularize** the missions; that is, it took the mission lands away from the control of the Catholic Church. By lessening the power of the priests, the Mexicans hoped to lessen loyalty to Spain.

The government widened its support among the people by a system of land grants. Most mission lands—and their hundreds of thousands of cattle—were assigned to rancheros. To gain a land grant, a ranchero made a diseño (*dih SEH nyoh*), a drawing that identified the rancho. Each land grant was enormous, measured in square miles rather than acres.

Although the ranchos were like

small kingdoms, the main house was usually a simple building of adobe (bricks of sun-dried clay) with dirt floors. On the wealthier ranchos, skilled horsemen called vaqueros (*vah KAIR ohs*) did most of the work for the rancheros. In springtime, the vaqueros rounded up and branded the newly born calves. In the fall, they rounded up full-grown cattle to slaughter for their hides and meat.

Yankee traders sailed their ships into the ports at San Diego, Monterey, and San Francisco. There they bought the cured hides and shipped them to New England shoe factories. In addition to hides, the ships took on tallow, a cattle by-product used in making soap and candles.

The hide trade was profitable but irregular. In the winter of 1835–1836, Richard Henry Dana, the writer—in an account of his voyage from Boston around Cape Horn to California—reported that the port of San Francisco was nearly deserted. ■

*A*ll around was the stillness of nature. . . . To the westward of the landing-place, were dreary sandhills, with little grass to be seen, and few trees, and beyond them higher hills, steep and barren, their sides gullied [worn away] by the rains. Some five or six miles beyond the landing-place, to the right, was a ruinous presidio, and some three or four miles to the left was the Mission of Dolores, as ruinous as the presidio, almost deserted.

■ *How did taking the missions away from the church change life in California?*

U.S. Citizens Go West

Although California and the east coast of the United States were linked by trade, California was a Mexican possession. Most westward-moving people from the United States headed for Oregon.

Overland to Oregon

The United States and Britain both claimed the Oregon country. The U.S. interest went back to the Lewis and Clark expedition. Hudson's Bay, a powerful British fur-trading company, competed with the fur-trading post set up by American John Jacob Astor. When Britain and the United States could not agree on the boundary between Oregon and Canada, they decided to let people from both countries settle in Oregon.

In 1835, the American Board for Foreign Missions strengthened the American claim by sending missionaries to the Northwest. Marcus and Narcissa Whitman and Henry and Eliza Spalding set up churches, schools, and mills, showed people of the Cayuse and Nez Perce tribes how to irrigate land, and taught them Christian ideas.

The descriptions by explorers, missionaries, and settlers helped to attract other U.S. citizens. By 1845, over 5,000 Americans had settled in Oregon. At his inauguration as President in 1845, Polk proclaimed that the United States had a "clear and unquestionable" title to Oregon. The following year Great Britain and the United States agreed to set the Oregon boundary at Latitude 49°N. Some expansionists had demanded a boundary at Latitude 54°40'N, but Polk did not feel the added territory was worth

▼ *Californios traded tanned hides of the type shown below. At right is a carpetbag, the "suitcase" used by many pioneers.*

a dispute with Britain.

By 1847, the increasing number of white settlers was beginning to alarm the Cayuse and Nez Perce. When some settlers arrived with measles, the disease proved fatal to large numbers of the Cayuse because they had no immunity to it. Convinced the missionaries had poisoned their children, the Cayuse killed 14 white people, including the Whitmans. To protect other settlers, Congress made Oregon a territory in 1848.

The Mormon Promised Land

The Whitmans and Spaldings went west for religious reasons—to establish Protestant missions and to convert the Indians to Christianity. A group known as the Mormons also went west for religious reasons.

The Mormons were founded by a young New Englander named Joseph Smith. From the age of 15 on, Smith experienced religious visions. He believed he was chosen to head a new and purified Christian church. In 1830, he formally founded the Church of Jesus Christ of Latter-day Saints at

Fayette, New York. Smith and his followers later moved west.

Smith's followers, known as Mormons, often met with hostility. People of other faiths objected to some practices such as the Mormons having several wives. Nevertheless, the Mormons built thriving communities in Ohio, Missouri, and Illinois. In Nauvoo, Illinois, Smith served as both mayor and religious leader. The Mormon community grew to 20,000, making Nauvoo the largest city in the state.

In 1844, however, some Mormons accused Smith of treason. This disagreement encouraged some anti-Mormons to attack the settlement at Nauvoo. An angry mob burst into the jail where Smith was held and murdered him and his brother Hyrum.

The horrified Mormons, led by Brigham Young, fled west, looking for a place to live that was outside the United States. The desert west of the Rockies, known as the Great Basin, seemed ideal.

Lured by the opportunity to worship freely, thousands of Mormons trekked west to the Great Basin and

▲ *Some Mormon families included several wives, a practice that stopped in 1890. Note the spinning wheel and butter churn. What do these tools tell you about the pioneers' way of life?*

Like Great Salt Lake, Pyramid Lake in Nevada has no outlet. Compare the modern photograph (top) *with the sketch made by Charles Preuss, Frémont's mapmaker, in 1844.*

■ *Briefly describe how U.S. settlements developed in Oregon.*

established a Mormon state named Deseret in 1849. By the next year the settlement at Great Salt Lake had over 11,000 inhabitants, most of them farmers. Their hard labor and discipline, combined with Young's irrigation scheme, made the desert blossom.

Other people admired the Mormons for their hard work and farming skills. But they were disturbed that Mormon religious leaders also headed the government. In the United States, in contrast, the Constitution called for separation of church and state. For more than 40 years the close relation-

ship of Mormon religion and politics caused opposition to admitting the Mormon state to the Union. Utah did not become a state until 1896.

Early U.S. Settlers in California

U.S. citizens began settling in Mexico's colony of California in the 1820s. Occasionally sailors left ship to try ranching or storekeeping or to work as tinsmiths, carpenters, or lumberjacks. Some U.S. trappers drifted into the colony and settled down.

Among the early non-Mexican settlers was Swiss immigrant John Augustus Sutter, who arrived by way of Hawaii. Sutter convinced the Mexican government that he would build a fort to protect the colony. His settlement on the American River became a goal for people traveling to California. Soon it would play a major role in California's history. ■

REVIEW

1. **FOCUS** Why did U.S. citizens begin to settle in the lands west of the Mississippi River?

2. **CONNECT** How did the Mexican War influence Polk's position on Oregon?

3. **ECONOMICS** How did Yankee traders and California rancheros supply one another's needs?

4. **CULTURE** In what way were the motives of the Oregon missionaries and the Mormons similar? different?

5. **CRITICAL THINKING** Apply the concept of Manifest Destiny to California. How might U.S. expansion affect the rancheros?

6. **ACTIVITY** Imagine you are in charge of a group of people about to settle in Oregon. Plan a colony and decide what the settlers will need. Think of problems they may face and their economic and cultural needs. Write your plan in the form of an outline.

Chapter 8

L E S S O N   4

Surviving on the Frontier

On the morning of January 24, 1848, carpenter James Marshall was working at Sutter's sawmill on the American River in California. "My eye was caught by something shining in the bottom of the ditch," said Marshall. "I reached my hand down and picked it up; it made my heart thump, for I was certain it was gold. . . . Then I saw another."

News of Marshall's discovery spread slowly. Then, on May 12, Mormon storekeeper Sam Brannan went to San Francisco. Grasping a bottle full of gold dust, he shouted words that electrified his listeners: "Gold! Gold! Gold from the American River!"

Fired by gold fever, thousands of men rushed off to the gold fields. "The whole country," reported the weekly newspaper *Californian,* "resounds to the sordid cry of gold, gold, GOLD! while the field is left half planted, the house half built and everything neglected but the manufacture of shovels and pickaxes."

THINKING FOCUS

What impact did the discovery of gold have on the West?

Key Terms

- ghost town
- regionalism

The Gold Fields

By 1849, people of every social class and occupation were rushing to California from all over the world, certain they would strike it rich. They traveled on foot, on horseback, by coach or wagon—even by ship.

The Journey West

Those bitten by the gold bug on the East Coast often decided to travel west by sea. Some sailed 13,000 miles around South America, braving the storms and lashing waves of Cape Horn. Others crossed the fever-ridden jungles of Panama to catch a ship on the Pacific shore. Passengers on either route were jammed together for weeks of monotonous travel and seasickness. The food—in very meager amounts—was often inedible.

Many forty-niners, as they were called, traveled overland on the routes blazed by the mountain men. By 1849, the routes to South Pass were well marked. Beyond that point, however, instructions tended to be vague. Many travelers got lost. Some never made it

▼ *Why was a 100-day voyage attractive to many forty-niners?*

241

Across Time & Space

The California gold rush came back to life in 1987 when a group of divers found the wreck of the S.S. Central America, a paddlewheel steamer that sank off the coast of Charleston, South Carolina, in 1857. Inside the wreck was California gold on its way from San Francisco to banks in New York. The value of the gold then was $1.2 million. Today it is worth about $450 million.

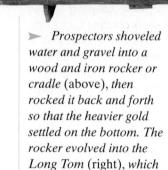

➤ *Prospectors shoveled water and gravel into a wood and iron rocker or cradle* (above), *then rocked it back and forth so that the heavier gold settled on the bottom. The rocker evolved into the Long Tom* (right), *which made working a claim easier.*

across the waterless loose sands and alkali flats west of Great Salt Lake.

The trail up into the Sierra Nevada, which rose to the west of the Great Basin, became steeper and steeper. Many travelers wondered if they would ever reach its end. Then, wrote Sarah Royce, who accompanied her husband to the gold fields in 1849, "I looked *down*, far over constantly descending hills, to where a soft haze sent up a warm, rosy glow that seemed to me a smile of welcome." The gold fields of California were in sight.

Tales of Riches

Once in California the forty-niners rushed off to the gold fields. Tales abounded of gold discoveries. There was the angry miner who kicked a rock in disgust and found a gold nugget underneath it. Another prospector—one who seeks valuable natural deposits such as gold—claimed to have found gold under his doorstep. Not to be outdone was the miner who shot a bear and found gold where the animal had fallen onto a ledge. Strange as it may sound, some of the stories were actually true!

Mining Camps

The mining camps were usually makeshift towns inhabited largely by single men. Life was often disorderly and rough. Brawls could break out at any time over claim jumping—taking over another miner's claim. The failure to strike it rich wore on tempers made short by the terrible living conditions at the gold fields.

Since all supplies were carried in from San Francisco and other places, prices were outrageous. The cost of a shovel went from $1 to $50 in a month. A $2 cradle—the device used to separate gold from sand and pebbles—cost $100 at the mines.

Fresh vegetables and fruit were rare. The miner's usual diet consisted of flapjacks or pancakes, sourdough bread, beans, and pickled or fried pork. One miner's song lamented, "I've lived on swine till I grunt and squeal." With such a poor diet, many men came down with diseases.

In mining areas, towns seemed to appear almost overnight. In November 1848, there was not a house in

Sacramento. In 1849, it became a supply center for the gold fields. Its population soared to 12,000 people.

Mining towns might die out overnight. When miners heard of a rich strike somewhere else, they grabbed their belongings and left. Within weeks, their town might become a **ghost town**, a deserted place. Silence replaced the bustle. ■

■ *Why did few mining towns become permanent settlements?*

Hardships of the Overland Trail

In 1849, 30,000 people traveled the Overland Trail. The next year the number rose to 55,000. Numbers decreased after that year but by 1860, 145,000 more people had moved to the West.

These men, women, and children all shared the hardships of life on the trail. Their journey began with the emotional strain of parting with familiar places and loved ones. One pioneer woman mourned, "I am leaving my home, my early friends and associates, never to see them again."

Looking like ships against the rolling plains, the canvas-covered wagons, each about ten feet long, followed one another in a train that might stretch out over two to five miles.

An experienced scout such as Kit Carson guided the wagon train. Usually everyone rode horseback or walked beside the team of oxen pulling the wagon. Since each wagon might weigh a ton or more when loaded, it needed three or four pair of oxen to pull it. Wagons contained tools, clothing, a few family treasures, and food for the journey.

A guidebook suggested pioneers carry 200 pounds of flour, 150 pounds of bacon, 10 pounds each of coffee and salt, and 20 pounds of sugar. To these staples the pioneers added dried fruit and beans. Slung beneath the wagon were spare wagon tongues, axles, spokes, and wheels for making the repairs that were often necessary.

Demanding Daily Chores

Travel by wagon train was physically taxing. The Overland Trail from Independence, Missouri, to Sutter's Fort in California was 2,000 miles

long. Since wagons traveled only about two miles an hour, the trip took several months to complete. The map on the next page shows one man's journey across the United States.

During the trip, people had little privacy and no sanitary facilities. The journey was especially hard for the women because they were expected to cook, wash and mend clothes and the wagon canvas, take care of the children, and doctor the family. Women and children also spent part of the day walking in the choking dust behind the wagons, picking up dried buffalo droppings, called buffalo chips, to use in place of wood for fuel.

For a pregnant woman, it was even harder. One woman said, "It all seems like a jumble of jolting wagon, crying baby, dust, sagebrush, and the never ceasing pain."

▲ *C. C. A. Christensen painted this group of pioneers crossing the plains on foot and hauling their possessions in handcarts. Many Mormons used this method of traveling west.*

243

In 1853, Charlotte Stearns Pengra recorded some routine evening chores she did:

> *I hung out what things were wet in the wagon, made griddle cakes, stewed berries, and made tea for supper. After that was over made two loaves of bread, stewed a pan of apples, prepared potatoes and meat for breakfast, and mended a pair of pants for Wm. pretty tired.*

She neglected to add that she unpacked the wagon when they halted and repacked it when they went on. Men's chores included repairing harnesses and wagons, caring for their animals, planning routes with the wagon train captain, hunting game, and standing guard at night.

Hazards of the Journey

Some of the pioneers, both men and women, were unable to bear the hardships of the trail and turned back to civilization. Others became sick and died from diseases such as cholera and smallpox and dysentery that was brought on by poor diets.

At all times the pioneers were at the mercy of the weather. They lost time waiting to ford flooded streams or stopping to find cattle that had stampeded during a storm. As they crossed Oregon in 1847, Elizabeth Smith Geer wrote the following:

> *It rains and snows. We start this morning around the falls with our wagons. . . . I carry my babe and lead, or rather carry another through snow, mud and water, almost to my knees.*

Since heavy wagon loads could not be carried across the mountains, items such as furniture often had to be discarded. Some people died of dehydration (lack of water) on the sands of scorching deserts. Other unfortunates found out too late that the water hole they had drunk from was poisonous. Sometimes Indian attacks were a threat.

▼ *On February 8, 1849, V. E. Geiger left Staunton, Virginia, and headed for California. How long did his journey take?*

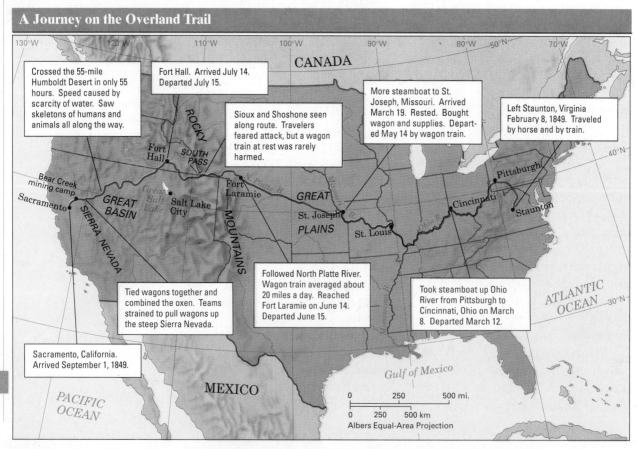

A Journey on the Overland Trail

Crossed the 55-mile Humboldt Desert in only 55 hours. Speed caused by scarcity of water. Saw skeletons of humans and animals all along the way.

Fort Hall. Arrived July 14. Departed July 15.

More steamboat to St. Joseph, Missouri. Arrived March 19. Rested. Bought wagon and supplies. Departed May 14 by wagon train.

Left Staunton, Virginia February 8, 1849. Traveled by horse and by train.

Sioux and Shoshone seen along route. Travelers feared attack, but a wagon train at rest was rarely harmed.

Tied wagons together and combined the oxen. Teams strained to pull wagons up the steep Sierra Nevada.

Followed North Platte River. Wagon train averaged about 20 miles a day. Reached Fort Laramie on June 14. Departed June 15.

Took steamboat up Ohio River from Pittsburgh to Cincinnati, Ohio on March 8. Departed March 12.

Sacramento, California. Arrived September 1, 1849.

CANADA
MEXICO
ATLANTIC OCEAN
PACIFIC OCEAN
Gulf of Mexico

ROCKY
SOUTH PASS
Fort Hall
Bear Creek mining camp
Sacramento
GREAT BASIN
SIERRA NEVADA
Great Salt Lake
Salt Lake City
Fort Laramie
MOUNTAINS
GREAT PLAINS
N. Platte R.
Missouri R.
St. Joseph
St. Louis
Mississippi R.
Ohio R.
Cincinnati
Pittsburgh
Staunton

0   250   500 mi.
0   250   500 km
Albers Equal-Area Projection

◄ *"The Prairie Schooner Family" shows pioneers enjoying an evening meal on the Overland Trail. What made the preparation of meals difficult?*

The settlers learned quickly that their trips must be well planned. Lack of food or equipment could be fatal.

Life on the Frontier

The hardships did not end when the pioneers reached their goal. It was difficult to part with the friends they had made while crossing the country. The pioneers missed those they had left behind. Because of the length of the trip, most pioneers reached Oregon or California in the fall. Despite their exhaustion, they had to build a shelter and start clearing fields.

Even for those who were experienced farmers, the new climate and growing conditions caused problems. The workday was a long one that ran from dawn to after dusk. Children matured quickly; they were expected to feed livestock, work in the fields, and care for younger sisters and brothers. A pioneer woman might stay up all night mending, making candles, preserving food, or caring for a sick family member. Men worked in their fields, helped others with farm chores, and took part in building the community school or church. ■

■ *What problems of weather and geography did the pioneers face?*

Impact of the Westward Movement

The hardships shared by people on the frontier gave them a sense of **regionalism**, of belonging to a distinct area. Gradually settlements grew into communities and then into towns with doctors, storekeepers, lawyers, sheriffs, and deputies. Towns that had existed before settlers from the United States arrived were often transformed.

In 1859, Richard Henry Dana returned to the port of San Francisco. Compare the following description of the port with his earlier account on page 238.

*W*e bore round the point towards the old anchoring-ground of the hide ships, and there, covering the sand-hills and the valleys, stretching from the water's edge to the base of the great hills, and from the old presidio to the mission, flickering all over with the lamps of its streets and houses, lay a city of one hundred thousand inhabitants. Clocks tolled the hour of midnight, . . . but the city was alive from the salute of our guns.

Richard Henry Dana, *Twenty Years After*, 1859

The West

The common experiences of the people who settled the West suggest they might have formed a region that is somehow distinct from other regions in the country. What exactly is a region? How are its borders determined? Do the same regions that were forming in 1850 still exist today?

Defining a Region

A country as immense as the United States can be divided up in many ways, on the basis of geography, economics, or culture. A region is an area that shares some set of defined characteristics. Geographical division, for example, groups together states with similar physical features such as mountains or plains. A geographical division may also emphasize transportation routes, such as river systems. Economic division stresses local agriculture, such as the citrus belt; or manufacturing; or markets—who trades with whom.

In addition to these indicators, regions may also be defined by the people who live in an area. This can be termed *cultural regionalism*. People might live in similar areas and use the land differently. For example, the Great Plains stretches from the Dakotas into Texas. The people who live in the north tend to be descendants of New Englanders and of Scandinavians, interested in cooperative ventures. The people who live in the south are apt to be small-scale, independent farmers who probably migrated there from the South.

Culture, as you know, includes all learned behavior—all the kinds of knowledge and skills that are passed on from one generation to another. In looking at cultural variations across the country, you would want to consider a group's religion, politics, housing styles, and special ways of speaking. You might also look at a group's preferences in music, literature, food, and social behavior.

Cultural Variations

Let's look at some examples of regional cultural variations. Some of the most interesting are differences in dialects—how people speak. Many people who live in New England, New York City, the South, and Texas use the same words but pronounce them in different ways. Do you pronounce the letter "a" in "pass" like the "a" in "pat" or like the broad "a" in "father"? Do you sound the "r" in "car" or "hard" or do you let it drop ("cah" or "hahd")? If you do, there is a good chance that you live in New England or that you moved from there recently.

Differences in dialects can also be traced through the choice of words. In the North people carry water in a "pail"; in the Midwest and in the South water is carried in a "bucket." Researchers can draw a line on a map of the United States dividing those who say "barn lot" and those who call it a "barnyard."

Spread of Cultures

The spread of cultures across the United States parallels the migration of people in the late 1700s from the first

coastal settlements inwards. The independent farmers of the Southern colonies were in the forefront of the migrants who entered Kentucky and Tennessee. The settlers on the Kentucky frontier, still restless, were among the first to travel along the Oregon Trail.

California in some ways is the most Americanized of all the states because its population is so diverse. Spaniards and Mexicans were of course the first to arrive. The explosive growth following the discovery of gold brought in settlers from every part of the country. Added to this were immigrants from both east and west—Irish and Chinese. Though in the East, immigrants typically headed for the big cities, in California many immigrants settled in the countryside to farm.

The Future of Regionalism

Some observers have predicted that regionalism is becoming less of a force in this country because of the achievements in transportation and in mass communication. They say that the distinctions between North, South, West, and East, are becoming blurred.

Others disagree. They point to the increased interest in folk cultures and in ethnic origins. Backing up this point of view are polls that suggest regional differences are even stronger among the population under 40 years of age than among the older population. Pride in regional variations, according to this point of view, will lead naturally to renewed pride in the country as a whole.

Impact on Inhabitants

A major impact of the westward movement was on the people already living there—the Mexican citizens of the Southwest and California and the many Indians. The Treaty of Guadalupe Hidalgo guaranteed the rights of Mexican citizens living on the lands ceded to the United States in 1848. Many Mexicans decided to stay and automatically became U.S. citizens. When thousands of forty-niners rushed to California, however, the Californios, as the Mexican inhabitants were called, had difficulty keeping their land. Some prospectors simply moved in and took possession. Under U.S. law, landholders had to provide positive proof that the land belonged to them. The boundaries of the land grants, however, were often vague and ownership was not clear. Rancheros who contested white settlers' claims in court usually lost their land. Within a few years most of the great California ranchos were gone. Rancheros in New Mexico also lost their land grants. Many were reduced to working as hired hands on the lands they once owned.

The Indian peoples of the West grew increasingly alarmed as the waves of pioneers flooded through their hunting lands. They attacked some wagon trains and an occasional settlement. However, because the pioneers did not stop in the Great Plains, no major confrontation occurred between the Plains Indians and white people. That clash would come later.

Impact on Pioneers

Those who journeyed west found that the mountains were higher than those elsewhere in the nation, the plains more vast, the rivers more turbulent. In overcoming these obstacles, the pioneers learned to be tough, resourceful, and frugal. The experience of the trail was a forge on which they hammered out their character.

The common hardships the pioneers had shared in the journey westward and in settling the frontier gave them a sense of community. They learned to cooperate in building homes, schools, and churches. At the same time, Westerners were self-reliant individualists used to solving their own problems and supplying their own needs. People in other parts of the United States also developed a sense of belonging to a particular region. ■

William Henry Jackson, a photographer with U.S. surveyors, also made some watercolor sketches. In this scene he shows a family just getting settled on the frontier.

■ *How did the westward movement affect those who already lived there?*

R E V I E W

1. **FOCUS** What impact did the discovery of gold have on the West?
2. **CONNECT** Compare and contrast the reasons why people moved west after 1848 with the reasons why the Whitmans and the Mormons had earlier moved to Oregon and Utah.
3. **SOCIAL** Describe the hardships people faced on the Overland Trail. How did life on the frontier differ from those hardships? How was it similar?
4. **CRITICAL THINKING** Review the concept of Manifest Destiny. What elements of Manifest Destiny can be seen in the way the Californios were treated after 1848?
5. **WRITING ACTIVITY** Imagine that the year is 1848 and that you are at Sutter's sawmill on the American River in California when Marshall discovered gold. Interview the people who are there. How did they react at first? What did they do when they learned that Marshall had really found gold?

247

The Oregon Trail

Francis Parkman

Francis Parkman (1823-1893) was a historian known for his vivid descriptions. In 1846, he journeyed to Wyoming on the Oregon Trail, part of which followed the route of Lewis and Clark. For several months he lived with the Sioux, gathering information about American Indian customs. The excerpt reprinted below is taken from the book of his observations entitled The Oregon Trail. *As you read Parkman's narrative, ask yourself "How does the description of the land add to the narrator's fear of being lost?"*

As you learned in Chapter 8, pioneers bound for the West followed routes, such as the Oregon Trail, that had been discovered by explorers and mountain men.

I looked about for some indications to show me where I was, and what course I ought to pursue; I might as well have looked for landmarks in the midst of the ocean. How many miles I had run, or in what direction, I had no idea; and around me the prairie was rolling in steep swells and pitches, without a single distinctive feature to guide me. I had a little compass hung at my neck; and, ignorant that the Platte at this point diverged considerably from its easterly course, I thought that by keeping to the northward I should certainly reach it. So I turned and rode about two hours in that direction. The prairie changed as I advanced, softening away into easier undulations, but nothing like the Platte appeared, nor any sign of a human being: the same wild endless expanse lay around me still; and to all appearance I was as far from my object as ever. I began now to think myself in danger of being lost, and, reining in my horse, summoned the scanty share of woodcraft that I possessed (if that term is applicable upon the prairie) to extricate me. It occurred to me that the buffalo might prove my best guides. I soon found one of the paths made by them in their passage to the river: it ran nearly at right angles to my course; but turning my horse's head in the direction it indicated, his freer gait and erected ears assured me that I was right.

But in the meantime my ride had been by no means a solitary one. The face of the country was dotted far and wide with countless hundreds of buffalo. They trooped along in files and columns, bulls, cows, and calves, on the green faces of the declivities in front. They scrambled away over the hills to the right and left; and far off, the pale blue swells in the extreme distance were dotted with innumerable specks. Sometimes I surprised shaggy old bulls grazing alone, or sleeping behind the ridges I ascended. They would leap up at my approach, stare stupidly at me through their tangled manes, and then gallop heavily away. The antelope were very numerous; and as they are always bold when in the neighborhood of buffalo, they would approach to look at me, gaze intently with their great round eyes, then suddenly leap aside, and

undulations wavelike surface

extricate get out of a bind

declivities downward slopes

stretch lightly away over the prairie, as swiftly as a race horse. Squalid, ruffian-like wolves sneaked through the hollows and sandy ravines. Several times I passed through villages of prairie dogs, who sat, each at the mouth of his burrow, holding his paws before him in a supplicating attitude, and yelping away most vehemently, whisking his little tail with every squeaking cry he uttered. Prairie dogs are not fastidious in their choice of companions; various long checkered snakes were sunning themselves in the midst of the village, and demure little gray owls, with a large white ring around each eye, were perched side by side with the rightful inhabitants. The prairie teemed with life. Again and again I looked toward the crowded hillsides, and was sure I saw horsemen; and riding near, with a mixture of hope and dread, for Indians were abroad, I found them transformed into a group of buffalo. There was nothing in human shape amid all this vast congregation of brute forms.

When I turned down the buffalo path, the prairie seemed changed; only a wolf or two glided by at intervals, like conscious felons, never looking to the right or left. Being now free from anxiety, I was at leisure to observe minutely the objects around me; and here, for the first time, I noticed insects wholly different from any of the varieties found farther to the eastward. Gaudy butterflies fluttered about my horse's head; strangely formed beetles, glittering with metallic luster, were crawling upon plants that I had never seen before; multitudes of lizards, too, were darting like lightning over the sand.

I had run to a great distance from the river. It cost me a long ride on the buffalo path, before I saw, from the edge of a sand hill, the pale surface of the Platte glistening in the midst of its desert valley, and the faint outline of the hills beyond waving along the sky. From where I stood, not a tree nor a bush nor a living thing was visible throughout the whole extent of the sun-scorched landscape.

supplicating pleading

Further Reading

The Story of the Oregon Trail. Conrad R. Stein.

Third Girl From the Left. Ann Turner. A young woman leaves Maine for harsh Montana as a mail-order bride and her adventures begin as she is left a widow with a 2,000 acre ranch to run.

Walking Up a Rainbow. Theodore Taylor. In 1852, a courageous Iowa orphan embarks on a westward journey full of hardship, adventure, intrigue, and danger.

Chapter Review

Reviewing Key Terms

annex (p. 232)
buffer zone (p. 231)
continental divide (p. 226)
expansionist (p. 230)
ghost town (p. 243)

Manifest Destiny (p. 227)
mountain man (p. 226)
regionalism (p. 245)
rendezvous (p. 226)
secularize (p. 237)

A. Define each of the following terms in your own words. Then use the term in a sentence that clearly shows the meaning of the term.
1. continental divide
2. Manifest Destiny
3. annex
4. expansionist
5. secularize
6. mountain man

B. Based on what you have read in the chapter, decide whether each of the following statements is true or false. If it is false, rewrite the sentence so that it is true.
1. A mountain man would spend much of the year in the wilderness and become a skilled tracker and pathfinder.
2. No settlers were allowed to go to Texas, which was a buffer zone between Mexico and the United States.
3. The Mexican government began to secularize the missions by putting them under the control of priests.
4. A ghost town only came alive at night, when the miners returned from the gold fields.

Exploring Concepts

A. On a separate sheet of paper, make a chart like the one shown below. Fill in the chart with information from the chapter. In the first column of your chart, list the areas explored or settled, along with dates of exploration or settlement. Then complete the chart by listing in the second column the reasons for the exploration or settlement. Write a short paragraph outlining the explorations and settlements that developed the West.

B. On your paper, answer each of the following questions in complete sentences.
1. What were the major effects of the Lewis and Clark expedition?
2. How did the work of the mountain men help later settlers?
3. How did Mexico's agreement to give free land to U.S. settlers in Texas backfire?
4. How did Texans turn the defeats at the Alamo and Goliad into victories?

Explorer/Settler	Dates and Territories Expanded/Settled	Reasons for Exploration/Settlement
Meriwether Lewis and William Clark		
Jedediah Smith		
Brigham Young		
Zebulon Pike		
Stephen Austin		
John C. Frémont		

Reviewing Skills

1. Outlines use roman numerals, capital letters, and numbers to note the difference between topics and details. Identify which parts of an outline use roman numerals, which use capital letters, and which use numbers.

2. Copy the outline on page 228. Decide whether the facts below are subtopics (S) or details (D), and put them in the correct order under the heading "III. Results of the Lewis and Clark Expedition."

   • New species were recorded, such as buffalo and Pacific salmon.
   • The expedition's samples of plants, animals, and rocks showed that the Louisiana Purchase territory was rich in natural resources.
   • The expedition catalogued in detail thousands of different plants and animals.

3. Zebulon Pike was exploring the upper Mississippi River at about the same time as the Lewis and Clark expedition. Use the information below to complete this outline:

   I. Zebulon Pike's Explorations
      A. Rocky Mountain Region
         1. Pike's Peak named after him.

   • Pike gives the government information about the number and kinds of troops Spain has in the New Mexico area.
   • New Mexico and Northern Mexico Region
   • Pike describes the wide sandy deserts of the Southwest.

4. Use the outline on page 228 to create a timeline of the Lewis and Clark expedition. Conduct your own research on the expedition, and add any information you find to your timeline.

Using Critical Thinking

1. In President Polk's inaugural address, he said, "None can fail to see the danger to our safety and future peace if Texas remains an independent state or becomes an ally . . . of some foreign nation." What do you think was the danger that Polk feared? Does that fear affect the United States' relationships with nearby countries today? Give examples to support your answer.

2. The Texans' defeat at the Alamo became one of our country's proudest stories. Why do you think a defeat became such a precious memory? Why are Texans and all Americans proud of it?

3. One historian has written of the Mexican War, "The vanquished Mexicans have never forgotten, or will they soon forget, that the northern 'gringos' tore away half of their country." Do you think the war was justified? What other means might have been used to settle the dispute?

Preparing for Citizenship

1. **WRITING ACTIVITY** Tales of the mountain men and their exploits became part of American folklore. Read through current newspapers and magazines, and identify people you think may become a part of our folklore. Write a short paper explaining what these people have done and how you think they will be seen by future generations.

2. **WRITING ACTIVITY** Many of the pioneers who made the journey across the plains kept diaries or wrote letters home. In the library, find some of these firsthand accounts. Write your favorite quotations in a notebook, and share them with the class.

3. **ART ACTIVITY** Draw a map of North America that shows how the idea of Manifest Destiny changed the boundaries in the Western United States during the 1800s.

4. **COLLABORATIVE LEARNING** The West was the frontier for Americans in the 1800s. The frontier for Americans today is outer space. Divide into groups and imagine that you are preparing to homestead on a new planet. What will you bring with you? What hardships might you face? Are your concerns different from or similar to those of the nineteenth-century pioneers? Compare your decisions with those of the other groups in your class.

Chapter 9

The North

One man built an entire mill from memory. Another man turned a "folly" into the first successful steam-powered boat. Women filled the factories and mills. The North was alive with invention and progress. Cities thrived and everywhere the character of Northern life was changing.

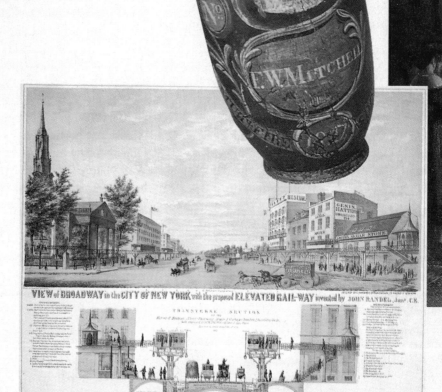

Cities grow quickly as canals, railroads, and telegraphs connect the nation. New York City even has elevated trains for mass transportation.

VIEW of BROADWAY in the CITY OF NEW YORK with the proposed ELEVATED RAIL-WAY invented by JOHN RANDEL, Junr. C.E.

1790	1800	1810	1820

Presidents

1789-1797
Washington

1797-1801
J. Adams

1801-1809
Jefferson

1809-1817
Madison

1817-1825
Monroe

1790

1827 Growing cities demand fire and police services. At right is a decorated hat worn by a firefighter in a parade. An equally ornate fire bucket from 1827 is shown at the top, left.

1860 Artist Henry Mosler depicts the bustling Canal Market in Cincinnati.

1830

1840

1850

1860

1825-1829
J. Q. Adams

1829-1837
Jackson

1837-1841
Van Buren

1841-1845
Tyler

1841
W. Harrison

1845-1849
Polk

1849-1850
Taylor

1850-1853
Fillmore

1853-1857
Pierce

1857-1861
Buchanan

1860

LESSON 1

The Industrial Revolution

How did the inventions of the Industrial Revolution change the way people lived, worked, and traveled?

Key Terms

- Industrial Revolution
- raw materials

➤ *Among a shoemaker's tools were knives for cutting leather, foot-shaped wooden casts for shaping leather, and hammers for tacking on the heels of shoes.*

R andolph, Massachusetts, 1830. Gideon Howard awakes each morning to his new life as an independent craftsman. In earlier days, he was a farmer who made shoes in his spare time for extra money. Now Howard makes his living as a cordwainer, or shoemaker.

Because more people want to buy shoes, Howard needs help to make enough pairs. He does some of the skilled work himself and supervises the other workers. One cuts the leather for the uppers (the top of the shoe); another stretches the leather over a wooden mold shaped like a foot. A stitcher attaches the upper to the sole, and another worker tacks on the heels. The completed shoes are

then taken to a store to be sold.

Individual shoemakers like Howard did a good business until the mid-1800s. Then the demand for shoes rose so rapidly they could not make shoes fast enough. Individual craftspeople lost business, and production moved from small shops to factories that used stitching machines and other new inventions. In the factories, each worker tended a machine that might do several tasks once done by skilled craftspeople working by hand. These advances made it possible to produce more shoes in a shorter time.

Howard's story illustrates how factories largely replaced craftspeople in the 1800s. A new industrial economy was emerging in America. Its growth was especially strong in the North.

Chapter 9

Revolution in Industry

The shift to factories in the United States grew out of a process that began in the British textile industry. In the late 1700s, British inventors developed machines to do tasks that had been done by hand. The spinning jenny, run by water power, replaced the spinning wheel, and the power loom replaced the hand loom. Because these machines were too expensive for most individuals, manufacturing moved from people's homes and shops to factories. This change in producing goods was so far-reaching and had such widespread effects that it is known as the **Industrial Revolution**. It changed not only the way goods were produced, but also how people lived and worked.

Americans copied, then modified, British industrial methods. To limit competition, however, British factory owners refused to allow any machinery or plans of machines to leave England. An ambitious British textile worker named Samuel Slater outwitted them by memorizing the plans. In 1790, Slater built a spinning mill in Pawtucket, Rhode Island, using machines based on these plans. It began a revolution in U.S. industry.

The use of the newest machinery and the newest techniques helped American industry succeed. One new method was the use of standard parts. Eli Whitney, a Connecticut inventor, developed tools and machinery to make parts that were exactly alike. For example, the bolt for one of Whitney's rifles would fit any of his rifles. Having interchangeable parts speeded up production and reduced costs.

Also important in America's success was its store of natural resources. Wood from its forests, coal and iron ore from its mines, and abundant water power were all vital in early industry.

Last, but certainly not least, were the American people. Skilled and resourceful, they provided the labor, the business leadership, and the inventiveness that made the United States an industrial leader. ◼

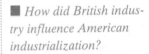

◼ *How did British industry influence American industrialization?*

◀ *As the Industrial Revolution swept the North, mills such as this one in Massachusetts were established. Americans began to make goods for themselves.*

Building a Transportation Network

The enormous size of the young nation meant that transportation was difficult and expensive. The United States needed easier, quicker, and cheaper methods of transportation.

A System of Roads

In 1794, the Lancaster Turnpike, linking Philadelphia and Lancaster, Pennsylvania, became the first hard-surfaced road in the United States. In the following years, more than 10,000 miles of roads were built to link the major commercial centers of the North. Many roads were built by private companies which charged a toll, or fee, for their use. Although tolls were used for upkeep, the roads were rough. Travelers jounced and bumped over the uneven surfaces. They welcomed the development of canals.

A Canal Network

In 1825, the state of New York completed the Erie Canal, a 363-mile waterway joining Buffalo on Lake Erie with Troy and Albany on the Hudson River. The new waterway linked the Atlantic Coast to all of the Great Lakes for the first time. Ships sailed from New York City up the Hudson River to Albany; then their cargo and passengers shifted to canal boats. The canal helped New York become the nation's most important city.

The Erie Canal made travel into the heart of the country easier and less expensive. Goods that cost $100 a ton by road cost only $10 a ton by canal—and the trip was only a third as long. Western **raw materials**—products in their natural state, such as iron ore or cotton—were shipped by canal to the East. Manufactured goods were shipped to the western frontier.

The enormous success of the Erie Canal encouraged an era of canal building. By 1840, over 3,000 miles of canals had been built. Yet, within a few years, canal building virtually ended. Canals could not compete with less costly kinds of transportation.

New inventions and advances in technology helped fuel the growth of U.S. industry.

The First Industrial Revolution, 1790–1860

1790, U.S. Patent Office opens, issuing the first patent to Samuel Hopkins for a new kind of fertilizer ingredient.

1794, Eli Whitney's patent for the cotton gin is granted. Whitney's idea is stolen and copied by others despite his patent.

1816, Althrough Philadelphia tested street lights earlier, Baltimore becomes the first city to light its streets with gas lamps.

1790　　　1800　　　1810　　　1820

1807, Robert Fulton's steamboat *Clermont* makes its maiden voyage on the Hudson River, traveling from New York City to Albany.

1825, Water keg from which Gov. Clinton of New York poured water from Lake Erie into the Atlantic Ocean November 25, 1825, symbolizing the completion of the Erie Canal.

Speedy Clipper Ships

When trade with England was cut off during the War of 1812, New England merchants developed a highly profitable trade with Asia. Lean, fast clipper ships with sails billowing in the wind, sped southeast from Salem and Boston and plunged through the raging waters of Cape Horn at the tip of South America. On the northwest coast of North America they traded blankets and trinkets for furs brought by Indian peoples. The furs were exchanged in China for silk, tea, and fine porcelain. On the return journey, the American ships took on California hides for New England shoemakers (see Chapter 8).

Both the dumpy canal barges and the sleek clippers were important to trade. Yet neither could compete with new vehicles powered by steam—the steamboat and the railroad.

Travel by Steamboat

Credit for making the steamboat a success goes to inventor Robert Fulton. He launched the *Clermont*, the first commercially successful steamboat, on the Hudson River in 1807. Soon steamboats were puffing along U.S. rivers and lakes. They dominated transportation on American waterways from 1815 to 1860. Eventually, however, their use declined. They were replaced by the steam railroad, which did not depend on the fixed routes of natural waterways.

▲ *Horses and mules walked along the towpath beside a canal, towing boats and barges. This painting shows the Erie Canal at Pittsford, New York.*

1847, The first official U.S. gummed postage stamps are issued. Senders began to pay the costs of sending letters.

1853, The Crystal Palace Exhibition is held in New York to display and demonstrate new American inventions and industrial advances.

1830	1840	1850	1860

1833, Samuel Colt invents and patents this six-shooter revolver, the first gun that could be used effectively by a person on hourseback.

1844, The first telegraph message is sent from the U.S. Supreme Court in Washington, D.C. to Baltimore, Md. by Samuel Morse, inventor of the telegraph. A printing telegraph invented by David Hughes is shown here.

1851, Amelia Jenks Bloomer, editor of the women's rights magazine, *Lily,* gains attention by wearing trousers, later known as *bloomers.*

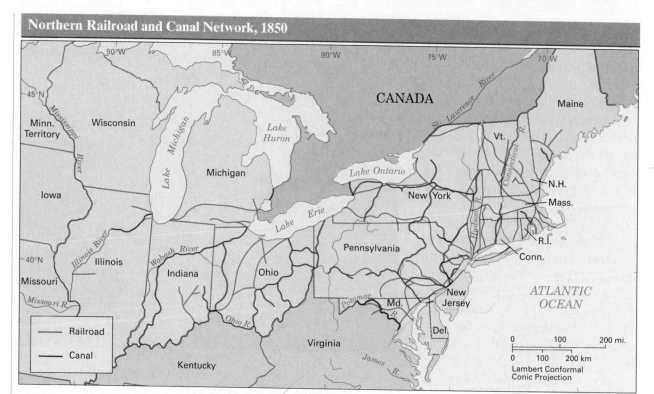

Northern Railroad and Canal Network, 1850

Railroad
Canal

▲ *In 1790, an order sent from Boston to Philadelphia took two weeks to arrive. By 1836, because of expanded railroad services, a similar order took only 36 hours.*

■ *What changes occurred in transportation in the 1800s?*

Across Time & Space

Workers in the 1800s felt machines threatened their jobs. In the 1950s factories began to use electronic robots for boring or dangerous jobs. Some people fear that such machines will put them out of work; others say they create new jobs.

Railroads Revolutionize Travel

Railroads developed first in Britain but grew most dramatically in the United States. Between 1828 and 1840, American workers laid about 3,300 miles of track. By 1860, trains clattered over an incredible 30,626 miles of track.

Train travel was speedy but uncomfortable. Cinders from the wood-burning engine blew into people's eyes, and black soot covered their clothing. The train lurched and jolted over uneven tracks. Yet, because railroads could be built almost anywhere, growing numbers of people used them.

Railroads offered fast, direct, and dependable service. The newly invented telegraph, developed in 1837 by Samuel F. B. Morse, helped control train traffic.

Railroads also provided job opportunities. Unskilled workers, many of them immigrants, laid the tracks and maintained the rail lines. Factory workers manufactured the locomotives and rails needed.

Steamboats and railroads used a new kind of power—steam. By the mid-1800s, steam power was transforming industry as well as transportation in the United States. ■

Production Revolutionized

For the most part, industrialization took place in the Northeast. The region had abundant water that could be used for power. The poor, stony soil of its hilly farms discouraged some farmers and sent them to the cities looking for work. Also New England already had a thriving trade by sea.

The New England textile mills were long brick buildings, three or four stories high, built beside a river

that supplied power for the machines. Inside the factories, workers cared for machines that clattered and hummed as they spun thread and wove fabric.

In 1814, a Boston merchant named Francis Cabot Lowell founded a textile mill at Waltham, Massachusetts. In this mill, Lowell combined all the steps of textile production—from spinning the raw cotton into thread to weaving the finished cloth—under one roof for the first time.

Lowell had hoped to build an entire community around his mill, but died before he could complete his plan. After his death, a city based on his ideas was built by the falls on the broad Merrimack River. Named Lowell in his honor, by 1855 it had some 52 mills that employed more than 13,000 people. These mills produced over one million yards of cotton cloth each week. In a year that was "nearly enough to belt the globe twice over." Lowell and the other Merrimack River towns—nearby Lawrence and Merrimack, New Hampshire—were the center of the textile industry in New England.

Women Enter the Factories

During the early 1800s, most farm women remained at home, rearing the children and performing household tasks. This pattern began to change in about 1820. New England farmers found it difficult to compete with Western farmers who could grow grain and other crops more cheaply. Many farmers' sons left New England and headed for the more fertile farms in the West. Farm daughters tried to help their families by going to work in the textile factories.

Most American factory owners welcomed these young women. They were used to hard work on the farms, and the factory owners hoped they would prove to be a dependable, obedient work force.

To avoid the poverty and crime found in British factory towns, the owners paid wages in cash, set up company-run boarding houses, and provided social and cultural opportunities. Although the boarding houses had strict rules, they gave the young women a place to live where someone looked after their well-being.

Lowell "Mill Girls"

Factory work tended to be repetitious and dull. Lucy Larcoom, who worked in the Lowell mills at a machine called a dressing frame, told how the machines sometimes seemed to overwhelm the workers.

> It had to be watched in a dozen directions every minute . . . it was always getting itself and me into trouble. I felt as if the half-live creature . . . was aware of my incapacity to manage it.

The women in the Lowell mills worked an average of 12 hours a day, six days a week. Men held all the

▲ Water power was used to operate mills. Flowing water turned a large, outdoor wheel. Gears then turned pulleys and belts that moved the factory's machines.

259

Lowell "mill girls" faced long work days for little pay.

■ *What made New England the center of the textile industry?*

supervisory positions and received higher pay. In 1836, men's daily wages ranged between 85 cents and $2, while women earned from 40 cents to 80 cents. A worker could be fined or denied work for being late, working too slowly, or challenging a supervisor's authority. To increase production, some mills had each worker take care of more machines or speeded up the rate at which machines worked. Workers had little choice but to work faster if they wanted to keep their jobs.

Despite these disadvantages, the New England "mill girls" saw factory work as a chance to learn about a world that was different from their familiar rural surroundings. Most enjoyed meeting other young people, going to theaters and museums, and shopping in a variety of stores. They found the bustling throngs of the city an exciting change from the isolation of farm life.

Most "mill girls" looked on facto-ry work as temporary. Most young women intended to work in the mills only until they married. When they felt conditions were too difficult, they left. In the mid-1800s, many farm women grew dissatisfied. Their place was taken by immigrant workers, most of them from Ireland.

Industry Inland

Not all the industrial cities were near the coast. When steam began to be used in factories as well as in transportation, industry could be set up closer to raw materials or markets. Pittsburgh, Pennsylvania, for example, was an inland city that grew up near supplies of coal and iron ore and cheap water transportation.

The Pittsburgh factories concentrated on metal working. The first factories made nails. Added to these were a steam engine factory and a mill using iron ore. At first, slabs of iron were rolled flat by hammers driven by country streams. In 1819, the Union Rolling Mill introduced a process that allowed the iron to be rolled in the factory. By making iron production more efficient, Pittsburgh became America's "Iron City."

The wave of industrial development sent ripples through every level of society in the United States. Centuries' old traditions were transformed as Americans faced new challenges of adjusting to city life. The country and the world would never again be the same. ■

R E V I E W

1. **FOCUS** How did the inventions of the Industrial Revolution change the way people lived, worked, and traveled?

2. **CONNECT** How was settlement of the West spurred by the expansion of the railroad and canal networks?

3. **GEOGRAPHY** What factors determined where factories were built during the early 1800s?

4. **CRITICAL THINKING** What do you think are the advantages and disadvantages of products assembled by hand?

Of manufactured goods?

5. **CRITICAL THINKING** "Mill girls" were subject to highly supervised, highly regulated work and social lives. Do you think this was an effective way to ensure productivity? Give reasons for your opinion.

6. **ACTIVITY** Ask your parents or other adults to tell you about their memories of a roadway being built. Ask them to explain how the road's construction affected the area in which it was built.

L E S S O N 2

The Urban North

> *I think our governments will remain virtuous for many centuries as long as they are chiefly agricultural; and this will be as long as there shall be vacant lands in any part of America. When they get piled upon one another in large cities, as in Europe, they will become corrupt as in Europe.*
>
> Thomas Jefferson to James Madison, 1787

Thomas Jefferson believed that cities were a threat to American values. In Jefferson's mind, America was meant to be a land of sturdy, independent farmers (see Chapter 8). The land would be free of the factories, industrial cities, and crowds of people found in Europe.

By 1816, growing cities and spreading industrialism pointed to sweeping change in the nation's political, social, and economic life. Jefferson declared, "we must now place the manufacturer by the side of the agriculturalist." He had come to recognize that the United States was becoming an industrial nation.

Many Americans welcomed the shift toward an urban society. In 1833, Amasa Walker, a follower of Andrew Jackson, remarked that a time would come when cities would become "great fountains of healthful moral influence, sending forth streams that shall fertilize and bless the land."

THINKING FOCUS

How did the growth of cities affect American society?

Key Term

- municipal

Urban Growth

During the 1700s, American business had been based on trade with other countries. The major colonial cities in the North were located on the Atlantic Coast and their economy depended on shipping.

In the 1800s, advances in technology and transportation shifted the economic emphasis from trade to industry. This shift changed the way Americans lived and worked.

City Populations Grow

U.S. cities grew very quickly during the 1840s, their population expanded due to immigrants and people moving from the farms. In 1820, only 12 cities in the United States had populations of more than 10,000 peo-

ple. By 1860, the United States had 101 cities of more than 10,000 people each. Eight of them were home to more than 100,000 people; one—New York City—had already topped one million inhabitants.

As the urban populations grew, city governments faced a number of problems. Housing the increase in people and protecting them were obviously important issues. The expanding cities also needed their own transportation systems.

Providing Housing

An important innovation in urban construction was the "balloon frame" house, introduced in the 1830s. Wood was sawed into thin pieces that were nailed together to make a relatively light, inexpensive frame. Traditional structures used heavy jointed timbers in their frames and needed skilled carpenters to build them.

The balloon frame did not require special skills. It allowed people to build whole neighborhoods quickly and economically. This technique was especially useful farther west, where the cities had plenty of space to spread outward.

In the older areas of the Northeast, cities grew upward instead of outward. The wooden frames that were most commonly used could not support the weight of buildings that were over a few stories high.

To solve this problem, some architects combined cast-iron columns with stone buildings. James Bogardus pioneered this method in 1848 when he built a five-story factory in New York. Later, he used iron to make entire frames for buildings. Iron, however, was heavy, and it limited the height of buildings. Taller buildings were not possible until new technology came along in the late 1800s.

➤ On this map the circles represent population, not the areas of the city. What cities had grown to over 300,000 people by 1860?

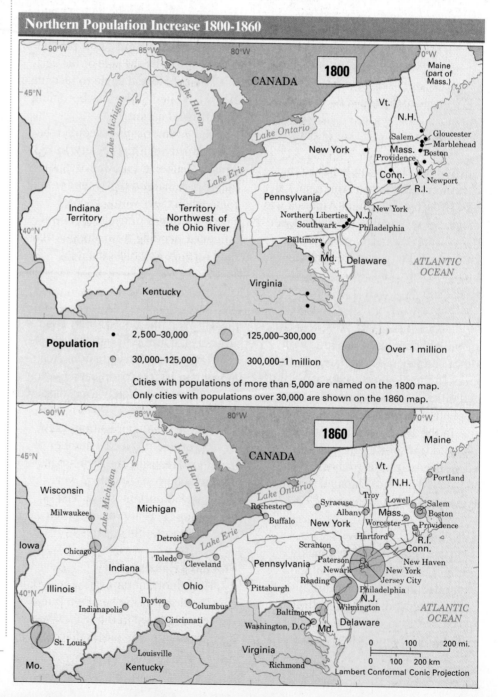

Northern Population Increase 1800-1860

Cities with populations of more than 5,000 are named on the 1800 map.
Only cities with populations over 30,000 are shown on the 1860 map.

Moving City People Around

In most cities before 1840, people could easily walk from one place to another. As these cities grew, the distances between different parts increased, and cities began to develop public transportation systems. Within the cities, horse-drawn vehicles called horsecars came into use in about 1850. Horsecars traveled on specific routes around the city, taking people from their homes to the places where they worked and shopped. By 1866, New York City had 16 horsecars with 800 cars and 8,000 horses to pull them. They carried about 35 million passengers a year.

As cities grew more crowded, however, the horsecars became less practical. Author Mark Twain commented that the cars were "getting left behind by fast walkers." He added that the cars were so crowded that "you will have to hang on by your eyelashes and your toenails."

Transportation was one **municipal**, or city-run, service. As city populations grew, the need increased for municipal services.

Protecting People

One problem facing the growing cities was a rising rate of crime. The part-time law officers were little more than watchmen who made scheduled rounds of the city. They were not organized or trained to enforce law and order. To protect law-abiding citizens, full-time municipal police forces were needed. In 1845, New York City set up the first modern police force. Philadelphia and Boston soon followed New York's example.

City dwellers also needed protection from fire. The large number of wooden frame buildings and the use of candles, fireplaces, and wood-burning stoves caused frequent fires. In the crowded cities these fires spread quickly and killed many people. At first, crews of volunteer firemen rushed through the streets pulling hose wagons and hand pumps. As cities grew, these volunteers were replaced by full-time professional firemen. About the same time, steam-powered pumps came into use. When the fire alarm sounded, horses dashed through the streets pulling steam pumps.

Another important concern in the cities were health problems. Most cities had no sanitation systems, and streets were clogged with garbage. Polluted water caused epidemics of deadly diseases. After a cholera epidemic in 1866, New York City set up the Metropolitan Board of Health. To make the city a more healthful place to

This 1803 painting, A Large View of Baltimore, shows one of the rapidly growing American cities.

live, it limited the number of people living in a room, banned throwing garbage in the streets, and required better ventilation of rooms and better connections between buildings and the city's sewer system. ■

People in the Cities

Most Americans considered the growth of cities a sign of success. Urban growth was so rapid, however, that it created numerous problems for people, especially the poor.

Social Classes

Within the cities lived wealthy factory owners and bankers, middle-class shopkeepers, and poor workers. The middle class included mill supervisors, shopkeepers, craftspeople, ministers, and school teachers. (The telegraph operator in A Moment in Time on page 265 was a member of the middle class.) Educated free blacks, usually ministers or teachers, made up a small proportion of the middle class.

The working poor included people who had moved from rural areas to the cities, immigrants, and unskilled free blacks. In the 1840s, over four million immigrants entered the United States; most of them settled in cities as unskilled laborers. Eventually some of the immigrants, through hard work

and education, moved up into the middle class.

In many typical mill cities, the workers lived in crowded apartments or company-owned housing a short walk from the factories where they worked. They depended on the factory whistle to tell them the time of day. The middle class were scattered throughout the city. Many used the horsecars to travel about. On the outskirts of the city, or on hills overlooking the mills, stood the mansions of the wealthy. Private horse-drawn carriages took them around the city.

Changing Social Relationships

Although the same social classes had existed before, industrialism changed the relationships between them. The gap between the classes grew steadily wider. Factory owners, bankers, and railroad owners grew wealthier as their businesses prospered. People in the middle class also benefited.

➤ *This painting, entitled* Sidewalks of New York *or* Rich Girl, Poor Girl, *illustrates the different social classes that developed in the urban North.*

A Telegraph Operator

10:34 A.M., August 29, 1852
Office of the Pittsburgh, Cincinnati,
and Louisville Telegraph Company
in Pittsburgh, Pennsylvania

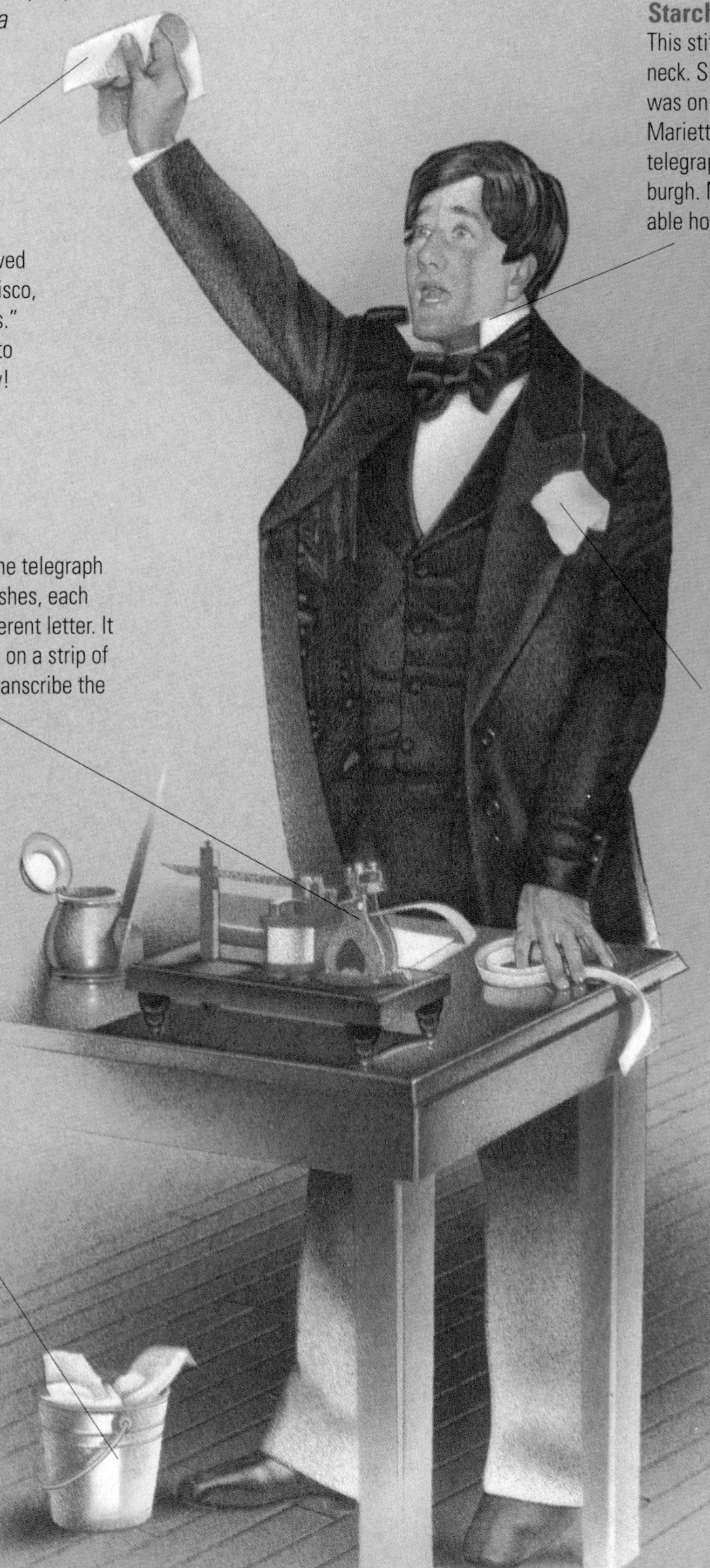

Starched Collar
This stiff collar irritates his neck. Six months ago he was on his family's farm in Marietta, Ohio. Now he's a telegraph operator in Pittsburgh. No more comfortable homespun shirts.

Message
"Largest gold shipment received in New York from San Francisco, worth over $2 million dollars." Someone run this message to the newspaper editor—now!

Telegraph
Dot, Dash, Dot . . . The telegraph taps out dots and dashes, each code signaling a different letter. It records the message on a strip of paper. His job is to transcribe the code into English.

Handkerchief
The summer air in the office is musty and hot. He reaches for this when the smells of oil lamps and ink make him sneeze.

Lunch Pail
With any luck, the boarding house matron packed him a big lunch. He came in at 6:00 this morning, and with all the excitement, he may be here until 9:00 tonight.

The poor, however, faced a new situation. Before industrialization, they had worked on farms or in shops for their board and room. They usually lived where they worked or nearby. If poor workers became ill or could not work, their employer often helped them out.

With the coming of industrialization, workers received wages that had to be spent for rent, food, clothing, medicine, and other expenses. They lost their income if they lost their jobs. They had no unemployment benefits or health insurance to protect them. They might receive aid from private charities, such as church groups, but there were no government programs of aid. Unemployment was a real threat. Urban workers had little choice but to work 10 to 12 hours a day, plus six hours on Saturdays, for very little pay.

■ How did industrialization change the relationship between social classes?

➤ Social reformer Dorothea Dix worked throughout her lifetime to improve life for people who were mentally ill.

Beginnings of Reform

The problems that faced people in the industrializing cities led to several reform movements. At first, these were carried out by individuals or private groups. One individual who worked for reform was Dorothea Dix, a Massachusetts school teacher. When she visited a women's prison in 1841, she found several mentally ill women among the inmates. To help these unfortunate women became Dix's lifelong cause.

For the next 40 years she urged states to build more hospitals for the mentally ill. She was so persuasive that the number of state mental hospitals increased from 13 in 1843 to 123 in 1880.

Dorothea Dix had concentrated on a single area that needed reform. Other reformers became involved in wider social issues. ■

REVIEW

1. **FOCUS** How did the growth of cities affect American society?

2. **CONNECT** How did developments in transportation contribute to the rapid industrialization of the North?

3. **ECONOMICS** How did the move from an economy based on commerce and trade to one based on manufacturing affect the way Americans lived and worked?

4. **CRITICAL THINKING** Why are municipal services performed by city governments rather than private organizations?

5. **CRITICAL THINKING** How did the experience of the working poor in cities differ from that of the wealthy and middle classes?

6. **WRITING ACTIVITY** Imagine you are a factory worker who has moved from a rural area to find a job in the city. Write two or three short diary entries that describe your first impressions of city life.

L E S S O N 3

Seeking a Better Way

> "We hold these truths to be self-evident: that all men and women are created equal..."
>
> Declaration of Sentiments,
> *Women's Rights Convention*,
> Seneca Falls, New York, 1848

These words sound familiar, but they are not the ones Thomas Jefferson wrote for the Declaration of Independence. Jefferson had mentioned only men when he wrote of equality. By the mid-1800s, some women were beginning to challenge this limitation of rights.

In 1848, no woman had the right to vote, and most women were denied property rights. If a woman was divorced, her husband had the unchallenged right to take the children.

In July 1848, more than 300 women met at the Wesleyan Methodist Church in Seneca Falls, New York. Their aim was to discuss "the social, civil, and religious condition and rights of women."

Among the organizers of the convention were Lucretia Mott and Elizabeth Cady Stanton. Both were active in the fight to end slavery. Their articles against slavery were welcomed by men who worked to end slavery. Yet, because they were women, they had not been allowed to make public speeches at the world antislavery convention in 1840. Angered by this rejection, Mott and Stanton decided to work to improve the status of women.

Some men supported the movement for women's rights. Most men, however, agreed with a male editor who called the Seneca Falls meeting "the most shocking and unnatural incident ever recorded in the history of womanity."

Despite this opposition, the movement for women's rights continued. In 1841, Elizabeth Cady Stanton met Susan B. Anthony, who was active in the antislavery movement. (To read more about Susan B. Anthony, see page 276.) The women became close friends and worked together for women's rights. This movement was just one of the social reforms that developed in the 1800s.

THINKING
FOCUS

What types of social reform movements developed in the 1800s?

Key Terms

- temperance
- utopia

◄ *Elizabeth Cady Stanton, a homemaker in upstate New York, organized the women's rights meeting in Seneca Falls. Many people still consider Seneca Falls as the birthplace of the women's rights movement in the United States.*

Reform Takes Many Shapes

Americans both welcomed and feared the rapid changes society was undergoing during the 1800s. Certainly industrialization and the growth of cities offered many new opportunities. However, many people wondered about the cost of industrial progress. Problems such as alcoholism, illiteracy, and poor working conditions cried out for action.

Reformers attempted to solve these problems in various ways. The movements they started were largely an outgrowth of the Second Great Awakening (see Chapter 6), which sought to create a better society. Their ideal was expressed by lawyer and educator Horace Mann: "Be ashamed to die until you have won some victory for humanity."

The Temperance Movement

Reformers had the most success in their attempts to decrease alcoholism. Although alcohol abuse had existed throughout American history, the problem became more severe with industrialization. Many workers felt resentment because their lives seemed to be regulated by machines. Instead of feeling proud of the products they made, many workers grew bored from doing the same, repetitive task. They feared unemployment, illness, and old age. In despair, many workers sought to escape their misery with alcohol.

Alcoholism led to physical abuse and broke up many families. Recognizing this destructiveness of alcoholism, reformers called for **temperance**—giving up all drinking of alcoholic beverages. By 1833, there were 5,000 local temperance societies with a combined membership of over one million people. Members signed a pledge promising they would never drink alcoholic beverages.

In line with the ideals of the Second Great Awakening, temperance leaders looked on alcoholism as a moral problem rather that a social problem or an illness. To them, alcoholics were sinners who spent the Sabbath in drinking rather than in worship. Through the efforts of these temperance societies, alcoholism declined sharply in the 1840s.

Women played a major role in the temperance movement. First, they were expected by tradition to set a

▲ Social reformer Susan B. Anthony was active in the antislavery, temperance, and women's rights movements. Anthony pledged her life insurance money to the University of Rochester in Rochester, New York, so that women could attend the school.

➤ Through drawings and posters that illustrated the results of alcoholism, temperance societies persuaded many to sign the pledge.

moral example for other family members. Second, women had firsthand experience of excessive drinking. Many had suffered physical and mental abuse at the hands of drunken fathers or husbands. Third, women wanted to stop men from spending on alcohol the money that their families needed.

Education for Women

In addition to urging temperance, many women sought expanded educational opportunities for themselves. In the process, they helped bring about public education for all.

One of the early reformers was Emma Willard, who believed women should be allowed to study mathematics, science, and philosophy—subjects traditionally restricted to male students. Willard founded the Troy Female Seminary in Troy, New York, in 1821. Other pioneers in this area included Sarah Josepha Hale, one of the first female magazine editors in the United States, and Mary Lyon, who founded Mount Holyoke Female Seminary (later Mount Holyoke College) in 1837.

Through the efforts of people such as these, women became better educated and more aware of the world outside their homes. Many, however, continued to believe that a woman's

place was in the home. Jobs such as teaching were seen as temporary positions that a woman would leave when she married.

Establishing Public Education

Before the 1820s, few children had the opportunity to go to school. From an early age they worked at trades or on the farm. The few public schools that did exist were understaffed; teachers were poorly paid and received little training. Students of all ages and abilities were crowded into one room. Schools had little money for textbooks or other supplies.

In 1837, lawyer Horace Mann became head of the newly formed Massachusetts State Board of Education. For the next 11 years, Mann worked with other reformers to establish a public educational system. Mann believed education was essential to democracy: "If we do not prepare children to become good citizens, if we do not develop their capacities, . . . then our republic must go down to destruction." His argument reinforced the idea that American constitutional democracy required citizens who were well informed.

Public education, Mann believed, would give children values—thrift, a sense of order, discipline, respect for authority—that would be useful in

The booming cities of the late nineteenth century had their share of problems: crime, fires, garbage, disease. But cities also had their share of pleasures. City-dwellers were less isolated than people living in the country. City people were able to get together to share ideas, entertainment, and common creative interests. Because the large populations were necessary to support libraries, theaters, museums, and art galleries, these cultural institutions first developed as part of the trend toward urbanization.

Reading Societies and Lyceums

The earliest cultural institutions weren't museums or concerts; they were discussion groups that met to exchange ideas and encourage learning. Benjamin Franklin started such a group, called the Junto, in the 1720s. Writer and critic Margaret Fuller also organized a group called "Conversations" in Boston from 1839 through 1844.

Discussions that featured a key speaker, often a famous figure, were known as lyceums. Begun in 1836 by Josiah Holbrook, lyceums offered the public the chance to hear lectures and debates. Later, the American Lyceum paid fees to lecturers who traveled around the entire country. Well-known speakers included Henry David Thoreau, Nathaniel Hawthorne, and Susan B. Anthony. Instead of gathering around the TV or going out to see a movie, as people do today, city-dwellers of the 1800s often spent a social evening at a public lecture.

Libraries

Some of these discussion groups and lyceums were known as "reading societies" because their members loaned each other books from their private collections. In this way, the meeting rooms became the earliest versions of public libraries. In 1731, for example, Benjamin Franklin started the Library Company of Philadelphia, a subscription library in which members' dues purchased books that members shared.

Other libraries began near colleges. For example, in 1638, John Harvard willed about 400 volumes to a newly formed school in Massachusetts, and the Harvard College Library was born. Today, this oldest U.S. library boasts over 11 million volumes.

The nation's commitment to free public education led naturally to its commitment to free public libraries. The first tax-supported public library opened in Peterborough, New Hampshire in 1833. In 1881, Andrew Carnegie, a leader in the steel industry, used part of his vast fortune to build more than 1,700 public libraries throughout the United States.

After the formation of the American Library Association in 1876, the institutions multiplied. Today, Americans have the opportunity to borrow books from over 6,000 public libraries across the country.

During the urbanization of the Industrial Revolution, people worked hard to improve the quality of their lives. This improvement included efforts to extend education beyond the confines of the schoolroom, into meeting places and libraries. In a sense, libraries were a small piece of the longed-for ideal city that actually became reality for cities and towns all across the nation.

industrialized society.

Massachusetts set aside tax money for public education and made it compulsory for children to attend elementary school. To meet the need for better trained teachers, Mann established the first of the normal schools (now called teacher's colleges). Other states followed his example, and public education became widely available.

Men Protest Working Conditions

The roots of labor reform came during the early 1800s as skilled craftsmen such as carpenters, shoemakers, and printers formed "trade societies." They called for higher wages, shorter hours, and better working conditions.

In 1835, the Philadelphia trade societies called a citywide strike —that is, they stopped work until their demands were met. Their slogan, "6 to 6," called for a workday running from 6 A.M. to 6 P.M., with an hour for breakfast and an hour for lunch.

Woman Workers Organize

The trade unions did not include women, since most labor organizers felt women did only unskilled work. Women therefore formed unions of their own. New York seamstresses established a union in 1825. In the 1830s, a Philadelphia organization represented women working in a variety of occupations.

Like men, women workers also used strikes to make their demands clear. In 1828, when textile mill owners in Dover, New Hampshire, issued rules that women workers found unacceptable, the women went on strike. The huge textile factories in Lowell, Massachusetts, stood idle when women went on strike in 1834 to protest a wage cut of 25 percent. Another strike occurred in 1836 when Lowell boarding houses raised the rent they charged. Workers gained little through these early strikes. The mill owners could easily replace the strikers with newly arrived immigrants who would work for lower wages. For most workers, conditions improved little until the late 1800s.

In 1844, five mill workers set up the Lowell Female Reform Association, an influential labor group. In one year, about 500 women joined. The association led the way in the fight to win a 10-hour workday. Their agitation led to the first government investigation of working conditions. ■

▲ *This list shows the strict regulations mill owners set for their workers.*

■ *What part did women play in the reform movements of the 19th century?*

Utopian Societies

Most of the reform movements were practical attempts to improve life by eliminating such problems as poverty, illiteracy, and alcoholism. Other reform groups felt that a new society was needed. These groups tried to set up communities known as **utopias** *(yoo TOW pee uhz)*. The name came from Thomas More's book *Utopia*, published in 1516, which describes a perfect place where all people are equal, prosperous, educat-

271

ed, and wise. Since utopia comes from Greek words meaning "no where," it clearly describes a place that does not exist. Nevertheless, many people in the 19th century believed perfection could be attained.

Utopian societies usually held ideas that differed greatly from those of the rest of the population. For example, many utopians were disturbed by the widening gap between rich and poor. Most utopians believed that people should set aside their private interests and work for the good of the community as a whole. They would thus share in both the work and the income of the community.

The Shakers

The Shakers, founded by Ann Lee in England, were the most famous of the religious utopian communities. Shaker ideals included purity, love, peace, and justice. In 1774, Ann Lee, known as Mother Ann, led eight followers to America. After the Shakers settled in upstate New York, they made many converts.

The largest Shaker community was founded in 1787 in New Lebanon, New York. The Shakers believed that all people were equal and should share in the benefits and responsibilities of life. Among the Shakers, property was owned by the community as a whole, not by the individual. Also, Shakers did not believe in marriage or bearing children. They therefore had to rely on converts to increase their numbers. By 1850, the number of Shakers had grown to about 6,000 people. Within a few years, however, the appeal of the Shakers diminished, and the number of their colonies declined. Today, only a handful of Shakers remain in New Hampshire and Maine.

Brook Farm

Some utopias were an attempt to create communities where people combined physical labor with intellectual curiosity. These communities were supposed to be "pure" compared to the cities. Though the structures and rules of groups varied, most consisted of members from several families living together and sharing the work.

The most famous of these utopian experiments was Brook Farm, established in 1841 in West Roxbury, Massachusetts. Brook Farm was planned as a community of thoughtful people who would lead harmonious lives by avoiding competition and greed.

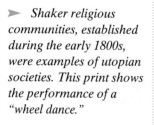

➤ *Shaker religious communities, established during the early 1800s, were examples of utopian societies. This print shows the performance of a "wheel dance."*

Individuals became members of Brook Farm by buying shares of stock. Each member had one vote. Community members worked the same number of hours for the same wages and paid the same room and board. Brook Farm was noted for its fine school, which stressed personal responsibility and encouraged students to have questioning minds.

The most famous shareholder, author Nathaniel Hawthorne, served for a time as the colony's director of agriculture. Hawthorne's fictional account, *The Blithedale Romance*, describes the goal of the colonists as the desire to breathe "air that had not been spoken into words of falsehood, formality and error, like all the air of the dusky city!"

Like other utopian communities, Brook Farm failed, closing in 1847. Utopians claimed the failure was financial, but Hawthorne pointed out that life in a utopian community had as many problems as life in a city. By the mid-1800s, the North was characterized by industrial cities joined to one another by an efficient transportation network. The outlooks and reform movements that colored the region were responses to rapid industrialization and the problems it created. These problems were quite different from those faced by the agricultural South. ■

■ *What were the goals of utopian societies?*

REVIEW

1. **FOCUS** What types of social reform movements developed in the 1800s?
2. **CONNECT** How did the rapid growth of cities and industries spark the move for social reform in the United States?
3. **CITIZENSHIP** How did utopians attempt to create a new social order?
4. **HISTORY** Why did so many women become involved in the temperance movement?
5. **CRITICAL THINKING** Why do you think social reformers considered public education to be so important?
6. **ACTIVITY** Imagine you are seeking to create a modern-day utopia. Prepare and deliver a short speech about how your community would be organized. Mention the ideals that would govern it and how it would provide food, jobs, and shelter for its members.

Using Computerized Sources

Here's Why

In order to make use of all possible resources when doing research, you need to understand and use computerized reference information. We are living in an age of "information explosion." Books, magazines, newspapers, radio, and television produce more and more information every day. In order to keep track of all that information, many libraries now use computerized systems to add to, or even to take the place of, the card catalog system.

Suppose you want to write a research paper on Mary Lyon, one of the educational leaders you have read about in this chapter. You could use a computer data bank to locate your reference material quickly and efficiently.

Here's How

A number of computerized reference systems are available today. Although they may vary in detail, most of them use menus and screens to organize the location and presentation of information. The following example uses features that are common to these systems. It does not show the detailed operations of an actual system, but instead serves as a guide for using these systems.

To begin your search on a computer data bank, you need to understand that the computer "interacts" with you. That is, information appears on the screen, you select what you want to know, and the computer

screen changes as you make those selections.

When you begin the search, the computer screen will show a main "menu," or list of items for you to select. Look at the sample "Main Menu" shown on this page. This menu presents you with five choices.

Your first choice should be number 1 because you want to give the computer your topic first. When you type the number 1, the screen titled "Enter Key Words" will appear.

Now type the first word or phrase of your topic on the first line. Type "Mary Lyon" and then press Enter. Remember that the computer will match exactly what you type. If you misspell your key word, the computer will not be able to find exactly what you are looking for.

When you finish with this screen, press the escape key, and the computer will return to the "Main Menu" again. Now choose number 2, "Set Search

```
MAIN MENU

Functions:
1. Enter Keyword(s)
2. Set Search Options
3. Search
4. Print
5. Exit


Type the number of the function.
```

```
ENTER KEYWORDS

Keyword(s): _____

            _____

            _____

            _____

            _____

Type one word or phrase on each line.
Press the <Esc> key to return to MAIN MENU.
```

Option." The next screen that appears will give you a choice of three different ways to search for information—by title, by topic, or by text. That is, you can look for items that have your key word in the title, for items about your key word, or for items in which your key word appears in the text.

At this point, you may choose number 1 to look for items that have "Mary Lyon" in the title, number 2 to look for items that are about Mary Lyon, or number 3 to choose items that have the name Mary Lyon anywhere in their text. In this case, you would choose either number 1 or 2, since you want items that are specifically about Mary Lyon, not articles that may refer to her. Type the number 1, and press Escape to return to the "Main Menu" again.

This time you will want to choose number 3 to perform the search. The computer will search through its data to locate articles that match your key words and search options. If you typed number 1 in the "Set Search Option" menu, the next screen that appears will provide you with a list of sources in the library whose titles contain the key words "Mary Lyon."

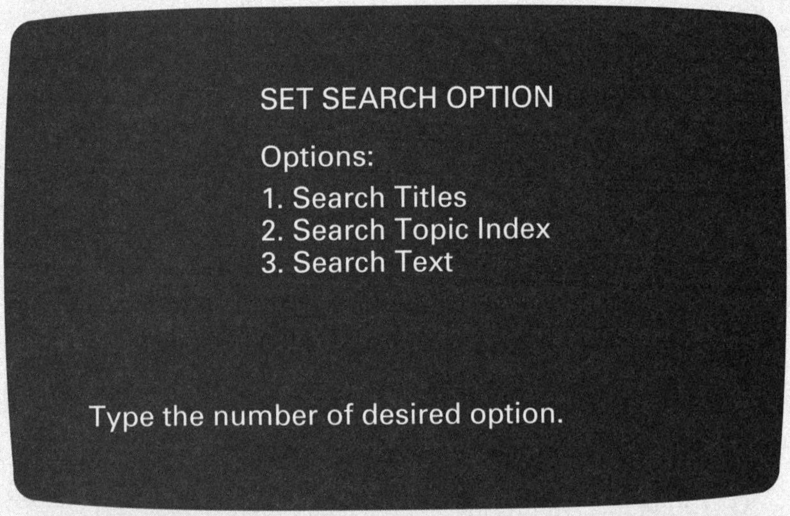

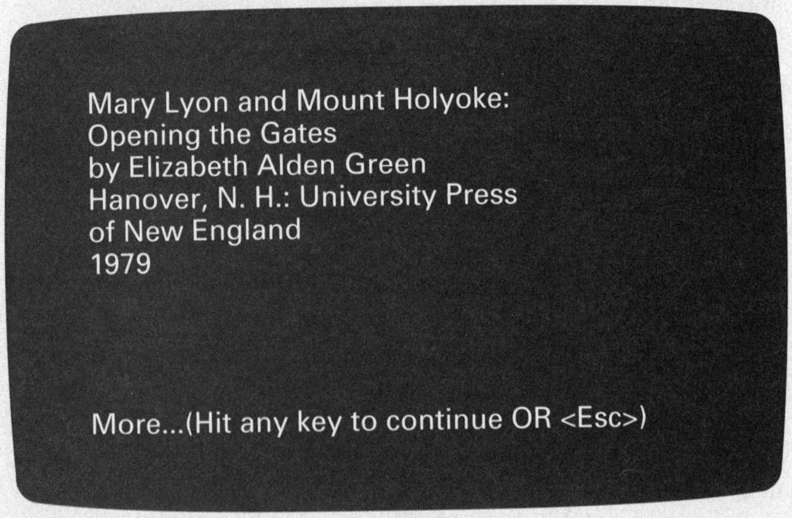

Your search is complete: you now know that the library has a book about Mary Lyon. At this point you can return to the main menu. You can type number 4 to print a copy of the information for your own reference, or you can type number 5 to exit from the system.

Try It

Suppose you wanted to research the Seneca Falls conference. Write down three words you could use to look for entries about your topic in a data bank. Then use a computer reference system in a library near you to do the research. Locate at least two entries on your topic using the computer.

Apply It

Think of a topic that you would like to learn about. Write down three ways you could look for information on this topic in a computerized reference system. Then use that system to locate one article on this topic.

```
SET SEARCH OPTION

Options:
1. Search Titles
2. Search Topic Index
3. Search Text




Type the number of desired option.
```

```
Mary Lyon and Mount Holyoke:
Opening the Gates
by Elizabeth Alden Green
Hanover, N. H.: University Press
of New England
1979




More...(Hit any key to continue OR <Esc>)
```

Susan's Trial

William Jay Jacobs

William Jay Jacobs' book Mother, Aunt Susan, and Me *tells the story of Elizabeth Cady Stanton (1815-1902) and Susan B. Anthony (1820-1906), and their organization of the women's suffrage movement. This move led to the introduction of the Nineteenth Amendment, which gave women the right to vote. As part of the struggle for this right, Anthony broke the law by voting in the 1872 presidential election and was subsequently arrested. This excerpt from* Mother, Aunt Susan, and Me *tells the story of Susan's trial. As you read, ask yourself, "Why would Susan B. Anthony be willing to break the law?"*

Justice Ward Hunt presided as trial judge. Henry B. Selden served as Susan B. Anthony's chief attorney. Mr. Selden said that when Susan voted she thought she had a right to vote. So what she did could not be considered a crime. She was putting her idea to a test. Susan B. Anthony was no criminal. Moreover, women legally did have the right to vote, he said, according to the Constitution.

Mr. Selden's speech was clear, logical, and to the point. For more than three hours he spoke eloquently.

But Judge Hunt hardly listened at all. Instead, he read a statement that he had prepared before coming into court–before he had heard the argument for the defense.

Then he ordered the all-male jury to find Susan B. Anthony guilty as charged.

Mr. Selden jumped to his feet. "I object! I object!" he shouted. "No judge has a right in a criminal case to tell a jury what to decide. I demand that the members of the jury be allowed to vote."

But Judge Hunt dismissed the jury without letting one of its members speak.

The next day Susan's lawyers asked for a new trial. Judge Hunt turned down the request. He then ordered Susan to stand for sentencing. "Has the prisoner anything to say why sentence shall not be pronounced?" asked Judge Hunt.

Susan, dressed in black except for a trimming of white lace at her neckline, paused for an instant. Then she spoke firmly and forcefully.

"Yes, Your Honor, I have many things to say: for in your ordered verdict of guilty you have trampled under foot every vital principle of our government. My natural rights, my civil rights, my political rights, my judicial rights are all alike ignored."

Judge Hunt, impatient, interrupted. Pointing at the accused, he declared, "The Court cannot allow the prisoner to go on."

In Lesson 3, you read about Susan B. Anthony's involvement in various reform movements of the 1800s. Here is a story about her fight for women's suffrage.

But Susan would not stop. Since the day of her arrest she had been given no chance to defend herself. Judge Hunt had not even allowed her to be a witness for herself at the trial.

"The prisoner must sit down–the Court cannot allow it," bellowed Judge Hunt.

Susan continued: "Had Your Honor submitted my case to the jury, as was clearly your duty, even then I should have had just cause of protest, for not one of those men was my peer; but native or foreign born, white or black, rich or poor, educated or ignorant, sober or drunk, each and every man of them was my political superior. . . . Under such circumstances a commoner in England, tried before a jury of lords, would have far less cause to complain than have I, a woman, tried before a jury of men."

"The Court must insist," Judge Hunt interrupted again. "The prisoner has been tried according to the established forms of the law."

"Yes, Your Honor," answered Susan, "but by forms of law all made by men, interpreted by men, in favor of men, and against women."

"The Court orders the prisoner to sit down. It will not allow another word!" shouted Judge Hunt, banging his gavel for order.

Susan had a final word. She had expected, she said, a fair trial and justice. "But failing to get this justice . . . I ask not leniency at your hands but rather the full rigor of the law."

"The Court must insist . . ."started Judge Hunt. At that point Susan sat down.

"The prisoner will stand up," directed the judge.

Again she rose.

"The sentence of the Court is that you pay a fine of one hundred dollars and the costs of prosecution."

"May it please Your Honor," began Susan. "I will never pay a dollar of your unjust penalty. All I possess is a debt of ten thousand dollars incurred by publishing my paper–*The Revolution*–the sole object of which was to educate all women to do precisely as I have done, rebel against your man-made, unjust, unconstitutional forms of law, which tax, fine, imprison, and hang women, while denying them the right of representation in the government."

Susan, remaining calm, but with her voice rising in defiance, then concluded: "I will work on with might and main to pay every dollar of that honest debt, but not a penny shall go to this unjust claim. And I shall earnestly and persistently continue to urge all women to the practical recognition of the old Revolutionary maxim, 'Resistance to tyranny is obedience to God.'"

For a moment the courtroom was hushed in silence. Later we heard that even some members of the jury said they had felt like applauding, perhaps even cheering out loud.

Further Reading

The Story of the 19th Amendment. Conrad Stein. This book presents an overview of the women's suffrage movement with attention to the work of Elizabeth Stanton, Lucretia Mott, and Susan B. Anthony.

Sports in the United States

Did Abner Doubleday invent baseball? Or did baseball in fact develop from a game played by Egyptians in time of the Pharaohs? If you could ride a time machine back to the early days of your favorite game, you would probably find some surprises.

Get Ready

Take a trip to your local library and explore the history of a sport that interests you. Some sports you might consider exploring, besides football and baseball, include archery, billiards, auto racing, gymnastics, roller skating, basketball, or the sport originally played by the Indians, lacrosse.

Before you begin your research, decide which sport you will investigate and think of interesting questions to ask. You might seek answers to such questions as: Where did this sport come from? Who invented it? Who played it in the past? How has the game changed? You might also consider how this sport reflects certain American values. Then collect the

tools you will need: a notebook and a pen or pencil.

Find Out

Stories about any sport are easy to come by, but remember—not all the stories you might read about or hear are true. For example, according to one popular story, a man named Abner Doubleday invented baseball in Cooperstown, New York. Supposedly, he did this one day in 1839. Historical records, however, show that baseball developed out of a British game called rounders, which was played at least as far back as the 1500s. Rounders, in turn, developed from other, older games. Some sources suggest that baseball may in fact have come from a game played by Egyptians in the time of the pharaohs!

Lacrosse, a ball game played all across the United States and Canada, was invented centuries ago by the Huron Indians, who called it *bagataway*. The game was called *jeu de la crosse (zhe deh lah KRAWS)*, French for "game of the hooked stick" by a French Jesuit priest who saw the game played in 1636. In both *bagataway* and lacrosse, two teams try to hurl a ball into each others' goals, using nets attached to sticks. Huron versions of the game sometimes involved hundreds of players and lasted for days. Modern lacrosse is played by two teams of 10 players each and lasts for one hour.

In 1891, James Naismith, a physical education teacher at the School for Christian Workers (now called Springfield College) in Massachusetts needed an indoor game for his students to play in times of bad weather. He hung some peach baskets on a gym rail and had his students compete to toss soccer balls into them. Naismith had just invented basketball. He would hardly recognize the fast-paced acrobatic game as it is played in the United States today, not just by professional, college, and high school teams, but by amateurs on playgrounds across the nation.

Separating fact from folklore takes research that is based on reliable sources. Begin by reading articles about your sport in some good encyclopedias. If the articles end with lists of recommended books on the subject, write down the titles and check for them in the card catalog. Also look for other books in the card catalog under under the category "sport" and under the name of the particular sport you are investigating. As you read, remember to jot down all interesting facts.

Move Ahead

Organize your notes in categories such as Original Game Form, Changes in Game Form, and Famous Players. If any other students have researched the same sport as you, compare your findings with theirs. Then work together to produce an oral report about your sport, complete with diagrams, pictures, and other interesting visuals.

Explore Some More

History doesn't just happen in the past. Changes like those of the past are happening right now. If you pay attention to sports news, you might see that the sport you have researched is changing today. (You might also want to consider how news coverage has influenced your sport.)

Take notes on changes you might see on television, hear on radio, or read about in newspapers or magazines that relate to the sport you are researching. If you play the sport yourself, notice what bothers you and your friends about the way it is set up. Your complaints may be the first signs of changes to come.

As you collect this information, compare the way the sport has evolved to the way it is changing now. Then shine your light into the future: write a description of the game as you predict it will be played 100 years from now.

Chapter Review

Reviewing Key Terms

Industrial Revolution (p. 255)   temperance (p. 268)
municipal (p. 263)   utopia (p. 271)
raw materials (p. 256)

A. The sentences below have been started for you. Complete each sentence so that the meaning of the key term is clear.
1. The Industrial Revolution . . .
2. The temperance movement . . .
3. The idea of a utopia today . . .
4. Raw materials from the West . . .
5. A municipal . . .

B. Based on what you have read in the chapter, decide whether each of the following statements is accurate. Write an explanation of each decision.
1. Supporters of the temperance movement wanted to encourage the use of alcoholic beverages.
2. Some nineteenth-century reformers tried to create a utopia by starting new communities in which all people were considered equal.
3. The increase in city populations decreased the need for municipal services.
4. Factory workers often took home the raw materials left at the end of a day of work in the textile mills.
5. The Industrial Revolution that swept through the North in the early 1800s was the result of an earlier revolution in Britain.

Exploring Concepts

A. Copy the following paragraph onto a separate sheet of paper. Fill in the blank spaces with information from the chapter.

In order to avoid competition with the United States, British factory owners refused to allow _____ to leave England. However, _____ managed to build a spinning mill in Pawtucket, Rhode Island, that marked the start of a new Industrial Revolution. New machinery and _____ contributed to the success of America's industries. Transportation was another key to the Industrial Revolution. Clipper ships, steamboats, a system of _____ and networks of _____ and _____ helped move goods more easily. In addition, the nation's natural resources, like _____ power, helped revolutionize production.

B. On a separate sheet of paper, answer the following questions in complete sentences.
1. How did the role of women change with the rise of industry in the Northeast?
2. What municipal services did cities need to provide for their growing populations?
3. What were some of the changes made in public education after the 1820s, and what were the reasons for the changes?

C. Support each of the following statements with facts and details from the chapter.
1. When the Industrial Revolution occurred in the United States, Americans adapted and improved British industrial methods.
2. The Industrial Revolution led to improvements in transportation in the United States.
3. The Lowell mill owners took several steps to avoid the poverty and moral decay that had occurred in British industrial towns.
4. Industries no longer needed to be located near the nation's coasts.
5. New methods of construction helped cities to grow.
6. There was a wide gap between the lifestyles of the rich and poor in American cities.
7. The condition of the urban poor gave rise to many reform movements.
8. People who sought to create utopian societies had two different motives.
9. Women played a major role in many of the reform movements.

Reviewing Skills

1. Explain why libraries are increasing their use of computer data banks.
2. When conducting a search by computer, why is it important to define and enter your key words very carefully?
3. Look at the sample computer screen at right. What information should you type onto the computer screen after you have pressed key number 1?
4. After you have entered the exact title of a book that you need for your research, which key should you select to begin your search?
5. Look at the timeline on page 256. When was the first patent issued? When was gaslight first used to light city streets?
6. Suppose you were using a computerized refer-

```
MAIN MENU

Functions:
1. Enter Keyword(s)
2. Set Search Options
3. Search
4. Print
5. Exit

Type the number of the function.
```

ence system. Although you searched for your key words under titles, topics, and text, no references were located. What information would you need to continue your search?

Using Critical Thinking

1. Private charitable groups took on the burden of caring for the needs of the poor during the early 1800s. Since the 1930s, the federal government has played a major part in helping the poor, but recently some politicians have said that private groups should do the job. Who do you think is better suited for this work—government agencies or private groups? Explain your answer.
2. Fanny Wright claimed that the wide gap between rich and poor contradicted the idea that all men are created equal. "The man possessed of a dollar feels himself to be, not merely 100 cents richer but also 100 cents better than the man who is penniless," she wrote. Do you agree with her? Explain your answer.
3. Many people recognized the need for universal education of both men and women. One teacher wrote, "Give the people knowledge . . . and you give them power. Education must ever be the grand safeguard of our liberties." Do you agree? Would our system of government be weakened if many people remained poorly educated? How?

Preparing for Citizenship

1. WRITING ACTIVITY Some Americans still live in communities that resemble utopias, in which people share tasks, grow their own food, and reject machinery. Research such groups as the Amish or Mennonites, and write a report on their beliefs and way of life.
2. COLLECTING INFORMATION Find out if there are any religious or charitable groups in your community that have programs to help those in need. Interview a person connected with the group to find out what they do. Are there any activities that the class can help with? Report on your findings.
3. COLLECTING INFORMATION Ask older people such as your parents or grandparents to describe the changes that have occurred in their community since they were children. What new buildings, roads, factories, shopping centers, or other changes have been made? Do they feel these changes have improved or harmed the community? Why? Compare your findings with those of other students.
4. COLLABORATIVE LEARNING Take a class trip through your community by walking or using public transportation. Look at different neighborhoods and parts of the community. Take notes on how your community is laid out in terms of housing, industry, parks, and municipal facilities. When you return, discuss what changes, if any, you would make to improve municipal services.

Chapter 10

The South

The South presented a peaceful, rural landscape of wide fields, elegant mansions, and small mountain farms. Down slow, winding rivers, boats carried cotton to ports on the coast. In the South, cotton was King. Grown by slave labor, cotton brought a thriving economy and a desire for more land.

The large, elegant home of a Southern landowner graces the rural landscape.

1790	1800	1810	1820

Presidents

| 1789-1797 Washington | 1797-1801 J. Adams | 1801-1809 Jefferson | 1809-1817 Madison | 1817-1825 Monroe |

1790

Mountain people cleared the land, built log cabins, and protected their fields with split-rail fences. The soft, sweet music of the Appalachian dulcimer accompanied the folk music of the mountain people.

1840 The port of New Orleans bustles with trade to far off places.

1830

1840

1850

1860

1825-1829
J. Q. Adams

1829-1837
Jackson

1837-1841
Van Buren

1841-1845
Tyler

1841
W. Harrison

1845-1849
Polk

1849-1850
Taylor

1850-1853
Fillmore

1853-1857
Pierce

1857-1861
Buchanan

1860

LESSON 1

The Cotton Kingdom

How did the cotton gin change the economy and the landscape of the South between 1790 and 1860?

Key Terms

- plantation
- antebellum
- cash crop

➤ *Cotton grows in a pod or boll that pops open when it is ripe. Southern planters grew two kinds of cotton. Sea-island cotton was easy to clean but grew well only along the coast. Upland cotton had a wider growing range but was difficult to clean.*

In 1792, wealthy Southerners gathered at Mulberry Grove, Georgia, the home of Catharine Littlefield Greene, widow of the Revolutionary War hero General Nathanael Greene. Imagine the scene: candles glowed in tall silver holders, a floral centerpiece lightly perfumed the air.

The dinner guests talked with animation of hunting, fine horses, and cotton, always cotton. Eli Whitney, a young tutor from the North, listened closely to their talk. The men's eyes sparkled when they described how machinery was changing the textile industry in New England and Britain. Since the mills needed more and more cotton, it looked like good times for the South.

One of the cotton growers brought the conversation back to reality. It was all very well to talk about possible profits, he said. But how were they to meet the demand for cotton? Their slaves could barely clean enough cotton by hand to meet the present needs of industry.

The growers did have machines to clean cotton. However, these machines did not work well with upland cotton, which was the kind most of them grew. The seeds stuck to the fiber so that slaves had to finish the cleaning by hand.

Whitney, who loved to tinker with machines, was intrigued. He wrote his father:

I heard much said of the extreme difficulty of ginning Cotton, that is, separating it from its seeds. There were a number of very respectable gentlemen at Mrs. Greene's who all agreed that if a machine could be invented which could clean the cotton with expedition, it would be a great thing both to the Country and to the inventor. I involuntarily happened to be thinking on the Subject, and struck out a plan of a Machine in my mind. . . . In about ten days I made a little model. . . which required the labor of one man to turn it. . . . One man and a horse will do more than fifty men with the old machines.

Whitney's cotton gin (gin is a shortened form of engine) was just what the Southern cotton growers needed. It rapidly cleaned the seeds from the short, sticky fibers of upland cotton, the variety that grew all over the South. The process was simple: a roller carried raw cotton along wooden slats. Sharp metal teeth thrust through the slats and quickly pulled the fibers from the seeds.

In 1794 Whitney obtained a patent—a license granting sole rights to make, use, or sell an invention—for his cotton gin. He himself earned little from his invention. The machine was so simple that manufacturers copied it without permission or paying a fee.

Chapter 10

The Cotton Revolution

The cotton gin caused great changes in the Southern economy. Once cotton growers began using Whitney's invention, production soared. In the years after 1812, raw cotton accounted for one-third of all exports from the United States. By 1830, cotton had increased to half of all U.S. exports.

Because cotton was so valuable, planters (farmers who owned 20 slaves or more) put all their efforts into growing it. They cleared large areas in the western part of the South. Known as the "New South," this area included Arkansas, Louisiana, Mississippi, Alabama, western Georgia, and northern Florida (see map, page 288).

The long, hot summers and the rich soil of the river valleys in the "New South" created ideal conditions for growing cotton. **Plantations**—large farms on which crops were grown by slaves—produced ever larger amounts of cotton. This revived slavery, which had declined after the tobacco market shrank in the late 1700s.

Toiling in the Fields

Cotton needed a great deal of labor during the year. The backbreaking work was done by slaves—men, women, and children—who worked from dawn to dark under a broiling sun. They planted the fields in April and tended them constantly.

In his book *Twelve Years as a Slave* (1853) Solomon Northup, a free black man who had been kidnapped and sold into slavery, described labor in the cotton fields:

Slaves carried a long sack which they slung over the head and one shoulder and filled with cotton. A skilled picker moved between two rows of cotton, deftly twisting the cotton bolls from the plant with each hand.

*D*uring all [the] hoeings the overseer or driver follows the slaves on horseback with a whip. . . . The fastest hoer takes the lead row. He is usually about a rod in advance of his companions. If one of them passes him, he [the fastest hoer] is whipped. If one falls behind or is a moment idle, he is whipped. In fact, the lash is flying from morning until night. . . .

When a new hand, one unaccustomed to [picking cotton], is sent for the first time into the field, he is whipped up smartly, and made for that day to pick as fast as he can possibly. At night [what he has picked] is weighed, so that his capability in cotton picking is known. He must bring in the same weight each night following. . . . The hands are required to be in the cotton field as soon as it is light in the morning, and, with the exception of 10 or 15 minutes, which is given them at noon to swallow their allowance of cold bacon, they are not permitted to be a moment idle until it is too dark to see.

Solomon Northup, *Twelve Years As a Slave*

HAULING THE WHOLE WEEKS PICKING

▲ *William Henry Brown combined cutouts and watercolors to create this scene of slaves hauling cotton to the gin.*

Other Plantation Chores

After the field work ended for the day, each slave still had tasks to do. "One feeds the mules," Northup wrote, "another the swine—another cuts the wood." Even then, the day was not over for the slaves. Evening was the only time they could return to their cabins and care for their families. Before they could sleep, they had to prepare the food they would need in the fields the next day.

Masters did make their slaves work hard. Although some planters punished slaves to get more work out of them, other masters used a system of rewards. Slaves who produced more got more food and earned some privileges. Slaves were valuable and could not be replaced easily because the United States had ended the slave trade in 1808.

After picking the cotton, slaves loaded it onto wagons to haul the crop to a nearby gin. The ginned cotton was pressed into bales—400-pound bundles covered with coarse cloth and held together with rope. Each of the cotton gins at a ginning mill processed three or four bales a day.

The bundles were then shipped to factories in Europe or in the North where the cotton was made into cloth. In 1814, Southern planters shipped 150,000 bales of cotton. By 1825, the planters were shipping 600,000 bales a year.

Rural South, Industrial North

The plantation South differed greatly from the industrial North. In the 1700s, both the North and the South depended mainly on farming. The North began to develop industries in the early 1800s. In the **antebellum** period—the time before the Civil War—the South remained agricultural. Eighty percent of the labor force worked in farming. Planters dominated the Southern economy. In the North, on the other hand, the farm population dropped from 70 to 40 percent of the total labor force.

As their industries grew, Northerners built a canal and railroad system to carry raw materials and manufactured goods to the growing cities. Northerners also harnessed the rivers to get power for industry. In the South, planters were content to send their crops to market on the slow-flowing rivers and the waterways along the coast. Few were interested in developing factories or using water for power.

Because farming remained the chief economy, few cities developed in the South. The cities that did grow had very little industry. Small, scattered towns served as centers of marketing or transportation, mainly in the fall and winter when crops were being shipped. Southern industries tended to be small—cabinet making or iron-working or cotton ginning—and devoted to local needs. Southern towns were rarely manufacturing centers. The difference between South and North could be seen in the way people talked of the place where they lived. While Northerners spoke of living in or near a town, Southerners talked of their county.

Some Southern leaders worried that their economy was not varied enough. They thought that Southern income depended too heavily on cotton. Although other crops—tobacco, rice, sugar cane, corn, and other grains—were grown, cotton brought in the most money.

Other Southern leaders noted that the South depended on the North not only for manufactured goods, but also for much of its transportation. The South had few ocean-going ships. Its produce was shipped to New England and Europe in Northern vessels. Joseph W. Lesesne, an Alabama plantation owner, complained in 1847, "Our whole commerce except a small fraction is in the hands of Northern men. . . . financially we are more enslaved than our negroes."

Impact of the Cotton Economy

Between 1830 and 1860, new machinery in the textile industry made it possible to produce cloth more quickly. This advance increased the demand for raw cotton. As a result, the South's economy relied on cotton production and the need for slave labor to grow it.

Cotton was a **cash crop**—one grown mainly to sell for money. An economy based on a single cash crop can yield a high income. However, if the crop fails or market prices for it drop, there is nothing to fall back on.

For greater security, many farmers diversify. They grow several money-making crops. If something goes wrong with one crop, the others will still bring in income.

Growing a variety of crops is especially important in cotton-growing areas, because cotton wears out the

▼ *Compare the factories and transportation in Springfield, Massachusetts, with those in New Orleans, Louisiana.*

Comparing the North and the South, around 1850

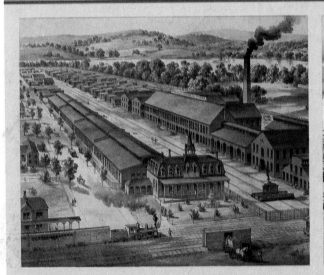

The North
- Transportation by railroads and canals
- Industrial economy, factories using water power
- Variety of manufactured products, textiles, and steel goods
- Voluntary labor force, many immigrants, low wages
- Few large cities and many mill towns

The South
- Transportation by steamboats on natural inland rivers
- Agricultural economy, centered on plantations
- Major crop concentration on cotton
- Slave labor force
- Few cities; river towns busy during harvest for shipping

287

The South

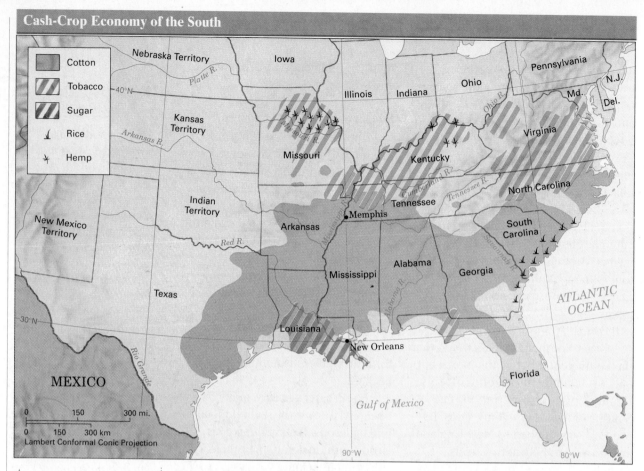

Cash-Crop Economy of the South

Legend:
- Cotton
- Tobacco
- Sugar
- Rice
- Hemp

▲ What cash crops were grown in the antebellum South? Coastal areas in the South are humid. What does that tell you about the rice and sugar cane grown there?

■ Why did cotton cultivation require back-breaking field work during most of the year?

soil rapidly. The land becomes useless unless it rests for a year between crops. Or soil can be improved by adding fertilizer or by alternating cotton with other crops. Before the 1830s, when planters began to use more fertilizer, they would abandon worn out fields and move to new land farther west.

Political Impact of Cotton

As planters in the "New South" turned more and more land to growing cotton, the economy could support more people. In 1790, the South had roughly one million white people, 657,000 black slaves, and 32,000 free black people. By 1860, some eight million white people, almost four million black slaves, and 262,000 free black people lived in the South. (Compare the Atlas maps on page 704 showing U.S. population density in 1790 and 1870.)

The rise in population brought statehood to the Southern territories. New states joined the Union in quick succession: Louisiana in 1812, Mississippi in 1817, Alabama in 1819, Arkansas in 1836, and Florida and Texas in 1845. The admission of these states greatly increased the power of the South in the United States Congress. ■

Proslavery Movement

Even white Southerners who did not own slaves took a proslavery stand during the antebellum years. Since most white Southerners benefited either directly or indirectly from the economy based on King Cotton, they supported slavery. Economic security was one powerful reason for the proslavery position in the South.

Some white Southerners also supported slavery out of fear. They believed that if slaves were freed and given legal rights, they would take control and white people would lose their property and even be in physical danger.

Arguments Defending Slavery

Many people defended slavery by pointing out that the Bible recognized the existence of slavery. These people said that slavery had been accepted worldwide for thousands of years. They also noted that, by introducing Christianity to their slaves, planters had thereby saved their souls.

Defenders of slavery also claimed that Northern industrial workers were little better off than slaves. They were badly paid, worked long hours, and lived in poverty. Some pointed out that slaves got food, clothing, and shelter from their masters while Northern industrial workers often went hungry and cold.

Others who supported slavery claimed that black people were inferior to whites. In 1832, Thomas R. Dew, a professor at William and Mary College in Virginia, wrote the first full-length book to defend slavery in the South. Dew argued that slavery was a "positive good." He looked on black people as children who thrived under the discipline and care of their masters.

James H. Hammond, a South Carolina planter and politician, said that every civilization had a "mud sill" class of laborers. (A mud sill is the lowest level of a building and supports the entire structure.) Slaves, claimed Hammond, were the ideal mud sill class.

Impact of Antislavery Movement

Antislavery activity in the North helped strengthen Southern support for slavery. Of course, not all Southerners supported slavery, nor did all Northerners oppose it. Yet antislavery feelings were on the rise in the North. Some Northerners were helping Southern slaves to escape. Alarmed and resentful of Northern interference, Southerners defended slavery more firmly. Extreme supporters of slavery even wanted to go back to importing slaves from Africa.

Few white Southerners went to such an extreme. Their concern lay in maintaining the plantation system as it existed. ■

▲ *Slaves outside their homes on a South Carolina plantation share some time together. Those supporting slavery used pictures such as this as evidence of a master's concern for the slaves' well-being.*

■ *List at least three arguments people gave in support of slavery.*

R E V I E W

1. **FOCUS** How did the cotton gin change the economy and the landscape of the South between 1790 and 1860?
2. **GEOGRAPHY** What made the "New South" suitable for growing cotton?
3. **CONNECT** What did Southern slaves harvest before 1790? What did they harvest after that date?
4. **ECONOMICS** Use the map on page 288 to make a chart listing each Southern state and its major cash crop(s).
5. **CRITICAL THINKING** If Whitney had not invented a practical cotton gin, what might have happened to slavery in the South? Explain your answer.
6. **WRITING ACTIVITY** Write a news story about the invention of the cotton gin. Include imaginary interviews with Eli Whitney and a plantation owner in your story.

L E S S O N 2

Life on the Plantation

Key Term

- cultural heritage

On the highest ground stood a large and handsome mansion. . . . the whole plantation, including the swamp land around it, and owned with it, covered several square miles. It was four miles from the settlement to the nearest neighbor's house. There were between thirteen and fourteen hundred acres under cultivation with cotton, corn, and other hoed crops, and two hundred hogs running at large in the swamp. . . . There were 135 slaves, big and little, of which 67 went to the field regularly. . . . We found in the field thirty ploughs [plows], moving together, turning the earth from the cotton plants, and from 30 to 40 hoers, the latter mainly women.

Frederick Law Olmsted published this account of a plantation after a Southern trip he made in 1856. Olmsted was a Northern journalist and travel writer who later became famous as the designer of Central Park in New York City.

A large plantation was not just cotton fields and a stately mansion at the end of a tree-lined road. It included many other buildings: the smokehouse where meat was preserved, the henhouse where poultry was raised, the barn where dairy cows and work animals were kept, and various buildings for storing tools, grain, and other goods. Stables sheltered purebred horses. In workshops, slaves made barrels and horseshoes, furniture, and cloth for use on the plantation.

Some plantations included a private chapel and a school for the planter's children. The kitchen was separate from the planter's home—known as the Big House—so that kitchen fires would not burn down the mansion. The Big House often had formal gardens. Vegetables and herbs were grown in other gardens for use in cooking and for herbal remedies.

Slave cabins were always separate from the Big House. A number of plantations included slave infirmaries, or hospitals, and a nursery where slave infants were cared for.

The Slave South

Olmsted's description of grand plantations with over 100 slaves continues to dominate most people's picture of the antebellum South. However, this portrait was the exception rather than the rule. Of the 50,000 plantations in the South in 1860, only 2,300 were owned by planters who held more than 100 slaves.

Most Southern farmers owned small farms and did not hold slaves. Nevertheless, these farmers tended to support slavery. They also acted as if they felt superior to all black people. Their support allowed the owners of large plantations to run the government and dominate the economy of the South.

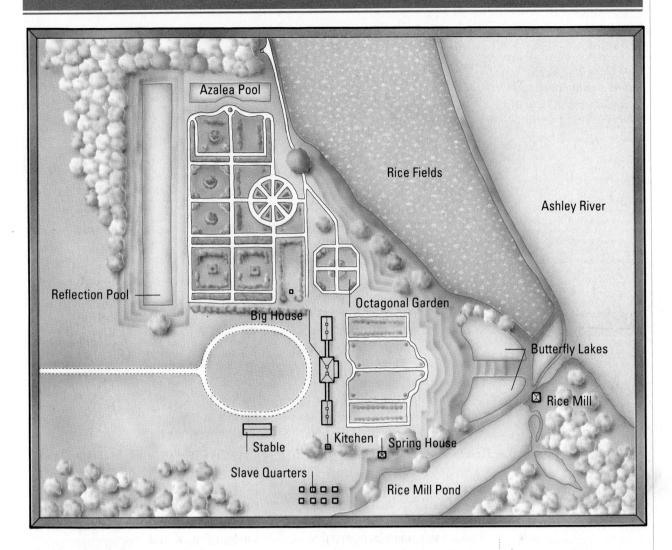

Azalea Pool

Rice Fields

Ashley River

Reflection Pool

Big House

Octagonal Garden

Butterfly Lakes

Rice Mill

Kitchen

Stable

Spring House

Slave Quarters

Rice Mill Pond

Master of the Land

A plantation was a self-contained world in which everyone—the planter, his wife and family, perhaps hired white workers, and slaves—played an important role.

The plantation master had final authority over his land, his slaves, and his family. When problems arose among his slaves, the master could act as judge and jury. If a slave wanted to marry, the master had to grant permission. Planters had almost total power over their slaves. The way they treated slaves, however, was tempered by the realization that slaves were valuable possessions. Planters did overwork slaves and sometimes treated them brutally—whipping them for failing to do their work, branding them, or otherwise disfiguring them. A planter might punish a particularly difficult

slave by selling the slave away from his or her family.

Planters also took the law into their own hands in arguments with other white gentlemen. They lived by a "code of honor," settling disputes by "pistols at ten paces," in duels that were often deadly.

Some masters believed they had a duty to teach their slaves about Christianity. A planter might take his slaves to Sunday services with him, but they were seated in their own special section in the back of the church or in a separate balcony. Other masters hired preachers to hold services on the plantation or took it upon themselves to read the Bible to their slaves.

Plantations had a strict ranking system. Although the planter ruled the entire estate, he might hire a white overseer to supervise work in the

This diagram is based on Middleton Plantation in South Carolina. What buildings can you identify? Why were gardens important?

➤ *This photograph shows a group of plantation mistresses with some of their servants.*

How Do We Know?

HISTORY *Letter writing was very important in the 19th century. Many plantation mistresses wrote daily or weekly letters to friends and family. Historians have found much detailed information about plantation society in such letters.*

fields. Some planters used trusted slaves as drivers, supervisors who made sure that the field hands kept up a fast pace.

The plantation mistress—the planter's wife—was second only to her husband in authority. However, she was expected to obey him without question.

Life in the Big House

The Big House was a visible symbol of a planter's wealth. It was usually a large two- or three-storied mansion. A wide entrance hall led into the dining room, parlor, library, and sitting room. Fine furniture, paintings, tapestries, and other fine objects, often imported from Europe, decorated the large, high-ceilinged rooms.

A wide staircase led to the second floor where there were several large bedrooms for family members and guests. In many homes the beds had headboards that were removed during hot weather. Because windows had no screens, mosquito netting was hung over beds to protect sleepers from the

insects that thrived in the humid climate.

Nurseries for the planter's children were on upper floors and could be reached by servants' stairs at the back of the house. On an upper balcony, slaves used a loose board that was attached to two sawhorses for "joggling" cranky infants or bored toddlers.

Running the Big House was the responsibility of the plantation mistress. She not only cared for her own family, but also took on responsibility for the physical and spiritual well-being of her "slave family." She was considered the "Christian conscience" of the South. Besides seeing that the slaves had food, clothing, shelter, and medical attention, she sometimes offered them advice and provided religious instruction.

The plantation mistress organized all food preparation, including curing meat, churning butter, and baking. She grew herbs, blended medicines, and nursed the slaves when they were ill. In addition, she was usually left in charge of the entire plantation whenever her husband was absent.

Many women took on the responsibilities of a plantation mistress at a young age. Daughters of planters usually married by age 22, and brides of 14 or 15 were not uncommon. Most young women had very little training for their new duties. They often learned their tasks from slaves on the plantation. One plantation wife told of her distress when she realized "for the first time the responsibilities. . . [of] the mistress of a large plantation and [of] the nights of sorrow and tears these thoughts had given her." ■

■ *What were some of the skills a plantation owner's bride needed to learn when she became mistress of the plantation?*

The Slave Community

Although slaves were a constant presence in the white household, they did not look on the master's house as their home. Rather, they found comfort and identity within their own slave community.

Slave Life

Myths about plantation life promote the idea that house slaves, slaves who did household chores such as cooking and caring for the planter's children, were too proud to do field work. In reality, most slaves were sent to the fields at harvest time. Only those who were too old or too young escaped working from sunup to sundown. Even the male slaves who were chosen to be drivers worked hard.

House slaves and drivers were set apart from the rest of the slave community. They had better food and clothing than field hands, but the costs were great. For example, a slave mother working in the Big House might be separated from her own child and have to sleep outside the door of her mistress's room. A driver might be forced to whip a member of his own family or a close friend.

When slaves were originally captured in Africa, they were separated from their families before being sold in America. To survive such inhumane treatment they often replaced their lost African families by "adopting" kin from among the slaves with whom they were shipped to America. Many of the slaves who suffered the journey to America together became as close as a real family.

Slave Culture

Slaves strengthened their sense of identity by carefully preserving the African cultural heritage. A people's **cultural heritage** includes customs, language, art, and beliefs. For example, since slaves could not legally marry, they often performed a ceremony adapted from an African custom. By "jumping the broom," a couple was united in the eyes of the slave community. Such customs gave slaves support and helped them to resist and struggle against their condition.

Many slaves had two names: the English names that their masters assigned them at birth, and African names used only among fellow slaves.

During the revival movements of the "Great Awakening" in the 1740s

Slave cabins were a stark contrast to the elegant Big House. These cabins are on Boone Plantation in South Carolina. They are reported to be the only remaining row of slave cabins in the United States. Today they are visited by tourists.

293

The South

➤ *This quilt, one of two surviving coverlets made by former slave Harriet Powers, uses a West African technique known as appliqué—cutting out pieces of one material and sewing them to another.*

Across Time & Space

In the early 1900s black Americans created a new sound in music. Based on the folk music of Southern slaves, it was transformed into a new style that came to be known as jazz. It remains America's greatest contribution to the world of music.

■ *Give three examples of cultural activities, separate from the white culture, in which plantation slaves participated.*

and the "Second Great Awakening" in the early 1820s, slaves were converted to Christianity by the thousands. Their church services combined African ritual with forms of American Protestantism. For example, the use of the ring shout echoed African ceremonies. Joyfully singing hymns, clapping, and stamping, worshipers circled in a shuffling dance, swaying to the rhythm of the music.

African cures for the sick sometimes proved more effective than white practices. For example, some white doctors used treatments that could be dangerous. Sometimes they drew blood from a patient, making the sick person weaker.

Slaves, on the other hand, tended to rely on natural cures and herbal medicines. For aches and pains they might use asper-root. It had an effect similar to that of today's aspirin.

Slaves also preserved African musical traditions. They created banjos and drums similar to African instruments by using hollowed gourds and stretched animal skins.

Slave work songs and spirituals combined African rhythms and musical tones with American hymns. From them grew new musical forms, such as spirituals, blues, and the forerunners of ragtime, Dixieland, and jazz.

Folktales, like music, provided relief. For example, the folktale character "Brer Rabbit" used his wits to outsmart his enemy. A symbol of the slaves' own condition, the rabbit stood for the dream of triumphing over slavery. You can read part of an account of one former slave's life on page 296. ■

Resistance to Slavery

Slaves found many ways to resist white control. Most forms of resistance were passive.

Passive Resistance

Slaves used songs not only to express their longings to be free, but also as a means of resisting slavery. For example, slaves might spread the news of a secret meeting by singing the refrain of the spiritual "Steal Away to Jesus":

"Steal away, steal away,
Steal away to Jesus.
Steal away, steal away home."

Made-up verses then indicated the place for a secret night meeting. White people who overheard the song were unaware of its special meaning.

Individual slaves resisted the planter's authority in various ways. Some pretended to be sick; some purposely broke tools; others worked as slowly as possible. Some slaves ran away often, even though they knew they would probably be caught and punished. By running away they were temporarily depriving the planter of their labor. Other slaves ran away to be with family members who did not live on their plantation.

Punishment for disobedience was harsh. Almost all runaways were whipped, some were branded, and some were actually maimed by having a leg tendon cut so that they could not run away again. For arson—the act of deliberately setting a fire—a slave might be hanged.

Although such punishments were brutal, they were not restricted to the South. It was said that the treatment of slaves differed little from the punishment that disobedient sailors received on ships owned by Northerners.

Slave Rebellions

Knowledge of plants might tempt a house slave to poison the master's food. This form of rebellion caused widespread fear among white Southerners. The most feared form of resistance, however, was organized, violent rebellion by a number of slaves.

Three major slave rebellions shook the South during the antebellum era, although only one of the three was an actual uprising. In 1800, white people in Richmond, Virginia, discovered a plot for a slave rebellion. Gabriel Prosser, a black preacher and blacksmith who had been freed, was plotting a general slave uprising. Betrayed by a slave, Prosser and 35 others were hanged.

In 1822, Denmark Vesey, a free black carpenter in Charleston, South Carolina, planned to lead a rebellion on July 14, the anniversary of the French Revolution. He too was betrayed by a slave and was executed along with 35 other black men. Thirty-seven more were deported from the city.

The most sensational rebellion of the era was Nat Turner's revolt in 1831. A slave preacher, Turner led 70 black men in an uprising in Southampton, Virginia. Before the three-day revolt was put down, 57 white people had been killed. White Southerners were in a panic. It was several weeks before Turner was caught, tried, and executed.

Most slaves did not revolt, and planters claimed they ruled their slaves generously. Although slaveholders were a minority in the South, they convinced millions of white Southerners to support slavery. ■

The shackles indicate the harsh treatment slaves often received. What does the poster suggest about the value of slaves?

■ *Describe passive methods that slaves used to resist the master's authority.*

R E V I E W

1. **FOCUS** Describe the responsibilities of the plantation owner, his wife, and the slaves they controlled.
2. **ECONOMICS** Explain why the plantation could be called a "self-contained world." How was this different from the way people in the North lived and worked?
3. **CULTURE** Identify the African traditions that slaves preserved. Explain how those traditions helped slaves maintain a sense of identity.
4. **CONNECT** Compare the labor system in the Northern factories in Chapter 9 with the Southern plantation system.
5. **CRITICAL THINKING** Why do you think planters dominated Southern life?
6. **WRITING ACTIVITY** Write two short accounts of an event occurring on a plantation. One account should reflect the point of view of someone living in the Big House; the other should be from a slave's viewpoint.

Slave Life

Frederick Douglass

In Lesson 2 you read about daily life on a Southern plantation. This selection is a firsthand account of slave life.

Frederick Douglass (1817?-1895) was a leading crusader for the rights of black Americans in the 1800s. An escaped slave, he knew the horrors of slavery and recorded his impressions in an autobiography, Narrative of the Life of Frederick Douglass. *His lifework included founding a newspaper, lecturing against slavery and inequality, and assisting with the Underground Railroad. As you read the selection, think about why the narrator feels both delight and sadness at seeing sailing ships.*

point of endurance: breaking point

fodder food for live-stock

cunning skill at tricks

I lived with Mr. Covey one year. During the first six months, of that year, scarce a week passed without his whipping me. I was seldom free from a sore back. My awkwardness was almost always his excuse for whipping me. We were worked fully up to the point of endurance. Long before day we were up, our horses fed, and by the first approach of day we were off to the field with our hoes and ploughing teams. Mr. Covey gave us enough to eat, but scarce time to eat it. We were often less than five minutes taking our meals. We were often in the field from the first approach of day till its last lingering ray had left us; and at saving-fodder time, midnight often caught us in the field binding blades.

Covey would be out with us. The way he used to stand it, was this. He would spend the most of his afternoons in bed. He would then come out fresh in the evening, ready to urge us on with his words, example, and frequently with the whip. Mr. Covey was one of the few slaveholders who could and did work with his hands. He was a hard-working man. He knew by himself just what a man or a boy could do. There was no deceiving him. His work went on in his absence almost as well as in his presence; and he had the faculty of making us feel that he was ever present with us. This he did by surprising us. He seldom approached the spot where we were at work openly, if he could do it secretly. He always aimed at taking us by surprise. Such was his cunning, that we used to call him, among ourselves, "the snake." When we were at work in the cornfield, he would sometimes crawl on his hands and knees to avoid detection, and all at once he would rise nearly in our midst, and scream out, "Ha, ha! Come, come! Dash on, dash on!" This being his mode of attack, it was never safe to stop a single minute. . . .

If at any one time of my life more than another, I was made to drink the bitterest dregs of slavery, that time was during the first six months of my stay with Mr. Covey. We were worked in all weathers. It was never too hot or too cold; it could never rain, blow, hail, or snow, too hard for us to work in the field. Work, work, work, was scarcely more the order of the day than of the night. The longest days were too short for him, and the shortest nights too long for him. I was somewhat unmanageable when I first went there, but a few months of this discipline tamed me. Mr. Covey succeeded in breaking me. I was broken in body, soul, and spirit. My natural elasticity was crushed, my intellect languished, the disposition to read departed, the cheerful spark that lingered about my eye died; the dark night of slavery closed in upon me; and behold a man transformed into a brute!

languish to go unused

Sunday was my only leisure time. I spent this in a sort of beast-like stupor, between sleep and wake, under some large tree. At times I would rise up, a flash of energetic freedom would dart through my soul, accompanied with a faint beam of hope, that flickered for a moment, and then vanished. I sank down again, mourning over my wretched condition. I was sometimes prompted to take my life, and that of Covey, but was prevented by a combination of hope and fear. My sufferings on this plantation seem now like a dream rather than a stern reality.

Our house stood within a few rods of the Chesapeake Bay, whose broad bosom was ever white with sails from every quarter of the habitable globe. Those beautiful vessels, robed in purest white, so delightful to the eye of freedom, were to me so many shrouded ghosts, to terrify and torment me with thoughts of my wretched condition. I have often, in the deep stillness of a summer's Sabbath, stood all alone upon the lofty banks of that noble bay, and traced, with saddened heart and tearful eye, the countless number of sails moving off to the mighty ocean. The sight of these always affected me powerfully. My thoughts would compel utterance; and there, with no audience but the Almighty, I would pour out my soul's complaint, in my rude way, with an apostrophe to the moving multitude of ships:—

shrouded covered

utterance speech

"You are loosed from your moorings, and are free; I am fast in my chains, and am a slave! You move merrily before the gentle gale, and I sadly before the bloody whip! You are freedom's swift-winged angels, that fly round the world; I am confined in bands of iron! O that I were free! . . ."

Further Reading

Narrative of the Life of Frederick Douglass. Frederick Douglass. In this famous autobiography, Douglass gives a vivid account of his life as a slave, his escape to freedom, and his work as an abolitionist.

Frederick Douglass and the Fight for Freedom. Shalman Russell. The story of Frederick Douglass comes to life in this thoughtful biography.

LESSON 3

The Other Souths

Key Terms

- yeoman farmer
- artisan

► *George Caleb Bingham did a series of paintings about Southern political life. Why did he omit women?*

Imagine the excitement as the people living in a small county in Georgia gathered at the town square on a Saturday morning in 1835. A robust man with a red face, white hair, and a booming voice stood on a tree stump and called out "Welcome! Welcome! Help yourself to our fresh-pressed cider, roast pig, and all the fixin's. We're gonna have a great time today! It will give you a taste of the great future for you all once I'm elected!"

The speaker, owner of the largest plantation in the county, looked out over the faces gathering around the stump he stood on, and smiled. Most of the people in his county had small farms. They lived far from one another in the scrubby pine woods. For them, a trip to the county seat (the town where government offices were located) was a major event. A full day of free food and entertainment would probably persuade most of the farmers to vote for this candidate.

The barbecue continued throughout the day with games, dances, and the constant hum of people gossiping with neighbors they hadn't seen for weeks. By nightfall, the plantation owner had shaken hands with each person in the crowd, kissed every baby in sight, and made sure that even those who couldn't read or write would be able to mark the ballot with an X beside his name.

Although this account is imaginary, it describes a common event in the South. Since most farm families had no slaves for large projects, they would get together at day-long parties to build barns or husk corn. Politicians in rural areas depended on such gatherings to gain political support. In this way, white Southerners mixed pleasure with politics or with cooperative labor.

Chapter 10

The Neglected Majority

The majority of white Southerners did not own slaves. They included **yeoman farmers**—owners of small farms—and mountain settlers. The mountain people lived by hunting, fishing, and gathering wild vegetables as well as by maintaining small farms. In addition, there were some very poor rural white people who owned no land and earned their living in whatever way they could.

Yeoman Farmers

Yeoman farmers usually grew an acre or so of cotton or another cash crop. They also grew crops and raised livestock for their own needs. The farmer and the farmer's family performed the work, perhaps with the help of a few hired white laborers. During the planting and harvesting seasons they might borrow several slaves. And, as noted, neighboring farm families shared work on large projects such as building a house.

Many yeoman farmers, although illiterate, had a strong oral tradition of songs and folk stories. The church played an important part in their social life, and many could quote long passages from the Bible.

Although they were not slaveholders and did not directly benefit from the slave economy, yeoman farmers generally supported the proslavery position of the ruling minority of planters.

Appalachian Culture

The people of the Appalachians—from the Smoky Mountains of Virginia to the Cumberland region of Tennessee—had much in common. Unlike yeoman farmers who might grow a small cash crop, these families often were completely cut off from the market economy. Most were hunters who managed to grow enough food for their family, but not enough for

trade. Although mountain families lived isolated lives, they enjoyed a rich culture.

A Closer Look shows some of the objects the mountain people used. Music was important in their lives. Many of the earliest settlers came to the United States from England, Wales, and the Scottish Highlands, where ancient ballads and dances were handed down from one generation to the next. Mountain musicians played the dulcimer (a stringed instrument), the fiddle, the bagpipe, and a small instrument known as the "mouth harp."

People in the mountains enjoyed opportunities to get together. Church meetings, harvest suppers, and Fourth of July celebrations provided a chance to display folk dances. Monthly county court sessions also served as a social event. Women met there to exchange recipes while men talked politics.

▲ *The mists formed by a humid atmosphere gave the Great Smoky Mountains (above) their name. Mountain people built their sturdy cabins with long sloping roofs that provide protection from the damp climate.*

Appalachian Crafts

Travel into the Appalachians—over hills and streams to cabins nestled in forests and grassy knolls. One observer commented, "Everywhere you go, it's climb, scramble, clamber down, and climb again." Here, people use what nature gives them to craft charming and practical items.

"Dipper gourds" are perfect for scooping water out of a stream, and "bottle gourds" are handy for storing seeds. Nimble fingers turn corn husks into useful articles: hats, shopping bags, doormats, or pretty painted dolls.

Friendship quilts such as this one often combine squares made by many different people. Each seamstress designs her own patch and may even sew her name onto it. The quilt might be a gift for a wedding or a farewell.

The Appalachian dulcimer is a Southern mountain folk instrument. The right hand strums or plucks the strings while the left hand stops or frets. The dulcimer is held on the lap and produces a soft, sad sound.

Snakes slither through folk-tales and folk art. A whittler had a good time carving this one on a walking stick.

Cornhusks, willow wands, cattail leaves, and honeysuckle vines all make fine baskets. These baskets are woven from oak splints shaved off an oak log with an axe. Basket dyes are made from roots and barks, such as walnut, willow, and sassafras.

301

■ How did the lives of yeoman farmers and mountain settlers differ from life on the plantations?

At county fairs people exhibited their best quilts, vegetables, and livestock, and sold stock at fairs and "mule days." Horse races gave the mountain people another chance for social contact, as well as an opportunity to show off the thoroughbred horses for which the South was famous. ■

The Urban South

The South was overwhelmingly rural. Social life in the rural South usually took place on the great plantations. Small Southern towns were active during the fall harvest and shipping season, but offered no year-round amusements such as theaters, lecture halls, or even inns for temporary hospitality. Only the larger cities could be called true metropolitan cultural centers.

Southern towns grew slowly, although there were some exceptions: Louisville, Kentucky, and New Orleans, Louisiana, almost doubled in size in the 10 years preceding the Civil War. The population of Mobile, Alabama, grew by 155 percent.

Urban Centers

Cities such as Savannah in Georgia, Richmond in Virginia, Charleston in South Carolina, and New Orleans had as varied a lifestyle as any Northern city. Planters and their wives often spent part of the year in cities. White **artisans**—workers trained in skilled trades such as printing and cabinet making—lived in the cities. So did most former slaves, who had either been granted their freedom or had bought it.

Many Southern cities had a diverse society. St. Augustine, Florida, had Spanish roots; Jamestown, Virginia, had been settled by the English. New Orleans, which had been settled by the French, gained Spanish colonists during the years it was ruled by Spain. The influence of these origins persisted and blended with the cultures of such later arrivals as white and black Southerners and German and Irish immigrants. Farmers from the Ohio River Valley and the South shipped their produce down the Mississippi through the busy port at its mouth. By 1860 New Orleans was the largest city in the South, and the fifth largest in the United States.

➤ *Eastman Johnson called this painting "Old Kentucky Home." The actual scene was the backyard of his father's home in Washington, D.C.*

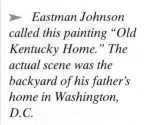

Southern Education

Cities such as New Orleans had fine colleges, and wealthy white people in the South were generally well-educated. They were tutored at home or were sent to private boarding schools or military academies. In 1850, the Southern states led the nation in number of private schools. The first state universities in the United States were the University of North Carolina, founded in 1795, and the University of Georgia, opened in 1808. Many Southern colleges were large by comparison with Northern schools. In 1856, for example, the University of Virginia had 568 students to the 361 at Harvard in Massachusetts.

Public education in the South, however, lagged behind the North, and many Southerners could not read and write. Many rural schools were open only those few months a year when children could be released from farm work. Southern farmers, like farmers in the North, did not feel formal education was a necessity for farm work.

Education for Black People

Slaves were forbidden to read or write, although some did so in defiance of their masters and the state. Slaveholders feared education would unite slaves and teach them dangerous ideas about freedom. In fact, two of the three major slave revolts were launched in cities, where more black men and women were literate. Some free black people who gained an education taught others to read and write. Among them was Frederick Douglass, who was born a slave on a Maryland plantation.

Douglass taught himself to write by copying letters marked on timber in the shipyard where he worked. Eventually he became one of the greatest leaders in the struggle for black freedom. In his autobiography, he explains how he cleverly expanded his knowledge. ■

◄ *Frederick Douglass escaped slavery in Maryland by running away to Massachusetts.*

*W*hen I met any boy who I knew could write, I would tell him I could write as well as he. The next word would be, "I don't believe you. Let me see you try it." I would then make the letters which I had been so fortunate as to learn and ask him to beat that. In this way I got a good many lessons in writing, which it is quite possible I should never have gotten in any other way.

During this time, my copybook was the board fence, brick wall, and pavement; my pen and ink was a lump of chalk. . . . By this time my little master Thomas had gone to school and learned how to write and had written over a number of copybooks. . . . When left [to take care of the house], I used to spend the time in writing in the places left in Master Thomas' copy-book, copying what he had written.

Narrative of the Life of Frederick Douglass, 1845

■ *What made most Southern cities different from cities in the North during the antebellum period?*

303

The South

Free Blacks

Thousands of free blacks—slaves who had been granted or had bought their freedom—lived in the cities below the Mason-Dixon line—the line that divided the North from the South. Some free black Southerners were able to climb the social ladder; some even held land and slaves.

Job Opportunities

Many free blacks used the skills they had learned as slaves to earn a living as blacksmiths, carpenters, masons, barbers, and tailors. In 1860, for example, free black men made up 40 percent of the tailors and 25 percent of the carpenters in Charleston, South Carolina.

The majority of free blacks in Southern towns and cities were women. By 1850, some cities had as many as 125 free black women for every 100 free black men. These women usually faced harsher lives than free black men because they lacked skills that paid well. Some

UNDERSTANDING SOCIAL CLASSES

Southern society in the 1860s was not just one society but was made up of several social classes that stood in a clear order of rank to one another. A social class is a group of people that share similar economic and cultural characteristics.

Southern Class Structure

Not everyone in white Southern society owned slaves, but because ownership of slaves indicated property and thus wealth, most everyone wanted to. A social hierarchy means that one social class is ranked above another. At the top of the white Southern hierarchy were the small number—about 2,300—who owned 100 or more slaves. Below them were the slightly larger group who owned from 10 to 50 slaves. By far the largest group—about 270,000 families—owned fewer than 10 slaves.

Three-quarters of Southern families, the yeoman farmers, did not own slaves. Yet they supported the right to own slaves, and might have if they could have afforded to buy and care for slaves. Slave ownership was simply not economically profitable for small landowners.

At the bottom of this white social hierarchy were the very poor who owned no land at all. In a way, they had the most to gain from the institution of slavery. While slavery existed, there was someone else who was worse off than they. On the other hand, the existence of slavery allowed plantation holders to accumulate large holdings of land, and made it harder for the landless to own property.

Other Class Hierarchies

The social ranking of white Southern society was not as rigid as the hierarchy of feudal society. Moving into a new rank was in principle easier in the South than in feudal times.

Yet, there were important differences between Southern society and feudal society. Although medieval serfs, or peasants, could not leave the land, they could not be sold. Their families could not be split up between masters, as happened with slave families.

The Class of Slaves

Without slaves, the social structure of the South could not have existed. A part of the American social philosophy then—as now—had been that everyone shared the same opportunity for social and economic advancement. In theory, the landless could come to own land, the nonslaveholders could one day buy a slave, and the small planters could become large plantation owners. All, that is, except the slaves. With very few exceptions, no slaves in the South in 1860 could break out of the system that they made work.

worked as laundresses and nurses, and a large number ran small boarding houses. Free black women did not usually work as domestic servants, a role reserved for slave women.

Restrictions on Free Blacks

Despite their status, free blacks were subject to harsh laws. They were not allowed to vote. When they attended theaters or other public performances, they had to sit in special areas. Their travel was restricted by state laws, and their houses could be searched for runaway slaves at any time.

When Virginia prisons became too crowded in 1822, the state decided not to imprison free blacks accused of crimes. Instead, officials whipped them or sold them into slavery as punishment for serious crimes.

Although masters often granted freedom to a faithful servant, white Southerners continued to be fearful and suspicious of the influence of free blacks on slaves. This attitude made it dangerous for blacks to socialize with one other and for free black people to gain full acceptance among their own people.

In the early 1800s many white Southerners supported the idea of shipping freed slaves to Africa. Colonization societies were formed to accomplish this goal. Many slaves, however, were third-generation Americans with no desire to "return" to Africa. By the late antebellum period, it was clear that this plan did not work. By the 1850s, the high demand for slaves and white fear of free blacks caused many planters to resist granting freedom to their slaves.

Resistance to Freeing Slaves

Slavery created ties that bound together the many Souths. The system of servitude provided the foundation for plantation life, fueled the cotton revolution, enriched New England mill owners, and helped to keep the Southern economy rural. White Southerners also tended to support slavery out of fear. The slave rebellions of the early 1800s created alarm at the possibilities that freed slaves might gain power and destroy the Southern plantation system.

As the South's dependence on slavery increased between 1790 and 1860, the gulf between the Southern cotton economy and the industrial economy of the North widened. The opposing goals and needs of the North and the South would create a deeper conflict—a conflict that would eventually lead to war. ■

◄ *Tags such as these were worn by free blacks as well as by slaves whom their masters hired out for work. What different jobs do these tags represent?*

■ *In what ways were free blacks' rights limited?*

R E V I E W

1. **FOCUS** What groups made up the majority of Southerners who lived outside the plantation system?
2. **CONNECT** How did the lives of Southern free blacks differ from those of slaves? In what ways were their lives similar?
3. **GEOGRAPHY** How did the mountain people's crafts reflect the natural surroundings?
4. **CRITICAL THINKING** Why do you think schooling did not seem as important to yeoman farmers in the rural South as it did to the working classes of the urban North?
5. **ACTIVITY** Draw a picture of an Appalachian event such as a harvest supper, a Fourth of July celebration, or a county fair. Be sure to include distinctly Appalachian objects and activities.

Choosing Appropriate Graphs

Here's Why

Graphs are an excellent way to present numerical information so that it is easier to understand. It is much easier to "see" what was happening over a certain time period by looking at graphs rather than at lists of numbers.

For example, in this chapter you have read about the dramatic increase in cotton production after the invention of the cotton gin. Suppose you wanted to show this information with a graph. In order to determine which kind of graph—line, bar, or circle graph—would be most appropriate, you first need to understand what each of these graphs does.

Here's How

Look at each of the graphs on this page and on the next. Bar graphs, like the one below, show information in columns and are best for presenting numbers and comparing quantities. Circle graphs, like the one on the right, indicate percentages and are useful for showing the relationship between parts and the whole. You also can use two or more circle graphs to compare different subjects, such as products or groups of people, or to show the difference in percentages over a period of time. The graphs on page 307 are line graphs, which are best for presenting statistics over a period of time. By reading the plotted points on a line graph, you can follow the curve to determine a trend in the information being given.

In order to choose which of these graphs is most appropriate for your purposes, you can follow the steps outlined below:

1. Ask yourself, "What is the main point I wish to communicate?"
2. Decide whether this point involves comparing the quantities of similar things (bar graph), showing percentages or the relationship of parts to a whole (circle graph), or showing a change or trend over time (line graph).
3. Choose the type of graph that can most effectively convey your information based on your answer in step two.

Look at the bar graph, which shows the growth of the nation's urban and rural populations in the North and South. This graph is effective in showing the overall growth in population from 1820 to 1860, but if you just wanted to show this change, you could use a line

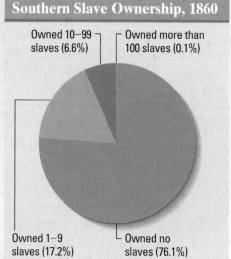

Southern Slave Ownership, 1860

Owned 10–99 slaves (6.6%)
Owned more than 100 slaves (0.1%)
Owned 1–9 slaves (17.2%)
Owned no slaves (76.1%)

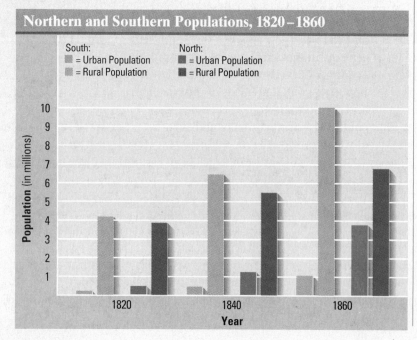

Northern and Southern Populations, 1820–1860

South:
■ = Urban Population
■ = Rural Population

North:
■ = Urban Population
■ = Rural Population

Population (in millions)

Year
1820   1840   1860

graph. By using different colored columns for urban and rural populations, this graph emphasizes the actual population numbers and more specifically outlines the differences in the population growth between the North and the South. You can see that in 1820 each region had similar populations in rural areas and in urban areas. However by 1860, the urban population in the North was triple that of the South, and the South had ten times the amount of people living on farms as they did in the cities.

Look at the circle graph on page 306 showing what percentage of Southern white people owned slaves. Although it seems that many people before the Civil War owned slaves, you've read that few planters owned more than 100 slaves. A circle graph is effective here since it gives you a dramatic picture of what those numbers mean and shows that three-quarters of the Southern white population owned no slaves at all.

Next look at the line graphs, which show cotton production and slave population from 1800 to 1860. Here the emphasis is in showing not just the numbers or quantities for these subjects, but also the trends over a period time that these figures represent. By comparing two graphs of the same kind, you can see whether these two sets of statistics follow the same trend.

The cotton production graph shows growth, or an

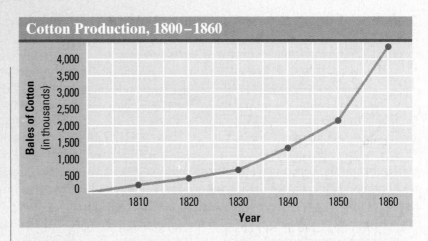

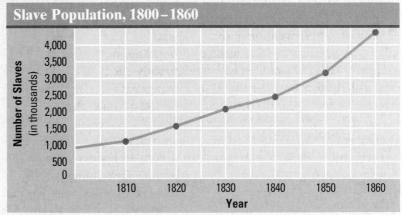

upward trend, since production increased from over 73,000 bales in 1800 to almost four million in 1860. You will notice an upward trend in the slave population graph as well, since the number of slaves rose significantly from 1800 to 1860. By comparing these two line graphs, you can see whether there was a relationship between cotton production and slavery.

Try It

Now go back to Lesson 1 of this chapter, and find the statistics about how many white people, slaves, and free blacks lived in the South in 1790 and in 1860. Following the process outlined on page 306, decide which type of graph—line, bar, or circle—is most appropriate to show this information, and then create that graph.

Apply It

You may look forward to the weekend all week long, but then once the weekend arrives, the hours just fly by. Suppose you wanted an accurate account of how you spend that free time. Write down how many hours of your weekend days you spend on different activities like sleeping, eating, studying, watching television, playing sports, or visiting with friends. Then choose two different graphs to present this information, and create those graphs, noting the difference in how this information is presented in each graph.

Chapter Review

Reviewing Key Terms

antebellum (p. 286)   cultural heritage (p. 293)
artisan (p. 302)   plantation (p. 285)
cash crop (p. 287)   yeoman farmer (p. 299)

A. In each of the following pairs, the two terms are related in some way. Write a sentence for each pair that clearly explains the meaning of the two terms.
1. artisan, yeoman farmer
2. cash crop, plantation
3. cultural heritage, antebellum

B. Based on what you have read in the chapter, decide whether each of the following sentences is accurate. Write an explanation of each decision.
1. The antebellum South grew quite rapidly in the years after the Civil War.
2. A yeoman farmer usually lived on a large plantation and spent all his time running it.
3. The cultural heritage of the South can be determined by studying the language, art, and beliefs of the people who lived there.
4. A yeoman farmer usually owned many slaves.
5. An artisan was an unskilled worker who traveled from place to place.
6. Some free blacks worked as artisans in the North and South before the Civil War.
7. In a cash crop economy, most farmers grow food for their own use and for sale to their neighbors.
8. Southern plantations were working farms with large, elegant homes for the white owners.

Exploring Concepts

A. Copy the following paragraph onto a separate sheet of paper. Fill in the blank spaces with information from the chapter.

With the invention of the _____ , cotton became the single most important crop of the South. Because growing cotton required many workers, the Southern economy became more dependent on _____ . Though most Southern whites were _____ with few or no slaves, large planters controlled the _____ and economy of the South. The master of a _____ had final authority over his land, his slaves, and his family. The life of a slave was one of constant work, but slaves _____ their masters in various ways. Even though slaves were brutally _____ , some worked as slowly as possible or _____ from the plantation. Slaves were not allowed to learn to read or write, for their masters thought that would encourage _____ . Laws even restricted the activities of _____ blacks, because whites feared their influence on _____ .

B. Support each of the following statements with facts and details from the chapter.
1. Whitney's cotton gin revolutionized the economy of the antebellum South.
2. The South's economy depended on the North.
3. The South became important in the United States Congress because the expansion of cotton growing territories increased the number of Southern representatives in Congress.
4. Southerners used both economic and religious arguments to defend slavery.
5. Everyone on a plantation played a specific role in this self-contained world.
6. Slaves had many ways of preserving their sense of identity and culture.
7. The majority of Southern whites were not owners of large plantations, but made up a diverse mix of people.
8. Most free blacks in the South were deprived of their full rights as citizens.

Reviewing Skills

1. The table at right gives U.S. population figures for 1800-1860. Decide which kind of graph—circle, line, or bar—would be the most appropriate way to present this information. Then draw the graph of your choice.
2. If you wanted to show the percentage of tailors who were free blacks in Charleston, South Carolina in 1860, what kind of graph would you choose?
3. Look at the quilt on page 294. What kind of a primary source is it? Make a list of all the infor-

Northern and Southern Populations, 1800–1860				
	1800	1820	1840	1860
North	2,636,000	4,360,000	6,761,000	10,594,000
South	2,622,000	4,419,000	6,951,000	11,133,000

mation you can gather from that source.

4. In what kind of publications would you find graphs that present statistics on currency rates, population trends, and budget figures?

Using Critical Thinking

1. In 1835, the governor of South Carolina said of the slaves, "There is not upon the face of the earth any class of people, high or low, so perfectly free from care and anxiety. . . . Our slaves are cheerful, contented, and happy, [unlike] the general condition of the human race." Put yourself in the place of a slave. How would you respond to this statement? Do people today still claim that the disadvantaged are content with their lives? Explain your answer?
2. An ex-slave recalled the religious teaching of his master, "Be nice to massa and missus; don't be mean; be obedient, and work hard. That was all the Sunday school lesson they taught us." Why do you think slaveowners sought to use religion as justification for slavery? How did the slaves respond?
3. Alexis de Tocqueville claimed that whites in the slave states were not as industrious as those in free states. In his opinion, slavery had a bad effect on the slaveholders, making them lazy and interested only in pleasure. Using examples from the chapter, explain why you agree or disagree with Tocqueville's statement.
4. Abraham Lincoln suggested that if "A" could enslave "B," then it stood to reason that "B" could enslave "A." If color were the reason for slavery, he went on, then "you are to be slave to the first man you meet with a fairer skin than your own." How would Southerners answer this argument? What was their main justification for slavery? Are there any places in the world where this argument is still used?

Preparing for Citizenship

1. WRITING ACTIVITY Many ex-slaves wrote about their experiences. Find some accounts of slavery in your library. Write a report describing the life of a slave.
2. ART ACTIVITY Look at the site plan for the plantation shown on page 291. Design your own plan, taking into account all that you have learned about the working and living conditions on large Southern plantations. If you choose, you may design a modern plantation, adding any modern conveniences that you think would have replaced slavery had the plantation culture survived.
3. ART ACTIVITY Both the white Appalachian mountain families of the South and the slaves created music that is part of American culture today. Find some recordings of mountain music or black spirituals and play them for the class. Discuss how they reflect the culture of the people who created them. Which kinds do you enjoy most? Why? Make up your own dances to perform with the music.
4. COLLABORATIVE LEARNING Create a short skit of a day in the life of a large plantation. Use details described in the chapter to role-play the people who lived there. Each student should have a chance to be a master, a mistress, an overseer, and a slave. Does your attitude toward the project change as your role changes?

The Nation Divides and Reunites

The issue of slavery wouldn't disappear. Just as it had endangered the Constitutional Convention, the debate over slavery threatened to break the young nation apart in the early 1800s. For a time, the North and the South were able to postpone the conflict through a series of fragile compromises, but the problem remained unresolved. It would take a long and bloody Civil War to end slavery and preserve the Union. When the war ended, the nation began the long, difficult process of healing its wounds.

1820

Augustus Saint-Gaudens. Bronze bas-relief of colonel Robert Shaw and the black 54th and 55th infantries of the Union Army. Boston, Massachusetts. Photograph by Jerome Liebling.

1877

Chapter 11

Causes of the Civil War

Slave or free? For decades, politicians from the North and the South tried to resolve the slavery issue through compromise. Now, new lands gained through purchase and battle brought the question into even sharper focus: Slave or free? The compromises failed. The antislavery movement gained momentum. And tensions grew.

Harriet Tubman, at the far left of the photograph opposite, helped hundreds of slaves escape to freedom through the Underground Railroad.

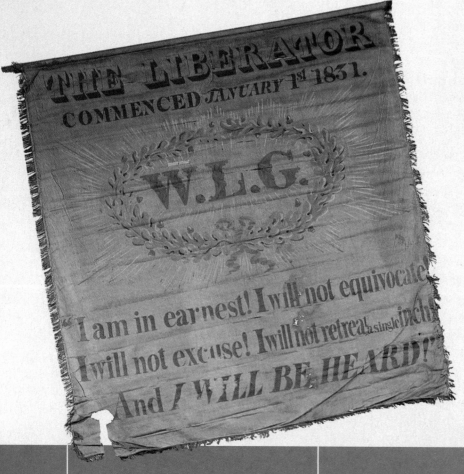

THE LIBERATOR

COMMENCED JANUARY 1st 1831.

W.L.G.

"I am in earnest! I will not equivocate! I will not excuse! I will not retreat a single inch! And *I WILL BE HEARD!*"

1831 Antislavery activists demand an immediate and no-compromise end to slavery. This banner shows the devotion of William Lloyd Garrison—publisher of the antislavery newspaper, *The Liberator*—to the cause.

1815	1825	1835

Presidents

1817-1825
Monroe

1825-1829
J. Q. Adams

1829-1837
Jackson

1837-1841
Van Buren

1820

1860 Democrat Stephen A. Douglas and Republican Abraham Lincoln run for the Senate. Slavery in the new territories is a main issue. Douglas favors letting the people decide; Lincoln wants to end slavery in the territories. Douglas wins, but the issue remains.

1845

1855

1865

1841–1845
Tyler

1845–1849
Polk

1850–1853
Fillmore

1857–1861
Buchanan

1853–1857
Pierce

1841
W. Harrison

1849–1850
Taylor

1861

L E S S O N   1

The Sectional Conflict

Why was compromise necessary between the North and the South as the United States expanded into western territories?

Key Term

- free labor

> W e have the wolf by the ears, and we can neither hold him, nor safely let him go. Justice is in one scale and self-preservation in the other.
>
> Thomas Jefferson

The fearsome "wolf" to which Thomas Jefferson referred in 1820 was slavery in the United States. Politicians had tried to maintain a balance between slaveholding and nonslaveholding states. Expansion into the West, however, deepened disagreement between North and South. When the territory of Missouri applied for admission to the Union in 1819, it was assumed that this slaveholding territory would become a slave state.

Instead, a full-scale congressional debate began in which slavery became a question of sectional, or regional, power.

The retired Jefferson, who had owned slaves all his life, saw both the good sense and the danger in ending slavery. "The Missouri debate, like a firebell in the night, awakened and filled me with terror," he wrote to a Massachusetts congressman who had requested the elder statesman's advice. The same man who penned the Declaration of Independence 44 years earlier, declaring "all men are created equal," could offer no solutions to the slavery issue. Politicians were faced with the great challenge of compromise in handling this growing national problem.

Different Regions, Different Needs

The North and the South of the early 1800s differed greatly in their economies and ways of life. Busy commercial regions filled with cities and factories characterized the North. Immigrants joined the Northern workforce, settling in cities and farmlands. Northern workers received pay for their labor, as well as the chance to improve their lives. They had the right to leave their employers and jobs for better opportunities. This system of work was called **free labor**.

In the South, the thriving cotton economy depended on slave labor. Owners of large and small plantations saw little reason to change a system that brought great profit. Talk among

Northerners of new farming methods, growing cities, and improved manufacturing must have sounded foolish to white Southerners. The South wanted new land for cotton—not a plan for remodeling its economy based on Northern ideas about industry.

Most white Southerners, even those who owned few slaves or none, believed in the economic need for slavery. And as the United States expanded into the territories it gained from the Louisiana Purchase, it was clear that the different interests of the two regions would cause serious conflict. How would Northerners and Southerners ever agree on such an important issue? ■

■ *Why did white Southerners resist the system of work called free labor?*

A Delicate Balance

When Missouri sought admission to the Union in 1819, it proposed a state constitution that would protect slavery. At the time, there were exactly as many slave states as free states in the Union. The House of Representatives was dominated by the North, and Southerners stood to gain control of the Senate if Missouri was admitted as a slave state. Most important, however, was the issue of extending slavery to the West.

Before the Missouri debate began, Congress used the Northwest Ordinance, legislation adopted in 1787 under the old Articles of Confederation, to prohibit slavery north and west of the Ohio River.

Now the political balance was in danger of being upset. Although the balance had been upset before, it had been easy to decide whether states east of the Mississippi should be slave or free. Mason and Dixon's line and the Ohio River had formed a natural and easily defined boundary between the two sections. But a line had not been drawn west of the Mississippi River. To complicate matters further, parts of the Missouri Territory lay to the north of the Ohio River, while other parts lay to the south.

Forging a Compromise

The debate in Congress grew heated. Some lawmakers wanted to forbid slavery in the new state. Others believed the Congress should not have authority over such matters. As the debate continued, Maine (then a northern portion of Massachusetts) applied for statehood.

In 1820, the Missouri Compromise was worked out and gained congressional approval, in part because of statesman Henry Clay's support. Missouri was to be admitted as a slave state. Maine would enter the Union as a free state. The balance had been preserved. The Compromise also pro-hibited slavery in other American territories west of the Mississippi River and north of Missouri's southern boundary.

While Northerners and Southerners had each gained from the Compromise, people from both regions remained concerned. Southerners grew more distrustful of Northerners and feared further legislation against slavery. An angry editorial in the *Richmond Enquirer* remarked about the Compromise, "We scarcely ever recollect to ever have tasted a bitterer cup. . . . What is a territorial restriction today becomes a state restriction tomorrow."

Thomas Jefferson, reflecting on the need to draw boundaries,

▲ *Statesman Henry Clay lent his support to the Missouri Compromise.*

▼ *The balance of slave and free states was threatened in 1819 when the Missouri Territory sought admission to the Union.*

Missouri Compromise

■ = Original Thirteen States
■ = States entering the Union, 1791–1819
■ = States entering after the Missouri Compromise

Slave States		Free States	
Missouri	(1821)	Maine	(1820)
Alabama	(1819)	Illinois	(1818)
Mississippi	(1817)	Indiana	(1816)
Louisiana	(1812)	Ohio	(1803)
Tennessee	(1796)	Vermont	(1791)
Kentucky	(1792)	Pennsylvania	
Georgia		New Jersey	
South Carolina		New York	
North Carolina		Connecticut	
Virginia		Rhode Island	
Maryland		Massachusetts	
Delaware		New Hampshire	

Causes of the Civil War

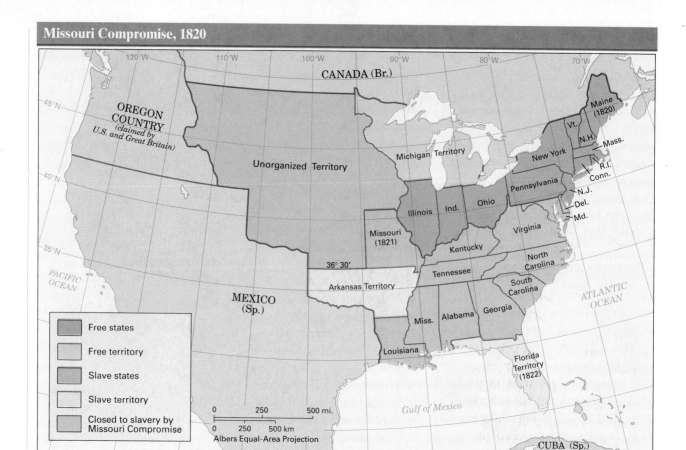

The map legend:
- Free states
- Free territory
- Slave states
- Slave territory
- Closed to slavery by Missouri Compromise

▲ *The United States acquired new territories with the Louisiana Purchase. White Southerners wished to extend slavery to the western territories, but Northerners opposed the idea. The Missouri Compromise was an attempt to strike a balance.*

■ *The Missouri Compromise ensured a senatorial balance between North and South. Why then did the Compromise frustrate and anger Southerners?*

observed, "A geographical line, coinciding with a marked principle, moral and political, once conceived and held up to the angry passions of men, will never be obliterated; and every new irritation will mark it deeper and deeper." Jefferson's remark predicted the bitter struggle that was yet to come.

South Relies on Senatorial Power

From 1820 to 1850 the South fought to maintain equality with the North in the Senate, and the two sections kept a delicate balance in that lawmaking body. As the South sought to bring new slave states into the Union, this balance in the Senate provided the basis of the South's political power.

The North, because of its larger population, controlled the House of Representatives. It seemed only a matter of time before the North would control the nation's entire political process, including the Senate. This appeared especially true since the North could expand into the area north and west of Missouri—the area

that would eventually become Minnesota, Iowa, the Dakotas, Montana, Idaho, Kansas, Nebraska, and Wyoming. The South, it seemed, could expand only into Florida, Arkansas, and Oklahoma.

South Eyes Texas for Slavery

In the early 1800s, Texas was a part of Mexico, although many American settlers lived there. These settlers considered themselves Americans, not Mexicans, and declared their independence in 1836.

As you learned in Chapter 8, Texans then set up their expansive Southern region as a slaveholding republic and sought to join the Union. But the United States, realizing the threat of war with Mexico, refused to annex, or take over, Texas. To do so would mean stirring resentment in Mexico and creating a new slave state, a step the North was eager to avoid. Mexico still did not accept the independence of Texas. In 1845, however, Congress bowed to Southern pressure and passed a bill allowing annexation. ■

UNDERSTANDING SECTIONALISM

*B*y the mid-1800s, the United States had grown through the addition of the Louisiana Purchase, Florida, Texas, the Oregon Territory, and the territory ceded by Mexico. With an area of 2,992,620 square miles, the United States was enormous compared to such nations as Great Britain, France, and Spain.

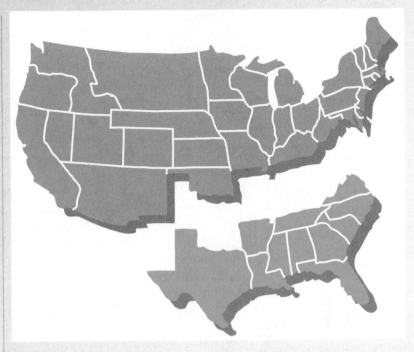

How could such a huge nation be ruled by one government? How could people living thousands of miles away from each other agree on political and social issues? The truth is that they often didn't. Citizens in various parts of the country developed their own interests, economies, and causes. The result was sectionalism, the devotion to the political and economic interest of a region or section of the country. Unlike regionalism, which divides the country culturally, sectionalism divides it politically and economically—often with serious consequences.

Early Sectionalism

Although sectionalism rose to a peak during the years before the Civil War, it was apparent even to the writers of the Constitution. There was strong sectional debate during the Constitutional Convention. The debate involved several issues, including ending the slave trade, passing export taxes, and giving Congress the power to allow only American ships to carry goods to and from America's ports.

Delegates from the Southern states objected to all of these measures. The region depended on slaves, the delegates argued. The South also wanted no taxes or shipping laws to interfere with their profitable exports. Delegates from the Northern states favored these measures, and the seeds of sectionalism were sown.

At the Constitutional Convention, delegates worked out a compromise. The slave trade would remain, they decided, but after 20 years it would again be put to a vote. Congress was given the power to tax imports, but export taxes were forbidden. Throughout American history, compromises such as this often solve sectional differences in constructive ways.

Sectionalism Continues

By the 1850s, sectionalism manifested itself almost entirely in the issues of slavery and states' rights. The North and the South were bitter enemies, rather than two parts of one whole. During these bitter years, citizens' loyalties to their section seemed more fierce than their loyalties to their nation.

America's regions have continued to clash politically and economically. In the late 1800s, the farmers in the West and the South joined together to form the Populist party. The Populists aimed to compete against what they saw as overwhelming northeastern and industrial political groups.

Even today, this sectionalism can be seen in the halls of Congress. Representatives of largely agricultural areas of the South and the West compete against the more industrial areas of the country for federal money. Despite their disagreements, however, there is little doubt that today's conflicts will never be as bitter or the result as serious as a Civil War that cost the nation hundreds of thousands of lives.

Sectionalism Deepens

In March 1845, Mexico, angered by the plan to annex Texas, broke diplomatic relations with the United States. By May 1846, Mexico and the United States were engaged in battle. President James Polk believed wholeheartedly that American settlers should expand westward. Some people suspected that his desire to gain new territory made him exaggerate reports of border conflicts and push for war with Mexico.

The Mexican-American War lasted until 1848, ending in an American victory. During these two years, the United States acquired vast territories. The new U.S. lands included areas that today make up California, Arizona, New Mexico, Utah, Nevada, and parts of Colorado.

Americans held strong views on the Mexican-American War. Support split along party lines and geographic lines. Democrats generally supported the war as a necessary step in the nation's westward expansion, but Northern Democrats were in a difficult position. They believed, with the rest of their party, in a policy of territorial expansion. But support of the war might appear to be support of slavery. Whigs tended to oppose becoming involved in a battle with Mexico.

North Backs the Wilmot Proviso

Congressman David Wilmot, a Pennsylvania Democrat and previous Polk supporter, had an answer to the dilemma of Northern Democrats. In 1846, he introduced the Wilmot Proviso, an amendment to a bill to finance the war. The amendment prohibited slavery in any territories won from Mexico. It allowed Northern Democrats to support the war without appearing to be proslavery. The amendment easily passed in the

▼ *The United States gained new lands from the Mexican-American War. These new territories sparked more disagreement over westward expansion and slavery.*

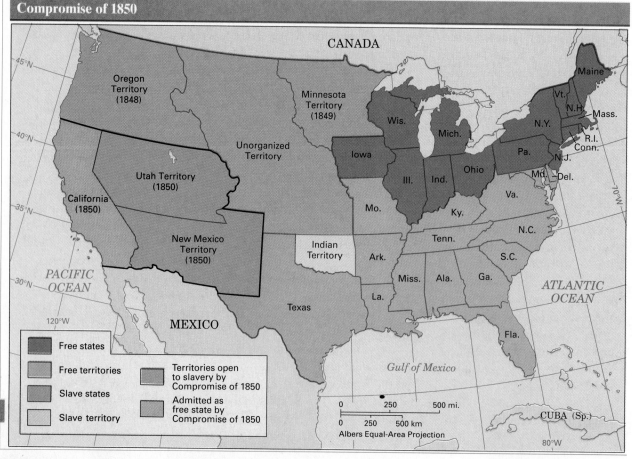

Compromise of 1850

Legend:
- Free states
- Free territories
- Slave states
- Slave territory
- Territories open to slavery by Compromise of 1850
- Admitted as free state by Compromise of 1850

House, thanks to the support of Northern Whigs and Democrats. But it failed in the Senate. This voting pattern was repeated in 1847. The South had won a legislative victory. But the voting—along rigid geographical lines—told another story, that of a nation where the hope of peace seemed lost.

Compromise of 1850 Reopens Wounds

Should the lands won from Mexico be open to slavery? By 1850, this question paralyzed national politics. Southerners said yes; they wanted more land for cotton cultivation. Northerners said no; their free labor system could not compete with slave labor in the territories. They insisted that if slavery took root in the territories, Northerners would be unable to settle there.

Meanwhile, another controversy developed. In the 1842 Prigg Decision, the Supreme Court relieved Northern law officials of the responsibility of catching runaway slaves. Southerners were furious. As many as 1,000 slaves escaped each year. Slaveholders needed a stronger federal law to regain their "property." Congress addressed these issues in a series of bills supported by Daniel Webster, Henry Clay, and Stephen A. Douglas. The Compromise of 1850 handed the South a new, harsher Fugitive Slave Law and created two slave territories: Utah and New Mexico.

The Compromise of 1850 offered the admission of California as a free state. It also ended the public sale of slaves in Washington, D. C. Now, for the first time since the Missouri Compromise, the free states outnumbered the slave states in the Senate.

The harsher Fugitive Slave Law created great hostility in the North and even led to violent riots. Northerners refused to help slaveholders capture runaway slaves. The North's failure to comply with the law only made the South more intent on defending its way of life. ∎

Fugitive Slave Bill.

CAUTION!! COLORED PEOPLE OF BOSTON, ONE & ALL, You are hereby respectfully CAUTIONED and advised, to avoid conversing with the Watchmen and Police Officers of Boston, For since the recent ORDER OF THE MAYOR & ALDERMEN, they are empowered to act as KIDNAPPERS AND Slave Catchers, And they have already been actually employed in KIDNAPPING, CATCHING, AND KEEPING SLAVES. Therefore, if you value your LIBERTY, and the Welfare of the Fugitives among you, Shun them in every possible manner, as so many HOUNDS on the track of the most unfortunate of your race. Keep a Sharp Look Out for KIDNAPPERS, and have TOP EYE open.

Notices appeared in Boston to warn citizens of the harsh Fugitive Slave Act. Northerners strongly opposed the law and refused to obey its orders.

The Compromise of 1850 gave the South a tougher fugitive slave law and two new territories. The North gained a free state. Why did both sides feel the Compromise was unacceptable?

REVIEW

1. **FOCUS** Why was compromise necessary between the North and the South as the United States expanded into western territories?

2. **CONNECT** Why did the North develop into an industrial economy while the South remained an agricultural economy?

3. **GEOGRAPHY** What effect did the Mexican-American War have on the acquisition of new land?

4. **CRITICAL THINKING** Why did the Missouri Compromise of 1820 fail to resolve the slavery debate?

5. **CRITICAL THINKING** What was the aim of the Wilmot Proviso?

6. **WRITING ACTIVITY** Write a "Letter to the Editor" from a Northerner, and another from a Southerner, stating your views on the Compromise of 1850. Do you approve or disapprove?

Causes of the Civil War

LESSON 2

The Antislavery Movement

THINKING FOCUS

How did the abolitionist movement contribute to the ongoing conflict between the North and the South?

Key Term

• abolitionism

▲ *Sojourner Truth, a famous activist in the antislavery movement, helped hundreds of slaves to escape.*

Outrageous! Dangerous! High treason! These were the typical reactions of Southern whites who read a pamphlet that mysteriously appeared in Southern cities. "How would they like for us to hold them in cruel slavery, and murder them as they do to us?" the publication demanded.

People all over the South were shocked when, in 1830, they were faced with such questions in a pamphlet titled *Appeal to the Colored Citizens of the World.* David Walker, a free black man who worked as a tailor in Boston, published the piece in 1829. It was not long afterward that the state of Georgia offered a $1,000 reward for Walker's arrest. Georgia enacted laws that made it a crime to hand out such incendiary, or inflammatory, publications. Teaching blacks to read or write became a crime in Georgia. Walker continued his mission, but died mysteriously in 1830,

the possible victim of murder.

Born a free man in the slave state of North Carolina, Walker had witnessed blacks being bought and sold as human property. He considered the supporters of slavery "avaricious [greedy] and unmerciful wretches."

Many of Walker's customers were sailors, and he would slip copies of his *Appeal* inside their duffel bags. Then his pamphlets would be carried to Southern port cities, where they would be passed along. In this way, Walker's bold call to insurrection, or open revolt, spread to slaves and slaveholders alike. Walker's message was the topic of many religious sermons in the South. The antislavery movement had found an urgent and compelling voice in David Walker. But his *Appeal* was just one of the many ways that abolitionists, those opposed to slavery, presented their views. Soon, men and women across the nation would be working for the antislavery movement.

Antislavery Movement Speaks with Many Voices

Many slaves sought their freedom at every opportunity. They tried risky escapes, they disobeyed their day-to-day orders, and they occasionally rose up violently against the slaveholders. Nat Turner's violent revolt of 1831 in Virginia, together with scores of smaller uprisings, made slaveowners fear their own slaves. Southerners' distrust of the North also grew because they

believed that antislavery agitation in the North encouraged slave rebellions.

Northern free blacks launched a crusade to liberate their "brothers" and "sisters" from slavery. One of the most famous activists was Sojourner Truth, who discarded her slave name of Isabella Baumfree. Expressing her belief that people best show love for God by love and concern for others, she helped hundreds of slaves escape and spread her word throughout the North. She even visited President Abraham Lincoln at the White House to deliver her message personally.

Antislavery Roots

Before the 1830s, the white antislavery movement was disorganized and ineffective. One group, the American Colonization Society, proposed to send free blacks and emancipated slaves to settle in the African land of Liberia. The first settlement of American blacks took place there in 1822. This group posed no threat to slaveholders who were happy to get rid of free blacks and troublesome slaves. Other groups believed that slavery should be ended gradually.

Then, on New Year's Day of 1831, a new and fiery brand of antislavery was born. On that day Boston publisher William Lloyd Garrison began a newspaper called the *Liberator*. The *Liberator* supported **abolitionism**, a movement that demanded an immediate and no-compromise end to slavery.

In 1834, Garrison helped found the American Antislavery Society. This new group worked to spread the abolition movement across the nation through the mails, lectures, and petitions to Congress.

Louder Voices

Among the many voices speaking against slavery during the 1800s was that of Frederick Douglass. A former slave from Maryland, Douglass became a leading spokesman for black freedom. He was a gifted writer and speaker who devoted his life to ending slavery and fighting for black rights.

Born Frederick Augustus Washington Bailey, he fled his Baltimore, Maryland, master as a young man in 1838. He settled in New Bedford, Massachusetts, and changed his name to avoid being captured. Douglass found work in a shipyard, but other men refused to work with

him because he was black. He found other jobs collecting trash and digging cellars.

At a meeting of the Massachusetts Antislavery Society in 1841, Douglass described what freedom meant to him. His speech impressed the audience and he was hired by the society to lecture about his experiences as a slave. In addition to lecturing, Douglass actively protested the racial segregation that was common in public places, even churches. He was once dragged from a railroad car reserved for white people.

In 1845, Douglass published the first of two autobiographies, or life accounts, *Narrative of the Life of Frederick Douglass.* You have already read two stories from this book in Chapter 10. Fearing that his identity as a runaway slave would be revealed, Douglass went to England for two years. While there, he continued to speak against slavery. When he returned to America in 1847, he founded an antislavery newspaper, the *North Star,* in Rochester, New York. ■

■ *What techniques did abolitionists Sojourner Truth, William Lloyd Garrison, and Frederick Douglass use to gain support for the antislavery movement?*

◄ *William Lloyd Garrison published a newspaper, the* Liberator, *to support the abolitionist movement.*

Women Play a Crucial Role

From the beginning of the abolition movement, women joined in large numbers. At first, they had to work in separate women's organizations. Many people believed that it was improper for women and men to work together. Some of the women's duties included organizing social gatherings to recruit new members and to circulate petitions. Some women even hid runaway slaves in their homes.

Early in the abolition movement, women saw their work as a religious crusade against the "sinful" and "un-Christian" slaveholders. Over time, however, many began to think of abolitionism as a broader movement toward equal rights—not only for blacks but for women as well.

The Grimké sisters, Angelina and Sarah, were two Southerners who went against all notions of "proper behavior" for women. They dared to lecture against slavery, not just to other women, but to audiences of both men and women—a practice unheard of in those days. "My idea," wrote Angelina, "is that whatever is morally right for a man to do is morally right

for a woman to do."

Lucretia Mott and Elizabeth Cady Stanton traveled overseas in 1840 to attend the World Antislavery Convention in London. As women, they were required to sit apart from the men at meetings. And in all the Convention's plans, they noticed that women were forced into secondary roles.

Of all the women fighting slavery, perhaps the most forceful voice came from a woman named Harriet Beecher Stowe.

Uncle Tom's Cabin Stirs the Nation

Imagine a Northern family in the 1850s, gathered around the fireplace, listening to a tale of incredible cruelty and unhappiness. They are reading a novel about the horrors of slavery. The main character, Tom, a slave, has just been sold. The novel that stirred the country was *Uncle Tom's Cabin,* written by Harriet Beecher Stowe and published in 1852. Stowe hated slavery and was especially appalled by the harsh new Fugitive Slave Act of 1850, which called on Northerners to help catch runaway slaves. Even worse, the

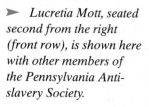
➤ *Lucretia Mott, seated second from the right (front row), is shown here with other members of the Pennsylvania Anti-slavery Society.*

A Quaker Abolitionist

5:47 P.M., October 29, 1839
On a path in the woods in Union, Ohio

Bonnet
It would be improper for her to leave home with her head uncovered. Hats are signs of modesty for Quaker women.

Woolen Shawl
As she walks to a meeting of the Union Female Antislavery Society, the shawl shields her from the wind. Like other Quaker women, she dresses plainly and practically.

Antislavery Petition
At tonight's meeting, her petition signed by 18 of her neighbors will be mailed with other petitions to President Van Buren.

Coins
Saved from her teaching pay, 17 cents is tucked in her dress pocket. Tonight, she'll give the coins to the Antislavery pamphlet fund. The money will help mail pamphlets to U.S. Senators.

Bread
This morning, she picked herbs from her garden to bake into the loaf. Tomorrow, it will be sold with many others at the Society Fair.

Newspaper
This copy of *The Liberator*, published in Boston by William Lloyd Garrison, contains antislavery articles she will share at the meeting.

Muddy Shoes
She just finished feeding vegetable scraps to the pigs. Mud from the pen sticks to her shoes. No matter—there are plenty of puddles between home and the meeting house.

➤ *Harriet Beecher Stowe hoped her novel,* Uncle Tom's Cabin, *would help bring about a peaceful end to slavery. Published in 1852, the book was very popular.*

135,000 SETS, 270,000 VOLUMES SOLD.

UNCLE TOM'S CABIN

FOR SALE HERE.

AN EDITION FOR THE MILLION, COMPLETE IN 1 Vol., PRICE 37 1-2 CENTS.
" IN GERMAN, IN 1 Vol. PRICE 50 CENTS.
" IN 2 Vols., CLOTH, 6 PLATES, PRICE $1.50.
SUPERB ILLUSTRATED EDITION, IN 1 Vol. WITH 153 ENGRAVINGS,
PRICES FROM $2.50 TO $5.00.

The Greatest Book of the Age.

act did not allow accused runaways to defend themselves in court.

Stowe decided to "write something that would make this whole nation feel what an accursed thing slavery is." Within days after the book came out, 10,000 people had bought copies.

Within a year, readers had bought 300,000 copies of *Uncle Tom's Cabin*. A dramatic play inspired by the book was performed in New York, London, and Paris. Audiences were moved to tears. Popular skits loosely based on the book were widely performed in towns throughout the North. Everywhere the book went, *Uncle Tom's Cabin* carried its powerful message of the evils of slavery.

Through this work of fiction, millions learned of the nightmare that individual slaves lived. People who had paid little attention to Garrison's political pleas read each word of Stowe's more emotional appeal. Many Americans became convinced that slavery was a great national sin.

Stowe had hoped that her book would bring a peaceful end to slavery, but instead, it just seemed to bring the nation closer to war. Northerners hated the South more than ever, and Southerners considered the book an elaborate lie, an unforgivable insult to their way of life. ■

■ *Why did women join the abolitionist movement? How did their reasons change in time?*

*T*om rose up meekly, to follow his new master, and raised up his heavy box on his shoulder. His wife took the baby in her arms to go with him to the wagon, and the children, still crying, trailed on behind.

Mrs. Shelby, walking up to the trader, detained him for a few moments, talking with him in an earnest manner; and while she was thus talking, the whole family party proceeded to a wagon, that stood ready harnessed at the door. A crowd of all the old and young hands on the place stood gathered around it, to bid farewell to their old associates. Tom had been looked up to, both as a head servant and a Christian teacher, by all the place, and there was much honest sympathy and grief about him, particularly among the women.

Harriet Beecher Stowe, *Uncle Tom's Cabin*

R E V I E W

1. **FOCUS** How did the abolitionist movement contribute to the ongoing conflict between the North and the South?
2. **CONNECT** What social, political, and economic forces led the nation to question slavery?
3. **CITIZENSHIP** Name some of the methods people used in their fight against slavery.
4. **HISTORY** Why did slave rebellions make Southerners distrust Northerners?
5. **CRITICAL THINKING** Why do you think Harriet Beecher Stowe's novel was so effective in demonstrating to the American public the evils of slavery?
6. **WRITING ACTIVITY** Write a news story that describes a white Southerner's reactions to finding a copy of David Walker's Appeal. Write it as a Southern reporter might view the experience.

LESSON 3

The Road to Bleeding Kansas

Crack! Crack! Congressman Brooks's wooden cane landed its solid blows across the back of Senator Sumner's head. Crack! Crack! Again and again, Brooks brandished his cane against his victim. Onlookers felt helpless because a friend of Brooks held them off with a pistol. Crack! Crack! The cane broke, yet Brooks kept swinging.

Sumner sat trapped behind his desk, which stood bolted to the floor. He couldn't move to defend himself. Finally, Sumner ripped his desk out of its very bolts and arose. He stumbled groggily and collapsed as the enraged Brooks kept swinging the broken walking stick. A few men at last rushed in to stop the savage beating. Why would a congressman attack a United States senator?

It was May 1856. Two days earlier Senator Charles Sumner of Massachusetts, one of the most outspoken enemies of slavery, had given a seething antislavery speech. Proslavery Congressman Preston Brooks of South Carolina became angered because the speech targeted Brooks's uncle, Senator Andrew Butler. Both the issue of slavery and Brooks's family honor were at stake. Brooks had at last found a chance to vent his rage at Senator Sumner.

Brooks's shocking attack symbolized the nation's growing split over slavery. No longer, it seemed, could lawmakers negotiate or compromise on this explosive issue. No longer could the nation hope for a peaceful solution to the conflict over slavery.

THINKING FOCUS

In what ways did the slavery issue continue to affect the American political process?

Key Terms

- popular sovereignty
- guerrilla

How Do We Know?

HISTORY *Newspapers from the past give historians and students alike a valuable, first-hand view of history. Most large libraries have extensive microfilm files of newspapers. How can we find out, for example, about the South's view of the attack on Senator Sumner? In a Southern proslavery newspaper, the beating was called "an elegant and effectual [effective] caning."*

The Kansas-Nebraska Act Paves the Way

The strain between North and South that exploded in the Senate also continued to affect the race to settle new territories. By the late 1840s, a westward migration had pushed past the Mississippi River and the lands bordering it. The rich, fertile lands of Kansas and Nebraska drew thousands of farmers onto the prairies. Many other settlers flocked to California for gold. Politicians saw that the growing nation needed to be linked by a transcontinental railroad that would stretch from Chicago to California.

Lawmakers knew that a bill was needed to set up a territorial government for Kansas. And in order to build the railroad, land had to be set aside for the railroad companies.

Yet the issue of slavery blocked these promising plans. Kansas and Nebraska were both closed to slavery under the Missouri Compromise of 1820. Southerners would not go along with the railroad unless they saw hope for slavery in these territories. They felt they had to overturn the Missouri Compromise.

325

Causes of the Civil War

A Northerner, Democratic Senator Stephen A. Douglas of Illinois, started the new debate rolling. Douglas introduced the Nebraska Bill in 1854 to organize a territorial government, which could then open the way to lay down railroad tracks. Southern senators, however, balked at any bill that would allow the ban on slavery in the territories to continue.

Douglas reworked his bill. His new proposal divided the area into two territories: that of Kansas and that of Nebraska. It was implied, but not stated, that Kansas would become a slave state, and Nebraska would be free of slavery. Douglas also proposed an idea called **popular sovereignty**, or the right of the voters in each territory to decide whether to become a free or slave state. The new bill rendered the Missouri Compromise meaningless.

Congress passed the Kansas-Nebraska Act in 1854. Antislavery people, Democrats and Whigs included, held rallies, demonstrations, and meetings throughout the North to condemn the Kansas-Nebraska Act. These gatherings helped to form a new political party. (The chart below will help your understanding of the many political parties and their beliefs during this time period.)

The Republican party was established in 1854 as the result of an "anti-Nebraska" meeting, and attracted members from many different groups.

Republicans Oppose Slavery

In February 1854, even before the Kansas-Nebraska Act passed, an "anti-Nebraska" meeting assembled in Ripon, Wisconsin. The participants called it a "Republican" meeting. The name was then kept when a new political party grew out of this meeting and was joined by many similar groups emerging throughout the North.

Antislavery people of all sorts joined the Republican Party. People who had supported the antislavery Free Soil Party in 1848 joined, as did many members of the Whig Party. Some Democrats embraced Republicanism, splitting from the proslavery forces in their own party.

As members of the Whigs and Democrats shifted to the Republican Party, another party—the Know-Nothings—grew in power for a short time. The Know-Nothing Party was dedicated to stopping immigration into the United States. Most Know-Nothing party members eventually joined the Republican party.

With the rise of the Republican Party, the nation's widening split became official. Their slogan—"Free Soil, Free Labor, Free Speech, Free Men" clearly identified Republicans as the antislavery party.

Self-Government for States?

Democrats needed an issue to strengthen their identity, an issue that would win the vote of the South. Yet they could not appear to be proslavery for fear of losing Northern votes.

The Democrats rallied behind

Political Parties	
Party	**Platform**
Democratic Formed in 1830	• Members mainly Southerners • Proslavery • Favored Western expansion, popular sovereignty, and states' rights
Whig Popular during 1840s–1850s	• Members mainly Easterners • Opposed Mexican War • Most opposed slavery in Western territories • Many joined Republican Party
American (Know-Nothing) Popular during 1850s	• Members promoted interests of native-born Americans • Anti-immigration • Opposed slavery • Ceased after 1856 election; many joined Republican Party
Republican Formed in 1854	• Members mainly Northerners • Antislavery • Favored Western expansion, strong federal government • Attracted Whigs and Know-Nothings

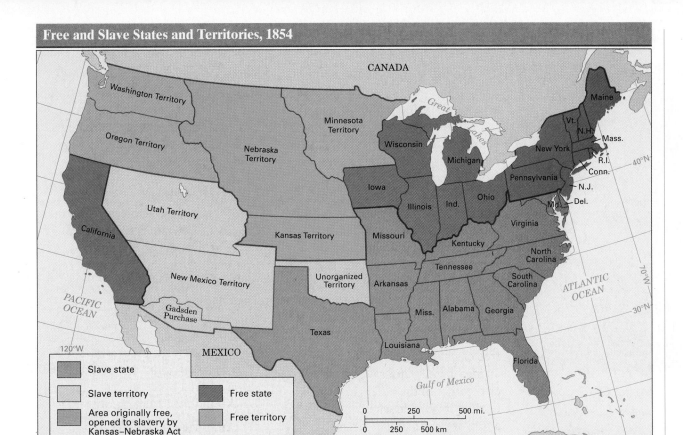

CANADA

Washington Territory

Oregon Territory

Minnesota Territory

Nebraska Territory

Wisconsin

Michigan

Maine

Vt.

N.H.

Mass.

New York

R.I.

Conn.

Pennsylvania

N.J.

Iowa

Illinois   Ind.   Ohio

Md. Del.

Utah Territory

California

Kansas Territory

Missouri

Virginia

Kentucky

North Carolina

New Mexico Territory

Unorganized Territory

Arkansas

Tennessee

South Carolina

ATLANTIC OCEAN

PACIFIC OCEAN

Gadsden Purchase

Miss. Alabama Georgia

Texas

Louisiana

Florida

MEXICO

Gulf of Mexico

40°N

70°W

30°N

120°W

Legend:
- Slave state
- Slave territory
- Area originally free, opened to slavery by Kansas–Nebraska Act
- Free state
- Free territory

0   250   500 mi.
0   250   500 km
Albers Equal Area Projection

CUBA
80°W

popular sovereignty, which allowed the settlers of any new territory to decide for themselves, through the vote, whether or not slavery would exist in that territory.

With this issue, the Democrats hoped to appeal to the age-old American ideal of self-government. Popular sovereignty truly seemed like an idea that all Americans could understand and support.

Split Over Popular Sovereignty

Southerners doubted that anyone would oppose the right of Western settlers to have a voice in their own government. Yet they also knew the concrete rewards of this "patriotic" idea. Popular sovereignty gave Southerners the opportunity to extend slavery westward. This was still an important concern for white Southerners who wanted more land for cotton.

Many Northerners scoffed at popular sovereignty. They would never agree to slavery in the territories, even if Western settlers had voted for it. Northerners believed that slave territories would turn away free laborers who were looking for new opportunities. Popular sovereignty, they feared, would close off new territories to settlers who did not have slaves. Settlement of the western territories was important to the Northern free labor economy as well. With such different economic concerns, and ways of life that seemed worlds apart, how could the North and the South avoid an all-out conflict? ■

▲ *The slavery issue caused many problems in settling new western territories. The Kansas-Nebraska Act of 1854 overturned the Missouri Compromise.*

■ *The Kansas-Nebraska Act implied that Congress could no longer decide whether or not a state or territory would allow slavery. How did this Act conflict with the earlier Missouri Compromise?*

Kansas Bleeds Under Western Expansion

The battle over slavery extended to the sprawling wheat fields and cattle country of Kansas. This time, however, the opposing forces used guns, swords, and cannons. Antislavery fighters carried rifles known as "Beecher's Bibles," named for Henry Ward Beecher (Harriet Beecher Stowe's brother). Beecher was a leading antislavery minister who helped to raise money to send guns to the antislavery settlers in Kansas.

327

Causes of the Civil War

John Brown took matters into his own hands when he led a violent four-month fight in Kansas against pro-slavery forces.

The battle erupted over settlement of the vast new territory. Each side wanted to populate Kansas. Yet few slaveowners actually moved to Kansas. They preferred raising cotton in the warmer South or Southwest. Northerners flocked to the area to start small farms on the territory's rich soil. By 1855, the majority of settlers in Kansas were from the North. Popular sovereignty, it seemed, would surely make Kansas a free state. But Southerners had a plan.

During the first territorial election in 1854, Kansans were to elect nonvoting delegates to Congress. Before the elections, 1,700 proslavery men stormed into Kansas from neighboring Missouri.

These "border ruffians" came to cast illegal votes and frighten the antislavery voters. The next year 5,000 border ruffians voted for the territorial legislature. Their votes elected a proslavery government.

The election was illegal, yet proslavery forces took over the territory and wrote slavery into the constitution. Antislavery forces felt cheated.

They banded together and formed their own government, representing the majority of Kansas. The territory now had two opposing governments. Kansas had become a powder keg, ready to explode.

Kansans Shed Blood

The antislavery forces, based in the city of Lawrence, armed themselves against the border ruffians. At first small skirmishes broke out, but both sides avoided a major battle. Then in May 1856, seven hundred proslavery men from Missouri and Kansas attacked Lawrence. These raiders burned the hotel, destroyed two newspaper offices, and looted the stores.

Abolitionist John Brown and his sons immediately staged a raid on proslavery settlers along the Pottawatomie River. Brown's men killed five settlers, splitting their heads open with swords.

Brown's raid launched four months of **guerrilla**, or independent, war in Kansas. As the violence dragged on, "Bleeding Kansas"

This photograph shows "free-staters" in Kansas preparing for battle.

became a slogan for antislavery forces around the nation.

Finally, federal troops were sent to end the fighting in Kansas. In just a few months, two hundred people had died fighting over slavery. And while "Bleeding Kansas" was no longer bleeding, the issue of slavery in the territories, the future of Kansas and the future of the nation were far from certain.

Violence Erupts in Congress

Perhaps some Americans could shrug off the violence in Kansas because it took place so far from their own homes. Perhaps they felt that such rugged frontier areas always attracted desperadoes, gunfighters, and other violent sorts. But they couldn't ignore the shocking attack that took place on the floor of the United States Senate. It took Senator Sumner three years to recover from the beating. Meanwhile, the statesman of Massachusetts left his Senate seat empty, a symbol of the aggressive and dangerous nature of "slave power."

The guerrilla warfare in Kansas and the violence in the Senate showed that Americans were clearly unable to resolve the debate over slavery. Northerners and Southerners alike held out little hope for a peaceful solution. Nevertheless, the political debate continued as the 1856 presidential election drew near. ■

■ *More than two hundred fighters died during the skirmishes in "Bleeding Kansas." Why was this territory fought over so violently?*

Buchanan Gains a Narrow Victory

The presidential election of 1856 became a three-way race over the issue of slavery in the territories. Republicans nominated John C. Frémont, a famous western explorer. Democrats named James Buchanan as their candidate. The Know-Nothing Party nominated former President Millard Fillmore.

The Republicans, a party of the North, stood firmly against slavery in the territories. The Democrats hoped to win Northern and Southern votes by standing for the "patriotic" popular sovereignty.

The Democrats won the election, but the Republicans made a very strong showing. Democrat Buchanan won only 45 percent of the popular vote, and the Republicans finished far ahead of the third-place Know-Nothing candidate.

The South appeared to have won this election—the nation had supported popular sovereignty. Yet the vote did little to heal the nation's wounds. Antislavery forces, inspired by the strong Republican showing, were ready to fight even harder. ■

◄ *Democrat James Buchanan won the 1856 presidential election.*

■ *The Republicans lost the presidential election of 1856. Yet in many ways the campaign was a success for them. How can a losing election campaign still benefit a candidate or party?*

R E V I E W

1. **FOCUS** In what ways did the slavery issue continue to affect the American political process?

2. **CONNECT** Make a list of all the factors that led to the overturn of the Missouri Compromise. What was the reason it was overturned?

3. **CITIZENSHIP** Give a description of someone who might have joined the Republican Party. What were some of the ideas the party supported?

4. **BELIEF SYSTEMS** How were "Bleeding Kansas" and the violence that erupted in Congress linked?

5. **CRITICAL THINKING** Why do you think that the presidential election of 1856 was not a simple two-way race between a proslavery and an antislavery candidate?

6. **WRITING ACTIVITY** Imagine you are a white Southern Democrat in the 1850s. Write a speech defending the idea of popular sovereignty.

329

Causes of the Civil War

LESSON 4

The House Divided

THINKING FOCUS

What events during the 1850s revealed that the conflict between the North and the South would never be resolved peacefully?

Key Term

- Underground Railroad

► *This oil painting by Thomas Hovenden is entitled* The Last Moments of John Brown. *Brown's death inspired strong antislavery feelings in the North.*

From the jail emerged a man of distinguished features. With head held high, the prisoner walked unhesitantly on a cool Virginia morning in 1859 to the field where he was to be hanged.

"This is a beautiful country," he declared. "I have never had the pleasure of seeing it before." A few minutes later, he was dead.

To antislavery supporters, John Brown's massacre of five slaveholders in Kansas in 1856 and his bold defense of the antislavery town of Osawatomie had been heroic acts.

John Brown had angrily witnessed victory after victory for the proslavery forces—in the courts, in Congress, and in the territories. He decided to fight back with a vengeance. In October 1859, with 21 of his followers, Brown raided a federal arsenal at Harpers Ferry with plans to seize guns stored there and to pass out guns and ammunition to slaves in the area. The success of his rebellion depended almost entirely on the help of slaves.

At first Brown and his men were able to hold the arsenal. They even held off the local militia throughout the next day and night. Yet no local slaves came to Brown's aid. Few had even heard of his revolt. U.S. marines soon stormed the arsenal. After losing many men, including two of his sons, Brown surrendered. Brown was tried and convicted for insurrection, treason, and murder. The sentence called for his speedy death. He was hanged on December 2, 1859. His death touched off a wave of sympathy and admiration in the North.

Now the hangman and soldiers guarding him looked on at the man who was soon to become legend. The words he had written in a note to his jailer would prove all too true: "The crimes of this guilty land will never be purged away, but with blood."

330

Slavery Battled on All Fronts

John Brown's bloody raid at Harpers Ferry angered many people. But events during the late 1850s convinced passionate abolitionists that they had to take matters into their own hands.

The Dred Scott Case

Two days after President Buchanan's inauguration in 1857, the Supreme Court released its decision in an important case known as *Dred Scott* v. *Sandford*. Dred Scott had been the slave of John Emerson, an army doctor from Missouri. During his military career, Emerson had taken Scott with him as a personal servant. On one assignment, Emerson lived at Fort Snelling in the present-day state of Minnesota. At that time, Fort Snelling was in a part of the territories declared free by the Missouri Compromise. After more than a year, the two men returned to Missouri.

When Emerson died in 1846, Scott was determined to gain his freedom. Some white friends helped Scott find a lawyer, and the slave sued for his freedom in the courts. He argued that he had become free the moment his master brought him into the territory designated nonslavery by the Missouri Compromise.

A Missouri court agreed with Scott's argument and declared him free. The Missouri Supreme Court, however, reversed the decision. Dred Scott then took his case to the United States Supreme Court.

The Supreme Court Decision

In 1857, the Supreme Court voted 7 to 2 that Scott must remain a slave. Writing the Supreme Court's opinion on the Dred Scott case, Chief Justice Roger B. Taney reached two important conclusions. Blacks, he insisted, had no right to sue in the federal courts because they could never be considered citizens of the United States. Even when the Constitution was written, Taney argued, blacks could not vote and had no rights. Taney was mistaken. Free blacks could in fact vote in 8 of the 13 states.

The Supreme Court decision against Dred Scott strengthened the harsh Fugitive Slave Law.

Taney and the Court also asserted that the Missouri Compromise was unconstitutional because it denied white Southerners the right to take their human property with them into the territories. In addition, Taney stated, Congress had no power to pass such a law for the territories. The Dred Scott case seemed to open all federal territories to slavery.

Republicans, now the majority party in the North, shook their heads in disbelief and anger. They considered Taney's opinion unjust and unsound. The one-sided, proslavery decision shattered their confidence in the Supreme Court.

Southerners and many Northern Democrats, however, applauded Taney's decision. They hoped it would finally end the great controversy over slavery in the territories. But the decision only added more fuel to the burning issue of slavery.

Kansans Create a Constitution

The debate over slavery still raged in Kansas, where fraudulent elections had been held and where an illegal proslavery legislature reigned. In 1857, this legislature called for a constitutional convention to make Kansas a slave state. The convention, meeting at the town of Lecompton, wrote a proslavery constitution.

Antislavery Kansas settlers refused to participate in the vote for the new constitution, but their action backfired. With only proslavery people voting, the constitution passed easily.

President Buchanan didn't want to anger Southern Democrats. He accepted this fraudulent "Lecompton Constitution," and the Senate, with its large Democratic majority, passed a Kansas statehood bill. The House, however, defeated it. The issue of slavery in Kansas remained unsettled. ■

■ *Why didn't Chief Justice Taney's rulings dissolve the anti-slavery movement?*

Antislavery Movement Forges Ahead

Despite setbacks in the courts, antislavery forces continued their work. Neither the harsh Fugitive Slave Act of 1850 nor the Dred Scott Decision could stop the movement.

Proslavery resistance was powerful. In 1854, the federal government spent almost $100,000 to return just one fugitive slave, Anthony Burns, from Boston. Burns's master later sold the slave for $905. Such was the determination of the proslavery forces.

Northerners argued that the whole Fugitive Slave Act was unfair. Marshals often seized accused slaves secretly and hurried them off to a commissioner before anyone knew what had happened. The accused person usually had no lawyer. Just the word of the slaveholder was often enough to settle the case. The alleged fugitive slave could not testify at all. Antislavery forces stood up to resist such unfair laws.

Picture this scene. Onto the streets of Christiana, Pennsylvania, in 1851, walk a group of black men, escaped slaves. They are cautious and are armed with pistols and rifles. Their former owner is now close on the trail of the runaways. The fugitives, finally in Pennsylvania, feel that their former master has surely given them up for lost.

But he hasn't. Suddenly, in Christiana, he and his men appear. In a flash, guns blaze. The slaves are determined to die before they will return. When the smoke clears, the slaveholder himself lies dead. His former slaves head for Canada and freedom.

In a number of Northern cities there were similar shootouts and crowd actions to prevent the return of fugitive slaves. Often the mobs included whites and blacks side by side. These actions made Southerners distrust the North more than ever. ■

■ *Why did Northerners think the Fugitive Slave Act was unfair?*

▼ *Southern states held 70 percent of the nation's total slave population in 1860.*

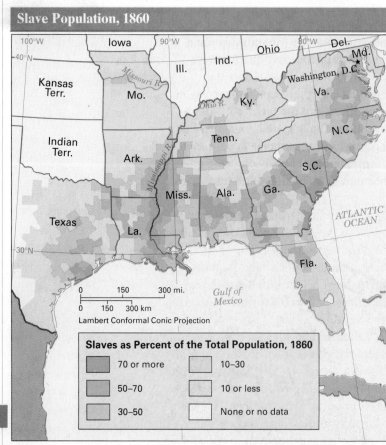

Slave Population, 1860

Iowa, Kansas Terr., Indian Terr., Texas, Mo., Ark., Ill., Ind., Ohio, Ky., Tenn., Miss., Ala., La., Va., N.C., S.C., Ga., Fla., Del., Md., Washington, D.C.

Missouri R., Ohio R., Mississippi R.

Gulf of Mexico, ATLANTIC OCEAN

0 150 300 mi.
0 150 300 km
Lambert Conformal Conic Projection

Slaves as Percent of the Total Population, 1860

- 70 or more
- 50–70
- 30–50
- 10–30
- 10 or less
- None or no data

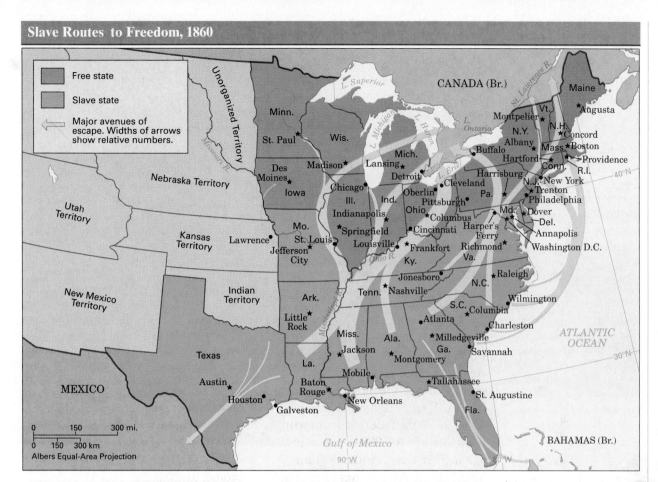

Free state

Slave state

Major avenues of escape. Widths of arrows show relative numbers.

CANADA (Br.)

L. Superior

Minn.

St. Paul

Wis.

Maine

Augusta

Montpelier

Vt.

N.H.

Concord

N.Y.

Albany

Mass.

Boston

Unorganized Territory

Des Moines

Madison

Lansing

Mich.

Detroit

L. Erie

Buffalo

Hartford

Conn.

Providence

R.I.

Harrisburg

Nebraska Territory

Iowa

Chicago

Ill.

Ind.

Oberlin

Cleveland

Pa.

New York

Trenton

N.J.

Pittsburgh

Philadelphia

Utah Territory

Indianapolis

Ohio

Columbus

Md.

Dover

Del.

Springfield

Cincinnati

Harper's Ferry

Annapolis

Kansas Territory

Lawrence

Mo.

St. Louis

Louisville

Frankfort

Richmond

Va.

Washington D.C.

Jefferson City

Ohio R.

Ky.

New Mexico Territory

Indian Territory

Ark.

Tenn.

Nashville

Jonesboro

Raleigh

N.C.

Wilmington

Little Rock

S.C.

Columbia

Atlanta

Charleston

ATLANTIC OCEAN

Texas

Miss.

Jackson

Ala.

Ga.

Milledgeville

Savannah

40°N

La.

Montgomery

30°N

MEXICO

Austin

Baton Rouge

Mobile

Tallahassee

Houston

Galveston

New Orleans

St. Augustine

Fla.

0   150   300 mi.

0   150   300 km

Albers Equal-Area Projection

Gulf of Mexico

90°W

80°W

BAHAMAS (Br.)

Slaves Ride the Underground Railroad

Antislavery forces did more than protect and rescue runaway slaves. In fact, they helped many slaves escape. A secret network known as the **Underground Railroad** guided some 100,000 fugitive slaves to freedom between 1780 and 1865.

What was the Underground Railroad? It was not a railroad, and it did not move underground. The Underground Railroad was a complex system of about 3,000 people—both blacks and whites—who helped transport escaped slaves. Under the cover of night, "conductors" led runaways to freedom, providing food and safe hiding places. They risked great danger in aiding slaves.

The means of transportation in the Underground Railroad varied. Slaves traveled on foot, in covered wagons, in boxes shipped by rail or in small boats gliding silently through the water by night. At the stations, slaves hid in attics, barns, cellars, and even secret rooms. Finally, at the end of the perilous journey, the runaway slave would settle in one of the 14 free states or in Canada.

Probably the most famous Underground Railroad "conductor" was a heroic black woman named Harriet Tubman, who had herself escaped from slavery. Harriet Tubman guided more than 300 slaves to freedom.

▲ *The Underground Railroad relied on thousands of "conductors" operating secretly throughout the North and the South.*

◄ *Harriet Tubman was known to blacks as "Moses." Like that Old-Testament leader, she brought her people out of slavery.*

■ *How did some abolitionists break the law to help the slaves?*

333

Causes of the Civil War

The woman shown below is Lear Green. She escaped slavery by shipping herself to Philadelphia in a sailor's chest. Many other slaves faced the danger of being caught while trying to escape.

■ *How did some abolitionists break the law to help the slaves?*

The raids, the rescues, and the Underground Railroad all convinced the South even more that the North was their enemy. But the raids and the Underground Railroad were not enough to topple slavery. The abolitionist movement alone did not have that much power.

Instead, antislavery forces needed a powerful spokesperson to state their case in the political arena. During the late 1850s just such a leader emerged. He was a country lawyer with just one term in Congress to his credit. His name was Abraham Lincoln. ■

Lincoln Inspires the Republicans

What should have been a routine election took a surprising turn. It was 1858, time for Illinois voters to reelect Democrat Stephen A. Douglas to the U.S. Senate. (Actually, the voters selected a state legislature, which then selected the senator.) Douglas's Republican opponent, Abraham Lincoln, had little political experience compared with Douglas.

Lincoln had an exciting idea. He would challenge the senator to a series of debates. Crowds who came to hear Douglas would also see and hear the less well known Lincoln.

Lincoln's focus in the debates was on slavery in the territories. Douglas, he insisted, did not care if slavery was

voted "up" or "down" in the territories. Lincoln, however, voiced strong opposition to the spread of slavery. Throughout Illinois in the summer and fall of 1858, crowds were fascinated by the spirited exchanges between the two chief candidates. Lincoln's speaking abilities particularly impressed the audience.

Lincoln lost the election of 1858. But the Republicans now had a forceful leader who had shown up well against the likely Democratic presidential candidate of 1860.

When the 1860 presidential campaign got under way, the Republicans did indeed nominate Lincoln as their candidate. The Democrats broke into

◄ *South Carolina rebels fired on Fort Sumter near Charleston, South Carolina on April 12, 1861. This action triggered the secession of four states and the start of the Civil War.*

two groups. Northern Democrats nominated Stephen A. Douglas. Southern Democrats chose their own candidate, John C. Breckenridge. A third party, the Constitutional Union Party, nominated John Bell.

Lincoln won the four-way race, sweeping the Northern states. Although he won only 39 percent of the popular vote, he gained more than enough electoral votes. Antislavery forces had elected a President, and white Southerners were horrified.

The South Chooses Secession

White Southerners did not want to be part of a nation that could elect Lincoln as its President. They called the new President a "black radical Republican" and a "friend of John Brown." Even before Lincoln took office, South Carolina, Mississippi,

Florida, Alabama, Georgia, Louisiana, and Texas had decided to **secede**, or leave the Union. These states even proposed starting their own government, the Confederate government.

War seemed unavoidable. Then, on April 12, 1861, Southern rebel forces fired on a federal outpost, Fort Sumter, in the harbor of Charleston, South Carolina. Immediately, the Southern states of Virginia, Arkansas, Tennessee, and North Carolina seceded and joined the Confederates. The tragic "firebell in the night" imagined by Jefferson had finally rung. The Missouri Compromise had failed. Proslavery and antislavery civilians clashed in the streets and took up arms. Thousands of Northerners and Southerners alike were to die for their beliefs. The Civil War had begun. The states were at war with each other. ■

■ *Abraham Lincoln lost the senatorial race of 1858 in Illinois but won the presidential election in 1860. Who elected him president?*

R E V I E W

1. **FOCUS** What events during the 1850s revealed that the conflict between the North and the South would never be resolved peacefully?
2. **CONNECT** How did the political system fail to resolve the slavery issue?
3. **GEOGRAPHY** Look at the map on page 333 of this lesson. List two routes the Underground Railroad used in bringing runaway slaves to freedom.
4. **BELIEF SYSTEMS** What conclusions were a result of the

Dred Scott case? How did Northerners react?
5. **CRITICAL THINKING** What event marked the beginning of the Civil War? Why were Southern states so determined to secede?
6. **WRITING ACTIVITY** Imagine you are a Northerner who refuses to obey the Fugitive Slave Act of 1850. Write a diary entry that plans the route of escape you would take from your home if a runaway slave were to approach you for help.

Causes of the Civil War

Analyzing Viewpoints on Slavery

Here's Why

Learning how to recognize the point of view that shapes a piece of writing helps us to know what influenced the writer to present information in a certain way. That knowledge can then help us to determine the extent to which the piece is based on the writer's emotional response to the subject.

Objective information is based on facts—statements that record an event without inserting personal opinion. Points of view, on the other hand, are subjective. That means that they involve the writer's opinions, attitudes, beliefs, or feelings. Historians are careful to analyze point of view when studying documents from the past. It is important for you, as a student, to recognize bias (personal preference) when you read any historical document.

In this chapter you learned that differences over slavery were so severe that they led to war between the North and South. You read that abolitionists demanded an immediate end to slavery, and that most white Southerners believed slavery to be a good and economically necessary way of life. First-person accounts and artifacts from that time period allow you to expand the knowledge you gained from the chapter. The actual written words of those who supported and those who opposed slavery offer an opportunity to learn how real people felt about the issue.

Suppose you are researching two very different documents that relate to slavery. Identifying and understanding the point of view of each document will help you to decide how the writers reached their conclusions.

Here's How

Read the following passages, and follow the steps to identify and analyze point of view. Be sure to look up any unfamiliar words.

1. **What is the subject?**
   The subject of both passages is slavery.

2. **Who is the writer?**
   The writer of the first passage is Lucretia Mott, a spokesperson for the abolitionist movement. The second passage is taken from an artifact. The author of the second passage is unknown; it appears on the

We have watched the accounts that had been furnished—some in the daily papers and some in letters and communications directly to us, and in personal visits of the cruelty that has been practiced in the South; and those accounts have come to us with the express desire that we should keep on and not resign the organization. They have told that the time has not come, while the slave in so many instances is only nominally and legally free, while in fact the almost unlimited power of his oppressor continues; and that in many parts of our Southland large numbers of families of slaves are still actually held in bondage, and their labor extorted from them by the lash, as formerly; that while, so far as the law is concerned, they may no longer be publicly bought and sold, yet they have been actually sold and transferred from place to place. All these facts show the necessity of our cause, and the continued existence of the Anti-Slavery Society, notwithstanding the legal abolition of the accursed system. All this has kept us on the watch, and has kept our interest alive in the great cause.

Lucretia Mott

This picture represents the Negro Quarters of a plantation, as taken in 1860. It is a true picture of life on a well organized Plantation in South Carolina. Old and young are assembled after the heads of the families have finished their tasks, to partake of their meals, prepared by those selected for that purpose by their owner, in consequence of their inability to do field work. The task of the industrious and provident slave was often finished by mid-day. After which they were permitted to work for themselves in a garden patch attached to their quarters. Many frequently made considerable sums of money in this way, which the more provident appropriated to the purchase of useful atricles, whilst others squandered theirs on things of no value, either for comfort or luxury.

Anonymous

back of the photograph shown on page 289.

3. **Who is the audience? That is, for whom is the piece written?**
Lucretia Mott was writing for fellow abolitionists. The passage is part of a speech she gave in September 1858 in Yardleyville, Pennsylvania.

The second passage describes a photograph of comfortable slaves on a plantation. It appears to have been written for pro-slavery white people.

4. **What is the purpose?**
Lucretia Mott's speech was written to convince people to join the fight against slavery. The other passage was written to convince people that slaves had a good life.

5. **What is the writer's attitude, or tone? Is it angry, sympathetic, humorous, or serious?**
Lucretia Mott's speech is urgent. She does not feel that there is any room for more than one opinion on slavery, but declares it is a "sin." She speaks of the "necessity of our cause."

The other writer takes a tone of authority, presenting all of the information in the description as fact. For instance, the phrase, "many frequently made considerable sums of money" is not backed by any examples, but the tone makes it sound like a well-researched fact. This piece also has a critical tone. When the writer says that "others squandered theirs on things of no value, either for comfort or luxury," a criticism of slaves is implied.

Try It

Now read the passage below. It is Abraham Lincoln's response to the demands of the abolitionists.

Use the five questions listed above to analyze the point of view in Lincoln's reply. Compare and contrast his point of view with that of the other two writers. What differences or similarities do you find?

My [foremost] object in this struggle is to save the Union. . . . if I could save the Union without freeing any slave, I would do it; if I could save it by freeing all the slaves, I would do it; and if I could save it by freeing some and leaving others alone, I would also do that.

Abraham Lincoln

Apply It

Locate a first-person account of a contemporary event or issue, such as a political rally, a debate, or a proposed law. Follow the steps outlined above to identify the writer's point of view. Analyze the information, and write a short paragraph outlining the writer's point of view.

337

Chapter Review

Reviewing Key Terms

abolitionism (p. 321)   popular sovereignty (p. 326)
free labor (p. 314)   Underground Railroad (p. 333)
guerrilla (p. 328)

A. The sentences below have been started for you. Use the key terms above to complete each sentence correctly.
1. Northern workers were paid . . .
2. William Lloyd Garrison and Lucretia Mott were people who . . .
3. Allowing voters in new territories . . .
4. John Brown's raid in Kansas . . .
5. Harriet Tubman worked . . .

B. Based on what you have read in the chapter, decide whether each of the following statements is accurate. Write an explanation of each decision.
1. Blacks feared that abolitionism would deny them their right to freedom.
2. The free labor economy in the North allowed workers to change jobs whenever they wanted.
3. Those who favored popular sovereignty felt that Congress should decide the issue of slavery for the nation.
4. The Underground Railroad was the first inter-continental railroad.
5. Frederick Douglass spoke out against slavery and was a strong proponent of abolitionism.

Exploring Concepts

A. On a separate sheet of paper, copy the timeline below. Use the events listed below to complete your timeline. Insert each event in the correct time position, and give the date it occurred (two of the events have been entered on the timeline as examples.)

- *Uncle Tom's Cabin* published
- Missouri Compromise
- Raid on Lawrence, Kansas
- Attack on Fort Sumter
- Texas becomes a state
- Kansas-Nebraska Act
- Dred Scott decision
- John Brown's raid on Harpers Ferry
- Lincoln elected president
- Fugitive Slave Act

B. Support each of the following statements with facts and details from the chapter.
1. In the early 1800s, the North and South differed greatly in their economies and their ways of life.
2. The Missouri Compromise settled one dispute, but contained a provision that began another battle.
3. The issue of the Mexican War divided the North and South.
4. The Compromise of 1850 further added to the divisions within the nation.
5. During the 1830s, several events frightened Southerners who supported slavery.
6. Women played a crucial role in the antislavery movement.
7. The Supreme Court's decision in the Dred Scott case was a great victory for slavery.

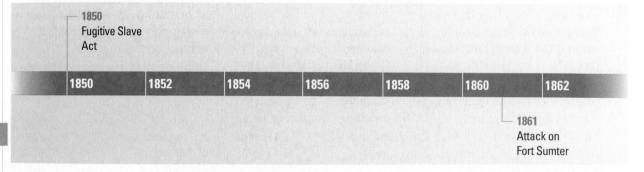

Reviewing Skills

I n the South, where slavery still exists, the Negroes are less carefully kept apart; they sometimes share the labors and the recreations of the whites; the whites consent to intermix with them to a certain extent, and although legislation treats them more harshly, the habits of the people are more tolerant and compassionate. In the South the master is not afraid to raise his slave to his own standing, because he knows that he can in a moment reduce him to the dust at pleasure. In the North the white no longer distinctly perceives the barrier that separates him from the degraded race, and he shuns the Negro with the more pertinacity [stubbornness] since he fears lest they should some day be confounded [mixed] together.

Alexis de Tocqueville, *Democracy in America*

1. Read the above passage from *Democracy in America* by Alexis de Tocqueville. Tocqueville was a French politician who was sent by his government in 1831 to study the prison system in the United States. He became so fascinated with the social structure of the United States that he wrote two volumes about it.

2. Look up any unfamiliar terms that you find in the passage. In your own words, explain what Tocqueville is saying in the passage.

3. What difference does Tocqueville point out between the way Northerners and Southerners treat black people?

4. Study the table on page 315 that shows Slave States and Free States after the Missouri Compromise. Use the information provided in that table to create two pie charts. One chart should show the percentages of free and slave states after the Missouri Compromise. The other should show the percentages of original states, states that entered the union between 1791 and 1819, and states that entered after the Missouri Compromise.

Using Critical Thinking

1. At the time of the Missouri Compromise, former President John Quincy Adams said that it would have been wiser to hold a new constitutional convention to outlaw slavery. He said, "This would have produced a new Union of 13 or 14 states, unpolluted with slavery." The slave states would have formed a separate government. How would Adams's plan have changed the history of the United States? What would the United States be like today?

2. William Lloyd Garrison said that even the states that had outlawed slavery were "involved in the guilt of slavery" because they allowed it to exist in the slave states. Do you agree or disagree? Explain your reasons.

3. People who disobeyed the Fugitive Slave Act by helping runaway slaves were breaking the law. They argued that the law was so unjust that they did not have to obey it. Do you think they were right or wrong? Explain your response.

Preparing for Citizenship

1. **WRITING ACTIVITY** William Lloyd Garrison's newspaper, *The Liberator*, was published in order to support abolitionism. Identify a current newspaper or magazine that is pubished in order to support a cause. Read the publication and choose an article on a subject that interests you. Write a letter to the editor in response to the article.

2. **WRITING ACTIVITY** Our system of law is based on precedent. That is, lawyers look at previous court decisions and use them to support their cases. Groups such as the abolitionists have tried to set a precedent by winning a court case, such as the Dred Scott case, in order to change the laws. Interest groups today still support individual legal cases in order to promote their point of view. Identify a current lawsuit in which an individual or group of individuals is trying to make a change through the courts. Write a brief outline of their cause and the case they are taking to court.

3. **COLLABORATIVE LEARNING** Stage a class debate on one of the issues in the Lincoln-Douglas debates, role-playing the two candidates. Then take a class vote to decide which side "won" the debate.

Chapter 12

A Nation Divided

*Lincoln became President. The Southern states left the
Union. Soon a bloody conflict ripped the nation apart.
Both sides were confident of a quick victory. But just as the
slavery issue offered no easy answers, this war yielded no
easy victories. The war dragged on for four years, leaving
hundreds of thousands dead and a way of life destroyed.*

Before the war, either a
Northern or a Southern
soldier could have worn
this U.S. Army hat.
Once the war began,
only Northerners would
wear it.

1861 Soldiers, such as the Northern soldier shown
here with his wife and children, faced the first "modern
war." New developments in military technology caused
massive injuries and thousands of deaths.

1860	1861	1862

Presidents

1861-1865
Lincoln

1860

Confederate soldiers, though fewer in number than Union soldiers, proved to be powerful opponents in a war that would pit brother against brother.

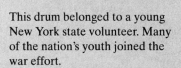

This drum belonged to a young New York state volunteer. Many of the nation's youth joined the war effort.

1863   1864   1865

1865

LESSON 1

North Versus South

THINKING

F O C U S

What advantages and disadvantages did each side have as it prepared to fight the Civil War?

Key Terms

- Confederacy
- secede

➤ *In the painting (above right) General Robert E. Lee is sitting astride his horse, Traveller. Lee considered "duty" the most important word in the English language.*

The battle cry echoed across the many fields and cities of the North and South: "The Confederates have taken Fort Sumter!" On April 12, 1861, the day of the attack, Col. Robert E. Lee faced a painful choice. Earlier, he had called slavery "a moral and political evil in any society." Lee had to decide whether to defend states' rights and slavery by defending his homeland, the South.

President Lincoln had hoped to use Lee's military skills, and with good reason. Lee had 30 years of experience in the United States Army. He had heroically defended his country in the Mexican-American War, and his friendship with fellow officers went back to his college years at the military academy at West Point, New York. For generations his family had been deeply patriotic.

Yet Lee's Southern loyalties also ran deep. Both his family and his wife's family had lived and prospered in Virginia since the 1600s. From 1791 to 1794, Lee's father governed the state. The thought of a divided nation pained him.

Which had the greater claim on his loyalty: state or nation? Lee found it difficult to decide the matter. Then on April 19, 1861, he learned that Virginia was planning to leave the Union. That evening, in a letter to his son, he resolved: "I shall return to my native state and share the miseries of my people." Lee took command of the military and naval forces of Virginia. He was to prove an able and much respected military leader.

Build-Up of Southern Forces

Lee faced the difficult task of building a large army from scratch for a war that had already started. Enlisting enough men was the easiest part, because war fever ran high. Lee soon filled his quota of 51,000. Many of the best officers from the United States Army—some of whom had fought in the Mexican-American war—joined the forces of the **Confederacy,** those Southern states that separated from the United States.

Thousands of Confederate recruits lacked experience, however, and had to be trained rapidly. Gathering supplies posed an even greater challenge. Heavy artillery was scarce, and the Confederacy had little money to provide equipment and uniforms. Volunteers furnished their own clothes and brought along their own hunting guns. Most of the cavalry even supplied their own horses. Amazingly, Lee's army was functioning within a month.

The Southern Viewpoint

In the three months that followed the election of President Lincoln in 1860, the seven cotton-growing states of the Deep South decided to **secede,** or withdraw formally, from the Union. These states were South Carolina, Mississippi, Florida, Alabama, Georgia, Louisiana, and Texas.

Jefferson Davis, the President of the new Southern Confederacy, had to establish not only an army but also a government. The fact that Southern

states seceded one at a time over a six-month period did not make these tasks easy. The Confederacy had to pull these states together to form a solid government.

The states of Virginia, Arkansas, and North Carolina remained in the Union until after the Confederates captured Fort Sumter in Charleston, South Carolina, on April 14, 1861. Tennessee did not join the Confederacy until June 1861. Many from Tennessee and from the western part of Virginia were pro-Union (they supported the government), and thousands of people from these states fought for the Union.

The states of Maryland, Delaware, Kentucky, and Missouri never seceded, although great numbers of their citizens fought for the South. Family loyalties in the slave states that did not secede were often divided.

▼ *Eleven Southern states decided to form their own government and call themselves the Confederate States of America.*

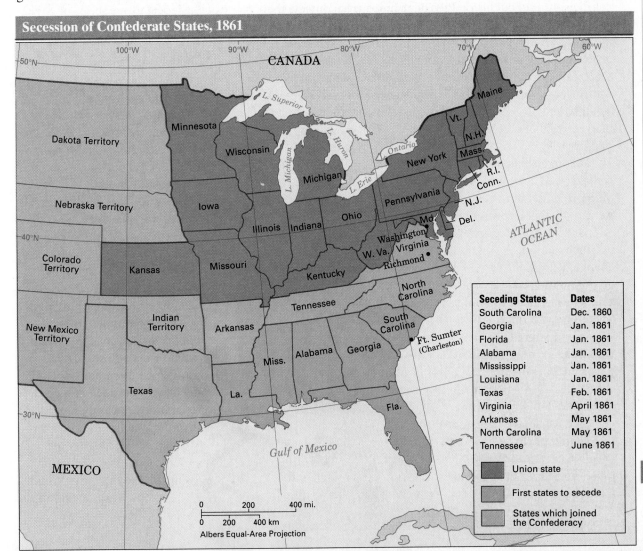

Secession of Confederate States, 1861

Seceding States	Dates
South Carolina	Dec. 1860
Georgia	Jan. 1861
Florida	Jan. 1861
Alabama	Jan. 1861
Mississippi	Jan. 1861
Louisiana	Jan. 1861
Texas	Feb. 1861
Virginia	April 1861
Arkansas	May 1861
North Carolina	May 1861
Tennessee	June 1861

Union state

First states to secede

States which joined the Confederacy

0   200   400 mi.
0   200   400 km
Albers Equal-Area Projection

343

Alexander Stephens, the Vice-president of the Confederacy called the conflict the "War Between the States." This name emphasized the Southern view that the Confederacy was based on a deep appreciation of states' rights. In U.S. government records, the conflict was called the "War of Rebellion," reflecting the Northern view that the Confederates had no right to secede and were therefore rebels. However, most Americans know the war best as the Civil War.

America has suffered only one civil war, but the term applies in a broad sense to many conflicts throughout history. We use the term civil war to refer to any war between two organized groups seeking power within the same nation. In this way, a civil war is clearly different from wars that involve violent conflict between two or more different nations.

Distinguishing between a civil war and a revolution is a bit more difficult. In general, we can say that a revolution is a particular kind of civil war in which one side is seeking to change the nation's system of government. However, not all civil wars are revolutions. Sometimes the opposing sides are fighting for power within the existing system of government.

Civil Wars Throughout History

Civil wars have occurred throughout history whenever a group of citizens organizes a rebellion against the government in power. In China,

for example, regional military leaders often battled for the right to establish a new dynasty. In the 1600s, a civil war took place in England. In that war the common people, or Parliamentarians, fought the ruling class of the English court, or Royalists. Eventually, the king was executed and the power shifted to the Parliamentarians for a brief period.

In the twentieth century, the Spanish Civil War foreshadowed World War II. From 1936 to 1939, Republicans staged a military revolt against the Nationalists who were then in power. As sometimes happens in civil war, each side received support from outside their nation. The Soviet Union and many volunteers from Europe and the United States supported the Republicans, while the Nationalists received aid from

Nazi Germany and Italy. Eventually, the Nationalists won the war and drove the Republicans from Spain.

Civil Wars Today

Sometimes it's hard to tell when an internal conflict becomes a full-fledged civil war. Throughout the world today, many violent conflicts are raging. At least some of these conflicts may be classified as civil wars.

In El Salvador, for example, an army of guerrillas drawn mainly from the nation's large population of impoverished people has fought a civil war since the late 1970s. They have battled against a series of governments, which they see as representing the interests of the military and the nation's wealthy elite. Also, in South Africa, a civil war rages between those who uphold the racial policies that allow whites to rule and those who oppose such policies.

Sadness of Civil War

All wars are terrible and destructive. However, civil wars are perhaps the saddest of human conflicts because they pit brother against brother. They determine the future of countries and usually bring about dramatic change, no matter who wins or loses. Their resolutions are often unclear and may leave a heritage of hatred. Generations remember and relive the war. Today, more than 120 years after the U.S. Civil War, the bitterness left by the war has not yet totally disappeared.

The family of President Lincoln's wife, Mary Todd Lincoln, had brothers, sisters, and other relatives who were loyal to the South. In fact, President Lincoln himself was forced to make an official denial that any member of his family was loyal to the South.

The North was a mighty opponent. It had the advantages of a much larger population and greater economic strength. Even so, at the start of the war, Southerners were self-confident. They compared themselves to the small number of colonists in the Revolutionary War who had defeated the vast powers of Great Britain.

Southerners, in fact, did have advantages. First, they were fighting on their own ground. This meant they were familiar with the land and accustomed to the climate. They were also nearer to their sources of supply and could count on local inhabitants for help. And they had a very important reason to fight. They were defending their families, their homes, and their way of life.

White Southerners believed in being prepared to defend themselves. Military schools across the South supported this tradition by training men to be skilled and daring soldiers.

Officers and Gentlemen

The Confederacy had reason to pride itself on its officers. After the war, both Northerners and Southerners could agree that Confederate Generals Robert E. Lee and Thomas "Stonewall" Jackson were among the greatest strategists of all time.

A close-knit corps of officers who had been trained at West Point as well as at military schools in the South provided valuable support. In addition, soldiers shared a friendship and deep pride that helped them to fight, and often to win, against overwhelming odds. ■

▲ *President Davis and his generals are, from left: P. G. T. Beauregard, Thomas "Stonewall" Jackson, Jefferson Davis, Jeb Stuart, and Joe Johnston. Downhill, to the right of the figures, an encampment is pictured.*

■ *What challenges did the South face in preparing for war?*

The Powerful North

Because of the Union's superior size and economic strength, both Northern leaders and the populace were convinced that they could defeat the Confederacy within a few months. They believed that democracy, both at home and abroad, would be threatened unless America was reunified. The North, in fact, appeared to have many real advantages over their opponents.

Strength in Numbers

The population of the 22 Union states was almost three times that of the 11 states of the Confederacy. Furthermore, one-third of the South's population were slaves, who were not allowed to serve in battle. Over the course of the war, these figures translated to some 2 million men who fought for the Union, compared with 800,000 for the Confederacy.

Although the Union army and navy were poorly prepared for war, they were strong compared with the armed troops of the Confederate forces, which at first had no navy. The North also had a larger fleet of ships and more shipyards. A strong Union navy enabled the North to block Southern ports, preventing Confeder-

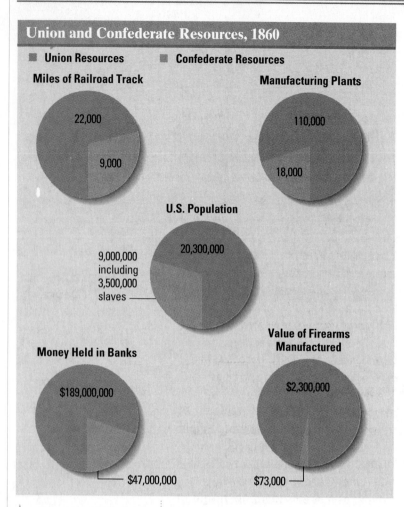

Union and Confederate Resources, 1860

■ Union Resources   ■ Confederate Resources

Miles of Railroad Track
22,000
9,000

Manufacturing Plants
110,000
18,000

U.S. Population
20,300,000
9,000,000 including 3,500,000 slaves

Money Held in Banks
$189,000,000
$47,000,000

Value of Firearms Manufactured
$2,300,000
$73,000

▲ *Although the North had more supplies and resources than the South, both sides felt confident about winning the war.*

■ *Why was a strong navy so important to the North's military success?*

ate ships from moving goods and trading with Europe.

Upper Hand in Industry

In the 1860s, the North produced most of the nation's manufactured goods, while the South remained mainly agricultural. The South's economy had always depended on the sale of farm products to Europe and the North in exchange for manufactured goods. These markets were cut off as a result of the war, causing the South severe shortages of all kinds.

Control of all rail and water traffic was vital to both sides to move supplies and troops. When the war began, the North had 70 percent of all the railroads. The North's naval strength also enabled it to take charge of much of the Southern river traffic.

The Financial Edge

Prior to the war, the South had also depended on the North's experience in handling money and business matters. During the war, both North and South issued their own paper money to pay expenses. But many people felt that these paper bills were less valuable than silver and gold. The paper dollar in the North was worth only about 50 cents. Toward the end of the war, the Southern dollar had a value of three cents. By the spring of 1864, prices in the South were 46 times higher than pre-war levels. For instance, it took five Confederate dollars to buy a cup of coffee. Many Southerners found it hard to feed their families.

At the beginning of the war, the Confederates hoped for support from Great Britain because it needed Southern cotton for its textile mills. Britain, however, was not prepared to become involved in the war. This denied the Confederacy the help of Britain's powerful navy to break the crippling Northern blockade.

In 1861, a quick and easy victory seemed possible to Northerners. Their optimism proved totally false. Four years of destruction were to pass before the North forced the South to surrender. ■

R E V I E W

1. **FOCUS** What advantages and disadvantages did each side have as it prepared to fight the Civil War?
2. **CONNECT** How did the North and South's inability to compromise on slavery lead to the Civil War?
3. **CITIZENSHIP** Why was Robert E. Lee so torn about which side to defend in the war?
4. **CRITICAL THINKING** Secession divided America into two

separate governments. Why do you think President Lincoln feared foreign reaction to secession?

5. **ACTIVITY** Create a drawing or political cartoon showing the firing at Fort Sumter as though you witnessed the event. In a caption, describe how this attack brings the nation to war, and summarize the positions of both the North and the South.

L E S S O N   2

The Nation at War

Sunday, July 21, 1861, was a steamy midsummer day in Washington, D.C., but the nation's capital was festive. For more than a week, thousands of Union and Confederate troops had gathered in northern Virginia. Now the greatest battle yet to take place on American soil was about to begin. Politicians, along with hundreds of other Washingtonians, expected that Union troops would crush the rebel forces. They loaded their horse-drawn buggies and headed for the battle site, ready for a picnic and an exciting and brief battle.

The Confederate troops, headed by General P. G. T. Beauregard, awaited the Yankees near Manassas Junction on the river of Bull Run. Both the Confederate and Union troops had employed almost 30,000 troops on the field. Few of these men had battle experience.

The soldiers on both sides had been up since before dawn. By noon, when the main battle began, they were hungry, thirsty, and tired. As the black smoke from cannons thickened and round after round of bullets battered the soldiers, neither side was at an advantage. Confederate troops held their ground, however, and General Thomas J. Jackson earned his nickname, "Stonewall," because his men held the line "like a stone wall."

By 4:30 that afternoon, the inexperienced Union troops retreated, shocked by the fighting ability of their opponent. Union soldiers struggled back toward Washington. Even sightseers ran for their lives. Several, including a congressman, were captured by the Confederates.

However, the Confederates were too exhausted and disorganized to chase the enemy to Washington and capture the Union capital. Some 600 men on each side died or were mortally wounded. Clearly, this war was going to be more of a struggle than either side had anticipated.

THINKING FOCUS

How did ideas about the nature of war change from the First Battle of Bull Run in 1861 to the Battle of Gettysburg of 1863?

Key Terms

- moderate
- emancipation

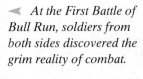

◄ *At the First Battle of Bull Run, soldiers from both sides discovered the grim reality of combat.*

347

A Nation Divided

Two Commanders-in-Chief Take Stock

In 1861, Presidents Abraham Lincoln (top) and Jefferson Davis were challenged to provide strong leadership for their governments.

▼ This photograph shows the living quarters of General McClellan at his military camp at Yorktown, Virginia.

In 1861, as the war began, the leadership of both governments was disorganized, just as their armies were. Confederate President Jefferson Davis faced the enormous challenge of having to quickly build a new Confederate government. President Lincoln had the difficult task of uniting a number of groups within the Union government.

The two Presidents came from very different backgrounds. Lincoln came from a poor frontier family. Davis grew up on his father's large Mississippi cotton plantation and became a successful planter himself. Lincoln was largely self-educated and began his career as a country lawyer. Davis graduated from West Point and had a distinguished military career. However, while their backgrounds and points of view were totally opposed, they shared a position as **moderates,** people who disapproved of extreme political views within their own political parties.

Davis's Challenge

Davis was elected President of the Confederacy as a compromise candidate. As a moderate, he had always supported the idea of states' rights. Now he also had to form a strong, united government if the Confederacy was going to survive the war. This meant gathering troops, forming battle plans, and raising taxes to run the war. Opponents of Davis said that he was limiting states' rights rather than saving and strengthening the ideas for which the South was fighting.

Davis's cold manner caused resentment in his Confederate Congress and led many people to resign. His strongest critics accused Davis of taking part in military business without really knowing much about the battlefield.

Lincoln's Task

Lincoln also had troubles in running the war, especially in the early years. Both political and military problems demanded the Union President's attentions.

Following the First Battle of Bull Run, Lincoln replaced General Irwin McDowell, whom Lincoln believed was too cautious, with General George B. McClellan, who had cleared western Virginia of Confederate troops. The following year, howev-

er, Lincoln removed General McClellan for his lack of forcefulness. Although an excellent organizer, McClellan, who was known as the "Little Napoleon" of the Civil War, was often slow—too slow at times—in making decisions.

Not until early 1864, when Lincoln put Ulysses S. Grant in charge of all Union forces, did the President feel he had found a bold and competent military leader. Grant's fighting ability pushed him to the rank of lieutenant general—a rank which, in the past, was held only by President George Washington. His bold and daring leadership also earned him the name "Unconditional Surrender" Grant.

Political problems also troubled the Union President. Early in his administration, Lincoln said that the war was a fight to save the nation rather than to end slavery. This idea angered the abolitionists, people working to end slavery in the United States.

Lincoln did not want to anger Democrats and people in border states by taking a total stand against slavery. At the same time, Lincoln supported Congress in freeing the District of Columbia slaves, which angered proslavery groups. With great caution, and after weighing proslavery and abolitionist arguments, Lincoln gained antislavery support by saying slavery was morally wrong. He made this bold move at a time when most of the nation still did not want to free the slaves. ■

◄ *The Confederate troops carried flags like this one into battle.*

Across Time & Space

What issues should be regulated, or controlled by the federal government? Today, issues such as gun control and the death penalty are covered by state-based legislation.

■ *What were the similarities and differences between President Lincoln and President Davis?*

Major Battles of the Civil War

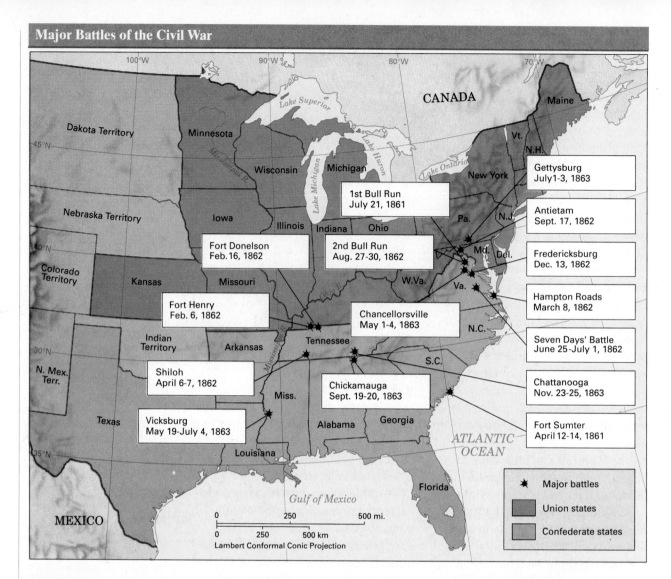

Major Battles of the Civil War

Battle	Significance	Battle	Significance
Fort Sumter April 12–14, 1861	Opening shots fired. Civil War declared.	**Second Bull Run** August 27–30, 1862	Grant's army forced to retreat to Washington.
First Bull Run July 21, 1861	First Civil War battle; Confederates prove their strength.	**Antietam** September 17, 1862	Bloodiest one-day battle of the Civil War: combined casualties of 23,000.
Fort Henry February 6, 1862	Grant's new ironclad gunboats batter and flood the fort.	**Fredericksburg** December 13, 1862	Confederate gunfire forces Union troops to retreat from attempts to cross river.
Fort Donelson February 16, 1862	Union victory. Grant demands "immediate and unconditional surrender."	**Chancellorsville** May 1–4, 1863	"Stonewall" Jackson wages successful offensive, but later dies from wounds.
Hampton Roads March 8, 1862	First major U.S. naval encounter: the North's *Monitor* fought the South's *Merrimac*.	**Vicksburg** May 19–July 4, 1863	Union victory. Opens Mississippi R. supply route to Union.
Battle of Shiloh April 6–7, 1862	Union victory. Heavy combined casualties; 23,000 soldiers killed.	**Gettysburg** July 1–3, 1863	Union victory. "Pickett's Charge" exposes Confederate troops to heavy fire.
Seven Days' Battle June 25–July 1, 1862	Confederates launch seven-day offensive; suffer heavy casualties, but save Richmond.	**Chickamauga** September 19–20, 1863	Confederate victory. Union army retreats to Chattanooga.
		Chattanooga November 23–25, 1863	Union reinforcements arrive by railroad and are victorious.

War Rages On

By the fall of 1862, the war had been raging for over a year, with no end in sight. On September 17, 1862, at Antietam Creek in Maryland, one of the bloodiest battles of the war took place. In a single day of fighting, the combined death counts of Confederate and Union men numbered over 20,000. This number exceeds the deaths from the War of 1812, the Mexican War, and the Spanish-American War combined.

Although Lincoln claimed Antietam as a victory for the North, in truth, neither side was victorious. The day after the slaughter, the Union forces under McClellan did not attack, and the Confederate troops, hungry and tired, retreated to Virginia.

Brother Against Brother

Both sides suffered much loss of life and property and of family unity. For example, Franklin Buchanan, commander of the Confederate ship *Merrimac*, sank the Union ship *Congress* on March 8, 1862. His brother, McKean Buchanan, drowned on the *Congress*. Major General George Crittenden served in the Confederate army, while his brother, Major General Thomas L. Crittenden, defended the Union.

The struggle between family and national loyalties affected women as well as men. Mary Vaughan, a Missouri woman, became a prisoner of the Union government, who accused her of being a Confederate sympathizer. Speaking in her own defense, she said: "Except [for] my own sons and son-in-law, whom I willingly fed I never willingly furnished the rebels anything. . . . I have tried hard to act as a loyal woman."

Mary Todd Lincoln was not the only First Lady whose family disagreed about the war. The brother of Varina Howell Davis, the Confederate President's wife, fought for the Union. ■

▼ *Uniforms, like the well-worn jacket shown here, were among the Confederate supplies that were hard to obtain.*

■ *Evaluate how the battle at Antietam helped to convince citizens that the nature of the Civil War would be neither glorious nor short-lived.*

◄ *Alexander Gardner took this photograph of Abraham Lincoln and General McClellan at Antietam, Maryland, in October 1862. A month later, Lincoln removed McClellan from his command.*

A Nation Divided

The President Proclaims an End to Slavery

Following the bloodshed at Antietam, Lincoln needed to broaden the reasons for remaining at war. He was still very serious about saving the Union, but now he took a firm stand on slavery as well. Linking the Union with the abolition of slavery in the South would strengthen his support in the North by pointing out the need to protect the country and to make it a country where freedom held great value. On September 22, 1862, he issued his first **Emancipation** (the act of freeing) Proclamation.

➤ *A young black man is shown as a slave (left) and in his Union uniform (right) after the Emancipation Proclamation.*

The Emancipation Proclamation would free "all slaves in areas still in rebellion." It was a statement of intent instead of a law, and slaveholders refused to accept it. But the Proclamation caused many people to realize that, along with moral reasons, other good reasons existed for freeing the four million slaves in the Confederacy. Emancipation would take away the South's major source of labor and give Union forces a new source of troops.

The proclamation did not affect slaveholders in the Union nor in parts of the Confederacy in Union hands. However, it would become effective in the regions that remained rebellious on January 1, 1863. When the Confederacy failed to agree, Lincoln signed a second Proclamation on New Year's Day. Many blacks took advantage of the proclamation and other Union antislavery policies to go to Union lines and freedom.

Blacks Can Enlist

The proclamation allowed former slaves to join the armed troops and opened the way for Northern free blacks to join the army. The army was already unofficially using both Northern blacks and escaped slaves to do low-paying jobs, and sometimes to fight. Large numbers of free blacks signed up, both because they wanted to support their country and because they needed work. At first they were paid less than white soldiers, but after they protested this discrimination, the pay was made equal.

During the war, 186,000 blacks served in the Union army and 29,000 in the Union navy. Sixteen blacks earned the Congressional Medal of Honor, the nation's highest military award. Overall, black military service created great pride among black citizens. Many Northern whites felt a debt of thanks to blacks as well. ■

■ *With the enactment of the Emancipation Proclamation, blacks could enlist in the military. How did this new policy influence the North's military strength?*

The Hinge of Fate

In the summer of 1863, the South began to back off before the powerful and persistent Union troops. Until then, the Confederacy had held its own despite limited resources. In 1861 and 1862, the two sides had each won and lost major battles, and, in many instances, there was no clear winner.

Basic military plans used by the South and the North differed widely. The South's plan called for its troops to protect its home soil and fight until the North gave up the idea of winning and accepted secession.

Union plans focused on blocking all major waterways used by the South and capturing Richmond, Virginia, the Confederate capital. In April 1862, Grant's Union troops began a bold campaign at Shiloh, Tennessee, in which the South lost its last chance for an important victory in the West. In July, Lee held back Union troops attempting to capture Richmond. In September, Lee's march into Maryland was stopped at Antietam.

Then in December 1862, the Confederates won a victory against General Joseph Hooker and his men at Fredericksburg, Virginia, and again in May 1863 at Chancellorsville, Virginia. At the battle of Chancellorsville General Thomas "Stonewall" Jackson was accidentally shot and killed by one of his own men.

Meanwhile, in April 1862 on the western front, Union Admiral David Farragut captured New Orleans and continued up the Mississippi River, taking Baton Rouge, Louisiana, and Natchez, Mississippi. He was not, however, able to take Vicksburg, Mississippi. In June, the navy succeeded in capturing Memphis, Tennessee. Only Vicksburg prevented the Union from controlling the entire river.

The Battle of Vicksburg

Union attempts to overtake Vicksburg by land at the end of 1862 also failed. Situated on high bluffs above the river, the city was seemingly impossible to capture. In the spring of 1863, Union General Grant surrounded the city by land, while his navy attacked it from the river.

Beginning May 22, Grant bombarded Vicksburg day and night for six weeks. The townspeople lived in quickly dug caves and many had to eat rats to survive. Vicksburg surrendered

▲ *This doll was used to smuggle medicine across state borders.*

▼ *The seventeen battle-scarred acres that became Cemetery Hill today have a peaceful air, as in this contemporary photograph.*

> *A Confederate sharpshooter is killed while defending his post.*

on July 4, 1863. This major victory for the Union enabled Union troops to blockade crucial Southern trade along the Mississippi River.

The Battle of Gettysburg

On the same day that the Union won a victory at Vicksburg in the west, it won another great battle in the east. In July 1863, General Lee invaded the North for the second time, crossing the Potomac River and ranging into Pennsylvania. On July 1, his army met the Union army under General George Meade at the town of Gettysburg. Lee succeeded in driving Meade back from the town. Unfortunately for Lee, Union forces took up a strong position along a high ridge of land.

For three days, Lee's men, time after time, charged up from the valley toward the Union lines above them, and were forced back. At the end of the third day, 23,000 Union men lay dead or wounded. The Confederates suffered 25,000 casualties.

On July 4 in a rainstorm, Lee's men faced the fire of Union forces and the shattered Confederate army stumbled back across the Potomac.

The number of dead resulting from the bloody Gettysburg battle reached 7,000 more than had died in the Revolutionary War and the War of 1812 combined. The Union was slowly headed for victory. (For a view of the battle of Gettysburg, read the literature selection on page 370.) ■

> ■ *Why were the battles at Vicksburg and Gettysburg referred to as "the Hinge of Fate"?*

R E V I E W

1. **FOCUS** How did ideas about the nature of the war change from the First Battle of Bull Run in 1861 to the Battle at Gettysburg in 1863?

2. **CONNECT** Why did Southerners see their role in the Civil War as similar to that of the colonists in the Revolutionary War?

3. **CIVIC VALUES, RIGHTS, AND RESPONSIBILITIES** What difficulties did Presidents Lincoln and Davis face as leaders during the Civil War?

4. **CRITICAL THINKING** What might have been President Lincoln's reason(s) for allowing Union slaveholders to keep their slaves under the terms of the Emancipation Proclamation?

5. **WRITING ACTIVITY** Imagine two people in the same family who support opposite sides in the Civil War. Write a letter from the point of view of each person, in which that person explains his/her opinions and feelings about the war to the other.

Chapter 12

L E S S O N   3

War on the Homefront

ollowing the Battle of
Gettysburg, a group of
Pennsylvanians made a
cemetery out of part of the
battleground to honor both Union
and Confederate soldiers who died
there. On November 19, 1863, a
ceremony was held to dedicate the
cemetery. Edward Everett, a prominent scholar and politician, made
a two-hour speech.

Then President Lincoln rose and
gave the Gettysburg Address. He
spoke for just two minutes, but that
speech, printed below, is still thought
to be one of the greatest speeches in
American history.

THINKING
FOCUS

*What major changes took
place in American society
as a result of the Civil
War?*

Key Terms

- civil rights
- draft

▲ *In defending the Civil
War, President Lincoln
urged Americans to
"make common cause to
save the good old ship of
the Union."*

ourscore and seven years ago our fathers brought forth upon this continent a new nation, conceived in liberty, and dedicated to the proposition that all men are created equal.

Now we are engaged in a great civil war, testing whether that nation,
or any nation so conceived and so dedicated, can long endure. We are met on a
great battlefield of that war. We have come to dedicate a portion of that field as
a final resting place for those who here gave their lives that that nation might
live. It is altogether fitting and proper that we should do this.

But in a larger sense we cannot dedicate, we cannot consecrate,
we cannot hallow this ground. The brave men, living and dead, who
struggled here, have consecrated it, far above our poor power to add or
detract. The world will little note, nor long remember what we say here;
but it can never forget what they did here. It is for us, the living, rather
to be dedicated here to the unfinished work which they who fought here have
thus far so nobly advanced. It is rather for us to be here dedicated to the
great task remaining before us, that from these honored dead we take increased
devotion to that cause for which they gave the last full measure of devotion;
that we here highly resolve that these dead shall not have died in vain;
that this nation, under God, shall have a new birth of freedom, and the
government of the people, by the people, and for the people shall not perish
from the earth.

–The Gettysburg Address, delivered by Abraham Lincoln, November 19, 1863

Crisis of Wartime Leadership

Lincoln's stirring speech at Gettysburg called for "a new birth of freedom." That was easier said than done. True, some slaves had been freed, but their freedom was still very limited because of racial prejudice. In addition, the **civil rights** of Union citizens had been greatly restricted by Lincoln and Congress in their push to win the war. Civil rights are the rights and freedoms (including freedom of speech, of the press, and of religion) of people as citizens. Freedom of the people of the Confederacy had also been limited by the need to keep economic and social order in a time of war.

▲ *These bills are an example of the variety of privately-issued paper money in use in the early war years. In 1863, the National Bank Act made Confederate money worthless.*

War Taxes Create Dissent

Federal spending rose to new heights during the war. The government imposed heavy taxes, which Union citizens deeply disliked. People paid these taxes every time they bought, sold, or distributed goods. In addition, Congress started an income tax to help raise money. It was small compared to today's taxes: 3 percent on income over $800. But this figure rose to 10 percent on incomes over $10,000 by the end of the war.

Confederate citizens paid even heavier taxes. In addition to creating income and sales taxes, the government took a percentage of all food crops. When these supplies rotted in warehouses because of the lack of transportation, hungry citizens and angry farmers became upset.

Civil Liberties Threatened

In wartime, governments often restrict civil rights. They did so during the Civil War. In April 1861, Lincoln first suspended the writ of habeas corpus—a law that protected people from being arrested and held without a trial—in certain parts of the Union.

By September 1862, the suspension applied to the whole nation. Lincoln said that the Constitution gave him the power to take any steps he needed for the nation during wartime. Under Lincoln's order, the Union military could arrest "all Rebels and Insurgents, their aiders and abettors within the United States." They could also arrest "all persons discouraging volunteer enlistments, resisting the militia **draft** [a call to military service], or guilty of any disloyal practice." This especially affected newspapers and politicians who disliked the draft and Southern sympathizers in the border states.

In 1863, soldiers arrested Clement L. Vallandigham, a popular congressman from Ohio, for his antigovernment positions as leader of the Peace Democrats. (Opponents, who did not trust the Peace Democrats, called them "Copperheads" after the poisonous snake.) However, government law was not always enforced. Vallandigham's supporters raised an outcry over his arrest, and he was merely released to the Confederacy.

Southerners Accused as Spies

Thousands of civilian men and women in the South faced arrest for suspected spying or for aiding the enemy. Once arrested, they could be sent to jail, without ever being officially charged. Feeding or caring for guerrillas—bands of civilians who fought against the Union—carried the risk of being arrested as a spy.

Guerrilla bands controlled whole areas in the South and sometimes destroyed enemy communications and supply lines. For the most part, however, they were considered outlaws. They often attacked citizens who were not directly involved in the war. Deserters often joined these bands.

Draft Riots Rage

Riots against the draft were the most violent reactions to wartime limitations on civil rights. The Union Draft Law of March 3, 1863, made every male citizen between 20 and 45 subject to the draft. What enraged the working classes across the country was that a man could avoid serving in the army by paying $300. This discriminated against the laborers whose pay averaged about $500 a year.

Draft riots broke out across the country between the police and the poor in Chicago, Pennsylvania, and Vermont. The worst riots happened in New York City on July 13, 1863. The rioters were mostly Irish immigrants from the city's poorest neighborhoods. The violence began with the burning of a recruiting office and spread throughout the city. The rioters' rage over the draft was mixed with their distrust of black Americans, whom they said wanted to take their jobs. The rioters torched abolitionists' houses and burned a black orphanage. A dozen blacks were hanged at the hands of a such rioters.

Police and firefighters, many of whom were Irish, fought the rioters with great bravery but could not stop them. Army troops arrived from Gettysburg, including an all-Irish unit, to calm the large groups of rioters. In the four days of rioting, over one hundred people were killed and several thousand wounded—most of them rioters.

People felt horror at the brutality of the riots, but many agreed with the rioters that allowing the rich to pay the poor to fight was unfair. The government finally ended exemptions in exchange for money. (Read about another problem with the draft in Making Decisions on page 360.)

Wartime Life in the South

Tensions also mounted in the South, in response to wartime policies. The Confederate government also started a draft in which substitutes could be hired to fight. The writ of habeas corpus was suspended for about a year. An exemption that allowed slaveowners with more than 20 slaves exemption from the draft caused great resentment. Again, people accused the government of favoring the rich. Many Confederate soldiers chose to desert their fighting posts. Civilians living in the path of the enemy lost their animals. Union soldiers often burned Confederate homes and took personal property. Homeless women and children had little money or food. The war affected every level of life in the South.

◄ In this etching from 1863, fire sweeps the Coloured Orphan Asylum as angry crowds react to the provisions of the draft. The day before the riots began, names of those drafted had been listed in the Sunday newspaper.

A Nation Divided

Food shortages caused rioting in cities throughout the eastern Confederacy. In 1863, bread riots rocked the capital of Richmond. Most of the rioters were women who were desperate to feed their families. They looted stores and even hijacked goods from trains. In addition, gangs of deserters raided trains and attacked supply depots.

In the last year of the war, desertions increased alarmingly. Soldiers were barefoot, hungry, and discouraged by their military losses. In ever-increasing numbers, soldiers deserted in order to go home to save their families from starvation and from being forced off their farms. ■

■ *Why did both Northern and Southern citizens resent the terms of the draft? What caused citizens to riot?*

Draft Sends Youth to War

The Civil War was fought by the young: 60 percent of the soldiers and sailors on both sides were 25 years of

➤ *About 5 percent of those fighting for the Confederacy were under 18 years of age.*

age or younger. The ranks also included many boys under the legal enlistment age of 18.

Drummer boys of 10 or 12 served in both armies. Young boys in both navies carried gunpowder to the men firing the cannon. Nicknamed "powder monkeys," they could scramble quickly down the narrow ship ladders to where the powder was stored.

In addition, young soldiers held dangerous and exhausting jobs. Boys of 13 and 14 often marched all day, slept on the ground, and faced enemy fire along with the men. Once a boy entered the armed forces, regardless of his age, he received no special treatment.

Some teenagers became high-ranking officers, commanding men

twice their age. Arthur MacArthur entered the Union army at 18 as a color-bearer, carrying the flag into battle, and rose to the high rank of lieutenant general.

Fifteen-year-old Union Private Nathaniel Gwynne lost an arm in battle and received the Medal of Honor for his bravery. David O. Dodd was 17 when the Union Army arrested him on Christmas 1863. He admitted that he was a Confederate spy but refused to earn a pardon in exchange for giving information. He was tried and sentenced to be hanged on January 8, 1864. On the morning of the hanging, he wrote to his parents and sisters: "I was sentenced to be hung [hanged] today at 3 o'clock. The time is fast approaching, but, thank God: I am prepared to die." Dodd was hanged on a tree on the lawn of the same school where he had been a student. ■

■ *What kinds of jobs were held by the young in the Civil War?*

Chapter 12

War Creates New Roles for Women

While men fought the Civil War, women's traditional roles as wives, homemakers, and mothers were expanded to include new social, political, and economic duties. Over the course of the war, thousands of homemakers were forced to support and protect themselves and their families while their husbands were in military service. A very heavy burden fell on those whose husbands were killed or wounded.

Many jobs that had been for men only before the war were opened to women. They worked as printers, blacksmiths, and farmers. Hundreds filled previously all-male government jobs, including important executive positions. Frances Spinner became Treasurer of the United States. Sally Tomkins was made a captain in the Confederate army. Women also directly helped the war effort by working in munitions factories where they made weapons and ammunition. Mary Livermore formed the U.S. Sanitary Commission, which aided sick Union soldiers and their families.

Women were employed by both armies as cooks and laundresses. Three thousand women became Army and Navy nurses—jobs previously restricted to men. Mary Bickerdyke, known as "Mother Bickerdyke," ran one of the more successful Union hospitals. In the South, Phoebe Yates Pember ran a hospital for Confederate soldiers.

More than 400 women, disguised as men, served as soldiers. Ellen Goodridge chose to join the army with her Union fiancé. Sarah Edmonds served as a nurse with the Second Michigan Calvary under the name Franklin Thompson. Amy Clark continued to fight after her Confederate soldier husband was killed at Shiloh. Most of these women were discovered when they were wounded in battle. Southern women, like women in the North, most often posed as men so they could be with their husbands.

▼ *During the Civil War, women filled factory jobs that were previously held by men.*

Women also served as spies. Dr. Mary Walker served the Union as a doctor but was also captured for spying. Rose O'Neal Greenhow, a Southern society hostess, became a famous Confederate figure in 1864 when she drowned while returning from a mission to Europe. Union spy Pauline Cushman, an actress, passed information to Union officers during theatrical tours and was put in jail as a spy. ◼

◼ *How did many women, who were not allowed to fight in the Civil War, find a way to help the war effort?*

REVIEW

1. **FOCUS** What major changes took place in American society as a result of the Civil War?

2. **CONNECT** How did the response of angry Northerners forced to pay high taxes during the Civil War differ from the response of colonists forced to pay a tax on British tea?

3. **HISTORY** In what way did the Civil War provide an opportunity for women to participate in the work force?

4. **CRITICAL THINKING** Was President Lincoln justified in suspending the writ of habeas corpus to maintain order during wartime? Offer support for your opinion.

5. **WRITING ACTIVITY** Write a short essay on the employment of the very young in the military, stating why you think this should or should not be allowed. Use one of the descriptions of a boy soldier in this chapter as an example in your argument.

A Nation Divided

The Shakers and the Civil War

A s we have received the grace of God in Christ, by the gospel, and are called to follow peace with all men, we cannot, consistent with our faith and conscience, bear the arms of war, for the purpose of shedding the blood of any, or do anything to justify or encourage it in others.

Joseph Meacham, Shaker elder

Y ou [the Shakers] ought to be made to fight. We need regiments of just such men as you.

President Abraham Lincoln

Background

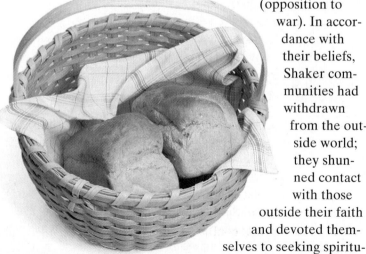

Shakers valued well-crafted items such as the basket below.

When George Ingels, a member of the Shaker society in North Union, Ohio, was drafted in 1862, he and his fellow community members faced a crisis. During the Civil War, nearly 6,000 Shakers lived scattered across the country in approximately 20 settlements from Maine to Ohio, supporting pacifism (opposition to war). In accordance with their beliefs, Shaker communities had withdrawn from the outside world; they shunned contact with those outside their faith and devoted themselves to seeking spiritu-al perfection. When the country went to war and the government started a military draft, Shakers who were summoned to military service had to choose between the dictates of their conscience and obedience to the law. All Shakers opposed slavery. But their opposition to war was stronger. Shaker elders (church leaders and policy makers) had taken a firm stand against participation in the military from the era of the Revolution well into the 1800s. Indeed, Shaker elders repeatedly petitioned state legislatures to repeal any taxes levied for military purposes.

Shakers wanted to avoid even indirect support of bloodshed. The Union government, however, was fighting the Civil War to abolish slavery and to preserve the Union. It needed every able-bodied man it could enlist, and it needed more funds to support the war effort.

Conflict Between Conscience and Country

When several young Shakers were threatened with being drafted, elders responded by sending representatives to Washington to appeal directly to the President. They presented Lincoln with a petition that clearly outlined their philosophical reasons for refusing to participate in the war effort. The Shakers were not content with ordinary status as conscientious objectors (those who refuse military service on religious or moral grounds). They wanted a total exemption from any support of the war, even indirect financial aid.

Secretary of War Stanton believed that although the Union might respect Shaker beliefs and not make them fight, the government could hardly let the Shakers avoid financial obligations in support of the war. To resolve this conflict, Elder Frederick Evans made the following proposal. The U.S. government still owed pension payments to veterans who had become Shakers after fighting in the War of 1812. If the federal government would agree not to draft Shaker men, the Shakers would forgive the debt. The government agreed to this proposal.

Later, when more Shakers were drafted, Secretary of War Stanton exempted them from service and ordered that other conscientious objectors also be exempted. Throughout the rest of the Civil War, Shakers neither bore arms nor paid fees for others to fight in their place.

Shakers avoided military service, but those who lived in the border states could not entirely escape the war. They lost money and property. The community at South Union, Kentucky, alone lost over $100,000 worth of property and had to feed 50,000 meals to invading soldiers—from both sides. Shakers considered this a small price to pay for the knowledge that they had upheld their principles and had not betrayed their country.

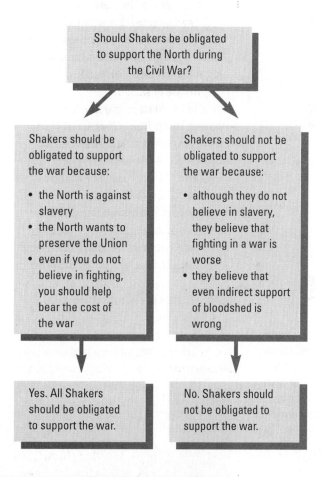

Should Shakers be obligated to support the North during the Civil War?

Shakers should be obligated to support the war because:
- the North is against slavery
- the North wants to preserve the Union
- even if you do not believe in fighting, you should help bear the cost of the war

Shakers should not be obligated to support the war because:
- although they do not believe in slavery, they believe that fighting in a war is worse
- they believe that even indirect support of bloodshed is wrong

Yes. All Shakers should be obligated to support the war.

No. Shakers should not be obligated to support the war.

Decision Point

1. Why did the Shakers refuse to pay for substitutes to fight in their place during the war?
2. Why did Lincoln let Shakers avoid the draft when the country needed soldiers so badly?
3. What alternatives did Lincoln have?
4. What else could the Shakers have done? What would another compromise position have been?
5. Can you think of any contemporary situations in which there has been opposition to fighting a war? How was that conflict resolved?

L E S S O N   4

The Long March to Surrender

THINKING
F O C U S

What events led to General Lee's surrender at Appomattox?

Before the invention of photography, war was often shown as a series of heroic fights between handsome, elegantly dressed soldiers riding sleek, prancing horses.

This romantic image was changed forever by thousands of Civil War photographs of battlefields. Gory depictions of the bodies of dead soldiers and the carcasses of skinny horses showed the reality.

Photographers, such as Matthew Brady, moved their heavy cameras and equipment in specially designed wagons that also served as darkrooms.

The cameras of the time were too slow to take action shots, so photographers focused instead on post-battle pictures. Often, bodies were arranged to show more shocking images.

Techniques for copying photographs in newspapers did not exist. However, weekly magazines printed woodcuts and engravings copied from war photographs. Hand-held viewers, called stereoscopes, turned single images into three-dimensional views. Thousands of people nationwide gathered to view exhibits of war photographs depicting death and the ruined lands and buildings.

➤ *Wartime photography showing the military in various states: at ease and guarding their commands. Photography changed the romantic images of war.*

The Final Tally

The horrors of three years of fighting, so clearly illustrated in battle photographs, increased a great deal in the last months of the war. Throughout the war, the North tried to hurt the South economically, politically, and morally. Yet in the third year of war, it was clear that a new instrument of war was necessary to end the conflict. The new approach, "psychological warfare," involved destroying the hopes of the entire South. General Sherman said, "We cannot change the hearts of those people of the South, but we can make war so terrible . . . that generations would pass away before they would again appeal to it."

In March 1864, Lincoln appointed Ulysses S. Grant head of all Union forces. With Grant's strong support, General Sherman in the west and General Sheridan in the east planned new tactics of destruction to bring the war to a close. No one would be spared the effects of "total war." The army burned houses and fields; people starved to death—all in the name of forcing the South to surrender.

Shocking Losses

Even without these harsh military tactics, the war was taking a tremendous toll in human suffering. Although doctors and nurses provided medical and social services to wounded soldiers, the science of medicine had advanced little since the Revolutionary War. Doctors came to the battlefield without much formal training. The importance of clean medical tools was unknown to them, and many patients survived surgery only to die later of infection. Amputation was seen as the only treatment for injury to the bone and was a common procedure. Seventy-five percent of soldiers suffering chest and stomach wounds died from their injuries.

However, some medical breakthroughs did take place during the

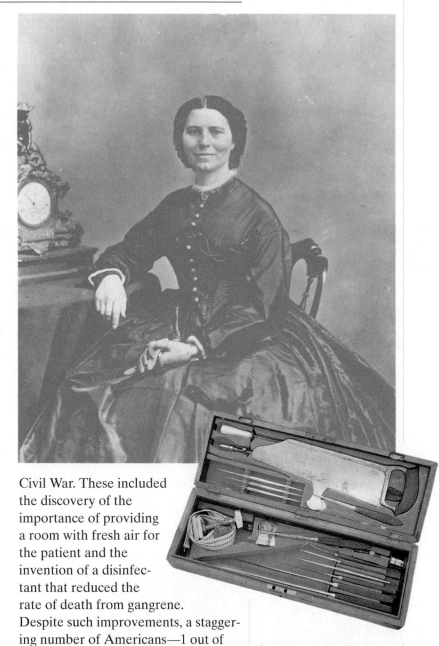

Civil War. These included the discovery of the importance of providing a room with fresh air for the patient and the invention of a disinfectant that reduced the rate of death from gangrene. Despite such improvements, a staggering number of Americans—1 out of every 50—died in the Civil War.

One important figure in medical care was Clara Barton. During the war, Barton risked her life to carry supplies to Union soldiers and to nurse the wounded on the battlefield. She was known as "the Angel of the Battlefield."

New weapon technology also added to the shocking death tolls of Northern and Southern soldiers. The next two pages show you a Closer Look at Civil War technology.

Nurse Clara Barton introduced battlefield emergency care and later founded the American Red Cross. Doctors performed surgery with instruments such as the ones featured in the medic's kit.

A Nation Divided

Civil War Technology

Rifles cracked. Cannons roared. Observation balloons hung over fields; and silent, ironclad ships floated on the waterways. Technology introduced in the Civil War would change the way war was waged. It was called the first modern war.

Just bad aim? Hot air balloons were used by the Union during the war to drop messages, sketch maps, and watch enemy maneuvers. Not one was ever shot down.

CHARLESTON

MERCURY

EXTRA:

Passed unanimously at 1.15 o'clock, P. M., December 20th, 1860.

AN ORDINANCE

To dissolve the Union between the State of South Carolina and other States united with her under the compact entitled "The Constitution of the United States of America."

We, the People of the State of South Carolina, in Convention assembled, do declare and ordain, and it is hereby declared and ordained,

That the Ordinance adopted by us in Convention, on the twenty-third day of May, in the year of our Lord one thousand seven hundred and eighty-eight, whereby the Constitution of the United States of America was ratified, and also, all Acts and parts of Acts of the General Assembly of this State, ratifying amendments of the said Constitution, are hereby repealed; and that the union now subsisting between South Carolina and other States, under the name of "The United States of America," is hereby dissolved.

THE

UNION
IS
DISSOLVED!

Bring out the big guns! The largest cannons ever made up to the Civil War were produced by the North. They rotated on huge circular tracks.

This .44 caliber Colt revolver contained six ammunition chambers. The Colt was famous for rapid fire in close combat. Confederate soldiers often used Colts they had stolen from Union cavalry.

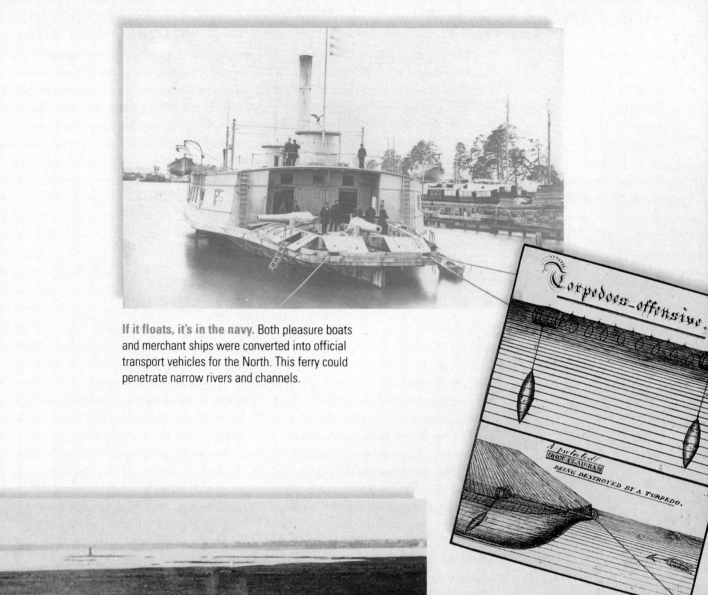

If it floats, it's in the navy. Both pleasure boats and merchant ships were converted into official transport vehicles for the North. This ferry could penetrate narrow rivers and channels.

A Confederate "torpedo" blew up the U.S.S. *Cairo* in 1862. It was the first time an underwater mine ever sank a warship. Some "torpedoes" with trigger mechanisms floated underwater. The bottom of a boat would brush the trigger and Kaboom!

The repeater rifle allowed for shooting from longer distances and firing without stopping to reload. The machine gun was also introduced in the Civil War, along with water mines, flame throwers, and gas shells. Although these weapons can be viewed as technological advances, such devices also brought about tremendous loss of human life.

Sherman Marches to the Sea

Throughout the summer of 1864, the Union army of 60,000 men led by General William Tecumseh Sherman made its way east through Georgia. In September, Sherman's men captured Atlanta, an important city in the Southern railroad network. Union forces destroyed or took anything of use to the Confederates. Sherman and his troops then forced all the people to leave Atlanta and burned the city to the ground. Sherman's army, with almost no opposition, marched through Georgia toward Savannah on the Atlantic coast. The troops lived off the countryside, eating whatever they could take from citizens' homes. They also destroyed and then burned a 50-mile-wide strip of land along their way. After the destruction of Atlanta and Sherman's march across the Georgia countryside, the citizens of Savan-nah were so frightened they quickly surrendered. Following the Union army was a large group of slaves who freed themselves from their Confederate owners. The sight of free black men and women marching through the streets frightened many Southerners. They feared the ex-slaves would seek a bloody revenge for their treatment by slave owners.

Savannah fell to Sherman in December 1864. He then turned north to South Carolina. In February, his men took the state capital of Columbia. Sherman then moved on into North Carolina on his drive toward Richmond, Virginia. However, before he reached the Confederate capital, the war was over.

The North Empties the Breadbasket

While Sherman was cutting his path of destruction through the Deep South, Union General Philip Henry Sheridan was destroying the Shenandoah Valley in Virginia. Farms in this area provided most of the food for Lee's hungry army. Grant instructed Sheridan to lay waste to the valley so that even a crow crossing it would have to bring its food supply from elsewhere. Sheridan also destroyed the Confederate army of the Shenandoah despite its brave efforts to resist. ■

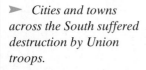

■ *Why did Grant and his generals believe that "total war" was necessary?*

➤ *Cities and towns across the South suffered destruction by Union troops.*

Surrender at Appomattox

By the spring of 1865, the South was broken and discouraged. General Lee's army of Virginia, reduced to 35,000 men, retreated from troops led by General George G. Meade, who commanded the army of the Potomac. Meade's troops numbered 80,000 strong. Sherman's army would soon arrive to separate Lee from the rest of the South.

On April 3, President Davis fled Richmond. As Lee's retreating troops departed, they set fire to army installations and warehouses. The fire spread quickly, leaving the Confederate capital in ashes.

Lee's men, ragged and barefoot, had been surviving on dried corn. They were about to run out of ammunition. Yet even at this desperate hour they held on. Seldom in history has a general enjoyed such respect from his men.

He said to his officers, "There is nothing left for me to do but go and see General Grant, and I would rather die a thousand deaths." Lee then wrote to Grant, requesting a meeting to discuss terms of the South's surrender. Lee's only choice was to save what was left of the South by surrendering immediately.

That meeting took place on April 9, 1865, at the town of Appomattox Court House, Virginia, where General Robert E. Lee surrendered to General Ulysses S. Grant. Lee was wearing his dress uniform and gold-mounted sword. Grant's personal belongings had not been sent ahead to him. He wore a faded shirt and his mud-caked battlefield boots.

Grant's appearance was shabby, but his terms were generous. He set free Lee's troops, provided them with food, and allowed them to take home their horses and mules, which they themselves had provided (most of the South's farm animals had been slaughtered for food). "The war is over," Grant reminded his troops, as he forbade them to fire their guns in celebration of the victory.

Grant wrote in his memoirs how sad he had felt at Lee's surrender. He hated to see "the downfall of a foe who had fought so long and valiantly, and had suffered so much for a cause though that cause was . . . one of the worst for which a people ever fought." ■

▼ *At the home of William McLean, in the village of Appomattox Court House, Virginia, Robert E. Lee and Ulysses S. Grant brought four years of bloody war to an end.*

JAMESTOWN JOURNAL.
EXTRA.
Jamestown, April 7th—2 P. M.
MORE
GOOD NEWS!
Gen. LEE
AND THE WHOLE
Rebel Army
SURRENDER

The following important news is just received:
Washington, April 7th—10:30 A. M.
To Gen. DIX, New York:
General Lee and whole Army have surrendered.
Signed,
E. M. STANTON,
Secretary of War.

■ *What terms did Grant set for Lee's surrender?*

R E V I E W

1. **FOCUS** What events led to General Lee's surrender at Appomattox?
2. **CONNECT** How did advances in weapon technology make the fighting of the Civil War different from previous wars?
3. **ECONOMICS** How did Sherman's march make it economically impossible for the South to remain at war?
4. **CRITICAL THINKING** Do you think that General Grant should have offered additional aid to the South after the war? Offer support for your answer.
5. **WRITING ACTIVITY** Write a short essay describing all the aspects of a war that you think need to be represented in photographs to fully illustrate the impact of war on soldiers and civilians. Explain your choices.

Reporting on Antietam

Here's Why

In our society, reports are the main way people gather and distribute important information in school and in business. Reports can answer questions, give a point of view on a subject, or identify a problem. Knowing how to prepare a report is a skill you will use in many different ways throughout your life.

Reports from the battlefront were the only way President Lincoln was able to determine the outcome of the Battle of Antietam, one of the bloodiest battles of the Civil War. Lincoln claimed that it was a victory for the North. However, most historians believe that evidence shows neither side won the battle decisively.

Suppose you wanted to decide for yourself which side actually won, or show that there was, in fact, no clear winner. Suppose also that you wanted to convince your class that your findings were valid. Combining the skills you learned in previous chapters—use of primary and specialized sources, note and bibliography cards, and outline development—will help you to prepare a written report.

Here's How

Follow these steps:

1. **Identify your purpose.**
   Is your report meant to inform, to convince, or does it have some other purpose? All of the information you present should support your purpose. In this case your report is meant to convince the reader that your research on the Battle of Antietam shows who did or did not win the battle.

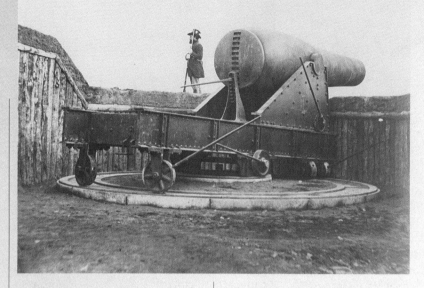

2. **Identify your audience.**
Who will read your report? If you are writing a report that will be read by someone who knows the subject well, you may be able to concentrate only on your specific topic. If it will be read by someone who does not know the subject well, you might need to provide more background information. Decide how much information you need to provide in order to convince your classmates that your decision on the outcome of the Battle of Antietam is correct.

3. **Choose a topic.**
Make your topic clear and specific, and put it in the form of a question you will answer. For this report your topic may be: Who won the Battle of Antietam?

4. **Locate sources.**
Use reference systems such as the library card catalogue or a computerized reference system to locate books. Use *The Readers' Guide to Periodical Literature* to find magazine articles. Refer to pages 274–275 in Chapter 9 on how to use computerized resources.

5. **Use index cards.**
Take notes, create bibliography cards, and record exact quotations from primary sources (noting the book and page number).

6. **Determine point of view in any quotations.**
Refer to the pages 88 and 89 to determine which of your sources are primary sources. For any primary sources, you should review pages 336 and 337 to determine the point of view.

7. **Organize the information into an outline.**
You may want to re-read pages 228 and 229 to review outlines.

8. **Prepare a bibliography.**
Alphabetize the bibliography cards that you created while taking notes, and use them to create a bibliography page.

9. **Write the report.**
Expand your outline into paragraphs. Each paragraph should have a topic sentence that states one main idea, followed by sentences that add details to develop the main idea.

10. **Write an introduction.**
Your introduction should interest your readers in your topic and explain what the report is about.

11. **Write a conclusion.**
Your conclusion should restate the main ideas you have presented and should complete the report.

Try It
Choose a major Civil War battle described in this chapter, and research it for a two-page written report. Follow the steps listed above to prepare the report.

Apply It
Choose a current topic that is heavily debated, such as gun control. Research both sides of the issue, and then write a topic question that your report will answer. Locate sources in your library, prepare bibliography cards, and develop an outline.

The Slopes of War

Norah A. Perez

N.A. Perez is the author of The Slopes of War *(1984), from which this selection is taken, as well as several other historical novels. On a trip to Gettysburg, Perez was moved to write about the human suffering endured by the townspeople of Gettysburg and the soldiers who fought there. Many authors who have written about war never set foot on a battlefield. What do you think such authors need to do in order to create a vivid and convincing account of war?*

In this chapter, you read about the important Northern victory at the Battle of Gettysburg and about the battle's terrible death toll for both sides. In this fictional account, the events of that battle are told from General Lee's perspective.

militia citizen army
skirmish a minor encounter in war

dysentery a stomach disorder

artillery large firing weapons

At Chambersburg General Lee tried to make sense out of the reports coming in to him. On Tuesday Pettigrew's men had headed into Gettysburg to find some desperately needed shoes; they had seen a few enemy uniforms and had reported back to General Heth. Convinced that what they had seen was probably the local militia, Heth had agreed to let Pettigrew return for the shoes the next morning. That was how it had started. Now a little skirmish had developed into something bigger.

As he pressed Traveller to reach Gettysburg quickly, Lee hoped that the Old Soldier's Disease, which was draining his energy, wouldn't be a nuisance to him much longer. He was feeling his age these days. It was as if his body, once fit and healthy and uncomplaining, nagged him for attention. First the heart and the troubling shortness of breath, and then this annoying dysentery. It worried him not to be in peak condition. A victory here and it was possible the war might end.

A. P. Hill, the commander of the Third Corps, was waiting, his bearded face blotched with red, twitching nervously above the collar of the crimson shirt he liked to wear into battle. He admitted that the brigades had met some surprising resistance on their shopping trip to town that morning. "But I have another division ready to go in and back up Heth. Dorsey Pender's men . . . good fellows." Hill was usually unsettled during military operations, but on this bright July morning Lee thought the man really looked quite ill as he repeated that he had men ready to go in. "With your permission, sir."

"Wait. Wait. . . ." Lee would not be rushed into this. He moved to and fro on his horse, listening to the familiar crack of muskets and the steady rumble of artillery, straining to understand what lay behind it. Heavy casualty reports were coming in now, and word had arrived that General Archer had been taken prisoner. In spite of his composure a hot cone of anger against his cavalry burned in his chest. No, he was not angry with them, but with his favorite, Jeb Stuart, the officer who had let him down. He had known that the marvelous man had flaws, that he was sometimes too buoyant and reckless, but this time he was unforgivably late, and Lee felt like a blinded man. He did not know what the danger was or where it was located. For all he knew, the soldiers scrambling through the woods and fields northwest of town might be involved with the whole Army of the Potomac. A spy had reported columns of the enemy in the area, but he knew he wasn't ready yet for a major encounter, not until all of his troops had arrived.

Hill said, "Just give me the word, sir. Pender will clear the road for us in no time."

"Not yet." The general never minded taking risks when he had to, but he refused to be stupid. "Let's wait and see just what it is we're up against."

And so a lull occurred, a little yawn in time, even as the snap of musketry went on and shells continued to burst and blossom white against the innocent blue sky. Time for parched soldiers to swallow tepid water and exhausted gun crews to reposition batteries and replenish ammunition, as a long slow scarf of yellow smoke drifted across the damaged ground.

Then, abruptly, things began to happen again. The murky puzzle that was baffling Lee came together sharply with a sudden shape and clear design. Five brigades of Rodes's division appeared north of the pike on Oak Hill in exactly the right position to swoop down on the tired blue troops that faced the west. If Pender drove in now with his fresh supports, and Rodes's men slammed down hard from the hill, the Union line would have to give. Integral parts clicked smoothly into place as if they had been planned. General Lee, his instincts for opportunity humming, gave the orders.

Yet Federal gears were whirring, too. The Eleventh Corps had just arrived, men fresh for battle hurrying double-quick along the pike and fanning out north of town. It was a hard luck unit, the scapegoat of the army because of its large number of immigrant recruits, but this time it was fortunate. The Confederates rushing down from Oak Hill came too fast, too eagerly, and the Eleventh hurled them back and forced them to regroup. Now the war machine boomed heavily across the landscape, knocking down fence rails, blasting wildflowers, smashing thousands of men under as it rumbled through the sultry summer afternoon.

buoyant enthusiastic
reckless without regard to outcome

tepid slightly warm

integral needed for functioning

scapegoat a person or group bearing the blame for others

Further Reading

Thunder at Gettysburg. Patricia L. Gauch. The Battle of Gettysburg is seen through the eyes of 14-year-old Tillie, who becomes involved in the tragic battle that takes place near her town.

Chapter Review

Reviewing Key Terms

civil rights (p. 356) emancipation (p. 352)
Confederacy (p. 342) moderate (p. 348)
draft (p. 356) secede (p. 343)

A. The sentences below have been started for you. Complete each sentence so that the meaning of the key term is clear.
1. The Emancipation Proclamation . . .
2. The Confederacy was a group of states that . . .
3. Both Abraham Lincoln and Jefferson Davis were moderates because . . .
4. In the effort to win the war, Lincoln and the Congress changed people's civil rights by . . .
5. By September 1862, President Lincoln declared that anyone who resisted the draft . . .

B. Based on what you have read in the chapter, decide whether each of the following statements is accurate. Write an explanation of each decision.
1. Each Southern state in favor of slavery became a confederacy.
2. Several slave states refused to secede, and stayed within the Union.
3. The moderates in Lincoln's party took the most extreme positions on slavery.
4. Emancipation made it possible for women to serve in the army.
5. During the Civil War, President Lincoln ordered the Union military to arrest anyone who resisted the draft.
6. All United States citizens are protected by civil rights.

Exploring Concepts

A. On a separate sheet of paper, make two tables modeled on the ones shown below. Complete the tables by filling in the advantages and disadvantages that the North and South faced in waging war against each other.

South	Advantages	Disadvantages
Economic		
Geographic		
Military		

North	Advantages	Disadvantages
Economic		
Geographic		
Military		

B. Support each of the following statements with facts and details from the chapter.
1. The South's economy was its greatest weakness.
2. President Davis faced many challenges in holding the Confederacy together.
3. President Lincoln also faced problems in carrying the war to a successful conclusion.
4. The Emancipation Proclamation benefited the North in several ways.
5. Lincoln restricted civil rights in the North during the war.
6. The many hardships of war drove people to riot in both the North and South.
7. The war gave women new opportunities in many fields.
8. Several factors contributed to the high casualty rate among soldiers who fought in the war.
9. Military leaders in the North used psychological warfare to wear down the South.

Reviewing Skills

1. Read the section about the battle of Gettysburg in this chapter, and make note cards on the information.
2. Based on the notes you have taken, write a topic question for a report on the battle of Gettysburg.
3. Use your note cards to create an outline for a report that will clearly answer your topic question. Be sure to include subtopics and supporting details.
4. Create a timeline for the major events that were presented in this chapter.
5. Suppose you wanted to write a report on different types of weapons used during the Civil War. What process would you follow to put the report together?

Using Critical Thinking

1. General Sherman wrote, "I say with the press unfettered [unchained; free to publish all news], we are defeated to the end of time. 'Tis folly to say the people must have news." Do you agree that some rights must be suspended in times of war or other dangers? For example, do you think that the government has the right to prohibit the publication of school newspapers during times of conflict?
2. Lincoln said, "If I could save the Union without freeing any slave, I would do it; and if I could do it by freeing all the slaves, I would do it; and if I could save it by freeing some and leaving others alone, I would also do that." What did he mean by that statement? Do you think the Emancipation Proclamation was consistent with that statement?
3. Some historians have said that given the South's lack of industries and its smaller population, it could never have won the war. Do you agree or disagree? Give reasons for your answer.

Preparing for Citizenship

1. **WRITING ACTIVITY** The Civil War was a war that affected every single household in both the North and the South. Part of the recovery process for a society that survives such horrors is to create art from history. Novels, plays, and paintings depicting a war usually become very popular in the years afterward. Identify movies or novels that are based on more recent wars. View one of these movies or read one of these novels, and write a short report about it.
2. **WRITING ACTIVITY** The Gettysburg Address is considered one of the most beautiful, moving speeches ever written. Lincoln wrote the speech to dedicate a cemetery. It is thus a eulogy, or formal praise, for those who died in the battle at Gettysburg. Read the account of Sherman's March to the Sea on page 366 and write a short eulogy for those who fell in his path.
3. **ART ACTIVITY** Clara Barton was the founder of the American division of the International Red Cross. She began her career during the Civil War by advertising in newspapers and urging officials to make sure that soldiers received necessary medical supplies. Look up information on the Red Cross today. Create a poster that identifies current medical needs.
4. **COLLABORATIVE LEARNING** One way a nation can come to terms with a painful past is to create movies and novels based on the disruptive periods of its history, such as the Civil War. *Gone With the Wind*, a movie about the effects of the Civil War on the Southern way of life, has become a classic. During its production the public was fascinated by the two-year search for exactly the right actor to play each role in the movie. As a class, create a list of major Civil War characters to be cast in a documentary about the North and South during the war. Read through previous chapters to include people such as Harriet Beecher Stowe and Harriet Tubman who played important parts in the events leading up to the war. Cast the characters from among current actors, explaining why each actor fits the part chosen for him or her.
5. **COLLABORATIVE LEARNING** "Dixie," "Battle Hymn of the Republic," "Tenting Tonight," and "Tramp! Tramp! Tramp!" were some of the songs that became popular during the Civil War. In small groups, look up the background of these songs, and give a presentation to the class.

Chapter 13
Reconstruction

Houses, streets, railroads, even entire cities lay in ruins. The war was over. It was a time to rebuild. New laws would help to rebuild peoples' lives. New schools would bring education and increased opportunities to all.

1865 The rebuilding of Richmond, Virginia, symbolizes the country's desire to heal its war wounds and move forward.

1865	1869
Presidents	
1865-1869 A. Johnson	1869-1877 Grant

1865

Adults and children alike learned in newly established freedmen's schools.

FREEDMEN SCHOOL

Documents called family records helped black families reconstruct their past.

FAMILY RECORD

BEFORE THE WAR — AND — SINCE THE WAR.

1873

1877

1877

A Time for Reconciliation

THINKING FOCUS

What social, political, and economic challenges faced the South following the Civil War?

Key Terms

- sharecropping
- Reconstruction
- amnesty
- segregated

Today your father, a Confederate soldier, is coming home. The war is over. General Robert E. Lee has surrendered to General Ulysses S. Grant. You are relieved to know that your father is not among the thousands of men killed in the war. As you wait and watch, you wonder what your father will say when he sees your home and the empty fields. Before the war, your father was a cotton farmer —just like his father—but now all that remains is one cow and an apple tree.

Your mother's sister from Atlanta lives with you now. Her husband was killed in the war and her son was captured by the enemy. Her home was burned during Sherman's March, and she had nowhere else to go. She arrived without money or possessions.

Your own home was spared, but you've seen your crops destroyed. Northerners drove the livestock off your land. For months you have survived on what little you could grow in a small garden patch. Supper often meant squirrels or rabbits or rats. Once a neighbor shared some mule meat he had stolen.

The war is over. Your father, once a proud farmer and soldier, will return to find only destruction and an uncertain future.

The Southern Way of Life Is Destroyed

The South in 1865 faced extreme poverty. The Civil War crippled Southern agriculture, which was the foundation of its economy. Burned-out plantations, weed-filled fields, and plundered homes left many Southerners without shelter, crops, or money.

The widespread destruction of roads, bridges, farm buildings, and machinery meant that the process of rebuilding the South would be slow and difficult. Confederate money issued during the war was worthless. White planters were ruined financially. Farmers could not get credit to buy seeds and plant new crops. Without money, many Southerners resorted to

a barter system, or trading of one kind of goods for another.

The loss of human life would also affect the effort to rebuild the South. Nearly 290,000 men—over one-fifth of the adult male population in the South—died for the Confederate cause. Some 37,000 blacks, most of whom were from the South, died serving in the Union army.

Nearly four million freed blacks, called freedmen, fled the plantations in search of a better life. To attract workers back to the fields, many plantation owners offered freedmen land to farm in return for a portion of the crop. This practice was called **sharecropping**. ■

■ How did the widespread destruction of the South affect agriculture?

Lincoln Plans for Reconstruction

President Lincoln had led the nation through the Civil War, the nation's bloodiest conflict. He eagerly sought a plan to reunite the nation in a peaceful way. This plan to bring the 11 Confederate states back into the Union was called **Reconstruction.** The Reconstruction period lasted from 1865 to 1877. The whole process would raise enormous questions about the nation's political, economic, and social future.

Proclamation of Amnesty

During the war, Lincoln worried about the conditions under which the South would rejoin the Union. "I do not want to hurt the hair of a single man in the South if it can possibly be avoided," he said. He wanted to help the South rebuild its cities and homes. Richmond, Virginia, once the Confederate capital, now lay in ruins. See A Closer Look on pages 380–381 about efforts to rebuild this city.

In those Southern states policed by Union troops, Lincoln organized new state governments. Fair treatment of Southerners in occupied areas, he felt, would discourage the remaining Confederate states from resisting. He also hoped it would bring about a more comfortable peace when the war finally ended.

On December 8, 1863, Lincoln presented to Congress his Proclamation of Amnesty and Reconstruction. **Amnesty** meant that every Southerner who then took an oath of loyalty to the United States would be pardoned. Any Confederate state could form a new government and adopt a new constitution. Ten percent of those who had voted in the presidential election of 1860 simply had to take the oath of loyalty to the United States. While the proclamation prohibited slavery, it did nothing about civil rights for blacks. Their right to vote and to have rights in society were not ensured. Several states took advantage of the plan. By 1864, they had reorganized new civilian governments.

The Wade-Davis Bill

When the war ended, Lincoln's party, the Republicans, had two main branches: the Radicals and the Moderates. Radical Republicans thought that Lincoln's plan should be more forceful. They believed that the federal government should take an active role in protecting the rights of blacks and loyal whites in the South.

In July 1864, the Radicals in Congress passed their own plan, the

▼ *In this 1865 cartoon by Thomas Nast, a woman symbolizes the Union. She considers whether to pardon the Confederates as Robert E. Lee kneels before her.*

Wade-Davis bill. The bill required that the majority (instead of 10 percent) of a state's 1860 voters in each Southern state swear allegiance to the United States and take part in drafting a new constitution. Only then could that state could be readmitted to the Union. The bill demanded that Confederates swear past and present loyalty.

The Wade-Davis bill also required the new state constitutions to outlaw slavery and declare the Confederate debt unpayable. Confederate bonds and money thus became worthless.

Republican Moderates in Congress agreed with Lincoln's easier terms for Reconstruction. However, the bill gained support because it gave Congress a strong role in forming Reconstruction policy. Members of Congress were unwilling to let the President single-handedly determine the course of Reconstruction.

With the support of Moderates, Congress passed the Wade-Davis bill. Congress then adjourned, however, and Lincoln refused to sign the bill. This defeated the Wade-Davis bill and angered many congressmen. In January 1865, Lincoln compromised by proposing the Thirteenth Amendment to outlaw slavery. Former Confederate states were required to ratify, or formally approve, the amendment before rejoining the Union.

The struggles between Lincoln and Congress reflected different views, even among Republicans, about what Reconstruction should mean. Radical Republicans hoped to reshape the South in the image of the North and to weaken the plantation system. Moderates, on the other hand, wanted to establish the power of the federal government and equality before the law for blacks and whites. ■

Lincoln Assassinated

Lincoln's popularity and his skill at handling Congress might have allowed him to carry out his plans. But on April 14, 1865, an assassin's bullet would silence the strongest voice for generous treatment of the South.

That evening, the President and Mrs. Lincoln went to a play at Ford's Theatre in Washington. Shortly after ten o'clock, John Wilkes Booth, a fanatically pro-Southern actor, slipped undetected into the President's private box and shot him in the back of the head. Booth then jumped over the railing onto the stage, crying, *"Sic semper tyrannis"* ("Thus always to tyrants"). Booth escaped from the theater on

horseback. Later, federal troops cornered and killed the President's assassin in a Virginia barn.

President Lincoln was carried to a nearby house. Doctors could only wash his wounds and try to make him comfortable. Secretary of War Edwin Stanton arrived and sent an officer to notify the Vice President, Andrew Johnson.

When word spread, crowds of people gathered around the house. The people waited for hours, remaining even when rain began to fall. Lincoln never regained consciousness and died the next morning. "Now he belongs to the ages," Stanton said.

News of Lincoln's death, just six days after Lee's surrender, stunned the North. For two days his body lay in state in the Capitol where thousands of people filed past his coffin. Then a special train carried his body back to Illinois for burial. Seven million people lined the route, waiting for hours to pay their final respects.

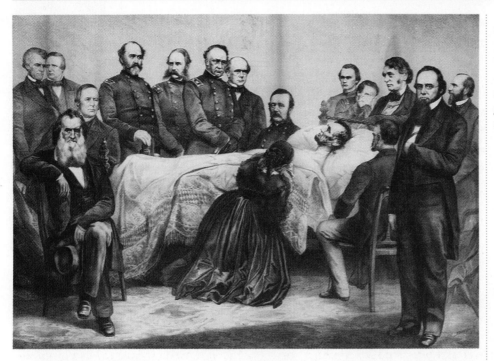

On his deathbed, President Lincoln was surrounded by leaders from his Cabinet and administration.

Johnson Takes the Reins

Hours after Lincoln's death, Chief Justice Salmon P. Chase went to Vice President Andrew Johnson's hotel to administer the oath of office. Johnson was a Southern Democrat who had remained loyal to the Union after his state, Tennessee, had seceded. He was well known for hating Southern aristocrats and wishing to punish those in the South who were guilty of treason. White Southerners naturally feared what Johnson's Reconstruction policy might bring.

Yet Johnson was once a slave owner. He strongly believed in states' rights. He did not believe the federal government had a right to control the society of the South, as long as its people accepted the abolition of slavery. However, Johnson came up short on political and diplomatic skills. He did not share Lincoln's ability to negotiate. Unfortunately, he found compromise impossible.

Johnson made public his plan for Reconstruction in May 1865. Its goal was to encourage the white South to renew its loyalty voluntarily. The plan disappointed the Radicals because it looked like Lincoln's 10 percent plan. Johnson set easy terms for the states to form new governments and send representatives to Congress. Johnson gave back voting rights to most whites, but he only encouraged new states to allow freedmen to vote.

Black Codes Keep Slavery Alive

The Southern states followed Johnson's policies, but not happily. None gave blacks the right to vote. Instead, the new state governments tried to bring back slavery in all but name. They used laws known as the Black Codes.

Enacted from 1865 to 1866, the Black Codes varied from state to state. But everywhere the laws were meant to keep blacks from being free. In Mississippi, black orphans or children whose parents could not raise them could be forced to work as apprentices, often for their former owners.

In Louisiana, freedmen had to sign yearly labor contracts that bound them to their place of work. South Carolina forbade blacks to hold any job except that of farmer or servant, unless they paid from $10 to $100 for a license. Plantation workers could only leave the grounds with permission from their "masters." ■

▲ President Andrew Johnson, a Southern Democrat from Tennessee, angered both white Southerners and Radical Republicans with his moderate Reconstruction policies.

■ How did the Black Codes keep freed blacks in virtual slavery?

The Rebuilding of Richmond

In the dead of the night, on April 2, 1865, Confederate soldiers, upon hearing that Union troops were approaching, torched their capital of Richmond, Virginia. As arsenals exploded, red-hot embers rained on the city. People stood on their rooftops, coughing from the black smoke, fanning away sparks to protect their homes.

Why torch your own capital? The Confederates wanted to prevent Northerners from taking valuable military supplies and equipment.

Hammering and chipping could be heard all over Richmond in the days that followed the fire. Chain gangs of convicts helped clear the rubble from streets and vacant lots. Rebuilding began as soon as the fire was under control.

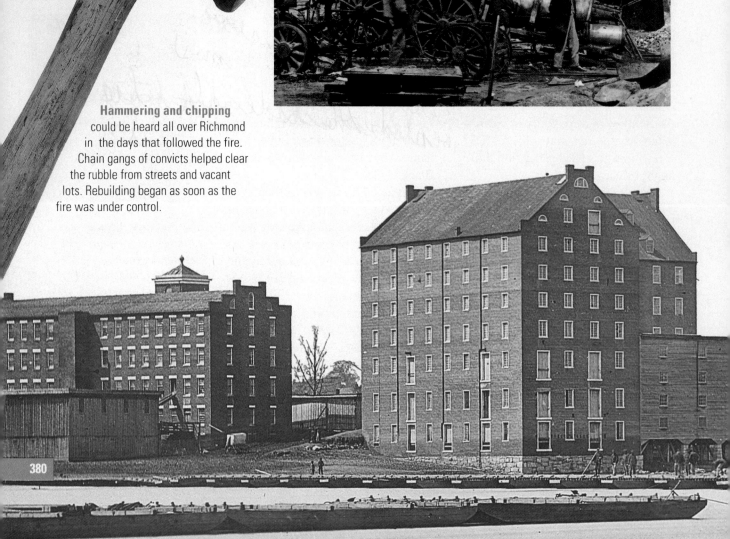

The Confederates left timed charges to explode after the Union soldiers arrived. Explosions around 2:00 A.M. shattered most of the city's mirrors and windows and killed more than a dozen people. Riots broke out. Union prisoners escaped, and panic-stricken dogs and thousands of squealing rats dashed through the streets.

Rebuilding transformed Main Street into a modern downtown area. This time around, builders used bricks and mortar instead of wood. The building boom provided many Richmonders with jobs, as new structures rose four or five stories high.

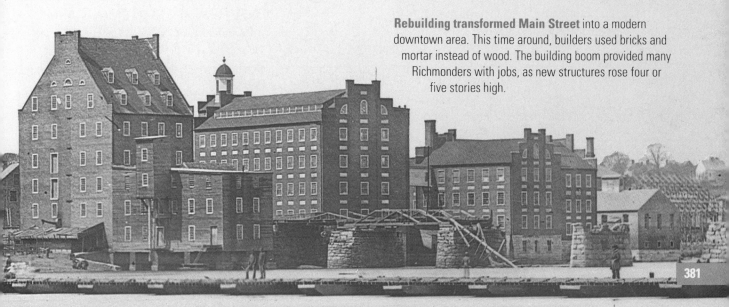

Freed People Struggle for Rights

Despite the Black Codes, former slaves rejoiced in their new freedom. Many had served in the Union army and were determined to have the rights they had fought to gain. Emancipation would not rid the opposition of Southern whites to ending slavery. But it did offer blacks the chance to travel, worship, and earn a living as their own masters. Under slavery, blacks were required to carry passes. Emancipation ended the pass system. Soon, freedmen were leaving plantations in search of better opportunities.

Cities and towns across the South experienced a great influx of blacks during and just after the Civil War. Between 1865 and 1870, the black population of the South's 10 largest cities doubled. Black institutions such as schools, churches, and social organizations were available to the newcomers. The Union Army's presence in cities also gave a measure of protection against the violence that blacks had suffered in the rural areas of the South.

Blacks were also now free to look for family members who had been sold to other masters. In 1865, a Northern reporter met a black man who had walked nearly 600 miles from Georgia to North Carolina to look for his wife and children. Some were not able to find missing relatives and faced crushing disappointment. Still others were able to reestablish the family ties that had been broken by the bonds of slavery. A Union officer wrote to his wife: "I wish you could see [these] people as they step from slavery into

▼ *In this engraving, black Americans in Washington, D.C., turn out to celebrate their freedom.*

Chapter 13

freedom. Men are taking their wives and children, families which had been for a long time broken up are reunited and oh! such happiness. I am glad I am here."

Freedmen's Bureau Provides Aid

Just before the war's end, Congress established the Freedmen's Bureau to give aid and support to newly freed blacks. For emergency relief, the Bureau distributed food to the needy of both races. Finding jobs for former slaves was one of the Bureau's first tasks. To help those returning to plantations, it drew up contracts that guaranteed rights and payment. In addition, the Bureau performed thousands of marriages for freed blacks. Unfortunately, Congress failed to set aside money for the Freedmen's Bureau. Its programs were often short-lived, lasting only a year or two.

Equality Through Education

Blacks set out to get better jobs and an education. They also sought the right to own property and the right to vote. Before the war ended, blacks had been kept by law from learning to read and write. They had long seen education as their ticket to indepen-

dence. Northern charitable and church groups and the Freedmen's Bureau helped in the effort to educate blacks. The American Missionary Association founded seven colleges, including Fisk and Atlanta universities, between 1866 and 1869. The Freedmen's Bureau helped to establish Howard University in 1867. The chief function of Howard is to train black students, but it is open to all students, regardless of race, sex, or color.

While advanced education was considered important, it was also necessary to provide very basic education to both freed blacks and poor whites. The Freedmen's Bureau set up more than 4,000 schools. Charlotte Forten, a free black woman from Philadelphia, taught in one of them. She wrote, "I never before saw children so eager to learn. . . . They come here as other children go to play. . . . Many of the grown people are [also] desirous of learning to read."

After 1868, state governments assumed responsibility for education and set up the first public school systems in the South. Though the schools were **segregated**, or separated by race, blacks and many poor whites were able to get an education.

◄ *Located in Washington, D.C., Howard University* (left) *is one of the largest chiefly black universities in the United States. It is supported by both federal and private funds. The university was named in honor of the Freedmen's Bureau's white administrator, General Oliver O. Howard* (above).

383

➤ *Guaranteeing civil rights for black Americans has proved difficult. Each of these amendments solved some problems, but it was over 100 years later, in the 1960s, that true equal rights were guaranteed by the United States government.*

Thirteenth Amendment

Date passed by Congress: 1865

Prohibited slavery in the United States

Fourteenth Amendment

Date passed by Congress: 1866

1) Defined national citizenship.

2) Permitted representation in Congress to be reduced if a state interfered with a citizen's right to vote.

3) Denied former Confederate officials the right to hold office.

4) Declared Confederate debts invalid.

Fifteenth Amendment

Date passed by Congress: 1869

Prohibited denial of the right to vote because of race or previous servitude.

Fourteenth Amendment Passes

After the Southern states reorganized under President Johnson's plan, they elected representatives to Congress. Northerners were outraged to find that many representatives had been former Confederate leaders. Congress refused to admit them. The stage was set for a battle between Congress and the President.

In December 1865, Congress set up a Joint Committee on Reconstruction to form its own program, which

■ *What led to the passing of an amendment to the Constitution, rather than a bill, to guarantee federal citizenship to black Americans?*

would grant full citizenship to blacks. The Republican Moderates were less interested in black rights. They cooperated with the Radicals only because they wanted to maintain a Republican majority in Congress.

In April 1866, Congress passed a bill that guaranteed federal citizenship to blacks. Johnson vetoed it, but Congress overrode him. However, fearing that the Supreme Court might overturn the law, the Republicans passed a Constitutional amendment. The Fourteenth Amendment forbade states to deny political rights to any citizen. It gave for the first time a definition of "citizen": anyone born or naturalized in the United States. The amendment also declared that no state shall deprive any person of the rights of life, liberty, or property, without due process of law.

The amendment did not directly give blacks the right to vote. It did provide a penalty for states that denied the right to vote to male citizens. The Fourteenth Amendment also excluded from federal or state office any high-ranking Confederate who had taken an oath of loyalty to the United States before the war.

In providing federal protection of individual and property rights, the Fourteenth Amendment is a cornerstone of American political freedom. Although it was at first intended to protect black rights in particular, the amendment has become a lasting and important legacy from the Reconstruction. ■

R E V I E W

1. **FOCUS** What social, political, and economic changes faced the South following the Civil War?

2. **CONNECT** What were the terms of surrender for the South after the Civil War? How did the surrender affect the South?

3. **BELIEF SYSTEMS** Why was it so difficult for white Southerners to accept the idea of free labor?

4. **CRITICAL THINKING** What caused President Johnson's unpopularity with both Southerners and Radical Republicans? How do you think he could have gained more support for his programs?

5. **CRITICAL THINKING** Why was education such an important goal of the Freedmen's Bureau? Why did they also aim to educate poor whites?

6. **ACTIVITY** Read the text of the Fourteenth Amendment on page 649. With several classmates, list situations in which citizens' rights would change if this amendment were no longer in place.

L E S S O N   2

Radical Reconstruction

"M r. Senator Ross, how say you? Is the respondent Andrew Johnson guilty or not guilty of a high misdemeanor as charged in this article?" asked the Chief Justice of the Supreme Court Salmon P. Chase. The setting was a trial to remove President Andrew Johnson from office. All eyes fastened on the Republican senator from Kansas, Edmund G. Ross. His vote would determine the outcome of Johnson's presidency.

Ross had refused to state his decision earlier during a preliminary poll. For this he was branded a traitor to the Republican cause. By the time of the actual vote in May 1868, not one person in the Senate chamber knew how the young senator from Kansas

would vote. He later remarked, "I almost literally looked down into my open grave. Friendships, position, fortune, everything that makes life desirable to an ambitious man were about to be swept away by the breath of my mouth, perhaps forever."

"Not guilty," he replied. The President was saved, and the conviction lost, by just one vote. But Johnson's effectiveness as President was over.

Reflecting on his role in the trial of the President, Ross later told his wife, "Millions of men cursing me today will bless me tomorrow for having saved the country from the greatest peril through which it has ever passed, though none but God can ever know the struggle it has cost me."

THINKING FOCUS

What were the effects of Radical Reconstruction on the South, and how did Southerners respond to the changes?

Key Terms

- martial law
- impeachment
- carpetbagger
- scalawag

◄ *This print shows Edmund G. Ross, fourth from the left, announcing his vote, at the impeachment trial of President Andrew Johnson.*

385

Congress Challenges Johnson

Across Time & Space

In 1974, the Judiciary Committee of the House of Representatives met to consider charges against President Richard M. Nixon. Nixon was accused of having misused his office and of obstructing justice by covering up the Watergate affair. A majority of the committee voted to recommend impeachment. Before the House could vote, Nixon resigned.

Before his trial, Johnson constantly opposed a congressional role in Reconstruction policy. This led to a long battle with the Radicals. The President urged former Confederate states to reject the Fourteenth Amendment. During the 1866 congressional campaign, Johnson asked voters to defeat the Radicals and to elect candidates who backed his Reconstruction plan. But Johnson's quick temper made him unpopular on the campaign trail. Race riots in New Orleans and Memphis convinced many in the North that Johnson's moderate policies had not worked. On election day, the Radicals won a huge victory.

Military Reconstruction Acts

The Radicals now had enough votes in both houses of Congress to override the President's vetoes and to take control of Reconstruction policy. They threw out Johnson's Reconstruction plan and put in one of their own—Radical Reconstruction.

In 1867, Congress passed a series of Military Reconstruction acts. These acts dissolved the governments of all the Confederate states except Tennessee, which had ratified the Fourteenth Amendment. The rest of the South was divided into five military districts. These states would be subject to **martial law**, or rule by the military.

Martial law would end only after the states met certain conditions set by Congress. The Southern states had to call constitutional conventions to set up state governments. These conventions had to ratify the Fourteenth Amendment and guarantee blacks the right to vote. Former Confederate officials and army officers—about one out of ten people in the South's population—were not allowed to vote, however.

Republican Party Sweeps the South

Federal military officials began to register voters in the South and helped to set up state conventions. Radical Republicans ruled these conventions

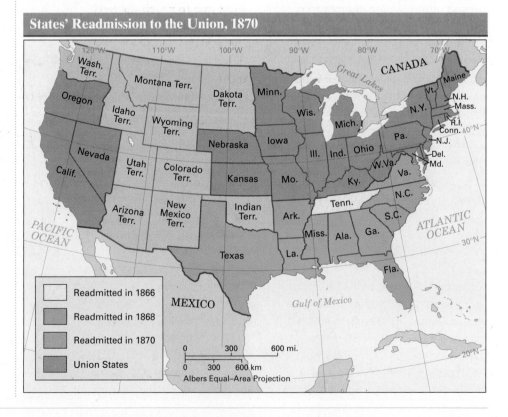

States' Readmission to the Union, 1870

➤ As this map shows, all Southern states were readmitted to the Union by 1870.

Legend:
- Readmitted in 1866
- Readmitted in 1868
- Readmitted in 1870
- Union States

0   300   600 mi.
0   300   600 km
Albers Equal-Area Projection

HARPER'S WEEKLY.

A JOURNAL OF CIVILIZATION

and blacks responded with enthusiasm. Nearly all eligible black voters registered. Of course, most gave their votes to the Republican Party. Political groups such as the Union League joined both freedmen and white unionists in a strong Republican voting force. A British visitor noted that the conventions reflected "the mighty revolution that had taken place in America."

Republicans swept into power, gaining control of all the governorships and state legislatures. The new state constitutions had to be approved by a majority of registered voters. Many white Southerners decided to stay away from the polls in protest. By refusing to vote, they hoped to defeat Reconstruction policies. ■

◄ *This November 16, 1867, cover of* Harper's Weekly *shows black men casting their votes for political representation.*

■ *How did Congress respond to Johnson's attempts to take control of Reconstruction policy?*

Johnson Stands Trial

President Johnson challenged the authority of Congress to decide and to enforce Reconstruction policy. He gave orders that limited the powers of military governors and supported officials who allowed disqualified Confederates to vote. He further angered Congress by trying to fire Secretary of War Edwin Stanton. He did so in direct opposition to the Tenure of Office Act. This bill took from the President the power to fire officials the Senate had approved.

Johnson's resistance to Congress caused great hostility. On February 24, 1868, the House of Representatives passed a resolution of **impeachment**. This formal charge of misconduct or wrongdoing was meant to remove Johnson from office.

Two other attempts to impeach Johnson had failed. The President was clearly in danger. Republicans were committed to granting blacks full political rights. Johnson's moderate policies, however, had restored the power of white Southerners who could not stand the idea of black rights.

Now, Johnson's presidency rested with the Senate, which served as a jury for his impeachment trial. All the elements of high courtroom drama were present, except Johnson himself, who did not attend the trial. Some one thousand tickets were sold to people who came to watch the trial.

With 54 members in the Senate, a two-thirds majority, (36 votes) was needed to convict Johnson. The 42 Republicans knew they could afford to lose only six votes if Johnson was to be removed from office. Six Republicans had already said that the facts presented were not enough to convict Johnson. Nineteen votes were needed to acquit Johnson. Then Senator Edmund G. Ross of Kansas cast his vote. He had refused to announce his verdict during the preliminary poll. Tension mounted. When Ross gave his vote of "Not guilty," Johnson's presidency was saved. ■

▼ *Like most political scandals, Johnson's impeachment created great curiosity. People came from all over the country to get a seat at the trial.*

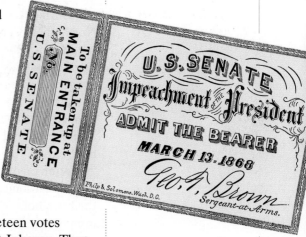

To be taken up at MAIN ENTRANCE

№ U.S. SENATE

U.S. SENATE

Impeachment of the President

ADMIT THE BEARER

MARCH 13 1868

Geo. T. Brown
Sergeant-at-Arms.

Philp & Solomons, Wash. D.C.

■ *How did President Johnson's resistance to Congressional authority lead to his impeachment?*

African Americans Enter Politics

■ *How do you think white Southerners regarded black officeholders?*

With the federal army protecting voters, nearly three hundred black delegates (elected or appointed officials in the House of Representatives) served in the constitutional conventions during the winter of 1867–1868. In Louisiana and South Carolina, they formed a majority of the delegates, and in Florida about 40 percent.

Blacks were able to elect many of their own candidates to office. They served as lieutenant governors, treasurers, secretaries of state, and superintendents of public education. In South Carolina, the cradle of the Confederacy, blacks gained the majority of legislative offices.

In many plantation counties, freedmen formed the majority of the population. They took control of local governments, helping to ensure the rights of rural blacks.

Blacks also won election to the U.S. Congress, with 16 serving in the House of Representatives, and two in the Senate. Hiram Revels, a college graduate, became the first black senator in 1870, when the Mississippi legislature named him to finish the term begun by Jefferson Davis before the Civil War. Blanche K. Bruce of Mississippi was the first black to serve a full term as senator. But white leaders still dominated the Republican Party in the South, and no black governors were elected to office. ■

Reshaping the South

During Reconstruction, many Northerners went to the South for political or financial opportunities. Southern whites called them **carpetbaggers** because of their carpetbags, or suitcases. The bags seemed deep enough to hold all the loot that would be stolen from the South. Southerners believed that the carpetbaggers came "to fatten on our misfortunes." And it is true that some Northerners used their positions in Reconstruction governments to their own advantage.

However, carpetbaggers included teachers, ministers, and officials of the Freedmen's Bureau. They and others went to the South to help gain full rights for blacks. Many had long fought against slavery. Now they sought to build a freer and more equal society in the South. For the most part, carpetbaggers probably combined the desire for personal gain with a commitment to modernizing the South. In short, they wanted to take part in the effort "to substitute the civilization of freedom for that of slavery."

Many other carpetbaggers were Union veterans who were drawn by economic opportunities in the South. Many bought cotton land or opened businesses in the cities. More than 60 won election to Congress, and nine served as governors.

Albion Tourgée, a carpetbagger from Ohio who settled in North Carolina, was dedicated to the antislavery cause. He published a novel after his return to the North in 1879. The novel's main character, Comfort Servosse, shared the early optimism of other Northerners. They felt that the South could be changed to be more like the North.

> *O*h, he replied, there must be great changes of course! Slavery has been broken up, and things must turn into new grooves; but I think the country will settle rapidly, now that slavery is out of the way. Manufactures will spring up, immigration will pour in, and it will be just the pleasantest part of the country.
>
> Albion Tourgée,
> *A Fool's Errand*

Southern white conservatives also used the term **scalawags** to describe native white Southerners who had opposed secession and who had cooperated with the Republicans. Most scalawags were poor whites who lived in small towns and on farms. They supported Reconstruction. Some gave their loyalty to the North for political favors. They also resented the plantation owners who had dominated the economy and politics of the South before the war. Scalawags looked to the new state governments to provide educational and job opportunities. Many of those who remained loyal to the Confederate cause thought of scalawags as traitors to the South.

A number of other scalawags, however, were powerful, well-educated whites. Some had been judges, Congressmen, and local officials before the war. Confederate veteran Charles Hays came from one of the wealthiest plantation families in Alabama. He joined the Republicans in 1867 and later served in Congress. Scalawags helped blacks get the vote. But their main interest was in the benefits they would get by guiding the South away from its past. ■

▲ *The cartoon* (above) *shows "The Solid South" carrying General Ulysses S. Grant in a giant carpetbag.*

■ *Why were some Southerners angry at carpetbaggers and scalawags?*

Rebuilding the South

White Southerners used charges of political corruption to discredit Republican policies. They insisted that corruption was caused by greedy carpetbaggers and by allowing blacks to hold office.

To be sure, corruption in many forms did exist. Some government officials got bribes from people who wanted contracts for public projects. Officials in charge of railroad building, for example, received stock in new railroad lines for their help. Money for schools and public services was also stolen. State budgets grew, and the demands placed on them increased as well. Officials were handling large amounts of money, corporations were competing for business, and communities were seeking prosperity. These

389

Reconstruction

► *This print shows a parade held in celebration of the Fifteenth Amendment, which gave blacks the right to vote.*

conditions encouraged a "get rich quick" spirit. Many officials saw nothing wrong with looking out for their own interests in the process.

In the postwar years, corruption was taking over in Northern as well as Southern state and local governments. Democrats and Republicans alike were deep in their plans to gain money through fraud.

Amendment Passed amid Turmoil

The Radicals knew the right of blacks to vote was important to keep Republicans in office in the South. To make sure blacks could vote, they pushed for passage of the Fifteenth Amendment.

In 1869, Congress approved the new amendment. It declared that neither the federal government nor any state could deny a citizen the right to vote "on account of race, color, or previous condition of servitude." The following year, the states ratified the amendment.

Many Southerners were horrified. Democrats argued that this new amendment made blacks a favored race. Yet some Radicals believed the Fifteenth Amendment had not gone far enough. It did not set up standard voting requirements for all states. Some states would later take advantage of this omission to restrict the voting rights of blacks and others on grounds other than race. ■

■ *Review the arguments for and against the Fifteenth Amendment. Why did Republicans think an amendment was necessary?*

REVIEW

1. **FOCUS** What were the effects of Radical Reconstruction on the South, and how did Southerners respond to the changes?

2. **CONNECT** How did the black freedmen experience change following the passage of the Fourteenth and Fifteenth Amendments?

3. **POLITICAL SYSTEMS** Explain how the Republicans' need for a strong party in the South led the Radicals to support voting rights for blacks.

4. **CRITICAL THINKING** What differences of opinion led to the bitter hostility between President Johnson and Republican members of Congress?

5. **CRITICAL THINKING** What was the purpose of martial law under the Military Reconstruction acts? Under what conditions would martial law be lifted?

6. **ACTIVITY** Imagine you are a carpetbagger who has just arrived in the postwar South. Write a diary entry that describes your expectations.

LESSON 3

Southern Life Under Reconstruction

Mary Virginia Montgomery was a slave for the first 14 years of her life, but after the war, the Montgomery family took on a different role at her home, Davis Bend. Mary Virginia's parents, Benjamin and Mary, had been slaves on a plantation of Joseph Davis, older brother of Confederate President Jefferson Davis and owner of Hurricane and Brierfield plantations just south of Vicksburg, Mississippi. After the war, the Montgomery family returned to Davis Bend from Cincinnati, Ohio, where they had lived during the war.

Benjamin Montgomery and his family established a community of black tenant farmers at Davis Bend. This extraordinary community was successful in raising cotton and food crops. On February 3, 1872, Mary noted in her diary, "The sun shines beautifully today. I am so proud of the prospect of a flower yard and the orchard improvement that I feel like one just embracing the threshold of a new life. I feel now the study of agriculture most necessary."

Freedmen at Davis Bend formed a self-governing colony with elected sheriffs and justices of the peace. As an all-black community, Davis Bend was an exceptional example of how much blacks could achieve when freed from slavery and prejudice.

Mary Virginia was a talented and well-educated woman who eventually taught school at Davis Bend. But white conservatives regained control of Mississippi. After floods, then droughts, the Montgomery family's fortunes declined. After Benjamin and Mary Montgomery died, the land went back to Jefferson Davis and the grandchildren of Joseph Davis.

THINKING
FOCUS

How did Reconstruction policies end in mixed results?

Key Terms

- redeem
- vigilante

◄ *Davis Bend, Mississippi, July 4, 1865. The Union Army had just freed these blacks. They stayed on to farm the land themselves.*

Forty Acres and a Mule

In January 1865, Secretary of War Stanton went to Savannah, Georgia, which was then in Union hands. Stanton met with leaders of the blacks who had followed General Sherman's army on its march through Georgia. Stanton asked the blacks how the government could support their families in freedom. "The way we can best take care of ourselves," they said, "is to have land, and . . . till it by our labor." Blacks dreamed that with "forty acres and a mule" they could become economically independent.

General Sherman responded by setting aside for blacks large areas of the land under his control. Every head of a family received 40 acres of land. Freed blacks quickly resettled on these lands and by mid-1865, forty thousand freed people were living in new locations. One former slaveowner visited his old plantation in Beaufort, South Carolina, and received friendly and polite treatment. But his former slaves "firmly and respectfully" told him that "we own this land now. Put it out of your head that it will ever be yours again."

Later, Congress gave the Freedmen's Bureau control of "abandoned" land in the South. The Bureau was to rent this land to freedmen for a period of three years. After that time, they could buy it.

Congress did not actually hold legal title to much of this land. Therefore, when President Johnson restored the legal rights of white Southerners, they reoccupied their land, which meant blacks lost what little property they had gained.

Truly "abandoned" land was likely to be too dry, underwater, or hard to get to. The Freedmen's Bureau gave blacks seeds to plant for crops. But in most cases black farmers were not able to survive on such small farms. Davis Bend, while it lasted, was an exception. But even that farm failed and eventually went back to the original white owners.

Black Codes Backlash

Cotton plantations had depended entirely on slave labor. Plantation owners therefore tried to take away other chances for employment for blacks. The Black Codes were passed in an effort to make African Americans accept the same conditions under which they had labored before the war. People who were now supposed to be free were made to carry passes, keep to a curfew, live in housing supplied by landowners, and give up the right to live on an equal basis with whites.

In fact, white Southerners agreed to do away with slavery only in order to get back into the Union. But they

Sharecropping changed the pattern and rhythm of life for many freed black families. This plow and the pitchfork on the facing page are typical farm tools of the time.

also wanted to keep a forced labor system. They fought long and hard to keep blacks from gaining any new freedoms. Reconstruction policy was fighting against the same social, political, and economic forces that had led the South into war. No amount of political idealism from the North would convince white Southerners that freeing blacks would ever work to their advantage.

Sharecropping

Some plantation owners paid their black workers a small wage. But the new plantation system that took shape in the South was the practice known as sharecropping. The white landowner broke up his estate into small units and set up a freed black family on each unit. In addition to the land, the black family was sometimes provided with housing, seeds, tools, and animals. The sharecroppers (black families) could keep part of what they grew as their pay. This share ranged between one-tenth and one-half of the crop.

Landowners would have liked to use the wage system, but blacks refused. They liked the independence of share cropping. It made them the masters of their own time and gave them an interest in their work.

However, when drought or other natural causes cut down on the year's harvest, a sharecropper's share was too small to feed a family. Businessmen got rich by giving credit to sharecroppers in return for part of next year's crop. Many sharecroppers found they could not get out of debt. Despite its financial drawbacks, this new labor system offered blacks an escape from constant supervision by whites.

Poorer whites—including some of the Confederate soldiers—sometimes became sharecroppers too. But whites, unlike blacks, could find many other ways to earn a living. ■

The poverty of these sharecroppers is clear in this photograph from about 1880.

■ *Why did many blacks become sharecroppers?*

The Reaction of White Southerners

Though Southerners had lost the war, they refused to accept the position of a conquered people. They bitterly resisted the efforts of the North to change the political and social life of their region.

Fighting Back with States' Rights

White Southerners who had resisted surrender to the North gradually regained the right to vote. Some took the oaths of loyalty; others reached voting age in the years after the war. They began to exercise their political power by electing Democratic majorities to state legislatures.

Democrats in the South had a strong message: they promised to **redeem,** or recover, the region and restore "Home Rule." Redeemers revived the argument that the states had the right to resist or ignore federal laws. Democrats claimed that the states were not "morally bound" by postwar constitutional amendments.

As Redeemers took control of politics, they passed laws to make sure they would remain in power. They targeted black voters, who were almost exclusively Republican. Although it was illegal to bar voters because of race, they found other kinds of restrictions that served equally well.

In the early 1870s, Tennessee and Georgia adopted the poll tax—a tax that a citizen had to pay in order to vote. Many blacks (and poor whites) could not afford to pay the poll tax, and thus they were denied the right to vote. Other states gerrymandered, or rearranged, voting districts to reduce the political power of blacks.

Outside the Law: Secret Societies

Some Southerners resorted to violence. Secret societies such as the Knights of the White Camelia, the White Brotherhood, and the Ku Klux Klan spread fear throughout the South. The Klan, or KKK, begun in 1866, claimed to be an organization of "chivalry, humanity, mercy, and patriotism." But it was clearly designed to maintain white supremacy in the Southern states. By 1870, KKK groups had formed in every Southern state. The white robes and hoods they wore were meant to frighten blacks into thinking they were ghosts of Confederate soldiers. The hoods also hid the faces of the Klansmen during raids.

The Klan launched a reign of terror against Republican office-holders, both black and white. Klan mobs killed an Arkansas congressman and three members of the South Carolina legislature. Black Republican leaders were dragged from their homes, beaten, whipped, even lynched. The KKK burned black schools and churches, terrorizing or killing white and black teachers. A black teacher's library was burned. The Klan threatened to strike out against any black person who tried to obtain books.

Blacks faced Klan violence simply because they were prosperous. Freedmen saw the rewards of their hard work destroyed before their eyes.

As Southern white resistance to Reconstruction grew, the KKK—begun as a Confederate veterans organization—became a **vigilante** group. It took the law into its own hands. Upper-class Southern whites rarely opposed the Klan's activities. Either they were afraid or they supported the Klan's lawless efforts to interfere with Reconstruction. Republican state officials declared that Klan violence was a local matter. They avoided dealing directly with the vigilante groups. ■

Across Time & Space

In 1871, Congress passed the Ku Klux Klan Act, making it a crime to use force, threat, or intimidation to deny citizens their rights. In later years, the Klan attacked Jews and Catholics as well as blacks. Today, organizations such as the National Association for the Advancement of Colored People (NAACP) and the Anti-Defamation League (ADL) fight the Klan.

➤ *White hoods like this have come to symbolize the terror tactics of the KKK.*

■ *How did Southern whites seek to counter the effects of the Fifteenth Amendment?*

The End of Reconstruction

The South's refusal to accept Reconstruction finally wore down the North. Southern intimidation of blacks weakened the voting strength of the Republicans. The North was unwilling to send enough federal troops to enforce the rights of black voters. With the deaths of Congressmen Thaddeus Stevens and Charles Sumner, the cause of black rights lost two of its most powerful supporters.

Many Northerners, sick of the long, drawn-out struggle, wanted national harmony in order to promote economic growth. One businessman expressed the feeling: "What the South needs now is capital to develop her resources. . . . We have tried this long enough. Now let the South alone."

In the 1876 presidential election, Republican Rutherford B. Hayes ran against the Democrat Samuel J. Tilden. Tilden won more popular votes than Hayes but was one electoral vote short of a majority. Disputed election returns in three Southern states—Florida, South Carolina, and Louisiana—held the key to victory.

Congress named a special electoral commission to decide which claims were valid. Democrats and Republicans had an equal number of seats on the commission. In order to win the election, Hayes had to receive all the disputed electoral votes.

As inauguration day drew near, the commission members struck a bargain. The Democrats agreed to give the disputed votes to the Republican Hayes in return for the Republicans' promise to remove all federal troops from the South.

This so-called Compromise of 1877 left blacks with no federal protection. A former South Carolina governor exclaimed: "[The agreement] consists in the abandonment of the Southern Republicans, and especially the colored race." The bargain to elect Hayes in return for the withdrawal of federal troops assured the victory of Home Rule in the South. Reconstruction was over. ■

■ *How and why did Reconstruction end?*

▼ *Reconstruction absorbed much of the nation's attention for nearly twelve years.*

Reconstruction, 1865–1877

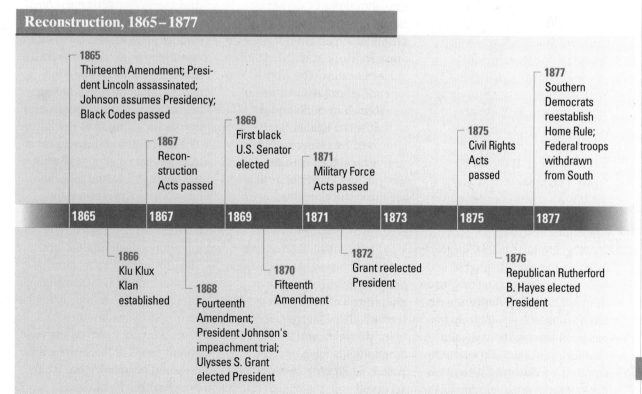

1865
Thirteenth Amendment; President Lincoln assassinated; Johnson assumes Presidency; Black Codes passed

1867
Reconstruction Acts passed

1869
First black U.S. Senator elected

1871
Military Force Acts passed

1875
Civil Rights Acts passed

1877
Southern Democrats reestablish Home Rule; Federal troops withdrawn from South

| 1865 | 1867 | 1869 | 1871 | 1873 | 1875 | 1877 |

1866
Klu Klux Klan established

1868
Fourteenth Amendment; President Johnson's impeachment trial; Ulysses S. Grant elected President

1870
Fifteenth Amendment

1872
Grant reelected President

1876
Republican Rutherford B. Hayes elected President

Reconstruction

That the Civil War occurred at all has been called the greatest failure of the Constitution. Despite checks and balances between federal and states' rights, and between majority rule and minority rights, the Constitution was unable to prevent the attempt at secession from the Union.

Yet the Constitution, its strength and its flexibility, played an important role in the preservation of the Union and in the reconstruction following the war. Together, the Thirteenth, Fourteenth, and Fifteenth Amendments redefined the protective powers of the federal government toward the individual citizen.

Rights of Individuals

During the writing of the Constitution, the protection of the rights of the individual from the potential tyranny of a centralized government provoked much discussion. With the passing of these three amendments, the government became the guardian of individual rights, rather than a threat to them. Basic civil rights were guaranteed under the law for everyone, no matter what their race, color, or past conditions of slavery.

The United States Constitution is the world's longest such surviving written constitution. No other nation has a written document to guide it that has been used without suspension for more than 200 years. A key to the Constitution's success is its capacity for amendment.

The Process of Change

During the writing of the Constitution, careful thought was given to the process of amendment. A major problem with the Articles of Confederation was that it required the approval of every state legislature before any alterations could be made. Thus James Madison suggested to the Constitutional convention a process of amending that could be initiated by a two-thirds majority of Congress. An amendment must then be ratified by a three-fourths majority of the states. Once ratified, the amendment is law and cannot be overturned by any branch of government. It can only be replaced or revoked by another amendment.

The importance of Article V defining the amendment process became immediately evident during the period of ratification of the Constitution. Initial opposition to the Constitution stemmed from its lack of any specific guarantee of individual liberties. The first 10 amendments to the Constitution, which became known as the Bill of Rights, were approved by Congress only a year after the Constitution itself was ratified. North Carolina accepted the Constitution only after the Bill of Rights was proposed by Congress, in 1789.

The somewhat laborious process of amendment ensures that the Constitution is not altered too easily to meet short-term or ill-considered interests. Over the years, more than 2,000 amendments have been proposed, while only 26 have been accepted and put into effect.

Change Without Amendment

The Constitution is not a rigid document. Because of imprecise language in some sections, it is open to interpretation. Most historians feel that this is more of a strength than a weakness. A level of interpretation is ensured, while another level can be reinterpreted by successive generations. One observer noted that there are two official ways to change the Constitution and two unofficial ways.

The two official ways are by the two-thirds and three-fourths process of amendment discussed above, or by a Constitutional Convention called for by two-thirds of the state legislatures. The second method has never been used.

By unofficial methods is meant, first, the Supreme Court's interpretation of the Constitution, which differs sometimes from court to court, depending on the views of new justices. The second unofficial method is by disregard on the part of the public. The Eighteenth Amendment, which introduced nation wide prohibition, is an example of the failure of a Constitutional amendment to effect social change. Because the amendment and legislation based on it was ignored by many people, Congress finally gave in and repealed it by passing another amendment, the Twenty-first, 14 years later.

Because of the Constitution's ability to change, it can be expected to last another 200 years. Having survived the turbulent times of Reconstruction, it should be able to face whatever changes lie ahead.

Legacies of Reconstruction

The Reconstruction period brought great changes in the nation. With the defeat of the Confederacy, slavery vanished forever. The federal government had established its authority. The Fourteenth and Fifteenth Amendments set a constitutional basis for many civil and political rights. In the South, many black citizens received education and some measure of economic and social rights.

Yet enormous challenges remained for blacks in taking on citizenship. When federal troops pulled out from the South, blacks lost much of their freedom. White legislatures passed laws that replaced slavery with segregation, a legally enforced separation of the races. Republicans had supported black voting rights to strengthen the Republican party. After Reconstruction, the South would remain solidly Democratic for nearly a century.

To escape poverty and racism, Southern blacks began moving elsewhere. Some went west, homesteading on the new frontier. In the early 1900s, thousands of blacks migrated to Northern cities such as Chicago and New York. There too they faced prejudice, but many found new opportunities in urban areas.

FROM THE PLANTATION TO THE SENATE.

◄ *The political opportunities for blacks, even those who had not been slaves, rose and fell during Reconstruction. This poster celebrates the height of black participation in the government of the Reconstruction Era.*

The ideals behind Radical Reconstruction—such as the attempt to enforce black suffrage—would not die. Amendments passed during Reconstruction would be used to attack other forms of injustice. The civil rights movement of the 1950s and 1960s, sometimes called the Second Reconstruction, continued the work that Reconstruction had begun. ■

■ *Would you say that Reconstruction was a failure or a success? Explain your answer.*

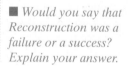

REVIEW

1. **FOCUS** How did Reconstruction policies end in mixed results?

2. **CONNECT** How did the new black freedom contribute to the dissatisfaction with sharecropping and the desire for "forty acres and a mule"?

3. **CITIZENSHIP** What was meant by Home Rule, and why did Southern Democrats promise to redeem the South?

4. **CULTURE** Who were the earliest members of the Ku Klux Klan, and what was the basis of their support? What tactics did they use to terrorize and intimidate their victims?

5. **CRITICAL THINKING** Attempts at enforcing Reconstruction ended in 1876 after the election of Rutherford B. Hayes. How might history have been different if Democrats had not reestablished Home Rule and if Republican governments had remained in the South after the election?

6. **ACTIVITY** Prepare and give a five-minute presentation on the goals and accomplishments of the Reconstruction Era. Conclude your presentation with mention of the work that was left to be done to ensure the rights of black Americans.

Analyzing the Civil War

Here's Why

Everything happened at once. The dog grabbed at your lunch, your mother called out "You'll miss your bus," while your sister picked up a pile of books and ran on ahead. When you got to class you discovered that you had left your report at home. What was the cause and what was the effect?

In this case, the dog, your sister, and running for the bus were all contributing causes. A lower grade on your report predictably is an immediate, or short-term effect. A lower semester grade is a possible long-term effect.

Knowing how to sort out multiple causes and effects, main causes and contributing causes, and short-term and long-term effects helps you understand why things happened as they did. This skill can be applied to forgotten school reports. The skills can also be applied to understanding the Civil War and the Reconstruction period following the war.

Here's How

You already know that if two events are related and if one happens before the other, the first may be the cause of the second. The diagram below shows that sometimes events result in a chain reaction. What was the effect of the first event becomes the cause of a second event, and so on.

The diagram below analyzes the effects of Lincoln's assassination on the post-war South. Lincoln's freeing the slaves was only one factor among the many complex events that led to his death. It could thus be called a contributing cause. The main cause of course was a bullet fired by John Wilkes Booth.

The diagram shows that Lincoln's death was in turn the cause of Andrew Johnson's succession as President. You will notice that the diagram labels this as a short-term effect because the change in presidency happened immediately after Lincoln's death. Johnson's moderate reconstruction plan resulted in the passage by Southern legislatures of the Black Codes. So the black Codes might be termed long-term effects of Lincoln's death.

Now look at the diagram on the next page. It analyzes the multiple causes--both main causes and contributing causes-- of the Civil War. It also shows the multiple effects of the war. The firing on Fort Sumter is frequently given as the immediate cause of the war. But as you know from your reading of Chapter 13, Fort Sumter was not an isolated event. What would you consider to be the main cause? Or do you think one cause can be singled out as the main cause of the Civil War?

The immediate effect of the war was that about 638,000 northern and southern soldiers were killed. But certainly the main effect was the preservation of the Union. Are there any effects of the Civil War, short-term or long-term, that you think should be added to the diagram?

Try It

Re-read the section on "Freed People Struggle for Rights" on pages 382-383. Using emancipation as your theme, see how long a cause-and-effect chain reaction you can create.

Now create a multiple

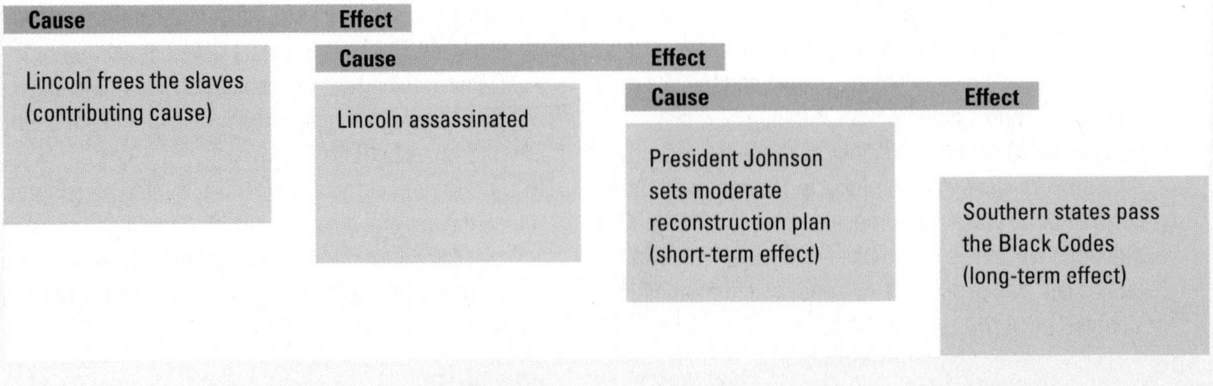

Cause	Effect
Lincoln frees the slaves (contributing cause)	

Cause	Effect
Lincoln assassinated	

Cause	Effect
President Johnson sets moderate reconstruction plan (short-term effect)	

Cause	Effect
	Southern states pass the Black Codes (long-term effect)

cause-and-effect diagram placing the passing of the Fourteenth Amendment at the center of your diagram. Which of the causes would you label as main causes and which contributing causes? Which effects would you label immediate and which long-term?

Apply It

Think of a recent event, such as an earthquake, a military conflict, or a change of government. Write down the event as the center of a multiple cause-and-effect diagram. Then complete the diagram, labeling the main cause, contributing causes, immediate or short-term effects, and long-term effects.

Multiple Causes

Antislavery sentiments build in the North

North and South develop differing economic policies

New states admitted to the Union

Civil War

Confederacy forms and secedes from the Union

Fort Sumter fired upon (immediate cause)

Multiple Effects

Slaves freed

Southern economy crippled

Reconstruction programs established

638,000 killed (immediate effect)

Union preserved (main effect)

The Lincoln Poems

Walt Whitman

Walt Whitman (1819-1892) published several editions of Leaves of Grass, *the collection of poems from which these selections are taken. During the Civil War, Whitman assisted in military hospitals and wrote poetry about his experiences of aiding wounded soldiers. After Lincoln's assassination, Whitman wrote several poems about his beloved President. As you read these poems, think about the three different ways Whitman portrayed Lincoln.*

O Captain! My Captain!

O Captain! my Captain! our fearful trip is done,
The ship has weather'd every rack, the prize we sought is won,
The port is near, the bells I hear, the people all exulting,
While follow eyes the steady keel, the vessel grim and daring;
But O heart! heart! heart!
O the bleeding drops of red,
Where on the deck my Captain lies,
Fallen cold and dead.

O Captain! my Captain! rise up and hear the bells;
Rise—for you the flag is flung—for you the bugle trills,
For you bouquets and ribbon'd wreaths—for you the shores a-crowding,
For you they call, the swaying mass, their eager faces turning;
Hear Captain! dear father!
This arm beneath your head!
It is some dream that on the deck,
You've fallen cold and dead.

My Captain does not answer, his lips are pale and still,
My father does not feel my arm, he has no pulse nor will,
The ship is anchor'd safe and sound, its voyage closed and done,
From fearful trip the victor ship comes in with object won;
Exult O shores, and ring O bells!
But I with mournful tread,
Walk the deck my Captain lies,
Fallen cold and dead.

In Lesson 1, you read about how President Lincoln was assassinated just days after the end of the Civil War. His death was devastating, because the nation had counted on him to guide it into peace.

rack storm condition
exulting celebrating
keel central structure of a ship
vessel boat

Hush'd Be the Camps To-day
(May 4, 1865)

Hush'd be the camps to-day,
And soldiers let us drape our war-worn weapons,
And each with musing soul retire to celebrate,
Our dear commander's death.

No more for him life's stormy conflicts,
Nor victory, nor defeat—no more time's dark events,
Charging like ceaseless clouds across the sky.

But sing poet in our name,
Sing of the love we bore him—because you, dweller in camps, know it
    truly.

As they invault the coffin there,
Sing—as they close the doors of earth upon him—one verse,
For the heavy hearts of soldiers.

musing deep in thought

ceaseless without stop

invault bury

This Dust Was Once the Man

This dust was once the man,
Gentle, plain, just and resolute, under whose cautious hand,
Against the foulest crime in history known in any land or age,
Was saved the Union of these States.

resolute determined

Further Reading

Abraham Lincoln: The Prairie Years and the War Years. Carl Sandburg. This is one volume of Sandburg's classic six-volume study of Lincoln.

Abraham Lincoln and the First Shot. R. N. Current. This book recounts Lincoln's years at the beginning of the Civil War.

It Was a Glorious Day!

Charlotte Forten

*In Lesson 1 you read
about Charlotte Forten's
involvement with the
Freedmen's Bureau's
efforts to provide a basic
education to freed black
slaves and poor whites.*

*Union ships captured Port Royal Harbor on the South Carolina
coast late in 1861. The local slaveowners escaped, leaving behind their many
slaves, who were now free. The U.S. government decided to send teachers south
to educate these freedmen. The next spring 53 teachers arrived from the North,
set themselves up on the plantations, and started to teach the former slaves how
to read and write.*

*In the fall of 1862, young Charlotte Forten (1837-1914) from
Philadelphia, the first black teacher, arrived just as the army had begun to raise
an all-black regiment from the young freedmen. Forten was invited to the army
camp to watch the celebration of Emancipation Day, January 1, 1863. She
recorded the events in her diary. What seems to have impressed her the most?*

New Year's Day, Emancipation Day, was a glorious one to
us. General Saxton and Colonel Higginson had invited
us to visit the camp of the First Regiment of South Carolina Volunteers on that day, "the greatest day in the nation's history." We
enjoyed perfectly the exciting scene on board the steamboat *Flora*. There
was an eager, wondering crowd of the freed people, in their holiday
attire, with the gayest of headkerchiefs, the whitest of aprons, and the
happiest of faces. The band was playing, the flags were streaming, and
everybody was talking merrily and feeling happy. The sun shone bright-
ly, and the very waves seemed to partake of the universal gayety, for
they danced and sparkled more joyously than ever before. Long before
we reached Camp Saxton, we could see the beautiful grove and the ruins
of the old fort near it.

grove small wooded
area

Some companies of the First Regiment were drawn up in line under
the trees near the landing, ready to receive us. They were a fine, soldier-
ly looking set of men, and their brilliant dress made a splendid appearance among the trees. It was my good fortune to find an old friend
among the officers. He took us over the camp and showed us all the
arrangements. Everything looked clean and comfortable; much neater,
we were told, than in most of the white camps. . . .

The ceremony in honor of Emancipation took place in the beautiful
grove of live-oaks adjoining the camp. I wish it were possible to describe
fitly the scene which met our eyes, as we sat upon the stand, and looked
down on the crowd before us. There were the black soldiers in their blue
coats and scarlet pantaloons; the officers of the First Regiment, and of
other regiments, in their handsome uniforms; and there were crowds of
lookers-on, men, women, and children, of every complexion, grouped in
various attitudes, under the moss-hung trees. The faces of all wore a

pantaloons pants

complexion   skin tone

happy, interested look.

The exercises commenced with a prayer by the chaplain of the regiment. An ode, written for the occasion, was then read and sung. President Lincoln's Proclamation of Emancipation was then read, and enthusiastically cheered. The Rev. Mr. French presented Colonel Higginson with two very elegant flags, a gift to the First Regiment, from the Church of the Puritans, in New York. He accompanied them by an appropriate and enthusiastic speech. As Colonel Higginson took the flags, before he had time to reply to the speech, some of the colored people, of their own accord, began to sing,—

> "My country, 'tis of thee,
> Sweet land of liberty,
> Of thee we sing!"

It was a touching and beautiful incident, and sent a thrill through all our hearts. The Colonel was deeply moved by it. He said that reply was far more effective than any speech he could make. But he did make one of those stirring speeches which are "half battles." All hearts swelled with emotion as we listened to his glorious words, "stirring the soul like the sound of trumpet." His soldiers are warmly attached to him, and he evidently feels toward them all as if they were his children.

General Saxton spoke also, and was received with great enthusiasm. Throughout the morning, repeated cheers were given for him by the regiment, and joined in heartily by all the people. They knew him to be one of the best and noblest men in the world. His unfailing kindness and consideration for them, so different from the treatment they have sometimes received at the hands of United States officers, have caused them to have unbounded confidence in him.

At the close of Colonel Higginson's speech, he presented the flags to the color bearers, Sergeant Rivers and Sergeant Sutton, with an earnest charge, to which they made appropriate replies.

Mrs. Gage uttered some earnest words, and then the regiment sang John Brown's Hallelujah Song.

After the meeting was over, we saw the dress-parade, which was a brilliant and beautiful sight. An officer told us that the men went through the drill remarkably well, and learned the movements with wonderful ease and rapidity. To us it seemed strange as a miracle to see this regiment of blacks, the first mustered into the service of the United States, thus doing itself honor in the sight of officers of other regiments, many of whom doubtless came to scoff. The men afterward had a great feast, ten oxen having been roasted whole, for their especial benefit.

chaplain a clergyman

scoff mock

Further Reading

Journal. Charlotte Forten. The author describes more of her experiences in the Civil War era in this book of diary entries.

Lincoln: A Photobiography. Russell Friedman. A detailed account of the Emancipation Proclamation is put into perspective with a series of excellent pictures.

Chapter Review

Reviewing Key Terms

amnesty (p. 377) redeem (p. 394)
carpetbagger (p. 388) scalawag (p. 389)
impeachment (p. 387) segregated (p. 383)
martial law (p. 386) sharecropping (p. 376)
Reconstruction (p. 377) vigilante (p. 394)

A. The sentences below have been started for you. Complete each sentence so that the meaning of the key term is clear.

1. During Reconstruction, the United States tried to . . .
2. A vigilante . . .
3. President Johnson was the first United States president to face impeachment because . . .
4. Carpetbaggers moved into the South to . . .
5. Martial law was used to . . .
6. A scalawag . . .

B. Based on what you have read in the chapter, decide whether each of the following statements is accurate. Write an explanation of each decision.

1. A sharecropper generously offered to share his harvest with those who were in need of food.
2. The federal government's Reconstruction policies created bitter feelings among Southerners.
3. The Freedmen's Bureau asked for a martial law to legalize the marriages of slaves.
4. The impeachment process gave the South a new crop that gradually replaced cotton.
5. The vigilantes to a state convention voted to set up a new state constitution.
6. Wealthy landowners sometimes rented out their farmland to carpetbaggers.
7. A vigilante reported violations of laws to the local sheriff or police chief.

Exploring Concepts

A. On a separate sheet of paper, make a chart like the one shown below. In the second column, list the requirements for re-admission of states to the Union. In the third column, list the provisions for black citizens' rights.

B. Answer each of the following questions in one or two complete sentences.

1. What were the principal purposes of the Thirteenth Amendment?
2. Why were the Black Codes issued?

3. How did free blacks show that they were ready to take their place as full citizens of the United States?
4. What were the principal provisions of the Fourteenth Amendment?
5. Why did Congress try to force President Johnson from office?
6. What were the main reasons for the passage of the Fifteenth Amendment?
7. Why were free blacks generally unsuccessful in setting up their own farms?

Reconstruction Plans	Requirements for Re-admission of States	Provisions for Black Citizens' Rights
President Lincoln's Plan		
Wade-Davis Bill		
President Johnson's Plan		
Radical Reconstruction		

Reviewing Skills

1. Identify the different kinds of causes and effects, and explain how they are related.
2. How do you determine the difference between a contributing cause and a main cause?
3. If President Lincoln had not signed the Emancipation Proclamation, would that have made a significant change in the causes and effects of the Civil War? Explain.
4. Following the chart on page 399, create a cause-and-effect diagram for Reconstruction. Note the political, social, and economic causes and effects of Reconstruction.
5. Read the words of Albion Tourgee on page 389. Determine the point of view in the selection, and write a short paragraph outlining your findings.
6. Suppose you wanted to determine the causes and effects of the American Revolution. What information would you need? What process would you follow?

Using Critical Thinking

1. Historians have said that when John Wilkes Booth assassinated Lincoln, he killed the South's most powerful friend. In what ways might Reconstruction have been different if Lincoln had lived? Why?
2. Just as it followed the American Civil War, a period of reconstruction for the defeated side follows every war. What should the goal of reconstruction be? Why might the victors want to follow a policy of revenge and punishment, as many Northerners did after the Civil War?
3. A Mississippi law written after the Civil War stated that "The negro is free, whether we like it or not. . . . To be free, however, does not make him a citizen or entitle him to social or political equality with the white man." Based on the wording of that law, what hardships do you think the newly freed blacks faced?
4. Frederick Douglass wrote that after the Civil War, African Americans were "free from the individual master but a slave to society." What did he mean by that statement? Do you agree or disagree with his conclusion? Explain your answer.

Preparing for Citizenship

1. WRITING ACTIVITY Imagine that you are a Northerner in 1866, and that the local newspaper has asked for a "man on the street" reaction to the following question: What should we (the Union) do with Robert E. Lee and other high-ranking Confederate soldiers? Write your response, making sure you cite specific reasons for your answer.
2. WRITING ACTIVITY Abraham Lincoln was a much-loved President. His death has been the subject of many books, paintings and poems. Read the Lincoln poems in this chapter and look up the following poems: *Abraham Lincoln Walks at Midnight* by Vachel Lindsay and *Lincoln, the Man of the People* by Edwin Markham. Write a short essay comparing how these poets present Lincoln.
3. COLLECTING INFORMATION In President John F. Kennedy's book *Profiles in Courage*, he described the courage of Senator Edmund G. Ross in voting not to impeach President Johnson. Find the book in your library and read the section on Ross. Write a short report on Ross's reasons for voting as he did.
4. ART ACTIVITY There have been a number of nations that have had to deal with the after-effects of a civil war. Look up recent accounts of such situations, and prepare a bulletin board display on the process of Reconstruction. Use pictures, maps, newspaper articles, and songs to provide a visual overview of the recovery process for such a nation.
5. COLLABORATIVE LEARNING During Reconstruction, people with different goals argued over how to heal the nation's wounds. As a class, choose Reconstruction roles. For example, you may be a defeated Confederate soldier, a member of the Radical Republicans, an ex-slave, a carpetbagger, a scalawag, or a worker in the Freedmen's Bureau. Prepare a speech that describes how you view your role in the process of Reconstruction and that provides your opinion on how Reconstruction ought to proceed.

A Time of Transformation

The changes that swept the United States in the decades following the Civil War were nothing short of revolutionary. Factories and cities experienced booming growth, immigrants poured in from Europe in record numbers, and technological advances in transportation and communication transformed the way Americans lived. The opening of the Brooklyn Bridge in 1883 symbolized America's movement from a rural agricultural nation to an urban, industrial power.

1850

Currier and Ives lithograph (detail). The Grand Opening of the Brooklyn Bridge on May 24, 1883. The Metropolitan Museum of Art, Bequest of Edward W. C. Arnold, 1954.

1920

Chapter 14

Reshaping the Great Plains

Between 1848 and 1900, change
swept across the Great Plains,
completely transforming the region.
The railroad, barbed wire, ranching,
and farming radically altered the
landscape. But the people and
animals who lived on these plains for
thousands of years experienced the
most shattering changes of all.

Railroads attracted
settlers to the Great
Plains by offering them
free land in the 1860s.

1850	1860	1870

Presidents

1850-1853
Fillmore

1853-1857
Pierce

1857-1861
Buchanan

1861-1865
Lincoln

1865-1869
A. Johnson

1869-1877
Grant

1850

Plains Indians and white
settlers struggled for control
of the Great Plains.

1889 People rush to claim land
when the U.S. government opens
former American Indian territory
to white settlement.

1890 Plains Indians settle
on lands set aside for them
by treaties with the U.S.
government.

1880

1890

1900

1877-1881
Hayes

1881-1885
Arthur

1881
Garfield

1885-1889
Cleveland

1889-1893
B. Harrison

1893-1897
Cleveland

1897-1901
McKinley

1900

LESSON 1

A Time of Change

THINKING FOCUS

How did people's view of the Great Plains change after 1860?

Key Terms

- transcontinental
- bonanza
- boom town

Two miles beyond South Pass City we saw for the first time that mysterious marvel which all Western untraveled boys have heard of and fully believe in, but are sure to be astounded at when they see it with their own eyes, nevertheless—banks of snow in dead summertime. We were now far up toward the sky, and knew all the time that we must presently encounter lofty summits clad in the "eternal snow"…yet when I did see it glittering in the sun on stately domes in the distance and knew the month was August and that my coat was hanging up because it was too warm to wear it, I was full as much amazed as if I never had heard of snow in August before. . . .

We were perched upon the extreme summit of the great range of the Rocky Mountains, toward which we had been climbing, for days and nights together—and about us was gathered a convention of Nature's kings that stood ten, twelve, and even thirteen thousand feet high. . . . It seemed that we could look around and abroad and contemplate the whole great globe, with its dissolving views of mountains, seas, and continents stretching away through the mystery of the summer haze. . . .

Monstrous rags of cloud hung low and swept along right over the spectator's head, swinging their tatters so nearly in his face that his impulse was to shrink when they came closest. In the one place I speak of, one could look below him upon a world of diminishing crags and canyons leading down, down, and away to a vague plain with a thread in it which was a road, and bunches of feathers in it which were trees.

Mark Twain, *Roughing It*

➤ *Travelers today, just as in Mark Twain's time, marvel to see snow capping the Rocky Mountains in summer. This condition shows the effect of altitude—height above sea level—on temperature. The higher a person climbs, the lower the temperature becomes.*

Variety of the West

Mark Twain wrote the preceding description of the Rocky Mountains while traveling west by stagecoach in 1861. On his journey Twain passed through several regions.

Varied Landforms

West of the Mississippi River stretch gently rolling grasslands called prairie. In this region of endless horizons, painter John Noble wrote, "You look on, on, on, out into space, out almost beyond time itself. You see nothing but the rise and swell of land and grass—the monotonous endless prairie!" Often compared to the sea, the grassland rises so gradually from east to west that it seems flat. From North Dakota to the foothills of the Rockies, this region is known as the Great Plains.

West of the Rockies lies a broad intermountain zone, a mixture of desert, basins, canyons, and plateaus. This region is mostly arid, or very dry.

Mountains between this area and the Pacific coast cut off the moist air from the ocean. Here, strikingly beautiful natural formations such as the Grand Canyon alternate with barren desert.

Beyond the intermountain zone and running parallel to the Rockies are the Cascade Mountains and the Sierra Nevada, their steep slopes covered with forests and dotted with mountain lakes. Fertile valleys lie between these ranges and the mountains along the north Pacific Coast.

Climates of the West

The Great Plains are a region of climatic extremes—sweltering heat, frigid cold, severe drought when water supplies are exhausted, raging blizzards, and spectacular thunderstorms. Early white settlers looked on the treeless, windswept prairie as a hostile environment and called it the "Great American Desert." Land that did not support trees, people reasoned, must

Geographical Regions of the West

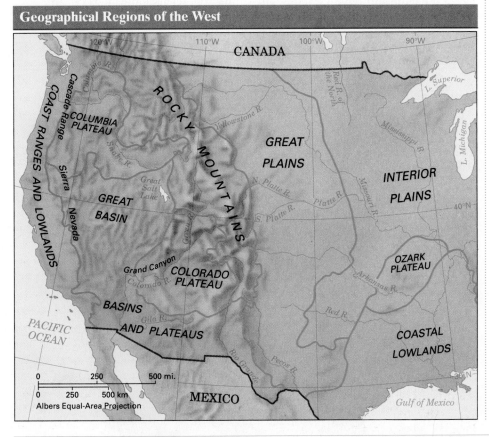

◄ *This map shows the major landforms west of the Mississippi River. What are the major rivers? What mountains divide the Great Plains from the Great Basin?*

411

be unfit for agriculture. In 1820, explorer Stephen H. Long wrote: "I do not hesitate in giving the opinion that [the prairie] is almost wholly unfit for cultivation, and of course uninhabitable by a people depending upon agriculture for their subsistence."

Impact of the Rivers

When Europeans first reached North America, most Indians of the Great Plains lived along the river systems—the Missouri, Platte, Arkansas, and Red rivers. These rivers all flow from the Rockies toward the Mississippi. They furnished water and transportation routes used by Indians, early explorers, and settlers.

Much of the West, however, lacked waterways that could be used for transportation. Although the Colorado River and Rio Grande provided water in a dry region, roaring rapids made them largely unusable and dangerous for travel. In the Great Basin—an area of 210,000 square miles—the rivers flow inland toward sinks or low places such as the Great Salt Lake instead of toward the sea. Often the water of these rivers is unfit to drink.

Because of the lack of water transportation, early pioneers traveled on horseback or by wagon train or stagecoach (Chapter 8). The building of railroads brought major changes to this region. ■

> ■ *Explain why the West is said to have a variety of environments.*

Railroads Arrive

In May 1869, with an echoing ring, railroad officials hammered a golden spike into the railroad ties at Promontory (*PROM uhn tawr ee*) Point, near Ogden, Utah. The ceremony marked the linking of the Central Pacific and Union Pacific railroads. It also marked the completion of the first **transcontinental** rail link in the world—the first railroad to cross an entire continent (see map).

In 1863, workers for the Central Pacific Railroad had begun laying tracks east from Sacramento, California. Two years later Union Pacific workers started to move west from

> ➤ *The map shows the major railroad lines in 1893. Locate the first transcontinental line. What other lines connect it with other parts of the West?*

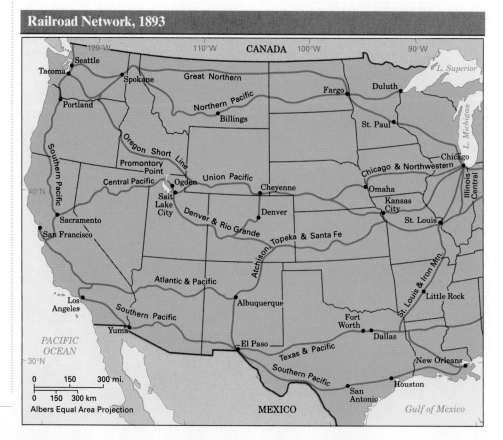

Railroad Network, 1893

Omaha, Nebraska. By 1868, the two crews were racing to see who would lay the most track.

The Central Pacific hired thousands of young Chinese men. They faced the task of building the stretch over the Sierra Nevada and across the Great Basin. Braving avalanches and blizzards and often lacking food and shelter, the Chinese laid 689 miles of track. In the swirling red dust of summer it took 10 days for a crew of 300 to cut a pass through the mountain and lay a single mile of track. Lowered in a basket, a worker chipped holes in the sheer face of a cliff, inserted dynamite, and was pulled up before the explosion went off.

The workers also dug tunnels through the mountains. Working through one of the coldest winters in western history, the Chinese struggled to tunnel as much as a foot a day. Nevertheless, they managed to complete their part of the railroad on time.

Working westward on the Union Pacific Railroad were hundreds of European immigrants, many of them Irish. Their part of the mammoth project involved laying tracks across the Great Plains and over the Rockies. In addition to extremes in temperature, they faced attacks by American Indians. Nevertheless, these workers laid an incredible 1,086 miles of track westward from Omaha, Nebraska.

By 1900, four other railroad lines linked the Atlantic and Pacific coasts. ■

▲ *The train trestle at Georgetown, Colorado, built in 1881–1882, rises 85 feet above the canyon floor. It gives a vivid idea of some of the obstacles overcome by the railroad workers.*

■ *Describe some of the problems faced by the men who built the transcontinental railroad.*

Mining Develops

The railroads opened the West to settlement on a massive scale. They also made it possible to move western minerals to cities where the ore was used in industry. In California and Nevada, mining developed before the railroads were built. In other areas, railroads promoted the development of mines. The combination of natural resources and railways to move them changed the face of the West.

The Silver Boom

Following the gold rush in California (described in Chapter 8), prospectors roamed the West looking for gold. In Nevada in 1859, they found an immensely rich vein of silver that became known as the Comstock Lode. (A lode is a vein of valuable ore within common rock such as granite.)

Most of the Comstock silver was deeply embedded in hard quartz rock. Heavy equipment was needed to cut shafts through rock, carry minerals to the surface, and crush the ore-bearing stone. Such machinery was too expensive for individual prospectors, so large companies took over mining. They brought in heavy equipment and hired experienced hard rock miners—Cornish and Welsh from Britain and Germans from the German States.

The miners had to cut through layers of *borrasca* (Spanish for "barren rock") to reach the **bonanza**, or rich rock. The Big Bonanza, encountered at a depth of more than 1,000 feet, yielded $26 million in 1876. The Comstock Lode paid over $292

▲ *This silver bar from the Comstock Lode is marked 999.5, indicating that it is nearly pure silver.*

413

This photograph shows Anaconda, Montana, famous for its rich copper ore. The bare hills were once covered with trees. What uses would miners have for lumber?

■ *Why was mining after 1850 often undertaken by large companies rather than by individual prospectors?*

for example, became Montana's capital city of Helena.

The most remarkable boom town, Virginia City, Nevada, sprang to life next to the Comstock Lode in 1859. By 1876, over 20,000 people, mostly single men who worked in the mines, lived in Virginia City and neighboring Gold Hill.

Mining equipment, together with most of the food, clothing, building materials, and even drinking water, had to be hauled from San Francisco to Virginia City. Yet the minerals extracted were so valuable that the city prospered.

Large mansions, decorated with the finest furniture, china, and paintings, lined the steep streets. People dined on expensive food; theaters drew leading performers from Europe and the East.

After 1882, however, the Virginia City bonanza gave out. Government demand for silver decreased, and silver prices fell. It was no longer profitable to mine ore that was not of the highest grade. By 1898, the miners had deserted Virginia City. The once-lively city was a virtual ghost town, with most of its buildings abandoned. Dust covered the goods in the stores, and mice ran through the rooms of once-elegant homes.

The presence of the miners hinted at the white settlement that would take place in the Western lands. In 1860, however, those lands were mainly occupied by many different American Indian peoples. ■

million between 1859 and 1882, making it one of the richest in the West.

Boom Town to Ghost Town

Miners rushed to the Comstock Lode. Their shelters, writes J. Ross Browne, included the following:

> *Frame shanties, pitched together as if by accident; tents of canvas, of blankets, of brush, of potato-sacks and old shirts; … smokey hovels of mud and stone; coyote holes in the mountain side forcibly seized and held by men; pits and shafts with smoke issuing from every crevice.*

Communities such as Cripple Creek, Goldfield, Poverty Gulch, Tombstone, and Last Chance Gulch appeared so rapidly they were known as **boom towns**. Some boom towns grew into cities. Last Chance Gulch,

---

R E V I E W

1. **FOCUS** How did people's view of the Great Plains change after 1860?

2. **CONNECT** In what parts of the West did people from the United States settle before 1860? What attracted them to each place?

3. **GEOGRAPHY** Name and briefly describe the major geographical regions of the West. Include major mountain ranges and river systems.

4. **ECONOMICS** Why is an efficient transportation system,

such as the network of railroad lines, important to both farmers and factory owners?

5. **CRITICAL THINKING** What caused some boom towns to turn into ghost towns while others grew into cities? Consider geographical factors as well as economic reasons.

6. **WRITING ACTIVITY** Prepare to interview participants at the ceremony marking the completion of the first transcontinental railroad. Draw up a list of questions to ask. Be sure to include workers as well as officials.

L E S S O N   2

Culture of the Plains Indians

"What is life?" asked the Blackfoot hunter Crowfoot as he lay dying in 1890. "It is the flash of a firefly in the night. It is the breath of a buffalo in the winter time." Crowfoot's reference suggests that the buffalo played an important part in the life of the Plains Indians.

White settlers moving westward across the Great Plains in the 1840s told of immense herds of buffalo that stretched as far as they could see. For the Indians who lived on the Plains, the buffalo were much more than an awe-inspiring spectacle. The great shaggy beasts provided them with food, clothing, weapons, tools, and shelter. Season after season the Indians followed the herds from one grazing ground to another.

Each part of the buffalo had its use. Hair and hide, hoofs, horns, bones—nothing was wasted. Buffalo meat that was not eaten right away was dried for later use. Bones were carved into weapons, tools, and ornaments; horns were used to make cups, ladles, and spoons. From the hides came clothing, bedding, moccasins, shields, and covers for tepees (also spelled *tipis*). "The tipi," said Chief Flying Hawk of the Oglala Sioux, "is much better to live in [than a house]; always clean, warm in winter, cool in summer; easy to move."

THINKING FOCUS

What are four characteristics of the Plains Indians' lives?

Hunters of the Buffalo

The Indians' dependence on the buffalo, however, did not become typical of the Great Plains until after Europeans arrived in North America. When the Indians began to obtain guns and horses from the white people, their way of life changed radically.

Settled Farmers

Before the Europeans arrived, many of the Plains Indians farmed the fertile land along the rivers, growing corn, beans, and squash. They varied their diet with game they hunted on foot. These Plains people included the Mandan whom Lewis and Clark had met on their expedition. They lived settled lives for much of the year. Their houses were rounded lodges built of earth and sturdy poles and were not meant to be moved. From

Plains Indian clothing, such as this shirt owned by Kicking Bear, was often beautifully decorated.

415

their villages, small hunting parties went out on the Plains to hunt the buffalo as the herds migrated to new pasture.

The sedentary Indians traded their surplus food for skins and meat from hunting tribes such as the Comanche and Kiowa, who stalked game on foot. They usually traveled no more than a very short distance each day because the dogs they used could only pull a limited weight.

A Nomadic Way of Life

Toward the end of the 1600s, this sedentary way of life changed dramatically with the introduction of two critical items—the gun and the horse. European fur traders from what is now Canada gave guns to the Chippewa in exchange for furs. Once the Chippewa used these guns against the Sioux, the Indians quickly realized what an advantage guns provided.

About the same time, Indians in

Plains Indian Culture

As they moved in search of buffalo, the Plains Indians carried along their art. They expressed their love of beauty by decorating nearly everything they used, from weapons to cookware.

Ceremonial headdresses such as this were worn by the most distinguished men of the tribe on special occasions. They included special feathers indicating brave deeds.

This hide is an artist's canvas, depicting warriors, tepees, and the all-important buffalo—the Indians' source of food, shelter, and clothing.

A horse's mask? This Cheyenne horse mask is made from thousands of porcupine quills colored with vegetable dyes, and sewn onto buckskin. Warriors decorated their horses for special occasions.

New Mexico revolted against Spanish settlers. Horses that the fleeing Spaniards left behind in 1680 were quickly adopted by Indians such as the Apache and Comanche. Soon horses became the symbol of wealth.

Guns from the north and horses from the south spread rapidly across the Great Plains, altering the lives of Indian peoples. Tribes on the Plains and in nearby regions competed to obtain them, for they made travel

faster and hunting easier. Many Plains Indians became nomads who followed the vast herds of buffalo. The Closer Look below shows some articles the Plains Indians created as part of their nomadic lifestyle.

The Kiowa and Blackfoot, who already lived on the Plains, were joined by other tribes (see map, page 419). The Cheyenne and the Arapaho moved south and west from what is now Minnesota. The Comanche, a

Hide moccasins such as these were decorated with beads. A woman might bead a leather shirt like this for her husband.

Even containers were decorated. Folded pieces of rawhide such as this were used to carry a variety of objects. Women decorated them with abstract geometrical designs.

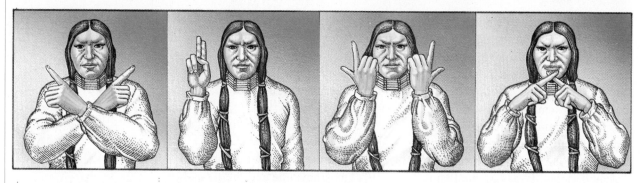

▲ *The signs this Indian is making read (from left to right):* trade, friend, buffalo, and tepee.

■ *How did the horse and gun transform the life of the Plains Indians?*

branch of the Shoshone, traveled southeast from the Rockies to the plains of Texas, where horses were plentiful. From the Minnesota-Wisconsin area came the various Dakota tribes. The Crow—hostile to the Sioux, Cheyenne, and Arapaho alike— moved west from the Missouri.

The nomadic way of life followed by the Plains Indians lasted only a short time. However, it provided what became the familiar image of Indian life—the mounted warrior wearing a feathered headdress. ■

Tribal Status

To obtain the horses on which their way of life depended, Plains Indians raided one another's herds. They also raided isolated settlements of pioneers and sometimes attacked wagon trains moving westward. Success in raids and warfare increasingly defined a man's status, or standing in the tribe.

Steps in Achieving Status

Although customs varied from tribe to tribe, the Plains Indians looked on certain actions as determining tribal status. A boy attained status by accompanying the men on a hunt. One improved his rank by stealing horses, fighting as a warrior, and leading a hunt or war party. This type of behavior became more common after the introduction of guns and horses. After a young man proved his ability to endure hardship in a demanding ceremony, he was eligible to become a tribal leader or chief. A man's rank reflected his bravery in warfare and in counting coup [*koo*]. A coup is a daring deed accomplished against heavy odds. What counted as a coup varied from tribe to tribe, but it always involved a daring act.

The greater the danger, the greater the coup. A major coup was to steal a rival chief's special horses, which were usually carefully guarded. In some tribes, the greatest coup was to ride into an enemy camp, touch the chief, and return unharmed.

After counting coup, a man might paint his face and body and also his wife's as part of the celebration held when he returned to the tribe. One Crow woman boasted:

I t was my face that he painted when he had gained that right by saving a Crow warrior's life in battle. And it was I who rode his warhorse and carried his shield. Ahh, I felt proud when my man painted my face.

Governing by Advice

Most Indians of the Plains were governed by a council of elders. These leaders discussed problems facing the tribe and tried to reach agreement on what action to take. The title *chief,* which white people equated with head of government, simply referred to a man who was a daring fighter or an experienced leader. A tribe might thus have several chiefs. The person leading the tribe at any one time depended on what the tribe was doing. One chief might be the leader in time of war, another might be chief of the hunt.

Beliefs and Ceremonies

The Plains Indians shared certain beliefs. They believed humans should respect the land and use its resources wisely. Their concept of land ownership differed greatly from that of white people. In 1855, when the U.S. government offered to buy land from the Dwamish tribe in Washington, Chief Seattle wrote President Franklin Pierce the following letter. His words reflect the feelings of many American Indian people:

H ow can you buy or sell the sky—the warmth of the land? The idea is strange to us. We do not own the freshness of the air or the sparkle of the water. How can you buy them from us?...
Every part of this earth is sacred to my people. Every shining pine needle, every sandy shore, every mist in the dark woods, every clearing and humming insect is holy in the memory and experience of my people.

The Plains Indians' lives were enriched with numerous ceremonies. One important ceremony for some nomadic tribes was the Sun Dance, performed as a solemn ritual to ensure spiritual growth and tribal renewal. For three or four days, participants went without food and water, dancing

American Indian Lands in 1850

Indian lands ceded before 1850
Remaining Indian lands, 1850

0   150   300 mi.
0   150 300 km
Albers Equal-Area Projection

to the beat of drums and the shrill piping of eagle-bone whistles. A few achieved a trancelike state. If they had a vision, it was believed to give them mystical power that would bring them success during the buffalo hunt or on a raid.

Eventually the U.S. government prohibited the Sun Dance in an effort to make the Indians give up their traditional ways. After the Civil War, the native peoples lost their lands and became dependent on the government for food and shelter. ■

In 1850, American Indians were the only inhabitants of most of the land west of the Mississippi River. In what parts of the West had white American people settled by 1850?

■ How did a man on the Plains acquire status in his tribe?

R E V I E W

1. **FOCUS** What are four characteristics of the Plains Indians' lives?

2. **CONNECT** What contacts did most Plains Indians have with white people before 1850?

3. **ECONOMICS** What constituted wealth among the Plains Indians? How was it acquired?

4. **POLITICAL SYSTEM** Why did many white people misunderstand the function and status of Indian chiefs?

5. **CRITICAL THINKING** How might a Plains Indian tribe react if gold or silver were found near its favorite hunting grounds? Why?

6. **ACTIVITY** Plains Indians often decorated their tepee covers with scenes of their life or important deeds. Draw a tepee and illustrate it with scenes from this lesson. You may wish to include some of the designs shown in A Closer Look (pages 416–417).

Reshaping the Great Plains

The World of the Buffalo Comes to an End

An Indian Legend

The Plains Indian culture depended on the buffalo, and the extinction of this great animal brought an end to the Plains Indian way of life. In this legend, Old Lady Horse (Spear Woman), a Kiowa, describes the extinction of the buffalo. Her story is told in American Indian Mythology *by Alice Marriott and Carol K. Rachlin. As you read, ask yourself whether there is anything in your everday life that is as important to you as the buffalo was to the Indians.*

Settlement of the Great Plains offered new, exciting opportunities to many people. In the process, though, an American Indian way of life was destroyed.

And now we come to the end of a world. The end of the buffalo was the end of Plains Indian life. And before the white man's superior technology, the buffalo succumbed. This is one story of why there are no more buffalo in the world.

Everything the Kiowas had came from the buffalo. Their tipis were made of buffalo hides, so were their clothes and moccasins. They ate buffalo meat. Their containers were made of hide, or of bladders or stomachs. The buffalo were the life of the Kiowas.

Most of all, the buffalo was part of the Kiowa religion. A white buffalo calf must be sacrificed in the Sun Dance. The priests used parts of the buffalo to make their prayers when they healed people or when they sang to the powers above.

So, when the white men wanted to build railroads, or when they wanted to farm or raise cattle, the buffalo still protected the Kiowas. They tore up the railroad tracks and the gardens. They chased the cattle off the ranges. The buffalo loved their people as much as the Kiowas loved them.

There was war between the buffalo and the white men. The white men built forts in the Kiowa country, and . . . shot the buffalo as fast as they could, but the buffalo kept coming on, coming on, even into the post cemetery at Fort Sill. Soldiers were not enough to hold them back.

Then the white men hired hunters to do nothing but kill the buffalo. Up and down the plains those men ranged, shooting sometimes as many as a hundred buffalo a day. Behind them came the skinners with their wagons. They piled the hides and bones into the wagons until they were full, and then took their loads to the new railroad stations that were being built, to be shipped east to the market. Sometimes there would be a pile of bones as high as a man, stretching a mile along the railroad track.

The buffalo saw that their day was over. They could protect their people no longer. Sadly, the last remnant of the great herd gathered in council, and decided what they would do.

The Kiowas were camped on the north side of Mount Scott, those of them who were still free to camp. One young woman got up very early in the morning. The dawn mist was still rising from Medicine Creek, and as she looked across the water, peering through the haze, she saw the last buffalo herd appear like a spirit dream.

Straight to Mount Scott the leader of the herd walked. Behind him came the cows and their calves, and the few young males who had survived. As the woman watched, the face of the mountain opened.

Inside Mount Scott the world was green and fresh, as it had been when she was a small girl. The rivers ran clear, not red. The wild plums were in blossom, chasing the red buds up the inside slopes. Into this world of beauty the buffalo walked never to be seen again.

Further Reading

The Mythology of North America. John Bierhorst. The author has prepared an invaluable guide to stories of the gods and heroes of Indian nations from the Arctic to the Southwest.

Anpao: An American Indian Odyssey. Jamake Highwater. The tale of the brave Anpao is taken from generations of Plains Indians' legends and includes revealing encounters with white men.

Indian Tales. Jaime de Angulo. This book is packed with Indian folklore, jokes, ceremonial rituals, games, and adventures.

L E S S O N   3

Indian Lands Lost

THINKING FOCUS

What factors combined to end the Plains Indians' nomadic way of life?

Key Terms

- annuity
- reservation
- assimilate

➤ *In June 1876, the Sioux chiefs Sitting Bull and Crazy Horse led the Indians in the Battle of Little Big Horn, in which Colonel George A. Custer and his men were defeated. An unknown Indian artist painted this version of the battle.*

It was July 4, 1876. All over the nation people were celebrating America's centennial, its hundredth birthday. In Philadelphia, where the Declaration of Independence had been adopted, thousands thronged to the grand opening of the Centennial Exposition. Throughout the nation flags flew, bands played patriotic marches, and fireworks delighted young and old alike.

The mood of jubilation, however, abruptly ended on the morning of July 6. At 3 A.M., telegraph messages from the West reached the Eastern newspapers. The content was brief but shocking. "Bismarck, Dakota Territory, July 5, 1876," they read. ". . . Custer attacked the Indians June 25, and he with every officer and man in five companies [was] killed."

Custer's defeat and the death of over 200 soldiers stunned people throughout the nation. They were aware that, for several years, clashes had taken place between the Indian peoples of the Plains and the U.S. army. However, they found it hard to believe troops representing a nation of 40 million had been destroyed.

Indians and White Settlers Clash

Before the gold rush of 1849, few clashes had occurred between the pioneers and the Plains Indians. In fact, several pioneers praised the Indians for the help that they had offered. In 1851, the northern Plains Indians—Assiniboine, Atsina, Arikara, Crow, Shoshone, Cheyenne, Arapaho, and Sioux—met U.S. government agents in a peace conference. They agreed to let pioneers pass through their lands unharmed. A similar agreement was made with southern tribes two years later.

Increasing Hostility

As more and more white settlers moved into the West, however, their oxen and horses ate the grass on which the buffalo depended. In addition, the settlers shot buffalo for food. Alarmed by the decreasing herds and attracted by the chance to gain horses, Indians attacked small groups of pioneers and isolated settlements.

Sometimes treaties between the U.S. government and the Indian peoples created problems. When U.S. officials made agreements with one or two chiefs in a tribe, they tended to think the agreement applied to the entire tribe. Some government officials failed to enforce the treaties that set aside areas for hunting. Revisions in the treaty with the Comanche, for example, gradually reduced their hunting grounds from 300 million acres to 3 million acres.

Dependent on Government Help

In exchange for Indian promises to allow pioneers to pass in peace, the U.S. government promised to supply the tribes with an **annuity**, a yearly provision of food, clothing, and other necessary items. The intention was to provide food only until the Indians learned to support themselves by farming or by a trade. The government agents who supplied the annuity, however, were often corrupt. They provided wormy flour, shoddy blankets, and defective guns—when they provided any supplies at all.

By the mid-1860s, white settlers from both East and West were closing in on Indian lands like a tightening vise. Once the transcontinental railroad was completed in 1869, the rush onto Indian lands became a stampede. At the same time hordes of hunters traveled west to shoot buffalo for hides or simply for sport. By 1880, only a few buffalo remained of the millions that had roamed the plains before 1850. Faced with starvation, Indians became dependent on annuities.

Sioux Uprising

Events in 1862 foreshadowed what would happen in the next quarter of a century. The Santee Sioux in

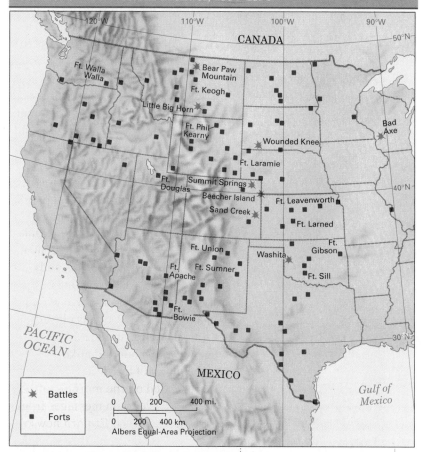

Conflict on the Western Frontier, 1864–1890

Minnesota, although not living on the Plains, were part of the annuity system. By 1862, they were on the verge of starvation because government agents had failed to deliver their annuity. Upset by white settlers who had moved onto their lands, the Sioux massacred several hundred white settlers (the exact number is unknown). Thousands of settlers fled their homes and refused to return. Army troops finally drove many of the Sioux out of Minnesota and onto the Great Plains.

Sand Creek Massacre

The Sioux uprising was the beginning of the bloodiest period in the history of the West. The map above shows where some of the clashes took place. In 1864, the Cheyenne and their Arapaho allies left their lands at Sand Creek in Colorado because the tribe was starving. They began to raid ranches and attack travelers.

The Indians who opposed war

Battles between Indians and the U.S. army were often a series of skirmishes rather than formal warfare. Find three places on the map where battles were fought.

423

obeyed when they were ordered back to the reservation. In November, however, Colonel John Chivington led a surprise attack. His command was to "kill and scalp all." Between 200 and 450 Indian men, women, and children were massacred. (The total depends on who was reporting the incident.) ■

■ *Why did the U.S. government want to settle the Plains Indians on reservations?*

Policies That Changed Indian Life

Although the U.S. Commissioner of Indian Affairs denounced the Sand Creek massacre, the U.S. government continued its efforts to make the Plains Indians give up their nomadic lifestyle. As you learned in Chapter 7, resettlement of the Indian peoples dated back to the 1830s, when the southeastern tribes were moved to Indian Territory (in what is now the state of Oklahoma).

The Move to Reservations

After the Civil War, the government began to move the Plains tribes to **reservations**, land set aside for a particular tribe and off limits to white settlers. Many of these reservations were in Indian Territory. To make room for the new arrivals, tribes who were already there, such as the Cherokee and Creek, were forced to give up some of their lands.

UNDERSTANDING ECOLOGY

Between 1870 and 1900, American settlers took control of the lands of the West, and they were often irresponsible caretakers. They cut millions of acres of timberlands, choked streams with slag from mines, and crisscrossed great sweeps of plain with railroads. In short, humans permanently altered the relationship of living things to each other and to their environment. Biologists refer to this relationship as ecology.

American settlers believed that the resources of the West were limitless. Because these settlers believed that nature existed for their benefit, they molded the land to meet their short-term interests.

The Indian View

In contrast to settlers, American Indians respected the land and its animals. They lived in harmony with nature and they believed that they were servants of the land, not the other way around. The following passage from a letter by Chief Seattle of the Duwamish tribe to President Franklin Pierce expresses this view:

"The white man must treat the beasts of this land as his brothers. All things are connected . . . If we sell you our land, love it as we've loved it. Care for it as we've cared for it. Hold in your mind the memory of the land, as it is when you take it. And with all your might, and with all your strength, and with all your heart —preserve it for your children."

Ecology Today

The European settlers did not heed Chief Seattle's advice. Today, people throughout the world are still upsetting ecological balances. In Brazil, for example, companies are cutting down the Amazon rain forests to clear land for cattle ranching to satisfy the world's huge appetite. Poor people desperate for land are also clearing forests, burning the remains to plant crops. Entire species of animals who only live in these special regions are losing their habitats and facing extinction. Even the world's climate is being altered by this huge loss of plant life.

The question of humankind's place in the environment is a difficult one. In the United States, we are blessed with a diversity of land and climate that matches the diversity of our people. We must not waste it. Perhaps we can learn from the American Indians who sought to live in harmony with nature. Like them, we must learn to see ourselves as part of a larger ecological system.

Once the Indian peoples were on reservations (see map), government officials believed they would be ready to **assimilate**, or adapt to white culture and give up their traditional beliefs and ways.

Futile Resistance

After 1870, all the Indians faced the choice of accepting peace on the U.S. government's terms or being exterminated. The U.S. Army had new rapid-fire guns and many more soldiers, could move troops quickly by train, and took advantage of tribal rivalries to overcome the Indian peoples. For example, the army used Pawnee, Crow, and Shoshone scouts to track down the Sioux.

Nevertheless, some Indians still resisted being moved to a reservation. The Nez Percé, who had always maintained peaceful relations with the United States, were ordered to move onto a reservation in 1877. In the process, some angry young Nez Percé killed 13 settlers. Pursued by army troops, their leader, Chief Joseph, led his people on a desperate retreat that covered more than 1,300 miles. He finally surrendered with a moving speech:

> It is cold, and we have no blankets. The little children are freezing to death. . . . Hear me, my chiefs! I am tired. My heart is sick and sad. From where the sun now stands I will fight no more forever.

The Nez Percé were sent to Indian Territory. Their request to return to the Northwest was granted in 1885.

New Landholding Policies

In 1871, Congress ended the practice, in effect since 1789, of treating Indian tribes as separate nations. Indian peoples were regarded as under the protection of the government. They could no longer make treaties, yet they were not U.S. citizens. They had

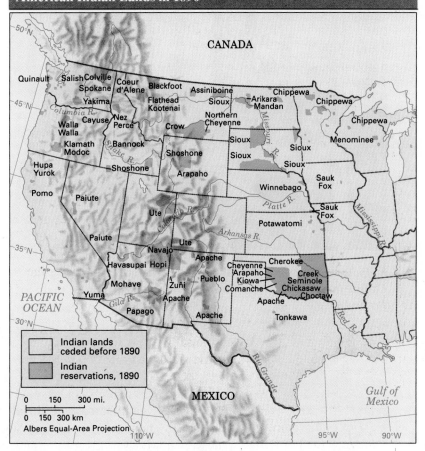

American Indian Lands in 1890

Indian lands ceded before 1890

Indian reservations, 1890

0   150   300 mi.
0   150   300 km
Albers Equal-Area Projection

Compare this map with the one on page 419 showing Indian lands in 1850. What major change took place between 1850 and 1890?

to obey U.S. laws, but they enjoyed none of the rights of other Americans.

In 1887, the Dawes Act divided Indian reservation land, which was held by the entire tribe, into grants of 160 acres for individual Indian families. Any surplus land was opened to settlement by white pioneers.

Well-intentioned reformers hoped the Dawes Act would encourage assimilation. They tried to teach the Indians a new way of life. But the result was disastrous. Few Plains Indians had any background in farming. Many went into debt and lost their land. Others sold their lands to white settlers for pitifully small sums.

Assimilation by Education

Another method the government used in an attempt to assimilate the Indians was to send Indian children to day schools or sometimes special boarding schools. Well-meaning teachers replaced the Indian children's trib-

Reshaping the Great Plains

▲ *Indian students at Carlisle Indian School in Pennsylvania.*

➤ *This Ghost Dance shirt comes from Wounded Knee. Many Ghost Dance shirts had designs that were believed to protect the wearer from bullets.*

■ *Explain how the Dawes Act and government education programs were used as part of the assimilation policy.*

al clothing with modern dress, gave them new names, and forced them to speak English. The schools taught the Indians the Christian religion and the customs of white society.

Generally, assimilation failed. Students often encountered discrimination, missed their parents, and wanted to go home. Even if they did well, few jobs were available in the vocations they were taught—printing, baking, drafting, and bricklaying. Those who adapted to white society often felt like misfits.

The Indian Response

Going from security to poverty, from freedom to confinement, and from power to humiliation was degrading to the Plains Indian peoples. Some of them turned to the teachings of a Paiute named Wovoka. Wovoka claimed that all Indians, living and dead, would be reunited in a reborn world. His followers performed a ritual known as the Ghost Dance.

The Sioux in Dakota, who were starving on the reduced lands of their reservation, called for active resistance. Fearing an uprising, U.S. troops attempted to round up the Sioux, resulting in the death of Sitting Bull. The Sioux were taken to Wounded Knee, South Dakota in 1890. When fighting broke out, the soldiers turned their rapid-firing guns on the Sioux, killing or wounding 200. Another hundred froze to death in the snow after they fled.

Resettled on reservations, their way of life gone, the Plains Indians faced decades of poverty and humiliation. Yet they never lost their pride in their heritage. They learned to adapt to new conditions. They also continued to practice their old beliefs and rituals, but also proved to be flexible and adaptable to change. For example, when the government approved a gathering on the Fourth of July, Indians set up tepees, dressed in ceremonial clothing, and performed traditional dances.

The massacre at Wounded Knee marked the end of Indian resistance. The land from which they had been removed could now be settled by white farmers and ranchers. ■

R E V I E W

1. **FOCUS** What factors combined to end the Plains Indians' nomadic way of life?

2. **CONNECT** How did the attempt to assimilate the Indians reflect the concept of Manifest Destiny?

3. **HISTORY** Trace the policies the U.S. government followed in its attempts to remove the Indians from the Great Plains.

4. **CRITICAL THINKING** Why might some Indians choose to adopt some aspects of white society? How might they use an American education to help their people?

5. **ACTIVITY** With a classmate, prepare a dialogue between a Plains Indian leader and a U.S. army commander about moving the tribe to a reservation. Be sure to present both points of view in a convincing way.

LESSON 4

Resettlement of the Land

When Charles Ingalls, the father of author Laura Ingalls Wilder, tried to file a claim for land in the Dakota Territory, he slept all night on the doorstep of the land office to be sure he got his claim. He told his family:

> *I* t looks like the whole country's trying to file on land. When I showed up at the land office, I couldn't get anywheres near the door.
>
> I've bet Uncle Sam $14.00 against a 160 acres of land, that we can make out to live on the claim for five years. Going to help me win the bet?

After the Civil War, thousands of people like the Ingalls family eagerly took advantage of the opportunity offered by the Homestead Act of 1862. It allotted a settler 160 acres of government-owned land. The only cost for the land was the few dollars needed to record a claim. Anyone could **homestead**, that is, file a claim for land, build a house there, and work the land for five years. If these conditions were met, the homesteader became the owner of the property.

The Homestead Act seemed to offer opportunity to people who had never even dreamed they could own land. Thousands of people, including recently freed slaves and white settlers seeking a better life, moved West and filed homestead claims.

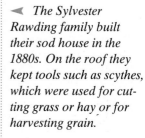

THINKING
FOCUS

In what ways did ranching and farming transform the American West?

Key Terms

• homestead

◄ *The Sylvester Rawding family built their sod house in the 1880s. On the roof they kept tools such as scythes, which were used for cutting grass or hay or for harvesting grain.*

427

Reshaping the Great Plains

Ranching on the Plains

Some homesteaders became farmers; others turned to ranching. Settlers who went to Texas and the Southwest found a long tradition of cattle ranching. About 1690, Mexican vaqueros brought cattle north to Texas. These cattle had little commercial value and were left to roam freely over the range. By the early 1800s, there were hundreds of thousands of wild longhorns.

The long-legged longhorns were tough animals that thrived on buffalo grass and did not need as much water as other breeds. Their meat, however, was lean, stringy, and tough. Gradually ranchers replaced them with pure-bred cattle imported from Britain. These cattle produced better meat and brought a higher price in the market.

Ranchers needed more than the 160 acres of a homestead for their herds. In the arid Plains each steer needed about 15 acres of grazing land. Ranchers used the public lands owned by the government for part of their cattle range. Several ranchers might use the same range. At roundup time their cowboys herded all the cattle together. Each owner's cattle were identified by a brand—a special symbol such as the owner's initials—burned into the animal's hide. Mounted on nimble-footed horses, the cowhands separated cattle bearing the same brand from the main herd.

On the Trail

After the roundup, cattle that were to be sold were driven to market. The trail boss hired 10–12 cowhands —usually single young men—to herd 2,000 or more cattle along the trail. The most experienced riders rode at the point or head of the herd. Riders farther back kept the herd moving and

▲ *Cowboys used branding irons* (above) *to identify cattle. The brand was registered with local officials; this helped ranchers trace lost or stolen stock.*

➤ *The California vaquero and the Texas cowboy had much in common. Many words used by cowboys were originally Spanish, reflecting the origins of cattle ranching.*

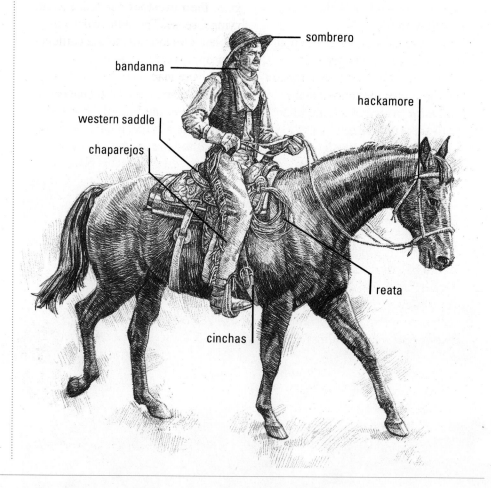

sombrero
bandanna
hackamore
western saddle
chaparejos
reata
cinchas

stopped cattle from straying. At the back of the herd, in the clouds of dust the cattle kicked up, rode the least experienced cowboys.

During the two to three months of the trail drive, cowboys rose before dawn and were in the saddle as long as 18 hours a day. The cowboy's job was tough, dirty, tiring, and dangerous. The slightest thing could panic a herd. A sudden clap of thunder might cause a frenzied stampede. Up and down hills and through brush the cowboys would gallop their horses in a frantic race to turn the terrified herd. If a cowboy fell, he might be dragged by his horse or run over by the cattle. There was no doctor to set broken limbs or sew up wounds.

During night watch the cowboys rode around the herd, calming the restless cattle by singing songs they made up about their lives. One such song, "Git Along, Little Dogies," appears below. (A dogie is a steer.)

The Cattle Boom

Early ranchers raised cattle mainly for their hides and tallow. After the Civil War, however, the growing population in the East demanded more beef. Men returning from the Civil War saw the wild Texas herds as a way to obtain desperately needed Northern dollars. Ranchers began rounding up the wild herds, branding them as

their own, and driving them to towns on the railroad lines. Cattle cars then carried them to markets farther east.

The first herds of Texas longhorns were driven north to cow towns in Missouri. As farmers moved west, however, they objected to herds of cattle trampling their crops, eating the grass their livestock needed, and carrying disease. The state legislature passed laws that forced the cattlemen to use trails farther west.

As the map on page 430 shows, trails from southern and western Texas met at the Red River. They formed the Chisholm Trail, which was opened in 1867 to reach the newly built railroad in Abilene, Kansas.

In 1869, more than 350,000 cattle

The word rodeo *comes from the Spanish word for* roundup. *At rodeos today, cowboys compete in riding and roping events. Cowboys usually smoothed the points of spurs (below) so they would not hurt their horses.*

Across Time & Space

In 1872, newspaper publisher Julius Sterling Morton persuaded Nebraska homesteaders to plant young trees. When they matured, the trees served as windbreaks and helped conserve moisture in the soil. Today, most states in the United States have set aside Arbor Day, a special day for planting trees.

A s I walked out one morning for pleasure,
  I met a cowpuncher a-jogging along.
  His hat was thrown back and his spurs was a-jingling,
And as he advanced he was singing this song.
Sing hooplio get along my little dogies,
For Wyoming shall be your new home.
Its hooping and yelling and cursing those dogies
To our misfortune but none of your own.

In the Springtime we round up the dogies,
Slap on the brands and bob off their tails.
Then we cut herd and herd is inspected,
And then we throw them on the trail.

John Avery Lomax, *Cowboy Songs and Other Frontier Ballads,* 1910

Reshaping the Great Plains

In cattle towns, large corrals held cattle to be fattened.

■ *How did barbed wire change ranching?*

▼ *Trace the route a shipment of beef might have taken from San Antonio to New York.*

tana, Wyoming, Colorado, and North and South Dakota. Within three years, the number of cattle in Montana increased from 250,000 to 600,000.

Once Eastern businessmen became aware that a steer worth $5 on the range could bring $45–60 on the market, cattle ranching became a big business. People in the East and in England and Scotland organized and financed cattle companies. By the mid-1880s, some of these companies had ranches, each of which covered an area larger than the entire New England states.

The rancher was king for only a short period, however. Unusually harsh winters in 1885–1886 and 1886–1887 took a terrible toll of livestock. Falling prices for beef made ranching unprofitable. The introduction of barbed wire fences limited the open range. Ranchers had to rent or buy the public lands they had used at little or no cost. By the 1890s, the ranches that remained were operated as large, fenced-in livestock farms, and cowboys were as likely to be mending fences as roping steers. ■

were driven along the Chisholm Trail. Two years later, the number had doubled. After that year, however, the trail drives gradually shifted to the Western Trail, which ended at Dodge City, Kansas.

The growth of the railroad network and new methods of meat packing and refrigeration helped to meet the demand for Western beef. As raising cattle became more profitable, ranching spread from Texas to Mon-

Moving Western Beef to Market

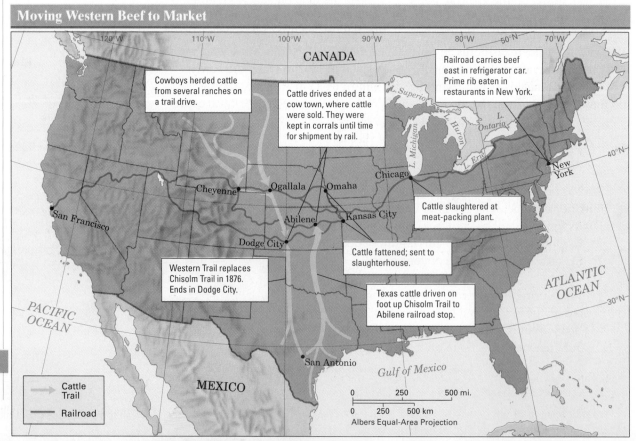

Cowboys herded cattle from several ranches on a trail drive.

Cattle drives ended at a cow town, where cattle were sold. They were kept in corrals until time for shipment by rail.

Railroad carries beef east in refrigerator car. Prime rib eaten in restaurants in New York.

Cattle slaughtered at meat-packing plant.

Cattle fattened; sent to slaughterhouse.

Western Trail replaces Chisolm Trail in 1876. Ends in Dodge City.

Texas cattle driven on foot up Chisolm Trail to Abilene railroad stop.

CANADA
L. Superior
L. Michigan
L. Huron
L. Ontario
L. Erie
New York
Chicago
Omaha
Ogallala
Cheyenne
Abilene
Kansas City
Dodge City
San Francisco
San Antonio
MEXICO
Gulf of Mexico
PACIFIC OCEAN
ATLANTIC OCEAN

→ Cattle Trail
— Railroad

0   250   500 mi.
0   250   500 km
Albers Equal-Area Projection

Farming on the Plains

When barbed wire was invented in the 1860s, farmers hailed it as a cheap way to fence their land. Ranchers, however, feared that homesteaders would fence their claims and keep cattle from water supplies. Thus, the big ranchers began to fence in the range, including the government land. When farmers and small stockholders complained to the government, they were told they had the right to cut the fences. A rash of fence-cutting followed, often leading to violence. In 1885, Congress made it a crime to fence in government lands. Since ranchers did not hold legal title to most of these lands, farmers could move in and establish claims.

Homesteaders Settle the Plains

Completion of the transcontinental railroad brought a torrent of settlers onto the Plains. Between 1862 and 1900, some 500,000 families moved west. Advertisements by railroads, territorial and state governments, and businesses made the Plains seem like a paradise. Lured by such advertising, by the Homestead Act's promise of free land, and by access to the railroad, single farmers and families had settled most of the available land in eastern Kansas and Nebraska by 1875.

Each year new settlers pushed farther west onto the Plains. They staked out claims in areas where the climate is too arid for conventional farming.

The first tasks of a homesteading family were to build a shelter and obtain water. On the treeless plain, most settlers made dugouts or houses of sod—soil held together by the roots of grass—like that on page 427.

Homesteaders dug wells for their water, drawing it up by bucket or by a hand pump. For fuel they gathered dried buffalo droppings or cut grass and made twists of it when it dried.

The prairie farmers were often called sodbusters because they broke up the sod to plant crops. If they failed to get a crop the first fall, they risked starving during the winter. All but the smallest children worked on the homestead. With hard work and favorable weather a family could build up a successful farm in five years. Each year they would try to break more ground and plant more crops, using the cash they earned from their harvest to buy machinery.

Farming Methods

Homesteaders had to learn new techniques to be successful farmers. Irrigation, such as that used by the Mormons in Utah, was one solution to the arid climate, but it required a reliable source of water and money for building an irrigation system. Water on the Plains was rarely adequate.

Many homesteaders turned to dry farming techniques. Each year they left half the land unplanted to preserve the moisture in the soil. Other fields were plowed deeply, and fewer seeds were planted per acre than in a wetter climate. Wheat was especially suited for the dry climate. The introduction of a hardy strain of wheat from Russia helped turn the Great Plains into one of the world's great wheat-producing areas.

Windmills were a necessity on the Plains because water sources were deep underground. The nearly constant wind about which early pioneers had complained turned the blades of these windmills, pumping up water for the home or a small garden or for watering livestock.

Problems of Homesteading

For many homesteaders, the dream of acquiring land turned into a nightmare. Many had started their claims without any extra money. Often they had to borrow funds to buy machinery, seed, and livestock. No

▲ *The hardships endured by homesteaders can be seen in the faces of this woman and her children.*

Reshaping the Great Plains

Horse-drawn combines harvest wheat on the Great Plains. Combines cut the wheat, threshed or separated the grain from the straw, and cleaned the grain.

matter how hard they worked, they could not make enough to pay off their debts. Wealthy people who bought land to sell for a profit forced up the value of land.

As taxes rose, the small homesteader fell further into debt. Many had to sell some or all of their land to pay back loans. Others lost their land to the banks whose loans they could not repay.

Technology Transforms Farming

Some farmers who were able to invest in the new technology met with astounding success. In 1874, the Northern Pacific Railroad and a Minnesota wheat grower named Oliver Dalrymple cooperated on a farming project in the Dakotas. Dalrymple used a mechanical sower to plant seeds; self-binding reapers to cut, gather, and bind the stalks of wheat; and steam-powered threshers to separate the wheat kernels from the husks and straw. He made a profit of more than 100 percent in the first year.

Impressed by these results, Eastern bankers formed companies that bought nearly all the land in the fertile Red River Valley of North Dakota. Using expensive equipment, they created huge factory-style farms that were so profitable they were called bonanza farms. Their success attracted thousands of settlers, increasing North Dakota's population from 2,400 in 1870 to almost 191,000 in 1890.

As settlers poured into the Red River Valley, railroad lines were built to reach the northern part of the Great Plains. This railroad network linked Plains farmers to the rest of the country. It allowed farmers to ship their produce East. The transcontinental railroad lines made prairie farmers part of the nation's economy. Aided by the machines manufactured in the industrial cities, they produced much of the food on which people in those cities depended. Three great regions of the nation—West, Great Plains, and East—had been joined together. ■

■ *What methods did farmers use to grow crops successfully on the Great Plains?*

REVIEW

1. **FOCUS** In what ways did ranching and farming transform the American West?

2. **CONNECT** How did U.S. government policy toward the Indians benefit other Americans?

3. **GEOGRAPHY** What geographical problems did farmers and ranchers face on the Great Plains?

4. **ECONOMICS** Explain how Western farming and ranching

became part of the national economy.

5. **CRITICAL THINKING** Did the Homestead Act achieve its aims? Explain.

6. **WRITING ACTIVITY** Write a review of a Western you have read or watched on TV or in the movies. How does it describe the cowboy's life? How does the information differ from what you have learned about the real West?

Tracing Routes West

Here's Why

Knowing how to relate transportation routes to the topography of the land and its resources can help you understand the development of an area.

As you have read, the completion of the transcontinental railroad changed our nation forever. The railroads were built to connect major cities and to reach new resources such as gold and silver. In addition, the routes had to accommodate vast changes in the landscape.

Suppose you wanted to understand how these ideas are presented on a map. Reading a topographic map is one way to relate what you have read with what you see on a map.

Here's How

Look at the map on this page that combines topographical information with the railroad routes. Follow the path of the Central Pacific Railroad from San Francisco to Ogden. You'll see that the route must go through many geographic regions—the Central Valley, the Sierra Nevada, and the Great Basin. It curves dramatically since it must allow for natural land formations like mountains, canyons, and rivers.

Now find the Denver & Rio Grande line. It winds as it crosses the Rockies, not just to cut through the mountain passes, but also to connect with the mining towns of Leadville and Cripple Creek. You can see here that the choice of routes

depended as much upon the location of natural resources as it did on the lay of the land.

Try It

Trace the route of the Northern Pacific Railroad from Fargo to Seattle, and answer the following questions. What major geographic regions does this route cross? Between which two cities is it straightest? What might this tell you about the land there?

What section is the route crossing when it starts to curve noticeably? What does this tell you about the landscape there? What two major mines did this railway pass? Identify major cities along the route. How do

you think the geographical features affected the way people settled this part of the country? How do you think the resources available affected the route of the railroads?

Apply It

Now go back to the map of the First Roads West in Chapter 7. What natural feature does the Nashville Road follow directly west of Richmond? Explain why the Wilderness Road does not go in a straight line from North Carolina to Boonesborough, Kentucky. What do these two maps tell you about the effect of topography on the development of the routes in the East and the West?

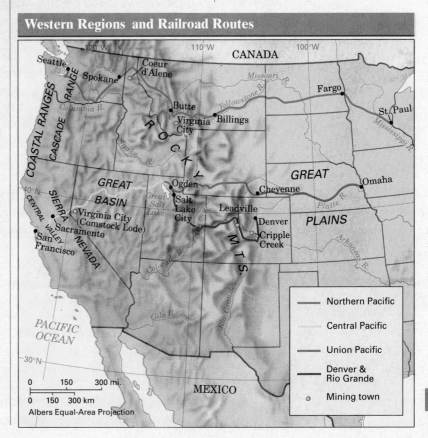

Western Regions and Railroad Routes

Legend:
— Northern Pacific
— Central Pacific
— Union Pacific
— Denver & Rio Grande
○ Mining town

0 150 300 mi.
0 150 300 km
Albers Equal-Area Projection

433

A New Home

Willa Cather

You have read about the hundreds of thousands of homesteaders who settled the Great Plains. This selection tells of how one young boy experienced his new home.

Willa Cather (1873-1947) grew up in Nebraska among immigrant families. My Antonia *is the story of a Czech family is struggling to maintain its farm in hard economic times. In this excerpt Jim Burden, the novel's narrator, sees the land for the first time. As you read, consider the details Jim sees and how he describes his new home.*

Early the next morning I ran out-of-doors to look about me. I had been told that ours was the only wooden house west of Black Hawk—until you came to the Norwegian settlement, where there were several. Our neighbors lived in sod houses and dugouts—comfortable, but not very roomy. Our white frame house, with a storey and half-storey above the basement, stood at the east end of what I might call the farmyard, with the windmill close by the kitchen door. From the windmill the ground sloped westward, down to the barns and granaries and pig-yards. This slope was trampled hard and bare, and washed out in winding gullies by the rain. Beyond the corn-cribs, at the bottom of the shallow draw, was a muddy little pond, with rusty willow bushes growing about it. The road from the post-office came directly by our door, crossed the farmyard, and curved round this little pond, beyond which it began to climb the gentle swell of unbroken prairie to the west. There, along the western sky-line it skirted a great cornfield, much larger than any field I had ever seen. This cornfield, and the sorghum patch behind the barn, were the only broken land in sight. Everywhere, as far as the eye could reach, there was nothing but rough, shaggy, red grass, most of it as tall as I.

North of the house, inside the ploughed fire-breaks, grew a thick-set strip of box-elder trees, low and bushy, their leaves already turning yellow. This hedge was nearly a quarter of a mile long, but I had to look very hard to see it at all. The little trees were insignificant against the grass. It seemed as if the grass were about to run over them, and over the plum-patch behind the sod chicken-house.

As I looked about me I felt that the grass was the country, as the water is the sea. The red of the grass made all the great prairie the colour of wine-stains, or of certain seaweeds when they are first washed up. And there was so much motion in it; the whole country seemed, somehow, to be running.

I had almost forgotten that I had a grandmother, when she came out, her sunbonnet on her head, a grain-sack in her hand, and asked me if I did not want to go to the garden with her to dig potatoes for dinner.

The garden, curiously enough, was a quarter of a mile from the house, and the way to it led up a shallow draw past the cattle corral. Grandmother called my attention to a stout hickory cane, tipped with copper, which hung by a leather thong from her belt. This, she said, was her rattlesnake cane. I must never go to the garden without a heavy stick or a corn-knife; she had killed a good many rattlers on her way back and forth. A little girl who lived on the Black Hawk road was bitten on the ankle and had been sick all summer.

draw ditch

I can remember exactly how the country looked to me as I walked beside my grandmother along the faint wagon-tracks on that early September morning. Perhaps the glide of long railway travel was still with me, for more than anything else I felt motion in the landscape; in the fresh, easy-blowing morning wind, and in the earth itself, as if the shaggy grass were a sort of loose hide, and underneath it herds of wild buffalo were galloping, galloping . . .

Alone, I should never have found the garden—except, perhaps, for the big yellow pumpkins that lay about unprotected by their withering vines—and I felt very little interest in it when I got there. I wanted to walk straight on through the red grass and over the edge of the world, which could not be very far away. The light air about me told me that the world ended here: only the ground and sun and sky were left, and if one went a little farther there would be only sun and sky, and one would float off into them, like the tawny hawks which sailed over our heads making slow shadows on the grass. While grandmother took the pitchfork we found standing in one of the rows and dug potatoes, while I picked them up out of the soft brown earth and put them into the bag, I kept looking up at the hawks that were doing what I might so easily do.

When grandmother was ready to go, I said I would like to stay up there in the garden awhile.

She peered down at me from under her sunbonnet. "Aren't you afraid of snakes?"

"A little," I admitted, "but I'd like to stay, anyhow."

"Well, if you see one, don't have anything to do with him. The big yellow and brown ones won't hurt you; they're bull-snakes and help to keep the gophers down. Don't be scared if you see anything look out of that hole in the bank over there. That's a badger hole. He's about as big as a big 'possum, and his face is striped, black and white. He takes a chicken once in a while, but I won't let the men harm him. In a new country a body feels friendly to the animals. I like to have him come out and watch me when I'm at work."

Grandmother swung the bag of potatoes over her shoulder and went down the path, leaning forward a little. The road followed the windings of the draw; when she came to the first bend, she waved at me and disappeared. I was left alone with this new feeling of lightness and content.

Further Reading

O, Pioneers. Willa Cather. This novel tells another tale of a hardy immigrant woman who matches her determination against the harsh, lonely life of the Nebraska prairie.

Where the Buffalo Roam

B uffalo Bill, Buffalo Bill
Never missed and never will;
Always aims and shoots to
kill
And the company pays his
buffalo bill.

Popular jingle in the late 1800s
about "Buffalo Bill" Cody

I moved up a dead buffalo and got
in several good shots . . . I
moved again, on through the dead
ones, to the farthermost one, and
fired three more shots and quit. As I
walked back through where the carcasses lay the thickest, I could not
help but think that I had done
wrong to make such a slaughter for
the hides alone.

John Cook, buffalo hunter

Background

Between 50 and 70 million buffalo roamed the Great Plains during the early 1800s. By the early 1870s, only 7 million remained.

During the early 1800s, enormous herds of buffalo roamed the Great Plains of America. Daniel Boone followed a buffalo trail through the Appalachian Mountains. This trail became the National Road, or so-called Cumberland Trail, which opened up the American West to settlement. As settlers moved slowly westward, they used buffalo meat as a source of food, buffalo hides for clothing and shelter, and buffalo droppings for heat and cooking fuel.

The buffalo helped in other ways as well. Guides and scouts used the trails of migratory buffalo to identify water holes as well as shallows in rivers where the settlers' heavy wagons could cross. Occasionally, a ribbon of greener, taller, grass fertilized by buffalo droppings marked the path to a water hole.

Western settlers were often amazed at the size of buffalo herds. One traveler in Kansas reported driving a wagon for 25 miles through one continuous herd. (Scientists estimate that the total number of buffalo in the early 1800s was between 50 and 70 million animals.) A great buffalo slaughter, however, began in 1871.

A Resource or a Nuisance?

There were so many buffalo the supply must have seemed endless. Often settlers would shoot several buffalo weighing 1,800 pounds and take only 50 or 75 pounds of meat from each animal. One hunter could kill over 100 buffalo in an hour while standing in one spot. The invention of the Sharp's rifle in 1871 made shooting buffalo even easier, since now the buffalo could be shot from a greater distance.

As the plains became more settled, farming and ranching brought further harm to the buffalo. In order to keep buffalo away from their cattle and crops, farmers used barbed wire. This also served to cut the buffalo off from their water supply.

Buffalo were no longer regarded as a resource, but as a nuisance. Migrating herds often blocked shipping on rivers for days as they swam across, or stopped railroads in their tracks. Angry buffalo bulls were capable of overturning a locomotive. Professional hunters were hired by the railroad companies to guard water holes, shooting the animals when they came to drink.

By 1865, there were only 15 million buffalo remaining, and by 1872 only 7 million. In 1883, a herd of 10,000 animals, the largest in Montana, was exterminated in just a few days. It was while working as such a professional buffalo hunter that William Cody earned his nickname, "Buffalo Bill."

Realizing that the buffalo were in danger of extinction, Walking Coyote, an Indian of the Pend d'Oreille tribe, captured, protected, and bred two pair of buffalo. They became the basis for two herds living in Montana today.

In 1905, Theodore Roosevelt and others founded the American Bison Society to create a buffalo sanctuary. Today, 35,000 buffalo live under government protection in the U.S. and Canada. Although this is a tiny fraction of their former number, they are no longer in danger of extinction.

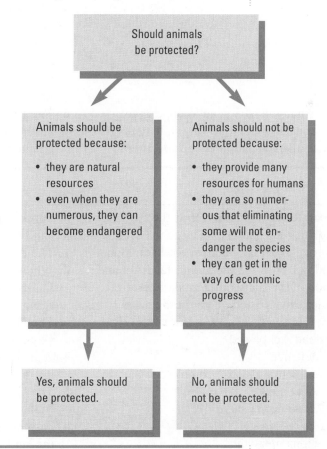

Should animals be protected?

Animals should be protected because:

- they are natural resources
- even when they are numerous, they can become endangered

Animals should not be protected because:

- they provide many resources for humans
- they are so numerous that eliminating some will not endanger the species
- they can get in the way of economic progress

Yes, animals should be protected.

No, animals should not be protected.

Decision Point

1. Compare the goals and values of those who wanted to protect the buffalo with those who hunted the buffalo.
2. Buffalo herds require enormous amounts of range land—land that could be used for farming or ranching. Which use is more important? Can you think of a compromise to allow for both?
3. Identify an issue in your state or region that involves a conflict between protecting wildlife and meeting peoples' needs. Collect news articles about the issue and discuss it in class.

Chapter Review

Reviewing Key Terms

annuity (p. 423)
assimilate (p. 425)
bonanza (p. 413)
boom town (p. 414)

homestead (p. 427)
reservation (p. 424)
transcontinental (p. 412)

A. In each of the following pairs, the two terms are related in some way. Write a sentence for each pair that clearly explains the relationship between the two terms.

1. bonanza, boom town
2. reservation, annuity
3. assimilate, reservation
4. transcontinental, boom town

B. Based on what you have read in the chapter, decide whether each of the following statements is accurate. Write an explanation of each decision.

1. Before homesteaders could settle on the prairie, they had to cut down the forests.
2. The transcontinental railroad connected the East Coast of North America with the West Coast.
3. Miners had to cut through layers of rock in order to reach the bonanza that contained silver or gold.
4. The opportunity to homestead enabled many people to start their own farms and ranches.
5. In order to allow people to pass safely through Indian territory, the government offered to supply tribes with food, clothing, and other necessities.
6. The government's efforts to assimilate the Indians by sending them to government schools was a failure.

Exploring Concepts

A. On a separate sheet of paper, copy the timeline below. Complete your timeline by using the events listed below (one event has been entered as a model for you to follow). How did the Homestead Act and the completion of the transcontinental railroad affect the other events listed on your timeline?

- Homestead Act passed
- Custer defeated
- Transcontinental railroad completed
- Dawes Act passed
- Wounded Knee massacre
- Nez Perce resistance
- Santee Sioux uprising

B. Support each of the following statements with facts and details from the chapter.

1. The American West has a variety of landforms.
2. When white settlers first crossed the Great Plains, they didn't settle there for a number of reasons.
3. The Plains Indians used the buffalo in many ways.
4. Many factors kept the Plains Indians from uniting into a single people.
5. The U.S. government sought to destroy the Indians' traditional way of life.
6. Farmers and ranchers had conflicting needs for the land.

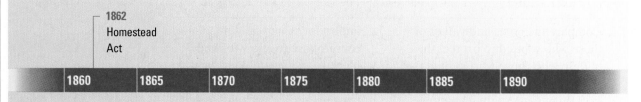

1862
Homestead
Act

| 1860 | 1865 | 1870 | 1875 | 1880 | 1885 | 1890 |

438

Reviewing Skills

1. Look at the map of Routes of Western Explorers on page 227, and trace the route of Lewis and Clark. Determine how their path followed the natural features of the land.

2. Follow the route of the Union Pacific Railroad in the map on page 433. What natural feature did it follow west of Omaha? What regions of the country did it cover? How does this information relate to what you already know about the difficulties faced by the men who built the railroad? Note the photo at right of the "loop" at Georgetown, Colorado where the railroad crosses Clear Creek, 85 feet above another set of tracks.

3. Based on what you have read in this chapter, determine the causes and effects of the Santee Sioux uprising. Write a paragraph explaining your determination.

4. Suppose you wanted to plan a hiking trip across the Cascade Mountains that would take

you across in the straightest line with the least difficulty. What kind of map (or maps) would you need to consult before you made such a trip?

Using Critical Thinking

1. The U. S. government loaned the companies that built the transcontinental railroads between $16,000 and $48,000 for each mile of track they built. The government also gave them vast tracts of public land along the rails. Why do you think the government did this? What effects did it have?

2. Black Elk, a Sioux Indian, wrote in 1886: "Once we were happy in our own country and we were seldom hungry, for then the two-leggeds and the four-leggeds lived together like relatives, and

there was plenty for them and for us." What do you think he meant by that statement? What do you think he would have said about the white settlers who took over his lands?

3. It has been said that the settlement of the Great Plains was made possible by the killing of the buffalo, the development of the transcontinental railroads, and the introduction of the windmill. Why was each of those actions important to the settlement of the plains? Would you add any items to that list? Explain your answer.

Preparing for Citizenship

1. **WRITING ACTIVITY** Just as many people who live in America today have very different lifestyles, the Plains Indians and the white settlers had very different ways of living. Make a table comparing the two cultures in the following areas: (a) forms of government, (b) beliefs about owning land, (c) types of shelter, (d) religious beliefs, and (e) ways of making a living. Write a short report explaining how the conflicts between these two cultures were resolved. Include your opinion on whether there could have been a better way for the Indians to have become a part of the United States society.

2. **ART ACTIVITY** Imagine you are working for the government or a railroad company in the late 1800s. Design a poster or video advertisement encouraging settlers to move West.

3. **COLLABORATIVE LEARNING** As a class, form committees that have the goal of attracting more people to your area. Each committee should design advertisements explaining different aspects of the benefits of life in your area. You might stress such things as climate, scenic landscape, good transportation, recreational and cultural opportunities, job opportunities, and the availability of schools.

Chapter 15

Industry and Workers

After the Civil War, a new America was in the making. New building techniques transformed the nation's cities. Immigrants expanded the nation's workforce. Together with new inventions, new methods of manufacturing, and new ways to sell products, the United States became an industrial leader.

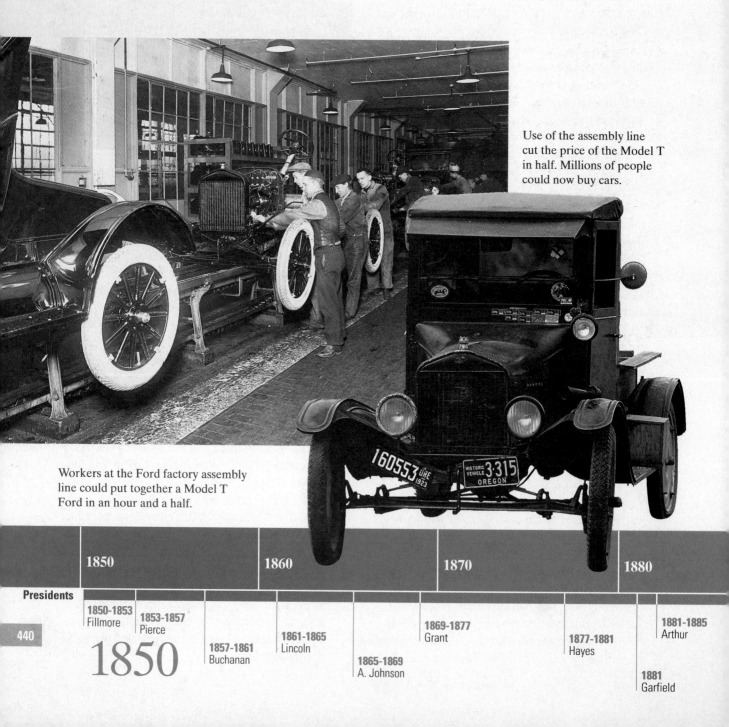

Use of the assembly line cut the price of the Model T in half. Millions of people could now buy cars.

Workers at the Ford factory assembly line could put together a Model T Ford in an hour and a half.

Presidents	1850			1860		1870		1880	
	1850-1853 Fillmore	1853-1857 Pierce		1861-1865 Lincoln		1869-1877 Grant			1881-1885 Arthur
			1857-1861 Buchanan		1865-1869 A. Johnson		1877-1881 Hayes	1881 Garfield	

1850

Immigrants throng to factories in industrial cities such as Cleveland, seeking new jobs and a new life in America.

1888 The lantern slide projector is one of the many inventions that provide Americans with new kinds of entertainment.

Advertisers used pictures of stylishly dressed women and children to promote labor-saving devices for the home.

THE LEONARD DRY AIR CLEANABLE REFRIGERATOR

BUCKEYE LAWN MOWER

| 1890 | 1900 | 1910 | 1920 |

1885-1889
Cleveland

1889-1893
B. Harrison

1893-1897
Cleveland

1897-1901
McKinley

1901-1909
T. Roosevelt

1909-1913
Taft

1913-1921
Wilson

1920

LESSON 1

Building the American Dream

THINKING FOCUS

What caused the massive economic growth that occurred in the United States following the Civil War?

Key Terms

- entrepreneur
- capital
- profit
- philanthropist

➤ *The 1876 Centennial Exposition in Philadelphia attracted eight million people. Visitors gathered to see America's latest technological advances.*

As the sun reached noon that May day in 1876, a chorus broke into the soaring music of Handel's "Hallelujah Chorus," a hundred guns boomed, steam whistles blew, bells rang, and swarms of people cheered. The occasion? It was the Centennial Exhibition in Philadelphia, a gigantic fair celebrating 100 years of American independence.

Over the next six months, eight million people jammed the exhibition grounds, jostling to see the exhibits. They marveled at animated wax figures, an automated baby feeder, and a gas-heated iron. They sampled bread made with a new kind of yeast, the products from a cheese factory, and foods from many countries. What impressed them most, however, were the wondrous new machines.

These machines were put into motion when President Ulysses S. Grant started the gigantic Corliss steam engine. Forty feet high, the Corliss engine operated 13 acres of machinery. Humming textile machines combed wool, spun cotton, and sewed cloth. Clattering presses printed newspapers and stamped wallpaper. Other machines sawed logs, pumped water, and carved wood.

Commented Western poet Joaquin Miller, "How the American's heart thrills with pride and love of his land as he contemplates the vast exhibition of art and prowess here." He then predicted, "Great as it seems today, it is but the acorn from which shall grow the wide-spreading oak of a century's progress."

The Centennial did indeed herald the world of the future. It announced America's coming of age as one of the great industrial nations of the world.

Amazing Inventions

Between 1870 and 1920, U.S. inventors came up with many mechanical and scientific innovations. Ranging from impractical gadgets to major innovations, their inventions poured into the U.S. Patent Office, where new inventions are registered. Between 1860 and 1900 alone, some 676,000 patents were filed. Many of these inventions became part of daily life everywhere.

One of the most influential inventions, a practical electric light, radically changed the face of cities. Lighted streets discouraged crime and invited people to stroll through the city after dark. Blinking lights on theater entrances caught public attention. By replacing oil and gas lamps, electric lights eliminated the danger of fires in theaters, factories, and homes.

The Electric Spark

Thomas Alva Edison, one of the greatest inventors in history, developed the first practical electric light. He also developed the generating system needed to produce electricity as well as hundreds of other useful inventions.

Edison is an outstanding example of a person whose curiosity and imagination brought him great success. Educated largely by his schoolteacher mother and motivated by boundless curiosity, Edison at the age of nine was busy conducting chemistry experiments. In later life, he performed as many as 10,000 experiments for a single project.

Impatient to try out new ideas, he often worked around the clock, stopping only for brief naps in a corner of his workroom. "Genius," Edison said, "is one percent inspiration and ninety-nine percent perspiration." In addition to the electric light, Edison's phonograph and improved motion pictures helped change the way people spent their leisure time.

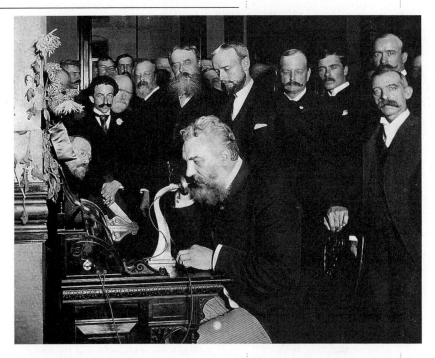

Faster Communications

Almost equaling the electric light in importance was the telephone invented by Alexander Graham Bell. Like his father, who taught the hearing-impaired to speak, Scottish-born Bell was fascinated by the mechanics of speech. Bell developed the idea of transmitting speech by electric waves and worked 10 years to devise the necessary machinery.

In March 1876, Bell patented the telephone, and within a year the first telephone company was founded. Businesses everywhere wanted this new invention. By 1900, about 1.5 million telephones were in use in the United States. The age of modern communications had begun.

Two other innovations that made business operations easier were the typewriter and the linotype machine. In 1872, the first commercially produced keyboard typewriter was developed by Christopher Latham Sholes in Milwaukee, Wisconsin. Businesses enthusiastically welcomed the new machine, which

Alexander Graham Bell is seated at the New York end of the first New York-Chicago telephone connection in 1892.

Bell's first model of his 1875 telephone was exhibited at the Centennial Exhibition in 1876.

443

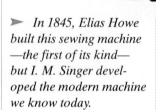

➤ *In 1845, Elias Howe built this sewing machine —the first of its kind— but I. M. Singer developed the modern machine we know today.*

■ *How did Edison's and Bell's inventions change American industry?*

➤ *Advertisements for the Singer sewing machine such as the one shown here boasted about the convenience of the cabinet table where the machine could be stored.*

helped productivity. Author Mark Twain commented, "One may lean back in his chair and work it. It piles up an awful stack of words on one page. It don't muss things or scatter ink blots around."

The introduction of the linotype machine in 1884 by German-born Ottmar Mergenthaler revolutionized the publishing industry. Instead of positioning each line of type manually letter by letter, an operator used a typewriter-like keyboard to set a whole line of type automatically. A full page of type was then inked and run through the rotary press (in use since 1846). This invention greatly speeded the production of newspapers, magazines, and books.

In addition to the telephone, typewriter, and linotype machine, adding machines and cash registers increased the speed of business transactions. All these machines helped to transform communications and production in American business.

From Invention to Industry

Another invention that revolutionized an industry was the sewing machine. Since the 1700s, inventors had experimented with crude mechanical sewing devices. But the first practical sewing machine was not patented until 1846.

While working in a factory that made machinery for the cotton industry, Elias Howe realized that sewing was the only part of the process still done by hand. For the next five years he labored to invent a sewing machine. Howe demonstrated the new machine's speed by competing with five girls sewing by hand. Although Howe held the patent on the sewing machine, the marvelous device came to be associated with a machinist named I. M. Singer.

In 1851, Singer was given a sewing machine to fix. He immediately saw how it could be improved, and within a short time he set up a company that used a unique system to manufacture sewing machines. An organizational genius and innovator, Singer was the first person to spend one million dollars a year on advertising.

By 1880, the Singer Manufacturing Company was manufacturing over 500,000 sewing machines each year and shipping them to homes and factories all over the world. By continually adopting new technological developments and using energetic promotion, the company grew into the world's largest manufacturer of a single product. ■

Chapter 15

The Economy Transformed

Singer started his business with very little money. Through innovative manufacturing and efficient business methods he built a huge industry. He is an example of the **entrepreneur** *(ahn truh pruh NUR)*, a farsighted, ambitious person who organizes and assumes the risk of a business venture. Between 1870 and 1920, entrepreneurs built companies that helped to transform the United States into an industrial giant.

Building Bigger Businesses

Efficient, large-scale production like Singer's depended on large amounts of **capital** or wealth—money or property used in a business. Capital is used to build factories, then to buy raw materials and to hire employees. Some money came from the government. For example, to promote the building of railroads, the government granted the railroad companies huge tracts of free land for the tracks. The companies could then sell the adjoining property to raise money. Other funds came from banks and individual investors. Banker J. Pierpont Morgan, for example, loaned money to companies manufacturing steel, farm equipment, telephones, and electricity. Each loan was repaid with interest. The amount left over after all expenses had been paid was **profit**.

Often entrepreneurs combined several small businesses to form larger companies. Well organized and efficiently operated, these huge companies repaid investors several times over.

Because large companies often made high profits, banks did not hesitate to lend them money. In this way big companies tended to get bigger. Soon men like John D. Rockefeller, one of the founders of the U.S. oil industry, banker J. Pierpont Morgan, and railroad entrepreneur Cornelius Vanderbilt became fabulously wealthy and earned the nickname "Captains of Industry." ■

■ *Explain how early entrepreneurs operated in the business world.*

▼ *For thousands of readers, Horatio Alger's heroes represented the American Dream.*

Realizing the American Dream

Many successful entrepreneurs rose to their positions of power from great poverty. These wealthy people represented "the American Dream." Young people were taught to believe that they could be financially wealthy, no matter how humble their beginnings, if only they would work hard enough. The popular writer Horatio Alger promoted this idea in his many novels with the theme of rags-to-riches. The heroes in his novels were poor boys who achieved wealth, a high social position, and power through hard work, virtuous living, and an unusual amount of luck.

The American Dream Achieved

Perhaps there is no better example of someone achieving the American Dream than Andrew Carnegie. The son of a Scottish weaver, Carnegie came to America at the age of 12 and began working for low wages at a cotton mill near Pittsburgh. By age 17, he was private secretary to the president of the Pennsylvania Railroad.

Carnegie became rich from an oil well he bought in his mid-twenties. He moved into steel production and introduced the newly invented blast furnace. It used a process in which a blast of air was introduced as iron ore melted. The oxygen in the air

FACING THE WORLD

BY HORATIO ALGER JR.

The Carnegie Library in Pittsburgh is one of many libraries established by philanthropist Andrew Carnegie.

■ *What does the term "rags to riches" mean? Give an example of someone who "realized" the American Dream.*

combined with the carbon in the iron, leaving the steel nearly pure. The new process was so efficient that Carnegie's factory produced more steel than all the other U.S. mills combined. The cost of a ton of steel dropped from $100 to $12.

Despite this lower price, demand and Carnegie's profits soared because of the many new ways in which steel was being used. These uses included rails for railroads, frames for buildings and bridges, and everyday wire, nails, and bolts. Soon Carnegie owned not only steel mills and the pig iron and coal used to make steel but also the railroads and ships that carried the finished product to market. By 1900, the company's yearly profits had reached $40 million. Carnegie had become one of the world's richest men.

Carnegie was quick to defend the accumulation of great wealth. He believed that business benefited when a few industrialists controlled the wealth, because such leaders were interested in promoting efficiency and good organization.

The Gospel of Wealth

In later life, Carnegie became a famous **philanthropist**—a person who promotes human welfare by funding beneficial public institutions. Though he himself had almost no formal education, Carnegie believed that access to books was a key to success. He therefore established libraries in towns throughout the United States. He also gave large sums to set up many scholarships, to construct public buildings, and to found the Endowment for International Peace.

Carnegie's great generosity sprang from his belief that those who acquired great wealth had a responsibility to give a portion of it back to society. In 1889, he wrote a series of essays expressing this idea. Known as the "Gospel of Wealth," Carnegie's ideas reflected his belief that hard work brought success. ■

R E V I E W

1. **FOCUS** What caused the massive economic growth that occurred in the United States following the Civil War?

2. **CONNECT** How do you think the railroad contributed to the development of American cities?

3. **CULTURE** How did inventions change the way Americans lived and worked?

4. **ECONOMICS** How did new developments in transportation, communications, and production affect business?

5. **CRITICAL THINKING** What does the term *American Dream* mean?

6. **WRITING ACTIVITY** Imagine how different your life would be without a telephone. Write a short essay describing how an average day would be different if you couldn't use a phone.

Chapter 15

L E S S O N   2

Moving into Industrial Cities

A popular legend says that a cow kicked over a lantern and started the great fire that burned down much of Chicago in October 1871.

Whether the cow actually ignited the blaze is unknown. Historians are sure, however, that the flames first appeared in the O'Leary barn. High winds fanned the fire through block after block of wooden buildings. The blaze, an eyewitness later wrote, devoured "the most stately and massive buildings as though they had been the cardboard playthings of a child."

Fleeing before the flames, terrified crowds plunged into the icy waters of Lake Michigan. The fire raged for over 24 hours, destroying 18,000 buildings. Firefighters had to dynamite entire city blocks in order to deprive the fire of fuel and bring it under control.

The fire's toll was staggering: 300 people died, and 90,000 people—nearly a third of the city's population—lost their homes. Property damage amounted to $200 million.

Yet the disaster did not destroy the spirit of the people, who immediately began to rebuild the city. The massive reconstruction attracted some of the nation's best architects as well as thousands of laborers, many of them immigrants. Within a year Chicago was well on its way to becoming the second largest city in the United States and revolutionizing American architecture in the process.

THINKING FOCUS

How did industrial development and the growth of cities change American life during the late 1800s and early 1900s?

Key Terms

- urban society

◄ *This lithograph by Currier and Ives shows Chicago's great fire of October 1871.*

447

Industrial Cities Develop

The rebirth of Chicago was part of a dramatic industrial expansion that caused incredible growth in the nation's cities. Between 1850 and 1900, the population of many American cities doubled and then doubled again. As the map on page 452 shows, many of today's large cities grew from towns to cities during this period. Such growth heralded the birth of a new **urban society**, a society based on city life.

Industry Creates Cities

Before the Civil War, most factories were built along lakes or rivers in order to harness water power and to take advantage of the low cost of water transportation. As oil and electricity began to power the machines of industry, these factory towns experienced tremendous growth. Cities that were centrally located became junctions for many railroad lines.

Cleveland, Ohio, was one of the cities that made the dramatic change from a commercial to an industrial center. Located on Lake Erie, Cleveland was a busy town of 6,000 people in the early 1800s. In 1851, when the railroad connected it with Columbus, the state capital, Cleveland was transformed into a thriving city. By 1900, nearly 290,000 people lived there.

Railroad connections brought iron ore from Minnesota and coal from Pennsylvania, helping Cleveland become a major producer of locomotives and other iron products. During this period the city also became the chief refining center for Pennsylvania oil. In 1870, John D. Rockefeller organized the Standard Oil Company in Cleveland.

A traveler entering Cleveland passed bustling steel factories and oil refineries on the outskirts. The poor part of the city housed thousands of immigrants—Hungarians, Poles, Lithuanians, and Russians—who worked in the mills. Most lived in shabby houses where several families were crowded together. Few houses had any plumbing, and the stench of wastes

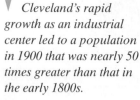

Cleveland's rapid growth as an industrial center led to a population in 1900 that was nearly 50 times greater than that in the early 1800s.

and garbage mixed with factory smoke, choking the air. Sludge from industries and sewage from homes were dumped into Lake Erie, contributing to widespread disease.

Yet a traveler could also feel a sense of excitement in Cleveland. On every side new buildings were going up; horse-drawn wagons, trolley cars (vehicles powered by an overhead wire), and pedestrians crowded the streets. Vendors sold vegetables, coal, ice, and fish. Newspaperboys such as the one shown on page 450 yelled the day's headlines. In the city's center, shoppers thronged to the new department stores, where they could buy everything from shoes to china.

Cities That Specialized

Cleveland's main industry was building locomotives for the nation's busy railroads. Other cities that specialized in one regional product were Pittsburgh, Pennsylvania (steel); Minneapolis, Minnesota (flour from midwestern wheat); Schenectady, New York (electrical goods); Corning, New York (glass); Memphis, Tennessee (cottonseed oil); Birmingham, Alabama (iron and steel); Denver, Colorado (mining); and Portland, Oregon (metal processing).

Chicago, with the largest manufacturing base of all, also enjoyed a strategic location. Located between the East and the Great Plains, Chicago was linked to the Atlantic Ocean by the Great Lakes and the St. Lawrence River. A canal joining it to the Illinois and Mississippi rivers connected it with New Orleans and the Gulf of Mexico. Chicago's superior transportation system linked it to resources and markets all over the country. The city quickly became the hub, or center, of U.S. railroad traffic.

New Uses for Steel

In the growing industrial cities, space became increasingly valuable. For decades, architects had dreamed of lofty buildings that would tower into the sky, but such buildings had been impossible to build with wood, brick, and stone. Those materials could not support the enormous weight of many stories. The use of steel frames as interior skeletons solved this problem. In Chicago, William LeBaron Jenney designed the Home Insurance building, the first skyscraper constructed with a metal frame, in 1884.

Steel frames also made the suspension bridge possible. The bridge's roadway is suspended by thick cables, and is strong enough to support trains and other traffic.

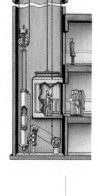

▲ *The Reliance building, constructed in 1895 in Chicago, is an example of steel frame construction. Electric elevators moved people to the upper stories. Multistory buildings changed the American cityscape forever.*

A Chicago Newsboy

8:16 A.M., November 9, 1904
On a busy street corner in Chicago

Newspaper
"Roosevelt Re-elected!" he shouts.
"Winner by a Landslide!" He'll
yell this headline for about five
hours today.

Bruised Cheek
Because newsboys sell more
papers on busy corners, they
often fight for the best spots.
This morning, he won the corner,
but came away with a bruise.

Badge
Children who are less than 10
years old cannot sell papers
on the streets. They must be
in school. This badge tells
settlement workers that this
boy is old enough to work.

Secret Pocket
"Only 3 cents!" He keeps a
penny for each paper he
sells. The money, stashed in
this hidden pocket, helps
pay for food, rent, and coal
for his family.

Bundles of Papers
Each morning and evening, he
carries two bundles—about 30
pounds each—from a corner
three blocks away where the
delivery man drops them.

Shoes
These worn out "hand-me-
downs" are from his dad.
Too big for his feet, the
shoes are tied on with string
from his bundles.

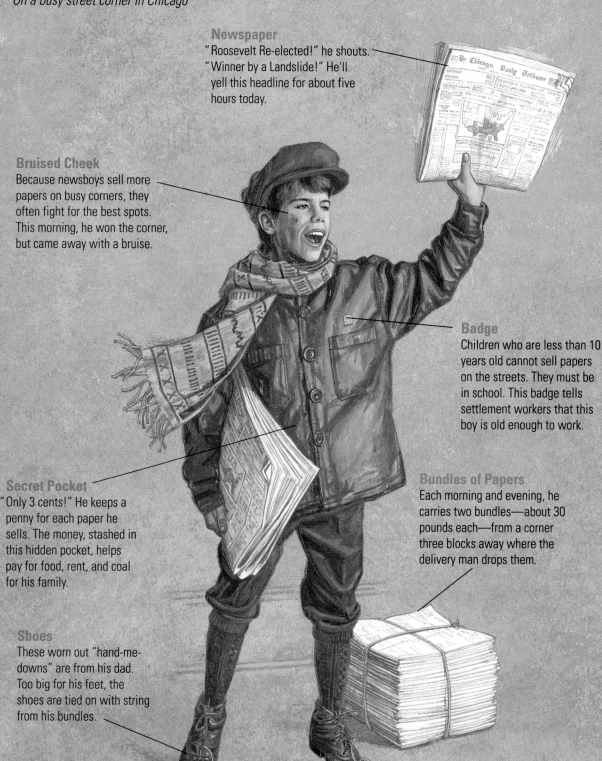

German immigrant John A. Roebling, a pioneer in the field, employed a steel framework in his design for the Brooklyn Bridge. The bridge was completed in 1883, and spanned the East River, connecting Brooklyn, New York to the island of Manhattan. With a span of 1,595 feet, the bridge was the longest of its kind in the world at that time. ■

■ *How did the new uses of steel change ways of constructing buildings? How did such changes aid transportation?*

Rural People Migrate to Cities

Just as the gold fields had lured settlers westward, the promise of a glowing future drew millions of rural Americans into the cities. In 1860, only one person in five lived in a city. By 1915, urban centers contained fully one-half the population of the United States.

Cheap Transportation

In 1850, cross-country travel had been a major undertaking lasting months. The railroads drastically reduced travel time. For far less money, and in relative comfort and safety, a family could travel to a distant state in only a few days. By 1900, cheap, practical transportation had created a more mobile society in which people could pack up and follow the trail of opportunity. This trail most often led to the cities, where people hoped they would find employment.

The Job-Seekers

Chicago's industrial boom changed many lives. In his novel, *Sister Carrie*, author Theodore Dreiser described how the great promise of opportunity and excitement attracted people to the city of Chicago. A passage from the novel appears below.

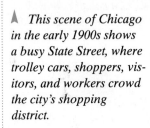

Some rural people moved to the cities in search of a new life. Many, however, were forced to move because they had lost their jobs when new inventions mechanized farming. With a single machine capable of doing the work formerly done by a dozen people using horse-drawn implements, the need for farm workers declined. Other rural workers lost their jobs when large businesses drove foundries, sawmills, and other small rural industries out of business. By 1910, a third of those living in cities had come from farms and small towns in the countryside. ■

▲ *This scene of Chicago in the early 1900s shows a busy State Street, where trolley cars, shoppers, visitors, and workers crowd the city's shopping district.*

*C*hicago had the peculiar qualifications of growth which made . . . adventuresome pilgrimages even on the part of young girls plausible. Its many and growing commercial opportunities gave it widespread fame, which made of it a giant magnet, drawing to itself, from all quarters, the hopeful and the hopeless—those who had their fortune yet to make and those whose fortunes and affairs had reached a disastrous climax elsewhere. It was a city of over 500,000, with the ambition, the daring, the activity of a metropolis of a million.

■ *What led people living on farms and in small towns to move to cities?*

451

Southern Blacks Move North

Northern cities also attracted many Southern blacks. They sought not only economic opportunity but also an escape from the unfair and often brutal treatment they received at the hands of Southern whites.

Although African Americans had been freed from slavery, many whites still considered them inferior. Persecuted by violent racist organizations such as the Ku Klux Klan, tens of thousands of blacks left the South after 1877.

Despite this wave of migration, in 1880, nine out of ten of America's 6.6 million blacks still worked on Southern farms or as domestic servants. Some of them enrolled in the abandoned Alabama church where Booker T. Washington had established Tuskegee Institute in 1881. At Tuskegee, blacks learned vocational, or trade-related, skills and took courses in teaching. Washington was convinced that blacks could improve their lives by learning practical skills or by becoming teachers. Instead of demanding that blacks seek social

➤ *Before the Civil War, fewer than one in five Americans lived in cities. By 1920, industrial centers across the country drew increasing numbers of people seeking better opportunities. America's population became almost equally divided between urban and rural areas.*

Across Time & Space

In contrast to 19th-century cities, modern cities are beginning to run out of space. Consequently, architects like Paolo Soleri design cities for the future that will occupy very small areas. Apartments, stores, robot-run factories, businesses, schools, and theaters will be grouped around parks and walkways in order to provide land for crops, woodland, and environmental preservation.

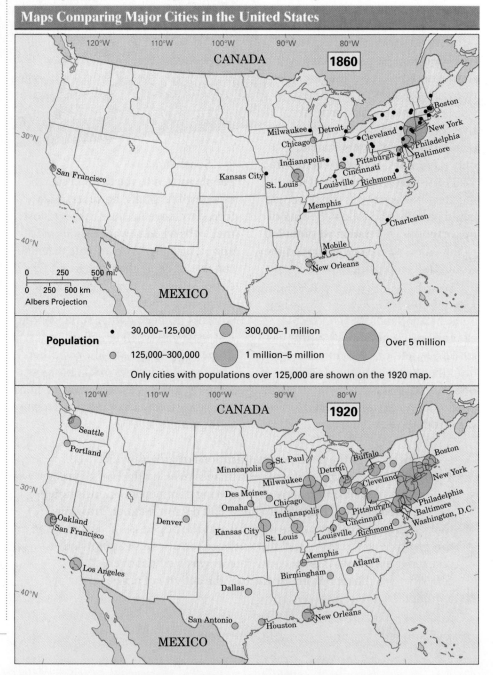

Maps Comparing Major Cities in the United States

Population
- 30,000–125,000
- 125,000–300,000
- 300,000–1 million
- 1 million–5 million
- Over 5 million

Only cities with populations over 125,000 are shown on the 1920 map.

equality, Washington focused on economic opportunity rather than political status. This was a view that most blacks rejected.

Washington and his followers did help African Americans make some gains. Yet poverty and bigotry, or intolerance, remained. In the 1890s, with lynchings at an all-time high, a second wave of blacks migrated to Northern cities.

The largest black migration to cities in this period occurred during World War I, when European immigration to America ceased. According to the Census Bureau, 330,000 Southern blacks moved to the North and West from 1910 to 1920. Crop failures and economic hardship in the South forced many to make the move. A growing need for factory workers also offered blacks opportunities in industrial cities.

Help for Black Migrants

The move north gave many African Americans opportunities they had never known before. But adjusting to a completely different way of life proved difficult. Several groups stepped in to help rural blacks adjust to urban life. Black churches, which had provided aid during the long years of slavery, supplied information about jobs and housing.

The largest organization offering assistance to blacks was the National Urban League. Founded in 1911, it provided blacks with temporary housing, information about work, and training for industrial jobs.

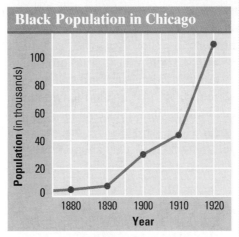

Black Population in Chicago

(Graph: Population (in thousands) vs. Year. Values rise from near 0 in 1880 and 1890 to about 30 in 1900, about 45 in 1910, and about 110 in 1920.)

▲ *As an industrial center, the city of Chicago attracted thousands of Southern blacks in search of jobs and better lives. This Southern family is shown arriving in Chicago.*

◄ *This graph shows the dramatic increase in the migration of Southern black people to urban areas.*

With the help of such organizations, blacks were able to make a place for themselves in Northern cities. There they, like other American workers, found themselves competing for jobs with newly arrived immigrants from Europe and Asia. ■

■ *How did black communities help people adjust to city life?*

R E V I E W

1. **FOCUS** How did industrial development and the growth of cities change American life during the late 1800s and early 1900s?

2. **CONNECT** Why did black Americans leave the South and migrate north and west after Reconstruction? What new challenges did they face?

3. **HISTORY** How did industrialization affect rural workers? Why would a farmer have moved to a large city?

4. **ECONOMICS** What effect did cheap transportation have on American business?

5. **CRITICAL THINKING** How did technological improvements change the lives of Americans?

6. **WRITING ACTIVITY** You are a farmer who has moved to the city to work in a factory. Write two or three diary entries that describe the sights and sounds of city and factory.

453

Industry and Workers

Comparing Population Maps

Here's Why

A thematic map presents a specific kind of information about the area it shows. Comparing thematic maps from different time periods will help you understand historical trends.

One such trend that has played an important role throughout American history is the movement of people from one area to another. From 1900 to 1920 the United States experienced rapid change as the economy shifted from agriculture to industry. This shift was reflected in the rapid growth of cities.

Suppose you wanted to see the changes in both population and industry of an area over a particular period of time. Comparing thematic maps is one way to do that.

Here's How

Look at the maps below of the midwestern United States. Note the key for population size and industrial areas. In 1900, Chicago was the largest city on the map, having a population of over one million. St. Louis and Pittsburgh were the only other cities over 500,000. Now look at the 1920 map. Chicago is still the largest city, but notice how many other cities—Detroit, Cleveland, and Buffalo—are now as large as St. Louis and Pittsburgh. Such comparisons show that Americans moved into these cities quite rapidly in only 20 years.

Look at the two maps again. This time compare the shaded parts that represent major industrial areas. Notice how those areas changed from 1900 to 1920.

Try It

Look at the maps again. How does the number of cities on the 1920 map compare with the number on the 1900 map? How does the change in industrial areas compare with the change in the number of cities? What relationship can you see between the change in the number and size of cities and the change in the industrial areas?

Apply It

Look at the U. S. population maps on pages 704 and 705. Compare the population density of the West Coast in 1870 to that of 1910. Which areas grew to have over 45 people per square mile? Which areas on the 1980 map now have more than 90 people per square mile? How has West Coast population changed in this century?

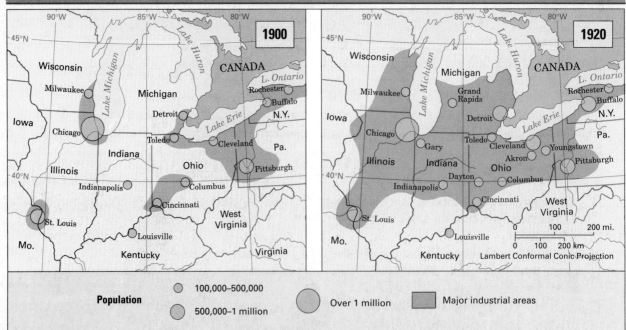

Development of Industrial Cities, 1900-1920

Population 100,000–500,000 500,000–1 million Over 1 million Major industrial areas

L E S S O N   3

The Workers' Changing World

Our machines were on long tables in large rooms, and we operators sat on both sides of the tables. At last I was where I wanted to be, and here I worked for ten years." Thus Agnes Nestor begins her account of life in a glove-making shop. Five feet tall, blue eyed, and delicate because of her poor health, Agnes started work when she was 17. "To drown the monotony of work," she continued, "we used to sing. This was allowed because the foreman could see that the rhythm kept us going at high speed. We sang 'A Bicycle Built for Two' and other popular songs.

"Before we began to sing we used to talk very loudly so as to be heard above the roar of the machines. We knew we must not stop our work just to hear what someone was saying; to stop work even for a minute meant a reduction in pay."

The women did piecework—that is, they were paid not by the hour but according to the number of pieces that they completed. The more gloves they sewed, the more they earned. They therefore had to work as fast as they could. However, Agnes pointed out, "There were always pace makers, a few girls who could work faster than the rest. . . . Their rate of work had to be the rate for all of us, if we were to earn a decent wage. It kept us tensed to continual hurry." This was known as "the sweating system," and the shops were known as "sweatshops."

Although their wages were pitifully small, Agnes noted that the women had to pay for some of the equipment they used. "We were charged fifty cents a week for the power furnished our machines. . . . We were obliged, besides, to buy our own needles. If you broke one, you were charged for a new one to replace it. We had, also, to buy our own machine oil."

THINKING FOCUS

How did changes in production affect the way in which Americans lived and worked during the late 1800s and early 1900s?

Key Terms

- assembly line
- strike
- labor union

◄ *Henry Bergman photographed these German immigrant seamstresses in a Wisconsin clothing factory around 1890.*

Production Speeds Up

Across Time & Space

When Americans and Canadians take the first Monday in September as a holiday, they are celebrating Labor Day, the day that honors all working people. The Australian version is called Eight-Hour Day, which honors workers' success in gaining a shorter working day. Appropriately, Labor Day was first suggested by two American workers—machinist Matthew Maguire and carpenter Peter McGuire.

▼ *Workers leave the Ford Motor Company factory in Detroit, Michigan. The plant covers more than 47 acres of floor space. Each worker specializes in one part of assembling an automobile.*

Women did not work under such conditions by choice. Like many rural migrants, they lacked job training and could only work as unskilled laborers. As factories became more mechanized, however, the need for unskilled labor grew.

Assembly Line

In 1913–1914 Henry Ford introduced the first moving **assembly line** in his automobile plant in Detroit, Michigan. A continuously moving belt carried parts past workers, each of whom performed one specific task in the assembly process. Wrote Ford, "The idea came . . . from the overhead trolley that the Chicago packers used in dressing—that is, cutting up—beef."

Ford envisioned an automobile that almost anyone could afford. The assembly line helped him meet his goal. Before Ford's innovation, a car body took twelve and a half hours to assemble. The cost of this labor helped make cars expensive. By reducing the time to a mere hour and a half, the assembly line process allowed Ford to sell cars for less money.

Assembly-line techniques were quickly applied to other industries.

Floor space in manufacturing plants was arranged so that one step followed another in a logical sequence, eliminating wasted movements.

Mass Production

The assembly line permitted mass production—that is, the manufacture of large quantities of the same item. Mass production allowed manufacturers to turn out products more quickly, more cheaply, and in larger amounts than ever before.

Mass production not only speeded up manufacturing; it also increased the investor's profit. The new system allowed factory managers to order raw materials in large quantities. As a result, costs were reduced. Producing many of the same items meant that machines could be used over and over for the same job. Such use of machines also reduced costs.

Improved communications and transportation networks also contributed to faster production. Between 1870 and 1920, railroads and steamships provided a cheap means of transporting goods. The telephone and telegraph helped manufacturers keep

in touch with current trends in industry. Electric lighting made it possible to operate factories for a full 24-hour period, thus increasing production.

Machine-tending workers provided the labor for much of the work done in factories. As more efficient machines were invented, fewer skills were needed to run them. Previously, one person might have been involved in several stages of production. Under the system known as division of labor, the different stages were divided among several workers. Each worker performed a single operation. For example, every 20 seconds the worker might pull down a lever so a machine could punch a hole in a steel plate. The punched plate then slid along a moving belt and a new one replaced it. The worker pulled the lever again, repeating the process, over and over, for 10 hours a day. Besides being repetitious, such jobs paid very low wages, causing workers to change jobs frequently. This turnover contributed to the increasing call for unskilled labor. ■

■ *Explain how the assembly line changed production.*

The Workers Struggle

Workers shared few of the increased profits of mechanized production. The fear of losing their jobs made workers endure abuses and made it easy for managers to take advantage of them.

Working Conditions

Young, inexperienced workers or those who could not speak English suffered most, but nearly all industrial laborers felt the effects of harsh working conditions. Andrew Carnegie described how he himself was exploited when he was a boy working in the cotton mills. He worked in "the dark cellar running a steam engine at two dollars a week, begrimed with coal dirt, without a trace of the elevating influences of life" (such as books, music, art, and recreation).

Factories often paid low wages; unskilled workers in the 1880s might earn an average daily wage of $1.50. They worked six days a week, earning $9 a week, $36 a month with no vacation time. Since rent for a single room might cost $10 a month, such a worker had only $26 left each month to buy food and clothing for the family and fuel for heat and cooking. Nothing was left over for medical emergencies. The need for more income made it necessary for as many members of the family to work as much as possible.

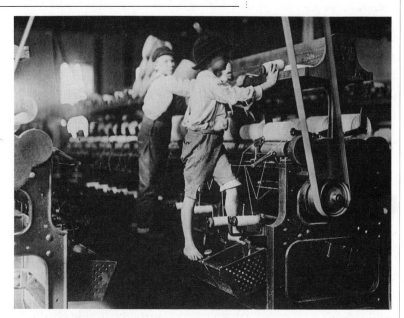

▲ *This photograph, taken by Lewis Hine in the early 1900s, shows young workers in a Georgia cotton mill.*

Workers could not afford to refuse when employers demanded they work 10 to 12 hours each day.

The piecework system forced people to work as quickly as possible, sometimes to the point of exhaustion, in order to earn decent wages. When business was good, employers expected their employees to take extra work home. When business dropped off, however, the same boss laid off workers without pay.

Workers also faced many hazards in the workplace. They were often exposed to high temperatures and poisonous gases; many lost fingers and other limbs in machines that lacked

Industry and Workers

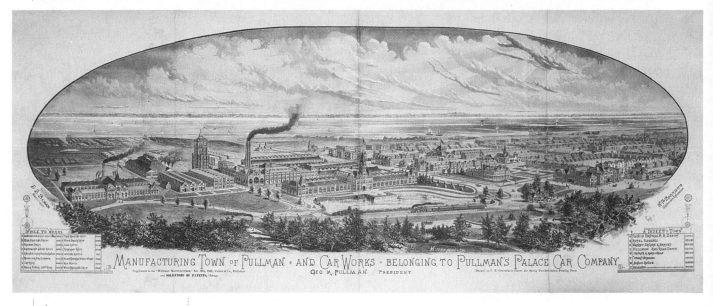

MANUFACTURING TOWN OF PULLMAN · AND CAR WORKS · BELONGING TO PULLMAN'S PALACE CAR COMPANY
GEO. M. PULLMAN   PRESIDENT.

▲ *This 1881 view of the Pullman community appeared in a supplement to the* Western Manufacturer. *George Pullman hoped his company town would help workers live happier, healthier, and more productive lives.*

■ *What factors contributed to the poor working conditions in most industries?*

safety devices. No programs existed to help the unemployed, the sick, the injured, or the families of those killed in industrial accidents.

Life in Company Towns

Some businesses set up company towns. The Pullman Palace Car Company in Chicago, which manufactured sleeping and dining cars for railroads, built a company town (named Pullman) in Illinois. George Pullman approved of the neat rows of brick houses, each with a flower garden, because he believed keeping his workers happy and healthy would make them work harder. At the time, Pullman workers were the best housed workers in the country, and the town was regarded as a landmark in city planning. It contained a church, a

school, a bank, a hotel, a theater, and a shopping area.

To Pullman's surprise, the workers were not pleased. One worker complained that the company had too much control over their lives. He commented, "We are born in a Pullman house, fed from the Pullman shop, taught in the Pullman school, catechized in the Pullman church, and when we die we shall be buried in the Pullman cemetery."

Often workers fell in debt because their wages were not enough to cover their expenses. The pastor of the church noted, "After deducting rent the men invariably had only from one to six dollars or so on which to live for two weeks. One man has a pay check in his possession of two cents [left] after paying rent." ■

Unions Develop

As abuses continued year after year, workers grew increasingly bitter. The growing discontent of millions of people could not be contained for long. But workers found their individual complaints were ignored. They began to organize so that they would be heard. Agnes Nestor, for example, persuaded the women sewing gloves to go on **strike**—to stop working—in order to get better wages. They not

only succeeded but also gained the right to join together in a **labor union,** a workers' organization that would try to obtain better wages and better working conditions.

Early Unions

Small, isolated attempts to organize trade unions dated back to the 1700s. The formation of the short-lived Philadelphia Mechanics Union in the 1820s, however, marked the beginning of the modern labor movement. The first influential union in the United States was the Knights of Labor, founded in 1869. The Knights had the idealistic goal of organizing all workers in society. They supported equal pay for men and women who did the same job and did not discriminate on the basis of race or religion. The group's motto was "An injury to one is the concern of all."

Although the Knights of Labor included 700,000 members by 1886, the union was troubled with internal disagreements and weak leadership. More successful was the American Federation of Labor (AFL), founded in 1886. Its first president was a Dutch-Jewish immigrant named Samuel Gompers.

A cigar maker since the age of 13, Gompers knew about working conditions from his own experience. He took a practical approach to unionization, seeking gradual improvement in the workers' welfare. The focus was on shorter hours, better wages, and improved working conditions. He avoided involvement in politics. Gompers created a lasting organization. The AFL did not try to enlist

unskilled workers. It concentrated on organizing skilled workers into thousands of local unions separated according to specific skills or occupations.

Gompers believed that organized workers had the right to strike. He also felt that strikes could be avoided if union leaders and employers met to work out agreements on such matters as wages and hours. If an agreement could not be reached, Gompers supported the use of boycotts—the refusal of union members to buy or use a company's products—as a form of protest. ■

▲ *Women picket a New York factory during the Ladies' Tailors strike in 1910.*

■ *How did workers use strikes and boycotts to change their working conditions?*

▼ *Samuel Gompers was AFL president almost continuously from 1886 until 1924. The chief weapon of the AFL was the strike.*

Unions Meet Opposition

The AFL succeeded in gaining higher wages for its members. More and more workers, however, belonged to the unskilled labor force, and they saw little improvement in their pay or working conditions. As discontent grew, major strikes occurred. Management's reactions to these strikes revealed their fear of organized labor.

On May 3, 1886, strikers at Chicago's McCormick Harvester Company fought with strikebreakers trying to enter the plant. Strikebreakers were people hired to work in place of those on strike. The police rushed in, and in the confusion four strikers were killed. The next day crowds gathered at Hay-

market Square to protest the incident. Ordered by the police to end the meeting, the speaker began to step down. Suddenly a bomb went off, killing 7 officers and injuring 67 others. The frightened police fired into the crowd, wounding over 50 people and killing 10. No one ever found out who had tossed the bomb, but the unions, particularly the Knights of Labor, were blamed.

Despite this setback, unions continued to work for better conditions. In 1892, the AFL steelworkers at Carnegie's plant in Homestead, Pennsylvania, asked for a raise. In response, the manager locked out the workers.

Before labor unions were formed, wage earners were at the mercy of their employer. They had no voice in determining their wages, work hours, or working conditions. Nor did they have anyone to represent them. Because work was a necessity to clothe, feed, and house themselves, workers were forced to accept the conditions of their employment.

Until the early 1800s, workers in the United States tended to act as individuals rather than as a group when dealing with their employers. During these years, factory management held most of the power. Bosses could ask workers to put in long hours for six days a week. They could offer low wages, few benefits, and little job security. Conditions in the factories and foundries were often dismal, even dangerous. Management was often in complete control.

The establishment of labor unions enabled workers to gain some control over their working conditions. A labor union is an organization of employees whose purpose is to obtain, through bargaining with an employer, better working conditions, pay, and benefits. The idea behind unions is that banding together gives workers power that they do not have as individuals.

Over the years, unions have achieved many gains for workers, including the outlawing of child labor, the adoption of health and safety regulations for the workplace, and the establishment of federal minimum hourly wage rates. Other important union achievements include a work day of eight hours (or fewer), a five-day work week, overtime pay, and paid vacations and holidays.

Kinds of Labor Unions

Since the start of the labor movement in the 1800s, workers in the United States have formed three main kinds of unions. These types of unions are craft unions, industrial unions, and public employee unions.

Membership in a craft union is limited to workers skilled in a particular craft or trade, such as carpenters or brick layers. The American Federation of Labor (AFL), organized in 1886, was made up of craft unions consolidated into a single group. Within the AFL, however, each craft union continued to govern itself—that is, each had a constitution, rules, and steps for dealing with employers.

Membership in industrial unions is open to skilled, semiskilled, and unskilled workers in mass-producing industries, such as the automobile and steel industries. Industrial unions started in the late nineteenth century when machinery and mechanical power began to drive the production process. The Knights of Labor, organized in 1869, and the Industrial Workers of the World (IWW), begun in 1905, were the first two unions to make a serious attempt to organize unskilled industrial workers. Since its founding in 1935, the Congress of Industrial Organizations (CIO) has numbered among its members auto, electric, mine, steel, and textile workers.

Membership in public employee unions consists of municipal employees, such as firefighters and police officers. Unlike unions dealing with private industries, public employee unions do not have the right to strike. They sometimes do strike, however, as the Professional Air Traffic Controllers did in 1981. As a result, President Reagan fired 11,500 controllers and broke up the union.

Unions Today

In 1955, the AFL and the CIO merged into the AFL-CIO, which today is the nation's major labor organization. For the last 40 years, the percentage of U.S. workers who belong to a union has been slowly declining. From a peak of about 25 percent around 1950, union membership has fallen to about 15 percent today. Despite this decline in the number of union members, the unions remain an important force in the nation's economy. And millions of nonunion workers also benefit from the higher wages and improved working conditions won through union efforts.

One steelworker commented that the union had only 800 members but that the lockout caused 3,000 unskilled workers to join them. The plant manager then sent for Pinkerton detectives to act as strikebreakers. A steelworker described how the Pinkerton guards arrived on barges at dawn and how shooting began when they tried to step ashore. The fighting continued for hours before the guards retreated. The Pinkertons were replaced by the National Guard, who protected the plant and the men hired to take the strikers' jobs. The union finally had to admit defeat.

Another union defeat occurred in 1892 when miners in Coeur d'Alene, Idaho rejected a wage reduction. The striking miners were locked out and replacements were brought in under armed guard. Soon violence erupted between the miners and company gunmen. State militia and federal troops were called in and the violence was ended. Although the miners at Coeur d'Alene experienced defeat, a new militant organization, the Western Federation of Miners, was established in 1893.

Strike at Pullman

In 1894, a strike at the Pullman plant led to bloodshed. When orders for new rail cars fell off and then stopped altogether, Pullman cut wages by about a third without lowering rent or prices in the company stores. To protest, the workers went on strike. Pullman then shut down the plant.

Acting in sympathy with the strikers, railroad workers refused to handle Pullman cars. This action halted most rail traffic.

Claiming that this action interfered with trade and with the U.S. mails, which were carried on the railroad, the courts issued an order to end the strike. Federal troops were sent to Pullman to enforce the court's ruling. Although the strikers at first fought the militia, they soon realized they could not go on, and the Pullman strike ended. However, the order and use of federal troops had set an example. In the years to come, such court orders would be used again and again as a means of halting strikes, but it would always be bitterly resented and opposed by the unions. ■

▲ *Troops were called in to settle a labor dispute at Andrew Carnegie's steel plant in Homestead, Pennsylvania. What started as a strike of 800 workers ended with 3,000 people locked out of their jobs.*

■ *What methods were used in the Pullman and Homestead strikes to stop unions from influencing workers?*

REVIEW

1. **FOCUS** How did changes in production affect the way in which Americans lived and worked during the late 1800s and early 1900s?

2. **CONNECT** What types of new work became available with the growth of industry?

3. **ECONOMICS** What effect did mass production have on the cost of business in the United States?

4. **ECONOMICS** Why did workers unionize? How did employers react to unions?

5. **CRITICAL THINKING** Do you think that unions can help or hurt the cause of workers? Do you believe all workers should belong to unions? Be sure to explain your reasons in detail.

6. **ACTIVITY** Imagine you are a union member in the early 1900s. Draw a creative poster or political cartoon that protests poor working conditions, such as long hours.

1850   1860
1870   1920

L E S S O N   4

Destination: America

THINKING
F O C U S

How did the influx of immigrants during the late 1800s affect American society?

"Happy journey!" "God help you!" "Good-bye!" These were the shouts that echoed in Mary Antin's ears in 1894 as she and her family joined the thousands of Russian Jews fleeing religious persecution.

Mary's father had immigrated to Boston, Massachusetts, several years earlier. Now 12-year-old Mary, her mother, her brother, and her sisters were on their way to join him.

At the Russian border, their passports were taken from them. A friendly German helped them cross the border. They then journeyed in crowded railroad cars to Hamburg, Germany. There they were locked up for two weeks because the Germans feared they might be carrying cholera, the deadly disease then raging in Russia. (See column 2 for Mary's recollection of the quarantine.)

Finally, the Antin family boarded a steamship bound for Boston. For 16

Quarantine, they called it, and there was a great deal of it—two weeks of it. Two weeks within high brick walls, several hundred of us herded in half a dozen compartments, . . . sleeping in rows, like sick people in a hospital; with roll-call morning and night, and short rations three times a day; with never a sign of the free world beyond our barred windows; with anxiety and longing and homesickness in our hearts, and in our ears the unfamiliar voice of the invisible ocean, which drew and repelled us at the same time.

days they sailed westward.

"And so suffering, fearing, brooding, rejoicing," wrote Mary, "we crept nearer and nearer to the coveted shore until, on a glorious May morning, . . . our eyes beheld the Promised Land, and my father received us in his arms."

Promise of America

Mary and her family were but a few of the thousands of immigrants who poured into the United States after the Civil War. Between 1860 and 1900, 14 million people arrived. Eight million more came between 1901 and 1910.

New Immigrants from Europe

Until 1880, three-fourths of the Europeans who immigrated to the United States had come from Britain, Ireland, Germany, and Scandinavia.

By 1890, the majority were from southern and eastern Europe. Most numerous were the Jews, who emigrated to escape poverty and religious persecution. Other immigrants fled from political turmoil. The vast majority, however, were escaping the ravages of poverty. They came from Italy, Poland, and Russia. They arrived from Austria-Hungary, Greece, Turkey, and Serbia. Most of these immigrants landed at Ellis Island in New York harbor. There, as many as

462

Chapter 15

5,000 newcomers were processed in a single day. As the Closer Look on pages 464–465 shows, the country had to find a way to process all these people. Ellis Island in New York harbor became the East Coast reception center for immigrants.

Immigrants from Europe who had friends and relatives already in the United States were encouraged to join them. Many of the young, single men, however, did not expect to stay. They planned to make as much money as they could and then return to their homelands to start a business or raise a family. A large percentage of these return migrants were farmers. Organizations such as the Sons of Italy and the Polish Women's Alliance helped newcomers to find housing and jobs.

Advertisements from steamship companies and low fares helped to lure immigrants to the United States. Further encouragement came from the governments of some states and from industries seeking cheap labor. Some companies even sent recruiters abroad to urge people to come to the United States.

Asian Immigrants

At the same time that Europeans were arriving on the East Coast, thousands of Asians were arriving on the West Coast of the United States. The majority of these Asian immigrants were Chinese.

Between 1865 and 1882, 320,000 Chinese immigrated to the United States. They fled from southern China where warfare, overpopulation, and a failing economy had left millions near starvation.

The first major wave of Chinese came after the discovery of gold in California in 1849. By 1852, visions of Gum Shan, the Mountain of Gold, had lured 20,000 Chinese to San Francisco. As you learned in Chapter 14, the demand for workers on the Union Pacific railroad later brought many Chinese to the Pacific coast.

In addition, the Japanese and the Filipinos immigrated to the United States. Like southern China, Japan was overpopulated and was suffering from economic hardships. In 1885, the Japanese emperor decreed that people could emigrate.

▼ *From 1870 to 1920, thousands of immigrants from European and Asian countries joined the American workforce.*

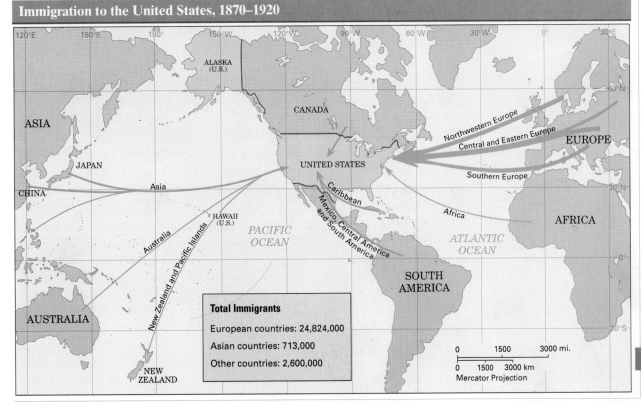

Immigration to the United States, 1870–1920

Total Immigrants

European countries: 24,824,000

Asian countries: 713,000

Other countries: 2,600,000

0   1500   3000 mi.

0 1500   3000 km

Mercator Projection

Industry and Workers

Ellis Island Immigrants

Welcome to the United States—get in line! The Statue of Liberty towered over a big waiting room for thousands of immigrants who arrived in the early 1900s. In fact, the waiting could even begin offshore. Even ships lined up in New York Harbor for days until space was available on Ellis Island.

What would you bring?
Many immigrants had only one small suitcase. Children brought toys and books. People like this Italian family brought bedding, a few dishes, maybe a violin, or a favorite photograph.

Red Star Line
Inspection Card
(Immigrants and Steerage Passengers)

Port of departure:
Date of departure: ANTWERP Apr 28th
Name of ship:
Name of Immigrant: Basilkin Poe
Last permanent residence:

Inspected and

To assist Inspection in New York Harbour, Passengers are requested to attach this Card to their Clothing.

INSPECTION CARD.
(Immigrants and Steerage Passengers.)

Port of Departure, GLASGOW. Date of Departure, 23 MAR 1912
Name of Ship, CALEDONIA
Name of Immigrant, Breitman Nikolej
Last residence,

passed at

U.S. port of

Berth No.

13 11

You've passed inspection!
Immigrants had to pass inspections and answer dozens of questions. A story goes that when one flustered German was asked his name, he answered, "Ich hab's vergessen" ("I forgot!"). The official wrote down his name as "Ferguson" and it stuck.

After weeks of seasickness, these Russian Jews smile with relief. More than 1 million Jews came to Ellis Island in the early 1900s. Men usually traveled ahead of their families, to secure housing and work.

All Aboard! 75% of those leaving Ellis Island headed for New York City, but others bought tickets for Chicago, Cleveland, and St. Louis. Railroad agents pinned numbered tags to the immigrants' clothing if they couldn't speak English. The numbers told other agents where the families were destined.

As a result, thousands of Japanese migrated to Hawaii, where they worked on American sugar plantations. When the islands of Hawaii became a United States territory in 1898, many Japanese moved on to the U.S. mainland. By 1900, more than 10,000 Japanese were living in the United States, mostly on the Pacific coast. ■

Immigrants Become Americans

Although welcomed by employers as cheap labor, the hard-working European and Asian immigrants often encountered fear and prejudice. Most had to learn a new language as well as to adjust to a new culture. Their dress and accents were often ridiculed; in many instances their religious beliefs met with intolerance. Most of the new immigrants were poor, uneducated, and untrained in any skilled labor. They could find only backbreaking, poorly paid jobs and had little choice but to live in dirty, crowded slums where disease and crime were common.

Facing Discrimination

Most immigrants dreamed of becoming true Americans—of adopting American dress and customs, as well as speaking the English language. However, some—particularly the older immigrants—clung to the traditions of their past, to the customs they had cherished all their lives. Their cultural differences were often viewed with suspicion by native-born Americans. Because immigrants would work for lower wages than the native-born, they were resented by the workers who were trying so hard to raise their own wages and standard of living.

As more and more immigrants arrived, the tide of nativism—a policy of favoring native-born inhabitants over immigrants—gained wide support. Nativists claimed that immigrants would exhaust American resources and endanger American culture with their foreign beliefs and "exotic" customs.

Foremost among these groups was the American Protective Association. Shouting "America for Americans," APA members tried to bar Catholics from entering the United States and opposed immigration generally.

In addition to facing discrimination in finding jobs and housing, immigrants sometimes encountered violence. Despite the problems they faced, the immigrants' new lives were

➤ *Asians, such as this Chinese family in California, faced discrimination in finding jobs and housing during the late 1800s and early 1900s.*

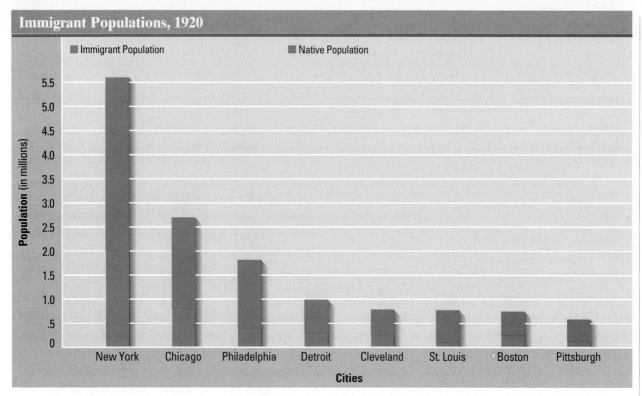

Immigrant Populations, 1920

■ Immigrant Population ■ Native Population

Population (in millions)

Cities: New York, Chicago, Philadelphia, Detroit, Cleveland, St. Louis, Boston, Pittsburgh

usually better than the ones they had left behind. Few other countries offered the freedom and opportunities that were available to immigrants in the United States.

Contributions of Immigrants

Immigrants such as Carnegie, Gompers, and Bell made lasting contributions to industry and labor. Other immigrants made outstanding contributions to the United States between 1870 and 1920. English-born William Mayo set up an emergency hospital that evolved into the world-famous Mayo Clinic. Swiss-born Mayer Guggenheim rose from a peddler selling lace door-to-door to make a fortune in mining. Hungarian-born Joseph Pulitzer, a newspaper editor, used his fortune to establish a graduate school of journalism at Columbia University. He also established the

Pulitzer Prizes that are awarded annually for outstanding achievement in journalism, art, literature, history, and music. Two Chinese men helped develop popular fruits—the Bing cherry, named for Ah Bing, and the Lue Gim Gon Mediterranean Valencia orange.

Perhaps the greatest contributions came from the thousands of anonymous immigrants who helped to transform the United States into an industrial giant. As the immigrants and their children became part of American society, they enriched it with their food, their music and art, and their ideas and visions of a better world. The great economic growth that took place between 1870 and 1920 owed an enormous debt to the hard work and talent of the millions who came to the United States from other lands. ■

▲ *Despite hardships, immigrants continued to settle in major urban centers. Which cities had the largest immigrant populations in 1920? Why do you think so many immigrants lived in New York City?*

■ *What problems did immigrants face in becoming Americans?*

R E V I E W

1. **FOCUS** How did the influx of immigrants during the late 1800s affect American society?

2. **CONNECT** Why did companies send recruiters abroad to encourage people to come to America?

3. **CULTURE** How did American workers react to competition from immigrants?

4. **CRITICAL THINKING** Why did the promise of America lead so many people to immigrate to this country?

5. **ACTIVITY** Prepare a short presentation on what opportunities were available to immigrants when they arrived in the United States.

Chapter Review

Reviewing Key Terms

assembly line (p. 456) philanthropist (p. 446)
capital (p. 445) profit (p. 445)
entrepreneur (p. 445) strike (p. 458)
labor union (p. 458) urban society (p. 448)

A. In each of the following pairs, the two terms are related in some way. Write a sentence for each pair that clearly explains the relationship between the two terms.
1. capital, profit
2. assembly line, mass production
3. labor union, strike
4. profit, entrepreneur
5. philanthropist, urban society

B. Based on what you have read in the chapter, decide whether each of the following statements is true or false. If a sentence is false, rewrite it so that it is true.
1. An entrepreneur was careful not to take risks.
2. Only a wealthy person could be an important philanthropist.
3. As more people took up farming, they moved from cities to rural areas, and the United States became an urban society.
4. Employers used children on assembly lines because they worked for lower wages.
5. Washington D.C. is the capital of the United States.

Exploring Concepts

A. On a separate sheet of paper, copy the chart below. In the second column, list the inventor of each invention. In the third column, briefly describe the impact that each invention had on society.

Invention	Inventor	Impact on society
Lightbulb		
Sewing machine		
Phonograph		
Telephone		
Linotype		
Generator		

B. Support each of the following statements with facts and details from the chapter.
1. Immigrants added much to American society during the late nineteenth century.
2. New inventions revolutionized American life between 1870 and 1920.
3. Efficient methods of manufacturing helped to create new businesses.
4. Improved transportation helped cities to grow.
5. There were many reasons why people moved from farms to the cities during this time.
6. Workers did not benefit from mass production methods.
7. Workers' discontent with job conditions had several effects.
8. In the cities, several groups helped newcomers such as Southern black people and immigrants.
9. The rising tide of immigrants caused resentment among native-born Americans.
10. The American Dream was an idea that appealed to all Americans, no matter what their income level.
11. Steel changed the way cities were designed and built in the nineteenth century.
12. Andrew Carnegie was an excellent example of the new American philanthropist.

Reviewing Skills

1. Look at the map of the Development of Industrial Cities, 1900–1920, on page 454. What was the population of Detroit in 1900? In 1920? Name three cities that were not on the 1900 map but had populations of at least 100,000 by 1920.
2. Turn to the thematic maps of U.S. climate and precipitation on pages 706 and 707. Look at the southeastern states. How do the climate and precipitation of this area relate to one another? Now look at the southern part of Florida. How do the climate and precipitation of this area differ from the rest of the Southeast?
3. Find a road map and a topographic map of your state. Trace a route from your town to the state capital or another large city. What type of terrain does the road cover? Write a short paragraph explaining what this tells you about

how transportation routes developed in your area.

4. Suppose you wanted to use a computerized reference system to research the background of a particular invention, such as the telephone shown on this page. Write down three topics you could use to begin your search.

Using Critical Thinking

1. Thomas Edison said "Genius is 1 percent inspiration and 99 percent perspiration." What did he mean by this? How does his statement reflect the values of many Americans, both in the late 1800s and today?
2. Do you think black Americans have faced obstacles other ethnic groups—including the immigrants discussed in this chapter—did not have to face? Explain your answer.
3. Many immigrants coming to the United States today face forms of discrimination. Based on what you know about the hardships earlier immigrants faced, why do you think some Americans still respond negatively to immigrants?
4. The right of entrepreneurs to make a profit by investing in new businesses is part of the economic system called capitalism. Do you think the new businesses described in this chapter could have developed if they had depended only on the government for support? Explain your answer.

Preparing for Citizenship

1. **WRITING ACTIVITY** Today, unions represent professional groups as well as labor groups. Interview someone who is a member of a union. Find out in what ways belonging to a union has been of benefit to them. Write a short report on your findings.
2. **WRITING ACTIVITY** Research the growth of your city or of a nearby large city. Find out when it was founded and how fast its population increased. When did it grow most rapidly? What accounted for this growth? What were, and are, its principal industries? Write a newspaper profile of the town or city, based on your research.
3. **ART ACTIVITY** Create a poster display on the evolution of one of the inventions mentioned in this chapter. Find as many pictures of different versions of the invention as you can. Use advertisements from old newspapers and magazines to find out how much examples of the invention cost long ago. Compare those advertisements and prices with current advertisements and prices for modern versions of the invention.
4. **COLLABORATIVE LEARNING** Assume that the class is a textile company. Divide into two groups, one representing management and one representing the union. Draw up a list of demands for each side, based on nineteenth-century working conditions. As a group, work out a compromise to keep the company running.

Chapter 16
The Gilded Age

gild: *to cover in a thin layer of either fake or real gold, usually done to make things look better than they really are*

The years following the Civil War offered many business opportunities. Plentiful resources, cheap labor, and government connections helped some Americans become wealthy on a truly grand scale. Business people became some of the nation's new heroes. Not everyone, though, was blinded to the problems beneath the gilded surface of power and money.

1880 Many wealthy Americans want to have the social standing of royal families in Europe. In this 1880 family portrait, the beautiful clothes and the fine furnishings make a royal impression. This carved rocking horse would make a fine toy for these children.

1868	1874	1880

Presidents

1869-1877
Grant

1877-1881
Hayes

1881-1885
Arthur

1881
Garfield

1868

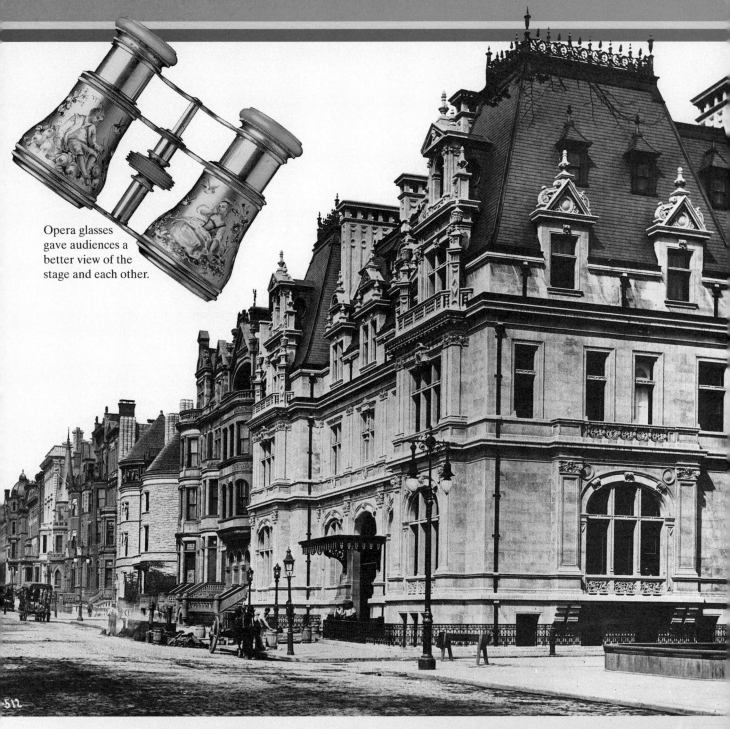

Opera glasses gave audiences a better view of the stage and each other.

1898 The Astor mansion dominates this block of fine homes on New York City's Fifth Avenue. The Astors are at the center of wealthy New York society.

1886

1892

1898

1885-1889
Cleveland

1889-1893
B. Harrison

1893-1897
Cleveland

1898

LESSON 1

The Politics of Corruption

Key Terms

- kickback
- patronage
- political machine
- graft

► *The millions James Fisk made in dishonest deals paid for expensive clothes, a mansion, and lavish parties.*

James ("Big Jim") Fisk died of a gunshot wound when he was only 37 years old, but he made a lot of mischief during his short life. He smuggled cotton from the South to the North in the Civil War. He printed and sold phony bonds to get control of the profitable Erie Railroad. He bribed government officials to interfere with justice on his behalf. And in the most sensational financial scandal in U.S. history, he helped take control of the gold market in 1869.

Fisk's personal life was as shady as his business dealings. Fisk's New York City office, on the top floors of his Opera House, was the scene of wild parties. "Some people are born to be good, other people are born to be bad. I was born to be bad," the huge and jovial Fisk said. Fisk loved to make a splash in everything he did. For example, he had the boats of his shipping line painted lavender and yellow, and dressed in a fancy, custom-made uniform to see them off. He was well liked, despite public knowledge of his corrupt ways. Thousands of Fisk's friends, enemies, and employees attended his lavish funeral. One newspaper even compared Fisk's funeral with that of Abraham Lincoln.

Big Jim's delight in being caught in scandals was unusual among business leaders, who generally sought to avoid bad publicity. However, Fisk's disregard for law and ethics was not unusual among the men who dominated American business and politics from about 1870 to 1900.

The writer Mark Twain called this period the "Gilded Age." It was a time when the glamorous lives of the rich and powerful hid the dishonest ways in which many of them made their money.

Big Business Attempts to Influence Politics

The Civil War had created many profitable opportunities for business leaders who had government contracts for war materials. Very often, businesses took advantage of the government's need for supplies to charge very high prices. Businesses also bribed congressmen and government officials to get contracts. These shady relationships didn't stop after the war. At the same time, as corporations became larger and more complex, it became harder to find out about such dishonest practices.

People who gained fortunes by illegal means were popularly known as "robber barons." Rich and powerful men like James Fisk, Jay Gould, and John D. Rockefeller often bribed or threatened congressional representatives and judges to write and interpret the law to suit their business needs. They bought votes and helped elect politicians whose decisions they could control. In this atmosphere of corruption, government officials used their positions to make money rather than to serve the public good.

The robber barons represented a new social class that became famous for showing off wealth in public. Even men from humble backgrounds like railroad giant Cornelius Vanderbilt found that, with enough money, they could buy their way into exclusive social circles.

Vanderbilt started the trend of building huge castle-like houses on New York's Fifth Avenue. Many of the wealthy also built mansions they called "summer cottages" in Newport, Rhode Island, and in other resort communities. To impress society further, they threw outrageously expensive parties. Some cost as much as $200,000. (The average worker earned $10 a week.) A small replica of the Palace of Versailles was built for one party. At another, thousands of orchids decorated the walls, and a layer of rose petals covered the floor. At a party in Newport, guests used silver shovels to dig for diamonds, sapphires, and rubies in a sandbox.

▼ *One way to upgrade one's social standing was to be seen at cultural events. At the opera, one could draw attention by the use of fold-out glasses* (above). *Children of the rich were indulged in many ways. Here* (below) *a group of girls attend a dog show.*

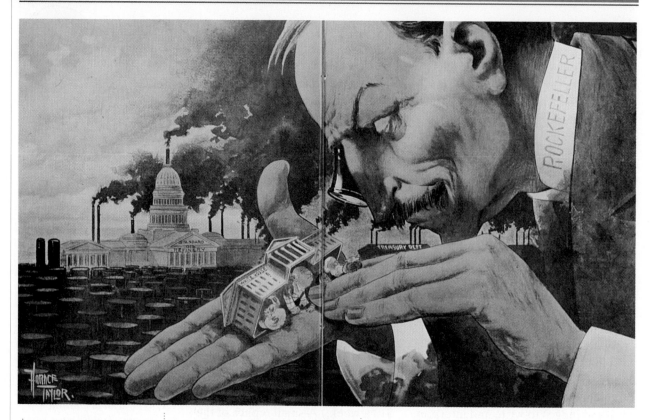

▲ *This famous cartoon suggested that oil baron John D. Rockefeller was the real power behind the United States government.*

■ *How did business influence politics during the Gilded Age?*

Many Americans were upset and spoke out against the widespread corruption and public display of wealth.

Among those speaking out against corruption was Walt Whitman—poet, essayist, and journalist.

> I say we had best look our times and lands searchingly in the face, like a physician diagnosing some deep disease. Never was there, perhaps, more hollowness at heart than at present here in the United States. . . . We live in an atmosphere of hypocrisy throughout. An acute and candid person in the revenue department in Washington, who regularly visits the cities to investigate frauds, had talked much with me about his discoveries. The depravity of the business classes of our country is not less than has been supposed, but infinitely greater. The official services of America, national, state, and municipal, in all their branches and departments are deep in corruption, bribery, and falsehood.
>
> Walt Whitman, 1871.

Scandals Plague Grant's Presidency

Ulysses S. Grant had no political experience before he ran for President. However, his friends felt that he would win in 1868 because of his popularity as a Civil War hero.

As President, Grant remained loyal to his friends. As it turned out, they were mostly dishonest and corrupt. Although Grant himself was an honest man, he was easily influenced by scoundrels in his political party.

Many took advantage of their political positions.

The Credit Mobilier Scandal

In 1872, during Grant's campaign for reelection, a New York newspaper reported that leaders of the Union Pacific Railroad had persuaded a number of government leaders to cooperate in a multimillion-dollar fraud. At the time, the Union Pacific was receiving millions of dollars in government money to build a transcontinental railroad. To steal some of this money, the Union Pacific's managers formed a railroad construction company called the Credit Mobilier *(cray DEE mo bee YAY)*. To cut off any political opposition, Massachusetts Congressman Oakes bribed selected congressmen with stock in this phony company.

No railroad track was ever laid with the public money that Congress set aside for Credit Mobilier. The money went instead into the pockets of the Union Pacific's managers and the Congressional representatives they had bribed. Grant's Vice President, Schuyler ("Smiler") Colfax, and Congressman James A. Garfield, later President, took part in the fraud.

More Corruption

The Credit Mobilier scandal was only the beginning of a string of embarrassing exposés about the Grant administration. In 1873, it was revealed that Secretary of War William Belknap had received **kickbacks**, or payoffs, for helping to cheat American Indian people out of rights to their trading posts. That same year, Grant's personal secretary, Orville Babcock, used blackmail to get more than $25,000 from whiskey makers who had not been paying excise taxes to the federal government. Among the favors received by Babcock was a $2,400 diamond shirt stud. The chief clerk of the Treasury also received money in the Whiskey Ring scandal.

Congress Tarnishes Its Reputation

Shortly after the Credit Mobilier scandal broke, Congress voted itself a 50 percent pay raise, including two years of back pay at the higher rate. This act raised salaries from $5,000 to $7,500, and gave each Congressman a gift of $5,000. Public outcry over this "back-pay steal" forced the legislators to back down. ■

■ In what ways did members of Grant's administration use their positions for their personal gain?

Machine Politics Develop

During Grant's presidency, serious urban problems arose that many city governments could not fix. Overwhelmed by immigrants from both rural areas and foreign countries, cities were overcrowded, dirty, and riddled with poverty and violence.

Expanding at the rapid pace set by industrial growth and immigration, cities required water, sewer, fire, police, and social services. But most city governments lacked the money, leadership, staff, and organization to meet these needs. Some people took

◄ This photograph was taken in New York in 1885. Corrupt political machines did little to solve the serious urban problems of the period.

The Gilded Age

➤ *This Thomas Nast cartoon clearly shows what the artist felt was on the mind of William "Boss" Tweed.*

Across Time & Space

HISTORY *Political cartoons like this one often help historians understand more about a political period. For instance, Thomas Nast helped dethrone William "Boss" Tweed of Tammany Hall with cartoons that pictured Tweed and his associates as vultures or smiling tricksters. "I don't care so much what the papers write about me," Tweed said, "My constituents can't read. But... they can see pictures."*

■ *In what sense were machine politics a direct response to conditions in American cities during the Gilded Age?*

advantage of this situation to gain political power.

Big City Political Bosses

Political bosses were usually men who had grown up in the neighborhoods they served. Bosses gained power by supplying basic needs to poor workers and immigrant families. Food baskets, loans, and job opportunities gave these people hope and a sense of belonging. In return, the bosses expected votes and other political support. Bosses also exchanged political favors, such as city jobs or work contracts, for money or votes. This system was called **patronage**.

A political organization known as the **political machine** grew out of the patronage system. Eventually, because of the personal loyalty the bosses commanded, their machines gained more control of the city. Bosses controlled jobs in the public schools, public works projects, and virtually every other aspect of city government. Often bosses did not even hold office themselves, but directed a city's government from a political club.

Once in power, bosses and their machines rewarded themselves with **graft**, money stolen from the city treasury. They also demanded kickbacks from contractors and companies who wanted the city's business. As a result, the cost of running the city skyrocketed.

The Tweed Ring

The most famous and possibly the most corrupt political boss of the Gilded Age was William Marcy Tweed.

Although he had little formal education, Tweed established and controlled New York's Democratic political machine. His political operation was called the Tammany Society. Its home was Tammany Hall. Tweed and his friends in the Tweed Ring stole about $200 million from New York City between 1868 and 1871. One of Tweed's friends named Garvey, who received $3 million for plastering, came to be known as the "Prince of Plasterers." Tweed was arrested, tried, convicted and imprisoned. But his political machine carried on.

Many reformers tried to rid their cities of machine politics—of bribery and corruption. Their efforts were not really effective, however, until the Progressive era in the early 1900s. ■

R E V I E W

1. **FOCUS** What were some of the characteristics of American politics in the decades following the Civil War?

2. **CONNECT** How did the Civil War encourage corruption in the federal government?

3. **HISTORY** Summarize the scandals that arose during Grant's presidency.

4. **CRITICAL THINKING** In what ways did machine politics ease some problems and aggravate others in American cities during the Gilded Age?

5. **WRITING ACTIVITY** Make a list of the basic facilities and services the local government provides in your city or hometown.

L E S S O N   2

The Reforming Impulse

Charles Guiteau waited nervously for President James Garfield at the train station in Washington, D.C., on July 2, 1881. He held a gun in his hand. As the President strolled into the station, Guiteau stepped forward and fired. Garfield fell to the ground, wounded. For another two months, he clung to life.

"I did it and will go to jail for it!" Guiteau screamed, "I am a Stalwart and [Vice President] Arthur will be President!"

At the time of the shooting, President Garfield was in a bitter fight with the Stalwarts, a group of people in his own Republican party. Stalwarts like Guiteau claimed that Garfield had not rewarded them enough for their hard work in his campaign. The Stalwarts wanted to control key political offices. The President, however, was weary of the "spoils system," in which the people with the best political connections got the best government jobs.

Even before President Garfield was shot, people were dissatisfied with the spoils system. Critics pointed out that the government was filled with unqualified people who had gotten their jobs in return for political support. Critics also claimed that the system barred the best workers from public service. Honest and capable people couldn't get government jobs unless they were also known as loyal party members.

When the President was assassinated by a Stalwart who had not received his "spoils," Americans demanded a change in the way government offices were filled. The corruption of the Gilded Age had finally inspired a call for reform.

THINKING FOCUS

What political and business practices did reformers in the 1870s and 1880s want to change? Why?

Key Terms

- Mugwumps
- civil service
- regulate
- monopoly
- trust

◄ *This engraving of the assassination of President Garfield accompanied newspaper accounts of his death. The technology to print photographs was not available to newspapers until the late 1890s.*

The Mugwumps Seek Reform

From the end of Reconstruction in 1877 to the turn of the century, American politics suffered from a stalemated condition. The two major parties largely agreed on economic, political, and social issues. They differed only in their constituencies, the people they represented. The Repub-

licans were mostly Northern white Protestants. The Democrats were most often Southerners, Catholics, and immigrants. Since the two parties were balanced in the number of their supporters, presidential elections—as shown in A Closer Look below—were won by only a few thousand votes.

Gilded Age Elections

After the Reconstruction Era, neither the Republicans nor the Democrats enjoyed a clear majority. The result: the four presidential elections of the Gilded Age were "fifty-fifty" races. Unfortunately for the voters, the campaigns were often reduced to little more than name-calling matches.

Elections were "gilded,"—ornate, but lacking substance. In the election of 1884, which pitted Republican James Blaine *(left)* against Democrat Grover Cleveland *(right)*, rumors and false accusations flew.

Donkeys and elephants became the popular symbols of the two parties. Cartoonist Thomas Nast sent Democrats hee-hawing and Republicans stampeding through the editorial pages at the turn of the century. The symbols have lasted to the present day.

The President and the federal government did not use the powers or take the responsibilities that they do today. The main goal of each party was to control offices and jobs, not to create new policies. The most time-consuming duty of the President was to make the political appointments—nearly one hundred thousand—required by the spoils system. This period of corruption and stalemate eventually inspired public pressure for reform.

One of the strongest forces for change following the Civil War were the **Mugwumps**, a group of Republicans who supported reform. Taking their name from an American Indian word meaning "big chiefs," the Mugwumps condemned the spoils system.

Four years later, in 1892, Harrison and Cleveland ran against each other again. This time Cleveland won. In this painting titled *The Lost Bet,* a Harrison supporter pulls a Cleveland supporter on a float, in order to settle their bet.

The people's choice? In 1888, Democrat Grover Cleveland gained 90,000 more popular votes than Republican Benjamin Harrison. But Harrison won the electoral vote and the presidency. Key states such as New York swung the election away from Cleveland.

They favored a fair and honest relationship between the North and South. They also wanted to reduce the protective tariff. (A tax on imports, the tariff was meant to encourage Americans to buy U.S. goods.)

Mugwumps were a powerful and well-educated group. Their leaders included cartoonist Thomas Nast, magazine editors E. L. Godkin and George W. Curtis, and Carl Schurz, the German-American senator from Missouri. Senator Schurz was a long-time advocate of reform. He often spoke out against the spoils system in Congress as well as in the press.

■ *Who were the Mugwumps and what features of the American political system did they seek to reform?*

Attacking the Spoils System

Mugwumps and other political reformers wanted a **civil service** system to replace the spoils system. Under their plan, government jobs would no longer be given out in exchange for party loyalty. Instead, people who wanted to work for the government had to prove their abilities by taking a test. This civil service examination would weed out unskilled people.

Reformers also had some selfish reasons for making a change in the way that government jobs were filled. Most of them were white middle-class Protestants. Just as much as they disliked the spoils system, they resented the immigrants and party boosters

▼ *Job-seekers wait to see the President. It was with dread that Presidents faced the endless lines of applicants. Few job-seekers were qualified for the jobs they obtained.*

480

who shared in the spoils.

Nevertheless, reformers had strong evidence to support their case. The spoils system had deep roots in American government. Since Andrew Jackson's day, people who could not read or write had held clerical jobs. Some officials put their family members and pets on the government payroll. American diplomats were often untrained and poorly educated.

Hayes Investigates the Customs House

The New York Customs House represented the spoils system at its worst. The customs house collected taxes levied on foreign goods that entered the United States through the port of New York. One of the most corrupt centers of patronage in the nation in the 1870s, it was run by New York Senator Roscoe Conkling. He was known as an arrogant man who sported dazzling, expensive clothes. Conkling used the customs house to run and finance his political machine. Fiercely opposed to reform, Conkling called the civil service the "snivel service."

Conkling met his match in President Rutherford B. Hayes, who was elected President in 1876. Hayes wanted no part of the scandal and corruption that had run wild in the Grant administration. In 1878, Hayes launched an investigation of the New York Customs House. The investigation found that more than 200 people who did no work for the customs

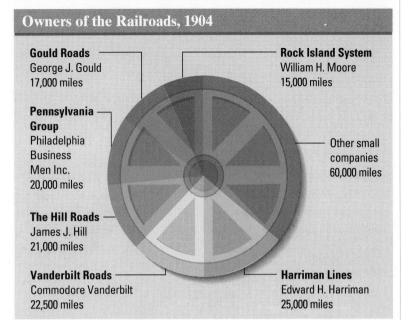

Owners of the Railroads, 1904

Gould Roads
George J. Gould
17,000 miles

Pennsylvania Group
Philadelphia Business Men Inc.
20,000 miles

The Hill Roads
James J. Hill
21,000 miles

Vanderbilt Roads
Commodore Vanderbilt
22,500 miles

Rock Island System
William H. Moore
15,000 miles

Other small companies
60,000 miles

Harriman Lines
Edward H. Harriman
25,000 miles

house were on its payroll. Over Conkling's loud objections, President Hayes fired two senior customs house officials.

The Civil Service Act of 1883

In the wake of President Garfield's assassination and the Customs House investigation, Congress passed the Civil Service Act of 1883. President Chester Arthur signed this act into law just two years after Garfield's death. An important step toward reform, the new law set aside about 15,000 federal jobs to be filled through a competitive test. Only persons who proved their abilities on the civil service test could be hired. The act also forbade elected officials to fire civil service workers because of their political views. ■

▲ This graph shows the ownership of the leading railroads in 1904. Because transportation was an important factor in the industrial growth of the nation, the owners of the large railroads became powerful national leaders in this period.

■ Why did reformers want to replace the spoils system with a civil service?

Regulating the Railroads

Following the Civil War the federal government gave millions of acres of land and millions of dollars to the railroad companies to lay new track. It made political and economic sense to connect the huge country with railroads. But after misusing these privileges for many years, the big railroad companies became the next targets of reform.

Railroad Abuses Cause Outrage

"What do I care about the law? Hain't I got the power?" growled Cornelius Vanderbilt, the most powerful of the railroad owners. Vanderbilt meant what he said. He and several other railroad owners with enormous holdings conspired to squeeze out smaller competitors. They charged more for short hauls, which farmers

"Who owns the locomotives and the cars. . .?" asked a Republican delegate to the 1878 California Constitutional Convention. "Are they not private property?. . . And yet you propose to hand over that property. . . to [government regulators] just as if you proposed to take from the gentleman his homestead and give it to me."

In firm agreement, the railroad owners took the regulators to court. Their lawyers intended to prove that regulation was unconstitutional. However, in the 1877 case of *Munn* v. *Illinois*, the Supreme Court ruled in favor of state regulation. Reformers were pleased, but their victory was short-lived. The Court reversed itself nine years later. Then it ruled that only Congress, and not state commissions, had the power to regulate interstate commerce, or the movement of goods across state lines.

The Interstate Commerce Act of 1887

The Supreme Court's ruling against state regulation of railroads forced the federal government to address mounting public demands for regulation. In 1887, Congress passed the Interstate Commerce Act. This act outlawed many of the unfair practices that railroad companies had used. It also set up an Interstate Commerce Commission (ICC) to enforce the new regulations.

The Interstate Commerce Act, however, had little power in regulating railroads in the years after its passage. Between 1887 and 1906, the Supreme Court ruled in favor of the railroad companies in almost every case raised by the ICC. Railroads found they could also count on long and expensive court proceedings to discourage their opponents. Nonetheless, the Interstate Commerce Act was an important achievement. It established the government's right to regulate business and paved the way for more effective regulation in later years. ■

▲ *William Henry Vanderbilt, son of Cornelius Vanderbilt, took over his father's railroads. He is shown here towering over two other railroad men, Jay Gould on his left, and Jim Fisk on his right.*

■ *For what reasons did the big railroad companies become targets of reform?*

required for their produce, than for the long hauls that manufacturers needed. Large shippers also received secret discounts for giving their business to the railroads.

For many years, railroad owners used bribes and threats to keep politicians from interfering with their shady business dealings. However, in the 1870s, some state governments passed laws against the unfair business practices of railroad companies. Many conservatives did not want government to **regulate**, or set rules for, the railroads. They argued that regulation was a violation of the Fifth Amendment protection of private property.

Restraining the Trusts

In the same way that reformers wanted to control the power of the railroads, they also wanted to curb the power of monopolies. A **monopoly** is a company that completely controls the market for one product or service. A **trust** is a combination of companies that work together to control the market. In the years after the Civil War, monopolies and trusts threatened to take control of the American economy.

The Power of the Monopolies

The story of oil baron John D. Rockefeller shows why reformers wanted to fight monopolies. A financial genius, Rockefeller began his career as a bookkeeper but soon built a great fortune in oil. He saw early in his career that the person who controlled the oil refineries—the places where "crude oil" from the ground was made into fuel—could control the entire oil industry. Rockefeller started buying oil companies as fast as he could.

Rockefeller was almost always able to force other owners to sell their companies to him. When he met resistance to his offer, he often resorted to bribery and intimidation. In one case, Standard Oil officials bribed the mechanic at another refinery to arrange for a small explosion there.

Rockefeller didn't need to buy every oil company in the country in order to control the industry. The trust, devised by his lawyer Samuel Dodd, enabled Rockefeller to control companies that he did not own. Through the Standard Oil trust, nine "trustees," led by Rockefeller, controlled 77 companies. Stockholders in those companies traded their stock for "trust certificates." They kept their share of the profits but lost their say in how their company was run.

From the beginning, reformers feared the power of the trusts. Journalist Ida Tarbell once described the Standard Oil trust as "an organization having no legal existence, independent of all authority, able to do anything it wanted anywhere....You could no more grasp it than you could an eel."

▼ *Oil fields, such as this one in Los Cerritos, California, helped John D. Rockefeller gain complete control over the oil business* (bottom left). *Ida Tarbell* (below) *wrote a book exposing the unfair practices of the Standard Oil Company.*

UNDERSTANDING MONOPOLIES

You may have played the board game Monopoly. The object of the game is to buy as much property as possible and to drive your opponents to bankruptcy—that is, to take all of their money. In the late 1800s and early 1900s, during the reign of such industrial giants as the United States Steel Corporation, this wasn't a game—it was a business.

A monopoly exists when one company or group controls the means of producing or selling a particular product or service. For example, John D. Rockefeller's Standard Oil Trust controlled over 90 percent of the oil business in the United States in the late 1800s.

Forming a Monopoly

A monopoly can control the price of a good or service by withholding or increasing supplies. At first, a monopoly may lower prices to drive its competitors out of business. Because of its vast resources, the monopoly can afford to charge less for a while. Smaller competitors, however, cannot afford the losses caused by lower prices.

Once a company has eliminated its competition, it is free to raise prices. In this way, a company with a monopoly can earn huge profits by selling the product or service at a high price. Such monopoly control not only raises costs for consumers but also limits their choice of a product or service.

The opposite of monopoly is competition, in which many sellers (often small companies) compete to produce and sell a certain kind of good or service. In a competitive market, so many sellers are competing that no one company can control the selling price.

You can tell how competitive a certain industry is by finding out how many separate companies supply similar products. If there is only one provider of a good or service, that company probably has a monopoly in that particular market. If there are that many suppliers, chances are that a high degree of competition exists in that industry.

Regulating Monopolies

In 1890, Congress passed the Sherman Antitrust Act to limit the negative effects of monopolies and to encourage competition. Although the act was not very effective at first, it did establish the precedent for government regulation of monopolies and trusts. These powers were later extended by the Clayton Antitrust Act and the Federal Trade Commission Act, both passed in 1914. Throughout most of the twentieth century, these laws have been strictly enforced to prohibit mergers that would create companies with a monopoly in a particular industry.

In regulating monopolies, governments must always balance the interests of competitors and consumers against the efficiency with which the economy operates. In some extreme cases, it would be highly inefficient for more than one firm to provide a good or service. Economists refer to this situation as a natural monopoly. A good example is local telephone service. It would be very costly and inefficient for more than one company to wire all the homes and businesses in a community. Other utilities such as those that provide electricity and natural gas are also natural monopolies. To protect the interests of consumers and to oversee the operation of these monopolies, state and local governments establish utility commissions.

Recent Trends

During the administration of President Ronald Reagan in the 1980s, the U.S. government modified its approach to the enforcement of antitrust laws. Basically, the government chose not to oppose most mergers because it felt they did not pose a threat to fair competition or the interests of consumers. As a result, the 1980s saw a new wave of huge mergers, particularly in such industries as airlines, food products, and publishing.

Although they have not created monopolies, many of these mergers have resulted in a large concentration of economic power in certain corporations. Today, as in the late 1800s, the debate continues over whether this concentration of economic power is good or bad for the nation.

Trusts based on the Standard Oil model soon arose in other industries. By 1900, trusts controlled the sugar, liquor, cattle, tobacco, nail, salt, leather, and bicycle industries.

The Sherman Antitrust Act of 1890

The extraordinary profits made by trusts were available only to a handful of owners. As trusts took over in more sections of the economy, they nearly wiped out their competitors. No governmental regulations restricted their behavior. As a result, prices rose, but the quality of goods and services often declined. Also, resources were wasted, and working conditions worsened. Many people became disgusted by the excesses of the trusts. Across the nation, both states and individuals looked to Congress to bring about a change.

"Congress alone can deal with the trusts," Ohio Senator John Sherman said, "and if we are unwilling or unable, there will soon be a trust for every production and a master to fix the price for every necessity of life." Sherman's speech as well as years of effort by reformers finally brought about the passage of the Sherman Antitrust Act in 1890. Its purpose was to limit the power of the trusts.

The language of the act suggested that monopolies would be banished from the American economy. "Every contract, combination in the form of trust or otherwise," it read, "or conspiracy in restraint of trade or commerce . . . is hereby declared to be illegal." Enforcing the law, however, proved another matter altogether.

The bill failed to define its terms clearly. Loopholes prevented the law from fulfilling its purpose.

Rockefeller's lawyers immediately devised a legal substitute for the trust called the holding company. A holding company didn't actually make or sell

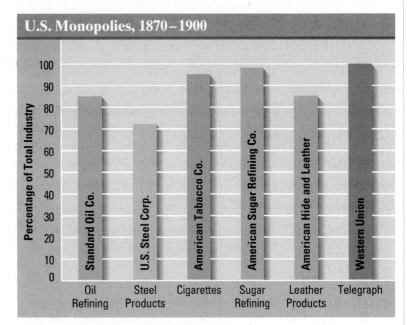

▼ *This chart shows the percentage of the markets that six powerful monopolies controlled in 1904.*

U.S. Monopolies, 1870–1900

Percentage of Total Industry (y-axis: 0, 10, 20, 30, 40, 50, 60, 70, 80, 90, 100)

- Standard Oil Co. — Oil Refining
- U.S. Steel Corp. — Steel Products
- American Tobacco Co. — Cigarettes
- American Sugar Refining Co. — Sugar Refining
- American Hide and Leather — Leather Products
- Western Union — Telegraph

anything. Its purpose was to gain control of other companies by buying their stock. Twenty-five holding companies were created in the first five years after the Sherman law was passed. In addition, the Supreme Court gave a narrow interpretation of the act in the 1895 case of *United States* v. *E. C. Knight Company*. The Court's ruling further weakened the law's effectiveness. Even so, the Sherman Antitrust Act laid an important legal foundation. This law enabled a willing president, Theodore Roosevelt, to break up many monopolies in the early 1900s. ■

■ *In what way did monopolies and trusts act against the best interests of the people?*

R E V I E W

1. **FOCUS** What political and business practices did reformers in the 1870s and 1880s want to change? Why?

2. **CONNECT** Explain how political bribery might have affected government efforts to regulate business.

3. **POLITICAL SYSTEMS** How did the civil service method of filling government jobs differ from the spoils system method?

4. **CRITICAL THINKING** Could the actions of monopolies and trusts during the Gilded Age be described as undemocratic? Why or why not?

5. **ACTIVITY** Make a cartoon about one of the political or economic problems of the Gilded Age, such as the spoils system, the railroads, or the trusts. Choose a specific issue, and use real characters if possible.

The Gilded Age

LESSON 3

The Populist Revolt

THINKING FOCUS

Why did American farmers decide to form their own political party in the 1890s?

Key Terms

- Populism
- cooperative

➤ *William Jennings Bryan is shown here on the presidential campaign trail in 1896. Bryan lost to William McKinley in the election.*

The Democrats were sharply divided over the issue of money when they gathered in Chicago for their 1896 convention. Some felt that the value of American money should be based on the gold held by the government. Others supported American farmers in the belief that only an unlimited money supply would solve the country's economic woes.

None of the delegates knew what to expect when a young congressman from Nebraska stepped up to the platform on the evening of July 7. Only 36 years old at the time, William Jennings Bryan was often called the "Great Commoner" because he championed the cause of the common people. In particular, Bryan supported many of the goals of America's discontented farmers, who in the 1890s were demanding sweeping political changes. In his speech at the 1896 Democratic convention, Bryan—an unknown figure to many—electrified the delegates.

Illinois poet Edgar Lee Masters heard Bryan's speech and described its effects: "The delegates arose and marched for an hour, shouting, weeping, rejoicing. They lifted this orator upon their shoulders and carried him as if he had been a god." The next day the Democrats nominated Bryan for President.

> The sympathies of the Democratic party, as shown by the platform, are on the side of the struggling masses who have ever been the foundation of the Democratic party. . . . You come to us and tell us that the great cities are in favor of the gold standard. We reply that the great cities rest upon our broad and fertile prairies. Burn down your cities and leave our farms, and your cities will spring up again as if by magic. But destroy our farms, and the grass will grow in the streets of every city in the country.
>
> If the gold delegates dare to defend the gold standard as a good thing, we will fight them to the uttermost. Having behind us the producing masses of this nation and the world, supported by the commercial interests, the laboring interests, and the toilers everywhere, we will answer their demand for a gold standard by saying to them: You shall not press down upon the brow of labor this crown of thorns, you shall not crucify mankind upon a cross of gold!
>
> William Jennings Bryan, July 7, 1896

The Roots of Populism

Bryan's 1896 presidential campaign marked the high point of a farmers' movement known as **Populism**. Although Populism did not emerge until the early 1890s, the movement had its roots in the economic and social conditions that developed following the Civil War.

Hard Times for Farmers

In the 1870s and 1880s, American farmers were caught in a trap. They faced increasing costs for growing and shipping grain at a time when grain prices were falling sharply. High interest rates, property taxes, and shipping charges drained their profits. Because farmers depended on the nearest railroad to get their grain to market, they had no way to protect themselves from increases in shipping charges. Railroad companies took advantage of the farmers by raising rates higher and higher for the short hauls they used. Frank Norris's novel *The Octopus* shows just how angry farmers were about railroads:

*W*e're cinched already. It all amounts to just this: You can't buck against the railroad. We've tried it and tried it, and we are stuck every time . . . Shelgrim [railroad owner] owns the courts. . . . He's got the Governor of the State in his pocket. He keeps a million-dollar lobby at Sacramento every minute of the time the legislature is in session; he's got his own men on the floor of the United States Senate. He has the whole thing organized like an army corps. What are you going to do?

Another major reason for the increased cost of farming was industrialization. Mechanical reapers, planters, and combines had become available by the 1880s. Farmers had to buy the new farm machinery if they wanted to grow more grain. Since these machines were expensive, farmers had to borrow large amounts of money

▼ *Farmers like these suffered from many social and political problems created by the economics of the Gilded Age.*

together to reduce costs and raise prices. In some places, Grangers pooled their money and bought farm machinery directly from manufacturers to avoid the extra retail costs. Grangers also pooled their crops. Such pooling allowed them to set their own prices, to sell directly to large merchants, and to avoid paying a commission to "middlemen."

Greenback-Labor Party

The value of paper money is a complex issue. Nowadays, the worth of paper currency is largely a measure of the confidence people have in the government and in the economy. In the 1870s, however, laws were passed guaranteeing that the value of paper money should depend on the amount of gold in the government's reserves.

People have always debated over what the worth of money should be. During and after the Civil War, the government issued paper money, called "greenbacks" because of their color, that could not be redeemed for gold. Farmers disagreed with bankers about how much money should be circulated and about whether its value should continue to be based on the price of gold.

Increasing the quantity of any item on the market, including money, lowers its value. Farmers believed that the government should put more dollars into circulation. This step would decrease the value of the money they owed the banks, making their loans easier to repay. They wanted the government to increase the money supply by printing more "greenbacks" and by introducing the unlimited, or "free," coinage of silver.

Bankers liked "hard" money, that

▲ *This poster from the 1870s summarizes some of the goals and ideals of the Grangers.*

Across Time & Space

In the 1970s, as in the 1890s, the cost of farming rose as the prices for crops fell. In 1983, farmers drove their tractors to Washington and parked them on the lawn of the Capitol to protest the government's agricultural policy. Farmers also organized numerous benefits around the country, donating the proceeds to families who were in danger of losing their farms.

from banks in order to buy them. Because the banks saw farming as a risky business, they charged high interest rates.

As the cost of farming increased, the prices that farmers could get for their crops fell. Ironically, the ability to produce more food by machines was largely to blame. The price that people would pay for crops fell as the supply of corn, wheat, potatoes, and other agricultural products on the market increased. This economic principle is called the law of supply and demand.

The Grange Movement

A single farmer could do little to raise the price of crops or to reduce the cost of farming. But there was much that farmers could do together. In 1867, Oliver Kelley—described by his friends as "an engine with too much steam"—founded an organization of farmers know as the Grange. The Grange gave farmers the opportunity to discuss the large economic and political issues that affected their lives. It also encouraged them to work

is, money based on the gold standard. The gold standard was an assurance that money would keep its value. Bankers feared that a sharp rise in prices would occur if there were more dollars in circulation than there was gold in the U.S. Treasury. They wanted to keep the dollars in circulation equal to the value of the government's gold. This "hard money" policy became law in 1875.

The Greenback-Labor Party was formed in 1878 to support an increased money supply and "free silver." Its members were farmers, laborers, and a few businessmen. With the help of farmers, the "Greenbacks" elected 14 members to Congress in 1878. Participating in the Greenback-Labor Party helped farmers realize the power they had to shape state law and influence national affairs. ■

■ *What economic and political factors led to the rise of the Populist movement?*

Farmers Establish the Populist Party

This is a nation of inconsistencies. The Puritans fleeing from oppression became oppressors. We fought England for our liberty and put chains on four million blacks. We wiped out slavery and by our tariff laws and national banks began a system of white wage slavery worse than the first....

We were told . . . to go to work and raise a big crop . . . and we raised the big crop that they told us to; and what came of it? Eight-cent corn . . . two-cent beef, and no price at all for butter and eggs—that's what came of it.

With statements like these, Kansas orator and reformer Mary Elizabeth Lease persuaded many farmers to join a Farmers' Alliance. The alliances of the 1880s were similar to, but more radical than, the Grange. As the wealth of robber barons and men like "Big Jim" Fisk increased, so did the discontent of the farmers. Led by the well-organized Southern Farmers' Alliance, the goal of these organizations was to fight for lower farming costs and higher crop prices. They tried out several kinds of farming cooperatives. In these **cooperatives**, farmers pooled their resources to save money on farm machinery and shipping costs. Although farming was their biggest concern, the farmers' alliances supported other causes. They wanted

regulation of railroads and monopolies, improved public schools, and greater rights for women. The alliances also published newspapers and sent out speakers like Lease to spread their message.

Ocala sets Agenda

In 1889, the two biggest alliances, the Northwestern Farmers' Alliance and the Southern Farmers' Alliance, merged. The next year the new National Farmers' Alliance held a meeting at Ocala, Florida. There they developed a platform for sweeping political reform. To lower the cost of farming, the Ocala Platform urged government loans for farmers and called for strict railroad regulation. To raise the price of farm crops, the plat-

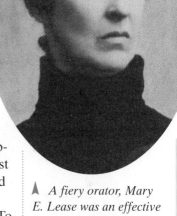

▲ *A fiery orator, Mary E. Lease was an effective spokesperson for the Populists.*

A PARTY OF PATCHES
Grand Balloon Ascension—Cincinnati, May 20th, 1891.

◄ *This cartoon expresses the view that the Populist party was a patchwork of special interest groups.*

form called for a larger money supply through the minting of silver coins.

Farmers Support Populists

In the 1890 election, National Farmers' Alliance members supported candidates in both major parties who expressed support for agricultural reform. Once elected, however, most of these "reformers" broke the promises they had made to farmers. In some states, farmers responded by organizing their own political party.

In 1892, farmers held another national convention, this time in Omaha, Nebraska. The convention officially established the Populist Party. The delegates, Populist leaders in their local communities, had colorful nicknames like "Sockless Jerry" Simpson and "Pitchfork Ben" Tillman.

At their 1892 convention, the Populists nominated James B. Weaver for President. Although Weaver lost the election badly, he received a record number of popular votes for a national third-party candidate. The Populists also won 2 governorships and 14 seats in the Congress.

Farmers Favor "Free Silver"

As you read earlier, farmers supported the Greenback-Labor Party in the 1870s. They believed that a larger money supply would lower the value of the money they owed and improve their chances of paying off their debts. Although the Greenback Party declined after 1879, farmers in the Populist Party continued to argue for "free silver," the unrestricted production of silver coins. Bankers and business people repeated their opposition. They argued that the amount of money in circulation must never exceed the nation's reserves of gold. ■

■ What measures did farmers take to lessen some of their economic hardships?

▼ *These campaign materials are from the election of 1896. Notice the gold bug which undoubtedly adorned the clothes of gold standard supporters.*

Populism Peaks and Fades

After 1892, Populists continued to call for an end to the abuse of wealth and power and for economic justice. From their founding convention in 1892 to the presidential election of 1896, Populists quickly made significant gains.

The Depression of 1893

A financial collapse in 1893 gave Populism a big boost. With about 2.5 million people out of work and many others unable to buy basic necessities, Americans lost confidence in Democratic President Grover Cleveland. Some Democrats began to wonder whether the prescriptions of the Populists for the economy might work after all.

Further, President Cleveland showed little caring for unemployed people during the depression. In 1894, businessman Jacob Coxey led a march of 500 unemployed people from Massillon, Ohio, to Washington, D.C., to protest Cleveland's economic policy. Police, acting on the President's orders, welcomed Coxey's "army" with clubbings and arrests.

The Election of 1896

In 1896, the Democrats abandoned Cleveland and nominated William Jennings Bryan, who supported "free silver," for President. By nominating Bryan, a "silverite," the Democrats stole an important issue from the Populists and made their party more attractive to farmers. After bitter infighting, the Populists decided to throw their support to Bryan as well.

The Populists did not fare well with Bryan. In the national campaign against the Republican candidate, William McKinley, Bryan distanced

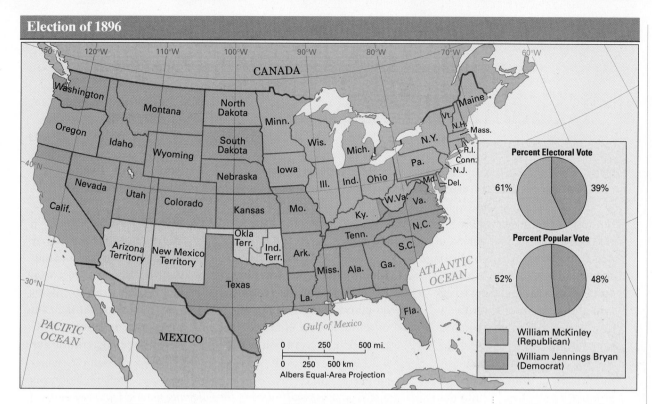

Election of 1896

CANADA

Percent Electoral Vote

61%   39%

Percent Popular Vote

52%   48%

William McKinley
(Republican)

William Jennings Bryan
(Democrat)

PACIFIC OCEAN

MEXICO

Gulf of Mexico

ATLANTIC OCEAN

0   250   500 mi.

0   250   500 km

Albers Equal-Area Projection

---

himself from the Populists. Many Americans thought that the Populists were too radical. And even though he had the support of two major parties, Bryan failed to earn the votes of workers. Workers were afraid that free silver would decrease the value of their wages.

Bryan campaigned at a frantic pace. He traveled a total of 18,000 miles and gave as many as 20 speeches a day. Meanwhile, McKinley sat on his front porch and read speeches to key political supporters, who did the traveling for him. The Republican campaign chest was full of contributions from the trusts, large banks, and railroads. A gift of $250,000 from Standard Oil nearly equaled the whole Democratic campaign chest. On election day, McKinley defeated Bryan by a comfortable margin.

The Decline of Populism

Bryan's defeat marked the end of the Populist Party. Several events guaranteed its fall. First, the economy began to boom after McKinley's election. The Republicans took the credit for the change. Second, the discovery of gold in Alaska in 1898 increased the nation's gold reserves. This brought about the inflation of currency that the Populists had been calling for. Finally, the Populists had not gained any support outside of the farming community.

The collapse of the Populist Party did not mark the end of their ideals. These were taken up by the major parties, and later, by Progressive reformers. The income tax and government regulation of transportation and utilities are all Populist goals that we take for granted today. ■

The popular vote in the 1896 presidential election was close, but McKinley clearly triumphed in the electoral vote—271 to Bryan's 176. What regions of the country did McKinley carry? What regions did Bryan carry?

■ *What factors contributed to the decline of the Populist Party?*

R E V I E W

1. **FOCUS** Why did American farmers decide to form their own political party in the 1890s?

2. **CONNECT** How did the rise of railroad monopolies hurt farmers?

3. **ECONOMICS** Why did farmers want the government to increase the money supply?

4. **CRITICAL THINKING** Why do you think it is difficult for a

"third" party such as the Populist party to compete against established political parties?

5. **WRITING ACTIVITY** Imagine that you are the editor of a Populist newspaper. Write an editorial encouraging farmers to form cooperatives. Or as a private citizen, write a letter to the editor urging farmers to come together on an issue that is dividing them.

491

The Gilded Age

Reading Mark Twain

Here's Why

Some pieces of literature are called "period pieces" because they are such clear reflections of the time period in which they were written. Historians read novels, short stories, and essays written during a certain period in order to learn how writers of the time viewed their society.

Knowing how to make inferences, or draw conclusions, about a society from what you read in the literature of that society, can provide you with a fuller view of history.

Mark Twain (the pen name for Samuel Langhorne Clemens) is best known for his novel *The Adventures of Huckleberry Finn.* However, Twain was also known for his humorous stories and novels about the society of his time.

Suppose you wanted to learn more about the Gilded Age from the perspective of someone who wrote about it. Reading "between the lines" of Twain's humor is an amusing way to do that.

Here's How

Twain's book *Innocents Abroad* pokes fun at Americans traveling through Europe in the late 1800s. At that time many wealthy people assumed that a year abroad was a necessary part of one's education.

In this passage from his book, Twain relates how he waited for and finally boarded his exclusive ship.

Read the passage from Twain's novel, and follow these steps to draw conclusions about American society during the Gilded Age.

1. **Identify the style of writing.** Is the work you are reading an autobiography, a novel, or another kind of literature? The excerpt below is from one of Twain's humorous novels.

2. **Identify how the style affects the subject matter.** In humor, you can assume that the writer may be exaggerating in order to entertain the reader. At the same time, you can assume that his or her exaggerations are

Occasionally, *during the following month, I dropped in at 117 Wall Street to inquire how the repairing and refurnishing of the vessel was coming on, how additions to the passenger list were averaging, how many people the committee were decreeing not "select" every day and banishing in sorrow and tribulation. I was glad to know that we were to have a little printing press on board and issue a daily newspaper of our own. I was glad to learn that our piano, our parlor organ, and our melodeon were to be the best instruments of the kind that could be had in the market. I was proud to observe that among our excursionists were three ministers of gospel, eight doctors, sixteen or eighteen ladies, several military and naval chieftains with sounding titles, an ample crop of "Professors" of various kinds and a gentleman who had "COMMISSIONER OF THE UNITED STATES OF AMERICA TO EUROPE, ASIA, AND AFRICA" thundering after his name in one awful blast! . . .*

During that memorable month I basked in the happiness of being for once in my life drifting with the tide of a great popular movement. Everybody was going to Europe—I, too, was going to Europe. Everybody was going to the famous Paris Exposition—I, too, was going to the Paris Exposition. The steamship lines were carrying Americans out of the various ports of the country at the rate of four or five thousand a week in the aggregate. If I met a dozen individuals during that month who were not going to Europe shortly, I have no distinct remembrance of it now . . .

In the fullness of time the ship was ready to receive her passengers. I was introduced to the young gentleman who was to be my roommate, and found him to be intelligent, cheerful of spirit, unselfish, full of generous impulses, patient, considerate, and wonderfully good-natured. Not any passenger that sailed in the Quaker City [ship's name] will withhold his endorsement of what I have just said. We selected a stateroom forward of the wheel, on the

based on activities or events that the audience would accept as rather common.

3. **Look for specific details that support general ideas.**
   When Twain makes general statements such as "steamship lines were carrying Americans out of the country at the rate of four or five thousand a week," look for details that illustrate his statement. He says, "If I met a dozen individuals during that month who were not going to Europe shortly, I have no distinct remembrance of it now. . ." It seemed to him as if everyone he met was going to Europe.

4. **Look for general ideas that can be drawn from specific details.**
   Note Twain's list of passengers: "three ministers of gospel, eight doctors, sixteen or eighteen ladies, several military and naval chieftains with sounding titles, an ample crop of 'Professors' of various kinds. . . . " In his amusing way he gives you a good idea of the kind of people who were traveling abroad at that time: professional, upper class people.

5. **Draw a conclusion.**
   In this passage from his novel, Twain exaggerates general ideas but gives specific information about a way of life. This piece of literature presents an amusingly close look at how one level of society lived during the Gilded Age.

Try It

Read the passage from *East River* on page 522. Use the steps above to make inferences about the life the writer describes.

Apply It

Choose one of the literature excerpts presented in this book, such as the excerpt from *My Antonia*. Read through the passage, and write a brief paragraph explaining how the literature enhances the history discussed in the chapter.

starboard side, "below decks." It had two berths in it, a dismal deadlight, a sink with a washbowl in it, and a long, sumptuously cushioned locker, which was to do service as a sofa—partly—and partly as a hiding place for our things. Notwithstanding all this furniture, there was still room to turn around in, but not to swing a cat in, at least with entire security to the cat. However, the room was large, for a ship's stateroom, and was in every way satisfactory.

The vessel was appointed to sail on a certain Saturday early in June . . .

Finally, above the banging, and rumbling, and shouting, and hissing of steam rang the order to "cast off!"—a sudden rush to the gangways—a scampering ashore of visitors—a revolution of the wheels, and we were off—the picnic was begun! Two very mild cheers went up from the dripping crowd on the pier; we answered them gently from the slippery decks; the flag made an effort to wave, and failed; the "battery of guns" spake not—the ammunition was out.

We steamed down to the foot of the harbor and came to anchor. It was still raining. And not only raining, but storming. "Outside" we could see, ourselves, that there was a tremendous sea on. We must lie still, in the calm harbor, till the storm should abate. Our passengers hailed from fifteen states; only a few of them had ever been to sea before; manifestly it would not do to pit them against a full-blown tempest until they had got their sea legs on. Toward evening the two steam tugs that had accompanied us with a rollicking champagne party of young New Yorkers on board who wished to bid farewell to one of our number in due and ancient form departed, and we were alone on the deep. On deep five fathoms, and anchored fast to the bottom. And out in the solemn rain at that. This was pleasuring with a vengeance . . .

Mark Twain, *Innocents Abroad*

Chapter Review

Reviewing Key Terms

civil service (p. 480)
cooperative (p. 489)
graft (p. 476)
kickback (p. 475)
monopoly (p. 483)
Mugwump (p. 479)

patronage (p. 476)
political machine (p. 476)
Populism (p. 487)
regulate (p. 482)
trust (p. 483)

A. In each of the following pairs, the two terms are related in some way. Write a sentence for each pair that clearly explains the meaning of the two terms.

1. kickback, graft
2. patronage, political machine
3. monopoly, regulate
4. Mugwumps, civil service
5. graft, civil service

B. Based on what you have read in the chapter, decide whether each of the following statements is accurate. Write an explanation of each decision.

1. Some officials received kickbacks for helping to cheat people out of their means of earning money.
2. Mugwumps were immigrants who came to America to work on the railroad.
3. In a cooperative, railroads and large shippers teamed up to keep the prices of farm products low.
4. Populism never gained much support outside farming areas.

Exploring Concepts

A. Copy the outline below onto a separate sheet of paper. Complete the outline with details from the chapter.

I. The Rise of Populism
A. Reasons for Farmer's Discontent
1. Increased Costs 2.
B. Farmer's Movements
1. 2. 3. 4.
C. Leaders of the Populist Movement
1. 2.
D. Reasons for Decline of Populism
1. 2. 3.

B. On a separate sheet of paper, write the answer to the following questions. Support your answers with facts and details from the chapter.

1. How did the robber barons influence government officials?
2. Which of President Grant's personal qualities encouraged corruption in his administration?
3. What was the main difference between the two major political parties in the period from 1877 to 1900?
4. How did the owners of trusts get around the restrictions of the Sherman Anti-Trust Act?
5. How did the introduction of new farm machinery hurt the farmers?
6. What was the main reason why farmers wanted a larger money supply?
7. Why was this period in the history of the United States called the Gilded Age?
8. Why was the Interstate Commerce Act important despite the fact that it was ineffective in regulating the railroads?
9. Why did bankers and business people oppose the idea of unrestricted production of silver coins?

Reviewing Skills

1. O. Henry was a short story writer who used the slang of his day in his writing. Find a copy of his classic short story "The Gift of the Magi," which first appeared in the *New York Sunday World* on December 10, 1905. Read the story, paying particular attention to the dialogue and the details. What does this story tell you about the way some people lived in the early twentieth century?

2. Read the passage from Frank Norris's novel *The Octopus* on page 487. Write a short paragraph explaining how that passage relates to the events in this chapter.

3. Create a timeline of the important events you have read about in this chapter. Write a short paragraph explaining what conclusions you can draw from the timeline.

4. Suppose you wanted to find out how people today view teenagers. Can you identify a particular piece of writing that you would consider a "period piece"? Explain your choice: what kind of writing is it, and why do you think it presents a contemporary view of teenagers?

Using Critical Thinking

1. Corruption in government did not end with the Grant administration. How do wealthy people and groups attempt to influence elected officials today? What can ordinary citizens do about it?

2. The debate over how much money to put into circulation still goes on today. Though the value of U.S. money no longer depends on gold or silver, the Federal Reserve Board decides how much money to put into circulation. What are the dangers of having too little money in circulation? What are the dangers of having too much money in circulation?

3. Farmers, unlike the members of labor unions, have never successfully used a strike to win higher prices for their labor. However, during the Depression they destroyed animals and crops to protest the low prices of their products. How do you think that affected the nation?

Preparing for Citizenship

1. **WRITING ACTIVITY** The two major parties, Republican and Democratic, still control American politics. Interview an adult who votes Republican and another who votes Democratic. Ask them to explain the reasons for their choice. Compare the results of your interviews, and decide if there are major differences between the parties today. Write a brief report on your findings.

2. **ART ACTIVITY** The Mugwump cartoonist Thomas Nast was the first one to use the elephant to represent the Republicans and the donkey to represent the Democrats (Note the cartoon at right.) Those symbols are still used today. Look through newspapers and magazines for cartoons or drawings that use those symbols. Create a "Republican" collage or a "Democrat" collage of your findings.

3. **COLLABORATIVE LEARNING** Advertising has always been an important part of politics. It is one way people have gained public attention and support of their beliefs. Divide the class into two groups, one representing big business and one representing independent farmers. Have each group develop a strategy for promoting its cause. Each group may create posters, write editorials, develop videos, or use other forms of contemporary communication. Present the advertising campaigns to another class, and ask the viewers to evaluate how well each campaign succeeds in presenting its group's beliefs.

Chapter 17

The Reform Era

Overcrowding. Hunger. Dangerous working conditions. By 1900, social problems fueled by immigration and industrial growth troubled America's cities. These problems inspired a new generation of reformers to fight to improve the quality of American life.

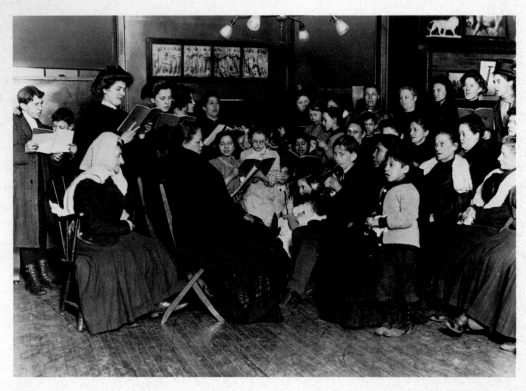

Immigrants and the poor find hope and help in social and educational centers set up by reformers.

1889-1893
B. Harrison

1893-1897
Cleveland

1897-1901
McKinley

1901-1909
T. Roosevelt

1910 The cities are overwhelmed with new residents. The photograph above shows an immigrant family in New York City. The small room serves as their living room, kitchen, and bedroom.

Journalist Nellie Bly, who earned fame for her shocking stories about jails and mental institutions, turned to travel. In this boardgame, Americans recreated her record-setting journey around the world .

1910

1920

1913-1921
Wilson

1909-1913
Taft

1920

L E S S O N   1

The Shame of the Cities

THINKING FOCUS

What caused the social problems and political corruption that were common features of American cities between 1890 and 1920?

Key Terms

- laissez faire
- Progressivism
- muckraker
- tenement
- zoning law

➤ *The Triangle Shirt-waist factory was typical of overcrowded, unsafe workplaces at the turn of the century. Newspaper reports helped create pressure for reform.*

When smoke and flames started to pour out of the eighth-floor windows of the Triangle Shirtwaist Factory in New York City on March 26, 1911, a passerby quickly contacted the fire department. The events that followed shocked and horrified the nation.

Out of the windows of the upper floors and off the roof of the 10-story building, workers—mostly young women—began leaping to their deaths on the sidewalks below. As the flames shot higher and higher, more workers jumped. Some held hands with friends as they plummeted to the ground. When the blaze ended only half an hour later, 146 of the 500 workers in the building had died in the fire or had leapt to their deaths. Only one outside fire escape, required by law, provided a way out of the building. An investigation revealed that the factory own-ers had locked the doors to the fire escape to prevent the workers from "loafing" on the stairs.

The tragedy of the Triangle Shirt-waist fire caused an uproar against health- and life-threatening conditions in American factories and sweatshops. One observer blamed the Triangle tragedy on "the greed of man." The observer mourned that "we might have foreseen it, and some of us did; we might have controlled it, but we chose not to do so."

Ironically, those who died in the fire had replaced women who had joined unions and struck for better working conditions. When the owners of the factory came to trial for the deaths of their workers, however, they were sentenced only to pay a small fine. The Triangle fire soon came to symbolize the indifference of business and government to the lives of ordinary workers.

A Time for Change

The United States has always had a capitalistic economy in which people are free to make or sell goods and services for a profit. The French term **laissez faire** *(LESS ay fair)* means "let it be." It refers to the economic policy that advocates no government interference in business. Its theory is that free trade and open competition stimulate production. America had a laissez-faire policy before the 1893 depression.

During the depression, monopolies raised prices even though there was less demand for their goods. At the same time, they cut the pay of their workers despite the fact that they were making more money than ever. The monopolies were placing their own greed above the public good. Many people became angry.

A popular movement arose in the late nineteenth and early twentieth centuries that called for the reform of unfair business practices. Reform movements were already under way in other areas of U.S. society. The "good government" movement had begun in the 1870s while Grant was President. It aimed to get rid of government corruption and inefficiency through civil service reform. The social welfare movement had begun before the Civil War. It fought for better education and safe housing. It also aimed to stop both the sale of alcohol and the use of child labor. Labor unions fought the conditions in sweatshops such as the sweatshop shown in A Closer Look on pages 500–501.

The depression of 1893 was severe. Many people feared that the economy and the government might collapse. In this time of uncertainty, reformers were able to bring together the separate reform movements. A broadly based nationwide reform movement emerged. Named **Progressivism** around 1905, the movement sought basic social, economic, and governmental reforms. It favored regulation by the government of big business, women's right to vote, and the establishment of child labor laws.

The Progressive movement was made up mainly of people from the middle class. They were well educated, and eager to change society to fit their values. On some issues, Progressives also came from the working class, the upper class, and all political parties.

Progressives often did not agree about how to achieve reform. Some did not trust government and felt that volunteer groups would be enough to solve social problems. Some wanted government to watch over business. A few wanted public ownership of monopolies. Progressives were united, however, in believing that society needed to change. They tried to find a vision or direction to guide society away from the unfairness they saw in laissez-faire capitalism.

Members of the Ash Can School were famous for their realistic paintings of urban life. George Bellows completed this painting of a city slum in 1913.

499

Sweatshops

Their name says it all. Men, women, and children worked 14-hour days in hot, stuffy upper-story apartments. The more pieces you made, the more you were paid. But the pay for each piece was low. So you had to work fast—and sweat.

Children worked in the sweatshops with their families. An entire family such as this might work 70 hours a week and earn only $3.00. The goal of the owners was to produce as much as possible, as cheaply as possible.

Italian and Jewish immigrants made up most of the sweatshop workforce. The more skilled work, such as operating sewing machines, required an apprenticeship period in which workers would not even be paid while they trained.

Making artificial flowers was a strenuous task. Sharp wires could cause cuts and punctures. Close detail work caused eyestrain.

Ready-made clothing was the most common sweatshop product. A family might make 12 dozen pairs of pants in one week.

Sweatshop rooms had no heat in the winter and only two small gas lights.

Often, six to twenty workers crowded into tight spaces.

This family assembles jackets in a windowless attic.

Families could rent rooms for a nickel a night.

Finished dry goods go straight to market. The sweatshop owner owns the whole building.

501

▲ *Jane Addams* (above) *not only sought to improve conditions in urban slums, she also urged women to find new social outlets for their energies and talents. In the shop* (top), *boys are learning skills that will help them find jobs later.*

■ *What were the main social and economic conditions during the period 1890 to 1920 that inspired reformers?*

Muckrakers Inspire Reform

Around 1900, a new generation of journalists began investigating and writing about the corruption, business abuses, and human misery in the nation's cities. Reporter Nellie Bly, for example, had herself committed to a mental institution. She later wrote a shocking account of the conditions there. Lincoln Steffens exposed bribery in the city government of St. Louis in his 1904 book *The Shame of the Cities*. Ida M. Tarbell wrote the *History of the Standard Oil Company* the same year. Other writers followed the example of these pioneers.

Theodore Roosevelt called these journalists **muckrakers** because they wrote about evil and corruption. Muckrakers found that monopolies were exploiting the public and keeping prices artificially high. Monopolies often sold poor and even harmful products. Muckrakers also exposed businesses that made their employees work in dangerous and unhealthful workplaces. These stories not only shocked the nation but also won strong support for many important reforms.

Settlement Houses Nourish the Poor

The misery of the cities and the cause of feminist liberation changed Jane Addams, a polite young woman from a well-to-do family, into a tough social reformer. Addams introduced the settlement house to America in 1889. A settlement house was a community center in an urban neighborhood. It provided childcare, education, and other services to immigrants and the poor.

Addams began Hull House in Chicago's poverty-stricken 19th ward. It became the model for the 50 settlement houses that were established by 1895. Hull House grew to take up a full city block. It offered a nursery, boys' clubs, a theater, a playground, a gym, classes in English, health, and nutrition, a pottery workshop, and a book bindery.

On the whole, Progressives were well educated. They recognized that scientifically gathered facts would strengthen their arguments for reform. They were also interested in finding scientific, efficient ways to distribute the services they offered.

Addams and her friends made scientific studies of American cities. They used the studies to fight child labor and workplace abuses. Addams also helped to put in place the nation's first factory inspection law and its first juvenile court.

Despite the major contributions of the settlement houses to the lives of the immigrants and the poor, Addams remained unsatisfied. She believed that private gifts and volunteer work were "totally inadequate to deal with the vast numbers of the city's [poor]." Like many other Progressives, she felt that the help of the government was needed to solve the nation's serious social problems. ■

UNDERSTANDING REFORM

What does the photograph on this page tell you about life in a New York City tenement at the turn of the century? Can you understand why many people who were concerned about the welfare of the city poor became Progressive reformers in the early 1900s? The reformers attacked not only the problems of the poor but also a wide range of problems at the city, state, and national levels.

In the two decades of the Progressive Era, American citizens participated in and witnessed some of the most important and creative reforms in U.S. history. But what exactly does reform mean? Basically, reform is a movement that tries to improve social, political, or other conditions without revolutionary changes. As you will read later in this chapter, there were others during this period who sought to make radical political changes. But the Progressive reformers wanted to improve the system, not overthrow it. Most of the reform leaders were from the middle class and college-educated, and so they had strong interests in preserving but improving the social and political system.

Varieties of Reform

Reform efforts can take a variety of approaches. In some cases, reformers are seeking to eliminate corruption, or the abuse of power. This is the type of reform that Progressives brought to city and state governments. In other cases, reformers simply seek improved ways of doing things. For example, Progressives sought to change educational methods to make schools more effective. Finally, reform may take the form of remedying problems by providing services and resources that no one else has supplied. Jane Addams's work through Hull House is a good example of this third kind of reform.

Reform Today

Of course, the Progressive movement did not solve all the nation's ills. Today, many people are working to bring about reforms similar to those carried out at the beginning of the century. For example, educational reform is once again a major goal at both the state and national levels. In addition, other reformers seek to enact ethics ordinances and other measures to curb corruption in government. People across the nation are also concerned with issues such as the lack of affordable housing, alcohol and drug abuse, pollution, and reducing crime in the nation's urban centers.

Educational Reform

▼ *Traditional classrooms of the 1800s would never have allowed the students to study together or to leave their seats.*

Progressives did not think highly of the traditional American school of the 1800s, which emphasized rote learning. Under this system, teachers dictated a lesson that the class then wrote down and memorized. Not

allowed to talk or move, students also sat in desks that were bolted to the floor.

Many Americans at this time did not know how to read or write English. Progressive reformers wanted

more people to be able to get a basic education. Middle-class Progressives also wanted schools to have an "Americanizing" function. They thought immigrants would pick up middle-class values as they learned to read, write, and speak English.

Following the lead of the Progressives, many businesses found that they benefited from having workers who could read. These businesses helped "Americanize" their employees by sending them for English lessons and job training. This business-sponsored educational is known as "industrial education."

Led by John Dewey, a Columbia University philosopher, Progressive educators began teaching students through participation. The Progressive curriculum also brought in subject matter important to students' lives. Job training and health education helped the poor get better jobs. School desks were unbolted from the floor to allow flexible use of the classroom. Nurseries, kindergartens, and playgrounds in which children learn through play became a new standard. Many of these reforms have become familiar traditions today. ■

■ *What features of 19th century American education did the Progressive movement reform?*

City Planning

The state of American cities in the late 1800s and early 1900s could be seen in Chicago. There pigs roamed the streets, and open sewers ran down the alleyways. In one section, six out of ten babies died in their first year. In some cities, elevated railroads coughed ashes, fouled the air with smoke, and shook buildings as they rumbled by. People in **tenements**— cheaply made apartments—lived as many as ten to each windowless room. The journalist Jacob Riis reported on the squalor and the terrible conditions of New York City slums in his 1890 book, *How the Other Half Lives*:

S wine roamed the streets and gutters as their principal scavengers. The death of a child in a tenement was registered at the Bureau of Vital Statistics as "plainly due to suffocation in the foul air of an unventilated apartment," and the Senators, who had come down from Albany to find out what was the matter with New York, reported that "there are annually cut off from the population by disease and death enough human beings to people a city...."

American cities had grown wildly, many without planning. Many politicians either did not care about or could not deal with the problems that resulted.

Urban Progressives believed that cities could be pleasant, livable, even beautiful places. They called for zoning laws and city planning. **Zoning laws** restricted the kinds of buildings and businesses that could be developed in a given place. Smoke-belching factories could then be separated from houses and markets. Traffic jams and crowding could also be prevented.

The Progressives' plans for the cities included safe apartment buildings to replace cheaply built tenements. In many cities Progressives also won tough housing laws. These laws required landlords to build safe buildings with fire escapes and a window in each room for light and air.

Hull House built the first public playground in 1892. In 1906, Progressives founded the National Playground Association of America. Its goal was to encourage cities to build public parks and playgrounds for children.

The grandest goal of the urban-planning movement was to improve cities with beautiful architecture. The "city beautiful" movement counted steel millionaire Andrew Carnegie among its members. With his support, the movement helped to build new libraries, museums, and government buildings. Many of these grand buildings were modeled after the most beautiful buildings in Europe. They became monuments to the "city beautiful" campaign to improve American urban life. ■

Reforming City Politics

The squalor of a city's darkest slum was often reflected in the corruption of the city's politics. Many cities across the country were still run by the "boss" system described in Chapter 16. Reports by muckrakers revealed the dishonesty and greed at the heart of this system. Businesses bribed city officials for government contracts; the railroads "bought" favorable legislation; and machine politicians stuffed the ballot boxes with illegal votes.

505

Commission Plan

Voters Elect

Board of Commissioners
acts as a city council
(one chosen to be mayor)

*Each commissioner heads
a department*

Fire, Finance
Police, Public works,
Public Welfare

City Manager Plan

Voters Elect

Council

Manager
Employed By Council

*Manager
directs departments*

Fire, Finance
Police, Public works,
Public Welfare

▲ *These charts show the structure of the commission and the city manager forms of government.*

■ *How did corrupt politicians increase the social and economic problems of the cities?*

Life in the cities depended upon efficient police, sanitation, and human services provided by city governments. Political corruption often put unqualified and incompetent people in jobs of great importance. As a result, these people could not deliver important services. Poor sanitation in Pittsburgh, for instance, endangered citizens when the city's water became contaminated with dysentery, cholera, and typhoid germs.

The Mechanics of Corruption

Before Progressive reform, most city governments organized elections by wards, or districts. In each district, each political party hired a ward heeler. This person told the people in that district whom to vote for and saw to it that they got to the polls on voting day. Political parties earned the loyalty of the voters by finding jobs, food, and housing, and by granting other favors for them. The efficiency of this political system is recognized in the term *party machine*.

Many immigrants were unskilled and could not speak English very well. They were willing to trade their votes for the practical rewards that the party machines offered them. On the larger scale, however, the machines bred unfair political practices and deep-seated corruption.

Forms of Government

Reformers used commissions and investigations to expose the corruption in city government and to take control of city hall. Reform politicians then changed the way the city did its business. Except in the biggest cities, they did away with the ward system and the political machines based in the neighborhoods. Instead, they had city-wide elections. These were easier to supervise and cut down on cheating.

Progressive reformers were ready to capture and reform city government whenever they had a chance. Their boldest success in city government blew in on the winds of a hurricane in September 1900.

That year, a powerful storm charged off the Gulf of Mexico and smashed Galveston, Texas. The city government could not manage the severe crisis that followed. Leading citizens threw the city government out. They replaced it with a small elected commission consisting of five members who were given executive and legislative power.

The commission form of government proved to be very effective. In this government, each of the commissioners took charge of one department of the city, such as roads, utilities, schools, and police. The system was soon adopted in Houston, Des Moines, and many other cities around the country.

The city manager form of government was a refinement of the commission. It was first used in Staunton, Virginia, in 1908. In this model, elected city officials hire a professional city manager, who has no political connections, to run the city. Hundreds of other American cities also adopted this efficient model. ■

REVIEW

1. **FOCUS** What caused the social problems and political corruption that were common features of American cities between 1890 and 1920?

2. **CONNECT** What were some of the reform movements that began before the Civil War?

3. **HISTORY** What steps did the Progressives take in the early 1900s to reform city government? Were their reform efforts successful?

4. **CRITICAL THINKING** Why do you think that Jane Addams and many other Progressives believed that private charity was not enough to solve the serious social problems in American cities at the turn of the century?

5. **ACTIVITY** Plan a neighborhood. Draw a map of a neighborhood where you would like to live. Show where you would locate apartments, factories, stores, parks, and roads.

L E S S O N   2

Progressive Reform

*T*here was never the least attention paid to what was cut up for sausage.... There would be meat that had tumbled out on the floor, in the dirt and sawdust, where the workers had tramped and spit uncounted billions of consumption [tuberculosis] germs. There would be meat stored in great piles in rooms; and the water from leaky roofs would drip over it, and thousands of rats would race about on it. . . . These rats were nuisances, and the packers would put poisoned bread out for them; they would die, and then rats, bread, and meat would go into the [sausage] together. This is no fairy story and no joke; the meat would be shoveled into carts, and the man who did the shoveling would not trouble to lift out a rat even when he saw one—there were things that went into the sausage in comparison with which a poisoned rat was a tidbit. . . .

Upton Sinclair, The Jungle

THINKING FOCUS

What kinds of changes in state and federal government resulted from Progressive reform?

Key Terms

- initiative
- referendum
- recall
- conservation

Muckraking journalist Upton Sinclair wrote this account of the Chicago meatpacking industry for his novel *The Jungle*, published in 1906. Sinclair had worked his way through City College in New York writing cheap novels. An urge to expose the exploitation of workers led Sinclair to the stockyards of Chicago. There he talked to workers and took notes on what he saw. Sinclair intended his book to inspire labor reform.

When *The Jungle* was published, however, readers were more shocked by the descriptions of meatpacking than by the difficult life of workers. After President Theodore Roosevelt read *The Jungle*, he shoved his breakfast sausages away and ordered a study of the meat industry. The study was used to support the Meat Inspection Act of 1906, which provided for government inspection of all meat shipped from one state to another.

State Government Reform

Progressives found that changes at the city level were often blocked by state governments. They set out to win control of state government to carry out their programs. Many Progressive reforms were intended to make state governments more responsive to the citizens who elected them. The most remarkable instance of this reform process was carried out in the state of Wisconsin.

Robert La Follette's Wisconsin Idea

Robert M. La Follette of Wisconsin was the first and most radical reformer of state politics and one of the most extraordinary figures of the early 1900s. "Now his face was calm; now a thundercloud; now full of sorrow," one journalist wrote of this energetic politician. A lawyer and former congressman, La Follette led an alliance of Wisconsin farmers, labor-

507

railroads. The new program gained fame across the country as the "Wisconsin idea."

The Revolt Spreads

Beginning in 1905, a wave of scandals in state governments led to reforms based on those in Wisconsin. Of all the states to reform themselves, California made the most significant changes. Governor Hiram Johnson introduced constitutional reforms that wiped out the political machines. The once-powerful Southern Pacific Railroad withdrew from politics and accepted state regulation. Reformers in most states brought in several new instruments of "direct" democracy.

The secret ballot replaced the old colored ballots. Sometimes called the Australian ballot, secret ballots reduced fraud and violence at voting places. The **initiative** gave voters in each state the power to start a bill with a simple petition. The **referendum** allowed a direct vote on a bill or law already passed by the legislature. The **recall** gave voters the power to remove an elected official from office at any time.

Not all the reforms were so democratic. Many white middle-class Progressives thought it was dangerous to give political power to the poor and minorities. In many Southern states, Progressives passed laws that took voting power away from blacks. In Louisiana, for instance, the number of registered black voters dropped from 130,000 in 1896 to 1,000 in 1904. ■

▲ *Wisconsin Governor "Battling Bob" La Follette was a powerful speaker as well as an effective reformer.*

ers, and immigrants who had been hurt by the depression of 1893.

La Follette was elected governor in 1900. He stormed into office, promising to take the government away from the bosses and give it "back to the people."

He quickly won passage of a law that provided direct primary elections. This change allowed voters, instead of political bosses, to choose candidates for political office. He reformed civil service so that appointments were based on ability, not patronage. He pushed through a law that prohibited business contributions to political parties. And he persuaded the state legislature to set up public commissions to watch over the utilities and the powerful

■ *How did Robert La Follette's "Wisconsin Idea" spur reform of state governments?*

The Federal Government Responds

When President McKinley was assassinated in Buffalo, New York, on September 6, 1901, 42-year-old Theodore Roosevelt became President. Progressivism soon became a strong, widespread movement. Roosevelt was drawn to Progressive ideas. He encouraged many reforms at the federal level. In order to get the reforms he wanted, Roosevelt dramatically expanded the power of the presidency and of the federal government.

Roosevelt promised Americans "a square deal" from the government. By "square deal" he meant protection from unfair business practices.

The Meat Inspection Act of 1906 shows how Roosevelt won passage of laws to regulate irresponsible businesses. The Pure Food and Drug Act of the same year followed a like pattern.

A series of articles by muckraker Samuel Hopkins Adams uncovered the fraud in ordinary medicines. Most medicines on the market until 1906 were mixtures of alcohol, addictive drugs like opium, and other harmful additives. Even medicine for crying babies contained opium.

Adams's articles inspired the Pure Food and Drug Act. This law banned the use of harmful additives in food and medicine and the use of false advertising. The federal government was taking on a new role as the regulator of American businesses.

Busting the Trusts

At the turn of the century, powerful corporations often joined together to form giant trusts. Then they ran their competitors out of business. President Roosevelt was not opposed to all monopolies, but he would not allow one that took unfair advantage of the public. "We do not wish to destroy corporations," he said, "but we do wish to make them subserve the public good."

One of Roosevelt's earliest acts as President was to file suit against the Northern Securities Company. This company had been created to control railroads in the Northwest. The suit shocked the business world but pleased Progressives. Roosevelt won the case after two years in court, and the monopoly was dissolved. Government became a power for business to reckon with.

▲ Before the passage of the Pure Food and Drug Act in 1906, Americans spent millions of dollars on quack remedies.

▼ In this political cartoon, the giant king represents the monopolies. The long line of various types of working people bring tributes, or gifts, to King Monopoly. What point do you think the cartoonist was trying to make?

509

President Theodore Roosevelt (at right) *rides with his friend, conservationist John Muir, at Yosemite National Park in California.*

Conservation

Roosevelt had a lifelong love for America's wilderness. By the time he became President, it was clear that the natural resources of the United States, once thought to be inexhaustible, had actually been wastefully reduced. Influenced by his friends John Muir, the naturalist, and Gifford Pinchot, the head of the U.S. Forest Service, Roosevelt instituted a program of **conservation,** or protection and efficient use of natural resources. The program included reform of public land use. In all, he set aside 148 million acres of land for forests, parks, and national monuments, including Pinnacles National Monument and Muir Woods in California.

Giving the Senate to the People

Amendments were added to the Constitution in 1913. They aided Progressive reform at the national level. These were the Sixteenth Amendment and the Seventeenth Amendment.

The Sixteenth Amendment provided for a federal income tax. This changed the way the government was funded and allowed for a more powerful federal government. A government with greater capabilities was needed to carry out Progressive reforms.

Before the Seventeenth Amendment, Americans did not directly elect U.S. Senators. Instead, state legislatures chose them. As a result, Senate seats were often handed over to the friends of political bosses and business leaders. Such senators were more loyal to those who put them in power than they were to the voters. The Senate seemed to be a political club whose members sold their votes.

David Graham Phillips, a muckraking journalist, exposed the buying and selling of Senate appointments in his 1906 article "The Treason of the Senate." A reform movement grew up around the issue. State after state passed provisions for an amendment to the Constitution to require the direct election of senators. The Senate itself refused to consider such an amendment. Finally, when even more scandals erupted, the Senate lost its credibility. It offered no more opposition to election reform. The Seventeenth Amendment required that U.S. Senators be elected directly by the voters of each state. ■

■ *What government reforms did Theodore Roosevelt institute at the federal level?*

The Bull Moose Party

Roosevelt had promised to limit himself to two terms as President. Accordingly, he announced in 1908 that he would not run again.

Roosevelt chose Secretary of War William Howard Taft to take his place as the Republican nominee. Taft easily won the presidency.

A former federal judge from Cincinnati and a friend of Roosevelt, Taft was quiet and politically unsure of himself. He did not have Roosevelt's energy and leadership ability. Taft preferred his courtroom to the White House. He believed that government should not be too active in the nation's affairs.

Taft did, however, make some strong reform moves. He established the Children's Bureau and became an even more active trustbuster than Roosevelt. But he became more conservative as his presidency wore on. He turned more and more to the "Old Guard" faction of the Republican Party. After a while, he lost the support and friendship of Roosevelt.

By the time of the 1912 elections, Roosevelt had decided to try to reclaim the presidency. Roosevelt's bid split the Republican Party into two angry, warring factions: conservatives who supported Taft and Progressives who supported Roosevelt. Although Roosevelt beat Taft in the primaries, the powerful conservatives who controlled the party still gave Taft the nomination.

Roosevelt and his supporters stormed out of the convention and started a third party. They called it the "Bull Moose Party," because Roosevelt had said, "I'm as strong as a bull moose."

The new Bull Moose Party split the Republican vote. This division gave the election to the Democratic nominee, a scholarly, inspiring man named Woodrow Wilson.

Although Roosevelt lost, the election was still a clear victory for the Progressives. Both Wilson and Roosevelt had campaigned on Progressive platforms. Woodrow Wilson took office in March 1913. ■

Democratic candidate Woodrow Wilson benefited from the split in the Republican Party in the election of 1912.

■ *How did Roosevelt's "Bull Moose Party" contribute to a Progressive victory in the 1912 election?*

▼ *Although Roosevelt easily outdistanced Taft in the 1912 election, he still lost the presidency to Woodrow Wilson by a wide margin.*

Election of 1912

Percent Electoral Vote

82%   16.5%   1.5%

Percent Popular Vote

42%   23%   7.5%   27.5%

- Woodrow Wilson (Democrat)
- Theodore Roosevelt (Progressive)
- William Howard Taft (Republican)
- Minor candidates

0   250   500 mi.
0   250   500 km
Albers Equal-Area Projection

The Reform Era

Wilson Continues Reform Efforts

Woodrow Wilson was an unlikely politician. An intellectual, he had been the president of Princeton University. Born and raised in Virginia, he was also the first Southerner to serve in the White House since 1846. As governor of New Jersey (1910–1912), Wilson had gained a reputation as a Progressive

▲ Few U.S. Presidents have had such strong academic credentials as Woodrow Wilson, formerly president of Princeton University.

■ What were President Woodrow Wilson's successes and failures in advancing Progressive causes?

politician. He supported many reforms that increased "direct democracy" in that state.

As President, Wilson launched one of the most ambitious programs of legislation in American history. He spoke eloquently in support of a reform program he called the "New Freedom." It was aimed at protecting the rights of individuals from economically powerful companies and banks.

Wilson's first target was tariff reform. Tariffs kept prices on foreign goods high and protected American manufacturers. But farmers and consumers in this country wanted lower tariffs so that prices would go down. Wilson won the first meaningful tariff reduction since the Civil War when Congress passed the Underwood Tariff Act in 1913.

Wilson turned next to banking reform. The banking system then in place was entirely private and was not very stable. Nearly everyone agreed that it did not meet the nation's need for a stable supply of money and credit. Wilson's answer was the Federal Reserve Act, which established the first national banking system since Andrew Jackson's presidency.

The 1913 act set up 12 Federal Reserve Banks and a Federal Reserve Board appointed by the President. The new banks regulated credit and the amount of money in circulation and provided services for banks.

The Federal Reserve Act was followed by the Clayton Antitrust Act of 1914. Like the Sherman Antitrust Act of 1890, the Clayton Act put restraints on monopolies. The Clayton bill prohibited a list of business practices used by monopolies. In 1914, Wilson also prodded Congress into creating the Federal Trade Commission. This agency had the power to investigate and prevent "unfair trade practices" by American businesses.

As a reformer, Wilson had blind spots. He allowed segregation by race in the federal government. He also withheld support for the women's suffrage amendment until passage seemed certain. But, on the whole, Wilson's contribution to Progressivism was impressive. ■

R E V I E W

1. **FOCUS** What kinds of changes in state and federal government resulted from Progressive reform?

2. **ECONOMICS** List and explain the importance of two economic reforms of the Progressive Era.

3. **CONNECT** In what sense did Roosevelt's trustbusting activities continue the reform efforts of an earlier era?

4. **CRITICAL THINKING** Do you think the new state reforms championed by Progressives improved democracy in America? Why or why not?

5. **ACTIVITY** Read your local newspaper for several days and choose the article that most closely resembles muckraking journalism. Share this article with your class.

L E S S O N   3

Competing Crusades

She must have looked like the angel of death swooping down for a visit: The saloon door swings open, and she shoves through it, almost six feet tall, a hatchet hanging from her waist, her long black dress nearly dragging on the floor as she walks. She plants herself squarely in the middle of the saloon, challenging anyone to try to stop her.

Then she attacks. Raising her hatchet, she destroys row after row of liquor bottles. Broken glass and liquor spray across the bar. Spinning around, she delivers a crashing blow to a bar chair, splintering the back. She then storms from one end of the saloon to the other, leaving a broad path of devastation behind her.

This was Carry Amelia Moore Nation on another mission to close down a saloon, or "joint," as they were then called. Nothing short of arrest or physical force would stop her. More than once she was beaten up and thrown into the street. She even spent time in jail. She soon became a national figure and helped to rally an army of supporters for the outlawing of alcohol.

Carry Nation began her famous mission after her first husband died of alcoholism. She was, no doubt, the most radical —and the most dramatic—anti-saloon crusader in a land full of fiery supporters of temperance. Nation spent three years attacking saloons. She was widely admired but publicly criticized by the Women's Christian Temperance Union (WCTU) for her unusual tactics. Replicas of her hatchet were sold in the thousands. The words on each hatchet seemed to sum up her story: "Carry Nation, Joint Smasher."

THINKING
FOCUS

What other social movements attempted to change American society during the Progressive Era, and what were their goals?

Key Terms

- prohibition
- socialist
- anarchist
- enfranchise

◄ *Although many prohibitionists disagreed with her tactics, Carry Nation was one of the best known and most colorful figures in the temperance movement.*

513

The Reform Era

Moral Reform

Across Time & Space

Some child labor is still practiced in the United States. In 1987, over 800,000 children had jobs as migrant farm workers. Worldwide, between 100 million and 200 million children are at work. In developing countries, many children work a 12-hour day for as little as 17 cents a day. Most will never go to school.

▼ *Lewis Hine took this photograph in a Carolina cotton mill in 1909.*

Carry Nation was not a lonely crusader. The country was full of women battling for change in American life. Throughout the 1800s and into the 1900s, women were a major force in almost every leading movement for moral reform. The temperance movement was also headed by women.

The Call for Prohibition

Born in the 1830s as the "temperance movement," the crusade against alcohol achieved some early successes. **Prohibition** laws in more than a dozen states made it illegal to buy alcohol.

The Anti-Saloon League was founded in 1895. The ASL grew into one of the strongest reform groups in American history. Joining with the Women's Christian Temperance Union, it publicized the link between alcohol and health problems, family problems, and poverty.

Marching in the streets, armies of women protested the sale and manufacture of alcohol. Success for the prohibitionists finally came. In 1917, the Eighteenth Amendment, prohibiting the manufacture or sale of alcohol, was passed by Congress. It was ratified by the necessary three-fourths of the states in 1919.

The Fight Against Child Labor

Nothing made Progressives angrier than the sight of children working in front of dangerous machinery. Children worked for long hours, their bodies limp with fatigue and their faces grim with pain. Children as young as 6 years old breathed the dust of coal mines and sweated in textile mills. In Southern cotton mills, 6-year-olds worked 12-hour days. They made 10 cents a day. Farther north, some went to work at 5 P.M. and sweated for 12 hours in front of the glass blowers' furnaces. These children earned less than a dollar a day.

Child laborers suffered more industrial accidents than adults. Thou-

sands of working children were killed or maimed each year. Throughout most of the 1800s, hard work was considered good for children. Poor families always needed the extra money their children earned.

Progressives like Florence Kelley set out to restrict child labor. Kelley came from a well-to-do Philadelphia family. She went to Hull House in the early 1890s, where she found her life's work in the fight against child labor. When no attorney would argue a child labor case for her, she earned a law degree and argued the case herself. Kelley and other child labor reformers took many cases to court. They were responsible for the enactment of state laws in Illinois that prohibited child labor and limited working hours for women. In 1904, Kelley helped to form the National Child Labor Committee to begin a campaign for state child labor laws. Between 1905 and 1907, nearly two-thirds of the states enacted some child labor reforms. But few states prohibited child labor outright, and many had no labor restrictions at all.

Aware of the limitations of state laws, child labor reformers first persuaded Congress to establish a Children's Bureau in the Department of Labor in 1912. The Child Labor Act, passed in 1916, banned interstate trade in goods made with child labor. Two years later, the Supreme Court struck this law down because it took from children the right to "sell" their labor.

Because of legal loopholes and court decisions, the Progressives' fight against child labor was largely ineffective. In the end, school attendance laws and changes in technology drained the profit out of child labor. The Supreme Court did not uphold laws against child labor until 1938. ∎

■ *Why didn't the Child Labor Act work?*

Radical Political Movements

Many social activists believed that the liberal reforms of the Progressives were not enough. These people didn't want to reform the American political and economic system. They wanted to replace it with something entirely different.

Eugene V. Debs and the Socialists

"The issue is Socialism versus Capitalism," pronounced Eugene V. Debs. "I am for Socialism because I am for humanity."

Debs, who had helped start a union for railroad workers in the 1890s, joined with other reformers in 1901 to establish the Socialist Party of America. The **Socialists** believed that capitalism was destroying small-scale businesses, that it denied workers the chance to earn fair wages and caused depressions and unemployment. The Socialists wanted workers or government to control the "means of production," that is, the factories and other facilities of America's industries. Their final goal was that all the people should enjoy equally the wealth produced by the nation.

In his run for the presidency in 1904, Eugene V. Debs received

▼ *A strong supporter of equality and social justice, Eugene V. Debs ran five times as the Socialist candidate for President.*

400,000 votes. The Socialist Party continued to gain power through the election of 1912. Debs earned almost a million votes that year, and Americans elected 79 Socialist mayors in 24 states.

During World War I, the federal government used patriotic feelings to hush public criticism of the war. Debs was thrown in jail for making an anti-war speech. Nonetheless, he won nearly a million votes from his prison cell in the 1920 presidential election. After the war, the government harassed radicals even more. Many were arrested. Socialist party membership declined. The party never recovered its former size or influence.

Anarchists and Radical Unionists

Among the most feared political radicals of their time were **anarchists**, because of their belief that all social structures, such as governments, are unnecessary and should be abolished. Some anarchists advocated violence to reach their goals. Emma Goldman, a famous anarchist, was thrown in jail because she told workers to steal bread if they were starving. Goldman eventually stopped believing in violence, but went on supporting anarchy. There were never very many anarchists, however, and anarchism died out as a movement by the 1940s.

A similar end was in store for the radical wing of the American labor movement. In 1905, workers unhappy with the traditional trade unions formed the Industrial Workers of the World (IWW). Its aim was "to abolish the wage system." The IWW often used threatening language, but it never started a fight. It tried to unionize both skilled and unskilled workers. It welcomed immigrants, women, and blacks. Most other unions, such as the American Federation of Labor (AFL), built their membership only among skilled white males.

The IWW's leader, William "Big Bill" Haywood, showed its aggressive spirit. Cowboy, miner, prospector, Haywood had lost an eye and mangled a hand as a young worker. He was a big, forceful man who impressed workers and businessmen alike. Haywood led the IWW in a successful strike for higher pay in the textile mills of Lawrence, Massachusetts, in 1912.

During World War I, the federal government attacked the IWW by imprisoning its leaders or deporting them to Russia. The union was no longer a force in the labor movement after the 1920s. ■

➤ *The Industrial Workers of the World used posters, songs, and poems to spread its message of radical unionism.*

THE **I.W.W.** is COMING!

JOIN THE ONE BIG UNION

■ *How did the goals of radical political movements differ from those of the Progressives?*

Women's Rights

As you learned in Chapter 9, in 1848 in Seneca, New York, Elizabeth Cady Stanton and Lucretia Mott organized a convention at which they called for women's suffrage, claiming that women had a right to vote. But by the beginning of the Progressive Era, the women's suffrage movement was split and badly demoralized. And though the Fifteenth Amendment had **enfranchised,** or given the vote to, black men in 1870, women were still not allowed to participate in the democratic system.

The idea of women voting seemed outrageous to many men and women in the 1800s. Strong opposition came from all over. The Catholic Church argued that a woman's place was in the home. The liquor industry feared women would vote in favor of prohibition. Political bosses were afraid women would vote to remove them from power. Stiff opposition also came from more conservative women's groups. Many of their members believed that their interests would be best protected by leaving politics to men.

Progress came rather slowly. Women presented a more united front when both the National and the American Suffrage Associations merged in 1890. Under the presidency of Carry Chapman Catt, the National American Women's Suffrage Association (NAWSA) testified at legislative hearings and carried on state-by-state campaigns. Eleven states had given women the right to vote by the year 1910.

Over time, more women began to see that the vote was the only way they could fully participate in Ameri-can society. Even conservative women's organizations were convert-ed. By 1914, the last of the major women's organizations had joined the suffrage campaign.

About a year earlier, Alice Paul, a Quaker with strong convictions and little patience with NAWSA's conservative methods, left NAWSA and started the militant Congressional Union. In the election of 1916, it became the National Women's Party (NWP). In 1917, the National Women's Party posted members around Woodrow Wilson's White House, holding a round-the-clock watch. Wilson's reaction was extreme. He had the protesters arrested. When some of them began a hunger strike, prison authorities let them be force-fed. Reports of the event in national newspapers helped the women's cause.

Wilson was driven by this confrontation to give his support to NAWSA, which had rejected the radical ways of the NWP. But still Congress would not budge.

Then two developments boosted the cause of women's suffrage. First, states began to pass suffrage legisla-

Women marched for suffrage in this parade in New York City in 1912. Several Western states had already given women the vote.

tion, putting pressure on the Congress. Second, the country went to war. Women very successfully took over the home front during the war. Their performance may have done more than anything else to convince the public and Congress that women deserved the right to vote.

Finally, in 1919, Congress passed a constitutional amendment that gave women nationwide the right to vote. In 1920, the Nineteenth Amendment became law when Tennessee became the thirty-sixth state to ratify it. ■

Progressivism for Whites Only

Even before the end of Reconstruction in 1877, violence against black Americans was taking place. Racist organizations such as the Ku Klux Klan attacked and killed blacks and were never brought to justice.

Blacks also suffered legal oppression. Most Southern states passed laws meant to keep blacks from using their right to vote. These laws set up qualifications that applied to most blacks but to few whites. Often the states would not allow anyone to vote who could not read and write. In addition, voters had to pay an annual poll tax of $1 or $2. Many poor blacks could not afford to pay the tax.

"Jim Crow" laws required "separate but equal" treatment for blacks. (They were named for an obedient, uncomplaining black character from a minstrel show.) These laws led to separate schools, restrooms, restaurants, and trains for white and black Americans.

A black man named Homer Plessy boarded a train in Louisiana on June 7, 1892, and sat in a "whites only" coach to challenge these laws. He was arrested and tried. His case went all the way to the Supreme Court. The court declared that "separate but equal" was a reasonable use of state powers. The 1896 case, *Plessy* v. *Ferguson*, approved a system of segregation that lasted for years. A few years later, the black poet Paul Laurence Dunbar wrote about the effects of discrimination in his poem, "Sympathy," two stanzas of which appear below.

The rise of Jim Crow laws contributed to a time of terrible racial hatred and violence. From 1895 to 1912, lynchings averaged nearly one every three days.

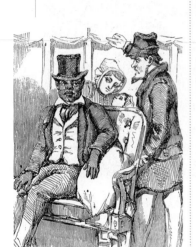

NEGRO EXPULSION FROM RAILWAY CAR, PHILADELPHIA.

▲ *This illustration shows one of the effects of "Jim Crow" laws: a white man orders a black man out of the "white" section of the train.*

I know what the caged bird feels, alas!
   When the sun is bright on the upland slopes;
   When the wind stirs soft through the springing grass,
And the river flows like a stream of glass;
   When the first bird sings and the first bud opes,
And the faint perfume from its chalice steals—
I know what the caged bird feels!

. . . .

I know why the caged bird sings, ah me,
   When his wing is bruised and his bosom sore,—
When he beats his bars and he would be free;
It is not a carol of joy or glee,
   But a prayer that he sends from his heart's deep core,
But a plea, that upward to Heaven he flings—
I know why the caged bird sings!

Paul Laurence Dunbar *Sympathy*

Ida B. Wells, the daughter of a slave, began to write against lynchings in her newspaper, the *Memphis Free Speech.* Her outspoken attitude led to death threats and to the bombing of her newspaper's office while she was away speaking in the North. Wells did not return to the South. She set herself up in Chicago where she went on writing and speaking against lynching.

Lynching was not only a Southern crime, however. In Springfield, Illinois, the home of President Lincoln, whites rioted in 1908. They were bent on driving blacks out of their town. The mob lynched a black man.

This terrible act seared the consciences of a number of Northern Progressives including Jane Addams and John Dewey. They helped organize a protest on the centennial of the birth of Abraham Lincoln in 1909. In 1910, a group of black leaders and Northern Progressives joined together to found the National Association for the Advancement of Colored People (NAACP), which has fought to defend black Americans against discrimination ever since.

W. E. B. Du Bois helped to found the NAACP. He was a Harvard-educated writer who went on to become the moral and intellectual leader of the black movement. Unlike his Southern predecessor, Booker T. Washington, Du Bois urged black Americans to demand their civil rights. ■

▲ *W.E.B. DuBois* (left) *felt that black Americans should speak out constantly against discrimination. Writer and educator Ida B. Wells* (right) *worked much of her life to end the vicious practice of lynching.*

■ *What impact did the Progressive movement have on the lives of black Americans?*

REVIEW

1. **FOCUS** What other social movements attempted to change American society during the Progressive Era, and what were their goals?

2. **CONNECT** Black men won the right to vote during Reconstruction. How was this right restricted by the 1890s?

3. **CITIZENSHIP** Name three events that contributed to the passage of the women's suffrage amendment.

4. **CRITICAL THINKING** Why do you think American businesses fought so hard to defeat child labor laws during the Progressive Era?

5. **WRITING ACTIVITY** Imagine that you are a prohibitionist, a socialist, a member of the IWW, a supporter of antilynching laws, or a supporter of the women's right to vote. Write a one-page statement in which you try to persuade others to join your cause.

Analyzing Historical Photographs

Here's Why

Photography is a powerful art. People say "the camera doesn't lie." Therefore people often believe that what they see is accurate. However, photographers always make choices about how to use the camera in order to create the kind of image they want.

A painter interprets the world around him or her by selecting certain colors, brushes and even style to convey a particular viewpoint. In the same way, a photographer decides what to photograph and how to present it.

Lighting can be used to highlight an object or person, or to create a certain mood or feeling. Sometimes a photographer will pose people or objects in a scene in order to communicate an idea. In addition the photographer can change the image in the process of developing it. By using such techniques, a photographer can sometimes create an image on paper that looks very different from the actual scene that was photographed.

As you have learned in this chapter, Jacob Riis and Lewis W. Hine used photography to inform the public of the terrible working and living conditions that many people faced in the late 1900s. Riis and Hine chose their subjects very carefully, highlighting the depressing surroundings and the emotions of hopelessness and despair in the people. They were able to use their art to influence how the camera reflected what they saw. In that way they were able to get their viewpoints across to the public. The public reacted to the grim scenes in their photos by pushing for reforms.

Knowing how to recognize the different ways in which the photographer can interpret an image will help you to analyze historical photographs.

Here's How

There are four steps that will help you analyze historical photographs:

1. If possible, identify the date when the photograph was taken and the location where it was shot.
2. Identify the subject of the photograph.
3. Identify any special photographic techniques the photographer may have used, such as a flash or a fake background.
4. Determine what the photographer was trying to show in the photograph.

Study the photograph on page 520. It was taken in Cleveland, Ohio, in 1908. The date tells you that this photograph was taken at a time when photographic equipment was rather simple. Therefore you can assume that the photographer was limited in the number of techniques available. There was no color photography at that time, and cameras were not equipped with zoom lenses.

The photographer has taken this photo from a point above the scene, from which the viewer can look across the beach at many people and activities. It is a daytime scene that uses normal light, and does not focus on one particular object. The people do not appear posed. Rather, the photographer seems to have wanted to show people enjoying a leisurely day at the beach.

Try It

Now study the photograph on this page of Hester Street, New York City, in 1905. Identify the subject and possible photographic techniques. What information does the photograph provide? Based on your analysis of the photograph, write a short paragraph outlining what you think the photographer was trying to show by taking the photograph.

Apply It

Look through a contemporary news magazine, and choose two photographs of people your age. They can be of people at home, at school, or at play. Approach these photographs as if you were a historian and you wanted to find out about our culture. Following the steps listed above, compare and contrast the two photographs. Write a paragraph describing how these images depict everyday life and what they say about today's culture.

Summer in New York

Sholem Asch

In his book East River, *Sholem Asch describes life in an immigrant neighborhood on 48th Street in New York City. As you read this excerpt think about how Asch uses details to create a picture of what life was like in a big city in the late 1800s.*

In Chapter 16 you read about Tammany Hall. This excerpt shows how political bosses did favors for their immigrant voters.

*T*he evening brought no relief from the oppressive heat. On the contrary, the walls of the buildings, having absorbed the heat all day, now began to throw it back into the street. The air was so humid that the people of the neighborhood had the feeling they were wrapped in a damp sheet which hampered their movements and from which they were unable to free themselves. It was impossible to stay indoors. The walls, the ceilings, the floors sweated with heat; the dampness filled the rooms and made it impossible to breathe. The heavy smells of food, sweat, and clothing, and the stale smell of mattresses and bedclothes added to the oppressiveness. The heat seemed to make bodies enormous and cumbersome. It sapped the energy and tortured the limbs.

The block dwellers swarmed out of their rooms, searching for a relieving gust of air. They crowded the fire escapes, the steps in front of doors, and the sidewalks.

Most of all they sought relief in the cool winds that came once in a while over the East River. But direct approach to the river shore was blocked to them. The streets ended in "dead ends" hemmed in by fences erected by the owners of the feed storehouses and stables. In a couple of places, however, there was an old unused dock, the planks water-soaked and rotted. From these docks one could hear the splashing of children swimming close to the shore, driven to find relief from the overpowering heat, disregarding the perils of the holes and falling timbers of the dock.

Other entrances to the waterfront were provided by the stables on the river shore. By climbing over fences and scrambling over the stable roofs it was possible to get down to the water's edge.

But 48th Street had two yards that opened on the river, and of these the people of the adjoining blocks were properly jealous. One of them was Harry's, to which, naturally, only his intimate friends, the people of his own block, who were interested in his pigeons, had admission. The other belonged to a private real-estate firm. Tammany had taken over the use of it so that the legitimate dwellers on 48th Street could come there to take their ease on the hot summer nights. With Judge Greenberg's help Uncle Maloney had managed to get permission to keep the property open to the Tammany members in the block. There was a lot of competition for the privilege among the inhabitants of the street. The yard stretched to the river shore, and the general belief was that cool winds blew there. Everyone in the neighborhood besieged the office of the Tammany captain for tickets of admission. The first tickets, naturally enough, went to the members in good standing of the local Tammany club; Maloney knew all of them. But in time everyone on the block came to feel that he or she had special rights to the place, even Heimowitz, the socialist, who had little enough to do with Tammany in other matters.

The yard was full of people; men, women, and children of the neighborhood. They had brought with them mattresses, blankets, pillows, cans of cold tea or beer or ice water, ready to spend half the night there, until the tenement rooms got cool enough to return to.

The river lay motionless in its broad bed, its dark patches of oily scum reflecting the star-studded sky. Now and then a light blinked from a slowly moving coal barge. A heavy silence lay over the river.

From time to time the hoarse blast of a freight boat cut through the air. The morbid prison shadows of Blackwell's Island in the middle of the river pressed on the water's surface. The dimly lighted mist that hung over the island seemed to oppress the spirit and burden the heart more than it served to lighten the darkness. Involuntarily, everyone who saw the lights gleaming through the island's mist would think of the poor devils sent "across the river." The melancholy which the sight of the island brought to every one of Manhattan's dwellers fell like a pall on the group gathered in the Tammany yard to escape the unbearable heat. How could anyone of them know what the morrow might bring? Poverty ruled their lives and—who could know?—might drive them relentlessly to a similar fate. The same melancholy drove them to find escape in sleep, to find a rest from all the cares and worries of the day.

morbid somber

Some of them sprawled out on blankets they had brought with them from their homes. Others, the Slavs, for instance, talked with animation about the old country, about the boats that floated down its rivers; the nearness of the East River had brought it to their minds. Yes, along the Vistula, the Bug, and the Volga enormous rafts of logs floated; people would live on them all summer. They talked about horses being led in the night to graze on the green plains.

animation excitement

"Another year's work in the slaughterhouse, and I'll save enough, and then back home, back to Czezov. I'll buy my brother's share and take over my father's farm, eight acres and ten head of cattle." Choleva let his fantasy roam. His speech was a mixture of Polish, Russian, and English.

"It'll be no good. You'll use up your few dollars in the old country and then you'll come back to America. Everybody comes back. One smell of the American air , and it draws you back. There's some kind of magic in it," someone said.

Further Reading

The New Immigrants. Carol Olsen Day and Edmond Day. This book describes the conditions of immigrants in the United States today.

A Tree Grows in Brooklyn. Betty Smith. The story of Francie Nolan, a young girl growing up in an immigrant neighborhood in the early 1900s.

Chapter Review

Reviewing Key Terms

anarchist (p. 516)
conservation (p. 510)
enfranchise (p. 516)
initiative (p. 508)
laissez faire (p. 499)
muckraker (p. 502)
Progressivism (p. 499)

prohibition (p. 514)
recall (p. 508)
referendum (p. 508)
socialist (p. 515)
tenement (p. 504)
zoning law (p. 505)

A. In each of the following pairs, the two terms are related in some way. Write a sentence for each pair that clearly explains the meaning of the two terms.
1. Progressivism, muckraker
2. recall, referendum
3. socialist, anarchist

B. Based on what you have read in the chapter, decide whether each of the following statements is accurate. Write an explanation of each decision.

1. Laissez-faire policies allowed businesses to operate without government restriction.
2. The tenement house was one of the reforms introduced by Jane Addams.
3. A zoning law allowed poor people to live in any area of the city they could afford.
4. Through the initiative, voters could propose laws that they felt were necessary.
5. Conservation programs were part of the government's effort to control railroad monopolies.
6. Anarchists proposed change through gradual social reforms.
7. The purpose of the Nineteenth Amendment was to enfranchise women by prohibiting them from voting.
8. Supporters of prohibition felt that giving women the right to vote would give them too much freedom.

Exploring Concepts

A. On a separate sheet of paper, copy the timeline below. Place each of the following items in the correct time position on the timeline.

- *The Shame of the Cities*
- *How the Other Half Lives*
- *The Jungle*
- Meat Inspection Act
- Pure Food and Drug Act
- Sixteenth Amendment ratified
- Seventeenth Amendment ratified
- Federal Reserve Act
- Eighteenth Amendment ratified
- Nineteenth Amendment ratified

B. Support each of the following statements with facts and details from the chapter.
1. Muckrakers identified three serious abuses of power by business monopolies.
2. The Progressive movement resulted in many improvements in children's lives.
3. The public supported women's right to vote.
4. Under Robert La Follette, Wisconsin provided many new ideas for state governments.
5. Progressive reforms at the state level gave voters more influence.
6. Theodore Roosevelt expanded the power of the presidency and the federal government.

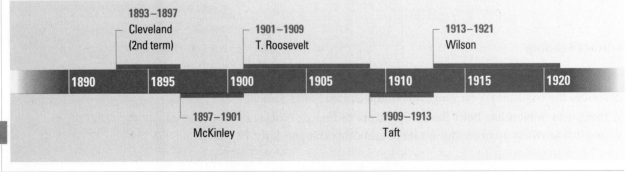

1893–1897
Cleveland
(2nd term)

1901–1909
T. Roosevelt

1913–1921
Wilson

1890   1895   1900   1905   1910   1915   1920

1897–1901
McKinley

1909–1913
Taft

Reviewing Skills

1. What are four steps that will help you analyze historical photographs?

2. What are some choices that a photographer makes before actually taking a photograph?

3. As you learned in Chapter 6, political cartoons are pictures that communicate a strong message. Photographers like Jacob Riis and Lewis Hine also communicated strong political messages in their photographs. In what way are political cartoons different from photographs?

4. Look at the photograph at the right taken by Jacob Riis. Using the four steps you already know, analyze this photograph. What do you think Riis was trying to say about living conditions in New York tenements?

5. Read the literature selection in this chapter on pages 522-523. Identify the style of writing, and explain how that style affects the subject of the selection.

6. Suppose you wanted to study the Progressive Era by examining photographs from that time period. What would you need to know about photography to be able to use it as a research tool for this project?

Using Critical Thinking

1. Theodore Roosevelt called the presidency a "bully pulpit." (*Bully* was slang for *very good.*) He meant that the president, like a national preacher, can make his views widely known to influence opinion. Identify methods that presidents use today to gain support for their policies. Do you think any of those methods have been successful? Explain.

2. Thomas Jefferson once said that a free press was the most important right Americans had. How did this right contribute to the Progressive movement's success? Does the media today carry on the tradition of exposing problems in business and government? Explain your answer.

3. Progressive reforms in education have been criticized by people who believe they made the schools too easy and did not require students to memorize facts or to learn things that were important but "boring." How do you feel about today's Progressive-influenced school system? Does it help you to learn things that are relevant to your life? Do you think the system could be improved? If so, how?

Preparing for Citizenship

1. **WRITING ACTIVITY** Be a muckraker! Identify a problem that you think exists in business, society, or government today. Write an article in which you try to convince others that this problem is serious. Describe what action you think should be taken to correct the problem.

2. **WRITING ACTIVITY** Find out if your state allows the initiative, referendum, and recall. If so, find out when they have been used recently, and write a report on how they were used and whether they were successful. If not, write a letter to a state official asking why those methods are not used.

3. **COLLABORATIVE LEARNING** Make a classroom display of the benefits of the Progressive movement. Choose one of the major areas from the chapter in which Progressives worked to improve their nation and communities. You could choose, for example, the area of government, food, conservation, labor, schools, or banking. Work with others who chose the same subject. Your display may include photographs, drawings, clay models, or any other means of displaying the results of Progressivism in today's world.

The Reform Era

Chapter 18

America Emerges as a World Power

By the late 1800s, the United States had pushed its boundaries westward and settled the nation. U.S. farms and factories produced more than enough food and goods for the country. Americans looked to foreign shores for new markets and resources. This activity brought the nation into competition with other countries, and conflicts resulted.

Lieutenant Colonel Theodore Roosevelt leads the "Rough Riders" during the Battle of San Juan Hill. Later, as President, Roosevelt continues to involve the United States in international affairs.

1850			1860		1870		1880	
1850-1853 Fillmore	1853-1857 Pierce		1861-1865 Lincoln		1869-1877 Grant	1877-1881 Hayes		1881-1885 Arthur
		1857-1861 Buchanan		1865-1869 A. Johnson			1881 Garfield	

1850

This map from the Spanish-American War shows the Caribbean islands that were a source of international conflict.

During World War I, the Purple Heart medal (left) and the Victory medal (right) were awarded to soldiers who distinguished themselves in battle.

1917 This poster of "Uncle Sam" introduced a highly successful media campaign, the first of its kind, to recruit soldiers and to promote patriotism during World War I.

1890	1900	1910	1920

1885-1889
Cleveland

1889-1893
B. Harrison

1893-1897
Cleveland

1897-1901
McKinley

1901-1909
T. Roosevelt

1909-1913
Taft

1913-1921
Wilson

1920

International Expansion

What social and economic factors led the United States to pursue a policy of international expansion after the Civil War?

Key Terms

- protectorate
- abdicate

W riting in 1885, minister Josiah Strong captured the new mood that was sweeping the United States in the 1880s and 1890s when he made the following prediction:

> T his Anglo-Saxon [Western European] race of unequaled energy, with all the majesty of numbers and the might of wealth behind it, will spread itself . . . down upon Mexico, down upon Central and South America, out upon the islands of the sea, over upon Africa and beyond."

Strong believed that Americans had a special responsibility to bring progress to people on other continents who, in his view, were primitive and uncivilized. In an 1899 campaign speech, Senator Albert Beveridge of Indiana echoed Strong's sentiments when he claimed that Americans would become:

> T he master organizers of the world . . . American factories are making more than the American people can use; American soil is producing more than they can consume. Fate has written our policy for us; the trade of the world must and shall be ours.

Reverend Strong and Senator Beveridge were among many people who envisioned a new role for the United States in world affairs. Before the Civil War, the United States had spent much of its energy expanding across North America. During the decades following the war, however, more Americans became interested in the world beyond their own borders. Many of these people—including foreign policy makers, bankers, ministers, and people in business—believed that the United States had a "divine" or God-given right to dominate the continent and the world.

Justifying Expansion

People like Strong and Beveridge drew support for their views from the world of science. In 1858, British biologist Charles Darwin published a new idea. Through his extensive travels and studies, Darwin had collected evidence that all species of living things have gradually evolved, or changed, over time. According to the theory

Darwin developed, some plants and animals are more fit to survive than other members of their species. They have physical features that help them to live longer and healthier lives. These plants and animals are more likely to survive and reproduce, while the less fit tend to die off.

For some people, the "survival of

the fittest" seemed to be the law of nations as well as the law of nature. They claimed that, just as the best-adapted animals dominate in the natural world, the strongest nations will and should dominate nations that are weaker. This idea became known as social Darwinism.

Social Darwinists believed that people with power and wealth had certain obligations, including the "improvement" of the "lower classes." Since most social Darwinists were white, this obligation became known as the "White Man's Burden." Some people said this view was not scientific and was racist. Social Darwinists countered that these critics were being misguided by their feelings. William Graham Sumner, a professor at Yale University and an enthusiastic advocate of the social Darwinist theory, proclaimed: "If we do not like the survival of the fittest, we have only one possible alternative, and that is survival of the unfittest." ■

■ *How did social Darwinism influence America's outlook on the world in the last half of the 19th century?*

Planning for Expansion

As you learned in chapter 8, in the 1840s Americans believed that it was the manifest destiny, or God-given right, of the United States to expand to the Pacific Ocean. In the late 1800s, Americans used the philosophy of social Darwinism to justify international expansion. Through trade, diplomacy, and conquest, America was determined to gain power around the world.

Businesses Seek New Opportunities

After the Civil War, American farmers produced more milk, cheese, corn, and wheat than Americans could eat. Miners dug out more copper and iron than the nation's businesses could use. And factories made more goods than Americans could buy.

The market in the United States had become saturated. That is, the supply of goods was greater than the demand for them. American businesses had to find somewhere to trade their goods. They began to look to foreign markets.

The desire to sell goods was not the only interest American businesses and banks had in other lands. Americans were also attracted by the raw materials of other countries. For example, they saw huge profits waiting for them in the sugar, fruits, oil, minerals, and rubber found in parts of Latin America and in Asia.

American Foreign Trade, 1876–1914

— = Export   — = Import

Value (millions of dollars)

2,800
2,400
2,000
1,600
1,200
800
400

1880   1890   1900   1910

Year

Seward Envisions Vast Empire

William H. Seward, secretary of state under President Abraham Lincoln, was a well-known and respected Republican. After the Civil War, Seward dreamed of establishing a huge American empire that would include Canada, the Caribbean, Cuba, Central America, Mexico, Hawaii, and Iceland. In Seward's vision, a canal across Central America would connect this vast empire geographically. A telegraph system

▲ *During the period of economic expansion following the Civil War, U.S. imports and exports grew at a rapid rate.*

The construction of the Great White Fleet in the 1890s transformed the United States into a naval power.

would allow people in all parts of the empire to communicate with each other.

Although Seward did not succeed in building an empire, he did expand America's territory. His most famous achievement as secretary of state was the 1867 purchase of Alaska from Russia for $7.2 million. Some representatives in Congress thought Alaska was nothing but an ice-covered wasteland. They ridiculed the purchase as "Seward's Folly," and they called the land itself "the Polar Bear Garden" or "Walrussia."

But Seward had the last laugh. As it turned out, Alaska contained rich deposits of copper, gold, and other minerals. Sea otters, seals, and whales filled its coastal waters, and its vast interior was a land of unique beauty.

Mahan's Powerful Navy

During the 1870s, the U.S. Navy was badly equipped. It was not able to support American plans for interna-

tional expansion. Civil War veteran and naval historian Captain Alfred T. Mahan was a social Darwinist. He claimed that stronger nations like the United States had a duty to dominate weaker ones. In his 1890 book, *The Influence of Sea Power upon History, 1660-1783,* Mahan called for the United States to obtain defensive overseas bases and later to establish foreign colonies. He also argued that a strong navy would be needed to protect these distant American territories.

Even before Mahan wrote his book, Congress had taken steps to build a "New Navy" in the 1880s. Presidents Chester A. Arthur, Grover Cleveland, and Benjamin Harrison had all given their support. One by one, wooden sailing ships were replaced with steam-powered vessels made of steel. Congress also authorized the construction of a fleet of big, modern battleships during this period. By 1895, the "Great White Fleet" was nearly finished. ■

■ *What impact did economic conditions at home have on America's foreign trade in the late 1800s?*

Expanding Trade with Asia

America's desire for economic expansion first became clear in the nation's relations with Asia. Long before the Civil War, the United States had tried to establish good trade relations with the countries of East Asia. As America's economy became more industrial, its interest in Asian markets grew steadily.

The China Trade

By the early 19th century, American trade with China was already brisk and profitable. American merchants made huge fortunes trading cloth, iron products, and fur for Chinese porcelain, tea, silk, jade, and other goods.

In 1842, the British forced China to give them extensive trading rights. Afraid Britain might keep China for itself, the United States demanded and received similar rights two years later. Trade between America and China continued to grow in the following decades.

When China lost a war with Japan in 1895, European nations saw a chance for even more economic gain. Right away France, Great Britain, Germany, and Russia divided China into trading areas, or "spheres of influence." But the plan removed the United States, not yet a world power, from the China trade.

The U.S. government would not let China be carved up into European colonies. Consequently, in 1898, the United States persuaded the Europeans to accept an Open Door Policy. This policy allowed China to remain independent while trading with all nations on an equal basis.

Opening Japan and Korea

On July 8, 1853, residents of Edo (now Tokyo) who looked out at the ocean stopped and rubbed their eyes in disbelief. Four black warships were sailing into the bay—against the prevailing winds.

Commodore Matthew C. Perry commanded these steam-powered vessels. Perry was faced with the difficult task of persuading the rulers of Japan to agree to open its ports to trade. The Japanese government had steadily refused almost all communications with other nations for more than two hundred years.

Impressed by Perry's ships, Japanese authorities accepted a letter from President Franklin Pierce asking Japan for friendship and trading privileges. Upon his return in early 1854, Perry negotiated for the United States the first trading agreement that Japan had ever signed with a Western nation. Japan's ports were opened to the commerce of the Western world.

Nearly 30 years later the United States signed a similar trading agreement with the nearby nation of Korea. Compared with Japan, Korea had been at least as cut off from the world.

▼ *An unknown Japanese artist painted this watercolor of Admiral Perry's 1853 landing in Japan.*

531

■ *Why did the United States seek to establish trade relations with Asian countries?*

It was known for much of the 19th century as the "Hermit Kingdom." But in 1876, Japan—by then an imperialist nation—forced Korea into a trade relationship. By this time,

American businesses were aggressively seeking out new markets for their extra goods. As a result, the United States established a trading agreement with Korea in 1882. ■

Moving into the Pacific

As the end of the 19th century approached, U.S. foreign policy officials decided that America needed some "stepping stones" to China and Japan. To achieve this goal, the United States claimed the Midway Islands in 1867 and acquired a naval station in the Samoan Islands in 1878. But the stepping stone the American government most wanted to get hold of was Hawaii.

By the end of the 1800s, the population of Hawaii included large numbers of wealthy American sugar planters. They owned much of the land in the islands. Native Hawaiians objected to the growing wealth and power of the Americans.

In 1891, Queen Liliuokalani (*lee lee oo oh kah LAH nee*) ascended the throne in Hawaii. A strong nationalist, she was determined to cut down foreign influence in the islands. "Hawaii for the Hawaiians" was her slogan.

At about the same time, the U.S. Congress placed a tariff on sugar imported from Hawaii to the United States. This policy made Hawaiian

sugar more expensive than American sugar. That hurt the fortunes of American planters in Hawaii. The planters knew, however, that if Hawaii became part of the United States, the tariff would no longer apply. Consequently, they plotted to overthrow Queen Liliuokalani. They would then declare Hawaii an American **protectorate,** a country or territory controlled by another nation.

John L. Stevens, the American minister to Hawaii, supported the planters. Stevens had U.S. marines surround the Hawaiian royal palace in January 1893. The queen and her army were not able to resist the marines. The planters forced the queen to **abdicate,** or give up, her throne. A treaty calling for the annexation of Hawaii was drafted.

In 1893, newly-elected President Grover Cleveland became upset over the matter and called for an investigation. He then rejected the planters' revolution and offered to reinstate Queen Liliuokalani. Cleveland abandoned the matter, however, when the angry queen said that she would cut off the heads of the revolutionists. Five years later, in 1898, Congress annexed the Hawaiian Islands through a joint resolution. ■

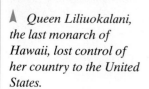

▲ *Queen Liliuokalani, the last monarch of Hawaii, lost control of her country to the United States.*

■ *In what way were smaller nations in the Pacific important to American expansionist plans?*

R E V I E W

1. **FOCUS** What social and economic factors led the United States to pursue a policy of international expansion after the Civil War?

2. **CONNECT** In what ways was the philosophy of social Darwinism similar to the earlier concept of Manifest Destiny?

3. **ECONOMICS** After the Civil War, "supply exceeded demand" in the United States. Why did this overproduc-

tion lead to the desire to create a worldwide American empire?

4. **CRITICAL THINKING** What assumptions did many Americans have about the peoples of Asia and Latin America in the late 1800s?

5. **ACTIVITY** Using the world map on pages 694–695, locate Hawaii, Samoa, and the Midway Islands.

532

L E S S O N   2

Conflict and Conquest

When French Emperor Napoleon III saw a chance to expand his empire at the United States' expense, he didn't hesitate. With the Union and the Confederacy bogged down in a bloody Civil War, he decided to extend his country's influence into the Americas.

The Monroe Doctrine clearly warned against European colonization in North and South America. But Napoleon III took advantage of the American Civil War to occupy Mexico in 1863. He wanted to set up a "puppet" government—one that would appear to be independent but would follow Napoleon III's orders. The emperor chose Archduke Maximilian of Austria to be the head of this government. Maximilian went to Mexico. With the help of Mexicans who supported Napoleon III, he took the throne offered him.

Secretary of State Seward immediately protested the move. He took no further action, however, because he did not want to bring France into open alliance with the Confederacy. But when the Civil War ended, Seward quickly sent an army of 50,000 Union troops to the Mexican border. Preoccupied with tensions in Europe, Napoleon III did not want war with America. He immediately abandoned his puppet empire. The Mexicans quickly overthrew the government and executed the ill-fated Maximilian.

THINKING FOCUS

What steps did U.S. Presidents take in the late 19th and early 20th centuries to keep European nations away from Latin America and to extend U.S. control over the region?

Key Terms

- yellow journalism
- imperialism

Policing the Hemisphere

Latin America was not only a source of profitable trade for the United States. It also acted as a defense against invasion by foreign countries. Through the use of diplomacy and military force, the United States maintained its leading role in the region during the last half of the 19th century. The American government used the Monroe Doctrine to explain its position.

In spite of the Monroe Doctrine, European nations went on trying to establish claims in Latin America. In 1878, for example, the French made plans to build a canal through Panama. "A canal under American control, or no canal," President Rutherford B. Hayes declared. He sent two warships into Panamanian waters to enforce his resolve.

Similarly, in 1895, Venezuela

THE PANAMA CANAL—THE LION IN THE PATH

◄ *This 1889 political cartoon shows Uncle Sam invoking the Monroe Doctrine against European governments that wanted to participate in the building of a canal through Panama.*

533

America Emerges as a World Power

■ *Under what circumstances did the United States invoke the Monroe Doctrine in the late 1800s?*

asked the United States to take its side in a dispute with Great Britain over the boundary between British Guiana (now Guyana) and Venezuela. Secretary of State Richard Olney urged Britain to choose a neutral nation to resolve the dispute. The British refused. They said that the United States had no right to step in. In the end, however, Britain backed down and agreed to arbitration. Once again, the United States had shown it was determined to enforce the Monroe Doctrine. ■

Conflict with Spain

America's desire for Cuba was the main factor that led to armed conflict between the United States and Spain. With its profitable sugar cane crops and well-situated harbors, Cuba was a prize worth winning. During the 1800s, the United States tried several times to take the island away from Spain. Although the attempts failed, they reflected a widely held desire by Americans for expansion.

The Pressure for War Builds

The Cuban people eventually tried to cast off Spanish rule in 1895. To punish the Cubans, Spanish General Valerano Weyler—called the "Butcher" in Cuba—sent hundreds of thousands of Cuban civilians to "concentration" camps. Nearly one quarter of Cuba's population died of starvation or disease in those deadly camps.

Most Americans sympathized with the Cubans' fight for independence. When reports of the horrible suffering in Weyler's camps began to reach the United States, the public's sympathy turned to outrage. American newspapers kept this sense of outrage alive with exaggerated stories of Spanish cruelty. "The old, the young, the weak, the crippled—all are

UNDERSTANDING IMPERIALISM

*I*n the late 1800s and early 1900s, a handful of countries took control of less powerful nations all over the globe. France, Germany, and Great Britain established colonies in Asia and Africa. Following their lead, the United States set up colonies in Latin America and the Pacific. By 1930, the United States and European nations controlled about 84 percent of the land surface of the world. The term *imperialism* is the name we give this policy of extending a nation's power by gaining economic and political control of other nations.

Why Expand?

The chief motivation behind imperialism is usually economic gain. Powerful nations can establish new markets for their manufactured goods. In addition, less developed nations often provide huge sources of inexpensive labor and raw materials.

Despite the importance of economics, Americans usually cited other reasons to justify their imperialism. Many Americans believed that they had a right and obligation to extend what they considered their superior culture to people less fortunate than themselves. In some cases, religious and humanitarian goals lead to imperialistic action. Many imperialists believed that they had a God-given mission to spread Christianity. In the process, they often brought schools, modern medicine, and advanced technologies to the countries they controlled.

What Happened to Colonies?

Colonies all over the globe sought independence from imperialist powers in the 1900s. After World War II, the United States and Europe let go of colonies as their peoples demanded freedom.

534

butchered without mercy," reported the New York *World*.

Newspapers such as Joseph Pulitzer's *World* and William Randolph Hearst's New York *Journal* developed a new kind of reporting called **yellow journalism**. Featuring huge headlines and melodramatic stories, the yellow press twisted facts in order to influence public opinion and to attract readers.

In February 1898, an American warship named the *Maine* blew up in Havana harbor. Two hundred sixty-two officers and sailors were killed. The official investigation proved inconclusive. Still, the yellow press blamed Spain for the tragedy. Newspapers stirred up the public with the cry, "Remember the *Maine*!" Over the next two months the calls for war grew steadily louder. Finally, on April 19, 1898, Congress declared Cuba's independence and authorized President McKinley to use force to drive Spain from the island.

The Spanish-American War

The dispute over Cuba directly set off the Spanish-American War. The first battles of the war, however, took place on the other side of the world in the Spanish-controlled Philippine Islands. Two months before the war began, Assistant Secretary of the Navy Theodore Roosevelt had alerted Commodore George Dewey, who was stationed near the Philippines, to be ready for war.

As soon as the war began, Dewey set off from Hong Kong for the Philippines. On April 30, less than a week after the United States' official declaration of war, Dewey arrived at Manila Bay. The next morning at dawn he opened fire and sank Spain's entire Pacific fleet in the battle of Manila. He then requested additional troops from President McKinley. With the help of Filipino rebels, he took complete control of the Philippines by early August.

Dewey's great naval victory in the Philippines increased the American public's excitement about what Secretary of State John Hay called a "splendid little war." Future U.S. President Theodore Roosevelt viewed war as an adventure and a challenge. When the conflict with Spain began, he quickly resigned as Assistant Secretary of the Navy. He became second in command of a ragtag group of volunteers called the Rough Riders.

Made up of cowboys, miners, college students, and society men, the Rough Riders embodied the frontier spirit and "joy in battle" that Roosevelt so dearly loved. Roosevelt became a national hero when he led the Rough Riders to victory in a charge up San Juan Hill.

The fighting in Cuba proved to be as one-sided as the fighting in the Philippines had been. On July 3, two days after the Rough Riders took San Juan Hill, the U.S. Navy destroyed the Spanish Caribbean fleet in Santiago Harbor. Spain could hardly keep fighting after that. On August 12, 1898, the defeated Spanish government signed a truce.

But while victory came quickly and only 379 Americans died in actual combat, the Spanish-American War was far from splendid. Because of the army's bad management and poor planning, many American

▼ *The yellow press was quick to blame Spain for the sinking of the* Maine. *William Randolph Hearst's* New York Journal *offered a $50,000 reward for evidence explaining the disaster.*

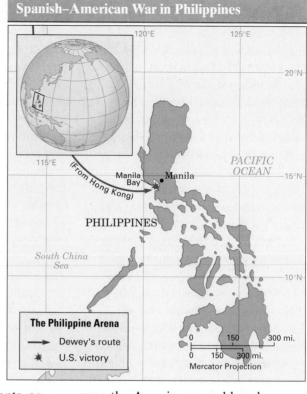

The Cuban Arena

→	Spanish Fleet
→	U.S. Fleet
---→	U.S. Army
▲ ▲ ▲	Blockade
✷	U.S. victory

0   150   300 mi.
0   150   300 km
Trimetric Projection

The Philippine Arena

→	Dewey's route
✷	U.S. victory

0   150   300 mi.
0   150   300 mi.
Mercator Projection

▲ *The Spanish-American War was fought on two fronts on opposite sides of the world; nevertheless, the United States defeated Spain in just three months.*

soldiers did not have guns, tents, or blankets. Food was often in short supply. Much worse, more than 5,400 Americans died of food poisoning, malaria, dysentery, and yellow fever.

Under the provisions of the peace treaty signed on December 10, 1898, Spain gave up Puerto Rico, Guam, and the Philippines to the United States. Although Cuba received its independence, the United States refused to withdraw its army. The United States wanted the Cubans to incorporate the Platt Amendment of 1901 into their new constitution. This amendment gave the United States the right to ensure "a government adequate for the protection of life, property, and individual liberty." Between 1901 and 1934, when the U.S. Congress finally repealed the Platt Amendment, the United States sent troops into Cuba several times to protect American business interests on the island.

Filipinos Fight for Independence

Filipino rebels helped the United States to defeat Spain in the summer of 1898. These Filipinos, who were fighting to secure their own independence, thought that once the war was

over, the Americans would pack up and go home. When Spain had been defeated, however, the American government decided it wanted to keep control of the islands for military and economic reasons.

A small but outspoken group of Americans, calling themselves the Anti-Imperialist League, argued against the takeover of the Philippines. The League's members included such well-known and influential people as Mark Twain, William Jennings Bryan, Jane Addams, Samuel Gompers, and Andrew Carnegie. They were against all forms of **imperialism,** the attempt to control other nations by economic or political means. They also believed that seizing the Philippines went against the political ideals on which America had been founded:

W*e hold that the policy known as imperialism is hostile to liberty and tends toward militarism, an evil from which it has been our glory to be free. . . . We insist that the subjugation of any people is "criminal aggression" and open disloyalty to the distinctive principles of our government.*

536

Chapter 18

To the imperialists, the idea that the United States might do something wrong was inconceivable. Convinced by social Darwinism of America's superiority, they swept aside all opposing arguments and annexed the Philippines in 1899. President McKinley declared it was America's duty to "educate the Filipinos, and uplift and civilize and Christianize them."

The resulting war against the Philippines (1899–1902) proved to be longer and more difficult than the war against Spain. In a total about-face, the United States became the unwelcome oppressor of an unwilling colony. About 70,000 American troops spent two years fighting in the jungles of the Philippines, and 5,000 of them died there. Eight thousand Filipinos—men, women, and children—died in the first year of the war alone. After a bitter struggle, the Filipinos finally surrendered in early 1902. They did not gain their independence until July 4, 1946. ■

■ *What events led the United States to declare war on Spain?*

Building the Panama Canal

Victory over the Spanish fueled American desire to rule the Western Hemisphere. To advance this goal and to improve their access to markets in Asia and Latin America, American businesses planned to build a canal through Central America. Theodore Roosevelt, who had become President after McKinley's assassination in 1901, quickly acted on this plan.

In 1903, Panama was still a province of Colombia. That year the Colombian government refused to sell the strip of land in Panama that the United States needed to build a canal. President Roosevelt was furious.

In Panama, however, many people were eager for the money that would pour into their region if the canal were built. They staged a revolution with unofficial encouragement from the United States government. No one died in the revolt, which soon ended with a Panamanian victory and a declaration of independence. Fifteen days later, on November 18, 1903, the United States secured the right to build and operate a canal through Panama. The Closer Look on the following two pages examines the difficulties involved in building the canal.

In 1904, the President added the "Roosevelt Corollary" to the Monroe Doctrine. He claimed the right to intervene in the internal affairs of Latin American nations to ensure that the United States had "stable, orderly, and prosperous neighbors."

THE WORLD'S CONSTABLE.

◄ *This political cartoon portrays Teddy Roosevelt as the police officer of the world. The "big stick" came to symbolize Roosevelt's foreign policy.*

Building the Panama Canal

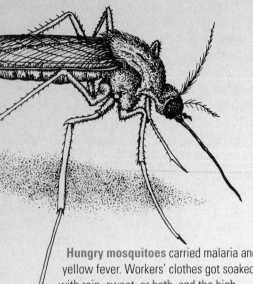

The French had tried to build a canal across Panama in the 1880s, but bad planning and widespread disease forced them to give up. After the United States secured the rights to build a canal through Panama, Americans arrived in droves. They brought dreams of hefty wages and high adventure. But for them too, the challenges of living and working in a hot, wet jungle soon set in.

Hungry mosquitoes carried malaria and yellow fever. Workers' clothes got soaked with rain, sweat, or both, and the high humidity let nothing dry. Books, shoes, and knapsacks grew mold overnight.

From north to south, ships journey through an elaborate system of locks that raise and lower the water level. As the map and drawing below show, they also travel through various channels and lakes on the 50-mile journey that connects the Atlantic and Pacific Oceans.

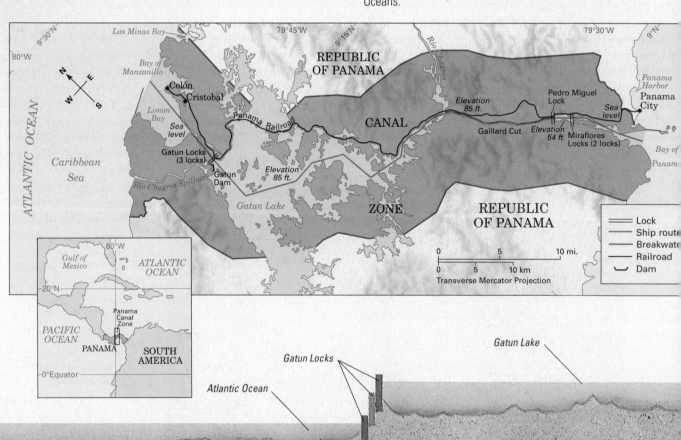

"**They are eating steadily into the ground.**" This was President Roosevelt's comment when he saw the construction work. Engineers studied and sketched, but during the rainy season, whole sides of mountains collapsed into the newly formed ditches. Construction took ten years, and costs were astronomical: $352 million and 5,609 lives.

Since its opening on August 15, 1914, the waterway has saved thousands of miles of sea travel. Today's traffic includes nearly 70 ships each day. Including waiting time, each ship takes about 15 hours to journey through the canal, and each one pays over $7,000 in tolls.

Pedro Miguel Lock

Miraflores Locks

Pacific Ocean

■ *What was the importance of the Panama Canal to the United States?*

As a result of this corollary, Roosevelt was known to "speak softly and carry a big stick" in foreign affairs.

Between 1904 and 1917, American Presidents invoked the Roosevelt Corollary on numerous occasions. The United States sent troops at one time or another to Haiti, Panama, Cuba, Nicaragua, Mexico, and the Dominican Republic, both to put down political revolts and to protect U.S. citizens and businesses. ■

Tension with Mexico

A revolution in Mexico in 1911 overthrew dictator Porfirio Diaz and established a democratic government. Two years later, however, General Victoriano Huerta, head of the Mexican army, murdered the new President and seized power. President Woodrow Wilson refused to recognize Huerta's regime and vowed to remove the "government of butchers."

On April 9, 1914, Mexican officials arrested members of the USS *Dolphin* in Tampico for landing their boat without authorization. This incident gave Wilson the excuse he wanted to intervene in Mexican affairs. The President ordered the U.S. Navy to take the Mexican port of Vera Cruz. Nineteen Americans and 126 Mexicans died in the battle that followed. Huerta's government fell soon afterwards, but the Mexican people were outraged by America's intervention.

➤ *Mexican revolutionary leader "Pancho" Villa eluded the American troops that President Woodrow Wilson sent to capture him in 1916.*

In August 1914, the American-supported candidate, Venustiano Carranza, became President of Mexico. However, many Mexicans continued to resent American interference in their nation's affairs. One of these Mexicans, a rebel general named Francisco "Pancho" Villa, held up a train in Chihuahua, took 16 American passengers hostage, and killed them. In a separate raid, he killed 19 Americans in New Mexico.

Furious, President Wilson sent troops under the command of General John J. Pershing into Mexico in 1916, but they failed to capture Villa. The Carranza government immediately protested this intervention. Tension between the two nations was nearing the breaking point when the United States abruptly withdrew its troops in January 1917. Wilson had more pressing concerns: German submarine attacks on U.S. ships were triggering American involvement in World War I. ■

■ *Why did the United States intervene in Mexican affairs on several occasions between 1914*

R E V I E W

1. **FOCUS** What steps did U.S. Presidents take in the late 19th and early 20th centuries to keep European nations away from Latin America and to extend U.S. control over the region?

2. **CONNECT** In what way did the 1823 Monroe Doctrine play an important role in American foreign affairs in the late 1800s?

3. **HISTORY** Why did the United States want a canal through Panama? What challenges did the United States have to overcome to build the canal?

4. **CRITICAL THINKING** Why did President Theodore Roosevelt claim for the United States the right to intervene in the internal affairs of Latin American countries?

5. **ACTIVITY** Read the Monroe Doctrine on pages 668–669. Think about how this document influenced events in the late 1800s.

L E S S O N   3

America at War

It is a fearful thing to lead this great peaceful people into war, into the most terrible and disastrous of all wars," said President Woodrow Wilson on April 2, 1917. His audience of Congressional representatives, Supreme Court justices, Cabinet officers, and diplomats rose to its feet in a long round of cheering and handclapping.

President Wilson thought it strange that America had received his message—which spelled certain death for many of its young men—with applause. Late that night, the President laid his head on the long table in the Cabinet room and cried.

Ironically, Wilson had won reelection just a few months earlier as the peace candidate. In fact, his slogan during the 1916 campaign was, "He kept us out of war!" The message was one that Americans wanted to hear in the fall of 1916.

However, within months of Wilson's victory, German submarines sank five American ships. With a heavy heart, the "peace candidate" declared that America would enter the First World War.

THINKING

FOCUS

What kept the United States out of World War I initially, and what prompted it to enter the war in 1917 on the side of the Allies?

Key Terms

- mobilize
- armistice

◄ *This photograph shows one of President Woodrow Wilson's campaign trucks in the 1916 election. Although Wilson won reelection as the "peace" candidate, he led the United States into World War I a few months later.*

War Sweeps Europe

By the time the United States became involved in 1917, the war in Europe had been going on for three years. Powerful European countries were always aware that their colonized people could start a war in order to gain independence. In addition, the competition for colonies had created intense rivalries that could spark war between European powers.

The nations of Europe tried to create some security for themselves by

541

America Emerges as a World Power

building up huge military forces and making agreements called alliances. The members of an alliance agreed to fight on the side of any other member that was attacked. In 1914, before the outbreak of war, there were two major European alliances: the Triple Alliance, made up of Germany, Austria-Hungary, and Italy, and the Triple Entente, made up of Britain, France, and Russia.

On June 28, 1914, Archduke Francis Ferdinand, heir to the Austro-Hungarian throne, and his wife Sophie led a parade through the streets of Sarajevo, capital of Bosnia. Many Bosnians resented Austria for taking their province from the kingdom of Serbia in 1908. As the Archduke's open car drew up beside a barber shop, an 18-year-old student who belonged to a Serbian nationalist society called "Union or Death" fired into the cab. The Archduke and his wife were instantly killed.

Austria immediately declared war on Serbia, whom it blamed for the assassination. Germany, in accordance with its promise, supported Austria; Russia came to the aid of Serbia. Within weeks, all the powers of Europe were at war. ■

■ *What factors and events led to the outbreak of World War I?*

Entering the War

President Wilson at first succeeded in keeping the nation out of World War I. Eventually, however, the United States was forced to choose sides.

American Neutrality

When war broke out in Europe in 1914, President Wilson promoted neutrality, the policy of not taking sides in a war. Although Wilson also discouraged American citizens from taking sides in the war, most Americans were sympathetic toward the Allied Powers: chiefly Britain, France, and Russia. Many Americans had English ancestors, and the French had helped in the American Revolution.

Other Americans, many of German descent, sided with the Central Powers: chiefly Germany and Austria-Hungary (Italy had withdrawn its support.) Regardless of their sympathies, most Americans did not want to enter the war on either side.

The End of Neutrality

Throughout the war, President Wilson made efforts to establish a peace agreement. Neither side would agree to negotiate. Each side thought it would soon win the war and be able to name its own terms.

Eventually, Americans got caught in the crossfire of British and German ocean warfare. In 1916, Britain tried to starve the Germans into surrender by preventing ships of any nation from delivering food and raw materials to Germany. The Germans fought Britain's naval blockade with a new weapon: the U-boat, or submarine. German submarines attacked both passenger ships and warships in their attempt to break the British blockade.

Germany had warned early in 1915 that it would attack any ship that entered a war zone around Britain. Americans protested that the policy was brutal and unfair. Germany countered that many "neutral" vessels were in fact carrying American-made weapons to the British.

On May 7, 1915, while sailing

▲ *World War I was the first war in which airplanes played an important role in the fighting.*

from New York to Liverpool, the British passenger ship *Lusitania* was attacked and sunk by a German submarine. The death toll of more than 1,200 people included 128 Americans. Although the United States did not enter the war as a result of this incident, pressure mounted on President Wilson to change his policy from one of neutrality to one of military preparation.

America finally decided to enter the war in February 1917. That month Britain intercepted and conveyed to American officials a secret message from the German foreign secretary, Arthur Zimmermann, to the German minister in Mexico. The "Zimmermann Telegram" asked Mexico to fight with Germany against the United States if the United States abandoned its policy of neutrality and entered the war. In exchange for its support, Germany promised to win for Mexico the territory it had lost to the United States in 1848 in Texas, New Mexico, and Arizona.

Faced with such concrete evidence of Germany's hostile attitude toward the United States, President Wilson could hold out no longer. On April 2, 1917, he delivered the speech that you read about at the beginning of this lesson. On April 6, the Congress of the United States officially declared war on Germany. ■

NOTICE!

TRAVELLERS intending to embark on the Atlantic voyage are reminded that a state of war exists between Germany and her allies and Great Britain and her allies; that the zone of war includes the waters adjacent to the British Isles; that, in accordance with formal notice given by the Imperial German Government, vessels flying the flag of Great Britain, or of any of her allies, are liable to destruction in those waters and that travellers sailing in the war zone on ships of Great Britain or her allies do so at their own risk.

IMPERIAL GERMAN EMBASSY
WASHINGTON, D. C., APRIL 22, 1915.

37 AMERICANS IN 1214 LUSITANIA LOSS

▲ *Before sinking the* Lusitania, *the German government published a warning in American newspapers to people considering an Atlantic crossing.*

■ *What caused President Wilson to turn his back on neutrality and declare war on Germany?*

Fighting the War

Now the American government faced the problem of how to **mobilize,** or assemble, an army that could help the Allies. President Wilson had started to strengthen the nation's army in 1916. He also had a powerful navy ready for battle. But when America entered the war, rifles, machine guns, and artillery pieces were in short supply. Clearly a large army would have to be recruited and trained at short notice, and industry would have to start producing war materials. By the end of 1917, every part of American society was focused on the war effort.

Mobilizing an Army

Shortly after the United States entered the war, Congress passed a Selective Service Act, which required all men between 21 and 30 years of

THE NAVY NEEDS YOU! DON'T READ AMERICAN HISTORY— MAKE IT !

U·S·NAVY RECRUITING STATION
34 EAST 23rd ST., NEW YORK

◄ *The government used dramatic posters like this one to encourage the public to purchase war bonds, to do volunteer service, and to enlist in the military.*

America Emerges as a World Power

Back our
girls over there
Y.W.C.A.
United War Work Campaign

ST IN
FIGHT—
ALWAYS
FAITHFUL—
A U.S. MARINE!

▲ *Posters encouraged women and men alike to aid in the war effort.*

▼ *In this 1917 photograph, American soldiers on their way to the war in France bid farewell to their loved ones.*

ported the war. By June 1917, nearly 10 million men had registered for the draft. By the end of the war, close to 5 million men were serving in the armed forces.

Women were not required to register for the draft, but several thousand served voluntarily in the armed forces. Many other women volunteered as nurses and ambulance drivers overseas, serving in such organizations as the Red Cross, Salvation Army, and U.S. Army Signal Corps.

A New Kind of War

The use of deadly new weapons—machine guns, poison gas, submarines, torpedoes, tanks, and airplanes—made World War I the bloodiest confrontation in human history. Submarines destroyed huge ships with one or two torpedoes. Machine guns mowed down whole companies of soldiers. And mustard gas, the deadliest of the chemical weapons used in the war, burned its victims' lungs and blistered their exposed flesh. Those soldiers who lived through heavy artillery attacks often suffered from shell shock, which left them unable to speak or

age to register for military service. Some people feared that the draft would produce riots. But the response of young men eligible for the draft was very positive. Urged on by government posters and popular songs, they stood in long lines to enlist. The Literature Selection on page 554 contains several of the patriotic songs that sup-

move for hours, days, or weeks.

The war was fought from rat-infested trenches 8 to 12 feet deep. From 1914 to 1917, neither the Allies nor the Central Powers were able to gain control of the Western Front, where thousands of men died to secure only a few yards of territory. At the 1916 Battle of the Somme, 60,000 men died in the first day of fighting. Altogether, more than a million British, French, and German sol-

▲ *Trench warfare and poison gas were two of the chief horrors of World War I. Soldiers lived, ate and slept in trenches. With shells exploding around them, soldiers rarely left the trench, except to retreat or attack. At left, soldiers who have been temporarily blinded by mustard gas await medical treatment.*

How Do We Know?

HISTORY *Many participants in World War I wrote diaries, letters, histories, biographies, poetry, and novels about their experiences. Chroniclers of World War I have used these records to describe daily life in the trenches.*

Suddenly the nearer explosions cease. The shelling continues but it has lifted and falls behind us, our trench is free. We seize the hand-grenades, pitch them out in front of the dug-out and jump after them. The bombardment has stopped and a heavy barrage now falls behind us. The attack has come.

No one would believe that in this howling waste there could still be men; but steel helmets now appear on all sides out of the trench, and fifty yards from us a machine-gun is already in position and barking.

The wire entanglements are torn to pieces. Yet they offer some obstacle. We see the storm-troops coming. Our artillery opens fire. Machine-guns rattle, rifles crack. The charge works its way across. Haie and Kropp begin with the hand-grenades. They throw as fast as they can, others pass them, the handles with the strings already pulled. Haie throws seventy-five yards, Kropp sixty, it has been measured, the distance is important. The enemy as they run cannot do much before they are within forty yards.

We recognize the smooth distorted faces, the helmets: they are French. They have already suffered heavily when they reach the remnants of the barbed wire entanglements. . . . The forward trenches have been abandoned. Are they still trenches? They are blown to pieces, annihilated—there are only broken bits of trenches, holes linked by cracks, nests of craters, that is all.

Erich Maria Remarque, from *All Quiet on the Western Front*, 1929

545

America Emerges as a World Power

The Western Front, 1918

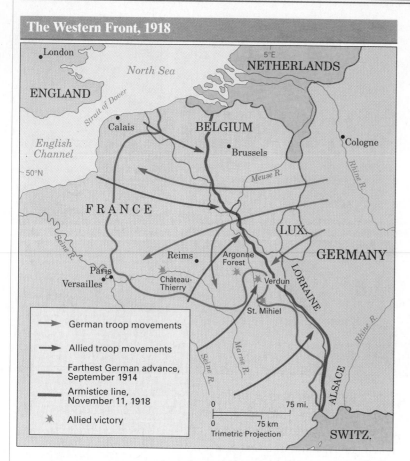

North Sea

London

ENGLAND

Strait of Dover

Calais

English Channel

50°N

Seine R.

FRANCE

Paris

Versailles

Reims

Château-Thierry

5°E

NETHERLANDS

BELGIUM

Brussels

Meuse R.

Argonne Forest

Verdun

St. Mihiel

Marne R.

Seine R.

Cologne

Rhine R.

LUX.

GERMANY

LORRAINE

Rhine R.

ALSACE

SWITZ.

→ German troop movements

→ Allied troop movements

— Farthest German advance, September 1914

— Armistice line, November 11, 1918

✷ Allied victory

0 — 75 mi.
0 — 75 km
Trimetric Projection

▲ *Although World War I lasted for four years, neither side gained much territory during that time, as the map above shows.*

■ *What impact did the United States' entry into the war have on the fighting in Europe?*

diers lost their lives in this one battle.

Troops that ventured from their trenches were cut down by machine gun fire. Those who remained in the trenches did not fare much better. Many soldiers died from drowning in the water-logged trenches or from diseases spread by mosquitoes and other insects in the polluted trench waters.

Two antiwar novels related the horrors of trench warfare and the pointlessness of war. *Under Fire* was published in 1916 by French novelist Henri Barbusse. *All Quiet on the Western Front* was published in 1929 by German author Erich Maria

Remarque. (See page 545 for an extract from Remarque's work.)

An Allied Victory

When American soldiers reached the scenes of battle in 1917, three years of fighting had drained the Allies of men and war supplies. The arrival of fresh American troops and supplies made the difference that enabled the Allies to win.

The first American contribution to the war took place on the seas. The German U-boat blockade hurt Britain badly. The U.S. Navy foiled the U-boats by guarding large convoys of supply ships with American destroyers and cruisers. The U.S. Navy also placed mines in the sea lanes around German ports, creating danger for U-boats entering or leaving Germany.

American soldiers were inexperienced but enthusiastic. The typical American soldier was a young white draftee, about 22 years old, who had never attended high school. Because of short training periods and early shortages of guns, many soldiers had never handled their weapons before they went to the front.

Nevertheless, Americans distinguished themselves in the fighting. Sergeant Alvin York earned fame and the Medal of Honor for his single-handed defeat of 160 German troops. In the fall of 1918, over one million Americans took part in the final Allied offense that broke the German army and ended the war. A temporary peace agreement called an **armistice** was signed by both sides on November 11, 1918. ■

R E V I E W

1. **FOCUS** What kept the United States out of World War I initially and what prompted it to enter the war in 1917 on the side of the Allies?

2. **CONNECT** In what earlier American wars did naval blockades play an important role?

3. **HISTORY** How did World War I differ from all wars that had preceded it?

4. **CRITICAL THINKING** How were both the Spanish-American War and World War I the result of imperialist rivalries?

5. **ACTIVITY** Look at the map of Europe in the Atlas and locate the nations in the Triple Alliance and the Triple Entente. Then, with a classmate, debate which group of nations was in a better geographical position from which to fight the war.

L E S S O N   4

Impact of the War

During the depression of 1893, a young Russian-born woman named Emma Goldman spoke to a huge gathering of unemployed workers in New York City. "If your children need food," the 24-year-old woman told the crowd, "go into the grocery stores and take it!"

When the United States entered the war in 1917, Goldman spoke out against the draft. She had earlier given up her support of violence. She was now opposed to the use of military or police force for any reason. Because Goldman expressed her antiwar views publicly, government agents arrested her for violating the Sedition Act, a law that restricted free speech during the war.

As an admitted radical and critic of the wartime government, Emma Goldman—and thousands of others like her—faced harsh punishment. After the war was over, the U.S. government deported Goldman and many other radicals to Russia.

During World War I, the United States would not tolerate criticism. Anyone who did not fully support the war was considered "anti-American"

for speaking his or her views. Many brave and patriotic people served jail or prison sentences for not agreeing with the U.S. government's position on the war.

President Wilson claimed the war would make the world "safe for democracy." Emma Goldman replied, "Poor as we are in democracy, how can we give of it to the world?"

THINKING
F O C U S

What impact did World War I have on American society during and after the war?

Key Terms

* dissent
* reparations
* isolationism

◄ *During World War I, the U.S. government imprisoned antiwar activists such as Emma Goldman.*

War at Home

In contrast to outspoken critics of the war such as Goldman, most Americans got behind the war effort. At the government's request, they grew their own food in backyard "victory gardens." They also responded to newspaper editorials and government

pamphlets encouraging them to scrimp and save. At the urging of popular songs and posters, they bought large numbers of Liberty Bonds. Such purchases gave the government billions of dollars in loans for arms and military supplies. Patriotic Americans

America Emerges as a World Power

OVER THE TOP FOR YOU

Buy U.S. Gov't Bonds
THIRD LIBERTY LOAN

➤ Government posters like this one urged Americans who stayed at home to buy Liberty Bonds. The government used the money for the war effort.

Across Time & Space

The suspicion and hostility that white Americans of English-speaking ancestry demonstrated toward other Americans during World War I reemerged in World War II. In February 1942, President Franklin D. Roosevelt authorized the arrest of all Japanese-Americans on the West Coast. The U.S. Army sent 110,000 Japanese-Americans into camps, where they were imprisoned for three years.

The Supreme Court upheld the conviction of Debs.

In 1918, Congress passed another law, called the Sedition Act, which was also meant to put down **dissent,** or criticism. The Sedition Act made it a crime to speak disrespectfully of either the government or its symbols, including the flag, the Constitution, and the military uniform. Like the Espionage Act, the Sedition Act was most often enforced against Americans whose political views did not go along with the patriotic spirit of the day. Members of the Socialist party and the Industrial Workers of the World, a radical labor union, were singled out for prosecution.

Suspicion of Foreigners

During the war, Americans who did not have family roots in an English-speaking nation, especially those of German background, were often suspected and accused of being traitors. The attempt to eliminate all things German from American society symbolized this suspicion and fear of foreigners. Sauerkraut was renamed "liberty cabbage," and hamburger became "liberty sausage." High schools in various parts of the country even stopped teaching the German language.

Sometimes German-Americans were physically attacked. In the worst such incident, a mob caught a German-American named Robert Prager. The mob wrapped Prager in an American flag, marched him through the streets of St. Louis, and then lynched him. The Prager affair was an extreme case, but abuse of foreigners was a common occurrence during the war.

Expanding Opportunities

Some Americans indirectly benefited because of the war. With two million white men fighting in Europe and no new immigrants entering the country, many jobs in the United

gladly did without certain foods and products, but critics of the government and foreign-born Americans lost many of their civil liberties because of wartime legislation.

Attacking the Critics

In the summer of 1918, Eugene V. Debs gave an antiwar speech in Canton, Ohio. Debs, who won 12% of the vote as the Socialist Party candidate for President in 1912, spoke against American involvement in the war and for free speech. He was arrested and convicted under the Espionage Act, which Congress had passed in 1917. This act made it illegal to say anything that could discourage men from registering for the draft. During World War I, even the courts, which were designed to safeguard Americans' freedom from the excesses of Congress and of the President, bowed to the public pressure for conformity.

States became available to blacks and women for the first time.

Both groups proved their ability to do any kind of job. Women became railroad conductors, brick layers, and factory workers. Their presence in traditionally male workplaces produced many problems. Men were annoyed by women's higher productivity and willingness to work for lower pay. Working mothers were often criticized for leaving their families. But many women welcomed the responsibilities. "It was not until our men were called overseas," said one woman bank executive, "that we made any real onslaught on the realm of finance, and became tellers, managers of departments, and junior and senior officers."

Women who did not take jobs helped in the war effort in other ways. They made uniforms, rolled bandages, and campaigned for the sale of Liberty Bonds to help finance the war.

American manufacturers offered jobs to large numbers of black Americans for the first time as a result of the war. Most factories were located in the North. To take advantage of these new job opportunities, many black families moved from their homes in the South to Northern cities such as Pittsburgh, Cleveland, Buffalo, Chicago, and Detroit.

White Americans were of two minds about the role of black Americans in the war effort. On the one hand, black workers' ability to learn new jobs quickly and do them well strengthened the home front, and their fighting ability helped the Allies win the war. However, many whites did not want to acknowledge that blacks were capable, effective workers. White soldiers returning from the war had no desire to compete for jobs with blacks on equal terms. At the same time, many blacks were not willing to return to a lesser role once the war had ended. ■

■ *What was life like for different groups of Americans who stayed at home during the war?*

▼ *World War I gave many American women the opportunity to work in jobs traditionally held by men. The woman in the photograph at left is welding a bomb casing in a munitions factory. The women below are assembling wings for airplanes.*

The Treaty of Versailles

World War I had a major impact on the lives of Americans who remained at home. The war also shaped the peacetime world that soldiers and civilians would eventually inhabit.

Wilson's 14 Points

One of the reasons President Wilson made the painful decision to lead the United States into war was his desire to influence the peace terms. The President called his plan for peace the Fourteen Points. In the postwar world that Wilson envisioned, nations would settle their disputes by negotiations—never by war. President Wilson proposed an international body called the League of Nations, whose members would promise to respect the "territorial integrity," or boundaries, of all other members.

The President was sure that only he could persuade the other Allies to look past their desire for revenge against Germany to shape a just and lasting peace. He announced in November 1918 that he would head the American delegation to the Paris Peace Conference.

The Final Treaty

Because France and England had fought longer and lost more during the war, they played a larger role than the United States in shaping the peace settlement. They also had a different vision. Instead of a peace of equals, the European Allies wanted to reward themselves and punish Germany by

➤ *The Treaty of Versailles changed the map of Europe. Austria-Hungary and Russia lost the most territory as a result of the war.*

Europe after World War I

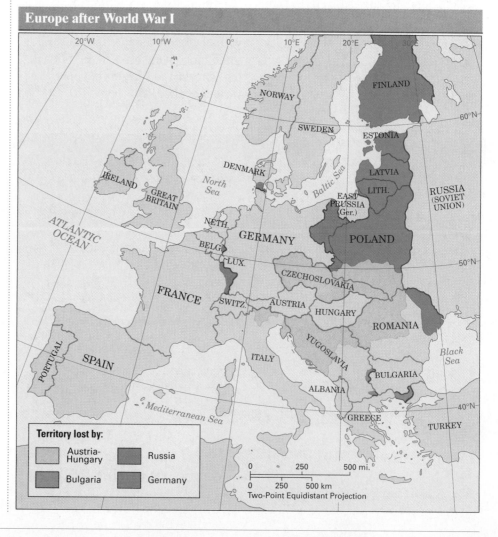

Territory lost by:
- Austria-Hungary
- Bulgaria
- Russia
- Germany

taking German territory and large sums of money called **reparations.**

The Treaty of Versailles fulfilled their hopes. Under the terms of the treaty, Germany was forced to accept total blame for the war, to give up 13 percent of its territory, and to pay $15 billion for damage to Allied property. The German government signed the treaty because it had no choice, but the German people never accepted it. Most Germans felt the terms were unfair and humiliating. Economically, they suffered terribly as a result of the conditions imposed by the treaty. The bitterness and resentment that the treaty inspired indirectly paved the way for World War II. ■

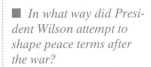
■ *In what way did President Wilson attempt to shape peace terms after the war?*

◄ *The Allied Powers met in the Hall of Mirrors at the Palace of Versailles to sign the 1919 peace treaty. President Woodrow Wilson is shown in the center of this painting holding the treaty.*

Retreating from World Affairs

President Wilson believed that the new League of Nations, whose charter was part of the peace treaty, would somehow make up for the harsh terms that Germany had received. Wilson also believed that the League of Nations would cut down on the risk of war. He hoped it would change the basis of international relations from competition to cooperation.

Rejecting the League

The Senate had other ideas. Most Democratic Senators voted to ratify the treaty. Senate Republicans, however, led by Henry Cabot Lodge, refused to give their support. Senator Lodge believed that the League of Nations would draw the United States into foreign wars. As proof he pointed to the provision that called for members of the League to regard a threat to any one of them as a threat to all. The Republicans' position had come to be known as **isolationism.**

When President Wilson saw that he could not get the votes he needed in the Senate, he took his case directly to the American people. He traveled across the country, explaining at each stop why he believed the treaty was so important. The American public responded to the President's words with enthusiasm. However, it was not the general public Wilson needed to convince but the Senators who had the power to ratify or kill the treaty.

Wilson's refusal to compromise with the Republican majority in the Senate and his high-handed methods

America Emerges as a World Power

led to defeat. After many votes on several versions, the Senate conclusively rejected the Treaty of Versailles in March 1920.

Wilson: A Broken Man

In 1919, on his cross-country trip to persuade Americans to preserve their hard-won peace through the League of Nations, Wilson collapsed from exhaustion. Shortly afterwards, he suffered a stroke that paralyzed his entire left side. He never fully regained his health, and for the rest of his presidency remained tired and depressed—a broken man.

Wilson's weakness symbolized the collapse of his dream for a world order based on lasting peace and justice. In his last months in office, President Wilson was greatly helped by his second wife, Edith Galt. An intelligent and strong-minded woman, she held the White House together during Wilson's long illness.

The League of Nations had to sink or swim without the United States. Promises of mutual defense, which members of the League had to make, had led many nations into the First World War.

Americans had had enough of "foreign" wars. In 1920, they looked inward once again. Isolationism, it was thought, would keep the United States safe. ■

■ *Why did the United States adopt a policy of isolationism after the war?*

The Aftermath of War

Having turned their backs on the world, Americans proceeded to fight bitterly against each other. From 1919 to 1920, people whose race, religion, or political views differed from those of the majority became the targets of violence and arrest.

A strong revival of the Ku Klux Klan sparked much violence. Based in the South, the Klan called for violence against anyone who was not white, Anglo-Saxon, and Protestant. It expanded rapidly into new areas, including the Midwest. At its postwar peak, it boasted five million members.

In addition, factory workers struck against low wages, long hours, and unsafe conditions. And both government officials and private citizens threatened the property and lives of political radicals.

Labor Unrest and Race Riots

In 1919, the year after the war, American silk workers, cigar makers, steel workers, carpenters, bakers,

➤ *The United States experienced a wave of strikes and protests at the end of World War I. This photograph shows striking steel workers in 1919.*

barbers, and police went out on strike. Over four million workers were involved. Many of them were working 12 hours a day, 6 days a week for pay that had not gone up as fast as the cost of living. Factory owners didn't believe that patriotic Americans would ever strike against their employers. They thought that radicals were stirring up labor unrest.

Meanwhile, in the summer of 1919, more than 25 race riots broke out across the nation. These riots resulted largely from the determination of white Americans to prevent blacks from keeping the economic gains they had made during the war. Mobs of whites lynched more than 70 African Americans. Stabbings, burning, and shootings took the lives of hundreds of Americans.

The Red Scare

On April 28, 1919, a package arrived at the home of Georgia Senator Thomas Hartwick. The bomb it contained badly injured the senator's maid. Two months later, another bomb exploded at the home of U.S. Attorney General A. Mitchell Palmer.

The bombings set off a year-long "Red Scare." During that time the Justice Department arrested over 6,000 Americans—many of them foreigners—on charges of plotting to overthrow the government. Almost none of those arrested were found guilty of the crimes with which they were charged.

The Bolshevik Revolution, which had established a Communist government in Russia in 1917, intensified Americans' fears of political radicals. During the war, Americans whose ancestors did not speak English were suspected of working with the enemy. After the war, anyone whose political views were different from those of the mainstream could earn himself or herself the label "radical." Immigrants from Russia or Eastern Europe were often suspected of being Communist spies.

The Return to "Normalcy"

By the presidential election of 1920, Americans were tired of both war and the fearful events of the postwar period. After eight years of Democratic rule, they were also ready for a change.

When the Republicans nominated a handsome and amiable Ohio Senator named Warren Harding, the public liked what it saw. Americans felt that the Republicans could return the nation to a time of, as Harding put it, "normalcy." The longing for peace and the desire to avoid foreign wars helped Harding to win a landslide victory in the 1920 election. His victory signaled the beginning of a new era of American history. ■

▲ *In his 1920 campaign for the presidency, Republican Senator Warren G. Harding promised Americans a "return to normalcy."*

■ *What internal problems disrupted American society in the postwar period?*

R E V I E W

1. **FOCUS** What impact did World War I have on American society during and after the war?
2. **CONNECT** How was the impact of World War I similar to and different from the impact of the American Revolution on women and black Americans?
3. **HISTORY** Why did America's European Allies reject President Wilson's Fourteen Points as a basis for peace?
4. **CRITICAL THINKING** Was the U.S. Congress justified in passing the Espionage and Sedition acts because of the threat of war? Why or why not?
5. **WRITING ACTIVITY** Make a chart that lists the pros and cons of the League of Nations. Then write a short statement for or against the plan.

American War Songs

Wars are fought not only by soldiers on the battlefields, but also in the hearts and minds of the civilian population. Songs like the ones reprinted below became very popular in World War I. Their rousing words and short verses were easy to remember, and their patriotic tone was encouraging and enthusiastic. For a population engaged in a world struggle, the songs promoted involvement and participation in the war effort. As you read these songs, ask yourself what kinds of images are used to arouse your patriotic impulses.

In Lesson 3 you read about how popular songs encouraged Americans to support the war effort during World War I. Keep this information in mind as you read the two songs reprinted here.

OVER THERE
George M. Cohan

Johnnie get your gun, get your gun, get your gun,
Take it on the run, on the run, on the run,
Hear them calling you and me,
Ev'ry son of liberty.
Hurry right away, no delay, go today,
Make your daddy glad to have had such a lad,
Tell your sweetheart not to pine,
To be proud her boy's in line.

pine suffer

CHORUS
Over there, over there,
Send the word over there
That the Yanks are coming,
The drums rum tumming ev'rywhere,
So prepare, say a prayer,
Send the word to beware,
We'll be over, we're coming over
And we won't come back till it's over,
Over there, over there.

Johnnie get your gun, get your gun, get your gun,
Johnnie, show the Hun you're a son of a gun,
Hoist the flag and let her fly,
Yankee Doodle do or die.
Pack your kit, show your grit, do your bit,
Yankees to the ranks from the towns and the tanks,
Make your mother proud of you
And the Red, White and Blue.

Hun negative term for German

554

UNCLE SAM
Edward Bushnell

So you've drawn your sword again, Uncle Sam!
You're lined up with fighting men, Uncle Sam!
For when freedom is at stake,
You will fight for honor's sake,
And you'll fight till tyrants quake, Uncle Sam!

We know war is not your game, Uncle Sam!
'Twas at peace you made your fame, Uncle Sam!
And 'tis always with regret
That you make a war-like threat;
But they've never whipped you yet, Uncle Sam!

We will sail on all the seas, Uncle Sam!
Without saying "if" or "please," Uncle Sam!
We'll not wear the Kaiser's tag,
And we'll fly no checkered rag,
For Old Glory is our flag, Uncle Sam!

Let the Eagle flap his wings, Uncle Sam!
These are sorry days for kings, Uncle Sam!
And the Kaiser and his crew
Will be missing when they're through
With the old Red, White and Blue, Uncle Sam!

Kaiser German emperor

Further Reading

Songs America Voted By. Irwin Silber. The author presents a collection of presidential compaign songs which, like the war songs, were designed to influence the course of current events.

Songs That Made America. James A. Warner. This book presents a broad regional, racial, and ethnic overview of the makers of America with folk-songs from all across the country.

Songs of Independence. Irwin Silber. This selection of ballads captures the spirit of the great battles and political struggles of the Colonial Era.

Supporting the War Effort

Here's Why

Knowing how to recognize and analyze propaganda is a useful way to learn about public opinion during a particular period. Propaganda is the use of words or familiar symbols to persuade a great number of readers to accept a certain point of view or to take a certain action.

Public interest groups use propaganda to promote their causes. The pamphlets you may see in a dentist's office urging you to brush your teeth daily are a form of propaganda.

During the first World War, the United States believed that Americans needed to think in new ways. In order to supply money for military goods, the people at home needed to be persuaded to buy bonds—a form of loaning their money to the government. The poster on the facing page was designed to make people want to buy bonds "For Home and Country." At the same time the government published numerous pamphlets in order to convince people of the need to support the war effort by making changes in their way of life.

Suppose you wanted to learn more about how the American government tried to influence people's opinions about World War I. Recognizing and analyzing written propaganda from that period would give you a great deal of information about how governments can use propaganda to affect people's lives.

Here's How

Look at the pamphlet below, which was published in the United States during the first World War. Ask the following questions to determine if it is propaganda:

1. Does it appeal to emotion or to reason? If it appeals to both, is the appeal to reason presented in emotional terms?
2. Does it include unsupported statements of opinion?
3. Does it call for a specific action on the part of the reader?
4. Does it make use of colorful language?

If the answer to some or all of these questions is "yes," you are probably reading propaganda. Specific answers to each question will tell you why. In this example, the answer to all four questions is "yes."

The man you love is fighting for your security and happiness. He is helping to bring this war to an early end—and to make another war like this impossible. He is doing something that HAS to be done for your sake. The more hopefully you write, the easier for him—and the quicker he comes back.

Of course his life is no bed of roses. Yet his discomforts are the discomforts of a red-blooded life in the open—the sort of life enjoyed by the cowboy of Arizona, by the mounted police of Canada, and by the adventurous spirits of all the world and of all times. . .

His fighting equipment, his bayonet, gas mask and ammunition embody every known advantage and improvement—American ingenuity has profited by all the past experience of our allies and the enemy as well. . . In all the history of the world no soldier has been so well equipped, so well taken care of as the American soldier. . .

The great majority of American soldiers will return stronger and more vigorous in body and in mind than when they joined the army.

Every conceivable condition contributes to his safety, comfort, and happiness EXCEPT ONE—The strong arm of Uncle Sam can do everything in the world for him—except control his thoughts of you. That one condition is entirely within your control.

His fighting power, his health, his chance of winning and living depend in the end upon WHAT YOU WRITE TO HIM. . .

So write him newsy, cheerful letters. Tell him the pleasant, treasured bits of gossip from home. . .

Do your part to maintain this spirit, this courage!

United States Gov't Comm. on Public Information

Back of every war activity lies—coal. Ships, shells, guns, transportation. For all these we must have—coal.

The more coal, the more shells with which to destroy the machine-gun nests of our enemies—and thereby save the lives of our own boys.

The larger the supply of coal—the shorter the war and fewer casualties....

Save coal....

If you feel that one shovel-ful of coal won't make any difference—think of it as a shell for the boys over there.

If you find yourself burning two lights when one will do—turn one out.

You, who have bought bonds and thrift stamps, you who have given of your money for war charities, given until you have felt the pinch, you whose sons and neighbors' sons are over there, will you not give up, too, just a bit of lazy, enervating comfort to help hurry along the job those brave boys have tackled?

Save light and heat, save coal.

United States Gov't Comm. on Public Information

as propaganda. Write a short paragraph explaining your answer.

Apply It

Choose a current issue and find out if there is a public interest group that has published pamphlets or posters about it. Analyze the writing of the group's documents to see if propaganda is used. Use the four-question format to decide whether or not it is propaganda.

Notice the appeal to emotion: Americans are assured that the soldiers are well taken care of. The pamphlet likens them to the cowboys of the West and describes their adventurous spirit. The appeals to reason are written to get an emotional reaction from the reader: "Every conceivable condition contributes to his safety, comfort, and happiness EXCEPT ONE . . . except control [of] his thoughts of you. That one condition is entirely within your control."

Notice the unsupported statements of opinion: "He is helping to bring this war to an early end—and to make another war like this impossible. He is doing something that HAS to be done for your sake." The piece presents no facts to back

up these statements.

Notice the call for action: American citizens are directed to write cheerful, uplifting letters to soldiers overseas in order to keep them happy and ready to fight for an early end to the war.

Notice the use of emotional language: the frequent use of italics, capital letters, and exclamation points adds a sense of urgency and excitement to the piece.

Try It

Now read the excerpt above, and use the four questions from the previous page to decide whether the excerpt is qualifies

For Home and Country

VICTORY LIBERTY LOAN

Chapter Review

Reviewing Key Terms

abdicate (p. 532)   mobilize (p. 543)
armistice (p. 546)   protectorate (p. 532)
dissent (p. 548)   reparations (p. 551)
imperialism (p. 536) yellow journalism (p. 535)
isolationism (p. 551)

A. Use each of the following terms in a complete sentence that clearly shows the meaning of the term.

1. dissent
2. yellow journalism
3. protectorate
4. imperialism
5. armistice
6. reparations

B. Based on what you have read in the chapter, decide whether each of the following statements is accurate. Write an explanation of each decision.

1. One way for a stronger nation to control a weaker nation is to declare the weaker nation a protectorate.
2. After the king abdicates, he is no longer the ruler of his nation.
3. Newspapers that practiced yellow journalism could be relied on to tell the truth.
4. After the armistice, nations built large supplies of arms and ammunition for war.
5. All the nations of Europe wanted to pay reparations to repair the war damage.
6. Those Americans who supported a policy of isolationism following World War I were generally strong supporters of the League of Nations.
7. After the United States declared war on Germany, President Woodrow Wilson decided not to mobilize American troops.
8. Imperialism was a policy large nations adopted in order to help small nations.

Exploring Concepts

A. On a separate sheet of paper, create two columns. In one column, list the terms shown below. In the other column, list the consequences of each item in the first column.

- Social Darwinism
- Roosevelt Corollary
- European Alliance System
- Zimmermann Telegram
- Sedition Act

B. Support each of the following statements with facts and details from the chapter.

1. Many Americans in the late 1800s used social Darwinism to justify the nation's economic and political expansion.
2. Americans sought new opportunities abroad because they wanted to both sell and buy goods.
3. The United States was determined that it alone should control a canal across Central America, and the American government took steps to protect its interests there.
4. Trade with Asian nations was important to the United States in the 1800s.
5. The United States was determined not to allow an unfriendly government to take power in Mexico.
6. American imperialist ambitions were among the causes of the Spanish-American War and were further fueled by the war's results.
7. Germany's actions overcame the desire most Americans had to remain neutral during World War I.
8. During and after World War I, the United States became increasingly intolerant of minorities and dissenters.
9. President Wilson failed to achieve his goal of constructing a fair and lasting peace after World War I.
10. The two-year period following World War I was a time of great social unrest in the United States.

Reviewing Skills

Look well at the loaf on your breakfast table and treat it as if it were real gold, because the British loaf is going to beat the German. . . . Women have done nobly in the war, but they must do still more. . . . Today the kitchen is the key to victory and is in the fighting line alongside our undying heroes of the trenches and our brave men of the sea.

Kennedy Jones, Director General
of Food Economy

1. What are the four questions you should ask in order to determine if a piece of writing qualifies as propaganda?

2. Read the passage at left written in London by the Director General of Food Economy, Kennedy Jones, during World War I. Do you think it is propaganda? Explain your answer.

3. Use the library to find a photograph from the World War I period. What information does the photograph you found provide about how people lived during that period? Write a short paragraph summarizing the information provided by the photograph.

4. Suppose you wanted to find out more about how the Vietnam War affected citizens of the United States. What source of information could you use?

Using Critical Thinking

1. Arthur Zimmermann insisted that Germany never sent the famous telegram bearing his name. If he was speaking the truth, what forces do you think might have been responsible for starting this rumor? What do you think their motives might have been?

2. Social Darwinism appealed to Americans who wanted their country to expand into an empire. To what extent did their dreams come true? Explain your answer.

3. According to Wilson, the most important of his Fourteen Points was the creation of a League of Nations. Do you believe such an organization could work? Explain your answer.

4. The 1918 Sedition Act made it a crime to speak disrespectfully of the government or its symbols. Do you think the government should restrict what people say during wartime? Explain your answer.

Preparing for Citizenship

1. **WRITING ACTIVITY** Look for examples of yellow journalism in a contemporary newspaper. Choose an article you think uses wild headlines and distorts the facts, and write a short report on the article, pointing out its use of facts and opinions.

2. **WRITING ACTIVITY** One of the great mysteries in American history is the question of who sank the battleship *Maine*. Investigate this subject and determine all of the possible forces behind the incident. Write a short article explaining what the incident might indicate about the role of public opinion in American foreign policy.

3. **ART ACTIVITY** Look at the sheet music cover at right. It is from the World War I song "Over There," which appears on page 554. Read the words to the song "Uncle Sam" on page 555, and then design a sheet music cover for that song.

4. **COLLABORATIVE LEARNING** Set up a class debate on this question: "Should the United States become involved in World War I?" Research both sides of the question, and conduct the debate according to Robert's Rules of Order. At the end of the debate, hold a vote on the issue.

America Emerges as a World Power

The Promise Continues

The U.S. Constitution promises Americans the "bless-ings of liberty." Over the decades, that promise has served as a beacon of hope for a steady stream of immi-grants seeking to escape poverty, injustice, and religious and political persecution. But for many years, the full benefits of American democracy were withheld from some groups of Americans. Only after a long and diffi-cult struggle were these people able to win all the rights of citizens as promised in the Constitution.

1789

Immigrants waiting to be processed at Ellis Island in the early 1900s. Culver Pictures.

2000

Chapter 19
Pluralism

Just as the New World drew the earliest explorers and settlers to its shores in search of a new life, the United States continues to attract people from all over the globe. Some have come seeking better jobs. Others have fled war-torn countries. All bring hopes and dreams of a better life. Their contributions have helped create a rich and vibrant society.

In the late 1800s and early 1900s, Ellis Island was the main reception center for immigrants.

These Chinese immigrants photographed in San Francisco's Chinatown around 1900, maintain their distinct "high class" dress. Colorful masks such as the one at the left are also a part of the Chinese tradition.

1775	1825	1875

1789

A small boat filled with Vietnamese refugees arrives in Hong Kong. Many Vietnamese people, fleeing war and its aftermath in their own land, try to seek refuge in the United States.

Japanese Americans honor their sons by flying banners shaped like carp, a fish noted for its strength.

Hispanic Americans, some of the nation's earliest immigrants, still celebrate customs that have their origins in Spain.

1925   1975   2025

2000

LESSON 1

A Land of Immigrants

THINKING FOCUS

How did U.S. immigration policy change between colonial days and 1960?

Key Terms

- quota
- asylum
- refugee

➤ *Americans celebrate the "birthday" of the Statue of Liberty. On the base of the statue are the words, "I lift my lamp beside the golden door." How might immigrants react to these words?*

In July 1986, more than two million people jammed New York harbor to celebrate the one-hundredth "birthday" of the Statue of Liberty. Americans young and old flocked to the event.

The four-day celebration included concerts, ethnic festivals, and the largest fireworks display in American history. On July 4, Chief Justice Warren Burger of the U.S. Supreme Court swore in 25,000 immigrants as citizens of the United States.

Lee Iacocca, the head of one of the largest U.S. automobile companies and an organizer of the event, felt a close bond to "Lady Liberty." The son

of poor immigrant parents, Iacocca considers himself proof of American opportunity. During the event, he recalled that millions of "people who sailed past the Lady with the Torch just before setting foot on Ellis Island always felt a special debt. She was their first sight of America and they never forgot her."

For many people, the Statue of Liberty remains the symbol of the United States. Perhaps one of the explanations for Americans' love of the statue is their common immigrant heritage. Every American is either an immigrant or the descendant of immigrants.

Coming to America

The very first American immigrants are lost in the mists of time. Thousands of years ago they crossed a narrow strip of land that at that time joined northeastern Asia and North America. Their descendants became known as the American Indians.

As you learned in Chapter 1, the next group of immigrants came from Spanish-held Mexico and arrived in what is now the southwestern United States in the late 1500s. In the early 1600s, men such as Champlain and Hudson explored parts of eastern North America, and eager European settlers soon followed.

Thousands more immigrants followed—decades, even centuries later. Many conditions drove people to leave their homes and to seek a new life in America. Some people fled starvation brought on by crop failures. Others were escaping revolutions or the power struggles among nations that caused unrest throughout their homelands. For still others, the United States offered the opportunity for economic success and social advancement—something that could not be found in Europe, where distinct lines were often drawn between different social classes.

Mixed Feelings About Newcomers

Even though they all share immigrant roots, Americans have always held mixed feelings about newcomers. Immigrants are often welcomed for the work they will do. They are often resented because they represent the new and unfamiliar—new cultures, new languages, and new ideas about life.

This conflict was expressed even in colonial times by George Washington, who commented on the one hand that: "the bosom of America is open to receive not only the [wealthy] and respectable stranger, but the oppressed and persecuted of all nations and religions whom we shall welcome

This drawing shows Germans boarding a ship to go to America. What does it suggest about the mood of the people?

to participate in all of our rights and privileges."

On the other hand, Washington was uneasy about immigrants: "I have no intention to invite immigrants, even if there are no restrictive acts against it. I am opposed to it altogether."

Other Americans, including Thomas Jefferson, feared that the political ideas of immigrants, most of whom had lived under the absolute rule of kings, would threaten the democratic principles of the United States. Leading Americans who agreed with these ideas proposed that only people born in the United States should be allowed to be citizens. One way to limit the political influence of immigrants, said Harrison Gray Otis of Massachusetts, was to "make a residence of forty or fifty years necessary before an alien should be entitled to citizenship."

A Welcome Mat in the Early Years

Despite some mixed feelings about immigration in the early years of the nation, newcomers steadily trickled into the United States and were generally welcomed. After all, the nation was huge and had vast lands to settle, lands that expanded

Pluralism

greatly after the Louisiana Purchase and the Mexican War, as you learned in Chapter 8.

To become a strong nation, the United States needed people to develop its resources, clear the land, grow crops and raise livestock, and build cities and ports. After the Civil War, when industry began to boom, thousands of people were needed to run the machines in factories, mine the ores needed in industry, and build the railroads to carry goods and people. Thousands more people were needed to produce the food for city workers and the materials used in industry. Immigrants, mainly from Europe, supplied this need. ■

■ Explain why the United States is called a land of immigrants.

Resistance to Immigration

Until 1880, most of the immigrants came from northern and western Europe. They spoke English or languages closely related to English, were mainly Protestant, and shared many of the ideals of the original colonists. Most of these immigrants quickly assimilated, or blended their cultures, into American society.

After 1880, however, increasing numbers of immigrants came from southern and eastern Europe. Many spoke Italian or one of the Slavic languages. Most were Roman Catholics, but significant numbers were Jews or Eastern Orthodox Christians, for example, Greeks and Russians. They came from countries governed by absolute rulers that granted few, if any, rights to their subjects. Many of these immigrants were fleeing oppression that restricted their freedom and threatened their lives.

These new immigrants came to a United States that had changed since the early 1800s. By this time, much of the frontier had been cleared and settled. The railroads had been built, and fewer jobs were available in industry. U.S. laborers saw the new immigrants as competitors because immigrants would work long hours and accept far lower wages than Americans.

Restrictions Begin

A sharp change in the attitude toward immigrants first became apparent in California. Chinese immigrants, who had come to work in the mines and later on the railroad (see Chapter 14), increased in number from 6,000 in 1880 to 30,000 in 1882.

Chinese people were brought in as contract workers who had pledged to work a certain period of time for Chinese labor contractors who sold the immigrants' labor to railroad or other projects. Most worked very hard for low wages, saved their money, and then returned to China.

The few Chinese who stayed often

▼ Many immigrants from eastern Europe were Slavic people from countries such as Poland and Russia.

faced scorn. Chinese customs, language, and beliefs were very different from those of Americans.

Up to this time the United States had done very little either to encourage or restrict immigration. Growing friction between American workers and Chinese immigrants, however, led to government restrictions on Asian immigration. In 1882, Congress passed the Chinese Exclusion Act, which banned contract laborers from China. In 1907, a Gentleman's Agreement with Japan placed similar limits on Japanese immigrants. Except for a few students and educated people, these measures effectively halted immigration from Asia until 1965.

Fear of Foreigners Grows

The 1890s were a period of renewed strength for the anti-immigration, or nativist movement, which had first appeared in the 1850s with the Know Nothing Party (Chapter 7).

At this time, immigration to the United States was reaching record levels. In fact, of all the immigrants in the world in the 19th century, 60 percent came to the United States. Some Americans began to insist on "America for Americans." These people attacked immigrants who differed in any way from Americans. Fears that the "new immigrants" would weaken or destroy treasured traditions led to new restrictions on immigrants.

The Immigration Act of 1891 ordered all new arrivals to be examined physically before they were allowed to enter the country. At Ellis Island in New York, doctors checked newcomers for diseases such as smallpox, tuberculosis, and cholera, which, if unchecked, could cause a deadly epidemic. A small proportion faced the disappointment of being labeled "undesirable" and were sent back to their native lands. Most, however, were admitted to the United States

Besides working in the mines and on the railroad, many Chinese people set up small businesses. Here some Chinese merchants are selling fish.

Over 12 million immigrants passed through the immigration center at Ellis Island between 1892 and 1922. Why was the experience both frightening and exciting?

■ Why did people in the United States tend to fear immigrants in the early 1900s?

and faced the challenge of finding jobs and housing and learning a new language and new customs. As you learned in Chapter 17, reformers worked to improve conditions for these immigrants, but many still had to overcome great hardships.

As the movement to organize labor grew, new fears arose. Business people welcomed the cheap labor immigrants provided, but feared the radical social ideas of some of them, especially the idea of labor unions. American business leaders were afraid that the immigrants would stir up trouble among American workers. These business owners wanted no more strikes like those at Homestead Steel Plant or Pullman Car Works (Chapter 15).

For their part, U.S. workers argued that cheap immigrant labor drove down wages and lowered the standard of living for the average American worker. Their resentment increased when immigrants were hired as strikebreakers.

Congress Passes Literacy Bill

During the early 1900s, the threat of war in Europe grew steadily and added to antiforeign feelings in the United States. In 1907, President Theodore Roosevelt set up the Dillingham Commission to study immigra-

tion. The commission's 42-volume report took four years to complete.

The report concluded that immigrants from southern and eastern Europe were less likely to become a part of American life than had the older groups from northern and western Europe. Immigration, the commission implied, should be restricted according to the nation of origin. In other words, the United States should decide how many immigrants it would accept from each foreign nation. The door to America was slowly beginning to close.

In 1914, just before the beginning of World War I in Europe, a number of American groups called for the immediate assimilation of immigrants. These groups joined President Woodrow Wilson in promoting the idea of "Americanization." They questioned the loyalties of immigrants, especially those from countries that did not have democratic governments. Across the nation, they encouraged immigrants to abandon their cultural heritage and embrace "100 percent Americanism."

Because of German attacks on France and Great Britain, German Americans faced particular hostility. They avoided speaking German in public places. Some changed their names to English-sounding names. For example, a person named Grünwald might change the name to Greenwood.

World War I all but halted immigration from Europe. Then, in 1917, Congress added a literacy test to its growing list of restrictions on immigrants. The test required an immigrant to be able to read his or her language in order to enter the United States. The restriction was aimed at newer immigrant groups such as Slavs, Italians, and Russians, who were coming to America in increasing numbers. Since illiteracy was generally declining, however, the literacy test had a limited effect. ■

Chapter 19

The Closing Door

After World War I ended in 1918, Europe was in a shambles. Hundreds of thousands of people had been uprooted by the war and by boundary changes after the war.

The Number of Immigrants Is Limited

Alarmed that new waves of immigrants would flood into the United States, Congress passed the Emergency Quota Act of 1921 (also called the Johnson Act). This law established a **quota**. It meant that only a certain number of people were allowed to immigrate to the United States. The quota limited each nationality to 3 percent of that group's foreign-born population living in the United States in 1910. For example, if 100,000 Italians lived in the United States in 1910, only 3,000 Italians would be allowed to immigrate in 1922.

The number of visas—official authorizations to live in a country—was restricted to a total of 350,000 immigrants. Many Americans felt the 1921 law was not fair. For many others, it was not strict enough.

In 1924, Congress replaced the Johnson Act with the National Origins Act, which reduced the quota from 3 percent to 2 percent of those present in 1890. By changing the base year from 1910 to 1890, the law favored the national groups that had arrived in the United States before 1890. It reduced or eliminated further immigration by eastern and southern Europeans, most of whom had immigrated to the United States after that date. The measure also reduced the total number of visas to about 150,000. The older group of immigrants—those from northern and western Europe—was entitled to three-quarters of these visas.

When a worldwide economic depression began in the late 1920s, immigration to the United States dropped severely. Thousands of Americans lost their jobs and could find no other work. Foreigners ceased to view America as the land of opportunity, and immigration reached its lowest level since 1820. The number dropped from over 800,000 in 1921 to less than 150,000 by 1929.

World War II Brings Exceptions

By the late 1930s, economic conditions slowly began to improve in the United States. Growing numbers of people in other nations applied for visas. During this period, widespread unrest was sweeping Europe and Asia. Some national groups feared for their lives because they were being blamed

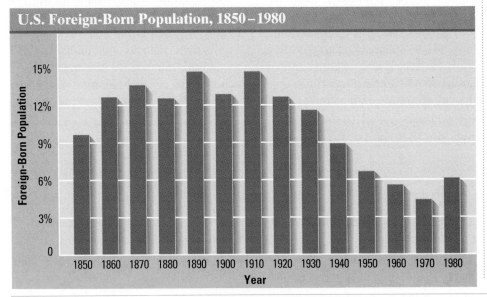

U.S. Foreign-Born Population, 1850–1980

◄ *In what two years did the U.S. population have the highest percentage of foreign born? In what year was the foreign-born population the lowest percentage of the total U.S. population?*

Pluralism

On October 1, 1940, Albert Einstein, his daughter Margot (right), and his secretary Helene Dukas were sworn in as citizens of the United States.

■ *What effect did the quota system have on immigration?*

for problems that beset their homelands. Most threatened were the Jews, who faced imprisonment and often death in Germany.

Recognizing the contributions that well-educated people, especially scientists, might make, the United States bent its quota rules. It offered **asylum**, or political protection, to highly educated Europeans, many of whom were Jewish writers and scholars. Several of these people made brilliant contributions to science and helped the United States become a leading power in the world.

One such scholar was a German Jew named Albert Einstein, winner of the Nobel Prize in Physics in 1921 and author of *The Meaning of Relativity* (1921). Einstein revolutionized modern science with his new theories about time, space, mass, and motion. Einstein, along with scientists Edward Teller from Hungary and Enrico Fermi from Italy, helped make the

United States the first nation with nuclear weapons.

Unfortunately, in order to maintain the immigration quotas during this time, the United States turned away many immigrants who were not distinguished people. Among them were Jews, millions of whom were brutally executed in the lands ruled by Germany during World War II.

Other Exceptions to the Quota System

The United States also made exceptions to its quota system after World War II ended in 1945. The country took in thousands of **refugees**, people who faced persecution because of their political beliefs. Many of these people came from eastern Europe, which had fallen under communist control. Since the United States opposed communism, it allowed many people from those countries to seek refuge in America.

When communist leader Fidel Castro took power in Cuba in 1959, thousands of Cubans sought refuge in the United States. Most of these immigrants were educated professionals who brought their skills and knowledge to the United States. Cuban immigrants became very successful in the United States.

In general, despite the restrictions, immigrants from many nations reached the United States between 1820 and 1960. Most became American citizens. Yet each group held on to some of its own customs and beliefs. In this way immigrants gave new meaning to the phrase *e pluribus unum*, which means, "Out of many, one." ■

R E V I E W

1. **FOCUS** How did U.S. immigration policy change between colonial days and 1960?

2. **CONNECT** Compare and contrast the patterns of immigration from 1840 to 1860 and after 1880.

3. **ECONOMICS** Explain how the quota system worked.

4. **CULTURE** How did exceptions to U.S. immigration laws fit with the attitude symbolized by the Statue of Liberty?

5. **CRITICAL THINKING** In a nation developed by immigrants, why are immigrants often unwelcome?

6. **WRITING ACTIVITY** Make a chart showing the different attitudes people have had toward immigrants. In one column, list the reasons in favor of immigration. List the reasons against immigration in a second column. You may wish to include years to indicate changing attitudes.

L E S S O N   2

America's Many Cultures

Early in the morning, grocers bustle about, arranging boxes of vegetables and fruits or displays of toys and curios from Asia. As they work, they chat with their neighbors and customers, talking about the weather and neighborhood events, wishing one another a good day. As the fog lifts from San Francisco Bay, tourists will be pouring through the dragon gates that mark the entrance to Chinatown.

Most of the residents here work in or close to their homes. The traditional good luck colors of gold and scarlet and the Chinese paper lanterns give the shops a festive air. Each shop identifies itself and tells of its goods in large Chinese characters. In the windows are T-shirts with fanciful dragons, hand-embroidered linens, delicate laces, silk clothing, hand-painted porcelain, lacquerware, enamelware, carvings of wood, stone, and ivory, and jewelry of jade, rose quartz,

and many other semiprecious stones.

One shop follows another, interrupted occasionally by restaurants serving barbecued chicken, dim sum, and the regional dishes of Szechwan, Hunan, and Canton as well as the traditional Mandarin cuisine. Along the side streets are small family-run groceries selling dried shrimp, pressed duck, fresh vegetables, dried or preserved fruit, spices, teas, and ginger.

San Francisco's Chinatown, the largest Chinese community outside Asia, is only one example of the kind of ethnic neighborhood that can be found in the United States today. Miami has its Little Havana, populated mainly by Cubans. Chicago's Pilsen neighborhood houses a huge Mexican population. Los Angeles has Koreatown. In playgrounds across the nation, many children speak a wide range of languages—Chinese, Spanish, Italian, Arabic, Hindu, and dozens more—often with a mixture of English.

THINKING FOCUS

What are some of the benefits and challenges of being an immigrant in the United States?

◄ *Why do many immigrant groups come together in communities like this one in San Francisco?*

571

Pluralism

From Melting Pot to Salad Bowl

▼ *The map shows major populations by county. Since Asians were not a major group in any county in 1980, they are not shown. Which ethnic groups appear in the industrial Northeast? In the Southwest?*

Every new arrival in the United States has faced the challenge of blending old and new. Remember the struggles faced by the Irish and German immigrants in Chapter 7. In Chapter 15 you read about the even greater challenges that faced people from southern and eastern Europe when they immigrated to the United States after 1880.

For many years, America was called the "melting pot," the country where the customs of new arrivals melted down and blended into one American culture. Many now believe this view is outdated. The United States is not made of one culture; it is made of many.

Today, many people compare the United States to a salad bowl. Like a salad, the United States is made of many different "ingredients" of peoples and cultures. Although they are mixed together, these varied ingredients remain separate. Just as each component in a salad bowl yields a separate taste, each cultural contribution adds to the variety and diversity of American life.

What Holds America Together?

When the immigrant culture and the local culture merge, each culture adapts in varying degrees to the customs of the other. Assimilation, or the process of taking on the language, customs and viewpoints of another culture, is a gradual process. Some people accomplish it much more readily than others, while some resist it altogether. Assimilation is largely a matter of choice.

As you read in Chapter 14, the U.S. government had little success when it tried to force the ways of white society onto the American Indians. Most immigrants, however, chose to blend into American culture, but hold on to vital aspects of their ethnic identity such as holiday celebrations.

The Hmong people, for example, immigrated to the United States from their war-torn country of Laos in Southeast Asia. These people have maintained many of their cultural traditions and crafts, including creative stitchery. This skilled work has also helped them to earn a living in the United States.

American Ancestry, 1980

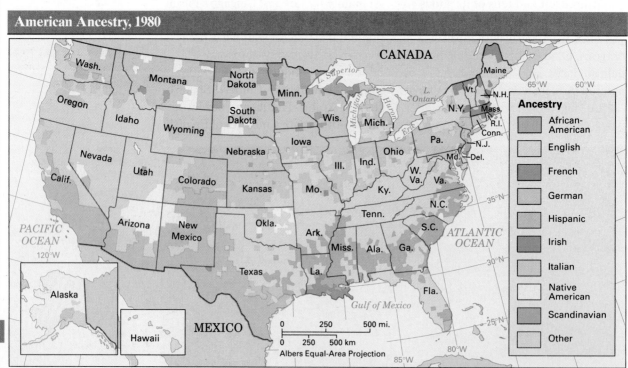

Ancestry
- African-American
- English
- French
- German
- Hispanic
- Irish
- Italian
- Native American
- Scandinavian
- Other

572

A Hmong Woman

3:07 p.m., May 16, 1985
In a small apartment in Fresno, California

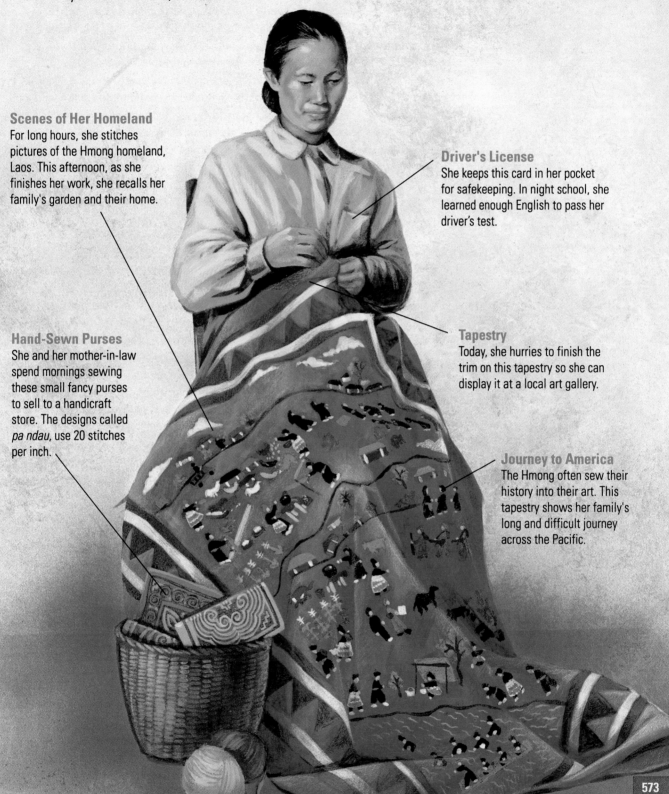

Scenes of Her Homeland
For long hours, she stitches pictures of the Hmong homeland, Laos. This afternoon, as she finishes her work, she recalls her family's garden and their home.

Driver's License
She keeps this card in her pocket for safekeeping. In night school, she learned enough English to pass her driver's test.

Hand-Sewn Purses
She and her mother-in-law spend mornings sewing these small fancy purses to sell to a handicraft store. The designs called *pa ndau*, use 20 stitches per inch.

Tapestry
Today, she hurries to finish the trim on this tapestry so she can display it at a local art gallery.

Journey to America
The Hmong often sew their history into their art. This tapestry shows her family's long and difficult journey across the Pacific.

573

T o support the family in America, Daddy tried various occupations—candy making, the ministry to which he was later ordained—but finally settled upon manufacturing men's and children's denim garments. He leased sewing equipment, installed machines in a basement where rent was cheapest, and there he and his family lived and worked. There was no thought that dim and airless quarters were terrible conditions for living and working, or that child labor was unhealthful. The only goal was for all in the family to work, to save, and to become educated. It was possible, so it would be done. . . .

I observed from birth that living and working were inseparable. My mother . . . was at her machine the minute housework was done, and she was the hardest working seamstress, seldom pausing, working after I went to bed. The hum of sewing machines continued day and night, seven days a week. . . . We knew that to overcome poverty, there were only two methods: working and education. It was our personal responsibility. Being poor did not entitle us to benefits.

Jade Snow Wong, Chinese American

▲ *Japanese Americans package fruit to ship to other parts of the United States.*

For Many, Hard Work Brings Success

In the passage above, Jade Snow Wong, who immigrated to the United States from China with her parents, describes her father's determination to succeed in his new homeland.

Work and education helped many immigrants to blend easily into American society. Older immigrants often accepted the fact that they themselves might never achieve the golden future they believed America promised. Yet they did not lose faith in the future. They were determined that their children would fulfill their dream.

To achieve that goal, they were willing to make enormous sacrifices —to work long hours at low-paying jobs, to spend little on themselves, and to save as much money as they could so that their children would have the opportunity to learn. Many immigrants believed that education served as the road to success in the United States.

Immigrants often struggled for years before they established themselves. Many achieved great personal and financial success. Their determination and achievements are all the more noteworthy in light of the hardships they had to overcome.

I.M. Pei is a Chinese-born American architect whose works include the John F. Kennedy Library in Boston, Massachusetts and the East Building of the National Gallery of Art in Washington, D.C. Pei said of his design for the National Gallery, "To make the visit a pleasant one . . . we built a circus." The design has a large central core of ramps, balconies and escalators covered by monumental skylights. The "big top", as it has been called, adds a sense of fun to the traditional idea of a museum, and is an example of one of the many ways American culture has benefited from the unique perspective immigrants can provide. ■

■ *What attitudes did many immigrants have toward education?*

Becoming an American

Adjusting to life in the United States is usually easier for children than for parents or grandparents. Adults often have more vivid memories of the people and places they left behind and can frequently be homesick. Children, on the other hand, have few memories of the old country. In school they quickly learn the language and customs of the new country and adapt quickly. In immigrant neighborhoods children often act as translators and interpreters for their parents when English is required.

The Generation Gap

Sometimes the attempt to balance old and new ways causes misunderstanding or sharp disagreement between children and their parents. Often the younger generation seems excited at discovering American culture. As they adapt to their new home, many young immigrants want to eat what Americans are eating and to have what their American peers have. They want hamburgers and hot dogs, designer jeans and the latest hairstyle.

UNDERSTANDING ASSIMILATION

Melting pot or salad bowl? How best to describe the United States? Should new immigrants discard their past ethnic identities to become 100 percent Americans? Or should they retain some features of their old culture, which then become part of the American "mix"?

How Assimilation Occurs

Assimilation means to be absorbed into the dominant culture. Assimilation is not the same as naturalization. If an immigrant fulfills all the requirements and takes an oath of allegiance, then he or she may become an American citizen. The action of the naturalization judge in conferring citizenship does not also include assimilation. That process may be immediate, or it may be a long, slow process that lasts a lifetime.

Factors that influence assimilation include the age of the newcomer, the motives that brought the person to America, and the degree of contact with people outside the new citizen's ethnic group. Also important are the criteria the dominant group—the Americans already here—use to judge assimilation.

Some examples may clarify this. Suppose a Filipino boy comes to this country with his parents and his widowed grandmother. The boy will probably learn a new language and new customs much faster than his parents or grandmother. For one thing, he has many more opportunities for learning—in the classroom, on the playground, around the neighborhood.

His parents, who came here because they wanted better jobs, also learn quickly. They know that a good knowledge of English will help them move ahead.

His grandmother, on the other hand, may have many fewer opportunities for meeting new people. Her English may be poor or even nonexistent. She may not be comfortable speaking with anyone except those who know the Filipino language. She is here only because she did not want to be left behind when her family decided to immigrate. She has less motivation to learn the English language and American ways.

Who Decides Assimilation

As noted above, the dominant culture—which usually means the majority—decides what constitutes assimilation. For example, the majority may decide that speaking English is an important part of being an American, but eating potatoes is not. Such a decision is not made by a vote, like electing a president. It's just something everyone knows.

➤ *Ethnic festivals usually provide a lively view of the culture and traditions of different groups in America's pluralistic society. This photo shows West Indians taking part in a parade.*

Their parents, on the other hand, feel they are cast adrift from their roots, and try to recreate the familiar world they once knew. They read newspapers and attend theaters in their native language, shop in stores selling their native foods, and join religious and social ethnic organizations to find companionship. Clubs and religious organizations also help the different groups of immigrants. Jews attend the local synagogue. Irish Americans join Irish social clubs. The Korean church helps to ease the sense of strangeness for immigrants from Korea.

The children often find themselves in difficult situations. At home, they are immigrants; at school, they are Americans. Thus, these children often have to hide one "identity" from the other.

■ *Why did some immigrants find it difficult to become assimilated?*

The United States Enriched

Immigrants have helped to broaden and deepen Americans' view of the world. Their presence helps Americans to appreciate different points of view. It also helps Americans realize how differently they themselves may appear to others. Immigrants have helped to shape the meaning of the word *American*. They have contributed to the varied foods Americans eat, and to all aspects of American life: politics, science, the theater, art, music, dance, literature, sports, medicine, and education.

Numerous immigrant groups have made their way to the United States with hope, faith, and determination. Although it is impossible to list the contributions all of these groups have made, the diversity of American life proudly tells their stories. ■

R E V I E W

1. **FOCUS** What are some of the benefits and challenges of being an immigrant in the United States?
2. **CONNECT** How did basing immigration quotas on national origins make it easier for immigrants to become assimilated after 1920?
3. **ECONOMICS** Why were immigrants willing to work at low-paying jobs?
4. **CRITICAL THINKING** What causes a gap between older and younger generations? What can be done to help bridge such a gap?
5. **ACTIVITY** Look through a large city's newspaper or a national magazine for evidence of immigrants in the United States. Look for announcements of ethnic festivals, recipes for ethnic food, reports on famous immigrants, and books or movies about the immigrant experience. Share your findings with the class.

Chapter 19

Conducting an Interview

Here's Why

Interviewing people who lived during a certain period is a good way to gather firsthand information about that time. Such oral histories are important primary sources for future historians.

In this chapter you have read about the experiences of different immigrant groups who came to the United States. Suppose you wanted to find out what life was like for the children of Mexican-American immigrants. One way to get that information firsthand would be to interview a child of Mexican-American immigrants.

Here's How

Before you interview someone, it is a good idea to find out as much about the person as you can. In addition, when you contact the person to set up the interview, you should tell them why you want to interview them, what you want to know, and how you plan to use the information.

> G rowing up, I could see all the injustices and I would think, "If only I could do something about it! If only there was somebody who could do something about it!" *That was always in the back of my mind. And after I was married, I cared about what was going on, but I felt I couldn't do anything. So I went to work, and I came home to clean the house, and I fixed the food for the next day, took care of the children and the next day went back to work. The whole thing over and over again. Politics to me was something foreign, something I didn't know about.*
>
> Jessie de la Cruz

Jessie de la Cruz (pictured at left) is the daughter of Mexican-American immigrants. Read the profile below to find out more about her:

Jessie de la Cruz grew up in a family that had immigrated from Mexico to California before World War II. After her father and grandfather died, the family became migrant farm workers. During her 30 years of migrant work, de la Cruz became active in changing the poor working conditions for migrant farmers. She was a union organizer, a delegate to the Democratic Party national convention, and the developer of a cooperative ranch. Today she is a living witness to the exploitation of immigrant families as farm laborers and has often been interviewed by historians.

Based on the information above, you can now make a list of 10 questions to ask de la Cruz if you were interviewing her about her experiences. The interview should begin with general questions and work toward specific questions that include the "five W's and an H" (who, what, when, where, why, and how) to make sure it covers all areas of information. Possible questions are:

1. What was it like growing up in an immigrant family?
2. When did your family first move to the United States?
3. Where did you live when you were growing up?
4. How did you get involved in union activities?

Try It

Above is a passage from an interview with de la Cruz. Read it, and make a list of five questions you would ask in order to gather more information.

Apply It

Each family has its own history. Decide which member of your family you would like to interview for an oral history project. Make a list of basic questions to ask. Write or call the person to set up an interview, and take notes or tape-record the interview.

L E S S O N   3

The Gates Reopened

THINKING
F O C U S

How did the pattern of immigration to the United States change after the 1960s?

Key Terms

- undocumented immigrant
- migrant worker
- bilingual education

> *S*o we got a private ship . . . not for money. The owner left Saigon already and everybody—maybe three thousand people, oh my!—just got on the ship. A lot of soldiers force themselves on. One of the people on the ship was a ship captain so he took the ship on the ocean. Others helped. Many times engine stopped. Stop. Stop. Stop. On the sea we run out of food and water. . . .
>
> We see a lot of small ships but they cannot help. We send message. Nobody answer. The engine was finished and ship almost sinking. Then we pretty lucky a Denmark ship see us and take us to Hong Kong. . . .
>
> Americans come to Hong Kong to interview. Everybody fill out a form and everybody happy, think that next day we go to the United States. But after that United States embassy don't come anymore to camp. A week later, a month later, nobody come. Everybody very depressed. We lucky, but we not very lucky. Then they change to let more people in and again they [the American embassy officials] interview.
>
> A Vietnamese Refugee, *Today's Immigrants, Their Stories*

This refugee's story reflects a growing problem in the world today. As nations around the globe have been torn by war, the number of refugees has increased. Although finding asylum may be difficult, the United States has struggled to offer fleeing people refuge. Yet, at the same time, the U.S. government must ensure that the needs of its own citizens are not neglected. How many people can the United States realistically accept? This issue remains as pressing today as it was in the early 1960s, when Congress introduced the laws reopening immigration to the United States.

Expanding Opportunities for Immigrants

On October 3, 1965, at the base of the Statue of Liberty, President Lyndon B. Johnson signed a new immigration law. He was carrying out a wish of his predecessor, President John F. Kennedy. A strong supporter of immigration, Kennedy had proposed a new immigration law. He was assassinated before his proposal could be passed.

The new law ended the quota system. It allowed each nation to send as many as 20,000 people to the United States in a single year, up to a total worldwide of 270,000 immigrants. The law was particularly concerned with reuniting families. Often families had been separated when the male head of the household immigrated to the United States in search of work. Moreover, many immigrants entered the United States illegally and could not send for their families.

Under the 1965 law, 74 percent of the available visas were allotted to the foreign relatives of American citizens and legal immigrants already in the country. President Johnson spoke of the new law in the following words:

> This bill . . . does repair a very deep and painful flaw in the fabric of American justice. It corrects a cruel and enduring wrong in the conduct of the American nation. . . . From this day forth those wishing to immigrate to America shall be admitted on the basis of their skills and their close relationship to those already here. This is a simple test and it is a fair test.

Although the new law treated foreigners more fairly than did the old, it still tended to prevent people from some nations from immigrating to the United States. Since it favored immigrants with relatives already in the United States, it discriminated against people from Asia, Africa, and Latin America. Most immigration from Asia had been banned altogether since the early 1900s, and only limited numbers of Latin Americans had been allowed under the old quota system.

Under the 1965 law, people from these regions could enter the United States only if they were professionals, technicians, or workers with other needed skills. By 1975, however, enough emigrants from Latin America and Asia had come to the United States that they were attracting large numbers of family members who wished to join them.

Admitting Soviet Jews

In 1974, the United States began to grant more visas when it was "in the interests of foreign policy." In other words, the United States increased the number of visas it allowed from a country in order to maintain good relations with that country or to get that country to make a desired change. For example, the United States offered to increase trade with the Soviet Union, provided the Soviet

government allowed more Jews to leave that country.

These policies also changed the immigration balance. Increasing the number of visas for people in one country required reducing visas for people in other countries. When the Soviet Union allowed more Jews to leave in the 1980s, the United States increased the number of visas for Soviet Jews. However, the total number of immigrants to the United States did not change. The increase in visas for Soviet Jews resulted in a decrease in visas for Asians.

Admission of Refugees

After 1960, U.S. immigration policies were affected by growing numbers of refugees. Congress defined a refugee as "any person outside his country, victimized by persecution on racial, religious, political, or social grounds."

In the 1970s and 1980s, thousands of Vietnamese, Cambodians, and Laotians fled their native countries during the Vietnam War and the later upheaval in Southeast Asia. They were known as "boat people" because they escaped in leaky, overcrowded boats, seeking asylum in a safer region. Up to 4,000 refugees fled each week.

President Jimmy Carter expressed

Vietnamese boat people use northward-blowing trade winds to reach Hong Kong. In 1989, the government there refused to admit more Vietnamese. Claiming they were looking for a better way of life rather than political asylum, the Hong Kong government threatened to send all the refugees who were then in Hong Kong back to Vietnam.

579

Pluralism

▲ *Vietnamese boat people arrive in Manila, the capital of the Philippines.*

■ *How did the immigration law of 1965 affect the people who immigrated to the United States?*

▼ *When did most immigrants from southern and eastern Europe come to the United States ? Where did most immigrants come from after 1981?*

the following view about American acceptance of refugees:

> Refugees are the living homeless casualties of our world's failure to live by the principles of peace and human rights. To help them is a simple human duty. As Americans, as a people made up largely of the descendants of refugees, we feel that duty with a special keenness.

Numbers of Refugees Increase

In 1980, about 130,000 Cubans sailed from Mariel, Cuba, to Florida. The United States was reluctant to welcome such a large group of foreigners, many of whom were suspected of being criminals or mentally or physically unfit. President Carter, however, called for "an open heart and open arms" for the Cubans, although most did not qualify as legal refugees.

Each year 10 million to 13 million people become refugees. The number has tripled since the 1970s. Most are innocent men, women, and children who are caught in regional wars— Southeast Asians such as the Cambodians and Vietnamese and Central Americans such as the Salvadorians.

The United States, with its tradition of welcoming the persecuted, has accepted many refugees—up to 94,000 a year. Thousands of refugees, however, remain in temporary camps around the world. Many other nations are not as welcoming as the United States in admitting refugees. ■

Undocumented Immigration

The line between refugee and immigrant is often blurred. An immigrant may come to the United States looking for a better life. A refugee, by definition, is a person who flees a country because his or her life is threatened. The United States does not always agree that people who say they are seeking protection in the United States are refugees.

Temporary Workers

During World War II, when U.S. soldiers were fighting in Europe and

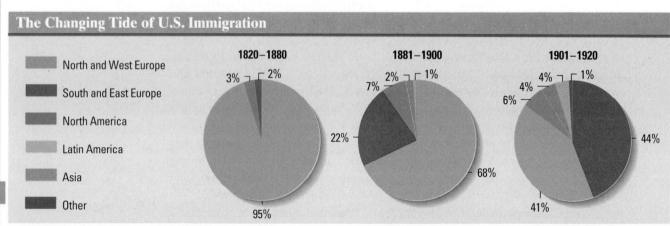

The Changing Tide of U.S. Immigration

- North and West Europe
- South and East Europe
- North America
- Latin America
- Asia
- Other

1820–1880
3% ⌐ 2%
22%
95%

1881–1900
2% ⌐ 1%
7%
68%

1901–1920
4% ⌐ 1%
4%
6%
44%
41%

Asia, the United States needed workers. It admitted many Mexicans as *braceros*—workers with temporary permits—to grow and harvest crops. The braceros had to return to Mexico when their permits expired.

About four million braceros entered the United States before 1964, when the program ended. Some returned to Mexico, but many stayed in the long-established Mexican-American communities. They became part of a growing underground community known as **undocumented immigrants** because they have no passports or visas to indicate their origins.

"Being illegal is nonexistence" said an Irish-born secretary who entered the United States illegally. "You've got no job security, no medical insurance, no right to open a bank account, and are an open target for landlords and employers."

Growing Number of Undocumented

Each year thousands of people enter the United States as undocumented immigrants. Living outside the law, they often work at seasonal jobs, such as growing and harvesting crops. Because they fear being caught and deported, they move frequently. In 1984, U.S. Customs agents found over one million undocumented immigrants; probably thousands more were not caught.

Many of these immigrants are desperately poor Mexicans seeking to survive. No one knows how many

Mexicans cross the 1,936-mile border between the two countries each year. The comments of one Mexican man reflect the thoughts of many of these undocumented immigrants:

> Even when there is work available back home, you're only making $2.25 for nine hours of work. You're working six days a week just to buy a pair of shoes. Compare that to the stupendous money you can make working in the United States, and you'll know why I'm here.

In recent years, increasing numbers of undocumented immigrants have been arriving from Central America, Ireland, Korea, the Philippines, and the Caribbean nations as

▲ *These migrant workers are picking celery in California.*

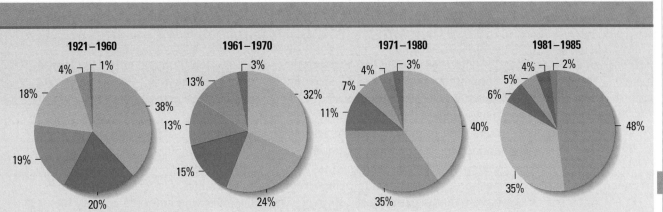

1921–1960
4% ⌐ 1%
18%
38%
19%
20%

1961–1970
3%
13%
32%
13%
15%
24%

1971–1980
4% ⌐ 3%
7%
11%
40%
35%

1981–1985
4% ⌐ 2%
5%
6%
48%
35%

Pluralism

Cesar Chávez founded the United Farm Workers, a union for migrant workers. He also organized sit-ins and national consumer boycotts of grapes and lettuce.

■ How did some undocumented workers gain the right to stay in the United States?

Across Time & Space

The on-going process of American immigration can be seen in the recently opened immigration center in San Antonio, Texas. Those immigrants who pass through its doors today, like their counterparts who went through Ellis Island in generations past, believe in the promise of a better life in the United States.

582

well as from Mexico. On an April day in 1989, for example, a young Korean tearfully greeted his wife. The Korean couple had been separated for eight years, ever since he became an undocumented immigrant to the United States. He did whatever work he could get, working for 70 hours each week. He sent as much money as he could to his family in Korea.

The Korean Association arranged the visit with his wife. He expected, however, that he would have to work at least three or four more years before he could send for his family permanently.

The Undocumented Create Tensions

Many Americans argue that undocumented immigrants take jobs away from U.S. citizens. Using undocumented immigrants, they say, allows U.S. employers to pay less and offer poor working conditions. They also claim that these immigrants are often supported by the welfare programs that are paid for by U.S. citizens.

Others argue that the undocumented take only those jobs that legal residents do not want. They point to statistics that seem to indicate that less than 20 percent of the undocumented immigrants depend on welfare money.

A Chance for a Pardon

In 1986, Congress passed the Immigration Reform and Control Act. The new law had three parts. It called for increasing the size of the United

States Border Patrol. People who knowingly hired undocumented workers faced fines and criminal penalties. Most important, the law granted amnesty, a general pardon, to all immigrants who had been in the United States illegally since 1982. Those who could prove they had been living in the United States continuously since January 1, 1982 were allowed to remain as legal immigrants.

Many undocumented workers, however, had purposely kept no records. Some found clever ways to prove they had been in the United States—a letter from a business, school records of their children, or magazine subscriptions. Other undocumented immigrants had arrived after the cut-off date and did not qualify for amnesty. They faced the loss of their jobs. Employers would no longer hire workers without papers because of the threat of fines.

Changes for Migrant Workers

Special measures were taken in 1986 for **migrant workers,** who traveled across the United States growing and harvesting crops as jobs became available. Farm workers who could prove they had spent at least 90 days in the United States between May 1, 1985, and May 1, 1986, could apply for permanent status. They had to pay $185, a large amount for people who often earned less than the minimum wage. Nevertheless, thousands of migrant workers applied for legal immigration. ■

Other Challenges of Immigration

The 1986 law did not decrease the flood of immigrants from Mexico and Central America. Although U.S. Customs agents caught many and sent them back to their own countries, most undocumented immigrants simply waited a while, and then tried to cross the border again. Unemployment and poverty in the nations of Latin America, as well as political unrest in Central America, made these people desperate for a new life in the United States.

Changing Tide of Immigration

Today, about 42 percent of the legal immigrants to the United States are Hispanics. The exact number of Hispanics who enter the country illegally is not known. By the year 2000, experts estimate, the U.S. population will include between 30 million and 35 million Hispanic Americans, making them the largest minority in the United States.

The number of Asian immigrants to the United States continues to increase also, particularly from Southeast Asia. Experts predict that the largest number will soon come from the Philippines, followed by China, Korea, Vietnam, and India.

Together, Asian and Latin American immigrants make up about 75 percent of the legal immigrants to the United States. In other words, the United States is undergoing a population shift similar to that caused by the immigration from southern and eastern Europe in the early 1900s.

The Hispanic population, in particular, seems more inclined to keep its native language than do most other immigrant groups in the United States. This reluctance to use English poses a problem for many U.S. institutions, including schools and governments.

The Language Question

An organization that wants English to be declared the official language of the country states: "Language is one of the few things we have in common in the U.S." The movement to make English the official U.S. language is in part a reaction to education presented in two languages, or **bilingual education**. In 1968, Congress passed the Bilingual Education Act. It called for teaching subject matter in the student's native language in addi-

tion to English. The bill's sponsors hoped that this process would help foreign-born students make an easy transition to using English.

Some people in the United States, however, feel that bilingual education is not really helping students learn

English. They argue that students should learn only English, claiming that bilingualism encourages a person to remain separate from the mainstream of U.S. society. They have called for laws making English the official U.S. language. Those who supported bilingual education, on the other hand, say that a person can be a U.S. citizen and still keep his or her cultural roots.

Although the United States continues to pride itself as a nation of immigrants, immigration patterns today continue to challenge U.S. public policy makers. Bilingual education and the problems of illegal immigration remain issues for Americans to resolve in the coming years. ■

▲ *In this second-grade classroom in Austin, Texas, the Pledge of Allegiance is written in Spanish as well as in English so that Hispanic students will have a better understanding of it.*

■ *What different views do people have on bilingual education?*

R E V I E W

1. **FOCUS** How did the pattern of immigration to the United States change after the 1960s?
2. **CONNECT** Compare the immigration law of 1965 with that of 1924.
3. **SOCIAL AND ECONOMICS** Why do people risk entering a country illegally?

4. **CRITICAL THINKING** What problems do growing numbers of immigrants pose to public services such as education, housing, fire and police protection, and health care?
5. **WRITING ACTIVITY** Imagine your family has moved to a country where English is not spoken. What problems might your family encounter? Describe those problems.

583

Pluralism

A Family Learns English

Richard Rodriguez

Immigrants in the United States have often felt torn between the culture of their homeland and their new American culture. In his memoir, Hunger of Memory, *Richard Rodriguez examines the sense of conflict he felt when he began to learn English. What impact did the process of learning English have on the Rodriguez family?*

A t first, it seemed a kind of game. After dinner each night, the family gathered to practice 'our' English. (It was still then *inglés*, a language foreign to us, so we felt drawn as strangers to it.) Laughing, we would try to define words we could not pronounce. We played with strange English sounds, often over-anglicizing our pronunciations. And we filled the smiling gaps of our sentences with familiar Spanish sounds. But that was cheating, somebody shouted. Everyone laughed. In school, meanwhile, like my brother and sister, I was required to attend a daily tutoring session. I needed a full year of special attention. I also needed my teachers to keep my attention from straying in class by calling out, *Rich-heard* — their English voices slowly prying loose my ties to my other name, its three notes, *Ri-car-do*. Most of all I needed to hear my mother and father speak to me in a moment of seriousness in broken — suddenly heartbreaking — English. The scene was inevitable: One Saturday morning I entered the kitchen where my parents were talking in Spanish. I did not realize that they were talking in Spanish however until, at the moment they saw me, I heard their voices change to speak English. Those *gringo* sounds they uttered startled me. Pushed me away. In that moment of trivial misunderstanding and profound insight, I felt my throat twisted by unsounded grief. I turned quickly and left the room. But I had no place to escape to with Spanish. (The spell was broken.) My brother and sisters were speaking English in another part of the house.

Again and again in the days following, increasingly angry, I was obliged to hear my mother and father: 'Speak to us *en inglés*.' (Speak.) Only then did I determine to learn classroom English. Weeks after, it happened: One day in school I raised my hand to volunteer an answer. I spoke out in a loud voice. And I did not think it remarkable when the entire class understood. That day, I moved very far from the disadvantaged child I had been only days earlier. The belief, the calming assurance that I belonged in public, had at last taken hold.

Shortly after, I stopped hearing the high and loud sounds of *los gringos*. A more and more confident speaker of English, I didn't trouble to listen to *how* strangers sounded, speaking to me. And there simply were

los gringos (Spanish)
the Yankees

too many English-speaking people in my day for me to hear American accents anymore. Conversations quickened. Listening to persons who sounded eccentrically pitched voices, I usually noted their sounds for an initial few seconds before I concentrated on *what* they were saying. Conversations became content-full. Transparent. Hearing someone's *tone* of voice — angry or questioning or sarcastic or happy or sad — I didn't distinguish it from the words it expressed. Sound and word were thus tightly wedded. At the end of the day, I was often bemused, always relieved, to realize how 'silent,' though crowded with words, my day in public had been. (This public silence measured and quickened the change in my life.)

At last, seven years old, I came to believe what had been technically true since my birth: I was an American citizen.

But the special feeling of closeness at home was diminished by then. Gone was the desperate, urgent, intense feeling of being at home; rare was the experience of feeling myself individualized by family intimates. We remained a loving family, but one greatly changed. No longer so close; no longer bound tight by the pleasing and troubling knowledge of our public separateness. Neither my older brother nor sister rushed home after school anymore. Nor did I. When I arrived home there would often be neighborhood kids in the house. Or the house would be empty of sounds.

Following the dramatic Americanization of their children, even my parents grew more publicly confident. Especially my mother. She learned the names of all the people on our block. And she decided we needed to have a telephone installed in the house. My father continued to use the word gringo. But it was no longer charged with the old bitterness or distrust. (Stripped of any emotional content, the word simply became a name for those Americans not of Hispanic descent.) Hearing him, sometimes, I wasn't sure if he was pronouncing the Spanish word *gringo* or saying gringo in English.

Matching the silence I started hearing in public was a new quiet at home. The family's quiet was partly due to the fact that, as we children learned more and more English, we shared fewer and fewer words with our parents. Sentences needed to be spoken slowly when a child addressed his mother or father. (Often the parent wouldn't understand.) The child would need to repeat himself. (Still the parent misunderstood.) The young voice, frustrated, would end up saying, 'Never mind' — the subject was closed. Dinners would be noisy with the clinking of knives and forks against dishes. My mother would smile softly between her remarks; my father at the other end of the table would chew and chew at his food, while he stared over the heads of his children.

sounded spoke with
eccentrically pitched
strangely high and low

Further Reading

The New Immigrants. Carol Olsen Day and Edmond Day. Describes the problems immigrants face and examines the controversies surrounding immigration today.

The Lower East Side

A Young Polish Girl

In this eyewitness account, which appears in America's Immigrants, *edited by Rhoda Hoff, a young Polish girl describes her life on New York's Lower East Side in the early 1900s. What does this selection show about life at the turn of the century for many immigrants?*

In Lesson 1 you read about the wave of new immigrants who came to the United States from eastern and southern Europe in the late 1800s. Now read one girl's story.

On rainy days we amused ourselves by writing our names backwards and holding the paper up to the mirror, to read forward; or to hum a song through tissue paper on a comb, or by crossing out names of boys and girls against our own to see if the letters remaining which were dissimilar would spell the words "I love you."

We used to tap melodies in the manner of telegraphy, on the window, using our fingers as drum sticks, keeping each beat exactly so, and then wonder if anyone would recognize the tune by the shortness and the slowness of each tap. We made scrap-books of important women or writers, of the day; of actors; of good pictures; or patriotic poems.

We played basket-ball in the yard of the school during the summer months and in the night school centers throughout the city; each week in a different center. We went to everything that was offered free. The concerts in the Mall in Central Park, where we heard Fritz Kreisler playing the violin. We experienced that choky feeling in our throats, to hear such heavenly music. We went to Central Park, to see the animals or to go rowing. Or to Prospect Park, to picnic. We went on hikes, and it was nothing out of the ordinary to take a short walk, say from 14th street to 110th street. We greatly appreciated the crowds in the streets; we did not feel lonely one bit. We enjoyed seeing a parade on Fifth Avenue as though it were a Grand Opera performance.

When the Hudson-Fulton celebration took place, Fifth Avenue was swarming with spectators. We went early in the dawn of the day, to find a place from which we could see the beautiful floats, depicting those two historical events: the day of the steamboat and the cotton gin. It was then a great swelling of pride in America came into being in our cultural life. Yet we went to see the Policemen's Parade with as much excitement.

Then we would go to the library, and enjoy the quiet and the enormous rooms (living rooms were then an unknown quantity among our people). We read books to escape reality; instead of thinking of ourselves we got into the spirit of the story we were reading and became a part of it, and forgot completely about the family and its problems.

Mother was having a Baby in an East Broadway Maternity Hospital.

So I became the cook. Also, standing on a box, I scrubbed the children's overalls and stockings. My dad was experiencing one of his idle periods.

He sat at his sewing machine, thinking of his father in the Old Country; he, too, had sat at just such a sewing-machine; and what did he make? Petticoats! So be it! If it was good enough for his father, it would be good enough for him! He took his last few dollars that he had saved to get mother out of the hospital, and bought some white calico and yards of white lace and began to make some petticoats. Perhaps he could sell them quickly before mother came home from the hospital; but who could sell them on a pushcart for him? He swallowed a dry tear in his throat and called me with downcast eyes.

"Here, take these down across the street and put them on a paper on the sidewalk. Whatever they offer you for them, take it; maybe 25¢ or 35¢ or even 15¢ but don't come back without money; don't come back till you sell them all."

I was dumbfounded. Me . . . did he mean me? I should sell them like a street peddler? What would my poor mother think, in the hospital there, if she knew? Mama! I screamed and ran down the steps, as though possessed. Hugging the bundle close to my heart, I flopped down on the last step in the dark hall—and thought to myself—Lillian, next door—she has no father, her mother has a pushcart, just downstairs — they eat every day—I saw them myself through the fire-escape window, yesterday. —They seemed happy, and unashamed, even proud! Lillian helps her mother sometimes at the pushcart, when her mother goes to buy chicken. How will my mother feel? She won't know. I whispered to myself; we must eat too . . . the kids are hungry and yesterday we made hamburgers; today I don't see any meat in the store.

Stoically I arose, put out my chest, and crossed the street, walked a few feet, lest someone who knew me should see me, and determined, set my wares on the ground. In a few minutes women began picking at them. "Such fine work! How much? Poor child, don't you know? I'll give you 20¢, but really you can get from someone else maybe 35¢; maybe even 50¢." I sold her two of them. A little more courageous, then, I sold some at 35¢ and eventually some with a little soil, at 15¢. Late into the night, I stood there, afraid to go home without a complete sell out; until it commenced to rain . . . Then I sold out at any price, and hurriedly pushed my way through the crowds, back across to my father. What his thoughts were while I was away, I cannot say. He said not a word, pocketed the money and the next day, he sent me for my mother. He was too proud to be annoyed by charity and could not bear the questions they asked. He just would not go and lower himself; that is all there was to it.

Further Reading

America's Immigrants: Adventures in Eyewitness History. Edited by Rhoda Hoff. This book contains the eyewitness account reprinted above along with many other firsthand stories told by immigrants.

Destination America. Maldwyn A. Jones. A study of immigrants who came to the United States between the years 1814 and 1914.

Chapter Review

Reviewing Key Terms

asylum (p. 570)
bilingual education (p. 583)
migrant worker (p. 582)
quota (p. 569)

refugee (p. 570)
undocumented
immigrant (p. 581)

come to America because they are unsafe in their own countries.

4. The Vietnamese boat people sought _____ when they escaped from their native country.

A. In each of the following pairs, the two terms are related in some way. Write a sentence for each pair that clearly explains the meaning of the two terms.
1. quota, undocumented immigrant
2. asylum, refugee
3. undocumented immigrant, migrant worker

B. Choose the key term that best completes each of the following sentences.
1. In order to assist new immigrants in their assimilation process to American culture, many schools offer _____ programs.
2. Because of _____ , which limit the number of immigrants allowed in the United States, many people live here as _____ .
3. The U.S. government allows many _____ to

C. Based on what you have read in the chapter, decide whether each of the following statements is accurate. Write an explanation of each decision.
1. Many undocumented immigrants find jobs as migrant workers, and work on farms across the United States.
2. Quotas allow for unrestricted immigration into the United States.
3. Refugees come to the United States because they cannot find employment in their home countries.
4. Classes taught only in English are part of this country's bilingual education program.
5. Undocumented immigrants often receive wages that are greater than the average American worker's wages.

Exploring Concepts

A. On a separate sheet of paper, copy the chart of immigration laws shown below. In the right-hand column, list the provisions of each law. Then write a

paragraph explaining how immigration laws have changed in the past century, from 1882 to 1965.

B. Support each of the following statements with facts and details from the chapter.
1. Between 1882 and 1924, Congress passed a series of laws aimed at restricting immigration.
2. There were many reasons why Americans resisted the new immigrants of the late nineteenth and early twentieth centuries.
3. Since 1960 the United States government has tried to make its immigration policy fairer.
4. Assimilation affected immigrants and American culture in many ways.
5. Opposition to immigrants has often resulted from the fear that they will take jobs away from other Americans.
6. Many immigrants come to the U.S. today because of economic and political desperation.

Immigration Laws	
Law and Year Enacted	**Provisions**
Chinese Exclusion Act–1882	
Gentleman's Agreement–1907	
Immigration Act of 1891	
Emergency Quota Act of 1921	
National Origins Act–1924	
Immigration Act of 1965	

Reviewing Skills

1. List the "five W's and an H" questions that interviews should cover.
2. What kind of preparations should you make before contacting a person to interview? What information should you give the person you wish to interview?
3. Read a newspaper or magazine interview with a person of interest to you, such as an actor, a sports figure, or a politician. Make a list identifying which information given in the interview answers the "five W's and an H" questions.
4. What could you learn from interviewing an immigrant or a child of immigrants that you could not learn from reading a history textbook?
5. Go back to the charts on United States Immigration on pages 580 and 581. What was the change in the percentage of immigrants from northern and western Europe from 1820-1860 to 1981-1985?
6. Suppose you wanted to interview your state representative. Make a list of guidelines you would follow in order to set up and conduct the interview. Then, if possible, arrange and conduct the interview.

Using Critical Thinking

Keep, ancient lands, your storied pomp!" cries she
With silent lips. "Give me your tired, your poor,
Your huddled masses yearning to breathe free,
The wretched refuse of your teeming shore.
Send these, the homeless, tempest-tost to me,
I lift my lamp beside the golden door!"

Emma Lazarus, 1883

1. The preceding verse is written on the base of the Statue of Liberty. According to this verse, what type of people does America welcome? In your opinion, has the American immigration policy been true to the words written on the Statue of Liberty?
2. Because earlier immigrants assimilated into American life by learning English, many people think that today's policy of bilingual education is unwise. Do you think that bilingual education helps or hurts new immigrants in their attempt to become a part of the American culture? Explain your response.
3. President Franklin Roosevelt once said, "All of our people—except full-blooded Indians—are immigrants, or descendents of immigrants." Assuming that this statement is true, why do you think Americans have so often treated immigrants badly?

Preparing for Citizenship

1. WRITING ACTIVITY Most of today's immigrants are from Asia or Latin America. Choose an Asian or Latin American country that interests you and write a report using the following questions as guidelines: (a) What conditions are people from this country trying to escape from? and (b) What kind of treatment are new immigrants from this country receiving in the United States?
2. WRITING ACTIVITY As you have read throughout this book, the history of the United States is a history of immigration. Imagine you are an immigrant, either today or at some point in history, and imagine that you are the first person in your family to arrive in the U.S. Write a letter to your family describing your new life and how it differs from life in your native land.
3. ART ACTIVITY Create a poster or a collage that illustrates the contributions the immigrant groups that arrived in the United States after 1880 have made to American culture. You may focus your collage on one area of contribution or on one country.
4. COLLABORATIVE LEARNING Divide into small groups. Write down as many ethnic foods offered in American restaurants and supermarkets as you can think of. Be sure to note each food's culture of origin. As a class, write on the board all of the foods you came up with. Which parts of the world are most represented?

Chapter 20

Modern American Democracy

The work and dedication of many people have helped to shape the social and political landscape of modern America. Unwilling to accept injustice and suffering, these women and men have spoken and acted on their dreams and beliefs. Their lives are proof that active, informed citizens are necessary to maintain a healthy democracy.

Frederick Douglass escaped slavery and began a lifelong fight against slavery, segregation, and racism.

A student of religion and government, James Madison proposed the system of checks and balances in our federal government.

| 1775 | 1825 | 1875 |

1789

Ida B. Wells, born a slave, began a crusade against lynchings of blacks. She spoke for women's suffrage and helped found the National Association for the Advancement of Colored People.

Cesar Chávez led the United Farm Workers union as it fought for reasonable pay and safe working conditions. He organized nationwide consumer boycotts of lettuce and grapes to attain these goals.

Social worker and reformer Jane Addams led in the development of research into social problems. An expert organizer and leader, she established social and educational services for the urban poor.

Rosa Parks, called by some the mother of the modern civil rights movement, challenged the system of racial segregation.

1925   1975   2025

2000

L E S S O N   1

A Government of Citizens

THINKING FOCUS

In what ways has the definition of citizenship and the rights associated with it expanded in the United States since 1787?

Key Terms

- citizen
- naturalization

N obody has to tell new Americans what it means to be a citizen. They have spent long hours studying the history and principles of the American democratic system. Many of them have had to learn a new language in the process. And all of them have had to wait years for the opportunity to stand before a judge and swear allegiance to their new country:

"I solemnly swear that I will support and defend the Constitution of the United States of America against all enemies, foreign and domestic, and that I will bear true faith and allegiance to the same, and that I take this obligation freely without any mental reservation or purpose of evasion; so help me God."

The entire ceremony lasts only five or ten minutes, but for many new citizens it is a moment they will never forget. After all, they have emigrated from their home countries, often leaving behind family, friends, and personal belongings. They have lived as strangers in a strange land, carrying a green card to prove their legal status as resident aliens. They have worked hard to learn the customs of a new country and waited patiently for the day when they could raise their right hands and take the oath of citizenship.

Most of us don't have to make such dramatic moves and sacrifices to become Americans. For us, citizenship is something we are born with, something we take for granted. But for those people who have struggled to become Americans, citizenship is a treasure worth the great effort they have made to attain it:

"Here, you have your rights," a new citizen of Palestinian origin named Rima Butros told the *New York Times*. "You finally belong some place. You're an American citizen."

➤ *At mass swearing-in ceremonies, such as the one pictured here, hundreds of immigrants take the oath of American citizenship at the same time.*

Citizenship Defined

"But what exactly does it mean to be a citizen?" you may be asking yourself. Technically, a **citizen** is a person who, by birth or naturalization, owes loyalty to and receives protection from a nation's government. As Rima Butros realized, however, being a citizen involves more than just loyalty and protection. Citizenship implies that a person has certain rights and privileges, which carry with them certain obligations and responsibilities. Citizenship also helps to bestow upon a person a sense of belonging.

A Government of the People

In 1776, the colonists declared their independence from England. Those who supported the Declaration of Independence chose to be united under a single government—to become the citizens of a new nation. Before this moment they had been subjects of the English king, owing their loyalty to him. Now they supported the idea that governments receive "their just powers from the consent of the governed."

The framers of the U.S. Constitution realized that a government must have the trust and loyalty of its citizens in order to be effective. They also understood that if people felt their government belonged to them, they would be more likely to develop that trust and loyalty. The framers captured their vision in the Preamble to the Constitution:

> We the people of the United States, in order to form a more perfect union, establish justice, insure domestic tranquility, provide for the common defense, promote the general welfare, and secure the blessings of liberty to ourselves and our posterity, do ordain and establish this Constitution for the United States of America.

"We the people...." With those three words, the framers signaled the kind of government they proposed to create. Theirs would be a government *of the people*. In other words, the power of the American government would come from the citizens of the United States. As citizens, they would be responsible for shaping and maintaining the kind of government they wanted. The new republic, as the framers envisioned it, was to be built on a foundation of its citizenry.

The 18th-century philosopher Jean Jacques Rousseau said it clearly:

> There can be no patriotism without liberty; no liberty without virtue; no virtue without citizens; create citizens and you will have everything you need....

Becoming a Citizen

You can become a citizen of the United States in one of three different ways: by birth, by blood, or by naturalization. To become a citizen by birth you must be born either in the United States or in an American embassy, ship, or airplane. If you are born to at least one parent who is an American citizen, on the other hand, you

593

Modern American Democracy

become a citizen by blood.

Or you can become a citizen by **naturalization**, the process by which a citizen of one nation becomes a citizen of another. To become a naturalized citizen, you must have lived in the United States for at least five years. If you can also prove you are literate and of "good moral character," understand the U.S. political system, and

■ *What does it mean to be a citizen of the United States?*

have never been a member of an organization advocating the overthrow of the U.S. government, you can apply for U.S. citizenship.

Today any person who meets the above qualifications can become an American citizen. Such was not always the case, however. For a long period of America's history, certain groups were excluded from citizenship. ■

Citizenship Expanded

Partly to avoid the thorny issue of slavery, the framers did not include a definition of citizenship in the Constitution. As a result, it was not clear whether states or the national government had the right to determine who qualified as a citizen.

➤ *The American flag has come to symbolize the basic freedoms of democracy promised by the Constitution.*

In 1790, the U.S. Congress passed the first law concerning citizenship. This law granted citizenship to any "free white person" who lived for over a year in a state, proved "good character," and took an oath "to support the Constitution of the United States." To look at it another way, however, the law also barred black Americans and American Indians from becoming U.S. citizens. In the early 1800s, many states also passed laws that effectively excluded most black and native peoples from American citizenship.

Even the U.S. Supreme Court supported the notion that certain groups

could be barred from citizenship. In the 1857 Dred Scott decision, which you read about in Chapter 11, the Supreme Court declared that slaves were property and were not to be considered American "citizens." Chief Justice Roger Taney wrote that the framers of the Constitution did not intend slaves to be included in the term *sovereign people.* Similarly, in the 1884 case *Elk* v. *Wilkins*, the Court ruled that a well-educated American Indian named John Elk did not have the right to vote because Indians were not American citizens.

In 1865, the Thirteenth Amendment to the Constitution finally abolished slavery. A subsequent campaign for black civil rights in the Congress resulted in both the 1866 Civil Rights Act and the Fourteenth Amendment.

Ratified in 1868, the Fourteenth Amendment added a concrete definition of citizenship to the Constitution for the first time:

A ll persons born or naturalized in the United States and subject to the jurisdiction thereof are citizens of the United States and of the state wherein they reside. No state shall make or enforce any law which shall abridge the privileges or immunities of citizens of the United States. . . .

As a result of the Fourteenth Amendment, black Americans won the right to be U.S. citizens just three years after winning their freedom.

Despite the broad language of the Fourteenth Amendment, American Indians were denied citizenship for another half century. Federal laws such as the Dawes Act of 1887 did give a few Indians the right to be citizens. However, it was not until the Indian Citizenship, or Snyder, Act of 1924, that all American Indians born in the United States were finally admitted to full citizenship. ■

■ *What groups of Americans have won their citizenship since 1787?*

Voting Rights Expanded

Today most Americans think of the right to vote as one of the most basic rights of a U.S. citizen. However, citizenship and voting have not always been so closely associated. During the first century of the nation's existence, for example, a large number of people who were American citizens could not vote.

Restricting Voting Rights

As you read in Chapter 4, many of the framers of the Constitution feared giving too much power to the people and encouraging mob rule. They felt that voting should be limited to white men who were landowners. Owning property, they believed, gave men a stake in society and made them more responsible citizens.

To check the power of the people, the framers created indirect methods of electing senators and Presidents. But they gave the states the power to decide which of their citizens should have the right to vote. As the framers hoped, most states did enact laws requiring some kind of property requirement—usually a certain amount of land—before allowing men to vote.

Fighting for the Vote

During the early 1800s, an increasing number of people began to see property requirements as unfair. Beginning with Ohio in 1802, state after state passed laws giving the vote to all white men, whether they owned property or not. By the late 1820s, most states had eliminated all property qualifications, though Virginia retained its requirement until 1851.

Although most white men had

▼ *The percentage of Americans who can become citizens and vote has expanded considerably since 1790.*

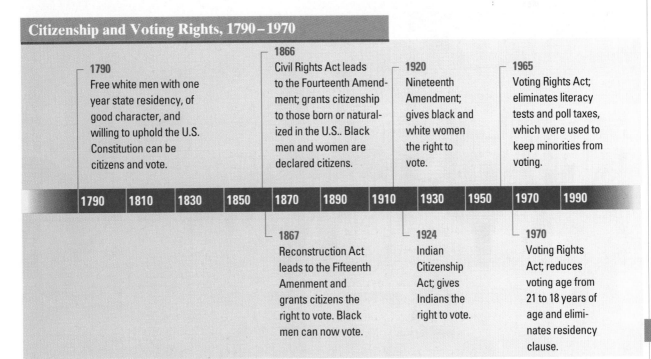

Citizenship and Voting Rights, 1790–1970

1790
Free white men with one year state residency, of good character, and willing to uphold the U.S. Constitution can be citizens and vote.

1866
Civil Rights Act leads to the Fourteenth Amendment; grants citizenship to those born or naturalized in the U.S.. Black men and women are declared citizens.

1920
Nineteenth Amendment; gives black and white women the right to vote.

1965
Voting Rights Act; eliminates literacy tests and poll taxes, which were used to keep minorities from voting.

| 1790 | 1810 | 1830 | 1850 | 1870 | 1890 | 1910 | 1930 | 1950 | 1970 | 1990 |

1867
Reconstruction Act leads to the Fifteenth Amenment and grants citizens the right to vote. Black men can now vote.

1924
Indian Citizenship Act; gives Indians the right to vote.

1970
Voting Rights Act; reduces voting age from 21 to 18 years of age and eliminates residency clause.

Modern American Democracy

How Do We Know?

HISTORY *Historians know that many of the framers supported property requirements for voting by studying James Madison's notes on the Constitutional Convention and by reading many of the framers' personal letters.*

■ *What groups of Americans have won the right to vote since 1787?*

▼ *Many women marched to win the right to vote (below right) in the early 1900s. In the 1960s and 1970s, women participated in marches again (below)—this time for peace and equal rights.*

won the right to vote by 1830, women had to wait another 90 years to achieve that right at the national level. As early as 1848, the women at the Seneca Falls Convention were demanding "immediate admission to all the rights and privileges which belong to them as citizens of the United States." Despite the gains they achieved in some areas, however, these women did not make much progress in winning the right to vote. And when Virginia Minor directly challenged the denial of the vote to women, the Supreme Court ruled in *Minor* v. *Happersatt* (1874) that voting was not a right protected by the U.S. Constitution.

In the late 1800s, many Western states began granting women the right to vote in state and local elections. A revived women's suffrage movement won this same right in many other states during the first two decades of the twentieth century. Finally, in 1920, the Nineteenth Amendment granted national suffrage: "The right of citizens of the United States to vote shall not be abridged by the United States or by any state on account of sex."

For black Americans and American Indians, the right to vote was more closely related to the winning of citizenship. Just two years after they became citizens, black Americans received the right to vote with the ratification of the Fifteenth Amendment:

> The right of citizens of the United States to vote shall not be denied or abridged by the United States or by any state on account of race, color, or previous condition of servitude.

American Indians gained their suffrage at exactly the same moment they won their citizenship—in 1924.

The most recent group of Americans to gain the right to vote were young men and women aged 18 to 20. If these young people were old enough to pay taxes and old enough to be sent to war, many argued, they should also be able to vote. With the ratification of the Twenty-Sixth Amendment in 1971, all American citizens aged 18 and older could vote. ■

Ideal Versus Reality

Unfortunately, legal rights are not always the same as actual rights. According to the law of the land, no American was denied citizenship or the right to vote on account of race, sex, religion, or country of origin by the year 1925. In reality, many Americans were denied their most basic rights as citizens as a result of prejudice and discrimination.

For example, in the years following Reconstruction, whites in the South devised several ways to strip black Americans of their suffrage. Poll taxes were imposed to sift the poor out of the voting population. The result was that most black citizens were unable to "pay" for their right to vote. In 1890, Mississippi became the first state to establish literacy tests as a further barrier against black people. Even educated blacks fell victim to these tests, since they were given questions that were purposely impossible to answer. In addition, a series of formal and informal laws called Jim Crow laws segregated Southern blacks from whites and denied them an equal opportunity to good schools and decent-paying jobs.

In practice, many American Indians lost the right to vote as the result of such barriers as education, transportation, and the prejudice of white election officials. Most American Indians lived on reservations that were miles from the nearest polling booth. When they did manage to get to town, white officials often made it difficult

◄ *The process of registering to vote, shown here, is a simple one, but for many decades discriminatory laws and practices prevented black Americans and American Indians from registering.*

for them to register or to vote.

Although no one prevented them from voting, women also discovered that gaining the right to vote did not end their treatment as second-class citizens. During the decades following 1920, women experienced discrimination in countless ways. They were denied entrance to certain professions, paid less than men for equal work, and prevented from advancing professionally to positions of leadership because of their sex.

Black Americans, American Indians, and women discovered that winning citizenship and the right to vote were only the first steps in their struggle for equal rights. In order to win that struggle, these and other groups of Americans who experienced discrimination needed a powerful ally. They found that ally in the United States Constitution. ■

■ *How have Americans sometimes been denied the rights legally guaranteed to them by the Constitution?*

REVIEW

1. **FOCUS** In what ways has the definition of citizenship and the rights associated with it expanded in the United States since 1787?

2. **CONNECT** How did their lack of citizenship put American Indians in a weaker position during the decades following the Civil War?

3. **HISTORY** How did being a citizen of the United States differ from being a subject of the king of England?

4. **CRITICAL THINKING** What does it reveal about the attitudes of many Americans before 1920 that women were one of the last major groups to win the right to vote?

5. **ACTIVITY** Construct a timeline on which you would indicate when different groups in American society won their citizenship and when they won the right to vote.

Analyzing Editorials

Here's Why

As a citizen of the United States, your beliefs about public affairs are important. Any democratic government relies on the judgment and participation of its citizens. If you simply believe whatever you read or hear about an issue, you have no power to make a reasoned judgment about it. If voters cannot make reasoned judgments of their own, the democratic process is weakened.

A free press is also necessary to democracy. Newspapers report important public occurrences. Newspapers also express their opinions in editorials, which are meant to persuade the reader to think or act in certain ways. No matter what position it takes, an editorial should be supported by facts and sound reasoning.

Today, as throughout our history, Americans are asked to vote on important issues. Suppose you want to decide how to vote on a certain issue. Reading newspaper editorials and determining the strength of their arguments would give you a closer understanding of the issue and the possible solutions. Then you could make up your own mind.

Here's How

Read the following editorial from the *New York Times*, of November 25, 1988, entitled "One Reason Voters Didn't Vote."

Analyze the strength of the argument using these steps:

1. Identify the issue.
The issue is the low voter turnout in the 1988 election.

2. Determine the writer's argument.
The argument is that voting should be made easier.

The final returns on voter turnout are as dismal as predicted: only half of America's eligible voters actually voted in the 1988 election, the lowest proportion since 1924. The figures offer no magic solution. But they argue strongly that more people would vote if voting could be made easier.

Who were the non-voters? According to a New York Times/CBS News post-election survey, they tended to be younger, poorer and less educated than voters. Would their votes have changed the outcome? No. If non-voters had voted, Vice President Bush might have won by 11 percentage points instead of 8—largely because of pro-Bush sentiment among younger non-voters.

Why didn't they vote? Seventeen percent didn't care or were too busy; 13 percent disliked the candidates. These numbers suggest apathy and dismay. But the largest group, 37 percent, said they didn't vote because they weren't registered. And the great majority of those said they would have voted if they could simply have showed up at the polls on Election Day.

There's disagreement about the importance of registration as an obstacle to turnout. The Committee for the Study of the American Electorate, for example, noted a decrease in voting this year even among registered voters. It also found that in two states with Election Day registration, Wisconsin and Minnesota, turnout has fallen below 1972 levels, when registration procedures were more complex. The real problem, those findings imply, is not onerous registration rules but an ominous reluctance to exercise the right to vote.

Yet the same study also suggests that simpler rules would add as many as 13 million voters to the rolls. It stands to reason, too, that simpler rules would boost turnout among the groups most conspicuously absent from this year's election—the poor and less educated, who are often deterred by complex procedures; and young people, who are more likely to have moved recently.

In this computer age, why not allow voters to establish their identities on Election Day with Social Security cards or driver's licenses? That won't remedy widespread voter apathy, and there may be argument about how much good it would do. But there's no argument that eliminating archaic barriers would be a sensible first step.

The New York Times, November 25, 1988

3. **Determine if the information presented is relevant to the argument.**

   The information presented has a direct relationship to the issue under debate. This editorial refers to voting figures in past elections, to surveys, and to data identifying nonvoters. One fact seems to be irrelevant: the writer refers to the present time as "this computer age," but does not say how that affects voting.

4. **See if the argument is supported by facts.**

   Does the information come from reliable, up-to-date sources? Is opinion presented as fact?

   The editorial cites two sources. It does not identify its source for voter turnout figures because these are easily verified. It cites a poll conducted by two reliable news organizations. The findings of a research agency are presented, but only in part. More information may be needed.

5. **Decide, based on the above steps, if the argument as a whole makes sense.** Does the conclusion match the evidence presented?

Try It

Read the excerpt above from an editorial by Mitofsky and Plissner. Decide which of these two editorials you think presents the stronger argument.

About 89 million Americans voted Tuesday, several million less than in 1984. . . . For the last three elections, the figures on voter turnout has hovered around 53 percent; this year, it appears to have dropped to about 49 percent. That does not mean, however, that approximately half the people in America who could have exercised their right to vote did not.

That 49 percent is assumed to be the percentage of "eligible voters" who go to the polls. But it isn't. Rather, it is the figure that results from dividing the total vote for President by the voting age population. Both of these numbers are suspicious.

The voting age population represents the number of people in the country who are at least 18 years old. It includes aliens, legal and illegal, many people confined to institutions and discharged felons—as much as 10 percent—who are plainly not eligible to vote.

The other part of the equation, the recorded vote for President, is also misleading. It excludes as much as 5 percent of the people who actually go to polls but for some reason—confusion over voting procedures, spoiled ballots or a decision not to vote for President—are not tallied in the Presidential vote. . . .The main reason people don't vote, however, has very little to do with the quality of the candidates or the campaign or the polls or the projections. Rather, it is the unique barriers to voting created by our archaic system of voter registration that keeps people from the polls.

The national election studies, conducted at the University of Michigan, show that in every Presidential election since 1964, at least 86 percent of those who are registered to vote do so. Thus, either universal registration or no registration would raise voter participation sharply.

Indeed, in countries whose high rates of voter participation are cited as models, such as Sweden, governments have active programs for seeking out and registering voters. They do not, as we do, rely on the voter to take the initiative to register well before the election takes place. . . .

Our country, with so many different systems for providing positive identification. . . could readily contrive standards for identifying persons eligible to vote without prior screening by a registration office.

Mitofsky and Plissner, *The New York Times*, November 10, 1988

Apply It

Find an editorial in your local newspaper that takes a stand on an issue that interests you. Analyze the strength of the editorial's argument and its relevance to the issue as a whole. Write a short paragraph outlining your findings. Do you agree with the editorial's view?

L E S S O N 2

Putting the Constitution to Work

Key Term

• sit-in

When a 42-year-old black seamstress named Rosa Parks boarded a bus in Montgomery, Alabama, in December 1955, she had no idea that she was about to make history. Tired after a hard day of work, Parks took a seat in the front of the bus, a section reserved according to Jim Crow laws for whites.

Moments later, Parks was asked to give up her seat to a white passenger and to move to the back of the bus. Although she had not intended to challenge the law that day, Parks suddenly decided she had had enough of being treated like a second-class citizen and refused to give up her seat. After warning her several times to move, local police arrested Parks and charged her with violating segregation laws.

Parks's action sparked a year-long boycott by blacks of Montgomery's bus system. Organized by such groups as the Alabama NAACP and the Women's Poitical Council, this boycott also witnessed the rise to prominence of a 27-year-old black minister of the Baptist church named Martin Luther King, Jr. Well educated and an inspiring speaker, King advocated nonviolent protest against unjust laws.

For 381 days, the black citizens of Montgomery refused to ride local buses. Instead, they organized car pools, accepted rides from sympathetic whites, or simply walked to their jobs—sometimes over long distances. Their actions cut the income of the bus company by 65 percent and hurt the business of downtown stores.

Finally, almost a year after the protest began, the U.S. Supreme Court ruled that segregation in public transportation was unconstitutional and therefore illegal. With the help of the Court, the black people of Montgomery had won a great victory against segregation. By a single act of courage, Rosa Parks had inspired the modern civil rights movement.

The Rights of Citizens

The U.S. Constitution guarantees American citizens certain basic freedoms. The Constitution also gives citizens—no matter what their age, race, income, sex, or religion—the right to seek enforcement of the law and to challenge unjust laws. Rosa Parks's effort to win the right to sit where she pleased is a good example of how citizens can use the Constitution to secure the fundamental rights it promises.

As you read in Chapter 4, critics of the newly drafted U.S. Constitution feared the powerful central government it established. They demanded that a bill of rights be added to the document to prevent this government from abusing individual liberties. Thus, one of the first acts of the new Congress in 1789 was to pass ten amendments to the Constitution that came to be known as the Bill of Rights.

The Bill of Rights spells out the basic freedoms guaranteed to every American citizen. It promises freedom of speech, religion, assembly, and the press. It protects citizens against "unreasonable" searches and seizures of property by government officials or the police. It assures citizens that they will receive a jury trial in criminal cases and a lawyer to defend them. And it guarantees due process of law — that is, the government must follow a set of fair, specific rules when a person is accused of and tried for a crime.

The original purpose of the Bill of Rights was to protect America's citizens from a tyrannical central government. But the Constitution said nothing about the states having to obey these amendments. The passing of the Fourteenth Amendment in 1868 completely changed this situation.

The Fourteenth Amendment declared that states could not "deprive any person of life, liberty, or property, without due process of law; nor deny to any person within its jurisdiction the equal protection of the law." What the amendment did, in effect, was to federalize the Bill of Rights. In other words, it affirmed that no government—federal, state, or local—could deny a citizen freedoms guaranteed in the Bill of Rights.

The Fourteenth Amendment was originally intended to protect the rights of America's black citizens. In the twentieth century, however, the Supreme Court has interpreted the amendment's language more broadly. Over the years, many other minority groups have turned to the Fourteenth Amendment to obtain or protect their basic liberties. ■

■ *In what ways does the Constitution guarantee American citizens certain basic rights?*

The Civil Rights Movement

The Montgomery bus boycott provided the civil rights movement with a set of tactics. However, the movement had its beginnings in a crucial Supreme Court case.

In its landmark 1954 decision, *Brown* v. *Board of Education of Topeka*, the Supreme Court completely reversed its ruling in the 1896 *Plessy* v. *Ferguson* case and rejected the idea of segregated public schools. "Separate educational facilities," the Court declared, "are inherently unequal" and have "no place in public education." In addition to rejecting the concept of "separate but equal" schools, the Court also ordered school integration to proceed immediately.

Challenging Segregation

The 1954 *Brown* decision shook the Southern institution of segregation to its foundation. It also provided civil rights leaders with a firm constitutional basis for future action.

Increasingly, the most important of these leaders was the Rev. Martin Luther King, Jr. With a deep, resonant voice and a charismatic presence, King spoke movingly from the pulpit about

▼ *Until the civil rights movement began to challenge segregation laws, black Americans often had to use separate and unequal facilities.*

The attorney who made the argument against segregation in Brown v. Board of Education of Topeka was a black lawyer named Thurgood Marshall. Thirteen years later, in 1967, Marshall became the first black American to be appointed to the U.S. Supreme Court.

the economic and social discrimination suffered by blacks. But King was also dedicated to nonviolence. "We must use the weapon of love," he told his followers. "We must have compassion and understanding for those who hate us."

In the late 1950s and early 1960s, many blacks and whites began to break segregation laws purposefully in order to challenge those laws in court. They swam in segregated swimming pools, worshiped in segregated churches, and rode on segregated buses. They participated in **sit-ins** at restaurants and lunch counters, refusing to leave until they were served.

Citing the Fourteenth Amendment, the Supreme Court ruled that segregation was illegal in case after case. But many Southerners did not accept those rulings quietly. Volunteers working on behalf of civil rights for blacks were jailed, beaten, and murdered across the South.

Throughout the civil rights movement, the relatively new medium of television kept Americans aware of unfolding events in the South. Many

Americans were startled and upset by the images that began to appear on the nightly news. As the nation looked on, young civil rights workers were dragged away from lunch counters and arrested, federal troops escorted black children to school past angry mobs, and law enforcement authorities turned police dogs and fire hoses on peaceful demonstrators. The brutality of the authorities and the courage of the protesters soon won the sympathy of much of the nation.

The March on Washington

In 1963, King and other civil rights leaders organized a demonstration in Washington, D.C., to protest the increasing violence in the South. The response was overwhelming. People from all over the nation, both black and white, poured into the capital to take part in the March on Washington.

On August 28, 1963, Martin Luther King, Jr., stood on the steps of the Lincoln Memorial, facing a crowd of 250,000 people. As millions more watched on television, King shared his dream with the American people:

So I say to you, my friends, that even though we must face the difficulties of today and tomorrow, I still have a dream. It is a dream deeply rooted in the American dream that one day this nation will rise up and live out the true meaning of its creed—we hold these truths to be self-evident, that all men are created equal.

I have a dream that one day on the red hills of Georgia, sons of former slaves and sons of former slave-owners will be able to sit down together at the table of brotherhood. . . .

I have a dream my four little children will one day live in a nation where they will not be judged by the color of their skin but by the content of their character. . . .

This will be the day when all of God's children will be able to sing with new meaning—"my country 'tis of thee; sweet land of liberty; of thee I sing; land where my father died, land of the pilgrim's pride; from every mountain side, let freedom ring"—and if America is to be a great nation, this must become true. . . .

And when we allow freedom to ring, when we let it ring from every village and hamlet, from every state and city, we will be able to speed up that day when all of God's children—black men and white men, Jews and Gentiles, Catholics and Protestants— will be able to join hands and to sing in the words of the old Negro spiritual, "Free at last, free at last; thank God Almighty, we are free at last."

The March on Washington

The Civil Rights movement of the early 1960s reached its peak with the March on Washington. On August 28, 1963, a quarter of a million Americans arrived in the nation's capital from almost every state in the union to make their demands known: "Jobs and Freedom!"

"**I have a dream** that one day my four little children will live in a nation where they will not be judged by the color of their skin but by the content of their character." Dr. King's inspiring speech stirred the nation.

Black, white, young, and old marched together. They came from every religion, every race, every profession, and every political party. The Washington Monument towers over their cause.

603

President John Kennedy responded to this unprecedented demonstration by quickly introducing a Civil Rights Act. When Kennedy was assassinated three months later, President Lyndon Johnson hurried the Civil Rights Act of 1964 through Congress as a memorial to the nation's slain leader. That same year the states abolished poll taxes by ratifying the Twenty-fourth Amendment to the Constitution. And just one year later, Congress passed the Voting Rights Act of 1965, which abolished state laws designed to prevent black Americans from exercising the right to vote.

Discrimination against blacks did not end in 1964. But through a series of Supreme Court decisions and major pieces of legislation, black Americans—basing their efforts on the Constitution—were able to obtain many rights long denied them. Their tactics and their successes inspired other groups of Americans to look to the Constitution for help. ■

■ *What strategies did black Americans use to win their civil rights?*

American Indians Make Gains

Though recognized as citizens and granted suffrage in 1924, American Indians had little control over their lives in the 1950s. The Bureau of Indian Affairs determined their education, livelihood, access to justice, and many aspects of their daily lives. Like black Americans, they still suffered prejudice and discrimination. Life on the reservations in the 1950s was bleak. Because of poor land and few economic opportunities, American Indians lived in appalling poverty and squalor. Alcoholism and infant mortality rates were high. Their average life expectancy was only half that of whites.

Angered at these conditions and inspired by the black civil rights movement, American Indians took bold action for political and social change in the 1960s and 1970s. Indian peoples across the nation formed political organizations, staged protest demonstrations, and pressured Congress and state legislatures for more Indian involvement in government programs affecting them.

American Indians benefited from the broad civil rights antipoverty programs in the 1960s. But in the late 1960s, Indian activists began to push for new laws aimed specifically at the problems of Indian peoples. Calling Indian citizens the "forgotten Americans," President Lyndon B. Johnson supported Congress in the passage of the Indian Civil Rights Act in 1968. This act guaranteed American Indians their basic rights and protection against the taking of their property without compensation.

In the early 1970s, American Indians made important gains. Under President Richard M. Nixon, they won 20 top appointments in the Bureau of Indian Affairs. In addition, the Indian Self-Determination and Education Assistance Act of 1975 gave Indian peoples more control of their reservations, their education, and the programs that affected them.

Like black Americans of the same period, American Indians turned to the courts to have their grievances heard and their claims resolved. For instance, in the mid-1970s, the Pas-

▼ *During the first half of the 20th century, Bureau of Indian Affairs schools, such as the one pictured below, attempted to assimilate American Indian students into the dominant white culture.*

During the early 1970s, American Indians participated in protests and marches demanding both an end to discrimination and respect for Indian cultures.

samaquoddy and Penobscot tribes of Maine went to court claiming that a huge area of land in Maine had been taken away from them by an illegal treaty in the 1800s. In the 1977 case of *Passamaquoddy Tribe* v. *Morton,* a federal judge ruled in favor of the state's Indians. Eventually the federal government negotiated a settlement in the form of the Maine Indian Claims Settlement Act of 1980. By the terms of this act, Maine's Indians received more than 300,000 acres of land and nearly $30 million in compensation.

Asserting their constitutional rights through appeal to the courts, American Indians won their land claims in case after case in the 1970s and 1980s. In 1971, for instance, after a long legal battle, President Nixon signed a bill returning to the Taos Pueblo their sacred Blue Lake

in New Mexico. A 1980 Supreme Court decision ordered the federal government to pay $117 million plus interest to the Sioux Indian Nation to compensate them for the loss of the Black Hills of South Dakota.

Despite these gains, life remains difficult on many American Indian reservations. Levels of unemployment, alcoholism, and suicide are still much higher than the national average. However, by skillful use of the American political and legal systems, American Indians have asserted their constitutional rights and corrected past injustices. Indian tribes have also invested money received from the federal government and provided new economic and educational opportunities for many of their people. ∎

■ How did American Indians win greater control over their lives and regain territory lost in the 18th and 19th centuries?

The Fight for Women's Rights

Although American women won suffrage in 1920, their struggle for equal rights continued. Shut out of many jobs, paid less than men for equal work, and portrayed as the "weaker sex" whose place was in the kitchen, women endured discrimination on a scale similar to that of minority groups for many decades.

The Rebirth of a Movement

In the 1960s, women joined the ranks of those Americans fighting to secure their equal rights. Many historians attribute the rebirth of the women's movement to a book published in 1963. In *The Feminine Mystique,* Betty Friedan claimed that women were as capable as men of

Modern American Democracy

▲ *In the early 1900s, women were expected to dress in certain ways and to perform narrowly defined roles.*

➤ *Today women work in a variety of fields once reserved for men. The woman on the left is a biologist. The woman on the right is a telephone repair person.*

doing any job and should be given the opportunity to fulfill "their unique possibilities as separate human beings."

Three years later, Friedan helped to found the National Organization for Women. "There is no civil rights movement to speak for women," the NOW organizers claimed, "as there has been for Negroes and other victims of discrimination." NOW's goal —and the goal of other women's organizations that sprang up in the late 1960s—was to fight for equal rights by lobbying for legislation and testing unjust laws in the courts.

The first major victory for the women's rights movement was accidental. In 1964, Southern Democrats offered an amendment to the proposed Civil Rights Act to prohibit discrimination on the basis of sex as well as race. They assumed this amendment would persuade more legislators to vote against the Civil Rights Act and thus help to defeat it. However, the amendment passed and became the basis for later attacks on sex discrimination.

Citing the Civil Rights Act and the Fourteenth Amendment, women won a series of judicial and legislative victories in the 1960s and 1970s. In one very important case, the Supreme Court ruled in 1971 that unequal treatment based only on gender violated the Fourteenth Amendment. Women used this ruling again and again to fight discriminatory laws and practices. In *Cleveland Board of Education* v. *Le Fleur* (1974), for example, the Supreme Court ruled that Jo Carol Le Fleur did not have to take leave without pay after a certain period of pregnancy and could return to work as soon as she wanted. Women won important legislative battles as well. The Educational Amendments of 1972 provided that college athletic programs for women receive financial support equal to those for men. That same year Congress passed the Equal Employment Opportunity Act, requiring equal pay to men and women for equal work. Other new

laws—both state and federal—ended many discriminatory practices and opened new career opportunities for women.

Despite an impressive list of achievements, the women's movement did experience one important defeat. In 1972, Congress passed an Equal Rights Amendment (ERA). More than 30 states quickly ratified this amendment, but then it ran into serious opposition from conservatives, who feared it would disrupt traditional family patterns and eliminate certain protections for women, such as exemption from military service. The amendment died in 1982.

New Roles for Women

Since the mid-1960s, the role of women in American society has changed immensely. More women now work in such traditional male occupations as computer scientists, business executives, truck drivers, engineers, pilots, car mechanics, architects, politicians, and psychiatrists. The two-career family, in which both husband and wife work, has increasingly become the norm.

The number of women entering the professions has skyrocketed during the past two decades. In the early 1970s, only 7 percent of the nation's physicians and 3 percent of its lawyers were women. By the mid-1980s, wo-

men accounted for 18 percent of all doctors and 20 percent of all lawyers in the United States.

Since 1980, two women have won seats in the United States Senate, and an increasing number have served in presidential cabinets. Sandra Day O'Connor was named the first woman Supreme Court Justice in 1981, and two years later, Sally Ride became the first woman astronaut to fly in outer space. The Democratic Party broke new ground in 1984 when it chose a woman, Representative Geraldine Ferraro, to serve as its vice-presidential candidate. Although some barriers and discrimination remain, women have clearly achieved a great deal in a very brief time. ■

The appointment of Sandra Day O'Connor to the Supreme Court in 1981 symbolized the gains women have made in recent decades.

■ What gains did women make as a result of the revival of the women's movement?

The Ongoing Struggle for Justice

Black Americans, American Indians, and women are not the only people who have turned to the Constitution when faced with discrimination and injustice. Since World War I, Asian Americans, Hispanic Americans, Jews, and a variety of religious groups have also fought, with the help of the Constitution and the courts, to obtain and protect their basic rights. More often than not, these groups have been successful in their charges of discrimination and prejudice. But

occasionally they have lost important battles.

During World War II, for example, Japanese Americans became the targets of hostility and suspicion. Many Americans, including defense officials, thought that these Japanese Americans might try to betray the United States to Japan. As a result, President Franklin Roosevelt granted the War Department the authority to relocate thousands of them.

With little warning, the govern-

607

► *Many Japanese Americans were selected out of relocation camps and drafted to serve in the U.S. Army in Europe. The men shown here are being sworn into service.*

ment moved Japanese Americans, two-thirds of whom were American citizens, into prison-like relocation camps. Most had to sell their houses, businesses, and personal possessions at great losses. But one of these Japanese Americans, Fred Korematsu, refused to obey the order to move. When he was arrested, tried, and convicted, he appealed his case to the U.S. Supreme Court.

In 1944, the Supreme Court upheld Korematsu's conviction in a 6-3 decision. The Court ruled that the relocation program was a "justifiable wartime measure."

Today, most Americans believe that the Supreme Court was wrong in 1944 and that the order to relocate Japanese Americans denied these people their most basic constitutional rights. In fact, Congress passed a law

in 1988 admitting that an injustice had been done and awarding financial compensation to Japanese Americans who lost their property as a result of the relocation order.

In the United States—as in all countries—there is sometimes a gap between the nation's political ideals and the reality of certain political and legal decisions. What the *Korematsu* case shows—as the *Plessy* v. *Ferguson* case did earlier—is that the system can sometimes fail the very people it is designed to protect. And because prejudice and discrimination still exist and people in positions of authority make mistakes, the struggle for equality and liberty is never-ending. For these reasons, it is important that American citizens know the Constitution, understand their rights, and get involved in the political process. ■

■ *In what sense is the effort to guarantee all Americans their constitutional rights a never-ending process?*

R E V I E W

1. **FOCUS** How have some groups of Americans used the Constitution to obtain the rights and freedoms previously denied them?
2. **CONNECT** In what sense did the civil rights movement of the 1950s and 1960s complete the work started during the period of Reconstruction?
3. **HISTORY** How did the Fourteenth Amendment make the

rights of all Americans more secure?
4. **CRITICAL THINKING** Do you think the spread of television ownership helped or hurt the civil rights movement? Explain.
5. **ACTIVITY** Make a list of at least three ways in which prejudice and discrimination have kept people from enjoying their full rights as American citizens.

Chapter 20

LESSON 3

Making a Difference

What do a 15-year-old high school sophomore named Tanja Vogt and Thomas Paine have in common? The answer is that both inspired major changes in their societies by writing an essay.

In October 1988, Vogt—a student at West Milford High School in New Jersey—read an article in her local newspaper that disturbed her. The article reported that the Board of Education had decided to use polystyrene trays in the lunchroom because they were less expensive than paper.

Vogt knew from her science class that polystyrene can have harmful effects on the environment. In the first place, it is not biodegradable, meaning that it can't be broken down by natural biological processes. In addition, some polystyrene products release gases called chlorofluorocarbons (CFCs) into the air. Scientific evidence indicates that these CFCs break down the protective ozone layer of the atmosphere.

Vogt decided to write a current events paper for her social studies class on the issue of polystyrene. Her teacher, Carl Stehle, read her paper to the class. After reminding students that Thomas Paine had had to persuade many hesitant colonists to support the American Revolution, Stehle challenged his class to do something about the polystyrene problem.

Vogt and her classmates immediately conducted a survey in the high school and middle school. They discovered that a large majority of students said they wanted to switch back to paper goods in the cafeteria. When they presented their findings to the Board of Education, the board's business administrator did a survey of his own. He found that roughly 80 percent of the students in the two schools would be willing to pay an extra nickel to eat their lunch from paper trays. As a result, the board voted in December to change to paper trays in all the township's schools as of February 1, 1989.

Having won their first battle and receiving national attention in the process, the students at West Milford's high school and middle school decided to expand their campaign. Since January 1989, they have written to more than 700 schools around New Jersey, urging them to eliminate polystyrene plates and trays from their cafeterias. They have also asked local businesses not to buy polystyrene products. And they are beginning to explore the idea of switching from paper to real plates that can be washed and used again, since paper products also add to the growing garbage problem and don't break down quickly in landfills.

In May 1989, Vogt and three other students participated in the International Youth Environmental Forum at the United Nations, where they explained their campaign to young people from other nations. In Vogt's view, it is all just a matter of common sense. "If you believe in something," she says, "it can be successful, because just one person has to start, and it will keep going."

THINKING FOCUS

Why is it important to be a responsible, active citizen?

Key Term

• glasnost

Citizens Who Made a Difference

In his 1961 inaugural address, President John F. Kennedy urged his fellow citizens to "ask not what your country can do for you; ask what you can do for your country." Kennedy knew that ordinary people can have a dramatic impact on society when they are inspired by a cause or an idea and become active in public affairs. As you have seen throughout this book, it was individuals—people like you—who made a difference in the history of America.

A Sense of Duty

Deborah Sampson, for example, was a heroic figure. A former teacher,

▼ *In addition to helping the poor, Jane Addams* (bottom right) *was involved in the effort to keep the United States out of World War I.*

she was determined to help in the fight for American independence. Disguising herself as a man, she joined the Continental Army and fought bravely for the cause of freedom in several battles.

A black slave, Frederick Douglass escaped to the North in 1838. Many people would have simply settled down and enjoyed their newly won freedom at this point. However, Douglass immediately threw himself into the abolition movement, lecturing and writing against slavery. In addition to describing the worst features of slavery in his eloquent autobiography (see pages 296–297), Douglass also helped to enlist black troops for the Union cause during the Civil War and spoke on behalf of women's rights.

One of the earliest and most important advocates of women's rights was a mother and homemaker named Elizabeth Cady Stanton. Although she cared deeply for her husband and children, Stanton also felt a responsibility to right social wrongs and improve the society in which she lived.

Originally involved in the abolition and temperance movements, Stanton helped organize the historic Seneca Falls Convention in 1848. She also drafted a Declaration of Sentiments—a variation on the Declaration of Independence—demanding that women "have immediate admission to all the rights and privileges which belong to them as citizens of the United States." Stanton remained active in the fight for women's rights until her death in 1902.

A well-educated but frail young woman named Jane Addams became one of the most important reformers of her time. Like Stanton, Addams considered it her duty to help those suffering from poverty and discrimination. In 1889, at the age of 29, she founded Hull House in one of the poorest slums of Chicago. Called a "settlement house," Hull House served as a school, a club, a counseling center, a political organization, a doctor's office, and a refuge from the small, crowded homes of many of Chicago's poor immigrants. It became the model for settlement houses all across the United States.

Samantha Smith's Dream

More recently, a 10-year-old American named Samantha Smith captured the nation's attention when she wrote a letter to then-Soviet leader Yuri V. Andropov. At the time, 1983, tension between the United States and the Soviet Union was high, and Smith confessed her worry "about Russia and the United States getting into a nuclear war." At Andropov's invitation, Smith visited the Soviet Union for two weeks. Though her trip did not reduce tensions between the two nations, her desire for friendship and cooperation did serve as a model for a different kind of relationship.

Samantha Smith died in a plane crash in 1985, but her dream of peace between the superpowers is much closer to realization today. The year Smith died, Mikhail Gorbachev became the new leader of the Soviet Union and called for *glasnost*, or a more open society. In 1987, the United States and the Soviet Union signed a new arms control agreement.

In 1989, citizen-led reform movements brought a greater measure of democracy to many countries in eastern Europe. In the fall of that year, East Germany dismantled the Berlin Wall. The two Germanies were united in 1990. The breakup of the Soviet Union in 1991 signaled the end of the Cold War.

Of course, Samantha Smith was not directly responsible for the improvement of relations between the United States and the former Soviet Union. But her vision of a more peaceful world touched the imagination of the nation and held out the promise of a better path. Like Sampson, and Douglass, Stanton, and Addams before her, Smith was willing to get involved and take action to promote America's highest ideals of peace and freedom. ■

▲ *Samantha Smith is shown here holding the letter from Yuri Andropov inviting her to the Soviet Union.*

■ *How have ordinary American citizens made the nation a better place in which to live?*

Rights Involve Responsibilities

At the end of the Constitutional Convention in 1787, someone asked the oldest delegate, Benjamin Franklin, "What have you created here?" Franklin answered sharply, "A republic, if we can keep it."

Franklin knew that a government whose power came from the people was only as good as its citizens. He also understood that, in order to survive, a democracy had to depend on its citizens to understand their government and know their rights, to participate in the political process, and to keep informed about the public issues of the day. Along with rights and freedoms, Franklin might have said, a citizen also has certain responsibilities.

Modern American Democracy

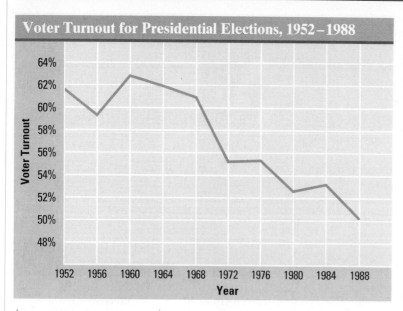

Voter Turnout for Presidential Elections, 1952–1988

▲ *Voter turnout in Presidential elections has declined steadily since a post-World War II high point in 1960.*

Today, however, many Americans are neither active nor informed. In recent surveys, for example, some American citizens have not been able to identify the Declaration of Independence or the United States Constitution. And in the presidential election of 1988, more than half of the eligible voters chose to remain at home.

Getting Involved

Either because they aren't interested or don't believe they can make a difference, some Americans have chosen not to take part in the democratic process. But as the students of West Milford, New Jersey, have proved, what Americans think—and what they do about what they think—can have a measurable impact on society.

Even though you may not be old enough to vote, you can still be active in politics and public affairs. Participating in your school's student government is one good way to learn about the nuts and bolts of the political process. You may also choose to take part in the model United Nations program at your school, if it has one, or start one if it doesn't.

In addition, students between the ages of 13 and 19 can join the youth organizations of various political parties, such as the Teen Age Republicans or the Young Democrats of America. Working through these organizations in local, state, and national elections, young people can learn how the political system works at the grass roots level. For example, club members might assist people in registering to vote, might pass out campaign flyers at shopping malls and on street corners, or might make phone calls to prospective voters.

Young people can have a voice in important issues of the day by joining organizations devoted to particular issues as well. Students Against Drunk Driving (SADD) offers programs to educate fellow teenagers about the dangers of drinking and driving. Amnesty International, on the other hand, works to support human rights. Its members write letters to oppressive governments around the world on behalf of political prisoners. The Audubon Society and the Sierra Club are dedicated to cleaning up and protecting the environment. For every important issue there usually exist several organizations with varying points of view about that issue.

Students can also become active in local affairs. They might volunteer to tutor in an illiteracy program or read for the blind. They could also organize a community effort to clean up a park or beach. They might write letters to city officials about the need for better public transportation or take part in petition campaigns to prohibit smoking in public places. They could also participate in walk-a-thons or read-a-thons to help raise money for the homeless.

Promises to Keep

Throughout American history, dedicated citizens have struggled to realize and expand the ideals set forth in the Constitution. They have fought to abolish slavery and segregation. They have worked to extend the right to vote to women and minorities, to

provide legal assistance to the poor, and to root out corruption in public office. They have called their government to account in the name of the people.

What has united them in these varying struggles is a simple but powerful idea: that the United States is a nation "of the people, by the people, and for the people." This idea has inspired people fighting for freedom in every part of the globe.

Throughout its history, the United States has held out a promise to all its citizens—the promise of a nation with "liberty and justice for all." During the 20th century, Americans have worked hard to fulfill that promise and have achieved many of their goals. But to provide liberty and justice for all, a nation needs informed and dedicated citizens. Keeping the promise of America will depend ultimately on you—the people. ■

▲ *In September, 1987, Americans gathered in front of the U.S. Capitol to celebrate the 200th anniversary of the Constitution. American democracy inspired the students who demonstrated in Tienanmen Square, Beijing, China, in the spring of 1989 (inset).*

■ *What responsibilities does being a good American citizen include?*

REVIEW

1. **FOCUS** Why is it important to be a responsible, active citizen?

2. **CONNECT** Name at least one reform or event in American history that was partly the result of a piece of writing by a concerned citizen.

3. **HISTORY** In what sense was Samantha Smith's letter to Yuri Andropov a foreshadowing of future events?

4. **CRITICAL THINKING** Why do you think it is dangerous for a democracy when a large number of citizens are neither active nor informed?

5. **ACTIVITY** Choose an important issue or event and follow how it is reported in two different newspapers, on two different television stations, and on two different radio stations. Report your findings to the class.

Modern American Democracy

Work Past and Present

How long has it been since you visited the shop of a slater, coach maker, tinner, teazle maker, razor strop maker, or bell founder? Probably not recently. These occupations and many others, once the work of thousands of Americans, disappeared long ago.

Get Ready

Changing times create new jobs and make others outdated. It will happen—it's happening right now—in your lifetime. To explore the ways in which work has changed over the years, you'll need to think about the kinds of work people used to do and what they do today. Then you can begin to ask questions about how and why work changes. You will also want to think about what types of work interest you.

Some of your exploring will be done at the local public library or at the school library. Some research can be done at home with your family or at school with your classmates. You may want to visit businesses in your community to learn firsthand about the work people do. You will need a notebook, and a pen or a pencil.

Find Out

Start your research by thinking about what types of work people have done in the past. Think about the types of work you have read about so far in this book. Make a list of the work people did in the 1800s and a separate list of the work people did in the past that is still done today.

Next, ask older members of your family—your parents, aunts, uncles, grandparents—what adults did to earn a living when they were young. Write their answers in your notebook, and note which types of work are still done today. Also note the kinds of work that interest you.

Now you are ready to make a list of the work that is done today by looking at the Yellow Pages of the telephone book. Make a list of present-day work by using the index or by looking at advertisements. Choose from your present-day inventory an occupation that interests you. Call a company or a person listed in the Yellow Pages under that occupa-

▼ *The Stock Exchange on Wall Street attracts people who are interested in business and finance.*

tion. Arrange to visit their workplace to talk with them about their work. Ask them about the educational requirements for their work, how they were trained, and what opportunities there are for young people today in that field. Prepare a report on your interview describing the work being done there and the products or services the company provides.

Move Ahead

Would you like to know something about the future of the occupation you've chosen? Arrange for a vocational counselor or the personnel director of a local company to visit your class. Find out from this person how young people can best prepare themselves for an occupation that interests them.

Explore Some More

The following list shows just a few of the hundreds of occupations listed in the Boston Directory for the year 1882. Look at the list and think about what each occupation might have been like. Also consider how work has changed throughout American history.

bill poster	ship bread baker
blacksmith	shipwright
carver	chimney sweep
troche maker	glass blower
washer woman	horse shoer
lamp wick maker	wharfinger
marble worker	wig maker
wood carver	lace weaver

Now turn your attention to the present and future by collecting articles from newspapers and magazines about occupations, professions, training programs, and schools, Look for predictions on jobs in the future, especially occupations that interest you. If one particular occupation interests you more than all the others, collect information for your notebook.

Here is a list of occupations that are common in today's job market. Do any of these appear in your present-day inventory? Compare this list with your inventory, and make notes relating to such factors as regions, natural resources, types of industry, and education.

accountant
plumber
teacher
cabinet maker
chef
photogragher
computer programmer
physician

Increasing numbers of women have joined the American work force in fields such as science {left} and business.

Industry provides employment for people with a variety of skills and backgrounds.

615

A Call for Civil Rights

John F. Kennedy

President Kennedy delivered this speech to the nation in June 1963, a time when violence in the South over civil rights issues was growing worse.

As you read this selection, keep in mind what you learned in Lesson 2 about the civil rights movement and the response in the South to civil rights protests and sit-ins.

reprisal   retaliation or revenge

I t ought to be possible for American consumers of any color to receive equal service in places of public accommodation, such as hotels and restaurants and theaters and retail stores, without being forced to resort to demonstrations in the street, and it ought to be possible for American citizens of any color to register and to vote in a free election without interference or fear of reprisal.

It ought to be possible, in short, for every American to enjoy the privileges of being American without regard to his race or his color. In short, every American ought to have the right to be treated as he would wish to be treated, as one would wish his children to be treated. But this is not the case.

The Negro baby born in America today, regardless of the section of the Nation in which he is born, has about one-half as much chance of completing a high school as a white baby born in the same place on the same day, one-third as much chance of completing college, one-third as much chance of becoming a professional man, twice as much chance of becoming unemployed, about one-seventh as much chance of earning $10,000 a year, a life expectancy which is seven years shorter, and the prospects of earning only half as much.

This is not a sectional issue. Difficulties over segregation and dis-crimination exist in every city, in every State of the Union, producing in many cities a rising tide of discontent that threatens the public safety.

partisan   devoted to a single political party or cause

Nor is this a partisan issue. In a time of domestic crisis men of good will and generosity should be able to unite regardless of party or politics. This is not even a legal or legislative issue alone. It is better to settle these matters in the courts than on the streets, and new laws are needed at every level, but law alone cannot make men see right.

We are confronted primarily with a moral issue. It is as old as the scriptures and is as clear as the American Constitution.

The heart of the question is whether all Americans are to be afforded equal rights and equal opportunities, whether we are going to treat our fellow Americans as we want to be treated. If an American, because his skin is dark, cannot eat lunch in a restaurant open to the public, if he cannot send his children to the best public school available, if he cannot vote for the public officials who represent him, if, in short, he cannot enjoy the full and free life which all of us want, then who among us would be content to have the color of his skin changed and stand in his place? Who among us would then be content with the counsels of patience and delay?

One hundred years of delay have passed since President Lincoln freed the slaves, yet their heirs, their grandsons, are not fully free. They are not yet freed from the bonds of injustice. They are not yet freed from social and economic oppression. And this Nation, for all its hopes and all its boasts, will not be fully free until all its citizens are free.

We preach freedom around the world, and we mean it, and we cherish our freedom here at home, but are we to say to the world, and much more importantly, to each other that this is a land of the free except for the Negroes; that we have no second-class citizens except Negroes; that we have no class or caste system, no ghettoes, no master race except with respect to the Negroes?

Now the time has come for this Nation to fulfill its promise. The events in Birmingham and elsewhere have so increased the cries for equality that no city or State or legislative body can prudently choose to ignore them.

The fires of frustration and discord are burning in every city, North and South, where legal remedies are not at hand. Redress is sought in the streets, in demonstrations, parades, and protests which create tensions and threaten lives.

We face, therefore, a moral crisis as a country and as a people. It cannot be met by repressive police action. It cannot be left to increased demonstrations in the streets. It cannot be quieted by token moves or talk. It is a time to act in the Congress, in your State and local legislative body and, above all, in all of our daily lives.

It is not enough to pin the blame on others, to say this is a problem of one section of the country or another, or deplore the fact that we face. A great change is at hand, and our task, our obligation, is to make that revolution, that change, peaceful and constructive for all.

Those who do nothing are inviting shame as well as violence. Those who act boldly are recognizing right as well as equality.

Next week I shall ask the Congress of the United States to act, to make a commitment it has not fully made in this century to the proposition that race has no place in American life or law. The Federal judiciary has upheld that proposition in a series of forthright cases. The executive branch has adopted that proposition in the conduct of its affairs, including the employment of Federal personnel, the use of Federal facilities, and the sale of federally financed housing.

But there are other necessary measures which only the Congress can provide, and they must be provided at this session. The old code of equity law under which we live commands for every wrong a remedy, but in too many communities, in too many parts of the country, wrongs are inflicted on Negro citizens and there are no remedies at law. Unless the Congress acts, their only remedy is in the street.

prudently wisely

redress satisfaction for wrong done

Further Reading

Why We Can't Wait. Martin Luther King. A collection of essays in which King explains why black Americans can no longer wait for their rights.

Dreams of Freedom

Langston Hughes

The most famous writer to emerge from the Harlem Renaissance of the 1920s, Langston Hughes published many volumes of poetry, fiction, and drama during his life. Much of his work captures the longing of black Americans for freedom and acceptance. The following poems are from Selected Poems of Langston Hughes.

In Lesson 2 you read about the rise and impact of the modern civil rights movement. Think about what you learned in that lesson as you read these two poems by Langston Hughes.

I, Too

I, too, sing America.
I am the darker brother.
They send me to eat in the kitchen
When company comes,
But I laugh,
And eat well,
And grow strong.

Tomorrow,
I'll be at the table
When company comes.
Nobody'll dare
Say to me,
"Eat in the kitchen,"
Then.

Besides,
They'll see how beautiful I am
And be ashamed—

I, too, am America.

Refugee in America

There are words like *Freedom*
Sweet and wonderful to say.
On my heart-strings freedom sings
All day everyday.

There are words like *Liberty*
That almost make me cry.
If you had known what I knew
You would know why.

Chapter Review

Reviewing Key Terms

glasnost (p. 611)
sit-in (p. 602)
citizen (p. 593)
naturalization (p. 594)

A. Use a dictionary to look up the derivation of each of the key terms listed above.

B. Use each of the terms above in a complete sentence that clearly explains the meaning of the term.

C. Based on what you have read in the chapter, determine if the following statements are true or false. If a statement is false, rewrite it to make it true.

1. Because of the Soviet Union's recent policy of *glasnost*, citizens of that country have fewer freedoms than they had before.
2. A person who is born in the United States is a naturalized citizen.
3. Civil rights workers organized sit-ins as part of their violent protest against the policy of segregation.
4. Citizens in a democratic society have an obligation to participate in the government.

Exploring Concepts

A. On a separate sheet of paper, copy the chart below. In the right-hand columns, list the groups that benefited from each amendment or Supreme Court action, as well as the important features of each amendment or action.

B. Support the following statements with facts and details from the chapter.
1. Many groups used the Fourteenth Amendment as a way to gain greater rights.
2. Property qualifications for voting were gradually removed.
3. Segregation was challenged in many different ways.
4. American Indians slowly gained rights using the courts and the Constitution.
5. Women have made many political and economic advances since the 1960s.
6. There are many ways that Americans can get involved in the Democratic process.
7. There are three ways to become a citizen of the United States.
8. Several of the constitutional amendments served to expand voting rights.

Action/Date	Groups Affected by Action	Important Features
14th Amendment—1868		
15th Amendment—1870		
19th Amendment—1920		
26th Amendment—1971		
Brown v. Board of Education—1954		
Indian Civil Rights Act—1968		

Reviewing Skills

1. What steps would you follow to evaluate the strength of a newspaper editorial or other argument?
2. For what reasons does a newspaper publish editorials?
3. How can a newspaper editorial help you make up your mind about an issue?
4. In the editorial on page 599, the two writers end by saying that current polls do not give accurate information on the actual number of Americans who vote. Find two facts within the editorial that support that conclusion.
5. The editorial of page 599 notes that the recorded vote for the President excluded as much as 5 percent of the people who go to the polls. Is this information relevant to the writers' argument? Explain your answer.
6. Reread "Understanding Point of View" on pages 336-337. Using what you know about point of view, analyze the editorials in this chapter.
7. Suppose electronic voting by telephone became a national issue. Where else might you find editorials on this subject other than in newspapers?

Using Critical Thinking

1. The U.S. Constitution states that no one but natural-born citizens, those born in the United States or to American parents, may be President. Which American citizens does this exclude from the Presidency? Do you think the law should be changed? Why or why not?
2. What was "the weapon of love" Martin Luther King, Jr. urged his followers to use in their protest against unjust laws? What effect do you think King's tactics had on public opinion? Explain your answer.
3. "In a democratic society, the citizens are responsible for the actions of their government." Do you agree or disagree with this statement? Why or why not?
4. In the democracy of ancient Athens, all eligible voters devoted some part of the year to civic duties. Do Americans have the same attitudes toward democratic responsibility?
5. President Johnson called Indian citizens the "forgotten Americans." What did he mean by that statement? Do you think it still holds true today? Explain your answer.
6. In 1848 the Seneca Falls Declaration said, "The history of mankind is a history of repeated injuries and usurpations [illegal authority over a person] on the part of man toward woman, having in direct object the establishment of an absolute tyranny over her. . . ." Compare those words with Abigail Adams's letter to her husband John on page 88. Based on those two writings, and on what you have read in this chapter, do you think women are now equal to men in the eyes of the law?

Preparing for Citizenship

1. WRITING ACTIVITY Rosa Parks is an example of an ordinary person who did extraordinary things. Do some research to find out what motivated her to make the stand she did in 1955. Then write a short report on who she was and how her actions have affected life in the United States today.
2. WRITING ACTIVITY Write a short newspaper article for each of the following headlines:
   • Brown Decision Declares Segregation Unconstitutional
   • Rosa Parks Arrested for Violating Segregation Laws
   • Indians Take Over Alcatraz
3. ART ACTIVITY People say that fashion follows politics. Look through the photos in this book to see how dress styles have changed throughout American history. Design outfits that you think may appear in the future.
4. COLLABORATIVE LEARNING Divide into groups, and choose an issue in society that you believe the government has not handled effectively. Form an imaginary organization, and write a statement of your beliefs, your organization's goals, and the tactics you will use to enact change. Did each group come up with the same tactics? Could you use these tactics in a non-democratic society?

Time/Space Databank

Our Constitution Today	622
Constitution	636
Declaration of Independence	656
Primary Sources	660
Columbus: *Discovery of the New World*	660
The Mayflower Compact	663
Patrick Henry: *"Give me Liberty or Give me Death"*	664
Thomas Paine: *Common Sense*	666
The Monroe Doctrine	668
Minipedia	670
Civil War	670
Indians, American	672
Lincoln, Abraham	673
Money	674
National Park System	678
Political party	680
President of the United States	682
Revolutionary War	684
United States	686
United States, Government of the	689
Washington, George	693

Atlas	694
World: Political	694
World: Physical	696
United States: Political	698
United States: Physical	700
North America: Political	702
North America: Physical	703
United States: Population Density, 1790	704
United States: Population Density, 1870	704
United States: Population Density, 1910	705
United States: Population Density, 1990	705
United States: Climate	706
United States: Vegetation	706
United States: Precipitation	707
United States: Land Use and Resources	707
World Gross National Product	708
United States: Time Zones	708
Gazetteer	709
Glossary of Geographic Terms	712
Biographical Dictionary	714
Glossary	718

OUR CONSTITUTION TODAY

I t took just under seventeen weeks for the delegates to the Convention to complete the Constitution. But in this short period of time, the delegates were able to establish the framework of a government that functions as well today as it did 200 years ago.

How could the framers of the Constitution—men from a rural, agricultural society—devise a system of government that could handle the problems of an industrial, technological society? How could this group of white male property owners foresee the vastly different political, economic, and social problems that the government would have to deal with 200 years later? Clearly they were men of vision. They knew that the nation would grow and change. The government that they created had to be able to respond to these changes. And it had to be designed so that no one person or group could gain total power. Their solution was a flexible constitution that could respond to a variety of problems.

PRINCIPLES OF LIMITED SELF-GOVERNMENT

▲ *The person who delivers your mail is an employee of the federal government.*

The framers of the Constitution were very distrustful of power. They had seen how the King and Parliament tried to control local matters in the colonies. The colonists had protested against this control and had fought a war to gain local self-government. Now the framers had the task of creating a new government. If they gave this new government too much power, a few people might take control. The framers also worried about taking powers away from the states. Each state jealously guarded its independence and individuality and feared the creation of a strong national government.

Yet the framers of the Constitution knew that the national government had to have certain powers. The United States could not defend itself and regulate its commercial activities without the authority to raise money and enforce laws.

Federalism Divides Powers

Part of the solution lay in the idea of a federal system of government. Under a federal system, the national government would be given the power to do certain things. But it would be carefully limited from having other powers. These other powers would either belong to the states or be shared between the states and the national government.

Article I, Section 8, of the Constitution explains what powers belong to the national government. For example, only the national government may declare war or make treaties. You can imagine what might happen if any state could declare war. A state at war with another country could draw the rest of the nation into war or cause a war between states.

The Constitution also delegates, or authorizes, the national government to print or coin money and to run the post office. Think of the confusion if every state had its own money system and post office. People doing business in more than one state would never be able to keep up with the local rates and laws.

Another very important power given to the national government is the power to regulate commerce among the states. In order to understand the importance of this power, you have to understand how the gov-ernment defines commerce. Commerce is much more than the buying and selling of goods. The courts have decided that commerce refers to all things that cross state borders—goods, persons, and even communications. It also includes the means used to move these goods across state borders such as trains, trucks, or airplanes. And commerce even includes the corporations and labor used to carry out these activities.

You can see that commerce has a very broad meaning for the government. This has given Congress the power to make laws covering a wide range of activities. As examples, Congress has made laws to regulate railroads and to improve harbors and transportation routes. It has made laws to regulate wages and work hours and to make air travel safe.

What about the states? What powers do they have? The Constitution tells more about what the states cannot do than what they can do. States cannot make treaties with other countries. They cannot print money or tax goods coming into or leaving the state. So what powers do the states have? The answer lies in the Tenth Amendment to the Constitution. It reads:

> The powers not delegated to the United States by the Constitution, nor prohibited by it to the states, are reserved to the states respectively, or to the people.

This amendment was added to the Constitution to prevent the federal government from taking powers away from the states. The Constitution reserves these powers to the states.

State governments use these reserved powers to make laws and regulations about all sorts of things. For example, your state runs its public school system. It sets the safety and

The Federal System

Powers Delegated to National Government

- Regulate interstate and foreign commerce
- Set standard weights and measures
- Coin money
- Regulate copyrights and patents
- Establish lower federal courts
- Declare war
- Create and maintain armed forces
- Make foreign policy
- Make laws governing citizenship

Powers Reserved to States

- Regulate commerce within states
- Establish local governments
- Maintain system of public schools
- Make laws about marriage and divorce
- Conduct elections
- Make laws for traffic
- Make laws governing corporations

Powers Shared by National Government and States

- Collect taxes
- Borrow money
- Charter banks
- Provide for general welfare
- Punish criminal offenses

◄ *This chart shows how the Constitution divides the powers between the national and state governments. Which one has the power to make foreign policy?*

➤ *It is the duty of the states to protect and promote public safety. This police officer works for the state government.*

are just a few of the many activities of state governments.

Separate Powers Given to the Three Branches

A national government must be able to make laws, carry out the laws, and interpret the laws. The framers of the Constitution did not want any one group to have all three of these powers. They wanted to prevent any group from becoming too powerful.

The Constitution does this by dividing the powers among three separate branches of government. The legislative branch makes the laws. This is our Senate and House of Representatives. The executive branch carries out the laws and runs the government on a day-to-day basis. The President, Cabinet, and federal agencies make up the executive branch. The judicial branch interprets the laws, usually by ruling on civil and criminal cases from lower courts.

This system is clearly different from a parliamentary system. In a parliamentary system, the powers are not divided among branches of government. In Great Britain, for example, Parliament is the central governing body. This body holds both the legisla-

educational standards for your school. It decides what courses you will study, and it certifies your teachers and principal. Each state has its own code of criminal laws to protect people and their property within the state. The police officers that you see on the highway are state police. They make sure that people obey the state laws and regulations. State programs give assistance to people who are unemployed, handicapped, or elderly. These

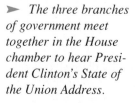

➤ *The three branches of government meet together in the House chamber to hear President Clinton's State of the Union Address.*

Checks and Balances

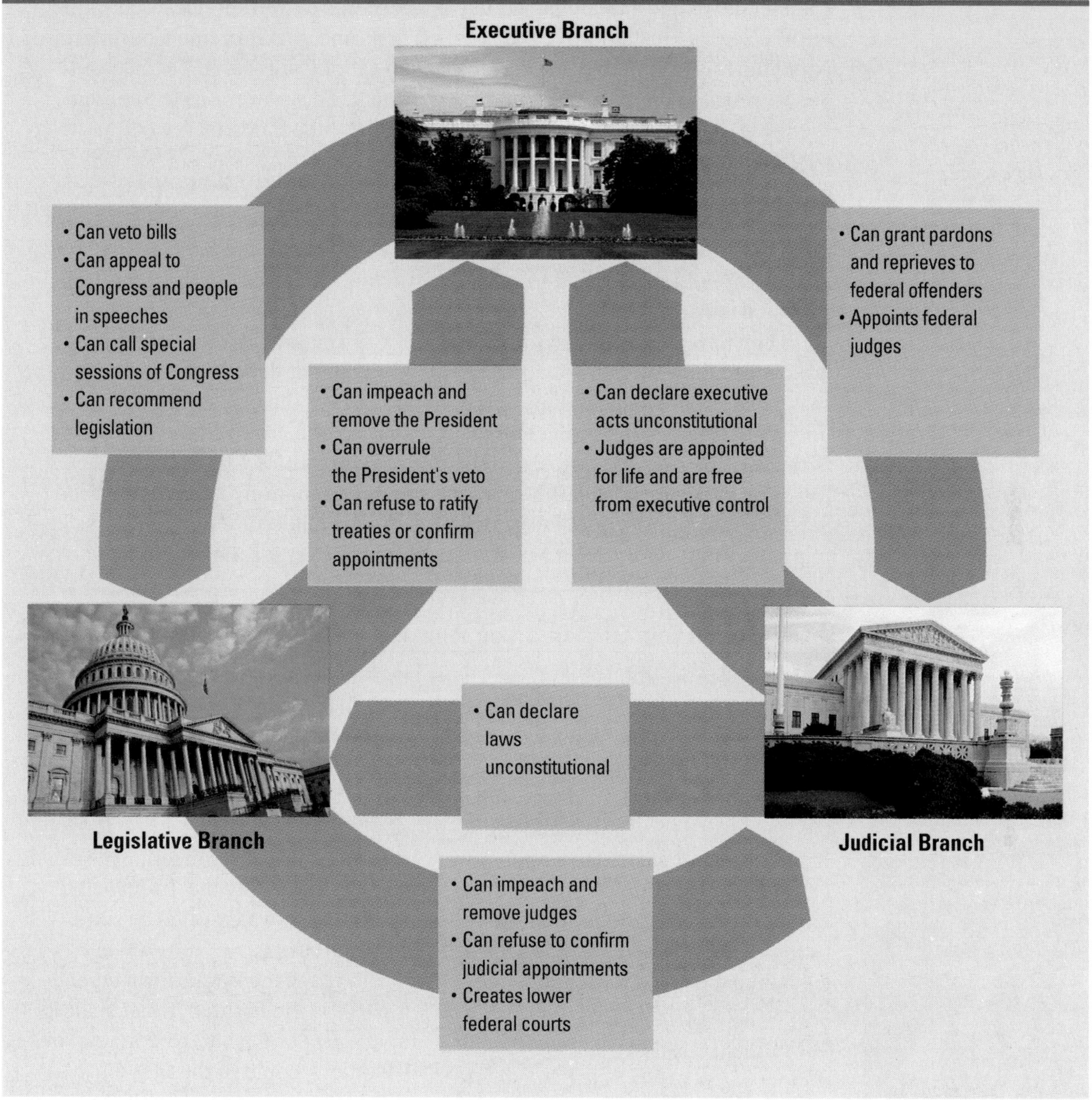

Executive Branch

- Can veto bills
- Can appeal to Congress and people in speeches
- Can call special sessions of Congress
- Can recommend legislation

- Can impeach and remove the President
- Can overrule the President's veto
- Can refuse to ratify treaties or confirm appointments

- Can declare executive acts unconstitutional
- Judges are appointed for life and are free from executive control

- Can grant pardons and reprieves to federal offenders
- Appoints federal judges

- Can declare laws unconstitutional

Legislative Branch

Judicial Branch

- Can impeach and remove judges
- Can refuse to confirm judicial appointments
- Creates lower federal courts

tive and the executive powers of the country. The executive—the British Prime Minister—is a member of the legislative branch. He or she is chosen by Parliament and is responsible to it.

Checks and Balances Provide Controls

The other way the Constitution prevents any one group from having total power is by making the three branches depend on each other for their authority. The legislative branch—the House of Representatives and the Senate—has the power to pass bills, that is, proposed laws. However, a bill must go to the President before it can become law. The President can veto, or reject, a bill that he or she believes is unwise. In turn, the House and Senate can reconsider the bill. If two-thirds of each house approve the vetoed law, it becomes law without the President's signature.

This diagram shows how each branch of government checks the activities of the other two branches.

The President nominates judges, Cabinet members, and ambassadors, but the Senate must approve the appointments. In one recent case, the Senate blocked the appointment of the President's nominee for a Cabinet position. The Senate investigated the candidate's qualifications and performance in previous jobs, and it decided that he wasn't the right person for the position. The President had to nominate someone else to fill the job.

The Supreme Court cannot make laws. It can, however, strike down laws that a majority of justices believe are unconstitutional—that is, in conflict with the principles and powers established by the Constitution. In Chapter 5, you read about the decision of the Supreme Court under John Marshall in the case *Marbury* v. *Madison*. This case was important because, for the first time, the Supreme Court declared an act of Congress to be unconstitutional. This power of the Supreme Court, called judicial review, has troubled some Americans. They believe that the Court is reaching too far into the lawmaking process. Most Americans, however, see judicial review as an important part of the American system of checks and balances.

By making the three branches of government depend on each other, the framers of the Constitution made sure that no one group could take control. And by carefully restricting the powers of the national government, the framers made sure that the states kept control over local matters.

A LIVING DOCUMENT

The Constitution is not a once-and-for-all listing of everything Americans need to govern themselves. The framers knew better than to do that. Instead, they designed a strong, flexible framework for a government. Knowing that the country would grow and change, the framers provided two important ways to add to the Constitution. They outlined a process for amending the Constitution, and they gave Congress the power to make any law that it deems "necessary and proper."

Amendments Allow Formal Changes

Realizing that people might want to make changes in the Constitution, the framers provided a way to amend it, or make formal changes. Then they made sure that these procedures had their own system of checks and balances.

A constitutional amendment can be proposed by a two-thirds vote of the Senate and the House of Representatives. It can also be proposed if two-thirds of the state legislatures vote to call a national convention (this has never happened). After Congress proposes an amendment, it must be ratified, or approved, by three-fourths of the state legislatures or by three-fourths of the states meeting in special conventions. Only the Twenty-first Amendment was ratified by state conventions.

Perhaps the best-known amendments are the first ten, which make up the Bill of Rights. As you read in Chapter 4, some of the first thirteen states were reluctant to ratify the Constitution. The first Congress proposed the Bill of Rights in response to the concerns of these states. The first three amendments secure rights that had been denied or threatened by the British. These include freedom of religion and speech and the right to assemble peacefully. Half of the Bill of Rights, in Amendments Four through Eight, deal with how trials and criminal investigations are to be carried out. The last two amendments in the

The First Amendment protects the right of these people to assemble peacefully.

◄ *These people are demonstrating their position on a public issue. Public assemblies such as this one must not disturb the peace or cause harm to anyone.*

Bill of Rights assure that individual and state rights will be preserved even if the Constitution does not mention them.

Approximately 9,000 resolutions for amending the Constitution have been proposed in Congress, but only 33 have been sent to the states for ratification. Just 26 amendments have been passed and made part of the Constitution.

Beyond the Bill of Rights, how has the amendment process been used? Here are some examples.

The framers did not see a need to raise money through an income tax. By the early years of this century, however, it was clear that the government had to find a way to raise more money. Income taxes were authorized by the Sixteenth Amendment, which was ratified in 1913.

Sometimes an amendment is needed to make something official that had been a custom before. George Washington, the first President, chose not to seek a third four-year term. The next thirty Presidents followed the custom. Franklin Roosevelt, however, was elected to a third and then a fourth term. A few years after he died, the Twenty-second Amendment set the maximum number of presidential terms at two.

On one occasion, Congress made an attempt to control social behavior. The Eighteenth Amendment outlawed the making, selling, or transporting of alcoholic beverages. This prohibition, as it was called, lasted from 1920 to 1933, when the Twenty-first Amendment repealed the Eighteenth Amendment. Why was the Eighteenth Amendment repealed? Primarily because it didn't work. Many people ignored the law by making their own alcoholic beverages or by buying it from "bootleggers" who made or imported the beverages illegally.

Laws Meet New Needs

You might wonder how a document as simple as the Constitution can be used to run a large country today. You might imagine that the limits placed on the federal government would have prevented it from responding to new issues.

One clause—just a few words—has been the source of almost all governmental growth. It is Article I,

627

Section 8, Clause 18, which gives Congress the power:

> To make all laws which shall be necessary and proper for carrying into execution the foregoing powers, and all other powers vested by this Constitution in the government of the United States, or in any department or officer thereof.

Read the clause again, slowly. It does not say exactly what Congress can do. Instead, this clause gives Congress implied powers, that is powers suggested indirectly. This means that, in addition to the clearly expressed powers given to it in the Constitution, Congress can pass laws that help it run the nation. Clause 18 allows Congress to stretch its powers as the needs of the country change. This is why it is sometimes called the "elastic clause."

▲ *The lawmaking powers of Congress affect a wide range of activities. These air traffic controllers are subject to federal legislation.*

The first use of implied powers under the elastic clause occurred in 1791. According to the Constitution, Congress has the power to tax, borrow money, and regulate commerce. Some members of Congress thought the government had to have a national bank in order to use these powers.

Congress used the elastic clause to justify setting up a national bank. It said that a national bank would help Congress to run the country.

Since 1791, Congress has used the elastic clause to pass laws in many different areas. One example is federal legislation in education. You might wonder why the federal government is involved in education. After all, the Constitution gives the states the authority to establish and maintain public schools. But the Constitution also gives Congress the power to "provide for the general welfare of the United States." Congress has stretched this power to include dealing with educational issues that affect large numbers of Americans. For example, many students in the United States have a native language other than English. Because this issue affects many Americans, the federal government has gotten involved in bilingual education. The Bilingual Education Act of 1968 provided federal aid for non-native speakers to receive instruction in both English and their native language.

A more recent example of the use of the elastic clause is the Federal Election Campaign Act passed in 1971. The purpose of this act is to control the use of money in federal elections. It requires detailed reporting of campaign contributions and spending by all candidates. The passage of the Federal Election Campaign Act reflects people's growing disgust with the "dirty tricks" used by political parties to get their candidates elected. The "last straw" in dirty tricks was the break-in of Democratic Party offices in the Watergate Hotel by Republican Party spies in the 1972 presidential election. President Richard Nixon's attempts to cover up the break-in forced him to resign the presidency. In response to the Watergate scandal, Congress also established the Federal Election Commission in 1974. This

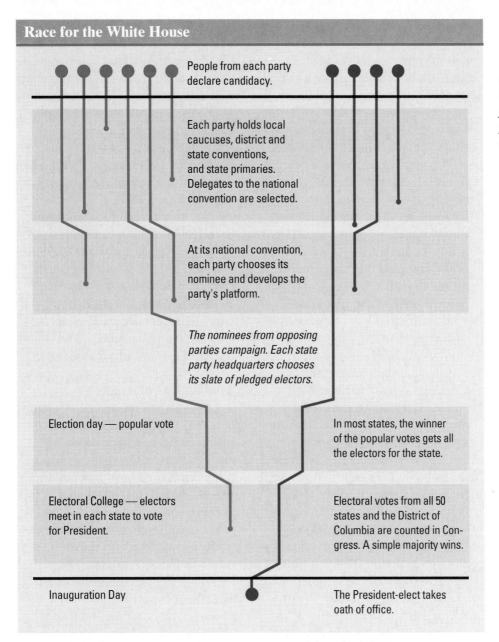

Race for the White House

People from each party declare candidacy.

Each party holds local caucuses, district and state conventions, and state primaries. Delegates to the national convention are selected.

At its national convention, each party chooses its nominee and develops the party's platform.

The nominees from opposing parties campaign. Each state party headquarters chooses its slate of pledged electors.

Election day — popular vote

In most states, the winner of the popular votes gets all the electors for the state.

Electoral College — electors meet in each state to vote for President.

Electoral votes from all 50 states and the District of Columbia are counted in Congress. A simple majority wins.

Inauguration Day

The President-elect takes oath of office.

◄ *The race to the White House begins when people from each political party declare their candidacy.*

independent agency in the executive branch makes sure that candidates and their supporters obey the law.

The Election System Evolves

Constitutional change, however, can take place by means other than formal amendment or congressional legislation. In some cases, custom and the actions of the political parties have also played a part in constitutional change. One example is the way in which the President and the Vice President are elected.

The framers of the Constitution disagreed about how the President should be elected. Some delegates thought that Congress should choose the President. Others thought that this would give Congress too much control over the President. Some of the delegates suggested that the states choose the President but others thought this would make the states too powerful. Then an idea was presented which the delegates agreed was the best solution. Each state would choose a special group of people called electors. The number of electors for each state would be equal in number to its repre-

OUR CONSTITUTION TODAY

sentatives in Congress. These electors would be free to use their own judgment in voting for a President. The electors, who together make up the electoral college, would cast their votes at their state capitals. Then their votes would be sent to Congress to be counted and the winner announced.

Why weren't people given the opportunity to vote directly? Because the delegates at the Constitutional Convention in 1787 distrusted the ability of the people to decide intelligently. Communications were poor at the time, and they thought it would be difficult for ordinary people to know the candidates.

With the development of political parties in the early 1800s, however, the electoral college system began to change. In our present system, each political party in each state chooses a slate, or list, of candidates for electors. At its national convention, each party also chooses its candidates for President and Vice President. The electors chosen by each party are no longer free to choose a President; they are pledged to vote for their party's candidates. When people go to the polls, they actually vote for the electors of the party whose presidential candidate they prefer; they do not vote for the presidential candidates themselves. In fact, at one time the names of the electors actually appeared on the ballot. But today most states list only the names of the presidential and vice-presidential candidates.

The electoral college system has its defects. In every state except Maine, the presidential election is a winner-take-all contest. Whichever slate of electors wins the popular vote—the majority of votes by the people—wins all of that state's electoral votes. It is possible for the presidential and vice-presidential candidate to win the popular vote overall but lose the electoral vote. For example, a slate of candidates could win by huge margins in small states and lose by just a few votes in the larger states. This has happened three times, in the elections of 1824, 1876, and 1888.

Another defect is that the entire presidential election can fail if no candidate gets a majority of votes in the electoral college. In such a case, the election is decided in the House of Representatives. If a strong third party grows, the House may not be able to achieve a majority. The country could be without a President.

Reforms Are Proposed

In every session since 1789, members of Congress have proposed constitutional amendments to change the election system. One logical proposal is the direct popular election of the President and Vice President. Each person's vote in the country would count equally across the whole country. The candidate with the most votes would become President.

Why hasn't a constitutional amendment been used to change the system? One reason is that three-fourths of the state legislatures would have to ratify the proposed amendment. Small states, which enjoy greater power than large states in the electoral college, would be reluctant to ratify an amendment that would take away their power.

The flexibility of the Constitution has permitted the government to cope with a wide variety of issues and problems. Because necessary changes can be made in the Constitution, it has survived more than 200 years as a workable framework of government.

Benjamin Harrison, the Republican presidential candidate in 1888, supported high tariffs to protect American industry. John F. Kennedy ran against Richard M. Nixon in the 1960 race to the White House.

OUR NATIONAL GOVERNMENT AT WORK TODAY

Today, the federal government functions very much as its designers intended more than 200 years ago. Each of the branches of the federal government has its specific duties and responsibilities. Together the three branches provide a system of checks and balances.

The President Acts As Chief Executive

Just as in any large company, the President's job is that of a chief, or leader. As chief executive, the President issues rules and directives for running the executive branch of the government. He or she can also grant reprieves or pardons to criminals or those accused of crimes.

The President is the chief of state, negotiating treaties and other international agreements (as President Jimmy Carter did in the Camp David accords between Israel and Egypt in 1978). As chief diplomat, the President appoints ambassadors to other countries and receives the ambassadors and ministers of other countries.

As chief administrator, the President chooses the heads of fourteen executive departments and many

The Executive Branch

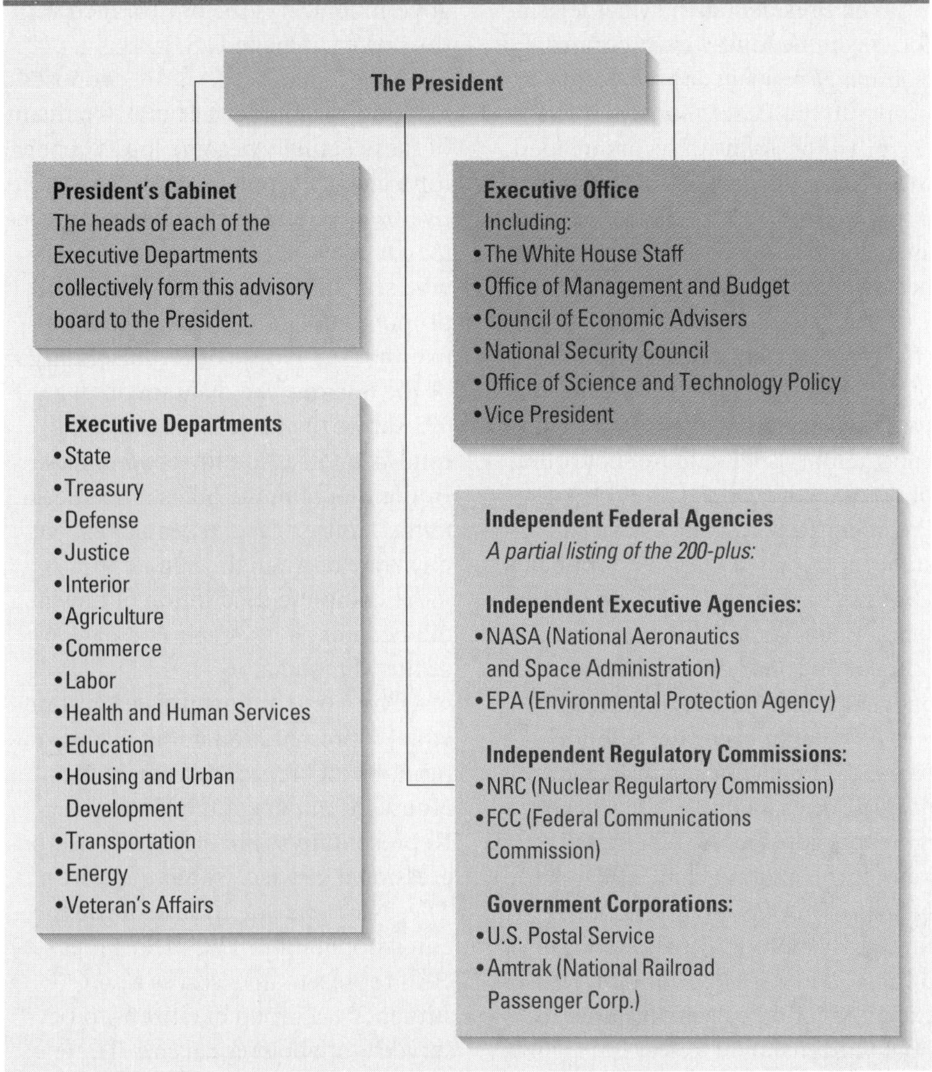

The President

President's Cabinet
The heads of each of the Executive Departments collectively form this advisory board to the President.

Executive Departments
- State
- Treasury
- Defense
- Justice
- Interior
- Agriculture
- Commerce
- Labor
- Health and Human Services
- Education
- Housing and Urban Development
- Transportation
- Energy
- Veteran's Affairs

Executive Office
Including:
- The White House Staff
- Office of Management and Budget
- Council of Economic Advisers
- National Security Council
- Office of Science and Technology Policy
- Vice President

Independent Federal Agencies
A partial listing of the 200-plus:

Independent Executive Agencies:
- NASA (National Aeronautics and Space Administration)
- EPA (Environmental Protection Agency)

Independent Regulatory Commissions:
- NRC (Nuclear Regulartory Commission)
- FCC (Federal Communications Commission)

Government Corporations:
- U.S. Postal Service
- Amtrak (National Railroad Passenger Corp.)

◄ *This chart shows the many agencies and departments in the Executive branch. Who makes up the President's Cabinet?*

631

➤ *Illinois Senator Carol Moseley-Braun takes part in the confirmation hearings of Supreme Court Justice Ruth Bader Ginsburg. The Senate has the job of confirming or rejecting the President's nominations to the Supreme Court and other high-level government offices.*

other agencies. If the Vice President dies or is otherwise removed from office, the President may choose a replacement.

The President is the chief legislator, recommending new programs. For example, President John F. Kennedy proposed the Peace Corps and President Lyndon Johnson recommended the War on Poverty. A President may also veto laws that he or she feels are against the national interest or his or her own beliefs.

The President is commander in chief of the armed forces. In times of war, he or she has the final authority. The President may also try to influence military spending by supporting or recommending certain programs. President Ronald Reagan, for instance, campaigned for the Strategic Defense Initiatives (S.D.I., or "Star Wars"). President Bill Clinton proposed an increase in the defense budget to raise military salaries.

As chief of his or her political party, the President can influence party policies and help other party members get elected. Finally, the President is the nation's chief citizen. He or she represents all other United States citizens at official meetings in other countries. The President is also expected to serve as an example to other citizens.

Congress Passes Laws

Congress—the House of Representatives and the Senate—is the legislative or lawmaking branch of the government. It is the only branch with the power to make U.S. laws.

Many ideas for laws are proposed to Congress, but fewer than 10 percent of these actually become law. The idea for a law may come from the executive branch, a congressional committee, or even from private individuals who see a need for a new law. These proposed laws are introduced as bills in either the House of Representatives or the Senate. The diagram on page 633 shows the basic steps that a bill follows on its route to becoming law. In this diagram, the bill is introduced in the House of Representatives, but bills may begin in the Senate too. A more complete description of how a bill becomes a law begins on page 690 of the Minipedia.

The Constitution gives each state equal representation in the Senate and proportional representation in the House. Members of the House of Representatives are elected from Congressional districts within the states. These districts are, by law, of roughly equal population. This means that each representative serves a constituency—a group of citizens to be served—of about equal size. There are

435 representatives in the House. The Constitution sets the minimum age of representatives at 25.

The Senate is much smaller than the House with just two senators from each state. Both senators are elected at large. In other words, their constituency consists of the entire population of their state. Senators must be at least 30 years old.

Because of its larger size, the House of Representatives imposes stricter rules on debate than does the Senate. Much of the House's work is done in committees, far from the House "floor," the chamber where actual laws are debated. In the Senate, debate can be much freer and can treat broader national issues. The Senate also depends heavily on committee work, but not as much as the House.

Senators were selected by state legislatures until 1913 when the Seventeenth Amendment was ratified. The only directly elected national officials had been members of the House.

A Bill Becomes Law

House of Representatives
- A new law is needed. A bill is drafted and sent to the House.
- The Clerk of the House sends the bill to a committee.
- The House committee studies the bill and makes revisions. The committee approves the bill and puts it on the House calendar.
- The Rules Committee decides to send the bill to the floor of the House.
- The bill is debated on the floor of the House. The House approves the bill and sends it to the Senate.

The Senate
- The clerk of the Senate sends the bill to the "presiding officer" who assigns the bill to a committee.
- The Senate committee studies the bill, makes several revisions, and approves it. The bill goes on the Senate calendar.
- The Senate majority leader chooses to send the bill to the Senate floor.
- The Senators debate the amended bill and approve it. The amended bill goes to a conference committee.

The Conference Committee
The conference committee, made up of members from both houses, works out differences between House and Senate versions. The revised bill goes back to both houses and is approved.

The President
- The bill goes to the President. If he does not act on the bill in 10 days, it becomes law.
- The President can approve the bill by signing it.
- The President can veto the bill. Congress can override the veto by a two-thirds vote.

◄ *A bill must go through many stages before it can become law. Follow the route of this bill as it moves through the legislative process.*

633

Today, senators are also elected by the people.

Both houses of Congress are involved in policing the ethics of government officials, including themselves. The Senate and House have

▲ *Much of the actual work of Congress is done in committees such as this Senate subcommittee.*

the power to investigate wrongdoing among government officials. They can also censure, or publicly condemn, any member for serious misdeeds.

The Supreme Court Guards Our Rights

The framers of the Constitution agreed on the need for a federal court system that would include a Supreme Court. They were clear about the types of cases that federal courts could hear. Beyond that, they didn't give many details. The task of organizing the court system was left to Congress.

What kinds of cases can the Supreme Court and lower federal courts hear? The answer is in Article III, Section 2, Clause 1, of the Constitution. For the most part, federal jurisdiction, or the authority to hear and decide a case, is limited to those cases in which the United States govern-

ment has a direct interest. These include cases in which states are in dispute or citizens from different states have sued each other. Any matter that is not mentioned in the Constitution is left to the various state court systems to decide.

A case usually ends up at the Supreme Court after it has traveled through at least one lower court. As you can see in the illustration on page 635, a case can go from a District Court through a Court of Appeals to the Supreme Court. The Supreme Court can also hear cases on appeal from the highest state courts. It can review the decisions of any of the state supreme courts if that decision has something to do with a question of federal law.

When the Supreme Court hears an appeal, it reviews the decisions of the lower court. It decides if the lower court's previous decision was based soundly on the principles of law and did not violate the Constitution. In these cases, the Supreme Court is said to have appellate jurisdiction, or authority to hear appeals. In a few special circumstances, the Supreme Court has original jurisdiction. This means that it can hear a case firsthand. This can happen in cases where two states disagree with each other or one state disagrees with the federal government.

About 5,000 cases are appealed to the Supreme Court each year. However, the Supreme Court agrees to hear only a small fraction of them. In many cases, the justices agree with the lower court's decision, and often the justices see no important point of law to be decided.

About 120 cases are actually reviewed by the Court every year. Most decisions are made and announced without giving reasons. For some cases, however, the justices may write long or short opinions explaining their decisions.

Only the most important cases from state and lower federal courts reach the Supreme Court. Sometimes the justices are called upon to interpret or defend important concepts of the Constitution. In this way, the Supreme Court guards our constitutional rights against laws or law enforcement methods that would ignore those rights or take them away.

The Supreme Court has made important decisions on many different issues. Here are a few significant cases. *NAACP* v. *Alabama* (1958) affirmed the First Amendment's guarantee of freedom of assembly by deciding that the state of Alabama could not force the National Association for the Advancement of Colored People to publish its membership list. In *Mapp* v. *Ohio* (1961), the Court upheld the Fourth Amendment prohibition against unreasonable search and seizure, saying that materials illegally seized in a raid could not be used as evidence. In 1963, the Court extended to everyone the right to legal counsel for those accused of serious crimes (*Gideon* v. *Wainwright*). The Fifth Amendment right against self-incrimination (testifying against oneself) was extended to suspects who had not yet been charged. In *Escobedo* v. *Illinois* and *Miranda* v. *Alabama*, the Court set guidelines for police questioning.

The Constitution Serves the People

Through interpretation by the Supreme Court, amendments, and legislation, the Constitution is a living piece of American history. Far more than just a yellowing piece of parchment, the Constitution is a daily guide for the U.S. government. It provides for a strong central government, assuring that national tasks such as defense will be carried out. It then limits the central government to just those essential tasks. The Constitution preserves the rights of individuals to determine their own destinies and to be treated fairly by their government. For more than 200 years, the Constitution has provided guidance and protection, yet is as fresh and vital today as it was when it was new.

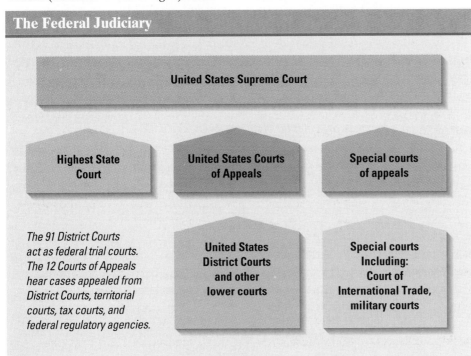

The Federal Judiciary

United States Supreme Court

Highest State Court

United States Courts of Appeals

Special courts of appeals

The 91 District Courts act as federal trial courts. The 12 Courts of Appeals hear cases appealed from District Courts, territorial courts, tax courts, and federal regulatory agencies.

United States District Courts and other lower courts

Special courts Including: Court of International Trade, military courts

◄ *The Supreme Court hears cases on appeal from the highest state courts, the U.S. Courts of Appeals, and from the special courts of appeal. In only a few special circumstances does a court case begin in the Supreme Court.*

★ ★ ★ ★ ★ ★ ★ ★ ★

The Constitution of the United States

PREAMBLE*

The Preamble states the purposes of the Constitution. The writers wanted to strengthen the national government and to secure peace for the United States. The Preamble makes it clear that the government's power comes from the people.

We the people of the United States, in order to form a more perfect union, establish justice, insure domestic tranquility, provide for the common defense, promote the general welfare, and secure the blessings of liberty to ourselves and our posterity, do ordain and establish this Constitution for the United States of America.

ARTICLE 1
LEGISLATIVE BRANCH

SECTION 1. CONGRESS

All legislative powers herein granted shall be vested in a Congress of the United States, which shall consist of a Senate and House of Representatives.

Section 1 gives Congress the power to make laws. Congress has two parts, the House of Representatives and the Senate. These two parts form the federal government's legislative branch.

SECTION 2. HOUSE OF REPRESENTATIVES

1. *Election and Term of Members* The House of Representatives shall be composed of members chosen every second year by the people of the several States, and the electors in each State shall have the qualifications requisite for electors of the most numerous branch of the State legislature.

Clause 1 Citizens elect the members of the House of Representatives every two years.

2. *Qualifications* No person shall be a representative who shall not have attained to the age of twenty-five years, and been seven years a citizen of the United States, and who shall not, when elected, be an inhabitant of that State in which he shall be chosen.

Clause 2 Representatives must be at least 25 years old. They must have been United States citizens for at least seven years. They must also live in the state they represent, but are not required to live in their district.

Clause 3 The number of representatives each state has is based on its population. The biggest states have the most representatives. Each state must have at least one representative. Congress has fixed the number of representatives in the House at 435 by a legislative act. The portion of the clause that states only three fifths of the slaves were to be counted for purposes of representation was overruled by the Thirteenth Amendment, which freed the slaves.

3. *Number of Representatives per State* Representatives ~~and direct taxes~~ shall be apportioned among the several States which may be included within this Union, according to their respective numbers, ~~which shall be determined by adding to the whole number of free persons, including those bound to service for a term of years, and excluding Indians not taxed, three-fifths of all other persons.~~** *The actual enumeration shall be made within*

* The titles of the Preamble, and of each article, section, clause, and amendment have been added to make the Constitution easier to read. These titles are not in the original document.

** Parts of the Constitution have been crossed out to show that they are not in force any more. They have been changed by amendments or they no longer apply.

three years after the first meeting of the Congress of the United States, and within every subsequent term of ten years, in such manner as they shall by law direct. The number of representatives shall not exceed one for every thirty thousand, but each State shall have at least one representative; and until such enumeration shall be made, the State of New Hampshire shall be entitled to choose three, Massachusetts eight, Rhode Island and Providence Plantations one, Connecticut five, New York six, New Jersey Four, Pennsylvania eight, Delaware one, Maryland six, Virginia ten, North Carolina five, South Carolina five, and Georgia three.

4. ***Vacancies*** *When vacancies happen in the representation from any State, the executive authority thereof shall issue writs of election to fill such vacancies.*

5. ***Special Powers*** *The House of Representatives shall choose their speaker and other officers, and shall have the sole power of impeachment.*

SECTION 3. SENATE

1. ***Number, Term, and Selection of Members*** *The Senate of the United States shall be composed of two senators from each State,* chosen by the legislature thereof, *for six years; and each senator shall have one vote.*

2. ***Overlapping Terms and Filling Vacancies*** *Immediately after they shall be assembled in consequence of the first election, they shall be divided as equally as may be into three classes.* The seats of the senators of the first class shall be vacated at the expiration of the second year, of the second class at the expiration of the fourth year, and of the third class at the expiration of the sixth year, *so that one-third may be chosen every second year;* and if vacancies happen by resignation, or otherwise, during the recess of the legislature of any State, the executive thereof may make temporary appointments until the next meeting of the legislature, which shall then fill such vacancies.

3. ***Qualifications*** *No person shall be a senator who shall not have attained to the age of thirty years, and been nine years a citizen of the United States, and who shall not, when elected, be an inhabitant of that State for which he shall be chosen.*

4. ***President of the Senate*** *The Vice President of the United States shall be President of the Senate, but shall have no vote, unless they be equally divided.*

5. ***Other Officers*** *The Senate shall choose their other officers, and also a President pro tempore, in the absence of the Vice President, or when he shall exercise the office of President of the United States.*

6. ***Impeachment Trials*** *The Senate shall have the sole power to try all impeachments. When sitting for that purpose, they shall be on oath or affirmation. When the President of the United States is tried, the Chief Justice shall preside: and no person shall be*

Clause 4 *Executive authority* refers to the governor of a state.

Clause 5 The speaker of the House is chosen by the party that has a majority in the House.

Clause 1 In each state, citizens elect two members of the Senate. This gives all states, whether big or small, equal power in the Senate. Senators serve six-year terms. The original Constitution specified that state legislatures choose the senators for their states. Today, however, people elect their senators directly. The Seventeenth Amendment made this change in 1913.

Clause 3 Senators must be at least 30 years old and United States citizens for at least nine years. Like representatives, they must live in the state they represent.

Clause 4 The Vice President of the United States acts as the President, or chief officer, of the Senate. The Vice President votes only in cases of a tie.

Clause 6 If the House of Representatives impeaches an official for a crime, the Senate conducts the trial. If two-thirds of the senators find the official guilty, then the person is removed from office. The only President ever impeached was Andrew Johnson in 1868. He was found not guilty.

Clause 7 The term judgment in this clause means conviction by the Senate.

Clause 1 Unless Congress acts, each state may decide where and when to hold elections. Today, as a result of an 1872 act of Congress, congressional elections are held in even-numbered years, on the Tuesday after the first Monday in November.

Clause 2 The Constitution requires Congress to meet at least once a year. In 1933, the Twentieth Amendment moved the required meeting date of Congress to January 3.

Clause 1 A quorum is the smallest number of members that must be present for an organization to hold a meeting. For each house of Congress, this number is the majority, or more than one-half, of its members.

Clause 2 Both Houses of Congress have developed detailed rules of procedure.

Clause 3 The Constitution requires each house to keep a record of its proceedings. *The Congressional Record* is published every day. It allows any person to look up the votes of his or her representative.

Clause 4 Both Houses of Congress must meet in the same place and remain in session for the same period of time.

Clause 1 Congress sets the salaries of its members, and they are paid by the federal government. No member can be arrested for anything he or she says while in office. This protection allows members to speak freely in Congress.

Clause 2 Emolument means salary. Members of Congress cannot hold other federal offices during their terms. This rule protects the checks and balances system set up by the Constitution.

★ ★ ★ ★ ★ ★ ★ ★ ★

convicted without the concurrence of two-thirds of the members present.

7. ***Penalties*** *Judgment in cases of impeachment shall not extend further than to removal from office, and disqualification to hold and enjoy any office of honor, trust or profit under the United States: but the party convicted shall nevertheless be liable and subject to indictment, trial, judgment and punishment, according to law.*

SECTION 4. ELECTIONS AND MEETINGS

1. ***Election of Congress*** *The times, places and manner of holding elections for senators and representatives shall be prescribed in each State by the legislature thereof; but the Congress may at any time by law make or alter such regulations, except as to the places of choosing senators.*

2. ***Annual Sessions*** *The Congress shall assemble at least once in every year,* ~~and such meeting shall be on the first Monday in December, unless they shall by law appoint a different day.~~

SECTION 5. RULES OF PROCEDURE

1. ***Organization*** *Each house shall be the judge of the elections, returns and qualifications of its own members, and a majority of each shall constitute a quorum to do business; but a smaller number may adjourn from day to day, and may be authorized to compel the attendance of absent members, in such manner, and under such penalties as each house may provide.*

2. ***Rules*** *Each house may determine the rules of its proceedings, punish its members for disorderly behavior, and, with the concurrence of two-thirds, expel a member.*

3. ***Journal*** *Each house shall keep a journal of its proceedings, and from time to time publish the same, excepting such parts as may in their judgment require secrecy; and the yeas and nays of the members of either house on any question shall, at the desire of one-fifth of those present, be entered on the journal.*

4. ***Adjournment*** *Neither house, during the session of Congress, shall, without the consent of the other, adjourn for more than three days, nor to any other place than that in which the two houses shall be sitting.*

SECTION 6. PRIVILEGES AND RESTRICTIONS

1. ***Pay and Protection*** *The senators and representatives shall receive a compensation for their services, to be ascertained by law, and paid out of the treasury of the United States. They shall in all cases, except treason, felony and breach of the peace, be privileged from arrest during their attendance at the session of their respective houses, and in going to and returning from the same; and for any speech or debate in either house, they shall not be questioned in any other place.*

2. ***Restrictions*** *No senator or representative shall, during the time for which he was elected, be appointed to any civil office under the authority of the United States, which shall have been created, or the emoluments thereof shall have been increased during such time; and*

no person holding any office under the United States shall be a member of either house during his continuance in office.

SECTION 7. MAKING LAWS

1. *Tax Bills All bills for raising revenue shall originate in the House of Representatives; but the Senate may propose or concur with amendments as on other bills.*

2. *Passing a Law Every bill which shall have passed the House of Representatives and the Senate, shall, before it becomes a law, be presented to the President of the United States; if he approve he shall sign it, but if not he shall return it, with his objections to that house in which it shall have originated, who shall enter the objections at large on their journal, and proceed to reconsider it. If after such reconsideration two-thirds of that house shall agree to pass the bill, it shall be sent, together with the objections, to the other house, by which it shall likewise be reconsidered, and if approved by two-thirds of that house, it shall become a law. But in all such cases the votes of both houses shall be determined by yeas and nays, and the names of the persons voting for and against the bill shall be entered on the journal of each house respectively. If any bill shall not be returned by the President within ten days (Sundays excepted) after it shall have been presented to him, the same shall be a law, in like manner as if he had signed it, unless the Congress by their adjournment prevent its return, in which case it shall not be a law.*

3. *Orders and Resolutions Every order, resolution, or vote to which the concurrence of the Senate and House of Representatives may be necessary (except on a question of adjournment) shall be presented to the President of the United States; and before the same shall take effect, shall be approved by him, or being disapproved by him, shall be repassed by two-thirds of the Senate and House of Representatives, according to the rules and limitations prescribed in the case of a bill.*

SECTION 8. POWERS DELEGATED TO CONGRESS

1. *Taxation The Congress shall have power to lay and collect taxes, duties, imposts, and excises, to pay the debts and provide for the common defense and general welfare of the United States; but all duties, imposts and excises shall be uniform throughout the United States;*

2. *Borrowing To borrow money on the credit of the United States;*

3. *Commerce To regulate commerce with foreign nations, and among the several States, and with the Indian tribes;*

4. *Naturalization and Bankruptcy To establish a uniform rule of naturalization, and uniform laws on the subject of bankruptcies through the United States;*

5. *Coins and Measures To coin money, regulate the value thereof, and of foreign coin, and fix the standard of weights and measures;*

6. *Counterfeiting To provide for the punishment of counterfeiting the securities and current coin of the United States;*

7. *Post Offices To establish post offices and post roads;*

Clause 1 *Revenue* is money raised by the government through taxes. Only the House of Representatives can introduce bills that tax the people.

Clause 2 A bill, or proposed law, must be passed by the majority of members in each house of Congress. Then it is sent to the President. If the President signs it, the bill becomes a law. If the President refuses to sign it and Congress is in session, the bill becomes law 10 days after the President receives it.

The President can also *veto*, or reject, a bill by sending it back to the house where it was introduced. However, if each house of Congress repasses the bill by a two-thirds vote, it becomes a law. Passing a law after the President has vetoed it is called overriding a veto. This process is an important part of the checks and balances system set up by the Constitution.

Clause 3 Congress can also pass orders and resolutions that have the same power as laws. Such acts are also subject to the President's veto. This clause prevents Congress from bypassing the President by calling bills by other names.

Clause 1 *Duties* are tariffs, *excises* are taxes on the production or sale of certain goods, and *imposts* are taxes in general. Only Congress has the power to collect taxes and spend tax money.

Clause 3 Congress controls trade with foreign countries and interstate trade.

Clause 4 *Naturalization* is the process by which a person from another country becomes a United States citizen. *Bankruptcy* is the condition in which an individual or business is unable to pay its debts. Congress has the power to pass laws on these two procedures.

★ ★ ★ ★ ★ ★ ★ ★ ★

Clause 8 A *copyright* protects an author's words. *Patents* allow inventors to profit from their work by keeping control over it for a certain number of years. Congress grants patents to encourage scientific research.

Clause 11 Only Congress can declare war on another country.
Clauses 12, 13, 14 Congress controls the army and navy. It has the power to decide the size of the armed forces and to write the laws that govern them.

Clause 15 Today the militia is called the National Guard. The National Guard often helps people after floods, tornadoes, and other disasters. Governors usually have control over the National Guard, though it can be placed under the command of the President.

Clause 17 Congress makes the laws for Washington, D.C., the nation's capital. In 1973, Congress gave residents of the District of Columbia the right to elect local officials.

Clause 18 This clause allows Congress to make laws on issues, such as television or radio, that are not mentioned in the Constitution. This clause is often called the *elastic clause* because it allows Congress to stretch its powers.

Clause 1 This clause was another compromise between the North and the South. It prevented Congress from regulating the slave trade for 20 years. Congress outlawed the slave trade in 1808.
Clause 2 A writ of habeas corpus requires the government to either charge a person in jail with a particular crime, or else let the person go free. Except in emergencies, Congress cannot deny the right of a person to a writ.

Clause 4 The Sixteenth Amendment gave Congress the power to tax income without regard to state populations.

8. *Copyrights and Patents* To promote the progress of science and useful arts by securing for limited times to authors and inventors the exclusive right to their respective writings and discoveries;

9. *Courts* To constitute tribunals inferior to the Supreme Court;

10. *Piracy* To define and punish piracies and felonies committed on the high seas, and offenses against the law of nations;

11. *Declaring War* To declare war, ~~grant letters of marque and reprisal~~, and make rules concerning captures on land and water;

12. *Army* To raise and support armies, but no appropriation of money to that use shall be for a longer term than two years;

13. *Navy* To provide and maintain a navy;

14. *Military Regulations* To make rules for the government and regulation of the land and naval forces;

15. *Militia* To provide for calling forth the militia to execute the laws of the Union, suppress insurrections and repel invasions;

16. *Militia Regulations* To provide for organizing, arming, and disciplining the militia, and for governing such part of them as may be employed in the service of the United States, reserving to the States respectively the appointment of the officers, and the authority of training the militia according to the discipline prescribed by Congress;

17. *National Capital* To exercise exclusive legislation in all cases whatsoever, over such district (not exceeding ten miles square) as may, by cession of particular States and the acceptance of Congress, become the seat of the government of the United States, and to exercise like authority over all places purchased by the consent of the legislature of the State in which the same shall be, for the erection of forts, magazines, arsenals, dockyards, and other needful buildings; and

18. *Necessary Laws* To make all laws which shall be necessary and proper for carrying into execution the foregoing powers, and all other powers vested by this Constitution in the government of the United States, or in any department or officer thereof.

SECTION 9. POWERS DENIED TO CONGRESS

1. *Slave Trade* ~~The migration or importation of such persons as any of the States now existing shall think proper to admit, shall not be prohibited by the Congress prior to the year one thousand eight hundred and eight, but a tax or duty may be imposed on such importation, not exceeding ten dollars for each person.~~

2. *Habeas Corpus* The privilege of the writ of habeas corpus shall not be suspended, unless when in cases of rebellion or invasion the public safety may require it.

3. *Special Laws* No bill of attainder or ex post facto law shall be passed.

4. *Direct Taxes* ~~No capitation, or other direct, tax shall be laid, unless in proportion to the census or enumeration herein before directed to be taken.~~

★ ★ ★ ★ ★ ★ ★ ★ ★

5. ***Export Taxes*** *No tax or duty shall be laid on articles exported from any State.*

6. ***Ports*** *No preference shall be given by any regulation of commerce or revenue to the ports of one State over those of another; nor shall vessels bound to, or from, one State be obliged to enter, clear, or pay duties in another.*

7. ***Regulations on Spending*** *No money shall be drawn from the treasury, but in consequence of appropriations made by law; and a regular statement and account of the receipts and expenditures of all public money shall be published from time to time.*

8. ***Titles of Nobility and Gifts*** *No title of nobility shall be granted by the United States: and no person holding any office of profit or trust under them, shall, without the consent of the Congress, accept of any present, emolument, office, or title, of any kind whatever, from any king, prince, or foreign State.*

SECTION 10. POWERS DENIED TO THE STATES

1. ***Complete Restrictions*** *No State shall enter into any treaty, alliance, or confederation; grant letters of marque and reprisal; coin money; emit bills of credit; make anything but gold and silver coin a tender in payment of debts; pass any bill of attainder, ex post facto law, or law impairing the obligation of contracts, or grant any title of nobility.*

2. ***Partial Restrictions*** *No State shall, without the consent of the Congress, lay any imposts or duties on imports or exports, except what may be absolutely necessary for executing its inspection laws: and the net produce of all duties and imposts laid by any State on imports or exports, shall be for the use of the treasury of the United States; and all such laws shall be subject to the revision and control of the Congress.*

3. ***Other Restrictions*** *No State shall, without the consent of Congress, lay any duty of tonnage, keep troops, or ships of war in time of peace, enter into any agreement or compact with another State, or with a foreign power, or engage in war, unless actually invaded, or in such imminent danger as will not admit of delay.*

ARTICLE II
EXECUTIVE BRANCH

SECTION 1. PRESIDENT AND VICE PRESIDENT

1. ***Term of Office*** *The executive power shall be vested in a President of the United States of America. He shall hold his office during the term of four years, and, together with the Vice President, chosen for the same term, be elected as follows:*

2. ***Electoral College*** *Each State shall appoint, in such manner as the legislature thereof may direct, a number of electors, equal to the whole number of senators and representatives to which the State may be entitled in the Congress; but no senator or representative, or person holding an office of trust or profit under the United States, shall be appointed an elector.*

Clause 5 Congress cannot tax exports.

Clause 6 When regulating trade, Congress must treat all states equally. Also, states cannot tax goods traveling between the states.

Clause 7 Congress controls the spending of public money. This clause checks the President's power.

Clause 8 Congress cannot award titles of nobility. Americans cannot accept titles of nobility unless Congress gives its consent.

Clause 1 The Constitution prevents the states from acting like individual countries. States cannot make treaties with foreign nations. They cannot issue their own money.
Clause 2 States cannot tax imports and exports without approval from Congress.

Clause 3 States cannot declare war. They cannot keep their own armies or navies.

Clause 1 The President has the power to carry out the laws passed by Congress. The President and the Vice President serve four-year terms.

Clause 2 A group of people called the Electoral College actually elect the President. Each state chooses electors, or delegates, to serve in the Electoral College. The number of electors each state receives equals the total number of its representatives and senators.

641

Clause 3 The Twelfth Amendment over-ruled this clause and changed the way the election process worked. Today, electors almost always vote for the candidate who won the popular vote in their states. In other words, the candidate who wins the popular vote in a state also wins its electoral votes.

3. *Election Process* The electors shall meet in their respective States, and vote by ballot for two persons, of whom one at least shall not be an inhabitant of the same State with themselves. And they shall make a list of all the persons voted for, and of the number of votes for each; which list they shall sign and certify, and transmit sealed to the seat of the government of the United States, directed to the President of the Senate. The President of the Senate shall, in the presence of the Senate and House of Representatives, open all the certificates, and the votes shall then be counted. The person having the greatest number of votes shall be the President, if such number be a majority of the whole number of electors appointed, and if there be more than one who have such majority, and have an equal number of votes, then the House of Representatives shall immediately choose by ballot one of them for President; and if no person have a majority, then from the five highest on the list the said house shall in like manner choose the President. But in choosing the President, the votes shall be taken by States, the representation from each State having one vote; a quorum for this purpose shall consist of a member or members from two-thirds of the States, and a majority of all the States shall be necessary to a choice. In every case, after the choice of the President, the person having the greatest number of votes of the electors shall be the Vice President. But if there should remain two or more who have equal votes, the Senate shall choose from them by ballot the Vice President.

4. *Time of Elections*. The Congress may determine the time of choosing the electors, and the day on which they shall give their votes; which day shall be the same throughout the United States.

Clause 4 Today, we elect our President on the Tuesday after the first Monday in November.

Clause 5 A President must be at least 35 years old, a United States citizen by birth, and a resident of the United States for at least 14 years.

5. *Qualifications* No person except a natural-born citizen, or a citizen of the United States at the time of the adoption of this Constitution, shall be eligible to the office of President; neither shall any person be eligible to that office who shall not have attained to the age of thirty-five years, and been fourteen years a resident within the United States.

Clause 6 If the President resigns, dies, or is impeached and found guilty, the Vice President becomes President.

6. *Vacancies* In case of the removal of the President from office, or of his death, resignation, or inability to discharge the powers and duties of the said office, the same shall devolve on the Vice President, and the Congress may by law provide for the case of removal, death, resignation, or inability, both of the President and Vice President, declaring what officer shall then act as President, and such officer shall act accordingly, until the disability be removed, or a President shall be elected.

Clause 7 The President receives a yearly salary that cannot be increased or decreased during his or her term. The President cannot hold any other government positions while in office.

7. *Salary* The President shall, at stated times, receive for his services a compensation, which shall neither be increased nor diminished during the period for which he shall have been elected, and he shall not receive within that period any other emolument from the United States, or any of them.

Clause 8 Every President must promise to uphold the Constitution. The Chief Justice of the Supreme Court usually administers this oath.

8. *Oath of Office* Before he enter on the execution of his office, he shall take the following oath or affirmation:—"I do solemnly swear

★ ★ ★ ★ ★ ★ ★ ★ ★

(or affirm) that I will faithfully execute the office of President of the United States, and will to the best of my ability, preserve, protect and defend the Constitution of the United States."

SECTION 2. POWERS OF THE PRESIDENT

1. ***Military Powers*** *The President shall be commander in chief of the army and navy of the United States, and of the militia of the several States, when called into the actual service of the United States; he may require the opinion, in writing, of the principal officer in each of the executive departments, upon any subject relating to the duties of their respective offices, and he shall have power to grant reprieves and pardons for offenses against the United States, except in cases of impeachment.*

Clause 1 The President is the leader of the country's military forces. The President is also in charge of state militias when they are called into national service. The military forces are under civilian, or nonmilitary, control.

2. ***Treaties and Appointments*** *He shall have power, by and with the advice and consent of the Senate, to make treaties, provided two-thirds of the senators present concur; and he shall nominate, and by and with the advice and consent of the Senate, shall appoint ambassadors, other public ministers and consuls, judges of the Supreme Court, and all other officers of the United States, whose appointments are not herein otherwise provided for, and which shall be established by law: but the Congress may by law vest the appointment of such inferior officers, as they think proper, in the President alone, in the courts of law, or in the heads of departments.*

Clause 2 The President can make treaties with other nations. However, treaties must be approved by a two-thirds vote of the Senate. The President can also make executive agreements with foreign governments that have the same force as treaties but do not need Senate approval. The President appoints Supreme Court Justices and ambassadors to foreign countries. The Senate must approve these appointments.

3. ***Temporary Appointments*** *The President shall have power to fill up all vacancies that may happen during the recess of the Senate, by granting commissions which shall expire at the end of their next session.*

SECTION 3. DUTIES

He shall from time to time give to the Congress information of the State of the Union, and recommend to their consideration such measures as he shall judge necessary and expedient; he may on extraordinary occasions, convene both houses, or either of them, and in case of disagreement between them with respect to the time of adjournment, he may adjourn them to such time as he shall think proper; he shall receive ambassadors and other public ministers; he shall take care that the laws be faithfully executed, and shall commission all the officers of the United States.

The President has the power to recommend legislation. The President must report to Congress at least once a year and make recommendations for laws. This report is known as the State of the Union Address. The President delivers it each January. The President can call special sessions of Congress in times of emergency.

SECTION 4. IMPEACHMENT

The President, Vice President and all civil officers of the United States, shall be removed from office on impeachment for, and conviction of, treason, bribery, or other high crimes and misdemeanors.

The President can be forced out of office only if found guilty of particular crimes. This clause protects government officials from being impeached for unimportant reasons.

ARTICLE III
JUDICIAL BRANCH

SECTION 1. FEDERAL COURTS

The judicial power of the United States shall be vested in one Supreme Court, and in such inferior courts as the Congress may from time to time ordain and establish. The judges, both of the Supreme and inferior courts, shall hold their offices during good behavior, and

The Supreme Court is the highest court in the nation. It makes the final decisions in all of the cases it hears. Today nine judges sit on the Supreme Court. Congress also has the power to set up a system of lower federal courts. All federal judges may hold their offices for as long as they live.

shall, at stated times, receive for their services, a compensation which shall not be diminished during their continuance in office.

SECTION 2. AUTHORITY OF THE FEDERAL COURTS

Clause 1 Federal Courts have authority in cases that involve the Constitution, federal laws, treaties, and disagreements between states. The Supreme Court established the right to judge whether a law is constitutional in *Marbury* v. *Madison* (1803). This right is known as *judicial review.*

1. ***General Jurisdiction*** *The judicial power shall extend to all cases, in law and equity, arising under this Constitution, the laws of the United States, and treaties made, or which shall be made, under their authority;—to all cases affecting ambassadors, other public ministers and consuls;—to all cases of admiralty and maritime jurisdiction;—to controversies to which the United States shall be a party;—to controversies between two or more States;— between a State and citizens of another State; between citizens of different States;—between citizens of the same State claiming lands under grants of different States, and between a State, or the citizens thereof, and foreign states, citizens or subjects.*

Clause 2 *Original jurisdiction* means the right to try a case before any other court hears it. *Appellate jurisdiction* means the right of a court to try cases appealed from lower federal and state courts.

2. ***The Supreme Court*** *In all cases affecting ambassadors, other public ministers and consuls, and those in which a State shall be party, the Supreme Court shall have original jurisdiction. In all the other cases before mentioned, the Supreme Court shall have appellate jurisdiction, both as to law and fact, with such exceptions, and under such regulations as the Congress shall make.*

Clause 3 The Constitution guarantees everyone the right to a trial by jury. The only exception is in impeachment cases, which are tried in the Senate.

3. ***Trial by Jury*** *The trial of all crimes, except in cases of impeachment, shall be by jury; and such trial shall be held in the State where the said crimes shall have been committed; but when not committed within any State, the trial shall be at such place or places as the Congress may by law have directed.*

SECTION 3. TREASON

Clause 1 People cannot be convicted of treason in the United States for what they think or say. To be guilty of treason, a person must rebel against the government by using violence or helping enemies of the country.

1. ***Definition*** *Treason against the United States shall consist only in levying war against them, or in adhering to their enemies, giving them aid and comfort. No person shall be convicted of treason unless on the testimony of two witnesses to the same overt act, or on confession in open court.*

Clause 2 Congress has the power to decide the punishment for treason, but it may not punish the children of convicted traitors.

2. ***Punishment*** *The Congress shall have power to declare the punishment of treason, but no attainder of treason shall work corruption of blood, or forfeiture except during the life of the person attainted.*

ARTICLE IV
RELATIONS AMONG THE STATES

SECTION 1. OFFICIAL RECORDS

Each state must accept the laws, acts, and legal decisions made by other states.

Full faith and credit shall be given in each State to the public acts, records, and judicial proceedings of every other State. And the Congress may by general laws prescribe the manner in which such acts, records, and proceedings shall be proved, and the effect thereof.

SECTION 2. PRIVILEGES OF THE CITIZENS

Clause 1 States must give the same rights to citizens from other states that they give to their own citizens.

1. ***Privileges*** *The citizens of each State shall be entitled to all privileges and immunities of citizens in the several States.*

★ ★ ★ ★ ★ ★ ★ ★ ★

2. Return of a Person Accused of a Crime *A person charged in any State with treason, felony, or other crime, who shall flee from justice, and be found in another State, shall on demand of the executive authority of the State from which he fled, be delivered up, to be removed to the State having jurisdiction of the crime.*

3. Return of Fugitive Slaves ~~No person held to service or labor in one State, under the laws thereof, escaping into another, shall, in consequence of any law or regulation therein, be discharged from such service or labor, but shall be delivered up on claim of the party to whom such service or labor may be due.~~

SECTION 3. NEW STATES AND TERRITORIES

1. New States *New States may be admitted by the Congress into this Union; but no new State shall be formed or erected within the jurisdiction of any other State; nor any State be formed by the junction of two or more States or parts of States, without the consent of the legislatures of the States concerned as well as of the Congress.*

2. Federal Lands *The Congress shall have power to dispose of and make all needful rules and regulations respecting the territory or other property belonging to the United States; and nothing in this Constitution shall be so construed as to prejudice any claims of the United States, or of any particular State.*

SECTION 4. GUARANTEES TO THE STATES

The United States shall guarantee to every State in this Union a republican form of government, and shall protect each of them against invasion; and on application of the legislature, or of the executive (when the legislature cannot be convened) against domestic violence.

ARTICLE V
AMENDING THE CONSTITUTION

The Congress, whenever two-thirds of both houses shall deem it necessary, shall propose amendments to this Constitution, or, on the application of the legislatures of two-thirds of the several States, shall call a convention for proposing amendments, which, in either case, shall be valid to all intents and purposes, as part of this Constitution, when ratified by the legislatures of three-fourths of the several States, or by conventions in three-fourths thereof, as the one or the other mode of ratification may be proposed by the Congress; provided ~~that no amendments which may be made prior to the year one thousand eight hundred and eight shall in any manner affect the first and fourth clauses in the ninth section of the first article, and~~ *that no State, without its consent, shall be deprived of its equal suffrage in the Senate.*

ARTICLE VI
GENERAL PROVISIONS

1. Public Debt *All debts contracted and engagements entered into, before the adoption of this Constitution, shall be as valid against the United States under this Constitution, as under the Confederation.*

Clause 2 If a person charged with a crime escapes to another state, he or she must be returned to the original state to go on trial. This act of returning someone from one state to another is called *extradition*.

Clause 3 The Thirteenth Amendment eliminated this clause, which required states to return runaway slaves to their owners.

Clause 1 Congress has the power to create new states out of the nation's territories. All new states have the same rights as the old states. This clause made it clear that the United States would not make colonies out of its new lands.

Clause 2 Congress has the power to make rules for the management of land owned by the United States government.

The federal government must defend the states from attacks by other countries and from rebellions.

An amendment to the Constitution may be proposed either by a two-thirds vote of each house of Congress or at the request of two-thirds of the states. To be ratified, or approved, an amendment must be supported either by three-fourths of the state legislatures or by three-fourths of special conventions held in each state.

Once an amendment is ratified, it becomes a part of the Constitution. Only a new amendment can change it. Amendments have allowed people to alter the Constitution to meet the changing needs of the nation.

Clause 1 The United States government agreed to pay all debts built up under the Articles of Confederation.

Clause 2 The Constitution is the highest law in the nation. Whenever a state law and a federal law conflict, the federal law must be obeyed.

Clause 3 All state and federal officials must promise to obey the Constitution. The use of religious qualifications for office holders is prohibited.

The framers provided that the Constitution would be approved as soon as nine of the thirteen states voted to accept it.

Each state held a special convention to debate the Constitution. The ninth state to approve the Constitution, New Hampshire, voted for ratification on June 21, 1788. The Constitution went into effect in March 1789.

★　★　★　★　★　★　★　★　★

2. *Federal Supremacy This Constitution, and the laws of the United States which shall be made in pursuance thereof; and all treaties made, or which shall be made, under the authority of the United States, shall be the supreme law of the land; and the judges in every State shall be bound thereby, anything in the constitution or laws of any State to the contrary notwithstanding.*

3. *Oaths of Office The senators and representatives before mentioned, and the members of the several State legislatures, and all executive and judicial officers, both of the United States, and of the several States, shall be bound by oath or affirmation to support this Constitution; but no religious test shall ever be required as a qualification to any office or public trust under the United States.*

ARTICLE VII
RATIFICATION

The ratification of the conventions of nine States shall be sufficient for the establishment of this Constitution between the States so ratifying the same.

Done in Convention by the unanimous consent of the States present the seventeenth day of September in the year of our Lord one thousand seven hundred and eighty-seven and of the independence of the United States of America the twelfth. In witness whereof we have hereunto subscribed our names.

George Washington, President and deputy from Virginia

DELAWARE
George Read
Gunning Bedford, Junior
John Dickinson
Richard Bassett
Jacob Broom

MARYLAND
James McHenry
Daniel of St. Thomas Jenifer
Daniel Carroll

VIRGINIA
John Blair
James Madison, Junior

NORTH CAROLINA
William Blount
Richard Dobbs Spaight
Hugh Williamson

SOUTH CAROLINA
John Rutledge
Charles Cotesworth Pinckney
Charles Pinckney
Pierce Butler

GEORGIA
William Few
Abraham Baldwin

NEW HAMPSHIRE
John Langdon
Nicholas Gilman

MASSACHUSETTS
Nathaniel Gorham
Rufus King

CONNECTICUT
William Samuel Johnson
Roger Sherman

NEW YORK
Alexander Hamilton

NEW JERSEY
William Livingston
David Brearley
William Paterson
Jonathan Dayton

PENNSYLVANIA
Benjamin Franklin
Thomas Mifflin
Robert Morris
George Clymer
Thomas FitzSimmons
Jared Ingersoll
James Wilson
Gouverneur Morris

★ ★ ★ ★ ★ ★ ★ ★ ★

AMENDMENT 1 (1791)*
BASIC FREEDOMS

Congress shall make no law respecting an establishment of religion, or prohibiting the free exercise thereof; or abridging the freedom of speech, or of the press; or the right of the people peaceably to assemble, and to petition the government for a redress of grievances.

AMENDMENT 2 (1791)
WEAPONS AND THE MILITIA

A well-regulated militia being necessary to the security of a free State, the right of the people to keep and bear arms shall not be infringed.

AMENDMENT 3 (1791)
HOUSING SOLDIERS

No soldier shall, in time of peace, be quartered in any house, without the consent of the owner, nor in time of war, but in a manner to be prescribed by law.

AMENDMENT 4 (1791)
SEARCH AND SEIZURE

The right of the people to be secure in their persons, houses, papers, and effects, against unreasonable searches and seizures, shall not be violated, and no warrants shall issue, but upon probable cause, supported by oath or affirmation, and particularly describing the place to be searched, and the persons or things to be seized.

AMENDMENT 5 (1791)
RIGHTS OF THE ACCUSED

No person shall be held to answer for a capital or otherwise infamous crime, unless on a presentment or indictment of a grand jury, except in cases arising in the land or naval forces, or in the militia, when in actual service in time of war or public danger; nor shall any person be subject for the same offense to be twice put in jeopardy of life or limb; nor shall be compelled in any criminal case to be a witness against himself, nor be deprived of life, liberty, or property, without due process of law; nor shall private property be taken for public use without just compensation.

AMENDMENT 6 (1791)
RIGHT TO A FAIR TRIAL

In all criminal prosecutions, the accused shall enjoy the right to a speedy and public trial, by an impartial jury of the State and district wherein the crime shall have been committed, which district shall have been previously ascertained by law, and to be informed of the nature and cause of the accusation; to be confronted with the witnesses against him; to have compulsory process for obtaining witnesses in his favor, and to have the assistance of counsel for his defense.

* The date beside each amendment is the year that the amendment was ratified.

The first 10 amendments to the Constitution are known as the Bill of Rights.

The First Amendment protects the five basic civil liberties: freedoms of religion, speech, press, assembly, and petition. The government cannot pass laws that favor one religion over another.

This amendment was included to prevent the federal government from taking away guns used by members of state militias.

The army cannot use people's homes to house soldiers unless it is approved by law. This amendment grew out of the colonial period when the British housed soldiers in private homes without the owners' permission.

This amendment protects people's privacy in their homes. The government cannot search or seize anyone's property without a warrant, or written order, from a court. A warrant must list the people and property to be searched and give reasons for the search.

No person may be tried for a capital crime (a crime punishable by death) or an *infamous crime* (a crime punishable by a prison term or other loss of rights) unless a *grand jury*, a panel of between 12 and 23 citizens, rules that there is enough evidence for a trial.

A person cannot be tried twice for the same crime. This amendment also protects a person from self-incrimination, or having to testify against himself or herself. In addition, a person accused of a crime is entitled to *due process of law*, meaning fair and equal treatment under the law.

Anyone accused of a crime is entitled to a quick and fair trial by jury. This right protects people from being kept in jail without being convicted of a crime. Also, the government must provide a lawyer for anyone accused of a crime who cannot afford to hire a lawyer.

Civil cases usually involve two or more people suing each other over money, property, or personal injury. A jury trial is guaranteed in lawsuits where the property in question is valued at more than $20.

Bail is money that the accused leaves with the court as a guarantee that he or she will appear for trial. Courts cannot treat people accused of crimes in ways that are unusually harsh.

The citizens keep all rights not listed in the Constitution.

Any rights not clearly given to the federal government by the Constitution belong to the states or the people.

A citizen from one state cannot sue the government of another state in a federal court. Such cases are decided in state courts.

Under the original Constitution, each member of the Electoral College voted for two candidates for President. The candidate with the most votes became President. The one with the second highest total became Vice President.

The Twelfth Amendment changed this system. Members of the electoral college distinguish between their votes for President and Vice President. This change was an important step in the development of the two-party system. It allows each party to nominate its own team of candidates. Under this system, however, it is possible for a candidate to win the popular vote and lose in the Electoral College. This happened in 1824, 1876, and 1888.

★ ★ ★ ★ ★ ★ ★ ★ ★

AMENDMENT 7 (1791)
JURY TRIAL IN CIVIL CASES

In suits at common law, where the value in controversy shall exceed twenty dollars, the right of trial by jury shall be preserved, and no fact tried by a jury shall be otherwise reexamined in any court of the United States, than according to the rules of the common law.

AMENDMENT 8 (1791)
BAIL AND PUNISHMENT

Excessive bail shall not be required, nor excessive fines imposed, nor cruel and unusual punishments inflicted.

AMENDMENT 9 (1791)
POWERS RESERVED TO THE PEOPLE

The enumeration in the Constitution of certain rights shall not be construed to deny or disparage others retained by the people.

AMENDMENT 10 (1791)
POWERS RESERVED TO THE STATES

The powers not delegated to the United States by the Constitution, nor prohibited by it to the States are reserved to the States respectively, or to the people.

AMENDMENT 11 (1795)
SUITS AGAINST STATES

The judicial power of the United States shall not be construed to extend to any suit in law or equity, commenced or prosecuted against one of the United States by citizens of another State, or by citizens or subjects of any foreign State.

AMENDMENT 12 (1804)
ELECTION OF THE PRESIDENT AND VICE PRESIDENT

The electors shall meet in their respective States, and vote by ballot for President and Vice President, one of whom, at least, shall not be an inhabitant of the same State with themselves; they shall name in their ballots the person voted for as President, and in distinct ballots the person voted for as Vice President, and they shall make distinct lists of all persons voted for as President, and of all persons voted for as Vice President, and of the number of votes for each, which lists they shall sign and certify, and transmit sealed to the seat of government of the United States, directed to the President of the Senate;—The President of the Senate shall, in the presence of the Senate and House of Representatives, open all the certificates and the votes shall then be counted;—The person having the greatest number of votes for President shall be the President, if such number be a majority of the whole number of electors appointed; and if no person have such majority, then from the persons having the highest numbers not exceeding three on the list of those voted for as President, the House of Representatives shall choose immediately, by ballot, the President. But in choosing the President, the votes shall be taken by States, the representation from each State having one vote; a quorum for this purpose shall consist of a member or members from two-thirds of the States, and a majority of all the States shall be necessary to a choice. And if the House of Representatives shall not choose a President whenever the right of choice shall devolve upon them, before the fourth day of March next following, then the Vice President shall act as President, as in the case of the death or other constitutional disability of the President. The person having the greatest number of votes as Vice President shall be the Vice President, if such number be a majority of the whole number of electors appointed, and if no person have a majority, then from the two highest numbers on the list, the Senate shall choose the Vice President; a quorum for the purpose shall consist of two-thirds of the whole number of senators, and a majority of the whole number shall be necessary to a choice. But no person constitutionally ineligible to the office of President shall be eligible to that of Vice President of the United States.

AMENDMENT 13 (1865)
END OF SLAVERY

SECTION 1. ABOLITION

Neither slavery nor involuntary servitude, except as a punishment for crime whereof the party shall have been duly convicted, shall exist within the United States, or any place subject to their jurisdiction.

Section 1 This amendment ended slavery in the United States. It was ratified right after the Civil War.

SECTION 2. ENFORCEMENT

Congress shall have power to enforce this article by appropriate legislation.

Section 2 Congress has the power to pass laws to carry out this amendment.

AMENDMENT 14 (1868)
RIGHTS OF CITIZENS

SECTION 1. CITIZENSHIP

All persons born or naturalized in the United States, and subject to the jurisdiction thereof, are citizens of the United States and of the State wherein they reside. No State shall make or enforce any law which shall abridge the privileges or immunities of citizens of the United States; nor shall any State deprive any person of life, liberty, or property, without due process of law; nor deny to any person within its jurisdiction the equal protection of the laws.

Section 1 This amendment defined citizenship for the first time in the Constitution. "Due process under law" means that no state may deny its citizens the rights and privileges they enjoy as United States citizens. The goal of this amendment was to protect the rights of the recently freed blacks.

SECTION 2. NUMBER OF REPRESENTATIVES

Representatives shall be apportioned among the several States according to their respective numbers, counting the whole number of persons in each State, excluding Indians not taxed. But when the right to vote at any election for the choice of electors for President and Vice President of the United States, representatives in Congress, the executive and judicial officers of a State, or the

Section 2 This clause replaced the Three-Fifths Compromise in Article 1. Each state's representation is based on its total population. Any state denying its male citizens over the age of 21 the right to vote will have its representation in Congress decreased.

CONSTITUTION

649

members of the legislature thereof, is denied to any of the male inhabitants of such State, being twenty-one years of age, and citizens of the United States, or in any way abridged, except for participation in rebellion, or other crime, the basis of representation therein shall be reduced in the proportion which the number of such male citizens shall bear to the whole number of male citizens twenty-one years of age in such State.

SECTION 3. PENALTY FOR REBELLION

No person shall be a senator or representative in Congress, or elector of President and Vice President, or hold any office, civil or military, under the United States, or under any State, who, having previously taken an oath, as a member of Congress, or as an officer of the United States, or as a member of any State legislature, or as an executive or judicial officer of any State, to support the Constitution of the United States, shall have engaged in insurrection or rebellion against the same, or given aid or comfort to the enemies thereof. But Congress may by a vote of two-thirds of each house, remove such disability.

SECTION 4. GOVERNMENT DEBT

The validity of the public debt of the United States, authorized by law, including debts incurred for payment of pensions and bounties for services in suppressing insurrection or rebellion, shall not be questioned. But neither the United States nor any State shall assume or pay any debt or obligation incurred in aid of insurrection or rebellion against the United States, or any claim for the loss or emancipation of any slave; but all such debts, obligations, and claims shall be held illegal and void.

SECTION 5. ENFORCEMENT

The Congress shall have power to enforce, by appropriate legislation, the provisions of this article.

AMENDMENT 15 (1870)
VOTING RIGHTS

SECTION 1. RIGHT TO VOTE

The right of citizens of the United States to vote shall not be denied or abridged by the United States or by any State on account of race, color, or previous condition of servitude.

SECTION 2. ENFORCEMENT

The Congress shall have power to enforce this article by appropriate legislation.

AMENDMENT 16 (1913)
INCOME TAX

The Congress shall have power to lay and collect taxes on incomes, from whatever source derived, without apportionment among the several States, and without regard to any census or enumeration.

Section 3 Officials who fought against the Union in the Civil War could not hold public office in the United States after the the war. This clause tried to keep Confederate leaders out of power. In 1872, Congress removed this ban.

Section 4 The United States paid all of the Union's debts from the Civil War. However, it did not pay any of the Confederacy's debts. This clause prevented the Southern states from using public money to pay for the rebellion or to pay citizens who lost their slaves.

Section 5 Congress has the power to pass laws to carry out this amendment. The Civil Rights Act of 1964 is an example of such a law.

Section 1 No state can deny its citizens the right to vote because of their race or previous condition of slavery. This amendment was designed to protect the voting rights of blacks.

Section 2 Congress has the power to pass laws to carry out this amendment. The Voting Rights Act of 1965 is an example of such a law.

Income Tax Congress has the power to tax personal incomes.

AMENDMENT 17 (1913)
DIRECT ELECTION OF SENATORS

SECTION 1. METHOD OF ELECTION

The Senate of the United States shall be composed of two senators from each State, elected by the people thereof, for six years; and each senator shall have one vote. The electors in each State shall have the qualifications requisite for electors of the most numerous branch of the State legislatures.

Section 1 In the original Constitution, the state legislatures elected senators. This amendment gave citizens the power to elect their senators directly. It made senators more responsible to the people they represented.

SECTION 2. VACANCIES

When vacancies happen in the representation of any State in the Senate, the executive authority of such State shall issue writs of election to fill such vacancies: Provided, that the legislature of any State may empower the executive thereof to make temporary appointments until the people fill the vacancies by election as the legislature may direct.

Section 2 If a Senate seat should become vacant for any reason, the governor of that state has the power to order a new election to fill the vacancy. A governor may also temporarily fill the vacant seat until an election can be held.

SECTION 3. EXCEPTION

This amendment shall not be so construed as to affect the election or term of any Senator chosen before it becomes valid as part of the Constitution.

Senators who had already been chosen by state legislatures were not affected by this amendment.

AMENDMENT 18 (1919)
BAN ON ALCOHOLIC DRINKS

SECTION 1. PROHIBITION

After one year from the ratification of this article the manufacture, sale, or transportation of intoxicating liquors within, the importation thereof into, or the exportation thereof from the United States and all territory subject to the jurisdiction thereof for beverage purposes is hereby prohibited.

Section 1 This amendment made it against the law to make or sell alcoholic beverages in the United States. This law was called Prohibition. Fourteen years later, the Twenty-First Amendment ended Prohibition.

SECTION 2. ENFORCEMENT

The Congress and the several States shall have concurrent power to enforce this article by appropriate legislation.

Section 2 Both Congress and the states had the power to pass laws to carry out this amendment.

SECTION 3. RATIFICATION

This article shall be inoperative unless it shall have been ratified as an amendment to the Constitution by the legislatures of the several States, as provided in the Constitution, within seven years from the date of the submission hereof to the States by the Congress.

Section 3 This amendment was the first one to include a time limit for ratification. To go into effect, the amendment had to be approved by three-fourths of the states within seven years.

AMENDMENT 19 (1920)
WOMEN'S SUFFRAGE

SECTION 1. RIGHT TO VOTE

The right of citizens of the United States to vote shall not be denied or abridged by the United States or by any State on account of sex.

Section 1 This amendment gave the right to vote to all women 21 years of age and older.

Section 2 Congress has the power to pass laws to carry out this amendment.

Section 1 The President and Vice President's terms begin on January 20 after being elected. The terms for senators and representatives begin on January 3. Before this amendment, an official defeated in a November election stayed in office until March. Such officeholders are known as *lame ducks*.

Section 2 Congress must meet at least once a year. The new session begins on January 3.

Section 3 A President who has been elected but has not yet taken office is called the President-elect. If the President-elect dies, the Vice President-elect becomes President. If neither the President-elect nor the Vice President-elect can take office, then Congress decides who will act as President.

Section 4 In the event that a candidate fails to win a majority in the Electoral College, and then dies while the election is being decided in the House of Representatives, Congress shall have the power to pass laws to resolve the problem. Congress has the same power in the event that a vice-presidential candidate dies while the election is in the Senate.

★ ★ ★ ★ ★ ★ ★ ★ ★

SECTION 2. ENFORCEMENT

The Congress shall have power to enforce this article by appropriate legislation.

AMENDMENT 20 (1933)
TERMS OF OFFICE

SECTION 1. BEGINNING OF TERMS

The terms of the President and Vice President shall end at noon on the twentieth day of January, and the terms of senators and representatives at noon on the third day of January, of the years in which such terms would have ended if this article had not been ratified; and the terms of their successors shall then begin.

SECTION 2. SESSIONS OF CONGRESS

The Congress shall assemble at least once in every year, and such meeting shall begin at noon on the third day of January, unless they shall by law appoint a different day.

SECTION 3. PRESIDENTIAL SUCCESSION

If, at the time fixed for the beginning of the term of the President, the President-elect shall have died, the Vice President-elect shall become President. If a President shall not have been chosen before the time fixed for the beginning of his term, or if the President-elect shall have failed to qualify, then the Vice President-elect shall act as President until a President shall have qualified; and the Congress may by law provide for the case wherein neither a President-elect nor a Vice President-elect shall have qualified, declaring who shall then act as President, or the manner in which one who is to act shall be selected, and such persons shall act accordingly until a President or Vice President shall have qualified.

SECTION 4. ELECTIONS DECIDED BY CONGRESS

The Congress may by law provide for the case of the death of any of the persons from whom the House of Representatives may choose a President whenever the right of choice shall have devolved upon them, and for the case of the death of any of the persons from whom the Senate may choose a Vice President whenever the right of choice shall have devolved upon them.

SECTION 5. EFFECTIVE DATE

Sections 1 and 2 shall take effect on the fifteenth day of October following the ratification of this article.

SECTION 6. RATIFICATION

This article shall be inoperative unless it shall have been ratified as an amendment to the Constitution by the legislatures of three-fourths of the several States within seven years from the date of its submission.

AMENDMENT 21 (1933)
END OF PROHIBITION

SECTION 1. REPEAL OF EIGHTEENTH AMENDMENT

The eighteenth article of amendment to the Constitution of the United States is hereby repealed.

Section 1 This amendment repealed, or ended, the Eighteenth Amendment. It made alcoholic beverages legal once again in the United States. Prohibition ended December 5, 1933.

SECTION 2. STATE LAWS

The transportation or importation into any State, territory, or possession of the United States for delivery or use therein of intoxicating liquors, in violation of the laws thereof, is hereby prohibited.

Section 2 States can still control or stop the sale of alcohol within their borders.

SECTION 3. RATIFICATION

This article shall be inoperative unless it shall have been ratified as an amendment to the Constitution by conventions in the several States, as provided in the Constitution, within seven years from the date of submission hereof to the States by the Congress.

AMENDMENT 22 (1951)
LIMIT ON PRESIDENTIAL TERMS

SECTION 1. TWO-TERM LIMIT

No person shall be elected to the office of the President more than twice, and no person who has held the office of President, or acted as President, for more than two years of a term to which some other person was elected President shall be elected to the office of the President more than once. But this article shall not apply to any person holding the office of President when this article was proposed by the Congress, and shall not prevent any person who may be holding the office of President, or acting as President, during the term within which this article becomes operative from holding the office of President or acting as President during the remainder of such term.

Section 1 Article II is silent on the number of terms a President may serve. In spite of this silence, George Washington set a precedent that Presidents should not serve more than two terms in office. However, Franklin Roosevelt broke the precedent. He was elected President four times between 1932 and 1944. Some people feared that a President holding office for this long could become too powerful. This amendment limits Presidents to two terms in office.

SECTION 2. RATIFICATION

This article shall be inoperative unless it shall have been ratified as an amendment to the Constitution by the legislatures of three-fourths of the several States within seven years from the date of its submission to the States by Congress.

AMENDMENT 23 (1961)
PRESIDENTIAL VOTES FOR WASHINGTON, D.C.

SECTION 1. NUMBER OF ELECTORS

The District constituting the seat of government of the United States shall appoint in such manner as the Congress may direct:

A number of electors of President and Vice President equal to the whole number of senators and representatives in Congress to which the District would be entitled if it were a State, but in no event more than the least populous State; they shall be in addition

Section 1 This amendment gives people who live in the nation's capital a vote for President. Washington, D.C.'s electoral votes are based on its population. However, it cannot have more votes than the state with the smallest population. Today Washington, D.C. has three electoral votes.

to those appointed by the States, but they shall be considered, for the purposes of the election of President and Vice President, to be electors appointed by a State; and they shall meet in the District and perform such duties as provided by the twelfth article of amendment.

SECTION 2. ENFORCEMENT

The Congress shall have power to enforce this article by appropriate legislation.

AMENDMENT 24 (1964)
BAN ON POLL TAXES

SECTION 1. POLL TAXES ILLEGAL

The right of citizens of the United States to vote in any primary or other election for President or Vice President, for electors for President or Vice President, or for senator or representative in Congress, shall not be denied or abridged by the United States or any State by reason of failure to pay any poll tax or other tax.

SECTION 2. ENFORCEMENT

The Congress shall have power to enforce this article by appropriate legislation.

AMENDMENT 25 (1967)
PRESIDENTIAL SUCCESSION

SECTION 1. VACANCY IN THE PRESIDENCY

In case of the removal of the President from office or of his death or resignation, the Vice President shall become President.

SECTION 2. VACANCY IN THE VICE PRESIDENCY

Whenever there is a vacancy in the office of the Vice President, the President shall nominate a Vice President who shall take office upon confirmation by a majority vote of both houses of Congress.

SECTION 3. DISABILITY OF THE PRESIDENT

Whenever the President transmits to the President pro tempore of the Senate and the speaker of the House of Representatives his written declaration that he is unable to discharge the powers and duties of his office, and until he transmits to them a written declaration to the contrary, such powers and duties shall be discharged by the Vice President as Acting President.

SECTION 4. DETERMINING PRESIDENTIAL DISABILITY

Whenever the Vice President and a majority of either the principal officers of the executive departments or of such other body as Congress may by law provide, transmit to the President pro tempore of the Senate and the speaker of the House of Representatives their written declaration that the President is unable to discharge the powers and duties of his office, the Vice President shall immediately

---

Section 2 Congress has the power to pass laws to carry out this legislation.

Section 1 A poll tax requires a person to pay a certain amount of money to register to vote. These taxes were used to stop poor blacks from voting. This amendment made any such taxes illegal in federal elections. The Supreme Court later ruled, in 1966, that poll taxes were illegal in state elections as well.

Section 1 In the event that the President dies, resigns, or is removed from office, the Vice President becomes President.
Section 2 If the Vice President becomes President, he or she may nominate a new Vice President. This nomination must be approved by both houses of Congress.

Secton 3 This section tells what happens if the President suddenly becomes ill or is seriously injured. The Vice President takes over as Acting President. When the President is ready to take office again, he or she must tell Congress.
Section 4 If the President is unconscious or refuses to admit to a disabling illness, the Vice President and the Cabinet have the right to inform Congress that the President is disabled. The Vice President then becomes acting President until the President as able to resume the duties of office. If there is a disagreement between the President and the Vice President and Cabinet about the President's ability to perform the duties of office, Congress has

assume the powers and duties of the office as Acting President.

Thereafter, when the President transmits to the President pro tempore of the Senate and the speaker of the House of Representatives his written declaration that no inability exists, he shall resume the powers and duties of his office unless the Vice President and a majority of either the principal officers of the executive departments or of such other body as Congress may by law provide, transmit within four days to the President pro tempore of the Senate and the speaker of the House of Representatives their written declaration that the President is unable to discharge the powers and duties of his office. Thereupon Congress shall decide the issue, assembling within forty-eight hours for that purpose if not in session. If the Congress, within twenty-one days after receipt of the latter written declaration, or, if Congress is not in session, within twenty-one days after Congress is required to assemble, determines by two-thirds vote of both houses that the President is unable to discharge the powers and duties of his office, the Vice President shall continue to discharge the same as Acting President; otherwise, the President shall resume the powers and duties of his office.

AMENDMENT 26 (1971)
VOTING AGE

SECTION 1. RIGHT TO VOTE

The right of citizens of the United States, who are eighteen years of age or older, to vote shall not be denied or abridged by the United States or by any State on account of age.

SECTION 2. ENFORCEMENT

The Congress shall have power to enforce this article by appropriate legislation.

the power to decide the issue. A two-thirds vote would be required to find the President unfit to perform his or her duties.

Section 1 This amendment gave the vote to all American citizens 18 years of age and older.

Section 2 Congress has the power to pass laws to carry out this amendment.

★ ★ ★ ★ ★ ★ ★ ★ ★

The Declaration of Independence

In Congress, July 4, 1776
The unanimous declaration of the thirteen united States of America

INTRODUCTION*

In the Declaration of Independence, the colonists explained why they were breaking away from Great Britain. They believed they had the right to form their own country.

powers of the earth other nations *station* place *impel* drive

When, in the course of human events, it becomes necessary for one people to dissolve the political bands which have connected them with another, and to assume, among the powers of the earth, the separate and equal station to which the laws of nature and of nature's God entitle them, a decent respect to the opinions of mankind requires that they should declare the causes which impel them to the separation.

BASIC RIGHTS

The opening part of the Declaration is very famous. It says that all people are equal. Everyone has certain basic rights that are unalienable. That means that these rights are so basic that they cannot be taken away. Governments are formed to protect these basic rights. If a government does not do this, then the people have a right to begin a new one.

endowed given *deriving* receiving *prudence* wisdom *transient* temporary *usurpations* seizing powers unjustly *absolute despotism* complete and unjust control *constrains* forces

We hold these truths to be self-evident: That all men are created equal, that they are endowed by their Creator with certain unalienable rights; that among these are life, liberty, and the pursuit of happiness; that, to secure these rights, governments are instituted among men, deriving their just powers from the consent of the governed; that whenever any form of government becomes destructive of these ends, it is the right of the people to alter or to abolish it, and to institute new government, laying its foundation on such principles, and organizing its powers in such form, as to them shall seem most likely to effect their safety and happiness. Prudence, indeed, will dictate that governments long established should not be changed for light and transient causes; and accordingly all experience hath shown that mankind are more disposed to suffer, while evils are sufferable, than to right themselves by abolishing the forms to which they are accustomed. But when a long train of abuses and usurpations, pursuing invariably the same object, evinces a design to reduce them under absolute despotism, it is their right, it is their duty, to throw off such government, and to provide new guards for their future security. Such has been the patient sufferance of these colonies; and such is now the necessity which constrains them to alter their former systems of government. The history of the present King of Great Britain is a history of repeated injuries and usurpations, all having in direct object the establishment of an absolute tyranny over these states. To prove this, let facts be submitted to a candid world.

Forming a new government meant ending the colonial ties to the king. The writers listed the wrongs of King George III to prove the need for their actions.

*Titles have been added to the Declaration to make it easier to read. These titles are not in the original document.

★ ★ ★ ★ ★ ★ ★ ★ ★

CHARGES AGAINST THE KING

He has refused his assent to laws, the most wholesome and necessary for the public good.

He has forbidden his governors to pass laws of immediate and pressing importance, unless suspended in their operation till his assent should be obtained; and, when so suspended, he has utterly neglected to attend to them.

He has refused to pass other laws for the accommodation of large districts of people, unless those people would relinquish the right of representation in the legislature, a right inestimable to them, and formidable to tyrants only.

He has called together legislative bodies at places unusual, uncomfortable, and distant from the depository of their public records, for the sole purpose of fatiguing them into compliance with his measures.

He has dissolved representative houses repeatedly, for opposing, with manly firmness, his invasions on the rights of the people.

He has refused for a long time, after such dissolutions, to cause others to be elected; whereby the legislative powers, incapable of annihilation, have returned to the people at large for their exercise; the state remaining, in the mean time, exposed to all the dangers of invasions from without and convulsions within.

He has endeavored to prevent the population of these states; for that purpose obstructing the laws for the naturalization of foreigners; refusing to pass others to encourage their migration hither, and raising the conditions of new appropriations of lands.

He has obstructed the administration of justice, by refusing his assent to laws for establishing judiciary powers.

He has made judges dependent on his will alone, for the tenure of their offices, and the amount of payment of their salaries.

He has erected a multitude of new offices, and sent hither swarms of officers to harass our people and eat out their substance.

He has kept among us, in times of peace, standing armies, without the consent of our legislatures.

He has affected to render the military independent of, and superior to, the civil power.

He has combined with others to subject us to a jurisdiction foreign to our constitution and unacknowledged by our laws, giving his assent to their acts of pretended legislation:

For quartering large bodies of armed troops among us;

For protecting them, by a mock trial, from punishment for any murders which they should commit on the inhabitants of these states;

For cutting off our trade with all parts of the world;

For imposing taxes on us without our consent;

For depriving us, in many cases, of the benefits of trial by jury;

Colonists said the king had not let the colonies make their own laws. He had limited the people's representation in their assemblies.

assent *agreement* **inestimable** *immeasurable* **formidable** *causing fear* **compliance** *giving in to a request or a demand*

The king had made colonial assemblies meet at unusual times and places. This made going to assembly meetings hard for colonial representatives.

In some cases the king stopped the assembly from meeting at all.

annihilation *complete destruction* **convulsions** *disturbances* **endeavored** *tried*

The king stopped people from moving to the colonies and into new western lands. **hither** *here* **appropriations** *grants* **judiciary powers** *system of law courts*

The king prevented the colonies from choosing their own judges. Instead, he sent over judges who depended on him for their jobs and salaries.

tenure *term* **multitude** *large number* **harass** *bother, cause trouble*

The king kept British soldiers in the colonies, even though the colonists had not asked for them.

render *make* **jurisdiction** *authority* **quartering** *providing housing for* **mock** *false* **imposing** *forcing* **depriving** *taking away*

The king and Parliament had taxed the colonists without their consent. This was one of the most important reasons the colonists were angry at Great Britain.

abolishing getting rid of **arbitrary** *tyran-nical* **fit instrument** *suitable tool* **invested** *having*

For transporting us beyond seas, to be tried for pretended offenses;

For abolishing the free system of English laws in a neighboring province, establishing therein an arbitrary government, and enlarging its boundaries, so as to render it at once an example and fit instrument for introducing the same absolute rule into these colonies;

For taking away our charters, abolishing our most valuable laws, and altering fundamentally the forms of our governments.

For suspending our own legislatures, and declaring themselves invested with power to legislate for us in all cases whatsoever.

The colonists felt that the king had waged war on them.

He has abdicated government here, by declaring us out of his protection and waging war against us.

abdicated given up **plundered** robbed

He has plundered our seas, ravaged our coasts, burned our towns, and destroyed the lives of our people.

The king had hired German soldiers and sent them to the colonies to keep order.

He is at this time transporting large armies of foreign mercenaries to complete the works of death, desolation, and tyranny already begun with circumstances of cruelty and perfidy scarcely paralleled in the most barbarous ages, and totally unworthy the head of a civilized nation.

mercenaries hired soldiers **desolation** *misery* **perfidy** *treachery* **barbarous** *uncivilized* **insurrection** *revolt*

He has constrained our fellow-citizens, taken captive on the high seas, to bear arms against their country, to become the executioners of their friends and brethren, or to fall themselves by their hands.

He has excited domestic insurrection among us, and has endeavored to bring on the inhabitants of our frontiers, the merciless Indian savages, whose known rule of warfare is an undistinguished destruction of all ages, sexes, and conditions.

RESPONSE TO THE KING

In every stage of these oppressions we have petitioned for redress in the most humble terms; our repeated petitions have been answered only by repeated injury. A prince, whose character is thus marked by every act which may define a tyrant, is unfit to be the ruler of a free people.

The colonists said that they had asked the king to change his policies, but he had not listened to them.

petitioned requested **redress** relief **unwar-rantable** unfair **magnanimity** generosity **conjured** requested earnestly **disavow** turn away from **consanguinity** kinship **acqui-esce** agree **denounces** condemns

Nor have we been wanting in our attentions to our British brethren. We have warned them, from time to time, of attempts by their legislature to extend an unwarrantable jurisdiction over us. We have reminded them of the circumstances of our emigration and settlement here. We have appealed to their native justice and magnanimity; and we have conjured them, by the ties of our common kindred, to disavow these usurpations, which would inevitably interrupt our connections and correspondence. They, too, have been deaf to the voice of justice and of consanguinity. We must, therefore, acquiesce in the necessity which denounces our separation, and hold them, as we hold the rest of mankind, enemies in war, in peace friends.

★ ★ ★ ★ ★ ★ ★ ★ ★ ★ ★ ★

INDEPENDENCE

We, therefore, the representatives of the United States of America, in General Congress assembled, appealing to the Supreme Judge of the world for the rectitude of our intentions, do, in the name and by the authority of the good people of these colonies, solemnly publish and declare, that these United Colonies are, and of right ought to be, FREE AND INDEPENDENT STATES; that they are absolved from all allegiance to the British crown, and that all political connection between them and the state of Great Britain is, and ought to be, totally dissolved; and that, as free and independent states, they have full power to levy war, conclude peace, contract alliances, establish commerce, and do all other acts and things which independent states may of right do. And for the support of this declaration, with a firm reliance on the protection of Divine Providence, we mutually pledge to each other our lives, our fortunes, and our sacred honor.

John Hancock

The writers declared that the colonies were free and independent states, equal to the world's other states. They had the powers to make war and peace and to trade with other countries.

rectitude moral rightness **absolved** freed **allegiance** loyalty **levy** declare **contract** make **mutually** together

The signers pledged their lives to the support of this Declaration. The Continental Congress ordered the Declaration of Independence to be read in all the states and to the army.

NEW HAMPSHIRE
Josiah Bartlett
William Whipple
Matthew Thornton

MASSACHUSETTS
John Adams
Samuel Adams
Robert Treat Paine
Elbridge Gerry

NEW YORK
William Floyd
Philip Livingston
Francis Lewis
Lewis Morris

RHODE ISLAND
Stephen Hopkins
William Ellery

NEW JERSEY
Richard Stockton
John Witherspoon
Francis Hopkinson
John Hart
Abraham Clark

PENNSYLVANIA
Robert Morris
Benjamin Rush
Benjamin Franklin
John Morton
George Clymer
James Smith
George Taylor
James Wilson
George Ross

DELAWARE
Caesar Rodney
George Read
Thomas McKean

MARYLAND
Samuel Chase
William Paca
Thomas Stone
Charles Carroll of Carrollton

NORTH CAROLINA
William Hooper
Joseph Hewes
John Penn

VIRGINIA
George Wythe
Richard Henry Lee
Thomas Jefferson
Benjamin Harrison
Thomas Nelson, Jr.
Francis Lightfoot Lee
Carter Braxton

SOUTH CAROLINA
Edward Rutledge
Thomas Heyward, Jr.
Thomas Lynch, Jr.
Arthur Middleton

CONNECTICUT
Roger Sherman
Samuel Huntington
William Williams
Oliver Wolcott

GEORGIA
Button Gwinnett
Lyman Hall
George Walton

★ ★ ★ ★ ★ ★ ★ ★ ★ ★ ★ ★ ★ ★ ★ ★ ★ ★ ★

Discovery of the New World

Christopher Columbus

Christopher Columbus (1451–1506) sailed from Spain in August 1492 in search of a shorter trade route to East Asia. But when he landed in the Bahamas in October, he discovered a land unknown to Europeans at that time. Columbus and his men explored several places they believed to be the "Indies," including such Caribbean islands as San Salvador, Cuba, and Hispaniola. They established trading posts and declared these islands to be Spanish possessions. On the trip home Columbus stopped at Lisbon, where he sent word of his success to Lord Raphael Sanchez, the treasurer of the expedition. In the letter reprinted below, dated March 23, 1493, Columbus describes both the land and the native people he found—people he called "Indians." Although he made three more trips to the New World—in 1493, 1498, and 1502—Columbus died in 1506 still believing he had reached the eastern shore of Asia.

K *nowing that it will afford you pleasure to learn that I have brought my undertaking to a successful termination, I have decided upon writing you this letter to acquaint you with all the events which have occurred in my voyage, and the discoveries which have resulted from it. Thirty-three days after my departure from [Gomera] I reached the Indian Sea, where I discovered many islands, thickly peopled, of which I took possession without resistance in the name of our most illustrious monarch, by public proclamation and with unfurled banners. To the first of these islands, which is called by the Indians Guanahani, I gave the name of the blessed Savior [San Salvador], relying upon whose protection I had reached this as well as the other islands; to each of these I also gave a name, ordering that one should be called Santa Maria de la Concepcion, another Fernandina, the third Isabella, the fourth Juana [Cuba], and so with all the rest. . . .*

As soon as we arrived at that, which as I have said was named Juana, I proceeded along its coast a short distance westward and found it to be so large and apparently without termination that I could not suppose it to be an island, but the continental province of Cathay. Seeing, however, no towns or populous places on the seacoast, but only a few detached houses and cottages, with whose inhabitants I was unable to communicate because they fled as soon as they saw us, I went further on, thinking that in my progress I should certainly find some city or village.

At length, after proceeding a great way and finding that nothing new presented itself and that the line of coast was leading us northward (which I wished to avoid because it was winter, and it was my intention to move southward, and because, moreover, the winds were contrary), I resolved not to attempt any further progress but rather to turn back and retrace my course to a certain bay that I had observed, and from which I afterward dispatched two of our men to ascertain whether there were a king or any cities in that province. These men reconnoitered the country for three days and found a most numerous population and great numbers of houses, though small and built without any regard to order; with which information they returned to us. In the meantime I had learned from some Indians whom I had seized that that country was certainly an island, and therefore I sailed toward the east, coasting to the distance of 322 miles, which brought us to the extremity of it; from this point I saw lying eastward another island, 54 miles distant from Juana, to which I gave the name Española [Hispaniola]. I went thither and steered my course eastward as I had done at Juana, even to the distance of 564 miles along the north coast. . . .

In that island also, which I have before said we named Española, there are mountains of very great size and beauty, vast plains, groves, and very fruitful fields, admirably adapted for tillage, pasture, and habitation. The convenience and excellence of the harbors in this island and the abundance of the rivers, so indispensable to the health of man, surpass anything that would be believed by one who had not seen it. The trees, herbage, and fruits of Española are very different from those of Juana, and, moreover, it abounds in various kinds of spices, gold, and other metals.

The inhabitants of both sexes in this island, and in all the others which I have seen or of which I have received information, go always naked as they were born, with the exception of some of the women, who use the covering of a leaf or small bough or an apron of cotton which they prepare for that purpose. None of them, as I have already said, are possessed of any iron, neither have they weapons, being unacquainted with and indeed incompetent to use them, not from any deformity of body (for they are well formed) but because they are timid and full of fear. They carry, however, in lieu of arms, canes dried in the sun, on the ends of which they fix heads of dried wood sharpened to a point, and even these they dare not use habitually; for it has often occurred when I have sent two or three of my men to any of the villages to speak with the natives, that they have come out in a disorderly troop and have fled in such haste at the approach of our men that the fathers forsook their children and the children their fathers. This timidity did not arise from any loss or injury that they had received from us; for, on the contrary, I gave to all I approached whatever articles I had about me, such as cloth and many other things, taking nothing of theirs in return; but they are naturally timid and fearful.

reconnoitered surveyed or inspected

indispensable essential

As soon, however, as they see that they are safe and have laid aside all fear, they are very simple and honest and exceedingly liberal with all they have; none of them refusing anything he may possess when he is asked for it, but, on the contrary, inviting us to ask them. They exhibit great love toward all others in preference to themselves. They also give objects of great value for trifles, and content themselves with very little or nothing in return. I, however, forbade that these trifles and articles of no value (such as pieces of dishes, plates, and glass, keys, and leather straps) should be given to them, although if they could obtain them, they imagined themselves to be possessed of the most beautiful trinkets in the world. It even happened that a sailor received for a leather strap as much gold as was worth three golden nobles, and for things of more trifling value offered by our men, especially newly coined blancas or any gold coins, the Indians would give whatever the seller required; as, for instance, an ounce and a half or two ounces of gold, or thirty or forty pounds of cotton, with which commodity they were already acquainted. Thus they bartered, like idiots, cotton and gold for fragments of bows, glasses, bottles, and jars, which I forbade as being unjust, and myself gave them many beautiful and acceptable articles which I had brought with me, taking nothing from them in return. I did this in order that I might the more easily conciliate them, that they might be led to become Christians and be inclined to entertain a regard for the King and Queen, our Princes, and all Spaniards, and that I might induce them to take an interest in seeking out and collecting and delivering to us such things as they possessed in abundance, but which we greatly needed. They practice no kind of idolatry, but have a firm belief that all strength and power, and indeed all good things, are in heaven, and that I had descended from thence with these ships and sailors, and under this impression was I received after they had thrown aside their fears. Nor are they slow or stupid, but of very clear understanding; and those men who have crossed to the neighboring islands give an admirable description of everything they observed; but they never saw any people clothed nor any ships like ours.

On my arrival at that sea, I had taken some Indians by force from the first island that I came to, in order that they might learn our language and communicate to us what they knew respecting the country; which plan succeeded excellently and was a great advantage to us, for in a short time, either by gestures and signs or by words, we were enabled to understand each other. These men are still traveling with me, and although they have been with us now a long time, they continue to entertain the idea that I have descended from heaven; and on our arrival at any new place they published this, crying out immediately with a loud voice to the other Indians, "Come, come and look upon beings of a celestial race"; upon which both women and men, children and adults, young men and old, when they got rid of the fear they at first entertained, would come out in throngs, crowding the roads to see us, some bringing food, others drink, with astonishing affection and kindness.

conciliate to gain the trust of
induce to persuade or convince

idolatry the worship of an image or object

The Mayflower Compact

The Pilgrims who sailed to the New World on the *Mayflower* had originally intended to settle in Virginia. When they landed in Massachusetts instead, in November 1620, they realized they were outside the jurisdiction of the Virginia Charter. To establish their own authority and to avoid a possible mutiny, the Pilgrim leaders drew up and signed an agreement known as the Mayflower Compact, which is reprinted below. The Mayflower Compact, which remained in effect until 1691, was the first written attempt at self-government in American history.

T*his day, before we came to harbor, observing some not well affected to unity and concord, but gave some appearance of faction, it was thought good there should be an association and agreement that we should combine together in one body, and to submit to such government and governors as we should by common consent agree to make and choose, and set our hands to this that follows word for word.*

In the name of God, Amen. We whose names are underwritten, the loyal subjects of our dread sovereign lord, King James, by the grace of God, of Great Britain, France, and Ireland, King, Defender of the Faith, etc.

Having undertaken for the glory of God, and advancement of the Christian faith and honor of our king and country, a voyage to plant the first colony in the northern parts of Virginia, do by these present, solemnly and mutually, in the presence of God and one of another, covenant and combine ourselves together into a civil body politic, for our better ordering and preservation and furtherance of the ends aforesaid; and by virtue hereof to enact, constitute, and frame such just and equal laws, ordinances, acts, constitutions, offices from time to time as shall be thought most meet and convenient for the general good of the colony; unto which we promise all due submission and obedience. In witness whereof we have hereunder subscribed our names, Cape Cod, 11th of November, in the year of the reign of our sovereign lord, King James, of England, France, and Ireland 18, and of Scotland 54. Anno Domini 1620.

concord harmony
faction internal conflict

covenant to promise by an agreement
body politic all the people of a politically organized state
meet suitable

★ ★

"Give Me Liberty, or Give Me Death"

Patrick Henry

Patrick Henry, a distinguished lawyer and politician, was one of the first colonial leaders to take a strong public stand against the Stamp Act in 1765. Ten years later, on March 23, 1775, he delivered his most famous speech to the Virginia Provincial Convention. At a time when tensions between England and the colonies were reaching the breaking point, Henry advocated the use of the Virginia militia in defending the colony against England. A portion of the speech is reprinted below in the version reconstructed by Henry's first biographer, William Wirt.

Mr. President," said he, "it is natural to man to indulge in the illusions of hope. We are apt to shut our eyes against a painful truth and listen to the song of that siren, till she transforms us into beasts. Is this," he asked, "the part of wise men, engaged in a great and *arduous* struggle for liberty? . . ."

"Is it that *insidious* smile with which our petition has been lately received? Trust it not, sir; it will prove a snare to your feet. Suffer not yourselves to be betrayed with a kiss. Ask yourselves how this gracious reception of our petition *comports* with those warlike preparations which cover our waters and darken our land. Are fleets and armies necessary to a work of love and reconciliation? Have we shown ourselves so unwilling to be reconciled that force must be called in to win back our love? Let us not deceive ourselves, sir. These are the implements of war and subjugation—the last arguments to which kings resort. I ask gentlemen, sir, what means this *martial* array, if its purpose be not to force us to submission? Can gentlemen assign any other possible motive for it? Has Great Britain any enemy in this quarter of the world to call for all this accumulation of navies and armies? No, sir, she has none. They are meant for us; they can be meant for no other. They are sent over to bind and rivet upon us those chains which the British Ministry have been so long forging.

"And what have we oppose to them? Shall we try argument? Sir, we have been trying that for the last two years. Have we anything new to offer upon the subject? Nothing. We have held the subject up in every light of which it is capable; but it has been all in vain. Shall we resort to entreaty and humble *supplication*? What terms shall we find which have

---

arduous difficult
insidious wicked or treacherous

comports agrees or corresponds

martial military

664

supplication begging or pleading

not been already exhausted? Let us not, I beseech you, sir, deceive ourselves longer. Sir, we have done everything that could be done to avert the storm which is now coming on. We have petitioned; we have remonstrated; we have supplicated; we have prostrated ourselves before the throne and have implored its interposition to arrest the tyrannical hands of the Ministry and Parliament. Our petitions have been slighted; our remonstrances have produced additional violence and insult; our supplications have been disregarded; and we have been spurned, with contempt, from the foot of the throne. In vain, after these things, may we indulge the fond hope of peace and reconciliation.

"There is no longer any room for hope. If we wish to be free; if we mean to preserve inviolate those inestimable privileges for which we have been so long contending; if we mean not basely to abandon the noble struggle in which we have been so long engaged, and which we have pledged ourselves never to abandon, until the glorious object of our contest shall be obtained; we must fight! I repeat it, sir, we must fight!! An appeal to arms and to God of hosts is all that is left us!

"They tell us, sir,. . . that we are weak, unable to cope with so formidable an adversary. But when shall we be stronger? Will it be the next week or the next year? Will it be when we are totally disarmed, and when a British guard shall be stationed in every house? Shall we gather strength by irresolution and inaction? Shall we acquire the means of effectual resistance by lying supinely on our backs and hugging the delusive phantom of hope, until our enemies shall have bound us hand and foot? Sir, we are not weak if we make a proper use of those means which the God of nature has placed in our power. Three millions of people armed in the holy cause of liberty and in such a country as that which we possess are invincible by any force which our enemy can send against us. . . .

"Besides, sir, we have no election. If we were base enough to desire it, it is now too late to retire from the contest. There is no retreat but in submission and slavery! Our chains are forged. Their clanking may be heard on the plains of Boston! The war is inevitable —and let it come! ! I repeat it, sir, let it come! ! !

"It is vain, sir, to extenuate the matter. Gentlemen may cry, peace, peace; but there is no peace. The war is actually begun! The next gale that sweeps from the north will bring to our ears the clash of resounding arms! Our brethren are already in the field! Why stand we here idle? What is it that gentlemen wish? What would they have? Is life so dear or peace so sweet as to be purchased at the price of chains and slavery?

"Forbid it, Almighty God—I know not what course others may take; but as for me," cried he, with both his arms extended aloft, his brows knit, every feature marked with the resolute purpose of his soul, and his voice swelled to its boldest note of exclamation—"give me liberty, or give me death!"

He took his seat. No murmur of applause was heard. The effect was too deep. After the trance of a moment, several members started from their seats. The cry, "To arms!" seemed to quiver on every lip and gleam from every eye.

remonstrated argued
prostrated thrown down
interposition intervention

inviolate untouchable or unspoiled
inestimable immeasurable

adversary opponent

supinely passively or lethargically
delusive false

extenuate downplay

★ ★ ★ ★ ★ ★ ★ ★ ★ ★ ★ ★ ★ ★ ★ ★ ★ ★ ★

Common Sense

Thomas Paine

After failing at various careers, Thomas Paine emigrated from England to America in 1774. Less than two years later he became one of the most important political writers of the revolutionary period. His pamphlet *Common Sense*, part of which is reprinted below, took the colonies by storm in the winter and spring of 1776. In clear, concise prose, Paine demanded a complete break from England and called for the establishment of an American republic. As Paine hoped, his pamphlet convinced thousands of colonists that a reconciliation with England was impossible. Paine's bold ideas also influenced such important figures as George Washington and Thomas Jefferson. During the American Revolution, Paine served in Washington's army and wrote a series of pamphlets entitled *The Crisis* that encouraged the Patriots in their fight for independence.

---

embarked entered

Volumes have been written on the subject of the struggle between England and America. Men of all ranks have embarked in the controversy, from different motives, and with various designs: but all have been ineffectual, and the period of debate is closed. Arms as a last resort decide the contest; the appeal was the choice of the king, and the continent has accepted the challenge. . . .

I have heard it asserted by some, that as America hath flourished under her former connection with Great Britain, the same connection is necessary towards her future happiness, and will always have the same effect. Nothing can be more fallacious than this kind of argument. We may as well assert that because a child has thriven upon milk, that it is never to have meat, or that the first twenty years of our lives is to become a precedent for the next twenty. But even this is admitting more than is true; for I answer roundly, that America would have flourished as much, and probably much more, had no European power taken any notice of her. The commerce by which she hath enriched herself are the necessaries of life, and will always have a market while eating is the custom of Europe. . . .

fallacious false

Alas! we have been long led away by ancient prejudices, and made large sacrifices to superstition. We have boasted the protection of Great Britain without considering that her motive was interest, not attachment; and that she did not protect us from our enemies on our account, but from her enemies on her own account. . . .

But Britain is the parent country, say some. Then the more shame upon her conduct. Even brutes do not devour their young, nor savages make war upon their families. . . . Europe, and not England, is the parent country of America. This new world hath been the asylum for the persecuted lovers of civil and religious liberty from every part of Europe. Hither have they fled, not from the tender embraces of a mother, but from the cruelty of the monster; and it is so far true of England, that the same tyranny which drove the first emigrants from home, pursues their descendants still. . . .

Europe is too thickly planted with kingdoms to be long at peace, and whenever a war breaks out between England and any foreign power, the trade of America goes to ruin, because of her connection with Britain. The next war may not turn out like the last, and should it not, the advocates of reconciliation now will be wishing for separation then, because neutrality in that case would be a safer convoy than a man of war. Everything that is right or natural pleads for separation. The blood of the slain, the weeping voice of nature cries, 'TIS TIME TO PART. . . .

But where, say some, is the king of America? I'll tell you, friend, he reigns above, and doth not make havoc of mankind like the Royal Brute of Great Britain. Yet that we may not appear to be defective even in earthly honors, let a day be solemnly set apart for proclaiming the charter; let it be brought forth placed on the divine law, the Word of God; let a crown be placed thereon, by which the world may know, that so far as we approve of monarchy, that in America THE LAW IS KING. For as in absolute governments the king is law, so in free countries the law ought to be king, and there ought to be no other. But lest any ill use should afterwards arise, let the crown at the conclusion of the ceremony be demolished, and scattered among the people whose right it is.

A government of our own is our natural right; and when a man seriously reflects on the precariousness of human affairs, he will become convinced, that it is infinitely wiser and safer to form a constitution of our own in a cool deliberate manner, while we have it in our power, than to trust such an interesting event to time and chance. . . .

O ye that love mankind! Ye that dare oppose not only the tyranny but the tyrant, stand forth! Every spot of the old world is overrun with oppression. Freedom hath been hunted round the globe. Asia and Africa have long expelled her. Europe regards her like a stranger, and England hath given her warning to depart. O receive the fugitive, and prepare in time an asylum for mankind.

asylum refuge

advocates supporters
convoy escort

absolute dictatorial

precariousness uncertainty

★ ★ ★ ★ ★ ★ ★ ★ ★ ★ ★ ★ ★ ★ ★ ★ ★ ★ ★

The Monroe Doctrine

James Monroe

During the first two decades of the 1800s, when many European nations were entangled in the Napoleonic Wars, a number of colonies in Latin America took advantage of the unrest in Europe to declare their independence. After these wars were over, it seemed that the mother countries intended to regain control of their former colonies, now such countries as Chile, Peru, Colombia, and Mexico. The United States supported the independence of these colonies and did not approve of Europe's intervention in the Americas. Consequently, in a message to Congress on December 2, 1823, President James Monroe warned the nations of Europe that the United States intended to protect all independent nations in the Western Hemisphere against European military intervention. The Monroe Doctrine, part of which is reprinted below, has remained an essential part of American foreign policy ever since.

A precise knowledge of our relations with foreign powers as respects our negotiations and transactions with each is thought to be particularly necessary. . . .

In the discussions to which this interest has given rise and in the arrangements by which they may terminate the occasion has been judged proper for asserting, as a principle in which the rights and interests of the United States are involved, that the American continents, by the free and independent condition which they have assumed and maintain, are henceforth not to be considered as subjects for future colonization by any European powers. . . .

It was stated at the commencement of the last session that great effort was then making in Spain and Portugal to improve the condition of the people of those countries and that it appeared to be conducted with extraordinary moderation. It need scarcely be remarked that the result has been so far very different from what was then anticipated. Of events in that quarter of the globe with which we derive our origin, we have always been anxious and interested spectators. The citizens of the United States cherish sentiments the most friendly in favor of the liberty and happiness of their fellow men on that side of the Atlantic. In the wars of

commencement
beginning

the European powers in matters relating to themselves we have never taken any part, nor does it comport with our policy so to do. It is only when our rights are invaded or seriously menaced that we resent injuries or make preparations for our defense.

With the movements in this hemisphere we are of necessity more immediately connected, and by causes which must be obvious to all enlightened and impartial observers. The political system of the allied powers is essentially different in this respect from that of America. This difference proceeds from that which exists in their respective governments; and to the defense of our own, which has been achieved by the loss of so much blood and treasure, and matured by the wisdom of their most enlightened citizens, and under which we have enjoyed unexampled felicity, this whole nation is devoted. We owe it, therefore, to candor and to the amicable relations existing between the United States and those powers to declare that we should consider any attempt on their part to extend their system to any portion of this hemisphere as dangerous to our peace and safety.

With the existing colonies or dependencies of any European power we have not interfered and shall not interfere. But with the governments who have declared their independence and maintained it, and whose independence we have, on great consideration and on just principles, acknowledged, we could not view any interposition for the purpose of oppressing them, or controlling in any other manner their destiny, by any European power in any other light than as the manifestation of an unfriendly disposition toward the United States. In the war between those new governments and Spain we declared our neutrality at the time of their recognition, and to this we have adhered, and shall continue to adhere, provided no change shall occur which, in the judgment of competent authorities of this government, shall make a corresponding change on the part of the United States indispensable to their security. . . .

Our policy with regard to Europe, which was adopted at an early stage of the wars which have so long agitated that quarter of the globe, nevertheless remains the same, which is not to interfere in the internal concerns of its powers; to consider the government de facto as the legitimate government for us; to cultivate friendly relations with it, and to preserve those relations by a frank, firm, and manly policy, meeting in all instances the just claims of every power, submitting to injuries from none. But in regard to those continents, circumstances are eminently and conspicuously different. It is impossible that the allied powers should extend their political system to any portion of either continent without endangering our peace and happiness; nor can anyone believe that our southern brethren, if left to themselves, would adopt it of their own accord.

It is equally impossible, therefore, that we should behold such interposition in any form with indifference. If we look to the comparative strength and resources of Spain and those new governments, and their distance from each other, it must be obvious that she can never subdue them. It is still the true policy of the United States to leave the parties to themselves, in the hope that other powers will pursue the same course.

comport agree

felicity happiness
candor straight-forwardness of expression
amicable friendly

interposition intervention

adhered continued to follow

indispensable essential

eminently clearly

Civil War

Uniforms of the Civil War

At the start of the Civil War, the militia units that largely made up the Union and Confederate armies wore a variety of uniforms. Both sides soon established regulation uniforms, such as the Union blue and Confederate gray examples shown below.

WORLD BOOK illustration by H. Charles McBarron, Jr.

North

Cavalry Corporal in Winter Overcoat

Infantry Private

Cavalry Captain in Full-Dress Uniform

South

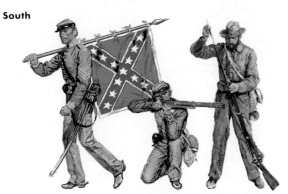

Cavalry Sergeant, 1862

Infantry Private, 1861-1862

Infantry Private, 1863-1865

Important events during the Civil War

1861

April 12 Confederate troops attacked Fort Sumter.
April 15 Lincoln issued a call for troops.
April 19 Lincoln proclaimed a blockade of the South.
May 21 Richmond, Va., was chosen as the Confederate capital.
July 21 Northern troops retreated in disorder after the First Battle of Bull Run (Manassas).

1862

Feb. 6 Fort Henry fell to Union forces.
Feb. 16 Grant's troops captured Fort Donelson.
March 9 The ironclad ships *Monitor* and *Merrimack (Virginia)* battled to a draw.
April 6-7 Both sides suffered heavy losses in the Battle of Shiloh, won by the Union.
April 16 The Confederacy began to draft soldiers.
April 18-25 Farragut attacked and captured New Orleans.
May 4 McClellan's Union troops occupied Yorktown, Va., and advanced on Richmond.
May 30 Northern forces occupied Corinth, Miss.
June 6 Memphis fell to Union armies.
June 25-July 1 Confederate forces under Lee saved Richmond in the Battles of the Seven Days.
Aug. 27-30 Lee and Jackson led Southern troops to victory in the Second Battle of Bull Run.
Sept. 17 Confederate forces retreated in defeat after the bloody Battle of Antietam (Sharpsburg).
Sept. 22 Lincoln issued a preliminary Emancipation Proclamation.
Oct. 8 Buell's forces ended Bragg's invasion of Kentucky in the Battle of Perryville.
Dec. 13 Burnside's Union forces received a crushing blow in the Battle of Fredericksburg.
Dec. 31-Jan. 2, 1863 Union troops under Rosecrans forced the Confederates to retreat after the Battle of Stones River (Murfreesboro).

1863

Jan. 1 Lincoln issued the Emancipation Proclamation.
March 3 The North passed a draft law.
May 1-4 Northern troops under Hooker were defeated in the Battle of Chancellorsville.
May 1-19 Grant's army defeated the Confederates in Mississippi and began to besiege Vicksburg.

July 1-3 The Battle of Gettysburg ended in a Southern defeat and marked a turning point in the war.
July 4 Vicksburg fell to Northern troops.
July 8 Northern forces occupied Port Hudson, La.
Sept. 19-20 Southern troops under Bragg won the Battle of Chickamauga.
Nov. 19 Lincoln delivered the Gettysburg Address.
Nov. 23-25 Grant and Thomas led Union armies to victory in the Battle of Chattanooga.

1864

March 9 Grant became general in chief of the North.
May 5-6 Union and Confederate troops clashed in the Battle of the Wilderness.
May 8-19 Grant and Lee held their positions in the Battle of Spotsylvania Court House.
June 3 The Union suffered heavy losses on the final day of the Battle of Cold Harbor.
June 20 Grant's troops laid siege to Petersburg, Va.
July 11-12 Early's Confederate forces almost reached Washington but retreated after brief fighting.
Aug. 5 Farragut won the Battle of Mobile Bay.
Sept. 2 Northern troops under Sherman captured Atlanta.
Sept. 19-Oct. 19 Sheridan led his troops on a rampage of destruction in the Shenandoah Valley.
Nov. 8 Lincoln was reelected President.
Nov. 15 Sherman began his march through Georgia.
Nov. 23 Hood invaded Tennessee.
Nov. 30 Schofield's Union forces inflicted heavy losses on Hood in the Battle of Franklin.
Dec. 15-16 The Battle of Nashville smashed Hood's army.
Dec. 21 Sherman's troops occupied Savannah, Ga.

1865

Feb. 6 Lee became general in chief of the South.
April 2 Confederate troops gave up Petersburg and Richmond.
April 9 Lee surrendered to Grant at Appomattox.
April 14 Lincoln was assassinated.
April 26 Johnston surrendered to Sherman.
May 4 Confederate forces in Alabama and Mississippi surrendered.
May 11 Jefferson Davis was captured.
May 26 The last Confederate troops surrendered.

Leading Civil War generals

National Archives
Ulysses S. Grant (North)

Valentine Museum, Richmond, Va.
Robert E. Lee (South)

Bettmann Archive
William T. Sherman (North)

Bettmann Archive
Stonewall Jackson (South)

Battles and campaigns of the Civil War

WORLD BOOK map

Excerpted from the Civil War article in *World Book*. Copyright © 1990 by World Book, Inc.

Indian, American

Where the Indians lived

The Indians of North and South America formed hundreds of tribes with many different ways of life. The location of many major tribes is shown below. Scholars divide the various tribes into groups of similar tribes that they call *culture areas*. Each culture area is shown as a different color.

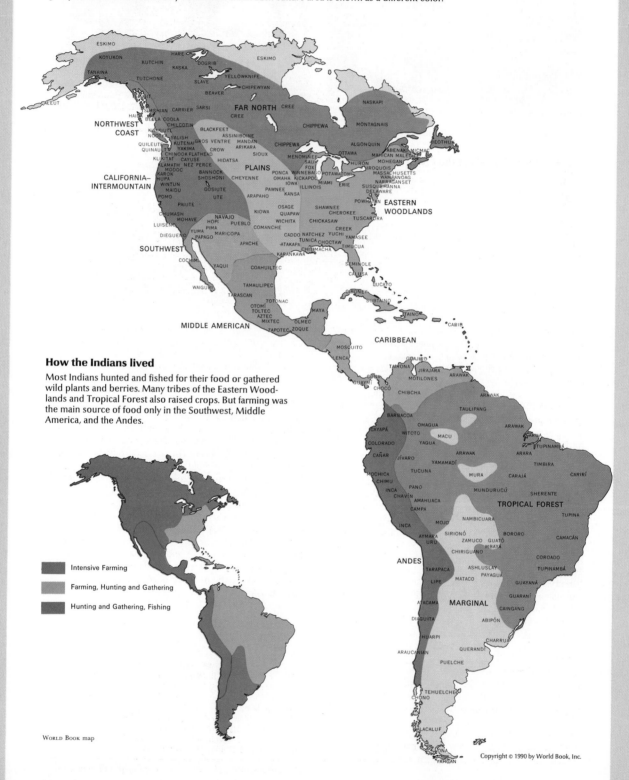

How the Indians lived

Most Indians hunted and fished for their food or gathered wild plants and berries. Many tribes of the Eastern Woodlands and Tropical Forest also raised crops. But farming was the main source of food only in the Southwest, Middle America, and the Andes.

Intensive Farming

Farming, Hunting and Gathering

Hunting and Gathering, Fishing

WORLD BOOK map

Copyright © 1990 by World Book, Inc.

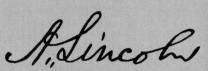

16th President of
the United States 1861-1865

Hannibal Hamlin
Vice President
1861-1865

Buchanan
15th President
1857-1861
Democrat

Lincoln
16th President
1861-1865
Republican

A. Johnson
17th President
1865-1869
Democrat

Andrew Johnson
Vice President
1865

Detail of an oil painting on canvas (1911) by Allen Tupper True; Henry E. Huntington Library and Art Gallery, San Marino, Calif.

Lincoln, Abraham (1809-1865), was one of the truly great men of all time. He led the United States during the Civil War (1861-1865), which was the greatest crisis in U.S. history. Lincoln helped end slavery in the nation and helped keep the American Union from splitting apart during the war. Lincoln thus believed that he proved to the world that democracy can be a lasting form of government. Lincoln's Gettysburg Address, second inaugural address, and many of his other speeches and writings are classic statements of democratic beliefs and goals. In conducting a bitter war, Lincoln never became bitter himself. He showed a nobility of character that has worldwide appeal. Lincoln, a Republican, was the first member of his party to become President. He was assassinated near the end of the Civil War and was succeeded by Vice President Andrew Johnson.

The American people knew little about Lincoln when he became President. Little in his past experience indicated that he could successfully deal with the deep differences between Northerners and Southerners over slavery. Lincoln received less than 40 per cent of the popular vote in winning the presidential election of 1860. But by 1865, he had become in the eyes of the world equal in importance to George Washington. Through the years, many people have regarded Lincoln as the greatest person in United States history.

During the Civil War, Lincoln's first task was to win the war. He had to view nearly all other matters in relation to the war. It was "the progress of our arms," he once said, "upon which all else depends." But Lincoln was a peace-loving man who had earlier described military glory as "that attractive rainbow, that rises in showers of blood—that serpent's eye that charms to destroy." The Civil War was by far the bloodiest war in U.S. history. In the Battle of Gettysburg, for example, the more

than 45,000 total *casualties* (people killed, wounded, captured, or missing) exceeded the number of casualties in all previous American wars put together.

Lincoln became a remarkable war leader. Some historians believe he was the chief architect of the Union's victorious military strategy. This strategy called for Union armies to advance against the enemy on all fronts at the same time. Lincoln also insisted that the objective of the Union armies should be the destruction of opposing forces, not the conquest of territory. Lincoln changed generals several times because he could not find one who would fight the war the way he wanted it fought. When he finally found such a general, Ulysses S. Grant, Lincoln stood firmly behind him.

Lincoln's second great task was to keep up Northern morale through the horrible war in which many relatives in the North and South fought against one another. He understood that the Union's resources vastly exceeded those of the Confederacy, and that the Union would eventually triumph if it remained dedicated to victory. For this reason, Lincoln used his great writing and speechmaking abilities to spur on his people.

Important dates in Lincoln's life

1809	(Feb. 12) Born near present-day Hodgenville, Ky.
1834	Elected to the Illinois General Assembly.
1842	(Nov. 4) Married Mary Todd.
1846	Elected to the U.S. House of Representatives.
1858	Debated slavery with Stephen A. Douglas.
1860	(Nov. 6) Elected President of the United States.
1864	(Nov. 8) Reelected President.
1865	(April 14) Shot by John Wilkes Booth.
1865	(April 15) Died in Washington, D.C.

Money

History of United States currency

In the American Colonies, money was scarce. England did not furnish coins and forbade the colonies to make them. The English hoped to force the colonies to trade almost entirely with England. One way of doing so was by limiting the money supply. Without money, the colonists could not do business with traders in other countries who demanded payment in cash. But the colonists could buy products from English traders with *bills of exchange.* They got these documents from other English traders in exchange for their own goods.

The American colonists used a variety of goods in place of money. These goods included beaver pelts, grain, musket balls, and nails. Some colonists, especially in the tobacco-growing colonies of Maryland and Virginia, circulated receipts for tobacco stored in warehouses. Indian wampum, which consisted of beads made from shells, was mainly used for keeping records. But Indians and colonists also accepted it as money.

The colonists also used any foreign coins they could get. English shillings, Spanish dollars, and French and Dutch coins all circulated in the colonies. Probably the most common coins were large silver Spanish dollars called *pieces of eight.* To make change, a person could

chop the coin into eight pie-shaped pieces called *bits.* Two bits were worth a quarter of a dollar, four bits a half dollar, and so on. We still use the expression *two bits* to mean a quarter of a dollar.

In 1652, the Massachusetts Bay Colony became the first colony to make coins. It produced several kinds of silver coins, including a *pine-tree shilling* and an *oak-tree shilling,* which were stamped with a tree design. Massachusetts continued to issue coins for 30 years in defiance of an English law that said only the monarch could issue them. The colony dated all coins 1652, no matter when they were made, probably to get around the law. In 1652, there was no monarch in England. Thus, the colonists could claim the coins were minted at a time when royal authority did not exist.

Massachusetts also became the first colony to produce paper money. In 1690, the colonial government issued notes called *bills of credit.* The bills were receipts for loans made by citizens to the colonial government. Massachusetts used the bills to help finance the first French and Indian war, a war between English and French colonists for control of eastern North America.

The first United States currency. During the mid-1700's, Great Britain tried to tighten its control over the American Colonies with new taxes, stricter trade regulations, and other laws. Friction between the Americans and the British mounted. In 1775, the Revolutionary War

Money in the American Colonies

Money was scarce in the American Colonies. Paper currency was seldom used, and the British did not allow the colonies to mint coins. As a result, the colonists used any foreign coins they could get. Indian wampum and other goods also circulated as money.

Wampum, which consisted of beads made from shells, was used by the Indians to decorate garments and keep records. The colonists, who had few coins, used it as money. Most wampum was made into necklaces or belts.

The oak-tree shilling was one of the first coins made in Massachusetts. The colony began to issue coins like the one above in 1660.

The escudo was used throughout the Americas. The 8-escudo coin above was minted in the reign of King Ferdinand VI of Spain.

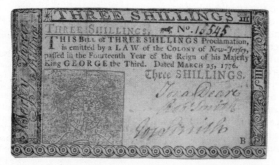

A 3-shilling note, *left,* was issued by the colony of New Jersey in 1776. A number of colonies issued their own paper currency.

674

broke out between the two sides. The next year, colonial leaders meeting as the Second Continental Congress declared independence and founded the United States of America. To help finance the war for independence, each state and the Continental Congress began to issue paper money.

As war expenses mounted, the states and Congress printed more and more money. Congress itself issued about $240 million in notes called *continentals*. So many continentals were printed that by 1780 they were almost worthless. Americans began to describe any useless thing as "not worth a continental." The experience with continentals was so bad that the U.S. government did not again issue paper currency for widespread use until the 1860's.

The United States won the Revolutionary War in 1783,

but the struggle left the American monetary system in disorder. Most of the currencies circulated by the states had little value. The U.S. Constitution, adopted in 1789, corrected this problem by giving Congress the sole power to coin money and regulate its value. In 1792, an act of Congress set up the first national money system in the United States. The act made the dollar the basic unit of money. It also put the nation on a system called the *bimetallic standard,* which meant that both gold and silver were legal money. The value of each metal in relation to the other was fixed by law. For years, 16 ounces (448 grams) of silver equaled 1 ounce (28 grams) of gold.

The act also established a national mint in Philadelphia. The mint produced $10 gold coins called *eagles,* silver dollars, and other coins.

Americans continued to use many foreign coins in ad-

Money in the new nation

Continental currency was issued by the Continental Congress to help finance the Revolutionary War (1775-1783). So many of these notes were printed that they became almost worthless.

The écu, a French coin, was one of many foreign coins that circulated in the United States after the nation won independence. A 1793 law made these coins part of the U.S. monetary system.

The Spanish dollar, or piece of eight, was another foreign coin that circulated in the new nation. The coin shown at the far left and center was minted in Mexico in 1790. These dollars could be chopped into eight pieces, called *bits,* or into quarters, *near left,* called *two bits.*

A $10 gold piece called an *eagle* was issued by the U.S. Mint from 1795 to 1933. The eagle shown above dates from 1795. It has a liberty cap on the front and an eagle on the back.

Bank notes were the most common paper money in the United States until the 1860's. Banks vowed to exchange their notes for gold or silver. The State Bank of Illinois issued this note in 1840.

Excerpted from the Money article in *World Book.* Copyright © 1990 by World Book, Inc.

Money

Later United States money

U.S. currency of the 1800's and early 1900's included silver coins, gold pieces, and various types of paper money. Many bills, including gold and silver certificates, could be exchanged for gold or silver coins on demand. The use of these two metals as money is called the *bimetallic standard*.

Silver dollar (1800)

U.S. Assay Office $50 gold piece (1851)

$20 gold double eagle (1865)

Confederate $10 bill (1861)

$5 legal tender note (about 1862)

$50 gold certificate (about 1882)

$20 national bank note (about 1882)

$50 silver certificate (about 1891)

Federal Reserve $10 bill (about 1914)

dition to their new currency. A law passed in 1793 made these coins part of the U.S. monetary system. The value of a foreign coin depended on how much gold or silver it had. In 1857, Congress passed a law removing foreign coins from circulation.

The rebirth of paper money. During the early 1800's, the only paper money in the United States consisted of hundreds of kinds of bank notes. Each bank promised to exchange its notes on demand for gold or silver coins. But numerous banks did not keep enough coins to redeem their notes. Many notes therefore were not worth their *face value*—that is, the value stated on them. As a result, people hesitated to accept bank notes.

The soundest bank notes of the early 1800's were issued by the two national banks chartered by the U.S. government. The First Bank of the United States was chartered by Congress from 1791 to 1811, and the Second Bank of the United States from 1816 to 1836. Both banks supported their notes with reserves of gold coins, and people considered the notes as good as gold.

Paper money as we know it today dates from the 1860's. To help pay the costs of the Civil War (1861-1865), the U.S. government issued about $430 million in paper money. The money could not be exchanged for gold or silver. The bills were called *legal tender notes* or *United States notes*. But most people called them *greenbacks* because the backs were printed in green. The government declared that greenbacks were *legal tender*—that is, money people must accept in payment of public and private debts. Nevertheless, the value of greenbacks depended on people's confidence in the government. That confidence rose and fell with the victories and defeats of the North in the Civil War. At one time, each greenback dollar was worth only 35 cents in gold coin. In the South, the Confederate States also issued paper money. It quickly became almost worthless.

In 1863 and 1864, Congress passed the National Bank Acts, which set up a system of privately owned banks chartered by the federal government. These national banks issued notes backed by U.S. government bonds.

Congress also taxed state bank notes to discourage banks from issuing them, and people from using them. As a result, national bank notes became the country's chief currency.

Some greenbacks also continued to circulate. The government announced that, beginning in 1879, it would pay gold coins for greenbacks. The U.S. Department of the Treasury gathered enough gold to redeem all the greenbacks likely to be brought in. But as soon as people knew they could exchange their greenbacks for gold, they were not anxious to do so. The fact that the Treasury paid out only gold coins meant the country was operating on an unofficial *gold standard,* rather than the bimetallic standard of the early 1800's. The gold standard is a system in which a nation defines its basic monetary unit as worth a certain quantity of gold and agrees to redeem its money in gold on demand.

The new national banks system eliminated the confusion that had existed when hundreds of different bank notes were in circulation. But the system did not provide for the federal government to increase the supply of money when needed. Shortages of money contributed to a series of economic slumps during the late 1800's. Many people called for the government to provide more money by coining unlimited amounts of silver. Such a policy was called *free silver,* and the argument over free silver became an important political issue.

The dispute reached a climax during the presidential election of 1896. The Republican candidate, William McKinley, favored the gold standard. McKinley defeated William Jennings Bryan, the Democratic candidate, who supported free silver. In 1900, Congress passed the Gold Standard Act, which officially put the nation on a gold standard. The United States went on and off the gold standard several times and finally abandoned it in 1971.

The United States suffered from repeated monetary difficulties until 1913, when Congress passed the Federal Reserve Act. This act created the Federal Reserve System, a central banking system that controls the nation's money supply.

United States currency today consists of coins and paper money. Under federal law, only the Department of the Treasury and the Federal Reserve System may issue U.S. currency. The Treasury issues all coins and a type of paper money known as *United States notes.* The Federal Reserve issues paper currency called *Federal Reserve notes.* All U.S. currency carries the nation's official motto, *In God We Trust.*

Coins come in six *denominations* (values): (1) penny, or 1 cent; (2) nickel, or 5 cents; (3) dime, or 10 cents; (4) quarter, or 25 cents; (5) half dollar, or 50 cents; and (6) $1. All coins are made of *alloys* (mixtures of metals). Pennies are copper-coated zinc. Nickels are a mixture of copper and nickel. Dimes, quarters, half dollars, and dollars are made of three layers of metal. The core is pure copper, and the outer layers are an alloy of copper and nickel.

Dimes, quarters, half dollars, and dollars have ridges called *reeding* or *milling* around the edge. Reeding helps blind people recognize certain denominations. For example, the reeding on a dime distinguishes it from a penny, which has a smooth edge.

Federal law requires that coins be dated with the year they were made. Coins also must bear the word *Liberty*

and the Latin motto *E Pluribus Unum,* meaning *out of many, one.* This motto refers to the creation of the United States from the original Thirteen Colonies.

Mints in Denver and Philadelphia make most coins for general circulation. Mints in San Francisco and West Point, N.Y., make mostly commemorative coins to mark special occasions, and gold and silver bullion coins for investors. People buy bullion coins for the value of the metal. Coins made in Denver are marked with a small *D.* A *P* appears on most coins made in Philadelphia. Some coins made in San Francisco are marked with an *S* and some in West Point with a *W.*

Chief features of a Federal Reserve note

Seal and letter of the Federal Reserve Bank that issued the note

Seal of the Department of the Treasury

Serial number

Serial number

Number of the Federal Reserve Bank that issued the note

Year when the note was designed

Printing plate identification numbers

Paper money. Federal Reserve notes make up nearly all the paper money issued in the United States today. About $195 billion of these notes were in circulation during the mid-1980's. They come in seven denominations: $1, $2, $5, $10, $20, $50, and $100. The notes are issued by the 12 Federal Reserve Banks in the Federal Reserve System. Each note has a letter, number, and seal that identify the bank which issued it. In addition, each note bears the words *Federal Reserve note* and a green Treasury seal. Until 1969, Federal Reserve Banks also issued notes in four large denominations: $500, $1,000, $5,000, and $10,000.

The only other paper money issued in the United States today consists of United States notes. The Treasury issues them in the $100 denomination only. These notes, which are the descendants of Civil War greenbacks, carry the words *United States note* and a red Treasury seal. The Treasury keeps about $323 million in United States notes in circulation. All Federal Reserve and United States notes bear the printed signatures of the secretary of the treasury and the treasurer of the United States.

Excerpted from the Money article in *World Book.* Copyright © 1990 by World Book, Inc.

Parklands of the National Park System

This map shows the location of the parklands in the National Park System. Because of space limitations, the parklands within the East Coast area outlined in black are not named on the map. Their names can be found by matching their numbers with those in the tables on the right of the map.

WORLD BOOK map

SAN JUAN ISLAND
NORTH CASCADES
OLYMPIC
ROSS LAKE
EBEY'S LANDING
LAKE CHELAN
KLONDIKE GOLD RUSH
GLACIER
COULEE DAM
MOUNT RAINIER
FORT CLATSOP
WASHINGTON
MOUNT SAINT HELENS
FORT VANCOUVER
WHITMAN MISSION
NEZ PERCE
FORT BENTON
FORT UNION TRADING POST
GRANT–KOHRS RANCH
MONTANA
T. ROOSEVELT
NORTH DAKOTA
JOHN DAY FOSSIL BEDS
BIG HOLE
KNIFE RIVER INDIAN VILLAGES
OREGON
IDAHO
YELLOWSTONE
CUSTER BATTLEFIELD
CRATER LAKE
BIGHORN CANYON
OREGON CAVES
CRATERS OF THE MOON
GRAND TETON
John D. Rockefeller, Jr., Memorial Parkway
DEVILS TOWER
SOUTH DAKOTA
REDWOOD
JEWEL CAVE
MOUNT RUSHMORE
LAVA BEDS
BADLANDS
WIND CAVE
WHISKEYTOWN-SHASTA-TRINITY
WYOMING
LASSEN VOLCANIC
GOLDEN SPIKE
FOSSIL BUTTE
FORT LARAMIE
AGATE FOSSIL BEDS
MISSOURI RIVER
POINT REYES
TIMPANOGOS CAVE
SCOTTS BLUFF
MUIR WOODS
DINOSAUR
NEBRASKA
JOHN MUIR, EUGENE O'NEILL
NEVADA
ROCKY MOUNTAIN
GOLDEN GATE
FORT POINT
YOSEMITE
HOMESTEAD
DEVILS POSTPILE
CALIFORNIA
COLORADO
PINNACLES
KINGS CANYON
CAPITOL REEF
ARCHES
BLACK CANYON
FLORISSANT FOSSIL BEDS
SEQUOIA
CEDAR BREAKS
CANYONLANDS
CURECANTI
UTAH
KANSAS
DEATH VALLEY
ZION
BRYCE CANYON
NATURAL BRIDGES
HOVENWEEP
YUCCA HOUSE
BENT'S OLD FORT
FORT LARNED
RAINBOW BRIDGE
PIPE SPRING
MESA VERDE
LAKE MEAD
GLEN CANYON
GREAT SAND DUNES
AZTEC RUINS
NAVAJO
CANYON DE CHELLY
GRAND CANYON
CAPULIN MOUNTAIN
WUPATKI
CHACO CULTURE
SUNSET CRATER
SANTA MONICA MOUNTAINS
WALNUT CANYON
HUBBELL TRADING POST
BANDELIER
FORT UNION
CHANNEL ISLANDS
JOSHUA TREE
TUZIGOOT
PECOS
LAKE MEREDITH
MONTEZUMA CASTLE
PETRIFIED FOREST
EL MORRO
CABRILLO
ARIZONA
ALIBATES FLINT QUARRIES
OKLAHOMA
HOHOKAM PIMA
TONTO
SALINAS
CASA GRANDE
GILA CLIFF DWELLINGS
NEW MEXICO
CHICKASAW
ORGAN PIPE CACTUS
SAGUARO
FORT BOWIE
WHITE SANDS
TUMACACORI
CHIRICAHUA
CORONADO
CARLSBAD CAVERNS
CHAMIZAL
GUADALUPE MOUNTAINS
TEXAS
FORT DAVIS
RIO GRANDE
LYNDON B. JOHNSON
BIG BEND
AMISTAD
SAN ANTONIO MISSIONS
PADRE ISLAND
PALO ALTO BATTLEFIELD

Alaska inset

CAPE KRUSENSTERN
NOATAK
GATES OF THE ARCTIC
BERING LAND BRIDGE
GATES OF THE ARCTIC
KOBUK VALLEY
ALASKA
YUKON-CHARLEY RIVERS
DENALI
DENALI
WRANGELL-ST. ELIAS
LAKE CLARK
LAKE CLARK
WRANGELL-ST. ELIAS
ALAGNAK
KLONDIKE GOLD RUSH
KATMAI
KENAI FJORDS
GLACIER BAY
ANIAKCHAK
KATMAI
GLACIER BAY
SITKA
ANIAKCHAK

0   200   400 Miles
0   200   400 Kilometers

Hawaii inset

U.S.S. ARIZONA
KALAUPAPA
HALEAKALA
PUUKOHOLA HEIAU
HAWAII
HAWAII VOLCANOES
KALOKO-HONOKOHAU
PU'UHONUA O HONAUNAU

0   200   400 Miles
0   200   400 Kilometers

Guam inset

GUAM
WAR IN THE PACIFIC

0   20 Miles
0   20 Kilometers

National Park System

Political party

The Democratic Party is the oldest existing political party in the United States. Some historians believe it began in the 1790's as Jefferson's Democratic-Republican Party. Most historians trace the party's origin to the campaign organization that formed after the 1824 presidential election to win the presidency for Jackson in 1828.

From 1828 to 1860, the Democratic Party won all but two presidential elections—those of 1840 and 1848—even though its members often disagreed on several issues. They fought, for example, over banking policies, the slavery issue, and tariff rates. Democrats also met bitter opposition from outside the party. About 1832, several groups that opposed Jackson combined to form the Whig Party. But the Whigs never united sufficiently to propose a program with as much popular appeal as that of the Democrats.

During the 1850's, the Democrats split over whether to oppose or support the extension of slavery. In 1860, the party even had two nominees for President—John C. Breckinridge and Stephen A. Douglas. Both lost to the Republican candidate, Abraham Lincoln.

From 1860 to 1932, only two Democrats won the presidency—Grover Cleveland in 1884 and 1892 and Woodrow Wilson in 1912 and 1916. The Republican Party had gained so much strength during the Civil War that the Democrats had great difficulty winning control of the government. In addition, the Republicans repeatedly charged the Democrats with having caused the war and having been disloyal to the Union.

The situation changed after 1929. Just as the Republicans had blamed the Democrats for the Civil War, so the Democrats blamed the Republicans for the stock market crash of 1929 and the Great Depression of the 1930's. The Democrats held the presidency from 1933 to 1953. During most of this period, they also controlled both houses of Congress. The Democrats kept control of both houses from 1955 to 1981. In 1981, the Republicans took over the Senate, though the Democrats held the House of Representatives. The Democrats regained control of both houses of Congress in the 1986 elections. However, since 1948, the Democrats have won the presidency only three times—in 1960, 1964, and 1976.

The Republican Party started as a series of antislavery political meetings in the Midwest in 1854. At that time, the Whig Party was breaking up. Many Whigs—as well as Northern Democrats—opposed the extension of slavery. The Republican Party represented this viewpoint and thus gained followers rapidly. The party's first presidential candidate, John C. Frémont, ran unsuccessfully in 1856, but he carried 11 Northern states.

From 1860, when Lincoln was elected, through 1928, the Republican Party won 14 of the nation's 18 presidential elections. Its policies appealed to many groups, including farmers, industrialists, and merchants. But financial scandals in Republican Ulysses S. Grant's presidency in the 1870's and economic unrest in the nation nearly cost the party the presidential election of 1876.

In 1912, President William Howard Taft was the leader of a divided Republican Party. Progressive Republicans wanted Theodore Roosevelt, who had been President from 1901 to 1909, to run again. But conservative Republicans renominated Taft at the party's 1912 national convention. Roosevelt then withdrew from the party and formed the Progressive, or "Bull Moose," Party. This split helped the Democratic candidate, Woodrow Wilson, win the election. The Republicans lost to Wilson again in 1916. They regained the presidency in 1920, and won in 1924 and 1928. But their popularity declined after the stock market crash of 1929.

During World War II (1939-1945), the Republicans began to show signs of recovery. In 1946, they won majorities in both houses of Congress for the first time since 1928. Then, in 1952, Dwight D. Eisenhower brought the Republicans their first presidential victory in 24 years. Eisenhower won again in 1956. But he had a Republican majority in both houses of Congress for only the first two of his eight years in office.

The Republicans lost to the Democrats in the 1960 and 1964 presidential elections. They regained the presidency in 1968 and held it in 1972, but the Democrats continued to control Congress. The Republicans lost the presidency to the Democrats in 1976 but regained it in 1980, when they also won control of the Senate. In the 1986 elections, the Democrats regained control of both houses of Congress. The Republicans held the presidency in 1984 and 1988.

Important political parties of the United States

This chart shows the time spans of some of the important political parties of the United States. A question mark means the date is disputed by political historians.

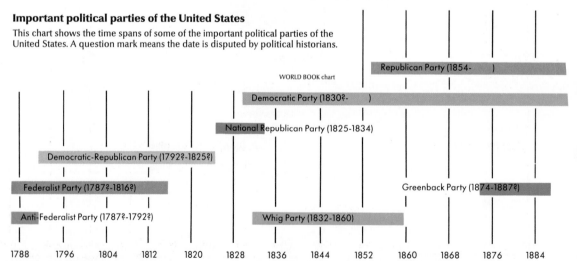

WORLD BOOK chart

Republican Party (1854-   )

Democratic Party (1830?-   )

National Republican Party (1825-1834)

Democratic-Republican Party (1792?-1825?)

Federalist Party (1787?-1816?)

Greenback Party (1874-1887?)

Anti-Federalist Party (1787?-1792?)

Whig Party (1832-1860)

1788   1796   1804   1812   1820   1828   1836   1844   1852   1860   1868   1876   1884

Administrations in office

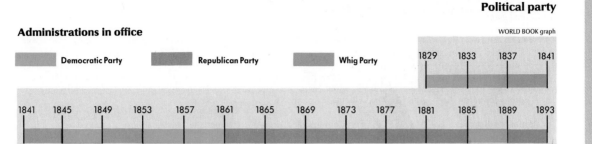

Democratic Party   Republican Party   Whig Party

| 1829 | 1833 | 1837 | 1841 |

| 1841 | 1845 | 1849 | 1853 | 1857 | 1861 | 1865 | 1869 | 1873 | 1877 | 1881 | 1885 | 1889 | 1893 |

| 1893 | 1897 | 1901 | 1905 | 1909 | 1913 | 1917 | 1921 | 1925 | 1929 | 1933 | 1937 | 1941 | 1945 |

| 1945 | 1949 | 1953 | 1957 | 1961 | 1965 | 1969 | 1973 | 1977 | 1981 | 1985 | 1989 | 1993 | 1997 |

Third parties. There have been many third parties in the United States. None of them ever won the presidency. But many of their proposals gained such widespread public support that the two major parties were forced to adopt them. These proposals included the convention system of nominating presidential candidates and the direct election of U.S. senators.

Third parties in the United States can be divided into five types, according to their origins and goals. The first type consists of groups that broke away from the two major parties. For example, the Liberal Republicans in 1872 and the Roosevelt Progressives in 1912 left the Republican Party. The Gold Democrats in 1896, the Dixiecrats in 1948, and the American Independent Party in 1968 split from the Democratic Party.

The second type of third party consists of organizations formed chiefly to help a specific group of people.

For example, debt-ridden farmers established the Greenback Party in the 1870's and the Populist Party in the 1890's.

The third type is made up of left wing protest groups. They include the Socialist Labor Party, formed in 1877; the Socialist Party, founded in 1901; the American Communist Party, organized in 1919; and the Socialist Workers Party, formed in 1938.

The fourth type consists of parties that have only one goal. These single-issue parties include the nation's oldest existing third party—the Prohibition Party, founded in 1869. This party seeks to prevent the manufacture and sale of alcoholic beverages in the United States.

The fifth type of third party consists of groups that have broad programs and attempt to gain national favor. Examples of this type of third party include the Progressive parties of 1924, 1948, and 1952.

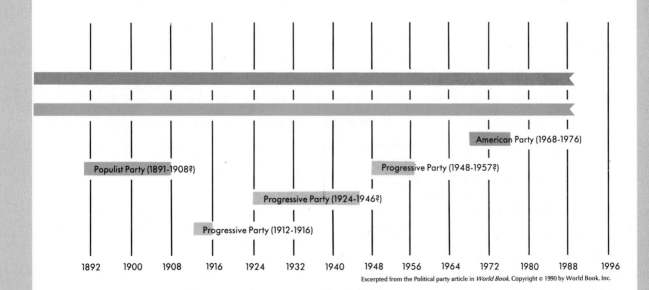

American Party (1968-1976)

Populist Party (1891-1908?)

Progressive Party (1948-1957?)

Progressive Party (1924-1946?)

Progressive Party (1912-1916)

| 1892 | 1900 | 1908 | 1916 | 1924 | 1932 | 1940 | 1948 | 1956 | 1964 | 1972 | 1980 | 1988 | 1996 |

Excerpted from the Political party article in *World Book*. Copyright © 1990 by World Book, Inc.

Presidents of the United States

President	Born	Birthplace	Political party	Age at inauguration	Served	Died	Age at death
1. George Washington ...	Feb. 22, 1732	Westmoreland County, Va.	None	57	1789-1797	Dec. 14, 1799	67
2. John Adams	Oct. 30, 1735	Braintree, Mass.	Federalist	61	1797-1801	July 4, 1826	90
3. Thomas Jefferson	Apr. 13, 1743	Albemarle County, Va.	Democratic-Republican	57	1801-1809	July 4, 1826	83
4. James Madison	Mar. 16, 1751	Port Conway, Va.	Democratic-Republican	57	1809-1817	June 28, 1836	85
5. James Monroe	Apr. 28, 1758	Westmoreland County, Va.	Democratic-Republican	58	1817-1825	July 4, 1831	73
6. John Quincy Adams	July 11, 1767	Braintree, Mass.	Democratic-Republican	57	1825-1829	Feb. 23, 1848	80
7. Andrew Jackson	Mar. 15, 1767	Waxhaw settlement, S.C. (?)	Democratic	61	1829-1837	June 8, 1845	78
8. Martin Van Buren	Dec. 5, 1782	Kinderhook, N.Y.	Democratic	54	1837-1841	July 24, 1862	79
9. William H. Harrison	Feb. 9, 1773	Berkeley, Va.	Whig	68	1841	Apr. 4, 1841	68
10. John Tyler	Mar. 29, 1790	Greenway, Va.	Whig	51	1841-1845	Jan. 18, 1862	71
11. James K. Polk	Nov. 2, 1795	near Pineville, N.C.	Democratic	49	1845-1849	June 15, 1849	53
12. Zachary Taylor	Nov. 24, 1784	Orange County, Va.	Whig	64	1849-1850	July 9, 1850	65
13. Millard Fillmore	Jan. 7, 1800	Locke, N.Y.	Whig	50	1850-1853	Mar. 8, 1874	74
14. Franklin Pierce	Nov. 23, 1804	Hillsboro, N.H.	Democratic	48	1853-1857	Oct. 8, 1869	64
15. James Buchanan	Apr. 23, 1791	near Mercersburg, Pa.	Democratic	65	1857-1861	June 1, 1868	77
16. Abraham Lincoln	Feb. 12, 1809	near Hodgenville, Ky.	Republican	52	1861-1865	Apr. 15, 1865	56
17. Andrew Johnson	Dec. 29, 1808	Raleigh, N.C.	Natl. Union†	56	1865-1869	July 31, 1875	66
18. Ulysses S. Grant	Apr. 27, 1822	Point Pleasant, Ohio	Republican	46	1869-1877	July 23, 1885	63
19. Rutherford B. Hayes ...	Oct. 4, 1822	Delaware, Ohio	Republican	54	1877-1881	Jan. 17, 1893	70
20. James A. Garfield	Nov. 19, 1831	Orange, Ohio	Republican	49	1881	Sept. 19, 1881	49
21. Chester A. Arthur	Oct. 5, 1829	Fairfield, Vt.	Republican	51	1881-1885	Nov. 18, 1886	57
22. Grover Cleveland	Mar. 18, 1837	Caldwell, N.J.	Democratic	47	1885-1889	June 24, 1908	71
23. Benjamin Harrison	Aug. 20, 1833	North Bend, Ohio	Republican	55	1889-1893	Mar. 13, 1901	67
24. Grover Cleveland	Mar. 18, 1837	Caldwell, N.J.	Democratic	55	1893-1897	June 24, 1908	71
25. William McKinley	Jan. 29, 1843	Niles, Ohio	Republican	54	1897-1901	Sept. 14, 1901	58
26. Theodore Roosevelt ...	Oct. 27, 1858	New York, N.Y.	Republican	42	1901-1909	Jan. 6, 1919	60
27. William H. Taft	Sept. 15, 1857	Cincinnati, Ohio	Republican	51	1909-1913	Mar. 8, 1930	72
28. Woodrow Wilson	Dec. 29, 1856	Staunton, Va.	Democratic	56	1913-1921	Feb. 3, 1924	67
29. Warren G. Harding	Nov. 2, 1865	near Blooming Grove, Ohio	Republican	55	1921-1923	Aug. 2, 1923	57
30. Calvin Coolidge	July 4, 1872	Plymouth Notch, Vt.	Republican	51	1923-1929	Jan. 5, 1933	60
31. Herbert C. Hoover	Aug. 10, 1874	West Branch, Iowa	Republican	54	1929-1933	Oct. 20, 1964	90
32. Franklin D. Roosevelt .	Jan. 30, 1882	Hyde Park, N.Y.	Democratic	51	1933-1945	Apr. 12, 1945	63
33. Harry S. Truman	May 8, 1884	Lamar, Mo.	Democratic	60	1945-1953	Dec. 26, 1972	88
34. Dwight D. Eisenhower	Oct. 14, 1890	Denison, Tex.	Republican	62	1953-1961	Mar. 28, 1969	78
35. John F. Kennedy	May 29, 1917	Brookline, Mass.	Democratic	43	1961-1963	Nov. 22, 1963	46
36. Lyndon B. Johnson	Aug. 27, 1908	near Stonewall, Tex.	Democratic	55	1963-1969	Jan. 22, 1973	64
37. Richard M. Nixon	Jan. 9, 1913	Yorba Linda, Calif.	Republican	56	1969-1974		
38. Gerald R. Ford‡	July 14, 1913	Omaha, Nebr.	Republican	61	1974-1977		
39. Jimmy Carter	Oct. 1, 1924	Plains, Ga.	Democratic	52	1977-1981		
40. Ronald W. Reagan	Feb. 6, 1911	Tampico, Ill.	Republican	69	1981-1989		
41. George H. W. Bush	June 12, 1924	Milton, Mass.	Republican	64	1989-		

†The National Union Party consisted of Republicans and War Democrats; Johnson was a Democrat.
‡Inaugurated Aug. 9, 1974, to replace Nixon, who resigned that same day.

Each President has a separate biography and picture in *World Book*.

College or university	Religion	Occupation or profession	Runner-up		Vice President	
1.	Episcopalian	Planter	John Adams	(1789, 1792)	John Adams	(1789-1797)
2. Harvard	Unitarian	Lawyer	Thomas Jefferson	(1796)	Thomas Jefferson	(1797-1801)
3. William and Mary	Unitarian*	Planter, lawyer	Aaron Burr / Charles C. Pinckney	(1800) / (1804)	Aaron Burr / George Clinton	(1801-1805) / (1805-1809)
4. Princeton	Episcopalian	Lawyer	Charles C. Pinckney / De Witt Clinton	(1808) / (1812)	George Clinton / Elbridge Gerry	(1809-1812) / (1813-1814)
5. William and Mary	Episcopalian	Lawyer	Rufus King / No opposition	(1816)	Daniel D. Tompkins	(1817-1825)
6. Harvard	Unitarian	Lawyer	Andrew Jackson	(1824)	John C. Calhoun	(1825-1829)
7.	Presbyterian	Lawyer	John Quincy Adams / Henry Clay	(1828) / (1832)	John C. Calhoun / Martin Van Buren	(1829-1832) / (1833-1837)
8.	Dutch Reformed	Lawyer	William H. Harrison	(1836)	Richard M. Johnson	(1837-1841)
9. Hampden-Sydney	Episcopalian	Soldier	Martin Van Buren	(1840)	John Tyler	(1841)
10. William and Mary	Episcopalian	Lawyer				
11. U. of N. Carolina	Methodist	Lawyer	Henry Clay	(1844)	George M. Dallas	(1845-1849)
12.	Episcopalian	Soldier	Lewis Cass	(1848)	Millard Fillmore	(1849-1850)
13.	Unitarian	Lawyer				
14. Bowdoin	Episcopalian	Lawyer	Winfield Scott	(1852)	William R. King	(1853)
15. Dickinson	Presbyterian	Lawyer	John C. Frémont	(1856)	John C. Breckinridge	(1857-1861)
16.	Presbyterian*	Lawyer	Stephen A. Douglas / Geo. B. McClellan	(1860) / (1864)	Hannibal Hamlin / Andrew Johnson	(1861-1865) / (1865)
17.	Methodist*	Tailor				
18. U.S. Mil. Academy	Methodist	Soldier	Horatio Seymour / Horace Greeley	(1868) / (1872)	Schuyler Colfax / Henry Wilson	(1869-1873) / (1873-1875)
19. Kenyon	Methodist*	Lawyer	Samuel J. Tilden	(1876)	William A. Wheeler	(1877-1881)
20. Williams	Disciples of Christ	Lawyer	Winfield S. Hancock	(1880)	Chester A. Arthur	(1881)
21. Union	Episcopalian	Lawyer				
22.	Presbyterian	Lawyer	James G. Blaine	(1884)	Thomas A. Hendricks	(1885)
23. Miami	Presbyterian	Lawyer	Grover Cleveland	(1888)	Levi P. Morton	(1889-1893)
24.	Presbyterian	Lawyer	Benjamin Harrison	(1892)	Adlai E. Stevenson	(1893-1897)
25. Allegheny College	Methodist	Lawyer	William J. Bryan	(1896, 1900)	Garret A. Hobart / Theodore Roosevelt	(1897-1899) / (1901)
26. Harvard	Dutch Reformed	Author	Alton B. Parker	(1904)	Charles W. Fairbanks	(1905-1909)
27. Yale	Unitarian	Lawyer	William J. Bryan	(1908)	James S. Sherman	(1909-1912)
28. Princeton	Presbyterian	Educator	Theodore Roosevelt / Charles E. Hughes	(1912) / (1916)	Thomas R. Marshall	(1913-1921)
29.	Baptist	Editor	James M. Cox	(1920)	Calvin Coolidge	(1921-1923)
30. Amherst	Congregationalist	Lawyer	John W. Davis	(1924)	Charles G. Dawes	(1925-1929)
31. Stanford	Friend (Quaker)	Engineer	Alfred E. Smith	(1928)	Charles Curtis	(1929-1933)
32. Harvard	Episcopalian	Lawyer	Herbert Hoover / Alfred M. Landon / Wendell L. Willkie / Thomas E. Dewey	(1932) / (1936) / (1940) / (1944)	John N. Garner / Henry A. Wallace / Harry S. Truman	(1933-1941) / (1941-1945) / (1945)
33.	Baptist	Businessman	Thomas E. Dewey	(1948)	Alben W. Barkley	(1949-1953)
34. U.S. Mil. Academy	Presbyterian	Soldier	Adlai E. Stevenson	(1952, 1956)	Richard M. Nixon	(1953-1961)
35. Harvard	Roman Catholic	Author	Richard M. Nixon	(1960)	Lyndon B. Johnson	(1961-1963)
36. Southwest Texas State	Disciples of Christ	Teacher	Barry M. Goldwater	(1964)	Hubert H. Humphrey	(1965-1969)
37. Whittier	Friend (Quaker)	Lawyer	Hubert H. Humphrey / George S. McGovern	(1968) / (1972)	Spiro T. Agnew / Gerald R. Ford**	(1969-1973) / (1973-1974)
38. Michigan	Episcopalian	Lawyer			Nelson A. Rockefeller§	(1974-1977)
39. U.S. Naval Academy	Baptist	Businessman	Gerald R. Ford	(1976)	Walter F. Mondale	(1977-1981)
40. Eureka	Disciples of Christ	Actor	Jimmy Carter / Walter F. Mondale	(1980) / (1984)	George H. W. Bush	(1981-1989)
41. Yale	Episcopalian	Businessman	Michael S. Dukakis	(1988)	Dan Quayle	(1989-)

*Church preference; never joined any church.

**Inaugurated Dec. 6, 1973, to replace Agnew, who resigned Oct. 10, 1973.
§Inaugurated Dec. 19, 1974, to replace Ford, who became President Aug. 9, 1974.

Revolutionary War

Important dates in the Revolutionary War

1775

April 19 Minutemen and redcoats clashed at Lexington and Concord.
June 15 The Congress named George Washington commander in chief of the Continental Army.
June 17 The British drove the Americans from Breed's Hill in the Battle of Bunker Hill.

1776

Feb. 27 The patriots defeated the Loyalists at Moore's Creek Bridge.
March 17 The British evacuated Boston.
July 4 The Declaration of Independence was adopted.
Aug. 27 The redcoats defeated the patriots on Long Island.
Sept. 15 The British occupied New York City.
Dec. 26 Washington mounted a surprise attack on Hessian troops at Trenton.

1777

Jan. 3 Washington gained a victory at Princeton.
Aug. 6 Loyalists and Indians forced the patriots back at Oriskany, but then withdrew.
Aug. 16 The patriots crushed the Hessians near Bennington.
Sept. 11 The British won the Battle of Brandywine.
Sept. 19 Gates's forces checked Burgoyne's army in the First Battle of Freeman's Farm.
Sept. 26 The British occupied Philadelphia.
Oct. 4 Washington's forces met defeat in the Battle of Germantown.
Oct. 7 The patriots defeated the British in the Second Battle of Freeman's Farm.
Oct. 17 Burgoyne surrendered at Saratoga.
Dec. 19 Washington's army retired to winter quarters at Valley Forge.

1778

Feb. 6 The United States and France signed an alliance.
June 28 The Battle of Monmouth ended in a draw.
Dec. 29 The redcoats took Savannah.

1779

Feb. 25 British defenders of Vincennes surrendered to George Rogers Clark.
June 21 Spain declared war on Great Britain.
Sept. 23 John Paul Jones's ship, the *Bonhomme Richard*, captured the British ship *Serapis*.

1780

May 12 Charleston fell after a British siege.
Aug. 16 The British defeated the Americans at Camden.
Oct. 7 American frontiersmen stormed the Loyalist positions on Kings Mountain.

1781

Jan. 17 The patriots won a victory at Cowpens.
March 15 Cornwallis clashed with Greene at Guilford Courthouse.
Sept. 5 A French fleet inflicted great damage on a British naval force at Chesapeake Bay.
Oct. 19 Cornwallis' forces surrendered at Yorktown.

1782

March 20 King George's chief minister, Lord North, resigned.
Nov. 30 The Americans and British signed a preliminary peace treaty in Paris.

1783

April 15 Congress ratified the preliminary peace treaty.
Sept. 3 The United States and Great Britain signed the final peace treaty in Paris.

Major battles of the Revolutionary War

Name	Place	Date	Commander		Dead and wounded*		Results
			American	British	American	British	
Bennington	Vermont	Aug. 16, 1777	Stark	Baum, Breymann	80	200	British defeat encouraged the patriots in their campaign against Burgoyne.
Brandywine	Pennsylvania	Sept. 11, 1777	Washington	Howe	700	540	An American retreat enabled the British to occupy Philadelphia.
Bunker Hill	Massachusetts	June 17, 1775	Prescott	Howe	400	1,000	The patriots were driven from their positions overlooking Boston.
Camden	South Carolina	Aug. 16, 1780	Gates	Cornwallis	1,000	300	The British crushed an American army.
Cowpens	South Carolina	Jan. 17, 1781	Morgan	Tarleton	70	330	Patriot victory encouraged Southern militiamen to come out and fight.
Freeman's Farm (First Battle)	New York	Sept. 19, 1777	Gates	Burgoyne	300	600	The British advance from Canada was halted.
Freeman's Farm (Second Battle)	New York	Oct. 7, 1777	Gates	Burgoyne	150	600	The patriots turned back a second attack.
Germantown	Pennsylvania	Oct. 4, 1777	Washington	Howe	650	550	An American attack turned into a loss and a retreat.
Guilford Courthouse	North Carolina	March 15, 1781	Greene	Cornwallis	250	650	The British decided to give up most of North Carolina.
Kings Mountain	South Carolina	Oct. 7, 1780	Campbell	Ferguson	100	300	The British advance into North Carolina was delayed.
Lexington and Concord	Massachusetts	April 19, 1775	Parker and others	Smith	90	250	The Revolutionary War in America began.
Long Island	New York	Aug. 27, 1776	Washington	Howe	250	400	The British forced the Americans from Long Island.
Monmouth	New Jersey	June 28, 1778	Washington	Clinton	250	400	A patriot attack ended in a draw.
Princeton	New Jersey	Jan. 3, 1777	Washington	Cornwallis	50	100	The British withdrew from western New Jersey.
Quebec	Quebec	Dec. 31, 1775	Arnold, Montgomery	Carleton	100	18	The Americans failed to seize the city of Quebec.
Trenton	New Jersey	Dec. 26, 1776	Washington	Rall	10	100	The patriots crushed the Hessians in a surprise assault.
Yorktown	Virginia	Oct. 6-19, 1781	Washington	Cornwallis	100	600	The British surrendered in the war's last major battle.

*Approximate totals. The figures listed are a compromise between several conflicting estimates.

Revolutionary War battles and campaigns

British strategy at first called for crushing the American Revolution in the North. After 1778, the fighting shifted to the South. In 1781, an American and French force defeated the British at Yorktown in the last major battle of the war. This map locates important battles and campaigns.

WORLD BOOK map

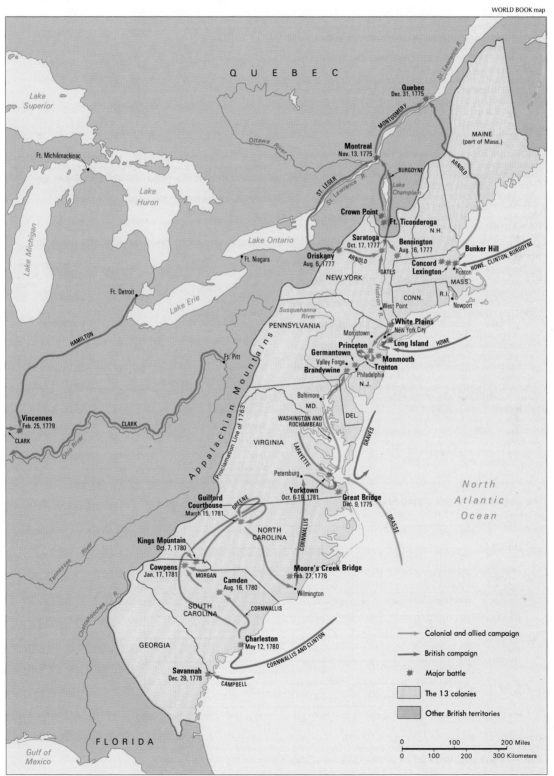

Lake Superior

Ft. Michilimackinac

Lake Huron

Lake Michigan

Ft. Detroit

Lake Erie

QUEBEC

Ottawa River

Quebec
Dec. 31, 1775

MONTGOMERY

St. Lawrence R.

MAINE
(part of Mass.)

Montreal
Nov. 13, 1775

BURGOYNE

ARNOLD

ST. LEGER

St. Lawrence R.

Lake Champlain

Crown Point

Ft. Ticonderoga
N.H.

Lake Ontario

Saratoga
Oct. 17, 1777

Bennington
Aug. 16, 1777

Bunker Hill

Ft. Niagara

Oriskany
Aug. 6, 1777

ARNOLD

GATES

Concord
Lexington

HOWE, CLINTON, BURGOYNE

Boston

MASS.

NEW YORK

Hudson R.

CONN.

R.I.

West Point

Newport

HAMILTON

Susquehanna River

PENNSYLVANIA

Morristown

White Plains
New York City

Long Island

HOWE

Ft. Pitt

Princeton

Germantown

Valley Forge

Brandywine

Monmouth

Trenton

Philadelphia

N.J.

Vincennes
Feb. 25, 1779

CLARK

CLARK

Ohio River

Appalachian Mountains

Proclamation Line of 1763

Baltimore

MD.

WASHINGTON AND
ROCHAMBEAU

DEL.

GRAVES

VIRGINIA

LAFAYETTE

North
Atlantic
Ocean

Tennessee River

Petersburg

Guilford
Courthouse
March 15, 1781

GREENE

Yorktown
Oct. 6-19, 1781

Great Bridge
Dec. 9, 1775

CORNWALLIS

GRASSE

Kings Mountain
Oct. 7, 1780

NORTH
CAROLINA

Chattahoochee R.

Cowpens
Jan. 17, 1781

MORGAN

Camden
Aug. 16, 1780

Moore's Creek Bridge
Feb. 27, 1776

Wilmington

SOUTH
CAROLINA

CORNWALLIS

GEORGIA

Charleston
May 12, 1780

CORNWALLIS AND CLINTON

Savannah
Dec. 29, 1778

CAMPBELL

FLORIDA

Gulf of
Mexico

→ Colonial and allied campaign

→ British campaign

✳ Major battle

The 13 colonies

Other British territories

0   100   200 Miles
0   100   200   300 Kilometers

United States

Facts in brief

Capital: Washington, D.C.

Form of government: Republic. For details, see **United States, Government of the.**

Area: 3,618,770 sq. mi. (9,372,571 km²), including 79,481 sq. mi. (205,856 km²) of inland water but excluding 60,788 sq. mi. (157,440 km²) of Great Lakes and Lake Saint Clair and 13,942 sq. mi. (36,110 km²) of coastal water. *Greatest distances excluding Alaska and Hawaii*—east-west, 2,807 mi. (4,517 km); north-south, 1,598 mi. (2,572 km). *Greatest distances in Alaska*—north-south, about 1,200 mi. (1,930 km); east-west, about 2,200 mi. (3,540 km). *Greatest distance in Hawaii*—northwest-southeast, about 1,610 mi. (2,591 km). *Extreme points including Alaska and Hawaii*—northernmost, Point Barrow, Alaska; southernmost, Ka Lae, Hawaii; easternmost, West Quoddy Head, Me.; westernmost, Cape Wrangell, Attu Island, Alaska. *Coastline*—4,993 mi. (8,035 km), excluding Alaska and Hawaii; 12,383 mi. (19,929 km), including Alaska and Hawaii.

Elevation: *Highest*—Mount McKinley in Alaska, 20,320 ft. (6,194 m) above sea level. *Lowest*—In Death Valley in California, 282 ft. (86 m) below sea level.

Physical features: *Longest river*—Mississippi, 2,348 mi. (3,779 km). *Largest lake within the United States*—Michigan, 22,300 sq. mi. (57,757 km²). *Largest island*—island of Hawaii, 4,038 sq. mi. (10,458 km²).

Population: *Estimated 1990 population*—250,372,000; density, 69 persons per sq. mi. (27 per km²); distribution, 74 per cent urban, 26 per cent rural. *1980 census*—226,545,805. *Estimated 1995 population*—259,259,000.

Chief products: *Agriculture*—beef cattle, chickens, corn, cotton, eggs, hogs, milk, soybeans, wheat. *Fishing industry*—crabs, salmon, shrimp. *Manufacturing*—airplanes, broadcasting equipment, cameras, computers and computer parts, fabricated metal products, gasoline, guided missiles, industrial chemicals, industrial machinery, motor vehicles, paper, pharmaceuticals, plastics, printed materials, processed foods, steel. *Mining*—coal, natural gas, petroleum.

Flag: Adopted June 14, 1777.

Motto: *In God We Trust,* adopted July 30, 1956.

National anthem: "The Star-Spangled Banner," adopted March 3, 1931.

Bird: Bald eagle, adopted June 20, 1782.

Flower: Rose, adopted Oct. 7, 1986.

Money: *Basic unit*—dollar.

Gross national product of the United States

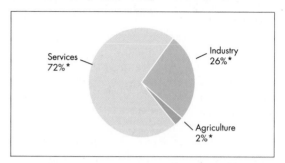

Services 72%*
Industry 26%*
Agriculture 2%*

The gross national product (GNP) is the total value of goods and services produced by a country in a year. The GNP measures a nation's total economic performance and can also be used to compare the economic output and growth of countries. The U.S. GNP was $4,526,700,000,000 in 1987.

Production and workers by economic activities

Economic activities	Per cent of GDP* produced	Employed workers Number of persons	Per cent of total
Manufacturing	19	19,065,000	17
Community, social, & personal services	18	24,196,000	22
Finance, insurance, & real estate	17	6,549,000	6
Wholesale & retail trade	16	24,381,000	22
Government	12	20,322,000	19
Communication & utilities	6	2,218,000	2
Construction	5	4,998,000	5
Transportation	3	3,166,000	3
Agriculture, forestry, & fishing	2	3,208,000	3
Mining	2	721,000	1
Total	100	108,825,000	100

*Based on gross domestic product (GDP). GDP is the total value of goods and services produced within the country in a year.
Sources: U.S. Bureau of Economic Analysis; U.S. Bureau of Labor Statistics.

The population of the United States

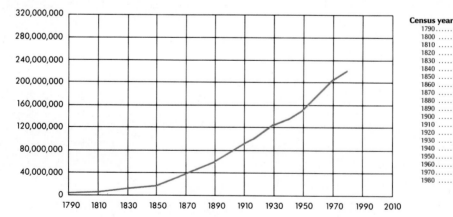

Census year	Population
1790	3,929,214
1800	5,308,483
1810	7,239,881
1820	9,638,453
1830	12,866,020
1840	17,069,453
1850	23,191,876
1860	31,443,321
1870	39,818,449
1880	50,155,783
1890	62,974,714
1900	75,994,575
1910	91,972,266
1920	105,710,620
1930	122,775,046
1940	131,669,275
1950	150,697,361
1960	179,323,175
1970	203,235,298
1980	226,545,805

Source: U.S. Bureau of the Census.

The population of the United States has risen steadily since the country's first census was taken in 1790. The above graph illustrates the country's population growth since the first census. The table at the right lists the population figure for each census year.

Regions of the United States

The map below shows the location of the seven regions of the continental United States. The table below the map lists the states within each region.

WORLD BOOK map

Symbols of the United States include the American flag and the Great Seal. The eagle holds an olive branch and arrows, symbolizing a desire for peace but the ability to wage war. The reverse side bears the Eye of Providence, representing God, and a pyramid dated 1776.

New England
Connecticut, Maine, Massachusetts, New Hampshire, Rhode Island, Vermont

Middle Atlantic States
New Jersey, New York, Pennsylvania

Southern States
Alabama, Arkansas, Delaware, Florida, Georgia, Kentucky, Louisiana, Maryland, Mississippi, North Carolina, South Carolina, Tennessee, Virginia, West Virginia

Midwestern States
Illinois, Indiana, Iowa, Kansas, Michigan, Minnesota, Missouri, Nebraska, North Dakota, Ohio, South Dakota, Wisconsin

Rocky Mountain States
Colorado, Idaho, Montana, Nevada, Utah, Wyoming

Southwestern States
*Arizona, *New Mexico, Oklahoma, Texas

Pacific Coast States
California, Oregon, Washington

*Arizona and New Mexico are often grouped with the Rocky Mountain States.

Main outlying areas of the United States

Name	Acquired	Status
American Samoa	*	Unorganized unincorporated territory
Baker Island and Jarvis Island	1856	Unincorporated territory
Guam	1898	Organized unincorporated territory
Howland Island	1856	Unincorporated possession
Johnston Island and Sand Island	1858	Unincorporated territory
Kingman Reef	1922	Unincorporated territory
Midway Island	1867	Unincorporated territory
Northern Mariana Islands	1947	Commonwealth
Palmyra Island	1898	Unincorporated possession
Puerto Rico	1898	Commonwealth
Trust Territory of the Pacific Islands	1947	UN trust territory (U.S. administration)
Virgin Islands of the United States	1917	Organized unincorporated territory
Wake Island	1898	Unincorporated possession

*Acquired in stages between 1900 and 1925.

The U.S. federal government dollar

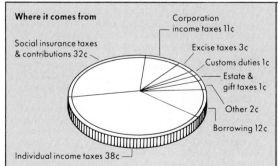

Where it comes from
Corporation income taxes 11¢
Social insurance taxes & contributions 32¢
Excise taxes 3¢
Customs duties 1¢
Estate & gift taxes 1¢
Other 2¢
Borrowing 12¢
Individual income taxes 38¢

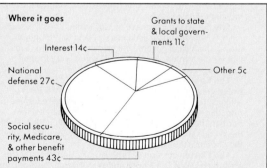

Where it goes
Grants to state & local governments 11¢
Interest 14¢
Other 5¢
National defense 27¢
Social security, Medicare, & other benefit payments 43¢

Proposals made by President George Bush in February 1989 for fiscal year Oct. 1, 1989-Sept. 30, 1990. Source: U.S. Office of Management and Budget.

United States

Major territorial acquisitions of the United States

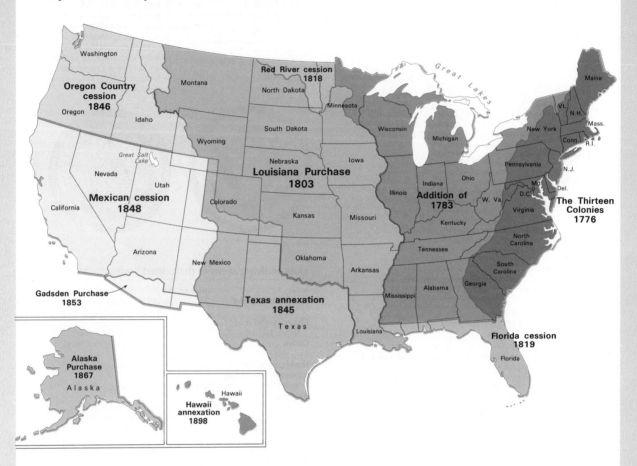

The United States added territory in a number of ways. It bought vast areas, gained others by treaty, and won much land through war. Following are brief descriptions of the major territorial acquisitions of the United States from 1776 to 1898.

The Thirteen Colonies occupied what became the original area of the United States. The 13 original states and parts of Maine, Vermont, and West Virginia were formed from this area.

The addition of 1783 extended the nation's boundaries north to the Great Lakes, south to the 31st parallel, and west to the Mississippi River. All or most of nine states were formed from this region, which more than doubled the territory of the United States.

The Louisiana Purchase of 1803 added 827,987 square miles (2,144,476 square kilometers) of land to the United States. The federal government paid France about $15 million for the territory. Part or all of 15 states were formed from the area.

The Red River cession was included in a treaty between the United States and Great Britain in 1818. Parts of Minnesota, North Dakota, and South Dakota were formed from this area. The treaty also made the 49th parallel the northern boundary of the United States between the Lake of the Woods and the high land in the Rocky Mountains called the *Continental Divide.*

The Florida cession of 1819 gave the United States the areas then called East Florida and West Florida. Parts of Loui-

siana, Mississippi, and Alabama and all of Florida were formed from this territory, which was ceded by Spain.

The Texas annexation of 1845 added what was then the nation's largest state. Most of the present boundaries of Texas were established in 1850, when the state gave up claims to western lands.

The Oregon Country cession extended the western border of the United States to the Pacific Ocean in 1846. This cession also established the 49th parallel as the nation's northern boundary in the area west of the Continental Divide. Idaho, Washington, and Oregon were formed from the Oregon region.

The Mexican cession of 1848 added over 525,000 square miles (1,360,000 square kilometers) of land to the United States. The government paid Mexico $15 million for a region that became the states of California, Nevada, and Utah. Parts of four other states were also formed from this region.

The Gadsden Purchase of 1853 gave the United States 29,640 square miles (76,770 square kilometers) of land in what is now Arizona and New Mexico. The United States paid Mexico $10 million for the land.

The Alaska Purchase of 1867 added 586,000 square miles (1,518,000 square kilometers) of territory to the country. The government paid Russia $7,200,000 for this region.

The Hawaii annexation of 1898 gave the United States its largest present overseas possession. The Hawaiian Islands cover 6,450 square miles (16,710 square kilometers).

Excerpted from the United States article in *World Book.* Copyright © 1990 by World Book, Inc.

United States, Government of the

How a bill becomes law in the United States

The drawings on this page and the next three pages show how federal laws are enacted in the United States. Thousands of bills are introduced during each Congress, which lasts two years, and hundreds become law. All bills not enacted by the end of the two-year period are killed.

WORLD BOOK illustrations by David Cunningham

Ideas for new laws come from many sources. The President, members of Congress, and other government officials may propose laws. Suggestions also come from individual citizens; special-interest groups, such as farmers, industry, and labor; newspaper editorials; and public protests. Congressional committees, in addition to lawyers who represent special-interest groups, actually write most bills and put them into proper legal form. Specialists called *legislative counsels* in both the Senate and House of Representatives also help prepare many bills for congressional action.

Individual citizens

Public protests

Newspaper editorials

Special-interest groups

The President

Members of Congress and other government officials

Each bill must be sponsored by a member of the House or Senate. Any number of senators or representatives may co-sponsor a bill. A bill may originate in either house of Congress unless it deals with taxes or spending. The Constitution provides that all such bills must be introduced in the House. The tradition that money bills must begin in the lower house came from England. There, the lower house—the House of Commons—is more likely to reflect the people's wishes because the people elect its members. They do not elect the upper house, the House of Lords. The rule has little meaning in the United States because voters elect both houses.

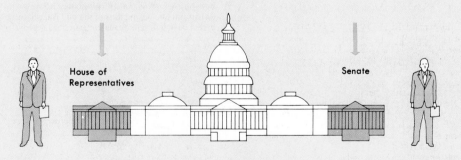

House of Representatives

Senate

United States, Government of the

How a bill goes through Congress

The drawings on this page and the next show the normal path of a bill introduced in the House of Representatives. The process is the same for a bill introduced in the Senate, except that the House action comes after the Senate action. A bill may die at almost any stage of the process if no action is taken on it. A majority of the bills introduced in Congress fail and never become law.

Introduction in the House. A sponsor introduces a bill by giving it to the clerk of the House or placing it in a box called the *hopper*. The clerk reads the title of the bill into the *Congressional Record* in a procedure called the *first reading*. The Government Printing Office prints the bill and distributes copies.

Assignment to committee. The speaker of the House assigns the bill to a committee for study. The House has about 20 *standing* (permanent) committees, each with jurisdiction over bills in a certain area.

The bill goes to the Senate to await its turn. Bills normally reach the Senate floor in the order that they come from committee. But if a bill is urgent, the leaders of the majority party might push it ahead.

Committee action. The committee or one of its subcommittees studies the bill and may hold hearings. The committee may approve the bill as it stands, revise the bill, or table it.

Assignment to committee. The Vice President of the United States, who is the presiding officer of the Senate, assigns the proposed law to a committee for study. The Senate has about 15 standing committees.

The Senate considers the bill. Senators can debate a bill indefinitely, unless they vote to limit discussion. When there is no further debate, the Senate votes. Most bills must have a simple majority to pass.

A conference committee made up of members of both houses works out any differences between the House and Senate versions of the bill. The revised bill is sent back to both houses for their final approval.

The committee studies the bill and hears testimony from experts and other interested persons. In some cases, a subcommittee conducts the study. The committee may release the bill with a recommendation to pass it, revise the bill and release it, or lay it aside so that the House cannot vote on it. Releasing the bill is called *reporting it out,* and laying it aside is called *tabling*.

The bill goes on a calendar, a list of bills awaiting action. The Rules Committee may call for quick action on the bill, limit debate, and limit or prohibit amendments. Otherwise, a bill might never reach the House floor.

Consideration by the House begins with a second reading of the bill, the only complete reading in most cases. A third reading, by title only, comes after any amendments have been added. If the bill passes by a *simple majority* (one more than half the votes), it goes to the Senate.

Introduction in the Senate. To introduce a bill, a senator must be recognized by the presiding officer and announce the introduction of the bill. A bill that has passed either house of Congress is sometimes called an *act,* but the term usually means legislation that has passed both houses and become law.

The bill is printed by the Government Printing Office in a process called *enrolling*. The clerk of the house of Congress that originated the bill certifies the final version.

The Speaker of the House signs the enrolled bill, and then the Vice President signs it. Finally, Congress sends the proposed new legislation to the White House for consideration by the President.

Action by the President

A bill passed by Congress goes to the President, who has 10 days—not including Sundays—to sign or veto it. The President may also let a bill become law by letting 10 days pass without acting.

Approval. After approving a bill, the President signs it, dates it, and often writes *approved* on it.

Veto. A vetoed bill must be returned to Congress with an explanation of the President's objections.

No action. The President might not veto the bill but may fail to sign it to show disapproval of some parts.

Reconsideration by Congress. If two-thirds of those members present approve the vetoed bill, it becomes law despite the veto.

Ten days pass. If the President holds the bill for 10 days—excluding Sundays—while Congress is in session, it becomes law without the signature of the chief executive. A bill that reaches the President fewer than 10 days—excluding Sundays—before Congress adjourns cannot become law without the President's signature. If the President fails to sign the proposed law, it dies. This procedure is called a *pocket veto*.

The bill becomes law and is given a number that indicates which Congress passed it. For example, a law enacted by the 95th Congress might be designated Public Law 95-250.

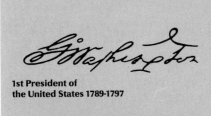

**1st President of
the United States 1789-1797**

Washington
1st President
1789-1797
No political
party

J. Adams
2nd President
1797-1801
Federalist

John Adams
Vice President
1789-1797

Oil painting on canvas (1796) by Gilbert Stuart; Jointly owned by the National Portrait Gallery, Smithsonian Institution, and the Museum of Fine Arts, Boston

Washington, George (1732-1799), won a lasting place in American history as the "Father of our Country." For nearly 20 years, he guided his country much as a father cares for a growing child.

In three important ways, Washington helped shape the beginning of the United States. First, he commanded the Continental Army that won American independence from Great Britain in the Revolutionary War. Second, Washington served as president of the convention that wrote the United States Constitution. Third, he was elected the first President of the United States.

The people of his day loved Washington. His army officers would have made him king if he had let them. From the Revolutionary War on, his birthday was celebrated each year throughout the country.

Washington lived an exciting life in exciting times. As a boy, he explored the wilderness. When he grew older, he helped the British fight the French and Indians. Many times he was nearly killed. As a general, he suffered hardships with his troops in the cold winters at Valley Forge, Pa., and Morristown, N.J. He lost many battles, but led the American army to final victory at Yorktown, Va. After he became President, he successfully solved many problems in turning the plans of the Constitution into a working government.

Washington went to school only until he was about 14 or 15. But he learned to make the most of all his abilities and opportunities. Washington's remarkable patience and his understanding of others helped him win people to his side in times of hardship and discouragement.

There are great differences between the United States of Washington's day and that of today. The new nation was small and weak. It stretched west only to the Mississippi River and had fewer than 4,000,000 people. Most people made their living by farming. Few children went to school. Few men or women could read or write. Transportation and communication were slow. It took Washington 3 days to travel about 90 miles (140 kilometers) from New York City to Philadelphia, longer than it now takes to fly around the world. There were only 11 states in the Union when Washington became President and 16 when he left office.

Important dates in Washington's life

1732	(Feb. 22) Born in Westmoreland County, Virginia.
1749	Became official surveyor for Culpeper County, Virginia.
1751	Went to Barbados Island, British West Indies.
1753	Carried British ultimatum to French in Ohio River Valley, as a major.
1754	Surrendered Fort Necessity in the French and Indian War, as a colonel.
1755	(July 9) With General Edward Braddock when ambushed by French and Indians.
1755-1758	Commanded Virginia's frontier troops, as a colonel.
1759	(Jan. 6) Married Mrs. Martha Dandridge Custis.
1774	Elected delegate to First Continental Congress.
1775	Elected delegate to Second Continental Congress.
1775	(June 15) Elected commander in chief of Continental Army.
1781	(Oct. 19) Victory at Yorktown.
1787	(May 25) Elected president of the Constitutional Convention.
1789	Elected first President of the United States.
1792	Reelected President of the United States.
1796	(Sept. 19) Published *Farewell Address,* refusing a third term.
1798	(July 4) Commissioned lieutenant general and commander in chief of new United States Army.
1799	(Dec. 14) Died at Mount Vernon at age 67.

Excerpted from the George Washington article in *World Book.* Copyright © 1990 by World Book, Inc.

WORLD: *Political*

ABBREVIATIONS

BOS. AND HERZ.
    Bosnia and Herzegovina
CEN. AFR. REP.
    Central African Republic
DEN. Denmark
FR. France
GR. Greece
IT. Italy
N. North, Northern
NETH. Netherlands
N.Z. New Zealand
PORT. Portugal
S. South
SP. Spain
U.A.E. United Arab
    Emirates
U.K. United Kingdom
U.S. United States
W. Western

—— National boundary

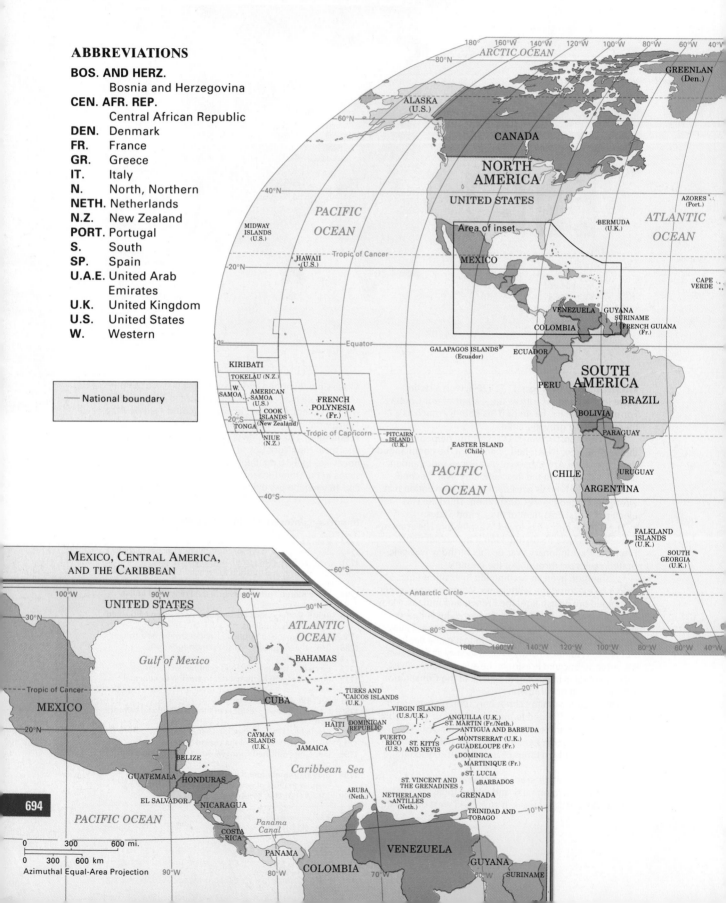

MEXICO, CENTRAL AMERICA, AND THE CARIBBEAN

0   300   600 mi.
0   300   600 km
Azimuthal Equal-Area Projection

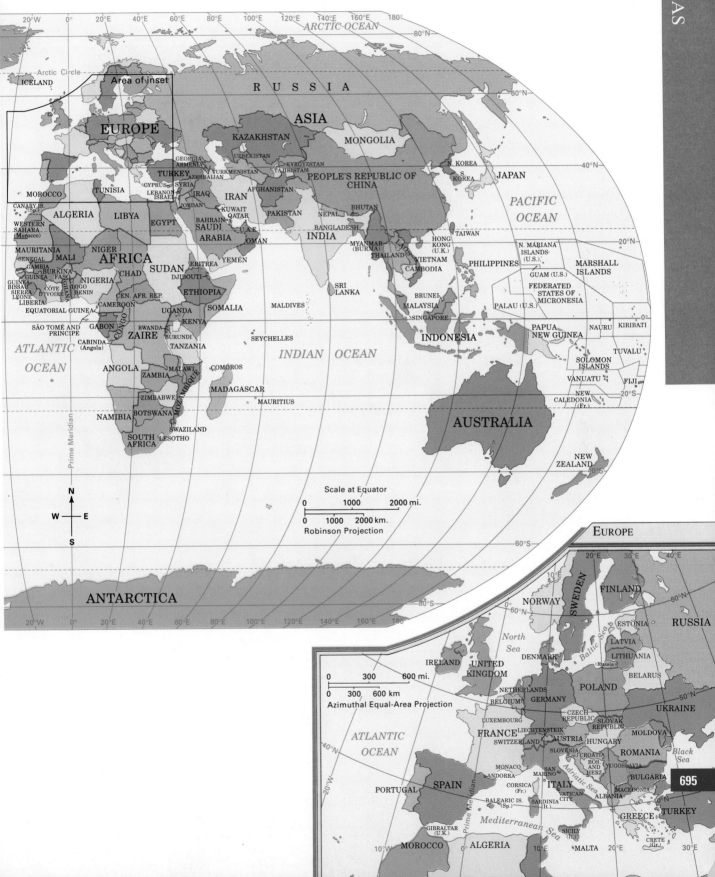

ARCTIC OCEAN

Beaufort Sea

GREENLAND

Baffin Bay

Mt. McKinley

Bering Sea

Gulf of Alaska

ALEUTIAN ISLANDS

ROCKY MOUNTAINS

NORTH AMERICA

Hudson Bay

NEWFOUNDLAND

GREAT PLAINS

Great Lakes

APPALACHIAN MTS.

AZORES

PACIFIC OCEAN

Mt. Whitney

Gulf of Mexico

BAHAMAS

BERMUDA

ATLANTIC OCEAN

Tropic of Cancer

HAWAIIAN ISLANDS

YUCATAN PEN.

CUBA

HISPANIOLA

WEST INDIES

CAPE VERDE ISLANDS

Caribbean Sea

CENTRAL AMERICA

GUIANA HIGHLANDS

Equator

GALAPAGOS ISLANDS

AMAZON BASIN

POLYNESIA

ANDES

SOUTH AMERICA

BRAZILIAN HIGHLANDS

Tropic of Capricorn

ATACAMA DESERT

PACIFIC OCEAN

Mt. Aconcagua

PAMPAS

PATAGONIA

FALKLAND ISLANDS

Cape Horn

Antarctic Circle

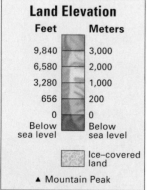

Land Elevation

Feet		Meters
9,840		3,000
6,580		2,000
3,280		1,000
656		200
0		0
Below sea level		Below sea level

Ice-covered land

▲ Mountain Peak

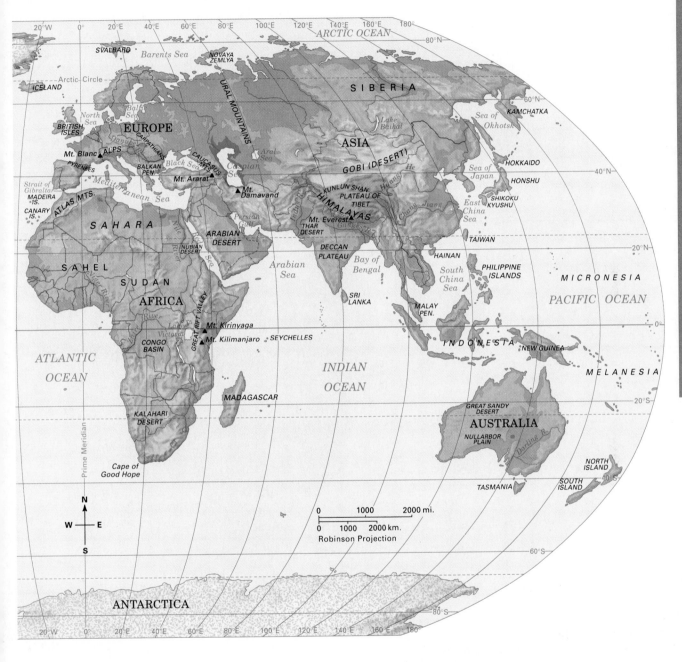

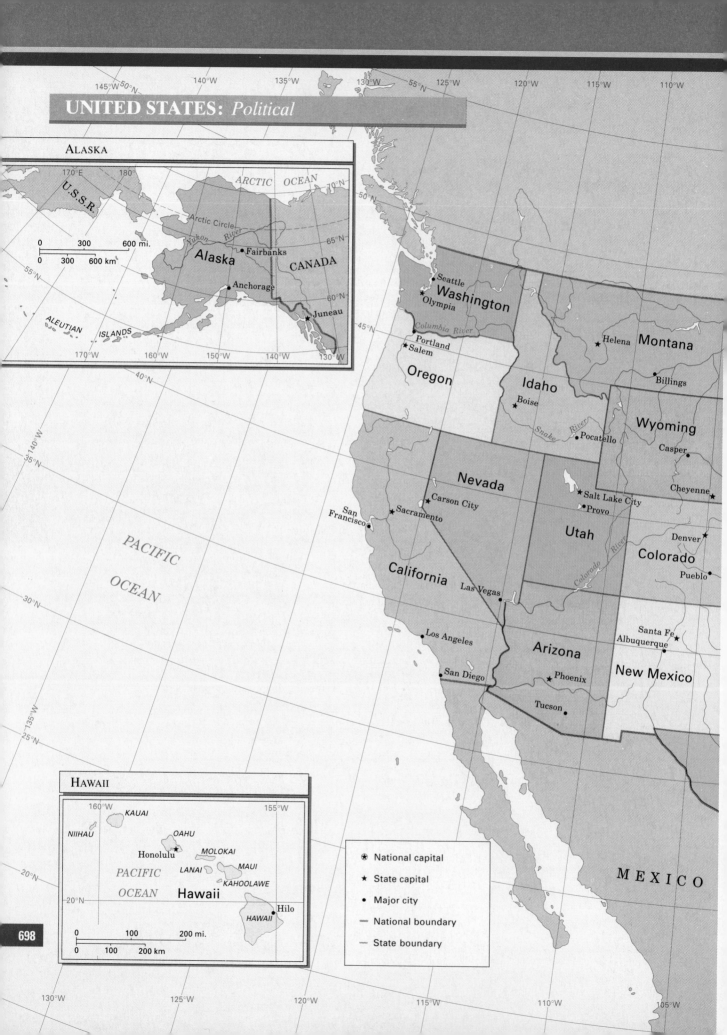

UNITED STATES: *Political*

ALASKA

ARCTIC OCEAN

U.S.S.R.

170°E   180   70°N

Arctic Circle
Yukon River

0   300   600 mi.
0   300   600 km

Alaska   • Fairbanks   65°N   CANADA

55°N

• Anchorage   60°N

ALEUTIAN   ISLANDS   ★ Juneau

170°W   160°W   150°W   140°W   130°W

PACIFIC

OCEAN

145°W 50°N   140°W   135°W   130°W   55°N   125°W   120°W   115°W   110°W

50°N

• Seattle
Washington
★ Olympia

45°N

★ Portland
★ Salem
Columbia River

Oregon

40°N

35°140°W

35°N

30°N

25°N

Idaho
• Boise
★

Snake   River

Nevada

★ Carson City
San
Francisco •   ★ Sacramento

California

Las Vegas

• Los Angeles

• San Diego

★ Helena   Montana

• Billings

Wyoming

• Pocatello   Casper •

★ Salt Lake City   Cheyenne ★
• Provo

Utah   Denver ★
Colorado
Colorado River   • Pueblo

Santa Fe
Albuquerque • ★

Arizona   • Phoenix   New Mexico

• Tucson

HAWAII

160°W   KAUAI   155°W

NIIHAU   OAHU

Honolulu ★   MOLOKAI
PACIFIC   LANAI   MAUI
20°N   KAHOOLAWE
OCEAN   Hawaii

• Hilo
HAWAII

0   100   200 mi.
0   100   200 km

MEXICO

✪	National capital
★	State capital
•	Major city
—	National boundary
—	State boundary

130°W   125°W   120°W   115°W   110°W   105°W

698

CANADA

105°W 100°W 95°W 90°W 85°W 80°W 75°W 70°W 65°W 60°W

55°N
50°N
45°N
40°N
35°N
30°N
25°N
20°N

Lake Superior

North Dakota
Bismarck
Fargo
Minnesota
Pierre
South Dakota
Sioux Falls
Minneapolis
St. Paul
Wisconsin
Madison
Milwaukee
Michigan
Lake Michigan
Lake Huron
Lansing
Detroit
Lake Erie
Lake Ontario

Maine
Augusta
Vermont
Burlington
Montpelier
New Hampshire
Portland
Concord
Boston
Albany
New York
Massachusetts
Providence
Hartford
Rhode Island
New Haven
Connecticut

Nebraska
Platte River
Missouri River
Omaha
Lincoln
Sioux City
Iowa
Des Moines
Chicago
Illinois
Indiana
Springfield
Indianapolis
Ohio
Columbus
Cleveland
Pennsylvania
Harrisburg
Pittsburgh
Wilmington
Philadelphia
New Jersey
Trenton
New York
Dover
Delaware
Baltimore
Annapolis
Maryland
Washington
West Virginia
Charleston
Virginia
Richmond
Norfolk

Kansas
Topeka
Wichita
Kansas City
Jefferson City
Missouri
St. Louis
Louisville
Frankfort
Kentucky
Evansville
Ohio River
Arkansas River
Nashville
Tennessee
North Carolina
Raleigh
Charlotte

Oklahoma
Oklahoma City
Tulsa
Fort Smith
Arkansas
Little Rock
Memphis
Mississippi River
South Carolina
Columbia
Charleston
Red River

Texas
Dallas
Austin
Houston
Rio Grande
Louisiana
Jackson
Baton Rouge
New Orleans
Mississippi
Greenville
Birmingham
Alabama
Montgomery
Atlanta
Georgia
Savannah
Tallahassee
Florida
Tampa
Miami

ATLANTIC OCEAN

Gulf of Mexico

N
W E
S

BAHAMAS

CUBA

70°W
75°W
80°W
85°W
90°W
95°W
100°W

0   200   400 mi.
0   200   400 km
Albers Equal-Area Projection

699

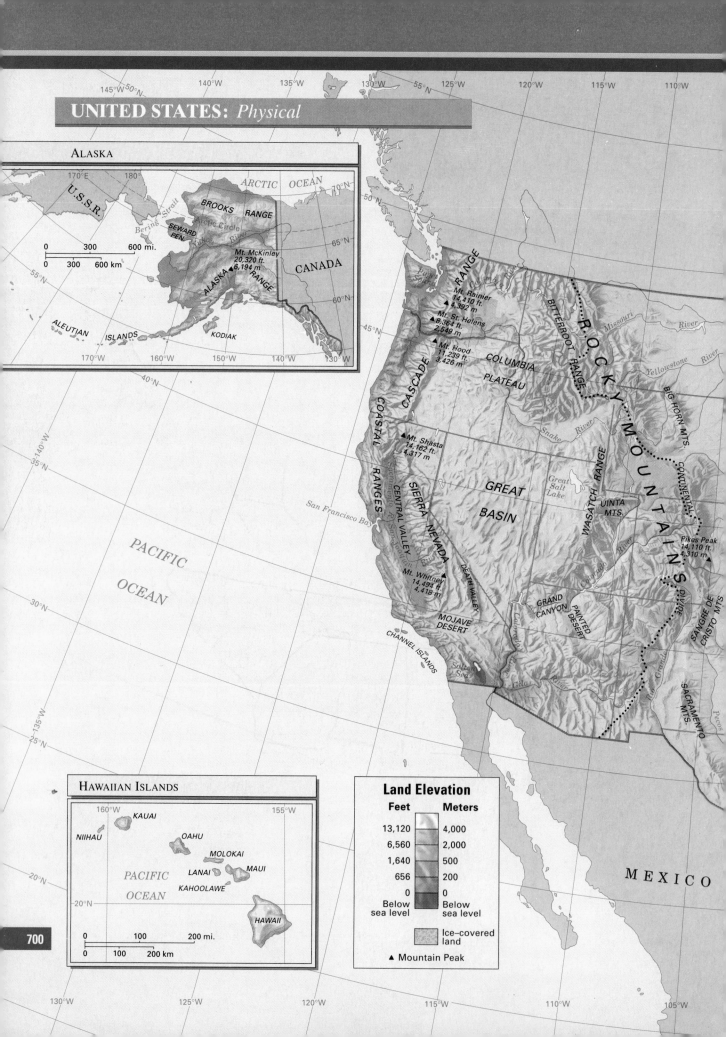

ALASKA

U.S.S.R.

ARCTIC OCEAN

BROOKS RANGE

Bering Strait

SEWARD PEN.

Arctic Circle

Yukon River

70°N

65°N

CANADA

Mt. McKinley
20,320 ft.
6,194 m

ALASKA RANGE

60°N

55°N

ALEUTIAN ISLANDS

KODIAK

| 0 | 300 | 600 mi. |
| 0 | 300 | 600 km |

170°E   180°   170°W   160°W   150°W   140°W   130°W

45°N

PACIFIC OCEAN

CANADA

COASTAL RANGE

Puget Sound

Mt. Rainier
14,410 ft.
4,392 m

Mt. St. Helens
8,364 ft.
2,549 m

Mt. Hood
11,239 ft.
3,426 m

CASCADE RANGE

COLUMBIA PLATEAU

BITTERROOT RANGE

ROCKY MOUNTAINS

Missouri River

Yellowstone River

BIG HORN MTS.

CONTINENTAL

Snake River

Mt. Shasta
14,162 ft.
4,317 m

COASTAL RANGES

Sacramento R.

CENTRAL VALLEY

San Joaquin R.

SIERRA NEVADA

GREAT BASIN

Great Salt Lake

WASATCH RANGE

UINTA MTS.

DIVIDE

Pikes Peak
14,110 ft.
4,310 m

San Francisco Bay

Mt. Whitney
14,494 ft.
4,418 m

DEATH VALLEY

GRAND CANYON

Colorado River

PAINTED DESERT

SANGRE DE CRISTO MTS

MOJAVE DESERT

CHANNEL ISLANDS

Salton Sea

Gila River

Rio Grande

SACRAMENTO MTS.

Pecos R.

MEXICO

HAWAIIAN ISLANDS

KAUAI

NIIHAU

OAHU

MOLOKAI

LANAI

MAUI

KAHOOLAWE

PACIFIC OCEAN

HAWAII

160°W   155°W

20°N

| 0 | 100 | 200 mi. |
| 0 | 100 | 200 km |

Land Elevation

Feet	Meters
13,120	4,000
6,560	2,000
1,640	500
656	200
0	0
Below sea level	Below sea level

Ice-covered land

▲ Mountain Peak

PACIFIC OCEAN

700

105°W 100°W 95°W 90°W 85°W 80°W 75°W 70°W 55°N 65°W 60°W

CANADA

Lake of the Woods

GREAT

MESABI RANGE

Lake Superior

50°N

St. Lawrence River

WHITE MTS.

▲ Mt. Washington
6,288 ft.
1,917 m

45°N

Lake Huron

Lake Michigan

BLACK HILLS

BADLANDS

Mississippi

Red River

Des Moines River

ADIRONDACK MTS.

CATSKILL MTS.

NANTUCKET

MARTHA'S VINEYARD

PLAINS

SAND HILLS

Missouri River

Lake Ontario

Lake Erie

Susquehanna River

Hudson R.

LONG ISLAND

40°N

Platte River

CENTRAL PLAINS

River

PLATEAU

ALLEGHENY PLATEAU

Delaware Bay

Arkansas River

OZARK PLATEAU

Ohio River

Wabash River

APPALACHIAN

Chesapeake Bay

35°N

CUMBERLAND PLATEAU

MOUNTAINS

BLUE RIDGE MTS.

FALL LINE

ATLANTIC

70°W

OUACHITA MOUNTAINS

Arkansas River

Tennessee River

▲ Mt. Mitchell
6,684 ft.
2,037 m

ATLANTIC COASTAL PLAIN

OCEAN

LLANO ESTACADO

Red River

Mississippi River

Savannah R.

30°N

EDWARDS PLATEAU

Brazos River

Sabine River

Red River

Tombigbee River

Alabama River

Pearl River

Chattahoochee River

Altamaha R.

Colorado River

Rio Grande

GULF COASTAL PLAIN

Mobile Bay

Pensacola Bay

Galveston Bay

N
W   E
S

Tampa Bay

Lake Okeechobee

BAHAMAS

25°N

Gulf of Mexico

EVERGLADES

FLORIDA KEYS

701

CUBA

0   200   400 mi.
0   200   400 km
Albers Equal-Area Projection

20°N

100°W 95°W 90°W 85°W 80°W 75°W

NORTH AMERICA: *Political*

EUROPE

ASIA

ARCTIC OCEAN

Bering Sea

Bering Strait

Beaufort Sea

Yukon River

QUEEN ELIZABETH ISLANDS

ELLESMERE ISLAND

GREENLAND (Denmark)

Baffin Bay

BANKS ISLAND

VICTORIA ISLAND

BAFFIN ISLAND

Arctic Circle

Gulf of Alaska

Anchorage

KODIAK ISLAND

ALEXANDER ARCHIPELAGO

Mackenzie River

QUEEN CHARLOTTE ISLANDS

Peace River

River

Hudson Bay

Labrador Sea

VANCOUVER ISLAND

Vancouver

Puget Sound

Seattle

Portland

Columbia R.

Edmonton

Calgary

CANADA

Winnipeg

NEWFOUNDLAND

PRINCE EDWARD ISLAND

CAPE BRETON ISLAND

Quebec

Montreal

Ottawa

St. Lawrence River

ATLANTIC OCEAN

Snake R.

Great Salt Lake

Salt Lake City

San Francisco

Sacramento

Oakland

San Jose

Denver

Missouri River

Platte R.

Colorado River

Minneapolis

St. Paul

Milwaukee

Chicago

Omaha

Kansas City

Wichita

L. Superior

L. Huron

Lake Michigan

Detroit

Cleveland

Lake Erie

Columbus

L. Ontario

Toronto

Boston

New York

Philadelphia

Baltimore

Washington

Richmond

Norfolk

St. Louis

Ohio River

Louisville

UNITED STATES

BERMUDA (U.K.)

Los Angeles

San Diego

Phoenix

Oklahoma City

Red River

Fort Worth

Dallas

Memphis

Nashville

Atlanta

Birmingham

Mississippi River

PACIFIC OCEAN

Ciudad Juárez

Chihuahua

Rio Grande

Austin

San Antonio

Houston

Mobile

New Orleans

Jacksonville

Tampa

Tropic of Cancer

Monterrey

MEXICO

Gulf of Mexico

Miami

Nassau

BAHAMAS

San Luis Potosí

Guadalajara

Tampico

Havana

CUBA

Santiago de Cuba

CAYMAN ISLANDS (U.K.)

JAMAICA

Kingston

Port-au-Prince

HAITI

DOMINICAN REPUBLIC

Santo Domingo

San Juan

PUERTO RICO (U.S.)

VIRGIN ISLANDS (U.S., U.K.)

ANGUILLA (U.K.)

ST. KITTS-NEVIS

DOMINICA

ANTIGUA AND BARBUDA

GUADELOUPE (Fr.)

MARTINIQUE (Fr.)

ST. LUCIA

BARBADOS

Mexico City

Cuernavaca

Veracruz

Puebla

Acapulco

Belmopan

BELIZE

GUATEMALA

Guatemala City

San Salvador

EL SALVADOR

HONDURAS

Tegucigalpa

NICARAGUA

Managua

Caribbean Sea

NETHERLANDS ANTILLES

ARUBA (Neth.)

NETHERLANDS ANTILLES (Neth.)

ST. VINCENT AND THE GRENADINES

GRENADA

TRINIDAD AND TOBAGO

N

W E

S

COSTA RICA

San José

Panama City

PANAMA

SOUTH AMERICA

Equator

⊛ National capital

● Major city

— National boundary

0   400   800 mi.

0   400   800 km

Azimuthal Equal-Area Projection

NORTH AMERICA: *Physical*

EUROPE

ASIA

ARCTIC OCEAN

Bering Sea

Bering Strait

BROOKS RANGE

Beaufort Sea

QUEEN ELIZABETH ISLANDS

ELLESMERE ISLAND

Baffin Bay

GREENLAND

BANKS ISLAND

Yukon River

Redoubt Volcano ▲ ALASKA RANGE
▲ Mt. McKinley

ALASKA PEN.

Gulf of Alaska

KODIAK ISLAND

VICTORIA ISLAND

BAFFIN ISLAND

Davis Strait

Foxe Basin

ALEXANDER ARCHIPELAGO

Great Bear Lake

Mackenzie River

Hudson Strait

Labrador Sea

QUEEN CHARLOTTE ISLANDS

Great Slave Lake

UNGAVA PENINSULA

VANCOUVER ISLAND

Peace River

LAURENTIAN SHIELD

LABRADOR

COAST MOUNTAINS

Hudson Bay

Puget Sound

River

R O C K Y

Mt. Rainier ▲

Columbia

Lake Winnipeg

NEWFOUNDLAND

Gulf of St. Lawrence

CAPE BRETON ISLAND

COLUMBIA PLATEAU

M O U N T A I N S

G R E A T

L. Superior

St. Lawrence River

SIERRA NEVADA

Snake R.

Great Salt Lake

BLACK HILLS

Missouri River

Lake Huron

L. Michigan

Ontario Niagara Falls

APPALACHIAN MTS.

Bay of Fundy

Cape Cod

GREAT BASIN

COAST RANGES

Mt. Whitney ▲
DEATH VALLEY

MOJAVE DESERT

P L A I N S

Platte R.

CENTRAL PLAINS

L. Erie

Ohio River

ATLANTIC COASTAL PLAIN

Cape Hatteras

BERMUDA

PACIFIC OCEAN

Colorado River

GRAND CANYON

Arkansas River

OZARK PLATEAU

Red River

Mississippi River

GULF COASTAL PLAIN

Cape Canaveral

ATLANTIC OCEAN

BAJA CALIFORNIA

Gulf of California

Rio Grande

SIERRA MADRE ORIENTAL

BAHAMAS

Straits of Florida

Cabo San Lucas

SIERRA MADRE OCCIDENTAL

Gulf of Mexico

CUBA

HISPANIOLA

PUERTO RICO

LESSER ANTILLES

LEEWARD IS.

PLATEAU OF MEXICO

GREATER ANTILLES

JAMAICA

WINDWARD ISLANDS

Popocatépetl ▲

YUCATÁN PENINSULA

Caribbean Sea

ISTHMUS OF TEHUANTEPEC

Tajumulco ▲

MOSQUITO COAST

Lago de Nicaragua

Panama Canal

Irazú ▲

ISTHMUS OF PANAMA

SOUTH AMERICA

Tropic of Cancer

Equator

Arctic Circle

Land Elevation

Feet	Meters
13,120	4,000
6,560	2,000
1,640	500
656	200
0	0
Below sea level	Below sea level

Ice–covered land

▲ Mountain Peak

N W E S

0   400   800 mi.
0 400 800 km

Azimuthal Equal-Area Projection

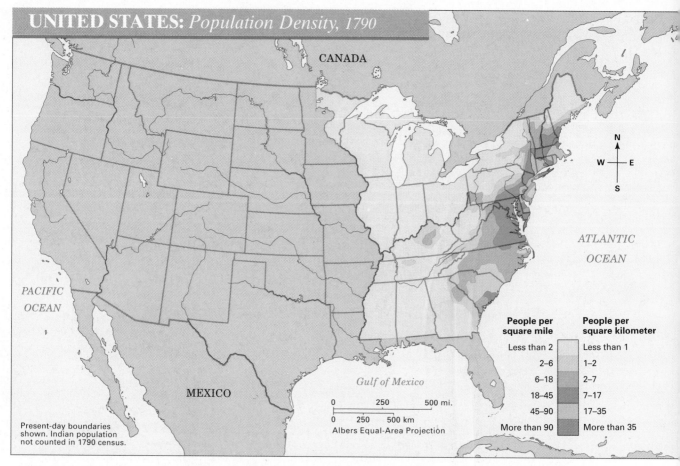

UNITED STATES: *Population Density, 1790*

CANADA

ATLANTIC OCEAN

PACIFIC OCEAN

MEXICO

Gulf of Mexico

N
W — E
S

People per square mile	People per square kilometer
Less than 2	Less than 1
2–6	1–2
6–18	2–7
18–45	7–17
45–90	17–35
More than 90	More than 35

0   250   500 mi.
0   250   500 km
Albers Equal-Area Projection

Present-day boundaries shown. Indian population not counted in 1790 census.

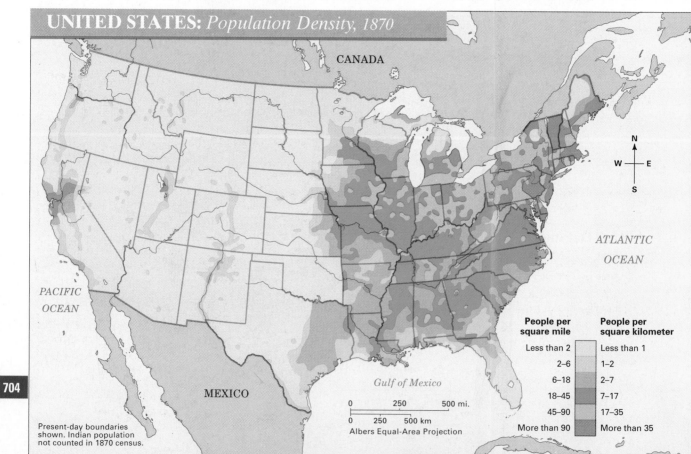

UNITED STATES: *Population Density, 1870*

CANADA

ATLANTIC OCEAN

PACIFIC OCEAN

MEXICO

Gulf of Mexico

N
W — E
S

People per square mile	People per square kilometer
Less than 2	Less than 1
2–6	1–2
6–18	2–7
18–45	7–17
45–90	17–35
More than 90	More than 35

0   250   500 mi.
0   250   500 km
Albers Equal-Area Projection

Present-day boundaries shown. Indian population not counted in 1870 census.

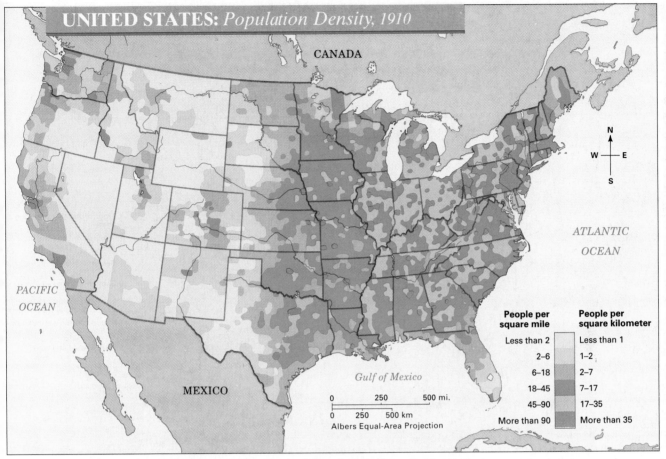

UNITED STATES: *Population Density, 1910*

CANADA

ATLANTIC
OCEAN

PACIFIC
OCEAN

MEXICO

Gulf of Mexico

People per square mile	People per square kilometer
Less than 2	Less than 1
2–6	1–2
6–18	2–7
18–45	7–17
45–90	17–35
More than 90	More than 35

0   250   500 mi.
0 250   500 km
Albers Equal-Area Projection

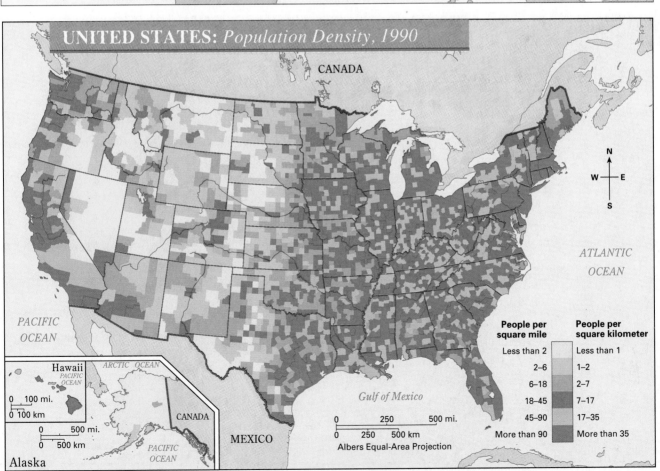

UNITED STATES: *Population Density, 1990*

CANADA

ATLANTIC
OCEAN

PACIFIC
OCEAN

Hawaii
PACIFIC OCEAN
ARCTIC OCEAN

0   100 mi.
0 100 km

0   500 mi.
0 500 km

CANADA

Alaska

MEXICO

Gulf of Mexico

PACIFIC
OCEAN

People per square mile	People per square kilometer
Less than 2	Less than 1
2–6	1–2
6–18	2–7
18–45	7–17
45–90	17–35
More than 90	More than 35

0   250   500 mi.
0 250   500 km
Albers Equal-Area Projection

705

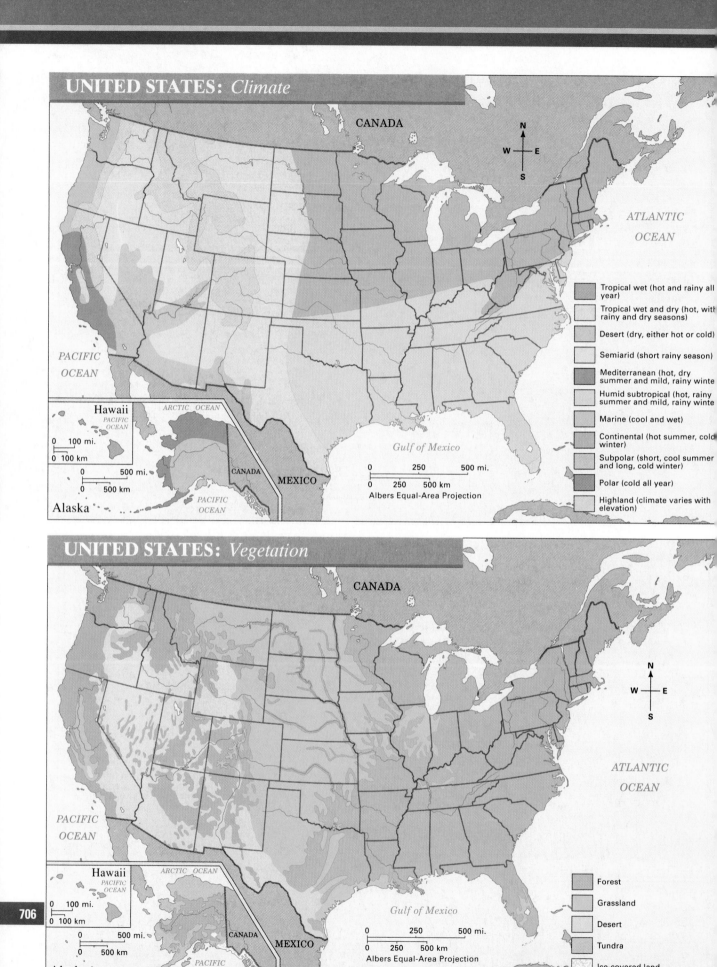

UNITED STATES: *Climate*

CANADA

N
W — E
S

ATLANTIC
OCEAN

PACIFIC
OCEAN

Tropical wet (hot and rainy all year)

Tropical wet and dry (hot, with rainy and dry seasons)

Desert (dry, either hot or cold)

Semiarid (short rainy season)

Mediterranean (hot, dry summer and mild, rainy winter)

Humid subtropical (hot, rainy summer and mild, rainy winter)

Marine (cool and wet)

Continental (hot summer, cold winter)

Subpolar (short, cool summer and long, cold winter)

Polar (cold all year)

Highland (climate varies with elevation)

Hawaii
ARCTIC OCEAN
PACIFIC OCEAN
0 100 mi.
0 100 km

0 500 mi.
0 500 km

CANADA
MEXICO

Alaska
PACIFIC OCEAN

Gulf of Mexico

0 250 500 mi.
0 250 500 km
Albers Equal-Area Projection

706

UNITED STATES: *Vegetation*

CANADA

N
W — E
S

ATLANTIC
OCEAN

PACIFIC
OCEAN

Hawaii
ARCTIC OCEAN
PACIFIC OCEAN
0 100 mi.
0 100 km

0 500 mi.
0 500 km

CANADA
MEXICO

Alaska
PACIFIC OCEAN

Gulf of Mexico

0 250 500 mi.
0 250 500 km
Albers Equal-Area Projection

Forest

Grassland

Desert

Tundra

Ice-covered land

UNITED STATES: *Precipitation*

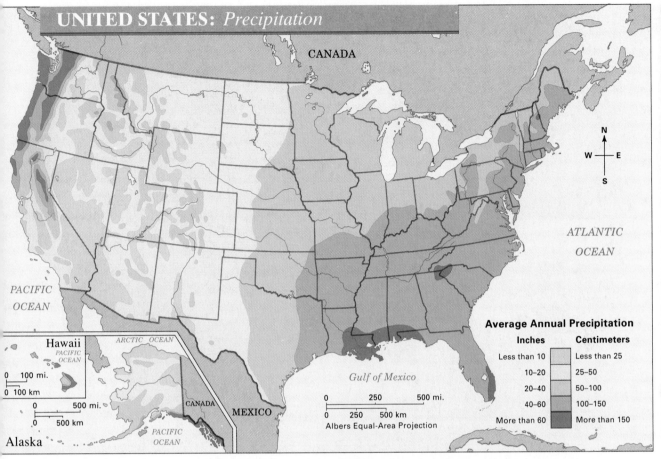

CANADA

N
W E
S

ATLANTIC
OCEAN

PACIFIC
OCEAN

Gulf of Mexico

Average Annual Precipitation

Inches	Centimeters
Less than 10	Less than 25
10–20	25–50
20–40	50–100
40–60	100–150
More than 60	More than 150

Hawaii
PACIFIC
OCEAN

0   100 mi.
0   100 km

ARCTIC OCEAN

0   500 mi.
0   500 km

CANADA

MEXICO

PACIFIC
OCEAN

Alaska

0   250   500 mi.
0   250   500 km
Albers Equal-Area Projection

UNITED STATES: *Land Use and Resources*

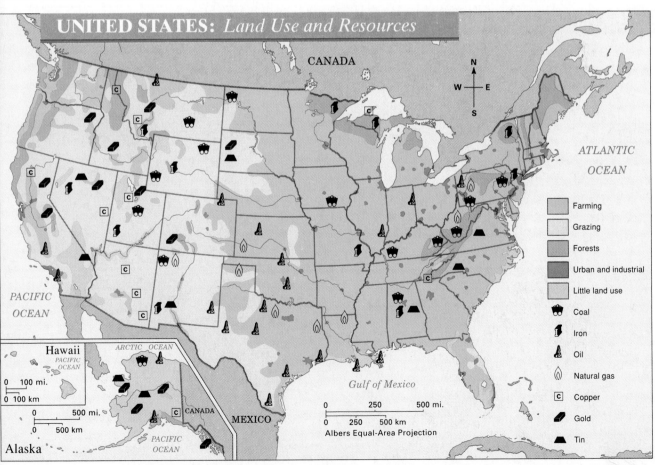

CANADA

N
W E
S

ATLANTIC
OCEAN

	Farming
	Grazing
	Forests
	Urban and industrial
	Little land use
Coal
Iron
Oil
Natural gas
C	Copper
Gold
Tin

PACIFIC
OCEAN

Hawaii
PACIFIC
OCEAN

0   100 mi.
0   100 km

ARCTIC OCEAN

0   500 mi.
0   500 km

CANADA

MEXICO

PACIFIC
OCEAN

Alaska

Gulf of Mexico

0   250   500 mi.
0   250   500 km
Albers Equal-Area Projection

WORLD: *Gross National Product*

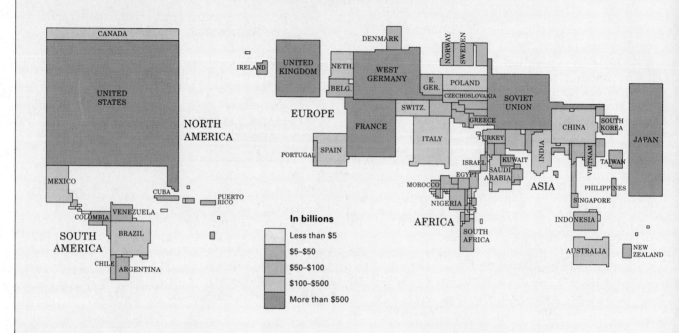

CANADA
UNITED STATES
NORTH AMERICA
MEXICO
CUBA
PUERTO RICO
COLOMBIA
VENEZUELA
BRAZIL
SOUTH AMERICA
CHILE
ARGENTINA

IRELAND
UNITED KINGDOM
NETH.
BELG.
EUROPE
FRANCE
PORTUGAL
SPAIN
DENMARK
WEST GERMANY
E. GER.
SWITZ.
ITALY
NORWAY
SWEDEN
POLAND
CZECHOSLOVAKIA
GREECE
TURKEY
MOROCCO
EGYPT
ISRAEL
NIGERIA
AFRICA
SOUTH AFRICA
SAUDI ARABIA
KUWAIT
SOVIET UNION
INDIA
CHINA
ASIA
VIETNAM
SOUTH KOREA
TAIWAN
PHILIPPINES
SINGAPORE
INDONESIA
AUSTRALIA
JAPAN
NEW ZEALAND

In billions
Less than $5
$5–$50
$50–$100
$100–$500
More than $500

Each country's size in the cartogram represents the size of its GNP (Gross National Product) compared with those of other countries in the world. Based on information in the *1986 Britannica World Data* (1986) and *The World Factbook, 1987*.

UNITED STATES: *Time Zones*

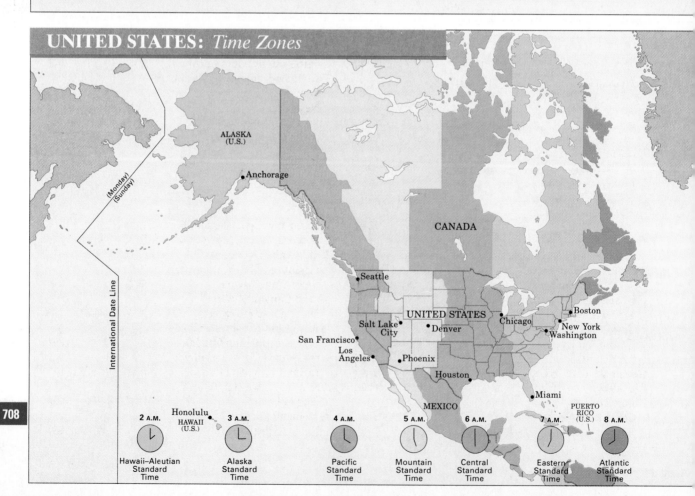

International Date Line
(Monday) (Sunday)
ALASKA (U.S.)
Anchorage
CANADA
Seattle
Salt Lake City
San Francisco
Los Angeles
Phoenix
Denver
UNITED STATES
Houston
Chicago
Boston
New York
Washington
Miami
MEXICO
PUERTO RICO (U.S.)

2 A.M.
Honolulu
HAWAII (U.S.)
Hawaii–Aleutian Standard Time

3 A.M.
Alaska Standard Time

4 A.M.
Pacific Standard Time

5 A.M.
Mountain Standard Time

6 A.M.
Central Standard Time

7 A.M.
Eastern Standard Time

8 A.M.
Atlantic Standard Time

This gazetteer will help you locate many of the places discussed in this book. Latitude and longitude given for large areas of land and water refer to the centermost point of the area; latitude and longitude of rivers refer to the river mouth. The page number tells you where to find each place on a map.

PLACE	LAT.	LONG.	PAGE
A			
Abilene (city in Kansas)	32°N	99°W	**430**
Annapolis (capital of Maryland)	39°N	76°W	**699**
Antietam (civil war battle site in Maryland)	39°N	78°W	**350**
Appalachian Mts. (range in eastern U.S.)	37°N	82°W	**701**
Atlanta (capital of Georgia)	33°N	84°W	**699**
B			
Badlands (dry area of South Dakota)	43°N	102°W	**700**
Baltimore (port city in Maryland)	39°N	76°W	**699**
Baton Rouge (capital of Louisiana)	30°N	91°W	**699**
Bering Strait (joins Pacific and Arctic Oceans)	66°N	168°W	**702**
Boston (capital of Massachusetts)	42°N	71°W	**69**
Buffalo (city in New York)	42°N	78°W	**262**
Bull Run (Civil War battle site in Virginia)	39°N	78°W	**350**
Bunker Hill (Revolutionary War battle site in Massachusetts)	42°N	71°W	**69**
C			
Canada (country in North America)	50°N	100°W	**702**
Cape Horn (southern tip of South America)	56°S	67°W	**696**
Cape of Good Hope (southern tip of Africa)	34°S	18°E	**697**
Caribbean Sea (part of Atlantic Ocean)	14°N	122°W	**694**
Cascade Mts. (range in western U.S.)	42°N	122°W	**700**
Central America (southernmost part of North America)	10°N	87°W	**694**
Charleston (port city in South Carolina)	32°N	79°W	**699**
Chesapeake Bay (waterway bordering Maryland and Virginia)	38°N	76°W	**701**
Chicago (largest city in Illinois)	41°N	87°W	**699**
Chisholm Trail (cattle trail of old Southwest)	35°N	94°W	**430**
Cincinnati (city in Ohio)	39°N	84°W	**262**
Cleveland (city in Ohio)	41°N	81°W	**699**
Colorado R. (in southwestern U.S.)	36°N	112°W	**700**

PLACE	LAT.	LONG.	PAGE
Columbia R. (in northwestern U.S.)	46°N	123°W	**698**
Concord (Revolutionary War battle site in Massachusetts)	42°N	71°W	**69**
Cuba (island country in Caribbean sea)	22°N	79°W	**536**
Cumberland Gap (pass through Blue Ridge Mts. in Tennessee)	35°N	85°W	**198**
D			
Dallas (city in Texas)	32°N	96°W	**699**
Delaware Bay (inlet between Delaware and New Jersey)	39°N	75°W	**701**
Des Moines (capital of Iowa)	41°N	93°W	**699**
Detroit (largest city in Michigan)	42°N	83°W	**452**
District of Columbia (seat of U.S. government)	38°N	77°W	**699**
Dodge City (city in Kansas)	37°N	100°W	**430**
E			
England (part of United Kingdom)	51°N	1°W	**695**
F			
Fort Sumter (Civil War harbor battle site in South Carolina)	32°N	79°W	**343**
Fort Ticonderoga (Revolutionary War battle site in northern New York)	43°N	73°W	**69**
Fredericksburg (Civil War battle site in Virginia)	38°N	77°W	**350**
G			
Gadsen Purchase (land U.S. purchased from Mexico)	32°N	110°W	**235**
Gatun Lake (Panama)	9°N	79°W	**538**
Gettysburg (Civil War battle site in Pennsylvania)	39°N	77°W	**350**
Grand Canyon (Colorado River gorge in Arizona)	36°N	112°W	**700**
Great Lakes (freshwater lakes between U.S. and Canada)			**701**
Great Plains (farm and range region in central U.S.)	45°N	104°W	**411**
Great Salt Lake (large salty lake in Utah)	41°N	112°W	**700**
Greenland (largest island in the world)	74°N	40°W	**694**

PLACE	LAT.	LONG.	PAGE
Gulf of Mexico (part of Atlantic, south of U.S., east of Mexico)	25°N	93°W	**701**
Gulf of St. Lawrence (inlet in northeast Canada)	48°N	62°W	**703**

H

PLACE	LAT.	LONG.	PAGE
Harpers Ferry (Civil War battle site in West Virginia)	39°N	77°W	**333**
Havana (capital of Cuba)	23°N	82°W	**536**
Hispaniola (island in West Indies)	17°N	73°W	**55**
Hudson Bay (inland sea in Canada)	64°N	80°W	**55**
Hudson River (north-south waterway in New York)	41°N	73°W	**701**

I

PLACE	LAT.	LONG.	PAGE
Indian Ocean (Body of water south of India)	0°	70°E	**697**
Ireland (Island country in western Europe)	0°	17°E	**550**
Isthmus of Panama (land separating Atlantic and Pacific Oceans)	9°N	81°W	**703**
Italy (country in southern Europe)	43°N	11°E	**550**

J

PLACE	LAT.	LONG.	PAGE
Jamaica (Caribbean island)	17°N	78°W	**55**
Jamestown (first English settlement in Virginia)	37°N	77°W	**21**
Japan (island country in East Asia)	36°N	133°E	**695**
Juneau (capital of Alaska)	58°N	134°W	**698**

K

PLACE	LAT.	LONG.	PAGE
Kansas City (City in Missouri)	39°N	94°W	**430**

L

PLACE	LAT.	LONG.	PAGE
Lake Champlain (borders Vermont and New York)	44°N	73°W	**69**
Lake Erie (Great Lake)	42°N	81°W	**699**
Lake Huron (Great Lake)	45°N	82°W	**699**
Lake Michigan (Great Lake)	43°N	87°W	**699**
Lake Ontario (Great Lake)	43°N	79°W	**699**
Lake Superior (Great Lake)	41°N	108°W	**699**
Lancaster (city in Pennsylvania)	40°N	76°W	**198**
Lexington (Revolutionary War battle site in Massachusetts)	42°N	71°W	**69**

PLACE	LAT.	LONG.	PAGE
Los Angeles (largest city in California)	34°N	118°W	**698**
Louisiana Purchase (land U.S. purchased from France)	35°N	92°W	**150**
Louisville (city in Kentucky)	38°N	85°W	**213**

M

PLACE	LAT.	LONG.	PAGE
Memphis (river port in Tennessee)	35°N	90°W	**452**
Mexican Cession (land ceded by Mexico to U.S.)			**235**
Mexico (North American country)	23°N	104°W	**702**
Milwaukee (city in Wisconsin)	43°N	87°W	**452**
Mississippi R. (one of longest rivers in central U.S.)	30°N	90°W	**150**
Missouri R. (tributary of Mississippi River)	40°N	96°W	**701**
Monterey (city in California)	36°N	123°W	**234**
Montgomery (capital of Alabama)	32°N	86°W	**699**
Montreal (largest city in Canada)	45°N	73°W	**702**

N

PLACE	LAT.	LONG.	PAGE
New Amsterdam (capital of New Netherlands, currently New York state)	41°N	74°W	**21**
New England (northeast section of U.S.)	42°N	71°W	**21**
Newark (city in New Jersey)	40°N	74°W	**262**
Newfoundland (Province of Canada)	48°N	56°W	**463**
New Orleans (port city in Louisiana)	30°N	90°W	**150**
Newport (port city in Rhode Island)	41°N	71°W	**262**
New Spain (North and Central American lands ruled by Spanish)	20°N	100°W	**21**
New York City (port city of New York)	40°N	73°W	**702**

O

PLACE	LAT.	LONG.	PAGE
Oakland (city in California)	37°N	122°W	**452**
Omaha (city in Nebraska)	41°N	95°W	**430**
Oregon Country (North American area claimed by U.S. and Canada)			**235**

PLACE	LAT.	LONG.	PAGE
Oregon Trail (explorers' route to northwest U.S.)	50°N	120°W	**227**

P

PLACE	LAT.	LONG.	PAGE
Painted Desert (dry region in southwestern U.S.)	36°N	111°W	**700**
Panama (Central American country)	8°N	81°W	**694**
Panama Canal (man-made waterway connecting Atlantic and Pacific Oceans)	9°N	81°W	**538**
Paris (capital of France)	48°N	2°E	**546**
Piedmont (upland region of eastern U.S.)	39°N	75°W	**701**
Philadelphia (largest city in Pennsylvania)	40°N	75°W	**112**
Philippines (island country in Southeast Asia)	14°N	125°E	**536**
Phoenix (capital of Arizona)	33°N	112°W	**698**
Pittsburgh (city in western Pennsylvania)	40°N	80°W	**699**
Platte R. (in north central U.S.)	40°N	100°W	**701**
Potomac R. (borders Maryland and Virginia)	38°N	77°W	**258**
Portugal (country in Europe)	38°N	8°W	**19**
Puerto Rico (island in West Indies, commonwealth of U.S.)	18°N	66°W	**702**

`Q

PLACE	LAT.	LONG.	PAGE
Quebec (province of Canada)	51°N	70°W	**83**

R

PLACE	LAT.	LONG.	PAGE
Richmond (capital of Virginia)	37°N	77°W	**198**
Rio Grande (river bordering Texas and Mexico)	24°N	93°W	**701**
Rocky Mts. (range in western North America)	50°N	114°W	**703**

S

PLACE	LAT.	LONG.	PAGE
Sacramento (capital of California)	38°N	121°W	**698**
St. Augustine (city in Florida; oldest city in U.S.)	29°N	81°W	**21**
St. Lawrence R. (waterway in northeast Canada)	48°N	70°W	**86**
St. Louis (largest city in Missouri)	38°N	90°W	**699**
Salt Lake City (capital of Utah)	40°N	111°W	**698**
San Antonio (city in Texas)	28°N	97°W	**430**

PLACE	LAT.	LONG.	PAGE
San Diego (port city in southern California)	32°N	117°W	**698**
San Francisco (port city in northern California)	37°N	122°W	**698**
Santa Fe (capital of New Mexico)	35°N	106°W	**698**
Savannah (port city in Georgia)	32°N	81°W	**333**
Seattle (largest city in Washington)	47°N	122°W	**702**
Sierra Nevada (mountain range in eastern California)	39°N	120°W	**227**
Spain (country in Europe)	40°N	3°W	**550**

T

PLACE	LAT.	LONG.	PAGE
Tenochtitlán (Aztec name for Mexico City)	19°N	99°W	**702**
Trenton (capital of New Jersey)	40°N	74°W	**699**

U

PLACE	LAT.	LONG.	PAGE
United Kingdom (countries of British Isles, except Ireland)	56°N	0°	**695**
United States (country in North America)	38°N	110°W	**702**

V

PLACE	LAT.	LONG.	PAGE
Virginia City (mining town in Nevada)	39°N	119°W	**433**
Vietnam (country in Southeast Asia)	18°N	107°E	**695**

W

PLACE	LAT.	LONG.	PAGE
Washington, D.C. (capital of United States)	38°N	77°W	**699**
West Indies (Islands in Caribbean Sea)	19°N	78°W	**702**

Y

PLACE	LAT.	LONG.	PAGE
Yorktown (Revolutionary War battle site in Virginia)	37°N	76°W	**69**

GLOSSARY OF GEOGRAPHIC TERMS

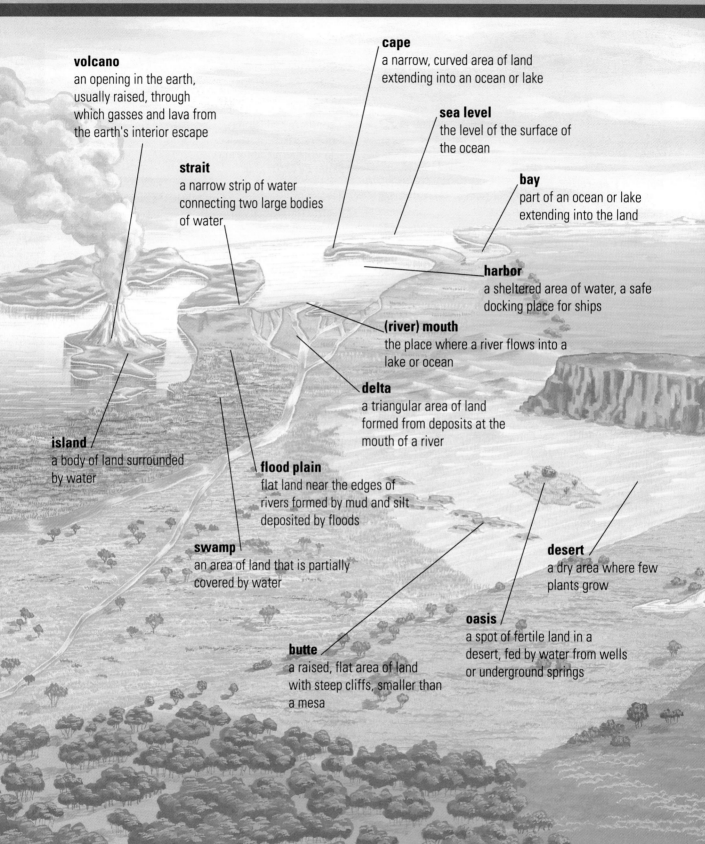

volcano
an opening in the earth, usually raised, through which gasses and lava from the earth's interior escape

strait
a narrow strip of water connecting two large bodies of water

cape
a narrow, curved area of land extending into an ocean or lake

sea level
the level of the surface of the ocean

bay
part of an ocean or lake extending into the land

harbor
a sheltered area of water, a safe docking place for ships

(river) mouth
the place where a river flows into a lake or ocean

delta
a triangular area of land formed from deposits at the mouth of a river

island
a body of land surrounded by water

flood plain
flat land near the edges of rivers formed by mud and silt deposited by floods

swamp
an area of land that is partially covered by water

butte
a raised, flat area of land with steep cliffs, smaller than a mesa

desert
a dry area where few plants grow

oasis
a spot of fertile land in a desert, fed by water from wells or underground springs

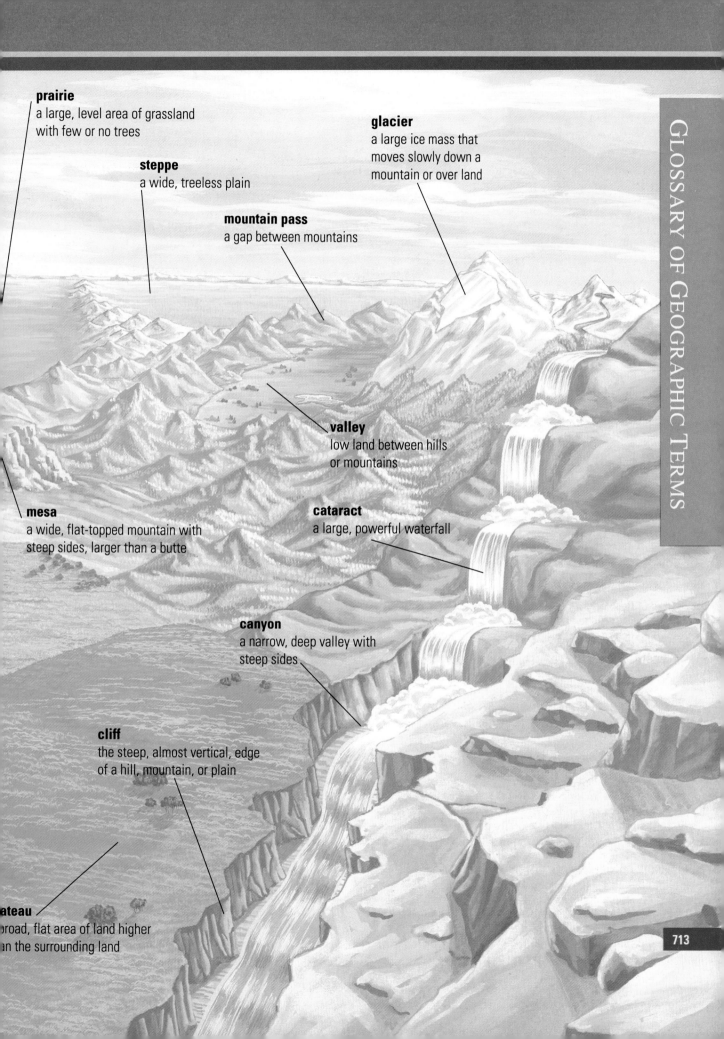

prairie
a large, level area of grassland
with few or no trees

steppe
a wide, treeless plain

mountain pass
a gap between mountains

glacier
a large ice mass that
moves slowly down a
mountain or over land

valley
low land between hills
or mountains

mesa
a wide, flat-topped mountain with
steep sides, larger than a butte

cataract
a large, powerful waterfall

canyon
a narrow, deep valley with
steep sides

cliff
the steep, almost vertical, edge
of a hill, mountain, or plain

ateau
oroad, flat area of land higher
an the surrounding land

GLOSSARY OF GEOGRAPHIC TERMS

Pronunciation Key

This chart presents the system of phonetic respellings used to indicate pronunciation in the Biographical Dictionary and in the chapters of this book.

Spellings	Symbol	Spellings	Symbol	Spellings	Symbol
pat	a	kick, cat, pique	k	thin, this	th
pay	ay	lid, needle	l	cut	uh
care	air	mum	m	urge, term, firm, word, heard	ur
father	ah	no, sudden	n		
bib	b	thing	ng	valve	v
church	ch	pot, horrid	ah	with	w
deed, milled	d	toe	oh	yes	y
pet	eh	caught, paw, for	aw	zebra, xylem	z
bee	ee	noise	oy	vision, pleasure, garage	zh
life, phase, rough	f	took	u		
gag	g	boot	oo	about, item, edible, gallop, circus	uh
hat	h	out	ow		
which	hw	pop	p	butter	ur
pit	ih	roar	r		
pie, by	eye, y	sauce	s	Capital letters indicate stressed syllables.	
pier	ihr	ship, dish	sh		
judge	j	tight, stopped	t		

A

Adams, John 1735–1826, 2nd U.S. President 1797–1801 (p. 84).

Adams, John Quincy 1767–1848, 6th U.S. President 1825–1829 (p. 183).

Addams, Jane 1860–1935, American social reformer (p. 502).

Allen, Ethan 1738–1789, Revolutionary leader at Fort Ticonderoga (p. 66).

Allen, Richard 1760–1831, African-American founder of an Episcopal Church (p. 195).

Anthony, Susan B. 1820–1906, American reformer (p. 268).

Attucks *(AT uhks),* **Crispus** 1723–1770, former slave killed in Boston Massacre (p. 58).

Austin, Stephen 1793–1836, political leader in Texas (p. 231).

B

Balboa, Vasco Nuñez de 1475–1517, Spanish discoverer of Pacific Ocean (p. 18).

Barton, Clara 1821–1912, founder of American Red Cross (p. 363).

Beecher, Catharine 1800–1878, American educator, antisuffragist (p. 192).

Beecher, Henry Ward 1813–1887, American clergyman, abolitionist (p. 190).

Bell, Alexander Graham 1847–1922, Scottish-born American inventor of telephone (p. 443).

Bonaparte, Napoleon 1769–1821, French emperor; sold Louisiana Territory to U.S. (p. 223).

Boone, Daniel 1734–1820, American frontiersman, helped settle Kentucky (p. 197).

Booth, John Wilkes 1838–1865, actor; assassinated Lincoln (p. 378).

Brady, Matthew 1823–1896, American Civil War photographer (p. 362).

Brown, John 1800–1859, American abolitionist; executed (p. 328).

Buchanan, James 1791–1868, 15th U.S. President 1857–1861 (p. 329).

Burgoyne *(bur GOYN),* **John** 1722–1792, English general, recaptured Fort Ticonderoga (p. 67).

Burr, Aaron 1756–1836, U.S. Vice President 1801–1805; killed Alexander Hamilton in duel (p. 147).

C

Cabot, John 1450–1498, Italian–born explorer (p. 20).

Carnegie, Andrew 1839–1919, Scottish-born American industrialist (p. 445).

Cartier *(kahr TYAY),* **Jacques** 1491–1557, French explorer (p. 20).

Catt, Carrie Chapman 1859–1947, American suffragist (p. 517).

Clark, George Rogers 1752–1818, American military leader (p. 68).

Clark, William 1770–1838, American explorer of the Northwest (p. 223).

Clay, Henry 1777–1852, American statesman (p. 315).

Cleveland, Grover 1837–1908, 22nd and 24th U.S. President 1885–1889; 1893–1897 (p. 532).

Columbus, Christopher 1451–1506, Italian discoverer of America (p. 18).

Cooper, James Fenimore 1789–1851, American writer of frontier novels (p. 197).

Cornwallis, Charles 1738–1805, British military leader in the Revolution (p. 68).

Cortés *(kawr TEHZ)*, **Hernando** 1485–1547, Spanish explorer (p. 19).

Crèvecoeur *(krehv KUR)*, **Michel de** 1735–1813, French agriculturalist (p. 180).

Crockett, Davy 1786–1836, American frontiersman; Tennessee Congressman (p. 197).

Custer, George Armstrong 1839–1876, American general killed at Little Big Horn (p. 422).

D

Davis, Jefferson 1808–1889, President of the Confederacy (p. 348).

Deere, John 1804–1886, American inventor of steel-bladed plow (p. 191).

Dewey, John 1859–1952, American philosopher and educator (p. 504).

Dix, Dorothea 1802–1887, American philanthropist, educator (p. 266).

Douglas, Stephen A. 1813–1861, American legislator (p. 326).

Douglass, Frederick 1817?–1895, former slave, anti-slavery leader (p. 321).

Dreiser *(DRY zur)*, **Theodore** 1871–1945, American author (p. 451).

DuBois *(doo BOYS)*, **W.E.B.** 1868–1963, American sociologist, founder of NAACP (p. 519).

E

Edison, Thomas Alva 1847–1931, American inventor (p. 443).

Edwards, Jonathan 1703–1758, American preacher of Great Awakening (p. 51).

Elskwatawa 1769–1834, called "The Prophet"; Shawnee leader (p. 204).

F

Fillmore, Millard 1800–1874, 13th U.S. President 1850–1853 (p. 329).

Ford, Henry 1863–1947, American automobile manufacturer (p. 456).

Franklin, Benjamin 1706–1790, American statesman, scientist (p. 82).

Frémont, John C. 1813–1890, American explorer (p. 226).

Fulton, Robert 1765–1815, American inventor of steamboat (p. 257).

G

Garfield, James A. 1831–1881, 20th U.S. President 1881 (p. 477).

Garrison, William Lloyd 1805–1879, American abolitionist (p. 321).

Gerry, Elbridge 1744–1814, Massachusetts governor; U.S. Vice President 1813–1814 (p. 113).

Gompers, Samuel 1850–1924, English–born American labor leader (p. 459).

Grant, Ulysses S. 1822–1885, 18th U.S. President 1869–1877; Union general (p. 442).

Greene, Nathanael 1742–1786, American Revolution general; defeated Cornwallis (p. 68).

H

Hamilton, Alexander 1757–1804, American states-man; killed by Aaron Burr in duel (p. 135).

Hancock, John 1737–1793, Signer of the Declaration of Independence (p. 66).

Harding, Warren 1865–1923, 29th U.S. President 1921–1923 (p. 553).

Harrison, William Henry 1773–1841, 9th U.S. President 1841 (p. 201).

Hayes, Rutherford B. 1822–1893, 19th U.S. President 1877–1881 (p. 481).

Hays, Mary Ludwig 1754–1832, known as Molly Pitcher; American Revolution heroine (p. 71).

Hearst, William Randolph 1863–1951, American newspaper publisher (p. 535).

Henry, Patrick 1736–1799, American Revolution leader; famous orator (p. 118).

Houston, Samuel 1793–1863, Texas general; President of Republic of Texas (p. 232).

Howe, Elias 1819–1867, American inventor of sewing machine (p. 444).

Howe, Sir William 1729–1814, British army commander-in-chief (p. 66).

Hudson, Henry d. 1611, English explorer (p. 20).

J

Jackson, Andrew 1767–1845, 7th U.S. President 1829–1837, called "Old Hickory" (p. 172).

Jackson, Thomas "Stonewall" 1824–1863, American Confederate general (p. 345).

Jay, John 1745–1829, American diplomat; signed treaty with England (p. 70).

Jefferson, Thomas 1743–1826, 3rd U.S. President 1801–1809; author of Declaration of Independence, scientist, architect, educator, diplomat (p. 147).

Johnson, Andrew 1808–1875, 17th U.S. President 1865–1869 (p. 379).

Joliet, Louis 1645–1700, French-Canadian explorer of America (p. 29).

K

Kelley, Florence 1859–1932, child labor activist (p. 515).

L

Lafayette, Marquis de 1757–1834, French leader in American Revolution (p. 70).

Lease, Mary E. 1850–1933, Populist leader (p. 489).

Lee, Ann 1736–1784, "Mother Ann"; English founder of American Shaker sect (p. 271).

Lee, Robert E. 1807–1870, American Confederate general; surrendered to Grant (p. 342).

Lewis, Meriwether 1774–1809, American Northwest explorer (p. 223).

Liliuokalani *(lee lee oo oh kah LAH nee)*, **Queen** 1838–1917, Hawaiian queen 1891–1893 (p. 532).

Lincoln, Abraham 1809–1865, 16th U.S. President 1861–1865; passed 13th Amendment; assassinated (p. 334).

Lincoln, Mary Todd 1818–1882, wife of Abraham Lincoln (p. 345).

Lowell, Francis 1775–1818, American textile producer (p. 259).

M

MacLeish, Archibald 1892–1982, American poet (p. 4).

Madison, Dolley 1768–1849, American First Lady, wife of James (p. 153).

Madison, James 1751–1836, 4th U.S. President 1809–1817 (p. 155).

Mann, Horace 1796–1859, American educator (p. 269).

Marion, Frances 1732?–1795, called "Swamp Fox"; American Revolution soldier (p. 68).

Marquette *(mahr KEHT)*, **Father Jacques** 1637–1675, French missionary and explorer (p. 29).

Marshall, James 1810–1885, American pioneer; started gold rush to California (p. 241).

Marshall, John 1755–1835, first Chief Justice of U.S. Supreme Court (p. 127).

Maximilian, Archduke 1832–1867, Austrian ruler and Emperor of Mexico 1864–1867 (p. 533).

McCormack, Cyrus 1809–1884, American inventor of reaper (p. 191).

McKinley, William 1843–1901, 25th U.S. President 1897–1901; assassinated (p. 491).

Monroe, James 1758–1831, 5th U.S. President 1817–1825 (p. 158).

Morgan, J. Pierpont 1867–1943, American financier (p. 445).

Morris, Robert 1734–1806, American Revolution financier (p. 91).

Mott, Lucretia Coffin 1793–1880, American social reformer (p. 322).

N

Nast, Thomas 1840–1902, German-born American cartoonist (p. 377).

Nation, Carry 1846–1911, American temperance reformer (p. 513).

O

Olmsted, Frederick Law 1822–1903, American landscape architect (p. 290).

P

Paine, Thomas 1737–1809, English-born American author of *Common Sense* (p. 65).

Paul, Alice 1885–1977, American social reformer (p. 517).

Penn, William 1644–1718, Quaker leader, settler of Pennsylvania (p. 30).

Perry, Matthew C. 1794–1858, American naval officer (p. 531).

Pierce, Franklin 1804–1869, 14th U.S. President 1853–1857 (p. 419).

Pike, Zebulon 1779–1813, American army officer and explorer (p. 226).

Polk, James K. 1795–1849, 11th U.S. President 1845–1849 (p. 234).

Prosser, Gabriel 1775?–1800, planner of slave rebellion (p. 295).

Pulitzer, Joseph 1847–1911, Hungarian-born American publisher (p. 467).

Pullman, George 1831–1897, American inventor of railroad sleeping cars (p. 458).

R

Raleigh *(RAW lee)*, **Sir Walter** 1552?–1618, English navigator, colonizer (p. 22).

Randolph, Edmund 1753–1813, American Revolutionary leader (p. 108).

Remarque *(ruh MAHRK)*, **Erich Maria** 1898–1970, German-born American novelist (p. 545).

Revels, Hiram 1827–1901, first African-American U.S. Senator (p. 388).

Revere, Paul 1735–1818, American Revolution patriot; silversmith (p. 58).

Riis *(rees)*, **Jacob A.** 1849–1914, Danish-born American reformer (p. 499).

Rockefeller, John D. 1839–1937, American industrialist and philanthropist (p. 474).

Roebling, John A. 1806–1869, German-born American engineer; built Brooklyn Bridge (p. 451).

Roosevelt, Theodore 1858–1919, 26th U.S. President 1901–1909; 1906 Nobel Peace Prize winner (p. 535).

Ross, John 1790–1866, Cherokee leader (p. 508).

S

Sacajawea *(sak uh juh WEE uh)* 1788?–1812, Shoshone Indian Guide, aided Lewis and Clark expedition (p. 222).

Santa Anna, Antonio de 1795?–1876, Mexican general and political leader during Mexican War (p. 232).

Schurz, Margaretha 1833–1876, German-born educator, started first U.S. kindergarten (p. 210).

Scott, Dred 1795?–1858, American slave involved in Supreme Court case (p. 331).

Sequoya *(sih KWOI uh)* 1760?–1843, leader of Cherokee Indians (p. 205).

Serra, Padre Junípero *(hoo NEE peh roh)* 1713–1784, Spanish missionary in California (p. 22).

Shays, Daniel 1747?–1825, American soldier at Bunker Hill (p. 95).

Sheridan, Philip Henry 1831–1888, American Union general (p. 366).

Sherman, William Tecumseh *(tih KUM suh)* 1820–1891, American Union general (p. 366).

Sinclair, Upton 1878–1968, American author; reformer (p. 507).

Singer, I.M. 1811–1875, American manufacturer of sewing machines (p. 444).

Slater, Samuel 1768–1835, English-born textile leader (p. 258).

Smith, Jedediah S. 1799?–1831, American fur trader, explorer (p. 226).

Smith, Joseph 1805–1844, American religious leader, founded Mormonism (p. 239).

Stanton, Elizabeth Cady 1815–1902, American feminist and social reformer (p. 322).

Stowe, Harriet Beecher 1811–1896, American novelist, author of *Uncle Tom's Cabin* (p. 322).

Stuart, Jeb 1833–1864, American Confederate general (p. 345).

Sumner, Charles 1811–1874, American politician; antislavery leader (p. 325).

Sumner, William Graham 1840–1910, American economist (p. 529).

Sutter, John Augustus 1803–1880, Swiss-born pioneer, found gold on his California land (p. 241).

T

Taney, Roger B. 1777–1864, American jurist involved in Dred Scott decision (p. 331).

Tarbell, Ida M. 1857–1944, American muckraking author (p. 502).

Taylor, Zachary 1784–1850, "Old Rough and Ready"; 12th U.S. President 1849–1850 (p. 234).

Tecumseh *(tih KUM suh)* 1768–1813, Shawnee Indian chief (p. 201).

Tocqueville *(TOHK vihl)*, **Alexis de** 1805–1859. French historian, author of *Democracy in America* (p. 181).

Trollope *(TRAHL uhp)*, **Frances** 1780–1863, English author on American manners (p. 179).

Truth, Sojourner 1797–1883, American abolitionist (p. 320).

Tubman, Harriet 1820–1913, American abolitionist (p. 333).

Turner, Nat 1800–1831, American leader of slave revolt (p. 295).

Twain, Mark (pen name of Samuel Clemens) 1835–1910, American author (p. 410).

V

Van Buren, Martin 1782–1862, 8th U.S. President 1837–1841 (p. 207).

Vanderbilt, Cornelius 1794–1877, American promoter of railroads (p. 407).

Verrazano, Giovanni *(joh VAH nee)* 1485?–1528? Italian explorer of Atlantic Coast (p. 20).

Vespucci *(vehs POOH chee)*, **Amerigo** 1454–1512, Italian navigator, explorer (p. 18).

W

Walker, David 1785–1830, American abolitionist (p. 320).

Walker, D. Mary 1832–1919, American physician and feminist (p. 359).

Warren, Mercy Otis 1728–1814, American author, historian (p. 74).

Washington, George 1732–99, 1st U.S. President 1789–1797; leader of Revolution (p. 134).

Webster, Daniel 1782–1852, American orator, Massachusetts politician (p. 178).

Webster, Noah 1758–1843, lexicographer; compiled first American dictionary (p. 164).

Weems, Mason 1759–1825, American clergyman; biographer of George Washington (p. 165).

Whitman, Marcus 1802–1847, American pioneer missionary in Oregon (p. 238).

Whitman, Walt 1819–1892, American poet (p. 474).

Whitney, Eli 1765–1825, American inventor of cotton gin (p. 284).

Wilder, Laura Ingalls 1867–1957, American author (p. 427).

Willard, Emma Hart 1787–1870, American author, favored women's education (p. 166).

Wilson, Woodrow 1856–1924, 28th U.S. President 1913–1921 (p. 541).

Y/Z

Young, Brigham 1801–1877, American Mormon leader in Utah (p. 239).

Zenger, John Peter 1697–1746, German-born colonial printer (p. 124).

GLOSSARY

Pronunciation Key

This chart presents the pronunciation key used in the Glossary. For a key to the phonetic respellings used to indicate pronunciation in the text of the chapters, see page 714.

Spellings	Symbol	Spellings	Symbol	Spellings	Symbol
pat	ă	kick, cat, pique	k	thin	th
pay	ā	lid, needle	l	this	*th*
care	âr	mum	m	cut	ŭ
father	ä	no, sudden	n	urge, term, firm,	ûr
bib	b	thing	ng	word, heard	
church	ch	pot, horrid	ŏ	valve	v
deed, milled	d	toe	ō	with	w
pet	ě	caught, paw, for	ô	yes	y
bee	ē	noise	oi	zebra, xylem	z
life, phase, rough	f	took	ŏŏ	vision, pleasure,	zh
gag	g	boot	ōō	garage	
hat	h	out	ou	about, item, edible,	ə
which	hw	pop	p	gallop, circus	
pit	ĭ	roar	r	butter	ər
pie, by	ī	sauce	s		
pier	îr	ship, dish	sh	Primary stress ´	
judge	j	tight, stopped	t	Secondary stress ´	

A

abdicate (ăb´ dĭ-kāt´) To formally give up power—such as a throne or a high office. (p. 532)

abolitionism (ăb´-ə-lĭsh´ ə-nĭz´ əm) Advocacy of the end of slavery in the United States. (p. 321)

administration (ăd-mĭn´ ĭ-strā´shən) The executive branch of the United States government, consisting of the President, his Cabinet, and the Vice President. (p. 134)

agrarian (ə-grâr´ ē-ən) Having to do with the land, its ownership, and its cultivation. (p. 136)

alien (ā´ lē-ən) An unnaturalized foreign resident of a country. (p. 139)

alliance (ə-lī´ əns) An organization or an agreement to promote common interests among an organization's members. (p. 27)

amendment (ə-mĕnd´mənt) Addition or change to the Constitution, made into law through the process of ratification. (p. 125)

amnesty (ăm´ nĭ-stē) A general pardon for offenders by a government, especially for political offenses. (p. 377)

anarchist (ăn´ ər-kĭst) A person who opposes all organized forms of government. (p. 516)

annex (ə-nĕks´) To increase the area in a country by incorporating other territory into it. (p. 232)

annuity (ə-nōō´ĭ-tē) Yearly provision of food, clothing, and other necessary items (provided to American Indians as part of an agreement with the United States government). (p. 423)

antebellum (ăn´ tē-bĕl´ əm) The time period before the Civil War. (p. 286)

Antifederalist (ăn´tē-fĕd´ ər-ə-lĭst) One who opposed ratifying the Constitution. (p. 119)

armistice (är´ mĭ-stĭs) A truce or temporary pause, agreed to by both sides, in a war or battle. (p. 546)

artisan (är´ tĭ-zən) A worker trained in a skilled trade such as cabinetmaking or printing. (p. 302)

assembly line (ə-sĕm´ blē lĭn) A continuously moving belt that moves parts past workers who each have a specific task. (p. 456)

assimilate (ə-sĭm´ ə-lāt´) To adopt a country's dominant culture. (p. 425)

asylum (ə-sī´ ləm) Political protection. (p. 570)

B

bilingual education (bī-lĭng´ gwəl ĕj´ ə-kā´ shən) Education presented in two languages. (p. 583)

bill of rights (bĭl ŭv rīts) A list of the basic liberties of citizens. (p. 113)

bonanza (bə-năn´ zə) A rich, valuable (ore-bearing) rock. (p. 413)

boom town (bōōm toun) A town that comes into existence suddenly. (p. 414)

boycott (boi´ kŏt´) An organized refusal to buy or use a product to express protest or to force a government, company, or person to take some action. (p. 57)

buffer zone (bŭf´ ər zōn) A territory separating two opposing powers. (p. 231)

C

Cabinet (kăb´ ə-nĭt) The advisory group selected by

the President, made up of the heads of the executive departments. (p. 134)

capital (kăp´ ĭ-tl) Material wealth, such as money or property, invested to produce more wealth. (p. 445)

carpetbagger (kär´ pĭt-băg´ ər) A Northerner who went to the South after the Civil War for political or financial advantage. (p. 388)

cash crop (kăsh krŏp) A single crop grown in large quantities for sale, often as an important source of income. (p. 287)

caucus (kô´ kəs) A closed meeting of political leaders to select candidates for office. (p. 175)

cede (sēd) To grant or surrender possession of something through a formal agreement. (p. 74)

checks and balances (chĕks ənd băl´ən-səz) A system in which branches of government balance each other in order to protect against abuses of power. (p. 108)

citizen (sĭt´ ĭ-zən) A person who, by birth or naturalization, owes loyalty to and receives protection from a nation's government. (p. 593)

civil rights (sĭv´ əl rīts) The personal freedoms belonging to a person by virtue of his or her status as a citizen or as a member of society. (p. 356)

civil service (sĭv´əl sûr´ vĭs) Jobs in federal, state, or local government that are awarded on the basis of merit rather than on political patronage. (p. 480)

commerce (kŏm´ ərs) The buying and selling of goods on a large scale. (p. 96)

Confederacy (kən-fĕd´ ər-ə-sē) The eleven Southern states that separated from the United States. (p. 342)

confederation (kən-fĕd´ ə-rā´ shən) A group of states joined loosely for a common purpose. (p. 84)

conquistador (kŏng-kē´ stə-dôr´) A Spanish word meaning "conqueror." (p. 18)

conservation (kŏn´ sûr-vā´ shən) The act or process of protecting and preserving natural resources and wilderness areas. (p. 510)

constitution (kŏn´ stĭ-tōō´ shən) A document that defines the main principles and framework of a government. (p. 83)

constitutional (kŏn´stĭ-tōō´ shə-nəl) In agreement with the principles established by the Constitution. (p. 151)

continental divide (kŏn´tə-nĕn´ tl dĭ-vīd´) Line that divides the rivers that flow west from those that flow east. (p. 226)

cooperative (kō-ŏp´ ər-ə-tĭv) An organization or association that is owned jointly by those who use its facilities or services. (p. 489)

cultural accommodation (kŭl´ chər-əl ə-kŏm´ə-dā´ shən) Reconciliation or compromise of opposing cultures. (p. 204)

cultural heritage (kŭl´ chər-əl hĕr´ ĭ-tĭj) The customs, language, and beliefs of a people's culture. (p. 293)

currency (kŭr´ ən-sē) Coins and paper bills that serve as money. (p. 73)

D

dissent (dĭ-sĕnt´) Disagreement or difference of opinion with established authority. (p. 548)

draft (drăft) A call to military service. (p. 356)

E

electoral vote (ĭ-lĕk´ tər-əl vōt) The ballot cast by the persons chosen by each state to elect the President. (p. 146)

emancipation (ĭ-măn´sə-pā´ shən) A condition of being freed from oppression, bondage, or restraint. (p. 352)

embargo (ĕm-bär´ gō) A ban on trade with another nation. (p. 59)

emigrate (ĕm´ ĭ-grāt´) To leave one country to settle permanently in another. (p. 211)

enfranchise (ĕn-frăn´ chīz´) To give the rights of citizenship, especially the right to vote. (p. 516)

entrepreneur (ŏn´ trə-prə-nûr´) A person who organizes and assumes the risk for a business venture. (p. 445)

estuary (ĕs´ chōō-ĕr´ ē) An arm of the sea that extends inland to meet the mouth of a river. (p. 6)

executive (ĭg-zĕk´ yə-tĭv) A person or group having administrative or managerial authority. (p. 85)

executive branch (ĭg-zĕk´ yə-tĭv brănch) The division of government led by the President. (p. 110)

expansionist (ĭk-spăn´ shən-ĭst) One who calls for increasing a nation's territory. (p. 230)

F

famine (făm´ ĭn) A drastic and wide-reaching shortage of food. (p. 211)

federal (fĕd´ ər-əl) Relating to a system of government that divides power between a central authority and a number of smaller states. (p. 84)

Federalist (fĕd´ ər-ə-lĭst) One who supported ratifying the Constitution and believed in a strong central government. (p. 119)

free labor (frē lā´ bər) System of work in which employees have the right to leave their employer and their job for better opportunities. (p. 314)

free press (frē prĕs) The right to publish anything, including criticism of the government. (p. 124)

G

ghost town (gōst toun) A town that has been totally abandoned. (p. 243)

glasnost (glăz´ nōst) A Russian word meaning openness. The term is used to describe a policy begun by Soviet leader Mikhail Gorbachev. (p. 611)

graft (grăft) Money gained by elected or appointed officials through dishonest or illegal means. (p. 476)

guerrilla (gə-rĭl´ ə) Irregular warfare by independent forces. (p. 328)

H

homestead (hōm´ stĕd´) Land claimed by a settler under the Homestead Act of 1862. (p. 424)

household economy (hous´ hōld´ĭ-kŏn´ ə-mē) Production of food and other necessary items by a family for use within the household or for exchange within the immediate community. (p. 164)

human geography (hyōō´ mən jē-ŏg´ rə-fē) The study of how human beings and places interact with and influence one another. (p. 5)

I

immigrant (ĭm´ ĭ-grənt) A person born in one country who moves into and takes up residence in another country. (p. 48)

impeachment (ĭm-pēch´ mənt) The procedure of charging an office-holding official with misconduct before a formal tribunal. (p. 387)

imperialism (ĭm-pîr´ ē-ə-lĭz´əm) The attempt to create an empire by controlling other countries through either economic or political means. (p. 536)

impressment (ĭm-prĕs´ mənt) The policy of forcing someone into military service. (p. 154)

indentured servant (ĭn-dĕn´ chərd sûr´ vənt) A person who agreed to work for a specified period of time in exchange for passage from Europe to the colonies. (p. 34)

Industrial Revolution (ĭn-dŭs´ trē-əl rĕv´ə-lōō´ shən) The social and economic changes that occurred when manufacturing shifted from people's homes and shops to factories. (p. 255)

inflation (ĭn-flā´ shən) A rapid rise in prices over a period of time. (p. 73)

initiative (ĭ-nĭsh´ ə-tĭv) A procedure that allows citizens to propose a new law or amendment for the approval of voters. (p. 508)

institution (ĭn´stĭ-tōō´ shən) An established organization dedicated to providing important social functions such as education. (p. 199)

isolationism (ī´sə-lā´ shə-nĭz´əm) The belief or policy that the United States should avoid alliance and minimize its involvement in the affairs of other nations. (p. 551)

J

judicial branch (jōō-dĭsh´ əl brănch) The division of government made up of the federal courts of law. (p. 110)

judicial review (jōō-dĭsh´ əl rĭ-vyōō´) The review of laws to determine whether or not they are constitutional. (p. 151)

K

kickback (kĭk´ băk´) A payment made to a person in return for political or business favors. (p. 475)

L

labor union (lā´ bər yōōn´yən) An organization of workers formed to serve workers' interests with respect to wages and working conditions. (p. 458)

laissez faire (lĕs´ā fār´) A policy that opposes governmental interference in or regulation of industry and the economy. (p. 499)

landform (lănd´ fôrm) A natural feature of the earth's surface, such as a mountain, hill, plateau, or plain. (p. 5)

legislative branch (lĕj´ ĭ-slā´tiv brănch) Congress, the division of government that passes laws. (p. 110)

legislature (lĕj´ ĭ-slā´ chər) Officially selected body responsible for making the laws for a political unit. (p. 85)

M

Manifest Destiny (măn´ ə-fĕst´ dĕst´ tə-nē) The nineteenth-century belief that the United States had the right and duty to expand throughout North America to spread white American culture. (p. 227)

market economy (mär´ kĭt ĭ-kŏn´ ə-mē) Production of food and other goods and services for cash sale, often in distant markets. (p. 166)

martial law (mär´ shəl lô) Temporary rule imposed on a civilian population by military authorities. (p. 386)

middle class (mĭd´ l klăs) Members of society with better-than-average education and income. (p. 192)

migrant worker (mī´ grənt wûr´ kər) A person who travels from place to place planting and harvesting crops as jobs are available. (p. 582)

migrate (mī´ grāt´) To move from one region and settle in another. (p. 197)

militia (mə-lĭsh´ ə) A group of armed citizens who are prepared for military service if called to defend their town, state, or country. (p. 63)

minuteman (mĭn´ ĭt-măn´) A member of the colonial Massachusetts militia who was ready to fight the British at a minute's notice. (p. 63)

mobilize (mō´ bə-līz´) To prepare or put into operation for war. (p. 543)

moderate (mŏd´ ər-ĭt) An individual opposed to radical or extreme views or measures in politics or religion. (p. 348)

monopoly (mə-nŏp´ə-lē) A company that completely controls the market for a particular commodity or service. (p. 483)

mountain man (moun´ tən măn) A fur trapper of the West during the early 1800s. (p. 226)

muckraker (mŭk´ rāk´ ər) A journalist who investigates and exposes political corruption and social problems in an effort to improve society. (p. 502)

Mugwumps (mŭg´ wŭmps´) A group of Republicans who sought to eliminate political corruption and business abuses during the Gilded Age. (p. 479)

municipal (myoō-nĭs´ ə-pəl) Of a city or urban political unit. (p. 263)

N

nativism (nā´ tĭ-vĭz´ əm) A policy favoring the interests of native-born inhabitants over those of immigrants. (p. 215)

naturalization (năch´ ə-rəl-ĭ-zā´ shən) The process by which the citizen of one country becomes the citizen of another country. (p. 594)

navigation (năv´ĭ-gā´ shən) The practice of plotting the course of a ship. (p. 17)

neoclassical (nē´ō-klăs´ ĭ-kəl) Pertaining to the revival of classical art forms. (p. 166)

neutrality (noō-trăl´ ĭ-tē) The state of being a nonparticipant in a war or other conflict. (p. 154)

nomad (nō´ măd´) One who moves from place to place rather than settling in one location. (p. 27)

nullify (nŭl´ ə-fī´) To refuse to recognize or enforce a law (a federal law within a state). (p. 178)

P

patronage (pā´ trə-nĭj) The practice of giving out government jobs in exchange for political support. (p. 476)

philanthropist (fĭ-lăn´ thrō-pĭst) A person who promotes human welfare through the funding of beneficial public institutions. (p. 446)

physical geography (fĭz´ ĭ-kəl jē-ŏg´ rə-fē) The study of the natural world, including the earth's climate, landforms, bodies of water, plants, animals, and resources. (p. 5)

plantation (plăn-tā´ shən) A large estate's farm on which crops are raised. (p. 285)

plateau (plă-tō´) An expanse of high, flat land. (p. 11)

pluralism (ploōr´ ə-liz´əm) A condition of society in which numerous distinct ethnic, religious, or cultural groups coexist within one nation. (p. 49)

political machine (pə-lĭt´ ĭ-kəl mə-shēn´) A powerful, tightly run political organization that developed in many American cities in the late 1800s and early 1900s. (p. 476)

popular sovereignty (pŏp´ yə-lər sŏv´-ər-ĭn-tē) The idea that voters in a territory should decide for themselves if their territory should allow slavery. (p. 326)

popular vote (pŏp´ yə-lər vōt) The total number of votes by the people within each state. (p. 174)

Populism (pŏp´ yə-lĭz´ əm) A member or supporter of the Populist Party, a political party that represented the interests of farmers in the 1890s. (p. 487)

prairie (prâr´ ē) An area of rolling grasslands. (p. 8)

precipitation (prĭ-sĭp´ ĭ-tā´shən) Moisture, condensed in the atmosphere, that falls to the earth in the form of rain or snow. (p. 8)

profit (prŏf´ ĭt) The gain from a business undertaking after all expenses have been paid for. (p. 445)

Progressivism (prə-grĕs´ ĭ-vĭz´əm) A broad reform movement that worked to correct political abuses and social problems during the early decades of the 1900s. (p. 499)

Prohibition (prō´ə-bĭsh´ ən) The forbidding by law of the manufacture, transportation, sale, and possession of alcoholic beverages. (p. 514)

protectorate (prə-tĕk´ tər-ĭt) A country or region that is protected and partially controlled by a more powerful country. (p. 532)

Q

quota (kwō´ tə) The largest number of immigrants who may enter a country in one year. (p. 568)

R

ratify (răt´ ə-fī´) To approve formally. (p. 120)

raw materials (rô mə-tĭr´ ē-əl) Unprocessed natural products used in manufacturing. (p. 256)

recall (rĭ-kŏl´) A special election that allows voters to remove an elected official from office before his or her term has expired. (p. 508)

Reconstruction (rē´kən-strŭk´ shən) The period (1865–1877) during which the former Confederate states were controlled by the federal government before being readmitted into the Union. (p. 377)

redeem (rĭ-dēm´) To recover or reclaim. (p. 394)

referendum (rĕf´ə-rĕn´ dəm) The process by which people can vote directly on a bill. (p. 508)

refugee (rĕf´yoō-jē´) Person who flees his or her country because of persecution for political beliefs. (p. 570)

regionalism (rē´ jə-nəl-ĭz´əm) A sense of belonging to a distinct region. (p. 245)

regulate (rĕg´ yə-lāt´) To control or manage business or other activities by established rules. (p. 482)

rendezvous (rän´ dā-voō´) French word meaning "meeting place." (p. 226)

reparations (rĕp´ə-rā´ shənz) Payments made by defeated nations as compensation for the damages they caused in war. (p. 551)

republic (rĭ-pŭb´ lĭk) A form of government in which the people exercise power through their chosen representatives. (p. 65)

reservation (rĕz´ ər-vā´ shən) Land that is set aside for American Indians. (p. 424)

revitalization (rē-vī´tl-ĭ-zā´ shən) The effort to bring new life and strength to a people or culture. (p. 204)

S

salutary neglect (săl´ yə-tĕr´ē nĭ-glĕkt´) The policy of weakly enforcing laws that England used in ruling the American colonies for much of the late 1600s and early 1700s. (p. 52)

satire (săt´ īr´) A literary work in which human faults are ridiculed through irony or wit. (p. 179)

scalawag (skăl´ ə-wăg´) A white Republican Southerner who had opposed secession and supported Radical Reconstruction. (p. 389)

secede (sĭ-sēd´) To withdraw formally from membership in an organization, association, or alliance. (p. 343)

sect (sĕkt) A small religious group that has formed a separate part of a larger denomination. (p. 21)

secularize (sĕk´ yə-lə-rīz´) To convert from religious use or ownership to civil use or ownership. (p. 237)

sedition (sĭ-dĭsh´ ən) Rebellion against the authority of the government. (p. 139)

segregated (sĕg´ rĭ-gāt´əd) The maintenance of separate facilities for members of different races or of facilities restricted to members of one race. (p. 383)

sharecropping (shâr´ krŏp´ĭng) A system of farming in which a tenant farmer gives a share of the crop to the farm owner instead of paying rent. (p. 376)

sit-in (sĭt=ĭn) A form of protest in which participants occupy a room or building until their demands are met. (p. 602)

social class (sō´ shəl klăs) A level of society characterized by certain cultural and economic traits. (p. 180)

socialist (sō´ shə-lĭst) A person who supports an economic system in which the workers have both political power and the means of producing and distributing goods. (p. 515)

sovereignty (sŏv´ ər-ĭn-tē) The supreme power or authority that an independent country or state has within its borders. (p. 91)

spoils system (spoilz sĭs´ təm) A system in which a winning candidate's supporters are rewarded with appointment to public office. (p. 175)

states' rights (stāts rīts) The idea that individual states could limit the power of the federal government. (p. 178)

strike (strīk) A temporary work stoppage in support of demands made on employers by workers. (p. 458)

subsistence farmer (səb-sĭs´ təns fär´ mər) A person who grows just enough food for his or her family's needs. (p. 35)

suffrage (sŭf´ rĭj) The right or privilege of voting. (p.169)

T

tariff (tăr´ ĭf) A duty imposed by a government on imported or exported goods. (p. 175)

temperance (tĕm´ pər-əns) The resolution not to drink any alcoholic beverages. (p. 268)

tenement (tĕn´ ə-mənt) An apartment building whose facilities barely meet or fail to meet minimum standards of sanitation, safety, and comfort. (p. 504)

term of office (tûrm ŭv ô´ fĭs) A limited period of time during which an elected official serves the public. (p. 92)

territory (tĕr´ ĭ-tôr´ē) An area belonging to the United States that is not a part of any existing state. (p. 96)

transcontinental (trăns´kŏn-tə-nĕn´ tl) Crossing a continent. (p. 412)

trust (trŭst) A combination of business firms formed by legal agreement, especially to reduce competition. (p. 483)

U

Underground Railroad (ŭn´ dər-ground´ rāl´ rōd´) A secret network that helped slaves escape to freedom. (p. 333)

undocumented immigrant (ŭn-dŏk´ yə-mənt´əd ĭm´ ĭ-grənt) A person who enters the United States without documented permission. (p. 581)

urban society (ŭr´ bən sə-sī´ ĭ-tē) A social structure that is based on city life. (p. 448)

Utopia (yōō-tō´ pē-ə) A community established to create social and political reform. (p. 271)

V

veto (vē´ tō) To prevent a legislative bill from becoming law by exercising executive authority. (p. 53)

vigilante (vĭj´ə-lăn´ tē) A group of citizens that, without authority, takes on itself powers such as pursuing and punishing those suspected of committing crimes. (p. 394)

W

working class (wûr´ kĭng klăs) Members of society who are employed for wages, usually in manual labor. (p. 192)

writs of assistance (rĭts ŭv ə-sĭs´ təns) Documents issued by the British government in the colonial period that allowed officials to conduct unrestricted searches. (p. 57)

Y

yellow journalism (yĕl´ ō jûr´ nə-lĭz´ əm) A style of newspaper reporting popular in the 1890s that featured exaggerated writing and sensational headlines. (p. 535)

yeoman farmer (yō´ mən fär´ mər) Owner of a small farm. (p. 299)

Z

zoning law (zōn´ ĭng lô) A law that restricts certain neighborhoods of a city to particular uses, such as residential, commercial, or industrial. (p. 505)

Italic numbers refer to pages on which illustrations appear; *quoted* refers to a quotation from a speech or writings of the person listed.

A

Abbot, John, 190, 198
Abolitionism, 321 *See also Antislavery*
Abominations, Tariff of, 177-178
Adams, Abigail, *88*
    quoted, 88
Adams, John, 65, 84, 91, 106
    midnight appointments of, 151
    as president, 146,
    quoted, 88
    as Vice President, 134, 135, 139
Adams, John Quincy, 158, 173-174
Adams, Samuel, 57-58, 75, 124-125
Adams, Samuel Hopkins, 509
Adams-Onís Treaty, 158
Addams, Jane, 502, *502,* 503, 519, 536, 610-611, *610*
Administration, 134
AFL-CIO, 460
African-Americans. *See Black Americans; Free blacks; Slavery; Slaves*
African Methodist Episcopal Church, 195, *195*
Agriculture. *See Farming*
Ah Bing, 467
Airplanes, in World War I, *542*
Alabama
    admission to union, 288
    in Civil War, 343
Alamo, Battle of, 232, 233, *233*
Alaska
    environment versus oil exploration in, 14-15, *15*
    purchase of, 530, 688
Alcoholism, *268*
Alger, Horatio, 445
Alien Act (1798), 139, 148
Allen, Ethan, 63, 66
Allen, Richard, 195, *195*
Alliances, 27, 542
Alligators, 7
All Quiet on the Western Front (Remarque), 545, 546
Amendments, 125. *See also Constitutional amendments; specific by number*
American Antislavery Society, 321
American Board for Foreign Missions, 238

American Colonization Society, 321
American Communist Party, 680
American English, evolution of, 51
American Federation of Labor (AFL), 459, 460, 516
American history, influence of geography on, 5-6
American identity, creation of, 164-166
American Independent Party, 680
American Indians. *See also specific tribes*
    assimilation of, 425-426
    citizenship of, 595
    civil rights for, 604-605, *605*
    culture areas of, *672*
    education of, 425-426, *426, 604*
    impact of disease on, 28
    and missionaries, 28-29
    relations with English colonists, 27-31
    removal of, to reservations, 424-426
    trade with, 29
    voting rights for, 596
    in War of 1812, 203-204
    and Western settlement, 202-207, *203, 419,* 422-424, *422, 423*
American Library Association, 270
American Missionary Association, 383
American Protective Association, 466
American Revolution
    battles of, 62, 63, 65, *65,* 66-70, *66, 69, 684, 685*
    black Americans in, 73-74
    British surrender at Yorktown, 70, *70*
    destruction in, 72-73, *72*
    economic consequences of, *73*
    end of, 70
    home front in, 71-73, *72*
    important dates in, *684*
    Loyalists versus Patriots in, 72
    minutemen in, 63, 64, *64*
    social impact of, 73-75
    start of, 62, *62*
    Treaty of Paris ending, 70
    weapons in, *68*
    women in, 71, 74-75, *74*

American West. *See West; Western settlement*
Anaconda, Montana, *414*
Anarchists, 516
Annapolis Convention (1786), 99
Annex, 232
Antebellum period, 286
Anthony, Susan B., 267, *268,* 270, 276-277
Anti-Defamation League (ADL), 394
Antietam, Battle of, 351, *368*
    reporting on, 368-369
Antifederalists, 119-120, 122
Anti-Imperialist League, 536
Antin, Mary, 462
Anti-Saloon League, 514
Antislavery movement, 320-322, *321, 322,* 332
    impact of, 289
    women in, 322-323, *323*
Apache Indians, 417
Appalachian culture, 299, 300-301, *300, 301,* 302
Appalachian Highlands, 7
Appalachian Mountains, 7
Appeal to the Colored Citizens of the World (Walker), 320
Appomattox, surrender at, 367, *367*
Arapaho Indians, 422
Arbor Day, 429
Architecture
    in colonial cities, 182, *182*
    neoclassicism, 168, *168*
    Republican, 165-166
    skyscrapers in, 449-450, *449*
Arctic National Wildlife Refuge (ANWR), 14-15, *14, 15*
Arikara Indians, 422
Arizona, acquisition of, 158
Arkansas
    admission to union, 288
    in Civil War, 343
Arkansas River, 11
Armistice, 546
Arnold, Benedict, 68
Art, neoclassical, 165-166
Arthur, Chester, 481
Articles of Confederation, 85-86, 90-92, 94
    land policy under, 96, 98, *98*
    weaknesses of, 95-96

"Articles of Confederation and Perpetual Union" (Franklin), 82

Artisans, 302

Asch, Sholem, 522-523

Ash Can School, 499

Asia
immigrants from, 463, 466, 572, 573, *573*
trade with, 531-532, *531*

Assembly line, 456

Assimilation, 572, 575
of American Indians, 425-426

Assiniboine Indians, 422

Astor, John Jacob, 238

Astrolabe, *17*

Asylum, 570

Atlanta, destruction of, 366

Atlanta University, 383

Atlas, historical, 32

Atsina Indians, 422

Attucks, Crispus, 58

Audubon Society, 612

Austin, Moses, 231

Australian ballot, 508

Aztecs, 27

B

Babcock, Orville, 475

Backcountry settlers, 37, 38

Bacon, Nathaniel, 31

Bacon's Rebellion, 31

Balboa, Vasco Núñez de, 18

Balloon frame house, 261-262

Baltimore, 197, *263*
free blacks in, 193
growth of, 193

Bank of the U.S.
First, 135, *135,* 675
Second, 176-177, *176, 177,* 675

Barbary Coast pirates, 96

Barbusse, Henri, 546

Barton, Clara, 363, *363*

Baseball, 278

Basketball, 279

Baumfree, Isabella, 320

Bayard, James, 147

Bear Flag Republic, 234

Beaumont, Gustave de, 181
sketchbook of, *183*

Beauregard, P. G. T., *345,* 347

Beecher, Catherine, 192, 200

Beecher, Henry Ward, 327

Belknap, William, 475

Bell, Alexander Graham, 443, *443, 467*

Bell, John, 335

Bellows, George, painting by, *499*

Benton, Jessie, 226-227

Benton, Thomas Hart, 226

Bergman, Henry, *455*

Beveridge, Albert, 528

Bibliography cards, 152

Bickerdyke, Mary, 359

Biddle, Nicholas, *177*

Bilingual education, 583

Bilingual Education Act (1968), 583, 628

Bill, process of becoming law, *689-692*

Bill of rights, 113, 124-127, *126,* 601, 626-627

Bimetallic standard, 675

Bingham, George Caleb, *painting by, 298*

Birmingham, Alabama, industry in, 449

Bishop Hill, *273*

Bison, *10*

Black Americans. *See also Free blacks; Slavery; Slaves*
in American Revolution, 73-74
and black codes, 379
challenge to segregation, 601-602
citizenship of, 594-595
in Civil War, 352, *352*
contributions of, 51
cultural heritage of, 293-294, *294*
in early America, 193-195
education of, 194-195, 303, 383, 452-453
and end of slavery, 382-383, *383*
free, 193-195, *193, 194, 195,* 305, 382-383, *383*
and Jim Crow laws, 518-519, 597, 600
and legacies of Reconstruction, 397, *397*
march on Washington, 602, 603, *603,* 604
migration of, to cities, *453*
in politics, 388, *388*
voting rights for, 390, *390,* 394, 508, 516, 596, 597

in World War I, 549

Black bears, *8*

Black Codes, 379, 392-393

Blackfoot Indians, 417

Black Freemasons, 194

Blaine, James, 478, *478*

"Bleeding Kansas," 328-329, *328*

Blithedale Romance, The (Hawthorne), 273

Bloomer, Amelia Jenks, 257

Bly, Nellie, 502

Bogardus, James, 262

Bolshevik Revolution, 553

Bonanza, 413

Boom towns, 414

Boone, Daniel, 197, 436

Booth, John Wilkes, 378

Boston, 39
closing of port of, by Great Britain, 59
colonial protests in, 54, *54,* 58-59
free blacks in, 193
growth of, 193

Boston African Society, 194

Boycott, 57

Braddock, Edward, 55

Braddock's Road, *198*

Bradford, William, 29

Brady, Matthew, 362

Branding iron, *428*

Breckenridge, John C., 335

Breed's Hill, 65

Brook Farm, 272-273

Brooklyn Bridge, 451

Brooks, Preston, 325

Brown, John, 328, *328,* 330, *330,* 331

Brown, William Henry, *painting by, 286*

Browne, J. Ross, *quoted,* 414

Brown v. Board of Education of Topeka (1954), 601, 602

Bruce, Blanche K., 388

Bryan, William Jennings, 486-487, *486,* 490-491, *491,* 536
quoted, 486

Buchanan, Franklin, 351

Buchanan, James, 329, *329*

Buchanan, McKean, 351

Buchanan's Station, 196

Buffalo, *10,* 26, *26*
hunting of, by Plains Indians, 415-416

as nuisance or resource, 436-437, *436, 437*
Buffer zone, 231
Bulfinch, Charles, 168
Bull Moose Party, 511
Bull Run, First Battle of, 347, *347,* 348
Bunker Hill, Battle of, 65, *65, 66,* 73
Buren, Martin Van, 207
Burger, Warren, 564
Burns, Anthony, 332
Burr, Aaron, 152, *152*
Bush, Barbara, 171, *171*
Bushnell, Edward, 555
Business
    entrepreneurs in, 445-446
    growth of big, 473
    and technology, 443-444, *443, 444*
Butros, Rima, 592

C

Cabinet, 134
    under Washington, 127, 134, 135
Cabot, John, 20, *20*
Cactus, 13
Calhoun, John, 177-178, *178*
California
    acquisition of, 158
    admission to union, 319
    as Bear Flag Republic, 234
    gold mining in, 241-243, *242*
    settlement of, 230, 236-238, *236, 237,* 240
"Call for Civil Rights, A" (Kennedy), 616-617
Camp David accords, 631
Camps, mining, 242-243
Canals, 256, *257*
Capital, 445
Caravel, 17
Carmel, New Spain, 22
Carnegie, Andrew, 270, 445, *446,* 457, 467, 505, 536
Carnegie Library, 446
Carpetbaggers, 388, *388*
Carranza, Venustiano, 540
Carson, Kit, 226, 243
Carter, Jimmy, 631
Cartier, Jacques, 20

Cascade Mountains, 11, 13
Cash crop, 287
Castro, Fidel, 570
Cather, Willa, 434-435
Catt, Carry Chapman, 517
Cattle ranching, 428-430, *429, 430*
Caucus, 175
Cayuga Indians, 27
Cayuse Indians, 238
Cede, 74
Cemetery Hill, *353*
Centennial Exhibition, 442, *442*
Central Pacific Railroad, 412
Central Plains, 9, 10
Central Valley, 12, 13
Chancellorsville, Battle of, 353
Charbonneau, Toussaint, 224
Charleston, South Carolina, 39, 302
    in American Revolution, 68
    growth of, 193
Chase, Salmon P., 379, 385
Chavez, Cesar, 582
Checks and balances, 108, 109, 625-626
Cherokee Indians
    in American Revolution, 74
    culture of, 205
    defeat of, 205-206, *206*
    and the Trail of Tears, 176, 206, *206,* 207, *207*
Cheyenne Indians, 422
Chicago
    great fire of 1871 in, 447, *447*
    growth of, 449, 451, *451*
    immigrants in, 213
    living conditions in, 504
    Pullman community in, 458, *458*
    skyscrapers in, 449-450, *449*
Child labor, 450, *450,* 500, *500,* 514, *514*
    reforms against, 514-515, *514*
Child Labor Act (1916), 515
Children's Bureau, 511, 515
Chillicothe, Ohio, 197
China
    relations with United States, 96
    trade with, 531
China-bound sailor, 97, *97*
Chinese Exclusion Act (1882), 567
Chinese immigrants, 566-567, *567*
    discrimination against, *466*
    restrictions on, 567

and railroad construction, 413
Chippewa Indians, 416
Chisholm Trail, 429-430
Chivington, John, 424
Christensen, C. C. A., painting by, *243*
Chronological outlining, 228-229
Chronologies, 32
Church, separation of, from state, 85
Cincinnati, *182*
    immigrants in, 213
Circuit riders, 200
Cities
    development of industrial, 448-451, *448, 452, 454*
    growth of, 182, *182,* 260-264
    housing in, 261-262
    immigrants in, 212-213, *212, 467*
    migration of rural people to, 451
    movement of blacks to, 452-453, *453*
    problems in late 1900s, 475-476, *475*
    protection of people in, 263-264
    reforms in, 266
    social classes in, 264, 266
    transportation in, 263
Citizens
    responsibilities of, 611-613
    rights of, 600-601
    ways of making a difference, 610-611
Citizenship, 592
    definition of, 593
    expansion of, 594-595
    methods of gaining, 593-594
    swearing in ceremony, *570, 592*
City government, forms of, 506, *506*
City manager form of city government, 506, *506*
City map, designing, 208-209, *209*
City planning, 504-505
City politics, reforming, 505-506
Civil liberties, in Civil War, 356
Civil rights, 356
Civil Rights Act (1866), 594
Civil Rights Act (1964), 604, 606
Civil Rights Act (1968), 604
Civil rights movement, 600, 601-603, *601, 603,* 604

for American Indians, 604-605, *605*
Civil Service Act (1883), 481
Civil service system, need for, 480-481, *480*
Civil War
  analyzing, 398-399
  battles and campaigns in, 347, *347*, *350*, 351, 353-354, *354*, *671*
  battle strategy in, 353, 363-364
  beginning of, 335, *335*
  blacks in, 352, *352*
  costs of, 363
  draft in, 356, 357, *357*, 358, 360-361
  economy during, 356
  and Emancipation Proclamation, *352*
  homefronts in, 355-359
  impact of, on South, 376
  important events during, *670*
  leadership in, 348-349
  Northern resources in, 345-346, *346*
  and secession of South, 335, *335*, 343, *343*
  and the Shakers, 360-361
  soldiers in, 358, *358*
  Southern resources in, 342-345, *346*
  surrender at Appomattox, *367*, 367, 376
  surrender of Lee in, 376
  technology in, 363, 364-365, 366
  uniforms of, *670*, *670*
  women in, 359, *359*
Civil wars, understanding, 344
Clark, Amy, 359
Clark, George Rogers, 68, 222, 223
Clark, William, 223
Clay, Henry, 175, 178, 315, *315*
  and Andrew Jackson, 184-185, *184*, *185*
  and Compromise of 1850, 319
  in election of 1824, 173
  in election of 1832, 176-177
  as secretary of state, 173
Clayton Antitrust Act (1914), 484, 512
Clermont, 256, 257
Cleveland, *448*
  growth of, 448-449

Cleveland, Grover, 490
  and acquisition of Hawaii, 532
  in election of 1888, 479, *479*
  in election of 1892, 479, *479*
Cleveland Board of Education v. *Le Fleur* (1974), 606
Climate, 7-8
  in American West, 12, 411-412
  in Central Heartland, 9-10
  in Eastern and Southern United States, 7-8
  in United States, 706
Clinton, George, 119, 127
Clinton, William, 632
Clipper ships, 257
Coeur d'Alene, Idaho, 461
Coffin Handbill, 174
Cohan, George, 554
Colonial government
  British influences on, 83-84, *84*
  influence of Enlightenment on, 82-83
Colonies
  post American Revolution, 75, 82-87
  British policies in, 56-59,
  ethnic population in, 48-49, *49*
  growth of, 48-49
  protests against British policies in, 54, *54*, 56-59, *57*
  slaves in, 49
Colorado Plateau, 11, 13
Colorado River, 11, 12
Colt, Samuel, 257
Colton, Walter, 236
Columbia River, 11, 12, 225
Columbus, Christopher, 17-18, *18*
  quoted, 660-662
Comanche Indians, 416, 417, 423
Commerce, 96
Commission form of city government, 506, *506*
Committee of Correspondence, 58
Committees of Safety, 72
Common Sense (Paine), 65, 82, 666-667
Communication, improvements in, 443-444, *443*, 456-457
Company towns, life in, 458, *458*
Compromise, reaching, 123
Compromise of 1850, *318*, 319, *319*
Compromise of 1877, 395
Computerized sources, 274-275

Comstock Lode, 413, *413*
Concord, Battle of, 62, 63, 66, 73
"Concord Hymm" (Emerson), 63
Confederacy, 342-345
Confederation, 84
Congress, 351
Congress, U.S., 632-634. *See also House of Representatives, U.S.; Senate, U.S.*
  first, 126
  and checks and balances, 625-626
  passage of bill by, *689-691*
Congress of Industrial Organizations (CIO), 460
Conkling, Roscoe, 481
Connecticut, 35
  colonial government in, 87
  ratification of constitution by, 120
Conquistadors, 18-19
Constitution
  definition of, 83
  origins of, 109
Constitution, U.S.
  amending, 626-627
  annotated, 636-657
  and limited self-government, 622-626
  as living document, 626-630
  ratification of, 118-122, *119*, *122*
  signing of, 112-113
Constitutional amendments, 396. *See also Bill of Rights; specific by number*
Constitutional Convention, 106
  Connecticut Compromise, 110, *110*
  delegates at, 107, *108*, *112*
  New Jersey Plan, 110
  reactions and counterproposals toVirginia Plan, 108
  sectionalism in, 317
  slavery issue at, 111
  Virginia Plan, 108, 110, 113
Constitutionality, of laws, 151
Constitutional Union Party, 335
Constitution, U.S.S., 155
Continental Army, 66-70
  black Americans in, 73-74
  women in, 74
Continental Association, 59

Continental Congress
    first, 59
    second, 65, 66, 68, 72, 73, 82, 84,
        85
Continental Divide, 11, 226
Continental dollar, 73, *73*, 675
Cook, John, *quoted*, 436
Coolidge, Calvin, *553*
Cooper, James Fenimore, 197
Cooperatives, farm, 489
Copley, John Singleton, portrait
    painted by, *74*
Copperheads, 356
Copper mining, *414*
Corning, New York, industry in,
    449
Cornwallis, Charles, 68, 70
Coronado, Francisco Vásquez de,
    19
Corruption
    in Gilded Age, 472-476, *472*, *474*,
        476
    under Reconstruction, 389-390
    and reform, 477-485
Cortés, Hernando, 19, 26
Cotton gin, 284, 285
Cotton production, 284-286, 288,
    288
Cowboys, 428-430, *428*, *429*
Coxey, Jacob, 490
Coxey's "army," 490
Coyotes, *9*
Crawford, William, 173
Crazy Horse, *422*
Credit mobilier scandal, 474-475
Crèvecoeur, Michel-Guillaume
    Jean de, 180
Crime, and the Ku Klux Klan, 394
Cripple Creek, 414
Critical thinking,
    cause and effect, analyzing the
        Civil War, 336-337
    editorials, analyzing, 598-599
    historical photographs, analyz-
        ing, 520-521
    period literature, reading Mark
        Twain, 492-493
    point of view, analyzing view-
        points on slavery, 336-337
    political cartoons, analyzing
        Jackson-Clay, 184-185
    primary sources, reading Abigail
        Adams's letters, 88-89

propaganda, analyzing, 556-557
Crittenden, George, 351
Crittenden, Thomas L., 351
Crockett, Davy, 197
Crow Indians, 422
Cuba
    immigrants from, 570
    Spanish-American War in, 535-
        536, *536*
    under Weyler, 534
Cultural accommodation, 204-205
Cultural heritage, 293
Cultural institutions, 270
Cultural regionalism, 246
Cumberland Gap, 7
Cumberland Road, *198*
Cumberland Trail, 436
Currency, 100-101, *100*, *101*, 674-
    677 *675*, *676*
    during American Revolution,
        73, *73*
    post American Revolution, 94,
        94
    gold standard for, 488-489, 677
    greenbacks, 488
Curtis, George W., 480
Cushman, Pauline, 359

D

Dall sheep, *14*
Dalrymple, Oliver, 432
Dana, Richard Henry, 238, 245
Darwin, Charles, 528-529
Daughters of Liberty, 57
Davis, Howell, 351
Davis, Jefferson, 343, *345*, 348, *348*,
    388, 391
Davis, Joseph, 391
Davis Bend, Mississippi, 391, *391*,
    392
Dawes Act (1887), 425
Debs, Eugene V., 515-516, *515*, 548
Decision making
    buffalos as resource or nuisance,
        436-437, *436*, *437*
    environment or energy, 14-15,
        14, *15*
    Shakers and the Civil War, 360-
        361
Declaration of Independence, 66,
    314
    annotated, 656-659

Declaration of Rights, 57
Deer, *8*
Deere, John, 191
    plow of, *191*
De la Cruz, Jesse, *577*
    quoted, 577
Delaware
    in Civil War, 343
    ratification of Constitution by,
        120
Delaware Indians, 202
Democracy in America: 1835-39
    (Tocqueville), 181, 183
Democratic Party, *326*, 680
    in Gilded Age, 478
    origin of, 174
Denver, Colorado, industry in, 449
Depression of 1893, 490, 499
Deseret, 240
Dew, Thomas R., 289
Dewey, George, 535
Dewey, John, 504, 519
Diaz, Portfirio, 540
Dickinson, Susanna, *232*
Dillingham Commission, 568
Dissent, 548
Dix, Dorothea, 266, *266*
Dodd, David O., 358
Dodd, Samuel, 483
Dodge City, Kansas, 430
Dolphin USS, 540
*Domestic Manners of the
    Americans* (Trollope), 178
Doubleday, Abner, 278
Doubloon, *94*
Douglas, Stephen A., 319, 326, 334-
    335
Douglass, Frederick, 296-297, 303,
    303, 321, 610
Downing, Jack, *177*
Draft
    in Civil War, 356, 357, *357*, 358,
        360-361
    in World War I, 543-544, *543*
Draft riots, 357, *357*
Dred Scott v. *Sandford*, 331, 594
Dreiser, Theodore, 451
Drinker, Elizabeth Sandwith, 71
Du Bois, W. E. B., 519
Due process amendment, 384
Dukas, Helene, *570*
Dunbar, Paul Laurence, *quoted*,
    518

Dunmore, Lord, 73-74
Dutch, exploration and settlement
  by, *19*, 20, *21*, 22

E

Eastern and Southern United
    States
  climate in, 7-8
  vegetation in, 8
  wildlife in, 8
Ecology, 424
Economy
  post American Revolution, 73,
    73, 92, 94-96, 99
  under Andrew Jackson, 177-178
  during Civil War, 346, 356
  in early Republic, 164-167, 191-
    193
  laissez faire, 499
  role of entrepreneurs in build-
    ing, 445-446
Edison, Thomas Alva, 443
Editorials, analyzing, 598-599
Edmonds, Sarah, 359
Education
  of American Indians, 425-426,
    426
  bilingual, 583
  of black Americans, 194-195,
    303, 383, 452-453
  establishing public, 269, 271
  reforms in, 504, *504*
  in South, 303
  start of first kindergarten, 210
  and western settlement, 199-200,
    200
  for women, 269, *269*
Educational Amendments (1972),
    606
Edwards, Jonathan, 52
Eighteenth Amendment, 514, 627
Eighteen year olds, voting rights
    for, 596
Eighth Amendment, 127
Eight-hour day, *456*
Einstein, Albert, 570, *570*
Einstein, Margot, *570*
Elastic clause, 628
Election(s)
  of 1789, 134
  of 1800, 146-147, *147*
  of 1808, 155

  of 1816, 158
  of 1824, 173-174
  of 1828, 173, 174, *175*
  of 1844, 234
  of 1856, 329
  of 1860, 334-335, 343
  of 1876, 395
  of 1884, 478, *478*
  of 1888, 479, *479*
  of 1890, 490
  of 1892, 479, *479*
  of 1896, 490-491, *490*, *491*
  of 1904, 515-516
  of 1908, 511
  of 1912, 511, *511*
  of 1916, 541, *541*
  of 1920, 553, *553*
Election system
  evolution of, 629-630
  proposed reforms for, 630
Electoral votes, 146
Elizabeth I (England), 22
Elk, *11*
Elk, John, 594
Elliot, Robert B., *388*
Ellis Island, 462-463, 567, *568*
  immigrants entering through,
    464-465, *464*, *465*
El Salvador, civil war in, 344
Elskwatawa (Prophet), 204, *204*
Emancipation Proclamation, 352,
    352
Embargo, 59
Embargo Act (1807), 154-155
Emergency Quota Act (1921), 569
Emerson, Ralph Waldo, 63
Emigration, 211
Endowment for International
    Peace, 446
Enfranchisement, 516
English, exploration and settle-
    ment by, *19*, 20, *21*, 22-23, *22*
English Bill of Rights, 83, *84*
English colonies, *38*
  farming in, 36-37, *36-37*
  government in, 52-53
  life in, 33-39, *33*, *35*
  religion in, 51-52, *52*
  relations with American Indians,
    29-31
Enlightenment, influence of, on
    colonial government, 82-83
Entrepreneurs, role of, in building

  economy, 445-446
Equal Employment Opportunity
    Act (1972), 606-607
Equal Rights Amendment (ERA),
    607
Erie Canal, 256, *257*
Escobedo v. Illinois, 635
Espionage Act, 548
Eurocentrism, 28
European exploration and settle-
    ment, 16-17
  contacts with American Indians,
    27-29
  by Dutch, *19*, 20, *21*, 22
  by English, *19*, 20, *21*, 22-23, *23*
  by French, *19*, 20, *21*, 22
  by Spanish, 17-19, *19*, 21-22, *21*,
    22
Evans, Frederick, 361
Executive branch, 110. *See also*
    President(s)
Expansionists, 230

F

Factories. *See also Industry*
  assembly-line in, 455, *455*, 456
  child labor in, 514-515, *514*
  first, *255*
  and mass production in, 456-457
  piecework system in, 455, 457
  women in, 259-260, *260*
  working conditions in, 457-458,
    457, 498, *498*, 500-501, *500*,
    501
Fallen Timbers, Battle of, 202
Fall line, 7
"Family Learns English, A"
    (Rodriguez), 584-585
Famine, 211
Famine (O'Flaherty), 212
Farmers' Alliance, 489
Farming
  cooperatives, 489
  in early America, 190-191
  in English colonies, 35, 36-37,
    36-37
  in Gilded Age, 487-488, *487*
  impact of technology in, 432
  improvements in, 191, *191*
  industrialization of, 487
  by Plains Indians, 415-416

sharecropping, 376, 392, *392*, *393*, *393*
  in South, 284-286, 288, *288*
  and Western settlement, 431-432, *432*
  of wheat, 190-191
Farragut, David, 353
Federal Election Campaign Act (1971), 628
Federalism, *136*
  opposition of, 135-137
  and separation of powers, 622-624
Federalist Papers, 121, *121*, 125
Federalist Party, 119, 120, 125, 134-135
  under Hamilton, 146
  and Hartford Convention, 158
  under Washington, 134-135
Federal Reserve Act (1913), 512
Federal Reserve note, 677, *677*
Federal Trade Commission, 512
Federal Trade Commission Act (1914), 484
Feminine Mystique (Friedan), 605-606
Ferdinand, Francis, assassination of, 542
Fermi, Enrico, 570
Ferraro, Geraldine, 606
Few, William, 199
Fifteenth Amendment, 390, *390*, 397, 516, 596
Fifth Amendment, 635
Fillmore, Millard, 329
Finney, Charles Grandison, 167, 169
Fire protection, in cities, 263
First Amendment, 126, 127
"First Day in Philadelphia" (Franklin), 114-117
First lady, role of, 170-171
Fisk, James "Big Jim," 472, *472*, 473, 489
Fisk University, 383
Florida
  acquisition of, 158, 688
  admission to union, 288
  in Civil War, 343
Flying Hawk, Chief, 415
Forbes Road, *198*
Force Bill, nullification of, 178
Ford, Henry, 456

Ford Motor Corporation, 456, *456*
Foreign policy
  acquisition of Alaska, 529-530
  acquisition of Pacific islands, 532
  under Articles of Confederation, 96
  imperialism as, 534, 536
  manifest destiny as 227, 230-235, *234*, *235*
  and Monroe Doctrine, 159, *159*, 533-534, *533*, 537
  and World War I, 542-546
  post World War I, 551-552
Forten, Charlotte, 383, 402-403
Fort Mandan, 224
Fort McHenry, 156, *156*
Fort Sumter, 343
Fort Ticonderoga, capture of, 63
Fort Wayne, Treaty of, 203
Forty-niners, 241-243, *241*, *242*
Fourteenth Amendment, 384, 397, 594, 601, 602, 606
Fourth Amendment, 127, 635
France
  exploration and settlement by, *19*, 20, *21*, 22
  North American claims of 1763, 55, *55*
  support for Americans in American
  Revolution, 68
  and War of 1812, 154-155
Franklin, Benjamin, *82*, 85, 91, 270, 611
  as colonial leader, 82, 86, 91, *91*
  and concept of perpetual union, 99
  at Constitutional Convention, 109, 112-113
  and negotiation of Treaty of Paris, 70
  quoted, 113
  writings of, 82, 114-117
Franklin, William, 85, *85*
Fredericksburg, Battle of, 353
Free African Society, 194
Free blacks, 304, 376
  job opportunities for, 304-305
  restrictions on, 305
  struggles of, 382-383, *382*
Freedmen's Bureau, 383, 388, 392
Freedom Journal, 321
Free labor, 314

Free press, 124
Free silver, 677
Free Soil Party, 326
Frémont, John C., 226-227, 329
French and Indian War, 55
French Revolution, 137
Friedan, Betty, 605-606
Frontier
  building institutions on, 199-200
  life on, 245, *245*
Fugitive Slave Act (1850), 319, *319*, 322, 332
Fugitive Slave Clause, in U.S. Constitution, 112
Fuller, Margaret, 270
Fulton, Robert, 256, 257

G

Gadsden Purchase (1853), 688
Gage, Thomas, 63, 65
Gardner, Alexander, photograph by, *351*
Garfield, James, 475
  assassination of, 477, *477*
Garrison, William Lloyd, 321, *321*
Gates, Horatio, 68
Geer, Elizabeth Smith, 244
Geography
  human, 5
  physical, 5
  relationship between history and, 4-6
George III (England), 59, 65, 66
Georgetown, Colorado, train trestle at, *413*
Georgia
  in Civil War, 343
  ratification of Constitution by, 120
Germans
  immigration of, to U.S., 210-211
  settlement of, in U.S., 212-213, *212*, *213*
Gerry, Elbridge, 113, 119, 124, *124*, 125
Gettysburg, Battle of, 354
Gettysburg Address, 355
Ghent, Treaty of (1814), 158
Ghost towns, 243, 414
Gideon v. *Wainwright* (1962), 635
Gilded Age, 472, 478-479, *478*, *479*

corruption in, 472-476, *472*, *474*, *476*

Glasnost, 611

Godkin, E. L., 480

Gold Democrats, 680

Gold fever, 241-243

Goldfield, 414

Goldman, Emma, 547, *547*

Gold standard, 488-489, 677

Gompers, Samuel, 459, *459*, 467, 536

Good government movement, 499

Goodridge, Ellen, 359

Gorbachev, Mikhail, 611

Gospel of Wealth, 446

Gould, Jay, 473

Government, forms of, 506, *506*

Government revenues, 93, *93*

Graft, 476

Grand Canyon, 11, 19

Grand Coulee Dam, 12

Grange movement, 488, *488*

Grant, Ulysses S., 442
 as general in Civil War, 349, 353, 367, *367*, 376, *389*, 670, 671
 scandals in administration of, 474-475

Graphs, choosing appropriate, 306-307, *306*, *307*

Great Awakening, 51-52, *52*, 293-294
 second, 167, 169, *169*, 268, 294

Great Basin, 11, 12, 412
 settlement of, 239-240

Great Britain
 in American Revolution, 66, 68, 70
 claims of, to Oregon, 238
 closing of Boston by, 59
 colonial policies of, 56-59
 colonial protests against policies of, 54, *54*, 56-59, *57*
 conflict with Venezuela, 533-534
 influences of, on American government, 83-84, *84*
 North American claims of 1763, 55, *55*
 surrender of, at Yorktown, 70, *70*
 and War of 1812, 154-158

Great Compromise, 110, *110*

Great Lakes, 10

Great Plains, 9

Great Salt Lake, 11

Great Smoky Mountains, *299*

Great Society, 632

Green, Lear, *334*

Greenback-Labor Party, 488-489, 490

Greenback Party, 488, 680

Greene, Catharine Littlefield, 284

Greene, Nathanael, 68, 70, 284

Greenhow, Rose O'Neal, 359

Green Mountain Boys, 63

Greenville, Treaty of, 202

Grenville, George, *57*

Grimké, Angelina, 322

Grimké, Sarah, 322

Griswold, Roger, *139*

Gross national product, of United States, *686*

Group skills,
 compromise, reaching a, 123

Guadalupe Hidalgo, Treaty of (1848), 235, 247

Guam, U.S. acquisition of, 536

Guerrière, 155

Guerrilla, 328-329

Guggenheim, Mayer, 467

Guiana (Guyana), 534

Guiteau, Charles, 477

Gulf of Mexico, 11

Gulf of St. Lawrence, *20*

Gwynne, Nathaniel, 358

H

Hale, Sarah Josepha, 269

Hamilton, Alexander, 99, 112, 120, 121
 as Federalist, 120, 146
 financial program of, 135, 136-137

Hamilton, Alexander Dr., 48

Hamilton, Andrew, 124

Hammond, James H., 289

Hancock, John, 63, 66, 124-125, *125*

Harding, Warren, election of, 553, *553*

Harper, Frances, *quoted*, 35

Harpers Ferry, 330

Harrison, William Henry, 155, 201, 204

Hart, Nancy Morgan, 71

Hartford Convention, 158

Harvard, John, 270

Harvard College Library, 270

Havenden, Thomas, painting by, *330*

Hawaii Islands, acquisition of, 532, 688

Hawthorne, Nathaniel, 270, 273

Hayes, Rutherford B., 210, 395, 481, 533

Haymarket Square riot, 459

Haynes, Robert Y., 178

Hays, Charles, 389

Hays, Mary Ludwig, 71

Haywood, William "Big Bill," 516

Health and sanitation, in cities, 263-264

Heard, Nathaniel, *85*

Helena, Montana, 414

Helpless Mouths, *211*

Henry, Patrick, 106, 122
 quoted, 664-665
 opposition of, to Constitution, 118, *118*

Hermitage, 173

Hervieu, Auguste de, 179

Hicks, William, painting by, *30*

Hine, Lewis, 520
 photographs by, *457*, 505, *514*

Historical atlas, 32

Historical photographs, analyzing, 520-521, *520*, *521*

History, relationship between geography and, 4-6

History of the Standard Oil Company (Tarbell), 502

Hmong people, 572, 573, *573*

Holbrook, Josiah, 270

Homestead, Pennsylvania, strike at, 458-460, *460*

Homestead Act (1862), 427

Homesteads, 427, *427*, 431-432, *431*

Hooker, Joseph, 353

Hoover Dam, 12

Hopkins, Samuel, 256

Household economy, 164-165

House of Burgesses, 85, 86, *87*

House of Representatives, U.S.
 See also Congress; Senate, U.S.
 determining numbers for, 111
 election of members of, 632, 633
 ethics rules for, 633
 passage of laws by, 633-634
 rules on debate in, 632

Houston, Sam, 234
Howard, Gideon, 254
Howard, Oliver O., *383*
Howard University, 383, *383*
Howe, Elias, 444, *444*
Howe, William, 66
How the Other Half Lives (Riis), 504
Hudson, Henry, 20, 22
Hudson-Mohawk Route, *198*
Hudson's Bay, 20
Hudson's Strait, 20
Huerta, Victoriano, 540
Hughes, Langston, 618
Hull House, 502, *502*, 503, 505, 515, 611
Human geography, 5
Hume, David, 109
"Hush'd Be the Camps To-day" (Whitman), 401
Hyrum, 239

I

"I, Too" (Hughes), 618
Illinois, 98
Immigrants
  ancestry of, *572*
  from Asia, 463, *463*, 466, 572, 573, *573*
  assimilation of, 572, 575
  changes in origin, *580*, 582-583
  in colonial America, 48-49, *49*
  contributions of, 51, 467, 576, *576*
  designation of, 214
  discrimination against, 466-467, *466*
  from eastern Europe, 566, *566*
  and Ellis Island, 464-465, *464, 465*
  establishment of, in cities, 212-213, *212, 467*
  expanding opportunities for, 578-580
  and growth of political bosses, 476
  from northern Europe, *463*
  prejudice against, 565
  refugees as, 579-580, *579*
  from southern Europe, 462-463, *463*
  Soviet Jews as, 579

travel of, to U.S., *212*
Immigration, 214
  and bilingual education, 583
  Federalist attempt to suppress, 139
  new wave of, 210-212, *212*
  quota system in, 569, 570
  reasons for, 214
  resistance to, 566-568
  restrictions on, 566-567, 569
  of temporary workers, 580-581, *581*
  undocumented, 580-582, *581*
  and World War II, 569-570
Immigration Act (1891), 567
Immigration Reform and Control Act (1986), 214, 582
Impeachment charges, against Richard Nixon, 386
Impeachment trial, of Andrew Johnson, 385, *385*, 387, *387*
Imperalism, 534, 536
Impressment, British policy of, 154, 156
Independence Hall, *75, 107*
Indiana, 98
Indian policies
  under Jackson, 176, *176*
  under Madison, 155
Indian Self-Determination and Education Assistance Act (1975), 604
Individual rights, as protected in Constitution, 396
Industrial Revolution, 254-255
  and growth of inland cities, 260
  impact of, on production, 258-260
  impact of, on transportation, 256-258, *256, 257, 258*
Industrial Workers of the World (IWW), 460, 516, *516*
Industry. *See also Factories*
  in early America, 192
  expansion of, post Civil War, 529
  and growth of big business, 473
  monopoly control of, 485
Inferences, making, from literature, 492-493
Inflation, 73
Influence of Sea Power upon History (Mahan), 530
Information organization, chrono-

logical outlining in, 228-229
Ingalls, Charles, 427
Ingels, George, 360
Initiative, 508
Institutions, building, on frontier, 199-200
Interchangeable parts, 255
Intermountain Region, 11
Interstate Commerce Act (1887), 482
Interstate Commerce Commission (ICC), 482
Interviewing, 577
Intolerable Acts (1774), 59
Inventions, 443-444, *443*
Irish
  immigration of, to U.S., 211-212, *211*
  settlement of, in U.S., 213, *213*
Iroquois Confederacy, in American Revolution, 74
Iroquois League, 27
Irving, Washington, 8, 140-145
Isolationism, 551
"It Was a Glorious Day!" (Forten), 402-403

J

Jack rabbit, *13*
Jackson, Andrew, *172*
  in Battle of New Orleans, 156, 158
  defeat of Red Sticks by, 203
  and federal bank, 176-177, *176, 177*
  and Henry Clay, 184-185, *184, 185*
  inauguration of, 172
  Indian policy of, 176, *176*, 205
  kitchen cabinet of, 175
  as member of House, 175
  spoils system under, 175
Jackson, Rachel, 174
Jackson, Thomas "Stonewall," 345, *345*, 347, 353, *671*
Jackson, William Henry, photograph by, *247*
Jacksonian politics, rise of, 173-175
Jacob, William Jay, 276-277
Jamestown, 23, *23*, 31, 302
Japan, trade with, 531-532, *531*
Japanese-Americans, 574, *574*

during World War I, 548
during World War II, 607-608,
    608
Jay, John, 70, 91, 120
Jefferson, Thomas, 65, 75, 91, 106,
    109, 147, 222
  as ambassador to France, 106,
    127
  as architect, 165, 168
  as author of Declaration of
    Independence, 66
  domestic policy of, 148-151
  in election of 1800, 146-147, *147*
  foreign policy of, 154-155, *154*
  inauguration of, 147-148
  influence of Enlightenment on,
    82
  and Lewis and Clark expedition,
    223-224
  and Louisiana Purchase, 149-
    151, *150*, 223
  quoted, 136, 261
  as secretary of state, 136
  views of, 85, 136, 199, 261, 314,
    315-316, 565
Jenney, William LeBaron, 449
"Jim Crow" laws, 518-519, 597, 600
John F. Kennedy Library, 574
Johnson, Andrew, *379*
  impeachment trial of, 385, *385*,
    387, *387*
  and passage of Fourteenth
    Amendment, 384
  Reconstruction under, 379
  as Vice President, 378
Johnson, Hiram, 508
Johnson, Lyndon B., 578, 604, 632
Johnson, Samuel, 51
Johnson Act (1921), 569
Johnston, Joe, *345*
Joliet, Louis, 29
Jones, Absalom, 195
Joseph, Chief, 425
Journalism
  and the muckrakers, 502
  yellow, 535, *535*
Judicial branch, 110
Judicial review, 151, *151*, 626
Jungle, The (Sinclair), 507

K

Kansas
  and Lecompton Constitution,
    332
  slavery issue in, 327-329, *328*
Kansas-Nebraska Act (1854), 325-
    327, *327*
Kelley, Florence, 515
Kennedy, John F., 578, 604, 616-
    617, 632
Kentucky, in Civil War, 343
Key, Francis Scott, 156
Kickbacks, 475
King, Martin Luther, Jr., 601, 602,
    603, *603*
  quoted, 602
King Philip's War, 31
Kiowa Indians, 416, 417
Kitchen cabinet, 175
Klamath Mountains, 11
Knights of Labor, 459, 460
Knights of the White Camelia, 394
Know-Nothing Party, 326, *326*, 567
Korea, trade with, 531-532
Korematsu, Fred, 608
Krans, Olof, painting by, *273*
Krimmel, John Lewis, painting by,
    111
Ku Klux Klan, 394, 452, 518, 552

L

Labor Day, *456*
Labor movement, 458, 460
  definition of, 458
  development of early, 458-459
  and the Industrial Workers of
    the World, 516, *516*
  opposition to, 459-460, *460*
  organization of migrant workers
    in, 582, *582*
  organization of women workers
    in, 271
  reforms fought for by, 499
  post World War I, 552-553, *552*
Lacrosse, 278-279
Lafayette, Marquis de, 70
La Follette, Robert M., 507-508,
    508
Laissez faire, 499
Lancaster Turnpike, 198, *198*, 256
Landforms, 5

Land Ordinance (1785), 199
Land policy, under Articles of
    Confederation, 96, 98, *98*
Land use, in United States, 707
Larcoom, Lucy, 259
Last Chance Gulch, 414
Latin America, and Monroe
    Doctrine, 159, *159*, 533-534,
    537, 668-669
Latrobe, Benjamin, 168
Leadership, concept of, 138
League of Nations, 551-552
Lease, Mary Elizabeth, 489, *489*
  quoted 489
Leatherstocking Tales, The
    (Cooper), 197
Lecompton Constitution, 332
Lee, Ann, 272
Lee, Robert E., 342, *342*, 345, 353,
    354, 367, *367*, 376, *671*
Le Fleur, Jo Carol, 606
Legislature, 85, 110. *See also*
    Congress, U.S.; House of
    Representatives, U.S.; Senate,
    U.S.
Lesesne, Joseph W., 287
Letters from an American Farmer
    (Crèvecoeur), 180
Lewis, Meriwether, 222, 223
Lewis and Clark expedition, 223-
    225, *225*
Lexington, Battle of, 62, *62*, 63, *66*,
    73
Liberal Republicans, 680
Liberator, 321, *321*
Liberia, 321
Liberty Bonds, 547, *548*
Libraries, 270
Liliuokalani, Queen, 532, *532*
Lincoln, Abraham, *348, 351*, 673,
    673
  assassination of, 378
  as commander-in-chief, 348-349
  on deathbed, *379*
  and Gettysburg Address, 355,
    355
  in election of 1858, 334
  in election of 1860, 334-335, 343
  as member of House of
    Representatives, 234
  and passage of Thirteen
    Amendment, 378
  poems about, 400-401

as president, 321
quoted, 355, 360
reconstruction plan of, 377
Lincoln, Mary Todd, 345, 351
Linotype machine, 444
Literacy Bill, 568
Literature
  in early 1800s, 179, 181, 183
  and Horatio Alger books, 445, *445*
  in late 1700s, 180
  making inferences from, 492-493
Little Big Horn, Battle of, *422*
Livermore, Mary, 359
Livingston, Robert, 150
Locke, John, 109
Lodge, Henry Cabot, 551
Lomax, John Avery, *quoted*, 429
Lone Star Republic, 232, 234
Los Cerritos, California, *483*
Louisiana
  admission to union, 288
  in Civil War, 343
Louisiana Purchase, 149-150, *149*, *150*, 314, 688
Louisiana Territory, exploration of, 222-225, *223*, *225*
Louisville, Kentucky, 302
Lowell, Francis Cabot, 258-259
Lowell Female Reform
    Association, 271
Lowell mill girls, 259-260, *260*
"Lower East Side, The," 586-587
Loyalists, 72
Lue Gim Gon, 467
Lusitania, 543
Lyceums, 270
Lyon, Mary, 269
Lyon, Matthew, *139*

M

MacArthur, Arthur, 358
Machine politics, 475-476
MacIntosh, Ebenezer, 54
Madison, Dolley, 153, *153*, *170*, 171
Madison, James, 106, 122, 125, 396
  at Annapolis Convention, 99
  as colonial leader, 86-87
  as congressman, 135
  at Constitutional Convention, 106, *106*, 107, 110, 111, 113
  domestic policy under, 155

as Federalist, 120
as secretary of state, 151
and War of 1812, 153, *153*, 155-156, 158
Magna Carta, 83, *84*
Maguire, Matthew, *456*
Mahan, Alfred T., 530
Maine, U.S.S., 535
Maine, admission to union, 315
Maine Indian Claims Settlement
    Act (1980), 605
Manifest Destiny, 227, 230-235, *234*, *235*
Mann, Horace, *268*, 269, 271
Manufacturing. *See Industry*
Mapp v. *Ohio (1961)*, 635
Map and globe skills,
  making maps, 208-209
  thematic maps, comparing population, 454
  topographical maps, interpreting, 433
Maps
  city, 208-209, *209*
  distance on, 208
  labels, 208
  orientation, 208
  population, 454, *454*
  scale on, 208
  symbols on, 208
  topographical, 433, *433*
Marbury, William, 151
Marbury v. *Madison*, 151, 626
Marion, Francis, 68
Market economy, 166-167
Marquette, Jacques, 29
Marshall, James, 241
Marshall, John, as chief justice, *127*, 151, 176, 205, 626
Marshall, Thurgood, 602
Martial law, 386
Martineau, Harriet, 181
Maryland
  in Civil War, 343
  and ownership of western lands, 86
Mason, George, 113, *113*, 124, 125
Massachusetts, 35
  abolition of slavery in, 194
  colonial government in, 85, 87
  opposition to ratification in, 124-125

ratification of Constitution by, 120
Massachusetts Bay Colony, 23, 29
Mass production, 456-457
Masters, Edgar Lee, 486
Maximilian of Austria, 533
Mayas, 27
Mayflower, 23, 83
Mayflower Compact, 83-84, *84*, 663
Mayo, William, 467
Mayo Clinic, 467
McClellan, George B., 348-349, *348*, *351*
McCormick Harvester Company, strike at, 459
McCormick Reaper, 191
McDowell, Irwin, 348
McGuire, Peter, *456*
McKinley, William, 490
  assassination of, 508, 537
  in election of 1896, 490-491, *491*
  and Spanish-American War, 535
Meacham, Joseph, *quoted*, 360
Meade, George, 354
Meat Inspection Act (1906), 507, 509
Medicine, in Civil War, 363, *363*
Memphis, Tennessee, industry in, 449
Mentally ill, treatment of, 266
Mergenthaler, Ottmar, 444
Merrimac, 351
Metacom's War, 31
Metes and bounds, 199
Mexican-American War, 342
Mexican cession (1848), 235, *235*, 688
Mexicans, immigration of, to U.S., 581-582
Mexican War, 234-235, *234*
Mexico
  independence of, 231
  revolution in, 540
  and the Zimmerman telegram, 543
Miami Indians, 202
Michigan, 98
Middle class, 192
Middle colonies, life in, 36-37
Midway Islands, acquisition of, 532
Migrant workers, 582
Migration, 197-198
Military Reconstruction Acts, 386

Militia, 63
Miller, Joaquin, 442
Milwaukee, immigrants in, 213
Mining
   of copper, *414*
   of gold, 241-243
   of silver, 413-414, *413*
Minneapolis, industry in, 449
Minnesota, 98
Minor, Virginia, 596
Minor v. *Happersatt* (1874), 596
Minutemen, 63, 64, *64*
Miranda v. *Alabama*, 635
Mississippi
   admission to union, 288
   in Civil War, 343
Missouri
   admission to union, 315
   in Civil War, 343
Missouri Compromise, 315, *315*, *316*, 325, 331, 335
Missouri River, 11
   exploration of, 225
Mobile, Alabama, 302
Moderates, 348
Money. *See Currency*
Monmouth, Battle of, 71
Monopoly, 483, 484
   control of industry by, *485*
   power of the, 483
Monroe, James, 127, 668-669
   quoted, 668-669
   in election of 1816, 158, *158*
   foreign policy under, 159, *159*
   and U.S. expansion, 150, 158
Monroe Doctrine, 159, *159*, 533, 668-669
   application of, 533-534, *533*
   Roosevelt Corollary to, 537
Montesquieu, Baron de, 109
Montgomery, Benjamin, 391
Montgomery bus boycott, 600, 601
Monticello, 165
Morgan, J. Pierpont, 445
Mormons, 239-240, *239*
Morris, Robert, 91, 92, 93, 94
Morse, Samuel F. B., 258
Morton, Julius Sterling, 429
Mott, Lucretia, 267, 322, *322*, *336*, 516
   quoted, 336
Mountain lions, *5*

Mountain men, 226-227, *226*
Mount Holyoke Female Seminary, 269
Mowawk Indians, 27
Muckrakers, reforms inspired by, 502
Mugwumps, 478-480
Muir, John, 510, *510*
Muir Woods, 510
Municipal, 263
Munn v. *Illinois*, 482
Music, spirituals, 51

N

NAACP v. *Alabama* (1958), 635
Naismith, James, 279
Napoleon, 156, 223
Narragansett Indians, 30-31
Narrative of the Life of Frederick Douglass (Douglass), 321
Nashville Road, *198*
Nast, Thomas, 480
   cartoon by, *377*, *476*, *478*, *478*
Nation, Carry, 513-514, *513*
National American Woman Suffrage Association (NAWSA), 517
National Association for the Advancement of Colored People (NAACP), 394, 519, 600
National Bank Acts (1863, 1864), 676-677
National Child Labor Committee, 515
National Farmers' Alliance, 489, 490
National Gallery of Art, 574
National Organization for Women (NOW), 606
National Origins Act (1924), 569
National Park System, *678-679*
National Playground Association of America, 505
National-Republican Party, 174-175
National Road, 166, *198*, 436
National Urban League, 453
National Women's Party (NWP), 517
Native Americans. *See American Indians; specific tribes*
Nativism, 215, 466

Naturalization, 594
Naturalization Act, 139
Nauvoo, Illinois, 239
Navigation, 17
Navy
   building of U.S., in 1890s, 530, *530*
   and Spanish American War, 535
   and War of 1812, 156
Neoclassicism, 165-166, 168, *168*
Nestor, Agnes, 455
Neutrality, 154
New Amsterdam, 22
Newburgh Conspiracy (1783), 94
New England colonies, 35-36, *35*
New Hampshire, 35
   ratification of Constitution by, 122
"New Home, A" (Cather), 434-435
New Jersey
   colonial government in, 85
   ratification of Constitution by, 120
New Jersey Plan, 110
New Lebanon, New York, 272
New Mexico
   acquisition of, 158
   settlement of, 230
New Netherland, 20
New Orleans, Battle of, 156, 157, *157*, 158, 173
New Orleans, Louisiana, *287*, 302
Newport, 39
Newsboy, 450, *450*
Newspapers
   antislavery, 321
   colonial, 124
New York, 39
   free blacks in, 193
   growth of, 193
   and ownership of western lands, 86
New York City, living conditions in, 504
New York Customs House, investigation of, 481
Nez Percé Indians, 225, 238, 425
Nina, 17
Nineteenth Amendment, 518, 596
Nixon, Richard, 604, 631
   impeachment charges against, 386

and Watergate scandal, 628-629
Nomads, 27
Non-Intercourse Act (1809), 155
Norris, Frank, 487
North
    in antebellum period, 314
    population growth of, *262*
    resources of, in Civil War, 345-
        346, *346*
North America
    European claims in 1763, 55, *55*
    physical map of, *703*
    political map of, *702*
North Carolina, 122
    in Civil War, 343
    colonial government in, 87
    colonial protests in, 59
    ratification of Constitution by,
        122
Northern Securities Company, 509
North Star, 321
Northup, Solomon, 285
    quoted, 285
Northwestern Farmers' Alliance,
    489
Northwest Ordinance (1787), 98,
    99, 200, 202
Northwest Passage, search for, 20
Nueces River, 234
Nullify, 178
Numismatics, 100-101

O

Ocala Platform, 489-490
"O Captain! My Captain!"
    (Whitman), 400
O'Connor, Sandra Day, 606, *606*
Octopus, The (Norris), 487
O'Flaherty, Liam, 212
Ohio, 98
Oil exploration, in Alaska, 14-15,
    15
Olive Branch Petition, 65
Oliver, Andrew, 54
Olmsted, Frederick Law, 290
Olney, Richard, 534
Oneida Indians, 27, 74
Onondaga Indians, 27
Open Door Policy, with China, 531
Oregon, settlement of, 238-239
Oregon country cession, 688
Oregon Trail, The (Parkman), 248-

249
O'Sullivan, John L., 230
Otis, Harrison Gray, 565
Outlining, chronological, 228-229
Overland Trail, hardships of, 243-
    245, *243, 244*
"Over There" (Cohan), 554
Ozark Highland, 10

P

Pacific Coast, 11-12, *12*
Pacific Northwest, 12
Pacific Ocean, 11, 18
Paine, Thomas, 82
    quoted, 65, 666-667
Painted Desert, 11
Panama, Isthmus of, 18
Panama Canal, building, 537-539,
    538, 539
Panic of 1837, 177
Paris, Treaty of (1763), 55
Paris, Treaty of (1783), 70
Park, Linton, painting by, *35*
Parkman, Francis, 248-249
Parks, Rosa, 600
"Parson's cause," *118*
Party machine, 506
Passamaquoddy Indians, 604-605
Passamaquoddy Tribe v. *Morton*
    (1977), 605
Patent, 284, 443
Patent Office, U.S., 256, 443
Paterson, William, 110
Patronage, 476
Paul, Alice, 517
Peace Corps, 632
Peace Democrats, 356
Pei, I.M., 574
Pember, Phoebe Yates, 359
Pengra, Charlotte Stearns, 244
Penn, William, 30, *30*
Pennsylvania
    abolition of slavery in, 194
    colonial government in, 87
    ratification of Constitution by,
        120
"Penny" societies, 169
Penobscot Indians, 605
Pequot Indians, 30
Pequot War, 30
Perez, Norah A., 370-371
Period literature, 492-493

Perry, Matthew C., 531, *531*
Perry, Oliver Hazard, 156
Petition of Rights (1628), *84*
Philadelphia, 39
    post American Revolution, 90,
        90
    Centennial Exhibition in, 422,
        442
    colonial, 48, *49*
    free blacks in, 193
    growth of, 193
Philadelphia Mechanics Union,
    458-459
Philanthropists, 446
Philippines
    fight for independence in, 536-
        537
    Spanish-American War in, 536,
        536
    U.S. acquisition of, 536
Phillips, David Graham, 510
Physical geography, 5
Piecework, 455
Piedmont, 7
Pierce, Franklin, 419, 424, 531, *531*
Pikes Peak, 226
Pilgrims, 23, 29
Pinchot, Gifford, 510
Pinckney, Charles C., 108, 146, 147
Pinckney, Eliza Lucas, 38
Pinnacles National Monument, 510
Pinta, 17
Pitcher, Molly, 71
Pittsburgh, industry in, 260, 449
Pizarro, Francisco, 19
Plains Indians, 26, *415*, 422
    beliefs of, 419
    buffalo hunting, 415
    ceremonies of, 419
    culture of, 416-417, *416, 417*
    farming by, 415-416
    as nomads, 416-418
    tribal status of, 418-419
    use of guns and horse by, 416-
        417
Plantations, 37-38, 285-286, 290-
    294, *291, 292, 293*
Plateau, 11
Platt Amendment (1901), 536
Platte River, 11
Plessy, Homer, 518
Plessy v. *Ferguson* (1896), 518, 601,
    608

Pluralism, 49, 50
Plymouth, 23
Poestenkill, New York, *180*
Point of view, on slavery, 336-337
Police protection, in cities, 263
Polish Women's Alliance, 463
Political cartoons, analyzing, 184-185, *184*
Political machine, 476
Political parties. *See also specific party*
  administrations in office, *680*
  Federalism versus Republicanism, *136*
  important U.S., *681*
  third parties, 680
Polk, James K., 168
  and Mexican War, 234
  and U.S. claim to Oregon, 238-239
Poll taxes, 394
Pontiac, 56
Popular sovereignty, 326, 327
Popular vote, 174
Population
  foreign-born, 48-49, *49*, *569*
  of U.S., *686*, *704-705*
Populism, 486
  decline of, 491
  peak of, 490-491
  roots of, 487-489
Populist Party, 489-490, *489*, 680
Portland, Oregon, industry in, 449
Postal system, colonial, *92*
Potawatomi Indians, 202
Poverty Gulch, 414
Prager, Robert, 548
Prairie, 8
Precipitation, 8. *See also Climate in United States, 707*
President(s), *682-683*
  action on legislation, *692*
  and checks and balances, 625-626
  as chief executive, 631–632
  term of office for, 627
Press, freedom of, 124
Preuss, Charles, sketch by, *240*
Prigg Decision (1842), 319
Primary sources
  Abraham Lincoln, Gettysburg Address, 355
  Carl Schurz, reminiscences, 210

The Constitution of the United States, 636–655
The Declaration of Independence, 656–659
Jade Snow Wong, on the Chinese immigrant experience, 574
James Madison, Franklin's "Rising Sun" speech, *113*
John and Abigail Adams, letters, 88
A Letter From Christopher Columbus, 660–662
Lucretia Mott, antislavery arguments, 336
Martin Luther King, excerpt from "I Have a Dream" speech, 602
Mary Lease, on Populism, 489
Mayflower Compact, 663
Monroe Doctrine, 668–669
Patrick Henry, "Give me Liberty or Give me Death," 664–665
Solomon Northup, on slavery, 285
Susan Smedes, diary, 378
Thomas Paine, *Common Sense*, 666–667
Unnamed Vietnamese refugee, journey to America, 578
Upton Sinclair, excerpt from *The Jungle*, 507
Walt Whitman, on government corruption, *474*
William Jennings Bryan, "Cross of Gold" speech, 486
Proclamation of 1763, 56
Professional Air Traffic Controllers, 460
Progressive movement, 503
  and black Americans, 518–519
  and city planning, 504–505
  and city politics, 505–506
  and education reform, 504, *504*
  and muckrakers, 502
  objectives of, 499
  origin of, 499
  and settlement houses, 502, *502*
Prohibition, 514
Prohibition Party, 680
Promontory Point, 412
Propaganda, 556–557
Prophet (Elskwatawa), 204, *204*

Proslavery movement, 288–289
Protestant Reformation, 16
Public interest groups, use of propaganda, 556–557
Publius, letters from, 120
Puerto Rico, U.S. acquisition of, 536
Pulitzer, Joseph, 467
Pulitzer Prizes, 467
Pullman community, *458*
Pullman Palace Car Company, 458
  strike at, 461
Pure Food and Drug Act (1906), 509
Putnam, Israel, 65
Pyramid Lake, *240*

Q

Quakers, 30, 48
Quartering Act, 56, 59
Quebec, 55
Quebec Act (1774), 59
Quilting bees, 36
Quota, 569–570

R

Railroads
  impact of, on travel, 258
  network of, 1893, *412*
  ownership of, *481*
  regulation of, 481–482
  transcontinental, 412–413, 423, 432
  in West, *433*
Raleigh, Sir Walter, 22
Ranchos, 237–238
Randolph, Edmund, 108, *108*, 113, 127
Ratification, of U.S. Constitution, 118–122, *119*, *122*
Reading societies, 270
Reagan, Ronald, 484, 632
Recall, 508
Reconstruction, 377, *395*
  congressional plan for, 384
  corruption under, 389–390
  end of, 395
  Johnson's plan for, 379
  legacies of, 397, *397*
  Lincoln's plan for, 377
  radical, 377–378, 385–390, *386*

second, 397
Southern life under, 388–395,
391, 397
Red Cross, 544
Redeem, 394
Red River cession, 688
"Red Scare," 553
Red Sticks, 203
Reference materials, using
primary sources, Abigail
Adams's letters as, 88–89
computerized sources, 274–275
specialized sources, 32
Referendum, 508
Reform, understanding, 503
Reform movements. *See also*
Progressivism
for child labor, 514–515, *514*
in cities, 266, 506, *506*
in education, 269–270, *269*
inspired by muckrakers, 502
of state government, 507–508
temperance, 268–269, *268*,
513–514
women's rights, 267, 516–518,
517, 605–607
and working conditions, 271
"Refugee in America" (Hughes),
618
Refugees, admission of, to U.S.,
579–580, *579*
Regionalism, 245, 246
Regions, in United States, 5, 6–13,
687
Reliance building, *449*
Religion
in English colonies, 51–52, *52*
and Western settlement, 200
Religious freedom, origin of, 49
Remarque, Erich Maria, 545, 546
Renaissance, 16
Rendezvous, 226
Report on Public Credit of 1790
(Hamilton), 135
Reports,
preparing,
bibliography cards, 152
chronological outlines,
228–229
conducting an interview, 577
writing,
reporting on Antietam,
368–369

Republic, 65
Republican architecture, 165–166
Republicanism (Jefferson),
136–137, 146–151, *136*
Republican motherhood, 166
Republican Party, *326*, 681
Republican Party
in Gilded Age, 478
and opposition to slavery, 326,
329
and Reconstruction, 386–387
Research skills
bibliography cards, 152
interviewing, 577
primary sources, 88–89, 378
Reservations, removal of Indians
to, 424–426
Revels, Hiram, 388
Revere, Paul, 63
engraving by, *58*
Revitalization, 204
Revival movements, 167, 169, *169*
Revolutionary War. *See American*
Revolution
Rhode Island, 35
abolition of slavery in, 194
colonial government in, 87
ratification of Constitution by,
122
Richmond, Virginia, 302
rebuilding of, 380–381, *380, 381*
ruin of, following Civil War, 377
Ridge, John, 207
Ridley, Colonel, 198
Riis, Jacob, 504, 520
photographs by, 505, *505*
Rio Grande River, 11
"Rip Van Winkle" (Irving),
140–145
Roads, and Western settlement,
198, 256
Roanoke, 22–23
Rockefeller, John D., 445, 473, *474*,
484
Rocky Mountains, 10–11, *11*, 13,
410, *410*, 411
Rodriguez, Richard, 584–585
Roebling, John A., 451
Roosevelt, Eleanor, 171, *171*
Roosevelt, Franklin D.
and relocation of Japanese
Americans, 607–608
term of office, 627

Roosevelt, Theodore
and Big Stick foreign policy,
537–538, *537*
and conservatism, 510, *510*
in election of 1912, 511, *511*
and election of senators, 510
and immigration, 568
and income taxes, 510
Progressivism under, 507–510,
680
and Rough Riders, 535
and trust busting, 509, *509*
Roosevelt Corollary to Monroe
Doctrine, 537
Ross, Edmund G., 385, *385*, 387
Ross, John, 205
Ross, Lewis, 205
Rotary press, 444
Rough Riders, 535
Rousseau, Jean Jacques, *quoted*,
593
Royce, Sarah, 242
Russia. *See also Soviet Union*
North American claims of 1763,
55, *55*

S

Sacajawea, 222, *222*, 224–225
Sacramento, 243
Sacramento River, 11
St. Augustine, Florida, 302
St. Lawrence River, 20
St. Louis, immigrants in, 213
Salem, Peter, 73
Salutary neglect, 52
Salvation Army, 544
Samoan Islands, acquisition of, 532
Samoset, 29
Sampson, Deborah, 74, 610
San Antonio de Bexar, 231
San Carlos de Rio Carmelo, *22*
Sand Creek massacre, 423–424
San Francisco, 238, 242
Chinatown in, 571, *571*
San Francisco Bay, 11
San Joaquin River, 11
San Salvador, 18
Santa Anna, Antonio López de,
232
Santa Fe, 234
Santa Maria, 17
Saratoga, Battle of, *66*

Satires, 179
Savannah, Georgia
   in American Revolution, 68
   in Civil War, 302, 366
Schenectady, New York, industry
   in, 449
Schurz, Carl, 210, 211, 480
   quoted, 210, 480
Schuyler, Colfax, 475
Scott, Dred, 331, *331*
Scott, Winfield, 234
Seals, *12*
Seattle, Chief, 424
Secession, of South, 335, *335, 343*
Second Reconstruction, 397
Sectionalism, 314–319, *316, 318*
Sects, 21
Secularize, 237
Sedition Act (1798), 139, 148
Sedition Act (1918), 548
Segregation, 383, 600–602
Selective Service Act (1940),
   543–544
Self–help books, 167
Seltze, Olaf, painting by, *225*
Senate, U.S.
   debate rules in, 632–633
   direct election of members, 510
   election of members, 632, 633
   ethics rules for, 633
   passage of laws by, 633–634
Seneca Falls Convention, 267, 596,
   610
Seneca Indians, 27
Separation of powers, 622–624
Sequoya, 205, *205*
Serra, Junipero, 22
Settlement houses, 502, *502*
"Seven Devils Mountains, The,"
   24–25
Seventeenth Amendment, 510
Seven Year's War, 55
Seward, William H., 529–530, 533
Sewing machines, 444
Shakers, 272, *272*
   and the Civil War, 360–361
Shame of the Cities, The (Steffens),
   502
Sharecropping, 376, 392, *392*, 393,
   393
Shawnee Indians, 202
Shays, Daniel, 95
Shays's Rebellion, 95, *95*, 99

Sheridan, Philip Henry, 366
Sherman, John, 485
Sherman, Roger, 84
Sherman, William, 363, 366, 392,
   671
Sherman Antitrust Act (1890), 484,
   485
Shiloh, Battle of, 353
Shoemaking, 254, *254*
Sholes, Christopher Latham, 443
Shoshone Indians, 225, 422
Sierra Club, 612
Sierra Nevada Mountains, 11, 13
Silver mining, 413–414, *413*
Simpson, "Sockless Jerry," 490
Sinclair, Upton, 507
   quoted, 507
Singer, I. M., 444, 445
Singer Manufacturing Company,
   444
Singer sewing machine, *444*
Sioux Indians, 416, 422, 423, 426
Sister Carrie (Dreiser), 451
Sit–ins, 602
Sitting Bull, *422*, 426
Sixteenth Amendment, 93, 510, 627
Sixth Amendment, 127
Skyscrapers, 449–450, *449*
Slater, Samuel, 255
Slave auction, *181*
"Slave Life" (Douglass), 296–297
Slave rebellions, 295
Slavery, *295*
   analyzing view points on,
      336–337
   arguments defending, 289
   and black codes, 379
   in early 1800s, 181, *181*
   end of, 382–383, *382*
   as issue at Constitutional
      Convention, 111
   on plantations, 285–286, *285,
      286, 289*
   and proslavery movement,
      288–289
   resistance to, 294–295
Slave(s)
   in colonial America, 49
   number of, *332*
   resistance to freeing, 305
   as social class, 193–194, 304
   in South, 290–295, *293*
   treatment of runaway, 295, *295*

Slave trade, 51
Slave Trade Clause, in U.S.
   Constitution, 112
Slopes of War, The (Perez),
   370–371
Smallpox, impact of, on American
   Indians, 28
Smedes, Susan Dabney, diary of,
   378
Smith, Jedediah, 226
Smith, Joseph, 239
Smith, Samatha, 611
Snyder Act (1924), 595
Social classes, 304
Social Darwinism, 528–529, 537
Socialist Labor Party, 680
Socialist Party, 548
Socialists, 515–516, *515*
Socialist Workers Party, 680
Sojourner Truth, 320–321, *320*
Soldiers, 73. *See also specific wars*
Soleri, Paolo, 452
Somme, Battle of, 545
Sons of Italy, 463
Sons of Liberty, 57
South. *See also Eastern and
      Southern United States*
   antebellum period in, 286, 288,
      288, 298–299, *298*, 302–305,
      302, 314
   class structure in, 304
   cotton production in, 284–288,
      288
   economy in, 287–288
   factories in, 287
   impact of Civil War on, 376
   Ku Klux Klan in, 394
   rebuilding after Civil War,
      380–381, *380, 381*, 388–390
   under Reconstruction, 391–395,
      391, 397
   resources of, in Civil War,
      342–345, *346*
   secession of, 335, *335*, 343, *343*
   slavery in, 290–295, 304
   transportation in, *287*
South Carolina
   abolition of slavery in, 194
   colonial protests in, 59
Southern colonies, 37–39
Southern Farmers' Alliance, 489
Southern Pacific Railroad, 508
Sovereignty, 91

Soviet Jews, admission of, to U.S., 579
Soviet Union. *See also Russia*
    Bolshevik Revolution in, 553
    glasnost in, 611
Spain
    exploration and settlement by, 17–19, *19,* 21–22, *21, 23*
    North American claims of 1763, 55, *55*
Spalding, Eliza, 238
Spalding, Henry, 238
Spanish–American War, 535–536, *536*
    in Cuba, 535–536, *536*
    end of, 536
    events leading to, 534–535
    in Philippines, 536, *536*
Speare, Elizabeth G., 40–43
Specialized resources, 32
Spinner, Frances, 359
Spinning jenny, 255
Spirituals, 51
Spoils system, 175
    attack on, 480–481, *480*
Sports, in the United States, 278–279
Springfield, Massachusetts, *287*
Squanto, 29
Stamp Act, 56
    protest of, 54, *54,* 56–57
    repeal of, 57, *57*
Stamp Act Congress, 56–57
Standard Oil Trust, 483, 484
Stanton, Edwin, 361, 378, 392
    Johnson's attempt to fire, 387
Stanton, Elizabeth Cady, 267, *267,* 322, 516, 610
"Star Spangled Banner," 156, *156*
State, separation of church from, 85
State government(s)
    emergence of, 86–87
    reforms in, 507–508
States' rights, doctrine of, 178
Statistical sources, 32
Statue of Liberty, 564, *564*
Steamboats, 257
Steffens, Lincoln, 502
Stevens, John L., 532
Stock exchange, *614*
Story, Joseph, 172
Stowe, Harriet Beecher, 322, 324,

324
    quoted, 324
Strategic Defense Initiative, 632
Strike, 458. *See also Labor movement*
    Homestead, 458–460, *460*
    McCormick, 459
    Pullman, 461
    by women workers, 271
Strong, Josiah, 528
Stuart, Jeb, *345*
Students Against Drunk Driving (SADD), 612
Submarines, in World War I, 542
Subsistence farmers, 35, 36–37, *36–37*
Suffrage. *See Voting rights*
"Summer in New York" (Asch), 522–523
Sumner, Charles, 325
Sumner, William Graham, 529
Supreme Court, U.S., 634–635
    and checks and balances, 626
    and judicial review, 151, *151,* 626
    under Marshall, 127, 151, 176
    role of, in interpreting constitution, 396
    under Taney, 331, 594
"Susan's Trial" (Jacob), 276–277
Sutter, John Augustus, 240
Swamp Fox, 68
Sweatshops, 500–501, *500, 501*

T

Taft, William Howard, 511
Tammany Hall, 476
Taney, Roger, 331, 594
Tarbell, Ida, 483, *483,* 502
Tariffs, 173
    of Abominations, 177–178
    of 1828, 178
    of 1832, 178
    under Wilson, 512
Taxes, 93, *93*
    income, 93, 510, 627
    whiskey, 137
Taylor, Zachary, 234
Tea Act (1773), 58–59
Technology
    in Civil War, 363, *364–365,* 366
    in farming, 432
    in World War I, 544–545, *545*

Tecumseh, 155, 201, *201,* 204
Teen Age Republicans, 612
Telegraph, 257, 258, 530
Telegraph operator, 265, *265*
Telephone, 443, *443*
Teller, Edward, 570
Temperance movement, 268–269, *268,* 513–514
Tenements, 504–505, *505*
Tennessee, in civil war, 343
Tenochtitlán, 19
Tenth Amendment, 623–624
Tenure of Office Act, 387
Term of office, 92
Territories, 96
Texas
    acquisition of, 158, 688
    admission to union, 288, 316
    in Civil War, 343
    independence of, 232
    as Lone Star Republic, 232–233
    and Mexican-American War, 318
    settlement of, 230–231, *231*
Thames, Battle of the, 204
Third parties, 680
Thirteenth Amendment, 378, 594
"This Dust Was Once the Man" (Whitman), 401
Thoreau, Henry David, 270
Three–Fifths Compromise, 111–112
Ticonderoga, Battle of, *66*
Tilden, Samuel J., 395
Tillman, "Pitchfork Ben," 490
Timelines,
    charting pre–Revolutionary events, 60–61, *61*
Time zones, in United States, *708*
Tippecanoe, Battle of, 155, 204
Tocqueville, Alexis de, 181, 183
Tombstone, 414
Tomkins, Sally, 359
Topographical maps, 433, *433*
Tories, 72
Torre, Thomas de la, 16
Tourgée, Albion, 388–389
    quoted, 389
Tour on the Prairies (Irving), 8
Town meetings, 85
Towns. *See also Cities*
    mapping and planning, 199, *199*
Townshend Acts (1767), 57

Townships, 96, 199
Trade. *See also Tariffs*
    and American Indians, 29
    under Articles of Confederation,
        96
    with Asia, 531–532, *531*
    foreign, 1876–1914, 529, *529*
Trail of Tears, 206, *206*, 207, *207*
Trans–Appalachian Frontier,
        196–200, *198*
Transcontinental Railroad,
        412–413, 423, 432
Transcontinental Treaty, 158
Transportation
    building network of, 256–258,
        256, 257, 258
    in cities, 263
    improvements in, 556
    and western settlement,
        198–199, *198*
Travis, William Barret, 232
"Treatise on Domestic Economy,
    A" (Beecher), 192
Tree line, 12
Trench warfare, in World War I,
        545, *545*
Trenton, Battle of, *66*
Triangle Shirtwaist Factory fire,
        498, *498*
Triple Alliance, and World War I,
        542
Triple Entente, and World War I,
        542
Trollope, Frances, 178, 180
Troy Female Seminary, 269
Trust(s), 483
    attempt to restrain, 483, 485
Trustbusting, under Theodore
        Roosevelt, 509, *509*
Tubman, Harriet, 333, *333*
Turner, Nat, 295, 320
Tuscaroras, in American
        Revolution, 74
Tuskegee Institute, 452–453
Twain, Mark, 263, 411, 444, 472,
        536
    quoted, 410, 492–493
Tweed, William Marcy, 476, *476*
Tweed Ring, 476
Twelve Years as a Slave (Northup),
        285
Twenty–First Amendment, 627
Twenty–Second Amendment, 627

Twenty–Sixth Amendment, 596
Typewriter, 443–444

U

U–boats, in World War I, 542, 546
"Uncle Sam" (Bushnell), 555
Uncle Tom's Cabin (Stowe), 322,
        323–324
Under Fire (Barbusse), 546
Underground Railroad, 333–334,
        334
Underwood Tariff Act (1913), 512
Union League, 387
Union Pacific Railroad, 412
    and Credit Mobilier scandal,
        474–475
Union Rolling Mill, 260
United Farm Workers, 582, *582*
United States
    climate in, *706*
    facts in brief, 686–688
    gross national product, *686*
    land use in, 707
    main outlying areas of, *687*
    major territorial acquisitions,
        688
    physical map of, *700–701*
    political map of, *698–699*
    population density in, *704–705*
    precipitation in, *707*
    production and workers by eco-
        nomic activity, *686*
    regions in, 5, 6–13, *687*
    symbols of, *99, 687*
    time zones in, *708*
    vegetation in, *706*
U.S. Army Signal Corps, 544
U.S. Capital, 147–148, *148*
U.S. Government, 84
    finances for, 93, *93, 687*
U.S. v. E. C. Knight Company, 485
University of Virginia, 165
Utah, settlement of, 239–240
Utopian societies, 271–272

V

Vallandigham, Clement L., 356
Vallejo, Mariano, 234
Valley Forge, 68
Van Buren, Martin, 177, *177*
Vanderbilt, Cornelius, 445, 473, 481

Vanderbilt, William Henry, *482*
Vaqueros, 238, *428*
Vaughan, Mary, 351
Vegetation
    in American West, 12–13
    in Central Heartland, 10
    in Eastern and Southern United
        States, 8
    in United States, *706*
Venezuela, conflict with Great
        Britain, 533–534
Vermont, abolition of slavery in,
        194
Verrazano, Giovanni da, 20
Versailles, Treaty of, 550–552, *550*
Vesey, Denmark, 295
Vespucci, Amerigo, 18
Veto, presidential, *692*
Vicksburg, Battle of, 353–354
Vietnamese–Americans, 574
Vietnamese boat people, *579, 580*
Vigilantes, 394
Villa, Francisco "Pancho," 540, *540*
Vincennes, 68
Virginia
    in Civil War, 343
    colonial government in, 85
    House of Burgesses in, 85, *87*
    and ownership of western lands,
        86
    ratification of Constitution by,
        122
Virginia, Mary, 391
Virginia City, 414
Virginia Plan, 108, 110
Visual learning,
    political cartoons, analyzing
        Jackson–Clay, 184–185, *184*
    historical photographs, analyz-
        ing 520–521, *520, 521*
Voter registration, *597*
Voter turnout, *174, 612*
Voting, reforms in, 508
Voting rights
    for American Indians, 596
    for black Americans, 390, *390*,
        394, 508, 516, 596, 597
    for 18–year olds, 596
    expansion of, 595–596, *595*
    and the poll tax, 394
    for white males, 169
    for women, *147*, 517–518, *517*,
        595–596, *596*

Voting Rights Act (1965), 604

W

Wade–Davis Bill, 378–379
Wagon train, travel by, 243–245,
    243
Walker, Amasa, 261
Walker, David, 320
Walker, Mary, 359
Wampanoag Indians, 31
War Hawks, and War of 1812, 155
War of 1812, 153, *153*
    and the Battle of New Orleans,
        157, *157*
    Indians in, *201*, 203–204
Warren, Mercy Otis, 74–75, *74*
Washington, Booker T., 452–453,
    519, *519*
Washington, D.C.
    burning of, in 1814, 153, *153*
    design of, 168
    end of slave sales in, 319
    march on, 602, 603, *603*, 604
    as new capital, 147–148, *148*
Washington, George, 66, 99, 565,
    693, *693*
    Cabinet of, 127, 134, 135
    as classical hero, 165, *165*
    as commander of Continental
        Army, 63, 66–70
    domestic policy under, 135, 137
    foreign policy under, 137, 154
    inauguration of, 134
    as leader, 138
    and Newburgh Conspiracy, 94
    as President, 134–135, 137
    as president of Constitutional
        Convention, 106, *108*
    in Seven Years' War, 55
    support of, for Constitution, 119
    term of office, 627
    and Whiskey Rebellion, 137,
        137
Washington, Martha, 170–171, *170*
Watergate scandal, 628–629
Water power, *259*
Wayne, Anthony, 202
Weaver, James B., 490
Webster, Daniel, 175, 178
    and Compromise of 1850, 319
Webster, Noah, 164
Weems, Mason, 165

Wells, Ida B., 519, *519*
West, *411. See also Western settle-
    ment*
    cattle ranching in, 428–430, *429,
        430*
    climate of, 411–412
    impact of river on, 412
    railroads in, *433*
    regions of, *411*
    resettlement of, 427
Western Federation of Miners, 461
Western lands
    conflict over ownership of, post
        American Revolution, 85–86, *86*
    expansion of, in early 1800s,
        166–167, *167*
    exploration of, 222–227, *223,
        225, 227*
    post War of 1812, 158
Western settlement, 236–240
    building schools and churches,
        199–200, *200*
    and development of mining,
        413–414, *414*
    and farming, 431–432, *432*
    homesteading in, 431–432, *431*
    impact of, 245–246, *246*
    and Indian policy, 202–207, *203*
    mapping and planning towns,
        199, *199*
    and Northwest Ordinance, 98,
        99
    railroads in, 412–413, *412*
    reasons for, 197–198
    response of Indians to, 204–205,
        422–424, *422, 423*
    routes of, 198–199, *198*
Weyler, Valeriano, 534
Wheat, farming of, 190–191
Whig Party, 174–175, *326*
Whiskey Ring scandal, 475
White, John, painting by, *27*
White Brotherhood, 394
Whitefield, George, 52
White House, 147
Whitman, Marcus, 238
Whitman, Narcissa, 238
Whitman, Walt, 400–401
    quoted, 474
Whitney, Eli, 255, 256, 284
Wilder, Laura Ingalls, 427
Wilderness Road, *198*
Wildlife

    in American West, 13
    in Central Heartland, 10
    in Eastern and Southern United
        States, 8
Willard, Emma Hart, 166, *166*, 269
Williams, Roger, 29–30
Wilmot, David, 318
Wilmot Proviso, 318
Wilson, Edith Galt, 171, *171*, 552,
    552
Wilson, Ellen, 171
Wilson, James, 110
Wilson, Woodrow, *512, 551*
    Fourteen Points of, 550
    in election of 1912, 511, *511*
    in election of 1916, 541, *541*
    illness of, 552
    and immigration, 568
    reforms under, 512
    tariffs under, 512
    and World War I, 542–543
Winslow, Hannah, 72
Wisconsin, 98
Wisconsin Idea, 507–508
Witch of Blackbird Pond, The
    (Speare), 40–43
Women
    in abolition movement, 322, *322,
        323*
    changing roles of, *606*, 607
    in Civil War, 359, *359*
    in early America, 166, 192
    education for, 269, *269*
    in English colonies, 38
    in factories, 259–260, *260*
    in frontier, 244, 245
    homemaking role of, 192, *192*
    in labor union, 271, *459*
    in revival movement, 169
    in temperance movement,
        268–269
    voting rights for, 517–518, *517,*
        595–596, *596*
    working conditions for, 455, *455,
        498, 498, 615*
    in World War I, 544, *544*, 549,
        549
Women's Christian Temperance
    Union (WCTU), 513, 514
Women's Political Council, 600
Women's rights movement, 267,
    516–518, *517*, 605–607
Wong, Jade Snow, 574

quoted, 574
Worcester v. *Georgia*, 176, 205
Work, explaining, 614–615, *614,
    615*
Workers, by economic activity in
    U.S., *686*
Working class, 192
Working conditions
    for children, 450, *450*, 500, *500*,
        514–515, *514*
    in cities, 266
    in factories, 259–260, *260*,
        457–458, *457*
    and reforms, 271, 514–515, *514*
    for women, 259–260, *260*, 455,
        455, 498, *498*, *615*
World
    gross national product through-
        out, 708
    physical map of, *696–697*
    political map of, *694–695*
"World of the Buffalo Comes to an
    End, The," 420–421
World War I
    allied victory in, 546
    black Americans in, 549
    causes of, 541–542
    draft for, 543–544, *543*
    in Europe, 541–542
    home front in, 547–549
    technology in, 544–545, *545*
    and Treaty of Versailles, 550–552
    U.S. entrance into, 542–544
    weapons used in, *542, 545*
    western front in, *546*
    women in, 544, *544*, 549, *549*
World War II
    effect of, on immigration,
        569–570
    treatment of
        Japanese–Americans in,
        607–608, *608*
Wounded Knee, South Dakota,
    426
Wovoka, 426
Writs of assistance, 57, *125*
Written arguments, editorials as,
    598–599

Y

Yamasee War, 31
Yellow journalism, 535, *535*

Yeoman farmers, 299
York, Alvin, 546
Yorktown, surrender of, 70, *70*
Yosemite National Park, *510*
Young, Brigham, 239
Young Democrats of America, 612

Z

Zebulon Pike, 226
Zenger, Anna, 124
Zenger, John Peter, 124
Zoning laws, 505

ACKNOWLEDGMENTS

Text *(continued from page iv)*

16 Adapted excerpt from Fray Francisco Ximenez, *Historia de la Provincia de San Vicente de Chiapas y Guatemala de la Orden de Predicadores, Prolog Del Lic. Antonio Villacorta*, C. 3 Vols., 1929. Extensive efforts to locate the rights holder were unsuccessful. If the rights holder sees this notice, he or she should contact the School Division Permissions Department, Houghton Mifflin Company, One Beacon Street, Boston, MA 02108. **24** from *Indian Legends of the Pacific Northwest* by Ella Clark. Published by the University of California Press. Copyright © 1953 by The Regents of the University of California; renewed 1981 by Ella E. Clark. Used by permission. **35** "The Slave Auction" by Frances E.W. Harper. Source: *Complete Poems of Frances E.W. Harper*, edited by Maryemma Graham. Copyright© 1988 by Oxford University Press, Inc. **40** Excerpts from *The Witch of Blackbird Pond* by Elizabeth George Speare. Copyright © 1958 by Elizabeth George Speare. Reprinted by permission of Houghton Mifflin Company. **166** From Willard, Emma Hart. *Education and the Weaker Sex*. 1819. **183** Excerpts from *Democracy in America* by Alexis de Tocqueville, translated by Henry Reeve, revised by Francis Bowen, and edited by Phillips Bradley. Copyright © 1945 and renewed 1973 by Alfred A. Knopf. Reprinted by permission of the publisher. **207** Quote by John G. Burnett from Perdue, Theda. *The Cherokee*. New York: Chelsea House Publishers, 1989. **211** From Macmanus, Seumas. *The Story of the Irish Race: A Popular History of Ireland*. New York: The Devin-Adair Co., 1921. **212** Excerpt from *Famine* by Liam O'Flaherty. Copyright 1937, 1965 by Liam O'Flaherty. Reprinted by permission of David R. Godine, Publisher. **232** From *The Texans*. New York: Time-Life Books, 1975. **241** Quote by James Marshall from Holliday, J.S. *The World Rushed In: The California Gold Rush Experience*. New York: Simon & Schuster, 1981. **242** Excerpt from *A Frontier Lady by Sarah Royce,* Copyright © 1932 byYale University Press, renewal Copyright © 1960 by Ralph Henry Gabriel. **242** From Paul, Rodman W. *Mining Frontiers of the Far West, 1848-1880*. The University of New Mexico Press, 1963. **243** Quotes by Elizabeth Goltra and anonymous woman from Clinton, Catherine. *The Other Civil War: American Women in the Nineteenth Century*. New York: Hill & Wang, 1984. **244** Quotes by Charlotte Stearns Pengra and Elizabeth Smith Geer from Schlisser, Lillian. *Women's Diaries of the Westward Journey*. New York: Schocken Books, 1982. **276** From *Mother, Aunt Susan and Me*, by William Jay Jacobs, Copyright © 1979 by William Jay Jacobs. Reprinted by permission of Coward-McCann. **284** From Hammond, M.B., ed. "Correspondence of Eli Whitney." *The American Historical Review,* 1897-98. **293** From Clinton, Catherine. *The Other Civil War: American Women in the Nineteenth Century*. New York: Hill & Wang, 1984. **370** From *The Slopes of War* by Norah A. Perez. Copyright © 1984 by N.A. Perez. Reprinted by permission of Houghton Mifflin Company. **389** Excerpt from *A Fool's Errand* by Albion W. Tourgee. Copyright © 1961 by the President and Fellows of Harvard College, renewed 1989 by John Hope Franklin. Reprinted by permission of Harvard University Press. **411** Quote by John Noble from *The American Magazine*, Aug., 1927. **414** From Watkins, T.H. *Gold and Silver in the West: The Illustrated History of an American Dream*. Palo Alto, CA: American West Publishing Co., 1971. **415** Excerpt from *Canadian Portraits, Brant, Crowfoot, Oronhyatekha, Famous Indians* by Ethel Brant Monture, Copyright © 1960 by Clarke, Irwin & Company, Ltd., Toronto. Reprinted by permission of Stoddart Publishing Co. Limited, 34 Lesmill Rd., Don Mills, Ontario, Canada. **418** From Linderman, Frank B. *Red Mother*. New York: John Day Co., 1932. **419** From "This Earth is Sacred" found in *Environmental Action*. Reprinted by permission of Environmental Action, Inc. 1525 New Hampshire Ave. N.W., Washington, D.C. 20036. **420** From *American Indian Mythology* by Alice Marriott and Carol K. Rachlin. Copyright © 1968 by Alice Marriott and Carol K. Rachlin. Published by Thomas Y. Crowell. Reprinted by permission of Harper & Row, Publishers, Inc. **425** McCreight, M.I. *Firewater and Forked Tongues, A Sioux Chief Interprets U.S. History*. Pasadena: Trail's End Publishing Co., 1947. **427** Excerpt from *By the Shores of Silver Lake* by Laura Ingalls Wilder. Text copyright 1939 by Laura Ingalls Wilder, copyright renewed 1967 by Roger L. MacBride. Reprinted by permission of Harper & Row, Publishers, Inc. **434** Excerpts from *My Antonia* by Willa Cather. Copyright 1918 by Willa Sibert Cather. Copyright renewed 1946 by Willa Sibert Cather. Copyright 1926 by Willa Sibert Cather.

Copyright renewed 1954 by Edith Lewis. Copyright 1949 by Houghton Mifflin Company. Copyright © renewed 1977 by Bertha Handlan. Reprinted by permission of Houghton Mifflin Company. **455** Nestor, Agnes. "I Become a Striker." *Woman's Labor Leader*. Rockford, Ill.: Bellevue Books, 1954. **474** From *Voices of Freedom: Sources in American History*. Englewood Cliffs, NJ: Prentice Hall Allyn & Bacon, 1987. **480** Georgia Historical Quarterly 35 (1951): 244-247 (July 31, 1865). **486** Quote by William J. Bryan from *The First Battle*, 1896. **487** Excerpt from *The Octopus: A Story of California* by Frank Norris. Copyright © 1958 by Kenneth S. Lynn. Reprinted by permission of Houghton Mifflin Company. **498** Quote by Stephen Wise from *Voices of Freedom: Sources in American History*. Englewood Cliffs, NJ: Prentice Hall Allyn & Bacon, 1987. **522** Excerpt from *East River* by Sholem Asch. Copyright 1946. **545** From *All Quiet on the Western Front* by Erich Maria Remarque. Copyright © 1928 by Ullstein A.G. Copyright © renewed 1956 by Erich Maria Remarque. Copyright © 1929, 1930 by Little, Brown and Co., copyright renewed © 1957, 1958 by Erich Maria Remarque. Reprinted by permission of the Estate of Erich Maria Remarque. **554** "Over There" by George M. Cohan. Copyright © 1917 (Renewed 1945) LEO FEIST, INC. All rights assigned to EMI CATALOGUE PARTNERSHIP. All rights Controlled and Administered by EMI FEIST CATALOG, INC. International Copyright Secured. Made in USA. All Rights Reserved. Reprinted by Permission. **555** Song, "Uncle Sam" by Edward Bushnell, copyright 1917 by Edward Bushnell. Extensive efforts to locate the rights holder were unsuccessful. If the rights holder sees this notice, he or she should contact the School Division Permissions Department, Houghton Mifflin Company, One Beacon Street, Boston, MA 02108. **556-557** From Vaughn, Stephen. *Holding Fast the Inner Lines: Democracy, Nationalism, and the Committee on Public Information*. Chapel Hill: The University of North Carolina Press, 1980. **559** From *A New England Girlhood: Outlined from Memory*, by Lucy Larcom. Copyright © 1924 by Houghton Mifflin Co. **564** From *Newsweek*, July 1986. **574** From "Puritans from the Orient: A Chinese Evolution" by Jade Snow Wong from*The Immigrant Experience* by Thomas Wheeler. Copyright © 1971 by Doubleday, a division of Bantam, Doubleday, Dell Publishing Group, Inc. Reprinted by permission of the publisher. **578, 580** From "I Get Homesick Every Day" from *Today's Immigrants, Their Stories* by Thomas Kessner and Betty Boyd Caroli. Copyright © 1981 by Thomas Kessner and Betty Boyd Caroli. Reprinted by permission of Oxford University Press. **580** Quote by Jimmy Carter from Kessner, Thomas and Betty Boyd Caroli. *Today's Immigrants, Their Stories*. New York: Oxford University Press, 1981. **581** "Working to Help Irish Immigrants Stay, Legally" by Marvine Howe and "Immigration Law is Failing to Cut Flow From Mexico" by Larry Rother, from *The New York Times*, November 27 and June 24, respectively. Copyright © 1988 by The New York Times Company. Reprinted by permission. **583** From *Time Magazine,* Dec, 5, 1988. **584** From *Hunger of Memory* by Richard Rodriguez. Copyright © 1982 by Richard Rodriguez. Reprinted by permission of David Godine, Publisher, Inc. **586** From *America's Immigrants* by Rhoda Hoff. Copyright © 1967 by Rhoda Hoff. Reprinted by permission of McIntosh and Otis, Inc. **598-599** "One Reason Voters Didn't Vote" (editorial); and "Low Voter Turnout? Don't believe it" by Warren J. Mitofsky and Martin Plissner, from *The New York Times,* November 25 and November 10, respectively. Copyright © 1988 by The New York Times Company. Reprinted by permission. **602** Excerpt from "I Have a Dream" speech, reprinted by permission of Joan Daves. Copyright © 1963 by Martin Luther King, Jr. **618** "I, Too" by Langston Hughes, from *Selected Poems of Langston Hughes*. Copyright 1926 by Alfred A. Knopf, Inc., and renewed 1954 by Langston Hughes. Reprinted by permission of Alfred A. Knopf, Inc. **618** "Refugee in America" by Langston Hughes from *Selected Poems of Langston Hughes*. Copyright 1943 by the Curtis Publishing Co. Reprinted by permission of Alfred A. Knopf, Inc.

Illustrations

Literature Border Design by Peggy Skycraft
Ligature 15, 50, 88, 89, 93, 109, 123, 161, 214, 228, 246, 274, 275, 281, 317, 361, 396, 398, 399, 437, 484, 598, 599 **Precision Graphics** 44, 49, 50, 61, 66, 67, 73, 76, 84, 92, 93, 102, 110, 122, 128, 136, 151, 160, 174, 186, 191, 209, 216, 217, 231, 250, 256, 257, 287, 306, 307, 309, 315, 326, 338, 346, 350, 372, 384, 395, 404, 438, 453, 467, 468, 481, 485, 494, 506, 524, 529,

569, 580, 581, 588, 595, 612, 619, 623, 625, 629, 631, 633, 635 **Brian Battles** 64 **Jeani Brunick** 573 **Susan David** 284 **Ebet Dudley** 538 **Randall Fleck** 538 **Hank Iken** 259,449 **Joe LeMonnier** 291 **Al Lorenz** 36,37,501 **Yoshi Miyake** 206 **Jim Needham** 211 **Rick Porter** 428,450 **Judy Reed** 127 **Joseph Scrofani** 418 **Richard Waldrep** 265 **Brent Watkinson** 323 **Paul Wenzel** 97

Maps

Mapping Specialists 19, 21, 38, 55, 69, 83, 86, 112, 150, 159, 167, 175, 194, 198, 203, 207, 213, 223, 227, 234, 235, 244, 258, 262, 288, 316, 318, 327, 332, 333, 343, 350, 386, 411, 412, 419, 423, 425, 430, 433, 452, 454, 463, 491, 511, 536, 538, 546, 550, 572

BA—Boston Athenaeum; **GC**—The Granger Collection; **INHP**—Independence National Historic Park Collection; **LC**—Library of Congress; **LPW**—Laurie Platt Winfrey, Inc.; **MMA**—The Metropolitan Museum of Art; **NYHS**—New-York Historical Society; **NYPL**—New York Public Library; **PC**—Private Collection; **SI**—Smithsonian Institution; **SM**—The Shelburne Museum, Shelburne, VT; **TIB**—The Image Bank

Photographs

Front Cover The Planet, Side wheel paddle steamer, courtesy of the Chicago Maritime Society and Museum; photo by Peter Bosy; **Back Cover** detail, New Jersey Historical Society, Newark; xviii–1 © Grant Heilman Photography; 2 John Carter Brown Library, Brown University, Providence, RI (bl); © Fred Maroon (br); 3 National Maritime Museum (t); Plimouth Plantation(b); 5 © Leonard Lee Rue III, Stock Boston; 6 © Jeff Gnass; 7 © Judy Canty, Stock Boston (t); © J.H. Carmichael Jr., TIB (br); © Art Wolfe (cr); 8 © Nick Pavloff, TIB (c); © James Tallon, Outdoor Exposures (tl); 9 © Art Wolfe (cr); © Grant Heilman, Grant Heilman Photography (b); 10 © Paul McCormick, TIB; 11 © Alan Becker, TIB (b); © Art Wolfe (cr); 12 © Dennis Stock, Magnum Photos, Inc. (t); © Jack Baker, TIB (bl); 13 © Jeff Gnass (tr); © James Tallon, Outdoor Exposures (c); 14 © Art Wolfe (c, bl); 15 © Jack Elness, COMSTOCK; 17 GC (tl); British Museum (br); 18 MMA (tl); British Museum, Newsweek Books (b); 20 GC; 22 The Fine Arts Museum of San Francisco, gift of Eleanor Martin; 23 U.S. Dept. of the Interior, Colonial National Historical Park; 25 © Joern Gerdts, Photo Researchers; 26 GC; 27 NYPL, Newsweek Books; 29 Schlowsky Photography; 30 LPW; 31 © C. Vic Maris, Earthshine; 32 Old Sturbridge Village, photo by Henry E. Peach; 33 Yale University Art Gallery, New Haven CT; 34 NYPL (b); GC (cl); 35 National Gallery of Art; 36 Old Sturbridge Village, photo by Henry E. Peach (tr, cr); Ralph Brunke (br); 37 Old Sturbridge Village, photo by Henry E. Peach; 38 The Library Company of Philadelphia; 39 PC; 46 National Gallery of Art, gift of Marian B. Maurice (cr); Colonial Williamsburg (cl); 47 The original painting hangs in the Selectmen's Meeting Room, Abbot Hall, Marblehead, MA (t); SI (b); 49 The Free Library of Philadelphia, photo by Joan Broderick; 51 GC; 52 American Antiquarian Society, Worcester, MA; 53 Concord Museum, Concord, MA; 54 LC; 56–7 Massachusetts Historical Society; 57 LC; 58 LC, LPW; 59 © Daughters of the American Revolution, Boston Tea Party Chapter; 60 Dover; 62 GC; 63 Concord Antiquarian Society, Concord, MA; 65 GC; 66 Dover (bc); Courtesy of The Bostonian Society/Old State House (bl); SI (br); 67 Dover (c); SI (b); 68 © FPG International; 70 Anne S.K. Brown Military Collection; 72 Connecticut Historical Society; 73 SI; 74 The Museum of Fine Arts, Boston, bequest of Winslow Warren, 1931; 75 Historical Society of Pennsylvania, Newsweek Books; 78–9 SM; 80 The Pennsylvania Academy of Fine Arts, Philadelphia (cr); The Free Library of Philadelphia, photo by Joan Broderick (cl); 81 The New Jersey Historical Society, Newark (tr); NYPL (l); 82 Yale University Art Gallery, New Haven, CT; 83 Her Majesty's Stationery Office, Newsweek Books; 85 GC; 87 Virginia State Library and Archives; 88 New York State Historical Association, Cooperstown; 90 The Free Library of Philadelphia, photo by Joan Broderick; 91 PC, Newsweek Books; 92 Steven A. Heassler; 94 GC (l); SI (c); 95 The Bettmann Archive; 96 Historical Society of Pennsylvania (c); Percival David Foundation, London, Newsweek Books (cl); 98 PC; 99 National Archives (tr); SI Numismatics (cr); 100 SI Numismatics (tr, bl); 101 Schlowsky Photography (tc, bl, bc, br); 104 Map Collection, The Free Library of Philadelphia, photo by Joan Broderick (c); 104–5 INHP (c); 105 NYHS (tr); INHP (br); 106 The Thomas Gilcrease Institute of American History and Art, Tulsa, OK (cr); 107 Courtesy National Park Service,

artist Lynn Gallagher; 108 INHP (t); LC (bc); 111 Toledo Museum of Art; 113 The Board of Regents of Gunston Hall, VA; 118 Virginia Historical Society; 119 NYHS; 121 American Antiquarian Society, Worcester, MA (cr); Schlowsky Photography (cl); Ralph J. Brunke (tr); American Antiquarian Society, Worcester, MA (bl, bc); 124 INHP; 125 GC; 126 GC; 130–1 Historical Society of Pennsylvania; 132 Museum of American Political Life, University of Hartford, photo by Sally Andersen-Bruce (tl, bl); NYHS (r); National Gallery of Art, LPW (c); 133 Courtesy National Geographic Society, photo by Pat Lanza Field; 135 Historical Society of Pennsylvania, Newsweek Books; 136 National Gallery of Art (b); LPW (t, c); 137 Henry Francis Dupont Winterthur Museum, Wilmington, DE; 139 LC; 141 SM; 143 NYHS, LPW; 146 The Historical Society of Pennsylvania, Newsweek Books; 147 The Bettmann Archive; 148 LC (tr); SI (bl); 149 Chicago Historical Society; 152 from *The True Aaron Burr*, by Charles Burr Todd, A.S. Barnes & Co., New York, 1902 (t, b); 153 GC (bl); NYHS (br); 154 Essex Institute, Salem, MA (bl); GC (cl); 155 © Eunice Harris, 1981, Photo Researchers (r); Henry Grosinski (b); 156 Maryland Historical Society (cl); GC (tl); 157 New Orleans Museum of Art (tl); Ralph J. Brunke (r, br); GC (cl); detail, New Orleans Museum of Art (cr); 158 LC; 162–3 © Donald Dietz, Stock Boston (bl); SM (c); 163 Photo by Tom Liddell (br); Abby Aldrich Rockefeller Folk Art Center, Colonial Williamsburg (tr); 164 GC; 165 Henry Francis Dupont Winterthur Museum, Wilmington, DE; 166 GC; 168 © Runk/Schoenberger, Grant Heilman Photography; 169 Old Dartmouth Historical Society; 170 PC (b); LPW (cl); 171 © Marvin Koner, Black Star (cl); LC (tr); © D. Staples, Black Star (bl); 172 NYPL; 173 NYHS (r); North Carolina Museum of Art (l); 176 Tennessee State Library & Archives (cl); LC (br); 177 NYHS; 178 Gibbes Museum of Art, Carolina Art Association; 179 GC; 180 MMA (cl); 181 Culver Pictures, Inc.; 182 Musée Jacquemart-André, Paris, Newsweek Books (br); Connecticut Historical Society (tr); Her Majesty's Stationery Office, Newsweek Books (bc); Cincinnati Historical Society (c); 183 Beinecke Library, Yale University, New Haven, CT; 184 NYHS; 185 Courtesy the Trustees of the Boston Public Library, Print Department; 188 Delaware Art Museum, Wilmington (cl); SM (br); 189 National Collection of Fine Arts, LPW; 190 Ralph J. Brunke; 191 SI; 192 from *Godey's Lady's Book*, 1859, courtesy Mark MacKay; 193 MMA; 195 The Free Library of Philadelphia (tl, tr); 196 GC; 197 GC (c); PC (br); 199 National Archives; 200 SI (tr); GC (tl); 201 GC; 202 © Kent & Donna Dannen 1980, Photo Researchers; 203 © Fort Malden National Historic Park, Amherstburg, Ontario; 204 LC; 205 NYPL; 210 NYPL; 211 Radio Times Hulton Picture Library; 212 The Edward W.C. Arnold Collection lent by MMA; 215 GC; 218–219 SM (l, c, r); 220 LC (br); INHP (c); SI (bl); 221 detail, MMA, photo by Geoffrey Clements; 222 State Historical Society of North Dakota; 224 Missouri Historical Society (bl); NYPL (bc); 225 The Thomas Gilcrease Institute of American History and Art, Tulsa, OK (tl); American Museum of Natural History, New York (cr); 226 Colorado Historical Society, Denver (tr, cl); 229 GC (tr, bl); 231 Courtesy of the San Antonio Museum Association, San Antonio, TX, on loan from Bexar County (tl); Barker Texas History Center (cr); 232 Courtesy the Alamo, The Daughters of the Republic of Texas; 233 NYPL (cr); © Steve Elmore, Tom Stack and Associates (b); Texas State Library (cl); Courtesy the Alamo, The Daughters of the Republic of Texas (c); © Jules Bucher, Photo Researchers (tr); 236 Seaver Center for Western History Research, LA County Museum of Natural History; 237 Bancroft Library, University of California at Berkeley; 238 The Oakland Museum History Department (cr, bl); 239 The Oakland Museum History Department; 240 © David Muench 1990 (tc); NYPL (cl); 241 American Antiquarian Society, Worcester, MA, courtesy Meyers Photo-Art; 242 Seaver Center for Western History Research, LA County Museum of Natural History (br); The Oakland Museum History Department (cl); 243 Church of Jesus Christ of Latter-Day Saints; 245 American Stanhope Collection; 247 National Park Service; 252 NYPL (b); Betty Willis Antiques, Marlborough, NH, photo by The Hansen Co. (c); 253 Cincinnati Historical Society (c); Betty Willis Antiques, Marlborough, NH, photo by The Hansen Co. (b); 254 Essex Institute, Salem, MA; 255 Wakefield Historical Society, Wakefield, MA; 256 NYPL (bl); NYHS (br); 257 Wide World (c); SI (bl, bc); PC (tr); GC (br); 260 Museum of American Textile History, Andover, MA; 263 Brooklyn Museum, Brooklyn, NY; 264 NYHS; 266 The Bettmann Archive; 267 National Portrait Gallery, SI, transfer from the National Museum of American

National American Woman's Suffrage Association through Mrs. Harriet Stanton Blatch, 1924, Washington, D.C.; 268 PC (b); Sophia Smith Collection, Smith College (tl); 269 Massachusetts Historical Society; 270 © Murray Alcosser, TIB; 271 SI; 272 Brown Brothers; 273 State of Illinois; 278 Schlowsky Photography (tr, cl); 279 Schlowsky Photography; (tr, br); 282 PC, Time-Life Books (c); 282–3 NYPL; 283 Courtesy Museum of Appalachia, Norris, TN, photo by Frank Hoffman (br); Courtesy National Park Service, photo by William A. Bake (cr); 285 Collection of John Ridley; 286 The Historic New Orleans Collection; 287 GC (bl, br); 289 William Gladstone Collection; 292 The Western Reserve Historical Society; 293 © Photography by Milt and Joan Mann, Cameramann International; 294 The Museum of Fine Arts, Boston, M. and M. Karolik Collection; 295 Culver Pictures, Inc. (t); GC (c); 298 Collection of Mr. & Mrs. Wilson Pile, photo by Clive Russ; 299 Great Smoky Mountain National Park (both); 300 Courtesy Museum of Appalachia, Norris, TN, photo by Frank Hoffman (tr, c, bl); 301 Courtesy Museum of Appalachia, Norris, TN, photo by Frank Hoffman (bl, t, r); 302 NYHS, Newsweek Books; 303 PC; 305 The Charleston Museum; 310–11 © Jerome Liebling; 312 Massachusetts Historical Society (cl); 312–13 Sophia Smith Collection, Smith College (tc); 313 Museum of American Political Life, University of Hartford, photo by Sally Andersen-Bruce; 315 NYHS; 319 Culver Pictures, Inc. (t); NYPL (c); 320 NYHS; 321 MMA (bc); NYPL (br); 322 GC; 324 Schlesinger Library of Historic Women, Radcliffe College, Cambridge, MA (l); MMA, Newsweek Books (t); 328 Kansas State Historical Society, Topeka (br); BA (tl); 329 PC; 330 MMA; 331 Missouri Historical Society; 333 GC; 334 NYPL (tl, tr); 335 LC; 336 National Portrait Gallery, SI, gift of Mrs. Alan Valentine; 340 Collection of Larry Williford (c); *The Civil War* series, *Decoying the Yanks,* photograph by Larry Sherer, © 1984, Time-Life Books, Inc. (bl); 341 Collection of Larry Williford (tc); *The Civil War* series, *20 Million Yankees,* photograph by Larry Sherer, © 1985, Time-Life Books, Inc. (br); 342 LC; 344 © Richard & Mary Magruder, TIB; 345 West Point Museum; 347 NYHS; 348 BA (tl, cl); 348–9 BA (b); 349 Museum of the Confederacy © Larry Sherer; 351 LC (bl); *The Civil War* series, *Confederate Ordeal,* photograph by Larry Sherer, © 1984, Time-Life Books, Inc. (cr); 352 U.S. Army Military History Institute, Carlisle Barracks, PA (cl, cr); 353 © David Muench (bc); *The Civil War* series, *Spies, Scouts, and Raiders,* photograph by Larry Sherer, © 1985, Time-Life Books, Inc. (tr); 354 BA; 355 Lincoln Library, Fort Wayne, IN; 356 *The Civil War* series, *Tenting Tonight,* photograph by Larry Sherer, © 1984, Time-Life Books, Inc.; 357 NYPL; 358 Cook Collection, Valentine Museum (cl); LC (cr); 359 GC; 360 Schlowsky Photography; 362 BA (bl, br); 363 National Archives (tr); © *The Civil War* series, *Decoying the Yanks,* photograph by Larry Sherer, © 1984, Time-Life Books, Inc. (cr); 364 BA (tr); *The Civil War* series, *20 Million Yankees,* photograph by Larry Sherer, © 1985, Time-Life Books, Inc. (bl); GC (cl); 365 BA (tc, b); Museum of the Confederacy, © Larry Sherer (cr); 366 LC; 367 National Archives (r); BA (l); 368 BA; 369 BA (t); *The Civil War* series, *20 Million Yankees,* photograph by Larry Sherer, © 1985, Time-Life Books, Inc. (b); 374–5 National Archives; 375 LC (b); William Gladstone Collection (t); 377 GC; 378 NYHS; 379 NYHS (tl); LC (cr); 380 Schlowsky Photography (cl); LC (cr); 380–1 LC (t, b); 381 Culver Pictures, Inc. (cr); The Andover Historical Society, Andover, MA (tl); 382 LC; 383 LC (tr); © Bill Howe, Photri/Marilyn Gartman Agency, Inc. (tl); 385 LC; 387 *Harper's Weekly,* November 16, 1867 (tl); LC (br); 388 Chicago Historical Society; 389 © Dick Spahr, Time-Life Books (cr); Culver Pictures, Inc. (tr); 390 LC; 391 Old Court House Museum, Eva W. Davis Memorial; 392 Old Sturbridge Village; 393 Brown Brothers (tc); John Deere Museum, photo by Boyd-Fitzgerald (cr); 394 Old Court House Museum, photo by Bob Pickett; 397 LC; 399 Collection of John Ridley; 406–7 MMA, Bequest of Edward W.C. Arnold, 1954; 408 GC; 408–9 Oklahoma Historical Society (c); 409 The University of Michigan Museum of Art (tr); Peabody Museum of Natural History, Yale University, New Haven, CT (br); 410 © Ann Duncan, Tom Stack and Associates; 413 Collection of John Ridley (tr); The Oakland Museum History Department (br); 414 LC; 415 GC; 416 © Justin Kerr (cl); Museum of the American Indian, Heye Foundation (bc); 417 Southwest Museum, Los Angeles, CA (l); Museum of the American Indian, Heye Foundation (tr); Peabody Museum of Anthropology, Harvard University, photo by Carmelo Guadagno (bl); Southwest Museum, Los Angeles, CA (tc); 420 Huntington Library and Art Gallery, San Marino, CA; 421 The Oakland Museum History Department; 422 GC; 426 LC (tl); GC (cr); 427 Solomon D. Butcher Collection, Nebraska State Historical Society, Lincoln; 428 Jane Libby; 429 Collection of John Ridley (tr); The Oakland Museum History Department (bc); 430 Collection of John Ridley; 431 LC; 432 State Historical Society of Wisconsin; 436 GC; 439 Collection of John

Ridley; 440 © D. Lowe, FPG International (br); Brown Brothers (cl); 441 Collection of Susan W. and Stephen D. Paine, photo by Sally Fox (br); Collection of Sally Fox (b); The Oakland Museum History Department (bl); The Bettmann Archive (t); 442 The Free Library of Philadelphia; 443 © American Telephone and Telegraph Co. (tr); SI (br); 444 NYHS (br); The Bettmann Archive (tl); 445 Culver Pictures, Inc.; 446 The Bettmann Archive (t); Collection of John Ridley (cl); 447 GC; 448 The Bettmann Archive; 451 Collection of John Ridley; 453 © University of Chicago Press; 455 State Historical Society of Wisconsin; 456 Collection of John Ridley; 457 George Eastman House Collection, LPW; 458 Chicago Historical Society; 459 AFL-CIO News (br); The Bettmann Archive (tr); 460 National Archives; 461 LC; 464 GC; 465 LC (tl); © Steve Elmore, Tom Stack and Associates (br); GC (bc); George Eastman House Collection (tr); National Park Service (c); George Eastman House Collection, LPW (cl); 466 Holt-Atherton Center for Western Studies, University of the Pacific; 469 SI; 470 The Oakland Museum History Department (cr); Museum of the City of New York (bl); 471 Museum of the City of New York (b); The Oakland Museum History Department (tl); 472 Brown Brothers; 473 The Oakland Museum History Department (tr); Brown Brothers (b); 474 NYPL; 475 Museum of the City of New York, Newsweek Books; 476 NYPL; 477 *Harper's Weekly,* July 8, 1881; 478 *Harper's Weekly,* Nov. 7, 1874 (b); Museum of American Political Life, University of Hartford, photo by Sally Andersen-Bruce (l, r); 479 GC (tl); Museum of American Political Life, University of Hartford, photo by Sally Andersen-Bruce (b); The Bettmann Archive (tr); 480 LC; 482 GC; 483 Security Pacific National Bank Historic Photograph Collection, Los Angeles Public Library (b); Culver Pictures, Inc. (cr); 486 LC; 487 State Historical Society of Wisconsin; 488 GC; 489 GC (cr, bc); 490 Stanley King Collection (b, bc); PC (b); 495 *Harper's Weekly,* Nov. 7, 1874; 496 George Eastman House Collection; 497 Brown Brothers (t); Collection of John Ridley (br); 498 Brown Brothers (b); GC (bl); 499 Los Angeles County Museum of Art; 500 The Jacob A. Riis Collection, Museum of the City of New York (tr, cl); Schlowsky Photography (bl); 502 Chicago Historical Society (tl); GC (cl); 503 LC; 504 Culver Pictures, Inc.; 505 Museum of the City of New York, Newsweek Books; 508 LC; 509 GC (tr); Culver Pictures, Inc. (b); 510 Theodore Roosevelt Collection, Harvard College Library; 511 Stanley King Collection; 512 Collection of John Ridley; 513 Brown Brothers; 514 George Eastman House Collection; 515 The Bettmann Archive; 516 National Archives; 517 LC; 518 LC; 519 NYPL (tr); © NAACP (tl); 520 LC; 521 GC; 525 Museum of the City of New York; 526 © Mort Kunstler, National Guard Bureau; 527 LC (tl); GC (r); Military Records, Commonwealth of MA, Natick (bl, bc); 530 GC; 531 United States Naval Academy Museum; 532 Culver Pictures, Inc.; 533 GC; 535 GC (br); Collection of John Ridley (cr); 537 GC; 538 National Archives; 539 Panama Canal Company or National Archives (c); 540 GC; 541 UPI/Bettmann Newsphotos; 542 © Photri/Marilyn Gartman Agency, Inc.; 543 The Press Museum (tr); GC (br); Brown Brothers (tc); 544 GC (tl, tc); National Archives (b); 545 GC (t); Imperial War Museum, London (tl); 547 Culver Pictures, Inc.; 548 GC; 549 GC (cl); The Bettmann Archive (b); 551 Imperial War Museum, Newsweek Books; 552 The Bettmann Archive (b); White House Collection (tl); 553 PC; 557 New Jersey Historical Society, Newark; 559 LC; 560–1 Culver Pictures, Inc.; 562 The Oakland Museum History Department (bc); California Historical Society, San Francisco (cr); George Eastman House Collection (cl); 563 © Eric Wheater, TIB (tl); © Bob Daemmrich, Stock Boston (bc); Reuters/Bettmann Newsphotos (tc); 564 © Al Satterwhite, TIB; 565 UPI/Bettmann Newsphotos, Newsweek Books; 567 California Historical Society; 568 Collection of John Ridley; 570 UPI/Bettmann Newsphotos; 571 © David Weintraub, 1985, Photo Researchers; 574 Elihu Blotnick; 576 © Joseph Rodriguez, Black Star; 577 Wide World; 579 UPI/Bettmann Newsphotos; 580 UPI/Bettmann Newsphotos; 581 © Grant Heilman Photography; 582 UPI/Bettmann Newsphotos; 583 © B. Daemmrich, Stock Boston; 590 PC (c); The Thomas Gilcrease Institute of American History and Art, Tulsa, OK (cl); 591 © Andrew Sacks, Black Star (br); University of Illinois at Chicago, The University Library, Jane Addams Memorial Collection (c); © Bob Riha, Gamma-Liaison (tr); NYPL (tc); 592 Wide World; 593 © David Marie/FOLIO; 594 © Grant Heilman Photography; 596 Wide World (b, l); 597 © R. Maiman, SYGMA; 601 NYPL; 603 UPI/Bettmann Newsphotos (tr, cl, br); 604 LC; 605 © Bob Fitch, Black Star (tl); © Frank Johnston, Black Star (tr); 606 © Gary Gladstone, TIB (bl); Brown Brothers (tl); © Lawrence Fried, 1980, TIB (br); 607 © Arthur Grace, SYGMA; 608 Toyo Miyatake, courtesy Elihu Blotnick; 610 Wallace Kirkland, Hull House; 611 Wide World; 613 UPI/Bettmann Newsphotos (t); © Eric Bouvet, Gamma-Liaison (tl); 614

© Marc Romanelli, TIB; 615 © Michael Melford, TIP (tc, br); © Alvis
Upitis, TIB (tr); 622 © Liane Enkelis, 1986, Stock Boston; 624 ©
Markel/Liaison International (b); © Cary Wolinsky, Stock Boston (tl);
625 © Garry D. McMichael, 1987, Photo Researchers (t); © Brian
Parker, Tom Stack and Associates (cl); © Bill Gutmann, Marilyn
Gartman Agency, Inc. (cr); 626 © Bob Daemmrich, Stock Boston; 627 ©
Gene Stein, Westlight; 628 © Susan Leavines, 1987, Photo Researchers;
630 The Bettmann Archive (t, c, b); 632 Wide World Photo; 634 © Ellis
Herwig, Stock Boston

Photo research by Carousel Research, Inc., Meyers-Photo Art, and
Pembroke Herbert/Picture Research Consultants